JOB SEEKERS GUIDE TO WALL STREET RECRUITERS

CHRISTOPHER W. HUNT

SCOTT A. SCANLON

John Wiley & Sons, Inc.

New York · Chichester · Weinheim · Brisbane · Singapore · Toronto

Copyright © 1998 by Hunt-Scanlon Publishing Company.
All rights reserved.
Published by John Wiley & Sons, Inc.

Published simultaneously in Canada.

Chapters 1, 2, and 3 consist of material adapted from
the following books by Richard H. Beatty: *The Resume Kit*,
The Perfect Cover Letter, and *The Five Minute Interview.*

This publication is designed to provide accurate and authoritative
information in regard to the subject matter covered. It is sold with
the understanding that the publisher is not engaged in rendering
professional services. If professional advice or other expert assistance is
required, the services of a competent professional person should be
sought.

Library of Congress Cataloging-in-Publication Data:

Hunt, Christopher W.
    Job seekers guide to Wall Street recruiters / Christopher W. Hunt,
Scott Scanlon.
        p.   cm.
    Includes index.
    ISBN 0-471-23994-1 (pbk. : alk. paper)
    1. Finance—Vocational guidance—United States.   2. Financial
services industry—Vocational guidance—United States.
    3. Executives—Recruiting—United States.   4. Job hunting—United
States.   I. Scanlon, Scott A.   II. Title.
    HG181.H845   1998
    332.6'023'73—dc21   97-44932
                                                              CIP

Printed in the United States of America

10 9 8 7 6 5 4 3 2 1

Contents

Introduction

Financial services make up one of the hottest employment sectors of the late 1990s, not just in the United States but around the world. Richard S. Lannamann of Russell Reynolds Associates stresses the importance of following developments in non-U.S. companies, because the biggest area of job expansion comes from developments like nonlocal hires by European and Asian banks engaged in global financial services. You may be a recently graduated MBA or you may be experienced in asset management or investment banking and ready to move on (and up) in a new and more rewarding employment situation. Searching for a job today can be a full-time job in itself—and fortune, as always, favors the prepared. You must highlight the skills and experience that will make you attractive to the companies you are targeting, and pursue your objectives energetically, imaginatively, and patiently. Realizing that you are the only one in control of your future can be frightening; however, career transitions, while difficult, are pivotal times of tremendous opportunity: The possibilities are infinite.

Even in the most turbulent economic times, one fact remains constant: To survive and grow, companies need innovative and dedicated people, and the right people are not always easy to find. This is particularly true in finance-related positions; there are more job opportunities than ever before. According to a recent article in the *New York Times*, "As securities, banking, insurance and money management industries continue their rapid consolidation some of the biggest names in finance are on the prowl for acquisitions on Wall Street—or have recently made the plunge. The main decision they all face is which firm will give them the biggest lift as they seek to build a global financial business." This merger and acquisition activity is having a profound effect on the employment ranks as well, providing new and numerous opportunities for professionals in this burgeoning market.

But in many finance-related positions opening up today the criteria have changed significantly. As Brian M. Sullivan of Sullivan & Company points out: "The new breed of Wall Streeter is extremely technologically proficient—they tend to have a business education or a strong quantitative education, like engineering, before they get into financial services. As a result, a significant number of people coming into financial services are very facile with numbers." Whatever your background and skill set, executive recruiters can be of assistance: giving you insights into your career and potential that you may not have considered, and matching you with opportunities that you may have been unaware of.

In an increasingly global environment, companies find their missions rapidly changing and the necessary skills redefined; the hundreds of resumes they receive in response to a classified ad don't tell them whether or not a candidate has the drive to succeed and the skills demanded. Recruiters help companies by examining their employment needs and then pre-screening and narrowing the field of potential candidates to present only those who seem to be a good fit. This works to your advantage: A search consultant can brief you on prospective companies and what sort of employees they are looking for, give you frank advice about your interview style, and prepare you for the sort of questions to expect. You can also be reassured that because the company has gone to the expense of contacting a recruiter, there is a genuine interest in filling the position promptly. Executive recruiters can also be helpful if you *don't* get a certain job: They can tell you why another candidate was chosen, and can coach you on how to improve for your next interview. Always remember: When an executive recruiter tries to contact you, take the call. It might be a new beginning for you.

THERE ARE TWO TYPES OF EXECUTIVE RECRUITERS

Although there are a number of ways to effectively market yourself, this book deals exclusively with executive recruiters, also known as headhunters or executive search consultants, who are seeking candidates not just for positions in the New York area but in other major financial centers throughout the country—and the world. What is an executive recruiter and what role can he or she play in your success? There are two basic types: retained and contingency. Both are paid by the companies that hire them, not by job seekers, but they differ in method, and sometimes the salary level, on which they operate.

Retained executive recruiters are headhunters who work on a contract with a client company. They are hired by companies to find a particular executive for a specific position and are subsequently paid a retainer fee (one-third at inception of the search, one-third at the halfway point, and one-third when the candidate is chosen and hired). These recruiters often handle the absolute crème de la crème. Major corporate figures such as Charles Brad Hintz, chief financial officer (CFO), Lehmann Brothers, Inc.; Michael Hogan, president, Wells Fargo Mutual Fund; C. Edward Carter, managing director and head of international banking, North America, Deutsche Morgan Grenfell; Barbara J. Kromsiek, president and chief executive officer (CEO), Calvert Group Ltd.; and Frank Newman, CEO, Bankers Trust Company, for example, were all placed by headhunters in this category. The average placement, however, is most often a rung or two lower. Though retained recruiters may be hired to fill a position with compensation in the millions or as low as $50,000, the average assignment generally runs between $75,000 and $125,000.

Contingency recruiters fill the gap between entry-level placements (generally handled by employment agency professionals) and those handled by the retained recruiter. The compensation level starts at about $30,000 and peaks at about $50,000. There are, however, exceptions, as a handful of contingency recruiters will place professionals with compensation levels exceeding $100,000. Recruiters in this category handle the bulk of lower to middle management and general management assignments. They are referred to as contingency recruiters because their fee is paid at the conclusion of the assignment or "contingent upon" the successful placement.

GETTING THEIR ATTENTION

Job seekers who wish to become part of recruiters' preferred lists (meaning that they deem you a strong candidate whom they will consider for any appropriate position) should employ certain steps in order to stand out from the rest of the crowd: Firms such as Korn/Ferry International, Spencer Stuart, Heidrick & Struggles, Russell Reynolds Associates, Management Recruiters International, Sullivan & Company, The Whitney Group, Highland Search Group, and others collectively receive in excess of one million resumes annually.

You should never, *ever* "cold-call" an executive recruiter—send a resume first. (It's fine to send a letter and resume by e-mail, because people in this area are very comfortable with this form of communication; but always mail in a hard copy too.) It might make a big difference, Brian Sullivan suggests, if you also attach to your resume "some type of study or analysis, paper, or critique" that emphasizes your qualifications for the finance-related job you are seeking in an industry that interests you.

Prior to sending your resume to any executive recruiter, make certain that you contact the search firm to see if it has real depth in handling finance-related placements, everything from positions in investment banking and venture capital firms to CFO and other corporate finance jobs. While many large search firms are labeled as generalist firms because they place executives in most functional disciplines and industries, they often have a practical area specializing in finance and financial services such as venture capital, the securities/brokerage industry, investment banking/investment management, banking, mutual funds, insurance, and accounting. Making sure that your resume is being sent to the appropriate recruiters is time well spent.

Also, don't discount numerous smaller firms, or specialty boutiques, which may prove to be an even better fit for someone with your background and experience in finance-related positions in the United States and other countries. For every type of finance-related position that exists on Wall Street, in banking or investment management, and in the corporate world, there seems to be a firm or recruiter that specializes in that area. This book focuses on positions in these and other areas in which finance-related experience is essential. Don't hesitate to call firms and ask them about their specialties if you have any questions. Again, a little digging on your part may pay off, saving you countless hours of following up with recruiters who are not able to help you, and on postage and paper as well! You can also check out the Web sites of companies that interest you. Even this book has its own Web site (job-seekers.com) that might be helpful to you.

NOW WHAT?

After you target recruiters or firms that specialize in your area of interest and experience in financial services, make certain that you are specific as to what you've done and what you are seeking. Don't generalize your credentials. The main question client companies have when reviewing resumes is, "What can this person do for us?" Answer that question on your resume by giving concrete examples of your accomplishments, and how your past companies have benefited from your contributions. Rather than simply saying you were a financial analyst responsible for implementing a new investment strategy for your firm, talk about the time you saved and the money you made for your company, and how you did it. It's impossible that you made no difference to your past company. Even if you feel your contribution was small, mention it. Think of your resume and cover letter as an outline for what you'll talk about when you meet a recruiter face-to-face.

Also use your resume, cover letter, and interview as chances to focus on what you expect to accomplish in the future. For example, if you are a CFO with a real understanding of and hands-on experience with management information systems (MIS), make sure that is clear in your cover letter and on your resume. The mistake that often plagues job seekers is trying to be everything to everyone. Also, if there are certain jobs that you are qualified for but are adamant about not doing, say so, and save your recruiter and yourself from arranging interviews for jobs that you wouldn't accept anyway. Another advantage to being specific about what you want is that if a client company calls with an opening that meets your criteria, the headhunter will be more likely to think of you.

Being realistic about your qualifications is helpful to both your headhunter and yourself. If you have 15 years of experience as a middle-management investment banking professional, it is not prudent to think that you will land a position as a CFO of an information technology company because you took a computer science course in college as well as a management accounting course. Instead, think through your capabilities and, for example, try to emphasize elements of your background that might make you attractive to one of the European or Asian banks or non-U.S. financial service companies that are looking for men and women with some international experience, people who are capable of thinking globally rather than locally. Recruiters like Gordon Grand of Russell Reynolds Associates feel that many of the exciting new finance-related job opportunities are to be found with international rather than U.S.-based operations. This means you may have to be prepared to live abroad. Would it be suitable for you or for your family? Is it the right long-term move? Or, if you have real people management skills, Richard Lannamann suggests you emphasize them, as they are increasingly important in many finance-related positions.

USE EVERY CONTACT AS AN OPPORTUNITY

One potential pitfall in the preparation of your credentials is the urge to stretch the truth. There is nothing wrong with highlighting or emphasizing various responsibilities or accomplishments. But in the desperation of trying to land a job, the temptation is strong to make certain "adjustments" to your credentials. A five-year stint at your last company may transform itself into seven years because the company you want to work for requires seven years' prior experience. Or in describing your position as director of a department in a large financial services operation you may state you increased your department's profit margin by 20 percent when the reality is that the increase was only 10 percent. Although you may think you're getting an edge by means of what you may perceive as inconsequential padding, the truth is that recruiters can smell these embellishments a mile away; detecting them is what they do for a living. Keep in mind that if you're caught lying, the recruiter will not deal with you again (if he or she does, perhaps you should be suspicious of the *recruiter's* integrity). Also, executive search is in many ways a close-knit community—there's a good chance that other recruiters may learn what you're up to. And, if you by some chance land the job anyway, you may find yourself in a position for which you are not qualified, which could, in an extreme case, mean lawsuits for you and possibly your headhunter.

Always return your recruiters' calls promptly and politely. Every contact as an opportunity to give them more confidence in you both as a candidate and as someone they'd like to help. And don't overlook the possibility that you can be helpful to them, too. If a recruiter mentions an opening that's inappropriate for you but might interest someone else you know, say so. Your honesty will be appreciated and remembered. Providing a valuable contact to a recruiter is not only a nice thing for you to do for someone but it may also be rewarding to you somewhere down the line.

If you are currently employed but are always keeping your eyes open for other career opportunities, the above suggestions certainly apply to you, but we would offer a few additional tips.

You may at some point in your professional life receive a call from a recruiter. It may come during a time when you are completely content with your career and the company you work for and you may not be interested in even taking the call. We would recommend that you not ignore a call from a recruiter for two reasons: First, although you are a happy camper, a recruiter might be considering you for an even better position. In fact, the only way you might be able to enhance your career is to change locations, as suggested above. And, second, the job the recruiter is considering you for may in fact not suit you. But it might be ideal for a colleague or friend with a finance or banking background who is unemployed or unhappy in his or her job.

Also, many employed executives are concerned about confidentiality if they decide to speak with a recruiter. Don't hesitate to mention this if it is a potential problem. Recruiters are used to these situations and know it is essential to maintain confidentiality. If your situation is highly sensitive, instruct your headhunter to leave messages on your home answering machine—just be sure to check your messages frequently during the day. If you reach the interview stage with a recruiter, the majority of meetings will naturally be held off-site, generally at the office of the recruiter or even perhaps at your residence. Discretion is the watchword for such meetings.

There is no doubt that finding a new job can be a challenging experience. Although executive search professionals should represent only a portion of your job search efforts, knowing how to utilize this valuable asset is essential. We hope that we have been able to provide you with a sense of the marketplace today, which recruiters are best for you, and how you can effectively work with them. Best of luck!

Chapter 1

Introduction to Resumes

The employment resume—its style, organization, and content—has long been a topic of considerable discussion and debate. Like religion and politics, this is a subject fraught with controversy. It is one of those topics where there are many "experts" who will provide you with considerable "professional" advice and counsel as long as you are willing to listen.

Should you wish to put this statement to the test, let me suggest that the next time you are at lunch or dinner with a group of friends or business colleagues, introduce the subject of "resume preparation" and ask a few of the following questions:

1. How long should a resume be?
2. What is the best resume format? How should it be organized?
3. Should there be a statement of job objective? If so, how should it be worded?
4. Should the resume contain personal data—age, height, weight, marital status, number of children?
5. Should hobbies and extracurricular activities be included?
6. How important is salary history? Should it be shown at all?
7. Where should education be described—near the end or the beginning of the resume?
8. What writing style is the most effective?
9. What is the best format for computer scanning and resume database search?

These, and similar questions, are guaranteed to spark a lively discussion punctuated with considerable difference of opinion. There will be those who claim that "Everyone knows that a resume should never be longer than a single page." Others will assert that "Two pages are quite acceptable." Still others will be adamant that "Two pages can never begin to do justice to 10 years of professional experience and accomplishment." All may use logical and persuasive arguments, with each sounding more convincing than the last. Who is right? Which argument should you believe? What works best?

As a consultant and executive with considerable employment experience, I can tell you that there are good answers to these questions. There is a right and a wrong way to prepare an employment resume. There are items that should definitely be included in the resume, and there are those that are best left out. There are resume formats that have consistently proven more effective than others, and there are those that should be avoided.

There are appropriate answers to these and many other questions associated with the subject of effective resume preparation. But you cannot expect to get expert advice on resume preparation over casual dinner conversation with a few friends whose expertise consists mainly of preparation of their first resume and a few articles read somewhere in a trade journal. This is hardly the type of advice that you need to prepare a resume that will be successful in launching you on a new and prosperous career track.

What I am about to share with you are the observations and advice of a human resources consultant and former personnel executive who has had considerable experience in the corporate employment function of a major Fortune 200 company. This is knowledge gleaned from years of employment experience—knowledge gained from the reading of thousands of employment resumes and the hiring of hundreds of employees at the professional, managerial, and executive level. This advice is based on firsthand observation of those resumes that resulted in job interviews and those that did not. This is advice based on "inside" knowledge of what makes professional employment managers tick—what motivates them to respond favorably to one resume and "turns them off" on the next. It will guide you in preparing a resume that will best display your qualifications and maximize your potential for landing interviews.

This chapter will provide you with an understanding of what happens in a typical company employment department. Where does your resume go? Who reads it? What is the basis for determining interest or lack of interest? What does the employment manager look for in a resume? How is the resume read? Who makes the final decision on your resume? Answers to these and similar questions should provide you with valuable insight that will enable you to design your resume to successfully compete for an employment interview. They will also serve as the basis for better understanding the recommendations made later in this chapter on such topics as resume format, content, style, appearance, and so on.

COMPETITION

In larger companies, it is not uncommon for the corporate employment department to receive as many as 40,000 to 50,000 resumes during the course of an average business year. Some receive considerably more. The annual employment volume of such firms typically runs in the range of 200 to 300 hires per year. Assuming an average of two to three interviews per hire, these firms will interview 400 to 900 employment candidates in meeting their employment requirements. This means that only 400 to 900 of the total 40,000 to 50,000 resumes received will result in an employment interview. In other words, only one or two out of every 100 resumes will result in an employment interview. Those are not very encouraging odds!

You are thus beginning your employment search at a decided statistical disadvantage. For every 100 resumes mailed to prospective employers, on the average you can expect only one or two interviews to result. These statistics alone should persuade you of the importance of a well-prepared and effective resume.

It is estimated that the average employment manager of a major corporation will read more than 20,000 resumes a year. Assuming no vacation time and 260 workdays in a year, this is equivalent to a weeknight workload of more than 75 resumes. Since employment managers must frequently travel, however, and most do take time off for holidays and vacations, it is estimated that this number is actually closer to 100. Since each resume averages 1½ pages in length, the employment manager has an average of 150 pages of reading to do each evening—a sizable chore!

Since the employment manager frequently spends the entire workday interviewing employment candidates, most resumes are normally read during the evening hours. Additionally, since evenings are often used by the manager to plan employment strategies, write recruitment advertising, and do other planning work necessary to the employment process, the amount of evening time left to read resumes may be only an hour or two.

In many cases, the employment manager is unable to read resumes until later in the evening. The early evening hours must often be used by the manager to make telephone calls to make job offers, follow up with candidates on outstanding offers, prescreen prospective candidates, and so on. These calls can usually be made only during the early part of the evening, leaving resume reading until later.

As you can well imagine, by 10 or 11 P.M. (following a full day of interviewing and several early evening phone calls) the typical employment manager is probably tired. He or she must now read an estimated 150 pages of resumes before retiring for the evening. You can well imagine how thoroughly these resumes will be read.

The technique used by most employment managers in reviewing resumes is not an in-depth, step-by-step reading process. Instead, it is a process of rapidly skimming the resume in a systematic way to determine whether or not the individual has qualifications and career interests consistent with the company's current employment requirements.

Considering all of these factors, resumes that are poorly prepared, sloppy, or in any other way difficult to read will receive very little consideration. Resumes are thought to be indicative of the overall personal style of the writer. Thus the inference that is frequently drawn from such poorly written resumes is that the applicant is likewise a sloppy, uncaring, of disorganized individual. Why then should the employment manager risk bringing this individual in for interviews? In such cases, the resume will more likely than not be stamped "no interest," and the employment manager will quickly move on to the next resume.

By now I hope that you are convinced that the general appearance of the resume is critical to its impact and effectiveness. It should be obvious that readability is likewise a major criterion for resume success. Resume organization and format are therefore extremely important factors to consider if your resume is to be successful in this difficult and competitive arena.

We now move on to a general discussion of the organization and operation of the typical company employment department. We carefully trace the steps through which your resume will likely pass, from the point of receipt by the department to final determination of application status.

RESUME PROCESSING

In the case of a company with a large employment department, the department is normally subdivided into functional specialties with each employment manager having accountability for a given area. For example, there may be an Administrative Employment Manager who has accountability for all administrative hiring: Accounting, Finance, Law, Data Processing, Human Resources, and so on. A Technical Employment Manager may also exist with accountability for all technical hiring: Research and Development, Central Engineering, Technical Services, Quality Control, and so on. Likewise, there may be an Operations Employment Manager with responsibility for all hiring related to manufacturing or plant operations. Marketing and Sales may also be represented by a separate employment manager.

As resumes are received by the employment department, there is usually one person who is designated to open and sort the mail into the appropriate categories for distribution to the individual employment managers. Once received by the employment manager's administrative assistant, the screening process will begin with the assistant "screening out" those resumes that are clearly not of interest to the employment manager. Thus if the employer is a steel company, the resumes of botanists, foresters, artists, and so forth are likely to be "screen out" at this point. Likewise, the administrative assistant may eliminate illegible, sloppy, or otherwise undesirable resumes.

The next step is for the employment manager to read the resume to determine whether there is an opening that is an appropriate match for the applicant's credentials. If not, the resume is usually marked "no interest," coded, and sent to Word Processing where an appropriate "no interest letter" is prepared and sent to the applicant. A copy of this letter along with the original resume is then returned to the employment department for filing and future reference.

At this point, "no interest" resumes are normally divided into two categories: (1) those in which the employer will probably have no future interest and (2) those having a high likelihood of interest at some future time ("future possibles"). Those in which the company is likely to have future interest are normally placed in an active file for future reference and review. In some cases, these "future interest" resumes are electronically scanned and stored on a computer resume data base. The remaining resumes are placed in a dead file with no possibility of future review.

When the employment manager determines that there is a reasonable match between the candidate's qualifications and the employment needs of a given department, the next step is a review of the resume by the hiring manager (the manager having the employment opening). Having reviewed the resume and determined that there is a probable match between the candidate's qualifications and interests and the requirements of the position, the hiring manager then notifies the employment manager of this interest and requests that the employment manager schedule the candidate for an interview. If, on the other hand, there is no interest, the hiring manager indicates this to the employment manager, and the resume is processed as described above.

In the case of the more sophisticated employers, there is usually one additional step in the process prior to extending an invitation for an interview. This step is referred to as the "telephone screen." This means that either the hiring manager or the employment manager will phone the candidate for the purpose of conducting a mini-interview. This telephone interview is intended to determine whether the candidate has sufficient qualifications and interest to warrant the time and expense of an on-site interview. Additionally, employers frequently use this preliminary interview to determine the validity of the information provided on the resume—a good reason to be factual in describing your qualifications and accomplishments!

There are three critical points in the resume-processing procedure at which your resume may be screened out and marked "no interest":

1. Administrative Assistant—screened for obvious incompatibility, incompleteness, sloppiness, or illegibility.
2. Employment Manager—screened for incompatibility with current openings and required candidate specifications.
3. Hiring Manager—screened for insufficient or inappropriate qualifications when compared with job requirements.

The highly competitive nature of the employment market, coupled with the thorough screening provided by the prospective employer, makes the preparation of a professional and effective resume an absolute must if one expects to be successful in the employment or job-hunting process! The resume cannot be left to chance. It must be carefully and deliberately designed if it is to successfully survive the rigors of the company's screening process.

Let's now take a closer look at the process used by the employment manager to screen resumes. How does he or she read a resume? What is the employment manager looking for? What will determine which resumes are screened out?

CANDIDATE SPECIFICATION

The very first step in the typical employment process is the preparation of an "employment requisition" by the hiring manager. This document is normally signed by the hiring manager's function head and human resources manager and is then forwarded to the appropriate employment manager. The purpose of the employment requisition is normally threefold:

1. Provides management authorization to hire.
2. Communicates basic data about the opening—title, level, salary range, reporting relationship, maximum starting salary, key job responsibilities, and so on.
3. Communicates basic or fundamental candidate specifications—type and level of education required, type and level of experience sought, technical and administrative skills required, and so forth.

Any good professional employment manager knows that the employment requisition seldom provides sufficient information to do a professional job of identifying and recruiting a well-qualified candidate. Considerably more information will usually be needed, and the employment manager is quick to arrange a meeting with the hiring manager to develop a more thorough and comprehensive candidate specification. The following are examples of typical "candidate specs."

Both of these candidate specs are highly detailed and very particular about the kind of qualifications that will satisfy the employment requirement. Very little has been left to chance. There is a clear understanding of both the educational and experience requirements for candidates who would receive serious consideration for employment.

Job Title: Chief Project Engineer
Job Level: 600 Points
Department: Central Engineering
Group: Mechanical
Education:
  Preferred: M.S. Mechanical Engineering
  Acceptable: B.S. Mechanical Engineering
Experience:
  Eight plus years experience in the design, development, installation, start-up, and debugging of Herrington Winders and auxiliary equipment. Demonstrated project leadership of projects in the eight to ten million range. Must have managed groups of five or more professionals.
Maximum Starting Salary: $85,000

Now let's look at another example.

Job Title: Director—Human Resources
Job Level: 1,200 Points
Department: Human Resources
Reporting Relationship: Sr. Vice President—Administration
Maximum Starting Salary: $100,000
Estimated Bonus: 20% to 30%
Education: Masters in Human Resources Management
Experience:

Requires a minimum 15 years experience in Human Resources in a corporation of 20,000 plus employees. Experience must include a broad range of Human Resources experience to include: Employment, Compensation & Benefits, Training & Development, and Employee Relations. Must be up-to-date with modern concepts in such areas as Human Resources Planning, Organization Effectiveness, and Executive Assessment. Experience must include demonstrated management leadership in the direction and guidance of decentralized, autonomous division Personnel functions in a multidivision and highly diversified company. Must have played key role in the development and execution of corporate-wide labor relations strategy in a multiunion setting. Must have managed a staff of at least 20 mid-management and professional level Human Resource professionals.

HOW RESUMES ARE READ

The candidate specification, as shown in the examples, is the basic tool of the employment manager when it comes to reading an employment resume. Actually the term "reading" is misleading when describing the process by which most employment managers review employment resumes. More precisely, the experienced employment manager rapidly scans for basic qualification highlights. The question that is constantly being asked by the employment manager is "Does this individual meet all of the critical qualifications of the candidate spec?"

The typical employment manager does not bother to read a resume in any degree of detail unless the preliminary scan indicates that the applicant has some of the essential skills and experience sought. In such cases, as key phrases and headings begin to match the candidate spec, the manager slows down and begins to read with a more critical eye. If several key criteria appear to be met, the employment professional will usually return to the beginning of the resume and begin a more thorough, detailed reading. To the contrary, if quick scanning of the resume indicates that few, if any, of the candidate's qualifications appear to match the current requirements, no time is lost in moving on to the next resume.

QUICK "KNOCKOUT" FACTORS

In scanning the employment resume, the employment manager is looking for key "knockout" factors—factors that clearly spell no interest and signal the employment manager to stop reading and move on to the next resume. Some of these quick knockout factors are:

1. Job objective incompatible with current openings
2. Inappropriate or insufficient educational credentials
3. Incompatible salary requirements
4. Geographic restrictions incompatible with current openings
5. Lack of U.S. citizenship or permanent resident status
6. Resume poorly organized, sloppy, or hard to read
7. Too many employers in too short a period of time
8. Too many pages—a book instead of a resume

Any of these factors quickly signals the employment manager that it would be a waste of time to read any further. These are generally sure knockout factors and warrant use of the no interest stamp. These same factors should be consciously avoided when preparing your employment resume.

CRITICAL READING

Having successfully passed the quick knockout factors test and avoided the no interest stamp, your resume must now undergo a more thorough and critical scanning. Concentration is now centered on the Work Experience section of the resume as the following questions are considered:

1. Are there sufficient years and level of experience?
2. Is experience in the appropriate areas?
3. Is the candidate missing any critical experience?
4. Does the candidate have sufficient breadth and depth of technical knowledge?
5. Does the applicant have sufficient management or leadership skills?
6. Are any technical or managerial skills missing?
7. Is there a solid record of accomplishment?
8. How does this candidate compare with others currently under consideration?
9. Based on overall qualifications, what are the probabilities that an offer would be made—50%, 75%, 90% (as measured against past candidates with similar credentials)?

There is little advice that can be given to the resume writer in this area. You are what you are, and the facts cannot be changed. You either have the qualifications and experience sought, or you don't. At best, you can hope that through diligent application of professional resume preparation techniques, you have done an excellent job of clearly presenting your overall skills, knowledge, accomplishments, and other pertinent professional qualifications.

There is nothing mysterious or mystical about the resume-reading process. It is essentially logical and straightforward. It is a process whereby the employment manager or hiring manager simply compares the candidate's qualifications and interests with the candidate's hiring spec in an effort to determine the candidate's degree of qualifications and the desirability of moving to the interview (or phone screen) step. Neatness, clarity, organization, style, and format are the key ingredients; they are critical to the impact and effectiveness of the employment resume.

Chapter 2

Introduction to Cover Letters

The cover letter that accompanies your employment resume is perhaps one of the most important letters you will ever write. Other than your resume, it is the single key document that will introduce you to a prospective employer and, if well-written, pave the way to that all-important job interview. It is an integral part of your overall job hunting campaign, and it can make or break you, depending upon how well it is written. Construction of this document should therefore be given very careful attention. The care that you give to writing this letter will certainly be a major factor in getting your job search off to an excellent start. Conversely, a poorly written letter will surely scuttle your campaign before it even begins.

THE PURPOSE OF THE COVER LETTER

Before you can expect to write an effective cover letter, you must understand its purpose. Without a clear understanding of what this letter is intended to accomplish, chances are it will be poorly designed, vague, and totally ineffective. On the other hand, understanding the purpose of this letter is truly paramount to maximizing its impact and effectiveness.

What is the purpose of the cover letter? What is it intended to do?

Well, first and foremost, it is a business letter used to transmit your resume to a prospective employer. So, it is a business transmittal letter. Second, it is a letter of introduction. It is used not only to transmit your resume but also to introduce you and your background to the employer. Third, and importantly, it is a sales letter, intended to convince the prospective employer that you have something valuable to contribute and that it will be worth the employer's time to grant you an interview.

To summarize, then, the purpose of a cover letter is:

1. To serve as a business transmittal letter for your resume.
2. To introduce you and your employment credentials to the employer.
3. To generate employer interest in interviewing you.

Certainly, knowing that these are the three main objectives of a well-written cover letter will provide you with some basic starting points. For now, it is important to simply keep these objectives in mind as we further explore the topic of effective cover letters.

FROM THE EMPLOYER'S PERSPECTIVE

When contemplating good cover letter design and construction, it is important to keep one very important fact in mind: The cover letter must be written from the employer's perspective.

Stated differently, good cover letter writing must take into consideration that the end result you seek is employer action. More specifically, you want the employer to grant you an interview, so it is important to understand those factors that will motivate an employer to do so.

To understand this important phenomenon, it is necessary to realistically address the following questions:

1. How does the employer read the cover letter?
2. What are the key factors the employer is looking for (and expects to find) in the cover letter?
3. What are the motivational factors that will pique the employer's curiosity and create a desire to interview you?

I think you will agree that these are some very important questions to ask if you are to be successful in designing cover letters that will be truly helpful to your job hunting program. You must pay close attention to the needs of the prospective employer, rather than just your own, if you expect to write cover letters that will motivate him or her to take action. Cover letters must, therefore, be "employer focused" rather than "job searcher focused" if you want to really maximize their overall effectiveness.

Top sales producers have always known that the most important principle in sales success, whether selling goods or services, is selling to the needs of the buyer. What is the customer really buying? Where are the priorities? What specific needs does he or she need to satisfy? Without knowing the answers to these questions, it is easy for the salesperson to emphasize product characteristics and attributes that have absolutely no relationship to the customer's real needs, and deemphasize characteristics and attributes that are truly important. The result—no sale!

In the ideal sense, therefore, it is important to research your target companies very well to determine what it is that they are buying (i.e., looking for in a successful employment candidate). If you are conducting a general broadcast campaign covering several hundred companies, such individual company research may simply not be feasible. If, on the other hand, you are targeting a dozen or so employers for whom you would really like to work, such research is not only feasible but should be considered an "absolute must." Careful advance research, in this case, will pay huge dividends, returning your initial investment of time and effort manyfold.

Even in the case of the general broadcast campaign, where you have targeted several hundred companies, there are clearly some things that you can do to focus your cover letters on the real needs of these employers. Here are some guidelines for conducting meaningful employer needs research:

1. Divide your target list of employers into industry groupings.
2. Using industry trade publications and key newspapers (available in most libraries), thoroughly research each industry grouping for answers to the following questions:
   a. What is the general state of this industry?
   b. What are the major problems faced by companies in this industry?
   c. What are the barriers or roadblocks that stand in the way of solving these problems
   d. What knowledge, skills, and capabilities are needed to address these problems and roadblocks?
   e. What major trends and changes are being driven by companies in this industry?
   f. What new knowledge, skills, and capabilities are needed to successfully drive these changes and trends?

Having conducted this research, you are now in a position to better focus your cover letter on key needs areas of interest to the majority of companies in each of your targeted industry groupings. This provides you with the opportunity to showcase your overall knowledge, skills, and capabilities in relation to those important needs areas. Such focusing substantially increases your chances for hitting the employer's bull's-eye, which will result in job interviews.

Where you can narrow your list to a dozen or so key companies, individual company research can have even greater payoff. Here, you have the opportunity to really zero in on the specific needs of the employer, and you can bring into play a number of research techniques for doing so. The research you do here can, in fact, be tailored to each individual firm; so you can substantially increase your probability of success and up by quite a bit the number of potential interview opportunities.

In many ways, the methodology used in conducting single-firm research is similar to that already described for industry-wide research. You will note some of these similarities as you review the following guidelines for researching the single firm.

1. Determine the firms you would like to target for individual research (firms for which you would really like to work).
2. Using industry trade publications and key newspapers (available at your local library) as well as annual reports, 10K forms, and product literature (available from the target firm's public affairs and marketing departments), thoroughly research for answers to the following questions:
   a. What is the general state of the company?
   b. How does it stack up against competition?
   c. What are the key problems and issues with which it is currently wrestling?
   d. What are the key barriers that must be removed in order to resolve these problems/issues?
   e. What knowledge, skills, and capabilities are needed to remove these key barriers?
   f. What are the company's strategic goals?
   g. What are the key changes that will need to come about for realization of these goals?
   h. What new knowledge, skills, and capabilities will be needed to bring about these critical changes?

Here, as with research of industry groupings, individual company research enables you to use the cover letter to highlight your knowledge, skills, and capabilities in areas that are of importance to the firm. In the case of individual firm research, however, there is the added advantage of being able to tailor the cover letter to target your qualifications to very specific, known needs of the employer. This can provide you with a substantial competitive advantage!

Another technique that you should employ when doing individual firm research is networking. If you don't already belong, you might consider joining specific industry or professional associations to which employees of your individual target firms belong. Using your common membership in these organizations as the basis, you can call these employees for certain inside information. Here are some questions you might consider asking:

1. Is the firm hiring people in your functional specialty?
2. Are there openings in this group now?
3. Who within the company is the key line manager (i.e., outside human resources) responsible for hiring for this group?
4. What are the key things this manager tends to look for in a successful candidate (e.g., technical knowledge, skills, style)?
5. What key problems/issues is the group currently wrestling with?
6. What kinds of skills and capabilities are they looking for to address these issues?
7. What are the major strategic changes this group is attempting to bring about?
8. What qualifications and attributes is the group seeking to help them orchestrate these strategic changes?

Answers to these questions can give you a tremendous competitive advantage when designing an effective cover letter and employment resume. You will have substantial ammunition for targeting and highlighting those qualifications of greatest interest to the employer. Here, you can make the most of your opportunity for successful self-marketing by focusing on the critical needs not only of the organization but of the functional hiring group as well. Clearly, this is a technique you should employ if you want to maximize your chances of getting hired!

The underlying principle behind this needs research methodology, whether industry grouping or individual company research, is that organizations are always looking for individuals who will be "value adding"—that is, individuals who can help them solve key problems and realize their strategic goals. These are the candidates who are seen as the value-adding change agents—the leaders who will help move the company ahead rather than cause it to stand still. Employer needs research will allow you to design effective cover letters that can truly set you apart from the competition and substantially improve your chances for landing interviews.

Chapter 3

Introduction to Interviewing

INTERVIEW THEORY

By definition, the employment interview is a two-way discussion between a job applicant and a prospective employer with the objective of exploring the probable compatibility between the applicant's qualifications and the needs of the employer, for the purpose of making an employment decision. It is the intent of both parties during this discussion to gain as much relevant information as possible on which to base this decision. Further, it is their intent to use the information obtained during the interview process to predict, with some level of accuracy, the probability for a successful match.

Modern interview theory subscribes to a single, universal theory around which almost all employment selection processes are designed. This theory is as follows:

Past performance and behavior are the most reliable factors known in predicting future performance and behavior.

With this theory in mind, it is important for the interviewee to know that the employer's basic interview strategy will be to use the interview discussion to uncover past performance and behavioral evidence in those areas that the employer considers important to successful job performance. These important areas are commonly known as selection criteria. It is against these criteria that the employer will be comparing the qualifications of prospective candidates, and eventually arriving at a final employment decision.

It should be evident that, as the candidate, it will be necessary for you to get some definition of these selection criteria if you expect to be successful in developing an effective counterstrategy. The key to accomplishing this is to force yourself to think as the employer does. Specifically, the question to ask is, "How does the employer go about developing candidate selection criteria?"

DEVELOPING THE CANDIDATE SPECIFICATION

The first step used by the employer in structuring an interview strategy is usually development of what is commonly known in professional employment circles as the candidate specification. This document typically describes the candidate sought by the employer in terms of such qualifications as knowledge, skills, experience, and other dimensions thought to be necessary to successful job performance. The candidate specification is normally prepared by the hiring manager, with occasional assistance provided by other department managers and/or the human resources department.

When well-prepared and carefully thought out, this specification can be a very valuable document. It frequently serves as the focal point for the employer's entire interview strategy. Advance knowledge of the contents of the document could prove equally as valuable to the interviewee, since it could be used as the basis for formulating an effective counterstrategy. Since this is not a practical consideration, the candidate must go through the same process as the employer in attempting to construct this specification.

When preparing the candidate specification, most hiring managers will review such things as the position description, current year's objectives, business plans, and so on. In essence, the manager is reviewing the general responsibilities of the position in an effort to determine the kind of person needed to meet these requirements. Such review typically results in a candidate specification that includes the following general categories: (1) education, (2) knowledge, (3) experience, (4) skills, and (5) personal attributes.

A typical candidate specification would probably read as follows:

Education.   BS degree in mechanical engineering preferred; degree in chemical engineering acceptable.

Knowledge.   Paper machine project engineering; wet end sheet formation.

Experience.   Two plus years in design, installation, and start-up of tissue and/or towel machines; twin wire-forming machine experience helpful.

Skills.   Solid engineering skills in mechanical design; project leadership of contractor personnel.

Personal Attributes.   Intelligent, articulate; able to work effectively in fast-paced construction/start-up environment; willing to work long hours, including frequent evenings and weekends; willing to travel at least 40 percent of the time, including weekend travel.

Although admittedly a fairly abbreviated description, this candidate specification is very similar to those used by most organizations.

The employer's strategy now becomes one of interviewing to determine how well the prospective candidate meets this specification. In my example, some of the candidate's qualifications for the position will be evident from a quick review of the applicant's resume. However, such areas as "level of engineering knowledge" and "level of intelligence" cannot be measured by using the applicant's resume. These can only be ascertained through the interview process.

INTERVIEWEE STRATEGY

Considering the employer's interview strategy, as defined earlier in this chapter, how can the interviewee formulate a meaningful counterstrategy? What steps can the interviewee take to maximize the potential for a favorable interview outcome?

In my judgment, there are a number of things you can do to duplicate fairly accurately the employer's thinking process, thereby allowing yourself to plan an effective counterstrategy that will allow you to "stack the deck" in your favor. Here are some of them:

Advance Information

You will want to obtain as much information as possible about the position, prior to the actual interview. Although much of this information is readily available just for the asking, it has always amazed me how few employment candidates ever bother to request it.

Don't be shy about requesting this information since many employers are willing to provide it to you if it is available. The strategic advantage of acquiring this information in advance of the interview far outweighs the risks of an employer politely declining your request.

Where available without too much difficulty, you should request the following in advance of your visit:

1. Position job description
2. Job objectives—current year
3. Department objectives—current year
4. Departmental or functional business plan
5. Annual report

Candidate Specification

During your initial telephone conversation with the employer, you should make it a point to ask for a verbal description of the kind of person they are seeking. Ask the employer to tell you not only what qualifications they are seeking, but also which of these qualifications they consider to be the most important. If time allows, and you can avoid sounding pushy, ask why these factors are considered to be important.

If the employer begins to balk, suggest that you need this information to determine whether or not you are interested in the position and whether you feel you have sufficient qualifications to warrant investing your time in further discussions. This should seem a reasonable request at this stage of the relationship and you will usually get what you want.

It is best to request answers to these questions at the beginning of your discussions, since you will lose considerable leverage once the employer has ascertained that you are interested in the position and are prepared to go to the next step.

Position Analysis

As with the employer, one of your first steps in formulating your interview strategy is to conduct an analysis of the position for which you will be interviewing. This procedure is similar to the employers' when they form the candidate specification. You will need to review the key responsibilities of the position in an effort to translate these into probable candidate selection criteria. The advance documents that you have collected from the employer should prove very helpful at this point.

The following set of questions should help you to walk through this process in a logical and thorough fashion. Space is provided for you to fill in your answers as you go along.

1. What are the *key ongoing responsibilities* of this position? (Job description should prove helpful here.) _____

_____

_____

_____

2. What are the *key technical problems* to be solved, and *challenges* to be met, in satisfying these ongoing responsibilities? _____

_____

_____

_____

3. What *technical* and/or *professional knowledge* does this suggest that a person must have in order to successfully solve these problems and meet these challenges? _____

_____

_____

_____

4. What are the *specific objectives* for this position for the *current year?* _____

_____

_____

_____

5. What are the *key technical challenges* that must be met and *problems* that must be solved if these objectives are to be successfully achieved? _____

_____

_____

_____

6. What *technical* and/or *professional knowledge* does this suggest that a person must have in order to successfully solve these problems and accomplish these objectives? _____

_____

Combined Candidate Specification

You now have two sources from which to construct a candidate specification. The first is the initial telephone conversation with the prospective employer, and the second is the position analysis that you have just completed.

Chances are, if you have done a particularly thorough job with your position analysis, you may well have given more thought to the qualifications necessary to successful job performance than has the employer with whom you will be interviewing. This could serve to place you at a decided strategic advantage during the interview, allowing you to highlight important aspects of your background that are critical to achievement of desired organizational results.

Be careful not to get carried away with your newfound power, however, since this could serve to alienate the interviewer and cause you to be labeled as a show-off or "know-it-all."

Now, pause for a moment to review the overall candidate requirements as defined by both you and the employer. With these requirements in mind, use the following set of questions to help you to translate these overall requirements into a combined candidate specification.

1. *Formal Education:* Considering the technical challenges of this position and the knowledge required, what formal education/training should the ideal candidate have (degree level and major)? Why? _____

    _____

    _____

2. *Training:* What informal education (training courses, seminars, etc.) would likely provide the required knowledge? _____

    _____

    _____

3. *Experience:* What level (number of years) and kind of experience would likely yield the depth and breadth of knowledge necessary for successful performance in this position? _____

    _____

    _____

4. *Related Experience:* What related or similar kinds of experience might yield the same kind of knowledge, and would therefore be an acceptable alternative?

    _____

    _____

    _____

5. *Skills:* What specific skills ar required by the position, and how might these be acquired? _____

    _____

    _____

6. *Personal Attributes:* What personal attributes and characteristics are probably important for successful performance of this position? _____

    _____

    _____

Job Seekers Guide to Wall Street Recruiters

Abbatiello, Christine Murphy — *Information Technology Recruiter*
Winter, Wyman & Company
1100 Circle 75 Parkway, Suite 800
Atlanta, GA 30339
Telephone: (770) 933-1525
Recruiter Classification: Contingency; **Lowest/Average Salary:** $30,000/$60,000; **Industry Concentration:** Generalist with a primary focus in Financial Services, Insurance; **Function Concentration:** Generalist

Abbott, Peter D. — *Partner*
The Abbott Group, Inc.
530 College Parkway, Suite N
Annapolis, MD 21401
Telephone: (410) 757-4100
Recruiter Classification: Retained; **Lowest/Average Salary:** $90,000/$90,000; **Industry Concentration:** Generalist with a primary focus in Venture Capital; **Function Concentration:** Generalist with a primary focus in Administration, Engineering, Finance/Accounting, General Management, Human Resources, Marketing, Research and Development

Abell, Vincent W. — *Executive Recruiter*
MSI International
8521 Leesburg Pike, Suite 435
Vienna, VA 22182
Telephone: (703) 893-5669
Recruiter Classification: Contingency; **Lowest/Average Salary:** $30,000/$75,000; **Industry Concentration:** Generalist with a primary focus in Financial Services; **Function Concentration:** Generalist with a primary focus in Administration, Engineering, Finance/Accounting, General Management, Marketing, Sales

Abernathy, Donald E. — *Accounting Recruiter*
Don Richard Associates of Charlotte
2650 One First Union Center
301 South College Street
Charlotte, NC 28202-6000
Telephone: (704) 377-6447
Recruiter Classification: Contingency, Executive Temporary; **Lowest/Average Salary:** $30,000/$50,000; **Industry Concentration:** Generalist with a primary focus in Financial Services; **Function Concentration:** Finance/Accounting

Abert, Janice — *Vice President*
Ledbetter/Davidson International, Inc.
101 Park Avenue
Suite 2508
New York, NY 10178
Telephone: (212) 687-6600
Recruiter Classification: Retained; **Lowest/Average Salary:** $90,000/$90,000; **Industry Concentration:** Financial Services; **Function Concentration:** Finance/Accounting, General Management, Human Resources, Marketing, Research and Development, Sales

Abramson, Roye — *Associate*
Source Services Corporation
379 Thornall Street
Edison, NJ 08837
Telephone: (908) 494-2800
Recruiter Classification: Contingency; **Lowest/Average Salary:** $30,000/$50,000; **Industry Concentration:** Financial Services; **Function Concentration:** Engineering, Finance/Accounting

Ackerman, Larry R. — *Vice President*
Spectrum Search Associates, Inc.
1888 Century Park East, Suite 320
Los Angeles, CA 90067
Telephone: (310) 286-6921
Recruiter Classification: Contingency; **Lowest/Average Salary:** $30,000/$50,000; **Industry Concentration:** Financial Services; **Function Concentration:** Finance/Accounting

Adams, Amy — *Associate Partner*
Richard, Wayne and Roberts
24 Greenway Plaza, Suite 1304
Houston, TX 77046-2493
Telephone: (713) 629-6681
Recruiter Classification: Retained; **Lowest/Average Salary:** $50,000/$90,000; **Industry Concentration:** Generalist with a primary focus in Financial Services; **Function Concentration:** Generalist with a primary focus in Finance/Accounting

Adams, Jeffrey C. — *Managing Principal*
Telford, Adams & Alexander/Jeffrey C. Adams & Co., Inc.
455 Market Street, Suite 1910
San Francisco, CA 94105
Telephone: (415) 546-4150
Recruiter Classification: Retained; **Lowest/Average Salary:** $50,000/$90,000; **Industry Concentration:** Generalist with a primary focus in Financial Services, Insurance; **Function Concentration:** Generalist

Adams, Len — *Executive Vice President*
The KPA Group
150 Broadway, Suite 1802
New York, NY 10038
Telephone: (212) 964-3640
Recruiter Classification: Contingency, Executive Temporary; **Lowest/Average Salary:** $20,000/$40,000; **Industry Concentration:** Financial Services; **Function Concentration:** Finance/Accounting, Human Resources

✓**Adler, Louis S.** — *President*
CJA - The Adler Group
17852 17th Street
Suite 209
Tustin, CA 92780
Telephone: (714) 573-1820
Recruiter Classification: Retained; **Lowest/Average Salary:** $50,000/$90,000; **Industry Concentration:** Generalist with a primary focus in Financial Services; **Function Concentration:** Generalist with a primary focus in Engineering, Finance/Accounting, General Management, Human Resources, Marketing, Research and Development, Sales

Afforde, Sharon Gould — *Executive Recruiter*
Jacobson Associates
150 North Wacker Drive
Suite 1120
Chicago, IL 60606
Telephone: (312) 726-1578
Recruiter Classification: Contingency; **Lowest/Average Salary:** $20,000/$50,000; **Industry Concentration:** Insurance; **Function Concentration:** Generalist

Agee, Jo Etta — *Account Executive*
Chrisman & Company, Incorporated
44 Montgomery Street, Suite 2360
San Francisco, CA 94104
Telephone: (213) 620-1192
Recruiter Classification: Retained; **Lowest/Average Salary:**
$75,000/$90,000; **Industry Concentration:** Financial Services;
Function Concentration: Generalist with a primary focus in
Finance/Accounting, General Management, Human Resources,
Women/Minorities

Akin, J.R. "Jack" — *President*
J.R. Akin & Company Inc.
7181 College Parkway, Suite 30
Fort Myers, FL 33907
Telephone: (941) 395-1575
Recruiter Classification: Retained; **Lowest/Average Salary:**
$90,000/$90,000; **Industry Concentration:** Generalist with a
primary focus in Insurance; **Function Concentration:**
Generalist with a primary focus in Administration, Engineering,
Finance/Accounting, General Management, Human Resources,
Marketing, Sales, Women/Minorities

Albert, Richard — *Associate*
Source Services Corporation
One CityPlace, Suite 170
St. Louis, MO 63141
Telephone: (314) 432-4500
Recruiter Classification: Contingency; **Lowest/Average Salary:**
$30,000/$50,000; **Industry Concentration:** Financial Services;
Function Concentration: Engineering, Finance/Accounting

Alexander, John T. — *Managing Principal*
Telford, Adams & Alexander
402 West Broadway, Suite 900
San Diego, CA 92101-3542
Telephone: (619) 238-5686
Recruiter Classification: Retained; **Lowest/Average Salary:**
$50,000/$75,000; **Industry Concentration:** Generalist with a
primary focus in Financial Services; **Function Concentration:**
Generalist with a primary focus in Administration,
Finance/Accounting, General Management, Human Resources,
Sales

Alford, Holly — *Associate*
Source Services Corporation
5429 LBJ Freeway, Suite 275
Dallas, TX 75240
Telephone: (214) 387-1600
Recruiter Classification: Contingency; **Lowest/Average Salary:**
$30,000/$50,000; **Industry Concentration:** Financial Services;
Function Concentration: Engineering, Finance/Accounting

✓**Allard, Susan** — *Partner*
Allard Associates
1059 Court Street, Suite 114
Woodland, CA 95695
Telephone: (800) 291-5279
Recruiter Classification: Retained; **Lowest/Average Salary:**
$75,000/$90,000; **Industry Concentration:** Financial Services;
Function Concentration: Generalist with a primary focus in
Administration, General Management, Marketing, Sales,
Women/Minorities

Allen, Jean E. — *Principal*
Lamalie Amrop International
200 Park Avenue
New York, NY 10166-0136
Telephone: (212) 953-7900
Recruiter Classification: Retained; **Lowest/Average Salary:**
$90,000/$90,000; **Industry Concentration:** Generalist with a
primary focus in Financial Services; **Function Concentration:**
Generalist

✓**Allen, Scott** — *Executive Recruiter*
Chrisman & Company, Incorporated
350 South Figueroa Street, Suite 550
Los Angeles, CA 90071
Telephone: (213) 620-1192
Recruiter Classification: Retained; **Lowest/Average Salary:**
$75,000/$90,000; **Industry Concentration:** Financial Services,
Insurance, Venture Capital; **Function Concentration:** Generalist
with a primary focus in Finance/Accounting, General
Management, Women/Minorities

Allen, Wade H. — *President*
Cendea Connection International
13740 Research Boulevard
Building 0-1
Austin, TX 78750
Telephone: (512) 219-6000
Recruiter Classification: Retained; **Lowest/Average Salary:**
$75,000/$90,000; **Industry Concentration:** Generalist with a
primary focus in Venture Capital; **Function Concentration:**
Generalist with a primary focus in General Management,
Marketing, Sales

Allen, William L. — *Vice President*
The Hindman Company
Browenton Place, Suite 110
2000 Warrington Way
Louisville, KY 40222
Telephone: (502) 426-4040
Recruiter Classification: Retained; **Lowest/Average Salary:**
$50,000/$90,000; **Industry Concentration:** Generalist with a
primary focus in Financial Services; **Function Concentration:**
Generalist with a primary focus in Engineering,
Finance/Accounting, General Management, Human Resources,
Marketing, Sales

Allgire, Mary L. — *Vice President*
Kenzer Corp.
625 North Michigan Avenue, Suite 1244
Chicago, IL 60611
Telephone: (312) 266-0976
Recruiter Classification: Retained; **Lowest/Average Salary:**
$50,000/$90,000; **Industry Concentration:** Financial Services,
Venture Capital; **Function Concentration:** Generalist with a
primary focus in Administration, Finance/Accounting, General
Management, Human Resources, Marketing, Research and
Development, Sales

Allred, J. Michael — *Director*
Spencer Stuart
One Atlantic Center, Suite 3230
1201 West Peachtree Street
Atlanta, GA 30309
Telephone: (404) 892-2800
Recruiter Classification: Retained; **Lowest/Average Salary:**
$90,000/$90,000; **Industry Concentration:** Financial Services,
Venture Capital; **Function Concentration:** Generalist with a
primary focus in General Management, Marketing, Sales

Alringer, Marc — *Associate*
Source Services Corporation
4510 Executive Drive, Suite 200
San Diego, CA 92121
Telephone: (619) 552-0300
Recruiter Classification: Contingency; **Lowest/Average Salary:** $30,000/$50,000; **Industry Concentration:** Financial Services; **Function Concentration:** Engineering, Finance/Accounting

Altreuter, Rose — *President Interim Professionals*
ALTCO Temporary Services
100 Menlo Park
Edison, NJ 08837
Telephone: (908) 549-6100
Recruiter Classification: Executive Temporary; **Lowest/Average Salary:** $20,000/$30,000; **Industry Concentration:** Financial Services; **Function Concentration:** Finance/Accounting, Human Resources, Marketing, Women/Minorities

Altreuter, Rose — *Manager Interim Professionals*
The ALTCO Group
100 Menlo Park, Ste. 214
Edison, NJ 08837
Telephone: (732) 549-6100
Recruiter Classification: Contingency; **Lowest/Average Salary:** $40,000/$50,000; **Industry Concentration:** Generalist with a primary focus in Financial Services, Insurance; **Function Concentration:** Generalist with a primary focus in Administration, Engineering, Finance/Accounting, Human Resources, Marketing, Research and Development

Amato, Joseph — *President*
Amato & Associates, Inc.
388 Market Street, Suite 500
San Francisco, CA 94111
Telephone: (415) 781-7664
Recruiter Classification: Contingency; **Lowest/Average Salary:** $50,000/$75,000; **Industry Concentration:** Insurance; **Function Concentration:** General Management, Marketing, Sales

Ambler, Peter W. — *President*
Peter W. Ambler Company
14651 Dallas Parkway, Suite 402
Dallas, TX 75240
Telephone: (972) 404-8712
Recruiter Classification: Retained; **Lowest/Average Salary:** $60,000/$90,000; **Industry Concentration:** Generalist with a primary focus in Financial Services; **Function Concentration:** Generalist with a primary focus in Engineering, Finance/Accounting, General Management, Human Resources, Marketing, Research and Development, Sales

Amico, Robert — *Associate*
Source Services Corporation
71 Spit Brook Road, Suite 305
Nashua, NH 03060
Telephone: (603) 888-7650
Recruiter Classification: Contingency; **Lowest/Average Salary:** $30,000/$50,000; **Industry Concentration:** Financial Services; **Function Concentration:** Engineering, Finance/Accounting

Amilowski, Maria — *Recruiter*
Highland Search Group
565 Fifth Avenue, 22nd Floor
New York, NY 10017
Telephone: (212) 328-1113
Recruiter Classification: Retained; **Lowest/Average Salary:** $90,000/$90,000; **Industry Concentration:** Financial Services, Insurance, Venture Capital; **Function Concentration:** Generalist with a primary focus in Administration, Finance/Accounting, General Management, Human Resources, Sales, Women/Minorities

Anderson, Maria H. — *Senior Consultant*
Barton Associates, Inc.
One Riverway, Suite 2500
Houston, TX 77056
Telephone: (713) 961-9111
Recruiter Classification: Retained; **Lowest/Average Salary:** $75,000/$90,000; **Industry Concentration:** Generalist with a primary focus in Financial Services; **Function Concentration:** Generalist with a primary focus in Administration, Finance/Accounting, General Management, Human Resources, Marketing, Research and Development, Women/Minorities

Anderson, Mary — *Managing Director*
Source Services Corporation
425 California Street, Suite 1200
San Francisco, CA 94104
Telephone: (415) 434-2410
Recruiter Classification: Contingency; **Lowest/Average Salary:** $30,000/$50,000; **Industry Concentration:** Financial Services; **Function Concentration:** Engineering, Finance/Accounting

Anderson, Matthew — *Associate*
Source Services Corporation
161 Ottawa NW, Suite 409D
Grand Rapids, MI 49503
Telephone: (616) 451-2400
Recruiter Classification: Contingency; **Lowest/Average Salary:** $30,000/$50,000; **Industry Concentration:** Financial Services; **Function Concentration:** Engineering, Finance/Accounting

Anderson, Richard — *Vice President*
Grant Cooper and Associates
795 Office Parkway, Suite 117
St. Louis, MO 63141
Telephone: (314) 567-4690
Recruiter Classification: Retained; **Lowest/Average Salary:** $60,000/$90,000; **Industry Concentration:** Generalist with a primary focus in Financial Services; **Function Concentration:** Generalist with a primary focus in Administration, Engineering, Finance/Accounting, General Management, Human Resources, Marketing, Sales

Anderson, Shawn — *Manager*
Temporary Accounting Personnel, Inc.
955 East Henrietta Road
Rochester, NY 14623
Telephone: (716) 427-9930
Recruiter Classification: Executive Temporary; **Lowest/Average Salary:** $20,000/$30,000; **Industry Concentration:** Generalist with a primary focus in Financial Services; **Function Concentration:** Finance/Accounting, Human Resources

Anderson, Steve — *Executive Recruiter*
CPS Inc.
One Westbrook Corporate Centre, Suite 600
Westchester, IL 60154
Telephone: (708) 531-8370
Recruiter Classification: Contingency; **Lowest/Average Salary:** $30,000/$50,000; **Industry Concentration:** Generalist with a primary focus in Financial Services, Insurance; **Function Concentration:** Engineering, Research and Development, Sales, Women/Minorities

Anderson, Terry — *Executive Director*
Intech Summit Group, Inc.
5075 Shoreham Place, Suite 280
San Diego, CA 92116
Telephone: (619) 452-2100
Recruiter Classification: Retained; **Lowest/Average Salary:** $60,000/$75,000; **Industry Concentration:** Generalist with a primary focus in Financial Services; **Function Concentration:** Generalist with a primary focus in Finance/Accounting, Marketing

Andre, Jacques P. — *Partner*
Ray & Berndtson
245 Park Avenue, 33rd Floor
New York, NY 10167
Telephone: (212) 370-1316
Recruiter Classification: Retained; **Lowest/Average Salary:** $90,000/$90,000; **Industry Concentration:** Financial Services; **Function Concentration:** Generalist

✔**Andujo, Michele M.** — *Executive Recruiter*
Chrisman & Company, Incorporated
350 South Figueroa Street, Suite 550
Los Angeles, CA 90071
Telephone: (213) 620-1192
Recruiter Classification: Retained; **Lowest/Average Salary:** $75,000/$90,000; **Industry Concentration:** Generalist with a primary focus in Financial Services, Insurance; **Function Concentration:** Generalist with a primary focus in Finance/Accounting, General Management, Human Resources, Marketing, Women/Minorities

Anwar, Tarin — *Managing Director*
Jay Gaines & Company, Inc.
450 Park Avenue
New York, NY 10022
Telephone: (212) 308-9222
Recruiter Classification: Retained; **Lowest/Average Salary:** $200,000/$400,000; **Industry Concentration:** Financial Services, Insurance; **Function Concentration:** Finance/Accounting, General Management, Marketing, Sales

Archer, Sandra F. — *Director*
Ryan, Miller & Associates Inc.
4601 Wilshire Boulevard, Suite 225
Los Angeles, CA 90010
Telephone: (213) 938-4768
Recruiter Classification: Contingency; **Lowest/Average Salary:** $50,000/$60,000; **Industry Concentration:** Generalist with a primary focus in Financial Services; **Function Concentration:** Generalist with a primary focus in Finance/Accounting

Argenio, Michelangelo — *Director*
Spencer Stuart
277 Park Avenue, 29th Floor
New York, NY 10172
Telephone: (212) 336-0200
Recruiter Classification: Retained; **Lowest/Average Salary:** $90,000/$90,000; **Industry Concentration:** Financial Services; **Function Concentration:** Generalist with a primary focus in Finance/Accounting, General Management, Marketing

Argentin, Jo — *Consultant*
Executive Placement Consultants, Inc.
2700 River Road, Suite 107
Des Plaines, IL 60018
Telephone: (847) 298-6445
Recruiter Classification: Contingency; **Lowest/Average Salary:** $40,000/$75,000; **Industry Concentration:** Generalist with a primary focus in Financial Services; **Function Concentration:** Finance/Accounting, Human Resources, Marketing

Arms, Douglas — *Legal Consultant*
TOPAZ International, Inc.
383 Northfield Avenue
West Orange, NJ 07052
Telephone: (201) 669-7300
Recruiter Classification: Contingency; **Lowest/Average Salary:** $40,000/$75,000; **Industry Concentration:** Financial Services; **Function Concentration:** Generalist with a primary focus in Women/Minorities

Arms, Douglas — *Legal Consultant*
TOPAZ Legal Solutions
383 Northfield Avenue
West Orange, NJ 07052
Telephone: (201) 669-7300
Recruiter Classification: Executive Temporary; **Lowest/Average Salary:** $40,000/$75,000; **Industry Concentration:** Financial Services; **Function Concentration:** Generalist with a primary focus in Women/Minorities

Aronin, Michael — *Senior Consultant*
Fisher-Todd Associates
535 Fifth Avenue, Suite 710
New York, NY 10017
Telephone: (212) 986-9052
Recruiter Classification: Contingency; **Lowest/Average Salary:** $50,000/$75,000; **Industry Concentration:** Generalist with a primary focus in Financial Services; **Function Concentration:** Generalist with a primary focus in Administration, General Management, Marketing, Research and Development, Sales, Women/Minorities

Aronow, Lawrence E. — *President*
Aronow Associates, Inc.
One Pennsylvania Plaza, Suite 2131
New York, NY 10119
Telephone: (212) 947-3777
Recruiter Classification: Contingency; **Lowest/Average Salary:** $50,000/$75,000; **Industry Concentration:** Financial Services; **Function Concentration:** Finance/Accounting, General Management, Marketing, Sales

Ascher, Susan P. — *President*
The Ascher Group
25 Pompton Avenue, Suite 310
Verona, NJ 07044
Telephone: (201) 239-6116
Recruiter Classification: Retained, Executive Temporary;
Lowest/Average Salary: $50,000/$90,000; **Industry
Concentration:** Generalist with a primary focus in Financial
Services, Insurance; **Function Concentration:** Generalist with a
primary focus in Administration, Finance/Accounting, General
Management, Human Resources, Marketing, Women/Minorities

Ashton, Edward J. — *President*
E.J. Ashton & Associates, Ltd.
P.O. Box 1048
Lake Zurich, IL 60047-1048
Telephone: (847) 540-9922
Recruiter Classification: Contingency; **Lowest/Average Salary:**
$30,000/$60,000; **Industry Concentration:** Insurance; **Function
Concentration:** Generalist with a primary focus in Administration,
Finance/Accounting, General Management, Marketing, Sales

Aston, Kathy — *Director*
Marra Peters & Partners
Millburn Esplanade
Millburn, NJ 07041
Telephone: (201) 376-8999
Recruiter Classification: Retained; **Lowest/Average Salary:**
$60,000/$90,000; **Industry Concentration:** Generalist with a
primary focus in Financial Services; **Function Concentration:**
Generalist with a primary focus in Administration, Engineering,
Finance/Accounting, General Management, Human Resources,
Marketing, Research and Development, Sales

Atkinson, S. Graham — *Principal*
Raymond Karsan Associates
522 East Genesee Street
Fayetteville, NY 13066
Telephone: (315) 637-4600
Recruiter Classification: Retained; **Lowest/Average Salary:**
$30,000/$90,000; **Industry Concentration:** Generalist with a
primary focus in Insurance; **Function Concentration:** Generalist

Attaway, Jana — *Project Manager*
Kaye-Bassman International Corp.
18333 Preston Road, Suite 500
Dallas, TX 75252
Telephone: (972) 931-5242
Recruiter Classification: Retained; **Lowest/Average Salary:**
$50,000/$90,000; **Industry Concentration:** Insurance

Attell, Harold — *Vice President*
A.E. Feldman Associates
445 Northern Boulevard
Great Neck, NY 11021
Telephone: (516) 466-4708
Recruiter Classification: Contingency; **Lowest/Average Salary:**
$60,000/$90,000; **Industry Concentration:** Generalist with a
primary focus in Financial Services, Venture Capital; **Function
Concentration:** Generalist with a primary focus in
Administration, General Management, Marketing, Sales

Atwood, Barrie — *Associate*
The Abbott Group, Inc.
530 College Parkway, Suite N
Annapolis, MD 21401
Telephone: (410) 757-4100
Lowest/Average Salary: $90,000/$90,000; **Industry
Concentration:** Generalist with a primary focus in Financial
Services; **Function Concentration:** Generalist with a primary
focus in Administration, Engineering, Human Resources,
Research and Development, Women/Minorities

Aubin, Richard E. — *Chairman*
Aubin International Inc.
281 Winter Street, #380
Waltham, MA 02154
Telephone: (617) 890-1722
Recruiter Classification: Retained; **Lowest/Average Salary:**
$90,000/$90,000; **Industry Concentration:** Generalist with a
primary focus in Venture Capital; **Function Concentration:**
Generalist

Austin Lockton, Kathy — *Senior Associate*
Juntunen-Combs-Poirier
600 Montgomery Street, 2nd Floor
San Francisco, CA 94111
Telephone: (415) 291-1699
Recruiter Classification: Retained; **Lowest/Average Salary:**
$90,000/$90,000; **Industry Concentration:** Financial Services;
Function Concentration: Finance/Accounting, General
Management, Marketing, Sales

Axelrod, Nancy R. — *Vice President*
A.T. Kearney, Inc.
225 Reinekers Lane
Alexandria, VA 22314
Telephone: (703) 739-4624
Recruiter Classification: Retained; **Lowest/Average Salary:**
$90,000/$90,000; **Industry Concentration:** Generalist with a
primary focus in Financial Services; **Function Concentration:**
Generalist with a primary focus in Engineering,
Finance/Accounting, General Management

Aydelotte, G. Thomas — *Partner*
Ingram & Aydelotte Inc./I-I-C Partners
430 Park Avenue, Suite 700
New York, NY 10022
Telephone: (212) 319-7777
Recruiter Classification: Retained; **Lowest/Average Salary:**
$150,000/$150,000; **Industry Concentration:** Generalist with a
primary focus in Financial Services, Insurance; **Function
Concentration:** Generalist with a primary focus in
Finance/Accounting, General Management, Marketing, Sales

Bacher, Judith — *Director*
Spencer Stuart
277 Park Avenue, 29th Floor
New York, NY 10172
Telephone: (212) 336-0200
Recruiter Classification: Retained; **Lowest/Average Salary:**
$50,000/$75,000; **Industry Concentration:** Financial Services;
Function Concentration: Finance/Accounting

Bader, Sam — *President*
Bader Research Corporation
6 East 45th Street
New York, NY 10017
Telephone: (212) 682-4750
Recruiter Classification: Contingency; **Lowest/Average Salary:**
$75,000/$100,000; **Industry Concentration:** Financial Services

Badger, Fred H. — *President*
The Badger Group
4125 Blackhawk Plaza Circle, Suite 270
Danville, CA 94506
Telephone: (510) 736-5553
Recruiter Classification: Retained; **Lowest/Average Salary:**
$90,000/$90,000; **Industry Concentration:** Generalist with a
primary focus in Financial Services; **Function Concentration:**
Generalist with a primary focus in Engineering,
Finance/Accounting, General Management, Human Resources,
Marketing, Research and Development, Sales

Baeder, Jeremy — *Vice President*
Executive Manning Corporation
3000 N.E. 30th Place, Suite 402/405/411
Fort Lauderdale, FL 33306
Telephone: (954) 561-5100
Recruiter Classification: Retained; **Lowest/Average Salary:**
$75,000/$90,000; **Industry Concentration:** Generalist with a
primary focus in Financial Services, Insurance; **Function
Concentration:** Generalist with a primary focus in
Administration, Engineering, General Management, Human
Resources, Research and Development, Sales,
Women/Minorities

Baer, Kenneth — *Associate*
Source Services Corporation
701 West Cypress Creek Road, Suite 202
Ft. Lauderdale, FL 33309
Telephone: (954) 771-0777
Recruiter Classification: Contingency; **Lowest/Average
Salary:** $30,000/$50,000; **Industry Concentration:** Financial
Services; **Function Concentration:** Engineering,
Finance/Accounting

Baglio, Robert — *Associate*
Source Services Corporation
8614 Westwood Center, Suite 750
Vienna, VA 22182
Telephone: (703) 790-5610
Recruiter Classification: Contingency; **Lowest/Average
Salary:** $30,000/$50,000; **Industry Concentration:** Financial
Services; **Function Concentration:** Engineering,
Finance/Accounting

Baier, Rebecca — *Associate*
Source Services Corporation
5429 LBJ Freeway, Suite 275
Dallas, TX 75240
Telephone: (214) 387-1600
Recruiter Classification: Contingency; **Lowest/Average
Salary:** $30,000/$50,000; **Industry Concentration:** Financial
Services; **Function Concentration:** Engineering,
Finance/Accounting

Bailey, Paul — *Vice President*
Austin-McGregor International
12005 Ford Road, Suite 720
Dallas, TX 75234-7247
Telephone: (972) 488-0500
Recruiter Classification: Retained; **Lowest/Average Salary:**
$50,000/$90,000; **Industry Concentration:** Generalist with a
primary focus in Financial Services, Venture Capital; **Function
Concentration:** Generalist

Bailey, Vanessa — *Recruiter*
Highland Search Group
565 Fifth Avenue, 22nd Floor
New York, NY 10017
Telephone: (212) 328-1113
Recruiter Classification: Retained; **Lowest/Average Salary:**
$90,000/$90,000; **Industry Concentration:** Financial Services,
Insurance, Venture Capital; **Function Concentration:** Generalist
with a primary focus in Administration, Finance/Accounting,
General Management, Human Resources, Sales,
Women/Minorities

Baje, Sarah — *Vice President Consulting Services*
Innovative Search Group, LLC
8097 Roswell Road
Suite C-101
Atlanta, GA 30350-3936
Telephone: (770) 399-9093
Recruiter Classification: Retained; **Lowest/Average Salary:**
$40,000/$90,000; **Industry Concentration:** Generalist with a
primary focus in Financial Services, Insurance; **Function
Concentration:** Generalist with a primary focus in Engineering,
Finance/Accounting, General Management, Human Resources,
Marketing, Research and Development, Sales, Women/Minorities

Baker, Bill — *Vice President Corporate
Development*
Kaye-Bassman International Corp.
18333 Preston Road, Suite 500
Dallas, TX 75252
Telephone: (972) 931-5242
Recruiter Classification: Retained; **Lowest/Average Salary:**
$75,000/$90,000; **Industry Concentration:** Insurance;
Function Concentration: Marketing, Sales

Baker, Gary M. — *Vice President*
Cochran, Cochran & Yale, Inc.
955 East Henrietta Road
Rochester, NY 14623
Telephone: (716) 424-6060
Recruiter Classification: Retained; **Lowest/Average Salary:**
$40,000/$60,000; **Industry Concentration:** Generalist with a
primary focus in Financial Services, Venture Capital; **Function
Concentration:** Generalist with a primary focus in Engineering,
Finance/Accounting, General Management, Human Resources,
Marketing, Sales, Women/Minorities

Baker, Gary M. — *President*
Temporary Accounting Personnel, Inc.
955 East Henrietta Road
Rochester, NY 14623
Telephone: (716) 427-9930
Recruiter Classification: Executive Temporary; **Lowest/Average
Salary:** $20,000/$30,000; **Industry Concentration:** Generalist
with a primary focus in Financial Services; **Function
Concentration:** Finance/Accounting, Human Resources

Baker, Gerry — *Vice President/Managing Director*
A.T. Kearney, Inc.
130 Adelaide Street West, Suite 2710
Toronto, Ontario, CANADA M5H 3P5
Telephone: (416) 947-1990
Recruiter Classification: Retained; **Lowest/Average Salary:**
$90,000/$90,000; **Industry Concentration:** Generalist with a
primary focus in Financial Services; **Function Concentration:**
Generalist with a primary focus in Engineering,
Finance/Accounting, General Management

Baker, Mark A. — *Senior Search Consultant*
Kaye-Bassman International Corp.
18333 Preston Road, Suite 500
Dallas, TX 75252
Telephone: (972) 931-5242
Recruiter Classification: Retained; **Lowest/Average Salary:**
$75,000/$90,000; **Industry Concentration:** Insurance;
Function Concentration: Sales

Bakken, Mark — *Associate*
Source Services Corporation
5429 LBJ Freeway, Suite 275
Dallas, TX 75240
Telephone: (214) 387-1600
Recruiter Classification: Contingency; **Lowest/Average Salary:** $30,000/$50,000; **Industry Concentration:** Financial Services; **Function Concentration:** Engineering, Finance/Accounting

Balbone, Rich — *Vice President*
Executive Manning Corporation
3000 N.E. 30th Place, Suite 402/405/411
Fort Lauderdale, FL 33306
Telephone: (954) 561-5100
Recruiter Classification: Retained; **Lowest/Average Salary:** $75,000/$90,000; **Industry Concentration:** Generalist with a primary focus in Financial Services, Insurance; **Function Concentration:** Generalist with a primary focus in Administration, Engineering, General Management, Human Resources, Research and Development, Sales, Women/Minorities

Balch, Randy — *Executive Recruiter*
CPS Inc.
One Westbrook Corporate Centre, Suite 600
Westchester, IL 60154
Telephone: (708) 531-8370
Recruiter Classification: Contingency; **Lowest/Average Salary:** $30,000/$50,000; **Industry Concentration:** Generalist with a primary focus in Financial Services, Insurance; **Function Concentration:** Engineering, Research and Development, Sales, Women/Minorities

Balchumas, Charles — *Managing Director*
Source Services Corporation
5343 North 16th Street, Suite 270
Phoenix, AZ 85016
Telephone: (602) 230-0220
Recruiter Classification: Contingency; **Lowest/Average Salary:** $30,000/$50,000; **Industry Concentration:** Financial Services; **Function Concentration:** Engineering, Finance/Accounting

Baldock, Robert G. — *Partner*
Ray & Berndtson/Lovas Stanley
Royal Bank Plaza, South Tower, Suite 3150
200 Bay Street, P.O. Box 125
Toronto, Ontario, CANADA M5J 2J3
Telephone: (416) 366-1990
Recruiter Classification: Retained; **Lowest/Average Salary:** $90,000/$90,000; **Industry Concentration:** Generalist with a primary focus in Financial Services; **Function Concentration:** Finance/Accounting, General Management

Ballantine, Caroline B. — *Partner*
Heidrick & Struggles, Inc.
233 South Wacker Drive
Suite 7000
Chicago, IL 60606-6402
Telephone: (312) 496-1000
Recruiter Classification: Retained; **Lowest/Average Salary:** $75,000/$90,000; **Industry Concentration:** Generalist with a primary focus in Financial Services; **Function Concentration:** Generalist

Baltaglia, Michael — *Search Consultant*
Cochran, Cochran & Yale, Inc.
955 East Henrietta Road
Rochester, NY 14623
Telephone: (716) 424-6060
Recruiter Classification: Retained; **Lowest/Average Salary:** $50,000/$75,000; **Industry Concentration:** Generalist with a primary focus in Financial Services, Venture Capital; **Function Concentration:** Generalist with a primary focus in Engineering, Finance/Accounting, General Management, Human Resources, Marketing, Sales, Women/Minorities

Balter, Sidney — *Associate*
Source Services Corporation
120 East Baltimore Street, Suite 1950
Baltimore, MD 21202
Telephone: (410) 727-4050
Recruiter Classification: Contingency; **Lowest/Average Salary:** $30,000/$50,000; **Industry Concentration:** Financial Services; **Function Concentration:** Engineering, Finance/Accounting

Banko, Scott — *Associate*
Source Services Corporation
3 Summit Park Drive, Suite 550
Independence, OH 44131
Telephone: (216) 328-5900
Recruiter Classification: Contingency; **Lowest/Average Salary:** $30,000/$50,000; **Industry Concentration:** Financial Services; **Function Concentration:** Engineering, Finance/Accounting

Baranowski, Peter — *Associate*
Source Services Corporation
71 Spit Brook Road, Suite 305
Nashua, NH 03060
Telephone: (603) 888-7650
Recruiter Classification: Contingency; **Lowest/Average Salary:** $30,000/$50,000; **Industry Concentration:** Financial Services; **Function Concentration:** Engineering, Finance/Accounting

Barbour, Mary Beth — *Consultant*
Tully/Woodmansee International, Inc.
524 6th Avenue, Suite 210
Seattle, WA 98119
Telephone: (206) 285-9200
Recruiter Classification: Retained; **Lowest/Average Salary:** $60,000/$90,000; **Industry Concentration:** Generalist with a primary focus in Financial Services; **Function Concentration:** Generalist with a primary focus in Engineering, Finance/Accounting, General Management, Human Resources, Marketing, Research and Development, Sales, Women/Minorities

Barch, Sherrie — *Principal*
Furst Group/MPI
555 S. Perryville Road
Rockford, IL 61108
Telephone: (815) 229-9111
Recruiter Classification: Retained; **Lowest/Average Salary:** $60,000/$90,000; **Industry Concentration:** Insurance; **Function Concentration:** Finance/Accounting, General Management, Human Resources, Marketing, Research and Development, Sales

Barger, H. Carter — *President*
Barger & Sargeant, Inc.
22 Windermere Road, Suite 500
P.O. Box 1420
Center Harbor, NH 03226-1420
Telephone: (603) 253-4700
Recruiter Classification: Retained; **Lowest/Average Salary:**
$90,000/$90,000; **Industry Concentration:** Generalist with a
primary focus in Financial Services, Insurance; **Function
Concentration:** Generalist with a primary focus in Engineering,
Finance/Accounting, General Management, Human Resources,
Marketing

Barlow, Ken H. — *Senior Vice President,
Southeast*
The Cherbonnier Group, Inc.
390 Towne Center Boulevard
Suite B
Ridgeland, MS 39157
Telephone: (601) 952-0020
Recruiter Classification: Retained; **Lowest/Average Salary:**
$75,000/$90,000; **Industry Concentration:** Generalist with a
primary focus in Financial Services, Venture Capital; **Function
Concentration:** Generalist with a primary focus in
Administration, Engineering, Finance/Accounting, General
Management, Marketing, Research and Development, Sales

Barnaby, Richard — *Associate*
Source Services Corporation
3 Summit Park Drive, Suite 550
Independence, OH 44131
Telephone: (216) 328-5900
Recruiter Classification: Contingency; **Lowest/Average Salary:**
$30,000/$50,000; **Industry Concentration:** Financial Services;
Function Concentration: Engineering, Finance/Accounting

Barnes, Gary — *Senior Partner*
Brigade Inc.
21483 Shannon Court
P.O. Box 1974
Cupertino, CA 95015-1974
Telephone: (408) 973-0600
Recruiter Classification: Retained; **Lowest/Average Salary:**
$90,000/$90,000; **Industry Concentration:** Financial Services,
Venture Capital; **Function Concentration:** Engineering,
Finance/Accounting, General Management, Human Resources,
Marketing, Women/Minorities

Barnes, Gregory — *Vice President*
Korn/Ferry International
1100 Louisiana, Suite 3400
Houston, TX 77002
Telephone: (713) 651-1834
Recruiter Classification: Retained; **Lowest/Average Salary:**
$100,000/$150,000; **Industry Concentration:** Generalist with a
primary focus in Financial Services, Insurance; **Function
Concentration:** Generalist

Barnes, Richard E. — *President*
Barnes Development Group, LLC
1017 West Glen Oaks Lane, Suite 108
Mequon, WI 53092
Telephone: (414) 241-8468
Recruiter Classification: Retained; **Lowest/Average Salary:**
$50,000/$75,000; **Industry Concentration:** Generalist with a
primary focus in Insurance; **Function Concentration:**
Generalist with a primary focus in Administration, Engineering,
Finance/Accounting, General Management, Human Resources,
Marketing, Research and Development, Sales

Barnes, Roanne L. — *Executive Vice President*
Barnes Development Group, LLC
1017 West Glen Oaks Lane, Suite 108
Mequon, WI 53092
Telephone: (414) 241-8468
Recruiter Classification: Retained; **Lowest/Average Salary:**
$50,000/$75,000; **Industry Concentration:** Generalist with a
primary focus in Financial Services, Insurance; **Function
Concentration:** Generalist with a primary focus in
Administration, Engineering, Finance/Accounting, General
Management, Human Resources, Marketing, Research and
Development, Sales

Barnette, Dennis A. — *Partner*
Heidrick & Struggles, Inc.
233 South Wacker Drive
Suite 7000
Chicago, IL 60606-6402
Telephone: (312) 496-1000
Recruiter Classification: Retained; **Lowest/Average Salary:**
$75,000/$90,000; **Industry Concentration:** Generalist with a
primary focus in Financial Services; **Function Concentration:**
Generalist

Barnum, Toni M. — *Partner*
Stone Murphy & Olson
5500 Wayzata Boulevard
Suite 1020
Minneapolis, MN 55416
Telephone: (612) 591-2300
Recruiter Classification: Retained; **Lowest/Average Salary:**
$75,000/$90,000; **Industry Concentration:** Generalist with a
primary focus in Financial Services, Insurance, Venture
Capital; **Function Concentration:** Generalist with a primary
focus in Finance/Accounting, General Management,
Marketing

Barrett, J. David — *Partner*
Heidrick & Struggles, Inc.
245 Park Avenue, Suite 4300
New York, NY 10167-0152
Telephone: (212) 867-9876
Recruiter Classification: Retained; **Lowest/Average Salary:**
$75,000/$90,000; **Industry Concentration:** Generalist with a
primary focus in Financial Services; **Function Concentration:**
Generalist with a primary focus in Finance/Accounting

Bartels, Fredrick — *Associate*
Source Services Corporation
4510 Executive Drive, Suite 200
San Diego, CA 92121
Telephone: (619) 552-0300
Recruiter Classification: Contingency; **Lowest/Average
Salary:** $30,000/$50,000; **Industry Concentration:** Financial
Services; **Function Concentration:** Engineering,
Finance/Accounting

Bartfield, Philip — *Associate*
Source Services Corporation
5 Independence Way
Princeton, NJ 08540
Telephone: (609) 452-7277
Recruiter Classification: Contingency; **Lowest/Average
Salary:** $30,000/$50,000; **Industry Concentration:** Financial
Services; **Function Concentration:** Engineering,
Finance/Accounting

Bartholdi, Ted — *Vice President*
Bartholdi & Company, Inc.
14 Douglass Way
Exeter, NH 03833
Telephone: (603) 772-4228
Recruiter Classification: Retained; **Lowest/Average Salary:**
$60,000/$90,000; **Industry Concentration:** Venture Capital;
Function Concentration: Generalist with a primary focus in
Engineering, Finance/Accounting, General Management,
Marketing, Research and Development, Sales

Bartholdi, Theodore G. — *President*
Bartholdi & Company, Inc.
10040 E. Happy Valley Road
Suite 244
Scottsdale, AZ 85255
Telephone: (602) 596-1117
Recruiter Classification: Retained; **Lowest/Average Salary:**
$60,000/$90,000; **Industry Concentration:** Venture Capital;
Function Concentration: Generalist with a primary focus in
Engineering, Finance/Accounting, General Management,
Marketing, Research and Development, Sales

Barton, Gary R. — *Partner*
Barton Associates, Inc.
One Riverway, Suite 2500
Houston, TX 77056
Telephone: (713) 961-9111
Recruiter Classification: Retained; **Lowest/Average Salary:**
$75,000/$90,000; **Industry Concentration:** Generalist with a
primary focus in Financial Services; **Function Concentration:**
Generalist with a primary focus in Administration,
Finance/Accounting, General Management, Human Resources,
Marketing, Sales

Barton, James — *Associate*
Source Services Corporation
1 Gatehall Drive, Suite 250
Parsippany, NJ 07054
Telephone: (201) 267-3222
Recruiter Classification: Contingency; **Lowest/Average Salary:**
$30,000/$50,000; **Industry Concentration:** Financial Services;
Function Concentration: Engineering, Finance/Accounting

Bason, Maurice L. — *President*
Bason Associates Inc.
11311 Cornell Park Drive
Cincinnati, OH 45242
Telephone: (513) 469-9881
Recruiter Classification: Retained; **Lowest/Average Salary:**
$60,000/$90,000; **Industry Concentration:** Generalist with a
primary focus in Financial Services, Insurance, Venture Capital;
Function Concentration: Generalist with a primary focus in
Administration, Engineering, Finance/Accounting, General
Management, Human Resources, Marketing, Research and
Development, Sales

Bass, M. Lynn — *Consultant*
Ray & Berndtson
One Allen Center
500 Dallas, Suite 3010
Houston, TX 77002
Telephone: (713) 309-1400
Recruiter Classification: Retained; **Lowest/Average Salary:**
$90,000/$90,000; **Industry Concentration:** Generalist with a
primary focus in Financial Services, Insurance; **Function
Concentration:** Generalist with a primary focus in Administration,
Finance/Accounting, General Management, Human Resources,
Marketing, Research and Development, Sales, Women/Minorities

Bass, Nate — *Managing Director*
Jacobson Associates
Five Neshaminy Interplex
Suite 113
Trevose, PA 19053
Telephone: (215) 639-5860
Recruiter Classification: Contingency; **Lowest/Average Salary:**
$60,000/$75,000; **Industry Concentration:** Financial Services,
Insurance; **Function Concentration:** Generalist with a primary
focus in Administration, Finance/Accounting, General
Management, Marketing, Research and Development, Sales

Bassler, John — *Managing Director Eastern
Region*
Korn/Ferry International
237 Park Avenue
New York, NY 10017
Telephone: (212) 687-1834
Recruiter Classification: Retained; **Lowest/Average Salary:**
$100,000/$150,000; **Industry Concentration:** Generalist with a
primary focus in Financial Services, Insurance; **Function
Concentration:** Generalist

Bassman, Robert — *Chairman and CEO*
Kaye-Bassman International Corp.
18333 Preston Road, Suite 500
Dallas, TX 75252
Telephone: (972) 931-5242
Recruiter Classification: Retained; **Lowest/Average Salary:**
$40,000/$60,000; **Industry Concentration:** Financial Services;
Function Concentration: Generalist

Bassman, Sandy — *Executive Vice President*
Kaye-Bassman International Corp.
18333 Preston Road, Suite 500
Dallas, TX 75252
Telephone: (972) 931-5242
Recruiter Classification: Executive Temporary; **Lowest/Average
Salary:** $40,000/$60,000; **Industry Concentration:** Financial
Services; **Function Concentration:** Generalist

Bates, Nina — *Senior Associate/Recruiter*
Allard Associates
44 Montgomery Street, Suite 500
San Francisco, CA 94104
Telephone: (800) 291-5279
Recruiter Classification: Retained; **Lowest/Average Salary:**
$50,000/$90,000; **Industry Concentration:** Financial Services;
Function Concentration: Marketing

Batte, Carol — *Associate*
Source Services Corporation
520 Post Oak Boulevard, Suite 700
Houston, TX 77027
Telephone: (713) 439-1077
Recruiter Classification: Contingency; **Lowest/Average Salary:**
$30,000/$50,000; **Industry Concentration:** Financial Services;
Function Concentration: Engineering, Finance/Accounting

Battles, Jonathan — *Principal*
Korn/Ferry International
2 Logan Square, Suite 2530
Philadelphia, PA 19103
Telephone: (215) 568-9911
Recruiter Classification: Retained; **Lowest/Average Salary:**
$100,000/$150,000; **Industry Concentration:** Generalist with a
primary focus in Financial Services, Insurance; **Function
Concentration:** Generalist

Bauman, Martin H. — *President*
Martin H. Bauman Associates, Inc.
375 Park Avenue, Suite 2002
New York, NY 10152
Telephone: (212) 752-6580
Recruiter Classification: Retained; **Lowest/Average Salary:**
$100,000/$250,000; **Industry Concentration:** Generalist with a
primary focus in Financial Services, Venture Capital; **Function
Concentration:** Generalist with a primary focus in
Administration, Engineering, Finance/Accounting, General
Management, Human Resources, Marketing, Research and
Development, Sales, Women/Minorities

Beall, Charles P. — *President/Managing Director*
Beall & Company, Inc.
535 Colonial Park Drive
Roswell, GA 30075
Telephone: (404) 992-0900
Recruiter Classification: Retained; **Lowest/Average Salary:**
$90,000/$90,000; **Industry Concentration:** Generalist with a
primary focus in Venture Capital; **Function Concentration:**
Generalist

Bearman, Linda — *Vice President*
Grant Cooper and Associates
795 Office Parkway, Suite 117
St. Louis, MO 63141
Telephone: (314) 567-4690
Recruiter Classification: Retained; **Lowest/Average Salary:**
$60,000/$90,000; **Industry Concentration:** Generalist with a
primary focus in Financial Services; **Function Concentration:**
Generalist with a primary focus in Administration, Engineering,
Finance/Accounting, General Management, Human Resources,
Marketing, Sales

Beaudin, Elizabeth C. — *Partner*
Callan Associates, Ltd.
2021 Spring Road, Suite 175
Oak Brook, IL 60521
Telephone: (708) 832-7080
Recruiter Classification: Retained; **Lowest/Average Salary:**
$90,000/$90,000; **Industry Concentration:** Generalist with a
primary focus in Financial Services; **Function Concentration:**
Generalist with a primary focus in Administration, Engineering,
Finance/Accounting, General Management, Human Resources,
Marketing, Research and Development, Sales, Women/Minorities

Beaulieu, Genie A. — *Director Communications*
Romac & Associates
183 Middle Street, 3rd Floor
P.O. Box 7040
Portland, ME 04112
Telephone: (207) 773-4749
Recruiter Classification: Executive Temporary; **Lowest/Average
Salary:** $60,000/$60,000; **Industry Concentration:** Financial
Services, Insurance; **Function Concentration:**
Finance/Accounting

Beaver, Bentley H. — *Managing Director*
The Onstott Group, Inc.
60 William Street
Wellesley, MA 02181
Telephone: (781) 235-3050
Recruiter Classification: Retained; **Lowest/Average Salary:**
$90,000/$90,000; **Industry Concentration:** Generalist with a
primary focus in Financial Services; **Function Concentration:**
Generalist with a primary focus in Engineering,
Finance/Accounting, General Management, Human Resources,
Marketing, Research and Development, Sales

Beaver, Robert — *Associate*
Source Services Corporation
1290 Oakmead Parkway, Suite 318
Sunnyvale, CA 94086
Telephone: (408) 738-8440
Recruiter Classification: Contingency; **Lowest/Average Salary:**
$30,000/$50,000; **Industry Concentration:** Financial Services;
Function Concentration: Engineering, Finance/Accounting

Becker, Elizabeth M. — *Recruiter*
Caliber Associates
125 Strafford Avenue
Suite 112
Wayne, PA 19087
Telephone: (610) 971-1880
Recruiter Classification: Retained; **Lowest/Average Salary:**
$75,000/$90,000; **Industry Concentration:** Venture Capital;
Function Concentration: Marketing, Research and
Development, Sales

Beckvold, John B. — *Principal*
Atlantic Search Group, Inc.
One Liberty Square
Boston, MA 02109
Telephone: (617) 426-9700
Recruiter Classification: Contingency; **Lowest/Average Salary:**
$20,000/$60,000; **Industry Concentration:** Generalist with a
primary focus in Financial Services, **Function Concentration:**
Finance/Accounting

Beer, John — *Vice President*
People Management Northeast Incorporated
One Darling Drive, Avon Park South
Avon, CT 06001
Telephone: (860) 678-8900
Recruiter Classification: Retained; **Lowest/Average Salary:**
$75,000/$90,000; **Industry Concentration:** Generalist with a
primary focus in Financial Services, Insurance; **Function
Concentration:** Generalist

Beeson, William B. — *Vice President*
Lawrence-Leiter & Co. Management Conultants
4400 Shawnee-Mission Parkway, Suite 204
Shawnee-Mission, KS 66205
Telephone: (913) 677-5500
Recruiter Classification: Retained; **Lowest/Average Salary:**
$50,000/$90,000; **Industry Concentration:** Generalist with a
primary focus in Financial Services, Insurance; **Function
Concentration:** Generalist

Belden, Charles P. — *Consultant*
Raymond Karsan Associates
2500 Mosside Boulevard, Suite 218
Monroeville, PA 15146
Telephone: (412) 373-5433
Recruiter Classification: Retained; **Lowest/Average Salary:**
$30,000/$90,000; **Industry Concentration:** Generalist with a
primary focus in Insurance; **Function Concentration:**
Generalist

Belden, Jeannette — *Associate*
Source Services Corporation
10220 SW Greenburg Road, Suite 625
Portland, OR 97223
Telephone: (503) 768-4546
Recruiter Classification: Contingency; **Lowest/Average Salary:**
$30,000/$50,000; **Industry Concentration:** Financial Services;
Function Concentration: Engineering, Finance/Accounting

Belin, Jean — *Consultant*
Boyden
500 East Broward Boulevard
Suite 1050
Ft. Lauderdale, FL 33394
Telephone: (954) 522-8885
Recruiter Classification: Retained; **Lowest/Average Salary:**
$90,000/$90,000; **Industry Concentration:** Generalist with a
primary focus in Financial Services; **Function Concentration:**
Generalist with a primary focus in Engineering,
Finance/Accounting, General Management, Human Resources,
Marketing, Sales, Women/Minorities

Bell, Lloyd W. — *Principal*
O'Brien & Bell
812 Huron Road, Suite 535
Cleveland, OH 44115
Telephone: (216) 575-1212
Recruiter Classification: Retained; **Lowest/Average Salary:**
$75,000/$90,000; **Industry Concentration:** Generalist with a
primary focus in Financial Services; **Function Concentration:**
Generalist with a primary focus in Engineering,
Finance/Accounting, General Management, Human
Resources, Marketing

Bell, Michael — *Director*
Spencer Stuart
One University Avenue
Suite 801
Toronto, Ontario, CANADA M5J 2P1
Telephone: (416) 361-0311
Recruiter Classification: Retained; **Lowest/Average Salary:**
$90,000/$90,000; **Industry Concentration:** Generalist with a
primary focus in Financial Services, Insurance; **Function
Concentration:** Generalist with a primary focus in Human
Resources

Bellano, Robert W. — *Director*
Stanton Chase International
10866 Wilshire Boulevard
Suite 870
Los Angeles, CA 90024
Telephone: (310) 474-1029
Recruiter Classification: Retained; **Lowest/Average Salary:**
$75,000/$90,000; **Industry Concentration:** Generalist with a
primary focus in Insurance, Venture Capital; **Function
Concentration:** Generalist with a primary focus in
Finance/Accounting, General Management, Human Resources,
Marketing, Sales

Bender, Alan — *President*
Bender Executive Search
45 North Station Plaza
Suite 315
Great Neck, NY 11021
Telephone: (516) 773-4300
Recruiter Classification: Retained; **Lowest/Average Salary:**
$75,000/$90,000; **Industry Concentration:** Generalist with a
primary focus in Financial Services; **Function Concentration:**
General Management, Marketing, Sales, Women/Minorities

Benjamin, Maurita — *Associate*
Source Services Corporation
8614 Westwood Center, Suite 750
Vienna, VA 22182
Telephone: (703) 790-5610
Recruiter Classification: Contingency; **Lowest/Average Salary:**
$30,000/$50,000; **Industry Concentration:** Financial Services;
Function Concentration: Engineering, Finance/Accounting

Bennett, Jo — *Vice President*
Battalia Winston International
300 Park Avenue
New York, NY 10022
Telephone: (212) 308-8080
Recruiter Classification: Retained; **Lowest/Average Salary:**
$90,000/$90,000; **Industry Concentration:** Generalist with a
primary focus in Insurance, Venture Capital; **Function
Concentration:** Generalist with a primary focus in Engineering,
Finance/Accounting, General Management, Human Resources,
Marketing, Sales, Women/Minorities

Benson, Edward — *Associate*
Source Services Corporation
1601 East Flamingo Road, Suite 18
Las Vegas, NV 89119
Telephone: (702) 796-9676
Recruiter Classification: Contingency; **Lowest/Average
Salary:** $30,000/$50,000; **Industry Concentration:** Financial
Services; **Function Concentration:** Engineering,
Finance/Accounting

Benson, Kate — *Associate*
Rene Plessner Associates, Inc.
375 Park Avenue
New York, NY 10152
Telephone: (212) 421-3490
Recruiter Classification: Retained; **Lowest/Average Salary:**
$75,000/$90,000; **Industry Concentration:** Generalist with a
primary focus in Insurance; **Function Concentration:**
Generalist with a primary focus in Administration,
Finance/Accounting, General Management, Human Resources,
Marketing, Research and Development, Sales

Beran, Helena — *Associate*
Michael J. Cavanagh and Associates
60 St. Clair Avenue East
Suite 905
Toronto, Ontario, CANADA M4T 1N5
Telephone: (416) 324-9661
Recruiter Classification: Retained; **Lowest/Average Salary:**
$80,000/$100,000; **Industry Concentration:** Generalist with a
primary focus in Venture Capital; **Function Concentration:**
Generalist with a primary focus in Administration, Engineering,
Finance/Accounting, General Management, Human Resources,
Marketing

Berger, Jeffrey — *Associate*
Source Services Corporation
10300 West 103rd Street, Suite 101
Overland Park, KS 66214
Telephone: (913) 888-8885
Recruiter Classification: Contingency; **Lowest/Average
Salary:** $30,000/$50,000; **Industry Concentration:** Financial
Services; **Function Concentration:** Engineering,
Finance/Accounting

Berk-Levine, Margo — *Executive Vice President*
MB Inc. Interim Executive Division
505 Fifth Avenue
New York, NY 10017
Telephone: (212) 661-4937
Recruiter Classification: Executive Temporary; **Lowest/Average
Salary:** $60,000/$75,000; **Industry Concentration:** Generalist
with a primary focus in Financial Services; **Function
Concentration:** Generalist with a primary focus in General
Management, Human Resources

Berman, Mitchell — *Partner*
Carlyle Group
625 N. Michigan Avenue
Suite 2100
Chicago, IL 60611
Telephone: (312) 587-3030
Recruiter Classification: Retained; **Lowest/Average Salary:**
$50,000/$90,000; **Industry Concentration:** Generalist with a
primary focus in Financial Services; **Function Concentration:**
Generalist

Bernard, Bryan — *Associate*
Source Services Corporation
520 Post Oak Boulevard, Suite 700
Houston, TX 77027
Telephone: (713) 439-1077
Recruiter Classification: Contingency; **Lowest/Average Salary:**
$30,000/$50,000; **Industry Concentration:** Financial Services;
Function Concentration: Engineering, Finance/Accounting

Bernas, Sharon — *Associate*
Source Services Corporation
3 Summit Park Drive, Suite 550
Independence, OH 44131
Telephone: (216) 328-5900
Recruiter Classification: Contingency; **Lowest/Average Salary:**
$30,000/$50,000; **Industry Concentration:** Financial Services;
Function Concentration: Engineering, Finance/Accounting

Berne, Marlene — *Vice President*
The Whitney Group
850 Third Avenue, 11th Floor
New York, NY 10022
Telephone: (212) 508-3500
Recruiter Classification: Retained; **Lowest/Average Salary:**
$90,000/$90,000; **Industry Concentration:** Financial Services,
Venture Capital; **Function Concentration:** Generalist with a
primary focus in Finance/Accounting, General Management,
Marketing, Sales

Berry, Harold B. — *Vice President*
The Hindman Company
Browenton Place, Suite 110
2000 Warrington Way
Louisville, KY 40222
Telephone: (502) 426-4040
Recruiter Classification: Retained; **Lowest/Average Salary:**
$50,000/$90,000; **Industry Concentration:** Generalist with a
primary focus in Financial Services; **Function Concentration:**
Generalist with a primary focus in Engineering,
Finance/Accounting, General Management, Human Resources,
Marketing, Sales

Bertoux, Michael P. — *Vice President*
Wilcox, Bertoux & Miller
100 Howe Avenue, Suite 155N
Sacramento, CA 95825
Telephone: (916) 977-3700
Recruiter Classification: Contingency; **Lowest/Average Salary:**
$40,000/$75,000; **Industry Concentration:** Financial Services;
Function Concentration: Administration, General Management

Bettick, Michael J. — *Professional Recruiter*
A.J. Burton Group, Inc.
120 East Baltimore Street, Suite 2220
Baltimore, MD 21202
Telephone: (410) 752-5244
Recruiter Classification: Contingency; **Lowest/Average Salary:**
$40,000/$75,000; **Industry Concentration:** Generalist with a
primary focus in Financial Services, Insurance; **Function
Concentration:** Generalist with a primary focus in Administration,
Finance/Accounting, General Management, Human Resources

Betts, Suzette — *Associate*
Source Services Corporation
520 Post Oak Boulevard, Suite 700
Houston, TX 77027
Telephone: (713) 439-1077
Recruiter Classification: Contingency; **Lowest/Average Salary:**
$30,000/$50,000; **Industry Concentration:** Financial Services;
Function Concentration: Engineering, Finance/Accounting

Bickett, Nicole — *Associate*
Source Services Corporation
111 Monument Circle, Suite 3930
Indianapolis, IN 46204
Telephone: (317) 631-2900
Recruiter Classification: Contingency; **Lowest/Average Salary:**
$30,000/$50,000; **Industry Concentration:** Financial Services;
Function Concentration: Engineering, Finance/Accounting

Biddix, Maryanne — *Consultant*
Tyler & Company
1000 Abernathy Road
Suite 1400
Atlanta, GA 30328-5655
Telephone: (770) 396-3939
Recruiter Classification: Retained; **Lowest/Average Salary:**
$75,000/$90,000; **Industry Concentration:** Insurance;
Function Concentration: Generalist

Bidelman, Richard — *Managing Director*
Source Services Corporation
1601 East Flamingo Road, Suite 18
Las Vegas, NV 89119
Telephone: (702) 796-9676
Recruiter Classification: Contingency; **Lowest/Average Salary:**
$30,000/$50,000; **Industry Concentration:** Financial Services;
Function Concentration: Engineering, Finance/Accounting

Bigelow, Dennis — *Vice President*
Marshall Consultants, Inc.
360 East 65th Street
New York, NY 10021
Telephone: (212) 628-8400
Recruiter Classification: Retained; **Lowest/Average Salary:**
$30,000/$50,000; **Industry Concentration:** Financial Services,
Insurance, Venture Capital; **Function Concentration:** Marketing

Biggins, J. Veronica — *Consultant*
Heidrick & Struggles, Inc.
One Peachtree Center
303 Peachtree Street, NE, Suite 3100
Atlanta, GA 30308
Telephone: (404) 577-2410
Recruiter Classification: Retained; **Lowest/Average Salary:**
$75,000/$90,000; **Industry Concentration:** Generalist with a
primary focus in Financial Services; **Function Concentration:**
Generalist

Billington, William H. — *Partner*
Spriggs & Company, Inc.
1701 East Lake Avenue
Suite 265
Glenview, IL 60025
Telephone: (708) 657-7181
Recruiter Classification: Retained; **Lowest/Average Salary:**
$60,000/$90,000; **Industry Concentration:** Generalist with a
primary focus in Financial Services; **Function Concentration:**
Generalist with a primary focus in General Management,
Human Resources, Marketing, Sales

Biolsi, Joseph — *Associate*
Source Services Corporation
15260 Ventura Boulevard, Suite 380
Sherman Oaks, CA 91403
Telephone: (818) 905-1500
Recruiter Classification: Contingency; **Lowest/Average Salary:** $30,000/$50,000; **Industry Concentration:** Financial Services; **Function Concentration:** Engineering, Finance/Accounting

Birkhead, Linda — *Associate*
Zwell International
300 South Wacker Drive, Suite 650
Chicago, IL 60606
Telephone: (312) 663-3737
Recruiter Classification: Retained; **Lowest/Average Salary:** $75,000/$90,000; **Industry Concentration:** Generalist with a primary focus in Financial Services; **Function Concentration:** Generalist with a primary focus in General Management, Human Resources, Sales

Birns, Douglas — *Associate*
Source Services Corporation
155 Federal Street, Suite 410
Boston, MA 02110
Telephone: (617) 482-8211
Recruiter Classification: Contingency; **Lowest/Average Salary:** $30,000/$50,000; **Industry Concentration:** Financial Services; **Function Concentration:** Engineering, Finance/Accounting

Bishop, Barbara — *Vice President*
The Executive Source
55 Fifth Avenue, 19th Floor
New York, NY 10003
Telephone: (212) 691-5505
Recruiter Classification: Executive Temporary; **Lowest/Average Salary:** $75,000/$90,000; **Industry Concentration:** Generalist with a primary focus in Financial Services, Insurance, Venture Capital; **Function Concentration:** Human Resources

Bladon, Andrew — *Vice President/Executive Director*
Don Richard Associates of Tampa, Inc.
100 North Tampa Street, Suite 1925
Tampa, FL 33602
Telephone: (813) 221-7930
Recruiter Classification: Contingency, Executive Temporary; **Lowest/Average Salary:** $20,000/$50,000; **Industry Concentration:** Generalist with a primary focus in Financial Services; **Function Concentration:** Generalist with a primary focus in Administration, Finance/Accounting, Research and Development

Blake, Eileen — *Senior Consultant*
Howard Fischer Associates, Inc.
1800 John F. Kennedy Boulevard, 7th Floor
Philadelphia, PA 19103
Telephone: (215) 568-8363
Recruiter Classification: Retained; **Lowest/Average Salary:** $90,000/$90,000; **Industry Concentration:** Financial Services, Insurance, Venture Capital; **Function Concentration:** Generalist

Blakslee, Jan H. — *President*
J: Blakslee International, Ltd.
49 Hillside Avenue
Mill Valley, CA 94941
Telephone: (415) 389-7300
Recruiter Classification: Retained; **Lowest/Average Salary:** $90,000/$90,000; **Industry Concentration:** Venture Capital; **Function Concentration:** Generalist with a primary focus in Engineering, Finance/Accounting, General Management, Human Resources, Marketing, Research and Development, Women/Minorities

Bland, Walter — *Associate*
Source Services Corporation
925 Westchester Avenue, Suite 309
White Plains, NY 10604
Telephone: (914) 428-9100
Recruiter Classification: Contingency; **Lowest/Average Salary:** $30,000/$50,000; **Industry Concentration:** Financial Services; **Function Concentration:** Engineering, Finance/Accounting

Blassaras, Peggy — *Associate*
Source Services Corporation
111 Monument Circle, Suite 3930
Indianapolis, IN 46204
Telephone: (317) 631-2900
Recruiter Classification: Contingency; **Lowest/Average Salary:** $30,000/$50,000; **Industry Concentration:** Financial Services; **Function Concentration:** Engineering, Finance/Accounting

Blecksmith, Edward L. — *Principal*
Larsen, Whitney, Blecksmith & Zilliacus
888 West 6th Street, Suite 500
Los Angeles, CA 90017
Telephone: (213) 243-0033
Recruiter Classification: Retained; **Lowest/Average Salary:** $75,000/$90,000; **Industry Concentration:** Financial Services; **Function Concentration:** Generalist

Blickle, Michael — *Associate*
Source Services Corporation
One South Main Street, Suite 1440
Dayton, OH 45402
Telephone: (513) 461-4660
Recruiter Classification: Contingency; **Lowest/Average Salary:** $30,000/$50,000; **Industry Concentration:** Financial Services; **Function Concentration:** Engineering, Finance/Accounting

Bliley, Jerry — *Senior Director*
Spencer Stuart
One University Avenue
Suite 801
Toronto, Ontario, CANADA M5J 2P1
Telephone: (416) 361-0311
Recruiter Classification: Retained; **Lowest/Average Salary:** $90,000/$90,000; **Industry Concentration:** Generalist with a primary focus in Financial Services; **Function Concentration:** Generalist with a primary focus in Finance/Accounting, General Management, Human Resources, Marketing, Sales

Blim, Barbara — *Principal*
JDG Associates, Ltd.
1700 Research Boulevard
Rockville, MD 20850
Telephone: (301) 340-2210
Recruiter Classification: Contingency; **Lowest/Average Salary:** $50,000/$90,000; **Industry Concentration:** Financial Services; **Function Concentration:** Engineering, Research and Development, Sales

Bloch, Suzanne — *Associate*
Source Services Corporation
701 West Cypress Creek Road, Suite 202
Ft. Lauderdale, FL 33309
Telephone: (954) 771-0777
Recruiter Classification: Contingency; **Lowest/Average Salary:** $30,000/$50,000; **Industry Concentration:** Financial Services; **Function Concentration:** Engineering, Finance/Accounting

Blocher, John — *Managing Director*
Source Services Corporation
10300 West 103rd Street, Suite 101
Overland Park, KS 66214
Telephone: (913) 888-8885
Recruiter Classification: Contingency; **Lowest/Average Salary:**
$30,000/$50,000; **Industry Concentration:** Financial Services;
Function Concentration: Engineering, Finance/Accounting

Bloomer, James E. — *Vice President*
L.W. Foote Company
110 110th Avenue N.E.
Suite 603
Bellevue, WA 98004-5840
Telephone: (206) 451-1660
Recruiter Classification: Retained; **Lowest/Average Salary:**
$75,000/$90,000; **Industry Concentration:** Generalist with a
primary focus in Venture Capital; **Function Concentration:**
Generalist with a primary focus in Administration, Engineering,
General Management, Marketing, Research and Development,
Sales

Blumenthal, Paula — *Partner*
J.P. Canon Associates
225 Broadway, Ste. 3602, 36th Fl.
New York, NY 10007-3001
Telephone: (212) 233-3131
Recruiter Classification: Contingency; **Lowest/Average Salary:**
$40,000/$75,000; **Industry Concentration:** Generalist with a
primary focus in Financial Services; **Function Concentration:**
Engineering

Boel, Werner — *Senior Associate*
The Dalley Hewitt Company
1401 Peachtree Street, Suite 500
Atlanta, GA 30309
Telephone: (404) 885-6642
Recruiter Classification: Retained; **Lowest/Average Salary:**
$50,000/$90,000; **Industry Concentration:** Generalist with a
primary focus in Financial Services, Insurance; **Function
Concentration:** Generalist with a primary focus in
Administration, Engineering, Finance/Accounting, General
Management, Human Resources, Marketing, Research and
Development, Sales

Bogansky, Amy — *Vice President*
Conex Incorporated
150 East 52nd Street, 2nd Floor
New York, NY 10022
Telephone: (212) 371-3737
Recruiter Classification: Retained; **Lowest/Average Salary:**
$75,000/$75,000; **Industry Concentration:** Generalist with a
primary focus in Financial Services; **Function Concentration:**
Generalist with a primary focus in Engineering, General
Management, Marketing, Research and Development, Sales

Bohn, Steve J. — *General Manager*
MSI International
2170 West State Road 434
Suite 454
Longwood, FL 32779
Telephone: (407) 788-7700
Recruiter Classification: Contingency; **Lowest/Average Salary:**
$30,000/$60,000; **Industry Concentration:** Generalist with a
primary focus in Financial Services; **Function Concentration:**
Generalist with a primary focus in Administration, Engineering,
Finance/Accounting, General Management, Marketing, Sales

Boltrus, Dick — *Partner*
Sink, Walker, Boltrus International
60 Walnut Street
Wellesley, MA 02181
Telephone: (617) 237-1199
Recruiter Classification: Retained; **Lowest/Average Salary:**
$90,000/$90,000; **Industry Concentration:** Financial Services;
Function Concentration: Engineering, General Management,
Research and Development, Sales

Bond, Robert J. — *Managing Partner*
Romac & Associates
125 Summer Street, Suite 1450
Boston, MA 02110
Telephone: (617) 439-4300
Recruiter Classification: Executive Temporary; **Lowest/Average
Salary:** $60,000/$60,000; **Industry Concentration:** Financial
Services, Insurance; **Function Concentration:**
Finance/Accounting

Bongiovanni, Vincent — *Senior Partner*
ESA Professional Consultants
141 Durham Road
Suite 16
Madison, CT 06443
Telephone: (203) 245-1983
Recruiter Classification: Retained; **Lowest/Average Salary:**
$50,000/$75,000; **Industry Concentration:** Venture Capital;
Function Concentration: Engineering, General Management,
Human Resources, Marketing, Research and Development,
Women/Minorities

Bonifield, Len — *Consultant*
Bonifield Associates
3003E Lincoln Drive West
Marlton, NJ 08053
Telephone: (609) 596-3300
Recruiter Classification: Contingency; **Lowest/Average Salary:**
$40,000/$60,000; **Industry Concentration:** Financial Services,
Insurance; **Function Concentration:** Generalist with a primary
focus in Administration, Finance/Accounting, General
Management, Human Resources, Marketing, Research and
Development, Sales

Bonnell, William R. — *President*
Bonnell Associates Ltd.
2960 Post Road, Suite 200
Southport, CT 06490
Telephone: (203) 319-7214
Recruiter Classification: Retained; **Lowest/Average Salary:**
$90,000/$90,000; **Industry Concentration:** Generalist with a
primary focus in Financial Services, Insurance; **Function
Concentration:** Generalist with a primary focus in
Finance/Accounting, General Management, Human Resources,
Marketing, Sales

Booth, Ronald — *Associate*
Source Services Corporation
5343 North 16th Street, Suite 270
Phoenix, AZ 85016
Telephone: (602) 230-0220
Recruiter Classification: Contingency; **Lowest/Average
Salary:** $30,000/$50,000; **Industry Concentration:** Financial
Services; **Function Concentration:** Engineering,
Finance/Accounting

Borden, Stuart — *Vice President*
M.A. Churchill & Associates, Inc.
Morelyn Plaza #307
1111 Street Road
Southampton, PA 18966
Telephone: (215) 953-0300
Recruiter Classification: Retained; **Lowest/Average Salary:**
$50,000/$75,000; **Industry Concentration:** Financial Services,
Insurance; **Function Concentration:** Marketing, Research and
Development, Sales

Borkin, Andrew — *President*
Strategic Advancement Inc.
242 Old New Brunswick Road
Suite 100
Piscataway, NJ 08854
Telephone: (908) 562-1222
Recruiter Classification: Retained; **Lowest/Average Salary:**
$50,000/$90,000; **Industry Concentration:** Financial Services,
Insurance; **Function Concentration:** Administration,
Engineering, Finance/Accounting, General Management,
Human Resources, Marketing, Research and Development

Borland, James — *Senior Vice President*
Goodrich & Sherwood Associates, Inc.
521 Fifth Avenue
New York, NY 10175
Telephone: (212) 697-4131
Recruiter Classification: Retained; **Lowest/Average Salary:**
$60,000/$90,000; **Industry Concentration:** Generalist with a
primary focus in Financial Services, Insurance, Venture Capital;
Function Concentration: Generalist with a primary focus in
Administration, Finance/Accounting, General Management,
Human Resources, Marketing, Sales

Bormann, Cindy Ann — *Manager*
MSI International
5215 North O'Connor Boulevard
Suite 1875
Irving, TX 75039
Telephone: (214) 869-3939
Recruiter Classification: Contingency; **Lowest/Average Salary:**
$30,000/$60,000; **Industry Concentration:** Generalist with a
primary focus in Financial Services; **Function Concentration:**
Generalist with a primary focus in Administration, Engineering,
Finance/Accounting, General Management, Marketing, Sales

Bosward, Allan — *Associate*
Source Services Corporation
1290 Oakmead Parkway, Suite 318
Sunnyvale, CA 94086
Telephone: (408) 738-8440
Recruiter Classification: Contingency; **Lowest/Average Salary:**
$30,000/$50,000; **Industry Concentration:** Financial Services;
Function Concentration: Engineering, Finance/Accounting

Bourrie, Sharon D. — *Director*
Chartwell Partners International, Inc.
275 Battery Street, Suite 2180
San Francisco, CA 94111
Telephone: (415) 296-0600
Recruiter Classification: Retained; **Lowest/Average Salary:**
$90,000/$90,000; **Industry Concentration:** Generalist with a
primary focus in Financial Services, Insurance, Venture Capital;
Function Concentration: Generalist with a primary focus in
Finance/Accounting, General Management, Human Resources,
Marketing, Women/Minorities

Bovich, Maryann C. — *Principal*
Higdon Prince Inc.
230 Park Avenue, Suite 1455
New York, NY 10169
Telephone: (212) 986-4662
Recruiter Classification: Retained; **Lowest/Average Salary:**
$150,000/$150,000; **Industry Concentration:** Generalist with a
primary focus in Financial Services, Venture Capital; **Function
Concentration:** Generalist with a primary focus in
Finance/Accounting, General Management, Human Resources,
Marketing, Sales, Women/Minorities

Bowden, Otis H. — *Managing Director*
BowdenGlobal, Ltd.
6450 Rockside Woods Boulevard
Suite 100
Cleveland, OH 44131
Telephone: (216) 328-2088
Recruiter Classification: Retained; **Lowest/Average Salary:**
$90,000/$90,000; **Industry Concentration:** Generalist with a
primary focus in Insurance; **Function Concentration:**
Generalist with a primary focus in Engineering,
Finance/Accounting, General Management, Human
Resources, Marketing, Research and Development,
Women/Minorities

Bowen, Tad — *Vice President*
Executive Search International
60 Walnut Street
Wellesley, MA 02181
Telephone: (617) 239-0303
Recruiter Classification: Retained; **Lowest/Average Salary:**
$75,000/$90,000; **Industry Concentration:** Generalist with a
primary focus in Financial Services; **Function Concentration:**
Generalist with a primary focus in General Management

Boyle, Russell E. — *Consultant*
Egon Zehnder International Inc.
350 Park Avenue
New York, NY 10022
Telephone: (212) 838-9199
Recruiter Classification: Retained; **Lowest/Average Salary:**
$90,000/$90,000; **Industry Concentration:** Generalist with a
primary focus in Financial Services; **Function Concentration:**
Generalist

Brackenbury, Robert — *Financial Recruiter*
Bowman & Marshall, Inc.
P.O. Box 25503
Overland Park, KS 66225
Telephone: (913) 648-3332
Recruiter Classification: Contingency; **Lowest/Average
Salary:** $30,000/$50,000; **Industry Concentration:** Financial
Services, Insurance; **Function Concentration:**
Finance/Accounting

Brackman, Janet — *Recruiter*
Dahl-Morrow International
12020 Sunrise Valley Drive
Reston, VA 20191
Telephone: (703) 860-6868
Recruiter Classification: Retained; **Lowest/Average Salary:**
$75,000/$90,000; **Industry Concentration:** Venture Capital;
Function Concentration: Generalist with a primary focus in
Engineering, Finance/Accounting, General Management,
Marketing, Sales

Bradley, Dalena — *Researcher*
Woodworth International Group
620 SW 5th Avenue, Suite 1225
Portland, OR 97204
Telephone: (503) 225-5000
Recruiter Classification: Retained; **Lowest/Average Salary:**
$60,000/$90,000; **Industry Concentration:** Generalist with a
primary focus in Financial Services, Insurance, Venture Capital;
Function Concentration: Generalist with a primary focus in
Engineering, Finance/Accounting, General Management,
Human Resources, Marketing, Research and Development,
Sales

Bradshaw, Monte — *Vice President*
Christian & Timbers
25825 Science Park Drive, Suite 400
Cleveland, OH 44122
Telephone: (216) 765-5868
Recruiter Classification: Retained; **Lowest/Average Salary:**
$100,000/$100,000; **Industry Concentration:** Generalist with a
primary focus in Financial Services, Venture Capital; **Function
Concentration:** Generalist with a primary focus in Engineering,
Finance/Accounting, General Management, Human Resources,
Marketing, Research and Development

Brady, Coloin — *Managing Director*
Johnson Smith & Knisely Accord
100 Park Avenue, 15th Floor
New York, NY 10017
Telephone: (212) 885-9100
Recruiter Classification: Retained; **Lowest/Average Salary:**
$90,000/$90,000; **Industry Concentration:** Financial Services;
Function Concentration: Human Resources, Sales

Brady, Dick — *Associate*
William Guy & Associates
Telephone: Unpublished
Recruiter Classification: Retained; **Lowest/Average Salary:**
$50,000/$90,000; **Industry Concentration:** Generalist with a
primary focus in Financial Services, Insurance, Venture Capital;
Function Concentration: Generalist with a primary focus in
Administration, Engineering, Finance/Accounting, General
Management, Human Resources, Research and Development,
Women/Minorities

Brady, Robert — *Executive Recruiter*
CPS Inc.
One Westbrook Corporate Centre, Suite 600
Westchester, IL 60154
Telephone: (708) 531-8370
Recruiter Classification: Contingency; **Lowest/Average Salary:**
$30,000/$50,000; **Industry Concentration:** Generalist with a
primary focus in Financial Services, Insurance; **Function
Concentration:** Engineering, Research and Development,
Sales, Women/Minorities

Brandeau, John — *Account Executive*
Chrisman & Company, Incorporated
44 Montgomery Street, Suite 2360
San Francisco, CA 94104
Telephone: (415) 352-1200
Recruiter Classification: Retained; **Lowest/Average Salary:**
$75,000/$90,000; **Industry Concentration:** Financial Services;
Function Concentration: Finance/Accounting,
Women/Minorities

Brandeis, Richard — *Executive Recruiter*
CPS Inc.
One Westbrook Corporate Centre, Suite 600
Westchester, IL 60154
Telephone: (708) 531-8370
Recruiter Classification: Contingency; **Lowest/Average Salary:**
$30,000/$50,000; **Industry Concentration:** Generalist with a
primary focus in Financial Services, Insurance; **Function
Concentration:** Engineering, Research and Development,
Sales, Women/Minorities

Brandenburg, David — *Staffing Consultant*
Professional Staffing Consultants
1331 Lamar, Suite 1459
Houston, TX 77010
Telephone: (713) 659-8383
Recruiter Classification: Retained; **Lowest/Average Salary:**
$50,000/$75,000; **Industry Concentration:** Generalist with a
primary focus in Financial Services; **Function Concentration:**
Generalist with a primary focus in Engineering,
Finance/Accounting, General Management, Human Resources

Brandjes, Michael J. — *Principal*
Brandjes Associates
16 South Calvert Street, Ste. 500
Baltimore, MD 21202
Telephone: (410) 547-6886
Recruiter Classification: Contingency; **Lowest/Average Salary:**
$50,000/$75,000; **Industry Concentration:** Financial Services;
Function Concentration: Generalist

Brandon, Irwin — *President*
Hadley Lockwood, Inc.
17 State Street, 38th Floor
New York, NY 10004
Telephone: (212) 785-4405
Recruiter Classification: Retained; **Lowest/Average Salary:**
$90,000/$90,000; **Industry Concentration:** Financial Services;
Function Concentration: Generalist

Brannon, Kathy — *Director of Life/Health
Underwriting*
Kaye-Bassman International Corp.
18333 Preston Road, Suite 500
Dallas, TX 75252
Telephone: (972) 931-5242
Recruiter Classification: Retained; **Lowest/Average Salary:**
$30,000/$50,000; **Industry Concentration:** Insurance

Brassard, Gary — *Associate*
Source Services Corporation
111 Monument Circle, Suite 3930
Indianapolis, IN 46204
Telephone: (317) 631-2900
Recruiter Classification: Contingency; **Lowest/Average Salary:**
$30,000/$50,000; **Industry Concentration:** Financial Services;
Function Concentration: Engineering, Finance/Accounting

Bratches, Howard — *Senior Partner*
Thorndike Deland Associates
275 Madison Avenue, Suite 1300
New York, NY 10016
Telephone: (212) 661-6200
Recruiter Classification: Retained; **Lowest/Average Salary:**
$100,000/$125,000; **Industry Concentration:** Generalist with a
primary focus in Financial Services, Insurance, Venture Capital;
Function Concentration: Generalist with a primary focus in
Finance/Accounting, General Management, Human Resources,
Marketing, Sales

Bremer, Brian — *Associate*
Source Services Corporation
5 Independence Way
Princeton, NJ 08540
Telephone: (609) 452-7277
Recruiter Classification: Contingency; **Lowest/Average Salary:**
$30,000/$50,000; **Industry Concentration:** Financial Services;
Function Concentration: Engineering, Finance/Accounting

Brennan, Patrick J. — *Managing Director and CEO*
Handy HRM Corp.
250 Park Avenue
New York, NY 10177-0074
Telephone: (212) 210-5600
Recruiter Classification: Retained; **Lowest/Average Salary:**
$90,000/$90,000; **Industry Concentration:** Financial Services,
Insurance, Venture Capital; **Function Concentration:** Generalist
with a primary focus in Administration, Finance/Accounting,
General Management, Human Resources, Marketing

Brenner, Mary — *Recruiter*
Prestige Inc.
P.O. Box 421
Reedsburg, WI 53959
Telephone: (608) 524-4032
Recruiter Classification: Contingency; **Lowest/Average Salary:**
$50,000/$90,000; **Industry Concentration:** Financial Services,
Insurance; **Function Concentration:** Generalist

Brewster, Edward — *Associate*
Source Services Corporation
9020 Capital of Texas Highway
Building I, Suite 337
Austin, TX 78759
Telephone: (512) 345-7473
Recruiter Classification: Contingency; **Lowest/Average Salary:**
$30,000/$50,000; **Industry Concentration:** Financial Services;
Function Concentration: Engineering, Finance/Accounting

Brieger, Steve — *Principal*
Thorne, Brieger Associates Inc.
11 East 44th Street
New York, NY 10017
Telephone: (212) 682-5424
Recruiter Classification: Retained; **Lowest/Average Salary:**
$90,000/$90,000; **Industry Concentration:** Generalist with a
primary focus in Financial Services; **Function Concentration:**
Generalist with a primary focus in Administration, Engineering,
Finance/Accounting, General Management, Human Resources,
Marketing, Research and Development, Sales

Brindise, Michael J. — *President*
Dynamic Search Systems, Inc.
3800 North Wilke Road, Suite 485
Arlington Heights, IL 60004
Telephone: (847) 259-3444
Recruiter Classification: Contingency; **Lowest/Average Salary:**
$30,000/$60,000; **Industry Concentration:** Generalist with a
primary focus in Financial Services, Insurance

Brinson, Robert — *Executive Recruiter*
MSI International
229 Peachtree Street, NE
Suite 1201
Atlanta, GA 30303
Telephone: (404) 659-5050
Recruiter Classification: Contingency; **Lowest/Average Salary:**
$30,000/$60,000; **Industry Concentration:** Generalist with a
primary focus in Financial Services; **Function Concentration:**
Administration, Engineering, Finance/Accounting, General
Management, Marketing, Sales

Britt, Stephen — *Recruiter*
Keith Bagg & Associates Inc.
85 Richmond St., W., Ste. 700
Toronto, Ontario, CANADA M5H 2C9
Telephone: (416) 863-1800
Recruiter Classification: Contingency; **Lowest/Average Salary:**
$40,000/$60,000; **Industry Concentration:** Generalist with a
primary focus in Insurance; **Function Concentration:**
Engineering, Research and Development

Broadhurst, Austin — *Partner*
Lamalie Amrop International
Metro Center, One Station Place
Stamford, CT 06902-6800
Telephone: (203) 324-4445
Recruiter Classification: Retained; **Lowest/Average Salary:**
$90,000/$90,000; **Industry Concentration:** Generalist with a
primary focus in Financial Services; **Function Concentration:**
Generalist

Brocaglia, Joyce — *Vice President*
Alta Associates, Inc.
8 Bartles Corner Road, Suite 021
Flemington, NJ 08822
Telephone: (908) 806-8442
Recruiter Classification: Retained; **Lowest/Average Salary:**
$50,000/$90,000; **Industry Concentration:** Generalist with a
primary focus in Financial Services, Insurance, Venture Capital;
Function Concentration: Finance/Accounting

Bronger, Patricia — *Associate*
Source Services Corporation
500 108th Avenue NE, Suite 1780
Bellevue, WA 98004
Telephone: (206) 454-6400
Recruiter Classification: Contingency; **Lowest/Average Salary:**
$30,000/$50,000; **Industry Concentration:** Financial Services;
Function Concentration: Engineering, Finance/Accounting

Brophy, Melissa — *President*
Maximum Management Corp.
420 Lexington Avenue
Suite 2016
New York, NY 10170
Telephone: (212) 867-4646
Recruiter Classification: Contingency, Executive Temporary;
Lowest/Average Salary: $30,000/$75,000; **Industry
Concentration:** Generalist with a primary focus in Financial
Services, Insurance; **Function Concentration:** Human Resources

Brother, Joy — *Vice President*
Charles Luntz & Associates. Inc.
14323 South Outer 40 Drive
Suite 400 South
Chesterfield, MO 63017-5734
Telephone: (314) 275-7992
Recruiter Classification: Retained; **Lowest/Average Salary:**
$40,000/$75,000; **Industry Concentration:** Financial Services;
Function Concentration: Generalist with a primary focus in
Administration, Engineering, Finance/Accounting, General
Management, Human Resources, Marketing, Sales

Brown, Buzz — *President*
Brown, Bernardy, Van Remmen, Inc.
12100 Wilshire Boulevard, Suite M-40
Los Angeles, CA 90025
Telephone: (310) 826-5777
Recruiter Classification: Contingency; **Lowest/Average Salary:**
$30,000/$75,000; **Industry Concentration:** Financial Services;
Function Concentration: Marketing

Brown, Charlene N. — *President*
Accent on Achievement, Inc.
3190 Rochester Road, Suite 104
Troy, MI 48083
Telephone: (248) 528-1390
Recruiter Classification: Contingency, Executive Temporary; **Lowest/Average Salary:** $30,000/$60,000; **Industry Concentration:** Generalist with a primary focus in Insurance, Venture Capital; **Function Concentration:** Finance/Accounting

Brown, Clifford — *Associate*
Source Services Corporation
111 Founders Plaza, Suite 1501E
Hartford, CT 06108
Telephone: (860) 528-0300
Recruiter Classification: Contingency; **Lowest/Average Salary:** $30,000/$50,000; **Industry Concentration:** Financial Services; **Function Concentration:** Engineering, Finance/Accounting

Brown, D. Perry — *Partner*
Don Richard Associates of Washington, D.C., Inc.
5 Choke Cherry Road, Suite 378
Rockville, MD 20850
Telephone: (301) 590-9800
Recruiter Classification: Contingency, Executive Temporary; **Lowest/Average Salary:** $30,000/$60,000; **Industry Concentration:** Financial Services; **Function Concentration:** Finance/Accounting

Brown, Daniel — *Associate*
Source Services Corporation
500 108th Avenue NE, Suite 1780
Bellevue, WA 98004
Telephone: (206) 454-6400
Recruiter Classification: Contingency; **Lowest/Average Salary:** $30,000/$50,000; **Industry Concentration:** Financial Services; **Function Concentration:** Engineering, Finance/Accounting

Brown, Franklin Key — *Executive Vice President and Managing Director*
Handy HRM Corp.
250 Park Avenue
New York, NY 10177-0074
Telephone: (212) 210-5609
Recruiter Classification: Retained; **Lowest/Average Salary:** $90,000/$90,000; **Industry Concentration:** Financial Services, Venture Capital; **Function Concentration:** Generalist with a primary focus in Finance/Accounting

Brown, Gina — *Partner*
Strategic Alliance Network, Ltd.
10901 Reed Hartman Highway
Suite 217
Cincinnati, OH 45242
Telephone: (513) 792-2800
Recruiter Classification: Retained, Contingency; **Lowest/Average Salary:** $30,000/$90,000; **Industry Concentration:** Financial Services; **Function Concentration:** Finance/Accounting, Marketing, Sales

Brown, Larry C. — *Managing Director*
Horton International
10 Tower Lane
Avon, CT 06001
Telephone: (860) 674-8701
Recruiter Classification: Retained; **Lowest/Average Salary:** $90,000/$90,000; **Industry Concentration:** Generalist with a primary focus in Insurance, Venture Capital; **Function Concentration:** Generalist with a primary focus in Administration, Finance/Accounting, General Management, Human Resources, Marketing, Sales, Women/Minorities

Brown, Lawrence Anthony — *Executive Recruiter*
MSI International
229 Peachtree Street, NE
Suite 1201
Atlanta, GA 30303
Telephone: (404) 659-5050
Recruiter Classification: Contingency; **Lowest/Average Salary:** $30,000/$60,000; **Industry Concentration:** Generalist with a primary focus in Financial Services; **Function Concentration:** Generalist with a primary focus in Administration, Engineering, Finance/Accounting, General Management, Marketing, Sales

Brown, S. Ross — *Managing Partner*
Egon Zehnder International Inc.
100 Spear Street, Suite 920
San Francisco, CA 94105
Telephone: (415) 904-7800
Recruiter Classification: Retained; **Lowest/Average Salary:** $90,000/$90,000; **Industry Concentration:** Generalist with a primary focus in Financial Services; **Function Concentration:** Generalist

Brown, Steffan — *Researcher*
Woodworth International Group
620 SW 5th Avenue, Suite 1225
Portland, OR 97204
Telephone: (503) 225-5000
Recruiter Classification: Retained; **Lowest/Average Salary:** $60,000/$90,000; **Industry Concentration:** Generalist with a primary focus in Financial Services, Insurance, Venture Capital; **Function Concentration:** Generalist with a primary focus in Engineering, Finance/Accounting, General Management, Human Resources, Marketing, Research and Development, Sales

Brown, Steve — *Recruiter*
K. Russo Associates
2 Greenwich Plaza, Suite 100
Greenwich, CT 06830
Telephone: (203) 622-3903
Recruiter Classification: Retained; **Lowest Salary:** $30,000; **Industry Concentration:** Financial Services, Insurance; **Function Concentration:** Human Resources

Brown, Steven — *Associate*
Source Services Corporation
5429 LBJ Freeway, Suite 275
Dallas, TX 75240
Telephone: (214) 387-1600
Recruiter Classification: Contingency; **Lowest/Average Salary:** $30,000/$50,000; **Industry Concentration:** Financial Services; **Function Concentration:** Engineering, Finance/Accounting

Browne, Michael — *Associate*
Source Services Corporation
20 Burlington Mall Road, Suite 405
Burlington, MA 01803
Telephone: (617) 272-5000
Recruiter Classification: Contingency; **Lowest/Average Salary:** $30,000/$50,000; **Industry Concentration:** Financial Services; **Function Concentration:** Engineering, Finance/Accounting

Bruce, Michael C. — *Director*
Spencer Stuart
10900 Wilshire Boulevard, Suite 800
Los Angeles, CA 90024-6524
Telephone: (310) 209-0610
Recruiter Classification: Retained; **Lowest/Average Salary:** $90,000/$90,000; **Industry Concentration:** Financial Services, Insurance; **Function Concentration:** Generalist

Brudno, Robert J. — *Managing Director*
Savoy Partners, Ltd.
1620 L Street N.W., Suite 801
Washington, DC 20036
Telephone: (202) 887-0666
Recruiter Classification: Retained; **Lowest/Average Salary:** $90,000/$90,000; **Industry Concentration:** Generalist with a primary focus in Financial Services, Venture Capital; **Function Concentration:** Generalist with a primary focus in Administration, Engineering, Finance/Accounting, General Management, Human Resources, Marketing, Sales, Women/Minorities

Brunner, Terry — *Associate*
Source Services Corporation
2000 Town Center, Suite 850
Southfield, MI 48075
Telephone: (810) 352-6520
Recruiter Classification: Contingency; **Lowest/Average Salary:** $30,000/$50,000; **Industry Concentration:** Financial Services; **Function Concentration:** Engineering, Finance/Accounting

Bruno, Deborah F. — *Vice President*
The Hindman Company
Browenton Place, Suite 110
2000 Warrington Way
Louisville, KY 40222
Telephone: (502) 426-4040
Recruiter Classification: Retained; **Lowest/Average Salary:** $50,000/$90,000; **Industry Concentration:** Generalist with a primary focus in Financial Services; **Function Concentration:** Generalist with a primary focus in Engineering, Finance/Accounting, General Management, Human Resources, Marketing, Sales, Women/Minorities

Bryant, Richard D. — *President*
Bryant Associates, Inc.
1390 The Point
Barrington, IL 60010
Telephone: (847) 382-0795
Recruiter Classification: Contingency; **Lowest/Average Salary:** $30,000/$60,000; **Industry Concentration:** Generalist with a primary focus in Financial Services; **Function Concentration:** Generalist with a primary focus in Engineering, Finance/Accounting, Human Resources, Marketing, Research and Development, Sales

Bryant, Shari G. — *Consultant*
Bryant Associates, Inc.
1390 The Point
Barrington, IL 60010
Telephone: (847) 382-0795
Recruiter Classification: Contingency; **Lowest/Average Salary:** $30,000/$60,000; **Industry Concentration:** Generalist with a primary focus in Financial Services; **Function Concentration:** Generalist with a primary focus in Engineering, Finance/Accounting, General Management, Marketing, Research and Development, Sales

Brzezinski, Ronald T. — *Associate*
Callan Associates, Ltd.
2021 Spring Road, Suite 175
Oak Brook, IL 60521
Telephone: (708) 832-7080
Recruiter Classification: Retained; **Lowest/Average Salary:** $90,000/$90,000; **Industry Concentration:** Generalist with a primary focus in Financial Services; **Function Concentration:** Generalist with a primary focus in Engineering, Finance/Accounting, General Management, Human Resources, Marketing, Research and Development, Sales, Women/Minorities

Buchalter, Allyson — *Vice President*
The Whitney Group
850 Third Avenue, 11th Floor
New York, NY 10022
Telephone: (212) 508-3500
Recruiter Classification: Retained; **Lowest/Average Salary:** $90,000/$90,000; **Industry Concentration:** Financial Services, Venture Capital; **Function Concentration:** Generalist with a primary focus in Finance/Accounting, General Management, Marketing, Sales

Buckles, Donna — *Recruiter*
Cochran, Cochran & Yale, Inc.
955 East Henrietta Road
Rochester, NY 14623
Telephone: (716) 424-6060
Recruiter Classification: Retained; **Lowest/Average Salary:** $50,000/$75,000; **Industry Concentration:** Generalist with a primary focus in Financial Services, Venture Capital; **Function Concentration:** Generalist with a primary focus in Engineering, Finance/Accounting, General Management, Human Resources, Sales, Women/Minorities

Buggy, Linda — *Senior Associate Recruiting*
Bonnell Associates Ltd.
2960 Post Road, Suite 200
Southport, CT 06490
Telephone: (203) 319-7214
Recruiter Classification: ; **Lowest/Average Salary:** $90,000/$90,000; **Industry Concentration:** Generalist with a primary focus in Financial Services, Insurance; **Function Concentration:** Generalist with a primary focus in Finance/Accounting, General Management, Human Resources, Sales, Women/Minorities

Bump, Gerald J. — *Executive Managing Director*
D.E. Foster Partners Inc.
303 Peachtree Street N.E., Suite 2000
Atlanta, GA 30308
Telephone: (404) 222-3440
Recruiter Classification: Retained; **Lowest/Average Salary:** $90,000/$90,000; **Industry Concentration:** Generalist with a primary focus in Financial Services, Insurance; **Function Concentration:** Generalist with a primary focus in Finance/Accounting, General Management, Human Resources, Marketing

Burch, Donald — *Associate*
Source Services Corporation
925 Westchester Avenue, Suite 309
White Plains, NY 10604
Telephone: (914) 428-9100
Recruiter Classification: Contingency; **Lowest/Average Salary:** $30,000/$50,000; **Industry Concentration:** Financial Services; **Function Concentration:** Engineering, Finance/Accounting

Burchard, Stephen R. — *President*
Burchard & Associates, Inc.
12977 North Outer Forty Drive
Suite 315
St. Louis, MO 63141
Telephone: (314) 878-2270
Recruiter Classification: Contingency; **Lowest/Average Salary:** $40,000/$60,000; **Industry Concentration:** Generalist with a primary focus in Financial Services; **Function Concentration:** Finance/Accounting, Human Resources

Burden, Gene — *Senior Vice President, Northwest*
The Cherbonnier Group, Inc.
1520 140th Avenue, N.E.
Suite 100
Bellevue, WA 67389
Telephone: (425) 644-9435
Recruiter Classification: Retained; **Lowest/Average Salary:**
$75,000/$90,000; **Industry Concentration:** Generalist with a
primary focus in Financial Services, Venture Capital; **Function
Concentration:** Generalist with a primary focus in
Administration, Engineering, Finance/Accounting, General
Management, Marketing, Research and Development, Sales

Burfield, Elaine — *Senior Vice President*
Skott/Edwards Consultants, Inc.
1776 On the Green
Morristown, NJ 07006
Telephone: (973) 644-0900
Recruiter Classification: Retained; **Lowest/Average Salary:**
$90,000/$90,000; **Industry Concentration:** Venture Capital;
Function Concentration: Finance/Accounting, General
Management, Marketing, Research and Development, Sales

Burke, John — *President*
The Experts
200 Reservoir Street
Needham, MA 02194
Telephone: (617) 449-6700
Recruiter Classification: Executive Temporary; **Lowest/Average
Salary:** $50,000/$90,000; **Industry Concentration:** Generalist
with a primary focus in Financial Services; **Function
Concentration:** Generalist with a primary focus in
Administration, Engineering, Finance/Accounting, General
Management, Human Resources, Marketing, Research and
Development, Sales

Burke, Karen A. — *Principal*
Mazza & Riley, Inc. (a Korn/Ferry International
affiliate)
55 William Street, Suite 120
Wellesley, MA 02181-4000
Telephone: (617) 235-7724
Recruiter Classification: Retained; **Lowest/Average Salary:**
$90,000/$90,000; **Industry Concentration:** Generalist with a
primary focus in Venture Capital; **Function Concentration:**
Generalist with a primary focus in Finance/Accounting,
General Management, Marketing, Sales

Burkhill, John — *President*
The Talley Group
P.O. Box 2918
Stanton, VA 24402
Telephone: (540) 248-7009
Recruiter Classification: Retained; **Lowest/Average Salary:**
$30,000/$60,000; **Industry Concentration:** Generalist with a
primary focus in Financial Services; **Function Concentration:**
Generalist with a primary focus in Engineering,
Finance/Accounting, Human Resources, Marketing, Sales

Burkland, Skott B. — *President*
Skott/Edwards Consultants, Inc.
1776 On the Green
Morristown, NJ 07006
Telephone: (973) 644-0900
Recruiter Classification: Retained; **Lowest/Average Salary:**
$90,000/$90,000; **Industry Concentration:** Venture Capital;
Function Concentration: Finance/Accounting, General
Management, Human Resources, Marketing, Research and
Development

Burnett-Stohner, Brendan G. — *Managing
Director*
Sullivan & Company
20 Exchange Place, 50th Floor
New York, NY 10005
Telephone: (212) 422-3000
Recruiter Classification: Retained; **Lowest/Average Salary:**
$90,000/$90,000; **Industry Concentration:** Generalist with a
primary focus in Financial Services; **Function Concentration:**
Generalist

Burns, Alan — *Partner*
The Enns Partners Inc.
70 University Avenue, Suite 410, P.O. Box 14
Toronto, Ontario, CANADA M5J 2M4
Telephone: (416) 598-0012
Recruiter Classification: Retained; **Lowest/Average Salary:**
$75,000/$90,000; **Industry Concentration:** Generalist with a
primary focus in Financial Services, Venture Capital; **Function
Concentration:** Generalist with a primary focus in
Administration, Finance/Accounting, General Management,
Human Resources, Marketing, Sales

Burns, Terence N. — *Managing Director*
D.E. Foster Partners Inc.
Peat Marwick Plaza
303 East Wacker Drive, 26th Floor
Chicago, IL 60601-5255
Telephone: (312) 938-1201
Recruiter Classification: Retained; **Lowest/Average Salary:**
$90,000/$90,000; **Industry Concentration:** Generalist with a
primary focus in Financial Services, Insurance; **Function
Concentration:** Generalist with a primary focus in
Administration, Finance/Accounting, General Management,
Human Resources, Marketing, Sales, Women/Minorities

Busch, Jack — *President*
Busch International
One First Street, Suite One
Los Altos, CA 94022-2754
Telephone: (650) 949-1115
Recruiter Classification: Retained; **Lowest/Average Salary:**
$90,000/$90,000; **Industry Concentration:** Venture Capital;
Function Concentration: Generalist with a primary focus in
Engineering, Finance/Accounting, General Management,
Marketing, Research and Development, Sales

Bush, R. Stuart — *Managing Director*
Russell Reynolds Associates, Inc.
1900 Trammell Crow Center
2001 Ross Avenue
Dallas, TX 75201-2977
Telephone: (214) 220-2033
Recruiter Classification: Retained; **Lowest/Average Salary:**
$90,000/$90,000; **Industry Concentration:** Financial Services;
Function Concentration: Generalist

Busterna, Charles — *Vice President*
The KPA Group
150 Broadway, Suite 1802
New York, NY 10038
Telephone: (212) 964-3640
Recruiter Classification: Contingency; **Lowest/Average Salary:**
$20,000/$40,000; **Industry Concentration:** Financial Services;
Function Concentration: Administration, Finance/Accounting,
Human Resources, Marketing

Butcher, Pascale — *Executive Recruiter*
F-O-R-T-U-N-E Personnel Consultants of Manatee
County
923 4th Street West
Palmetto, FL 34221
Telephone: (941) 729-3674
Recruiter Classification: Contingency; **Lowest/Average Salary:**
$30,000/$50,000; **Industry Concentration:** Financial Services;
Function Concentration: Finance/Accounting

Butler, Kirby B. — *President*
The Butlers Company Insurance Recruiters
2753 State Road 580, Ste. 103
Clearwater, FL 33761
Telephone: (813) 725-1065
Recruiter Classification: Contingency; **Lowest/Average Salary:**
$50,000/$90,000; **Industry Concentration:** Insurance; **Function
Concentration:** Generalist with a primary focus in
Administration, Finance/Accounting, General Management,
Human Resources, Marketing, Research and Development, Sales

Butterfass, Stanley — *Principal*
Butterfass, Pepe & MacCallan Inc.
P.O. Box 721
Mahwah, NJ 07430
Telephone: (201) 512-3330
Recruiter Classification: Retained; **Lowest/Average Salary:**
$60,000/$90,000; **Industry Concentration:** Generalist with a
primary focus in Financial Services, Insurance; **Function
Concentration:** Generalist with a primary focus in
Finance/Accounting, General Management, Human Resources,
Women/Minorities

Buttrey, Daniel — *Managing Director*
Source Services Corporation
100 North Tryon Street, Suite 3130
Charlotte, NC 28202
Telephone: (704) 333-8311
Recruiter Classification: Contingency; **Lowest/Average Salary:**
$30,000/$50,000; **Industry Concentration:** Financial Services;
Function Concentration: Engineering, Finance/Accounting

Buzolits, Patrick — *Associate*
Source Services Corporation
2000 Town Center, Suite 850
Southfield, MI 48075
Telephone: (810) 352-6520
Recruiter Classification: Contingency; **Lowest/Average Salary:**
$30,000/$50,000; **Industry Concentration:** Financial Services;
Function Concentration: Engineering, Finance/Accounting

Bye, Randy — *Managing Partner*
Romac & Associates
3200 Beechleaf Court
Suite 409
Raleigh, NC 27625
Telephone: (919) 878-4454
Recruiter Classification: Executive Temporary; **Lowest/Average
Salary:** $60,000/$60,000; **Industry Concentration:** Financial
Services, Insurance; **Function Concentration:** Finance/Accounting

Byrnes, Thomas A. — *Chairman*
The Search Alliance, Inc.
148 East Avenue, Suite 2L
Norwalk, CT 06851
Telephone: (203) 838-9936
Recruiter Classification: Retained; **Lowest/Average Salary:**
$90,000/$90,000; **Industry Concentration:** Generalist with a
primary focus in Financial Services, Insurance; **Function
Concentration:** Generalist with a primary focus in
Finance/Accounting, General Management, Human Resources,
Marketing, Research and Development, Sales, Women/Minorities

Cafero, Les — *Associate*
Source Services Corporation
425 California Street, Suite 1200
San Francisco, CA 94104
Telephone: (415) 434-2410
Recruiter Classification: Contingency; **Lowest/Average
Salary:** $30,000/$50,000; **Industry Concentration:** Financial
Services; **Function Concentration:** Engineering,
Finance/Accounting

Caldwell, C. Douglas — *Chairman*
The Caldwell Partners Amrop International
Sixty-Four Prince Arthur Avenue
Toronto, Ontario, CANADA M5R 1B4
Telephone: (416) 920-7702
Recruiter Classification: Retained; **Lowest/Average Salary:**
$60,000/$90,000; **Industry Concentration:** Generalist with a
primary focus in Financial Services, Insurance; **Function
Concentration:** Generalist

Caldwell, William R. — *Partner*
Pearson, Caldwell & Farnsworth, Inc.
One California Street, Suite 1950
San Francisco, CA 94111
Telephone: (415) 982-0300
Recruiter Classification: Retained; **Lowest/Average Salary:**
$90,000/$90,000; **Industry Concentration:** Financial
Services; **Function Concentration:** Administration,
Finance/Accounting, General Management, Human
Resources, Marketing, Sales

Calivas, Kay — *Professional Recruiter*
A.J. Burton Group, Inc.
120 East Baltimore Street, Suite 2220
Baltimore, MD 21202
Telephone: (410) 752-5244
Recruiter Classification: Contingency; **Lowest/Average Salary:**
$40,000/$75,000; **Industry Concentration:** Generalist with a
primary focus in Financial Services, Insurance; **Function
Concentration:** Generalist with a primary focus in
Administration, Finance/Accounting, General Management,
Human Resources

Call, David — *Manager*
Cochran, Cochran & Yale, Inc.
955 East Henrietta Road
Rochester, NY 14623
Telephone: (716) 424-6060
Recruiter Classification: Retained; **Lowest/Average Salary:**
$50,000/$75,000; **Industry Concentration:** Generalist with a
primary focus in Financial Services, Venture Capital; **Function
Concentration:** Generalist with a primary focus in Engineering,
Finance/Accounting, General Management, Human Resources,
Marketing, Sales, Women/Minorities

Callan, Robert M. — *Partner*
Callan Associates, Ltd.
2021 Spring Road, Suite 175
Oak Brook, IL 60521
Telephone: (708) 832-7080
Recruiter Classification: Retained; **Lowest/Average Salary:**
$90,000/$90,000; **Industry Concentration:** Generalist with a
primary focus in Financial Services; **Function Concentration:**
Generalist with a primary focus in Administration, Engineering,
Finance/Accounting, General Management, Human Resources,
Marketing, Research and Development, Sales,
Women/Minorities

Cameron, James W. — *President*
Cameron Consulting
1112 Austin Avenue
Pacific Grove, CA 93950
Telephone: (408) 646-8415
Recruiter Classification: Retained; **Lowest/Average Salary:**
$60,000/$90,000; **Industry Concentration:** Generalist with a
primary focus in Financial Services, Insurance; **Function
Concentration:** Generalist with a primary focus in
Engineering, Finance/Accounting, General Management,
Human Resources, Marketing, Research and Development,
Sales

Campbell, E. — *Associate*
Source Services Corporation
120 East Baltimore Street, Suite 1950
Baltimore, MD 21202
Telephone: (410) 727-4050
Recruiter Classification: Contingency; **Lowest/Average
Salary:** $30,000/$50,000; **Industry Concentration:** Financial
Services; **Function Concentration:** Engineering,
Finance/Accounting

Campbell, Gary — *Branch Manager*
Romac & Associates
Three Ravinia Drive
Suite 1460
Atlanta, GA 30346
Telephone: (404) 604-3880
Recruiter Classification: Executive Temporary; **Lowest/Average
Salary:** $60,000/$60,000; **Industry Concentration:** Financial
Services, Insurance; **Function Concentration:**
Finance/Accounting

Campbell, Jeff — *Associate*
Source Services Corporation
425 California Street, Suite 1200
San Francisco, CA 94104
Telephone: (415) 434-2410
Recruiter Classification: Contingency; **Lowest/Average
Salary:** $30,000/$50,000; **Industry Concentration:** Financial
Services; **Function Concentration:** Engineering,
Finance/Accounting

Campbell, Patricia A. — *Managing Director*
The Onstott Group, Inc.
60 William Street
Wellesley, MA 02181
Telephone: (781) 235-3050
Recruiter Classification: Retained; **Lowest/Average Salary:**
$90,000/$90,000; **Industry Concentration:** Generalist with a
primary focus in Financial Services; **Function Concentration:**
Generalist with a primary focus in General Management,
Human Resources, Marketing, Sales, Women/Minorities

Campbell, Robert Scott — *Principal*
Wellington Management Group
1601 Market Street, Suite 2902
Philadelphia, PA 19103-2499
Telephone: (215) 569-8900
Recruiter Classification: Retained; **Lowest/Average Salary:**
$90,000/$90,000; **Industry Concentration:** Generalist with a
primary focus in Financial Services, Venture Capital;
Function Concentration: Generalist with a primary focus in
Finance/Accounting, General Management, Marketing,
Sales

Campbell, Robert Scott — *Principal*
Wellington Management Group
5201 Great America Parkway
Suite 320
Santa Clara, CA 95054
Telephone: Unpublished
Recruiter Classification: Retained; **Lowest/Average Salary:**
$90,000/$90,000; **Industry Concentration:** Generalist with a
primary focus in Financial Services, Venture Capital;
Function Concentration: Generalist with a primary focus in
Finance/Accounting, General Management, Marketing,
Sales

Campbell, Thomas J. — *Partner*
Heidrick & Struggles, Inc.
2740 Sand Hill Road
Menlo Park, CA 94025
Telephone: (415) 234-1500
Recruiter Classification: Retained; **Lowest/Average Salary:**
$75,000/$90,000; **Industry Concentration:** Generalist with a
primary focus in Financial Services; **Function Concentration:**
Generalist

Campbell, W. Ross — *Consultant*
Egon Zehnder International Inc.
1 First Canadian Place
P.O. Box 179
Toronto, Ontario, CANADA M5X 1C7
Telephone: (416) 364-0222
Recruiter Classification: Retained; **Lowest/Average Salary:**
$90,000/$90,000; **Industry Concentration:** Generalist with a
primary focus in Financial Services; **Function Concentration:**
Generalist

Cannavino, John J. — *President*
Financial Resource Associates, Inc.
105 West Orange Street
Altamonte Springs, FL 32714
Telephone: (407) 869-7000
Recruiter Classification: Contingency; **Lowest/Average Salary:**
$40,000/$60,000; **Industry Concentration:** Financial Services;
Function Concentration: Generalist with a primary focus in
Finance/Accounting

Cannavino, Matthew J. — *Associate*
Financial Resource Associates, Inc.
105 West Orange Street
Altamonte Springs, FL 32714
Telephone: (407) 869-7000
Recruiter Classification: Contingency; **Lowest/Average
Salary:** $40,000/$60,000; **Industry Concentration:** Financial
Services; **Function Concentration:** Finance/Accounting,
Sales

Cannavo, Louise — *Managing Director*
The Whitney Group
850 Third Avenue, 11th Floor
New York, NY 10022
Telephone: (212) 508-3500
Recruiter Classification: Retained; **Lowest/Average Salary:**
$90,000/$90,000; **Industry Concentration:** Financial Services,
Venture Capital; **Function Concentration:** Generalist with a
primary focus in Finance/Accounting, General Management,
Marketing, Sales

Cannon, Alexis — *Associate Partner*
Richard, Wayne and Roberts
24 Greenway Plaza, Suite 1304
Houston, TX 77046-2493
Telephone: (713) 629-6681
Recruiter Classification: Retained; **Lowest/Average Salary:**
$50,000/$90,000; **Industry Concentration:** Generalist with a
primary focus in Financial Services; **Function Concentration:**
Generalist with a primary focus in Finance/Accounting

Capizzi, Karen — *Search Consultant*
Cochran, Cochran & Yale, Inc.
955 East Henrietta Road
Rochester, NY 14623
Telephone: (716) 424-6060
Recruiter Classification: Retained; **Lowest/Average Salary:**
$50,000/$75,000; **Industry Concentration:** Generalist with a
primary focus in Financial Services, Venture Capital; **Function
Concentration:** Generalist with a primary focus in Engineering,
Finance/Accounting, General Management, Human Resources,
Marketing, Sales, Women/Minorities

Cappe, Richard R. — *President*
Roberts Ryan and Bentley
1107 Kenilworth Drive, Suite 208
Towson, MD 21204
Telephone: (410) 321-6600
Recruiter Classification: Retained; **Lowest/Average Salary:**
$90,000/$90,000; **Industry Concentration:** Financial Services,
Insurance; **Function Concentration:** Administration, General
Management

Carideo, Joseph — *Partner*
Thorndike Deland Associates
275 Madison Avenue, Suite 1300
New York, NY 10016
Telephone: (212) 661-6200
Recruiter Classification: Retained; **Lowest/Average Salary:**
$100,000/$125,000; **Industry Concentration:** Generalist with a
primary focus in Financial Services, Insurance, Venture Capital;
Function Concentration: Generalist with a primary focus in
Finance/Accounting, General Management, Human Resources,
Marketing, Sales

Carlson, Eric — *Associate*
Source Services Corporation
500 108th Avenue NE, Suite 1780
Bellevue, WA 98004
Telephone: (206) 454-6400
Recruiter Classification: Contingency; **Lowest/Average Salary:**
$30,000/$50,000; **Industry Concentration:** Financial Services;
Function Concentration: Engineering, Finance/Accounting

Carlson, Judith — *Financial Recruiter*
Bowman & Marshall, Inc.
P.O. Box 25503
Overland Park, KS 66225
Telephone: (913) 648-3332
Recruiter Classification: Contingency; **Lowest/Average Salary:**
$30,000/$50,000; **Industry Concentration:** Financial Services,
Insurance; **Function Concentration:** Finance/Accounting

Carnal, Rick — *Associate*
Source Services Corporation
3 Summit Park Drive, Suite 550
Independence, OH 44131
Telephone: (216) 328-5900
Recruiter Classification: Contingency; **Lowest/Average Salary:**
$30,000/$50,000; **Industry Concentration:** Financial Services;
Function Concentration: Engineering, Finance/Accounting

Carrington, Timothy — *Principal*
Korn/Ferry International
303 Peachtree Street N.E.
Suite 1600
Atlanta, GA 30308
Telephone: (404) 577-7542
Recruiter Classification: Retained; **Lowest/Average Salary:**
$100,000/$150,000; **Industry Concentration:** Generalist with a
primary focus in Financial Services, Insurance; **Function
Concentration:** Generalist

Carro, Carl R. — *Managing Director*
Executive Search Consultants International, Inc.
330 Fifth Avenue
Suite 5501
New York, NY 10118
Telephone: (212) 333-1900
Recruiter Classification: Retained; **Lowest/Average Salary:**
$90,000/$90,000; **Industry Concentration:** Generalist with a
primary focus in Financial Services; **Function Concentration:**
Generalist with a primary focus in Finance/Accounting,
General Management, Human Resources, Marketing

Carrott, Gregory T. — *Managing Partner*
Egon Zehnder International Inc.
1 First Canadian Place
P.O. Box 179
Toronto, Ontario, CANADA M5X 1C7
Telephone: (416) 364-0222
Recruiter Classification: Retained; **Lowest/Average Salary:**
$90,000/$90,000; **Industry Concentration:** Generalist with a
primary focus in Financial Services; **Function Concentration:**
Generalist

Carter, Jon F. — *Consultant*
Egon Zehnder International Inc.
100 Spear Street, Suite 920
San Francisco, CA 94105
Telephone: (415) 904-7800
Recruiter Classification: Retained; **Lowest/Average Salary:**
$90,000/$90,000; **Industry Concentration:** Generalist with a
primary focus in Financial Services; **Function Concentration:**
Generalist

Carter, Linda — *Associate*
Source Services Corporation
5429 LBJ Freeway, Suite 275
Dallas, TX 75240
Telephone: (214) 387-1600
Recruiter Classification: Contingency; **Lowest/Average
Salary:** $30,000/$50,000; **Industry Concentration:** Financial
Services; **Function Concentration:** Engineering,
Finance/Accounting

Carvalho-Esteves, Maria — *Associate*
Source Services Corporation
379 Thornall Street
Edison, NJ 08837
Telephone: (908) 494-2800
Recruiter Classification: Contingency; **Lowest/Average
Salary:** $30,000/$50,000; **Industry Concentration:** Financial
Services; **Function Concentration:** Engineering,
Finance/Accounting

Cary, Con — *President*
Cary & Associates
P.O. Box 2043
Winter Park, FL 32790-2043
Telephone: (407) 647-1145
Recruiter Classification: Retained; **Lowest/Average Salary:**
$30,000/$75,000; **Industry Concentration:** Generalist with a
primary focus in Financial Services, Venture Capital; **Function
Concentration:** Generalist with a primary focus in
Administration, Engineering, Finance/Accounting, Human
Resources, Marketing, Sales

Casal, Daniel G. — *Executive Recruiter*
Bonifield Associates
3003E Lincoln Drive West
Marlton, NJ 08053
Telephone: (609) 596-3300
Recruiter Classification: Contingency; **Lowest/Average
Salary:** $40,000/$50,000; **Industry Concentration:** Financial
Services, Insurance; **Function Concentration:** Generalist with
a primary focus in Administration, Finance/Accounting,
General Management, Marketing, Research and
Development, Sales

Cashen, Anthony B. — *Senior Partner*
Lamalie Amrop International
200 Park Avenue
New York, NY 10166-0136
Telephone: (212) 953-7900
Recruiter Classification: Retained; **Lowest/Average Salary:**
$90,000/$90,000; **Industry Concentration:** Generalist with a
primary focus in Financial Services; **Function Concentration:**
Generalist with a primary focus in Finance/Accounting,
General Management, Marketing

Castillo, Eduardo — *Principal*
Korn/Ferry International
Daniel Zambrano 525
Col. Chepe Vera
Monterrey, N.L., MEXICO 11000
Telephone: (528) 348-4355
Recruiter Classification: Retained; **Lowest/Average Salary:**
$100,000/$150,000; **Industry Concentration:** Generalist with a
primary focus in Financial Services, Insurance; **Function
Concentration:** Generalist

Castine, Michael P. — *Partner*
Highland Search Group
565 Fifth Avenue, 22nd Floor
New York, NY 10017
Telephone: (212) 328-1113
Recruiter Classification: Retained; **Lowest/Average Salary:**
$90,000/$90,000; **Industry Concentration:** Financial Services,
Insurance, Venture Capital; **Function Concentration:** Generalist
with a primary focus in Administration, Finance/Accounting,
General Management, Human Resources, Sales,
Women/Minorities

Castle, Lisa — *Associate*
Source Services Corporation
379 Thornall Street
Edison, NJ 08837
Telephone: (908) 494-2800
Recruiter Classification: Contingency; **Lowest/Average
Salary:** $30,000/$50,000; **Industry Concentration:** Financial
Services; **Function Concentration:** Engineering,
Finance/Accounting

Castriota, Dominic — *Partner*
Rhodes Associates
555 Fifth Avenue
New York, NY 10017
Telephone: (212) 983-2000
Recruiter Classification: Retained; **Lowest/Average Salary:**
$90,000/$200,000; **Industry Concentration:** Financial
Services, Insurance, Venture Capital; **Function Concentration:**
Generalist

Caudill, Nancy — *Managing Director*
Webb, Johnson Associates, Inc.
280 Park Avenue, 43rd Floor
New York, NY 10017
Telephone: (212) 661-3700
Recruiter Classification: Retained; **Lowest/Average Salary:**
$90,000/$90,000; **Industry Concentration:** Generalist with a
primary focus in Financial Services; **Function Concentration:**
Generalist

Cavanagh, Michael J. — *President*
Michael J. Cavanagh and Associates
60 St. Clair Avenue East
Suite 905
Toronto, Ontario, CANADA M4T 1N5
Telephone: (416) 324-9661
Recruiter Classification: Retained; **Lowest/Average Salary:**
$80,000/$100,000; **Industry Concentration:** Generalist with a
primary focus in Venture Capital; **Function Concentration:**
Generalist with a primary focus in Administration, Engineering,
Finance/Accounting, General Management, Human Resources,
Marketing

Celenza, Catherine — *Executive Recruiter*
CPS Inc.
303 Congress Street, 5th Floor
Boston, MA 02210
Telephone: (617) 439-7950
Recruiter Classification: Contingency; **Lowest/Average Salary:**
$30,000/$50,000; **Industry Concentration:** Generalist with a
primary focus in Financial Services, Insurance; **Function
Concentration:** Engineering, Research and Development,
Sales, Women/Minorities

Cersosimo, Rocco — *Associate*
Source Services Corporation
Foster Plaza VI
681 Anderson Drive, 2nd Floor
Pittsburgh, PA 15220
Telephone: (412) 928-8300
Recruiter Classification: Contingency; **Lowest/Average Salary:**
$30,000/$50,000; **Industry Concentration:** Financial Services;
Function Concentration: Engineering, Finance/Accounting

Chamberlin, Brooks T. — *Managing Director*
Korn/Ferry International
237 Park Avenue
New York, NY 10017
Telephone: (212) 687-1834
Recruiter Classification: Retained; **Lowest/Average Salary:**
$100,000/$150,000; **Industry Concentration:** Generalist with a
primary focus in Financial Services, Insurance; **Function
Concentration:** Generalist

Chamberlin, Joan — *Associate*
William Guy & Associates
P.O. Box 57407
Sherman Oaks, CA 91413
Telephone: Unpublished
Recruiter Classification: Retained; **Lowest/Average Salary:** $50,000/$90,000; **Industry Concentration:** Generalist with a primary focus in Financial Services; **Function Concentration:** Generalist with a primary focus in Administration, Human Resources, Marketing, Sales, Women/Minorities

Chamberlin, Michael A. — *Executive Search Consultant*
Tower Consultants, Ltd.
4195 N.E. Hyline Drive
Jensen Beach, FL 34957
Telephone: (561) 225-5151
Recruiter Classification: Retained; **Lowest/Average Salary:** $60,000/$90,000; **Industry Concentration:** Generalist with a primary focus in Financial Services, Insurance; **Function Concentration:** Administration, Human Resources, Women/Minorities

Champion, Geoffrey — *Managing Vice President*
Advanced Technology
Korn/Ferry International
2180 Sand Hill Road
Menlo Park, CA 94025
Telephone: (415) 233-2733
Recruiter Classification: Retained; **Lowest/Average Salary:** $100,000/$150,000; **Industry Concentration:** Generalist with a primary focus in Financial Services, Insurance; **Function Concentration:** Generalist

Chan, Margaret — *Managing Director*
Webb, Johnson Associates, Inc.
280 Park Avenue, 43rd Floor
New York, NY 10017
Telephone: (212) 661-3700
Recruiter Classification: Retained; **Lowest/Average Salary:** $90,000/$90,000; **Industry Concentration:** Generalist with a primary focus in Financial Services; **Function Concentration:** Generalist

Chappell, Peter — *Managing Director*
The Bankers Group
10 South Riverside Plaza, Suite 1424
Chicago, IL 60606
Telephone: (312) 930-9456
Recruiter Classification: Contingency; **Lowest/Average Salary:** $50,000/$75,000; **Industry Concentration:** Generalist with a primary focus in Financial Services, Insurance, Venture Capital; **Function Concentration:** Generalist with a primary focus in Administration, Finance/Accounting, General Management, Human Resources, Marketing, Sales, Women/Minorities

Chappell, Peter — *Managing Director*
Robertson & Associates
10 South Riverside Plaza
Suite 1410
Chicago, IL 60606
Telephone: (312) 936-1958
Recruiter Classification: Retained; **Lowest/Average Salary:** $50,000/$75,000; **Industry Concentration:** Generalist with a primary focus in Financial Services, Insurance, Venture Capital; **Function Concentration:** Generalist with a primary focus in Finance/Accounting, Human Resources, Women/Minorities

Charles, Ronald D. — *Partner*
The Caldwell Partners Amrop International
Sixty-Four Prince Arthur Avenue
Toronto, Ontario, CANADA M5R 1B4
Telephone: (416) 920-7702
Recruiter Classification: Retained; **Lowest/Average Salary:** $60,000/$90,000; **Industry Concentration:** Generalist with a primary focus in Financial Services, Insurance; **Function Concentration:** Generalist

Chase, James — *Associate*
Source Services Corporation
1500 West Park Drive, Suite 390
Westborough, MA 01581
Telephone: (508) 366-2600
Recruiter Classification: Contingency; **Lowest/Average Salary:** $30,000/$50,000; **Industry Concentration:** Financial Services; **Function Concentration:** Engineering, Finance/Accounting

Chatterjie, Alok — *Executive Recruiter*
MSI International
8521 Leesburg Pike, Suite 435
Vienna, VA 22182
Telephone: (703) 893-5669
Recruiter Classification: Contingency; **Lowest/Average Salary:** $30,000/$75,000; **Industry Concentration:** Financial Services; **Function Concentration:** Generalist with a primary focus in Administration, Engineering, Finance/Accounting, General Management, Marketing, Sales

Chauvin, Ralph A. — *Partner*
The Caldwell Partners Amrop International
Sixty-Four Prince Arthur Avenue
Toronto, Ontario, CANADA M5R 1B4
Telephone: (416) 920-7702
Recruiter Classification: Retained; **Lowest/Average Salary:** $60,000/$90,000; **Industry Concentration:** Generalist with a primary focus in Insurance; **Function Concentration:** Generalist

Cheah, Victor — *Associate*
Source Services Corporation
20 Burlington Mall Road, Suite 405
Burlington, MA 01803
Telephone: (617) 272-5000
Recruiter Classification: Contingency; **Lowest/Average Salary:** $30,000/$50,000; **Industry Concentration:** Financial Services; **Function Concentration:** Engineering, Finance/Accounting

Cherbonnier, L. Michael — *President*
TCG International, Inc.
471 North Post Oak Lane
Houston, TX 77024
Telephone: (713) 960-9511
Recruiter Classification: Executive Temporary; **Lowest/Average Salary:** $75,000/$90,000; **Industry Concentration:** Generalist with a primary focus in Venture Capital; **Function Concentration:** Generalist with a primary focus in Engineering, Finance/Accounting, General Management, Marketing, Research and Development, Sales

Cherbonnier, L. Michael — *President*
The Cherbonnier Group, Inc.
3050 Post Oak Boulevard, Suite 1600
Houston, TX 77056
Telephone: (713) 688-4701
Recruiter Classification: Retained; **Lowest/Average Salary:** $75,000/$90,000; **Industry Concentration:** Generalist with a primary focus in Financial Services, Venture Capital; **Function Concentration:** Generalist with a primary focus in Administration, Engineering, Finance/Accounting, General Management, Human Resources, Marketing, Research and Development, Sales

Chndler, Brad J. — *Vice President*
Furst Group/MPI
8009 34th Avenue, Suite 1450
Minneapolis, MN 55425
Telephone: (612) 851-9213
Recruiter Classification: Retained; **Lowest/Average Salary:**
$60,000/$90,000; **Industry Concentration:** Generalist with a
primary focus in Insurance; **Function Concentration:**
Generalist with a primary focus in Finance/Accounting,
General Management, Human Resources, Marketing, Research
and Development, Sales

Cho, Ui — *Executive Recruiter*
Richard, Wayne and Roberts
24 Greenway Plaza, Suite 1304
Houston, TX 77046-2493
Telephone: (713) 629-6681
Recruiter Classification: Retained; **Lowest/Average Salary:**
$50,000/$90,000; **Industry Concentration:** Generalist with a
primary focus in Financial Services; **Function Concentration:**
Generalist with a primary focus in Finance/Accounting

Chrisman, Timothy R. — *Chief Executive Officer*
Chrisman & Company, Incorporated
350 South Figueroa Street, Suite 550
Los Angeles, CA 90071
Telephone: (213) 620-1192
Recruiter Classification: Retained; **Lowest/Average Salary:**
$75,000/$90,000; **Industry Concentration:** Generalist with a
primary focus in Financial Services, Insurance, Venture Capital;
Function Concentration: Generalist with a primary focus in
Marketing, Women/Minorities

Christenson, H. Alan — *Managing Partner*
Christenson & Hutchison
466 Southern Boulevard
Chatham, NJ 07928-1462
Telephone: (201) 966-1600
Recruiter Classification: Retained; **Lowest/Average Salary:**
$75,000/$90,000; **Industry Concentration:** Generalist with a
primary focus in Financial Services, Insurance; **Function
Concentration:** Generalist with a primary focus in
Finance/Accounting, General Management, Human Resources,
Marketing, Sales

Christian, Jeffrey E. — *President and CEO*
Christian & Timbers
25825 Science Park Drive, Suite 400
Cleveland, OH 44122
Telephone: (216) 765-5877
Recruiter Classification: Retained; **Lowest/Average Salary:**
$90,000/$90,000; **Industry Concentration:** Venture Capital;
Function Concentration: General Management, Marketing,
Sales, Women/Minorities

Christian, Philip — *Consultant*
Ray & Berndtson
One Allen Center
500 Dallas, Suite 3010
Houston, TX 77002
Telephone: (713) 309-1400
Recruiter Classification: Retained; **Lowest/Average Salary:**
$90,000/$90,000; **Industry Concentration:** Generalist with a
primary focus in Financial Services, Insurance; **Function
Concentration:** Generalist with a primary focus in
Administration, Finance/Accounting, General Management,
Human Resources, Marketing, Research and Development,
Sales, Women/Minorities

Christiansen, Amy — *Executive Recruiter*
CPS Inc.
One Westbrook Corporate Centre, Suite 600
Westchester, IL 60154
Telephone: (708) 531-8370
Recruiter Classification: Contingency; **Lowest/Average Salary:**
$30,000/$50,000; **Industry Concentration:** Generalist with a
primary focus in Financial Services, Insurance; **Function
Concentration:** Engineering, Research and Development,
Sales, Women/Minorities

Christiansen, Doug — *Executive Recruiter*
CPS Inc.
One Westbrook Corporate Centre, Suite 600
Westchester, IL 60154
Telephone: (708) 531-8370
Recruiter Classification: Contingency; **Lowest/Average Salary:**
$30,000/$50,000; **Industry Concentration:** Generalist with a
primary focus in Financial Services, Insurance; **Function
Concentration:** Engineering, Research and Development,
Sales, Women/Minorities

Christman, Joel — *Associate*
Source Services Corporation
525 Vine Street, Suite 2250
Cincinnati, OH 45202
Telephone: (513) 651-3303
Recruiter Classification: Contingency; **Lowest/Average Salary:**
$30,000/$50,000; **Industry Concentration:** Financial Services;
Function Concentration: Engineering, Finance/Accounting

Chronopoulos, Dennis — *Associate*
Source Services Corporation
20 Burlington Mall Road, Suite 405
Burlington, MA 01803
Telephone: (617) 272-5000
Recruiter Classification: Contingency; **Lowest/Average Salary:**
$30,000/$50,000; **Industry Concentration:** Financial Services;
Function Concentration: Engineering, Finance/Accounting

Citarella, Richard A. — *Vice President/Managing
Director*
A.T. Kearney, Inc.
1100 Abernathy Road, Suite 900
Atlanta, GA 30328-5603
Telephone: (770) 393-9900
Recruiter Classification: Retained; **Lowest/Average Salary:**
$90,000/$90,000; **Industry Concentration:** Generalist with a
primary focus in Financial Services; **Function Concentration:**
Generalist with a primary focus in Finance/Accounting,
Marketing, Sales

Citrin, James M. — *Director*
Spencer Stuart
Financial Centre
695 East Main Street
Stamford, CT 06901
Telephone: (203) 324-6333
Recruiter Classification: Retained; **Lowest/Average Salary:**
$90,000/$90,000; **Industry Concentration:** Generalist with a
primary focus in Financial Services; **Function Concentration:**
Generalist

Citrin, Lea — *Executive Vice President*
K.L. Whitney Company
6 Aspen Drive
North Caldwell, NJ 07006
Telephone: (201) 228-7124
Recruiter Classification: Retained; **Lowest/Average Salary:**
$75,000/$90,000; **Industry Concentration:** Financial Services;
Function Concentration: Marketing, Sales

Cizek, John T. — *Principal*
Cizek Associates, Inc.
2021 Midwest Road, Suite 200
Oak Brook, IL 60521
Telephone: (630) 953-8570
Recruiter Classification: Retained; **Lowest/Average Salary:**
$75,000/$90,000; **Industry Concentration:** Generalist with a
primary focus in Financial Services; **Function Concentration:**
Generalist with a primary focus in Administration, Engineering,
Finance/Accounting, General Management, Human Resources,
Marketing, Research and Development, Sales

Cizek, Marti J. — *President*
Cizek Associates, Inc.
2390 East Camelback Road, Suite 300
Phoenix, AZ 85016
Telephone: (602) 553-1066
Recruiter Classification: Retained; **Lowest/Average Salary:**
$75,000/$90,000; **Industry Concentration:** Generalist with a
primary focus in Financial Services; **Function Concentration:**
Generalist with a primary focus in Administration, Engineering,
Finance/Accounting, General Management, Human Resources,
Marketing, Research and Development, Sales,
Women/Minorities

Clake, Bob — *Principal*
Furst Group/MPI
555 S. Perryville Road
Rockford, IL 61108
Telephone: (815) 229-9111
Recruiter Classification: Retained; **Lowest/Average Salary:**
$60,000/$90,000; **Industry Concentration:** Insurance;
Function Concentration: Finance/Accounting, General
Management, Human Resources, Marketing, Research and
Development, Sales

Clarey, William A. — *Consultant*
Preng & Associates, Inc.
2925 Briarpark, Suite 1111
Houston, TX 77042
Telephone: (713) 266-2600
Recruiter Classification: Retained; **Lowest/Average Salary:**
$90,000/$90,000; **Industry Concentration:** Generalist with a
primary focus in Venture Capital; **Function Concentration:**
Generalist with a primary focus in Finance/Accounting,
General Management, Human Resources

Clark, Donald B. — *Industry Leader - Financial
Services*
Ray & Berndtson
Sears Tower, 233 South Wacker Drive, Suite 4020
Chicago, IL 60606-6310
Telephone: (312) 876-0730
Recruiter Classification: Retained; **Lowest/Average Salary:**
$90,000/$90,000; **Industry Concentration:** Financial Services;
Function Concentration: Generalist

Clark, Evan — *Vice President*
The Whitney Group
850 Third Avenue, 11th Floor
New York, NY 10022
Telephone: (212) 508-3500
Recruiter Classification: Retained; **Lowest/Average Salary:**
$90,000/$90,000; **Industry Concentration:** Financial Services,
Venture Capital; **Function Concentration:** Generalist with a
primary focus in Finance/Accounting, General Management,
Marketing, Sales

Clark, James — *Manager/Lab Recruiter*
CPS Inc.
363 East Lincoln Highway, Suite E
DeKalb, IL 60115
Telephone: (815) 756-1221
Recruiter Classification: Contingency; **Lowest/Average Salary:**
$30,000/$50,000; **Industry Concentration:** Generalist with a
primary focus in Financial Services, Insurance; **Function
Concentration:** Engineering, Research and Development,
Sales, Women/Minorities

Clark, Julie — *Contract Services Division
Recruiter*
Corporate Recruiters Ltd.
490-1140 West Pender Street
Vancouver, British Columbia, CANADA V6E 4G1
Telephone: (604) 687-5993
Recruiter Classification: Contingency; **Lowest/Average Salary:**
$30,000/$60,000; **Industry Concentration:** Generalist with a
primary focus in Financial Services, Insurance

Clark, Steven — *Partner*
D.A. Kreuter Associates, Inc.
1100 East Hector Street, Suite 388
Conshohocken, PA 19428
Telephone: (610) 834-1100
Recruiter Classification: Retained; **Lowest/Average Salary:**
$60,000/$90,000; **Industry Concentration:** Financial Services,
Insurance; **Function Concentration:** General Management,
Marketing, Sales

Clarke Smith, Jamie — *Executive Director*
Kaye-Bassman International Corp.
18333 Preston Road, Suite 500
Dallas, TX 75252
Telephone: (972) 931-5242
Recruiter Classification: Retained; **Lowest/Average Salary:**
$75,000/$90,000; **Industry Concentration:** Generalist with a
primary focus in Insurance; **Function Concentration:**
Generalist with a primary focus in Finance/Accounting,
General Management, Human Resources, Marketing, Sales,
Women/Minorities

Clauhsen, Elizabeth A. — *Senior Vice President*
Savoy Partners, Ltd.
1620 L Street N.W., Suite 801
Washington, DC 20036
Telephone: (202) 887-0666
Recruiter Classification: Retained; **Lowest/Average Salary:**
$90,000/$90,000; **Industry Concentration:** Generalist with a
primary focus in Financial Services, Venture Capital; **Function
Concentration:** Generalist with a primary focus in
Administration, Engineering, Finance/Accounting, General
Management, Human Resources, Marketing, Sales,
Women/Minorities

Clawson, Bob — *Managing Director*
Source Services Corporation
3701 West Algonquin Road, Suite 380
Rolling Meadows, IL 60008
Telephone: (847) 392-0244
Recruiter Classification: Contingency; **Lowest/Average
Salary:** $30,000/$50,000; **Industry Concentration:** Financial
Services; **Function Concentration:** Engineering,
Finance/Accounting

Clawson, Robert — *Managing Director*
Source Services Corporation
150 South Wacker Drive, Suite 400
Chicago, IL 60606
Telephone: (312) 346-7000
Recruiter Classification: Contingency; **Lowest/Average Salary:** $30,000/$50,000; **Industry Concentration:** Financial Services; **Function Concentration:** Engineering, Finance/Accounting

Clayton, Fred J. — *Executive Vice President*
Berkhemer Clayton Incorporated
Union Station
800 N. Alameda Street, Suite. 200
Los Angeles, CA 90012
Telephone: (213) 621-2300
Recruiter Classification: Retained; **Lowest/Average Salary:** $75,000/$90,000; **Industry Concentration:** Generalist with a primary focus in Financial Services; **Function Concentration:** Generalist with a primary focus in Administration, Finance/Accounting, General Management, Human Resources, Marketing, Women/Minorities

Clemens, Bill — *Director*
Spencer Stuart
Financial Centre
695 East Main Street
Stamford, CT 06901
Telephone: (203) 324-6333
Recruiter Classification: Retained; **Lowest/Average Salary:** $90,000/$90,000; **Industry Concentration:** Financial Services; **Function Concentration:** Generalist with a primary focus in Finance/Accounting

Cloutier, Gisella — *Vice President*
Dinte Resources, Inc.
8300 Greensboro Drive
Suite 880
McLean, VA 22102
Telephone: (703) 448-3300
Recruiter Classification: Executive Temporary; **Lowest/Average Salary:** $90,000/$90,000; **Industry Concentration:** Generalist with a primary focus in Financial Services; **Function Concentration:** Generalist with a primary focus in Finance/Accounting, General Management, Human Resources, Marketing, Sales

Cocchiaro, Richard — *Regional President*
Romac & Associates
20 North Wacker Drive
Suite 2420
Chicago, IL 60606
Telephone: (312) 263-0902
Recruiter Classification: Executive Temporary; **Lowest/Average Salary:** $60,000/$60,000; **Industry Concentration:** Financial Services, Insurance; **Function Concentration:** Finance/Accounting

Cocconi, Alan — *Associate*
Source Services Corporation
150 South Wacker Drive, Suite 400
Chicago, IL 60606
Telephone: (312) 346-7000
Recruiter Classification: Contingency; **Lowest/Average Salary:** $30,000/$50,000; **Industry Concentration:** Financial Services; **Function Concentration:** Engineering, Finance/Accounting

Cochran, Scott P. — *Vice President*
The Badger Group
4125 Blackhawk Plaza Circle, Suite 270
Danville, CA 94506
Telephone: (510) 736-5553
Recruiter Classification: Retained; **Lowest/Average Salary:** $90,000/$90,000; **Industry Concentration:** Generalist with a primary focus in Financial Services; **Function Concentration:** Generalist with a primary focus in Engineering, Finance/Accounting, General Management, Human Resources, Marketing, Research and Development, Sales

Cochrun, James — *Associate*
Source Services Corporation
9020 Capital of Texas Highway
Building I, Suite 337
Austin, TX 78759
Telephone: (512) 345-7473
Recruiter Classification: Contingency; **Lowest/Average Salary:** $30,000/$50,000; **Industry Concentration:** Financial Services; **Function Concentration:** Engineering, Finance/Accounting

Coe, Karen J. — *President*
Coe & Company International Inc.
1535 400-3rd Avenue SW
Center Tower
Calgary, Alberta, Canada T20 4H2
Telephone: (403) 232-8833
Recruiter Classification: Retained; **Lowest/Average Salary:** $75,000/$90,000; **Industry Concentration:** Financial Services; **Function Concentration:** Generalist with a primary focus in Engineering, Human Resources, Marketing, Sales

Coffman, Brian — *Vice President*
Kossuth & Associates, Inc.
800 Bellevue Way N.E., Suite 400
Bellevue, WA 98004
Telephone: (206) 450-9050
Recruiter Classification: Retained; **Lowest/Average Salary:** $50,000/$90,000; **Industry Concentration:** Venture Capital; **Function Concentration:** Generalist with a primary focus in Administration, Engineering, Finance/Accounting, General Management, Human Resources, Marketing, Research and Development, Sales, Women/Minorities

Cohen, Michael R. — *Chief Executive Officer*
Intech Summit Group, Inc.
5075 Shoreham Place, Suite 280
San Diego, CA 92116
Telephone: (619) 452-2100
Recruiter Classification: Retained; **Lowest/Average Salary:** $60,000/$90,000; **Industry Concentration:** Generalist with a primary focus in Financial Services, Insurance; **Function Concentration:** Generalist with a primary focus in Finance/Accounting, General Management, Human Resources

Cohen, Pamela — *Legal Consultant*
TOPAZ International, Inc.
383 Northfield Avenue
West Orange, NJ 07052
Telephone: (201) 669-7300
Recruiter Classification: Contingency; **Lowest/Average Salary:** $40,000/$75,000; **Industry Concentration:** Financial Services; **Function Concentration:** Generalist with a primary focus in Women/Minorities

Cohen, Pamela — *Legal Consultant*
TOPAZ Legal Solutions
383 Northfield Avenue
West Orange, NJ 07052
Telephone: (201) 669-7300
Recruiter Classification: Executive Temporary; **Lowest/Average Salary:** $40,000/$75,000; **Industry Concentration:** Financial Services; **Function Concentration:** Generalist with a primary focus in Women/Minorities

Cohen, Robert C. — *Chief Executive Officer*
Intech Summit Group, Inc.
5075 Shoreham Place, Suite 280
San Diego, CA 92116
Telephone: (619) 452-2100
Recruiter Classification: Retained; **Lowest/Average Salary:** $75,000/$90,000; **Industry Concentration:** Generalist with a primary focus in Financial Services, Insurance, Venture Capital; **Function Concentration:** Generalist with a primary focus in Administration, Engineering, Finance/Accounting, General Management, Human Resources, Marketing, Research and Development, Sales, Women/Minorities

Colasanto, Frank M. — *Principal*
W.R. Rosato & Associates, Inc.
61 Broadway, 26th Floor
New York, NY 10006
Telephone: (212) 509-5700
Recruiter Classification: Retained; **Lowest/Average Salary:** $90,000/$90,000; **Industry Concentration:** Financial Services; **Function Concentration:** Administration, Marketing, Research and Development, Sales

Cole, Kevin — *Partner*
Don Richard Associates of Washington, D.C., Inc.
8180 Greensboro Drive, Suite 1020
McLean, VA 22102
Telephone: (703) 827-5990
Recruiter Classification: Contingency, Executive Temporary; **Lowest/Average Salary:** $40,000/$60,000; **Industry Concentration:** Financial Services; **Function Concentration:** Finance/Accounting

Cole, Rosalie — *Associate*
Source Services Corporation
150 South Wacker Drive, Suite 400
Chicago, IL 60606
Telephone: (312) 346-7000
Recruiter Classification: Contingency; **Lowest/Average Salary:** $30,000/$50,000; **Industry Concentration:** Financial Services; **Function Concentration:** Engineering, Finance/Accounting

Coleman, J. Gregory — *Managing Director*
Korn/Ferry International
237 Park Avenue
New York, NY 10017
Telephone: (212) 687-1834
Recruiter Classification: Retained; **Lowest/Average Salary:** $100,000/$150,000; **Industry Concentration:** Generalist with a primary focus in Financial Services; **Function Concentration:** Generalist

Coleman, J. Kevin — *President*
J. Kevin Coleman & Associates, Inc.
416 Hermosa Place
So. Pasadena, CA 91030
Telephone: (818) 403-0704
Recruiter Classification: Retained; **Lowest/Average Salary:** $60,000/$90,000; **Industry Concentration:** Generalist with a primary focus in Venture Capital; **Function Concentration:** Generalist with a primary focus in Engineering, Finance/Accounting, General Management, Human Resources, Marketing

Coleman, Patricia — *Principal*
Korn/Ferry International
233 South Wacker
Chicago, IL 60606
Telephone: (312) 466-1834
Recruiter Classification: Retained; **Lowest/Average Salary:** $100,000/$150,000; **Industry Concentration:** Generalist with a primary focus in Financial Services, Insurance; **Function Concentration:** Generalist

Collard, Joseph A. — *Senior Director*
Spencer Stuart
1111 Bagby, Suite 1616
Houston, TX 77002-2594
Telephone: (713) 225-1621
Recruiter Classification: Retained; **Lowest/Average Salary:** $90,000/$90,000; **Industry Concentration:** Generalist with a primary focus in Insurance; **Function Concentration:** Generalist with a primary focus in Engineering, Finance/Accounting, General Management, Human Resources, Marketing, Sales

Collins, Scott — *Associate*
Source Services Corporation
5343 North 16th Street, Suite 270
Phoenix, AZ 85016
Telephone: (602) 230-0220
Recruiter Classification: Contingency; **Lowest/Average Salary:** $30,000/$50,000; **Industry Concentration:** Financial Services; **Function Concentration:** Engineering, Finance/Accounting

Collins, Stephen — *Managing Director*
The Johnson Group, Inc.
1 World Trade Center, Suite 4517
New York, NY 10048-0202
Telephone: (212) 775-0036
Recruiter Classification: Contingency; **Lowest/Average Salary:** $60,000/$75,000; **Industry Concentration:** Financial Services; **Function Concentration:** Finance/Accounting, Women/Minorities

Collis, Martin — *Consultant*
E.L. Shore & Associates Ltd.
1201-2 St. Clair Avenue E.
Toronto, Ontario, CANADA M4T 2T5
Telephone: (416) 928-9399
Recruiter Classification: Retained; **Lowest/Average Salary:** $60,000/$90,000; **Industry Concentration:** Generalist with a primary focus in Financial Services, Insurance; **Function Concentration:** Generalist

Colman, Michael — *President*
Executive Placement Consultants, Inc.
2700 River Road, Suite 107
Des Plaines, IL 60018
Telephone: (847) 298-6445
Recruiter Classification: Contingency; **Lowest/Average Salary:** $40,000/$75,000; **Industry Concentration:** Generalist with a primary focus in Financial Services; **Function Concentration:** Finance/Accounting, Human Resources, Marketing

Comai, Christine — *Associate*
Source Services Corporation
2000 Town Center, Suite 850
Southfield, MI 48075
Telephone: (810) 352-6520
Recruiter Classification: Contingency; **Lowest/Average Salary:**
$30,000/$50,000; **Industry Concentration:** Financial Services;
Function Concentration: Engineering, Finance/Accounting

Combs, Stephen L. — *Managing Director*
Juntunen-Combs-Poirier
600 Montgomery Street, 2nd Floor
San Francisco, CA 94111
Telephone: (415) 291-1699
Recruiter Classification: Retained; **Lowest/Average Salary:**
$90,000/$90,000; **Industry Concentration:** Financial Services,
Venture Capital; **Function Concentration:** Finance/Accounting,
Marketing, Sales

Combs, Thomas — *Associate*
Source Services Corporation
161 Ottawa NW, Suite 409D
Grand Rapids, MI 49503
Telephone: (616) 451-2400
Recruiter Classification: Contingency; **Lowest/Average Salary:**
$30,000/$50,000; **Industry Concentration:** Financial Services;
Function Concentration: Engineering, Finance/Accounting

Comstock, Rodger — *Managing Director*
Johnson Smith & Knisely Accord
100 Park Avenue, 15th Floor
New York, NY 10017
Telephone: (212) 885-9100
Recruiter Classification: Retained; **Lowest/Average Salary:**
$90,000/$90,000; **Industry Concentration:** Financial Services;
Function Concentration: General Management, Human
Resources, Sales

Cona, Joseph A. — *President*
Cona Personnel Search
625 South Second Avenue
Springfield, IL 62704-2500
Telephone: (217) 522-3933
Recruiter Classification: Contingency; **Lowest/Average Salary:**
$20,000/$50,000; **Industry Concentration:** Generalist with a
primary focus in Financial Services, Insurance; **Function
Concentration:** Generalist with a primary focus in Administration,
Engineering, Finance/Accounting, General Management

Conard, Rodney J. — *President*
Conard Associates, Inc.
74 Northeastern Boulevard, Suite 22A
Nashua, NH 03062
Telephone: (603) 886-0600
Recruiter Classification: Retained; **Lowest/Average Salary:**
$100,000/$125,000; **Industry Concentration:** Generalist with a
primary focus in Financial Services; **Function Concentration:**
Generalist with a primary focus in Finance/Accounting,
General Management, Marketing

Coneys, Bridget — *Associate*
Source Services Corporation
8614 Westwood Center, Suite 750
Vienna, VA 22182
Telephone: (703) 790-5610
Recruiter Classification: Contingency; **Lowest/Average Salary:**
$30,000/$50,000; **Industry Concentration:** Financial Services;
Function Concentration: Engineering, Finance/Accounting

Conley, Kevin E. — *Partner*
Lamalie Amrop International
10 Post Office Square
Boston, MA 02109-4603
Telephone: (617) 292-6242
Recruiter Classification: Retained; **Lowest/Average Salary:**
$90,000/$90,000; **Industry Concentration:** Generalist with a
primary focus in Financial Services; **Function Concentration:**
Generalist

Connaghan, Linda — *Financial Recruiter*
Bowman & Marshall, Inc.
P.O. Box 25503
Overland Park, KS 66225
Telephone: (913) 648-3332
Recruiter Classification: Contingency; **Lowest/Average Salary:**
$30,000/$50,000; **Industry Concentration:** Financial Services,
Insurance; **Function Concentration:** Finance/Accounting

Connelly, Kevin M. — *Director*
Spencer Stuart
401 North Michigan Avenue, Suite 3400
Chicago, IL 60611-4244
Telephone: (312) 822-0080
Recruiter Classification: Retained; **Lowest/Average Salary:**
$90,000/$90,000; **Industry Concentration:** Generalist with a
primary focus in Financial Services, Venture Capital;
Function Concentration: Generalist with a primary focus
in Administration, Finance/Accounting, General
Management

Conway, Maureen — *President*
Conway & Associates
1007 Church Street
Suite 408
Evanston, IL 60201
Telephone: (847) 866-6832
Recruiter Classification: Retained; **Lowest/Average Salary:**
$60,000/$90,000; **Industry Concentration:** Generalist with a
primary focus in Financial Services; **Function Concentration:**
Generalist with a primary focus in Administration,
Engineering, Finance/Accounting, General Management,
Human Resources, Marketing, Research and Development,
Sales

Cook, Charlene — *Associate*
Source Services Corporation
15260 Ventura Boulevard, Suite 380
Sherman Oaks, CA 91403
Telephone: (818) 905-1500
Recruiter Classification: Contingency; **Lowest/Average
Salary:** $30,000/$50,000; **Industry Concentration:** Financial
Services; **Function Concentration:** Engineering,
Finance/Accounting

Cook, Dennis — *Vice President*
A.T. Kearney, Inc.
130 Adelaide Street West, Suite 2710
Toronto, Ontario, CANADA M5H 3P5
Telephone: (416) 947-1990
Recruiter Classification: Retained; **Lowest/Average Salary:**
$90,000/$90,000; **Industry Concentration:** Generalist with a
primary focus in Financial Services; **Function Concentration:**
Generalist with a primary focus in Engineering,
Finance/Accounting, General Management

Cooke, Katherine H. — *Managing Director*
Horton International
10 Tower Lane
Avon, CT 06001
Telephone: (860) 674-8701
Recruiter Classification: Retained; **Lowest/Average Salary:** $90,000/$90,000; **Industry Concentration:** Generalist with a primary focus in Financial Services; **Function Concentration:** Generalist with a primary focus in Engineering, Finance/Accounting, General Management, Human Resources, Marketing, Sales

Corso, Glen S. — *Director*
Chartwell Partners International, Inc.
275 Battery Street, Suite 2180
San Francisco, CA 94111
Telephone: (415) 296-0600
Recruiter Classification: Retained; **Lowest/Average Salary:** $90,000/$90,000; **Industry Concentration:** Financial Services; **Function Concentration:** Generalist with a primary focus in Administration, Finance/Accounting, General Management, Marketing, Women/Minorities

Cortina Del Valle, Pedro — *Partner*
Ray & Berndtson
Palo Santo No. 6
Colonia Lomas Altas
Mexico City, D.F., MEXICO 11950
Telephone: (525) 570-7462
Recruiter Classification: Retained; **Lowest/Average Salary:** $90,000/$90,000; **Industry Concentration:** Generalist with a primary focus in Financial Services, Insurance; **Function Concentration:** Generalist with a primary focus in Administration, Finance/Accounting, General Management, Human Resources, Marketing, Research and Development, Sales, Women/Minorities

Costello, Lynda — *Executive Search Consultant*
Coe & Company International Inc.
1535 400-3rd Avenue SW
Center Tower
Calgary, Alberta, Canada T20 4H2
Telephone: (403) 232-8833
Recruiter Classification: Retained; **Lowest/Average Salary:** $75,000/$90,000; **Industry Concentration:** Financial Services; **Function Concentration:** Generalist with a primary focus in Administration, Engineering, Finance/Accounting, General Management, Human Resources, Marketing, Research and Development, Sales

Cotugno, James — *Associate*
Source Services Corporation
1 Gatehall Drive, Suite 250
Parsippany, NJ 07054
Telephone: (201) 267-3222
Recruiter Classification: Contingency; **Lowest/Average Salary:** $30,000/$50,000; **Industry Concentration:** Financial Services; **Function Concentration:** Engineering, Finance/Accounting

Coughlin, Stephen — *Associate*
Source Services Corporation
100 North Tryon Street, Suite 3130
Charlotte, NC 28202
Telephone: (704) 333-8311
Recruiter Classification: Contingency; **Lowest/Average Salary:** $30,000/$50,000; **Industry Concentration:** Financial Services; **Function Concentration:** Engineering, Finance/Accounting

Coulman, Karen — *Executive Recruiter*
CPS Inc.
One Westbrook Corporate Centre, Suite 600
Westchester, IL 60154
Telephone: (708) 531-8370
Recruiter Classification: Contingency; **Lowest/Average Salary:** $30,000/$50,000; **Industry Concentration:** Generalist with a primary focus in Financial Services, Insurance; **Function Concentration:** Engineering, Research and Development, Sales, Women/Minorities

Courtney, Brendan — *Vice President*
A.J. Burton Group, Inc.
120 East Baltimore Street, Suite 2220
Baltimore, MD 21202
Telephone: (410) 752-5244
Recruiter Classification: Contingency; **Lowest/Average Salary:** $40,000/$75,000; **Industry Concentration:** Generalist with a primary focus in Financial Services, Insurance; **Function Concentration:** Generalist with a primary focus in Administration, Finance/Accounting, General Management, Human Resources

Cox, William — *Vice President*
E.J. Ashton & Associates, Ltd.
P.O. Box 1048
Lake Zurich, IL 60047-1048
Telephone: (847) 540-9922
Recruiter Classification: Contingency; **Lowest/Average Salary:** $30,000/$60,000; **Industry Concentration:** Insurance; **Function Concentration:** Generalist with a primary focus in Administration, Finance/Accounting, General Management, Marketing, Sales

Coyle, Hugh F. — *Vice President*
A.J. Burton Group, Inc.
120 East Baltimore Street, Suite 2220
Baltimore, MD 21202
Telephone: (410) 752-5244
Recruiter Classification: Contingency, Executive Temporary; **Lowest/Average Salary:** $40,000/$75,000; **Industry Concentration:** Generalist with a primary focus in Financial Services, Insurance; **Function Concentration:** Generalist with a primary focus in Administration, Finance/Accounting, General Management, Human Resources

Cragg, Barbara R. — *Consultant*
Southwestern Professional Services
2451 Atrium Way
Nashville, TN 37214
Telephone: (615) 391-2722
Recruiter Classification: Contingency; **Lowest/Average Salary:** $30,000/$50,000; **Industry Concentration:** Generalist with a primary focus in Insurance; **Function Concentration:** Generalist with a primary focus in Engineering, Human Resources, Sales, Women/Minorities

Cramer, Paul J. — *Partner*
C/R Associates
1231 Delaware Avenue
Buffalo, NY 14209
Telephone: (716) 884-1734
Recruiter Classification: Contingency; **Lowest/Average Salary:** $20,000/$50,000; **Industry Concentration:** Generalist with a primary focus in Financial Services; **Function Concentration:** Administration, Finance/Accounting, Human Resources

Crane, Howard C. — *Director*
Chartwell Partners International, Inc.
275 Battery Street, Suite 2180
San Francisco, CA 94111
Telephone: (415) 296-0600
Recruiter Classification: Retained; **Lowest/Average Salary:**
$90,000/$90,000; **Industry Concentration:** Generalist with a
primary focus in Financial Services, Insurance; **Function
Concentration:** Generalist with a primary focus in
Finance/Accounting, General Management, Human Resources,
Marketing, Sales

Crath, Paul F. — *Partner*
Price Waterhouse
Suite 3000, Box 82 Royal Trust Tower
Toronto Dominion Centre
Toronto, Ontario, CANADA M5K 1G8
Telephone: (416) 863-1133
Recruiter Classification: Retained; **Lowest/Average Salary:**
$75,000/$90,000; **Industry Concentration:** Generalist with a
primary focus in Financial Services, Venture Capital; **Function
Concentration:** Generalist with a primary focus in Administration,
Engineering, Finance/Accounting, General Management, Human
Resources, Marketing, Research and Development, Sales

Crawford, Cassondra — *Associate*
Don Richard Associates of Washington, D.C., Inc.
1020 19th Street, NW, Suite 650
Washington, DC 20036
Telephone: (202) 463-7210
Recruiter Classification: Contingency; **Lowest/Average Salary:**
$20,000/$30,000; **Industry Concentration:** Financial Services;
Function Concentration: Finance/Accounting

Crecos, Gregory P. — *Managing Partner*
Gregory Michaels and Associates, Inc.
8410 West Bryn Mawr Avenue
Suite 400
Chicago, IL 60631
Telephone: (773) 380-1333
Recruiter Classification: Retained; **Lowest/Average Salary:**
$90,000/$90,000; **Industry Concentration:** Generalist with a
primary focus in Financial Services; **Function Concentration:**
Generalist with a primary focus in Finance/Accounting,
General Management, Human Resources, Marketing, Sales

Crist, Peter — *President*
Crist Partners, Ltd.
303 West Madison, Suite 2650
Chicago, IL 60606
Telephone: (312) 920-0609
Recruiter Classification: Retained; **Lowest/Average Salary:**
$300,000/$500,000; **Industry Concentration:** Generalist with a
primary focus in Financial Services, Insurance, Venture Capital;
Function Concentration: Generalist with a primary focus in
Finance/Accounting, General Management

Critchley, Walter — *President*
Cochran, Cochran & Yale, Inc.
5166 Main Street
Williamsville, NY 14221
Telephone: (716) 631-1300
Recruiter Classification: Retained; **Lowest/Average Salary:**
$50,000/$75,000; **Industry Concentration:** Generalist with a
primary focus in Financial Services, Venture Capital; **Function
Concentration:** Generalist with a primary focus in Engineering,
Finance/Accounting, General Management, Human Resources,
Marketing, Sales, Women/Minorities

Critchley, Walter — *Vice President*
Temporary Accounting Personnel, Inc.
955 East Henrietta Road
Rochester, NY 14623
Telephone: (716) 427-9930
Recruiter Classification: Executive Temporary;
Lowest/Average Salary: $20,000/$30,000; **Industry
Concentration:** Generalist with a primary focus in Financial
Services; **Function Concentration:** Finance/Accounting,
Human Resources

Cronin, Dolores — *President*
Corporate Careers, Inc.
1500 Quail Street, Suite 290
Newport Beach, CA 92660
Telephone: (714) 476-7007
Recruiter Classification: Contingency; **Lowest/Average Salary:**
$30,000/$60,000; **Industry Concentration:** Financial Services;
Function Concentration: General Management, Sales

Cruse, O.D. — *Senior Director*
Spencer Stuart
1717 Main Street, Suite 5300
Dallas, TX 75201-4605
Telephone: (214) 658-1777
Recruiter Classification: Retained; **Lowest/Average Salary:**
$90,000/$90,000; **Industry Concentration:** Venture Capital;
Function Concentration: Engineering, Finance/Accounting,
General Management, Marketing, Research and Development,
Sales, Women/Minorities

Cruz, Catherine — *Office Manager/Legal
Consultant*
TOPAZ Legal Solutions
383 Northfield Avenue
West Orange, NJ 07052
Telephone: (201) 669-7300
Recruiter Classification: Executive Temporary; **Lowest/Average
Salary:** $40,000/$75,000; **Industry Concentration:** Financial
Services; **Function Concentration:** Generalist with a primary
focus in Women/Minorities

Cruz, Catherine — *Office Manager/Legal
Consultant*
TOPAZ International, Inc.
383 Northfield Avenue
West Orange, NJ 07052
Telephone: (201) 669-7300
Recruiter Classification: Contingency; **Lowest/Average Salary:**
$40,000/$75,000; **Industry Concentration:** Financial Services;
Function Concentration: Generalist with a primary focus in
Women/Minorities

Crystal, Jonathan A. — *Senior Director*
Spencer Stuart
1111 Bagby, Suite 1616
Houston, TX 77002-2594
Telephone: (713) 225-1621
Recruiter Classification: Retained; **Lowest/Average Salary:**
$90,000/$90,000; **Industry Concentration:** Generalist with a
primary focus in Financial Services, Insurance; **Function
Concentration:** Generalist with a primary focus in
Administration, Finance/Accounting, General Management,
Marketing, Sales, Women/Minorities

Cuddihy, Paul — *Vice President*
Dahl-Morrow International
12020 Sunrise Valley Drive
Reston, VA 20191
Telephone: (703) 860-6868
Recruiter Classification: Retained; **Lowest/Average Salary:**
$75,000/$90,000; **Industry Concentration:** Venture Capital;
Function Concentration: Generalist with a primary focus in
Engineering, Finance/Accounting, General Management,
Marketing, Sales

Cuddy, Brian C. — *Managing Partner*
Romac & Associates
125 Summer Street, Suite 1450
Boston, MA 02110
Telephone: (617) 439-4300
Recruiter Classification: Executive Temporary; **Lowest/Average
Salary:** $60,000/$60,000; **Industry Concentration:** Financial
Services, Insurance; **Function Concentration:**
Finance/Accounting

Cuddy, Patricia — *Associate*
Source Services Corporation
379 Thornall Street
Edison, NJ 08837
Telephone: (908) 494-2800
Recruiter Classification: Contingency; **Lowest/Average
Salary:** $30,000/$50,000; **Industry Concentration:** Financial
Services; **Function Concentration:** Engineering,
Finance/Accounting

Cunningham, Lawrence — *Vice President,*
Bio-Pharmaceutical Division
Howard Fischer Associates, Inc.
1800 John F. Kennedy Boulevard, 7th Floor
Philadelphia, PA 19103
Telephone: (215) 568-8363
Recruiter Classification: Retained; **Lowest/Average Salary:**
$90,000/$90,000; **Industry Concentration:** Generalist with a
primary focus in Financial Services, Insurance, Venture Capital;
Function Concentration: Generalist with a primary focus in
Administration, Finance/Accounting, General Management,
Human Resources, Marketing, Research and Development,
Sales, Women/Minorities

Cunningham, Robert Y. — *Director Consulting*
Services
Goodrich & Sherwood Associates, Inc.
521 Fifth Avenue
New York, NY 10175
Telephone: (212) 697-4131
Recruiter Classification: Retained; **Lowest/Average Salary:**
$60,000/$90,000; **Industry Concentration:** Generalist with a
primary focus in Financial Services, Insurance, Venture Capital;
Function Concentration: Generalist with a primary focus in
Administration, Finance/Accounting, General Management,
Human Resources, Marketing, Sales

Curren, Camella — *Associate*
Source Services Corporation
4170 Ashford Dunwoody Road, Suite 285
Atlanta, GA 30319
Telephone: (404) 255-2045
Recruiter Classification: Contingency; **Lowest/Average
Salary:** $30,000/$50,000; **Industry Concentration:** Financial
Services; **Function Concentration:** Engineering,
Finance/Accounting

Curtis, Ellissa — *Search Consultant*
Cochran, Cochran & Yale, Inc.
955 East Henrietta Road
Rochester, NY 14623
Telephone: (716) 424-6060
Recruiter Classification: Retained; **Lowest/Average Salary:**
$50,000/$75,000; **Industry Concentration:** Financial Services,
Venture Capital; **Function Concentration:** Generalist with a
primary focus in Engineering, Finance/Accounting, General
Management, Human Resources, Marketing, Sales,
Women/Minorities

Cushman, Judith — *President*
Judith Cushman & Associates
1125 12th Avenue, NW
Suite B-1A
Issaquah, WA 98027
Telephone: (425) 392-8660
Recruiter Classification: Retained; **Lowest/Average Salary:**
$30,000/$90,000; **Industry Concentration:** Generalist with a
primary focus in Financial Services; **Function Concentration:**
Generalist

Cutka, Matthew — *Associate*
Source Services Corporation
2029 Century Park East, Suite 1350
Los Angeles, CA 90067
Telephone: (310) 277-8092
Recruiter Classification: Contingency; **Lowest/Average Salary:**
$30,000/$50,000; **Industry Concentration:** Financial Services;
Function Concentration: Engineering, Finance/Accounting

Czepiel, Susan — *Executive Recruiter*
CPS Inc.
303 Congress Street, 5th Floor
Boston, MA 02210
Telephone: (617) 439-7950
Recruiter Classification: Contingency; **Lowest/Average Salary:**
$30,000/$50,000; **Industry Concentration:** Generalist with a
primary focus in Financial Services, Insurance; **Function
Concentration:** Engineering, Research and Development,
Sales, Women/Minorities

D'Alessio, Gary A. — *President*
Chicago Legal Search, Ltd.
33 North Dearborn Street, Suite 2302
Chicago, IL 60602-3109
Telephone: (312) 251-2580
Recruiter Classification: Contingency; **Lowest/Average Salary:**
$50,000/$90,000; **Industry Concentration:** Venture Capital;
Function Concentration: Women/Minorities

D'Elia, Arthur P. — *Vice President*
Korn/Ferry International
237 Park Avenue
New York, NY 10017
Telephone: (212) 687-1834
Recruiter Classification: Retained; **Lowest/Average Salary:**
$100,000/$150,000; **Industry Concentration:** Generalist with a
primary focus in Financial Services; **Function Concentration:**
Generalist

Dabich, Thomas M. — *Vice President*
Robert Harkins Associates, Inc.
P.O. Box 236
1248 West Main Street
Ephrata, PA 17522
Telephone: (717) 733-9664
Recruiter Classification: Contingency; **Lowest/Average Salary:**
$40,000/$60,000; **Industry Concentration:** Generalist with a
primary focus in Financial Services; **Function Concentration:**
Generalist with a primary focus in Finance/Accounting

Danforth, W. Michael — *Executive Vice President*
Hyde Danforth Wold & Co.
5950 Berkshire Lane, Suite 1600
Dallas, TX 75225
Telephone: (214) 691-5966
Recruiter Classification: Retained; **Lowest/Average Salary:**
$50,000/$75,000; **Industry Concentration:** Generalist with a
primary focus in Financial Services; **Function Concentration:**
Generalist with a primary focus in Administration, General
Management, Human Resources, Sales

Daniels, Alfred — *Managing Director*
Alfred Daniels & Associates
5795 Waverly Avenue
La Jolla, CA 92037
Telephone: (619) 459-4009
Recruiter Classification: Contingency; **Lowest/Average
Salary:** $75,000/$90,000; **Industry Concentration:** Financial
Services; **Function Concentration:** Generalist with a primary
focus in Administration, Finance/Accounting, General
Management, Marketing, Research and Development,
Sales

Daniels, C. Eugene — *Vice President*
Sigma Group International
6551 South Revere Parkway
Suite 125
Englewood, CO 80111-6410
Telephone: (303) 792-9881
Recruiter Classification: Retained; **Lowest/Average Salary:**
$90,000/$90,000; **Industry Concentration:** Generalist with a
primary focus in Financial Services; **Function Concentration:**
Generalist with a primary focus in Administration, Engineering,
Finance/Accounting, General Management, Human Resources,
Marketing

Dankberg, Iris — *Associate*
Source Services Corporation
4170 Ashford Dunwoody Road, Suite 285
Atlanta, GA 30319
Telephone: (404) 255-2045
Recruiter Classification: Contingency; **Lowest/Average
Salary:** $30,000/$50,000; **Industry Concentration:** Financial
Services; **Function Concentration:** Engineering,
Finance/Accounting

Dannenberg, Richard A. — *Principal*
Roberts Ryan and Bentley
1107 Kenilworth Drive, Suite 208
Towson, MD 21204
Telephone: (410) 321-6600
Recruiter Classification: Retained; **Lowest/Average Salary:**
$90,000/$90,000; **Industry Concentration:** Financial
Services, Insurance; **Function Concentration:** Administration,
Marketing

Darter, Steven M. — *President*
People Management Northeast Incorporated
One Darling Drive, Avon Park South
Avon, CT 06001
Telephone: (860) 678-8900
Recruiter Classification: Retained; **Lowest/Average Salary:**
$75,000/$90,000; **Industry Concentration:** Generalist with a
primary focus in Financial Services, Insurance; **Function
Concentration:** Generalist

Davis, C. Scott — *Associate*
Source Services Corporation
7730 East Bellview Avenue, Suite 302
Englewood, CO 80111
Telephone: (303) 773-3700
Recruiter Classification: Contingency; **Lowest/Average Salary:**
$30,000/$50,000; **Industry Concentration:** Financial Services;
Function Concentration: Engineering, Finance/Accounting

Davis, Elease — *Associate*
Source Services Corporation
525 Vine Street, Suite 2250
Cincinnati, OH 45202
Telephone: (513) 651-3303
Recruiter Classification: Contingency; **Lowest/Average Salary:**
$30,000/$50,000; **Industry Concentration:** Financial Services;
Function Concentration: Engineering, Finance/Accounting

Davis, G. Gordon — *President*
Davis & Company
3419 Via Lido, Suite 615
Newport Beach, CA 92663
Telephone: (714) 376-6995
Recruiter Classification: Retained; **Lowest/Average Salary:**
$50,000/$75,000; **Industry Concentration:** Generalist with a
primary focus in Venture Capital; **Function Concentration:**
Generalist with a primary focus in Administration, Engineering,
Finance/Accounting, General Management, Human Resources,
Marketing, Research and Development, Sales

Davis, Joan — *Executive Recruiter*
MSI International
5215 North O'Connor Boulevard
Suite 1875
Irving, TX 75039
Telephone: (214) 869-3939
Recruiter Classification: Contingency; **Lowest/Average Salary:**
$30,000/$75,000; **Industry Concentration:** Generalist with a
primary focus in Financial Services; **Function Concentration:**
Generalist with a primary focus in Finance/Accounting

Davis, Steven M. — *Consultant*
Sullivan & Company
20 Exchange Place, 50th Floor
New York, NY 10005
Telephone: (212) 422-3000
Recruiter Classification: Retained; **Lowest/Average Salary:**
$90,000/$90,000; **Industry Concentration:** Generalist with a
primary focus in Financial Services; **Function Concentration:**
Generalist

Dawson, Joe — *Executive Recruiter*
S.C. International, Ltd.
1430 Branding Lane, Suite 119
Downers Grove, IL 60515
Telephone: (708) 963-3033
Recruiter Classification: Contingency; **Lowest/Average Salary:**
$30,000/$50,000; **Industry Concentration:** Insurance;
Function Concentration: Administration, Human Resources

Dawson, William — *Associate*
Source Services Corporation
8614 Westwood Center, Suite 750
Vienna, VA 22182
Telephone: (703) 790-5610
Recruiter Classification: Contingency; **Lowest/Average Salary:**
$30,000/$50,000; **Industry Concentration:** Financial Services;
Function Concentration: Engineering, Finance/Accounting

de Bardin, Francesca — *President*
F.L. Taylor & Company, Inc.
300 East 34th Street
New York, NY 10016
Telephone: (212) 679-4674
Recruiter Classification: Retained; **Lowest/Average Salary:**
$75,000/$90,000; **Industry Concentration:** Generalist with a
primary focus in Financial Services; **Function Concentration:**
Generalist with a primary focus in Human Resources,
Marketing, Sales

De Brun, Thomas P. — *Partner*
Ray & Berndtson
One Park Plaza, Suite 420
Irvine, CA 92614
Telephone: (714) 476-8844
Recruiter Classification: Retained; **Lowest/Average Salary:**
$90,000/$90,000; **Industry Concentration:** Generalist with a
primary focus in Financial Services, Insurance; **Function
Concentration:** Generalist with a primary focus in
Administration, Finance/Accounting, General Management,
Human Resources, Marketing, Research and Development,
Sales, Women/Minorities

de Cholnoky, Andrea — *Senior Director*
Spencer Stuart
277 Park Avenue, 29th Floor
New York, NY 10172
Telephone: (212) 336-0200
Recruiter Classification: Retained; **Lowest/Average Salary:**
$90,000/$90,000; **Industry Concentration:** Financial Services;
Function Concentration: Generalist with a primary focus in
Administration, Finance/Accounting, General Management,
Research and Development, Sales

de Palacios, Jeannette C. — *President*
J. Palacios & Associates, Inc.
P.O. Box 362437
San Juan, PR 00936-2437
Telephone: (787) 723-6433
Recruiter Classification: Retained; **Lowest/Average Salary:**
$50,000/$75,000; **Industry Concentration:** Financial Services;
Function Concentration: Generalist with a primary focus in
Engineering, Finance/Accounting, General Management,
Human Resources, Marketing, Sales

de Tuede, Catherine — *Senior Associate*
The Search Alliance, Inc.
148 East Avenue, Suite 2L
Norwalk, CT 06851
Telephone: (203) 838-9936
Recruiter Classification: Retained; **Lowest/Average Salary:**
$90,000/$90,000; **Industry Concentration:** Generalist with a
primary focus in Financial Services, Insurance; **Function
Concentration:** Generalist with a primary focus in General
Management, Human Resources, Marketing, Sales,
Women/Minorities

De Zara, Max — *President*
Carlyle Group
625 N. Michigan Avenue
Suite 2100
Chicago, IL 60611
Telephone: (312) 587-3030
Recruiter Classification: Retained; **Lowest/Average Salary:**
$50,000/$90,000; **Industry Concentration:** Generalist with a
primary focus in Financial Services; **Function Concentration:**
Generalist

Dean, Mary — *Principal Advanced Technology*
Korn/Ferry International
2180 Sand Hill Road
Menlo Park, CA 94025
Telephone: (415) 233-2733
Recruiter Classification: Retained; **Lowest/Average Salary:**
$100,000/$150,000; **Industry Concentration:** Generalist with a
primary focus in Financial Services, Insurance; **Function
Concentration:** Generalist

Deaver, Henry C. — *Consultant*
Ray & Berndtson
Sears Tower, 233 South Wacker Drive, Suite 4020
Chicago, IL 60606-6310
Telephone: (312) 876-0730
Recruiter Classification: Retained; **Lowest/Average Salary:**
$90,000/$90,000; **Industry Concentration:** Generalist with a
primary focus in Financial Services, Insurance; **Function
Concentration:** Generalist with a primary focus in
Administration, Finance/Accounting, General Management,
Human Resources, Marketing, Research and Development,
Sales, Women/Minorities

Debus, Wayne — *Associate*
Source Services Corporation
5343 North 16th Street, Suite 270
Phoenix, AZ 85016
Telephone: (602) 230-0220
Recruiter Classification: Contingency; **Lowest/Average
Salary:** $30,000/$50,000; **Industry Concentration:** Financial
Services; **Function Concentration:** Engineering,
Finance/Accounting

Deck, Jack — *Managing Director*
Source Services Corporation
One CityPlace, Suite 170
St. Louis, MO 63141
Telephone: (314) 432-4500
Recruiter Classification: Contingency; **Lowest/Average
Salary:** $30,000/$50,000; **Industry Concentration:** Financial
Services; **Function Concentration:** Engineering,
Finance/Accounting

DeCorrevont, James — *President*
DeCorrevont & Associates
225 Country Club Drive
Largo, FL 34641
Telephone: (312) 642-9300
Recruiter Classification: Contingency; **Lowest/Average Salary:**
$40,000/$90,000; **Industry Concentration:** Generalist with a
primary focus in Financial Services, Insurance; **Function
Concentration:** Generalist with a primary focus in
Administration, Finance/Accounting, Human Resources,
Marketing, Sales, Women/Minorities

DeCorrevont, James — *President*
DeCorrevont & Associates
1122 North Clark Street
Chicago, IL 60610
Telephone: (312) 642-9300
Recruiter Classification: Contingency; **Lowest/Average Salary:**
$40,000/$90,000; **Industry Concentration:** Generalist with a
primary focus in Financial Services, Insurance; **Function
Concentration:** Generalist with a primary focus in
Administration, Finance/Accounting, Human Resources,
Marketing, Sales, Women/Minorities

DeFuniak, William S. — *Managing Partner*
DeFuniak & Edwards
1602 Hidden Hills Trail
Long Beach, IN 46360
Telephone: (219) 878-9790
Recruiter Classification: Retained; **Lowest/Average Salary:**
$75,000/$90,000; **Industry Concentration:** Insurance;
Function Concentration: General Management

DeHart, Donna — *Vice President*
Tower Consultants, Ltd.
771 East Lancaster Avenue
Villanova, PA 19085
Telephone: (610) 519-1700
Recruiter Classification: Retained; **Lowest/Average Salary:**
$60,000/$90,000; **Industry Concentration:** Generalist with a
primary focus in Financial Services, Insurance; **Function
Concentration:** Administration, Human Resources,
Women/Minorities

Del Pino, William — *Insurance Consultant*
National Search, Inc.
2816 University Drive
Coral Springs, FL 33071
Telephone: (800) 935-4355
Recruiter Classification: Contingency; **Lowest/Average Salary:**
$30,000/$50,000; **Industry Concentration:** Insurance;
Function Concentration: Generalist with a primary focus in
Administration, Finance/Accounting, General Management,
Human Resources, Marketing, Research and Development,
Sales, Women/Minorities

Del Prete, Karen — *Vice President*
Gilbert Tweed/INESA
415 Madison Avenue
New York, NY 10017
Telephone: (212) 758-3000
Recruiter Classification: Retained; **Lowest/Average Salary:**
$90,000/$90,000; **Industry Concentration:** Generalist with a
primary focus in Financial Services, Venture Capital; **Function
Concentration:** Generalist

Delaney, Patrick J. — *Principal*
Sensible Solutions, Inc.
239 West Coolidge Avenue
Barrington, IL 60010
Telephone: (847) 382-0070
Recruiter Classification: Retained, Executive Temporary;
Lowest/Average Salary: $60,000/$90,000; **Industry
Concentration:** Generalist with a primary focus in Financial
Services; **Function Concentration:** Generalist with a primary
focus in Administration, Engineering, Finance/Accounting,
General Management, Human Resources, Marketing,
Sales

Della Monica, Vincent — *Account Executive*
Search West, Inc.
340 North Westlake Boulevard
Suite 200
Westlake Village, CA 91362-3761
Telephone: (805) 496-6811
Recruiter Classification: Contingency; **Lowest/Average
Salary:** $40,000/$60,000; **Industry Concentration:**
Insurance; **Function Concentration:** Administration,
Marketing

Delman, Charles — *Vice President*
Korn/Ferry International
237 Park Avenue
New York, NY 10017
Telephone: (212) 687-1834
Recruiter Classification: Retained; **Lowest/Average Salary:**
$100,000/$150,000; **Industry Concentration:** Generalist with a
primary focus in Financial Services; **Function Concentration:**
Generalist

Delmonico, Laura — *Professional Recruiter*
A.J. Burton Group, Inc.
120 East Baltimore Street, Suite 2220
Baltimore, MD 21202
Telephone: (410) 752-5244
Recruiter Classification: Contingency; **Lowest/Average Salary:**
$40,000/$75,000; **Industry Concentration:** Generalist with a
primary focus in Financial Services, Insurance; **Function
Concentration:** Generalist with a primary focus in
Administration, Finance/Accounting, General Management,
Human Resources

DeMarco, Robert — *Managing Director*
Source Services Corporation
1500 West Park Drive, Suite 390
Westborough, MA 01581
Telephone: (508) 366-2600
Recruiter Classification: Contingency; **Lowest/Average
Salary:** $30,000/$50,000; **Industry Concentration:** Financial
Services; **Function Concentration:** Engineering,
Finance/Accounting

Demchak, James P. — *Partner*
Sandhurst Associates
4851 LBJ Freeway, Suite 601
Dallas, TX 75244
Telephone: (214) 458-1212
Recruiter Classification: Retained; **Lowest/Average Salary:**
$75,000/$90,000; **Industry Concentration:** Generalist with a
primary focus in Financial Services, Insurance; **Function
Concentration:** Generalist with a primary focus in
Finance/Accounting, Human Resources, Marketing,
Sales

Desai, Sushila — *Search Consultant*
Sink, Walker, Boltrus International
60 Walnut Street
Wellesley, MA 02181
Telephone: (617) 237-1199
Recruiter Classification: Retained; **Lowest/Average Salary:**
$90,000/$90,000; **Industry Concentration:** Financial Services;
Function Concentration: Engineering, General Management,
Research and Development, Sales

Desgrosellier, Gary P. — *President*
Personnel Unlimited/Executive Search
25 West Nora
Spokane, WA 99205
Telephone: (509) 326-8880
Recruiter Classification: Contingency; **Lowest/Average
Salary:** $30,000/$60,000; **Industry Concentration:**
Generalist with a primary focus in Insurance; **Function
Concentration:** Generalist with a primary focus in
Engineering, Finance/Accounting, Human Resources,
Marketing, Sales

Desmond, Dennis — *Executive Vice President/Partner*
Beall & Company, Inc.
535 Colonial Park Drive
Roswell, GA 30075
Telephone: (404) 992-0900
Recruiter Classification: Retained; **Lowest/Average Salary:** $90,000/$90,000; **Industry Concentration:** Generalist with a primary focus in Financial Services, Insurance, Venture Capital; **Function Concentration:** Generalist with a primary focus in Administration, Engineering, Finance/Accounting, General Management, Human Resources, Marketing, Research and Development, Sales

Desmond, Mary — *Associate*
Source Services Corporation
150 South Wacker Drive, Suite 400
Chicago, IL 60606
Telephone: (312) 346-7000
Recruiter Classification: Contingency; **Lowest/Average Salary:** $30,000/$50,000; **Industry Concentration:** Financial Services; **Function Concentration:** Engineering, Finance/Accounting

Dever, Mary — *Associate*
Source Services Corporation
505 East 200 South, Suite 300
Salt Lake City, UT 84102
Telephone: (801) 328-0011
Recruiter Classification: Contingency; **Lowest/Average Salary:** $30,000/$50,000; **Industry Concentration:** Financial Services; **Function Concentration:** Engineering, Finance/Accounting

Devito, Alice — *Associate*
Source Services Corporation
925 Westchester Avenue, Suite 309
White Plains, NY 10604
Telephone: (914) 428-9100
Recruiter Classification: Contingency; **Lowest/Average Salary:** $30,000/$50,000; **Industry Concentration:** Financial Services; **Function Concentration:** Engineering, Finance/Accounting

deVry, Kimberly A. — *Executive Search Recruiter*
Tower Consultants, Ltd.
771 East Lancaster Avenue
Villanova, PA 19085
Telephone: (610) 519-1700
Recruiter Classification: Retained; **Lowest/Average Salary:** $60,000/$90,000; **Industry Concentration:** Generalist with a primary focus in Financial Services, Insurance; **Function Concentration:** Administration, Human Resources, Women/Minorities

deWilde, David M. — *Managing Director*
Chartwell Partners International, Inc.
275 Battery Street, Suite 2180
San Francisco, CA 94111
Telephone: (415) 296-0600
Recruiter Classification: Retained; **Lowest/Average Salary:** $90,000/$90,000; **Industry Concentration:** Generalist with a primary focus in Financial Services, Insurance, Venture Capital; **Function Concentration:** Finance/Accounting, General Management, Human Resources, Marketing, Women/Minorities

Dewing, Jesse J. — *Recruiter/Consultant*
Don Richard Associates of Charlotte
2650 One First Union Center
301 South College Street
Charlotte, NC 28202-6000
Telephone: (704) 377-6447
Recruiter Classification: Contingency; **Lowest/Average Salary:** $30,000/$50,000; **Industry Concentration:** Financial Services; **Function Concentration:** Finance/Accounting

Dezember, Steve — *Partner*
Ray & Berndtson
191 Peachtree Street, NE, Suite 3800
Atlanta, GA 30303-1757
Telephone: (404) 215-4600
Recruiter Classification: Retained; **Lowest/Average Salary:** $90,000/$90,000; **Industry Concentration:** Generalist with a primary focus in Financial Services, Insurance; **Function Concentration:** Generalist with a primary focus in Administration, Finance/Accounting, General Management, Human Resources, Marketing, Research and Development, Sales, Women/Minorities

Di Filippo, Thomas — *Associate*
Source Services Corporation
20 Burlington Mall Road, Suite 405
Burlington, MA 01803
Telephone: (617) 272-5000
Recruiter Classification: Contingency; **Lowest/Average Salary:** $30,000/$50,000; **Industry Concentration:** Financial Services; **Function Concentration:** Engineering, Finance/Accounting

DiCioccio, Carmen — *Search Consultant*
Cochran, Cochran & Yale, Inc.
5166 Main Street
Williamsville, NY 14221
Telephone: (716) 631-1300
Recruiter Classification: Retained; **Lowest/Average Salary:** $50,000/$75,000; **Industry Concentration:** Generalist with a primary focus in Financial Services, Venture Capital; **Function Concentration:** Generalist with a primary focus in Engineering, Finance/Accounting, General Management, Human Resources, Marketing, Sales, Women/Minorities

Dicker, Barry — *Managing Partner*
ESA Professional Consultants
141 Durham Road
Suite 16
Madison, CT 06443
Telephone: (203) 245-1983
Recruiter Classification: Retained; **Lowest/Average Salary:** $50,000/$75,000; **Industry Concentration:** Venture Capital; **Function Concentration:** Engineering, General Management, Human Resources, Women/Minorities

Dickerson, Scot — *Vice President*
Key Employment Services
1001 Office Park Road, Suite 320
West Des Moines, IA 50265-2567
Telephone: (515) 224-0446
Recruiter Classification: Contingency; **Lowest/Average Salary:** $30,000/$75,000; **Industry Concentration:** Insurance; **Function Concentration:** General Management

Dickey, Chester W. — *President and CEO*
Bowden & Company, Inc.
5000 Rockside Road, Suite 550
Cleveland, OH 44131
Telephone: (216) 447-1800
Recruiter Classification: Retained; **Lowest/Average Salary:**
$90,000/$90,000; **Industry Concentration:** Generalist with a
primary focus in Financial Services, Insurance, Venture Capital;
Function Concentration: Generalist

Dickey, Chester W. — *President and CEO*
Bowden & Company, Inc.
9420 Hunters Pond Drive
Tampa, FL 33647
Telephone: (813) 973-8592
Recruiter Classification: Retained; **Lowest/Average Salary:**
$90,000/$90,000; **Industry Concentration:** Generalist with a
primary focus in Financial Services, Insurance, Venture Capital;
Function Concentration: Generalist

Dickson, Duke — *Associate*
A.D. & Associates Executive Search, Inc.
5589 Woodsong Drive, Suite 100
Atlanta, GA 30338-2933
Telephone: (770) 393-0021
Recruiter Classification: Contingency; **Lowest/Average Salary:**
$50,000/$75,000; **Industry Concentration:** Generalist with a
primary focus in Financial Services; **Function Concentration:**
Generalist with a primary focus in Engineering,
Finance/Accounting, General Management, Human Resources,
Marketing, Research and Development, Sales,
Women/Minorities

Dieckmann, Ralph E. — *President*
Dieckmann & Associates, Ltd.
180 North Stetson, Suite 5555
Two Prudential Plaza
Chicago, IL 60601
Telephone: (312) 819-5900
Recruiter Classification: Retained; **Lowest/Average Salary:**
$90,000/$90,000; **Industry Concentration:** Generalist with a
primary focus in Financial Services, Insurance; **Function
Concentration:** Generalist with a primary focus in
Finance/Accounting, General Management, Women/Minorities

Diers, Gary — *Associate*
Source Services Corporation
10220 SW Greenburg Road, Suite 625
Portland, OR 97223
Telephone: (503) 768-4546
Recruiter Classification: Contingency; **Lowest/Average
Salary:** $30,000/$50,000; **Industry Concentration:** Financial
Services; **Function Concentration:** Engineering,
Finance/Accounting

Dietz, David S. — *Manager*
MSI International
201 St. Charles Avenue
Suite 2205
New Orleans, LA 70170
Telephone: (504) 522-6700
Recruiter Classification: Contingency; **Lowest/Average Salary:**
$30,000/$60,000; **Industry Concentration:** Generalist with a
primary focus in Financial Services; **Function Concentration:**
Generalist with a primary focus in Administration,
Engineering, Finance/Accounting, General Management,
Marketing, Sales

DiFilippo, James — *Vice President Retail*
Korn/Ferry International
237 Park Avenue
New York, NY 10017
Telephone: (212) 687-1834
Recruiter Classification: Retained; **Lowest/Average Salary:**
$100,000/$150,000; **Industry Concentration:** Generalist with a
primary focus in Financial Services, Insurance; **Function
Concentration:** Generalist

DiGiovanni, Charles — *President*
Penn Search
687 West Lancaster Avenue
Strafford, PA 19087
Telephone: (610) 964-8820
Recruiter Classification: Contingency; **Lowest/Average Salary:**
$30,000/$60,000; **Industry Concentration:** Generalist with a
primary focus in Financial Services, Insurance; **Function
Concentration:** Finance/Accounting

DiMarchi, Paul — *President*
DiMarchi Partners, Inc.
1225 17th Street, Suite 1460
Denver, CO 80202
Telephone: (303) 292-9300
Recruiter Classification: Retained; **Lowest/Average Salary:**
$90,000/$90,000; **Industry Concentration:** Generalist with
a primary focus in Venture Capital; **Function Concentration:**
Generalist with a primary focus in Engineering,
Finance/Accounting, General Management, Marketing, Sales

DiMarchi, Paul — *President*
DiMarchi Partners, Inc.
885 Arapahoe Avenue
Boulder, CO 80302
Telephone: (303) 415-9300
Recruiter Classification: Retained; **Lowest/Average Salary:**
$90,000/$90,000; **Industry Concentration:** Generalist with a
primary focus in Venture Capital; **Function Concentration:**
Generalist with a primary focus in Engineering,
Finance/Accounting, General Management, Marketing, Sales

Dingeldey, Peter E. — *Vice President*
Search Advisors International Corp.
777 South Harbour Island Boulevard
Suite 925
Tampa, FL 33602
Telephone: (813) 221-7555
Recruiter Classification: Retained; **Lowest/Average Salary:**
$75,000/$90,000; **Industry Concentration:** Generalist with a
primary focus in Financial Services, Insurance; **Function
Concentration:** Generalist with a primary focus in
Administration, Engineering, Finance/Accounting, General
Management, Human Resources, Marketing, Research and
Development, Sales, Women/Minorities

Dingman, Bruce — *President*
Robert W. Dingman Company, Inc.
650 Hampshire Road
Suite 116
Westlake Village, CA 91361
Telephone: (805) 778-1777
Recruiter Classification: Retained; **Lowest/Average Salary:**
$100,000/$145,000; **Industry Concentration:** Generalist with a
primary focus in Financial Services, Insurance; **Function
Concentration:** Generalist with a primary focus in
Administration, Engineering, Finance/Accounting, General
Management, Human Resources, Marketing, Sales

Dinte, Paul — *President*
Dinte Resources, Inc.
8300 Greensboro Drive
Suite 880
McLean, VA 22102
Telephone: (703) 448-3300
Recruiter Classification: Retained, Executive Temporary;
Lowest/Average Salary: $75,000/$90,000; **Industry
Concentration:** Generalist with a primary focus in Financial
Services; **Function Concentration:** Generalist with a primary
focus in Finance/Accounting, General Management, Human
Resources, Marketing

DiPiazza, Joseph — *Senior Vice President*
Boyden
375 Park Avenue, Suite 1509
New York, NY 10152
Telephone: (212) 980-6480
Recruiter Classification: Retained; **Lowest/Average Salary:**
$75,000/$90,000; **Industry Concentration:** Financial Services;
Function Concentration: Finance/Accounting

DiSalvo, Fred — *Vice President*
The Cambridge Group Ltd
161A John Jefferson Road
Williamsburg, VA 23185
Telephone: (757) 565-1150
Recruiter Classification: Contingency; **Lowest/Average Salary:**
$60,000/$75,000; **Industry Concentration:** Generalist with a
primary focus in Financial Services; **Function Concentration:**
Administration, Finance/Accounting, General Management,
Human Resources, Marketing, Research and Development,
Sales, Women/Minorities

Diskin, Rochelle — *Account Executive*
Search West, Inc.
340 North Westlake Boulevard
Suite 200
Westlake Village, CA 91362-3761
Telephone: (805) 496-6811
Recruiter Classification: Contingency; **Lowest/Average Salary:**
$40,000/$60,000; **Industry Concentration:** Financial Services;
Function Concentration: Administration, Finance/Accounting,
Marketing

Dittmar, Richard — *Associate*
Source Services Corporation
4200 West Cypress Street, Suite 101
Tampa, FL 33607
Telephone: (813) 879-2221
Recruiter Classification: Contingency; **Lowest/Average Salary:**
$30,000/$50,000; **Industry Concentration:** Financial Services;
Function Concentration: Engineering, Finance/Accounting

Divine, Robert S. — *Principal*
O'Shea, Divine & Company, Inc.
610 Newport Center Drive, Suite 1040
Newport Beach, CA 92660
Telephone: (714) 720-9070
Recruiter Classification: Retained; **Lowest/Average Salary:**
$75,000/$90,000; **Industry Concentration:** Generalist with a
primary focus in Financial Services; **Function Concentration:**
Generalist with a primary focus in Engineering,
Finance/Accounting, General Management, Human
Resources, Marketing, Research and Development,
Sales

Dixon, Aris — *Executive Recruiter*
CPS Inc.
One Westbrook Corporate Centre, Suite 600
Westchester, IL 60154
Telephone: (708) 531-8370
Recruiter Classification: Contingency; **Lowest/Average Salary:**
$30,000/$50,000; **Industry Concentration:** Generalist with a
primary focus in Financial Services, Insurance; **Function
Concentration:** Engineering, Research and Development,
Sales, Women/Minorities

Do, Sonnie — *Executive Recruiter*
Whitney & Associates, Inc.
920 Second Avenue South, Suite 625
Minneapolis, MN 55402-4035
Telephone: (612) 338-5600
Recruiter Classification: Contingency; **Lowest/Average Salary:**
$20,000/$50,000; **Industry Concentration:** Generalist with a
primary focus in Financial Services, Insurance, Venture Capital;
Function Concentration: Finance/Accounting

Dobrow, Samuel — *Associate*
Source Services Corporation
4170 Ashford Dunwoody Road, Suite 285
Atlanta, GA 30319
Telephone: (404) 255-2045
Recruiter Classification: Contingency; **Lowest/Average Salary:**
$30,000/$50,000; **Industry Concentration:** Financial Services;
Function Concentration: Engineering, Finance/Accounting

Doele, Donald C. — *Vice President*
Goodrich & Sherwood Associates, Inc.
One Independence Way
Princeton, NJ 08540
Telephone: (609) 452-0202
Recruiter Classification: Retained; **Lowest/Average Salary:**
$60,000/$90,000; **Industry Concentration:** Generalist with a
primary focus in Financial Services, Insurance, Venture Capital;
Function Concentration: Generalist with a primary focus in
Administration, Finance/Accounting, General Management,
Human Resources, Marketing, Sales

Doman, Matthew — *Executive Recruiter*
S.C. International, Ltd.
1430 Branding Lane, Suite 119
Downers Grove, IL 60515
Telephone: (708) 963-3033
Recruiter Classification: Contingency; **Lowest/Average Salary:**
$30,000/$50,000; **Industry Concentration:** Insurance;
Function Concentration: Administration, Human Resources

Donahue, Debora — *Associate*
Source Services Corporation
505 East 200 South, Suite 300
Salt Lake City, UT 84102
Telephone: (801) 328-0011
Recruiter Classification: Contingency; **Lowest/Average Salary:**
$30,000/$50,000; **Industry Concentration:** Financial Services;
Function Concentration: Engineering, Finance/Accounting

Donath, Linda — *Dahl-Morrow International*
Dahl-Morrow International
12020 Sunrise Valley Drive
Reston, VA 20191
Telephone: (703) 860-6868
Recruiter Classification: Retained; **Lowest/Average Salary:**
$75,000/$90,000; **Industry Concentration:** Venture Capital;
Function Concentration: Generalist with a primary focus in
Engineering, Finance/Accounting, General Management,
Marketing, Sales

Dong, Stephen — *Associate*
Executive Search, Ltd.
4830 Interstate Drive
Cincinnati, OH 45246
Telephone: (513) 874-6901
Recruiter Classification: Retained; **Lowest/Average Salary:**
$50,000/$75,000; **Industry Concentration:** Generalist with a
primary focus in Financial Services, Insurance

Donnelly, George J. — *Vice Chairman International*
Ward Howell International, Inc.
1000 Louisiana Street
Suite 3150
Houston, TX 77002
Telephone: (713) 655-7155
Recruiter Classification: Retained; **Lowest/Average Salary:**
$75,000/$90,000; **Industry Concentration:** Generalist with a
primary focus in Financial Services; **Function Concentration:**
Generalist with a primary focus in General Management

Donnelly, Patti — *Associate*
Source Services Corporation
150 South Warner Road, Suite 238
King of Prussia, PA 19406
Telephone: (610) 341-1960
Recruiter Classification: Contingency; **Lowest/Average Salary:**
$30,000/$50,000; **Industry Concentration:** Financial Services;
Function Concentration: Engineering, Finance/Accounting

Dorfner, Martin — *Associate*
Source Services Corporation
Foster Plaza VI
681 Anderson Drive, 2nd Floor
Pittsburgh, PA 15220
Telephone: (412) 928-8300
Recruiter Classification: Contingency; **Lowest/Average Salary:**
$30,000/$50,000; **Industry Concentration:** Financial Services;
Function Concentration: Engineering, Finance/Accounting

Dorsey, Jim — *Executive Recruiter*
Ryan, Miller & Associates Inc.
4601 Wilshire Boulevard, Suite 225
Los Angeles, CA 90010
Telephone: (213) 938-4768
Recruiter Classification: Contingency; **Lowest/Average Salary:**
$60,000/$75,000; **Industry Concentration:** Financial Services;
Function Concentration: Generalist

Dotson, M. Ileen — *Principal*
Dotson & Associates
412 East 55th Street, Suite 8A
New York, NY 10022
Telephone: (212) 593-4274
Recruiter Classification: Contingency; **Lowest/Average Salary:**
$75,000/$90,000; **Industry Concentration:** Generalist with a
primary focus in Financial Services, Insurance; **Function
Concentration:** General Management, Marketing, Sales,
Women/Minorities

Doukas, Jon A. — *Principal and Senior Consultant*
Professional Bank Services, Inc. D/B/A Executive
Search, Inc.
Suite 305, 6200 Dutchman's Lane
Louisville, KY 40205
Telephone: (502) 451-6633
Recruiter Classification: Retained; **Lowest/Average Salary:**
$20,000/$90,000; **Industry Concentration:** Financial Services;
Function Concentration: Generalist with a primary focus in
Administration, Finance/Accounting, General Management,
Human Resources

Dowdall, Jean — *Vice President*
A.T. Kearney, Inc.
225 Reinekers Lane
Alexandria, VA 22314
Telephone: (703) 739-4624
Recruiter Classification: Retained; **Lowest/Average Salary:**
$90,000/$90,000; **Industry Concentration:** Generalist with a
primary focus in Financial Services; **Function Concentration:**
Generalist with a primary focus in Engineering,
Finance/Accounting, General Management

Dowell, Chris — *Senior Vice President*
The Abbott Group, Inc.
1577 Spring Hill Road
Vienna, VA 22182
Telephone: (703) 790-0314
Recruiter Classification: Retained; **Lowest/Average Salary:**
$90,000/$90,000; **Industry Concentration:** Generalist with a
primary focus in Venture Capital; **Function Concentration:**
Generalist with a primary focus in Administration, Engineering,
Finance/Accounting, General Management, Human Resources,
Marketing, Research and Development

Dowell, Mary K. — *Principal*
Professional Search Associates
12459 Lewis Street, Suite 102
Garden Grove, CA 92640-6606
Telephone: (714) 740-0919
Recruiter Classification: Contingency; **Lowest/Average Salary:**
$40,000/$75,000; **Industry Concentration:** Generalist with a
primary focus in Financial Services; **Function Concentration:**
Finance/Accounting, General Management, Human Resources,
Marketing, Sales

Dowlatzadch, Homayoun — *Associate*
Source Services Corporation
4510 Executive Drive, Suite 200
San Diego, CA 92121
Telephone: (619) 552-0300
Recruiter Classification: Contingency; **Lowest/Average
Salary:** $30,000/$50,000; **Industry Concentration:** Financial
Services; **Function Concentration:** Engineering,
Finance/Accounting

Downs, James L. — *Principal*
Sanford Rose Associates
2915 Providence Road
Suite 300
Charlotte, NC 28211
Telephone: (704) 366-0730
Recruiter Classification: Contingency; **Lowest/Average Salary:**
$30,000/$75,000; **Industry Concentration:** Generalist with a
primary focus in Financial Services; **Function Concentration:**
Generalist

Downs, William — *Associate*
Source Services Corporation
4170 Ashford Dunwoody Road, Suite 285
Atlanta, GA 30319
Telephone: (404) 255-2045
Recruiter Classification: Contingency; **Lowest/Average
Salary:** $30,000/$50,000; **Industry Concentration:** Financial
Services; **Function Concentration:** Engineering,
Finance/Accounting

Doyle, James W. — *Managing Director*
Executive Search Consultants International, Inc.
330 Fifth Avenue
Suite 5501
New York, NY 10118
Telephone: (212) 333-1900
Recruiter Classification: Retained; **Lowest/Average Salary:**
$90,000/$90,000; **Industry Concentration:** Generalist with a
primary focus in Financial Services; **Function Concentration:**
Generalist with a primary focus in Finance/Accounting,
General Management, Human Resources, Marketing

Doyle, John P. — *Partner*
Ray & Berndtson
Sears Tower, 233 South Wacker Drive, Suite 4020
Chicago, IL 60606-6310
Telephone: (312) 876-0730
Recruiter Classification: Retained; **Lowest/Average Salary:**
$90,000/$90,000; **Industry Concentration:** Financial Services;
Function Concentration: Generalist with a primary focus in
Human Resources

Dreifus, Donald — *Account Executive*
Search West, Inc.
1888 Century Park East
Suite 2050
Los Angeles, CA 90067-1736
Telephone: (310) 284-8888
Recruiter Classification: Contingency; **Lowest/Average
Salary:** $40,000/$60,000; **Industry Concentration:** Generalist
with a primary focus in Financial Services; **Function
Concentration:** Generalist with a primary focus in
Administration, Finance/Accounting, General Management,
Marketing

Dressler, Ralph — *Senior Consultant*
Romac & Associates
1040 North Kings Highway
Suite 624
Cherry Hill, NJ 08034
Telephone: (609) 482-9677
Recruiter Classification: Executive Temporary; **Lowest/Average
Salary:** $60,000/$60,000; **Industry Concentration:** Financial
Services, Insurance; **Function Concentration:**
Finance/Accounting

Dromeshauser, Peter — *President*
Dromeshauser Associates
20 William Street
Wellesley, MA 02181
Telephone: (617) 239-0222
Recruiter Classification: Retained; **Lowest/Average Salary:**
$90,000/$90,000; **Industry Concentration:** Financial Services,
Venture Capital; **Function Concentration:** General
Management, Marketing, Sales

Drummond-Hay, Peter — *Managing Director*
Russell Reynolds Associates, Inc.
200 Park Avenue
New York, NY 10166-0002
Telephone: (212) 351-2000
Recruiter Classification: Retained; **Lowest/Average Salary:**
$90,000/$90,000; **Industry Concentration:** Generalist with a
primary focus in Financial Services; **Function Concentration:**
Generalist

Drury, James J. — *Managing Director*
Spencer Stuart
401 North Michigan Avenue, Suite 3400
Chicago, IL 60611-4244
Telephone: (312) 822-0080
Recruiter Classification: Retained; **Lowest/Average Salary:**
$90,000/$90,000; **Industry Concentration:** Generalist with a
primary focus in Venture Capital; **Function Concentration:**
Generalist with a primary focus in Administration,
Finance/Accounting, General Management, Human Resources,
Marketing, Sales

Dubbs, William — *President*
Williams Executive Search, Inc.
4200 Norwest Center
90 South 7th Street
Minneapolis, MN 55402
Telephone: (612) 339-2900
Recruiter Classification: Retained; **Lowest/Average Salary:**
$90,000/$90,000; **Industry Concentration:** Generalist with a
primary focus in Financial Services, Venture Capital;
Function Concentration: Generalist with a primary focus in
Finance/Accounting, General Management, Marketing,
Sales

Duckworth, Donald R. — *Managing Director*
Johnson Smith & Knisely Accord
600 Peachtree Street, Suite 3860
Atlanta, GA 30308
Telephone: (404) 874-2100
Recruiter Classification: Retained; **Lowest/Average Salary:**
$90,000/$90,000; **Industry Concentration:** Financial Services;
Function Concentration: General Management, Human
Resources, Sales

Ducruet, Linda K. — *Consultant*
Heidrick & Struggles, Inc.
51 Weaver Street
Greenwich Office Park #3
Greenwich, CT 06831-5150
Telephone: (203) 629-3200
Recruiter Classification: Retained; **Lowest/Average Salary:**
$75,000/$90,000; **Industry Concentration:** Generalist with a
primary focus in Financial Services; **Function Concentration:**
Generalist with a primary focus in Finance/Accounting

Dudley, Craig J. — *Managing Partner*
Ray & Berndtson
Palo Santo No. 6
Colonia Lomas Altas
Mexico City, D.F., MEXICO 11950
Telephone: (525) 570-7462
Recruiter Classification: Retained; **Lowest/Average Salary:**
$90,000/$90,000; **Industry Concentration:** Generalist with a
primary focus in Financial Services; **Function Concentration:**
Generalist

Duelks, John — *Associate*
Source Services Corporation
4170 Ashford Dunwoody Road, Suite 285
Atlanta, GA 30319
Telephone: (404) 255-2045
Recruiter Classification: Contingency; **Lowest/Average
Salary:** $30,000/$50,000; **Industry Concentration:** Financial
Services; **Function Concentration:** Engineering,
Finance/Accounting

Duggan, James P. — *Vice President*
Slayton International, Inc./I-I-C Partners
181 West Madison Street, Suite 4510
Chicago, IL 60602
Telephone: (312) 456-0080
Recruiter Classification: Retained; **Lowest/Average Salary:**
$90,000/$90,000; **Industry Concentration:** Generalist with a
primary focus in Venture Capital; **Function Concentration:**
Generalist with a primary focus in Engineering, General
Management, Sales

Dunbar, Marilynne — *Consultant*
Ray & Berndtson/Lovas Stanley
Royal Bank Plaza, South Tower, Suite 3150
200 Bay Street, P.O. Box 125
Toronto, Ontario, CANADA M5J 2J3
Telephone: (416) 366-1990
Recruiter Classification: Retained; **Lowest/Average Salary:**
$90,000/$90,000; **Industry Concentration:** Generalist with a
primary focus in Financial Services, Insurance, Venture Capital;
Function Concentration: Generalist with a primary focus in
Finance/Accounting, General Management, Human Resources,
Marketing, Women/Minorities

Duncan, Dana — *Associate*
Source Services Corporation
5429 LBJ Freeway, Suite 275
Dallas, TX 75240
Telephone: (214) 387-1600
Recruiter Classification: Contingency; **Lowest/Average
Salary:** $30,000/$50,000; **Industry Concentration:** Financial
Services; **Function Concentration:** Engineering,
Finance/Accounting

Dunkel, David L. — *Managing Partner*
Romac & Associates
120 Hyde Park Place
Suite 200
Tampa, FL 33606
Telephone: (813) 229-5575
Recruiter Classification: Executive Temporary; **Lowest/Average
Salary:** $60,000/$60,000; **Industry Concentration:** Financial
Services, Insurance; **Function Concentration:**
Finance/Accounting

Dunlow, Aimee — *Associate*
Source Services Corporation
5429 LBJ Freeway, Suite 275
Dallas, TX 75240
Telephone: (214) 387-1600
Recruiter Classification: Contingency; **Lowest/Average
Salary:** $30,000/$50,000; **Industry Concentration:** Financial
Services; **Function Concentration:** Engineering,
Finance/Accounting

Dunman, Betsy L. — *President*
Crawford & Crofford
15327 NW 60th Avenue, Suite 240
Miami Lakes, FL 33014
Telephone: (305) 820-0855
Recruiter Classification: Contingency, Executive Temporary;
Lowest/Average Salary: $30,000/$60,000; **Industry
Concentration:** Generalist with a primary focus in Financial
Services, Insurance; **Function Concentration:** Generalist with a
primary focus in Administration, Engineering,
Finance/Accounting, General Management, Marketing,
Research and Development, Sales

Dunn, Mary Helen — *Partner*
Ray & Berndtson
245 Park Avenue, 33rd Floor
New York, NY 10167
Telephone: (212) 370-1316
Recruiter Classification: Retained; **Lowest/Average Salary:**
$90,000/$90,000; **Industry Concentration:** Financial Services;
Function Concentration: Generalist

Dupont, Rick — *Chief Financial Officer*
Source Services Corporation
5580 LBJ Freeway, Suite 300
Dallas, TX 75240
Telephone: (214) 385-3002
Recruiter Classification: Contingency; **Lowest/Average
Salary:** $30,000/$50,000; **Industry Concentration:** Financial
Services; **Function Concentration:** Engineering,
Finance/Accounting

Durakis, Charles A. — *President*
C.A. Durakis Associates, Inc.
5550 Sterret Place, Suite 302
Columbia, MD 21044
Telephone: (410) 740-5590
Recruiter Classification: Retained; **Lowest/Average Salary:**
$90,000/$90,000; **Industry Concentration:** Generalist with a
primary focus in Financial Services, Venture Capital; **Function
Concentration:** Generalist with a primary focus in
Finance/Accounting, General Management, Human
Resources, Marketing

Dwyer, Julie — *Executive Recruiter*
CPS Inc.
One Westbrook Corporate Centre, Suite 600
Westchester, IL 60154
Telephone: (708) 531-8370
Recruiter Classification: Contingency; **Lowest/Average Salary:**
$30,000/$50,000; **Industry Concentration:** Generalist with a
primary focus in Financial Services, Insurance; **Function
Concentration:** Engineering, Research and Development,
Sales, Women/Minorities

Early, Alice C. — *Managing Director*
Russell Reynolds Associates, Inc.
200 Park Avenue
New York, NY 10166-0002
Telephone: (212) 351-2000
Recruiter Classification: Retained; **Lowest/Average Salary:**
$90,000/$90,000; **Industry Concentration:** Generalist with a
primary focus in Financial Services; **Function Concentration:**
Generalist

Eason, Jan C. — *Vice President*
Summit Group International
2171 West Park Court
Suite F
Stone Mountain, GA 30087
Telephone: (770) 469-3844
Recruiter Classification: Retained; **Lowest/Average Salary:**
$60,000/$75,000; **Industry Concentration:** Insurance;
Function Concentration: Generalist with a primary focus in
Engineering, Finance/Accounting, General Management,
Human Resources, Marketing, Sales

Ebeling, John A. — *Vice President*
Gilbert Tweed/INESA
155 Prospect Avenue
West Orange, NJ 07052
Telephone: (201) 731-3033
Recruiter Classification: Retained; **Lowest/Average Salary:**
$90,000/$90,000; **Industry Concentration:** Generalist with a
primary focus in Financial Services; **Function Concentration:**
Generalist with a primary focus in General Management,
Human Resources, Marketing, Research and Development,
Sales, Women/Minorities

Eddy, Terry — *Associate*
William Guy & Associates
P.O. Box 57407
Sherman Oaks, CA 91413
Telephone: Unpublished
Recruiter Classification: Retained; **Lowest/Average Salary:**
$50,000/$90,000; **Industry Concentration:** Generalist with a
primary focus in Financial Services, Insurance; **Function
Concentration:** Generalist with a primary focus in Engineering,
Finance/Accounting, General Management, Human Resources,
Marketing, Sales, Women/Minorities

Edwards, Dorothy — *Manager*
MSI International
800 Gessner, Suite 1220
Houston, TX 77024
Telephone: (713) 722-0050
Recruiter Classification: Contingency; **Lowest/Average Salary:**
$30,000/$75,000; **Industry Concentration:** Generalist with a
primary focus in Financial Services; **Function Concentration:**
Generalist with a primary focus in Administration,
Engineering, Finance/Accounting, General Management,
Marketing, Sales

Edwards, Douglas W. — *Consultant*
Egon Zehnder International Inc.
One Atlantic Center, Suite 3000
1201 West Peachtree Street N.E.
Atlanta, GA 30309
Telephone: (404) 875-3000
Recruiter Classification: Retained; **Lowest/Average Salary:**
$90,000/$90,000; **Industry Concentration:** Generalist with a
primary focus in Financial Services; **Function Concentration:**
Generalist

Edwards, Ned — *Partner*
Ingram & Aydelotte Inc./I-I-C Partners
430 Park Avenue, Suite 700
New York, NY 10022
Telephone: (212) 319-7777
Recruiter Classification: Retained; **Lowest/Average Salary:**
$150,000/$150,000; **Industry Concentration:** Generalist with a
primary focus in Financial Services; **Function Concentration:**
Generalist with a primary focus in Finance/Accounting,
General Management, Marketing

Edwards, Randolph J. — *Managing Partner*
DeFuniak & Edwards
960 Fell Street, Suite 317
Baltimore, MD 21231
Telephone: (410) 732-1521
Recruiter Classification: Retained; **Lowest/Average Salary:**
$50,000/$90,000; **Industry Concentration:** Insurance;
Function Concentration: General Management

Edwards, Robert — *Recruiter*
J.P. Canon Associates
225 Broadway, Ste. 3602, 36th Fl.
New York, NY 10007-3001
Telephone: (212) 233-3131
Recruiter Classification: Contingency; **Lowest/Average Salary:**
$40,000/$75,000; **Industry Concentration:** Generalist with a
primary focus in Financial Services; **Function Concentration:**
Engineering

Edwards, Verba L. — *President and CEO*
Wing Tips & Pumps, Inc.
P.O. Box 99580
Troy, MI 48099
Telephone: (810) 641-0980
Recruiter Classification: Contingency; **Lowest/Average Salary:**
$20,000/$60,000; **Industry Concentration:** Generalist with a
primary focus in Financial Services, Insurance; **Function
Concentration:** Generalist with a primary focus in
Administration, Engineering, Finance/Accounting, General
Management, Human Resources, Marketing, Research and
Development, Sales, Women/Minorities

Eggert, Scott — *Associate*
Source Services Corporation
1105 Schrock Road, Suite 510
Columbus, OH 43229
Telephone: (614) 846-3311
Recruiter Classification: Contingency; **Lowest/Average
Salary:** $30,000/$50,000; **Industry Concentration:** Financial
Services; **Function Concentration:** Engineering,
Finance/Accounting

Ehrgott, Elizabeth — *Associate Director*
The Ascher Group
25 Pompton Avenue, Suite 310
Verona, NJ 07044
Telephone: (201) 239-6116
Recruiter Classification: Retained, Executive Temporary;
Lowest/Average Salary: $50,000/$90,000; **Industry
Concentration:** Generalist with a primary focus in Financial
Services, Insurance; **Function Concentration:** Generalist with a
primary focus in Administration, Finance/Accounting, General
Management, Human Resources, Marketing,
Women/Minorities

Ehrhart, Jennifer — *Executive Recruiter/Manager*
ADOW's Executeam
10921 Reed Hartman Highway, Suite 225
Blue Ash, OH 45242-2830
Telephone: (513) 891-5335
Recruiter Classification: Executive Temporary; **Lowest/Average
Salary:** $60,000/$90,000; **Industry Concentration:** Generalist
with a primary focus in Financial Services; **Function
Concentration:** Generalist with a primary focus in
Administration, Engineering, Finance/Accounting, General
Management, Human Resources, Marketing,
Women/Minorities

Eiseman, Joe — *Managing Director*
Source Services Corporation
925 Westchester Avenue, Suite 309
White Plains, NY 10604
Telephone: (914) 428-9100
Recruiter Classification: Contingency; **Lowest/Average Salary:**
$30,000/$50,000; **Industry Concentration:** Financial Services;
Function Concentration: Engineering, Finance/Accounting

Eiseman, Joe — *Managing Director*
Source Services Corporation
1 Gatehall Drive, Suite 250
Parsippany, NJ 07054
Telephone: (201) 267-3222
Recruiter Classification: Contingency; **Lowest/Average Salary:**
$30,000/$50,000; **Industry Concentration:** Financial Services;
Function Concentration: Engineering, Finance/Accounting

Eiseman, Joe — *Managing Director*
Source Services Corporation
15 Essex Road, Suite 201
Paramus, NJ 07652
Telephone: (201) 845-3900
Recruiter Classification: Contingency; **Lowest/Average Salary:**
$30,000/$50,000; **Industry Concentration:** Financial Services;
Function Concentration: Engineering, Finance/Accounting

Elder, Tom — *Associate*
Juntunen-Combs-Poirier
111 Bayhill Drive, Suite 255
San Bruno, CA 94066
Telephone: (415) 635-0184
Recruiter Classification: Retained; **Lowest/Average Salary:**
$90,000/$90,000; **Industry Concentration:** Financial Services,
Venture Capital; **Function Concentration:** Engineering,
Finance/Accounting, General Management, Research and
Development

Eldridge, Charles B. — *Partner*
Ray & Berndtson
191 Peachtree Street, NE, Suite 3800
Atlanta, GA 30303-1757
Telephone: (404) 215-4600
Recruiter Classification: Retained; **Lowest/Average Salary:**
$90,000/$90,000; **Industry Concentration:** Generalist with a
primary focus in Financial Services, Insurance; **Function
Concentration:** Generalist with a primary focus in
Administration, Finance/Accounting, General Management,
Human Resources, Marketing, Research and Development,
Sales, Women/Minorities

Elli-Kirk, Matrice — *Director*
Spencer Stuart
1717 Main Street, Suite 5300
Dallas, TX 75201-4605
Telephone: (214) 658-1777
Recruiter Classification: Retained; **Lowest/Average Salary:**
$90,000/$90,000; **Industry Concentration:** Financial Services;
Function Concentration: Finance/Accounting

Ellis, David — *Recruiter/Co-Owner*
Don Richard Associates of Georgia, Inc.
3475 Lenox Road, Suite 210
Atlanta, GA 30326
Telephone: (404) 231-3688
Recruiter Classification: Executive Temporary; **Lowest/Average
Salary:** $60,000/$75,000; **Industry Concentration:** Financial
Services; **Function Concentration:** Finance/Accounting,
Human Resources

Ellis, Patricia — *Associate*
Source Services Corporation
7730 East Bellview Avenue, Suite 302
Englewood, CO 80111
Telephone: (303) 773-3700
Recruiter Classification: Contingency; **Lowest/Average Salary:**
$30,000/$50,000; **Industry Concentration:** Financial Services;
Function Concentration: Engineering, Finance/Accounting

Ellis, Ted K. — *Vice President - Bristol/Southeast*
The Hindman Company
325 Springlake Road
Bristol, VA 24201
Telephone: (540) 669-5006
Recruiter Classification: Retained; **Lowest/Average Salary:**
$50,000/$90,000; **Industry Concentration:** Generalist with a
primary focus in Financial Services; **Function Concentration:**
Generalist with a primary focus in Engineering,
Finance/Accounting, General Management, Human Resources,
Marketing, Sales

Ellis, William — *President*
Interspace Interactive Inc.
521 Fifth Avenue
New York, NY 10017
Telephone: (212) 867-6661
Recruiter Classification: Contingency; **Lowest/Average
Salary:** $50,000/$60,000; **Industry Concentration:**
Generalist with a primary focus in Financial Services;
Function Concentration: Generalist with a primary focus in
Engineering, Finance/Accounting, General Management,
Human Resources, Marketing, Sales, Women/
Minorities

Elster, Irv — *Executive Vice President*
Spectrum Search Associates, Inc.
1888 Century Park East, Suite 320
Los Angeles, CA 90067
Telephone: (310) 286-6921
Recruiter Classification: Contingency; **Lowest/Average Salary:**
$30,000/$50,000; **Industry Concentration:** Financial Services;
Function Concentration: Finance/Accounting

Emerson, Randall — *Managing Director*
Source Services Corporation
111 Monument Circle, Suite 3930
Indianapolis, IN 46204
Telephone: (317) 631-2900
Recruiter Classification: Contingency; **Lowest/Average
Salary:** $30,000/$50,000; **Industry Concentration:** Financial
Services; **Function Concentration:** Engineering,
Finance/Accounting

Emery, Jodie A. — *Principal*
Lamalie Amrop International
Metro Center, One Station Place
Stamford, CT 06902-6800
Telephone: (203) 324-4445
Recruiter Classification: Retained; **Lowest/Average Salary:**
$90,000/$90,000; **Industry Concentration:** Generalist with a
primary focus in Financial Services; **Function Concentration:**
Generalist

Engelbert, Kimberly S. — *Vice President*
Watson International, Inc.
25 West 43rd Street, Suite 914
New York, NY 10036-7406
Telephone: (212) 354-3344
Recruiter Classification: Retained; **Lowest/Average Salary:**
$90,000/$90,000; **Industry Concentration:** Financial Services;
Function Concentration: Generalist with a primary focus in
Administration, Finance/Accounting, General Management,
Human Resources, Marketing, Sales

England, Mark — *Vice President*
Austin-McGregor International
12005 Ford Road, Suite 720
Dallas, TX 75234-7247
Telephone: (972) 488-0500
Recruiter Classification: Retained; **Lowest/Average Salary:**
$50,000/$90,000; **Industry Concentration:** Generalist with a
primary focus in Venture Capital; **Function Concentration:**
Generalist with a primary focus in Engineering,
Finance/Accounting, General Management, Human Resources,
Marketing, Research and Development, Sales,
Women/Minorities

Engle, Bryan — *Managing Director*
Source Services Corporation
120 East Baltimore Street, Suite 1950
Baltimore, MD 21202
Telephone: (410) 727-4050
Recruiter Classification: Contingency; **Lowest/Average
Salary:** $30,000/$50,000; **Industry Concentration:** Financial
Services; **Function Concentration:** Engineering,
Finance/Accounting

Engler, Peter G — *Partner*
Lautz Grotte Engler
One Bush Street, Suite 550
San Francisco, CA 94104
Telephone: (415) 834-3100
Recruiter Classification: Retained; **Lowest/Average Salary:**
$90,000/$90,000; **Industry Concentration:** Generalist with a
primary focus in Financial Services; **Function Concentration:**
Generalist with a primary focus in Marketing

Enns, George — *Partner*
The Enns Partners Inc.
70 University Avenue, Suite 410, P.O. Box 14
Toronto, Ontario, CANADA M5J 2M4
Telephone: (416) 598-0012
Recruiter Classification: Retained; **Lowest/Average Salary:**
$75,000/$90,000; **Industry Concentration:** Generalist with a
primary focus in Financial Services, Venture Capital; **Function
Concentration:** Generalist with a primary focus in
Administration, Finance/Accounting, General Management,
Human Resources, Marketing, Sales

Epstein, Kathy J. — *Principal*
Lamalie Amrop International
10 Post Office Square
Boston, MA 02109-4603
Telephone: (617) 292-6242
Recruiter Classification: Retained; **Lowest/Average Salary:**
$90,000/$90,000; **Industry Concentration:** Generalist with a
primary focus in Financial Services; **Function Concentration:**
Generalist

Erder, Debra — *Vice President*
Canny, Bowen Inc.
200 Park Avenue
49th Floor
New York, NY 10166
Telephone: (212) 949-6611
Recruiter Classification: Retained; **Lowest/Average Salary:**
$90,000/$120,000; **Industry Concentration:** Generalist with a
primary focus in Financial Services, Venture Capital; **Function
Concentration:** Generalist with a primary focus in
Finance/Accounting, Human Resources, Marketing

Erickson, Elaine — *Executive Vice President*
Kenzer Corp.
777 Third Avenue, 26th Floor
New York, NY 10017
Telephone: (212) 308-4300
Recruiter Classification: Retained; **Lowest/Average Salary:**
$50,000/$90,000; **Industry Concentration:** Financial Services,
Venture Capital; **Function Concentration:** Generalist with a
primary focus in Administration, Finance/Accounting, General
Management, Human Resources, Marketing, Research and
Development, Sales

Erikson, Theodore J. — *President*
Erikson Consulting Associates, Inc.
230 Park Avenue
Suite 1000
New York, NY 10169
Telephone: (212) 808-3053
Recruiter Classification: Retained; **Lowest/Average Salary:**
$90,000/$90,000; **Industry Concentration:** Financial Services,
Venture Capital; **Function Concentration:** General
Management, Research and Development

Erlien, Nancy B. — *Executive Recruiter*
Jacobson Associates
150 North Wacker Drive
Suite 1120
Chicago, IL 60606
Telephone: (312) 726-1578
Recruiter Classification: Contingency; **Lowest/Average Salary:**
$20,000/$50,000; **Industry Concentration:** Insurance;
Function Concentration: Generalist

Ervin, Darlene — *Executive Recruiter*
CPS Inc.
One Westbrook Corporate Centre, Suite 600
Westchester, IL 60154
Telephone: (708) 531-8370
Recruiter Classification: Contingency; **Lowest/Average Salary:**
$30,000/$50,000; **Industry Concentration:** Generalist with a
primary focus in Financial Services, Insurance; **Function
Concentration:** Engineering, Research and Development,
Sales, Women/Minorities

Ervin, Russell — *Associate*
Source Services Corporation
10220 SW Greenburg Road, Suite 625
Portland, OR 97223
Telephone: (503) 768-4546
Recruiter Classification: Contingency; **Lowest/Average
Salary:** $30,000/$50,000; **Industry Concentration:** Financial
Services; **Function Concentration:** Engineering,
Finance/Accounting

Esposito, Mark — *Vice President*
Christian & Timbers
100 Park Avenue, 16th Floor
New York, NY 10017
Telephone: (212) 880-6446
Recruiter Classification: Retained; **Lowest/Average Salary:**
$90,000/$90,000; **Industry Concentration:** Generalist with a
primary focus in Financial Services, Insurance, Venture Capital;
Function Concentration: Generalist with a primary focus in
Finance/Accounting, Marketing, Research and Development,
Sales

Estes, Susan — *Recruiter*
The Talley Group
P.O. Box 2918
Stanton, VA 24402
Telephone: (540) 248-7009
Recruiter Classification: Retained; **Lowest/Average Salary:**
$30,000/$60,000; **Industry Concentration:** Financial Services

Eustis, Lucy R. — *Unit Manager*
MSI International
201 St. Charles Avenue
Suite 2205
New Orleans, LA 70170
Telephone: (504) 522-6700
Recruiter Classification: Contingency; **Lowest/Average Salary:**
$30,000/$60,000; **Industry Concentration:** Generalist with a
primary focus in Financial Services; **Function Concentration:**
Generalist with a primary focus in Administration, Engineering,
Finance/Accounting, General Management, Marketing, Sales

Evan-Cook, James W. — *Executive Recruiter*
Jacobson Associates
150 North Wacker Drive
Suite 1120
Chicago, IL 60606
Telephone: (312) 726-1578
Recruiter Classification: Contingency; **Lowest/Average Salary:**
$20,000/$50,000; **Industry Concentration:** Insurance;
Function Concentration: Generalist

Evans, David — *Vice President*
Executive Manning Corporation
3000 N.E. 30th Place, Suite 402/405/411
Fort Lauderdale, FL 33306
Telephone: (954) 561-5100
Recruiter Classification: Retained; **Lowest/Average Salary:**
$75,000/$90,000; **Industry Concentration:** Generalist with a
primary focus in Financial Services, Insurance; **Function
Concentration:** Generalist with a primary focus in
Administration, Engineering, General Management, Human
Resources, Research and Development, Sales,
Women/Minorities

Evans, Timothy — *Associate*
Source Services Corporation
1500 West Park Drive, Suite 390
Westborough, MA 01581
Telephone: (508) 366-2600
Recruiter Classification: Contingency; **Lowest/Average Salary:**
$30,000/$50,000; **Industry Concentration:** Financial Services;
Function Concentration: Engineering, Finance/Accounting

Fabbro, Vivian — *Vice President*
A.T. Kearney, Inc.
222 West Adams Street
Chicago, IL 60606
Telephone: (312) 648-0111
Recruiter Classification: Retained; **Lowest/Average Salary:**
$90,000/$90,000; **Industry Concentration:** Generalist with a
primary focus in Financial Services; **Function Concentration:**
Generalist with a primary focus in Finance/Accounting

Fagerstrom, Jon — *Associate*
Source Services Corporation
4510 Executive Drive, Suite 200
San Diego, CA 92121
Telephone: (619) 552-0300
Recruiter Classification: Contingency; **Lowest/Average Salary:**
$30,000/$50,000; **Industry Concentration:** Financial Services;
Function Concentration: Engineering, Finance/Accounting

Fales, Scott — *Associate*
Source Services Corporation
161 Ottawa NW, Suite 409D
Grand Rapids, MI 49503
Telephone: (616) 451-2400
Recruiter Classification: Contingency; **Lowest/Average Salary:**
$30,000/$50,000; **Industry Concentration:** Financial Services;
Function Concentration: Engineering, Finance/Accounting

Fancher, Robert L. — *Vice President*
Bason Associates Inc.
11311 Cornell Park Drive
Cincinnati, OH 45242
Telephone: (513) 469-9881
Recruiter Classification: Retained; **Lowest/Average Salary:**
$60,000/$90,000; **Industry Concentration:** Generalist with a
primary focus in Financial Services, Insurance, Venture Capital;
Function Concentration: Generalist with a primary focus in
Administration, Engineering, Finance/Accounting, General
Management, Human Resources, Marketing, Research and
Development, Sales

Fanning, Paul — *Associate*
Source Services Corporation
15260 Ventura Boulevard, Suite 380
Sherman Oaks, CA 91403
Telephone: (818) 905-1500
Recruiter Classification: Contingency; **Lowest/Average Salary:**
$30,000/$50,000; **Industry Concentration:** Financial Services;
Function Concentration: Engineering, Finance/Accounting

Farler, Wiley — *Managing Director*
Source Services Corporation
Foster Plaza VI
681 Anderson Drive, 2nd Floor
Pittsburgh, PA 15220
Telephone: (412) 928-8300
Recruiter Classification: Contingency; **Lowest/Average Salary:**
$30,000/$50,000; **Industry Concentration:** Financial Services;
Function Concentration: Engineering, Finance/Accounting

Farley, Leon A. — *Managing Partner*
Leon A. Farley Associates
468 Jackson Street
San Francisco, CA 94111
Telephone: (415) 989-0989
Recruiter Classification: Retained; **Lowest/Average Salary:**
$90,000/$90,000; **Industry Concentration:** Generalist with a
primary focus in Financial Services; **Function Concentration:**
Generalist with a primary focus in Engineering,
Finance/Accounting, General Management, Human Resources,
Marketing, Sales

Farnsworth, John A. — *Partner*
Pearson, Caldwell & Farnsworth, Inc.
One California Street, Suite 1950
San Francisco, CA 94111
Telephone: (415) 982-0300
Recruiter Classification: Retained; **Lowest/Average Salary:**
$90,000/$90,000; **Industry Concentration:** Financial Services;
Function Concentration: Administration, Finance/Accounting,
General Management, Human Resources, Marketing, Sales

Fawcett, Anne M. — *Managing Partner*
The Caldwell Partners Amrop International
Sixty-Four Prince Arthur Avenue
Toronto, Ontario, CANADA M5R 1B4
Telephone: (416) 920-7702
Recruiter Classification: Retained; **Lowest/Average Salary:**
$60,000/$90,000; **Industry Concentration:** Generalist with a
primary focus in Financial Services; **Function Concentration:**
Generalist

Fechheimer, Peter — *Associate*
Source Services Corporation
1290 Oakmead Parkway, Suite 318
Sunnyvale, CA 94086
Telephone: (408) 738-8440
Recruiter Classification: Contingency; **Lowest/Average
Salary:** $30,000/$50,000; **Industry Concentration:** Financial
Services; **Function Concentration:** Engineering,
Finance/Accounting

Feder, Gwen — *Consultant*
Egon Zehnder International Inc.
350 Park Avenue
New York, NY 10022
Telephone: (212) 838-9199
Recruiter Classification: Retained; **Lowest/Average Salary:**
$90,000/$90,000; **Industry Concentration:** Generalist with a
primary focus in Financial Services; **Function Concentration:**
Generalist

Federman, Jack R. — *Principal*
W.R. Rosato & Associates, Inc.
61 Broadway, 26th Floor
New York, NY 10006
Telephone: (212) 509-5700
Recruiter Classification: Retained; **Lowest/Average Salary:**
$90,000/$90,000; **Industry Concentration:** Financial Services;
Function Concentration: Administration, Marketing, Research
and Development, Sales

Fee, J. Curtis — *Senior Director*
Spencer Stuart
401 North Michigan Avenue, Suite 3400
Chicago, IL 60611-4244
Telephone: (312) 822-0080
Recruiter Classification: Retained; **Lowest/Average Salary:**
$90,000/$90,000; **Industry Concentration:** Generalist
with a primary focus in Financial Services; **Function
Concentration:** Generalist with a primary focus in
Finance/Accounting, General Management,
Marketing

Feldman, Abe — *President*
A.E. Feldman Associates
445 Northern Boulevard
Great Neck, NY 11021
Telephone: (516) 466-4708
Recruiter Classification: Contingency, Executive Temporary;
Lowest/Average Salary: $60,000/$90,000; **Industry
Concentration:** Generalist with a primary focus in Financial
Services, Venture Capital; **Function Concentration:** Generalist
with a primary focus in Administration, General Management,
Marketing, Sales

Feldman, Kimberley — *Consultant*
Atlantic Search Group, Inc.
One Liberty Square
Boston, MA 02109
Telephone: (617) 426-9700
Recruiter Classification: Contingency; **Lowest/Average Salary:**
$20,000/$60,000; **Industry Concentration:** Generalist with a
primary focus in Financial Services; **Function Concentration:**
Finance/Accounting

Fennell, Patrick — *Managing Director*
Korn/Ferry International
Scotia Plaza
40 King Street West
Toronto, Ontario, CANADA M5H 3Y2
Telephone: (416) 366-1300
Recruiter Classification: Retained; **Lowest/Average Salary:**
$100,000/$150,000; **Industry Concentration:** Generalist with a
primary focus in Financial Services, Insurance; **Function
Concentration:** Generalist

Ferguson, Kenneth — *Associate*
Source Services Corporation
4170 Ashford Dunwoody Road, Suite 285
Atlanta, GA 30319
Telephone: (404) 255-2045
Recruiter Classification: Contingency; **Lowest/Average
Salary:** $30,000/$50,000; **Industry Concentration:** Financial
Services; **Function Concentration:** Engineering,
Finance/Accounting

Ferneborg, Jay W. — *Vice President/Partner*
Ferneborg & Associates, Inc.
1450 Fashion Island Boulevard, Suite 650
San Mateo, CA 94404
Telephone: (415) 577-0100
Recruiter Classification: Retained; **Lowest/Average Salary:**
$90,000/$90,000; **Industry Concentration:** Generalist with a
primary focus in Financial Services, Venture Capital; **Function
Concentration:** Generalist with a primary focus in
Administration, Finance/Accounting, General Management,
Human Resources, Marketing, Sales

Ferneborg, John R. — *President*
Ferneborg & Associates, Inc.
1450 Fashion Island Boulevard, Suite 650
San Mateo, CA 94404
Telephone: (415) 577-0100
Recruiter Classification: Retained; **Lowest/Average Salary:**
$90,000/$90,000; **Industry Concentration:** Generalist with a
primary focus in Financial Services, Venture Capital; **Function
Concentration:** Generalist with a primary focus in
Administration, Finance/Accounting, General Management,
Human Resources, Marketing, Sales

Ferrara, David M. — *Senior Vice President*
Intech Summit Group, Inc.
5075 Shoreham Place, Suite 280
San Diego, CA 92116
Telephone: (619) 452-2100
Recruiter Classification: Retained; **Lowest/Average Salary:**
$90,000/$90,000; **Industry Concentration:** Financial
Services; **Function Concentration:** Research and
Development

Ferrari, S. Jay — *President/Senior Partner*
Ferrari Search Group
16781 Chagrin Boulevard, Suite 164
Cleveland, OH 44120
Telephone: (216) 491-1122
Recruiter Classification: Retained; **Lowest/Average Salary:**
$75,000/$90,000; **Industry Concentration:** Financial Services,
Insurance, Venture Capital; **Function Concentration:**
Finance/Accounting, Marketing, Sales

Field, Andrew — *Associate*
Source Services Corporation
7730 East Bellview Avenue, Suite 302
Englewood, CO 80111
Telephone: (303) 773-3700
Recruiter Classification: Contingency; **Lowest/Average Salary:**
$30,000/$50,000; **Industry Concentration:** Financial Services;
Function Concentration: Engineering, Finance/Accounting

Fields, Fredric — *Vice President and Director of Marketing*
C.A. Durakis Associates, Inc.
5550 Sterret Place, Suite 302
Columbia, MD 21044
Telephone: (410) 740-5590
Recruiter Classification: Retained; **Lowest/Average Salary:**
$90,000/$90,000; **Industry Concentration:** Generalist with a
primary focus in Financial Services, Insurance, Venture Capital;
Function Concentration: Generalist

Fienberg, Chester — *President*
Drummond Associates, Inc.
50 Broadway, Suite 1201
New York, NY 10004
Telephone: (212) 248-1120
Recruiter Classification: Contingency; **Lowest/Average Salary:**
$40,000/$75,000; **Industry Concentration:** Financial Services;
Function Concentration: Finance/Accounting

Fifield, George C. — *Consultant*
Egon Zehnder International Inc.
California Plaza II, Suite 3580
300 South Grand Avenue
Los Angeles, CA 90071
Telephone: (213) 621-8900
Recruiter Classification: Retained; **Lowest/Average Salary:**
$90,000/$90,000; **Industry Concentration:** Generalist with a
primary focus in Financial Services; **Function Concentration:**
Generalist

Finkel, Leslie — *Managing Director*
Source Services Corporation
150 South Warner Road, Suite 238
King of Prussia, PA 19406
Telephone: (610) 341-1960
Recruiter Classification: Contingency; **Lowest/Average
Salary:** $30,000/$50,000; **Industry Concentration:** Financial
Services; **Function Concentration:** Engineering,
Finance/Accounting

Finnerty, James — *Associate*
Source Services Corporation
20 Burlington Mall Road, Suite 405
Burlington, MA 01803
Telephone: (617) 272-5000
Recruiter Classification: Contingency; **Lowest/Average Salary:**
$30,000/$50,000; **Industry Concentration:** Financial Services;
Function Concentration: Engineering, Finance/Accounting

Fiorelli, Cheryl — *Recruiter/Researcher*
Tower Consultants, Ltd.
771 East Lancaster Avenue
Villanova, PA 19085
Telephone: (610) 519-1700
Recruiter Classification: Retained; **Lowest/Average Salary:**
$60,000/$75,000; **Industry Concentration:** Generalist with a
primary focus in Financial Services; **Function Concentration:**
Administration, Human Resources, Women/Minorities

Fischer, Adam — *Vice President, Telecommunications*
Howard Fischer Associates, Inc.
1800 John F. Kennedy Boulevard, 7th Floor
Philadelphia, PA 19103
Telephone: (215) 568-8363
Recruiter Classification: Retained; **Lowest/Average Salary:**
$90,000/$90,000; **Industry Concentration:** Generalist with a
primary focus in Financial Services, Insurance, Venture Capital;
Function Concentration: Generalist with a primary focus in
Administration, Finance/Accounting, General Management,
Human Resources, Marketing, Research and Development,
Sales, Women/Minorities

Fischer, Howard M. — *President and CEO*
Howard Fischer Associates, Inc.
1800 John F. Kennedy Boulevard, 7th Floor
Philadelphia, PA 19103
Telephone: (215) 568-8363
Recruiter Classification: Retained; **Lowest/Average Salary:**
$90,000/$90,000; **Industry Concentration:** Generalist with a
primary focus in Financial Services, Insurance, Venture Capital;
Function Concentration: Generalist with a primary focus in
Administration, Finance/Accounting, General Management,
Human Resources, Marketing, Research and Development,
Sales, Women/Minorities

Fischer, Janet L. — *Partner*
Boyden
2 Prudential Plaza, Suite 2500
180 North Stetson Avenue
Chicago, IL 60601
Telephone: (312) 565-1300
Recruiter Classification: Retained; **Lowest/Average Salary:**
$75,000/$90,000; **Industry Concentration:** Financial Services;
Function Concentration: Generalist with a primary focus in
Engineering, Finance/Accounting, General Management,
Human Resources, Marketing, Research and Development,
Sales, Women/Minorities

Fischer, John C. — *Office Managing Director*
Horton International
10 Tower Lane
Avon, CT 06001
Telephone: (860) 674-8701
Recruiter Classification: Retained; **Lowest/Average Salary:**
$90,000/$90,000; **Industry Concentration:** Generalist with a
primary focus in Venture Capital; **Function Concentration:**
Generalist with a primary focus in Finance/Accounting,
General Management, Sales

Fisher, Neal — *Principal*
Fisher Personnel Management Services
1219 Morningside Drive
Manhattan Beach, CA 90266
Telephone: (310) 546-7507
Recruiter Classification: Retained; **Lowest/Average Salary:**
$75,000/$75,000; **Industry Concentration:** Generalist with a
primary focus in Financial Services; **Function Concentration:**
Generalist with a primary focus in Engineering,
Finance/Accounting, General Management, Human
Resources, Marketing, Research and Development,
Sales

Fishler, Stu — *Vice President*
A.T. Kearney, Inc.
Biltmore Tower
500 South Grand Avenue, Suite 1780
Los Angeles, CA 90071
Telephone: (213) 689-6800
Recruiter Classification: Retained; **Lowest/Average Salary:**
$90,000/$90,000; **Industry Concentration:** Generalist with a
primary focus in Financial Services; **Function Concentration:**
Generalist with a primary focus in Engineering,
Finance/Accounting, General Management

Fitzgerald, Brian — *Associate*
Source Services Corporation
5429 LBJ Freeway, Suite 275
Dallas, TX 75240
Telephone: (214) 387-1600
Recruiter Classification: Contingency; **Lowest/Average
Salary:** $30,000/$50,000; **Industry Concentration:** Financial
Services; **Function Concentration:** Engineering,
Finance/Accounting

Fitzgerald, Diane — *Principal*
Fitzgerald Associates
21 Muzzey Street
Lexington, MA 02173
Telephone: (617) 863-1945
Recruiter Classification: Retained; **Lowest/Average Salary:**
$60,000/$90,000; **Industry Concentration:** Insurance;
Function Concentration: Generalist with a primary focus in
Finance/Accounting, General Management, Marketing,
Research and Development, Sales, Women/Minorities

Fitzgerald, Geoffrey — *Principal*
Fitzgerald Associates
21 Muzzey Street
Lexington, MA 02173
Telephone: (617) 863-1945
Recruiter Classification: Retained; **Lowest/Average Salary:**
$60,000/$90,000; **Industry Concentration:** Insurance;
Function Concentration: Generalist with a primary focus in
Finance/Accounting, General Management, Marketing,
Research and Development, Sales, Women/Minorities

Flanagan, Robert M. — *President*
Robert M. Flanagan & Associates, Ltd.
Fields Lane, JMK Building
North Salem, NY 10560-0339
Telephone: (914) 277-7210
Recruiter Classification: Retained; **Lowest/Average Salary:**
$90,000/$90,000; **Industry Concentration:** Generalist with a
primary focus in Financial Services, Insurance; **Function
Concentration:** Generalist with a primary focus in
Administration, Finance/Accounting, Human Resources,
Marketing, Sales

Fleming, Marco — *Executive Recruiter*
MSI International
2170 West State Road 434
Suite 454
Longwood, FL 32779
Telephone: (407) 788-7700
Recruiter Classification: Contingency; **Lowest/Average Salary:**
$30,000/$60,000; **Industry Concentration:** Generalist with a
primary focus in Financial Services; **Function Concentration:**
Generalist with a primary focus in Administration,
Engineering, Finance/Accounting, General Management,
Marketing, Sales

Fletcher, David — *Professional Recruiter*
A.J. Burton Group, Inc.
120 East Baltimore Street, Suite 2220
Baltimore, MD 21202
Telephone: (410) 752-5244
Recruiter Classification: Contingency; **Lowest/Average Salary:**
$40,000/$75,000; **Industry Concentration:** Generalist with a
primary focus in Financial Services, Insurance; **Function
Concentration:** Generalist with a primary focus in
Administration, Finance/Accounting, General Management,
Human Resources

Flood, Michael — *Managing Director*
Norman Broadbent International, Inc.
200 Park Avenue, 20th Floor
New York, NY 10166
Telephone: (212) 953-6990
Recruiter Classification: Retained; **Lowest/Average Salary:**
$90,000/$90,000; **Industry Concentration:** Financial Services,
Venture Capital; **Function Concentration:**
Finance/Accounting, General Management, Human
Resources, Marketing, Sales

Flora, Dodi — *Regional Director*
Crawford & Crofford
15327 NW 60th Avenue, Suite 240
Miami Lakes, FL 33014
Telephone: (305) 820-0855
Recruiter Classification: Contingency, Executive Temporary;
Lowest/Average Salary: $30,000/$60,000; **Industry
Concentration:** Financial Services, Insurance; **Function
Concentration:** Administration, Engineering,
Finance/Accounting, General Management, Human Resources,
Sales

Flores, Agustin — *Partner*
Ward Howell International, Inc.
Rexer Seleccion de Ejecutivos, S.C.
Blvd. Adolfo Lopez Mateos 20, Col. San Angel Inn
Mexico City, D.F., MEXICO 01060
Telephone: (525) 550-9180
Recruiter Classification: Retained; **Lowest/Average Salary:**
$75,000/$90,000; **Industry Concentration:** Financial Services;
Function Concentration: Generalist

Florio, Robert — *Associate*
Source Services Corporation
525 Vine Street, Suite 2250
Cincinnati, OH 45202
Telephone: (513) 651-3303
Recruiter Classification: Contingency; **Lowest/Average
Salary:** $30,000/$50,000; **Industry Concentration:** Financial
Services; **Function Concentration:** Engineering,
Finance/Accounting

Flynn, Jack — *Managing Partner*
Executive Search Consultants Corporation
8 South Michigan Avenue, Suite 1205
Chicago, IL 60603
Telephone: (312) 251-8400
Recruiter Classification: Contingency; **Lowest/Average Salary:**
$40,000/$60,000; **Industry Concentration:** Financial Services,
Insurance; **Function Concentration:** Administration, General
Management

Fogarty, Michael — *Executive Recruiter*
CPS Inc.
One Westbrook Corporate Centre, Suite 600
Westchester, IL 60154
Telephone: (708) 531-8370
Recruiter Classification: Contingency; **Lowest/Average Salary:**
$30,000/$50,000; **Industry Concentration:** Generalist with a
primary focus in Financial Services, Insurance; **Function
Concentration:** Engineering, Research and Development,
Sales, Women/Minorities

Fong, Robert — *Principal*
Korn/Ferry International
600 University Street, Suite 3111
Seattle, WA 98101
Telephone: (206) 447-1834
Recruiter Classification: Retained; **Lowest/Average Salary:**
$100,000/$150,000; **Industry Concentration:** Generalist with a
primary focus in Financial Services, Insurance; **Function
Concentration:** Generalist

Foote, Leland W. — *President*
L.W. Foote Company
110 110th Avenue N.E.
Suite 603
Bellevue, WA 98004-5840
Telephone: (206) 451-1660
Recruiter Classification: Retained; **Lowest/Average Salary:**
$75,000/$90,000; **Industry Concentration:** Generalist with a
primary focus in Venture Capital; **Function Concentration:**
Generalist with a primary focus in Administration, Engineering,
Finance/Accounting, General Management, Human Resources,
Marketing, Research and Development, Sales,
Women/Minorities

Ford, Sandra D. — *Managing Director*
The Ford Group, Inc.
485 Devon Park Drive, Suite 110
Wayne, PA 19087
Telephone: (610) 975-9007
Recruiter Classification: Retained; **Lowest/Average Salary:**
$90,000/$90,000; **Industry Concentration:** Financial Services;
Function Concentration: Finance/Accounting, General
Management, Human Resources, Marketing,
Women/Minorities

Foreman, David C. — *Senior Associate*
Koontz, Jeffries & Associates, Inc.
18-22 Bank Street
Summit, NJ 07901
Telephone: (908) 598-1900
Recruiter Classification: Retained; **Lowest/Average Salary:**
$60,000/$90,000; **Industry Concentration:** Generalist with a
primary focus in Financial Services; **Function Concentration:**
Generalist with a primary focus in Administration, Engineering,
Finance/Accounting, General Management, Human Resources,
Marketing, Research and Development, Sales,
Women/Minorities

Foreman, Rebecca — *Associate*
Aubin International Inc.
281 Winter Street, #380
Waltham, MA 02154
Telephone: (617) 890-1722
Recruiter Classification: Retained; **Lowest/Average Salary:**
$90,000/$90,000; **Industry Concentration:** Generalist with a
primary focus in Venture Capital; **Function Concentration:**
Generalist

Forestier, Lois — *Associate*
Source Services Corporation
2 Penn Plaza, Suite 1176
New York, NY 10121
Telephone: (212) 760-2200
Recruiter Classification: Contingency; **Lowest/Average Salary:**
$30,000/$50,000; **Industry Concentration:** Financial Services;
Function Concentration: Engineering, Finance/Accounting

Forgosh, Jack H. — *Senior Consultant*
Raymond Karsan Associates
170 So. Warner Road
Wayne, PA 19087
Telephone: (610) 971-9171
Recruiter Classification: Retained; **Lowest/Average Salary:**
$30,000/$90,000; **Industry Concentration:** Generalist with a
primary focus in Insurance; **Function Concentration:**
Generalist

Foster, Bradley — *Associate*
Source Services Corporation
2000 Town Center, Suite 850
Southfield, MI 48075
Telephone: (810) 352-6520
Recruiter Classification: Contingency; **Lowest/Average Salary:**
$30,000/$50,000; **Industry Concentration:** Financial Services;
Function Concentration: Engineering, Finance/Accounting

Foster, Brian Scott — *Director*
Don Richard Associates of Charlotte
2650 One First Union Center
301 South College Street
Charlotte, NC 28202-6000
Telephone: (704) 377-6447
Recruiter Classification: Contingency, Executive Temporary;
Lowest/Average Salary: $30,000/$60,000; **Industry
Concentration:** Financial Services; **Function Concentration:**
Finance/Accounting

Foster, Dwight E. — *Chairman/Executive
Managing Director*
D.E. Foster Partners Inc.
570 Lexington Avenue, 14th Floor
New York, NY 10022
Telephone: (212) 872-6232
Recruiter Classification: Retained; **Lowest/Average Salary:**
$90,000/$90,000; **Industry Concentration:** Generalist with a
primary focus in Financial Services, Insurance; **Function
Concentration:** Finance/Accounting, General Management

Foster, John — *Associate*
Source Services Corporation
8614 Westwood Center, Suite 750
Vienna, VA 22182
Telephone: (703) 790-5610
Recruiter Classification: Contingency; **Lowest/Average Salary:**
$30,000/$50,000; **Industry Concentration:** Financial Services;
Function Concentration: Engineering, Finance/Accounting

Fotia, Frank — *Principal*
JDG Associates, Ltd.
1700 Research Boulevard
Rockville, MD 20850
Telephone: (301) 340-2210
Recruiter Classification: Contingency; **Lowest/Average Salary:**
$50,000/$90,000; **Industry Concentration:** Financial Services;
Function Concentration: Engineering, Finance/Accounting,
Research and Development

Fowler, Edward D.C. — *Director*
Research/Associate
Higdon Prince Inc.
230 Park Avenue, Suite 1455
New York, NY 10169
Telephone: (212) 986-4662
Recruiter Classification: Retained; **Lowest/Average Salary:**
$150,000/$150,000; **Industry Concentration:** Generalist with a
primary focus in Financial Services, Venture Capital; **Function
Concentration:** Generalist with a primary focus in
Finance/Accounting, General Management, Human Resources,
Marketing, Sales, Women/Minorities

Fowler, Susan B. — *Managing Director*
Russell Reynolds Associates, Inc.
200 Park Avenue
New York, NY 10166-0002
Telephone: (212) 351-2000
Recruiter Classification: Retained; **Lowest/Average Salary:**
$90,000/$90,000; **Industry Concentration:** Generalist with a
primary focus in Financial Services; **Function Concentration:**
Generalist

Fowler, Thomas A. — *Vice President -
Dallas/Southwest*
The Hindman Company
Suite 200, The Tower at Williams Square
5215 North O'Connor Road
Irving, TX 75039
Telephone: (214) 868-9122
Recruiter Classification: Retained; **Lowest/Average Salary:**
$50,000/$90,000; **Industry Concentration:** Generalist with a
primary focus in Financial Services; **Function Concentration:**
Generalist with a primary focus in Engineering,
Finance/Accounting, General Management, Human Resources,
Marketing, Sales

Fox, Amanda C. — *Partner*
Ray & Berndtson
Sears Tower, 233 South Wacker Drive, Suite 4020
Chicago, IL 60606-6310
Telephone: (312) 876-0730
Recruiter Classification: Retained; **Lowest/Average Salary:**
$90,000/$90,000; **Industry Concentration:** Generalist with a
primary focus in Financial Services, Insurance; **Function
Concentration:** Generalist with a primary focus in
Finance/Accounting, Human Resources

Fox, Lucie — *Associate*
Allard Associates
44 Montgomery Street, Suite 500
San Francisco, CA 94104
Telephone: (800) 291-5279
Recruiter Classification: Retained; **Lowest/Average Salary:**
$50,000/$90,000; **Industry Concentration:** Financial Services;
Function Concentration: Marketing

Francis, Brad — *Managing Director*
Source Services Corporation
7730 East Bellview Avenue, Suite 302
Englewood, CO 80111
Telephone: (303) 773-3700
Recruiter Classification: Contingency; **Lowest/Average
Salary:** $30,000/$50,000; **Industry Concentration:** Financial
Services; **Function Concentration:** Engineering,
Finance/Accounting

Frantino, Michael — *Associate*
Source Services Corporation
379 Thornall Street
Edison, NJ 08837
Telephone: (908) 494-2800
Recruiter Classification: Contingency; **Lowest/Average
Salary:** $30,000/$50,000; **Industry Concentration:** Financial
Services; **Function Concentration:** Engineering,
Finance/Accounting

Frazier, John — *Manager*
Cochran, Cochran & Yale, Inc.
955 East Henrietta Road
Rochester, NY 14623
Telephone: (716) 424-6060
Recruiter Classification: Retained; **Lowest/Average Salary:**
$40,000/$60,000; **Industry Concentration:** Generalist with a
primary focus in Financial Services, Venture Capital; **Function
Concentration:** Generalist with a primary focus in Engineering,
Finance/Accounting, General Management, Human Resources,
Marketing, Sales, Women/Minorities

Frederick, Dianne — *Associate*
Source Services Corporation
525 Vine Street, Suite 2250
Cincinnati, OH 45202
Telephone: (513) 651-3303
Recruiter Classification: Contingency; **Lowest/Average
Salary:** $30,000/$50,000; **Industry Concentration:** Financial
Services; **Function Concentration:** Engineering,
Finance/Accounting

Freedman, Howard — *Vice President*
Korn/Ferry International
237 Park Avenue
New York, NY 10017
Telephone: (212) 687-1834
Recruiter Classification: Retained; **Lowest/Average Salary:**
$100,000/$150,000; **Industry Concentration:** Generalist with a
primary focus in Financial Services; **Function Concentration:**
Generalist

Freeh, Thomas — *Managing Director*
Source Services Corporation
4170 Ashford Dunwoody Road, Suite 285
Atlanta, GA 30319
Telephone: (404) 255-2045
Recruiter Classification: Contingency; **Lowest/Average
Salary:** $30,000/$50,000; **Industry Concentration:** Financial
Services; **Function Concentration:** Engineering,
Finance/Accounting

Freeman, Mark — *Partner*
ESA Professional Consultants
141 Durham Road
Suite 16
Madison, CT 06443
Telephone: (203) 245-1983
Recruiter Classification: Retained; **Lowest/Average Salary:**
$50,000/$75,000; **Industry Concentration:** Venture Capital;
Function Concentration: Engineering, General Management,
Human Resources, Marketing, Research and Development,
Women/Minorities

Freier, Bruce — *President*
Executive Referral Services, Inc.
8770 West Bryn Mawr, Suite 110
Chicago, IL 60631
Telephone: (773) 693-6622
Recruiter Classification: Contingency; **Lowest/Average Salary:** $30,000/$50,000; **Industry Concentration:** Generalist with a primary focus in Venture Capital; **Function Concentration:** Finance/Accounting, General Management, Marketing, Women/Minorities

French, William G. — *Partner*
Preng & Associates, Inc.
2925 Briarpark, Suite 1111
Houston, TX 77042
Telephone: (713) 266-2600
Recruiter Classification: Retained; **Lowest/Average Salary:** $90,000/$90,000; **Industry Concentration:** Financial Services, Venture Capital; **Function Concentration:** Generalist with a primary focus in Engineering, Finance/Accounting, General Management, Human Resources, Marketing, Research and Development

Frerichs, April — *Executive Recruiter*
Ryan, Miller & Associates Inc.
4601 Wilshire Boulevard, Suite 225
Los Angeles, CA 90010
Telephone: (213) 938-4768
Recruiter Classification: Contingency; **Lowest/Average Salary:** $40,000/$50,000; **Industry Concentration:** Generalist with a primary focus in Financial Services; **Function Concentration:** Generalist with a primary focus in Finance/Accounting

Fribush, Richard — *Professional Recruiter*
A.J. Burton Group, Inc.
120 East Baltimore Street, Suite 2220
Baltimore, MD 21202
Telephone: (410) 752-5244
Recruiter Classification: Contingency; **Lowest/Average Salary:** $40,000/$75,000; **Industry Concentration:** Generalist with a primary focus in Financial Services, Insurance; **Function Concentration:** Generalist with a primary focus in Administration, Finance/Accounting, General Management, Human Resources

Friedman, Deborah — *Associate*
Source Services Corporation
425 California Street, Suite 1200
San Francisco, CA 94104
Telephone: (415) 434-2410
Recruiter Classification: Contingency; **Lowest/Average Salary:** $30,000/$50,000; **Industry Concentration:** Financial Services; **Function Concentration:** Engineering, Finance/Accounting

Friedman, Donna L. — *President*
Tower Consultants, Ltd.
4195 N.E. Hyline Drive
Jensen Beach, FL 34957
Telephone: (561) 225-5151
Recruiter Classification: Retained; **Lowest/Average Salary:** $60,000/$90,000; **Industry Concentration:** Generalist with a primary focus in Financial Services, Insurance; **Function Concentration:** Administration, Human Resources, Women/Minorities

Friedman, Helen E. — *Partner*
McCormack & Farrow
695 Town Center Drive
Suite 660
Costa Mesa, CA 92626
Telephone: (714) 549-7222
Recruiter Classification: Retained; **Lowest/Average Salary:** $75,000/$90,000; **Industry Concentration:** Generalist with a primary focus in Financial Services; **Function Concentration:** Generalist with a primary focus in Administration, Finance/Accounting, General Management, Human Resources, Research and Development, Women/Minorities

Frock, Suzanne D. — *Principal*
Brandjes Associates
16 South Calvert Street, Ste. 500
Baltimore, MD 21202
Telephone: (410) 547-6886
Recruiter Classification: Contingency; **Lowest/Average Salary:** $50,000/$75,000; **Industry Concentration:** Financial Services; **Function Concentration:** Generalist

Frumess, Gregory — *Managing Director Financial Services Practice*
D.E. Foster Partners Inc.
570 Lexington Avenue, 14th Floor
New York, NY 10022
Telephone: (212) 872-6232
Recruiter Classification: Retained; **Lowest/Average Salary:** $90,000/$90,000; **Industry Concentration:** Financial Services, Insurance; **Function Concentration:** Finance/Accounting

Fuhrman, Dennis — *Managing Director*
Source Services Corporation
500 108th Avenue NE, Suite 1780
Bellevue, WA 98004
Telephone: (206) 454-6400
Recruiter Classification: Contingency; **Lowest/Average Salary:** $30,000/$50,000; **Industry Concentration:** Financial Services; **Function Concentration:** Engineering, Finance/Accounting

Fujino, Rickey — *Associate*
Source Services Corporation
1290 Oakmead Parkway, Suite 318
Sunnyvale, CA 94086
Telephone: (408) 738-8440
Recruiter Classification: Contingency; **Lowest/Average Salary:** $30,000/$50,000; **Industry Concentration:** Financial Services; **Function Concentration:** Engineering, Finance/Accounting

Fulger, Herbert — *Associate*
Source Services Corporation
3 Summit Park Drive, Suite 550
Independence, OH 44131
Telephone: (216) 328-5900
Recruiter Classification: Contingency; **Lowest/Average Salary:** $30,000/$50,000; **Industry Concentration:** Financial Services; **Function Concentration:** Engineering, Finance/Accounting

Fulton, Christine N. — *Recruiter*
Highland Search Group
565 Fifth Avenue, 22nd Floor
New York, NY 10017
Telephone: (212) 328-1113
Recruiter Classification: Retained; **Lowest/Average Salary:** $90,000/$90,000; **Industry Concentration:** Financial Services, Insurance, Venture Capital; **Function Concentration:** Generalist with a primary focus in Administration, Finance/Accounting, General Management, Human Resources, Research and Development, Sales, Women/Minorities

Furlong, James W. — *President*
Furlong Search, Inc.
634 East Main Street
Hillsboro, OR 97123
Telephone: (503) 640-3221
Recruiter Classification: Retained; **Lowest/Average Salary:**
$90,000/$90,000; **Industry Concentration:** Venture Capital;
Function Concentration: Generalist with a primary focus in
Engineering, Finance/Accounting, General Management,
Marketing, Research and Development, Sales

Furlong, James W. — *President*
Furlong Search, Inc.
550 Tyndall Street, Suite 11
Los Altos, CA 94022
Telephone: (415) 856-8484
Recruiter Classification: Retained; **Lowest/Average Salary:**
$90,000/$90,000; **Industry Concentration:** Venture Capital;
Function Concentration: Generalist with a primary focus in
Engineering, Finance/Accounting, General Management,
Marketing, Research and Development, Sales

Furlong, James W. — *President*
Furlong Search, Inc.
19312 Romar Street
Northridge, CA 91324
Telephone: (818) 885-7044
Recruiter Classification: Retained; **Lowest/Average Salary:**
$90,000/$90,000; **Industry Concentration:** Venture Capital;
Function Concentration: Generalist with a primary focus in
Engineering, Finance/Accounting, General Management,
Marketing, Research and Development, Sales

Fust, Sheely F. — *Partner*
Ray & Berndtson
2029 Century Park East, Suite 1000
Los Angeles, CA 90067
Telephone: (310) 557-2828
Recruiter Classification: Retained; **Lowest/Average Salary:**
$90,000/$90,000; **Industry Concentration:** Generalist with a
primary focus in Financial Services, Insurance; **Function
Concentration:** Generalist with a primary focus in
Administration, Finance/Accounting, General Management,
Human Resources, Marketing, Research and Development,
Sales, Women/Minorities

Fyhrie, David — *Associate*
Source Services Corporation
3701 West Algonquin Road, Suite 380
Rolling Meadows, IL 60008
Telephone: (847) 392-0244
Recruiter Classification: Contingency; **Lowest/Average Salary:**
$30,000/$50,000; **Industry Concentration:** Financial Services;
Function Concentration: Engineering, Finance/Accounting

Gabel, Gregory N. — *Vice President*
Canny, Bowen Inc.
200 Park Avenue
49th Floor
New York, NY 10166
Telephone: (212) 949-6611
Recruiter Classification: Retained; **Lowest/Average Salary:**
$90,000/$90,000; **Industry Concentration:** Generalist with a
primary focus in Venture Capital; **Function Concentration:**
Generalist with a primary focus in Engineering,
Finance/Accounting, General Management, Human Resources,
Marketing, Research and Development, Sales,
Women/Minorities

Gabler, Howard A. — *President*
G.Z. Stephens Inc.
One World Trade Center
Suite 1527
New York, NY 10048
Telephone: (212) 321-3040
Recruiter Classification: Retained; **Lowest/Average Salary:**
$90,000/$90,000; **Industry Concentration:** Financial Services;
Function Concentration: Generalist

Gabriel, David L. — *Managing Director*
The Arcus Group
100 North Central (At Main), Suite 1200
Dallas, TX 75201
Telephone: (214) 744-2100
Recruiter Classification: Retained; **Lowest/Average Salary:**
$90,000/$90,000; **Industry Concentration:** Generalist with a
primary focus in Financial Services, Insurance, Venture Capital;
Function Concentration: Generalist with a primary focus in
Administration, Engineering, Finance/Accounting, General
Management, Human Resources, Marketing, Research and
Development, Women/Minorities

Gaffney, Keith — *Managing Director Executive
Search*
Gaffney Management Consultants
35 North Brandon Drive
Glendale Heights, IL 60139-2087
Telephone: (630) 307-3380
Recruiter Classification: Retained; **Lowest/Average Salary:**
$60,000/$90,000; **Industry Concentration:** Generalist with a
primary focus in Venture Capital; **Function Concentration:**
Generalist with a primary focus in Engineering, General
Management, Research and Development,
Women/Minorities

Gaffney, Megan — *Associate*
Source Services Corporation
8614 Westwood Center, Suite 750
Vienna, VA 22182
Telephone: (703) 790-5610
Recruiter Classification: Contingency; **Lowest/Average Salary:**
$30,000/$50,000; **Industry Concentration:** Financial Services;
Function Concentration: Engineering, Finance/Accounting

Gaffney, William — *President*
Gaffney Management Consultants
35 North Brandon Drive
Glendale Heights, IL 60139-2087
Telephone: (630) 307-3380
Recruiter Classification: Retained; **Lowest/Average Salary:**
$60,000/$90,000; **Industry Concentration:** Generalist with a
primary focus in Venture Capital; **Function Concentration:**
Generalist with a primary focus in Engineering, General
Management, Research and Development,
Women/Minorities

Gaines, Jay — *President*
Jay Gaines & Company, Inc.
450 Park Avenue
New York, NY 10022
Telephone: (212) 308-9222
Recruiter Classification: Retained; **Lowest/Average Salary:**
$200,000/$500,000; **Industry Concentration:** Generalist with a
primary focus in Financial Services, Insurance; **Function
Concentration:** Generalist with a primary focus in
Finance/Accounting, General Management, Marketing, Sales

Gaines, Ronni L. — *President*
TOPAZ Legal Solutions
383 Northfield Avenue
West Orange, NJ 07052
Telephone: (201) 669-7300
Recruiter Classification: Executive Temporary; **Lowest/Average Salary:** $40,000/$75,000; **Industry Concentration:** Financial Services; **Function Concentration:** Generalist with a primary focus in Women/Minorities

Gaines, Ronni L. — *Partner*
TOPAZ International, Inc.
383 Northfield Avenue
West Orange, NJ 07052
Telephone: (201) 669-7300
Recruiter Classification: Contingency; **Lowest/Average Salary:** $40,000/$75,000; **Industry Concentration:** Financial Services; **Function Concentration:** Generalist with a primary focus in Women/Minorities

Galante, Suzanne M. — *Vice President*
Vlcek & Company, Inc.
620 Newport Center Drive
Suite 1100
Newport Beach, CA 92660
Telephone: (714) 752-0661
Recruiter Classification: Retained; **Lowest/Average Salary:** $90,000/$90,000; **Industry Concentration:** Generalist with a primary focus in Financial Services; **Function Concentration:** Generalist with a primary focus in Engineering, Finance/Accounting, General Management, Human Resources, Marketing, Sales, Women/Minorities

Galinski, Paul — *Assistant Vice President*
E.J. Ashton & Associates, Ltd.
P.O. Box 1048
Lake Zurich, IL 60047-1048
Telephone: (847) 540-9922
Recruiter Classification: Contingency; **Lowest/Average Salary:** $30,000/$60,000; **Industry Concentration:** Insurance; **Function Concentration:** Generalist with a primary focus in Administration, Finance/Accounting, General Management, Marketing, Sales

Gallagher, Terence M. — *Chief Operating Officer*
Battalia Winston International
120 Wood Avenue, South
Iselin, NJ 08830
Telephone: (908) 549-2002
Recruiter Classification: Retained; **Lowest/Average Salary:** $90,000/$90,000; **Industry Concentration:** Generalist with a primary focus in Financial Services, Insurance; **Function Concentration:** Generalist with a primary focus in Administration, Finance/Accounting, General Management, Human Resources, Marketing, Sales, Women/Minorities

Gamble, Ira — *Associate*
Source Services Corporation
1290 Oakmead Parkway, Suite 318
Sunnyvale, CA 94086
Telephone: (408) 738-8440
Recruiter Classification: Contingency; **Lowest/Average Salary:** $30,000/$50,000; **Industry Concentration:** Financial Services; **Function Concentration:** Engineering, Finance/Accounting

Gantar, Donna — *Senior Consultant*
Howard Fischer Associates, Inc.
1800 John F. Kennedy Boulevard, 7th Floor
Philadelphia, PA 19103
Telephone: (215) 568-8363
Recruiter Classification: Retained; **Lowest/Average Salary:** $90,000/$90,000; **Industry Concentration:** Generalist with a primary focus in Financial Services, Insurance, Venture Capital; **Function Concentration:** Generalist with a primary focus in Administration, Finance/Accounting, General Management, Human Resources, Marketing, Research and Development, Sales, Women/Minorities

Gardiner, E. Nicholas P. — *President*
Gardiner International
101 East 52nd Street
New York, NY 10022
Telephone: (212) 838-0707
Recruiter Classification: Retained; **Lowest/Average Salary:** $90,000/$90,000; **Industry Concentration:** Generalist with a primary focus in Financial Services, Insurance; **Function Concentration:** Generalist with a primary focus in Finance/Accounting, General Management, Marketing

Gardner, Michael — *Associate*
Source Services Corporation
2 Penn Plaza, Suite 1176
New York, NY 10121
Telephone: (212) 760-2200
Recruiter Classification: Contingency; **Lowest/Average Salary:** $30,000/$50,000; **Industry Concentration:** Financial Services; **Function Concentration:** Engineering, Finance/Accounting

Garfinkle, Steven M. — *Managing Director*
Battalia Winston International
20 William Street
Wellesley Hills, MA 02181
Telephone: (617) 239-1400
Recruiter Classification: Retained; **Lowest/Average Salary:** $90,000/$90,000; **Industry Concentration:** Generalist with a primary focus in Financial Services, Insurance, Venture Capital; **Function Concentration:** Generalist with a primary focus in Engineering, Finance/Accounting, General Management, Human Resources, Marketing, Research and Development, Sales, Women/Minorities

Garland, Dick — *President*
Dick Garland Consultants
31 E. 32nd Street
Suite 300
New York, NY 10016
Telephone: (212) 481-8484
Recruiter Classification: Retained; **Lowest/Average Salary:** $75,000/$90,000; **Industry Concentration:** Financial Services; **Function Concentration:** Finance/Accounting, Marketing, Sales

Garrett, Mark — *Associate*
Source Services Corporation
One CityPlace, Suite 170
St. Louis, MO 63141
Telephone: (314) 432-4500
Recruiter Classification: Contingency; **Lowest/Average Salary:** $30,000/$50,000; **Industry Concentration:** Financial Services; **Function Concentration:** Engineering, Finance/Accounting

Garzone, Dolores — *Executive Recruiter*
M.A. Churchill & Associates, Inc.
Morelyn Plaza #307
1111 Street Road
Southampton, PA 18966
Telephone: (215) 953-0300
Recruiter Classification: Retained; **Lowest/Average Salary:**
$50,000/$75,000; **Industry Concentration:** Financial Services;
Function Concentration: General Management, Marketing,
Sales

Gates, Lucille C. — *Principal*
Lamalie Amrop International
Chevron Tower
1301 McKinney Street
Houston, TX 77010-3034
Telephone: (713) 739-8602
Recruiter Classification: Retained; **Lowest/Average Salary:**
$90,000/$90,000; **Industry Concentration:** Generalist with a
primary focus in Financial Services; **Function Concentration:**
Generalist

Gauthier, Robert C. — *Managing Director*
Columbia Consulting Group
20 South Charles Street, 9th Floor
Baltimore, MD 21201
Telephone: (410) 385-2525
Recruiter Classification: Retained; **Lowest/Average Salary:**
$75,000/$90,000; **Industry Concentration:** Generalist with a
primary focus in Financial Services, Insurance; **Function
Concentration:** Generalist with a primary focus in
Finance/Accounting, General Management, Human Resources,
Marketing, Sales

Geiger, Jan — *Outplacement Manager*
Wilcox, Bertoux & Miller
100 Howe Avenue, Suite 155N
Sacramento, CA 95825
Telephone: (916) 977-3700
Recruiter Classification: Contingency; **Lowest/Average Salary:**
$40,000/$75,000; **Industry Concentration:** Financial Services;
Function Concentration: Administration, Finance/Accounting,
General Management

Gennawey, Robert — *Managing Director*
Source Services Corporation
One Park Plaza, Suite 560
Irvine, CA 92714
Telephone: (714) 660-1666
Recruiter Classification: Contingency; **Lowest/Average
Salary:** $30,000/$50,000; **Industry Concentration:** Financial
Services; **Function Concentration:** Engineering,
Finance/Accounting

George, Brenda — *Banking Recruiter*
Don Richard Associates of Charlotte
2650 One First Union Center
301 South College Street
Charlotte, NC 28202-6000
Telephone: (704) 377-6447
Recruiter Classification: Contingency; **Lowest/Average Salary:**
$30,000/$50,000; **Industry Concentration:** Financial Services;
Function Concentration: Sales

George, Delores F. — *President and Owner*
Delores F. George Human Resource Management
& Consulting Industry
269 Hamilton Street, Suite 1
Worcester, MA 01604
Telephone: (508) 754-3451
Recruiter Classification: Contingency; **Lowest/Average Salary:**
$60,000/$60,000; **Industry Concentration:** Generalist with a
primary focus in Financial Services, Insurance; **Function
Concentration:** Generalist with a primary focus in
Administration, Finance/Accounting, General Management,
Human Resources, Marketing, Research and Development,
Sales, Women/Minorities

Gerber, Mark J. — *Associate*
Wellington Management Group
1601 Market Street, Suite 2902
Philadelphia, PA 19103-2499
Telephone: (215) 569-8900
Recruiter Classification: Retained; **Lowest/Average Salary:**
$75,000/$90,000; **Industry Concentration:** Generalist with a
primary focus in Financial Services; **Function Concentration:**
Generalist with a primary focus in Administration,
Finance/Accounting, General Management

Germain, Valerie — *Managing Director*
Jay Gaines & Company, Inc.
450 Park Avenue
New York, NY 10022
Telephone: (212) 308-9222
Recruiter Classification: Retained; **Lowest/Average Salary:**
$200,000/$250,000; **Industry Concentration:** Generalist
with a primary focus in Financial Services, Insurance;
Function Concentration: Generalist with a primary focus in
Administration, General Management, Marketing, Sales

Gerster, J.P. — *Associate*
Juntunen-Combs-Poirier
111 Bayhill Drive, Suite 255
San Bruno, CA 94066
Telephone: (415) 635-0184
Recruiter Classification: Retained; **Lowest/Average Salary:**
$90,000/$90,000; **Industry Concentration:** Financial Services,
Venture Capital; **Function Concentration:** Engineering,
Finance/Accounting, General Management, Research and
Development

Gestwick, Daniel — *Search Consultant*
Cochran, Cochran & Yale, Inc.
5166 Main Street
Williamsville, NY 14221
Telephone: (716) 631-1300
Recruiter Classification: Retained; **Lowest/Average Salary:**
$50,000/$75,000; **Industry Concentration:** Generalist with a
primary focus in Financial Services, Venture Capital;
Function Concentration: Generalist with a primary focus in
Engineering, Finance/Accounting, General Management,
Human Resources, Marketing, Sales, Women/Minorities

Ghurani, Mac — *Associate*
Gary Kaplan & Associates
201 South Lake Avenue
Suite 600
Pasadena, CA 91101
Telephone: (818) 796-8100
Recruiter Classification: Retained; **Lowest/Average Salary:**
$75,000/$90,000; **Industry Concentration:** Generalist with a
primary focus in Financial Services, Insurance; **Function
Concentration:** Generalist with a primary focus in Engineering,
Finance/Accounting, General Management, Human Resources,
Marketing, Research and Development

Giacalone, Louis — *Associate*
Allard Associates
70 Pine Street, 60th Floor
New York, NY 10270
Telephone: (800) 291-5279
Recruiter Classification: Retained; **Lowest/Average Salary:**
$75,000/$90,000; **Industry Concentration:** Financial Services;
Function Concentration: Marketing

Gibbons, Ronald L. — *Vice President*
Flynn, Hannock, Incorporated
1001 Farmington Avenue
West Hartford, CT 06107
Telephone: (860) 521-5005
Recruiter Classification: Retained, Executive Temporary;
Lowest/Average Salary: $75,000/$90,000; **Industry
Concentration:** Generalist with a primary focus in Financial
Services, Insurance; **Function Concentration:** Generalist with a
primary focus in Administration, General Management,
Marketing, Sales

Gibbs, John S. — *Director*
Spencer Stuart
277 Park Avenue, 29th Floor
New York, NY 10172
Telephone: (212) 336-0200
Recruiter Classification: Retained; **Lowest/Average Salary:**
$90,000/$90,000; **Industry Concentration:** Generalist with a
primary focus in Financial Services, Insurance, Venture Capital;
Function Concentration: Generalist with a primary focus in
Administration, Finance/Accounting, General Management,
Human Resources, Marketing, Sales

Giesy, John — *Associate*
Source Services Corporation
1105 Schrock Road, Suite 510
Columbus, OH 43229
Telephone: (614) 846-3311
Recruiter Classification: Contingency; **Lowest/Average
Salary:** $30,000/$50,000; **Industry Concentration:** Financial
Services; **Function Concentration:** Engineering,
Finance/Accounting

Gilbert, Jerry — *Member Advisory Board*
Gilbert & Van Campen International
Graybar Building, 420 Lexington Avenue
New York, NY 10170
Telephone: (212) 661-2122
Recruiter Classification: Retained; **Lowest/Average Salary:**
$90,000/$90,000; **Industry Concentration:** Generalist with a
primary focus in Financial Services, Venture Capital; **Function
Concentration:** Generalist with a primary focus in
Finance/Accounting, General Management, Human Resources,
Marketing, Sales, Women/Minorities

Gilbert, Patricia G. — *Executive Director*
Lynch Miller Moore, Inc.
10 South Wacker Drive, Suite 2935
Chicago, IL 60606
Telephone: (312) 876-1505
Recruiter Classification: Retained; **Lowest/Average Salary:**
$75,000/$90,000; **Industry Concentration:** Generalist with a
primary focus in Financial Services, Venture Capital; **Function
Concentration:** Generalist with a primary focus in
Finance/Accounting, General Management, Human
Resources

Gilchrist, Robert J. — *Managing Director*
Horton International
10 Tower Lane
Avon, CT 06001
Telephone: (860) 674-8701
Recruiter Classification: Retained; **Lowest/Average Salary:**
$90,000/$90,000; **Industry Concentration:** Insurance;
Function Concentration: Generalist with a primary focus in
Engineering, Finance/Accounting, General Management,
Human Resources, Marketing

Gilinsky, David — *Associate*
Source Services Corporation
3 Summit Park Drive, Suite 550
Independence, OH 44131
Telephone: (216) 328-5900
Recruiter Classification: Contingency; **Lowest/Average
Salary:** $30,000/$50,000; **Industry Concentration:** Financial
Services; **Function Concentration:** Engineering,
Finance/Accounting

Gill, Patricia — *Managing Principal*
Columbia Consulting Group
P.O. Box 1483
Princeton, NJ 08542-1483
Telephone: (609) 466-8900
Recruiter Classification: Retained; **Lowest/Average Salary:**
$75,000/$90,000; **Industry Concentration:** Generalist with a
primary focus in Financial Services, Insurance, Venture Capital;
Function Concentration: Generalist with a primary focus in
Finance/Accounting, General Management, Human Resources,
Marketing, Sales

Gill, Susan — *Consultant*
Plummer & Associates, Inc.
231 Washington Avenue
Marietta, GA 30060
Telephone: (770) 429-9007
Recruiter Classification: Retained, Executive Temporary;
Lowest/Average Salary: $90,000/$90,000; **Industry
Concentration:** Financial Services, Venture Capital; **Function
Concentration:** Generalist with a primary focus in
Administration, Finance/Accounting, General Management,
Marketing

Gillespie, Thomas — *Contract Recruiter*
Professional Search Consultants
3050 Post Oak Boulevard, Suite 1615
Houston, TX 77056
Telephone: (713) 960-9215
Recruiter Classification: Executive Temporary; **Lowest/Average
Salary:** $50,000/$60,000; **Industry Concentration:** Generalist
with a primary focus in Financial Services; **Function
Concentration:** Generalist with a primary focus in Engineering,
Human Resources, Sales

Gilreath, James M. — *President*
Gilreath Weatherby, Inc.
P.O. Box 1483 - 3 Hidden Ledge Road
Manchester-by-the-Sea, MA 01944
Telephone: (508) 526-8771
Recruiter Classification: Retained; **Lowest/Average Salary:**
$75,000/$90,000; **Industry Concentration:** Generalist with a
primary focus in Venture Capital; **Function Concentration:**
Generalist with a primary focus in Engineering,
Finance/Accounting, General Management, Human Resources,
Marketing

Giries, Juliet D. — *Senior Consultant*
Barton Associates, Inc.
One Riverway, Suite 2500
Houston, TX 77056
Telephone: (713) 961-9111
Recruiter Classification: Retained; **Lowest/Average Salary:**
$75,000/$90,000; **Industry Concentration:** Generalist with a
primary focus in Financial Services; **Function Concentration:**
Generalist with a primary focus in Finance/Accounting, Human
Resources, Marketing, Research and Development, Sales

Glass, Lori — *Vice President*
The Executive Source
55 Fifth Avenue, 19th Floor
New York, NY 10003
Telephone: (212) 691-5505
Recruiter Classification: Executive Temporary; **Lowest/Average
Salary:** $75,000/$90,000; **Industry Concentration:** Generalist
with a primary focus in Financial Services, Insurance, Venture
Capital; **Function Concentration:** Human Resources

Glickman, Leenie — *Associate*
Source Services Corporation
20 Burlington Mall Road, Suite 405
Burlington, MA 01803
Telephone: (617) 272-5000
Recruiter Classification: Contingency; **Lowest/Average Salary:**
$30,000/$50,000; **Industry Concentration:** Financial Services;
Function Concentration: Engineering, Finance/Accounting

Gluzman, Arthur — *Associate*
Source Services Corporation
2000 Town Center, Suite 850
Southfield, MI 48075
Telephone: (810) 352-6520
Recruiter Classification: Contingency; **Lowest/Average Salary:**
$30,000/$50,000; **Industry Concentration:** Financial Services;
Function Concentration: Engineering, Finance/Accounting

Gnatowski, Bruce — *Associate*
Source Services Corporation
8614 Westwood Center, Suite 750
Vienna, VA 22182
Telephone: (703) 790-5610
Recruiter Classification: Contingency; **Lowest/Average Salary:**
$30,000/$50,000; **Industry Concentration:** Financial Services;
Function Concentration: Engineering, Finance/Accounting

Goar, Duane R. — *Partner*
Sandhurst Associates
4851 LBJ Freeway, Suite 601
Dallas, TX 75244
Telephone: (214) 458-1212
Recruiter Classification: Retained; **Lowest/Average Salary:**
$75,000/$90,000; **Industry Concentration:** Generalist with a
primary focus in Financial Services, Insurance; **Function
Concentration:** Generalist with a primary focus in
Finance/Accounting, Human Resources, Marketing, Sales

Gobert, Larry — *Chief Operating Officer*
Professional Search Consultants
3050 Post Oak Boulevard, Suite 1615
Houston, TX 77056
Telephone: (713) 960-9215
Recruiter Classification: Executive Temporary; **Lowest/Average
Salary:** $75,000/$75,000; **Industry Concentration:** Generalist
with a primary focus in Financial Services, Venture Capital;
Function Concentration: Generalist with a primary focus in
Finance/Accounting, General Management, Marketing

Goedtke, Steven — *Consultant*
Southwestern Professional Services
2451 Atrium Way
Nashville, TN 37214
Telephone: (615) 391-2722
Recruiter Classification: Contingency; **Lowest/Average Salary:**
$30,000/$50,000; **Industry Concentration:** Generalist with a
primary focus in Financial Services, Insurance; **Function
Concentration:** Sales

Gold, Donald — *Associate*
Executive Search, Ltd.
4830 Interstate Drive
Cincinnati, OH 45246
Telephone: (513) 874-6901
Recruiter Classification: Retained; **Lowest/Average Salary:**
$50,000/$75,000; **Industry Concentration:** Generalist with a
primary focus in Financial Services; **Function Concentration:**
Finance/Accounting

Goldberg, Susan C. — *President*
Susan C. Goldberg Associates
65 LaSalle Road
West Hartford, CT 06107
Telephone: (860) 236-4597
Recruiter Classification: Contingency; **Lowest/Average Salary:**
$40,000/$60,000; **Industry Concentration:** Insurance;
Function Concentration: Finance/Accounting

Golde, Lisa — *Consultant*
Tully/Woodmansee International, Inc.
1088 U.S. 27 North
Lake Placid, FL 33852
Telephone: (941) 465-1024
Recruiter Classification: Retained; **Lowest/Average Salary:**
$60,000/$90,000; **Industry Concentration:** Generalist with a
primary focus in Financial Services, Insurance; **Function
Concentration:** Generalist with a primary focus in Engineering,
Finance/Accounting, General Management, Marketing, Sales,
Women/Minorities

Goldenberg, Susan — *Senior Associate*
Grant Cooper and Associates
795 Office Parkway, Suite 117
St. Louis, MO 63141
Telephone: (314) 567-4690
Recruiter Classification: Retained; **Lowest/Average Salary:**
$60,000/$90,000; **Industry Concentration:** Generalist with a
primary focus in Financial Services, Insurance, Venture Capital;
Function Concentration: Generalist with a primary focus in
Administration, Engineering, Finance/Accounting, General
Management, Human Resources, Marketing, Research and
Development, Sales

Goldsmith, Joseph B. — *Associate*
Higdon Prince Inc.
230 Park Avenue, Suite 1455
New York, NY 10169
Telephone: (212) 986-4662
Recruiter Classification: Retained; **Lowest/Average Salary:**
$150,000/$150,000; **Industry Concentration:** Generalist with a
primary focus in Financial Services, Venture Capital; **Function
Concentration:** Generalist with a primary focus in
Finance/Accounting, General Management, Human Resources,
Marketing, Sales, Women/Minorities

Goldson, Bob — *Principal*
The McCormick Group, Inc.
20 Walnut Street, Suite 308
Wellesley Hills, MA 02181
Telephone: (617) 239-1233
Recruiter Classification: Retained; **Lowest/Average Salary:**
$60,000/$75,000; **Industry Concentration:** Insurance;
Function Concentration: Generalist

Goldstein, Gary — *President*
The Whitney Group
850 Third Avenue, 11th Floor
New York, NY 10022
Telephone: (212) 508-3500
Recruiter Classification: Retained; **Lowest/Average Salary:**
$90,000/$90,000; **Industry Concentration:** Financial Services,
Venture Capital; **Function Concentration:** Generalist with a
primary focus in Finance/Accounting, General Management,
Marketing, Sales

Goldstein, Steven G. — *President*
The Jonathan Stevens Group, Inc.
116 Village Boulevard
Suite 200
Princeton, NJ 08540-5799
Telephone: (609) 734-7444
Recruiter Classification: Retained; **Lowest/Average Salary:**
$40,000/$75,000; **Industry Concentration:** Generalist with a
primary focus in Financial Services; **Function Concentration:**
Generalist with a primary focus in Engineering,
Finance/Accounting, Human Resources, Marketing

Gonye, Peter K. — *Consultant*
Egon Zehnder International Inc.
350 Park Avenue
New York, NY 10022
Telephone: (212) 838-9199
Recruiter Classification: Retained; **Lowest/Average Salary:**
$90,000/$90,000; **Industry Concentration:** Generalist with a
primary focus in Financial Services; **Function Concentration:**
Generalist

Gonzalez, Kristen — *Professional Recruiter*
A.J. Burton Group, Inc.
120 East Baltimore Street, Suite 2220
Baltimore, MD 21202
Telephone: (410) 752-5244
Recruiter Classification: Contingency; **Lowest/Average Salary:**
$40,000/$75,000; **Industry Concentration:** Generalist with a
primary focus in Financial Services, Insurance; **Function
Concentration:** Generalist with a primary focus in
Administration, Finance/Accounting, General Management,
Human Resources

Gonzalez, Rafael — *Principal*
Korn/Ferry International
Montes Urales 641
Lomas De Chapultepec
Mexico City, D.F., MEXICO 11000
Telephone: (525) 202-0046
Recruiter Classification: Retained; **Lowest/Average Salary:**
$100,000/$150,000; **Industry Concentration:** Generalist with a
primary focus in Financial Services, Insurance; **Function
Concentration:** Generalist

Goodman, Dawn M. — *Project Associate*
Bason Associates Inc.
11311 Cornell Park Drive
Cincinnati, OH 45242
Telephone: (513) 469-9881
Recruiter Classification: Retained; **Lowest/Average Salary:**
$60,000/$90,000; **Industry Concentration:** Generalist with a
primary focus in Financial Services, Insurance, Venture Capital;
Function Concentration: Generalist with a primary focus in
Administration, Engineering, Finance/Accounting, General
Management, Human Resources, Marketing, Research and
Development, Sales

Goodman, Julie — *Account Executive*
Search West, Inc.
750 The City Drive South
Suite 100
Orange, CA 92668-4940
Telephone: (714) 748-0400
Recruiter Classification: Contingency; **Lowest/Average
Salary:** $40,000/$60,000; **Industry Concentration:** Financial
Services; **Function Concentration:** Administration,
Finance/Accounting

Goodridge, Benjamin — *Executive Recruiter*
S.C. International, Ltd.
1430 Branding Lane, Suite 119
Downers Grove, IL 60515
Telephone: (708) 963-3033
Recruiter Classification: Contingency; **Lowest/Average
Salary:** $30,000/$50,000; **Industry Concentration:**
Insurance; **Function Concentration:** Administration, Human
Resources

Goodwin, Gary — *Associate*
Source Services Corporation
2 Penn Plaza, Suite 1176
New York, NY 10121
Telephone: (212) 760-2200
Recruiter Classification: Contingency; **Lowest/Average
Salary:** $30,000/$50,000; **Industry Concentration:** Financial
Services; **Function Concentration:** Engineering,
Finance/Accounting

Goodwin, Tim — *Senior Director*
William Guy & Associates
P.O. Box 57407
Sherman Oaks, CA 91413
Telephone: Unpublished
Recruiter Classification: Retained; **Lowest/Average Salary:**
$50,000/$90,000; **Industry Concentration:** Financial Services,
Insurance; **Function Concentration:** Generalist with a primary
focus in Administration, Engineering, Finance/Accounting,
General Management, Research and Development,
Women/Minorities

Gordon, Gerald L. — *Senior Associate*
E.G. Jones Associates, Ltd.
1505 York Road
Lutherville, MD 21093
Telephone: (410) 337-4925
Recruiter Classification: Contingency; **Lowest/Average
Salary:** $20,000/$50,000; **Industry Concentration:** Generalist
with a primary focus in Financial Services; **Function
Concentration:** Generalist with a primary focus in
Administration, Finance/Accounting, General Management,
Marketing, Sales

Gordon, Teri — *Director*
Don Richard Associates of Washington, D.C., Inc.
8180 Greensboro Drive, Suite 1020
McLean, VA 22102
Telephone: (703) 827-5990
Recruiter Classification: Executive Temporary; **Lowest/Average**
Salary: $20,000/$30,000; **Industry Concentration:** Financial
Services; **Function Concentration:** Administration,
Finance/Accounting, Human Resources

Gorfinkle, Gayle — *Partner*
Executive Search International
60 Walnut Street
Wellesley, MA 02181
Telephone: (617) 239-0303
Recruiter Classification: Retained; **Lowest/Average Salary:**
$75,000/$90,000; **Industry Concentration:** Venture Capital;
Function Concentration: Generalist

Gorman, Patrick — *Associate*
Source Services Corporation
425 California Street, Suite 1200
San Francisco, CA 94104
Telephone: (415) 434-2410
Recruiter Classification: Contingency; **Lowest/Average Salary:**
$30,000/$50,000; **Industry Concentration:** Financial Services;
Function Concentration: Engineering, Finance/Accounting

Gorman, T. Patrick — *Vice President*
Techsearch Services, Inc.
6 Hachaliah Brown Drive
Somers, NY 10589
Telephone: (914) 277-2727
Recruiter Classification: Contingency; **Lowest/Average Salary:**
$50,000/$75,000; **Industry Concentration:** Financial Services;
Function Concentration: Finance/Accounting

Gotlys, Jordan — *Associate*
Stone Murphy & Olson
5500 Wayzata Boulevard
Suite 1020
Minneapolis, MN 55416
Telephone: (612) 591-2300
Recruiter Classification: Retained; **Lowest/Average Salary:**
$75,000/$90,000; **Industry Concentration:** Generalist with a
primary focus in Financial Services, Insurance; **Function**
Concentration: Generalist with a primary focus in
Finance/Accounting, General Management, Marketing, Sales

Gourley, Timothy — *Associate*
Source Services Corporation
155 Federal Street, Suite 410
Boston, MA 02110
Telephone: (617) 482-8211
Recruiter Classification: Contingency; **Lowest/Average Salary:**
$30,000/$50,000; **Industry Concentration:** Financial Services;
Function Concentration: Engineering, Finance/Accounting

Gow, Roderick C. — *Managing Partner*
Lamalie Amrop International
200 Park Avenue
New York, NY 10166-0136
Telephone: (212) 953-7900
Recruiter Classification: Retained; **Lowest/Average Salary:**
$90,000/$90,000; **Industry Concentration:** Generalist with a
primary focus in Financial Services, Insurance; **Function**
Concentration: Generalist with a primary focus in
Finance/Accounting, General Management, Marketing, Sales

Grado, Eduardo — *Associate*
Source Services Corporation
5429 LBJ Freeway, Suite 275
Dallas, TX 75240
Telephone: (214) 387-1600
Recruiter Classification: Contingency; **Lowest/Average**
Salary: $30,000/$50,000; **Industry Concentration:** Financial
Services; **Function Concentration:** Engineering,
Finance/Accounting

Graff, Jack — *Associate*
Source Services Corporation
5343 North 16th Street, Suite 270
Phoenix, AZ 85016
Telephone: (602) 230-0220
Recruiter Classification: Contingency; **Lowest/Average**
Salary: $30,000/$50,000; **Industry Concentration:** Financial
Services; **Function Concentration:** Engineering,
Finance/Accounting

Graham, Craig — *Partner*
Ward Howell International, Inc.
141 Adelaide Street West
Suite 1800
Toronto, Ontario, CANADA M5H 3L5
Telephone: (416) 862-1273
Recruiter Classification: Retained; **Lowest/Average Salary:**
$75,000/$90,000; **Industry Concentration:** Financial Services;
Function Concentration: Generalist

Graham, Dale — *Executive Recruiter*
CPS Inc.
One Westbrook Corporate Centre, Suite 600
Westchester, IL 60154
Telephone: (708) 531-8370
Recruiter Classification: Contingency; **Lowest/Average Salary:**
$30,000/$50,000; **Industry Concentration:** Generalist with a
primary focus in Financial Services, Insurance; **Function**
Concentration: Engineering, Research and Development,
Sales, Women/Minorities

Graham, Shannon — *Associate*
Source Services Corporation
7730 East Bellview Avenue, Suite 302
Englewood, CO 80111
Telephone: (303) 773-3700
Recruiter Classification: Contingency; **Lowest/Average Salary:**
$30,000/$50,000; **Industry Concentration:** Financial Services;
Function Concentration: Engineering, Finance/Accounting

Grand, Gordon — *Managing Director*
Russell Reynolds Associates, Inc.
200 Park Avenue
New York, NY 10166-0002
Telephone: (212) 351-2000
Recruiter Classification: Retained; **Lowest/Average Salary:**
$90,000/$90,000; **Industry Concentration:** Generalist with a
primary focus in Financial Services; **Function Concentration:**
Generalist

Grandinetti, Suzanne — *Associate*
Source Services Corporation
1500 West Park Drive, Suite 390
Westborough, MA 01581
Telephone: (508) 366-2600
Recruiter Classification: Contingency; **Lowest/Average Salary:**
$30,000/$50,000; **Industry Concentration:** Financial Services;
Function Concentration: Engineering, Finance/Accounting

Grant, Michael — *Vice President*
Zwell International
300 South Wacker Drive, Suite 650
Chicago, IL 60606
Telephone: (312) 663-3737
Recruiter Classification: Retained; **Lowest/Average Salary:**
$75,000/$90,000; **Industry Concentration:** Generalist with a
primary focus in Financial Services, Insurance, Venture Capital;
Function Concentration: Generalist with a primary focus in
Engineering, Finance/Accounting, General Management,
Human Resources, Marketing, Research and Development,
Sales

Grantham, John — *President*
Grantham & Co., Inc.
136 Erwin Road
Chapel Hill, NC 27514
Telephone: (919) 932-5650
Recruiter Classification: Retained; **Lowest/Average Salary:**
$85,000/$90,000; **Industry Concentration:** Generalist with a
primary focus in Financial Services, Insurance; **Function
Concentration:** Generalist with a primary focus in Engineering,
Finance/Accounting, General Management, Human Resources,
Marketing, Research and Development, Sales

Grantham, Philip H. — *Managing Principal*
Columbia Consulting Group
20 South Charles Street, 9th Floor
Baltimore, MD 21201
Telephone: (410) 385-2525
Recruiter Classification: Retained; **Lowest/Average Salary:**
$75,000/$90,000; **Industry Concentration:** Generalist with a
primary focus in Financial Services, Insurance, Venture Capital;
Function Concentration: Generalist with a primary focus in
Engineering, Finance/Accounting, Human Resources,
Marketing, Sales, Women/Minorities

Grasch, Jerry E. — *Vice President*
The Hindman Company
Browenton Place, Suite 110
2000 Warrington Way
Louisville, KY 40222
Telephone: (502) 426-4040
Recruiter Classification: Retained; **Lowest/Average Salary:**
$50,000/$90,000; **Industry Concentration:** Generalist with a
primary focus in Financial Services; **Function Concentration:**
Generalist with a primary focus in Engineering,
Finance/Accounting, General Management, Human Resources,
Marketing, Sales

Grassl, Peter O. — *President*
Bowman & Marshall, Inc.
P.O. Box 25503
Overland Park, KS 66225
Telephone: (913) 648-3332
Recruiter Classification: Contingency; **Lowest/Average Salary:**
$30,000/$50,000; **Industry Concentration:** Financial Services,
Insurance; **Function Concentration:** Finance/Accounting

Graves, Rosemarie — *Partner*
Don Richard Associates of Washington, D.C., Inc.
8201 Corporate Drive, Suite 620
Landover, MD 20785
Telephone: (301) 474-3900
Recruiter Classification: Contingency, Executive Temporary;
Lowest/Average Salary: $40,000/$60,000; **Industry
Concentration:** Financial Services; **Function Concentration:**
Finance/Accounting

Gray, Annie — *President and CEO*
Annie Gray Associates, Inc./The Executive Search
Firm
12400 Olive Boulevard, Suite 555
St. Louis, MO 63141
Telephone: (314) 275-4405
Recruiter Classification: Retained; **Lowest/Average Salary:**
$75,000/$90,000; **Industry Concentration:** Generalist with a
primary focus in Financial Services; **Function Concentration:**
Generalist with a primary focus in Administration, General
Management, Human Resources

Gray, Betty — *Executive Recruiter*
Accent on Achievement, Inc.
3190 Rochester Road, Suite 104
Troy, MI 48083
Telephone: (248) 528-1390
Recruiter Classification: Contingency; **Lowest/Average Salary:**
$30,000/$50,000; **Industry Concentration:** Generalist with a
primary focus in Financial Services; **Function Concentration:**
Finance/Accounting

Gray, Heather — *Associate*
Source Services Corporation
520 Post Oak Boulevard, Suite 700
Houston, TX 77027
Telephone: (713) 439-1077
Recruiter Classification: Contingency; **Lowest/Average Salary:**
$30,000/$50,000; **Industry Concentration:** Financial Services;
Function Concentration: Engineering, Finance/Accounting

Gray, Mark — *Vice President*
Executive Referral Services, Inc.
8770 West Bryn Mawr, Suite 110
Chicago, IL 60631
Telephone: (773) 693-6622
Recruiter Classification: Contingency; **Lowest/Average Salary:**
$30,000/$50,000; **Industry Concentration:** Venture Capital;
Function Concentration: Administration, Finance/Accounting,
General Management, Human Resources, Marketing, Research
and Development, Sales, Women/Minorities

Gray, Russell — *Associate*
Source Services Corporation
1290 Oakmead Parkway, Suite 318
Sunnyvale, CA 94086
Telephone: (408) 738-8440
Recruiter Classification: Contingency; **Lowest/Average Salary:**
$30,000/$50,000; **Industry Concentration:** Financial Services;
Function Concentration: Engineering, Finance/Accounting

Grayson, E.C. — *Senior Director*
Spencer Stuart
525 Market Street, Suite 3700
San Francisco, CA 94105
Telephone: (415) 495-4141
Recruiter Classification: Retained; **Lowest/Average Salary:**
$90,000/$90,000; **Industry Concentration:** Generalist with a
primary focus in Financial Services; **Function Concentration:**
Generalist

Graziano, Lisa — *Associate*
Source Services Corporation
1 Gatehall Drive, Suite 250
Parsippany, NJ 07054
Telephone: (201) 267-3222
Recruiter Classification: Contingency; **Lowest/Average Salary:**
$30,000/$50,000; **Industry Concentration:** Financial Services;
Function Concentration: Engineering, Finance/Accounting

Grebenschikoff, Jennifer R. — *Vice President*
Physician Executive Management Center
4014 Gunn Highway, Suite 160
Tampa, FL 33624
Telephone: (813) 963-1800
Recruiter Classification: Retained; **Lowest/Average Salary:**
$90,000/$90,000; **Industry Concentration:** Insurance;
Function Concentration: General Management

Grebenstein, Charles R. — *Senior Vice President*
Skott/Edwards Consultants, Inc.
1776 On the Green
Morristown, NJ 07006
Telephone: (973) 644-0900
Recruiter Classification: Retained; **Lowest/Average Salary:**
$90,000/$90,000; **Industry Concentration:** Venture Capital;
Function Concentration: Engineering, Finance/Accounting,
General Management, Marketing, Research and Development,
Sales

Greco, Patricia — *Co-Managing Director*
Howe-Lewis International
521 Fifth Avenue, 36th Floor
New York, NY 10175
Telephone: (212) 697-5000
Recruiter Classification: Retained; **Lowest/Average Salary:**
$90,000/$90,000; **Industry Concentration:** Insurance;
Function Concentration: General Management, Human
Resources, Marketing, Women/Minorities

Gresia, Paul — *Associate*
Source Services Corporation
8614 Westwood Center, Suite 750
Vienna, VA 22182
Telephone: (703) 790-5610
Recruiter Classification: Contingency; **Lowest/Average Salary:**
$30,000/$50,000; **Industry Concentration:** Financial Services;
Function Concentration: Engineering, Finance/Accounting

Griffin, Cathy — *Vice President*
A.T. Kearney, Inc.
153 East 53rd Street
New York, NY 10022
Telephone: (212) 751-7040
Recruiter Classification: Retained; **Lowest/Average Salary:**
$90,000/$90,000; **Industry Concentration:** Generalist with a
primary focus in Financial Services; **Function Concentration:**
Generalist with a primary focus in Engineering,
Finance/Accounting, General Management

Groban, Jack — *Vice President/Managing
Director*
A.T. Kearney, Inc.
Biltmore Tower
500 South Grand Avenue, Suite 1780
Los Angeles, CA 90071
Telephone: (213) 689-6800
Recruiter Classification: Retained; **Lowest/Average Salary:**
$90,000/$90,000; **Industry Concentration:** Generalist with a
primary focus in Financial Services; **Function Concentration:**
Generalist with a primary focus in Finance/Accounting

Groner, David — *Associate*
Source Services Corporation
150 South Wacker Drive, Suite 400
Chicago, IL 60606
Telephone: (312) 346-7000
Recruiter Classification: Contingency; **Lowest/Average Salary:**
$30,000/$50,000; **Industry Concentration:** Financial Services;
Function Concentration: Engineering, Finance/Accounting

Grossman, James — *Associate*
Source Services Corporation
10300 West 103rd Street, Suite 101
Overland Park, KS 66214
Telephone: (913) 888-8885
Recruiter Classification: Contingency; **Lowest/Average Salary:**
$30,000/$50,000; **Industry Concentration:** Financial Services;
Function Concentration: Engineering, Finance/Accounting

Grossman, Martin — *Associate*
Source Services Corporation
15600 N.W. 67th Avenue, Suite 210
Miami Lakes, FL 33014
Telephone: (305) 556-8000
Recruiter Classification: Contingency; **Lowest/Average Salary:**
$30,000/$50,000; **Industry Concentration:** Financial Services;
Function Concentration: Engineering, Finance/Accounting

Grotenhuis, Dirkten — *Executive Recruiter*
Chrisman & Company, Incorporated
350 South Figueroa Street, Suite 550
Los Angeles, CA 90071
Telephone: (213) 620-1192
Recruiter Classification: Retained; **Lowest/Average Salary:**
$75,000/$90,000; **Industry Concentration:** Generalist with a
primary focus in Financial Services, Insurance; **Function
Concentration:** Generalist with a primary focus in
Finance/Accounting, General Management, Human Resources,
Marketing, Sales

Grotte, Lawrence C. — *Partner*
Lautz Grotte Engler
One Bush Street, Suite 550
San Francisco, CA 94104
Telephone: (415) 834-3100
Recruiter Classification: Retained; **Lowest/Average Salary:**
$90,000/$90,000; **Industry Concentration:** Generalist with a
primary focus in Venture Capital; **Function Concentration:**
Generalist with a primary focus in Engineering,
Finance/Accounting, General Management, Human Resources,
Marketing, Sales

Grumulaitis, Leo — *Associate*
Source Services Corporation
5429 LBJ Freeway, Suite 275
Dallas, TX 75240
Telephone: (214) 387-1600
Recruiter Classification: Contingency; **Lowest/Average Salary:**
$30,000/$50,000; **Industry Concentration:** Financial Services;
Function Concentration: Engineering, Finance/Accounting

Grzybowski, Jill — *Executive Recruiter*
CPS Inc.
One Westbrook Corporate Centre, Suite 600
Westchester, IL 60154
Telephone: (708) 531-8370
Recruiter Classification: Contingency; **Lowest/Average Salary:**
$30,000/$50,000; **Industry Concentration:** Generalist with a
primary focus in Financial Services, Insurance; **Function
Concentration:** Engineering, Research and Development,
Sales, Women/Minorities

Guc, Stephen — *Associate*
Source Services Corporation
2000 Town Center, Suite 850
Southfield, MI 48075
Telephone: (810) 352-6520
Recruiter Classification: Contingency; **Lowest/Average Salary:**
$30,000/$50,000; **Industry Concentration:** Financial Services;
Function Concentration: Engineering, Finance/Accounting

Gudino, Richard — *Recruiter*
Keith Bagg & Associates Inc.
85 Richmond St., W., Ste. 700
Toronto, Ontario, CANADA M5H 2C9
Telephone: (416) 863-1800
Recruiter Classification: Contingency; **Lowest/Average Salary:**
$40,000/$50,000; **Industry Concentration:** Financial Services;
Function Concentration: Finance/Accounting

Gulian, Randolph — *Managing Director*
Strategic Executives, Inc.
Six Landmark Square
4th Floor
Stamford, CT 06901
Telephone: (203) 359-5757
Recruiter Classification: Retained; **Lowest/Average Salary:**
$90,000/$90,000; **Industry Concentration:** Generalist with a
primary focus in Financial Services; **Function Concentration:**
Generalist with a primary focus in General Management,
Marketing, Sales

Gurnani, Angali — *Consultant*
Executive Placement Consultants, Inc.
2700 River Road, Suite 107
Des Plaines, IL 60018
Telephone: (847) 298-6445
Recruiter Classification: Contingency; **Lowest/Average Salary:**
$40,000/$75,000; **Industry Concentration:** Generalist with a
primary focus in Financial Services; **Function Concentration:**
Generalist with a primary focus in Finance/Accounting, Human
Resources, Marketing

Gurtin, Kay L. — *Managing Partner*
Executive Options, Ltd.
910 Skokie Boulevard
Suite 210
Northbrook, IL 60068
Telephone: (708) 291-4322
Recruiter Classification: Executive Temporary; **Lowest/Average
Salary:** $40,000/$60,000; **Industry Concentration:** Generalist
with a primary focus in Financial Services; **Function
Concentration:** Generalist with a primary focus in
Finance/Accounting, General Management, Human Resources,
Marketing, Women/Minorities

Guthrie, Stuart — *Associate*
Source Services Corporation
One Park Plaza, Suite 560
Irvine, CA 92714
Telephone: (714) 660-1666
Recruiter Classification: Contingency; **Lowest/Average
Salary:** $30,000/$50,000; **Industry Concentration:** Financial
Services; **Function Concentration:** Engineering,
Finance/Accounting

Gutknecht, Steven — *Executive Recruiter*
Jacobson Associates
150 North Wacker Drive
Suite 1120
Chicago, IL 60606
Telephone: (312) 726-1578
Recruiter Classification: Contingency; **Lowest/Average Salary:**
$20,000/$50,000; **Industry Concentration:** Insurance;
Function Concentration: Generalist

Guy, C. William — *Managing Director*
William Guy & Associates
P.O. Box 57407
Sherman Oaks, CA 91413
Telephone: Unpublished
Recruiter Classification: Retained; **Lowest/Average Salary:**
$50,000/$90,000; **Industry Concentration:** Generalist with a
primary focus in Financial Services, Insurance; **Function
Concentration:** Generalist with a primary focus in
Administration, Engineering, Finance/Accounting, General
Management, Human Resources, Marketing, Research and
Development, Women/Minorities

Haas, Margaret P. — *President*
The Haas Associates, Inc.
443 West 24th Street
New York, NY 10011
Telephone: (212) 741-2457
Recruiter Classification: Retained; **Lowest/Average Salary:**
$60,000/$90,000; **Industry Concentration:** Financial
Services; **Function Concentration:** Administration,
Finance/Accounting, General Management, Human
Resources, Marketing, Sales

Habelmann, Gerald B. — *President*
Habelmann & Associates
P.O. Box 1186
Birmingham, MI 48012
Telephone: (313) 207-1815
Recruiter Classification: Retained; **Lowest/Average Salary:**
$60,000/$75,000; **Industry Concentration:** Generalist with a
primary focus in Financial Services; **Function Concentration:**
Generalist with a primary focus in Administration,
Finance/Accounting

Haberman, Joseph C. — *Vice President*
A.T. Kearney, Inc.
225 Reinekers Lane
Alexandria, VA 22314
Telephone: (703) 739-4624
Recruiter Classification: Retained; **Lowest/Average Salary:**
$90,000/$90,000; **Industry Concentration:** Generalist with a
primary focus in Financial Services; **Function Concentration:**
Generalist with a primary focus in Finance/Accounting,
General Management, Human Resources

Hacker-Taylor, Dianna — *Associate*
Source Services Corporation
525 Vine Street, Suite 2250
Cincinnati, OH 45202
Telephone: (513) 651-3303
Recruiter Classification: Contingency; **Lowest/Average
Salary:** $30,000/$50,000; **Industry Concentration:** Financial
Services; **Function Concentration:** Engineering,
Finance/Accounting

Haddad, Charles — *Managing Partner*
Romac & Associates
1770 Kirby Parkway
Suite 216
Memphis, TN 38138-7405
Telephone: (901) 756-6050
Recruiter Classification: Executive Temporary; **Lowest/Average
Salary:** $60,000/$60,000; **Industry Concentration:** Financial
Services, Insurance; **Function Concentration:**
Finance/Accounting

Hagerty, Kenneth — *Principal Advanced Technology*
Korn/Ferry International
Presidential Plaza
900 19th Street, N.W.
Washington, DC 20006
Telephone: (202) 822-9444
Recruiter Classification: Retained; **Lowest/Average Salary:** $100,000/$150,000; **Industry Concentration:** Generalist with a primary focus in Financial Services, Insurance; **Function Concentration:** Generalist

Hagglund, Karl H. — *Principal*
Simpson Associates, Inc.
1900 Minnesota Court
Suite 118
Mississauga, Ontario Canada, L5N 3C9
Telephone: (905) 821-2722
Recruiter Classification: Retained; **Lowest/Average Salary:** $75,000/$90,000; **Industry Concentration:** Generalist with a primary focus in Financial Services; **Function Concentration:** Generalist with a primary focus in Finance/Accounting, General Management

Haider, Martin — *Associate*
Source Services Corporation
7730 East Bellview Avenue, Suite 302
Englewood, CO 80111
Telephone: (303) 773-3700
Recruiter Classification: Contingency; **Lowest/Average Salary:** $30,000/$50,000; **Industry Concentration:** Financial Services; **Function Concentration:** Engineering, Finance/Accounting

Hailey, H.M. — *Vice President Operations*
Damon & Associates, Inc.
7515 Greenville Avenue, Suite 900
Dallas, TX 75231
Telephone: (214) 696-6990
Recruiter Classification: Contingency; **Lowest/Average Salary:** $30,000/$50,000; **Industry Concentration:** Generalist with a primary focus in Financial Services; **Function Concentration:** General Management, Marketing, Sales

Halbrich, Mitch — *Professional Recruiter*
A.J. Burton Group, Inc.
120 East Baltimore Street, Suite 2220
Baltimore, MD 21202
Telephone: (410) 752-5244
Recruiter Classification: Contingency; **Lowest/Average Salary:** $40,000/$75,000; **Industry Concentration:** Generalist with a primary focus in Financial Services, Insurance; **Function Concentration:** Generalist with a primary focus in Administration, Finance/Accounting, General Management, Human Resources

Hales, Daphne — *Associate*
Source Services Corporation
4170 Ashford Dunwoody Road, Suite 285
Atlanta, GA 30319
Telephone: (404) 255-2045
Recruiter Classification: Contingency; **Lowest/Average Salary:** $30,000/$50,000; **Industry Concentration:** Financial Services; **Function Concentration:** Engineering, Finance/Accounting

Hall, Peter V. — *Managing Director*
Chartwell Partners International, Inc.
275 Battery Street, Suite 2180
San Francisco, CA 94111
Telephone: (415) 296-0600
Recruiter Classification: Retained; **Lowest/Average Salary:** $90,000/$90,000; **Industry Concentration:** Generalist with a primary focus in Financial Services, Venture Capital; **Function Concentration:** Generalist with a primary focus in Finance/Accounting, General Management, Marketing, Sales, Women/Minorities

Halladay, Patti — *Principal*
Intersource, Ltd.
1509-A West 6th Street
Austin, TX 78703
Telephone: (512) 457-0883
Recruiter Classification: Retained; **Lowest/Average Salary:** $40,000/$75,000; **Industry Concentration:** Generalist with a primary focus in Financial Services; **Function Concentration:** Finance/Accounting, Human Resources

Hallagan, Robert E. — *President and CEO*
Heidrick & Struggles, Inc.
One Post Office Square
Suite 3570
Boston, MA 02109-0199
Telephone: (617) 423-1140
Recruiter Classification: Retained; **Lowest/Average Salary:** $75,000/$90,000; **Industry Concentration:** Generalist with a primary focus in Financial Services; **Function Concentration:** Generalist

Haller, Mark — *Associate*
Source Services Corporation
525 Vine Street, Suite 2250
Cincinnati, OH 45202
Telephone: (513) 651-3303
Recruiter Classification: Contingency; **Lowest/Average Salary:** $30,000/$50,000; **Industry Concentration:** Financial Services; **Function Concentration:** Engineering, Finance/Accounting

Hallock, Peter B. — *Senior Vice President*
Goodrich & Sherwood Associates, Inc.
401 Merritt Seven Corporate Park
Norwalk, CT 06851
Telephone: (203) 847-2525
Recruiter Classification: Retained; **Lowest/Average Salary:** $60,000/$90,000; **Industry Concentration:** Generalist with a primary focus in Financial Services, Insurance, Venture Capital; **Function Concentration:** Generalist with a primary focus in Administration, Finance/Accounting, General Management, Human Resources, Marketing, Sales

Hallstrom, Victoria — *Consultant*
The Whitney Group
850 Third Avenue, 11th Floor
New York, NY 10022
Telephone: (212) 508-3500
Recruiter Classification: Retained; **Lowest/Average Salary:** $90,000/$90,000; **Industry Concentration:** Financial Services, Venture Capital; **Function Concentration:** Generalist with a primary focus in Finance/Accounting, General Management, Marketing, Sales

Hamilton, John R. — *Partner*
Ray & Berndtson
245 Park Avenue, 33rd Floor
New York, NY 10167
Telephone: (212) 370-1316
Recruiter Classification: Retained; **Lowest/Average Salary:**
$90,000/$90,000; **Industry Concentration:** Generalist with a
primary focus in Financial Services, Insurance; **Function
Concentration:** Generalist with a primary focus in
Administration, Finance/Accounting, General Management,
Human Resources, Marketing, Research and Development,
Sales, Women/Minorities

Hamm, Gary — *Associate*
Source Services Corporation
5429 LBJ Freeway, Suite 275
Dallas, TX 75240
Telephone: (214) 387-1600
Recruiter Classification: Contingency; **Lowest/Average
Salary:** $30,000/$50,000; **Industry Concentration:** Financial
Services; **Function Concentration:** Engineering,
Finance/Accounting

Hamm, Mary Kay — *Managing Partner*
Romac & Associates
530 East Swedesford Road
Suite 202
Valley Forge, PA 19087
Telephone: (215) 687-6107
Recruiter Classification: Executive Temporary; **Lowest/Average
Salary:** $60,000/$60,000; **Industry Concentration:** Financial
Services, Insurance; **Function Concentration:**
Finance/Accounting

Hammond, Karla — *Vice President*
People Management Northeast Incorporated
One Darling Drive, Avon Park South
Avon, CT 06001
Telephone: (860) 678-8900
Recruiter Classification: Retained; **Lowest/Average Salary:**
$75,000/$90,000; **Industry Concentration:** Generalist with a
primary focus in Financial Services, Insurance; **Function
Concentration:** Generalist with a primary focus in
Finance/Accounting, General Management, Human Resources,
Marketing, Sales

Hampshire, Kay — *Associate*
Allard Associates
44 Montgomery Street, Suite 500
San Francisco, CA 94104
Telephone: (800) 291-5279
Recruiter Classification: Retained; **Lowest/Average Salary:**
$40,000/$75,000; **Industry Concentration:** Financial Services;
Function Concentration: Marketing

Hanes, Leah — *Partner*
Ray & Berndtson
2029 Century Park East, Suite 1000
Los Angeles, CA 90067
Telephone: (310) 557-2828
Recruiter Classification: Retained; **Lowest/Average Salary:**
$90,000/$90,000; **Industry Concentration:** Generalist with a
primary focus in Financial Services, Insurance; **Function
Concentration:** Generalist with a primary focus in
Administration, Finance/Accounting, General Management,
Human Resources, Marketing, Research and Development,
Sales, Women/Minorities

Hanley, Alan P. — *Partner*
Williams, Roth & Krueger Inc.
20 North Wacker Drive
Chicago, IL 60606
Telephone: (312) 977-0800
Recruiter Classification: Retained; **Lowest/Average Salary:**
$90,000/$90,000; **Industry Concentration:** Generalist with a
primary focus in Financial Services; **Function Concentration:**
Generalist with a primary focus in Engineering,
Finance/Accounting, General Management, Human Resources,
Marketing, Research and Development, Sales

Hanley, J. Patrick — *Senior Vice President*
Canny, Bowen Inc.
200 Park Avenue
49th Floor
New York, NY 10166
Telephone: (212) 949-6611
Recruiter Classification: Retained; **Lowest/Average Salary:**
$120,000/$120,000; **Industry Concentration:** Generalist with
a primary focus in Venture Capital; **Function Concentration:**
Generalist with a primary focus in Administration,
Finance/Accounting, General Management, Human
Resources

Hanley, Maureen E. — *Vice President*
Gilbert Tweed/INESA
155 Prospect Avenue
West Orange, NJ 07052
Telephone: (201) 731-3033
Recruiter Classification: Retained; **Lowest/Average Salary:**
$90,000/$90,000; **Industry Concentration:** Generalist with a
primary focus in Financial Services; **Function Concentration:**
Generalist with a primary focus in Finance/Accounting,
General Management, Human Resources, Marketing,
Sales

Hanley, Steven — *Associate*
Source Services Corporation
8614 Westwood Center, Suite 750
Vienna, VA 22182
Telephone: (703) 790-5610
Recruiter Classification: Contingency; **Lowest/Average
Salary:** $30,000/$50,000; **Industry Concentration:** Financial
Services; **Function Concentration:** Engineering,
Finance/Accounting

Hanna, Remon — *Associate*
Source Services Corporation
2029 Century Park East, Suite 1350
Los Angeles, CA 90067
Telephone: (310) 277-8092
Recruiter Classification: Contingency; **Lowest/Average
Salary:** $30,000/$50,000; **Industry Concentration:** Financial
Services; **Function Concentration:** Engineering,
Finance/Accounting

Hannock, Elwin W. — *President*
Flynn, Hannock, Incorporated
1001 Farmington Avenue
West Hartford, CT 06107
Telephone: (860) 521-5005
Recruiter Classification: Retained, Executive Temporary;
Lowest/Average Salary: $75,000/$90,000; **Industry
Concentration:** Generalist with a primary focus in Financial
Services, Insurance; **Function Concentration:** Generalist with a
primary focus in Administration, General Management,
Marketing, Sales

Hanson, Grant M. — *Associate Director*
Goodrich & Sherwood Associates, Inc.
6 Century Drive
Parsippany, NJ 07054
Telephone: (201) 455-7100
Recruiter Classification: Retained; **Lowest/Average Salary:**
$60,000/$90,000; **Industry Concentration:** Generalist with a
primary focus in Financial Services, Insurance, Venture Capital;
Function Concentration: Generalist with a primary focus in
Administration, Finance/Accounting, General Management,
Human Resources, Marketing, Sales

Hanson, Lee — *Consultant*
Heidrick & Struggles, Inc.
Four Embarcadero Center, Suite 3570
San Francisco, CA 94111
Telephone: (415) 981-2854
Recruiter Classification: Retained; **Lowest/Average Salary:**
$75,000/$90,000; **Industry Concentration:** Generalist with a
primary focus in Financial Services; **Function Concentration:**
Generalist with a primary focus in Finance/Accounting

Harbaugh, Paul J. — *Executive Vice President*
International Management Advisors, Inc.
516 Fifth Avenue
New York, NY 10036-7501
Telephone: (212) 758-7770
Recruiter Classification: Retained; **Lowest/Average Salary:**
$75,000/$90,000; **Industry Concentration:** Generalist with a
primary focus in Financial Services; **Function Concentration:**
Generalist with a primary focus in Engineering,
Finance/Accounting, General Management, Human Resources,
Marketing, Research and Development, Women/Minorities

Harbert, David O. — *Partner*
Sweeney Harbert & Mummert, Inc.
777 South Harbour Island Boulevard
Suite 130
Tampa, FL 33602
Telephone: (813) 229-5360
Recruiter Classification: Retained; **Lowest/Average Salary:**
$90,000/$90,000; **Industry Concentration:** Generalist with a
primary focus in Financial Services; **Function Concentration:**
Generalist with a primary focus in Engineering,
Finance/Accounting, General Management, Human Resources,
Marketing, Women/Minorities

Hardison, Richard L. — *President*
Hardison & Company
4975 Preston Park Boulevard, Suite 150
Plano, TX 75093
Telephone: (972) 985-6990
Recruiter Classification: Retained; **Lowest/Average Salary:**
$150,000/$180,000; **Industry Concentration:** Generalist with a
primary focus in Financial Services, Venture Capital; **Function
Concentration:** Generalist with a primary focus in Engineering,
Finance/Accounting, General Management, Human Resources,
Marketing, Women/Minorities

Hardy, Thomas G. — *Senior Director*
Spencer Stuart
277 Park Avenue, 29th Floor
New York, NY 10172
Telephone: (212) 336-0200
Recruiter Classification: Retained; **Lowest/Average Salary:**
$90,000/$90,000; **Industry Concentration:** Generalist with a
primary focus in Venture Capital; **Function Concentration:**
Generalist

Harelick, Arthur S. — *Office of the President*
Ashway, Ltd.
295 Madison Avenue
New York, NY 10017
Telephone: (212) 679-3300
Recruiter Classification: Contingency; **Lowest/Average
Salary:** $30,000/$90,000; **Industry Concentration:**
Insurance; **Function Concentration:** General
Management

Harfenist, Harry — *President*
Parker Page Group
12550 Biscayne Boulevard
Suite 209
Miami, FL 33181
Telephone: (305) 892-2822
Recruiter Classification: Executive Temporary; **Lowest/Average
Salary:** $30,000/$75,000; **Industry Concentration:** Generalist
with a primary focus in Financial Services; **Function
Concentration:** Generalist

Hargis, N. Leann — *Senior Associate*
Montgomery Resources, Inc.
555 Montgomery Street, Suite 1650
San Francisco, CA 94111
Telephone: (415) 956-4242
Recruiter Classification: Contingency; **Lowest/Average Salary:**
$30,000/$60,000; **Industry Concentration:** Financial Services,
Insurance, Venture Capital; **Function Concentration:**
Finance/Accounting

Harney, Elyane — *Senior Associate*
Gary Kaplan & Associates
201 South Lake Avenue
Suite 600
Pasadena, CA 91101
Telephone: (818) 796-8100
Recruiter Classification: Retained; **Lowest/Average Salary:**
$75,000/$90,000; **Industry Concentration:** Generalist with a
primary focus in Financial Services, Insurance; **Function
Concentration:** Generalist with a primary focus in
Engineering, Finance/Accounting, General Management,
Human Resources, Marketing, Research and
Development

Harp, Kimberly — *Associate*
Source Services Corporation
7730 East Bellview Avenue, Suite 302
Englewood, CO 80111
Telephone: (303) 773-3700
Recruiter Classification: Contingency; **Lowest/Average
Salary:** $30,000/$50,000; **Industry Concentration:** Financial
Services; **Function Concentration:** Engineering,
Finance/Accounting

Harrell, L. Parker — *Managing Director*
Korn/Ferry International
Presidential Plaza
900 19th Street, N.W.
Washington, DC 20006
Telephone: (202) 822-9444
Recruiter Classification: Retained; **Lowest/Average Salary:**
$100,000/$150,000; **Industry Concentration:** Generalist with a
primary focus in Financial Services; **Function Concentration:**
Generalist

Harris, Jack — *Vice President*
A.T. Kearney, Inc.
130 Adelaide Street West, Suite 2710
Toronto, Ontario, CANADA M5H 3P5
Telephone: (416) 947-1990
Recruiter Classification: Retained; **Lowest/Average Salary:**
$90,000/$90,000; **Industry Concentration:** Generalist with a
primary focus in Financial Services; **Function Concentration:**
Generalist with a primary focus in Engineering,
Finance/Accounting, General Management

Harris, Joe W. — *Executive Recruiter*
Cendea Connection International
13740 Research Boulevard
Building 0-1
Austin, TX 78750
Telephone: (512) 219-6000
Recruiter Classification: Retained; **Lowest/Average Salary:**
$75,000/$90,000; **Industry Concentration:** Generalist with a
primary focus in Venture Capital; **Function Concentration:**
Generalist with a primary focus in General Management,
Marketing, Sales

Harris, Julia — *Managing Director*
The Whitney Group
850 Third Avenue, 11th Floor
New York, NY 10022
Telephone: (212) 508-3500
Recruiter Classification: Retained; **Lowest/Average Salary:**
$90,000/$90,000; **Industry Concentration:** Financial Services,
Venture Capital; **Function Concentration:** Generalist with a
primary focus in Finance/Accounting, General Management,
Marketing, Sales

Harris, Seth O. — *Vice President*
Christian & Timbers
24 New England Executive Park
Burlington, MA 01803
Telephone: (617) 229-9515
Recruiter Classification: Retained; **Lowest/Average Salary:**
$90,000/$90,000; **Industry Concentration:** Generalist with a
primary focus in Venture Capital; **Function Concentration:**
Generalist with a primary focus in Engineering,
Finance/Accounting, General Management, Human Resources,
Marketing, Research and Development, Sales

Harrison, Joel — *Managing Partner*
D.A. Kreuter Associates, Inc.
1100 East Hector Street, Suite 388
Conshohocken, PA 19428
Telephone: (610) 834-1100
Recruiter Classification: Retained; **Lowest/Average Salary:**
$60,000/$90,000; **Industry Concentration:** Financial Services,
Insurance; **Function Concentration:** General Management,
Marketing, Sales

Harrison, Patricia — *Associate*
Source Services Corporation
5429 LBJ Freeway, Suite 275
Dallas, TX 75240
Telephone: (214) 387-1600
Recruiter Classification: Contingency; **Lowest/Average
Salary:** $30,000/$50,000; **Industry Concentration:** Financial
Services; **Function Concentration:** Engineering,
Finance/Accounting

Hart, Andrew D. — *Managing Director*
Russell Reynolds Associates, Inc.
200 Park Avenue
New York, NY 10166-0002
Telephone: (212) 351-2000
Recruiter Classification: Retained; **Lowest/Average Salary:**
$90,000/$90,000; **Industry Concentration:** Financial Services;
Function Concentration: Generalist

Hart, Crystal — *Associate*
Source Services Corporation
One Park Plaza, Suite 560
Irvine, CA 92714
Telephone: (714) 660-1666
Recruiter Classification: Contingency; **Lowest/Average Salary:**
$30,000/$50,000; **Industry Concentration:** Financial Services;
Function Concentration: Engineering, Finance/Accounting

Hart, David — *Executive Vice President*
Hadley Lockwood, Inc.
17 State Street, 38th Floor
New York, NY 10004
Telephone: (212) 785-4405
Recruiter Classification: Retained; **Lowest/Average Salary:**
$90,000/$90,000; **Industry Concentration:** Financial Services;
Function Concentration: Generalist

Hart, James — *Associate*
Source Services Corporation
One CityPlace, Suite 170
St. Louis, MO 63141
Telephone: (314) 432-4500
Recruiter Classification: Contingency; **Lowest/Average Salary:**
$30,000/$50,000; **Industry Concentration:** Financial Services;
Function Concentration: Engineering, Finance/Accounting

Hart, Robert T. — *Director*
D.E. Foster Partners Inc.
Stamford Square, 3001 Summer Street, 5th Floor
Stamford, CT 06905
Telephone: (203) 406-8247
Recruiter Classification: Retained; **Lowest/Average Salary:**
$90,000/$90,000; **Industry Concentration:** Generalist with a
primary focus in Financial Services; **Function Concentration:**
Generalist with a primary focus in Administration,
Finance/Accounting, General Management, Human Resources,
Marketing, Research and Development, Sales, Women/Minorities

Hartle, Larry — *Executive Recruiter*
CPS Inc.
One Westbrook Corporate Centre, Suite 600
Westchester, IL 60154
Telephone: (708) 531-8370
Recruiter Classification: Contingency; **Lowest/Average Salary:**
$30,000/$50,000; **Industry Concentration:** Generalist with a
primary focus in Financial Services, Insurance; **Function
Concentration:** Engineering, Research and Development,
Sales, Women/Minorities

Harty, Shirley Cox — *Consultant*
Ray & Berndtson
191 Peachtree Street, NE, Suite 3800
Atlanta, GA 30303-1757
Telephone: (404) 215-4600
Recruiter Classification: Retained; **Lowest/Average Salary:**
$90,000/$90,000; **Industry Concentration:** Generalist with a
primary focus in Financial Services; **Function Concentration:**
Generalist

Harvey, Mike — *President*
Advanced Executive Resources
3040 Charlevoix Drive, SE
Grand Rapids, MI 49546
Telephone: (616) 942-4030
Recruiter Classification: Retained; **Lowest/Average Salary:**
$30,000/$50,000; **Industry Concentration:** Generalist with a
primary focus in Financial Services; **Function Concentration:**
Generalist with a primary focus in Engineering,
Finance/Accounting, General Management, Human
Resources, Marketing, Research and Development, Sales,
Women/Minorities

Harwood, Brian — *Associate*
Source Services Corporation
111 Founders Plaza, Suite 1501E
Hartford, CT 06108
Telephone: (860) 528-0300
Recruiter Classification: Contingency; **Lowest/Average
Salary:** $30,000/$50,000; **Industry Concentration:** Financial
Services; **Function Concentration:** Engineering,
Finance/Accounting

Haselby, James — *Associate*
Source Services Corporation
10300 West 103rd Street, Suite 101
Overland Park, KS 66214
Telephone: (913) 888-8885
Recruiter Classification: Contingency; **Lowest/Average
Salary:** $30,000/$50,000; **Industry Concentration:** Financial
Services; **Function Concentration:** Engineering,
Finance/Accounting

Hasten, Lawrence — *Associate*
Source Services Corporation
15260 Ventura Boulevard, Suite 380
Sherman Oaks, CA 91403
Telephone: (818) 905-1500
Recruiter Classification: Contingency; **Lowest/Average
Salary:** $30,000/$50,000; **Industry Concentration:** Financial
Services; **Function Concentration:** Engineering,
Finance/Accounting

Haughton, Michael — *Senior Vice President*
DeFrain, Mayer LLC
6900 College Boulevard
Suite 300
Overland Park, KS 66211
Telephone: (913) 345-0500
Recruiter Classification: Retained; **Lowest/Average Salary:**
$50,000/$90,000; **Industry Concentration:** Generalist with a
primary focus in Financial Services, Insurance; **Function
Concentration:** Generalist with a primary focus in Engineering,
Finance/Accounting, General Management, Human Resources,
Marketing, Sales

Hauser, Martha — *Director*
Spencer Stuart
One Atlantic Center, Suite 3230
1201 West Peachtree Street
Atlanta, GA 30309
Telephone: (404) 892-2800
Recruiter Classification: Retained; **Lowest/Average Salary:**
$90,000/$90,000; **Industry Concentration:** Insurance;
Function Concentration: Generalist with a primary focus in
Finance/Accounting, General Management, Human Resources,
Sales, Women/Minorities

Havener, Donald Clarke — *Partner*
The Abbott Group, Inc.
530 College Parkway, Suite N
Annapolis, MD 21401
Telephone: (410) 757-4100
Recruiter Classification: Retained; **Lowest/Average Salary:**
$90,000/$90,000; **Industry Concentration:** Generalist with a
primary focus in Venture Capital; **Function Concentration:**
Generalist with a primary focus in Engineering,
Finance/Accounting, General Management, Human
Resources, Marketing, Research and Development

Hawksworth, A. Dwight — *President*
A.D. & Associates Executive Search, Inc.
5589 Woodsong Drive, Suite 100
Atlanta, GA 30338-2933
Telephone: (770) 393-0021
Recruiter Classification: Contingency; **Lowest/Average Salary:**
$50,000/$75,000; **Industry Concentration:** Generalist with a
primary focus in Financial Services; **Function Concentration:**
Generalist with a primary focus in Engineering,
Finance/Accounting, General Management, Human Resources,
Marketing, Research and Development, Sales,
Women/Minorities

Hawley, Robert E. — *Partner*
Hayden Group, Incorporated
One Post Office Square
Suite 3830
Boston, MA 02109
Telephone: (617) 482-2445
Recruiter Classification: Retained; **Lowest/Average Salary:**
$90,000/$90,000; **Industry Concentration:** Financial
Services

Hay, William E. — *President*
William E. Hay & Co.
20 South Clark Street, Suite 2305
Chicago, IL 60603
Telephone: (312) 782-6510
Recruiter Classification: Retained; **Lowest/Average Salary:**
$50,000/$75,000; **Industry Concentration:** Generalist with a
primary focus in Financial Services, Insurance; **Function
Concentration:** Generalist with a primary focus in
Finance/Accounting, General Management, Marketing,
Women/Minorities

Hayes, Lee — *Associate*
Source Services Corporation
3701 West Algonquin Road, Suite 380
Rolling Meadows, IL 60008
Telephone: (847) 392-0244
Recruiter Classification: Contingency; **Lowest/Average Salary:**
$30,000/$50,000; **Industry Concentration:** Financial Services;
Function Concentration: Engineering, Finance/Accounting

Haystead, Steve — *Executive Recruiter*
Advanced Executive Resources
3040 Charlevoix Drive, SE
Grand Rapids, MI 49546
Telephone: (616) 942-4030
Recruiter Classification: Retained; **Lowest/Average Salary:**
$30,000/$50,000; **Industry Concentration:** Generalist with a
primary focus in Financial Services; **Function Concentration:**
Generalist with a primary focus in Engineering,
Finance/Accounting, General Management, Human Resources,
Marketing, Research and Development, Sales,
Women/Minorities

Hazerjian, Cynthia — *Executive Recruiter*
CPS Inc.
303 Congress Street, 5th Floor
Boston, MA 02210
Telephone: (617) 439-7950
Recruiter Classification: Contingency; **Lowest/Average Salary:**
$30,000/$50,000; **Industry Concentration:** Generalist with a
primary focus in Financial Services, Insurance; **Function**
Concentration: Engineering, Research and Development,
Sales, Women/Minorities

Heafey, Bill — *Executive Recruiter*
CPS Inc.
One Westbrook Corporate Centre, Suite 600
Westchester, IL 60154
Telephone: (708) 531-8370
Recruiter Classification: Contingency; **Lowest/Average Salary:**
$30,000/$50,000; **Industry Concentration:** Generalist with a
primary focus in Financial Services, Insurance; **Function**
Concentration: Engineering, Research and Development,
Sales, Women/Minorities

Healey, Joseph T. — *Recruiter*
Highland Search Group
565 Fifth Avenue, 22nd Floor
New York, NY 10017
Telephone: (212) 328-1113
Recruiter Classification: Retained; **Lowest/Average Salary:**
$90,000/$90,000; **Industry Concentration:** Financial Services;
Function Concentration: Generalist with a primary focus in
Administration, Finance/Accounting, General Management,
Human Resources, Sales, Women/Minorities

Heaney, Thomas — *Vice President*
Korn/Ferry International
4816 IDS Center
Minneapolis, MN 55402
Telephone: (612) 333-1834
Recruiter Classification: Retained; **Lowest/Average Salary:**
$100,000/$150,000; **Industry Concentration:** Generalist with a
primary focus in Financial Services, Insurance; **Function**
Concentration: Generalist

Hebel, Robert W. — *President*
R.W. Hebel Associates
4833 Spicewood Springs Road, Suite 202
Austin, TX 78759-8404
Telephone: (512) 338-9691
Recruiter Classification: Retained; **Lowest/Average Salary:**
$90,000/$90,000; **Industry Concentration:** Venture Capital;
Function Concentration: Generalist with a primary focus in
Engineering, Finance/Accounting, General Management,
Human Resources, Marketing, Research and Development,
Sales

Hedlund, David — *President*
Hedlund Corporation
One IBM Plaza, Suite 2618
Chicago, IL 60611
Telephone: (312) 755-1400
Recruiter Classification: Contingency; **Lowest/Average Salary:**
$75,000/$90,000; **Industry Concentration:** Financial Services,
Insurance; **Function Concentration:** Engineering,
Finance/Accounting, Marketing

Heiken, Barbara E. — *President*
Randell-Heiken, Inc.
The Lincoln Building
60 East 42nd Street, Suite 2022
New York, NY 10165
Telephone: (212) 490-1313
Recruiter Classification: Retained; **Lowest/Average Salary:**
$60,000/$90,000; **Industry Concentration:** Generalist with a
primary focus in Financial Services, Insurance; **Function**
Concentration: Generalist with a primary focus in General
Management, Human Resources, Marketing, Sales,
Women/Minorities

Heinrich, Scott — *Associate*
Source Services Corporation
500 108th Avenue NE, Suite 1780
Bellevue, WA 98004
Telephone: (206) 454-6400
Recruiter Classification: Contingency; **Lowest/Average Salary:**
$30,000/$50,000; **Industry Concentration:** Financial Services;
Function Concentration: Engineering, Finance/Accounting

Heinze, David — *President*
Heinze & Associates, Inc.
3033 Excelsior Boulevard, Suite 300
Minneapolis, MN 55416
Telephone: (612) 924-2389
Recruiter Classification: Retained; **Lowest/Average Salary:**
$75,000/$90,000; **Industry Concentration:** Generalist with a
primary focus in Financial Services, Insurance, Venture Capital;
Function Concentration: Generalist with a primary focus in
Engineering, Finance/Accounting, General Management,
Human Resources, Marketing, Research and Development,
Sales

Hellebusch, Jerry — *President*
Morgan Hunter Corp.
6800 College Boulevard, Suite 550
Overland Park, KS 66211
Telephone: (913) 491-3434
Recruiter Classification: Contingency; **Lowest/Average**
Salary: $20,000/$30,000; **Industry Concentration:** Financial
Services, Insurance; **Function Concentration:**
Finance/Accounting

Heller, Steven A. — *Vice President*
Martin H. Bauman Associates, Inc.
375 Park Avenue, Suite 2002
New York, NY 10152
Telephone: (212) 752-6580
Recruiter Classification: Retained; **Lowest/Average Salary:**
$100,000/$250,000; **Industry Concentration:** Generalist with a
primary focus in Financial Services, Venture Capital; **Function**
Concentration: Generalist

Hellinger, Audrey W. — *Vice President*
Martin H. Bauman Associates, Inc.
625 North Michigan Avenue, Suite 500
Chicago, IL 60611-3108
Telephone: (312) 751-5407
Recruiter Classification: Retained; **Lowest/Average Salary:**
$100,000/$250,000; **Industry Concentration:** Generalist with a
primary focus in Financial Services, Venture Capital; **Function**
Concentration: Generalist with a primary focus in
Administration, Engineering, Finance/Accounting, General
Management, Human Resources, Marketing, Research and
Development, Sales, Women/Minorities

Helminiak, Audrey — *Executive Recruiter*
Gaffney Management Consultants
35 North Brandon Drive
Glendale Heights, IL 60139-2087
Telephone: (630) 307-3380
Recruiter Classification: Retained; **Lowest/Average Salary:**
$60,000/$90,000; **Industry Concentration:** Generalist with a
primary focus in Venture Capital; **Function Concentration:**
Generalist with a primary focus in Engineering, General
Management, Human Resources, Marketing, Research and
Development, Sales, Women/Minorities

Hendrickson, Jill E. — *Consultant*
Gregory Michaels and Associates, Inc.
8410 West Bryn Mawr Avenue
Suite 400
Chicago, IL 60631
Telephone: (773) 380-1333
Recruiter Classification: Retained; **Lowest/Average Salary:**
$90,000/$90,000; **Industry Concentration:** Generalist with a
primary focus in Financial Services; **Function Concentration:**
Generalist with a primary focus in Finance/Accounting,
General Management, Human Resources, Marketing, Sales

Heneghan, Donald A. — *Partner*
Allerton Heneghan & O'Neill
70 West Madison Street, Suite 2015
Chicago, IL 60602
Telephone: (312) 263-1075
Recruiter Classification: Retained; **Lowest/Average Salary:**
$90,000/$90,000; **Industry Concentration:** Generalist with a
primary focus in Financial Services; **Function Concentration:**
Generalist with a primary focus in Finance/Accounting,
General Management, Human Resources, Marketing, Research
and Development, Women/Minorities

Henn, George W. — *President*
G.W. Henn & Company
42 East Gay Street, Suite 1312
Columbus, OH 43215-3119
Telephone: (614) 469-9666
Recruiter Classification: Retained; **Lowest/Average Salary:**
$90,000/$90,000; **Industry Concentration:** Generalist with a
primary focus in Financial Services, Insurance; **Function
Concentration:** Generalist with a primary focus in Engineering,
Finance/Accounting, Human Resources, Marketing, Research
and Development

Henneberry, Ward — *Associate*
Source Services Corporation
500 108th Avenue NE, Suite 1780
Bellevue, WA 98004
Telephone: (206) 454-6400
Recruiter Classification: Contingency; **Lowest/Average Salary:**
$30,000/$50,000; **Industry Concentration:** Financial Services;
Function Concentration: Engineering, Finance/Accounting

Hennig, Sandra M. — *Executive Recruiter*
MSI International
229 Peachtree Street, NE
Suite 1201
Atlanta, GA 30303
Telephone: (404) 659-5050
Recruiter Classification: Contingency; **Lowest/Average Salary:**
$30,000/$60,000; **Industry Concentration:** Generalist with a
primary focus in Financial Services; **Function Concentration:**
Administration, Engineering, Finance/Accounting, General
Management, Marketing, Sales

Henry, Mary — *Vice President*
Conex Incorporated
150 East 52nd Street, 2nd Floor
New York, NY 10022
Telephone: (212) 371-3737
Recruiter Classification: Retained; **Lowest/Average Salary:**
$75,000/$75,000; **Industry Concentration:** Generalist with a
primary focus in Financial Services; **Function Concentration:**
Generalist with a primary focus in Engineering, General
Management, Marketing, Research and Development, Sales

Hensley, Bert — *Managing Director*
Morgan Samuels Co., Inc.
9171 Wilshire Boulevard
Suite 428
Beverly Hills, CA 90210
Telephone: (310) 278-9660
Recruiter Classification: Retained; **Lowest/Average Salary:**
$100,000/$150,000; **Industry Concentration:** Generalist with a
primary focus in Financial Services; **Function Concentration:**
Generalist with a primary focus in Finance/Accounting,
General Management, Human Resources

Hensley, Gayla — *Principal*
Atlantic Search Group, Inc.
One Liberty Square
Boston, MA 02109
Telephone: (617) 426-9700
Recruiter Classification: Contingency; **Lowest/Average Salary:**
$20,000/$60,000; **Industry Concentration:** Generalist with a
primary focus in Financial Services; **Function Concentration:**
Finance/Accounting

Hergenrather, Richard A. — *President and CEO*
Hergenrather & Company
401 West Charlton Avenue
Spokane, WA 99208-7246
Telephone: (509) 466-6700
Recruiter Classification: Retained; **Lowest/Average Salary:**
$60,000/$90,000; **Industry Concentration:** Generalist with a
primary focus in Financial Services; **Function Concentration:**
Generalist with a primary focus in Engineering,
Finance/Accounting, General Management, Human Resources,
Marketing, Research and Development, Sales

Herman, Pat — *Executive Recruiter*
Whitney & Associates, Inc.
920 Second Avenue South, Suite 625
Minneapolis, MN 55402-4035
Telephone: (612) 338-5600
Recruiter Classification: Contingency; **Lowest/Average Salary:**
$20,000/$50,000; **Industry Concentration:** Generalist with a
primary focus in Financial Services, Insurance, Venture Capital;
Function Concentration: Finance/Accounting

Herman, Shelli — *Senior Associate*
Gary Kaplan & Associates
201 South Lake Avenue
Suite 600
Pasadena, CA 91101
Telephone: (818) 796-8100
Recruiter Classification: Retained; **Lowest/Average Salary:**
$75,000/$90,000; **Industry Concentration:** Generalist with a
primary focus in Financial Services, Insurance; **Function
Concentration:** Generalist with a primary focus in Engineering,
Finance/Accounting, General Management, Human Resources,
Marketing, Research and Development

Hernandez, Ruben — *Associate*
Source Services Corporation
15600 N.W. 67th Avenue, Suite 210
Miami Lakes, FL 33014
Telephone: (305) 556-8000
Recruiter Classification: Contingency; **Lowest/Average Salary:** $30,000/$50,000; **Industry Concentration:** Financial Services; **Function Concentration:** Engineering, Finance/Accounting

Heroux, David — *Associate*
Source Services Corporation
15260 Ventura Boulevard, Suite 380
Sherman Oaks, CA 91403
Telephone: (818) 905-1500
Recruiter Classification: Contingency; **Lowest/Average Salary:** $30,000/$50,000; **Industry Concentration:** Financial Services; **Function Concentration:** Engineering, Finance/Accounting

Herzog, Sarah — *Associate*
Source Services Corporation
One Park Plaza, Suite 560
Irvine, CA 92714
Telephone: (714) 660-1666
Recruiter Classification: Contingency; **Lowest/Average Salary:** $30,000/$50,000; **Industry Concentration:** Financial Services; **Function Concentration:** Engineering, Finance/Accounting

Hetherman, Margaret F. — *Director Research*
Highland Search Group
565 Fifth Avenue, 22nd Floor
New York, NY 10017
Telephone: (212) 328-1113
Recruiter Classification: Retained; **Lowest/Average Salary:** $90,000/$90,000; **Industry Concentration:** Financial Services, Insurance, Venture Capital; **Function Concentration:** Generalist with a primary focus in Administration, Finance/Accounting, General Management, Human Resources, Research and Development, Sales, Women/Minorities

Hewitt, Rives D. — *Principal*
The Dalley Hewitt Company
1401 Peachtree Street, Suite 500
Atlanta, GA 30309
Telephone: (404) 885-6642
Recruiter Classification: Retained; **Lowest/Average Salary:** $50,000/$90,000; **Industry Concentration:** Generalist with a primary focus in Financial Services, Insurance; **Function Concentration:** Generalist with a primary focus in Administration, Engineering, Finance/Accounting, General Management, Human Resources, Marketing, Research and Development, Sales

Hewitt, W. Davis — *Principal*
The Dalley Hewitt Company
1401 Peachtree Street, Suite 500
Atlanta, GA 30309
Telephone: (404) 885-6642
Recruiter Classification: Retained; **Lowest/Average Salary:** $50,000/$90,000; **Industry Concentration:** Generalist with a primary focus in Financial Services, Insurance; **Function Concentration:** Generalist with a primary focus in Administration, Engineering, Finance/Accounting, General Management, Human Resources, Marketing, Research and Development, Sales

Higbee, Joan — *Principal*
Thorndike Deland Associates
275 Madison Avenue, Suite 1300
New York, NY 10016
Telephone: (212) 661-6200
Recruiter Classification: Retained; **Lowest/Average Salary:** $100,000/$125,000; **Industry Concentration:** Generalist with a primary focus in Financial Services, Venture Capital; **Function Concentration:** Generalist with a primary focus in Finance/Accounting, General Management, Human Resources, Marketing, Sales

Higdon, Henry G. — *Managing Director*
Higdon Prince Inc.
230 Park Avenue, Suite 1455
New York, NY 10169
Telephone: (212) 986-4662
Recruiter Classification: Retained; **Lowest/Average Salary:** $150,000/$150,000; **Industry Concentration:** Generalist with a primary focus in Financial Services, Venture Capital; **Function Concentration:** Generalist with a primary focus in Administration, Finance/Accounting, General Management, Human Resources, Marketing, Sales, Women/Minorities

Higgins, Donna — *Vice President, Bio-Pharmaceutical Division*
Howard Fischer Associates, Inc.
1800 John F. Kennedy Boulevard, 7th Floor
Philadelphia, PA 19103
Telephone: (215) 568-8363
Recruiter Classification: Retained; **Lowest/Average Salary:** $90,000/$90,000; **Industry Concentration:** Generalist with a primary focus in Financial Services, Insurance, Venture Capital; **Function Concentration:** Generalist with a primary focus in Administration, Finance/Accounting, General Management, Human Resources, Marketing, Research and Development, Sales, Women/Minorities

Higgins, William — *Associate*
William Guy & Associates
P.O. Box 57407
Sherman Oaks, CA 91413
Telephone: Unpublished
Recruiter Classification: Retained; **Lowest/Average Salary:** $50,000/$90,000; **Industry Concentration:** Generalist with a primary focus in Financial Services; **Function Concentration:** Generalist with a primary focus in Engineering, Human Resources, Research and Development, Sales, Women/Minorities

Hight, Susan — *Associate*
Source Services Corporation
150 South Warner Road, Suite 238
King of Prussia, PA 19406
Telephone: (610) 341-1960
Recruiter Classification: Contingency; **Lowest/Average Salary:** $30,000/$50,000; **Industry Concentration:** Financial Services; **Function Concentration:** Engineering, Finance/Accounting

Hilbert, Laurence — *Managing Director*
Source Services Corporation
9020 Capital of Texas Highway
Building I, Suite 337
Austin, TX 78759
Telephone: (512) 345-7473
Recruiter Classification: Contingency; **Lowest/Average Salary:** $30,000/$50,000; **Industry Concentration:** Financial Services; **Function Concentration:** Engineering, Finance/Accounting

Hildebrand, Thomas B. — *President*
Professional Resources Group, Inc.
1331 50th Street, Suite 102
West Des Moines, IA 50266-1602
Telephone: (515) 222-0248
Recruiter Classification: Executive Temporary; **Lowest/Average Salary:** $60,000/$90,000; **Industry Concentration:** Generalist with a primary focus in Financial Services, Insurance; **Function Concentration:** Generalist with a primary focus in Administration, Finance/Accounting, General Management, Human Resources, Marketing

Hilgenberg, Thomas — *Associate*
Source Services Corporation
1233 North Mayfair Road, Suite 300
Milwaukee, WI 53226
Telephone: (414) 774-6700
Recruiter Classification: Contingency; **Lowest/Average Salary:** $30,000/$50,000; **Industry Concentration:** Financial Services; **Function Concentration:** Engineering, Finance/Accounting

Hill, Emery — *Manager*
MSI International
4801 Independence Boulevard
Suite 408
Charlotte, NC 28212
Telephone: (704) 535-6610
Recruiter Classification: Contingency; **Lowest/Average Salary:** $30,000/$60,000; **Industry Concentration:** Generalist with a primary focus in Financial Services; **Function Concentration:** Generalist with a primary focus in Administration, Engineering, Finance/Accounting, General Management, Marketing, Sales

Hill, Michael D. — *Vice President*
Tyler & Company
1521 North Cooper Street, Suite 200
Dallas, TX 76011
Telephone: (817) 460-4242
Recruiter Classification: Retained; **Lowest/Average Salary:** $75,000/$90,000; **Industry Concentration:** Insurance; **Function Concentration:** Generalist

Hill, Randall W. — *Partner*
Heidrick & Struggles, Inc.
300 South Grand Avenue, Suite 2400
Los Angeles, CA 90071
Telephone: (213) 625-8811
Recruiter Classification: Retained; **Lowest/Average Salary:** $75,000/$90,000; **Industry Concentration:** Generalist with a primary focus in Financial Services; **Function Concentration:** Generalist

Hillen, Skip — *Vice President*
The McCormick Group, Inc.
20 Walnut Street, Suite 308
Wellesley Hills, MA 02181
Telephone: (617) 239-1233
Recruiter Classification: Retained, Contingency; **Lowest/Average Salary:** $50,000/$75,000; **Industry Concentration:** Generalist with a primary focus in Insurance; **Function Concentration:** Generalist with a primary focus in Engineering, General Management, Human Resources, Marketing, Sales

Hiller, Steve — *Consultant*
The McCormick Group, Inc.
20 Walnut Street, Suite 308
Wellesley Hills, MA 02181
Telephone: (617) 239-1233
Recruiter Classification: Retained; **Lowest/Average Salary:** $40,000/$75,000; **Industry Concentration:** Insurance; **Function Concentration:** Generalist

Hilliker, Alan D. — *Consultant*
Egon Zehnder International Inc.
350 Park Avenue
New York, NY 10022
Telephone: (212) 838-9199
Recruiter Classification: Retained; **Lowest/Average Salary:** $90,000/$90,000; **Industry Concentration:** Generalist with a primary focus in Financial Services; **Function Concentration:** Generalist

Hillyer, Carolyn — *Associate*
Source Services Corporation
10300 West 103rd Street, Suite 101
Overland Park, KS 66214
Telephone: (913) 888-8885
Recruiter Classification: Contingency; **Lowest/Average Salary:** $30,000/$50,000; **Industry Concentration:** Financial Services; **Function Concentration:** Engineering, Finance/Accounting

Himes, Dirk — *Vice President*
A.T. Kearney, Inc.
222 West Adams Street
Chicago, IL 60606
Telephone: (312) 648-0111
Recruiter Classification: Retained; **Lowest/Average Salary:** $90,000/$90,000; **Industry Concentration:** Generalist with a primary focus in Financial Services; **Function Concentration:** Generalist with a primary focus in Engineering, Finance/Accounting, General Management

Himlin, Amy — *Search Consultant*
Cochran, Cochran & Yale, Inc.
955 East Henrietta Road
Rochester, NY 14623
Telephone: (716) 424-6060
Recruiter Classification: Retained; **Lowest/Average Salary:** $50,000/$75,000; **Industry Concentration:** Financial Services, Venture Capital; **Function Concentration:** Generalist with a primary focus in Engineering, Finance/Accounting, General Management, Human Resources, Marketing, Sales, Women/Minorities

Hindman, Neil C. — *President*
The Hindman Company
Browenton Place, Suite 110
2000 Warrington Way
Louisville, KY 40222
Telephone: (502) 426-4040
Recruiter Classification: Retained; **Lowest/Average Salary:** $50,000/$90,000; **Industry Concentration:** Generalist with a primary focus in Financial Services; **Function Concentration:** Generalist with a primary focus in Engineering, Finance/Accounting, General Management, Human Resources, Marketing, Sales

Hinojosa, Oscar — *Associate*
Source Services Corporation
5429 LBJ Freeway, Suite 275
Dallas, TX 75240
Telephone: (214) 387-1600
Recruiter Classification: Contingency; **Lowest/Average Salary:** $30,000/$50,000; **Industry Concentration:** Financial Services; **Function Concentration:** Engineering, Finance/Accounting

Hobart, John N. — *Partner*
Ray & Berndtson
301 Commerce Street, Suite 2300
Fort Worth, TX 76102
Telephone: (817) 334-0500
Recruiter Classification: Retained; **Lowest/Average Salary:** $90,000/$90,000; **Industry Concentration:** Financial Services; **Function Concentration:** Generalist

Hochberg, Brian — *National Accounts Manager*
M.A. Churchill & Associates, Inc.
Morelyn Plaza #307
1111 Street Road
Southampton, PA 18966
Telephone: (215) 953-0300
Recruiter Classification: Retained; **Lowest/Average Salary:** $50,000/$75,000; **Industry Concentration:** Financial Services; **Function Concentration:** General Management, Marketing, Research and Development, Sales

Hochberg, Steven P. — *President*
Caliber Associates
125 Strafford Avenue
Suite 112
Wayne, PA 19087
Telephone: (610) 971-1880
Recruiter Classification: Retained; **Lowest/Average Salary:** $90,000/$90,000; **Industry Concentration:** Venture Capital; **Function Concentration:** Marketing, Research and Development, Sales

Hockett, William — *Principal*
Hockett Associates, Inc.
P.O. Box 1765
Los Altos, CA 94023
Telephone: (415) 941-8815
Recruiter Classification: Retained; **Lowest/Average Salary:** $100,000/$170,000; **Industry Concentration:** Generalist with a primary focus in Venture Capital; **Function Concentration:** Generalist with a primary focus in Finance/Accounting, General Management, Marketing, Research and Development, Sales

Hocking, Jeffrey — *Principal*
Korn/Ferry International
The Transamerica Pyramid
600 Montgomery Street
San Francisco, CA 94111
Telephone: (415) 956-1834
Recruiter Classification: Retained; **Lowest/Average Salary:** $100,000/$150,000; **Industry Concentration:** Generalist with a primary focus in Financial Services, Insurance; **Function Concentration:** Generalist

Hodge, Jeff — *Managing Partner*
Heidrick & Struggles, Inc.
Four Embarcadero Center, Suite 3570
San Francisco, CA 94111
Telephone: (415) 981-2854
Recruiter Classification: Retained; **Lowest/Average Salary:** $75,000/$90,000; **Industry Concentration:** Generalist with a primary focus in Financial Services; **Function Concentration:** Generalist with a primary focus in Finance/Accounting

Hoevel, Michael J. — *Partner*
Poirier, Hoevel & Co.
12400 Wilshire Boulevard, Suite 915
Los Angeles, CA 90025
Telephone: (310) 207-3427
Recruiter Classification: Retained; **Lowest/Average Salary:** $75,000/$90,000; **Industry Concentration:** Generalist with a primary focus in Financial Services, Insurance; **Function Concentration:** Generalist with a primary focus in Administration, Engineering, Finance/Accounting, Human Resources, Marketing, Sales, Women/Minorities

Hoffman, Stephen — *Managing Director*
Source Services Corporation
1290 Oakmead Parkway, Suite 318
Sunnyvale, CA 94086
Telephone: (408) 738-8440
Recruiter Classification: Contingency; **Lowest/Average Salary:** $30,000/$50,000; **Industry Concentration:** Financial Services; **Function Concentration:** Engineering, Finance/Accounting

Hoffmeir, Patti — *Vice President*
Tyler & Company
Chadds Ford Business Campus
Brandywine Two Building, Suite 208
Chadds Ford, PA 19317-9667
Telephone: (610) 558-6100
Recruiter Classification: Retained; **Lowest/Average Salary:** $75,000/$90,000; **Industry Concentration:** Insurance; **Function Concentration:** Generalist

Hofner, Andrew — *Associate*
Source Services Corporation
150 South Wacker Drive, Suite 400
Chicago, IL 60606
Telephone: (312) 346-7000
Recruiter Classification: Contingency; **Lowest/Average Salary:** $30,000/$50,000; **Industry Concentration:** Financial Services; **Function Concentration:** Engineering, Finance/Accounting

Hofner, Kevin E. — *Partner*
Lamalie Amrop International
Chevron Tower
1301 McKinney Street
Houston, TX 77010-3034
Telephone: (713) 739-8602
Recruiter Classification: Retained; **Lowest/Average Salary:** $90,000/$90,000; **Industry Concentration:** Generalist with a primary focus in Financial Services; **Function Concentration:** Generalist

Holland, John A. — *Vice President*
Holland, McFadzean & Associates, Inc.
2901 Tasman Drive
Suite 204
Santa Clara, CA 95054
Telephone: (408) 496-0775
Recruiter Classification: Retained; **Lowest/Average Salary:**
$90,000/$90,000; **Industry Concentration:** Financial Services;
Function Concentration: Generalist with a primary focus in
Engineering, Finance/Accounting, General Management,
Human Resources, Marketing, Research and Development,
Sales

Holland, Kathleen — *Legal Consultant*
TOPAZ International, Inc.
383 Northfield Avenue
West Orange, NJ 07052
Telephone: (201) 669-7300
Recruiter Classification: Contingency; **Lowest/Average Salary:**
$40,000/$75,000; **Industry Concentration:** Financial Services;
Function Concentration: Generalist with a primary focus in
Women/Minorities

Holland, Kathleen — *Legal Consultant*
TOPAZ Legal Solutions
383 Northfield Avenue
West Orange, NJ 07052
Telephone: (201) 669-7300
Recruiter Classification: Executive Temporary; **Lowest/Average
Salary:** $40,000/$75,000; **Industry Concentration:** Financial
Services; **Function Concentration:** Generalist with a primary
focus in Women/Minorities

Holland, Rose Mary — *Consultant*
Price Waterhouse
2401 Toronto Dominion Tower
Edmonton Centre
Edmonton, Alberta, CANADA T5J 2Z1
Telephone: (403) 493-8200
Recruiter Classification: Retained; **Lowest/Average Salary:**
$75,000/$75,000; **Industry Concentration:** Generalist with a
primary focus in Financial Services; **Function Concentration:**
Generalist with a primary focus in Administration, Engineering,
Finance/Accounting, General Management, Human Resources,
Marketing, Sales

Holmes, Lawrence J. — *Managing Director*
Columbia Consulting Group
20 South Charles Street, 9th Floor
Baltimore, MD 21201
Telephone: (410) 385-2525
Recruiter Classification: Retained; **Lowest/Average Salary:**
$75,000/$90,000; **Industry Concentration:** Generalist with a
primary focus in Financial Services, Insurance, Venture Capital;
Function Concentration: Generalist with a primary focus in
Finance/Accounting, General Management, Human Resources,
Marketing, Research and Development, Sales

Holodnak, William A. — *President*
J. Robert Scott
27 State Street
Boston, MA 02109
Telephone: (617) 720-2770
Recruiter Classification: Retained; **Lowest/Average Salary:**
$75,000/$90,000; **Industry Concentration:** Generalist with a
primary focus in Financial Services; **Function Concentration:**
Generalist with a primary focus in Finance/Accounting,
General Management, Human Resources

Holt, Carol — *Vice President*
Bartholdi & Company, Inc.
12020 Sunrise Valley Drive
Suite 160
Reston, VA 20191
Telephone: (703) 476-5519
Recruiter Classification: Retained; **Lowest/Average Salary:**
$60,000/$90,000; **Industry Concentration:** Venture Capital;
Function Concentration: Generalist with a primary focus in
Engineering, Finance/Accounting, General Management,
Marketing, Research and Development, Sales

Holzberger, Georges L. — *Partner*
Highland Search Group
565 Fifth Avenue, 22nd Floor
New York, NY 10017
Telephone: (212) 328-1113
Recruiter Classification: Retained; **Lowest/Average Salary:**
$90,000/$90,000; **Industry Concentration:** Financial Services,
Venture Capital; **Function Concentration:** Generalist with a
primary focus in Administration, Finance/Accounting, General
Management, Human Resources, Sales, Women/Minorities

Honer, Paul E. — *Partner*
Ingram & Aydelotte Inc./I-I-C Partners
430 Park Avenue, Suite 700
New York, NY 10022
Telephone: (212) 319-7777
Recruiter Classification: Retained; **Lowest/Average Salary:**
$150,000/$150,000; **Industry Concentration:** Generalist with a
primary focus in Financial Services, Venture Capital; **Function
Concentration:** Generalist with a primary focus in
Finance/Accounting, General Management

Honey, W. Michael M. — *Partner*
O'Callaghan Honey/Ray & Berndtson, Inc.
400-400 Fifth Avenue S.W.
Calgary, Alberta, CANADA T2P 0L6
Telephone: (403) 269-3277
Recruiter Classification: Retained; **Lowest/Average Salary:**
$90,000/$90,000; **Industry Concentration:** Generalist with a
primary focus in Financial Services; **Function Concentration:**
Generalist

Hoover, Catherine — *Associate*
J.L. Mark Associates, Inc.
2000 Arapahoe Street, Suite 505
Denver, CO 80205
Telephone: (303) 292-0360
Recruiter Classification: Retained; **Lowest/Average Salary:**
$60,000/$90,000; **Industry Concentration:** Generalist with a
primary focus in Financial Services, Insurance; **Function
Concentration:** Generalist with a primary focus in
Administration, Finance/Accounting, General Management,
Human Resources, Marketing, Research and Development, Sales

Hopkins, Chester A. — *Senior Vice President*
Handy HRM Corp.
250 Park Avenue
New York, NY 10177-0074
Telephone: (212) 557-0400
Recruiter Classification: Retained; **Lowest/Average Salary:**
$90,000/$90,000; **Industry Concentration:** Generalist with a
primary focus in Financial Services, Insurance; **Function
Concentration:** Generalist with a primary focus in
Administration, Finance/Accounting, General Management,
Human Resources, Marketing, Research and Development, Sales

Hopkinson, Dana — *Banking and Investment Services Recruiter*
Winter, Wyman & Company
101 Federal Street, 27th Floor
Boston, MA 02110-1800
Telephone: (617) 951-2700
Recruiter Classification: Contingency; **Lowest/Average Salary:** $30,000/$60,000; **Industry Concentration:** Financial Services, Venture Capital; **Function Concentration:** Finance/Accounting

Hopp, Lorrie A. — *Senior Consultant*
Gregory Michaels and Associates, Inc.
8410 West Bryn Mawr Avenue
Suite 400
Chicago, IL 60631
Telephone: (773) 380-1333
Recruiter Classification: Retained; **Lowest/Average Salary:** $90,000/$90,000; **Industry Concentration:** Generalist with a primary focus in Financial Services; **Function Concentration:** Generalist with a primary focus in Finance/Accounting, General Management, Human Resources, Marketing, Sales

Hopper, John W. — *Associate*
William Guy & Associates
P.O. Box 57407
Sherman Oaks, CA 91413
Telephone: Unpublished
Recruiter Classification: Retained; **Lowest/Average Salary:** $50,000/$90,000; **Industry Concentration:** Generalist with a primary focus in Financial Services; **Function Concentration:** Generalist with a primary focus in Administration, Engineering, Research and Development, Sales

Hoskins, Charles R. — *Managing Partner*
Heidrick & Struggles, Inc.
76 South Laura Street, Suite 2110
Jacksonville, FL 32202
Telephone: (904) 355-6674
Recruiter Classification: Retained; **Lowest/Average Salary:** $75,000/$90,000; **Industry Concentration:** Generalist with a primary focus in Financial Services; **Function Concentration:** Generalist

Hostetter, Kristi — *Associate*
Source Services Corporation
1105 Schrock Road, Suite 510
Columbus, OH 43229
Telephone: (614) 846-3311
Recruiter Classification: Contingency; **Lowest/Average Salary:** $30,000/$50,000; **Industry Concentration:** Financial Services; **Function Concentration:** Engineering, Finance/Accounting

Houchins, William M. — *Vice President*
Christian & Timbers
8840 Stanford Boulevard
Suite 25900
Columbia, MD 21045
Telephone: (410) 872-0200
Recruiter Classification: Retained; **Lowest/Average Salary:** $90,000/$90,000; **Industry Concentration:** Venture Capital; **Function Concentration:** Generalist with a primary focus in Engineering, Finance/Accounting, General Management, Human Resources, Marketing, Research and Development, Sales, Women/Minorities

Houterloot, Tim — *Associate*
Source Services Corporation
111 Monument Circle, Suite 3930
Indianapolis, IN 46204
Telephone: (317) 631-2900
Recruiter Classification: Contingency; **Lowest/Average Salary:** $30,000/$50,000; **Industry Concentration:** Financial Services; **Function Concentration:** Engineering, Finance/Accounting

Howard, Lee Ann — *Principal*
Lamalie Amrop International
Metro Center, One Station Place
Stamford, CT 06902-6800
Telephone: (203) 324-4445
Recruiter Classification: Retained; **Lowest/Average Salary:** $90,000/$90,000; **Industry Concentration:** Generalist with a primary focus in Financial Services; **Function Concentration:** Generalist

Howard, Leon — *Executive Recruiter*
Richard, Wayne and Roberts
24 Greenway Plaza, Suite 1304
Houston, TX 77046-2493
Telephone: (713) 629-6681
Recruiter Classification: Retained; **Lowest/Average Salary:** $50,000/$90,000; **Industry Concentration:** Generalist with a primary focus in Financial Services; **Function Concentration:** Generalist with a primary focus in Finance/Accounting

Howard, Susy — *Consultant*
The McCormick Group, Inc.
1400 Wilson Boulevard
Arlington, VA 22209
Telephone: (703) 841-1700
Recruiter Classification: Retained; **Lowest/Average Salary:** $40,000/$60,000; **Industry Concentration:** Generalist with a primary focus in Financial Services, Insurance; **Function Concentration:** Generalist

Howe, Theodore — *General Manager*
Romac & Associates
Commerce Tower, Suite 1700
P.O. Box 13264
Kansas City, MO 64199
Telephone: (816) 221-1020
Recruiter Classification: Executive Temporary; **Lowest/Average Salary:** $60,000/$60,000; **Industry Concentration:** Financial Services, Insurance; **Function Concentration:** Finance/Accounting

Howe, Vance A. — *Managing Director*
Ward Howell International, Inc.
2525 E. Arizona Biltmore Circle
Suite 124
Phoenix, AZ 85016
Telephone: (602) 955-3800
Recruiter Classification: Retained; **Lowest/Average Salary:** $75,000/$90,000; **Industry Concentration:** Generalist with a primary focus in Financial Services; **Function Concentration:** Generalist

Howell, Robert B. — *Principal*
Atlantic Search Group, Inc.
One Liberty Square
Boston, MA 02109
Telephone: (617) 426-9700
Recruiter Classification: Contingency; **Lowest/Average Salary:** $20,000/$60,000; **Industry Concentration:** Generalist with a primary focus in Financial Services; **Function Concentration:** Finance/Accounting

Howell, Robert B. — *Principal*
Atlantic Search Group, Inc.
One Liberty Square
Boston, MA 02109
Telephone: (617) 426-9700
Recruiter Classification: Contingency; **Lowest/Average Salary:**
$20,000/$60,000; **Industry Concentration:** Generalist with a
primary focus in Financial Services; **Function Concentration:**
Finance/Accounting

Hoyda, Louis A. — *Partner*
Thorndike Deland Associates
275 Madison Avenue, Suite 1300
New York, NY 10016
Telephone: (212) 661-6200
Recruiter Classification: Retained; **Lowest/Average Salary:**
$100,000/$125,000; **Industry Concentration:** Generalist with a
primary focus in Financial Services, Insurance, Venture Capital;
Function Concentration: Generalist with a primary focus in
Finance/Accounting, General Management, Human Resources,
Marketing, Sales

Hucko, Donald S. — *Senior Vice President*
Jonas, Walters & Assoc., Inc.
1110 North Old World Third St., Suite 510
Milwaukee, WI 53203-1102
Telephone: (414) 291-2828
Recruiter Classification: Retained; **Lowest/Average Salary:**
$50,000/$90,000; **Industry Concentration:** Generalist with a
primary focus in Financial Services, Insurance; **Function
Concentration:** Generalist with a primary focus in
Administration, Engineering, Finance/Accounting, General
Management, Human Resources, Marketing, Sales

Hudson, Reginald M. — *President*
Search Bureau International
P.O. Box 377608
Chicago, IL 60637
Telephone: (708) 210-1834
Recruiter Classification: Contingency; **Lowest/Average Salary:**
$40,000/$60,000; **Industry Concentration:** Generalist with a
primary focus in Financial Services, Insurance; **Function
Concentration:** Generalist with a primary focus in Engineering,
Finance/Accounting, General Management, Human Resources,
Marketing, Research and Development, Sales,
Women/Minorities

Hughes, Barbara — *Associate*
Source Services Corporation
1290 Oakmead Parkway, Suite 318
Sunnyvale, CA 94086
Telephone: (408) 738-8440
Recruiter Classification: Contingency; **Lowest/Average Salary:**
$30,000/$50,000; **Industry Concentration:** Financial Services;
Function Concentration: Engineering, Finance/Accounting

Hughes, Cathy N. — *Recruiter*
The Ogdon Partnership
375 Park Avenue, Suite 2409
New York, NY 10152-0175
Telephone: (212) 308-1600
Recruiter Classification: Retained; **Lowest/Average Salary:**
$90,000/$90,000; **Industry Concentration:** Generalist with a
primary focus in Venture Capital; **Function Concentration:**
Generalist with a primary focus in Administration,
Finance/Accounting, General Management, Human Resources,
Marketing, Sales, Women/Minorities

Hughes, David — *Recruiter*
Southwestern Professional Services
2451 Atrium Way
Nashville, TN 37214
Telephone: (615) 391-2722
Recruiter Classification: Contingency; **Lowest/Average Salary:**
$20,000/$20,000; **Industry Concentration:** Insurance;
Function Concentration: Sales

Hughes, Kendall G. — *Principal*
Hughes & Associates
718 Oakwood Trail
Fort Worth, TX 76112
Telephone: (817) 496-3650
Recruiter Classification: Contingency; **Lowest/Average Salary:**
$30,000/$60,000; **Industry Concentration:** Insurance;
Function Concentration: Generalist

Hughes, R. Kevin — *Senior Vice President*
Handy HRM Corp.
250 Park Avenue
New York, NY 10177-0074
Telephone: (212) 210-5625
Recruiter Classification: Retained; **Lowest/Average Salary:**
$90,000/$90,000; **Industry Concentration:** Generalist with a
primary focus in Financial Services, Insurance; **Function
Concentration:** Generalist with a primary focus in
Administration, Finance/Accounting, Human Resources,
Marketing, Sales

Hughes, Randall — *Associate*
Source Services Corporation
4200 West Cypress Street, Suite 101
Tampa, FL 33607
Telephone: (813) 879-2221
Recruiter Classification: Contingency; **Lowest/Average
Salary:** $30,000/$50,000; **Industry Concentration:** Financial
Services; **Function Concentration:** Engineering,
Finance/Accounting

Hult, Dana — *Associate*
Source Services Corporation
71 Spit Brook Road, Suite 305
Nashua, NH 03060
Telephone: (603) 888-7650
Recruiter Classification: Contingency; **Lowest/Average
Salary:** $30,000/$50,000; **Industry Concentration:** Financial
Services; **Function Concentration:** Engineering,
Finance/Accounting

Humphrey, Titus — *Associate*
Source Services Corporation
1290 Oakmead Parkway, Suite 318
Sunnyvale, CA 94086
Telephone: (408) 738-8440
Recruiter Classification: Contingency; **Lowest/Average
Salary:** $30,000/$50,000; **Industry Concentration:** Financial
Services; **Function Concentration:** Engineering,
Finance/Accounting

Hunter, Steven — *President*
Diamond Tax Recruiting
Two Pennsylvania Plaza, Suite 1985
New York, NY 10121
Telephone: (212) 695-4220
Recruiter Classification: Contingency; **Lowest/Average Salary:**
$50,000/$75,000; **Industry Concentration:** Financial Services;
Function Concentration: Finance/Accounting

Hurd, J. Nicholas — *Area Manager*
Russell Reynolds Associates, Inc.
Old City Hall, 45 School Street
Boston, MA 02108-3296
Telephone: (617) 523-1111
Recruiter Classification: Retained; **Lowest/Average Salary:**
$90,000/$90,000; **Industry Concentration:** Generalist with a
primary focus in Financial Services; **Function Concentration:**
Generalist

Hurtado, Jaime — *Associate*
Source Services Corporation
879 West 190th Street, Suite 250
Los Angeles, CA 90248
Telephone: (310) 323-6633
Recruiter Classification: Contingency; **Lowest/Average Salary:**
$30,000/$50,000; **Industry Concentration:** Financial Services;
Function Concentration: Engineering, Finance/Accounting

Hussey, Wayne — *Consultant Associate*
Krecklo & Associates Inc.
Scotia Plaza, Suite 4900
40 King Street West
Toronto, Ontario, CANADA M5H 4A2
Telephone: (416) 777-6799
Recruiter Classification: Retained; **Lowest/Average Salary:**
$75,000/$90,000; **Industry Concentration:** Generalist with a
primary focus in Insurance

Hutchison, William K. — *Partner*
Christenson & Hutchison
466 Southern Boulevard
Chatham, NJ 07928-1462
Telephone: (201) 966-1600
Recruiter Classification: Retained; **Lowest/Average Salary:**
$75,000/$90,000; **Industry Concentration:** Generalist with a
primary focus in Financial Services, Insurance; **Function
Concentration:** Generalist with a primary focus in
Finance/Accounting, General Management, Human Resources,
Marketing, Sales

Hutton, Thomas J. — *Vice President*
The Thomas Tucker Company
425 California Street, Suite 2502
San Francisco, CA 94104
Telephone: (415) 693-5900
Recruiter Classification: Retained; **Lowest/Average Salary:**
$90,000/$90,000; **Industry Concentration:** Generalist with a
primary focus in Insurance; **Function Concentration:** Generalist
with a primary focus in Engineering, General Management

Hybels, Cynthia — *Professional Recruiter*
A.J. Burton Group, Inc.
120 East Baltimore Street, Suite 2220
Baltimore, MD 21202
Telephone: (410) 752-5244
Recruiter Classification: Contingency; **Lowest/Average Salary:**
$40,000/$75,000; **Industry Concentration:** Generalist with a
primary focus in Financial Services, Insurance; **Function
Concentration:** Generalist with a primary focus in Administration,
Finance/Accounting, General Management, Human Resources

Hylas, Lisa — *Associate*
Source Services Corporation
15600 N.W. 67th Avenue, Suite 210
Miami Lakes, FL 33014
Telephone: (305) 556-8000
Recruiter Classification: Contingency; **Lowest/Average Salary:**
$30,000/$50,000; **Industry Concentration:** Financial Services;
Function Concentration: Engineering, Finance/Accounting

Hyman, Linda — *Vice President*
Korn/Ferry International
One Palmer Square
Princeton, NJ 08542
Telephone: (609) 921-8811
Recruiter Classification: Retained; **Lowest/Average Salary:**
$100,000/$150,000; **Industry Concentration:** Generalist with a
primary focus in Financial Services, Insurance; **Function
Concentration:** Generalist

Hypes, Richard G. — *Managing Director*
Lynch Miller Moore, Inc.
10 South Wacker Drive, Suite 2935
Chicago, IL 60606
Telephone: (312) 876-1505
Recruiter Classification: Retained; **Lowest/Average Salary:**
$75,000/$90,000; **Industry Concentration:** Generalist with a
primary focus in Financial Services, Venture Capital; **Function
Concentration:** Generalist with a primary focus in
Finance/Accounting, General Management, Marketing

Ikle, A. Donald — *Managing Director*
Ward Howell International, Inc.
99 Park Avenue, Suite 2000
New York, NY 10016-1699
Telephone: (212) 697-3730
Recruiter Classification: Retained; **Lowest/Average Salary:**
$75,000/$90,000; **Industry Concentration:** Insurance;
Function Concentration: Generalist with a primary focus in
General Management

Illsley, Hugh G. — *Managing Partner*
Ward Howell International, Inc.
141 Adelaide Street West
Suite 1800
Toronto, Ontario, CANADA M5H 3L5
Telephone: (416) 862-1273
Recruiter Classification: Retained; **Lowest/Average Salary:**
$75,000/$90,000; **Industry Concentration:** Financial Services,
Insurance; **Function Concentration:** Generalist

Imely, Larry S. — *Vice President*
Stratford Group
6120 Parkland Boulevard
Cleveland, OH 44124
Telephone: (216) 460-3232
Recruiter Classification: Retained; **Lowest/Average Salary:**
$90,000/$90,000; **Industry Concentration:** Generalist with a
primary focus in Financial Services, Insurance, Venture Capital;
Function Concentration: Engineering, General Management,
Sales, Women/Minorities

Imhof, Kirk — *Associate*
Source Services Corporation
505 East 200 South, Suite 300
Salt Lake City, UT 84102
Telephone: (801) 328-0011
Recruiter Classification: Contingency; **Lowest/Average Salary:**
$30,000/$50,000; **Industry Concentration:** Financial Services;
Function Concentration: Engineering, Finance/Accounting

Inger, Barry — *Associate*
Source Services Corporation
20 Burlington Mall Road, Suite 405
Burlington, MA 01803
Telephone: (617) 272-5000
Recruiter Classification: Contingency; **Lowest/Average Salary:**
$30,000/$50,000; **Industry Concentration:** Financial Services;
Function Concentration: Engineering, Finance/Accounting

Ingram, D. John — *Partner*
Ingram & Aydelotte Inc./I-I-C Partners
430 Park Avenue, Suite 700
New York, NY 10022
Telephone: (212) 319-7777
Recruiter Classification: Retained; **Lowest/Average Salary:**
$150,000/$150,000; **Industry Concentration:** Generalist with a
primary focus in Financial Services, Insurance; **Function
Concentration:** Generalist with a primary focus in General
Management, Human Resources, Marketing, Sales

Inguagiato, Gregory — *Manager*
MSI International
6345 Balboa Boulevard
Suite 335
Encino, CA 91316
Telephone: (818) 342-0222
Recruiter Classification: Contingency; **Lowest/Average Salary:**
$30,000/$60,000; **Industry Concentration:** Generalist with a
primary focus in Financial Services; **Function Concentration:**
Generalist with a primary focus in Administration, Engineering,
Finance/Accounting, General Management, Marketing, Sales

Inskeep, Thomas — *Associate*
Source Services Corporation
150 South Warner Road, Suite 238
King of Prussia, PA 19406
Telephone: (610) 341-1960
Recruiter Classification: Contingency; **Lowest/Average Salary:**
$30,000/$50,000; **Industry Concentration:** Financial Services;
Function Concentration: Engineering, Finance/Accounting

Intravaia, Salvatore — *Associate*
Source Services Corporation
2 Penn Plaza, Suite 1176
New York, NY 10121
Telephone: (212) 760-2200
Recruiter Classification: Contingency; **Lowest/Average Salary:**
$30,000/$50,000; **Industry Concentration:** Financial Services;
Function Concentration: Engineering, Finance/Accounting

Irish, Alan — *Executive Recruiter*
CPS Inc.
One Westbrook Corporate Centre, Suite 600
Westchester, IL 60154
Telephone: (708) 531-8370
Recruiter Classification: Contingency; **Lowest/Average Salary:**
$30,000/$50,000; **Industry Concentration:** Generalist with a
primary focus in Financial Services, Insurance; **Function
Concentration:** Engineering, Research and Development,
Sales, Women/Minorities

Irwin, Mark — *Associate*
Source Services Corporation
10220 SW Greenburg Road, Suite 625
Portland, OR 97223
Telephone: (503) 768-4546
Recruiter Classification: Contingency; **Lowest/Average Salary:**
$30,000/$50,000; **Industry Concentration:** Financial Services;
Function Concentration: Engineering, Finance/Accounting

Issacs, Judith A. — *Senior Associate*
Grant Cooper and Associates
795 Office Parkway, Suite 117
St. Louis, MO 63141
Telephone: (314) 567-4690
Recruiter Classification: Retained; **Lowest/Average Salary:**
$60,000/$90,000; **Industry Concentration:** Generalist with a
primary focus in Financial Services; **Function Concentration:**
Generalist with a primary focus in Administration, Engineering,
Finance/Accounting, General Management, Human Resources,
Marketing, Sales

Jablo, Steven A. — *Principal*
Dieckmann & Associates, Ltd.
180 North Stetson, Suite 5555
Two Prudential Plaza
Chicago, IL 60601
Telephone: (312) 819-5900
Recruiter Classification: Retained; **Lowest/Average Salary:**
$75,000/$90,000; **Industry Concentration:** Generalist with a
primary focus in Financial Services, Insurance, Venture Capital;
Function Concentration: Generalist with a primary focus in
Engineering, Finance/Accounting, General Management,
Marketing, Sales

Jackowitz, Todd — *Vice President*
J. Robert Scott
27 State Street
Boston, MA 02109
Telephone: (617) 720-2770
Recruiter Classification: Retained; **Lowest/Average Salary:**
$75,000/$90,000; **Industry Concentration:** Generalist with a
primary focus in Financial Services; **Function Concentration:**
Generalist

Jackson, Joan — *Vice President*
A.T. Kearney, Inc.
225 Reinekers Lane
Alexandria, VA 22314
Telephone: (703) 739-4624
Recruiter Classification: Retained; **Lowest/Average Salary:**
$90,000/$90,000; **Industry Concentration:** Generalist with a
primary focus in Financial Services; **Function Concentration:**
Generalist with a primary focus in Engineering,
Finance/Accounting, General Management

Jacobs, Martin J. — *Executive Vice
President/Recruiter*
The Rubicon Group
P.O. Box 2159
Scottsdale, AZ 85252-2159
Telephone: (602) 423-9280
Recruiter Classification: Contingency; **Lowest/Average Salary:**
$30,000/$60,000; **Industry Concentration:** Generalist with a
primary focus in Financial Services, Insurance; Function
Concentration: Generalist with a primary focus in
Administration, Engineering, Finance/Accounting, General
Management, Marketing, Research and Development

Jacobs, Mike — *Principal*
Thorne, Brieger Associates Inc.
11 East 44th Street
New York, NY 10017
Telephone: (212) 682-5424
Recruiter Classification: Retained; **Lowest/Average Salary:**
$90,000/$90,000; **Industry Concentration:** Generalist with a
primary focus in Financial Services, Insurance; Function
Concentration: Generalist with a primary focus in
Administration, Engineering, Finance/Accounting, General
Management, Human Resources, Marketing, Research and
Development, Sales

Jacobson, David — *President*
J. J. & H., Ltd.
150 North Wacker Drive
Chicago, IL 60606
Telephone: (312) 726-1578
Recruiter Classification: Retained; **Lowest/Average Salary:**
$50,000/$90,000; **Industry Concentration:** Insurance; Function
Concentration: Generalist

Jacobson, David N. — *President*
Jacobson Associates
150 North Wacker Drive
Suite 1120
Chicago, IL 60606
Telephone: (312) 726-1578
Recruiter Classification: Contingency; **Lowest/Average Salary:** $20,000/$50,000; **Industry Concentration:** Insurance; Function **Concentration:** Generalist

Jacobson, Gregory — *Executive Recruiter*
Jacobson Associates
1785 The Exchange, Suite 320
Atlanta, GA 30339
Telephone: (404) 952-3877
Recruiter Classification: Contingency; **Lowest/Average Salary:** $20,000/$50,000; **Industry Concentration:** Insurance;
Function Concentration: Generalist

Jacobson, Hayley — *Associate*
Source Services Corporation
2 Penn Plaza, Suite 1176
New York, NY 10121
Telephone: (212) 760-2200
Recruiter Classification: Contingency; **Lowest/Average Salary:** $30,000/$50,000; **Industry Concentration:** Financial Services; **Function Concentration:** Engineering, Finance/Accounting

Jacobson, Jewel — *Vice President*
Jacobson Associates
150 North Wacker Drive
Suite 1120
Chicago, IL 60606
Telephone: (312) 726-1578
Recruiter Classification: Contingency; **Lowest/Average Salary:** $20,000/$50,000; **Industry Concentration:** Insurance;
Function Concentration: Generalist

Jacobson, Rick — *President*
The Windham Group
114 Winchester Road
Fairlawn, OH 44333
Telephone: (330) 867-1075
Recruiter Classification: Retained; **Lowest/Average Salary:** $75,000/$90,000; **Industry Concentration:** Generalist with a primary focus in Financial Services, Insurance; **Function Concentration:** Generalist with a primary focus in Finance/Accounting, General Management, Human Resources, Marketing, Sales

Jadulang, Vincent — *Associate*
Source Services Corporation
One Park Plaza, Suite 560
Irvine, CA 92714
Telephone: (714) 660-1666
Recruiter Classification: Contingency; **Lowest/Average Salary:** $30,000/$50,000; **Industry Concentration:** Financial Services; **Function Concentration:** Engineering, Finance/Accounting

Jaedike, Eldron — *Recruiter*
Prestige Inc.
P.O. Box 421
Reedsburg, WI 53959
Telephone: (608) 524-4032
Recruiter Classification: Contingency; **Lowest/Average Salary:** $50,000/$90,000; **Industry Concentration:** Financial Services, Insurance; **Function Concentration:** Generalist

James, Richard — *President*
Criterion Executive Search, Inc.
5420 Bay Center Drive, Suite 101
Tampa, FL 33609-3402
Telephone: (813) 286-2000
Recruiter Classification: Contingency; **Lowest/Average Salary:** $40,000/$90,000; **Industry Concentration:** Generalist with a primary focus in Financial Services, Insurance; **Function Concentration:** Generalist with a primary focus in Administration, Engineering, Finance/Accounting, Research and Development, Women/Minorities

Janis, Laurence — *Partner*
Integrated Search Solutions Group, LLC
33 Main Street
Port Washington, NY 11050
Telephone: (516) 767-3030
Recruiter Classification: Retained; **Lowest/Average Salary:** $90,000/$90,000; **Industry Concentration:** Generalist with a primary focus in Financial Services; **Function Concentration:** Generalist with a primary focus in Human Resources, Marketing, Sales

Jansen, John F. — *President*
Delta Services
11711 Memorial Drive
Suite 252
Houston, TX 77024
Telephone: (713) 975-7725
Recruiter Classification: Retained; **Lowest/Average Salary:** $75,000/$90,000; **Industry Concentration:** Financial Services; **Function Concentration:** Engineering, Finance/Accounting, Human Resources, Marketing, Research and Development, Sales

Janssen, Don — *Consultant*
Howard Fischer Associates, Inc.
1800 John F. Kennedy Boulevard, 7th Floor
Philadelphia, PA 19103
Telephone: (215) 568-8363
Recruiter Classification: Retained; **Lowest/Average Salary:** $90,000/$90,000; **Industry Concentration:** Generalist with a primary focus in Financial Services, Insurance, Venture Capital; **Function Concentration:** Generalist with a primary focus in Administration, Finance/Accounting, General Management, Human Resources, Marketing, Research and Development, Sales, Women/Minorities

Januale, Lois — *Search Consultant*
Cochran, Cochran & Yale, Inc.
5166 Main Street
Williamsville, NY 14221
Telephone: (716) 631-1300
Recruiter Classification: Retained; **Lowest/Average Salary:** $50,000/$75,000; **Industry Concentration:** Generalist with a primary focus in Financial Services, Venture Capital; **Function Concentration:** Generalist with a primary focus in Engineering, Finance/Accounting, General Management, Human Resources, Marketing, Sales, Women/Minorities

Januleski, Geoff — *Associate*
Source Services Corporation
150 South Warner Road, Suite 238
King of Prussia, PA 19406
Telephone: (610) 341-1960
Recruiter Classification: Contingency; **Lowest/Average Salary:** $30,000/$50,000; **Industry Concentration:** Financial Services; **Function Concentration:** Engineering, Finance/Accounting

Jazylo, John V. — *Senior Vice President*
Handy HRM Corp.
250 Park Avenue
New York, NY 10177-0074
Telephone: (212) 210-5612
Recruiter Classification: Retained; **Lowest/Average Salary:**
$90,000/$90,000; **Industry Concentration:** Generalist with a
primary focus in Financial Services, Venture Capital; **Function
Concentration:** Finance/Accounting, General Management,
Marketing, Sales, Women/Minorities

Jazylo, John V. — *Senior Vice President*
Skott/Edwards Consultants, Inc.
1776 On the Green
Morristown, NJ 07006
Telephone: (973) 644-0900
Recruiter Classification: Retained; **Lowest/Average Salary:**
$90,000/$90,000; **Industry Concentration:** Financial Services;
Function Concentration: Generalist with a primary focus in
Administration, Finance/Accounting

Jeffers, Richard B. — *Principal*
Dieckmann & Associates, Ltd.
180 North Stetson, Suite 5555
Two Prudential Plaza
Chicago, IL 60601
Telephone: (312) 819-5900
Recruiter Classification: Retained; **Lowest/Average Salary:**
$90,000/$90,000; **Industry Concentration:** Generalist with a
primary focus in Financial Services, Insurance; **Function
Concentration:** Generalist with a primary focus in
Finance/Accounting, General Management, Marketing, Sales,
Women/Minorities

Jeltema, John — *Associate*
Source Services Corporation
One Park Plaza, Suite 560
Irvine, CA 92714
Telephone: (714) 660-1666
Recruiter Classification: Contingency; **Lowest/Average
Salary:** $30,000/$50,000; **Industry Concentration:** Financial
Services; **Function Concentration:** Engineering,
Finance/Accounting

Jensen, Robert — *Associate*
Source Services Corporation
3701 West Algonquin Road, Suite 380
Rolling Meadows, IL 60008
Telephone: (847) 392-0244
Recruiter Classification: Contingency; **Lowest/Average
Salary:** $30,000/$50,000; **Industry Concentration:** Financial
Services; **Function Concentration:** Engineering,
Finance/Accounting

Jernigan, Susan N. — *Principal*
Sockwell & Associates
227 West Trade Street, Suite 1930
Charlotte, NC 28202
Telephone: (704) 372-1865
Recruiter Classification: Retained; **Lowest/Average Salary:**
$90,000/$90,000; **Industry Concentration:** Generalist with a
primary focus in Financial Services; **Function Concentration:**
Generalist with a primary focus in Administration,
Finance/Accounting, General Management, Human Resources,
Marketing, Sales

Joffe, Barry — *Director Executive Search
Consulting*
Bason Associates Inc.
11311 Cornell Park Drive
Cincinnati, OH 45242
Telephone: (513) 469-9881
Recruiter Classification: Retained; **Lowest/Average Salary:**
$60,000/$90,000; **Industry Concentration:** Generalist with a
primary focus in Financial Services, Insurance, Venture Capital;
Function Concentration: Generalist with a primary focus in
Administration, Engineering, Finance/Accounting, General
Management, Human Resources, Marketing, Research and
Development, Sales

Johnson, Brian — *Professional Recruiter*
A.J. Burton Group, Inc.
120 East Baltimore Street, Suite 2220
Baltimore, MD 21202
Telephone: (410) 752-5244
Recruiter Classification: Contingency; **Lowest/Average Salary:**
$40,000/$75,000; **Industry Concentration:** Generalist with a
primary focus in Financial Services, Insurance; **Function
Concentration:** Generalist with a primary focus in
Administration, Finance/Accounting, General Management,
Human Resources

Johnson, Greg — *Managing Director*
Source Services Corporation
525 Vine Street, Suite 2250
Cincinnati, OH 45202
Telephone: (513) 651-3303
Recruiter Classification: Contingency; **Lowest/Average Salary:**
$30,000/$50,000; **Industry Concentration:** Financial Services;
Function Concentration: Engineering, Finance/Accounting

Johnson, Harold E. — *Senior Partner*
Lamalie Amrop International
200 Park Avenue
New York, NY 10166-0136
Telephone: (212) 953-7900
Recruiter Classification: Retained; **Lowest/Average Salary:**
$90,000/$90,000; **Industry Concentration:** Generalist with a
primary focus in Financial Services; **Function Concentration:**
Generalist

Johnson, John W. — *Managing Director*
Webb, Johnson Associates, Inc.
280 Park Avenue, 43rd Floor
New York, NY 10017
Telephone: (212) 661-3700
Recruiter Classification: Retained; **Lowest/Average Salary:**
$90,000/$90,000; **Industry Concentration:** Generalist with a
primary focus in Financial Services; **Function Concentration:**
Generalist with a primary focus in Administration, Engineering,
Finance/Accounting, General Management, Human Resources,
Marketing, Research and Development, Sales

Johnson, Julie M. — *Executive Recruiter*
International Staffing Consultants, Inc.
500 Newport Center Drive, Suite 300
Newport Beach, CA 92660-7003
Telephone: (714) 721-7990
Recruiter Classification: Contingency; **Lowest/Average Salary:**
$40,000/$60,000; **Industry Concentration:** Generalist with a
primary focus in Insurance; **Function Concentration:**
Generalist with a primary focus in Engineering, General
Management, Marketing, Research and Development, Sales

Johnson, Kathleen A. — *Partner*
Barton Associates, Inc.
One Riverway, Suite 2500
Houston, TX 77056
Telephone: (713) 961-9111
Recruiter Classification: Retained; **Lowest/Average Salary:**
$75,000/$90,000; **Industry Concentration:** Generalist with a
primary focus in Financial Services; **Function Concentration:**
Generalist with a primary focus in Administration,
Finance/Accounting, General Management, Human Resources,
Marketing, Sales

Johnson, Keith — *Managing Partner*
Romac & Associates
760 Pillsbury Center
200 South Sixth Street
Minneapolis, MN 55402
Telephone: (612) 334-5990
Recruiter Classification: Executive Temporary; **Lowest/Average
Salary:** $60,000/$60,000; **Industry Concentration:** Financial
Services, Insurance; **Function Concentration:**
Finance/Accounting

Johnson, Priscilla — *President*
The Johnson Group, Inc.
1 World Trade Center, Suite 4517
New York, NY 10048-0202
Telephone: (212) 775-0036
Recruiter Classification: Contingency; **Lowest/Average Salary:**
$60,000/$75,000; **Industry Concentration:** Generalist with a
primary focus in Financial Services, Insurance; **Function
Concentration:** Generalist with a primary focus in
Finance/Accounting, General Management, Human Resources,
Marketing, Sales, Women/Minorities

Johnson, Ronald S. — *President*
Ronald S. Johnson Associates, Inc.
11661 San Vicente Boulevard, Suite 400
Los Angeles, CA 90049
Telephone: (310) 820-5855
Recruiter Classification: Retained; **Lowest/Average Salary:**
$90,000/$90,000; **Industry Concentration:** Generalist with a
primary focus in Venture Capital; **Function Concentration:**
Generalist

Johnson, S. Hope — *Managing Director*
Boyden Washington, D.C.
2445 M Street N.W., Suite 250
Washington, DC 20037-1435
Telephone: (202) 342-7200
Recruiter Classification: Retained; **Lowest/Average Salary:**
$60,000/$90,000; **Industry Concentration:** Generalist with a
primary focus in Financial Services; **Function Concentration:**
Generalist with a primary focus in Administration,
Engineering, General Management, Human Resources,
Women/Minorities

Johnson, Stanley C. — *President*
Johnson & Company
11 Grumman Hill Road
Wilton, CT 06897
Telephone: (203) 761-1212
Recruiter Classification: Retained; **Lowest/Average Salary:**
$90,000/$90,000; **Industry Concentration:** Generalist with a
primary focus in Financial Services; **Function Concentration:**
Generalist with a primary focus in Engineering,
Finance/Accounting, General Management, Human Resources,
Marketing, Sales

Johnson, Valerie — *Executive Search Consultant*
Coe & Company International Inc.
1535 400-3rd Avenue SW
Center Tower
Calgary, Alberta, Canada T20 4H2
Telephone: (403) 232-8833
Recruiter Classification: Retained; **Lowest/Average Salary:**
$75,000/$90,000; **Industry Concentration:** Financial Services;
Function Concentration: Generalist with a primary focus in
Administration, Engineering, Finance/Accounting, General
Management, Human Resources, Marketing, Research and
Development, Sales

Johnston, James R. — *Principal*
The Stevenson Group of Delaware Inc.
836 Farmington Avenue, Suite 223
West Hartford, CT 06119-1544
Telephone: (860) 232-3393
Recruiter Classification: Retained; **Lowest/Average Salary:**
$75,000/$90,000; **Industry Concentration:** Financial Services,
Insurance; **Function Concentration:** Generalist

Johnstone, Grant — *Associate*
Source Services Corporation
520 Post Oak Boulevard, Suite 700
Houston, TX 77027
Telephone: (713) 439-1077
Recruiter Classification: Contingency; **Lowest/Average Salary:**
$30,000/$50,000; **Industry Concentration:** Financial Services;
Function Concentration: Engineering, Finance/Accounting

Jones, B.J. — *Principal*
Intersource, Ltd.
515 East Carefree Highway
P.O. Box 42033438
Phoenix, AZ 80080
Telephone: (602) 780-4540
Recruiter Classification: Retained; **Lowest/Average Salary:**
$30,000/$75,000; **Industry Concentration:** Generalist with a
primary focus in Financial Services; **Function Concentration:**
Finance/Accounting

Jones, Barbara J. — *Senior Vice President*
Kaye-Bassman International Corp.
18333 Preston Road, Suite 500
Dallas, TX 75252
Telephone: (972) 931-5242
Recruiter Classification: Executive Temporary; **Lowest/Average
Salary:** $40,000/$60,000; **Industry Concentration:** Financial
Services; **Function Concentration:** Generalist

Jones, Daniel F. — *Principal*
Atlantic Search Group, Inc.
One Liberty Square
Boston, MA 02109
Telephone: (617) 426-9700
Recruiter Classification: Contingency; **Lowest/Average Salary:**
$20,000/$60,000; **Industry Concentration:** Generalist with a
primary focus in Financial Services; **Function Concentration:**
Finance/Accounting

Jones, Edward G. — *President*
E.G. Jones Associates, Ltd.
1505 York Road
Lutherville, MD 21093
Telephone: (410) 337-4925
Recruiter Classification: Contingency; **Lowest/Average Salary:**
$90,000/$90,000; **Industry Concentration:** Venture Capital;
Function Concentration: Generalist

Jones, Herschel — *Vice President*
Korn/Ferry International
600 University Street, Suite 3111
Seattle, WA 98101
Telephone: (206) 447-1834
Recruiter Classification: Retained; **Lowest/Average Salary:**
$100,000/$150,000; **Industry Concentration:** Generalist with a
primary focus in Financial Services; **Function Concentration:**
Generalist

Jones, Jonathan C. — *Senior Vice President*
Canny, Bowen Inc.
200 Park Avenue
49th Floor
New York, NY 10166
Telephone: (212) 949-6611
Recruiter Classification: Retained; **Lowest/Average Salary:**
$90,000/$90,000; **Industry Concentration:** Financial Services;
Function Concentration: Finance/Accounting, Marketing,
Sales

Jones, Mark — *Senior Search Consultant*
Kaye-Bassman International Corp.
18333 Preston Road, Suite 500
Dallas, TX 75252
Telephone: (972) 931-5242
Recruiter Classification: Retained; **Lowest/Average Salary:**
$60,000/$75,000; **Industry Concentration:** Insurance

Jones, Rodney — *Associate*
Source Services Corporation
379 Thornall Street
Edison, NJ 08837
Telephone: (908) 494-2800
Recruiter Classification: Contingency; **Lowest/Average
Salary:** $30,000/$50,000; **Industry Concentration:** Financial
Services; **Function Concentration:** Engineering,
Finance/Accounting

Jordan, Jon — *Search Consultant*
Cochran, Cochran & Yale, Inc.
955 East Henrietta Road
Rochester, NY 14623
Telephone: (716) 424-6060
Recruiter Classification: Retained; **Lowest/Average Salary:**
$50,000/$75,000; **Industry Concentration:** Generalist with a
primary focus in Financial Services, Venture Capital;
Function Concentration: Generalist with a primary focus in
Engineering, Finance/Accounting, General Management,
Human Resources, Marketing, Sales, Women/
Minorities

Jordan, Stephen T. — *Acting G.E.O.*
Leader/Partner
Ray & Berndtson
Texas Commerce Tower
2200 Ross Avenue, Suite 4500W
Dallas, TX 75201
Telephone: (214) 969-7620
Recruiter Classification: Retained; **Lowest/Average Salary:**
$90,000/$90,000; **Industry Concentration:** Generalist with a
primary focus in Financial Services; **Function Concentration:**
Generalist

Jorgensen, Tom — *Vice President*
The Talley Group
P.O. Box 2918
Stanton, VA 24402
Telephone: (540) 248-7009
Recruiter Classification: Retained; **Lowest/Average Salary:**
$30,000/$60,000; **Industry Concentration:** Generalist with a
primary focus in Financial Services; **Function Concentration:**
Engineering, Finance/Accounting

Joys, David S. — *Partner*
Heidrick & Struggles, Inc.
245 Park Avenue, Suite 4300
New York, NY 10167-0152
Telephone: (212) 867-9876
Recruiter Classification: Retained; **Lowest/Average Salary:**
$75,000/$90,000; **Industry Concentration:** Generalist with a
primary focus in Financial Services; **Function Concentration:**
Generalist

Judge, Alfred L. — *President*
The Cambridge Group Ltd
1175 Post Road East
Westport, CT 06880
Telephone: (203) 226-4243
Recruiter Classification: Contingency; **Lowest/Average Salary:**
$60,000/$75,000; **Industry Concentration:** Generalist with a
primary focus in Financial Services; **Function Concentration:**
Administration, Finance/Accounting, General Management,
Human Resources, Marketing, Research and Development,
Sales, Women/Minorities

Judy, Otto — *Executive Recruiter*
CPS Inc.
One Westbrook Corporate Centre, Suite 600
Westchester, IL 60154
Telephone: (708) 531-8370
Recruiter Classification: Contingency; **Lowest/Average Salary:**
$30,000/$50,000; **Industry Concentration:** Generalist with a
primary focus in Financial Services, Insurance; **Function
Concentration:** Engineering, Research and Development,
Sales, Women/Minorities

Juelis, John J. — *Vice President*
Peeney Associates
141 South Avenue
Fanwood, NJ 07023
Telephone: (908) 322-2324
Recruiter Classification: Retained; **Lowest/Average Salary:**
$60,000/$90,000; **Industry Concentration:** Generalist with a
primary focus in Financial Services; **Function Concentration:**
Generalist with a primary focus in Administration, Engineering,
Finance/Accounting, General Management, Human Resources,
Marketing, Research and Development, Sales,
Women/Minorities

Juratovac, Michael — *Senior Associate*
Montgomery Resources, Inc.
555 Montgomery Street, Suite 1650
San Francisco, CA 94111
Telephone: (415) 956-4242
Recruiter Classification: Contingency; **Lowest/Average Salary:**
$30,000/$60,000; **Industry Concentration:** Financial Services,
Insurance, Venture Capital; **Function Concentration:**
Finance/Accounting

Juska, Frank — *Vice President*
Rusher, Loscavio & LoPresto
180 Montgomery Street, Suite 1616
San Francisco, CA 94104-4239
Telephone: (415) 765-6600
Recruiter Classification: Retained; **Lowest/Average Salary:**
$75,000/$90,000; **Industry Concentration:** Financial Services,
Venture Capital; **Function Concentration:** Administration,
Engineering, General Management

Kacyn, Louis J. — *Consultant*
Egon Zehnder International Inc.
One First National Plaza
21 South Clark Street, Suite 3300
Chicago, IL 60603-2006
Telephone: (312) 782-4500
Recruiter Classification: Retained; **Lowest/Average Salary:**
$90,000/$90,000; **Industry Concentration:** Generalist with a
primary focus in Financial Services; **Function Concentration:**
Generalist

Kader, Richard — *President*
Richard Kader & Associates
7850 Freeway Circle, Suite 201
Cleveland, OH 44130
Telephone: (440) 891-1700
Recruiter Classification: Contingency; **Lowest/Average Salary:**
$50,000/$60,000; **Industry Concentration:** Generalist with a
primary focus in Financial Services; **Function Concentration:**
Generalist with a primary focus in Administration,
Engineering, Finance/Accounting, Marketing, Sales,
Women/Minorities

Kaiser, Donald J. — *President*
Dunhill International Search of New Haven
59 Elm Street
New Haven, CT 06510
Telephone: (203) 562-0511
Recruiter Classification: Contingency; **Lowest/Average Salary:**
$30,000/$75,000; **Industry Concentration:** Generalist with a
primary focus in Financial Services; **Function Concentration:**
Generalist with a primary focus in Administration, Engineering,
Finance/Accounting, General Management, Human Resources,
Marketing, Sales

Kaiser, Elaine M. — *Consultant*
Dunhill International Search of New Haven
59 Elm Street
New Haven, CT 06510
Telephone: (203) 562-0511
Recruiter Classification: Contingency; **Lowest/Average Salary:**
$50,000/$75,000; **Industry Concentration:** Financial Services;
Function Concentration: Finance/Accounting, Marketing,
Sales

Kalinowski, David — *Search Consultant*
Jacobson Associates
Five Neshaminy Interplex
Suite 113
Trevose, PA 19053
Telephone: (215) 639-5860
Recruiter Classification: Contingency; **Lowest/Average
Salary:** $20,000/$40,000; **Industry Concentration:** Financial
Services, Insurance; **Function Concentration:** Generalist with
a primary focus in Administration, Finance/Accounting,
General Management, Marketing, Research and
Development, Sales

Kane, Frank — *Professional Recruiter*
A.J. Burton Group, Inc.
4550 Montgomery Avenue, Ste. 325 North
Bethesda, MD 20814
Telephone: (301) 654-0082
Recruiter Classification: Contingency, Executive Temporary;
Lowest/Average Salary: $40,000/$75,000; **Industry
Concentration:** Generalist with a primary focus in Financial
Services, Insurance; **Function Concentration:** Generalist with a
primary focus in Administration, Finance/Accounting, General
Management, Human Resources

Kane, Karen — *Consultant*
Howard Fischer Associates, Inc.
1800 John F. Kennedy Boulevard, 7th Floor
Philadelphia, PA 19103
Telephone: (215) 568-8363
Recruiter Classification: Retained; **Lowest/Average Salary:**
$90,000/$90,000; **Industry Concentration:** Generalist with a
primary focus in Financial Services, Insurance, Venture Capital;
Function Concentration: Generalist with a primary focus in
Administration, Finance/Accounting, General Management,
Human Resources, Marketing, Research and Development,
Sales, Women/Minorities

Kanovsky, Gerald — *Chairman*
Career Consulting Group, Inc.
1100 Summer Street
Stamford, CT 06905
Telephone: (203) 975-8800
Recruiter Classification: Contingency; **Lowest/Average Salary:**
$40,000/$75,000; **Industry Concentration:** Financial Services;
Function Concentration: Marketing, Sales

Kanovsky, Marlene — *President*
Career Consulting Group, Inc.
1100 Summer Street
Stamford, CT 06905
Telephone: (203) 975-8800
Recruiter Classification: Contingency; **Lowest/Average Salary:**
$40,000/$50,000; **Industry Concentration:** Financial Services;
Function Concentration: Marketing, Sales

Kantor, Richard — *Account Executive*
Search West, Inc.
340 North Westlake Boulevard
Suite 200
Westlake Village, CA 91362-3761
Telephone: (805) 496-6811
Recruiter Classification: Contingency; **Lowest/Average
Salary:** $40,000/$60,000; **Industry Concentration:** Financial
Services; **Function Concentration:** Administration,
Finance/Accounting

Kaplan, Gary — *President*
Gary Kaplan & Associates
201 South Lake Avenue
Suite 600
Pasadena, CA 91101
Telephone: (818) 796-8100
Recruiter Classification: Retained; **Lowest/Average Salary:**
$75,000/$90,000; **Industry Concentration:** Generalist with a
primary focus in Financial Services, Insurance; **Function
Concentration:** Generalist with a primary focus in
Engineering, Finance/Accounting, General Management,
Human Resources, Marketing, Research and Development,
Sales

Kaplan, Traci — *Associate*
Source Services Corporation
8614 Westwood Center, Suite 750
Vienna, VA 22182
Telephone: (703) 790-5610
Recruiter Classification: Contingency; **Lowest/Average Salary:**
$30,000/$50,000; **Industry Concentration:** Financial Services;
Function Concentration: Engineering, Finance/Accounting

Karalis, William — *Executive Recruiter*
CPS Inc.
One Westbrook Corporate Centre, Suite 600
Westchester, IL 60154
Telephone: (708) 531-8370
Recruiter Classification: Contingency; **Lowest/Average Salary:**
$30,000/$50,000; **Industry Concentration:** Generalist with a
primary focus in Financial Services, Insurance; **Function
Concentration:** Engineering, Research and Development,
Sales, Women/Minorities

Kasprzyk, Michael — *Associate*
Source Services Corporation
8614 Westwood Center, Suite 750
Vienna, VA 22182
Telephone: (703) 790-5610
Recruiter Classification: Contingency; **Lowest/Average Salary:**
$30,000/$50,000; **Industry Concentration:** Financial Services;
Function Concentration: Engineering, Finance/Accounting

Kassouf, Constance — *Senior Vice President*
The Whitney Group
850 Third Avenue, 11th Floor
New York, NY 10022
Telephone: (212) 508-3500
Recruiter Classification: Retained; **Lowest/Average Salary:**
$90,000/$90,000; **Industry Concentration:** Financial Services,
Venture Capital; **Function Concentration:** Generalist with a
primary focus in Finance/Accounting, General Management,
Marketing, Sales

Katz, Cyndi — *Account Executive*
Search West, Inc.
1888 Century Park East
Suite 2050
Los Angeles, CA 90067-1736
Telephone: (310) 284-8888
Recruiter Classification: Contingency; **Lowest/Average Salary:**
$40,000/$60,000; **Industry Concentration:** Generalist with a
primary focus in Financial Services; **Function Concentration:**
Administration

Kaye, Jeffrey — *President and COO*
Kaye-Bassman International Corp.
18333 Preston Road, Suite 500
Dallas, TX 75252
Telephone: (972) 931-5242
Recruiter Classification: Executive Temporary; **Lowest/Average
Salary:** $40,000/$60,000; **Industry Concentration:** Financial
Services; **Function Concentration:** Generalist

Keating, Pierson — *Partner*
Nordeman Grimm, Inc.
717 Fifth Avenue, 26th Floor
New York, NY 10022
Telephone: (212) 935-1000
Recruiter Classification: Retained; **Lowest/Average Salary:**
$90,000/$90,000; **Industry Concentration:** Generalist with a
primary focus in Financial Services, Venture Capital; **Function
Concentration:** Generalist with a primary focus in
Finance/Accounting, General Management, Human Resources,
Marketing, Research and Development, Sales

Keck, Jason B. — *Senior Search Consultant*
Kaye-Bassman International Corp.
18333 Preston Road, Suite 500
Dallas, TX 75252
Telephone: (972) 931-5242
Recruiter Classification: Retained; **Lowest/Average Salary:**
$40,000/$60,000; **Industry Concentration:** Insurance;
Function Concentration: Marketing, Sales

Kehoe, Mike — *Executive Recruiter*
CPS Inc.
One Westbrook Corporate Centre, Suite 600
Westchester, IL 60154
Telephone: (708) 531-8370
Recruiter Classification: Contingency; **Lowest/Average Salary:**
$30,000/$50,000; **Industry Concentration:** Generalist with a
primary focus in Financial Services, Insurance; **Function
Concentration:** Engineering, Research and Development,
Sales, Women/Minorities

Keitel, Robert S. — *Vice President*
A.T. Kearney, Inc.
3 Lagoon Drive, Suite 160
Redwood City, CA 94065
Telephone: (415) 637-6600
Recruiter Classification: Retained; **Lowest/Average Salary:**
$90,000/$90,000; **Industry Concentration:** Generalist with a
primary focus in Financial Services; **Function Concentration:**
Generalist with a primary focus in General Management

Keith, Stephanie — *Recruiter*
Southwestern Professional Services
9485 Regency Square Boulevard, Suite 110
Jacksonville, FL 32225
Telephone: (904) 464-0400
Recruiter Classification: Contingency; **Lowest/Average Salary:**
$40,000/$60,000; **Industry Concentration:** Financial Services;
Function Concentration: Finance/Accounting

Keller, Barbara E. — *Senior Consultant*
Barton Associates, Inc.
One Riverway, Suite 2500
Houston, TX 77056
Telephone: (713) 961-9111
Recruiter Classification: Retained; **Lowest/Average Salary:**
$75,000/$90,000; **Industry Concentration:** Generalist with a
primary focus in Financial Services; **Function Concentration:**
Generalist with a primary focus in Finance/Accounting,
General Management, Human Resources, Marketing, Sales

Keller, Peggy — *Consultant*
The McCormick Group, Inc.
20 Walnut Street, Suite 308
Wellesley Hills, MA 02181
Telephone: (617) 239-1233
Recruiter Classification: Retained; **Lowest/Average Salary:**
$50,000/$60,000; **Industry Concentration:** Insurance;
Function Concentration: Generalist

Kelly, Claudia L. — *Managing Director*
Spencer Stuart
Financial Centre
695 East Main Street
Stamford, CT 06901
Telephone: (203) 324-6333
Recruiter Classification: Retained; **Lowest/Average Salary:**
$90,000/$90,000; **Industry Concentration:** Generalist with a
primary focus in Financial Services; **Function Concentration:**
Generalist with a primary focus in Finance/Accounting,
Marketing, Women/Minorities

Kelly, Donna J. — *Vice President Placement*
Accountants Executive Search
535 Fifth Avenue, Suite 1200
New York, NY 10017
Telephone: (212) 682-5900
Recruiter Classification: Executive Temporary; **Lowest/Average Salary:** $40,000/$60,000; **Industry Concentration:** Generalist with a primary focus in Financial Services; **Function Concentration:** Finance/Accounting

Kelly, Elizabeth Ann — *Senior Associate*
Wellington Management Group
1601 Market Street, Suite 2902
Philadelphia, PA 19103-2499
Telephone: (215) 569-8900
Recruiter Classification: Retained; **Lowest/Average Salary:** $90,000/$90,000; **Industry Concentration:** Generalist with a primary focus in Venture Capital; **Function Concentration:** Generalist with a primary focus in General Management, Human Resources, Marketing, Sales, Women/Minorities

Kelly, Peter W. — *Partner*
R. Rollo Associates
725 South Figueroa Street, Suite 3230
Los Angeles, CA 90017
Telephone: (213) 688-9444
Recruiter Classification: Retained; **Lowest/Average Salary:** $90,000/$90,000; **Industry Concentration:** Generalist with a primary focus in Financial Services, Insurance, Venture Capital; **Function Concentration:** Generalist with a primary focus in Administration, Finance/Accounting, General Management, Human Resources, Marketing

Kelly, Robert — *Associate*
Source Services Corporation
100 North Tryon Street, Suite 3130
Charlotte, NC 28202
Telephone: (704) 333-8311
Recruiter Classification: Contingency; **Lowest/Average Salary:** $30,000/$50,000; **Industry Concentration:** Financial Services; **Function Concentration:** Engineering, Finance/Accounting

Kelso, Patricia C. — *Associate Partner*
Barton Associates, Inc.
One Riverway, Suite 2500
Houston, TX 77056
Telephone: (713) 961-9111
Recruiter Classification: Retained; **Lowest/Average Salary:** $75,000/$90,000; **Industry Concentration:** Generalist with a primary focus in Financial Services; **Function Concentration:** Generalist with a primary focus in Administration, General Management, Human Resources, Marketing, Sales

Kennedy, Craig — *Associate*
Source Services Corporation
10220 SW Greenburg Road, Suite 625
Portland, OR 97223
Telephone: (503) 768-4546
Recruiter Classification: Contingency; **Lowest/Average Salary:** $30,000/$50,000; **Industry Concentration:** Financial Services; **Function Concentration:** Engineering, Finance/Accounting

Kennedy, Michael — *Senior Partner*
The Danbrook Group, Inc.
14180 Dallas Parkway, Suite 400
Dallas, TX 75240
Telephone: (214) 392-0057
Recruiter Classification: Contingency; **Lowest/Average Salary:** $30,000/$50,000; **Industry Concentration:** Insurance; **Function Concentration:** Generalist with a primary focus in Administration, Finance/Accounting, General Management, Marketing, Sales

Kennedy, Paul — *Associate*
Source Services Corporation
One Park Plaza, Suite 560
Irvine, CA 92714
Telephone: (714) 660-1666
Recruiter Classification: Contingency; **Lowest/Average Salary:** $30,000/$50,000; **Industry Concentration:** Financial Services; **Function Concentration:** Engineering, Finance/Accounting

Kennedy, Walter — *Branch Manager*
Romac & Associates
111 North Orange Avenue
Suite 1150
Orlando, FL 32801
Telephone: (407) 843-0765
Recruiter Classification: Executive Temporary; **Lowest/Average Salary:** $60,000/$60,000; **Industry Concentration:** Financial Services, Insurance; **Function Concentration:** Finance/Accounting

Kennedy, Walter — *Managing Director*
Source Services Corporation
80 South 8th Street
Minneapolis, MN 55402
Telephone: (612) 332-6460
Recruiter Classification: Contingency; **Lowest/Average Salary:** $30,000/$50,000; **Industry Concentration:** Financial Services; **Function Concentration:** Engineering, Finance/Accounting

Kennedy, Walter — *Managing Director*
Source Services Corporation
8500 Normandale Lake, Suite 955
Bloomington, MN 55437
Telephone: (612) 835-5100
Recruiter Classification: Contingency; **Lowest/Average Salary:** $30,000/$50,000; **Industry Concentration:** Financial Services; **Function Concentration:** Engineering, Finance/Accounting

Kenney, Jeanne — *Associate*
Source Services Corporation
425 California Street, Suite 1200
San Francisco, CA 94104
Telephone: (415) 434-2410
Recruiter Classification: Contingency; **Lowest/Average Salary:** $30,000/$50,000; **Industry Concentration:** Financial Services; **Function Concentration:** Engineering, Finance/Accounting

Kenzer, Robert D. — *Chairman*
Kenzer Corp.
777 Third Avenue, 26th Floor
New York, NY 10017
Telephone: (212) 308-4300
Recruiter Classification: Retained; **Lowest/Average Salary:** $50,000/$90,000; **Industry Concentration:** Financial Services, Venture Capital; **Function Concentration:** Generalist with a primary focus in Administration, Finance/Accounting, General Management, Human Resources, Marketing

Keogh, James — *Principal*
Sanford Rose Associates
2625 Butterfield Road
Suite 107W
Oak Brook, IL 60521
Telephone: (708) 574-9405
Recruiter Classification: Contingency; **Lowest/Average Salary:** $30,000/$75,000; **Industry Concentration:** Generalist with a primary focus in Financial Services; **Function Concentration:** Generalist

Kern, Jerry L. — *Executive Vice President*
ADOW's Executeam
2734 Chancellor Drive, Suite 102
Crestview Hills, KY 41017-3443
Telephone: (606) 344-8600
Recruiter Classification: Executive Temporary; **Lowest/Average**
Salary: $60,000/$90,000; **Industry Concentration:** Generalist
with a primary focus in Financial Services; **Function**
Concentration: Generalist with a primary focus in
Administration, Engineering, Finance/Accounting, General
Management, Human Resources, Marketing, Research and
Development, Women/Minorities

Kern, Kathleen G. — *President*
ADOW's Executeam
36 East Fourth Street, Suite 1020
Cincinnati, OH 45202-3810
Telephone: (513) 721-2369
Recruiter Classification: Executive Temporary; **Lowest/Average**
Salary: $60,000/$90,000; **Industry Concentration:** Generalist
with a primary focus in Financial Services; **Function**
Concentration: Generalist with a primary focus in
Administration, Engineering, Finance/Accounting, General
Management, Human Resources, Marketing, Women/Minorities

Kershaw, Lisa — *Consultant*
Tanton Mitchell/Paul Ray Berndtson
710-1050 West Pender Street
Vancouver, British Columbia, CANADA V6E 3S7
Telephone: (604) 685-0261
Recruiter Classification: Retained; **Lowest/Average Salary:**
$75,000/$90,000; **Industry Concentration:** Generalist with a
primary focus in Financial Services, Insurance; **Function**
Concentration: Generalist with a primary focus in
Administration, Finance/Accounting, General Management,
Human Resources, Marketing, Sales

Keshishian, Gregory — *Senior Vice President,*
Executive Compensation Practice
Handy HRM Corp.
250 Park Avenue
New York, NY 10177-0074
Telephone: (212) 210-5650
Recruiter Classification: Retained; **Lowest/Average Salary:**
$90,000/$90,000; **Industry Concentration:** Generalist with a
primary focus in Financial Services, Insurance, Venture Capital; **Function Concentration:** Generalist with a primary focus in
Finance/Accounting, General Management, Human Resources

Kettwig, David A. — *Vice President*
A.T. Kearney, Inc.
222 West Adams Street
Chicago, IL 60606
Telephone: (312) 648-0111
Recruiter Classification: Retained; **Lowest/Average Salary:**
$90,000/$90,000; **Industry Concentration:** Generalist with a
primary focus in Financial Services; **Function Concentration:**
Generalist with a primary focus in Finance/Accounting,
General Management, Human Resources, Marketing, Sales

Keyser, Anne — *Vice President*
A.T. Kearney, Inc.
One Memorial Drive, 14th Floor
Cambridge, MA 02142
Telephone: (617) 374-2600
Recruiter Classification: Retained; **Lowest/Average Salary:**
$90,000/$90,000; **Industry Concentration:** Generalist with a
primary focus in Financial Services; **Function Concentration:**
Generalist with a primary focus in Engineering,
Finance/Accounting, General Management

Kien-Jersey, Tammy — *Director*
Spencer Stuart
Financial Centre
695 East Main Street
Stamford, CT 06901
Telephone: (203) 324-6333
Recruiter Classification: Retained; **Lowest/Average Salary:**
$90,000/$90,000; **Industry Concentration:** Financial
Services; **Function Concentration:** Finance/
Accounting

Kilcoyne, Pat — *Executive Recruiter*
CPS Inc.
One Westbrook Corporate Centre, Suite 600
Westchester, IL 60154
Telephone: (708) 531-8370
Recruiter Classification: Contingency; **Lowest/Average**
Salary: $30,000/$50,000; **Industry Concentration:**
Generalist with a primary focus in Financial Services,
Insurance; **Function Concentration:** Engineering,
Research and Development, Sales, Women/
Minorities

Kilcullen, Brian A. — *Partner*
D.A. Kreuter Associates, Inc.
1100 East Hector Street, Suite 388
Conshohocken, PA 19428
Telephone: (610) 834-1100
Recruiter Classification: Retained; **Lowest/Average Salary:**
$60,000/$90,000; **Industry Concentration:** Financial Services,
Insurance; **Function Concentration:** General Management,
Marketing, Sales

Kile, Robert W. — *Vice President*
Rusher, Loscavio & LoPresto
180 Montgomery Street, Suite 1616
San Francisco, CA 94104-4239
Telephone: (415) 765-6600
Recruiter Classification: Retained; **Lowest/Average Salary:**
$75,000/$75,000; **Industry Concentration:** Insurance;
Function Concentration: Administration, General
Management

Kiley, Phyllis — *Senior Insurance Consultant*
National Search, Inc.
2816 University Drive
Coral Springs, FL 33071
Telephone: (800) 935-4355
Recruiter Classification: Contingency; **Lowest/Average**
Salary: $30,000/$50,000; **Industry Concentration:**
Insurance; **Function Concentration:** Generalist with a
primary focus in Administration, Finance/Accounting,
General Management, Human Resources, Marketing,
Research and Development, Sales, Women/
Minorities

King, Bill — *Vice President Administration*
The McCormick Group, Inc.
1400 Wilson Boulevard
Arlington, VA 22209
Telephone: (703) 841-1700
Recruiter Classification: Retained; **Lowest/Average Salary:**
$50,000/$90,000; **Industry Concentration:** Financial Services,
Insurance; **Function Concentration:** Engineering,
Finance/Accounting, General Management, Human Resources,
Marketing, Sales

King, Margaret — *Vice President*
Christian & Timbers
20833 Stevens Creek Boulevard, Suite 200
Cupertino, CA 95014
Telephone: (408) 446-5440
Recruiter Classification: Retained; **Lowest/Average Salary:**
$90,000/$90,000; **Industry Concentration:** Venture Capital;
Function Concentration: Generalist with a primary focus in
Engineering, Finance/Accounting, General Management, Human
Resources, Marketing, Research and Development, Sales

King, Shannon — *Associate*
Source Services Corporation
4510 Executive Drive, Suite 200
San Diego, CA 92121
Telephone: (619) 552-0300
Recruiter Classification: Contingency; **Lowest/Average Salary:**
$30,000/$50,000; **Industry Concentration:** Financial Services;
Function Concentration: Engineering, Finance/Accounting

King, Steven — *Office of the President*
Ashway, Ltd.
295 Madison Avenue
New York, NY 10017
Telephone: (212) 679-3300
Recruiter Classification: Contingency; **Lowest/Average Salary:**
$30,000/$90,000; **Industry Concentration:** Insurance;
Function Concentration: General Management

King, Thomas — *Recruiter*
Morgan Hunter Corp.
6800 College Boulevard, Suite 550
Overland Park, KS 66211
Telephone: (913) 491-3434
Recruiter Classification: Contingency; **Lowest/Average Salary:**
$20,000/$30,000; **Industry Concentration:** Generalist with a
primary focus in Financial Services; **Function Concentration:**
Finance/Accounting

Kinser, Richard E. — *President*
Richard Kinser & Associates
919 Third Avenue, 10th Floor
New York, NY 10022
Telephone: (212) 593-5429
Recruiter Classification: Retained; **Lowest/Average Salary:**
$90,000/$90,000; **Industry Concentration:** Generalist with a
primary focus in Financial Services, Insurance; **Function
Concentration:** Generalist with a primary focus in Engineering,
Finance/Accounting, General Management, Human Resources,
Marketing, Research and Development

Kip, Luanne S. — *President*
Kip Williams, Inc.
355 Lexington Avenue, 11th Floor
New York, NY 10017-6603
Telephone: (212) 661-1225
Recruiter Classification: Retained; **Lowest/Average Salary:**
$75,000/$90,000; **Industry Concentration:** Generalist with a
primary focus in Venture Capital; **Function Concentration:**
Generalist with a primary focus in General Management,
Human Resources, Marketing, Sales, Women/Minorities

Kirschman, David R. — *President*
Physician Executive Management Center
4014 Gunn Highway, Suite 160
Tampa, FL 33624
Telephone: (813) 963-1800
Recruiter Classification: Retained; **Lowest/Average Salary:**
$90,000/$90,000; **Industry Concentration:** Insurance;
Function Concentration: General Management

Kirschner, Alan — *Associate*
Source Services Corporation
2 Penn Plaza, Suite 1176
New York, NY 10121
Telephone: (212) 760-2200
Recruiter Classification: Contingency; **Lowest/Average Salary:**
$30,000/$50,000; **Industry Concentration:** Financial Services;
Function Concentration: Engineering, Finance/Accounting

Kishbaugh, Herbert S. — *President*
Kishbaugh Associates International
2 Elm Square
Andover, MA 01810
Telephone: (508) 475-7224
Recruiter Classification: Retained; **Lowest/Average Salary:**
$75,000/$90,000; **Industry Concentration:** Generalist with a
primary focus in Financial Services; **Function Concentration:**
Generalist with a primary focus in Administration,
Finance/Accounting, General Management, Human Resources,
Marketing, Research and Development, Sales

Kkorzyniewski, Nicole — *Executive Recruiter*
CPS Inc.
One Westbrook Corporate Centre, Suite 600
Westchester, IL 60154
Telephone: (708) 531-8370
Recruiter Classification: Contingency; **Lowest/Average Salary:**
$30,000/$50,000; **Industry Concentration:** Generalist with a
primary focus in Financial Services, Insurance; **Function
Concentration:** Engineering, Research and Development,
Sales, Women/Minorities

Klages, Constance W. — *President*
International Management Advisors, Inc.
516 Fifth Avenue
New York, NY 10036-7501
Telephone: (212) 758-7770
Recruiter Classification: Retained; **Lowest/Average Salary:**
$75,000/$90,000; **Industry Concentration:** Generalist with a
primary focus in Financial Services; **Function Concentration:**
Generalist with a primary focus in Engineering,
Finance/Accounting, General Management, Human Resources,
Marketing, Research and Development, Women/Minorities

Klavens, Cecile J. — *President*
The Pickwick Group, Inc.
One Washington Street, Suite 111
Wellesley, MA 02181
Telephone: (617) 235-6222
Recruiter Classification: Executive Temporary; **Lowest/Average
Salary:** $40,000/$60,000; **Industry Concentration:** Generalist
with a primary focus in Financial Services; **Function
Concentration:** Generalist with a primary focus in
Finance/Accounting, General Management, Human Resources,
Marketing, Women/Minorities

Klein, Brandon — *Professional Recruiter*
A.J. Burton Group, Inc.
120 East Baltimore Street, Suite 2220
Baltimore, MD 21202
Telephone: (410) 752-5244
Recruiter Classification: Contingency; **Lowest/Average Salary:**
$40,000/$75,000; **Industry Concentration:** Generalist with a
primary focus in Financial Services, Insurance; **Function
Concentration:** Generalist with a primary focus in
Administration, Finance/Accounting, General Management,
Human Resources

Klein, Gary — *Vice President*
A.T. Kearney, Inc.
153 East 53rd Street
New York, NY 10022
Telephone: (212) 751-7040
Recruiter Classification: Retained; **Lowest/Average Salary:**
$90,000/$90,000; **Industry Concentration:** Generalist with a
primary focus in Financial Services; **Function Concentration:**
Generalist with a primary focus in Engineering,
Finance/Accounting, General Management

Klein, Lynn M. — *Managing Director*
Riotto-Jones Associates
600 Third Avenue
New York, NY 10016
Telephone: (212) 697-4575
Recruiter Classification: Retained; **Lowest/Average Salary:**
$90,000/$90,000; **Industry Concentration:** Financial Services;
Function Concentration: Administration, Finance/Accounting,
General Management, Marketing, Sales

Klein, Mary Jo — *Search Consultant*
Cochran, Cochran & Yale, Inc.
955 East Henrietta Road
Rochester, NY 14623
Telephone: (716) 424-6060
Recruiter Classification: Retained; **Lowest/Average Salary:**
$50,000/$75,000; **Industry Concentration:** Generalist with a
primary focus in Financial Services, Venture Capital; **Function
Concentration:** Generalist with a primary focus in Engineering,
Finance/Accounting, General Management, Human Resources,
Marketing, Sales, Women/Minorities

Klein, Mel — *President*
Stewart/Laurence Associates
P.O. Box 1156
Atrium Executive Park
Englishtown, NJ 07726
Telephone: (732) 972-8000
Recruiter Classification: Retained; **Lowest/Average Salary:**
$75,000/$90,000; **Industry Concentration:** Venture Capital;
Function Concentration: General Management, Marketing, Sales

Kleinstein, Jonah A. — *President*
The Kleinstein Group
33 Wood Avenue South
Metro Park Plaza
Iselin, NJ 08830
Telephone: (908) 494-7500
Recruiter Classification: Retained; **Lowest/Average Salary:**
$60,000/$90,000; **Industry Concentration:** Generalist with a
primary focus in Financial Services, Insurance; **Function
Concentration:** Generalist

Kleinstein, Scott — *Associate*
Source Services Corporation
150 South Wacker Drive, Suite 400
Chicago, IL 60606
Telephone: (312) 346-7000
Recruiter Classification: Contingency; **Lowest/Average Salary:**
$30,000/$50,000; **Industry Concentration:** Financial Services;
Function Concentration: Engineering, Finance/Accounting

Klusman, Edwin — *Associate*
Source Services Corporation
2000 Town Center, Suite 850
Southfield, MI 48075
Telephone: (810) 352-6520
Recruiter Classification: Contingency; **Lowest/Average Salary:**
$30,000/$50,000; **Industry Concentration:** Financial Services;
Function Concentration: Engineering, Finance/Accounting

Knight, Liz — *Consultant*
Plummer & Associates, Inc.
65 Rowayton Avenue
Rowayton, CT 06853
Telephone: (203) 899-1233
Recruiter Classification: Retained, Executive Temporary;
Lowest/Average Salary: $90,000/$90,000; **Industry
Concentration:** Venture Capital; **Function Concentration:**
Generalist

Knisely, Gary — *Chief Executive Officer*
Johnson Smith & Knisely Accord
100 Park Avenue, 15th Floor
New York, NY 10017
Telephone: (212) 885-9100
Recruiter Classification: Retained; **Lowest/Average Salary:**
$90,000/$90,000; **Industry Concentration:** Generalist with a
primary focus in Financial Services, Venture Capital; **Function
Concentration:** Generalist with a primary focus in
Administration, Finance/Accounting, General Management,
Human Resources, Marketing, Research and Development,
Sales, Women/Minorities

Knoll, Robert — *Associate*
Source Services Corporation
One CityPlace, Suite 170
St. Louis, MO 63141
Telephone: (314) 432-4500
Recruiter Classification: Contingency; **Lowest/Average
Salary:** $30,000/$50,000; **Industry Concentration:** Financial
Services; **Function Concentration:** Engineering,
Finance/Accounting

Koblentz, Joel M. — *Managing Partner*
Egon Zehnder International Inc.
One Atlantic Center, Suite 3000
1201 West Peachtree Street N.E.
Atlanta, GA 30309
Telephone: (404) 875-3000
Recruiter Classification: Retained; **Lowest/Average Salary:**
$90,000/$90,000; **Industry Concentration:** Generalist with a
primary focus in Financial Services; **Function Concentration:**
Generalist

Koczak, John — *Associate*
Source Services Corporation
525 Vine Street, Suite 2250
Cincinnati, OH 45202
Telephone: (513) 651-3303
Recruiter Classification: Contingency; **Lowest/Average
Salary:** $30,000/$50,000; **Industry Concentration:** Financial
Services; **Function Concentration:** Engineering,
Finance/Accounting

Koehler, Frank R. — *Principal*
The Koehler Group
P.O. Box 18156
Philadelphia, PA 19116
Telephone: (215) 673-8315
Recruiter Classification: Contingency; **Lowest/Average
Salary:** $60,000/$75,000; **Industry Concentration:**
Generalist with a primary focus in Financial Services,
Insurance; **Function Concentration:** Human
Resources

Kohn, Adam P. — *Vice President/Principle*
Christian & Timbers
25825 Science Park Drive, Suite 400
Cleveland, OH 44122
Telephone: (216) 765-5869
Recruiter Classification: Retained; **Lowest/Average Salary:**
$90,000/$90,000; **Industry Concentration:** Generalist with a
primary focus in Venture Capital; **Function Concentration:**
Generalist with a primary focus in Engineering,
Finance/Accounting, General Management, Human Resources,
Marketing, Sales, Women/Minorities

Kondra, Vernon J. — *Director Operations*
The Douglas Reiter Company, Inc.
1221 S.W. Yamhill, Suite 301A
Portland, OR 97205
Telephone: (503) 228-6916
Recruiter Classification: Executive Temporary; **Lowest/Average**
Salary: $75,000/$90,000; **Industry Concentration:** Generalist
with a primary focus in Financial Services; **Function**
Concentration: Generalist with a primary focus in
Administration, Engineering, Finance/Accounting, General
Management, Human Resources, Marketing

Konker, David N. — *Managing Director*
Russell Reynolds Associates, Inc.
1900 Trammell Crow Center
2001 Ross Avenue
Dallas, TX 75201-2977
Telephone: (214) 220-2033
Recruiter Classification: Retained; **Lowest/Average Salary:**
$90,000/$90,000; **Industry Concentration:** Generalist with a
primary focus in Financial Services; **Function Concentration:**
Generalist

Koontz, Donald N. — *President*
Koontz, Jeffries & Associates, Inc.
18-22 Bank Street
Summit, NJ 07901
Telephone: (908) 598-1900
Recruiter Classification: Retained; **Lowest/Average Salary:**
$75,000/$90,000; **Industry Concentration:** Generalist with a
primary focus in Financial Services; **Function Concentration:**
Generalist with a primary focus in Administration, Engineering,
Finance/Accounting, General Management, Human Resources,
Marketing, Research and Development, Sales,
Women/Minorities

Kopsick, Joseph M. — *Senior Director*
Spencer Stuart
401 North Michigan Avenue, Suite 3400
Chicago, IL 60611-4244
Telephone: (312) 822-0080
Recruiter Classification: Retained; **Lowest/Average Salary:**
$90,000/$90,000; **Industry Concentration:** Generalist with a
primary focus in Venture Capital; **Function Concentration:**
Generalist with a primary focus in Engineering,
Finance/Accounting, General Management, Human Resources,
Marketing, Research and Development, Sales

Kossuth, David — *Vice President International*
Kossuth & Associates, Inc.
800 Bellevue Way N.E., Suite 400
Bellevue, WA 98004
Telephone: (206) 450-9050
Recruiter Classification: Retained; **Lowest/Average Salary:**
$50,000/$90,000; **Industry Concentration:** Venture Capital;
Function Concentration: Generalist with a primary focus in
Engineering, Finance/Accounting, General Management, Human
Resources, Marketing, Research and Development, Sales

Kossuth, Jane — *President*
Kossuth & Associates, Inc.
800 Bellevue Way N.E., Suite 400
Bellevue, WA 98004
Telephone: (206) 450-9050
Recruiter Classification: Retained; **Lowest/Average Salary:**
$75,000/$90,000; **Industry Concentration:** Venture Capital;
Function Concentration: Generalist with a primary focus in
Engineering, Finance/Accounting, General Management,
Human Resources, Marketing, Research and Development,
Sales, Women/Minorities

Kotick, Maddy — *Consultant*
The Stevenson Group of New Jersey
560 Sylvan Avenue
Englewood Cliffs, NJ 07632
Telephone: (201) 568-1900
Recruiter Classification: Retained; **Lowest/Average Salary:**
$75,000/$90,000; **Industry Concentration:** Generalist with a
primary focus in Financial Services; **Function Concentration:**
Generalist with a primary focus in Finance/Accounting,
General Management, Human Resources, Marketing,
Sales

Kramer, Donald — *President*
Dunhill Professional Search of Tampa
4350 West Cypress Street, Suite 225
Tampa, FL 33607
Telephone: (813) 872-8118
Recruiter Classification: Contingency; **Lowest/Average Salary:**
$30,000/$100,000; **Industry Concentration:** Financial
Services, Insurance; **Function Concentration:**
Finance/Accounting

Kramer, Peter — *Vice President*
Dunhill Professional Search of Tampa
4350 West Cypress Street, Suite 225
Tampa, FL 33607
Telephone: (813) 872-8118
Recruiter Classification: Contingency; **Lowest/Average Salary:**
$30,000/$100,000; **Industry Concentration:** Financial
Services, Insurance; **Function Concentration:**
Finance/Accounting

Kratz, Steve — *Senior Vice President*
Tyler & Company
1000 Abernathy Road
Suite 1400
Atlanta, GA 30328-5655
Telephone: (770) 396-3939
Recruiter Classification: Retained; **Lowest/Average Salary:**
$75,000/$90,000; **Industry Concentration:** Insurance;
Function Concentration: Generalist

Krauser, H. James — *Senior Director*
Spencer Stuart
Financial Centre
695 East Main Street
Stamford, CT 06901
Telephone: (203) 324-6333
Recruiter Classification: Retained; **Lowest/Average Salary:**
$90,000/$90,000; **Industry Concentration:** Financial Services,
Insurance, Venture Capital; **Function Concentration:** Generalist
with a primary focus in Finance/Accounting, General
Management, Marketing

Krecklo, Brian Douglas — *President*
Krecklo & Associates Inc.
Le Cartier, 1115 Sherbrooke Street West
Suite 2401
Montreal, Quebec, CANADA H3A 1H3
Telephone: (514) 281-9999
Recruiter Classification: Retained; **Lowest/Average Salary:**
$60,000/$75,000; **Industry Concentration:** Generalist with a
primary focus in Insurance

Krejci, Stanley L. — *Managing Director and
Partner*
Boyden Washington, D.C.
2445 M Street N.W., Suite 250
Washington, DC 20037-1435
Telephone: (202) 342-7200
Recruiter Classification: Retained; **Lowest/Average Salary:**
$75,000/$90,000; **Industry Concentration:** Generalist with a
primary focus in Financial Services, Venture Capital; **Function
Concentration:** Generalist with a primary focus in Engineering,
Finance/Accounting, General Management, Human Resources,
Marketing, Research and Development, Sales,
Women/Minorities

Kreuch, Paul C. — *Senior Vice President*
Skott/Edwards Consultants, Inc.
500 Fifth Avenue, 26th Floor
New York, NY 10110
Telephone: (212) 382-1166
Recruiter Classification: Retained; **Lowest/Average Salary:**
$90,000/$90,000; **Industry Concentration:** Financial Services;
Function Concentration: Administration, Finance/Accounting,
General Management, Marketing, Sales

Kreuter, Daniel A. — *President*
D.A. Kreuter Associates, Inc.
1100 East Hector Street, Suite 388
Conshohocken, PA 19428
Telephone: (610) 834-1100
Recruiter Classification: Retained; **Lowest/Average Salary:**
$60,000/$90,000; **Industry Concentration:** Financial Services,
Insurance; **Function Concentration:** General Management,
Marketing, Sales

Kreutz, Gary L. — *President*
Kreutz Consulting Group, Inc.
585 North Bank Lane, Suite 2000
Lake Forest, IL 60045
Telephone: (847) 234-9115
Recruiter Classification: Retained; **Lowest/Average Salary:**
$75,000/$150,000; **Industry Concentration:** Generalist with
a primary focus in Financial Services; **Function
Concentration:** Finance/Accounting, General Management,
Marketing, Research and Development, Women/
Minorities

Krick, Terry L. — *Senior Associate*
Financial Resource Associates, Inc.
105 West Orange Street
Altamonte Springs, FL 32714
Telephone: (407) 869-7000
Recruiter Classification: Contingency; **Lowest/Average Salary:**
$40,000/$60,000; **Industry Concentration:** Financial Services;
Function Concentration: Generalist with a primary focus in
Finance/Accounting

Krieger, Dennis F. — *Managing Director*
Seiden Krieger Associates, Inc.
375 Park Avenue
New York, NY 10152
Telephone: (212) 688-8383
Recruiter Classification: Retained; **Lowest/Average Salary:**
$90,000/$90,000; **Industry Concentration:** Generalist with a
primary focus in Venture Capital; **Function Concentration:**
Generalist with a primary focus in Engineering,
Finance/Accounting, General Management, Human Resources,
Marketing, Research and Development, Sales,
Women/Minorities

Krueger, Kurt — *President*
Krueger Associates
100 Skokie Boulevard
Wilmette, IL 60091
Telephone: (847) 853-0550
Recruiter Classification: Retained; **Lowest/Average Salary:**
$90,000/$90,000; **Industry Concentration:** Generalist
with a primary focus in Insurance; **Function
Concentration:** Generalist with a primary focus in
Engineering, Finance/Accounting, General Management,
Human Resources, Marketing, Research and
Development

Kucewicz, William — *Account Executive*
Search West, Inc.
1888 Century Park East
Suite 2050
Los Angeles, CA 90067-1736
Telephone: (310) 284-8888
Recruiter Classification: Contingency; **Lowest/Average
Salary:** $40,000/$60,000; **Industry Concentration:**
Generalist with a primary focus in Insurance; **Function
Concentration:** Generalist with a primary focus in
Administration

Kuhl, Teresa — *Executive Recruiter*
Don Richard Associates of Tampa, Inc.
100 North Tampa Street, Suite 1925
Tampa, FL 33602
Telephone: (813) 221-7930
Recruiter Classification: Contingency, Executive Temporary;
Lowest/Average Salary: $20,000/$50,000; **Industry
Concentration:** Generalist with a primary focus in
Financial Services; **Function Concentration:** Generalist
with a primary focus in Administration, Finance/
Accounting, Human Resources, Research and
Development

Kunzer, William J. — *President*
Kunzer Associates, Ltd.
1415 West 22nd Street
Oak Brook, IL 60521
Telephone: (630) 574-0010
Recruiter Classification: Retained; **Lowest/Average Salary:**
$50,000/$90,000; **Industry Concentration:** Generalist with a
primary focus in Financial Services; **Function Concentration:**
Generalist with a primary focus in Engineering,
Finance/Accounting, General Management, Human
Resources, Marketing, Research and Development,
Sales

Kuo, Linda — *Senior Associate*
Montgomery Resources, Inc.
555 Montgomery Street, Suite 1650
San Francisco, CA 94111
Telephone: (415) 956-4242
Recruiter Classification: Contingency; **Lowest/Average Salary:**
$30,000/$60,000; **Industry Concentration:** Financial Services,
Insurance, Venture Capital; **Function Concentration:**
Finance/Accounting

Kurrigan, Geoffrey — *Partner*
ESA Professional Consultants
141 Durham Road
Suite 16
Madison, CT 06443
Telephone: (203) 245-1983
Recruiter Classification: Retained; **Lowest/Average Salary:**
$50,000/$75,000; **Industry Concentration:** Venture Capital;
Function Concentration: Engineering, General Management,
Human Resources, Marketing, Research and Development,
Women/Minorities

Kussner, Janice N. — *Partner*
Herman Smith Executive Initiatives Inc.
161 Bay Street, Suite 3600
Box 629
Toronto, Ontario, CANADA M5J 2S1
Telephone: (416) 862-8830
Recruiter Classification: Retained; **Lowest/Average Salary:**
$60,000/$75,000; **Industry Concentration:** Generalist with a
primary focus in Financial Services; **Function Concentration:**
Generalist with a primary focus in Engineering,
Finance/Accounting, General Management, Human Resources,
Marketing, Sales

Kvasnicka, Jay Allen — *Consultant Accounting
and Finance*
Morgan Hunter Corp.
6800 College Boulevard, Suite 550
Overland Park, KS 66211
Telephone: (913) 491-3434
Recruiter Classification: Contingency; **Lowest/Average Salary:**
$30,000/$50,000; **Industry Concentration:** Generalist with a
primary focus in Financial Services; **Function Concentration:**
Finance/Accounting

La Chance, Ronald — *Associate*
Source Services Corporation
15600 N.W. 67th Avenue, Suite 210
Miami Lakes, FL 33014
Telephone: (305) 556-8000
Recruiter Classification: Contingency; **Lowest/Average
Salary:** $30,000/$50,000; **Industry Concentration:** Financial
Services; **Function Concentration:** Engineering,
Finance/Accounting

Laba, Marvin — *President*
Marvin Laba & Associates
6255 Sunset Boulevard, Suite 617
Los Angeles, CA 90028
Telephone: (213) 464-1355
Recruiter Classification: Retained; **Lowest/Average Salary:**
$50,000/$75,000; **Industry Concentration:** Generalist with a
primary focus in Financial Services; **Function Concentration:**
Generalist with a primary focus in Finance/Accounting,
General Management, Human Resources, Marketing,
Sales

Laba, Stuart M. — *Senior Vice President*
Marvin Laba & Associates
250 Ridgedale Avenue, Suite #A-1
Florham Park, NJ 07932
Telephone: (201) 966-2888
Recruiter Classification: Retained; **Lowest/Average Salary:**
$50,000/$90,000; **Industry Concentration:** Generalist with a
primary focus in Financial Services; **Function Concentration:**
Generalist with a primary focus in Finance/Accounting,
General Management, Human Resources,
Sales

Labrecque, Bernard F. — *Managing Partner*
Laurendeau Labrecque/Ray & Berndtson, Inc.
1250 West Rene-Levesque Boulevard
Suite 3925
Montreal, Quebec, CANADA H3B 4W8
Telephone: (514) 937-1000
Recruiter Classification: Retained; **Lowest/Average Salary:**
$75,000/$90,000; **Industry Concentration:** Generalist with a
primary focus in Venture Capital; **Function Concentration:**
Finance/Accounting, General Management, Human Resources,
Marketing, Research and Development, Sales

Lachance, Roger — *Partner*
Laurendeau Labrecque/Ray & Berndtson, Inc.
1250 West Rene-Levesque Boulevard
Suite 3925
Montreal, Quebec, CANADA H3B 4W8
Telephone: (514) 937-1000
Recruiter Classification: Retained; **Lowest/Average Salary:**
$75,000/$90,000; **Industry Concentration:** Generalist with a
primary focus in Financial Services; **Function Concentration:**
Administration, Engineering, Finance/Accounting, General
Management, Human Resources, Marketing

Lache, Shawn E. — *Associate*
The Arcus Group
100 North Central (At Main), Suite 1200
Dallas, TX 75201
Telephone: (214) 744-2100
Recruiter Classification: Retained; **Lowest/Average Salary:**
$90,000/$90,000; **Industry Concentration:** Generalist with a
primary focus in Financial Services, Insurance, Venture Capital;
Function Concentration: Generalist with a primary focus in
Engineering, Finance/Accounting, General Management,
Marketing, Research and Development, Sales

Lacoste, Daniel — *Partner*
The Caldwell Partners Amrop International
1840 Sherbrooke Street West
Montreal, Quebec, CANADA H3H 1E4
Telephone: (514) 935-6969
Recruiter Classification: Retained; **Lowest/Average Salary:**
$60,000/$90,000; **Industry Concentration:** Generalist with a
primary focus in Financial Services; **Function Concentration:**
Generalist

Laderman, David — *Manager*
Romac & Associates
530 East Swedesford Road
Suite 202
Wayne, PA 19087
Telephone: (215) 687-6107
Recruiter Classification: Executive Temporary; **Lowest/Average
Salary:** $60,000/$60,000; **Industry Concentration:** Financial
Services, Insurance; **Function Concentration:**
Finance/Accounting

Laird, Cheryl — *Executive Recruiter*
CPS Inc.
One Westbrook Corporate Centre, Suite 600
Westchester, IL 60154
Telephone: (708) 531-8370
Recruiter Classification: Contingency; **Lowest/Average Salary:**
$30,000/$50,000; **Industry Concentration:** Generalist with a
primary focus in Financial Services, Insurance; **Function
Concentration:** Engineering, Research and Development,
Sales, Women/Minorities

Lamb, Angus K. — *Principal*
Raymond Karsan Associates
18 Commerce Way
Woburn, MA 01801
Telephone: (617) 932-0400
Recruiter Classification: Retained; **Lowest/Average Salary:**
$30,000/$90,000; **Industry Concentration:** Generalist with a
primary focus in Insurance; **Function Concentration:**
Generalist

Lamb, Peter S. — *Banking and Trust Recruiter*
Executive Resource, Inc.
553 South Industrial Drive
P.O. Box 356
Hartland, WI 53029-0356
Telephone: (414) 369-2540
Recruiter Classification: Contingency; **Lowest/Average Salary:**
$40,000/$60,000; **Industry Concentration:** Financial Services;
Function Concentration: Generalist with a primary focus in
Finance/Accounting

Lambert, William — *Associate*
Source Services Corporation
525 Vine Street, Suite 2250
Cincinnati, OH 45202
Telephone: (513) 651-3303
Recruiter Classification: Contingency; **Lowest/Average Salary:**
$30,000/$50,000; **Industry Concentration:** Financial Services;
Function Concentration: Engineering, Finance/Accounting

Lamia, Michael — *Associate*
Source Services Corporation
15600 N.W. 67th Avenue, Suite 210
Miami Lakes, FL 33014
Telephone: (305) 556-8000
Recruiter Classification: Contingency; **Lowest/Average Salary:**
$30,000/$50,000; **Industry Concentration:** Financial Services;
Function Concentration: Engineering, Finance/Accounting

Landan, Joy — *Executive Recruiter*
Jacobson Associates
150 North Wacker Drive
Suite 1120
Chicago, IL 60606
Telephone: (312) 726-1578
Recruiter Classification: Contingency; **Lowest/Average Salary:**
$20,000/$50,000; **Industry Concentration:** Insurance;
Function Concentration: Generalist

Lang, Sharon A. — *Consultant*
Ray & Berndtson
Sears Tower, 233 South Wacker Drive, Suite 4020
Chicago, IL 60606-6310
Telephone: (312) 876-0730
Recruiter Classification: Retained; **Lowest/Average Salary:**
$90,000/$90,000; **Industry Concentration:** Generalist with a
primary focus in Financial Services, Insurance; **Function
Concentration:** Generalist with a primary focus in
Administration, Finance/Accounting, General Management,
Human Resources, Marketing, Research and Development,
Sales, Women/Minorities

Lannamann, Richard S. — *Managing Director*
Russell Reynolds Associates, Inc.
200 Park Avenue
New York, NY 10166-0002
Telephone: (212) 351-2000
Recruiter Classification: Retained; **Lowest/Average Salary:**
$90,000/$90,000; **Industry Concentration:** Generalist with a
primary focus in Financial Services; **Function Concentration:**
Generalist

Lapat, Aaron D. — *Associate*
J. Robert Scott
27 State Street
Boston, MA 02109
Telephone: (617) 720-2770
Recruiter Classification: Retained; **Lowest/Average Salary:**
$75,000/$90,000; **Industry Concentration:** Generalist with a
primary focus in Financial Services; **Function Concentration:**
Generalist

LaPierre, Louis — *Managing Partner*
Romac & Associates
183 Middle Street, 3rd Floor
P.O. Box 7040
Portland, ME 04112
Telephone: (207) 773-4749
Recruiter Classification: Executive Temporary; **Lowest/Average
Salary:** $60,000/$60,000; **Industry Concentration:** Financial
Services, Insurance; **Function Concentration:**
Finance/Accounting

Lapointe, Fabien — *Associate*
Source Services Corporation
1500 West Park Drive, Suite 390
Westborough, MA 01581
Telephone: (508) 366-2600
Recruiter Classification: Contingency; **Lowest/Average Salary:**
$30,000/$50,000; **Industry Concentration:** Financial Services;
Function Concentration: Engineering, Finance/Accounting

Lardner, Lucy D. — *Consultant*
Tully/Woodmansee International, Inc.
9 Woody Lane
Sparta, NJ 07871
Telephone: (201) 726-8645
Recruiter Classification: Retained; **Lowest/Average Salary:**
$60,000/$90,000; **Industry Concentration:** Generalist with a
primary focus in Financial Services; **Function Concentration:**
Generalist with a primary focus in Engineering,
Finance/Accounting, General Management, Human Resources,
Marketing, Research and Development, Sales

Larsen, Bruce — *Manager Insurance/Healthcare
and Banking*
Prestige Inc.
P.O. Box 421
Reedsburg, WI 53959
Telephone: (608) 524-4032
Recruiter Classification: Contingency; **Lowest/Average Salary:**
$50,000/$90,000; **Industry Concentration:** Financial Services,
Insurance; **Function Concentration:** Generalist

Larsen, Richard F. — *President*
Larsen, Whitney, Blecksmith & Zilliacus
888 West 6th Street, Suite 500
Los Angeles, CA 90017
Telephone: (213) 243-0033
Recruiter Classification: Retained; **Lowest/Average Salary:**
$75,000/$90,000; **Industry Concentration:** Financial Services,
Insurance; **Function Concentration:** Generalist with a primary
focus in Finance/Accounting, General Management

Lasher, Charles M. — *President*
Lasher Associates
1200 South Pine Island Road, Suite 370
Fort Lauderdale, FL 33324-4402
Telephone: (305) 472-5658
Recruiter Classification: Retained; **Lowest/Average Salary:**
$75,000/$90,000; **Industry Concentration:** Generalist with a
primary focus in Financial Services, Insurance, Venture Capital;
Function Concentration: Generalist with a primary focus in
Engineering, Finance/Accounting, General Management, Human
Resources, Marketing, Research and Development, Sales

Laskin, Sandy — *Associate*
Source Services Corporation
925 Westchester Avenue, Suite 309
White Plains, NY 10604
Telephone: (914) 428-9100
Recruiter Classification: Contingency; **Lowest/Average Salary:**
$30,000/$50,000; **Industry Concentration:** Financial Services;
Function Concentration: Engineering, Finance/Accounting

Lauderback, David R. — *Vice President*
A.T. Kearney, Inc.
1200 Bank One Center
600 Superior Avenue, East
Cleveland, OH 44114-2650
Telephone: (216) 241-6880
Recruiter Classification: Retained; **Lowest/Average Salary:**
$90,000/$90,000; **Industry Concentration:** Generalist with a
primary focus in Financial Services; **Function Concentration:**
Generalist with a primary focus in Finance/Accounting,
General Management, Marketing, Sales

Laurendeau, Jean E. — *Partner*
Laurendeau Labrecque/Ray & Berndtson, Inc.
1250 West Rene-Levesque Boulevard
Suite 3925
Montreal, Quebec, CANADA H3B 4W8
Telephone: (514) 937-1000
Recruiter Classification: Retained; **Lowest/Average Salary:**
$75,000/$90,000; **Industry Concentration:** Generalist with a
primary focus in Financial Services, Insurance; **Function
Concentration:** Administration, Finance/Accounting, General
Management, Human Resources, Marketing

Lautz, Lindsay A. — *Partner*
Lautz Grotte Engler
One Bush Street, Suite 550
San Francisco, CA 94104
Telephone: (415) 834-3100
Recruiter Classification: Retained; **Lowest/Average Salary:**
$90,000/$90,000; **Industry Concentration:** Generalist with a
primary focus in Financial Services, Venture Capital; **Function
Concentration:** Generalist with a primary focus in
Administration, Engineering, Finance/Accounting, General
Management, Human Resources, Marketing, Sales,
Women/Minorities

LaValle, Michael — *Managing Partner*
Romac & Associates
Two Piedmont Plaza, Suite 701
2000 West First Street
Winston-Salem, NC 27104-4206
Telephone: (919) 725-1933
Recruiter Classification: Executive Temporary; **Lowest/Average
Salary:** $60,000/$60,000; **Industry Concentration:** Financial
Services, Insurance; **Function Concentration:**
Finance/Accounting

Laverty, William — *Associate*
Source Services Corporation
525 Vine Street, Suite 2250
Cincinnati, OH 45202
Telephone: (513) 651-3303
Recruiter Classification: Contingency; **Lowest/Average Salary:**
$30,000/$50,000; **Industry Concentration:** Financial Services;
Function Concentration: Engineering, Finance/Accounting

Lawrance, Susanne — *Specialist Insurance/Legal*
Sharrow & Associates
24735 Van Dyke
Center Line, MI 48015
Telephone: (810) 759-6910
Recruiter Classification: Contingency; **Lowest/Average Salary:**
$20,000/$40,000; **Industry Concentration:** Insurance;
Function Concentration: Administration, General
Management, Sales

Lazar, Miriam — *Associate*
Source Services Corporation
120 East Baltimore Street, Suite 1950
Baltimore, MD 21202
Telephone: (410) 727-4050
Recruiter Classification: Contingency; **Lowest/Average Salary:**
$30,000/$50,000; **Industry Concentration:** Financial Services;
Function Concentration: Engineering, Finance/Accounting

Lazaro, Alicia C. — *Managing Director*
The Whitney Group
850 Third Avenue, 11th Floor
New York, NY 10022
Telephone: (212) 508-3500
Recruiter Classification: Retained; **Lowest/Average Salary:**
$90,000/$90,000; **Industry Concentration:** Financial Services,
Venture Capital; **Function Concentration:** Generalist with a
primary focus in Finance/Accounting, General Management,
Marketing, Sales

Leahy, Jan — *Executive Recruiter*
CPS Inc.
One Westbrook Corporate Centre, Suite 600
Westchester, IL 60154
Telephone: (708) 531-8370
Recruiter Classification: Contingency; **Lowest/Average Salary:**
$30,000/$50,000; **Industry Concentration:** Generalist with a
primary focus in Financial Services, Insurance; **Function
Concentration:** Engineering, Research and Development,
Sales, Women/Minorities

Leblanc, Danny — *Associate*
Source Services Corporation
5429 LBJ Freeway, Suite 275
Dallas, TX 75240
Telephone: (214) 387-1600
Recruiter Classification: Contingency; **Lowest/Average Salary:**
$30,000/$50,000; **Industry Concentration:** Financial Services;
Function Concentration: Engineering, Finance/Accounting

LeComte, Andre — *Consultant*
Egon Zehnder International Inc.
1 Place Ville-Marie, Suite 3310
Montreal, Quebec, CANADA H3B 3N2
Telephone: (514) 876-4249
Recruiter Classification: Retained; **Lowest/Average Salary:**
$90,000/$90,000; **Industry Concentration:** Generalist with a
primary focus in Financial Services; **Function Concentration:**
Generalist

Ledbetter, Steven G. — *Executive Recruiter*
Cendea Connection International
13740 Research Boulevard
Building 0-1
Austin, TX 78750
Telephone: (512) 219-6000
Recruiter Classification: Retained; **Lowest/Average Salary:**
$75,000/$90,000; **Industry Concentration:** Generalist with a
primary focus in Venture Capital; **Function Concentration:**
Generalist with a primary focus in General Management,
Marketing, Sales

Lee, Everett — *Associate*
Source Services Corporation
5429 LBJ Freeway, Suite 275
Dallas, TX 75240
Telephone: (214) 387-1600
Recruiter Classification: Contingency; **Lowest/Average
Salary:** $30,000/$50,000; **Industry Concentration:** Financial
Services; **Function Concentration:** Engineering,
Finance/Accounting

Lee, Roger — *Partner*
Montgomery Resources, Inc.
555 Montgomery Street, Suite 1650
San Francisco, CA 94111
Telephone: (415) 956-4242
Recruiter Classification: Contingency, Executive Temporary;
Lowest/Average Salary: $30,000/$60,000; **Industry
Concentration:** Generalist with a primary focus in Financial
Services, Insurance, Venture Capital; **Function Concentration:**
Finance/Accounting

Leetma, Imbi — *Principal*
Stanton Chase International
10866 Wilshire Boulevard
Suite 870
Los Angeles, CA 90024
Telephone: (310) 474-1029
Recruiter Classification: Retained; **Lowest/Average Salary:**
$75,000/$90,000; **Industry Concentration:** Generalist with a
primary focus in Insurance, Venture Capital; **Function
Concentration:** Generalist with a primary focus in
Finance/Accounting, General Management, Human Resources,
Marketing, Sales

Leigh, Rebecca — *Associate*
Source Services Corporation
9020 Capital of Texas Highway
Building I, Suite 337
Austin, TX 78759
Telephone: (512) 345-7473
Recruiter Classification: Contingency; **Lowest/Average
Salary:** $30,000/$50,000; **Industry Concentration:** Financial
Services; **Function Concentration:** Engineering,
Finance/Accounting

Leighton, Mark — *Associate*
Source Services Corporation
1500 West Park Drive, Suite 390
Westborough, MA 01581
Telephone: (508) 366-2600
Recruiter Classification: Contingency; **Lowest/Average
Salary:** $30,000/$50,000; **Industry Concentration:** Financial
Services; **Function Concentration:** Engineering,
Finance/Accounting

Leighton, Nina — *Recruiter*
The Ogdon Partnership
375 Park Avenue, Suite 2409
New York, NY 10152-0175
Telephone: (212) 308-1600
Recruiter Classification: Retained; **Lowest/Average Salary:**
$90,000/$90,000; **Industry Concentration:** Generalist with a
primary focus in Insurance, Venture Capital; **Function
Concentration:** Generalist with a primary focus in Engineering,
Finance/Accounting, General Management, Human Resources,
Marketing, Sales

Leininger, Dennis — *Executive Vice
President/General Manager*
Key Employment Services
1001 Office Park Road, Suite 320
West Des Moines, IA 50265-2567
Telephone: (515) 224-0446
Recruiter Classification: Contingency; **Lowest/Average Salary:**
$30,000/$75,000; **Industry Concentration:** Financial Services,
Insurance; **Function Concentration:** Engineering,
Finance/Accounting, General Management, Human Resources,
Marketing, Research and Development, Sales, Women/Minorities

Lence, Julie Anne — *Unit Manager*
MSI International
201 St. Charles Avenue
Suite 2205
New Orleans, LA 70170
Telephone: (504) 522-6700
Recruiter Classification: Contingency; **Lowest/Average Salary:**
$30,000/$60,000; **Industry Concentration:** Generalist with a
primary focus in Financial Services; **Function Concentration:**
Generalist with a primary focus in Administration, Engineering,
Finance/Accounting, General Management, Marketing, Sales

Lennox, Charles — *Director*
Price Waterhouse
Suite 3000, Box 82 Royal Trust Tower
Toronto Dominion Centre
Toronto, Ontario, CANADA M5K 1G8
Telephone: (416) 863-1133
Recruiter Classification: Retained; **Lowest/Average Salary:**
$60,000/$90,000; **Industry Concentration:** Generalist with a
primary focus in Financial Services; **Function Concentration:**
Generalist

Leonard, Linda — *Senior Associate*
Harris Heery & Associates
40 Richards Avenue
One Norwalk West
Norwalk, CT 06854
Telephone: (203) 857-0808
Recruiter Classification: Retained; **Lowest/Average Salary:**
$75,000/$90,000; **Industry Concentration:** Financial Services,
Insurance; **Function Concentration:** General Management,
Marketing

Leslie, William H. — *Consultant*
Boyden/Zay & Company
Two Midtown Plaza, Suite 1740
1360 Peachtree Street, NE
Atlanta, GA 30309-3214
Telephone: (404) 876-9986
Recruiter Classification: Retained; **Lowest/Average Salary:**
$90,000/$90,000; **Industry Concentration:** Generalist with a
primary focus in Financial Services, Insurance, Venture Capital;
Function Concentration: Generalist with a primary focus in
Administration, Engineering, Finance/Accounting, General
Management, Human Resources, Marketing

Letcher, Harvey D. — *Partner*
Sandhurst Associates
4851 LBJ Freeway, Suite 601
Dallas, TX 75244
Telephone: (214) 458-1212
Recruiter Classification: Retained; Lowest/Average Salary:
$75,000/$90,000; Industry Concentration: Generalist with a
primary focus in Financial Services, Insurance; Function
Concentration: Generalist with a primary focus in
Finance/Accounting, Human Resources, Marketing, Sales

Levenson, Laurel — *Managing Director*
Source Services Corporation
4510 Executive Drive, Suite 200
San Diego, CA 92121
Telephone: (619) 552-0300
Recruiter Classification: Contingency; Lowest/Average Salary:
$30,000/$50,000; Industry Concentration: Financial Services;
Function Concentration: Engineering, Finance/Accounting

Levine, Alan M. — *President*
MB Inc. Interim Executive Division
505 Fifth Avenue
New York, NY 10017
Telephone: (212) 661-4937
Recruiter Classification: Executive Temporary; Lowest/Average
Salary: $75,000/$90,000; Industry Concentration: Generalist
with a primary focus in Financial Services; Function
Concentration: Finance/Accounting, General Management,
Marketing, Sales

Levine, Irwin — *Associate*
Source Services Corporation
2 Penn Plaza, Suite 1176
New York, NY 10121
Telephone: (212) 760-2200
Recruiter Classification: Contingency; Lowest/Average Salary:
$30,000/$50,000; Industry Concentration: Financial Services;
Function Concentration: Engineering, Finance/Accounting

Levine, Lawrence — *Partner*
Trebor Weldon Lawrence, Inc.
355 Lexington Avenue
New York, NY 10017
Telephone: (212) 867-0066
Recruiter Classification: Retained; Lowest/Average Salary:
$75,000/$90,000; Industry Concentration: Financial Services;
Function Concentration: General Management, Marketing, Sales

Levine, Lois — *Medical Consultant*
National Search, Inc.
2816 University Drive
Coral Springs, FL 33071
Telephone: (800) 935-4355
Recruiter Classification: Contingency; Lowest/Average Salary:
$30,000/$50,000; Industry Concentration: Insurance;
Function Concentration: Generalist with a primary focus in
Administration, Finance/Accounting, General Management,
Human Resources, Marketing, Research and Development,
Sales, Women/Minorities

Levine, Roberta — *Consultant*
Tyler & Company
Chadds Ford Business Campus
Brandywine Two Building, Suite 208
Chadds Ford, PA 19317-9667
Telephone: (610) 558-6100
Recruiter Classification: Retained; Lowest/Average Salary:
$75,000/$90,000; Industry Concentration: Insurance;
Function Concentration: Generalist

Levinson, Lauren — *Partner*
The Danbrook Group, Inc.
14180 Dallas Parkway, Suite 400
Dallas, TX 75240
Telephone: (214) 392-0057
Recruiter Classification: Contingency; Lowest/Average Salary:
$30,000/$50,000; Industry Concentration: Insurance;
Function Concentration: Generalist with a primary focus in
Administration, Finance/Accounting, General Management,
Marketing, Sales

Lewicki, Christopher — *Manager*
MSI International
8521 Leesburg Pike, Suite 435
Vienna, VA 22182
Telephone: (703) 893-5669
Recruiter Classification: Contingency; Lowest/Average Salary:
$30,000/$60,000; Industry Concentration: Generalist with a
primary focus in Financial Services; Function Concentration:
Administration, Engineering, Finance/Accounting, General
Management, Marketing, Sales

Lewis, Daniel — *Associate*
Source Services Corporation
2000 Town Center, Suite 850
Southfield, MI 48075
Telephone: (810) 352-6520
Recruiter Classification: Contingency; Lowest/Average
Salary: $30,000/$50,000; Industry Concentration: Financial
Services; Function Concentration: Engineering,
Finance/Accounting

Lewis, Jon A. — *Associate*
Sandhurst Associates
4851 LBJ Freeway, Suite 601
Dallas, TX 75244
Telephone: (212) 458-1212
Recruiter Classification: Retained; Lowest/Average Salary:
$75,000/$90,000; Industry Concentration: Generalist with
a primary focus in Financial Services, Insurance, Venture
Capital; Function Concentration: Generalist with a
primary focus in Administration, Finance/Accounting,
General Management, Human Resources, Marketing,
Sales

Lewis, Marc D. — *Senior Vice President*
Handy HRM Corp.
250 Park Avenue
New York, NY 10177-0074
Telephone: (212) 557-0400
Recruiter Classification: Retained; Lowest/Average Salary:
$90,000/$90,000; Industry Concentration: Generalist
with a primary focus in Financial Services; Function
Concentration: Finance/Accounting, Women/
Minorities

Lewis, Sean — *Leasing/Finance Specialist*
Southwestern Professional Services
2451 Atrium Way
Nashville, TN 37214
Telephone: (615) 391-2722
Recruiter Classification: Contingency; Lowest/Average Salary:
$90,000/$90,000; Industry Concentration: Generalist with a
primary focus in Financial Services; Function Concentration:
Sales

Lezama Cohen, Luis — *Partner*
Ray & Berndtson
Palo Santo No. 6
Colonia Lomas Altas
Mexico City, D.F., MEXICO 11950
Telephone: (525) 570-7462
Recruiter Classification: Retained; **Lowest/Average Salary:**
$90,000/$90,000; **Industry Concentration:** Generalist with a
primary focus in Financial Services, Insurance; **Function
Concentration:** Generalist with a primary focus in
Administration, Finance/Accounting, General Management,
Human Resources, Marketing, Research and Development,
Sales, Women/Minorities

Liebowitz, Michael E. — *Partner*
Highland Search Group
565 Fifth Avenue, 22nd Floor
New York, NY 10017
Telephone: (212) 328-1113
Recruiter Classification: Retained; **Lowest/Average Salary:**
$90,000/$90,000; **Industry Concentration:** Financial Services;
Function Concentration: Generalist with a primary focus in
Administration, Finance/Accounting, General Management,
Sales, Women/Minorities

Liebross, Eric — *Associate*
Source Services Corporation
1 Gatehall Drive, Suite 250
Parsippany, NJ 07054
Telephone: (201) 267-3222
Recruiter Classification: Contingency; **Lowest/Average
Salary:** $30,000/$50,000; **Industry Concentration:** Financial
Services; **Function Concentration:** Engineering,
Finance/Accounting

Lin, Felix — *Associate*
Source Services Corporation
879 West 190th Street, Suite 250
Los Angeles, CA 90248
Telephone: (310) 323-6633
Recruiter Classification: Contingency; **Lowest/Average
Salary:** $30,000/$50,000; **Industry Concentration:** Financial
Services; **Function Concentration:** Engineering,
Finance/Accounting

Lindberg, Eric J. — *President and CEO*
MSI International
2500 Marquis One Tower
245 Peachtree Center Ave.
Atlanta, GA 30303
Telephone: (404) 659-5236
Recruiter Classification: Contingency; **Lowest/Average Salary:**
$30,000/$60,000; **Industry Concentration:** Generalist with a
primary focus in Financial Services; **Function Concentration:**
Generalist with a primary focus in Administration, Engineering,
Finance/Accounting, General Management, Marketing, Sales

Lindholst, Kai — *Managing Partner*
Egon Zehnder International Inc.
One First National Plaza
21 South Clark Street, Suite 3300
Chicago, IL 60603-2006
Telephone: (312) 782-4500
Recruiter Classification: Retained; **Lowest/Average Salary:**
$90,000/$90,000; **Industry Concentration:** Generalist with a
primary focus in Financial Services; **Function Concentration:**
Generalist

Lindsay, M. Evan — *Partner*
Heidrick & Struggles, Inc.
One Peachtree Center
303 Peachtree Street, NE, Suite 3100
Atlanta, GA 30308
Telephone: (404) 577-2410
Recruiter Classification: Retained; **Lowest/Average Salary:**
$75,000/$90,000; **Industry Concentration:** Generalist with a
primary focus in Financial Services; **Function Concentration:**
Generalist

Line, Joseph T. — *Vice President*
Sharrow & Associates
24735 Van Dyke
Center Line, MI 48015
Telephone: (810) 759-6910
Recruiter Classification: Contingency; **Lowest/Average Salary:**
$30,000/$50,000; **Industry Concentration:** Insurance

Linney, George — *Consultant*
Tyler & Company
c/o Premier 4501 Charlotte Park
Charlotte, NC 28217
Telephone: (704) 529-3358
Recruiter Classification: Retained; **Lowest/Average Salary:**
$75,000/$90,000; **Industry Concentration:** Insurance;
Function Concentration: Generalist

Linton, Leonard M. — *President*
Byron Leonard International, Inc.
2659 Townsgate Road, Suite 100
Westlake Village, CA 91361
Telephone: (805) 373-7500
Recruiter Classification: Retained; **Lowest/Average Salary:**
$60,000/$90,000; **Industry Concentration:** Generalist with a
primary focus in Financial Services; **Function Concentration:**
Generalist with a primary focus in Administration, Engineering,
Finance/Accounting, General Management, Human Resources,
Marketing, Research and Development, Sales

Lipuma, Thomas — *Associate*
Source Services Corporation
1 Gatehall Drive, Suite 250
Parsippany, NJ 07054
Telephone: (201) 267-3222
Recruiter Classification: Contingency; **Lowest/Average Salary:**
$30,000/$50,000; **Industry Concentration:** Financial Services;
Function Concentration: Engineering, Finance/Accounting

Litt, Michele — *Vice President*
The Whitney Group
850 Third Avenue, 11th Floor
New York, NY 10022
Telephone: (212) 508-3500
Recruiter Classification: Retained; **Lowest/Average Salary:**
$90,000/$90,000; **Industry Concentration:** Financial Services,
Venture Capital; **Function Concentration:** Generalist with a
primary focus in Finance/Accounting, General Management,
Marketing, Sales

Little, Elizabeth A. — *Associate*
Financial Resource Associates, Inc.
105 West Orange Street
Altamonte Springs, FL 32714
Telephone: (407) 869-7000
Recruiter Classification: Contingency; **Lowest/Average Salary:**
$40,000/$60,000; **Industry Concentration:** Financial Services;
Function Concentration: Finance/Accounting, Sales

Little, Suzaane — *Executive Recruiter*
Don Richard Associates of Tampa, Inc.
100 North Tampa Street, Suite 1925
Tampa, FL 33602
Telephone: (813) 221-7930
Recruiter Classification: Contingency, Executive Temporary;
Lowest/Average Salary: $20,000/$50,000; **Industry**
Concentration: Generalist with a primary focus in
Financial Services; **Function Concentration:** Generalist
with a primary focus in Administration, Finance/
Accounting

Littman, Stephen — *Managing Partner*
Rhodes Associates
555 Fifth Avenue
New York, NY 10017
Telephone: (212) 983-2000
Recruiter Classification: Retained; **Lowest/Average Salary:**
$100,000/$200,000; **Industry Concentration:** Financial
Services, Insurance, Venture Capital; **Function Concentration:**
Generalist

Livingston, Peter R. — *President*
Livingston, Robert and Company Inc.
Two Greenwich Plaza
Greenwich, CT 06830
Telephone: (203) 622-4901
Recruiter Classification: Retained; **Lowest/Average Salary:**
$90,000/$90,000; **Industry Concentration:** Generalist with a
primary focus in Financial Services; **Function Concentration:**
Generalist

Loeb, Stephen H. — *President*
Grant Cooper and Associates
795 Office Parkway, Suite 117
St. Louis, MO 63141
Telephone: (314) 567-4690
Recruiter Classification: Retained; **Lowest/Average Salary:**
$60,000/$90,000; **Industry Concentration:** Generalist with a
primary focus in Financial Services; **Function Concentration:**
Generalist with a primary focus in Administration, Engineering,
Finance/Accounting, General Management, Human Resources,
Marketing, Sales

Loewenstein, Victor H. — *Managing Partner*
Egon Zehnder International Inc.
350 Park Avenue
New York, NY 10022
Telephone: (212) 838-9199
Recruiter Classification: Retained; **Lowest/Average Salary:**
$90,000/$90,000; **Industry Concentration:** Generalist with a
primary focus in Financial Services; **Function Concentration:**
Generalist

Lofthouse, Cindy — *Executive Recruiter*
CPS Inc.
One Westbrook Corporate Centre, Suite 600
Westchester, IL 60154
Telephone: (708) 531-8370
Recruiter Classification: Contingency; **Lowest/Average**
Salary: $30,000/$50,000; **Industry Concentration:**
Generalist with a primary focus in Financial Services,
Insurance; **Function Concentration:** Engineering,
Research and Development, Sales, Women/
Minorities

Lokken, Karen — *Technical Recruiter*
A.E. Feldman Associates
445 Northern Boulevard
Great Neck, NY 11021
Telephone: (516) 466-4708
Recruiter Classification: Contingency; **Lowest/Average**
Salary: $60,000/$90,000; **Industry Concentration:**
Generalist with a primary focus in Financial Services,
Venture Capital; **Function Concentration:** Generalist with a
primary focus in Administration, General Management,
Marketing, Sales

Lombardi, Nancy W. — *Vice President*
WTW Associates, Inc.
675 Third Avenue, Suite 2808
New York, NY 10017
Telephone: (212) 972-6990
Recruiter Classification: Retained; **Lowest/Average Salary:**
$75,000/$90,000; **Industry Concentration:** Generalist with a
primary focus in Financial Services; **Function Concentration:**
Generalist

Long, Helga — *Partner and Managing Director -
Global Markets*
Horton International
420 Lexington Avenue, Suite 810
New York, NY 10170
Telephone: (212) 973-3780
Recruiter Classification: Retained; **Lowest/Average Salary:**
$90,000/$90,000; **Industry Concentration:** Generalist
with a primary focus in Financial Services; **Function**
Concentration: Generalist with a primary focus in
Finance/Accounting, General Management, Human
Resources, Marketing, Research and Development, Sales,
Women/Minorities

Long, John — *Associate*
Source Services Corporation
4200 West Cypress Street, Suite 101
Tampa, FL 33607
Telephone: (813) 879-2221
Recruiter Classification: Contingency; **Lowest/Average**
Salary: $30,000/$50,000; **Industry Concentration:** Financial
Services; **Function Concentration:** Engineering,
Finance/Accounting

Long, Mark — *Associate*
Source Services Corporation
111 Monument Circle, Suite 3930
Indianapolis, IN 46204
Telephone: (317) 631-2900
Recruiter Classification: Contingency; **Lowest/Average**
Salary: $30,000/$50,000; **Industry Concentration:** Financial
Services; **Function Concentration:** Engineering,
Finance/Accounting

Long, Melanie — *Senior Medical Consultant*
National Search, Inc.
2816 University Drive
Coral Springs, FL 33071
Telephone: (800) 935-4355
Recruiter Classification: Contingency; **Lowest/Average Salary:**
$30,000/$50,000; **Industry Concentration:** Insurance;
Function Concentration: Generalist with a primary focus in
Administration, Finance/Accounting, General Management,
Human Resources, Marketing, Research and Development,
Sales, Women/Minorities

Long, Milt — *Associate*
William Guy & Associates
P.O. Box 57407
Sherman Oaks, CA 91413
Telephone: Unpublished
Recruiter Classification: Retained; **Lowest/Average Salary:**
$50,000/$90,000; **Industry Concentration:** Generalist with a
primary focus in Financial Services, Venture Capital; **Function
Concentration:** Generalist with a primary focus in
Administration, Engineering, General Management, Human
Resources, Women/Minorities

Long, Thomas — *Consultant*
Egon Zehnder International Inc.
1 First Canadian Place
P.O. Box 179
Toronto, Ontario, CANADA M5X 1C7
Telephone: (416) 364-0222
Recruiter Classification: Retained; **Lowest/Average Salary:**
$90,000/$90,000; **Industry Concentration:** Generalist with a
primary focus in Financial Services; **Function Concentration:**
Generalist

Long, William G. — *President*
McDonald, Long & Associates, Inc.
670 White Plains Road
Scarsdale, NY 10583
Telephone: (914) 723-5400
Recruiter Classification: Retained, Executive Temporary;
Lowest/Average Salary: $75,000/$90,000; **Industry
Concentration:** Generalist with a primary focus in Financial
Services, Insurance, Venture Capital; **Function Concentration:**
Generalist with a primary focus in Administration, Engineering,
Finance/Accounting, General Management, Human Resources,
Marketing, Sales, Women/Minorities

Lonneke, John W. — *Executive Recruiter*
MSI International
5215 North O'Connor Boulevard
Suite 1875
Irving, TX 75039
Telephone: (214) 869-3939
Recruiter Classification: Contingency; **Lowest/Average Salary:**
$30,000/$75,000; **Industry Concentration:** Generalist with a
primary focus in Financial Services; **Function Concentration:**
Generalist with a primary focus in Finance/Accounting

Looney, Scott — *Managing Director*
A.E. Feldman Associates
445 Northern Boulevard
Great Neck, NY 11021
Telephone: (516) 466-4708
Recruiter Classification: Contingency; **Lowest/Average Salary:**
$60,000/$90,000; **Industry Concentration:** Generalist with a
primary focus in Financial Services, Venture Capital; **Function
Concentration:** Generalist with a primary focus in
Administration, General Management, Marketing, Sales

Loper, Doris — *Regional Manager*
Mortgage & Financial Personnel Services
5850 Canoga Avenue, Suite 400
Woodland Hills, CA 91367
Telephone: (818) 710-7133
Recruiter Classification: Contingency, Executive Temporary;
Lowest/Average Salary: $30,000/$40,000; **Industry
Concentration:** Financial Services, Insurance; **Function
Concentration:** Finance/Accounting

Lopis, Roberta — *Executive Recruiter*
Richard, Wayne and Roberts
24 Greenway Plaza, Suite 1304
Houston, TX 77046-2493
Telephone: (713) 629-6681
Recruiter Classification: Retained; **Lowest/Average Salary:**
$50,000/$90,000; **Industry Concentration:** Generalist
with a primary focus in Financial Services; **Function
Concentration:** Generalist with a primary focus in
Finance/Accounting

LoPresto, Robert L. — *President - High
Technology*
Rusher, Loscavio & LoPresto
2479 Bayshore Road, Suite 700
Palo Alto, CA 94303
Telephone: (415) 494-0883
Recruiter Classification: Retained; **Lowest/Average Salary:**
$90,000/$90,000; **Industry Concentration:** Venture Capital;
Function Concentration: Administration, Engineering, General
Management, Marketing, Research and Development, Sales

Loscavio, J. Michael — *Executive Vice President*
Rusher, Loscavio & LoPresto
180 Montgomery Street, Suite 1616
San Francisco, CA 94104-4239
Telephone: (415) 765-6600
Recruiter Classification: Retained; **Lowest/Average Salary:**
$75,000/$90,000; **Industry Concentration:** Generalist with a
primary focus in Financial Services, Insurance; **Function
Concentration:** Generalist with a primary focus in General
Management, Research and Development

Lotufo, Donald A. — *Managing Partner*
D.A.L. Associates, Inc.
2777 Summer Street
Stamford, CT 06905
Telephone: (203) 961-8777
Recruiter Classification: Retained; **Lowest/Average Salary:**
$75,000/$90,000; **Industry Concentration:** Generalist with a
primary focus in Financial Services; **Function Concentration:**
Generalist with a primary focus in Administration, Engineering,
Finance/Accounting, General Management, Human Resources,
Marketing, Research and Development, Sales

Lotz, R. James — *Chairman*
International Management Advisors, Inc.
516 Fifth Avenue
New York, NY 10036-7501
Telephone: (212) 758-7770
Recruiter Classification: Retained; **Lowest/Average Salary:**
$75,000/$90,000; **Industry Concentration:** Generalist with a
primary focus in Financial Services; **Function Concentration:**
Generalist with a primary focus in Engineering,
Finance/Accounting, General Management, Human Resources,
Marketing, Research and Development, Women/Minorities

Loubet, Larry — *Partner*
Carlyle Group
625 N. Michigan Avenue
Suite 2100
Chicago, IL 60611
Telephone: (312) 587-3030
Recruiter Classification: Retained; **Lowest/Average Salary:**
$50,000/$90,000; **Industry Concentration:** Generalist with a
primary focus in Financial Services; **Function Concentration:**
Generalist

Lovas, W. Carl — *Managing Partner*
Ray & Berndtson/Lovas Stanley
Royal Bank Plaza, South Tower, Suite 3150
200 Bay Street, P.O. Box 125
Toronto, Ontario, CANADA M5J 2J3
Telephone: (416) 366-1990
Recruiter Classification: Retained; **Lowest/Average Salary:**
$90,000/$90,000; **Industry Concentration:** Generalist with a
primary focus in Financial Services; **Function Concentration:**
Generalist with a primary focus in Finance/Accounting,
General Management

Lovely, Edward — *Senior Vice President*
The Stevenson Group of New Jersey
560 Sylvan Avenue
Englewood Cliffs, NJ 07632
Telephone: (201) 568-1900
Recruiter Classification: Retained; **Lowest/Average Salary:**
$75,000/$90,000; **Industry Concentration:** Generalist with a
primary focus in Financial Services; **Function Concentration:**
Generalist with a primary focus in Finance/Accounting,
General Management, Human Resources, Marketing, Sales

Loving, Vikki — *President*
Intersource, Ltd.
72 Sloan Street
Roswell, GA 30075
Telephone: (770) 645-0015
Recruiter Classification: Retained; **Lowest/Average Salary:**
$90,000/$90,000; **Industry Concentration:** Generalist with a
primary focus in Financial Services, Insurance; **Function
Concentration:** Finance/Accounting, Human Resources,
Women/Minorities

Lucarelli, Joan — *Vice President and Principal*
The Onstott Group, Inc.
60 William Street
Wellesley, MA 02181
Telephone: (781) 235-3050
Recruiter Classification: Retained; **Lowest/Average Salary:**
$90,000/$90,000; **Industry Concentration:** Generalist with a
primary focus in Financial Services; **Function Concentration:**
Generalist with a primary focus in Engineering,
Finance/Accounting, General Management, Human Resources,
Marketing, Research and Development, Sales,
Women/Minorities

Lucas, Ronnie L. — *Manager*
MSI International
5215 North O'Connor Boulevard
Suite 1875
Irving, TX 75039
Telephone: (214) 869-3939
Recruiter Classification: Contingency; **Lowest/Average Salary:**
$30,000/$75,000; **Industry Concentration:** Generalist with a
primary focus in Financial Services; **Function Concentration:**
Generalist with a primary focus in Administration, Engineering,
Finance/Accounting, General Management, Marketing, Sales

Luce, Daniel — *Managing Director*
Source Services Corporation
520 Post Oak Boulevard, Suite 700
Houston, TX 77027
Telephone: (713) 439-1077
Recruiter Classification: Contingency; **Lowest/Average Salary:**
$30,000/$50,000; **Industry Concentration:** Financial Services;
Function Concentration: Engineering, Finance/Accounting

Lucht, John — *President*
The John Lucht Consultancy Inc.
The Olympic Tower
641 Fifth Avenue
New York, NY 10022
Telephone: (212) 935-4660
Recruiter Classification: Retained; **Lowest/Average Salary:**
$150,000/$150,000; **Industry Concentration:** Generalist with a
primary focus in Financial Services, Insurance, Venture Capital;
Function Concentration: Generalist with a primary focus in
Administration, Engineering, Finance/Accounting, General
Management, Human Resources, Marketing, Research and
Development, Sales, Women/Minorities

Ludder, Mark — *Associate*
Source Services Corporation
8614 Westwood Center, Suite 750
Vienna, VA 22182
Telephone: (703) 790-5610
Recruiter Classification: Contingency; **Lowest/Average
Salary:** $30,000/$50,000; **Industry Concentration:** Financial
Services; **Function Concentration:** Engineering,
Finance/Accounting

Ludlow, Michael — *Associate*
Source Services Corporation
One Park Plaza, Suite 560
Irvine, CA 92714
Telephone: (714) 660-1666
Recruiter Classification: Contingency; **Lowest/Average Salary:**
$30,000/$50,000; **Industry Concentration:** Financial Services;
Function Concentration: Engineering, Finance/Accounting

Ludlow, Paula — *Managing Director*
Horton International
420 Lexington Avenue, Suite 810
New York, NY 10170
Telephone: (212) 973-3780
Recruiter Classification: Retained; **Lowest/Average Salary:**
$90,000/$90,000; **Industry Concentration:** Generalist with a
primary focus in Financial Services, Insurance; **Function
Concentration:** Generalist with a primary focus in
Finance/Accounting, General Management, Human Resources,
Marketing, Sales

Lumsby, George N. — *Senior Consultant*
International Management Advisors, Inc.
516 Fifth Avenue
New York, NY 10036-7501
Telephone: (212) 758-7770
Recruiter Classification: Retained; **Lowest/Average Salary:**
$75,000/$90,000; **Industry Concentration:** Generalist with a
primary focus in Financial Services; **Function Concentration:**
Generalist with a primary focus in Engineering,
Finance/Accounting, General Management, Human Resources,
Marketing, Research and Development, Women/Minorities

Lundy, Martin — *Associate*
Source Services Corporation
20 Burlington Mall Road, Suite 405
Burlington, MA 01803
Telephone: (617) 272-5000
Recruiter Classification: Contingency; **Lowest/Average
Salary:** $30,000/$50,000; **Industry Concentration:** Financial
Services; **Function Concentration:** Engineering,
Finance/Accounting

Luntz, Charles E. — *President*
Charles Luntz & Associates. Inc.
14323 South Outer 40 Drive
Suite 400 South
Chesterfield, MO 63017-5734
Telephone: (314) 275-7992
Recruiter Classification: Retained; **Lowest/Average Salary:**
$40,000/$75,000; **Industry Concentration:** Generalist with a
primary focus in Financial Services, Insurance**; Function
Concentration:** Generalist with a primary focus in
Administration, Engineering, Finance/Accounting, General
Management, Human Resources, Marketing, Research and
Development, Sales, Women/Minorities

Lupica, Anthony — *Search Consultant*
Cochran, Cochran & Yale, Inc.
1333 W. 120th Avenue, Suite 311
Westminster, CO 80234
Telephone: (303) 252-4600
Recruiter Classification: Retained; **Lowest/Average Salary:**
$50,000/$75,000; **Industry Concentration:** Generalist with a
primary focus in Financial Services, Venture Capital**; Function
Concentration:** Generalist with a primary focus in Engineering,
Finance/Accounting, General Management, Human Resources,
Marketing, Sales, Women/Minorities

Lynam, Joseph V. — *Chief Financial and
Operations Officer*
Johnson Smith & Knisely Accord
100 Park Avenue, 15th Floor
New York, NY 10017
Telephone: (212) 885-9100
Recruiter Classification: Retained; **Lowest/Average Salary:**
$90,000/$90,000; **Industry Concentration:** Financial Services;
Function Concentration: Finance/Accounting

Lynch, Michael C. — *Managing Director*
Lynch Miller Moore, Inc.
10 South Wacker Drive, Suite 2935
Chicago, IL 60606
Telephone: (312) 876-1505
Recruiter Classification: Retained; **Lowest/Average Salary:**
$75,000/$90,000; **Industry Concentration:** Generalist with a
primary focus in Financial Services, Insurance, Venture Capital;
Function Concentration: Generalist with a primary focus in
Finance/Accounting, General Management, Marketing

Lynch, Sean E. — *Senior Consultant*
Raymond Karsan Associates
170 So. Warner Road
Wayne, PA 19087
Telephone: (610) 971-9171
Recruiter Classification: Retained; **Lowest/Average Salary:**
$30,000/$90,000; **Industry Concentration:** Generalist with a
primary focus in Insurance**; Function Concentration:**
Generalist

Lyon, Jenny — *Vice President*
Marra Peters & Partners
10612 Providence Road, Suite 305
Charlotte, NC 28277
Telephone: (704) 841-8000
Recruiter Classification: Retained; **Lowest/Average Salary:**
$60,000/$90,000; **Industry Concentration:** Generalist with a
primary focus in Financial Services; **Function Concentration:**
Generalist with a primary focus in Administration, Engineering,
Finance/Accounting, General Management, Human Resources,
Marketing, Research and Development, Sales

Lyons, Denis B.K. — *Senior Director*
Spencer Stuart
277 Park Avenue, 29th Floor
New York, NY 10172
Telephone: (212) 336-0200
Recruiter Classification: Retained; **Lowest/Average Salary:**
$90,000/$90,000; **Industry Concentration:** Generalist with a
primary focus in Financial Services; **Function Concentration:**
Generalist with a primary focus in Finance/Accounting,
General Management, Marketing

Lyons, J. David — *Managing Director*
Aubin International Inc.
281 Winter Street, #380
Waltham, MA 02154
Telephone: (617) 890-1722
Recruiter Classification: Retained; **Lowest/Average Salary:**
$90,000/$90,000; **Industry Concentration:** Generalist with a
primary focus in Venture Capital**; Function Concentration:**
Generalist with a primary focus in Engineering,
Finance/Accounting, General Management, Human Resources,
Marketing, Research and Development, Sales

Lyons, Michael — *Associate*
Source Services Corporation
4510 Executive Drive, Suite 200
San Diego, CA 92121
Telephone: (619) 552-0300
Recruiter Classification: Contingency; **Lowest/Average
Salary:** $30,000/$50,000; **Industry Concentration:** Financial
Services; **Function Concentration:** Engineering,
Finance/Accounting

Macan, Sandi — *Consultant*
Caliber Associates
125 Strafford Avenue
Suite 112
Wayne, PA 19087
Telephone: (610) 971-1880
Recruiter Classification: Retained; **Lowest/Average Salary:**
$75,000/$90,000; **Industry Concentration:** Venture Capital;
Function Concentration: Marketing, Research and
Development, Sales

MacCallan, Deirdre — *Principal*
Butterfass, Pepe & MacCallan Inc.
P.O. Box 721
Mahwah, NJ 07430
Telephone: (201) 512-3330
Recruiter Classification: Retained; **Lowest/Average Salary:**
$60,000/$90,000; **Industry Concentration:** Generalist with a
primary focus in Financial Services, Insurance**; Function
Concentration:** Generalist with a primary focus in
Finance/Accounting, General Management, Human Resources,
Women/Minorities

Macdonald, G. William — *President*
The Macdonald Group, Inc.
301 Route 17, Suite 800
Rutherford, NJ 07070
Telephone: (201) 939-2312
Recruiter Classification: Retained; **Lowest/Average Salary:**
$75,000/$90,000; **Industry Concentration:** Generalist with a
primary focus in Financial Services, Venture Capital;
Function Concentration: Generalist with a primary focus in
General Management, Human Resources, Research and
Development

MacDougall, Andrew J. — *Managing Director*
Spencer Stuart
One University Avenue
Suite 801
Toronto, Ontario, CANADA M5J 2P1
Telephone: (416) 361-0311
Recruiter Classification: Retained; **Lowest/Average Salary:** $90,000/$90,000; **Industry Concentration:** Financial Services, Insurance; **Function Concentration:** Generalist

MacIntyre, Lisa W. — *Partner*
Highland Search Group
565 Fifth Avenue, 22nd Floor
New York, NY 10017
Telephone: (212) 328-1113
Recruiter Classification: Retained; **Lowest/Average Salary:** $90,000/$90,000; **Industry Concentration:** Financial Services, Insurance, Venture Capital; **Function Concentration:** Generalist with a primary focus in Administration, Finance/Accounting, General Management, Human Resources, Sales, Women/Minorities

Mackenna, Kathy — *Consultant*
Plummer & Associates, Inc.
65 Rowayton Avenue
Rowayton, CT 06853
Telephone: (203) 899-1233
Recruiter Classification: Retained; **Lowest/Average Salary:** $90,000/$90,000; **Industry Concentration:** Generalist with a primary focus in Venture Capital; **Function Concentration:** Generalist with a primary focus in Administration, Finance/Accounting, General Management, Human Resources, Marketing

MacMillan, James — *Associate*
Source Services Corporation
100 North Tryon Street, Suite 3130
Charlotte, NC 28202
Telephone: (704) 333-8311
Recruiter Classification: Contingency; **Lowest/Average Salary:** $30,000/$50,000; **Industry Concentration:** Financial Services; **Function Concentration:** Engineering, Finance/Accounting

MacNaughton, Sperry — *President and Principal*
McNaughton Associates
3600 Lime Street, Suite 323
Riverside, CA 92501
Telephone: (909) 788-4951
Recruiter Classification: Retained; **Lowest/Average Salary:** $60,000/$90,000; **Industry Concentration:** Generalist with a primary focus in Financial Services; **Function Concentration:** Generalist with a primary focus in Administration, Engineering, Finance/Accounting, Human Resources, Marketing, Sales, Women/Minorities

Macomber, Keith S. — *Consultant*
Sullivan & Company
20 Exchange Place, 50th Floor
New York, NY 10005
Telephone: (212) 422-3000
Recruiter Classification: Retained; **Lowest/Average Salary:** $90,000/$90,000; **Industry Concentration:** Generalist with a primary focus in Financial Services; **Function Concentration:** Generalist

MacPherson, Holly — *Associate*
Source Services Corporation
425 California Street, Suite 1200
San Francisco, CA 94104
Telephone: (415) 434-2410
Recruiter Classification: Contingency; **Lowest/Average Salary:** $30,000/$50,000; **Industry Concentration:** Financial Services; **Function Concentration:** Engineering, Finance/Accounting

Macrides, Michael — *Associate*
Source Services Corporation
20 Burlington Mall Road, Suite 405
Burlington, MA 01803
Telephone: (617) 272-5000
Recruiter Classification: Contingency; **Lowest/Average Salary:** $30,000/$50,000; **Industry Concentration:** Financial Services; **Function Concentration:** Engineering, Finance/Accounting

Madaras, Debra — *Associate*
Financial Resource Associates, Inc.
105 West Orange Street
Altamonte Springs, FL 32714
Telephone: (407) 869-7000
Recruiter Classification: Contingency; **Lowest/Average Salary:** $40,000/$60,000; **Industry Concentration:** Financial Services; **Function Concentration:** Finance/Accounting

Maer, Harry — *Vice President, New York*
Kenzer Corp.
777 Third Avenue, 26th Floor
New York, NY 10017
Telephone: (212) 308-4300
Recruiter Classification: Retained; **Lowest/Average Salary:** $50,000/$90,000; **Industry Concentration:** Financial Services, Venture Capital; **Function Concentration:** Generalist with a primary focus in Administration, Finance/Accounting, General Management, Human Resources, Marketing, Research and Development, Sales

Magee, Harrison R. — *Vice President*
Bowden & Company, Inc.
5000 Rockside Road, Suite 550
Cleveland, OH 44131
Telephone: (216) 447-1800
Recruiter Classification: Retained; **Lowest/Average Salary:** $90,000/$90,000; **Industry Concentration:** Generalist with a primary focus in Financial Services, Insurance, Venture Capital; **Function Concentration:** Generalist

Maggio, Mary — *Associate*
Source Services Corporation
925 Westchester Avenue, Suite 309
White Plains, NY 10604
Telephone: (914) 428-9100
Recruiter Classification: Contingency; **Lowest/Average Salary:** $30,000/$50,000; **Industry Concentration:** Financial Services; **Function Concentration:** Engineering, Finance/Accounting

Maglio, Charles J. — *President*
Maglio and Company, Inc.
450 N. Sunny Slope Road
Brookfield, WI 53005
Telephone: (414) 784-6020
Recruiter Classification: Retained; **Lowest/Average Salary:** $50,000/$90,000; **Industry Concentration:** Generalist with a primary focus in Insurance; **Function Concentration:** Generalist with a primary focus in Engineering, Finance/Accounting, General Management, Human Resources, Marketing, Research and Development, Sales

Mahmoud, Sophia — *Associate*
Source Services Corporation
425 California Street, Suite 1200
San Francisco, CA 94104
Telephone: (415) 434-2410
Recruiter Classification: Contingency; **Lowest/Average Salary:**
$30,000/$50,000; **Industry Concentration:** Financial Services;
Function Concentration: Engineering, Finance/Accounting

Mahr, Toni — *Senior Consultant*
K. Russo Associates
2 Greenwich Plaza, Suite 100
Greenwich, CT 06830
Telephone: (203) 622-3903
Recruiter Classification: Retained; **Lowest/Average Salary:**
$30,000/$90,000; **Industry Concentration:** Financial Services,
Insurance; **Function Concentration:** Human Resources

Mainwaring, Andrew Brian — *Senior Consultant*
Executive Search Consultants Corporation
8 South Michigan Avenue, Suite 1205
Chicago, IL 60603
Telephone: (312) 251-8400
Recruiter Classification: Contingency; **Lowest/Average Salary:**
$40,000/$60,000; **Industry Concentration:** Generalist with a
primary focus in Insurance; **Function Concentration:**
Generalist with a primary focus in Administration,
Finance/Accounting, Human Resources, Women/Minorities

Mairn, Todd — *Associate*
Source Services Corporation
161 Ottawa NW, Suite 409D
Grand Rapids, MI 49503
Telephone: (616) 451-2400
Recruiter Classification: Contingency; **Lowest/Average Salary:**
$30,000/$50,000; **Industry Concentration:** Financial Services;
Function Concentration: Engineering, Finance/Accounting

Major, Susan — *Vice President*
A.T. Kearney, Inc.
222 West Adams Street
Chicago, IL 60606
Telephone: (312) 648-0111
Recruiter Classification: Retained; **Lowest/Average Salary:**
$90,000/$90,000; **Industry Concentration:** Generalist with a
primary focus in Financial Services; **Function Concentration:**
Generalist with a primary focus in Engineering,
Finance/Accounting, General Management

Makrianes, James K. — *Managing Director*
Webb, Johnson Associates, Inc.
280 Park Avenue, 43rd Floor
New York, NY 10017
Telephone: (212) 661-3700
Recruiter Classification: Retained; **Lowest/Average Salary:**
$90,000/$90,000; **Industry Concentration:** Generalist with a
primary focus in Financial Services; **Function Concentration:**
Generalist

Malcolm, Rod — *Vice President*
Korn/Ferry International
Scotia Plaza
40 King Street West
Toronto, Ontario, CANADA M5H 3Y2
Telephone: (416) 366-1300
Recruiter Classification: Retained; **Lowest/Average Salary:**
$100,000/$150,000; **Industry Concentration:** Generalist with a
primary focus in Financial Services, Insurance; **Function
Concentration:** Generalist

Mallin, Ellen — *Vice President*
Howard Fischer Associates, Inc.
1800 John F. Kennedy Boulevard, 7th Floor
Philadelphia, PA 19103
Telephone: (215) 568-8363
Recruiter Classification: Retained; **Lowest/Average Salary:**
$90,000/$90,000; **Industry Concentration:** Generalist with a
primary focus in Financial Services, Insurance, Venture Capital;
Function Concentration: Generalist with a primary focus in
Administration, Finance/Accounting, General Management,
Human Resources, Marketing, Research and Development,
Sales, Women/Minorities

Manassero, Henri J.P. — *Partner Hospitality*
International Management Advisors, Inc.
516 Fifth Avenue
New York, NY 10036-7501
Telephone: (212) 758-7770
Recruiter Classification: Retained; **Lowest/Average Salary:**
$75,000/$90,000; **Industry Concentration:** Generalist with a
primary focus in Financial Services; **Function Concentration:**
Generalist with a primary focus in Engineering,
Finance/Accounting, General Management, Human Resources,
Marketing, Research and Development, Women/Minorities

Mancino, Gene — *President*
Blau Mancino Schroeder
12 Roszel Road, Suite C-101
Princeton, NJ 08540
Telephone: (609) 520-8400
Recruiter Classification: Retained; **Lowest/Average Salary:**
$75,000/$75,000; **Industry Concentration:** Venture Capital;
Function Concentration: General Management, Marketing,
Research and Development

Mangum, Maria — *Vice President*
Thomas Mangum Company
1655 Hastings Ranch Drive
Pasadena, CA 91107
Telephone: (818) 351-0866
Recruiter Classification: Retained; **Lowest/Average Salary:**
$75,000/$100,000; **Industry Concentration:** Generalist with a
primary focus in Financial Services; **Function Concentration:**
Generalist with a primary focus in Administration, Engineering,
Finance/Accounting, General Management, Human Resources,
Marketing, Research and Development

Mangum, William T. — *President*
Thomas Mangum Company
1655 Hastings Ranch Drive
Pasadena, CA 91107
Telephone: (818) 351-0866
Recruiter Classification: Retained; **Lowest/Average Salary:**
$75,000/$100,000; **Industry Concentration:** Generalist with a
primary focus in Financial Services; **Function Concentration:**
Generalist with a primary focus in Administration, Engineering,
Finance/Accounting, General Management, Human Resources,
Marketing, Research and Development

Manns, Alex — *Executive Recruiter*
Crawford & Crofford
15327 NW 60th Avenue, Suite 240
Miami Lakes, FL 33014
Telephone: (305) 820-0855
Recruiter Classification: Contingency; **Lowest/Average Salary:**
$20,000/$50,000; **Industry Concentration:** Generalist with a
primary focus in Financial Services; **Function Concentration:**
Generalist with a primary focus in Administration, Engineering,
Finance/Accounting, General Management, Human Resources,
Marketing, Sales

Mansford, Keith — *Chairman Bio-Pharmaceutical Division*
Howard Fischer Associates, Inc.
1800 John F. Kennedy Boulevard, 7th Floor
Philadelphia, PA 19103
Telephone: (215) 568-8363
Recruiter Classification: Retained; **Lowest/Average Salary:** $90,000/$90,000; **Industry Concentration:** Financial Services, Insurance, Venture Capital; **Function Concentration:** Generalist with a primary focus in Administration, Finance/Accounting, General Management, Human Resources, Marketing, Research and Development, Sales, Women/Minorities

Manzo, Renee — *Consultant*
Atlantic Search Group, Inc.
One Liberty Square
Boston, MA 02109
Telephone: (617) 426-9700
Recruiter Classification: Contingency; **Lowest/Average Salary:** $20,000/$60,000; **Industry Concentration:** Generalist with a primary focus in Financial Services; **Function Concentration:** Finance/Accounting

Maphet, Harriet — *Vice President*
The Stevenson Group of New Jersey
560 Sylvan Avenue
Englewood Cliffs, NJ 07632
Telephone: (201) 568-1900
Recruiter Classification: Retained; **Lowest/Average Salary:** $75,000/$90,000; **Industry Concentration:** Generalist with a primary focus in Financial Services; **Function Concentration:** Generalist with a primary focus in Finance/Accounting, General Management, Human Resources, Marketing, Sales

Marino, Chester — *Manager*
Cochran, Cochran & Yale, Inc.
1333 W. 120th Avenue, Suite 311
Westminster, CO 80234
Telephone: (303) 252-4600
Recruiter Classification: Retained; **Lowest/Average Salary:** $50,000/$75,000; **Industry Concentration:** Generalist with a primary focus in Financial Services, Venture Capital; **Function Concentration:** Generalist with a primary focus in Engineering, Finance/Accounting, General Management, Human Resources, Marketing, Sales, Women/Minorities

Marino, Jory J. — *Managing Director*
Sullivan & Company
20 Exchange Place, 50th Floor
New York, NY 10005
Telephone: (212) 422-3000
Recruiter Classification: Retained; **Lowest/Average Salary:** $90,000/$90,000; **Industry Concentration:** Generalist with a primary focus in Financial Services; **Function Concentration:** Generalist

Mark, John L. — *Principal*
J.L. Mark Associates, Inc.
2000 Arapahoe Street, Suite 505
Denver, CO 80205
Telephone: (303) 292-0360
Recruiter Classification: Retained; **Lowest/Average Salary:** $60,000/$90,000; **Industry Concentration:** Generalist with a primary focus in Financial Services, Insurance; **Function Concentration:** Generalist with a primary focus in Administration, Finance/Accounting, General Management, Human Resources, Marketing, Research and Development, Sales, Women/Minorities

Mark, Lynne — *Partner*
J.L. Mark Associates, Inc.
2000 Arapahoe Street, Suite 505
Denver, CO 80205
Telephone: (303) 292-0360
Recruiter Classification: Retained; **Lowest/Average Salary:** $60,000/$90,000; **Industry Concentration:** Generalist with a primary focus in Financial Services, Insurance; **Function Concentration:** Generalist with a primary focus in Administration, Finance/Accounting, General Management, Human Resources, Marketing, Research and Development, Sales, Women/Minorities

Marks, Ira — *Principal*
Strategic Alternatives
3 Portola Road
Portola Valley, CA 94028
Telephone: (415) 851-2211
Recruiter Classification: Retained; **Lowest/Average Salary:** $75,000/$90,000; **Industry Concentration:** Generalist with a primary focus in Venture Capital; **Function Concentration:** Generalist with a primary focus in Engineering, General Management, Marketing, Research and Development, Sales, Women/Minorities

Marks, Russell E. — *Managing Director*
Webb, Johnson Associates, Inc.
280 Park Avenue, 43rd Floor
New York, NY 10017
Telephone: (212) 661-3700
Recruiter Classification: Retained; **Lowest/Average Salary:** $90,000/$90,000; **Industry Concentration:** Generalist with a primary focus in Financial Services; **Function Concentration:** Generalist with a primary focus in Administration, Engineering, Finance/Accounting, General Management, Human Resources, Marketing, Research and Development, Sales

Marks, Sarah J. — *Principal*
The Executive Source
55 Fifth Avenue, 19th Floor
New York, NY 10003
Telephone: (212) 691-5505
Recruiter Classification: Executive Temporary; **Lowest/Average Salary:** $75,000/$90,000; **Industry Concentration:** Financial Services, Insurance, Venture Capital; **Function Concentration:** Human Resources

Marra, John — *Partner*
Marra Peters & Partners
7040 West Palmetto Park Road, Suite 145
Boca Raton, FL 33433
Telephone: (407) 347-7778
Recruiter Classification: Retained; **Lowest/Average Salary:** $60,000/$90,000; **Industry Concentration:** Generalist with a primary focus in Financial Services; **Function Concentration:** Generalist with a primary focus in Administration, Engineering, Finance/Accounting, General Management, Human Resources, Marketing, Research and Development, Sales

Marra, John — *Partner*
Marra Peters & Partners
Millburn Esplanade
Millburn, NJ 07041
Telephone: (201) 376-8999
Recruiter Classification: Retained; **Lowest/Average Salary:** $60,000/$90,000; **Industry Concentration:** Generalist with a primary focus in Financial Services; **Function Concentration:** Generalist with a primary focus in Administration, Engineering, Finance/Accounting, General Management, Human Resources, Marketing, Research and Development, Sales

Marshall, E. Leigh — *Managing Director*
Norman Broadbent International, Inc.
200 Park Avenue, 20th Floor
New York, NY 10166
Telephone: (212) 953-6990
Recruiter Classification: Retained; **Lowest/Average Salary:**
$90,000/$90,000; **Industry Concentration:** Financial
Services; **Function Concentration:** Finance/
Accounting

Marsteller, Franklin D. — *Director*
Spencer Stuart
2005 Market Street, Suite 2350
Philadelphia, PA 19103
Telephone: (215) 851-6200
Recruiter Classification: Retained; **Lowest/Average Salary:**
$90,000/$90,000; **Industry Concentration:**
Financial Services, Insurance; **Function
Concentration:** Generalist

Martin, Jon — *Consultant*
Egon Zehnder International Inc.
1 First Canadian Place
P.O. Box 179
Toronto, Ontario, CANADA M5X 1C7
Telephone: (416) 364-0222
Recruiter Classification: Retained; **Lowest/Average Salary:**
$90,000/$90,000; **Industry Concentration:** Generalist with a
primary focus in Financial Services; **Function Concentration:**
Generalist

Marumoto, William H. — *Managing Director and
Partner*
Boyden Washington, D.C.
2445 M Street N.W., Suite 250
Washington, DC 20037-1435
Telephone: (202) 342-7200
Recruiter Classification: Retained; **Lowest/Average Salary:**
$75,000/$90,000; **Industry Concentration:** Generalist
with a primary focus in Financial Services, Venture
Capital; **Function Concentration:** Generalist with a
primary focus in Engineering, Finance/Accounting,
General Management, Human Resources, Marketing,
Research and Development, Sales, Women/
Minorities

Marwil, Jennifer — *Associate*
Source Services Corporation
One South Main Street, Suite 1440
Dayton, OH 45402
Telephone: (513) 461-4660
Recruiter Classification: Contingency; **Lowest/Average
Salary:** $30,000/$50,000; **Industry Concentration:** Financial
Services; **Function Concentration:** Engineering,
Finance/Accounting

Mashakas, Elizabeth — *Legal Consultant*
TOPAZ Legal Solutions
383 Northfield Avenue
West Orange, NJ 07052
Telephone: (201) 669-7300
Recruiter Classification: Executive Temporary; **Lowest/Average
Salary:** $40,000/$75,000; **Industry Concentration:** Financial
Services; **Function Concentration:** Generalist with a primary
focus in Women/Minorities

Mashakas, Elizabeth — *Legal Consultant*
TOPAZ International, Inc.
383 Northfield Avenue
West Orange, NJ 07052
Telephone: (201) 669-7300
Recruiter Classification: Contingency; **Lowest/Average Salary:**
$40,000/$75,000; **Industry Concentration:** Financial Services;
Function Concentration: Generalist with a primary focus in
Women/Minorities

Masserman, Bruce — *President*
Masserman & Associates, Inc.
191 Post Road West
Westport, CT 06880
Telephone: (203) 221-2870
Recruiter Classification: Retained; **Lowest/Average Salary:**
$60,000/$75,000; **Industry Concentration:** Generalist with a
primary focus in Financial Services, Insurance, Venture
Capital

Massey, R. Bruce — *Managing Director*
Horton International
330 Bay Street, Suite 1104
Toronto, Ontario, CANADA M5H 2S8
Telephone: (416) 861-0077
Recruiter Classification: Retained; **Lowest/Average Salary:**
$90,000/$90,000; **Industry Concentration:** Generalist with a
primary focus in Financial Services, Insurance, Venture
Capital; **Function Concentration:** Generalist with a primary
focus in Finance/Accounting, General Management, Human
Resources, Marketing, Research and Development,
Sales

Mather, David R. — *Vice President*
Christian & Timbers
20833 Stevens Creek Boulevard, Suite 200
Cupertino, CA 95014
Telephone: (408) 446-5440
Recruiter Classification: Retained; **Lowest/Average Salary:**
$90,000/$90,000; **Industry Concentration:** Generalist with a
primary focus in Venture Capital; **Function Concentration:**
Generalist with a primary focus in Engineering,
Finance/Accounting, General Management, Human
Resources, Marketing, Research and Development,
Sales

Mathias, Douglas — *Managing Director*
Source Services Corporation
10220 SW Greenburg Road, Suite 625
Portland, OR 97223
Telephone: (503) 768-4546
Recruiter Classification: Contingency; **Lowest/Average Salary:**
$30,000/$50,000; **Industry Concentration:** Financial Services;
Function Concentration: Engineering, Finance/Accounting

Mathias, Kathy — *Managing Director*
Stone Murphy & Olson
5500 Wayzata Boulevard
Suite 1020
Minneapolis, MN 55416
Telephone: (612) 591-2300
Recruiter Classification: Retained; **Lowest/Average Salary:**
$75,000/$90,000; **Industry Concentration:** Generalist with a
primary focus in Financial Services, Insurance; **Function
Concentration:** Generalist with a primary focus in Engineering,
Finance/Accounting, General Management, Human Resources,
Marketing, Sales, Women/Minorities

Mathis, Carrie — *Associate*
Source Services Corporation
5429 LBJ Freeway, Suite 275
Dallas, TX 75240
Telephone: (214) 387-1600
Recruiter Classification: Contingency; **Lowest/Average Salary:**
$30,000/$50,000; **Industry Concentration:** Financial Services;
Function Concentration: Engineering, Finance/Accounting

Mattes, Edward C. — *Recruiter*
The Ogdon Partnership
375 Park Avenue, Suite 2409
New York, NY 10152-0175
Telephone: (212) 308-1600
Recruiter Classification: Retained; **Lowest/Average Salary:**
$90,000/$90,000; **Industry Concentration:** Generalist with a
primary focus in Financial Services, Insurance, Venture Capital;
Function Concentration: Generalist with a primary focus in
Finance/Accounting, General Management, Marketing, Sales

Matthews, Corwin — *Associate*
Woodworth International Group
620 SW 5th Avenue, Suite 1225
Portland, OR 97204
Telephone: (503) 225-5000
Recruiter Classification: Retained; **Lowest/Average Salary:**
$60,000/$90,000; **Industry Concentration:** Generalist with a
primary focus in Financial Services, Insurance, Venture Capital;
Function Concentration: Generalist with a primary focus in
Engineering, Finance/Accounting, General Management, Human
Resources, Marketing, Research and Development, Sales

Matthews, Mary — *Principal*
Korn/Ferry International
237 Park Avenue
New York, NY 10017
Telephone: (212) 687-1834
Recruiter Classification: Retained; **Lowest/Average Salary:**
$100,000/$150,000; **Industry Concentration:** Generalist with a
primary focus in Financial Services, Insurance; **Function
Concentration:** Generalist

Mattingly, Kathleen — *Managing Director*
Source Services Corporation
2850 National City Tower
Louisville, KY 40202
Telephone: (502) 581-9900
Recruiter Classification: Contingency; **Lowest/Average Salary:**
$30,000/$50,000; **Industry Concentration:** Financial Services;
Function Concentration: Engineering, Finance/Accounting

Matueny, Robert — *Executive Recruiter*
Ryan, Miller & Associates Inc.
4601 Wilshire Boulevard, Suite 225
Los Angeles, CA 90010
Telephone: (213) 938-4768
Recruiter Classification: Contingency; **Lowest/Average Salary:**
$40,000/$50,000; **Industry Concentration:** Financial Services;
Function Concentration: Finance/Accounting

Mauer, Kristin — *Senior Associate*
Montgomery Resources, Inc.
555 Montgomery Street, Suite 1650
San Francisco, CA 94111
Telephone: (415) 956-4242
Recruiter Classification: Contingency; **Lowest/Average Salary:**
$30,000/$60,000; **Industry Concentration:** Financial Services,
Insurance, Venture Capital; **Function Concentration:**
Finance/Accounting

Maxwell, John — *Associate*
Source Services Corporation
1500 West Park Drive, Suite 390
Westborough, MA 01581
Telephone: (508) 366-2600
Recruiter Classification: Contingency; **Lowest/Average
Salary:** $30,000/$50,000; **Industry Concentration:** Financial
Services; **Function Concentration:** Engineering,
Finance/Accounting

Mayer, Thomas — *Associate*
Source Services Corporation
3 Summit Park Drive, Suite 550
Independence, OH 44131
Telephone: (216) 328-5900
Recruiter Classification: Contingency; **Lowest/Average
Salary:** $30,000/$50,000; **Industry Concentration:** Financial
Services; **Function Concentration:** Engineering,
Finance/Accounting

Mayes, Kay H. — *Director*
John Shell Associates, Inc.
115 Atrium Way, Suite 122
Columbia, SC 29223
Telephone: (803) 788-6619
Recruiter Classification: Contingency, Executive Temporary;
Lowest/Average Salary: $20,000/$40,000; **Industry
Concentration:** Generalist with a primary focus in Financial
Services, Insurance; **Function Concentration:**
Finance/Accounting

Maynard Taylor, Susan — *Executive Recruiter*
Chrisman & Company, Incorporated
350 South Figueroa Street, Suite 550
Los Angeles, CA 90071
Telephone: (213) 620-1192
Recruiter Classification: Retained; **Lowest/Average Salary:**
$75,000/$90,000; **Industry Concentration:** Generalist with a
primary focus in Financial Services, Insurance, Venture Capital;
Function Concentration: Generalist with a primary focus in
Finance/Accounting, General Management, Human Resources,
Marketing, Women/Minorities

Mazor, Elly — *Consultant*
Howard Fischer Associates, Inc.
1800 John F. Kennedy Boulevard, 7th Floor
Philadelphia, PA 19103
Telephone: (215) 568-8363
Recruiter Classification: Retained; **Lowest/Average Salary:**
$90,000/$90,000; **Industry Concentration:** Generalist with a
primary focus in Financial Services, Insurance, Venture Capital;
Function Concentration: Generalist with a primary focus in
Administration, Finance/Accounting, General Management,
Human Resources, Marketing, Research and Development,
Sales, Women/Minorities

Mazza, David B. — *Partner*
Mazza & Riley, Inc. (a Korn/Ferry International
affiliate)
55 William Street, Suite 120
Wellesley, MA 02181-4000
Telephone: (617) 235-7724
Recruiter Classification: Retained; **Lowest/Average Salary:**
$90,000/$90,000; **Industry Concentration:** Generalist with a
primary focus in Financial Services, Venture Capital;
Function Concentration: Generalist with a primary focus in
Finance/Accounting, General Management, Marketing,
Sales

Mazzuckelli, Katie — *Vice President*
Tyler & Company
1000 Abernathy Road
Suite 1400
Atlanta, GA 30328-5655
Telephone: (770) 396-3939
Recruiter Classification: Retained; **Lowest/Average Salary:**
$75,000/$90,000; **Industry Concentration:** Insurance;
Function Concentration: Generalist

McAndrews, Kathy — *Executive Recruiter*
CPS Inc.
One Westbrook Corporate Centre, Suite 600
Westchester, IL 60154
Telephone: (708) 531-8370
Recruiter Classification: Contingency; **Lowest/Average Salary:**
$30,000/$50,000; **Industry Concentration:** Generalist with a
primary focus in Financial Services, Insurance; **Function
Concentration:** Engineering, Research and Development,
Sales, Women/Minorities

McAteer, Thomas — *Partner*
Montgomery Resources, Inc.
555 Montgomery Street, Suite 1650
San Francisco, CA 94111
Telephone: (415) 956-4242
Recruiter Classification: Contingency, Executive Temporary;
Lowest/Average Salary: $30,000/$60,000; **Industry
Concentration:** Generalist with a primary focus in Financial
Services, Insurance, Venture Capital; **Function Concentration:**
Finance/Accounting

McBride, Jonathan E. — *President*
McBride Associates, Inc.
1511 K Street N.W., Suite 819
Washington, DC 20005
Telephone: (202) 638-1150
Recruiter Classification: Retained; **Lowest/Average Salary:**
$150,000/$150,000; **Industry Concentration:** Generalist
with a primary focus in Financial Services, Insurance,
Venture Capital; **Function Concentration:** Generalist
with a primary focus in Administration, Finance/
Accounting, General Management, Human Resources,
Marketing, Research and Development, Sales,
Women/Minorities

McBryde, Marnie — *Senior Director*
Spencer Stuart
277 Park Avenue, 29th Floor
New York, NY 10172
Telephone: (212) 336-0200
Recruiter Classification: Retained; **Lowest/Average Salary:**
$50,000/$75,000; **Industry Concentration:** Generalist
with a primary focus in Financial Services; **Function
Concentration:** Generalist with a primary focus in
Finance/Accounting, General Management,
Marketing, Sales

McCabe, Christopher — *Consultant*
Raymond Karsan Associates
2001 Westside Drive, Suite 130
Alpharetta, GA 30201
Telephone: (770) 442-8771
Recruiter Classification: Retained; **Lowest/Average Salary:**
$30,000/$90,000; **Industry Concentration:** Generalist with a
primary focus in Insurance; **Function Concentration:**
Generalist

McCallister, Richard A. — *Managing Director*
Boyden
2 Prudential Plaza, Suite 2500
180 North Stetson Avenue
Chicago, IL 60601
Telephone: (312) 565-1300
Recruiter Classification: Retained; **Lowest/Average Salary:**
$75,000/$90,000; **Industry Concentration:** Financial Services;
Function Concentration: Generalist with a primary focus in
Engineering, Finance/Accounting, General Management,
Human Resources, Marketing, Research and Development,
Sales, Women/Minorities

McCann, Cornelia B. — *Director*
Spencer Stuart
2005 Market Street, Suite 2350
Philadelphia, PA 19103
Telephone: (215) 851-6200
Recruiter Classification: Retained; **Lowest/Average Salary:**
$90,000/$90,000; **Industry Concentration:** Financial Services,
Venture Capital; **Function Concentration:** Generalist

McCarthy, Laura — *Associate*
Source Services Corporation
8614 Westwood Center, Suite 750
Vienna, VA 22182
Telephone: (703) 790-5610
Recruiter Classification: Contingency; **Lowest/Average Salary:**
$30,000/$50,000; **Industry Concentration:** Financial Services;
Function Concentration: Engineering, Finance/Accounting

McCarty, J. Rucker — *Partner*
Heidrick & Struggles, Inc.
One Peachtree Center
303 Peachtree Street, NE, Suite 3100
Atlanta, GA 30308
Telephone: (404) 577-2410
Recruiter Classification: Retained; **Lowest/Average Salary:**
$75,000/$90,000; **Industry Concentration:** Generalist with a
primary focus in Financial Services; **Function Concentration:**
Generalist

McClearen, V. Bruce — *Vice President*
Tyler & Company
1000 Abernathy Road
Suite 1400
Atlanta, GA 30328-5655
Telephone: (770) 396-3939
Recruiter Classification: Retained; **Lowest/Average Salary:**
$75,000/$90,000; **Industry Concentration:** Insurance;
Function Concentration: Generalist

McClement, John — *Principal*
Korn/Ferry International
237 Park Avenue
New York, NY 10017
Telephone: (212) 687-1834
Recruiter Classification: Retained; **Lowest/Average Salary:**
$100,000/$150,000; **Industry Concentration:** Generalist with a
primary focus in Financial Services; **Function Concentration:**
Generalist

McCloskey, Frank D. — *Managing Director*
Johnson Smith & Knisely Accord
181 West Madison Street, Suite 4850
Chicago, IL 60602
Telephone: (312) 920-9400
Recruiter Classification: Retained; **Lowest/Average Salary:**
$90,000/$90,000; **Industry Concentration:** Financial Services;
Function Concentration: Engineering, Finance/Accounting,
General Management, Human Resources, Marketing, Sales

McConnell, Greg — *Branch Manager/Information Technology Recruiter*
Winter, Wyman & Company
1100 Circle 75 Parkway, Suite 800
Atlanta, GA 30339
Telephone: (770) 933-1525
Recruiter Classification: Contingency; **Lowest/Average Salary:** $30,000/$60,000; **Industry Concentration:** Generalist with a primary focus in Financial Services, Insurance; **Function Concentration:** Generalist

McCool, Anne G. — *Senior Vice President*
Sullivan & Company
20 Exchange Place, 50th Floor
New York, NY 10005
Telephone: (212) 422-3000
Recruiter Classification: Retained; **Lowest/Average Salary:** $90,000/$90,000; **Industry Concentration:** Generalist with a primary focus in Financial Services, Insurance; **Function Concentration:** Generalist

McCormick, Brian — *Executive Vice President*
The McCormick Group, Inc.
1400 Wilson Boulevard
Arlington, VA 22209
Telephone: (703) 841-1700
Recruiter Classification: Retained; **Lowest/Average Salary:** $50,000/$90,000; **Industry Concentration:** Financial Services, Insurance; **Function Concentration:** Engineering, Finance/Accounting, General Management, Human Resources, Marketing, Sales

McCormick, Harry B. — *Partner*
Hayden Group, Incorporated
One Post Office Square
Suite 3830
Boston, MA 02109
Telephone: (617) 482-2445
Recruiter Classification: Retained; **Lowest/Average Salary:** $90,000/$90,000; **Industry Concentration:** Financial Services

McCormick, Joseph — *Associate*
Source Services Corporation
111 Founders Plaza, Suite 1501E
Hartford, CT 06108
Telephone: (860) 528-0300
Recruiter Classification: Contingency; **Lowest/Average Salary:** $30,000/$50,000; **Industry Concentration:** Financial Services; **Function Concentration:** Engineering, Finance/Accounting

McCreary, Charles "Chip" — *President*
Austin-McGregor International
12005 Ford Road, Suite 720
Dallas, TX 75234-7247
Telephone: (972) 488-0500
Recruiter Classification: Retained; **Lowest/Average Salary:** $50,000/$90,000; **Industry Concentration:** Generalist with a primary focus in Venture Capital; **Function Concentration:** Generalist with a primary focus in Engineering, Finance/Accounting, General Management, Human Resources, Marketing, Research and Development, Sales, Women/Minorities

McDermott, Jeffrey T. — *Consultant*
Vlcek & Company, Inc.
620 Newport Center Drive
Suite 1100
Newport Beach, CA 92660
Telephone: (714) 752-0661
Recruiter Classification: Retained; **Lowest/Average Salary:** $90,000/$90,000; **Industry Concentration:** Generalist with a primary focus in Financial Services; **Function Concentration:** Generalist with a primary focus in Engineering, Finance/Accounting, General Management, Human Resources, Marketing, Sales, Women/Minorities

McDermott, Richard A. — *Partner*
Ray & Berndtson
Sears Tower, 233 South Wacker Drive, Suite 4020
Chicago, IL 60606-6310
Telephone: (312) 876-0730
Recruiter Classification: Retained; **Lowest/Average Salary:** $90,000/$90,000; **Industry Concentration:** Insurance; **Function Concentration:** Generalist

McDonald, Scott A. — *Partner*
McDonald Associates International
234 Washington Road
Rye, NH 03870
Telephone: (603) 433-6295
Recruiter Classification: Retained; **Lowest/Average Salary:** $60,000/$90,000; **Industry Concentration:** Generalist with a primary focus in Financial Services, Insurance; **Function Concentration:** Generalist with a primary focus in Administration, Engineering, Finance/Accounting, General Management, Marketing, Sales, Women/Minorities

McDonald, Stanleigh B. — *Partner*
McDonald Associates International
1290 N. Western Avenue
Suite 209
Lake Forest, IL 60045
Telephone: (708) 234-6889
Recruiter Classification: Retained; **Lowest/Average Salary:** $60,000/$90,000; **Industry Concentration:** Generalist with a primary focus in Financial Services, Insurance; **Function Concentration:** Generalist with a primary focus in Administration, Engineering, Finance/Accounting, General Management, Human Resources, Marketing, Sales, Women/Minorities

McDowell, Robert N. — *Partner*
Christenson & Hutchison
466 Southern Boulevard
Chatham, NJ 07928-1462
Telephone: (201) 966-1600
Recruiter Classification: Retained; **Lowest/Average Salary:** $75,000/$90,000; **Industry Concentration:** Generalist with a primary focus in Financial Services, Insurance; **Function Concentration:** Generalist with a primary focus in Finance/Accounting, General Management, Human Resources, Marketing, Sales

McFadden, Ashton S. — *Partner*
Johnson Smith & Knisely Accord
100 Park Avenue, 15th Floor
New York, NY 10017
Telephone: (212) 885-9100
Recruiter Classification: Retained; **Lowest/Average Salary:** $90,000/$90,000; **Industry Concentration:** Financial Services, Insurance, Venture Capital; **Function Concentration:** Generalist with a primary focus in Administration, Finance/Accounting, General Management, Human Resources, Marketing, Research and Development, Sales

McFadzen,, James A. — *President*
Holland, McFadzean & Associates, Inc.
2901 Tasman Drive
Suite 204
Santa Clara, CA 95054
Telephone: (408) 496-0775
Recruiter Classification: Retained; **Lowest/Average Salary:**
$90,000/$90,000; **Industry Concentration:** Financial Services;
Function Concentration: Generalist with a primary focus in
Engineering, Finance/Accounting, General Management, Human
Resources, Marketing, Research and Development, Sales

McGinnis, Rita — *Associate*
Source Services Corporation
5429 LBJ Freeway, Suite 275
Dallas, TX 75240
Telephone: (214) 387-1600
Recruiter Classification: Contingency; **Lowest/Average Salary:**
$30,000/$50,000; **Industry Concentration:** Financial Services;
Function Concentration: Engineering, Finance/Accounting

McGoldrick, Terrence — *Associate*
Source Services Corporation
One South Main Street, Suite 1440
Dayton, OH 45402
Telephone: (513) 461-4660
Recruiter Classification: Contingency; **Lowest/Average Salary:**
$30,000/$50,000; **Industry Concentration:** Financial Services;
Function Concentration: Engineering, Finance/Accounting

McGuire, Pat — *Professional Recruiter*
A.J. Burton Group, Inc.
4550 Montgomery Avenue, Ste. 325 North
Bethesda, MD 20814
Telephone: (301) 654-0082
Recruiter Classification: Contingency; **Lowest/Average Salary:**
$40,000/$75,000; **Industry Concentration:** Generalist with a
primary focus in Financial Services, Insurance; **Function
Concentration:** Generalist with a primary focus in
Administration, Finance/Accounting, General Management,
Human Resources

McHugh, Keith — *Associate*
Source Services Corporation
879 West 190th Street, Suite 250
Los Angeles, CA 90248
Telephone: (310) 323-6633
Recruiter Classification: Contingency; **Lowest/Average Salary:**
$30,000/$50,000; **Industry Concentration:** Financial Services;
Function Concentration: Engineering, Finance/Accounting

McIntosh, Arthur — *Associate*
Source Services Corporation
5429 LBJ Freeway, Suite 275
Dallas, TX 75240
Telephone: (214) 387-1600
Recruiter Classification: Contingency; **Lowest/Average Salary:**
$30,000/$50,000; **Industry Concentration:** Financial Services;
Function Concentration: Engineering, Finance/Accounting

McIntosh, Tad — *Associate*
Source Services Corporation
5429 LBJ Freeway, Suite 275
Dallas, TX 75240
Telephone: (214) 387-1600
Recruiter Classification: Contingency; **Lowest/Average Salary:**
$30,000/$50,000; **Industry Concentration:** Financial Services;
Function Concentration: Engineering, Finance/Accounting

McKeown, Patricia A. — *Partner*
DiMarchi Partners, Inc.
1225 17th Street, Suite 1460
Denver, CO 80202
Telephone: (303) 292-9300
Recruiter Classification: Retained; **Lowest/Average Salary:**
$90,000/$90,000; **Industry Concentration:** Generalist
with a primary focus in Financial Services, Insurance,
Venture Capital; **Function Concentration:** Generalist
with a primary focus in Finance/Accounting, General
Management, Human Resources, Marketing, Sales,
Women/Minorities

McKinney, Julia — *Associate*
Source Services Corporation
100 North Tryon Street, Suite 3130
Charlotte, NC 28202
Telephone: (704) 333-8311
Recruiter Classification: Contingency; **Lowest/Average
Salary:** $30,000/$50,000; **Industry Concentration:** Financial
Services; **Function Concentration:** Engineering,
Finance/Accounting

McKnight, Amy E. — *Director*
Chartwell Partners International, Inc.
275 Battery Street, Suite 2180
San Francisco, CA 94111
Telephone: (415) 296-0600
Recruiter Classification: Retained; **Lowest/Average Salary:**
$90,000/$90,000; **Industry Concentration:** Generalist
with a primary focus in Financial Services; **Function
Concentration:** Generalist with a primary focus in
Finance/Accounting, Marketing, Sales, Women/
Minorities

McLaughlin, John — *Managing Partner*
Romac & Associates
180 Montgomery Street
Suite 1860
San Francisco, CA 94104
Telephone: (415) 788-2815
Recruiter Classification: Executive Temporary; **Lowest/Average
Salary:** $60,000/$60,000; **Industry Concentration:** Financial
Services, Insurance; **Function Concentration:**
Finance/Accounting

McLean, B. Keith — *Partner*
Price Waterhouse
Suite 3000, Box 82 Royal Trust Tower
Toronto Dominion Centre
Toronto, Ontario, CANADA M5K 1G8
Telephone: (416) 863-1133
Recruiter Classification: Retained; **Lowest/Average Salary:**
$90,000/$90,000; **Industry Concentration:** Generalist with a
primary focus in Insurance; **Function Concentration:**
Generalist

McLean, E. Peter — *Senior Director*
Spencer Stuart
277 Park Avenue, 29th Floor
New York, NY 10172
Telephone: (212) 336-0200
Recruiter Classification: Retained; **Lowest/Average Salary:**
$90,000/$90,000; **Industry Concentration:** Generalist with a
primary focus in Financial Services; **Function Concentration:**
Generalist with a primary focus in Finance/Accounting,
General Management

McMahan, Stephen — *Managing Director*
Source Services Corporation
71 Spit Brook Road, Suite 305
Nashua, NH 03060
Telephone: (603) 888-7650
Recruiter Classification: Contingency; **Lowest/Average Salary:**
$30,000/$50,000; **Industry Concentration:** Financial Services;
Function Concentration: Engineering, Finance/Accounting

McMahan, Stephen — *Managing Director*
Source Services Corporation
155 Federal Street, Suite 410
Boston, MA 02110
Telephone: (617) 482-8211
Recruiter Classification: Contingency; **Lowest/Average Salary:**
$30,000/$50,000; **Industry Concentration:** Financial Services;
Function Concentration: Engineering, Finance/Accounting

McManners, Donald E. — *President*
McManners Associates, Inc.
2525 Ontario Drive
San Jose, CA 95124
Telephone: (408) 559-9232
Recruiter Classification: Retained; **Lowest/Average Salary:**
$90,000/$90,000; **Industry Concentration:** Generalist with a
primary focus in Insurance, Venture Capital; **Function
Concentration:** Generalist with a primary focus in
Administration, Engineering, General Management, Human
Resources, Marketing, Research and Development,
Women/Minorities

McManus, Paul — *Principal*
Aubin International Inc.
281 Winter Street, #380
Waltham, MA 02154
Telephone: (617) 890-1722
Recruiter Classification: Retained; **Lowest/Average Salary:**
$90,000/$90,000; **Industry Concentration:** Generalist with a
primary focus in Venture Capital; **Function Concentration:**
Generalist

McMillin, Bob — *Director*
Price Waterhouse
601 West Hastings Street
Suite 1400
Vancouver, British Columbia, CANADA V6B 5A5
Telephone: (604) 682-4711
Recruiter Classification: Retained; **Lowest/Average Salary:**
$75,000/$75,000; **Industry Concentration:** Generalist with a
primary focus in Financial Services, Insurance; **Function
Concentration:** Generalist with a primary focus in
Administration, Engineering, Finance/Accounting, General
Management, Human Resources, Marketing, Sales

McNamara, Catherine — *Consultant*
Ray & Berndtson
Texas Commerce Tower
2200 Ross Avenue, Suite 4500W
Dallas, TX 75201
Telephone: (214) 969-7620
Recruiter Classification: Retained; **Lowest/Average Salary:**
$90,000/$90,000; **Industry Concentration:** Generalist with a
primary focus in Financial Services, Insurance; **Function
Concentration:** Generalist with a primary focus in
Administration, Finance/Accounting, General Management,
Human Resources, Marketing, Research and Development,
Sales, Women/Minorities

McNamara, Timothy C. — *Managing Director*
Columbia Consulting Group
20 South Charles Street, 9th Floor
Baltimore, MD 21201
Telephone: (410) 385-2525
Recruiter Classification: Retained; **Lowest/Average Salary:**
$75,000/$90,000; **Industry Concentration:** Generalist with a
primary focus in Financial Services, Insurance, Venture Capital;
Function Concentration: Generalist with a primary focus in
Engineering, Finance/Accounting, Human Resources,
Marketing, Research and Development

McNamara, Timothy Connor — *Managing
Director*
Horton International
111 S. Calvert Street, Suite 2700
Baltimore, MD 21202-3200
Telephone: (410) 385-5244
Recruiter Classification: Retained; **Lowest/Average Salary:**
$90,000/$90,000; **Industry Concentration:** Financial Services;
Function Concentration: Administration, Engineering, General
Management, Human Resources, Marketing

McNear, Jeffrey E. — *Operations
Manager/Barrettemps Search Division*
Barrett Partners
100 North LaSalle Street, Suite 1420
Chicago, IL 60602
Telephone: (312) 443-8877
Recruiter Classification: Contingency; **Lowest/Average Salary:**
$30,000/$50,000; **Industry Concentration:** Financial Services,
Insurance; **Function Concentration:** Engineering,
Finance/Accounting

McNichols, Walter B. — *Vice President*
Gary Kaplan & Associates
201 South Lake Avenue
Suite 600
Pasadena, CA 91101
Telephone: (818) 796-8100
Recruiter Classification: Retained; **Lowest/Average Salary:**
$75,000/$90,000; **Industry Concentration:** Generalist with a
primary focus in Financial Services, Insurance; **Function
Concentration:** Generalist with a primary focus in Engineering,
Finance/Accounting, General Management, Human Resources,
Marketing, Research and Development

McNulty, Kelly L. — *Consultant*
Gregory Michaels and Associates, Inc.
8410 West Bryn Mawr Avenue
Suite 400
Chicago, IL 60631
Telephone: (773) 380-1333
Recruiter Classification: Retained; **Lowest/Average Salary:**
$90,000/$90,000; **Industry Concentration:** Generalist with a
primary focus in Financial Services; **Function Concentration:**
Generalist with a primary focus in Finance/Accounting,
General Management, Human Resources, Marketing, Sales

McPherson, Stephen M. — *Managing Director*
Ward Howell International, Inc.
99 Park Avenue, Suite 2000
New York, NY 10016-1699
Telephone: (212) 697-3730
Recruiter Classification: Retained; **Lowest/Average Salary:**
$75,000/$90,000; **Industry Concentration:** Financial Services;
Function Concentration: Generalist

McQuoid, David — *Vice President*
A.T. Kearney, Inc.
8500 Normandale Lake Boulevard
Suite 1630
Minneapolis, MN 55437
Telephone: (612) 921-8436
Recruiter Classification: Retained; **Lowest/Average Salary:**
$90,000/$90,000; **Industry Concentration:** Generalist with a
primary focus in Financial Services; **Function Concentration:**
Generalist with a primary focus in Administration,
Finance/Accounting, Human Resources

McSherry, James F. — *Senior Vice President*
Midwest Region
Battalia Winston International
180 North Wacker Drive, Suite 600
Chicago, IL 60606
Telephone: (312) 704-0050
Recruiter Classification: Retained; **Lowest/Average Salary:**
$90,000/$90,000; **Industry Concentration:** Generalist with a
primary focus in Insurance, Venture Capital; **Function
Concentration:** Generalist with a primary focus in General
Management, Human Resources, Sales, Women/Minorities

Mead, James D. — *President*
James Mead & Company
164 Kings Highway North
Westport, CT 06880
Telephone: (203) 454-5544
Recruiter Classification: Retained; **Lowest/Average Salary:**
$90,000/$90,000; **Industry Concentration:** Venture Capital;
Function Concentration: General Management, Marketing,
Sales

Mead-Fox, David — *Vice President Healthcare*
Korn/Ferry International
One International Place
Boston, MA 02110-1800
Telephone: (617) 345-0200
Recruiter Classification: Retained; **Lowest/Average Salary:**
$100,000/$150,000; **Industry Concentration:** Generalist with a
primary focus in Financial Services, Insurance; **Function
Concentration:** Generalist

Meadows, C. David — *Managing Director*
Professional Staffing Consultants
1331 Lamar, Suite 1459
Houston, TX 77010
Telephone: (713) 659-8383
Recruiter Classification: Retained; **Lowest/Average Salary:**
$50,000/$75,000; **Industry Concentration:** Generalist with a
primary focus in Financial Services; **Function Concentration:**
Generalist with a primary focus in Engineering,
Finance/Accounting, General Management, Human
Resources

Meagher, Patricia G. — *Director*
Spencer Stuart
401 North Michigan Avenue, Suite 3400
Chicago, IL 60611-4244
Telephone: (312) 822-0080
Recruiter Classification: Retained; **Lowest/Average Salary:**
$90,000/$90,000; **Industry Concentration:** Generalist with a
primary focus in Insurance; **Function Concentration:**
Generalist with a primary focus in Administration,
Finance/Accounting, General Management, Human Resources,
Marketing, Sales, Women/Minorities

Meany, Brian M. — *Vice President*
Herbert Mines Associates, Inc.
399 Park Avenue, 27th Floor
New York, NY 10022
Telephone: (212) 355-0909
Recruiter Classification: Retained; **Lowest/Average Salary:**
$90,000/$90,000; **Industry Concentration:** Generalist
with a primary focus in Venture Capital; **Function
Concentration:** Generalist with a primary focus in
Administration, Finance/Accounting, General
Management, Human Resources, Marketing, Sales,
Women/Minorities

Meara, Helen — *Associate*
Source Services Corporation
5 Independence Way
Princeton, NJ 08540
Telephone: (609) 452-7277
Recruiter Classification: Contingency; **Lowest/Average
Salary:** $30,000/$50,000; **Industry Concentration:** Financial
Services; **Function Concentration:** Engineering,
Finance/Accounting

Medina-Haro, Adolfo — *Managing Partner*
Heidrick & Struggles, Inc.
Torre Chapultepec, Ruben Dario No. 281 Ofna.
1403
Col. Bosque de Chapultepec
Mexico City, D.F., MEXICO 11580
Telephone: (525) 280-5200
Recruiter Classification: Retained; **Lowest/Average Salary:**
$75,000/$90,000; **Industry Concentration:** Generalist with a
primary focus in Financial Services; **Function Concentration:**
Generalist

Meehan, John — *Associate*
Source Services Corporation
8614 Westwood Center, Suite 750
Vienna, VA 22182
Telephone: (703) 790-5610
Recruiter Classification: Contingency; **Lowest/Average
Salary:** $30,000/$50,000; **Industry Concentration:** Financial
Services; **Function Concentration:** Engineering,
Finance/Accounting

Meier, J. Dale — *Principal*
Grant Cooper and Associates
795 Office Parkway, Suite 117
St. Louis, MO 63141
Telephone: (314) 567-4690
Recruiter Classification: Retained; **Lowest/Average Salary:**
$60,000/$90,000; **Industry Concentration:** Generalist with a
primary focus in Financial Services; **Function Concentration:**
Generalist with a primary focus in Administration, Engineering,
Finance/Accounting, General Management, Human Resources,
Marketing, Sales

Meiland, A. Daniel — *Consultant*
Egon Zehnder International Inc.
350 Park Avenue
New York, NY 10022
Telephone: (212) 838-9199
Recruiter Classification: Retained; **Lowest/Average Salary:**
$90,000/$90,000; **Industry Concentration:** Generalist with a
primary focus in Financial Services; **Function Concentration:**
Generalist

Meltzer, Andrea Y. — *Managing Partner*
Executive Options, Ltd.
910 Skokie Boulevard
Suite 210
Northbrook, IL 60068
Telephone: (708) 291-4322
Recruiter Classification: Executive Temporary; **Lowest/Average Salary:** $40,000/$60,000; **Industry Concentration:** Generalist with a primary focus in Financial Services; **Function Concentration:** Generalist with a primary focus in Finance/Accounting, General Management, Human Resources, Marketing, Women/Minorities

Mendelson, Jeffrey — *Associate*
Source Services Corporation
2 Penn Plaza, Suite 1176
New York, NY 10121
Telephone: (212) 760-2200
Recruiter Classification: Contingency; **Lowest/Average Salary:** $30,000/$50,000; **Industry Concentration:** Financial Services; **Function Concentration:** Engineering, Finance/Accounting

Mendoza, Guadalupe — *Partner*
Ward Howell International, Inc.
Rexer Seleccion de Ejecutivos, S.C.
Blvd. Adolfo Lopez Mateos 20, Col. San Angel Inn
Mexico City, D.F., MEXICO 01060
Telephone: (525) 550-9180
Recruiter Classification: Retained; **Lowest/Average Salary:** $75,000/$90,000; **Industry Concentration:** Financial Services, Insurance; **Function Concentration:** Generalist

Mendoza-Green, Robin — *Associate*
Source Services Corporation
1 Gatehall Drive, Suite 250
Parsippany, NJ 07054
Telephone: (201) 267-3222
Recruiter Classification: Contingency; **Lowest/Average Salary:** $30,000/$50,000; **Industry Concentration:** Financial Services; **Function Concentration:** Engineering, Finance/Accounting

Menk, Carl — *Chairman*
Canny, Bowen Inc.
200 Park Avenue
49th Floor
New York, NY 10166
Telephone: (212) 949-6611
Recruiter Classification: Retained; **Lowest/Average Salary:** $90,000/$90,000; **Industry Concentration:** Generalist with a primary focus in Insurance; **Function Concentration:** Generalist with a primary focus in General Management, Human Resources, Marketing

Mercer, Julie — *Managing Principal*
Columbia Consulting Group
20 South Charles Street, 9th Floor
Baltimore, MD 21201
Telephone: (410) 385-2525
Recruiter Classification: Retained; **Lowest/Average Salary:** $75,000/$90,000; **Industry Concentration:** Generalist with a primary focus in Financial Services, Insurance, Venture Capital; **Function Concentration:** Generalist with a primary focus in Finance/Accounting, Human Resources, Marketing, Sales, Women/Minorities

Merrigan, Eileen M. — *Partner*
Lamalie Amrop International
200 Park Avenue
New York, NY 10166-0136
Telephone: (212) 953-7900
Recruiter Classification: Retained; **Lowest/Average Salary:** $90,000/$90,000; **Industry Concentration:** Generalist with a primary focus in Financial Services; **Function Concentration:** Generalist with a primary focus in Finance/Accounting, Marketing, Sales

Mertensotto, Chuck H. — *Executive Recruiter*
Whitney & Associates, Inc.
920 Second Avenue South, Suite 625
Minneapolis, MN 55402-4035
Telephone: (612) 338-5600
Recruiter Classification: Contingency, Executive Temporary; **Lowest/Average Salary:** $20,000/$50,000; **Industry Concentration:** Generalist with a primary focus in Financial Services, Insurance, Venture Capital; **Function Concentration:** Finance/Accounting

Messett, William J. — *President*
Messett Associates, Inc.
7700 North Kendall Drive, Suite 304
Miami, FL 33156
Telephone: (305) 275-1000
Recruiter Classification: Retained; **Lowest/Average Salary:** $75,000/$90,000; **Industry Concentration:** Generalist with a primary focus in Financial Services, Insurance; **Function Concentration:** Generalist with a primary focus in Administration, Engineering, Finance/Accounting, General Management, Human Resources, Marketing, Sales, Women/Minorities

Messina, Marco — *Associate*
Source Services Corporation
500 108th Avenue NE, Suite 1780
Bellevue, WA 98004
Telephone: (206) 454-6400
Recruiter Classification: Contingency; **Lowest/Average Salary:** $30,000/$50,000; **Industry Concentration:** Financial Services; **Function Concentration:** Engineering, Finance/Accounting

Mestepey, John — *Vice President/Managing Director*
A.T. Kearney, Inc.
First Union Financial Center, Suite 3500
200 South Biscayne Boulevard
Miami, FL 33131
Telephone: (305) 577-0046
Recruiter Classification: Retained; **Lowest/Average Salary:** $90,000/$90,000; **Industry Concentration:** Generalist with a primary focus in Financial Services; **Function Concentration:** Generalist with a primary focus in Administration, Finance/Accounting, General Management, Human Resources, Marketing, Sales

Meyer, Michael F. — *Shareholder*
Witt/Kieffer, Ford, Hadelman & Lloyd
432 North 44th Street
Suite 360
Phoenix, AZ 85008
Telephone: (602) 267-1370
Recruiter Classification: Retained; **Lowest/Average Salary:** $75,000/$90,000; **Industry Concentration:** Insurance; **Function Concentration:** Generalist with a primary focus in General Management, Human Resources

Meyer, Stacey — *Senior Associate*
Gary Kaplan & Associates
201 South Lake Avenue
Suite 600
Pasadena, CA 91101
Telephone: (818) 796-8100
Recruiter Classification: Retained; **Lowest/Average Salary:**
$75,000/$90,000; **Industry Concentration:** Generalist
with a primary focus in Financial Services, Insurance;
Function Concentration: Generalist with a primary
focus in Engineering, Finance/Accounting, General
Management, Human Resources, Marketing, Research
and Development

Meyers, Steven — *Senior Associate*
Montgomery Resources, Inc.
555 Montgomery Street, Suite 1650
San Francisco, CA 94111
Telephone: (415) 956-4242
Recruiter Classification: Contingency, Executive Temporary;
Lowest/Average Salary: $30,000/$60,000; **Industry
Concentration:** Generalist with a primary focus in Financial
Services, Insurance, Venture Capital; **Function Concentration:**
Finance/Accounting

Meza, Anna — *Executive Recruiter*
Richard, Wayne and Roberts
24 Greenway Plaza, Suite 1304
Houston, TX 77046-2493
Telephone: (713) 629-6681
Recruiter Classification: Retained; **Lowest/Average Salary:**
$50,000/$90,000; **Industry Concentration:** Generalist
with a primary focus in Financial Services; **Function
Concentration:** Generalist with a primary focus in
Finance/Accounting

Michaels, Joseph — *Executive Recruiter*
CPS Inc.
One Westbrook Corporate Centre, Suite 600
Westchester, IL 60154
Telephone: (708) 531-8370
Recruiter Classification: Contingency; **Lowest/Average Salary:**
$30,000/$50,000; **Industry Concentration:** Generalist with a
primary focus in Financial Services, Insurance; **Function
Concentration:** Engineering, Research and Development,
Sales, Women/Minorities

Michaels, Stewart — *Partner*
TOPAZ Legal Solutions
383 Northfield Avenue
West Orange, NJ 07052
Telephone: (201) 669-7300
Recruiter Classification: Executive Temporary; **Lowest/Average
Salary:** $40,000/$75,000; **Industry Concentration:** Financial
Services; **Function Concentration:** Generalist with a primary
focus in Women/Minorities

Michaels, Stewart — *Partner*
TOPAZ International, Inc.
383 Northfield Avenue
West Orange, NJ 07052
Telephone: (201) 669-7300
Recruiter Classification: Contingency; **Lowest/Average Salary:**
$40,000/$75,000; **Industry Concentration:** Financial Services;
Function Concentration: Generalist with a primary focus in
Women/Minorities

Milkint, Margaret Resce — *Executive Vice
President*
Jacobson Associates
150 North Wacker Drive
Suite 1120
Chicago, IL 60606
Telephone: (312) 726-1578
Recruiter Classification: Contingency; **Lowest/Average Salary:**
$20,000/$50,000; **Industry Concentration:** Insurance;
Function Concentration: Generalist

Miller, David — *Recruiter*
Temporary Accounting Personnel, Inc.
955 East Henrietta Road
Rochester, NY 14623
Telephone: (716) 427-9930
Recruiter Classification: Executive Temporary;
Lowest/Average Salary: $20,000/$30,000; **Industry
Concentration:** Generalist with a primary focus in Financial
Services; **Function Concentration:** Finance/Accounting,
Human Resources

Miller, David — *Search Consultant*
Cochran, Cochran & Yale, Inc.
955 East Henrietta Road
Rochester, NY 14623
Telephone: (716) 424-6060
Recruiter Classification: Retained; **Lowest/Average Salary:**
$50,000/$75,000; **Industry Concentration:** Generalist
with a primary focus in Financial Services, Venture Capital;
Function Concentration: Generalist with a primary
focus in Engineering, Finance/Accounting, General
Management, Human Resources, Marketing, Sales,
Women/Minorities

Miller, Harold B. — *Executive Recruiter*
MSI International
1050 Crown Pointe Parkway
Suite 1000
Atlanta, GA 30338
Telephone: (404) 394-2494
Recruiter Classification: Contingency; **Lowest/Average Salary:**
$30,000/$60,000; **Industry Concentration:** Generalist with a
primary focus in Financial Services; **Function Concentration:**
Finance/Accounting

Miller, Kenneth A. — *President*
Computer Network Resources, Inc.
28231 Tinajo
Mission Viejo, CA 92692
Telephone: (714) 951-5929
Recruiter Classification: Contingency; **Lowest/Average Salary:**
$60,000/$75,000; **Industry Concentration:** Insurance;
Function Concentration: Sales

Miller, Larry — *Associate*
Source Services Corporation
4200 West Cypress Street, Suite 101
Tampa, FL 33607
Telephone: (813) 879-2221
Recruiter Classification: Contingency; **Lowest/Average
Salary:** $30,000/$50,000; **Industry Concentration:** Financial
Services; **Function Concentration:** Engineering,
Finance/Accounting

Miller, Michael R. — *Managing Director*
Lynch Miller Moore, Inc.
10 South Wacker Drive, Suite 2935
Chicago, IL 60606
Telephone: (312) 876-1505
Recruiter Classification: Retained; **Lowest/Average Salary:**
$75,000/$90,000; **Industry Concentration:** Generalist with a
primary focus in Venture Capital; **Function Concentration:**
Generalist with a primary focus in Finance/Accounting,
General Management, Marketing

Miller, Roy — *Partner*
The Enns Partners Inc.
70 University Avenue, Suite 410, P.O. Box 14
Toronto, Ontario, CANADA M5J 2M4
Telephone: (416) 598-0012
Recruiter Classification: Retained; **Lowest/Average Salary:**
$75,000/$90,000; **Industry Concentration:** Generalist with a
primary focus in Financial Services, Venture Capital; **Function
Concentration:** Generalist with a primary focus in
Administration, Finance/Accounting, General Management,
Human Resources, Marketing, Sales

Miller, Timothy — *Associate*
Source Services Corporation
3 Summit Park Drive, Suite 550
Independence, OH 44131
Telephone: (216) 328-5900
Recruiter Classification: Contingency; **Lowest/Average Salary:**
$30,000/$50,000; **Industry Concentration:** Financial Services;
Function Concentration: Engineering, Finance/Accounting

Milligan, Dale — *Associate*
Source Services Corporation
4170 Ashford Dunwoody Road, Suite 285
Atlanta, GA 30319
Telephone: (404) 255-2045
Recruiter Classification: Contingency; **Lowest/Average Salary:**
$30,000/$50,000; **Industry Concentration:** Financial Services;
Function Concentration: Engineering, Finance/Accounting

Millonzi, Joel C. — *Senior Managing Director*
Johnson Smith & Knisely Accord
100 Park Avenue, 15th Floor
New York, NY 10017
Telephone: (212) 885-9100
Recruiter Classification: Retained; **Lowest/Average Salary:**
$90,000/$90,000; **Industry Concentration:** Financial Services,
Insurance, Venture Capital; **Function Concentration:** Generalist
with a primary focus in Administration, Finance/Accounting,
General Management, Human Resources, Marketing, Research
and Development, Sales

Mills, John — *Associate*
Source Services Corporation
1105 Schrock Road, Suite 510
Columbus, OH 43229
Telephone: (614) 846-3311
Recruiter Classification: Contingency; **Lowest/Average Salary:**
$30,000/$50,000; **Industry Concentration:** Financial Services;
Function Concentration: Engineering, Finance/Accounting

Milner, Carol — *Associate*
Source Services Corporation
One CityPlace, Suite 170
St. Louis, MO 63141
Telephone: (314) 432-4500
Recruiter Classification: Contingency; **Lowest/Average Salary:**
$30,000/$50,000; **Industry Concentration:** Financial Services;
Function Concentration: Engineering, Finance/Accounting

Milstein, Bonnie — *Executive Vice President*
Marvin Laba & Associates
6255 Sunset Boulevard, Suite 617
Los Angeles, CA 90028
Telephone: (213) 464-1355
Recruiter Classification: Retained; **Lowest/Average Salary:**
$50,000/$90,000; **Industry Concentration:** Financial
Services; **Function Concentration:** Generalist with a
primary focus in Finance/Accounting, General
Management, Human Resources, Marketing,
Sales

Mines, Herbert T. — *Chairman and CEO*
Herbert Mines Associates, Inc.
399 Park Avenue, 27th Floor
New York, NY 10022
Telephone: (212) 355-0909
Recruiter Classification: Retained; **Lowest/Average Salary:**
$300,000/$500,000; **Industry Concentration:** Venture Capital;
Function Concentration: Generalist with a primary focus in
Finance/Accounting, General Management, Human Resources,
Marketing

Mingle, Larry D. — *Managing Principal*
Columbia Consulting Group
185 Helios Drive
Jupiter, FL 33477
Telephone: (561) 748-0232
Recruiter Classification: Retained; **Lowest/Average Salary:**
$75,000/$90,000; **Industry Concentration:** Generalist with a
primary focus in Financial Services, Insurance, Venture
Capital; **Function Concentration:** Generalist with a primary
focus in Finance/Accounting, Human Resources, Marketing,
Sales

Miras, Cliff — *Managing Director*
Source Services Corporation
379 Thornall Street
Edison, NJ 08837
Telephone: (908) 494-2800
Recruiter Classification: Contingency; **Lowest/Average
Salary:** $30,000/$50,000; **Industry Concentration:** Financial
Services; **Function Concentration:** Engineering,
Finance/Accounting

Miras, Cliff — *Managing Director*
Source Services Corporation
5 Independence Way
Princeton, NJ 08540
Telephone: (609) 452-7277
Recruiter Classification: Contingency; **Lowest/Average
Salary:** $30,000/$50,000; **Industry Concentration:** Financial
Services; **Function Concentration:** Engineering,
Finance/Accounting

Mirtz, P. John — *Partner*
Mirtz Morice, Inc.
One Dock Street
Stamford, CT 06902
Telephone: (203) 964-9266
Recruiter Classification: Retained; **Lowest/Average Salary:**
$90,000/$90,000; **Industry Concentration:** Generalist with a
primary focus in Financial Services, Insurance; **Function
Concentration:** Generalist

Misiurewicz, Marc — *Search Consultant*
Cochran, Cochran & Yale, Inc.
955 East Henrietta Road
Rochester, NY 14623
Telephone: (716) 424-6060
Recruiter Classification: Retained; **Lowest/Average Salary:**
$50,000/$75,000; **Industry Concentration:** Generalist with
a primary focus in Financial Services, Venture Capital;
Function Concentration: Generalist with a primary
focus in Engineering, Finance/Accounting, General
Management, Human Resources, Marketing, Sales,
Women/Minorities

Mitchell, Jeff — *Professional Recruiter*
A.J. Burton Group, Inc.
4550 Montgomery Avenue, Ste. 325 North
Bethesda, MD 20814
Telephone: (301) 654-0082
Recruiter Classification: Contingency; **Lowest/Average Salary:**
$40,000/$75,000; **Industry Concentration:** Generalist with a
primary focus in Financial Services, Insurance; **Function
Concentration:** Generalist with a primary focus in
Administration, Finance/Accounting, General Management,
Human Resources

Mitchell, John — *Managing Partner*
Romac & Associates
Plaza of the Americas
700 North Pear St. #940
Dallas, TX 75201
Telephone: (214) 720-0050
Recruiter Classification: Executive Temporary; **Lowest/Average
Salary:** $60,000/$60,000; **Industry Concentration:** Financial
Services, Insurance; **Function Concentration:**
Finance/Accounting

Mitton, Bill — *Executive Vice President*
Executive Resource, Inc.
553 South Industrial Drive
P.O. Box 356
Hartland, WI 53029-0356
Telephone: (414) 369-2540
Recruiter Classification: Contingency; **Lowest/Average Salary:**
$30,000/$50,000; **Industry Concentration:** Generalist with a
primary focus in Financial Services; **Function Concentration:**
Finance/Accounting, Human Resources

Mittwol, Myles — *Associate*
Source Services Corporation
1 Gatehall Drive, Suite 250
Parsippany, NJ 07054
Telephone: (201) 267-3222
Recruiter Classification: Contingency; **Lowest/Average
Salary:** $30,000/$50,000; **Industry Concentration:** Financial
Services; **Function Concentration:** Engineering,
Finance/Accounting

Mochwart, Donald — *Vice President*
Drummond Associates, Inc.
50 Broadway, Suite 1201
New York, NY 10004
Telephone: (212) 248-1120
Recruiter Classification: Contingency; **Lowest/Average
Salary:** $40,000/$75,000; **Industry Concentration:** Financial
Services; **Function Concentration:** Finance/
Accounting

Mogul, Gene — *President*
Mogul Consultants, Inc.
380 North Broadway, Suite 208
Jericho, NY 11753-2109
Telephone: (516) 822-4363
Recruiter Classification: Contingency; **Lowest/Average
Salary:** $40,000/$75,000; **Industry Concentration:** Financial
Services, Insurance; **Function Concentration:** Generalist
with a primary focus in Engineering, General
Management, Marketing, Research and Development,
Sales

Mohr, Brian — *Executive Recruiter*
CPS Inc.
One Westbrook Corporate Centre, Suite 600
Westchester, IL 60154
Telephone: (708) 531-8370
Recruiter Classification: Contingency; **Lowest/Average Salary:**
$30,000/$50,000; **Industry Concentration:** Generalist with a
primary focus in Financial Services, Insurance; **Function
Concentration:** Engineering, Research and Development,
Sales, Women/Minorities

Molitor, John L. — *Manager Accounting/Financial
Search Division*
Barrett Partners
100 North LaSalle Street, Suite 1420
Chicago, IL 60602
Telephone: (312) 443-8877
Recruiter Classification: Contingency; **Lowest/Average Salary:**
$30,000/$50,000; **Industry Concentration:** Financial Services,
Insurance; **Function Concentration:** Engineering,
Finance/Accounting

Mollichelli, David — *Associate*
Source Services Corporation
One Park Plaza, Suite 560
Irvine, CA 92714
Telephone: (714) 660-1666
Recruiter Classification: Contingency; **Lowest/Average
Salary:** $30,000/$50,000; **Industry Concentration:** Financial
Services; **Function Concentration:** Engineering,
Finance/Accounting

Molnar, Robert A. — *Partner*
Johnson Smith & Knisely Accord
100 Park Avenue, 15th Floor
New York, NY 10017
Telephone: (212) 885-9100
Recruiter Classification: Retained; **Lowest/Average Salary:**
$90,000/$90,000; **Industry Concentration:** Financial Services,
Insurance, Venture Capital; **Function Concentration:**
Generalist

Mondragon, Philip — *Vice President*
A.T. Kearney, Inc.
Ruben Dario 281-Piso 15
Col. Bosques de Chapultepec
Mexico City D.F., MEXICO 11580
Telephone: (525) 282-0050
Recruiter Classification: Retained; **Lowest/Average Salary:**
$90,000/$90,000; **Industry Concentration:** Generalist with a
primary focus in Financial Services; **Function Concentration:**
Generalist with a primary focus in Engineering,
Finance/Accounting, General Management

Monogenis, Emanuel N. — *Partner*
Heidrick & Struggles, Inc.
245 Park Avenue, Suite 4300
New York, NY 10167-0152
Telephone: (212) 867-9876
Recruiter Classification: Retained; **Lowest/Average Salary:**
$75,000/$90,000; **Industry Concentration:** Generalist with a
primary focus in Financial Services; **Function Concentration:**
Generalist

Montgomery, James M. — *President*
Houze, Shourds & Montgomery, Inc.
Greater L.A. World Trade Center, Suite 800
Long Beach, CA 90831-0800
Telephone: (562) 495-6495
Recruiter Classification: Retained; **Lowest/Average Salary:**
$90,000/$90,000; **Industry Concentration:** Generalist with a
primary focus in Venture Capital; **Function Concentration:**
Generalist with a primary focus in Finance/Accounting, General
Management, Human Resources, Marketing, Women/Minorities

Moodley, Logan — *Vice President*
Austin-McGregor International
12005 Ford Road, Suite 720
Dallas, TX 75234-7247
Telephone: (972) 488-0500
Recruiter Classification: Retained; **Lowest/Average Salary:**
$50,000/$90,000; **Industry Concentration:** Generalist with a
primary focus in Financial Services, Venture Capital; **Function
Concentration:** Generalist

Moore, Craig — *Associate*
Source Services Corporation
20 Burlington Mall Road, Suite 405
Burlington, MA 01803
Telephone: (617) 272-5000
Recruiter Classification: Contingency; **Lowest/Average Salary:**
$30,000/$50,000; **Industry Concentration:** Financial Services;
Function Concentration: Engineering, Finance/Accounting

Moore, Dianna — *Associate*
Source Services Corporation
2850 National City Tower
Louisville, KY 40202
Telephone: (502) 581-9900
Recruiter Classification: Contingency; **Lowest/Average Salary:**
$30,000/$50,000; **Industry Concentration:** Financial Services;
Function Concentration: Engineering, Finance/Accounting

Moore, Janice E. — *Executive Recruiter*
MSI International
1050 Crown Pointe Parkway
Suite 1000
Atlanta, GA 30338
Telephone: (404) 394-2494
Recruiter Classification: Contingency; **Lowest/Average Salary:**
$30,000/$75,000; **Industry Concentration:** Generalist with a
primary focus in Financial Services; **Function Concentration:**
Generalist with a primary focus in Finance/Accounting

Moore, Mark — *Chairman and CEO*
Wheeler, Moore & Elam Co.
14800 Quorum Drive, Suite 200
Dallas, TX 75240
Telephone: (214) 386-8806
Recruiter Classification: Retained; **Lowest/Average Salary:**
$50,000/$75,000; **Industry Concentration:** Generalist with a
primary focus in Venture Capital; **Function Concentration:**
Generalist with a primary focus in Administration, Engineering,
Finance/Accounting, General Management, Human Resources,
Marketing, Research and Development, Sales

Moore, Suzanne — *Associate*
Source Services Corporation
8614 Westwood Center, Suite 750
Vienna, VA 22182
Telephone: (703) 790-5610
Recruiter Classification: Contingency; **Lowest/Average Salary:**
$30,000/$50,000; **Industry Concentration:** Financial Services;
Function Concentration: Engineering, Finance/Accounting

Moore, T. Wills — *Consultant*
Ray & Berndtson
191 Peachtree Street, NE, Suite 3800
Atlanta, GA 30303-1757
Telephone: (404) 215-4600
Recruiter Classification: Retained; **Lowest/Average Salary:**
$90,000/$90,000; **Industry Concentration:** Generalist with a
primary focus in Financial Services, Insurance; **Function
Concentration:** Generalist with a primary focus in
Administration, Finance/Accounting, General Management,
Human Resources, Marketing, Research and Development,
Sales, Women/Minorities

Moore, Vickie J. — *Partner*
Kirkman & Searing, Inc.
8045 Leesburg Pike
Suite 540
Vienna, VA 22182
Telephone: (703) 761-7020
Recruiter Classification: Retained; **Lowest/Average Salary:**
$90,000/$90,000; **Industry Concentration:** Financial Services,
Insurance; **Function Concentration:** General Management,
Marketing, Sales, Women/Minorities

Moran, Douglas — *Associate*
Source Services Corporation
10220 SW Greenburg Road, Suite 625
Portland, OR 97223
Telephone: (503) 768-4546
Recruiter Classification: Contingency; **Lowest/Average Salary:**
$30,000/$50,000; **Industry Concentration:** Financial Services;
Function Concentration: Engineering, Finance/Accounting

Morato, Rene — *Associate*
Source Services Corporation
15600 N.W. 67th Avenue, Suite 210
Miami Lakes, FL 33014
Telephone: (305) 556-8000
Recruiter Classification: Contingency; **Lowest/Average Salary:**
$30,000/$50,000; **Industry Concentration:** Financial Services;
Function Concentration: Engineering, Finance/Accounting

Morawetz, Justin A. — *Recruiter*
Keith Bagg & Associates Inc.
85 Richmond St., W., Ste. 700
Toronto, Ontario, CANADA M5H 2C9
Telephone: (416) 863-1800
Recruiter Classification: Contingency; **Lowest/Average Salary:**
$40,000/$60,000; **Industry Concentration:** Financial Services;
Function Concentration: Marketing, Sales

Moretti, Denise — *Associate*
Source Services Corporation
150 South Warner Road, Suite 238
King of Prussia, PA 19406
Telephone: (610) 341-1960
Recruiter Classification: Contingency; **Lowest/Average Salary:**
$30,000/$50,000; **Industry Concentration:** Financial Services;
Function Concentration: Engineering, Finance/Accounting

Morgan, David G. — *Principal*
Morgan Stampfl, Inc.
6 West 32nd Street
New York, NY 10001
Telephone: (212) 643-7165
Recruiter Classification: Contingency; **Lowest/Average Salary:**
$50,000/$90,000; **Industry Concentration:** Financial Services;
Function Concentration: Finance/Accounting

Morgan, Donald T. — *Vice President*
MSI International
1050 Crown Pointe Parkway
Suite 1000
Atlanta, GA 30338
Telephone: (404) 394-2494
Recruiter Classification: Contingency; **Lowest/Average Salary:**
$30,000/$60,000; **Industry Concentration:** Generalist with a
primary focus in Financial Services; **Function Concentration:**
Finance/Accounting

Morgan, Gary — *Insurance Consultant*
National Search, Inc.
2816 University Drive
Coral Springs, FL 33071
Telephone: (800) 935-4355
Recruiter Classification: Contingency; **Lowest/Average Salary:**
$30,000/$50,000; **Industry Concentration:** Insurance; **Function
Concentration:** Generalist with a primary focus in Administration,
Finance/Accounting, General Management, Human Resources,
Marketing, Research and Development, Sales, Women/Minorities

Morgan, Nancy — *Recruiter*
K. Russo Associates
2 Greenwich Plaza, Suite 100
Greenwich, CT 06830
Telephone: (203) 622-3903
Recruiter Classification: Retained; **Lowest/Average Salary:**
$30,000/$90,000; **Industry Concentration:** Financial Services,
Insurance; **Function Concentration:** Human Resources

Moriarty, Mike — *Associate*
Source Services Corporation
2850 National City Tower
Louisville, KY 40202
Telephone: (502) 581-9900
Recruiter Classification: Contingency; **Lowest/Average Salary:**
$30,000/$50,000; **Industry Concentration:** Financial Services;
Function Concentration: Engineering, Finance/Accounting

Morice, James L. — *Partner*
Mirtz Morice, Inc.
One Dock Street
Stamford, CT 06902
Telephone: (203) 964-9266
Recruiter Classification: Retained; **Lowest/Average Salary:**
$90,000/$90,000; **Industry Concentration:** Generalist with a
primary focus in Financial Services, Insurance; **Function
Concentration:** Generalist

Morris, David A. — *Managing Partner*
Heidrick & Struggles, Inc.
One Houston Center
1221 McKinney Street, Suite 3050
Houston, TX 77010
Telephone: (713) 237-9000
Recruiter Classification: Retained; **Lowest/Average Salary:**
$75,000/$90,000; **Industry Concentration:** Generalist with a
primary focus in Financial Services; **Function Concentration:**
Generalist

Morris, Paul T. — *President*
The Morris Group
1024 East Lancaster Avenue
P.O. Box 188
Bryn Mawr, PA 19010-0188
Telephone: (610) 520-0100
Recruiter Classification: Contingency; **Lowest/Average Salary:**
$40,000/$75,000; **Industry Concentration:** Generalist with a
primary focus in Financial Services, Insurance; **Function
Concentration:** Human Resources, Marketing, Research and
Development, Sales, Women/Minorities

Morris, Scott — *Associate*
Source Services Corporation
1105 Schrock Road, Suite 510
Columbus, OH 43229
Telephone: (614) 846-3311
Recruiter Classification: Contingency; **Lowest/Average Salary:**
$30,000/$50,000; **Industry Concentration:** Financial Services;
Function Concentration: Engineering, Finance/Accounting

Morrow, Melanie — *Associate*
Source Services Corporation
3 Summit Park Drive, Suite 550
Independence, OH 44131
Telephone: (216) 328-5900
Recruiter Classification: Contingency; **Lowest/Average Salary:**
$30,000/$50,000; **Industry Concentration:** Financial Services;
Function Concentration: Engineering, Finance/Accounting

Morse, Mary — *Vice President*
Travis & Company
325 Boston Post Road
Sudbury, MA 01776
Telephone: (508) 443-4000
Recruiter Classification: Retained; **Lowest/Average Salary:**
$90,000/$90,000; **Industry Concentration:** Financial Services;
Function Concentration: Generalist

Mortansen, Patricia — *Vice President*
Norman Broadbent International, Inc.
Sears Tower, Suite 9850
233 South Wacker Drive
Chicago, IL 60606
Telephone: (312) 876-3300
Recruiter Classification: Retained; **Lowest/Average Salary:**
$90,000/$90,000; **Industry Concentration:** Generalist with a
primary focus in Financial Services; **Function Concentration:**
Generalist with a primary focus in Finance/Accounting,
General Management, Human Resources, Marketing, Sales

Morton, Robert C. — *Senior Consultant*
Morton, McCorkle & Associates, Inc.
2190 South Mason Road, Suite 309
St. Louis, MO 63131-1637
Telephone: (314) 984-9494
Recruiter Classification: Retained; **Lowest/Average Salary:**
$60,000/$90,000; **Industry Concentration:** Generalist with a
primary focus in Insurance, Venture Capital; **Function
Concentration:** Generalist with a primary focus in Engineering,
Finance/Accounting, General Management, Human Resources,
Marketing, Research and Development, Sales

Moseley, Micahel A. — *Search Consultant*
Kaye-Bassman International Corp.
18333 Preston Road, Suite 500
Dallas, TX 75252
Telephone: (972) 931-5242
Recruiter Classification: Retained; **Lowest/Average Salary:**
$30,000/$60,000; **Industry Concentration:** Insurance;
Function Concentration: Marketing, Sales

Moskowitz, Marc — *Vice President and CFO*
Kenzer Corp.
777 Third Avenue, 26th Floor
New York, NY 10017
Telephone: (212) 308-4300
Recruiter Classification: Retained; **Lowest/Average Salary:**
$50,000/$90,000; **Industry Concentration:** Financial Services;
Function Concentration: Finance/Accounting

Mott, Greg — *Associate*
Source Services Corporation
5429 LBJ Freeway, Suite 275
Dallas, TX 75240
Telephone: (214) 387-1600
Recruiter Classification: Contingency; **Lowest/Average
Salary:** $30,000/$50,000; **Industry Concentration:** Financial
Services; **Function Concentration:** Engineering,
Finance/Accounting

Mowatt, Virginia — *Director*
Spencer Stuart
401 North Michigan Avenue, Suite 3400
Chicago, IL 60611-4244
Telephone: (312) 822-0080
Recruiter Classification: Retained; **Lowest/Average Salary:**
$90,000/$90,000; **Industry Concentration:** Generalist with a
primary focus in Financial Services; **Function Concentration:**
Generalist

Moyse, Richard G. — *Principal*
Thorndike Deland Associates
275 Madison Avenue, Suite 1300
New York, NY 10016
Telephone: (212) 661-6200
Recruiter Classification: Retained; **Lowest/Average Salary:**
$100,000/$125,000; **Industry Concentration:** Generalist
with a primary focus in Financial Services, Insurance;
Function Concentration: Generalist with a primary focus in
Sales

Msidment, Roger — *Associate*
Source Services Corporation
10300 West 103rd Street, Suite 101
Overland Park, KS 66214
Telephone: (913) 888-8885
Recruiter Classification: Contingency; **Lowest/Average
Salary:** $30,000/$50,000; **Industry Concentration:** Financial
Services; **Function Concentration:** Engineering,
Finance/Accounting

Mueller, Colleen — *Associate*
Source Services Corporation
5429 LBJ Freeway, Suite 275
Dallas, TX 75240
Telephone: (214) 387-1600
Recruiter Classification: Contingency; **Lowest/Average Salary:**
$30,000/$50,000; **Industry Concentration:** Financial Services;
Function Concentration: Engineering, Finance/Accounting

Mueller-Maerki, Fortunat F. — *Consultant*
Egon Zehnder International Inc.
350 Park Avenue
New York, NY 10022
Telephone: (212) 838-9199
Recruiter Classification: Retained; **Lowest/Average Salary:**
$90,000/$90,000; **Industry Concentration:** Generalist with a
primary focus in Financial Services; **Function Concentration:**
Generalist

Muendel, H. Edward — *Managing Director*
Stanton Chase International
100 East Pratt Street
Suite 2530
Baltimore, MD 21202
Telephone: (410) 528-8400
Recruiter Classification: Retained; **Lowest/Average Salary:**
$75,000/$90,000; **Industry Concentration:** Generalist with a
primary focus in Financial Services, Venture Capital; **Function
Concentration:** Generalist with a primary focus in
Administration, Engineering, Finance/Accounting, General
Management, Human Resources, Marketing, Research and
Development, Sales

Muller, Susan — *Recruiter*
Corporate Recruiters Ltd.
490-1140 West Pender Street
Vancouver, British Columbia, CANADA V6E 4G1
Telephone: (604) 687-5993
Recruiter Classification: Contingency; **Lowest/Average Salary:**
$30,000/$60,000; **Industry Concentration:** Financial Services,
Insurance

Mulligan, Robert P. — *Vice President/Managing
Director*
William Willis Worldwide Inc.
P.O. Box 4444
Greenwich, CT 06831-0408
Telephone: (203) 661-4500
Recruiter Classification: Retained; **Lowest/Average Salary:**
$90,000/$90,000; **Industry Concentration:** Generalist with a
primary focus in Financial Services, Insurance; **Function
Concentration:** Generalist with a primary focus in Engineering,
Finance/Accounting, General Management, Human Resources,
Marketing, Research and Development

Murphy, Corinne — *Associate*
Source Services Corporation
100 North Tryon Street, Suite 3130
Charlotte, NC 28202
Telephone: (704) 333-8311
Recruiter Classification: Contingency; **Lowest/Average Salary:**
$30,000/$50,000; **Industry Concentration:** Financial Services;
Function Concentration: Engineering, Finance/Accounting

Murphy, Cornelius J. — *Senior Vice President*
Goodrich & Sherwood Associates, Inc.
250 Mill Street
Rochester, NY 14614
Telephone: (716) 777-4060
Recruiter Classification: Retained; **Lowest/Average Salary:**
$60,000/$90,000; **Industry Concentration:** Generalist with a
primary focus in Financial Services, Insurance, Venture Capital;
Function Concentration: Generalist with a primary focus in
Administration, Finance/Accounting, General Management,
Human Resources, Marketing, Sales

Murphy, Erin — *Executive Recruiter*
CPS Inc.
One Westbrook Corporate Centre, Suite 600
Westchester, IL 60154
Telephone: (708) 531-8370
Recruiter Classification: Contingency; **Lowest/Average Salary:**
$30,000/$50,000; **Industry Concentration:** Generalist with a
primary focus in Financial Services, Insurance; **Function
Concentration:** Engineering, Research and Development,
Sales, Women/Minorities

Murphy, Gary J. — *Partner*
Stone Murphy & Olson
5500 Wayzata Boulevard
Suite 1020
Minneapolis, MN 55416
Telephone: (612) 591-2300
Recruiter Classification: Retained; **Lowest/Average Salary:**
$75,000/$90,000; **Industry Concentration:** Generalist with a
primary focus in Financial Services, Insurance; **Function
Concentration:** Human Resources

Murphy, James — *Associate*
Source Services Corporation
4170 Ashford Dunwoody Road, Suite 285
Atlanta, GA 30319
Telephone: (404) 255-2045
Recruiter Classification: Contingency; **Lowest/Average
Salary:** $30,000/$50,000; **Industry Concentration:** Financial
Services; **Function Concentration:** Engineering,
Finance/Accounting

Murphy, Patrick J. — *President*
P.J. Murphy & Associates, Inc.
735 North Water Street
Milwaukee, WI 53202
Telephone: (414) 277-9777
Recruiter Classification: Retained; **Lowest/Average Salary:**
$60,000/$90,000; **Industry Concentration:** Generalist with a
primary focus in Financial Services; **Function Concentration:**
Generalist with a primary focus in Administration,
Finance/Accounting, General Management, Human Resources,
Marketing, Sales

Murphy, Peter — *Principal*
Korn/Ferry International
One Landmark Square
Stamford, CT 06901
Telephone: (203) 359-3350
Recruiter Classification: Retained; **Lowest/Average Salary:**
$100,000/$150,000; **Industry Concentration:** Generalist with a
primary focus in Financial Services, Insurance; **Function
Concentration:** Generalist

Murray, Virginia — *Vice President*
A.T. Kearney, Inc.
130 Adelaide Street West, Suite 2710
Toronto, Ontario, CANADA M5H 3P5
Telephone: (416) 947-1990
Recruiter Classification: Retained; **Lowest/Average Salary:**
$90,000/$90,000; **Industry Concentration:** Generalist
with a primary focus in Financial Services; **Function
Concentration:** Generalist with a primary focus in
Engineering, Finance/Accounting, General
Management

Murry, John — *Associate*
Source Services Corporation
20 Burlington Mall Road, Suite 405
Burlington, MA 01803
Telephone: (617) 272-5000
Recruiter Classification: Contingency; **Lowest/Average
Salary:** $30,000/$50,000; **Industry Concentration:** Financial
Services; **Function Concentration:** Engineering,
Finance/Accounting

Mursuli, Meredith — *Consultant*
Lasher Associates
1200 South Pine Island Road, Suite 370
Fort Lauderdale, FL 33324-4402
Telephone: (305) 472-5658
Recruiter Classification: Retained; **Lowest/Average Salary:**
$75,000/$90,000; **Industry Concentration:** Generalist with a
primary focus in Financial Services, Insurance, Venture Capital;
Function Concentration: Generalist with a primary focus in
Engineering, Finance/Accounting, General Management,
Human Resources, Marketing, Research and Development,
Sales

Mustin, Joyce M. — *Vice President and Partner*
J: Blakslee International, Ltd.
49 Hillside Avenue
Mill Valley, CA 94941
Telephone: (415) 389-7300
Recruiter Classification: Retained; **Lowest/Average Salary:**
$90,000/$90,000; **Industry Concentration:** Venture Capital;
Function Concentration: Generalist with a primary focus in
Engineering, Finance/Accounting, General Management,
Human Resources, Marketing, Research and Development,
Women/Minorities

Mydlach, Renee — *Senior Division Manager*
CPS Inc.
One Westbrook Corporate Centre, Suite 600
Westchester, IL 60154
Telephone: (708) 531-8370
Recruiter Classification: Contingency; **Lowest/Average Salary:**
$30,000/$50,000; **Industry Concentration:** Generalist with a
primary focus in Financial Services, Insurance; **Function
Concentration:** Engineering, Research and Development,
Sales, Women/Minorities

Myers, Kay — *Recruiter*
Signature Staffing
6800 College Boulevard, Suite 550
Overland Park, KS 66211
Telephone: (913) 338-2020
Recruiter Classification: Executive Temporary; **Lowest/Average
Salary:** $30,000/$40,000; **Industry Concentration:** Generalist
with a primary focus in Financial Services, Insurance; **Function
Concentration:** Generalist with a primary focus in
Finance/Accounting, Marketing

Nabers, Karen — *Associate*
Source Services Corporation
9020 Capital of Texas Highway
Building I, Suite 337
Austin, TX 78759
Telephone: (512) 345-7473
Recruiter Classification: Contingency; **Lowest/Average
Salary:** $30,000/$50,000; **Industry Concentration:** Financial
Services; **Function Concentration:** Engineering,
Finance/Accounting

Nagle, Charles L. — *Senior Vice President*
Tyler & Company
1000 Abernathy Road
Suite 1400
Atlanta, GA 30328-5655
Telephone: (770) 396-3939
Recruiter Classification: Retained; **Lowest/Average Salary:**
$75,000/$90,000; **Industry Concentration:** Insurance;
Function Concentration: Generalist

Nagler, Leon G. — *Managing Director*
Nagler, Robins & Poe, Inc.
65 William Street
Wellesley Hills, MA 02181
Telephone: (617) 431-1330
Recruiter Classification: Retained; **Lowest/Average Salary:**
$90,000/$90,000; **Industry Concentration:** Generalist with a
primary focus in Financial Services, Venture Capital; **Function
Concentration:** Generalist with a primary focus in Engineering,
Finance/Accounting, General Management, Human Resources,
Marketing, Research and Development, Sales

Nagy, Les — *Managing Director*
Source Services Corporation
255 Consumers Road, Suite 404
North York, Ontario, CANADA M2J 1R1
Telephone: (416) 495-1551
Recruiter Classification: Contingency; **Lowest/Average Salary:**
$30,000/$50,000; **Industry Concentration:** Financial Services;
Function Concentration: Engineering, Finance/Accounting

Naidicz, Maria — *Consultant*
Ray & Berndtson
Sears Tower, 233 South Wacker Drive, Suite 4020
Chicago, IL 60606-6310
Telephone: (312) 876-0730
Recruiter Classification: Retained; **Lowest/Average Salary:**
$90,000/$90,000; **Industry Concentration:** Generalist with a
primary focus in Financial Services, Insurance; **Function
Concentration:** Generalist with a primary focus in
Administration, Finance/Accounting, General Management,
Human Resources, Marketing, Research and Development,
Sales, Women/Minorities

Nair, Leslie — *Vice President*
Zwell International
300 South Wacker Drive, Suite 650
Chicago, IL 60606
Telephone: (312) 663-3737
Recruiter Classification: Retained; **Lowest/Average Salary:**
$75,000/$90,000; **Industry Concentration:** Generalist with a
primary focus in Financial Services, Venture Capital; **Function
Concentration:** Generalist with a primary focus in Engineering,
General Management, Marketing, Sales

Nass, Martin D. — *Partner (Practice Leader - Real
Estate)*
Lamalie Amrop International
200 Park Avenue
New York, NY 10166-0136
Telephone: (212) 953-7900
Recruiter Classification: Retained; **Lowest/Average Salary:**
$90,000/$90,000; **Industry Concentration:** Generalist with a
primary focus in Financial Services; **Function Concentration:**
Generalist with a primary focus in Finance/Accounting,
General Management

Nathanson, Barry F. — *President*
Barry Nathanson Associates
40 Cutter Mill Road
Great Neck, NY 11021
Telephone: (516) 482-7222
Recruiter Classification: Retained; **Lowest/Average Salary:**
$90,000/$90,000; **Industry Concentration:** Generalist with a
primary focus in Financial Services; **Function Concentration:**
Generalist with a primary focus in Administration,
Finance/Accounting, General Management, Human Resources,
Marketing, Research and Development, Sales

Necessary, Rick — *Associate*
Source Services Corporation
111 Monument Circle, Suite 3930
Indianapolis, IN 46204
Telephone: (317) 631-2900
Recruiter Classification: Contingency; **Lowest/Average
Salary:** $30,000/$50,000; **Industry Concentration:** Financial
Services; **Function Concentration:** Engineering,
Finance/Accounting

Neckanoff, Sharon — *Account Executive*
Search West, Inc.
340 North Westlake Boulevard
Suite 200
Westlake Village, CA 91362-3761
Telephone: (805) 496-6811
Recruiter Classification: Contingency; **Lowest/Average
Salary:** $40,000/$60,000; **Industry Concentration:** Financial
Services; **Function Concentration:** Administration,
Finance/Accounting

Needham, Karen — *Associate*
Source Services Corporation
111 Founders Plaza, Suite 1501E
Hartford, CT 06108
Telephone: (860) 528-0300
Recruiter Classification: Contingency; **Lowest/Average
Salary:** $30,000/$50,000; **Industry Concentration:** Financial
Services; **Function Concentration:** Engineering,
Finance/Accounting

Neelin, Sharon — *Consultant*
The Caldwell Partners Amrop International
Sixty-Four Prince Arthur Avenue
Toronto, Ontario, CANADA M5R 1B4
Telephone: (416) 920-7702
Recruiter Classification: Retained; **Lowest/Average Salary:**
$60,000/$90,000; **Industry Concentration:** Generalist with a
primary focus in Financial Services, Insurance; **Function
Concentration:** Generalist

Nees, Eugene C. — *Partner*
Ray & Berndtson
245 Park Avenue, 33rd Floor
New York, NY 10167
Telephone: (212) 370-1316
Recruiter Classification: Retained; **Lowest/Average Salary:**
$90,000/$90,000; **Industry Concentration:** Generalist
with a primary focus in Financial Services, Insurance;
Function Concentration: Generalist with a primary
focus in Administration, Finance/Accounting, General
Management, Human Resources, Marketing,
Research and Development, Sales, Women/
Minorities

Neff, Herbert — *Associate*
Source Services Corporation
15600 N.W. 67th Avenue, Suite 210
Miami Lakes, FL 33014
Telephone: (305) 556-8000
Recruiter Classification: Contingency; **Lowest/Average
Salary:** $30,000/$50,000; **Industry Concentration:** Financial
Services; **Function Concentration:** Engineering,
Finance/Accounting

Neff, Thomas J. — *President*
Spencer Stuart
277 Park Avenue, 29th Floor
New York, NY 10172
Telephone: (212) 336-0200
Recruiter Classification: Retained; **Lowest/Average Salary:**
$90,000/$90,000; **Industry Concentration:** Generalist with a
primary focus in Financial Services, Insurance, Venture Capital;
Function Concentration: Generalist with a primary focus in
General Management

Neher, Robert L. — *Senior Executive Vice
President*
Intech Summit Group, Inc.
5075 Shoreham Place, Suite 280
San Diego, CA 92116
Telephone: (619) 452-2100
Recruiter Classification: Retained; **Lowest/Average Salary:**
$75,000/$90,000; **Industry Concentration:** Generalist with a
primary focus in Financial Services, Insurance, Venture Capital;
Function Concentration: Generalist with a primary focus in
Administration, Engineering, Finance/Accounting, General
Management, Human Resources, Marketing, Research and
Development, Sales, Women/Minorities

Nehring, Keith — *Consultant*
Howard Fischer Associates, Inc.
1800 John F. Kennedy Boulevard, 7th Floor
Philadelphia, PA 19103
Telephone: (215) 568-8363
Recruiter Classification: Retained; **Lowest/Average Salary:**
$90,000/$90,000; **Industry Concentration:** Generalist with a
primary focus in Financial Services, Insurance, Venture Capital;
Function Concentration: Generalist with a primary focus in
Administration, Finance/Accounting, General Management,
Human Resources, Marketing, Research and Development,
Sales, Women/Minorities

Neidhart, Craig C. — *Partner*
TNS Partners, Inc.
8140 Walnut Hill Lane
Suite 301
Dallas, TX 75231
Telephone: (214) 369-3565
Recruiter Classification: Retained; **Lowest/Average Salary:**
$90,000/$90,000; **Industry Concentration:** Generalist with a
primary focus in Venture Capital; **Function Concentration:**
Generalist with a primary focus in Engineering,
Finance/Accounting, General Management, Human Resources,
Marketing, Research and Development, Sales

Nelson, Hitch — *Associate*
Source Services Corporation
1290 Oakmead Parkway, Suite 318
Sunnyvale, CA 94086
Telephone: (408) 738-8440
Recruiter Classification: Contingency; **Lowest/Average Salary:**
$30,000/$50,000; **Industry Concentration:** Financial Services;
Function Concentration: Engineering, Finance/Accounting

Nelson, Mary — *Associate*
Source Services Corporation
8614 Westwood Center, Suite 750
Vienna, VA 22182
Telephone: (703) 790-5610
Recruiter Classification: Contingency; **Lowest/Average Salary:**
$30,000/$50,000; **Industry Concentration:** Financial Services;
Function Concentration: Engineering, Finance/Accounting

Nelson-Folkersen, Jeffrey — *Associate*
Source Services Corporation
4200 West Cypress Street, Suite 101
Tampa, FL 33607
Telephone: (813) 879-2221
Recruiter Classification: Contingency; **Lowest/Average
Salary:** $30,000/$50,000; **Industry Concentration:** Financial
Services; **Function Concentration:** Engineering,
Finance/Accounting

Nemec, Phillip — *Vice President Southeast Asia
Recruitment*
Dunhill International Search of New Haven
59 Elm Street
New Haven, CT 06510
Telephone: (203) 562-0511
Recruiter Classification: Contingency; **Lowest/Average Salary:**
$30,000/$60,000; **Industry Concentration:** Generalist with a
primary focus in Financial Services; **Function Concentration:**
Generalist with a primary focus in Engineering,
Finance/Accounting, General Management, Human Resources,
Marketing, Sales

Nephew, Robert — *Vice President*
Christian & Timbers
24 New England Executive Park
Burlington, MA 01803
Telephone: (617) 229-9515
Recruiter Classification: Retained; **Lowest/Average Salary:**
$90,000/$90,000; **Industry Concentration:** Financial Services,
Insurance, Venture Capital; **Function Concentration:** Generalist
with a primary focus in Engineering, Finance/Accounting,
General Management, Human Resources, Marketing, Research
and Development, Sales

Neri, Gene — *Executive Recruiter*
S.C. International, Ltd.
1430 Branding Lane, Suite 119
Downers Grove, IL 60515
Telephone: (708) 963-3033
Recruiter Classification: Contingency; **Lowest/Average
Salary:** $30,000/$50,000; **Industry Concentration:**
Insurance; **Function Concentration:** Administration,
Human Resources

Neuberth, Jeffrey G. — *Senior Vice
President/Director*
Canny, Bowen Inc.
200 Park Avenue
49th Floor
New York, NY 10166
Telephone: (212) 949-6611
Recruiter Classification: Retained; **Lowest/Average Salary:**
$120,000/$201,000; **Industry Concentration:** Generalist with a
primary focus in Financial Services, Venture Capital; **Function
Concentration:** Generalist with a primary focus in Engineering,
Finance/Accounting, General Management, Human Resources,
Marketing, Women/Minorities

Neuwald, Debrah — *Associate*
Source Services Corporation
1233 North Mayfair Road, Suite 300
Milwaukee, WI 53226
Telephone: (414) 774-6700
Recruiter Classification: Contingency; **Lowest/Average Salary:**
$30,000/$50,000; **Industry Concentration:** Financial Services;
Function Concentration: Engineering, Finance/Accounting

Newman, Jose L. — *Managing Partner*
Ward Howell International, Inc.
Rexer Seleccion de Ejecutivos, S.C.
Blvd. Adolfo Lopez Mateos 20, Col. San Angel Inn
Mexico City, D.F., MEXICO 01060
Telephone: (525) 550-9180
Recruiter Classification: Retained; **Lowest/Average Salary:**
$75,000/$90,000; **Industry Concentration:** Financial Services;
Function Concentration: Generalist

Newman, Lynn — *Associate*
Kishbaugh Associates International
2 Elm Square
Andover, MA 01810
Telephone: (508) 475-7224
Recruiter Classification: Retained; **Lowest/Average Salary:**
$75,000/$90,000; **Industry Concentration:** Generalist with a
primary focus in Financial Services; **Function Concentration:**
Generalist with a primary focus in Finance/Accounting,
General Management, Marketing, Research and Development,
Sales

Newpoff, Brad L. — *Furst Group*
Furst Group/MPI
555 S. Perryville Road
Rockford, IL 61108
Telephone: (815) 229-9111
Recruiter Classification: Retained; **Lowest/Average Salary:**
$60,000/$90,000; **Industry Concentration:** Generalist with a
primary focus in Insurance; **Function Concentration:**
Generalist with a primary focus in Finance/Accounting,
Human Resources, Marketing, Research and Development,
Sales

Nichols, Gary — *Senior Associate*
Koontz, Jeffries & Associates, Inc.
18-22 Bank Street
Summit, NJ 07901
Telephone: (908) 598-1900
Recruiter Classification: Retained; **Lowest/Average Salary:**
$60,000/$90,000; **Industry Concentration:** Generalist with a
primary focus in Financial Services; **Function Concentration:**
Generalist with a primary focus in Administration, Engineering,
Finance/Accounting, General Management, Human Resources,
Marketing, Research and Development, Sales,
Women/Minorities

Niejet, Michael C. — *Vice President*
O'Brien & Bell
812 Huron Road, Suite 535
Cleveland, OH 44115
Telephone: (216) 575-1212
Recruiter Classification: Retained; **Lowest/Average Salary:**
$75,000/$90,000; **Industry Concentration:** Financial Services;
Function Concentration: Generalist with a primary focus in
General Management, Marketing, Sales

Nielsen, Sue — *Recruiter*
Ells Personnel System Inc.
9900 Bren Road East, Suite 105 Opus Center
Minnetonka, MN 55343
Telephone: (612) 932-9933
Recruiter Classification: Contingency; **Lowest/Average Salary:**
$20,000/$20,000; **Industry Concentration:** Generalist with a
primary focus in Insurance; **Function Concentration:**
Generalist with a primary focus in Administration,
Finance/Accounting, Human Resources, Women/Minorities

Noebel, Todd R. — *President*
The Noebel Search Group, Inc.
14902 Preston Road, Suite 404-102
Dallas, TX 75240
Telephone: (972) 458-7788
Recruiter Classification: Retained; **Lowest/Average Salary:**
$60,000/$90,000; **Industry Concentration:** Generalist with a
primary focus in Financial Services, Insurance; **Function
Concentration:** Finance/Accounting, General Management,
Human Resources, Women/Minorities

Nolan, Robert — *Associate*
Source Services Corporation
150 South Warner Road, Suite 238
King of Prussia, PA 19406
Telephone: (610) 341-1960
Recruiter Classification: Contingency; **Lowest/Average
Salary:** $30,000/$50,000; **Industry Concentration:** Financial
Services; **Function Concentration:** Engineering,
Finance/Accounting

Nolen, Shannon — *Associate*
Source Services Corporation
2029 Century Park East, Suite 1350
Los Angeles, CA 90067
Telephone: (310) 277-8092
Recruiter Classification: Contingency; **Lowest/Average
Salary:** $30,000/$50,000; **Industry Concentration:** Financial
Services; **Function Concentration:** Engineering,
Finance/Accounting

Nolte, William D. — *Principal*
W.D. Nolte & Company
6 Middlesex Road
Darien, CT 06820
Telephone: (203) 323-5858
Recruiter Classification: Retained; **Lowest/Average Salary:**
$75,000/$90,000; **Industry Concentration:** Generalist with a
primary focus in Financial Services, Insurance, Venture Capital;
Function Concentration: Generalist with a primary focus in
Engineering, Finance/Accounting, General Management,
Human Resources, Marketing, Sales

Norman, Randy — *Vice President*
Austin-McGregor International
12005 Ford Road, Suite 720
Dallas, TX 75234-7247
Telephone: (972) 488-0500
Recruiter Classification: Retained; **Lowest/Average Salary:**
$50,000/$90,000; **Industry Concentration:** Generalist with a
primary focus in Venture Capital; **Function Concentration:**
Generalist with a primary focus in Engineering,
Finance/Accounting, General Management, Human Resources,
Marketing, Research and Development, Sales,
Women/Minorities

Normann, Amy — *Research Associate*
Robert M. Flanagan & Associates, Ltd.
Fields Lane, JMK Building
North Salem, NY 10560-0339
Telephone: (914) 277-7210
Recruiter Classification: Retained; **Lowest/Average Salary:**
$90,000/$90,000; **Industry Concentration:** Generalist with a
primary focus in Financial Services, Insurance; **Function
Concentration:** Generalist with a primary focus in
Administration, Finance/Accounting, Human Resources,
Marketing, Sales

Norris, Ken — *Vice President*
A.T. Kearney, Inc.
222 West Adams Street
Chicago, IL 60606
Telephone: (312) 648-0111
Recruiter Classification: Retained; **Lowest/Average Salary:**
$90,000/$90,000; **Industry Concentration:** Generalist
with a primary focus in Financial Services; **Function
Concentration:** Generalist with a primary focus in
Engineering, Finance/Accounting, General
Management

Norsell, Paul E. — *President*
Paul Norsell & Associates, Inc.
P.O. Box 6686
Auburn, CA 95604-6686
Telephone: (916) 269-0121
Recruiter Classification: Retained; **Lowest/Average Salary:**
$125,000/$135,000; **Industry Concentration:** Generalist with
a primary focus in Financial Services; **Function
Concentration:** Generalist with a primary focus in
Administration, Engineering, Finance/Accounting, General
Management, Human Resources, Marketing, Research and
Development, Sales

Norton, James B. — *Partner*
Lamalie Amrop International
191 Peachtree Street N.E.
Atlanta, GA 30303-1747
Telephone: (404) 688-0800
Recruiter Classification: Retained; **Lowest/Average Salary:**
$90,000/$90,000; **Industry Concentration:** Generalist with a
primary focus in Financial Services; **Function Concentration:**
Generalist

Nunziata, Peter — *Consultant*
Atlantic Search Group, Inc.
One Liberty Square
Boston, MA 02109
Telephone: (617) 426-9700
Recruiter Classification: Contingency; **Lowest/Average Salary:**
$20,000/$60,000; **Industry Concentration:** Generalist with a
primary focus in Financial Services; **Function Concentration:**
Finance/Accounting

Nutter, Roger — *Principal*
Raymond Karsan Associates
100 Merchant Street, Suite 220
Cincinnati, OH 45246
Telephone: (513) 771-7979
Recruiter Classification: Retained; **Lowest/Average Salary:**
$30,000/$90,000; **Industry Concentration:** Generalist with a
primary focus in Insurance; **Function Concentration:**
Generalist

O'Brien, Susan — *Associate*
Source Services Corporation
1105 Schrock Road, Suite 510
Columbus, OH 43229
Telephone: (614) 846-3311
Recruiter Classification: Contingency; **Lowest/Average
Salary:** $30,000/$50,000; **Industry Concentration:** Financial
Services; **Function Concentration:** Engineering,
Finance/Accounting

O'Connell, Mary — *Executive Recruiter*
CPS Inc.
303 Congress Street, 5th Floor
Boston, MA 02210
Telephone: (617) 439-7950
Recruiter Classification: Contingency; **Lowest/Average Salary:**
$30,000/$50,000; **Industry Concentration:** Generalist with a
primary focus in Financial Services, Insurance; **Function
Concentration:** Engineering, Research and Development,
Sales, Women/Minorities

O'Connell, Michael — *Partner*
Ryan, Miller & Associates Inc.
4601 Wilshire Boulevard, Suite 225
Los Angeles, CA 90010
Telephone: (213) 938-4768
Recruiter Classification: Contingency, Executive Temporary;
Lowest/Average Salary: $60,000/$60,000; **Industry
Concentration:** Financial Services; **Function Concentration:**
Finance/Accounting

O'Halloran, Robert — *Executive Recruiter*
MSI International
1050 Crown Pointe Parkway
Suite 1000
Atlanta, GA 30338
Telephone: (404) 394-2494
Recruiter Classification: Contingency; **Lowest/Average Salary:**
$30,000/$75,000; **Industry Concentration:** Generalist with a
primary focus in Financial Services; **Function Concentration:**
Generalist with a primary focus in Finance/Accounting

O'Hara, Daniel M. — *Managing Director*
Lynch Miller Moore, Inc.
10 South Wacker Drive, Suite 2935
Chicago, IL 60606
Telephone: (312) 876-1505
Recruiter Classification: Retained; **Lowest/Average Salary:**
$75,000/$90,000; **Industry Concentration:** Generalist with a
primary focus in Financial Services, Venture Capital; **Function
Concentration:** Generalist with a primary focus in
Administration, Finance/Accounting, General Management,
Human Resources, Marketing, Research and Development,
Sales

O'Maley, Kimberlee — *Director*
Spencer Stuart
525 Market Street, Suite 3700
San Francisco, CA 94105
Telephone: (415) 495-4141
Recruiter Classification: Retained; **Lowest/Average Salary:**
$90,000/$90,000; **Industry Concentration:** Generalist with a
primary focus in Financial Services; **Function Concentration:**
Generalist with a primary focus in Finance/Accounting,
General Management, Marketing, Sales

O'Neill, James P. — *Partner*
Allerton Heneghan & O'Neill
70 West Madison Street, Suite 2015
Chicago, IL 60602
Telephone: (312) 263-1075
Recruiter Classification: Retained; **Lowest/Average Salary:**
$90,000/$90,000; **Industry Concentration:** Generalist with a
primary focus in Financial Services, Insurance, Venture Capital;
Function Concentration: Generalist with a primary focus in
Finance/Accounting, General Management, Human Resources,
Women/Minorities

O'Neill, Stephen A. — *Senior Associate*
Harris Heery & Associates
40 Richards Avenue
One Norwalk West
Norwalk, CT 06854
Telephone: (203) 857-0808
Recruiter Classification: Retained; **Lowest/Average Salary:**
$75,000/$90,000; **Industry Concentration:** Financial Services,
Insurance; **Function Concentration:** Finance/Accounting,
General Management, Marketing

O'Reilly, John — *Director*
Stratford Group
445 Byers Road
Miamisburg, OH 45342
Telephone: (937) 859-6797
Recruiter Classification: Retained; **Lowest/Average Salary:**
$75,000/$90,000; **Industry Concentration:** Generalist with a
primary focus in Financial Services, Insurance; **Function**
Concentration: Generalist with a primary focus in
Finance/Accounting, General Management

Occhiboi, Emil — *Associate*
Source Services Corporation
925 Westchester Avenue, Suite 309
White Plains, NY 10604
Telephone: (914) 428-9100
Recruiter Classification: Contingency; **Lowest/Average**
Salary: $30,000/$50,000; **Industry Concentration:** Financial
Services; **Function Concentration:** Engineering,
Finance/Accounting

Ocon, Olga — *Principal*
Busch International
One First Street, Suite One
Los Altos, CA 94022-2754
Telephone: (650) 949-1115
Recruiter Classification: Retained; **Lowest/Average Salary:**
$90,000/$90,000; **Industry Concentration:** Venture Capital;
Function Concentration: Generalist with a primary focus in
Engineering, Finance/Accounting, General Management,
Marketing, Research and Development, Sales

Ogden, Dayton — *Senior Director*
Spencer Stuart
Financial Centre
695 East Main Street
Stamford, CT 06901
Telephone: (203) 324-6333
Recruiter Classification: Retained; **Lowest/Average Salary:**
$90,000/$90,000; **Industry Concentration:** Generalist
with a primary focus in Financial Services; **Function**
Concentration: Generalist with a primary focus in
General Management

Ogdon, Thomas H. — *President*
The Ogdon Partnership
375 Park Avenue, Suite 2409
New York, NY 10152-0175
Telephone: (212) 308-1600
Recruiter Classification: Retained; **Lowest/Average Salary:**
$90,000/$90,000; **Industry Concentration:** Generalist with a
primary focus in Financial Services, Insurance, Venture Capital;
Function Concentration: Generalist with a primary focus in
Administration, Finance/Accounting, General Management,
Human Resources, Marketing, Research and Development,
Sales

Ogilvie, Kit — *Vice President Bio-Pharmaceutical*
Division
Howard Fischer Associates, Inc.
1800 John F. Kennedy Boulevard, 7th Floor
Philadelphia, PA 19103
Telephone: (215) 568-8363
Recruiter Classification: Retained; **Lowest/Average Salary:**
$90,000/$90,000; **Industry Concentration:** Financial Services,
Insurance, Venture Capital; **Function Concentration:**
Generalist with a primary focus in Administration,
Finance/Accounting, General Management, Human
Resources, Marketing, Research and Development, Sales,
Women/Minorities

Ohman, Gregory L. — *Senior Vice President*
Skott/Edwards Consultants, Inc.
500 Fifth Avenue, 26th Floor
New York, NY 10110
Telephone: (212) 382-1166
Recruiter Classification: Retained; **Lowest/Average Salary:**
$90,000/$90,000; **Industry Concentration:** Financial Services;
Function Concentration: Administration, Finance/Accounting,
General Management, Human Resources

Oldfield, Theresa — *Partner*
Strategic Alliance Network, Ltd.
10901 Reed Hartman Highway
Suite 217
Cincinnati, OH 45242
Telephone: (513) 792-2800
Recruiter Classification: Retained; **Lowest/Average Salary:**
$30,000/$90,000; **Industry Concentration:** Financial Services;
Function Concentration: Finance/Accounting, Marketing,
Sales

Olin, Robyn — *Executive Recruiter*
Richard, Wayne and Roberts
24 Greenway Plaza, Suite 1304
Houston, TX 77046-2493
Telephone: (713) 629-6681
Recruiter Classification: Retained; **Lowest/Average Salary:**
$50,000/$90,000; **Industry Concentration:** Generalist
with a primary focus in Financial Services; **Function**
Concentration: Generalist with a primary focus in
Finance/Accounting

Olsen, Kristine — *Research Associate*
Williams Executive Search, Inc.
4200 Norwest Center
90 South 7th Street
Minneapolis, MN 55402
Telephone: (612) 339-2900
Recruiter Classification: Retained; **Lowest/Average Salary:**
$75,000/$75,000; **Industry Concentration:** Generalist with a
primary focus in Financial Services; **Function Concentration:**
Generalist

Olsen, Robert — *Associate*
Source Services Corporation
150 South Wacker Drive, Suite 400
Chicago, IL 60606
Telephone: (312) 346-7000
Recruiter Classification: Contingency; **Lowest/Average**
Salary: $30,000/$50,000; **Industry Concentration:** Financial
Services; **Function Concentration:** Engineering,
Finance/Accounting

Ongirski, Richard P. — *Principal*
Raymond Karsan Associates
170 So. Warner Road
Wayne, PA 19087
Telephone: (610) 971-9171
Recruiter Classification: Retained; **Lowest/Average Salary:**
$30,000/$90,000; **Industry Concentration:** Generalist with a
primary focus in Insurance; **Function Concentration:**
Generalist

Onstott, Joseph — *Managing Director*
The Onstott Group, Inc.
430 Cowper Street
Palo Alto, CA 94301
Telephone: (415) 617-4500
Recruiter Classification: Retained; **Lowest/Average Salary:**
$90,000/$90,000; **Industry Concentration:** Financial
Services, Venture Capital; **Function Concentration:**
Generalist with a primary focus in Administration,
Finance/Accounting, General Management, Human
Resources, Marketing, Sales

Onstott, Joseph E. — *Managing Director*
The Onstott Group, Inc.
60 William Street
Wellesley, MA 02181
Telephone: (781) 235-3050
Recruiter Classification: Retained; **Lowest/Average Salary:**
$90,000/$90,000; **Industry Concentration:** Generalist
with a primary focus in Financial Services, Venture
Capital; **Function Concentration:** Generalist with a
primary focus in Finance/Accounting, General
Management, Marketing, Sales

Oppedisano, Edward — *Chairman and CEO*
Oppedisano & Company, Inc.
370 Lexington Avenue, Suite 1200
New York, NY 10017
Telephone: (212) 696-0144
Recruiter Classification: Retained; **Lowest/Average Salary:**
$60,000/$90,000; **Industry Concentration:** Financial Services;
Function Concentration: Generalist with a primary focus in
Finance/Accounting

Orkin, Ralph — *Principal*
Sanford Rose Associates
26250 Euclid Avenue, Suite 629
Euclid, OH 44132
Telephone: (216) 731-0005
Recruiter Classification: Contingency; **Lowest/Average Salary:**
$30,000/$75,000; **Industry Concentration:** Generalist with a
primary focus in Financial Services; **Function Concentration:**
Generalist

Orkin, Sheilah — *Principal*
Sanford Rose Associates
26250 Euclid Avenue, Suite 629
Euclid, OH 44132
Telephone: (216) 731-0005
Recruiter Classification: Contingency; **Lowest/Average Salary:**
$30,000/$75,000; **Industry Concentration:** Generalist with a
primary focus in Financial Services; **Function Concentration:**
Generalist

Ornish, Cindy — *Senior Search Consultant*
Kaye-Bassman International Corp.
18333 Preston Road, Suite 500
Dallas, TX 75252
Telephone: (972) 931-5242
Recruiter Classification: Retained; **Lowest/Average Salary:**
$40,000/$75,000; **Industry Concentration:** Insurance;
Function Concentration: General Management, Marketing,
Sales

Ornstein, Robert — *Partner*
Trebor Weldon Lawrence, Inc.
355 Lexington Avenue
New York, NY 10017
Telephone: (212) 867-0066
Recruiter Classification: Retained; **Lowest/Average Salary:**
$75,000/$90,000; **Industry Concentration:** Financial Services;
Function Concentration: General Management, Marketing,
Sales

Orr, Stacie — *Associate*
Source Services Corporation
155 Federal Street, Suite 410
Boston, MA 02110
Telephone: (617) 482-8211
Recruiter Classification: Contingency; **Lowest/Average
Salary:** $30,000/$50,000; **Industry Concentration:** Financial
Services; **Function Concentration:** Engineering,
Finance/Accounting

Oswald, Mark G. — *Senior Vice President*
Canny, Bowen Inc.
101 Federal Street, Suite 1900
Boston, MA 02110
Telephone: (617) 292-6242
Recruiter Classification: Retained; **Lowest/Average Salary:**
$90,000/$90,000; **Industry Concentration:** Generalist with a
primary focus in Financial Services, Insurance; **Function
Concentration:** Generalist with a primary focus in General
Management, Human Resources, Marketing,
Women/Minorities

Ott, George W. — *President and CEO*
Ott & Hansen, Inc.
136 South Oak Knoll, Suite 300
Pasadena, CA 91101
Telephone: (818) 578-0551
Recruiter Classification: Retained; **Lowest/Average Salary:**
$75,000/$90,000; **Industry Concentration:** Generalist with a
primary focus in Financial Services, Venture Capital; **Function
Concentration:** Generalist with a primary focus in
Finance/Accounting, General Management, Human Resources,
Marketing, Sales

Ottenritter, Chris — *Executive Recruiter*
CPS Inc.
One Westbrook Corporate Centre, Suite 600
Westchester, IL 60154
Telephone: (708) 531-8370
Recruiter Classification: Contingency; **Lowest/Average
Salary:** $30,000/$50,000; **Industry Concentration:**
Generalist with a primary focus in Financial Services,
Insurance; **Function Concentration:** Engineering,
Research and Development, Sales, Women/
Minorities

Ouellette, Christopher — *Associate*
Source Services Corporation
155 Federal Street, Suite 410
Boston, MA 02110
Telephone: (617) 482-8211
Recruiter Classification: Contingency; **Lowest/Average Salary:** $30,000/$50,000; **Industry Concentration:** Financial Services; **Function Concentration:** Engineering, Finance/Accounting

Overlock, Craig — *Consultant*
Ray & Berndtson
Sears Tower, 233 South Wacker Drive, Suite 4020
Chicago, IL 60606-6310
Telephone: (312) 876-0730
Recruiter Classification: Retained; **Lowest/Average Salary:** $90,000/$90,000; **Industry Concentration:** Generalist with a primary focus in Financial Services, Insurance; **Function Concentration:** Generalist with a primary focus in Administration, Finance/Accounting, General Management, Human Resources, Marketing, Research and Development, Sales, Women/Minorities

Owen, Christopher — *Associate*
Source Services Corporation
8614 Westwood Center, Suite 750
Vienna, VA 22182
Telephone: (703) 790-5610
Recruiter Classification: Contingency; **Lowest/Average Salary:** $30,000/$50,000; **Industry Concentration:** Financial Services; **Function Concentration:** Engineering, Finance/Accounting

Pace, Susan A. — *Managing Director*
Horton International
10 Tower Lane
Avon, CT 06001
Telephone: (860) 674-8701
Recruiter Classification: Retained; **Lowest/Average Salary:** $90,000/$90,000; **Industry Concentration:** Generalist with a primary focus in Financial Services, Insurance; **Function Concentration:** Generalist with a primary focus in Engineering, Finance/Accounting, General Management, Human Resources, Marketing, Sales

Pachowitz, John — *Associate*
Source Services Corporation
1233 North Mayfair Road, Suite 300
Milwaukee, WI 53226
Telephone: (414) 774-6700
Recruiter Classification: Contingency; **Lowest/Average Salary:** $30,000/$50,000; **Industry Concentration:** Financial Services; **Function Concentration:** Engineering, Finance/Accounting

Padilla, Jose Sanchez — *Consultant*
Egon Zehnder International Inc.
Paseo de las Palmas No. 405-703
Co. Lomas de Chapultepec
Mexico City, D.F., MEXICO 11000
Telephone: (525) 540-7635
Recruiter Classification: Retained; **Lowest/Average Salary:** $90,000/$90,000; **Industry Concentration:** Generalist with a primary focus in Financial Services; **Function Concentration:** Generalist

Page, G. Schuyler — *Vice President*
A.T. Kearney, Inc.
Lincoln Plaza, Suite 4170
500 North Akard Street
Dallas, TX 75201
Telephone: (214) 969-0010
Recruiter Classification: Retained; **Lowest/Average Salary:** $90,000/$90,000; **Industry Concentration:** Generalist with a primary focus in Financial Services; **Function Concentration:** Generalist with a primary focus in Finance/Accounting

Palazio, Carla — *Vice President*
A.T. Kearney, Inc.
First Union Financial Center, Suite 3500
200 South Biscayne Boulevard
Miami, FL 33131
Telephone: (305) 577-0046
Recruiter Classification: Retained; **Lowest/Average Salary:** $90,000/$90,000; **Industry Concentration:** Generalist with a primary focus in Financial Services; **Function Concentration:** Generalist with a primary focus in Finance/Accounting, General Management

Paliwoda, William — *Associate*
Source Services Corporation
925 Westchester Avenue, Suite 309
White Plains, NY 10604
Telephone: (914) 428-9100
Recruiter Classification: Contingency; **Lowest/Average Salary:** $30,000/$50,000; **Industry Concentration:** Financial Services; **Function Concentration:** Engineering, Finance/Accounting

Pallman-David, Cynthia — *Senior Associate/Director of Research*
Bonnell Associates Ltd.
2960 Post Road, Suite 200
Southport, CT 06490
Telephone: (203) 319-7214
Recruiter Classification: Retained; **Lowest/Average Salary:** $90,000/$90,000; **Industry Concentration:** Generalist with a primary focus in Financial Services, Insurance; **Function Concentration:** Generalist with a primary focus in Finance/Accounting, General Management, Human Resources, Sales, Women/Minorities

Palma, Frank R. — *Executive Vice President*
Goodrich & Sherwood Associates, Inc.
6 Century Drive
Parsippany, NJ 07054
Telephone: (201) 455-7100
Recruiter Classification: Retained; **Lowest/Average Salary:** $60,000/$90,000; **Industry Concentration:** Generalist with a primary focus in Financial Services, Insurance, Venture Capital; **Function Concentration:** Generalist with a primary focus in Administration, Finance/Accounting, General Management, Human Resources, Marketing, Sales

Palmer, Carlton A. — *Senior Vice President/Partner*
Beall & Company, Inc.
535 Colonial Park Drive
Roswell, GA 30075
Telephone: (404) 992-0900
Recruiter Classification: Retained; **Lowest/Average Salary:** $90,000/$90,000; **Industry Concentration:** Generalist with a primary focus in Financial Services, Insurance, Venture Capital; **Function Concentration:** Generalist with a primary focus in Administration, Engineering, Finance/Accounting, General Management, Human Resources, Marketing, Research and Development, Sales

Palmer, James H. — *Vice President*
The Hindman Company
Browenton Place, Suite 110
2000 Warrington Way
Louisville, KY 40222
Telephone: (502) 426-4040
Recruiter Classification: Retained; **Lowest/Average Salary:**
$50,000/$90,000; **Industry Concentration:** Generalist with a
primary focus in Financial Services; **Function Concentration:**
Generalist with a primary focus in Engineering,
Finance/Accounting, General Management, Human Resources,
Marketing, Sales

Palmieri, Cathryn C. — *Vice President*
Korn/Ferry International
237 Park Avenue
New York, NY 10017
Telephone: (212) 687-1834
Recruiter Classification: Retained; **Lowest/Average Salary:**
$100,000/$150,000; **Industry Concentration:** Generalist with a
primary focus in Financial Services; **Function Concentration:**
Generalist

Panarese, Pam — *Consultant*
Howard Fischer Associates, Inc.
1800 John F. Kennedy Boulevard, 7th Floor
Philadelphia, PA 19103
Telephone: (215) 568-8363
Recruiter Classification: Retained; **Lowest/Average Salary:**
$90,000/$90,000; **Industry Concentration:** Generalist with a
primary focus in Financial Services, Insurance, Venture Capital;
Function Concentration: Generalist with a primary focus in
Administration, Finance/Accounting, General Management,
Human Resources, Marketing, Research and Development,
Sales, Women/Minorities

Panchella, Joseph J. — *Principal*
Wellington Management Group
1601 Market Street, Suite 2902
Philadelphia, PA 19103-2499
Telephone: (215) 569-8900
Recruiter Classification: Retained; **Lowest/Average Salary:**
$90,000/$90,000; **Industry Concentration:** Generalist with a
primary focus in Financial Services, Venture Capital; **Function
Concentration:** Generalist with a primary focus in
Finance/Accounting, General Management

Pankratz, Dennis — *Vice President*
Furst Group/MPI
555 S. Perryville Road
Rockford, IL 61108
Telephone: (815) 229-9111
Recruiter Classification: Retained; **Lowest/Average Salary:**
$60,000/$90,000; **Industry Concentration:** Generalist with a
primary focus in Insurance; **Function Concentration:** Generalist
with a primary focus in Finance/Accounting, General
Management, Marketing, Research and Development, Sales

Papasadero, Kathleen — *Associate*
Woodworth International Group
620 SW 5th Avenue, Suite 1225
Portland, OR 97204
Telephone: (503) 225-5000
Recruiter Classification: Retained; **Lowest/Average Salary:**
$60,000/$90,000; **Industry Concentration:** Generalist with a
primary focus in Financial Services, Insurance, Venture Capital;
Function Concentration: Generalist with a primary focus in
Engineering, Finance/Accounting, General Management, Human
Resources, Marketing, Research and Development, Sales

Papciak, Dennis J. — *President*
Temporary Accounting Personnel
2100 Wharton Street
Suite 710
Pittsburgh, PA 15203-1942
Telephone: (412) 488-9155
Recruiter Classification: Executive Temporary; **Lowest/Average
Salary:** $60,000/$90,000; **Industry Concentration:** Generalist
with a primary focus in Financial Services; **Function
Concentration:** Administration, Finance/Accounting

Papciak, Dennis J. — *President*
Accounting Personnel Associates, Inc.
2100 Wharton Street, Suite 710
Pittsburgh, PA 15203-1942
Telephone: (412) 481-6015
Recruiter Classification: Contingency; **Lowest/Average Salary:**
$20,000/$50,000; **Industry Concentration:** Financial Services;
Function Concentration: Administration, Finance/Accounting,
Women/Minorities

Papoulias, Cathy — *Vice President*
Pendleton James and Associates, Inc.
One International Place
Suite 2350
Boston, MA 02110
Telephone: (617) 261-9696
Recruiter Classification: Retained; **Lowest/Average Salary:**
$90,000/$90,000; **Industry Concentration:** Financial Services,
Venture Capital; **Function Concentration:** General
Management, Marketing, Sales, Women/Minorities

Pappas, Christina E. — *Executive Search
Consultant*
Williams Executive Search, Inc.
4200 Norwest Center
90 South 7th Street
Minneapolis, MN 55402
Telephone: (612) 339-2900
Recruiter Classification: Retained; **Lowest/Average Salary:**
$75,000/$90,000; **Industry Concentration:** Generalist with a
primary focus in Financial Services, Venture Capital; **Function
Concentration:** Generalist with a primary focus in
Finance/Accounting

Paradise, Malcolm — *Associate*
Source Services Corporation
71 Spit Brook Road, Suite 305
Nashua, NH 03060
Telephone: (603) 888-7650
Recruiter Classification: Contingency; **Lowest/Average
Salary:** $30,000/$50,000; **Industry Concentration:** Financial
Services; **Function Concentration:** Engineering,
Finance/Accounting

Pardo, Maria Elena — *Consultant*
Smith Search, S.C.
Barranca del Muerto No. 472, Col. Alpes
Mexico City, D.F., MEXICO 01010
Telephone: (525) 593-8766
Recruiter Classification: Retained; **Lowest/Average Salary:**
$60,000/$90,000; **Industry Concentration:** Generalist
with a primary focus in Financial Services, Venture
Capital; **Function Concentration:** Generalist with a primary
focus in Administration, Engineering, Finance/Accounting,
General Management, Human Resources, Marketing,
Sales

Parente, James — *Associate*
Source Services Corporation
925 Westchester Avenue, Suite 309
White Plains, NY 10604
Telephone: (914) 428-9100
Recruiter Classification: Contingency; **Lowest/Average Salary:**
$30,000/$50,000; **Industry Concentration:** Financial Services;
Function Concentration: Engineering, Finance/Accounting

Park, Dabney G. — *Senior Partner*
Mark Stanley/EMA Partners International
2121 Ponce de Leon Boulevard #630
P.O. Box 149071
Coral Gables, FL 33114
Telephone: (305) 444-1612
Recruiter Classification: Retained; **Lowest/Average Salary:**
$75,000/$90,000; **Industry Concentration:** Generalist with a
primary focus in Financial Services; **Function Concentration:**
Generalist with a primary focus in Finance/Accounting,
General Management, Human Resources, Sales

Parker, Gayle — *Partner*
Trebor Weldon Lawrence, Inc.
355 Lexington Avenue
New York, NY 10017
Telephone: (212) 867-0066
Recruiter Classification: Retained; **Lowest/Average Salary:**
$75,000/$90,000; **Industry Concentration:** Financial Services;
Function Concentration: General Management, Marketing,
Sales

Parker, P. Grant — *Principal*
Raymond Karsan Associates
170 So. Warner Road
Wayne, PA 19087
Telephone: (610) 971-9171
Recruiter Classification: Retained; **Lowest/Average Salary:**
$30,000/$90,000; **Industry Concentration:** Generalist with a
primary focus in Insurance; **Function Concentration:**
Generalist

Parkhurst, David R. — *Consultant*
Tyler & Company
1000 Abernathy Road
Suite 1400
Atlanta, GA 30328-5655
Telephone: (770) 396-3939
Recruiter Classification: Retained; **Lowest/Average Salary:**
$75,000/$90,000; **Industry Concentration:** Insurance;
Function Concentration: Generalist

Parroco, Jason — *Associate*
Source Services Corporation
2850 National City Tower
Louisville, KY 40202
Telephone: (502) 581-9900
Recruiter Classification: Contingency; **Lowest/Average Salary:**
$30,000/$50,000; **Industry Concentration:** Financial Services;
Function Concentration: Engineering, Finance/Accounting

Parry, William H. — *Vice President*
Horton International
24405 Chestnut Street, Suite 107
Santa Clarita, CA 91321
Telephone: (805) 222-2272
Recruiter Classification: Retained; **Lowest/Average Salary:**
$90,000/$90,000; **Industry Concentration:** Generalist with a
primary focus in Financial Services, Insurance; **Function
Concentration:** Generalist with a primary focus in General
Management, Human Resources, Marketing, Research and
Development, Sales

Parsons, Allison D. — *Senior Consultant*
Barton Associates, Inc.
One Riverway, Suite 2500
Houston, TX 77056
Telephone: (713) 961-9111
Recruiter Classification: Retained; **Lowest/Average Salary:**
$75,000/$90,000; **Industry Concentration:** Generalist with a
primary focus in Financial Services; **Function Concentration:**
Generalist with a primary focus in Administration, General
Management, Human Resources, Marketing

Pastrana, Dario — *Managing Partner*
Egon Zehnder International Inc.
Paseo de las Palmas No. 405-703
Co. Lomas de Chapultepec
Mexico City, D.F., MEXICO 11000
Telephone: (525) 540-7635
Recruiter Classification: Retained; **Lowest/Average Salary:**
$90,000/$90,000; **Industry Concentration:** Generalist with a
primary focus in Financial Services; **Function Concentration:**
Generalist

Patel, Shailesh — *Associate*
Source Services Corporation
925 Westchester Avenue, Suite 309
White Plains, NY 10604
Telephone: (914) 428-9100
Recruiter Classification: Contingency; **Lowest/Average Salary:**
$30,000/$50,000; **Industry Concentration:** Financial Services;
Function Concentration: Engineering, Finance/Accounting

Patence, David W. — *Senior Vice President*
Handy HRM Corp.
250 Park Avenue
New York, NY 10177-0074
Telephone: (212) 210-5633
Recruiter Classification: Retained; **Lowest/Average Salary:**
$90,000/$90,000; **Industry Concentration:** Financial Services;
Function Concentration: Finance/Accounting, Sales

Paternie, Patrick — *Associate*
Source Services Corporation
One Park Plaza, Suite 560
Irvine, CA 92714
Telephone: (714) 660-1666
Recruiter Classification: Contingency; **Lowest/Average Salary:**
$30,000/$50,000; **Industry Concentration:** Financial Services;
Function Concentration: Engineering, Finance/Accounting

Paul, Kathleen — *Associate*
Source Services Corporation
One CityPlace, Suite 170
St. Louis, MO 63141
Telephone: (314) 432-4500
Recruiter Classification: Contingency; **Lowest/Average Salary:**
$30,000/$50,000; **Industry Concentration:** Financial Services;
Function Concentration: Engineering, Finance/Accounting

Paul, Lisa D. — *Resource Manager*
Merit Resource Group, Inc.
7950 Dublin Boulevard, Suite 205
Dublin, CA 94568
Telephone: (510) 828-4700
Recruiter Classification: Executive Temporary; **Lowest/Average
Salary:** $75,000/$90,000; **Industry Concentration:** Generalist
with a primary focus in Financial Services, Venture Capital;
Function Concentration: Generalist with a primary focus in
Human Resources

Payette, Pierre — *Consultant*
Egon Zehnder International Inc.
1 Place Ville-Marie, Suite 3310
Montreal, Quebec, CANADA H3B 3N2
Telephone: (514) 876-4249
Recruiter Classification: Retained; **Lowest/Average Salary:**
$90,000/$90,000; **Industry Concentration:** Generalist with a
primary focus in Financial Services; **Function Concentration:**
Generalist

Paynter, Sandra L. — *Partner*
Ward Howell International, Inc.
141 Adelaide Street West
Suite 1800
Toronto, Ontario, CANADA M5H 3L5
Telephone: (416) 862-1273
Recruiter Classification: Retained; **Lowest/Average Salary:**
$75,000/$90,000; **Industry Concentration:** Financial Services,
Insurance; **Function Concentration:** Generalist

Peal, Matthew — *Associate*
Source Services Corporation
161 Ottawa NW, Suite 409D
Grand Rapids, MI 49503
Telephone: (616) 451-2400
Recruiter Classification: Contingency; **Lowest/Average Salary:**
$30,000/$50,000; **Industry Concentration:** Financial Services;
Function Concentration: Engineering, Finance/Accounting

Pearson, John R. — *Partner*
Pearson, Caldwell & Farnsworth, Inc.
One California Street, Suite 1950
San Francisco, CA 94111
Telephone: (415) 982-0300
Recruiter Classification: Retained; **Lowest/Average Salary:**
$90,000/$90,000; **Industry Concentration:** Financial Services;
Function Concentration: Administration, Finance/Accounting,
General Management, Human Resources, Marketing, Sales

Pease, Edward — *President/Co-Owner*
Don Richard Associates of Georgia, Inc.
3475 Lenox Road, Suite 210
Atlanta, GA 30326
Telephone: (404) 231-3688
Recruiter Classification: Executive Temporary; **Lowest/Average
Salary:** $60,000/$75,000; **Industry Concentration:** Financial
Services; **Function Concentration:** Finance/Accounting,
Human Resources

Pedley, Jill — *Executive Recruiter*
CPS Inc.
One Westbrook Corporate Centre, Suite 600
Westchester, IL 60154
Telephone: (708) 531-8370
Recruiter Classification: Contingency; **Lowest/Average Salary:**
$30,000/$50,000; **Industry Concentration:** Generalist with a
primary focus in Financial Services, Insurance; **Function
Concentration:** Engineering, Research and Development,
Sales, Women/Minorities

Peeney, James D. — *President*
Peeney Associates
141 South Avenue
Fanwood, NJ 07023
Telephone: (908) 322-2324
Recruiter Classification: Retained; **Lowest/Average Salary:**
$60,000/$90,000; **Industry Concentration:** Generalist with a
primary focus in Financial Services; **Function Concentration:**
Generalist with a primary focus in Administration, Engineering,
Finance/Accounting, General Management, Human Resources,
Marketing, Research and Development, Sales, Women/Minorities

Pelisson, Charles — *Vice President*
Marra Peters & Partners
Millburn Esplanade
Millburn, NJ 07041
Telephone: (201) 376-8999
Recruiter Classification: Retained; **Lowest/Average Salary:**
$60,000/$90,000; **Industry Concentration:** Generalist with a
primary focus in Financial Services; **Function Concentration:**
Generalist with a primary focus in Administration, Engineering,
Finance/Accounting, General Management, Human Resources,
Marketing, Research and Development, Sales

Pepe, Leonida R. — *Principal*
Butterfass, Pepe & MacCallan Inc.
P.O. Box 721
Mahwah, NJ 07430
Telephone: (201) 512-3330
Recruiter Classification: Retained; **Lowest/Average Salary:**
$60,000/$90,000; **Industry Concentration:** Generalist with a
primary focus in Financial Services, Insurance; **Function
Concentration:** Generalist with a primary focus in
Finance/Accounting, General Management, Human Resources,
Marketing, Women/Minorities

Percival, Chris — *Senior Legal Search Consultant*
Chicago Legal Search, Ltd.
33 North Dearborn Street, Suite 2302
Chicago, IL 60602-3109
Telephone: (312) 251-2580
Recruiter Classification: Contingency; **Lowest/Average Salary:**
$50,000/$90,000; **Industry Concentration:** Venture Capital;
Function Concentration: Women/Minorities

Peretz, Jamie — *Principal Global Financial
Services*
Korn/Ferry International
237 Park Avenue
New York, NY 10017
Telephone: (212) 687-1834
Recruiter Classification: Retained; **Lowest/Average Salary:**
$100,000/$150,000; **Industry Concentration:** Generalist with a
primary focus in Financial Services, Insurance; **Function
Concentration:** Generalist

Perkey, Richard — *Vice President*
Korn/Ferry International
303 Peachtree Street N.E.
Suite 1600
Atlanta, GA 30308
Telephone: (404) 577-7542
Recruiter Classification: Retained; **Lowest/Average Salary:**
$100,000/$150,000; **Industry Concentration:** Generalist with a
primary focus in Financial Services; **Function Concentration:**
Generalist

Pernell, Jeanette — *Vice President*
Norman Broadbent International, Inc.
Sears Tower, Suite 9850
233 South Wacker Drive
Chicago, IL 60606
Telephone: (312) 876-3300
Recruiter Classification: Retained; **Lowest/Average Salary:**
$90,000/$90,000; **Industry Concentration:** Generalist with a
primary focus in Financial Services, Insurance; **Function
Concentration:** Generalist with a primary focus in
Finance/Accounting, General Management, Human Resources,
Marketing, Sales, Women/Minorities

Peroff, Michael — *Principal*
Trebor Weldon Lawrence, Inc.
355 Lexington Avenue
New York, NY 10017
Telephone: (212) 867-0066
Recruiter Classification: Retained; **Lowest/Average Salary:**
$75,000/$90,000; **Industry Concentration:** Financial Services;
Function Concentration: General Management, Marketing,
Sales

Perry, Carolyn — *Associate*
Source Services Corporation
1 Gatehall Drive, Suite 250
Parsippany, NJ 07054
Telephone: (201) 267-3222
Recruiter Classification: Contingency; **Lowest/Average Salary:**
$30,000/$50,000; **Industry Concentration:** Financial Services;
Function Concentration: Engineering, Finance/Accounting

Perry, James — *Director*
Strategic Executives, Inc.
Six Landmark Square
4th Floor
Stamford, CT 06901
Telephone: (203) 359-5757
Recruiter Classification: Retained; **Lowest/Average Salary:**
$90,000/$90,000; **Industry Concentration:** Generalist with a
primary focus in Financial Services; **Function Concentration:**
Generalist with a primary focus in General Management,
Marketing, Sales

Peternell, Melanie — *Division Supervisor*
Signature Staffing
6800 College Boulevard, Suite 550
Overland Park, KS 66211
Telephone: (913) 338-2020
Recruiter Classification: Executive Temporary; **Lowest/Average**
Salary: $30,000/$40,000; **Industry Concentration:** Generalist
with a primary focus in Financial Services, Insurance; **Function**
Concentration: Generalist with a primary focus in
Finance/Accounting, Marketing

Peters, Kevin — *Associate*
Source Services Corporation
879 West 190th Street, Suite 250
Los Angeles, CA 90248
Telephone: (310) 323-6633
Recruiter Classification: Contingency; **Lowest/Average Salary:**
$30,000/$50,000; **Industry Concentration:** Financial Services;
Function Concentration: Engineering, Finance/Accounting

Petersen, Richard — *Associate*
Source Services Corporation
5343 North 16th Street, Suite 270
Phoenix, AZ 85016
Telephone: (602) 230-0220
Recruiter Classification: Contingency; **Lowest/Average Salary:**
$30,000/$50,000; **Industry Concentration:** Financial Services;
Function Concentration: Engineering, Finance/Accounting

Peterson, Eric N. — *Director*
Stratford Group
6120 Parkland Boulevard
Cleveland, OH 44124
Telephone: (216) 460-3232
Recruiter Classification: Retained; **Lowest/Average Salary:**
$90,000/$90,000; **Industry Concentration:** Generalist with a
primary focus in Financial Services; **Function Concentration:**
Generalist with a primary focus in Engineering,
Finance/Accounting, General Management, Human Resources,
Marketing, Sales

Peterson, John — *Executive Recruiter*
CPS Inc.
One Westbrook Corporate Centre, Suite 600
Westchester, IL 60154
Telephone: (708) 531-8370
Recruiter Classification: Contingency; **Lowest/Average Salary:**
$30,000/$50,000; **Industry Concentration:** Generalist with a
primary focus in Financial Services, Insurance; **Function**
Concentration: Engineering, Research and Development,
Sales, Women/Minorities

Pettibone, Linda G. — *Vice President*
Herbert Mines Associates, Inc.
399 Park Avenue, 27th Floor
New York, NY 10022
Telephone: (212) 355-0909
Recruiter Classification: Retained; **Lowest/Average Salary:**
$75,000/$90,000; **Industry Concentration:** Venture Capital;
Function Concentration: Generalist with a primary focus in
Administration, Finance/Accounting, General Management,
Human Resources, Marketing, Sales

Pettway, Samuel H. — *Director*
Spencer Stuart
One Atlantic Center, Suite 3230
1201 West Peachtree Street
Atlanta, GA 30309
Telephone: (404) 892-2800
Recruiter Classification: Retained; **Lowest/Average Salary:**
$90,000/$90,000; **Industry Concentration:** Financial Services,
Venture Capital; **Function Concentration:** Administration,
Finance/Accounting, General Management, Human Resources,
Marketing, Sales, Women/Minorities

Petty, J. Scott — *Associate*
The Arcus Group
15915 Katy Freeway, Suite 635
Houston, TX 77094
Telephone: (281) 578-3100
Recruiter Classification: Retained; **Lowest/Average Salary:**
$90,000/$90,000; **Industry Concentration:** Generalist with a
primary focus in Insurance, Venture Capital; **Function**
Concentration: Generalist with a primary focus in
Administration, Engineering, Finance/Accounting, Human
Resources, Marketing, Sales

Pfannkuche, Anthony V. — *Senior Director*
Spencer Stuart
10900 Wilshire Boulevard, Suite 800
Los Angeles, CA 90024-6524
Telephone: (310) 209-0610
Recruiter Classification: Retained; **Lowest/Average Salary:**
$40,000/$60,000; **Industry Concentration:** Venture Capital;
Function Concentration: Generalist with a primary focus in
Finance/Accounting, General Management

Pfau, Madelaine — *Partner*
Heidrick & Struggles, Inc.
2200 Ross Avenue, Suite 4700E
Dallas, TX 75201-2787
Telephone: (214) 220-2130
Recruiter Classification: Retained; **Lowest/Average Salary:**
$75,000/$90,000; **Industry Concentration:** Generalist with a
primary focus in Financial Services; **Function Concentration:**
Generalist

Pfeiffer, Irene — *Director*
Price Waterhouse
Esso Plaza - East Tower
1200 425 First Street S.W.
Calgary, Alberta, CANADA T2P 3V7
Telephone: (403) 267-1200
Recruiter Classification: Retained; **Lowest/Average Salary:**
$75,000/$75,000; **Industry Concentration:** Generalist with a
primary focus in Financial Services; **Function Concentration:**
Generalist with a primary focus in Administration, Engineering,
Finance/Accounting, General Management, Human Resources,
Marketing, Sales

Phillips, Donald L. — *Principal*
O'Shea, Divine & Company, Inc.
610 Newport Center Drive, Suite 1040
Newport Beach, CA 92660
Telephone: (714) 720-9070
Recruiter Classification: Retained; **Lowest/Average Salary:**
$75,000/$90,000; **Industry Concentration:** Generalist with a
primary focus in Financial Services; **Function Concentration:**
Generalist with a primary focus in Administration, Engineering,
Finance/Accounting, General Management, Human Resources,
Marketing, Sales, Women/Minorities

Phillips, James L. — *Partner*
Highland Search Group
565 Fifth Avenue, 22nd Floor
New York, NY 10017
Telephone: (212) 328-1113
Recruiter Classification: Retained; **Lowest/Average Salary:**
$90,000/$90,000; **Industry Concentration:** Financial Services,
Insurance, Venture Capital; **Function Concentration:** Generalist
with a primary focus in Administration, Finance/Accounting,
General Management, Human Resources, Sales,
Women/Minorities

Phillips, Richard K. — *Executive Vice President,
Financial Services*
Handy HRM Corp.
250 Park Avenue
New York, NY 10177-0074
Telephone: (212) 210-5636
Recruiter Classification: Retained; **Lowest/Average Salary:**
$90,000/$90,000; **Industry Concentration:** Financial Services,
Venture Capital; **Function Concentration:** Finance/Accounting,
Human Resources, Research and Development

Phipps, Peggy — *Researcher*
Woodworth International Group
620 SW 5th Avenue, Suite 1225
Portland, OR 97204
Telephone: (503) 225-5000
Recruiter Classification: Retained; **Lowest/Average Salary:**
$60,000/$90,000; **Industry Concentration:** Generalist with a
primary focus in Financial Services, Insurance, Venture Capital;
Function Concentration: Generalist with a primary focus in
Engineering, Finance/Accounting, General Management, Human
Resources, Marketing, Research and Development, Sales

Pickering, Dale — *President*
Agri-Tech Personnel, Inc.
3113 N.E. 69th Street
Kansas City, MO 64119
Telephone: (816) 453-7200
Recruiter Classification: Contingency; **Lowest/Average Salary:**
$30,000/$75,000; **Industry Concentration:** Financial Services;
Function Concentration: Engineering, Finance/Accounting,
General Management, Human Resources, Marketing, Research
and Development, Sales

Pickering, Dorothy C. — *Vice President*
Livingston, Robert and Company Inc.
Two Greenwich Plaza
Greenwich, CT 06830
Telephone: (203) 622-4902
Recruiter Classification: Retained; **Lowest/Average Salary:**
$90,000/$90,000; **Industry Concentration:** Generalist with a
primary focus in Financial Services; **Function Concentration:**
Generalist

Pickering, Rita — *Vice President*
Agri-Tech Personnel, Inc.
3113 N.E. 69th Street
Kansas City, MO 64119
Telephone: (816) 453-7200
Recruiter Classification: Contingency; **Lowest/Average Salary:**
$30,000/$75,000; **Industry Concentration:** Financial Services;
Function Concentration: Engineering, Finance/Accounting,
General Management, Human Resources, Marketing, Research
and Development, Sales

Pickford, Stephen T. — *President*
The Corporate Staff, Inc.
177 Bovet Road, Suite 600
San Mateo, CA 94402
Telephone: (415) 344-2613
Recruiter Classification: Executive Temporary;
Lowest/Average Salary: $40,000/$75,000; **Industry
Concentration:** Generalist with a primary focus in Financial
Services, Insurance; **Function Concentration:** Generalist
with a primary focus in Administration, Finance/
Accounting, General Management, Human Resources,
Marketing, Sales

Pierce, Mark — *Principal*
Korn/Ferry International
233 South Wacker
Chicago, IL 60606
Telephone: (312) 466-1834
Recruiter Classification: Retained; **Lowest/Average Salary:**
$100,000/$150,000; **Industry Concentration:** Generalist with a
primary focus in Financial Services, Insurance; **Function
Concentration:** Generalist

Pierce, Matthew — *Associate*
Source Services Corporation
One Park Plaza, Suite 560
Irvine, CA 92714
Telephone: (714) 660-1666
Recruiter Classification: Contingency; **Lowest/Average
Salary:** $30,000/$50,000; **Industry Concentration:** Financial
Services; **Function Concentration:** Engineering,
Finance/Accounting

Pierotazio, John — *Executive Recruiter*
CPS Inc.
One Westbrook Corporate Centre, Suite 600
Westchester, IL 60154
Telephone: (708) 531-8370
Recruiter Classification: Contingency; **Lowest/Average
Salary:** $30,000/$50,000; **Industry Concentration:**
Generalist with a primary focus in Financial Services,
Insurance; **Function Concentration:** Engineering,
Research and Development, Sales, Women/
Minorities

Pierpont-Engstrom, Elizabeth H. — *Associate*
Russell Reynolds Associates, Inc.
200 Park Avenue
New York, NY 10166-0002
Telephone: (212) 351-2000
Recruiter Classification: Retained; Lowest/Average Salary:
$90,000/$90,000; Industry Concentration: Generalist with a
primary focus in Financial Services; Function Concentration:
Generalist

Pierson, Edward J. — *Partner*
Johnson Smith & Knisely Accord
100 Park Avenue, 15th Floor
New York, NY 10017
Telephone: (212) 885-9100
Recruiter Classification: Retained; Lowest/Average Salary:
$90,000/$90,000; Industry Concentration: Financial Services,
Insurance, Venture Capital; Function Concentration: Generalist
with a primary focus in Administration, Finance/Accounting,
General Management, Human Resources, Marketing, Sales,
Women/Minorities

Pigott, Daniel — *Senior Partner*
ESA Professional Consultants
141 Durham Road
Suite 16
Madison, CT 06443
Telephone: (203) 245-1983
Recruiter Classification: Retained; Lowest/Average Salary:
$50,000/$75,000; Industry Concentration: Venture Capital;
Function Concentration: Engineering, General Management,
Human Resources, Marketing, Research and Development,
Women/Minorities

Pillow, Charles — *Associate*
Source Services Corporation
5429 LBJ Freeway, Suite 275
Dallas, TX 75240
Telephone: (214) 387-1600
Recruiter Classification: Contingency; Lowest/Average Salary:
$30,000/$50,000; Industry Concentration: Financial Services;
Function Concentration: Engineering, Finance/Accounting

Pineda, Rosanna — *Associate*
Source Services Corporation
2 Penn Plaza, Suite 1176
New York, NY 10121
Telephone: (212) 760-2200
Recruiter Classification: Contingency; Lowest/Average Salary:
$30,000/$50,000; Industry Concentration: Financial Services;
Function Concentration: Engineering, Finance/Accounting

Pinson, Stephanie L. — *President*
Gilbert Tweed/INESA
155 Prospect Avenue
West Orange, NJ 07052
Telephone: (201) 731-3033
Recruiter Classification: Retained; Lowest/Average Salary:
$90,000/$90,000; Industry Concentration: Generalist with a
primary focus in Insurance; Function Concentration:
Generalist

Pirro, Sheri — *Associate*
Source Services Corporation
1105 Schrock Road, Suite 510
Columbus, OH 43229
Telephone: (614) 846-3311
Recruiter Classification: Contingency; Lowest/Average Salary:
$30,000/$50,000; Industry Concentration: Financial Services;
Function Concentration: Engineering, Finance/Accounting

Pittard, Patrick S. — *North American Managing
Partner*
Heidrick & Struggles, Inc.
One Peachtree Center
303 Peachtree Street, NE, Suite 3100
Atlanta, GA 30308
Telephone: (404) 577-2410
Recruiter Classification: Retained; Lowest/Average Salary:
$75,000/$90,000; Industry Concentration: Generalist with a
primary focus in Financial Services; Function Concentration:
Generalist

Pitto, Lili — *Vice President*
Ryan, Miller & Associates Inc.
790 East Colorado, Suite 506
Pasadena, CA 91101
Telephone: (818) 568-3100
Recruiter Classification: Contingency; Lowest/Average Salary:
$40,000/$75,000; Industry Concentration: Financial Services;
Function Concentration: Generalist with a primary focus in
Finance/Accounting

Plant, Jerry — *Associate*
Source Services Corporation
1 Gatehall Drive, Suite 250
Parsippany, NJ 07054
Telephone: (201) 267-3222
Recruiter Classification: Contingency; Lowest/Average
Salary: $30,000/$50,000; Industry Concentration: Financial
Services; Function Concentration: Engineering,
Finance/Accounting

Platte, John D. — *Managing Director*
Russell Reynolds Associates, Inc.
200 Park Avenue
New York, NY 10166-0002
Telephone: (212) 351-2000
Recruiter Classification: Retained; Lowest/Average Salary:
$90,000/$90,000; Industry Concentration: Generalist with a
primary focus in Financial Services; Function Concentration:
Generalist

Plazza, Richard C. — *Principal*
The Executive Source
55 Fifth Avenue, 19th Floor
New York, NY 10003
Telephone: (212) 691-5505
Recruiter Classification: Executive Temporary;
Lowest/Average Salary: $75,000/$90,000; Industry
Concentration: Generalist with a primary focus in Financial
Services, Insurance, Venture Capital; Function Concentration:
Human Resources

Plessner, Rene — *President*
Rene Plessner Associates, Inc.
375 Park Avenue
New York, NY 10152
Telephone: (212) 421-3490
Recruiter Classification: Retained; Lowest/Average Salary:
$75,000/$90,000; Industry Concentration: Generalist
with a primary focus in Insurance; Function Concentration:
Generalist with a primary focus in Administration,
Finance/Accounting, General Management, Human
Resources, Marketing, Research and Development,
Sales

Plimpton, Ralph L. — *President*
R L Plimpton Associates
5655 South Yosemite Street, Suite 410
Greenwood Village, CO 80111
Telephone: (303) 771-1311
Recruiter Classification: Retained; **Lowest/Average Salary:**
$40,000/$75,000; **Industry Concentration:** Generalist with a
primary focus in Financial Services, Insurance; **Function**
Concentration: Finance/Accounting, General Management,
Human Resources, Research and Development

Pliszka, Donald J. — *Principal*
Praxis Partners
5004 Monument Avenue, Suite 102
Richmond, VA 23230
Telephone: (804) 739-5809
Recruiter Classification: Retained; **Lowest/Average Salary:**
$60,000/$90,000; **Industry Concentration:** Generalist with a
primary focus in Venture Capital; **Function Concentration:**
Generalist with a primary focus in Engineering,
Finance/Accounting, General Management, Human Resources,
Women/Minorities

Plummer, John — *President*
Plummer & Associates, Inc.
65 Rowayton Avenue
Rowayton, CT 06853
Telephone: (203) 899-1233
Recruiter Classification: Retained, Executive Temporary;
Lowest/Average Salary: $90,000/$90,000; **Industry**
Concentration: Venture Capital; **Function Concentration:**
Generalist with a primary focus in Finance/Accounting,
General Management, Human Resources, Marketing

Poirier, Frank — *Principal*
Juntunen-Combs-Poirier
111 Bayhill Drive, Suite 255
San Bruno, CA 94066
Telephone: (415) 635-0180
Recruiter Classification: Retained; **Lowest/Average Salary:**
$90,000/$90,000; **Industry Concentration:** Financial Services,
Venture Capital; **Function Concentration:** Engineering,
Finance/Accounting, General Management, Research and
Development

Poirier, Roland L. — *Partner*
Poirier, Hoevel & Co.
12400 Wilshire Boulevard, Suite 915
Los Angeles, CA 90025
Telephone: (310) 207-3427
Recruiter Classification: Retained; **Lowest/Average Salary:**
$75,000/$90,000; **Industry Concentration:** Generalist with a
primary focus in Financial Services, Insurance; **Function**
Concentration: Generalist with a primary focus in
Administration, Engineering, Finance/Accounting, General
Management, Human Resources, Marketing, Sales,
Women/Minorities

Polansky, Mark — *Vice President Advanced*
Technology
Korn/Ferry International
237 Park Avenue
New York, NY 10017
Telephone: (212) 687-1834
Recruiter Classification: Retained; **Lowest/Average Salary:**
$100,000/$150,000; **Industry Concentration:** Generalist with a
primary focus in Financial Services, Insurance; **Function**
Concentration: Generalist

Pomerance, Mark — *Executive Recruiter*
CPS Inc.
One Westbrook Corporate Centre, Suite 600
Westchester, IL 60154
Telephone: (708) 531-8370
Recruiter Classification: Contingency; **Lowest/Average Salary:**
$30,000/$50,000; **Industry Concentration:** Generalist with a
primary focus in Financial Services, Insurance; **Function**
Concentration: Engineering, Research and Development,
Sales, Women/Minorities

Pomeroy, T. Lee — *Consultant*
Egon Zehnder International Inc.
350 Park Avenue
New York, NY 10022
Telephone: (212) 838-9199
Recruiter Classification: Retained; **Lowest/Average Salary:**
$90,000/$90,000; **Industry Concentration:** Generalist with a
primary focus in Financial Services; **Function Concentration:**
Generalist

Poracky, John W. — *Partner*
M. Wood Company
10 North Dearborn Street, Suite 700
Chicago, IL 60602
Telephone: (312) 368-0633
Recruiter Classification: Retained; **Lowest/Average Salary:**
$60,000/$90,000; **Industry Concentration:** Generalist with a
primary focus in Financial Services, Insurance; **Function**
Concentration: Generalist with a primary focus in
Finance/Accounting, General Management, Sales

Poremski, Paul — *Professional Recruiter*
A.J. Burton Group, Inc.
120 East Baltimore Street, Suite 2220
Baltimore, MD 21202
Telephone: (410) 752-5244
Recruiter Classification: Contingency; **Lowest/Average Salary:**
$40,000/$75,000; **Industry Concentration:** Generalist with a
primary focus in Financial Services, Insurance; **Function**
Concentration: Generalist with a primary focus in
Administration, Finance/Accounting, General Management,
Human Resources

Porter, Albert — *Vice President*
The Experts
200 Reservoir Street
Needham, MA 02194
Telephone: (617) 449-6700
Recruiter Classification: Executive Temporary; **Lowest/Average**
Salary: $50,000/$90,000; **Industry Concentration:** Generalist
with a primary focus in Financial Services; **Function**
Concentration: Generalist with a primary focus in
Administration, Engineering, Finance/Accounting, General
Management, Human Resources, Marketing, Research and
Development, Sales

Poster, Lawrence D. — *Managing Director*
Catalyx Group
One Harkness Plaza, Suite 300
61 West 62nd Street
New York, NY 10023
Telephone: (212) 956-3525
Recruiter Classification: Retained; **Lowest/Average Salary:**
$90,000/$90,000; **Industry Concentration:** Venture Capital;
Function Concentration: Generalist with a primary focus in
General Management, Research and Development

Pototo, Brian — *Associate*
Source Services Corporation
1500 West Park Drive, Suite 390
Westborough, MA 01581
Telephone: (508) 366-2600
Recruiter Classification: Contingency; **Lowest/Average Salary:**
$30,000/$50,000; **Industry Concentration:** Financial Services;
Function Concentration: Engineering, Finance/Accounting

Potter, Mark W. — *Chief Operating Officer*
Highland Search Group
565 Fifth Avenue, 22nd Floor
New York, NY 10017
Telephone: (212) 328-1113
Recruiter Classification: Retained; **Lowest/Average Salary:**
$90,000/$90,000; **Industry Concentration:** Financial Services,
Insurance, Venture Capital; **Function Concentration:** Generalist
with a primary focus in Administration, Finance/Accounting,
General Management, Human Resources, Sales,
Women/Minorities

Potter, Steven B. — *Partner*
Highland Search Group
565 Fifth Avenue, 22nd Floor
New York, NY 10017
Telephone: (212) 328-1113
Recruiter Classification: Retained; **Lowest/Average Salary:**
$90,000/$90,000; **Industry Concentration:** Financial Services,
Venture Capital; **Function Concentration:** Generalist with a
primary focus in Administration, Finance/Accounting, General
Management, Human Resources, Sales, Women/Minorities

Powell, Danny — *Associate*
Source Services Corporation
520 Post Oak Boulevard, Suite 700
Houston, TX 77027
Telephone: (713) 439-1077
Recruiter Classification: Contingency; **Lowest/Average Salary:**
$30,000/$50,000; **Industry Concentration:** Financial Services;
Function Concentration: Engineering, Finance/Accounting

Powell, Gregory — *Associate*
Source Services Corporation
8614 Westwood Center, Suite 750
Vienna, VA 22182
Telephone: (703) 790-5610
Recruiter Classification: Contingency; **Lowest/Average Salary:**
$30,000/$50,000; **Industry Concentration:** Financial Services;
Function Concentration: Engineering, Finance/Accounting

Power, Michael — *Associate*
Source Services Corporation
3701 West Algonquin Road, Suite 380
Rolling Meadows, IL 60008
Telephone: (847) 392-0244
Recruiter Classification: Contingency; **Lowest/Average Salary:**
$30,000/$50,000; **Industry Concentration:** Financial Services;
Function Concentration: Engineering, Finance/Accounting

Powers Johnson, Allyson — *Vice President*
Skott/Edwards Consultants, Inc.
500 Fifth Avenue, 26th Floor
New York, NY 10110
Telephone: (212) 382-1166
Recruiter Classification: Retained; **Lowest/Average Salary:**
$90,000/$90,000; **Industry Concentration:** Financial Services,
Insurance; **Function Concentration:** Administration,
Finance/Accounting, Marketing, Sales

Pratt, Tyler P. — *Principal*
Furst Group/MPI
555 S. Perryville Road
Rockford, IL 61108
Telephone: (815) 229-9111
Recruiter Classification: Retained; **Lowest/Average Salary:**
$60,000/$90,000; **Industry Concentration:** Insurance;
Function Concentration: Generalist with a primary focus in
Finance/Accounting, General Management, Human Resources,
Marketing, Research and Development

Pregeant, David — *Associate*
Source Services Corporation
1290 Oakmead Parkway, Suite 318
Sunnyvale, CA 94086
Telephone: (408) 738-8440
Recruiter Classification: Contingency; **Lowest/Average Salary:**
$30,000/$50,000; **Industry Concentration:** Financial Services;
Function Concentration: Engineering, Finance/Accounting

Prencipe, V. Michael — *Principal*
Raymond Karsan Associates
1500 North Beauregard Street, Suite 110
Alexandria, VA 22311
Telephone: (703) 845-1114
Recruiter Classification: Retained; **Lowest/Average Salary:**
$30,000/$90,000; **Industry Concentration:** Insurance;
Function Concentration: Generalist

Press, Fred — *President*
Adept Tech Recruiting
219 Glendale Road
Scarsdale, NY 10583
Telephone: (914) 725-8583
Recruiter Classification: Contingency; **Lowest/Average Salary:**
$30,000/$75,000; **Industry Concentration:** Financial Services,
Insurance; **Function Concentration:** Administration,
Finance/Accounting

Preusse, Eric — *Associate*
Source Services Corporation
1500 West Park Drive, Suite 390
Westborough, MA 01581
Telephone: (508) 366-2600
Recruiter Classification: Contingency; **Lowest/Average Salary:**
$30,000/$50,000; **Industry Concentration:** Financial Services;
Function Concentration: Engineering, Finance/Accounting

Price, Andrew G. — *Associate*
The Thomas Tucker Company
425 California Street, Suite 2502
San Francisco, CA 94104
Telephone: (415) 693-5900
Recruiter Classification: Retained; **Lowest/Average Salary:**
$90,000/$90,000; **Industry Concentration:** Generalist with a
primary focus in Financial Services; **Function Concentration:**
Generalist with a primary focus in Engineering,
Finance/Accounting, General Management, Human Resources,
Marketing, Research and Development

Price, Carl — *Associate*
Source Services Corporation
3701 West Algonquin Road, Suite 380
Rolling Meadows, IL 60008
Telephone: (847) 392-0244
Recruiter Classification: Contingency; **Lowest/Average Salary:**
$30,000/$50,000; **Industry Concentration:** Financial Services;
Function Concentration: Engineering, Finance/Accounting

Price, Kenneth M. — *Vice President*
Messett Associates, Inc.
7700 North Kendall Drive, Suite 304
Miami, FL 33156
Telephone: (305) 275-1000
Recruiter Classification: Retained; **Lowest/Average Salary:**
$75,000/$90,000; **Industry Concentration:** Generalist with a
primary focus in Financial Services, Insurance; **Function
Concentration:** Generalist with a primary focus in
Administration, Engineering, Finance/Accounting, General
Management, Human Resources, Marketing, Sales,
Women/Minorities

Priem, Windle B. — *President North America*
Korn/Ferry International
237 Park Avenue
New York, NY 10017
Telephone: (212) 687-1834
Recruiter Classification: Retained; **Lowest/Average Salary:**
$100,000/$150,000; **Industry Concentration:** Generalist with a
primary focus in Financial Services; **Function Concentration:**
Generalist

Prince, Marilyn L. — *Managing Director*
Higdon Prince Inc.
230 Park Avenue, Suite 1455
New York, NY 10169
Telephone: (212) 986-4662
Recruiter Classification: Retained; **Lowest/Average Salary:**
$150,000/$150,000; **Industry Concentration:** Generalist with a
primary focus in Financial Services, Venture Capital; **Function
Concentration:** Generalist with a primary focus in
Finance/Accounting, General Management, Human Resources,
Marketing, Sales, Women/Minorities

Probert, William W. — *Partner*
Ward Howell International, Inc.
141 Adelaide Street West
Suite 1800
Toronto, Ontario, CANADA M5H 3L5
Telephone: (416) 862-1273
Recruiter Classification: Retained; **Lowest/Average Salary:**
$75,000/$90,000; **Industry Concentration:** Generalist with a
primary focus in Financial Services; **Function Concentration:**
Generalist

Proct, Nina — *Vice President*
Martin H. Bauman Associates, Inc.
375 Park Avenue, Suite 2002
New York, NY 10152
Telephone: (212) 752-6580
Recruiter Classification: Retained; **Lowest/Average Salary:**
$100,000/$250,000; **Industry Concentration:** Generalist with a
primary focus in Financial Services, Venture Capital; **Function
Concentration:** Generalist with a primary focus in
Administration, Engineering, Finance/Accounting, General
Management, Human Resources, Marketing, Research and
Development, Sales, Women/Minorities

Provus, Barbara L. — *Principal*
Shepherd Bueschel & Provus, Inc.
401 North Michigan Avenue, Suite 3020
Chicago, IL 60611-5555
Telephone: (312) 832-3020
Recruiter Classification: Retained; **Lowest/Average Salary:**
$150,000/$225,000; **Industry Concentration:** Generalist with a
primary focus in Venture Capital; **Function Concentration:**
Generalist with a primary focus in Sales

Pryor, Bill — *Executive Recruiter*
Cendea Connection International
13740 Research Boulevard
Building 0-1
Austin, TX 78750
Telephone: (512) 219-6000
Recruiter Classification: Retained; **Lowest/Average Salary:**
$75,000/$90,000; **Industry Concentration:** Generalist with a
primary focus in Venture Capital; **Function Concentration:**
Generalist with a primary focus in General Management,
Marketing, Sales

Puckett, Jennifer — *Associate*
Rene Plessner Associates, Inc.
375 Park Avenue
New York, NY 10152
Telephone: (212) 421-3490
Recruiter Classification: Retained; **Lowest/Average Salary:**
$75,000/$90,000; **Industry Concentration:** Generalist with a
primary focus in Insurance; **Function Concentration:**
Generalist with a primary focus in Administration,
Finance/Accounting, General Management, Human Resources,
Marketing, Research and Development, Sales

Pugrant, Mark A. — *Managing Director*
Grant/Morgan Associates, Inc.
7500 Old Georgetown Road
Suite 710
Bethesda, MD 20814
Telephone: (301) 718-8888
Recruiter Classification: Contingency; **Lowest/Average
Salary:** $30,000/$50,000; **Industry Concentration:** Financial
Services; **Function Concentration:** Administration,
Finance/Accounting

Rabinowitz, Peter A. — *President*
P.A.R. Associates Inc.
60 State Street, Suite 1040
Boston, MA 02109-2706
Telephone: (617) 367-0320
Recruiter Classification: Retained; **Lowest/Average Salary:**
$100,000/$125,000; **Industry Concentration:** Generalist with a
primary focus in Financial Services, Insurance; **Function
Concentration:** Generalist with a primary focus in
Administration, Finance/Accounting, General Management,
Marketing, Women/Minorities

Racht, Janet G. — *President*
Crowe, Chizek and Company, LLP
330 East Jefferson Boulevard
P.O. Box 7
South Bend, IN 46624
Telephone: (219) 232-3992
Recruiter Classification: Retained; **Lowest/Average Salary:**
$30,000/$50,000; **Industry Concentration:** Financial Services;
Function Concentration: Finance/Accounting, General
Management, Human Resources

Railsback, Richard — *Principal*
Korn/Ferry International
237 Park Avenue
New York, NY 10017
Telephone: (212) 687-1834
Recruiter Classification: Retained; **Lowest/Average Salary:**
$100,000/$150,000; **Industry Concentration:** Generalist with a
primary focus in Financial Services, Insurance; **Function
Concentration:** Generalist

Raines, Bruce R. — *President*
Raines International Inc.
1120 Avenue of the Americas
21st Floor
New York, NY 10036
Telephone: (212) 997-1100
Recruiter Classification: Retained; **Lowest/Average Salary:** $90,000/$90,000; **Industry Concentration:** Generalist with a primary focus in Financial Services, Insurance, Venture Capital; **Function Concentration:** Generalist with a primary focus in Administration, Finance/Accounting, General Management, Human Resources, Marketing, Research and Development, Sales, Women/Minorities

Ramler, Carolyn S. — *Vice President*
The Corporate Connection, Ltd.
7202 Glen Forest Drive
Richmond, VA 23226
Telephone: (804) 288-8844
Recruiter Classification: Contingency; **Lowest/Average Salary:** $20,000/$50,000; **Industry Concentration:** Generalist with a primary focus in Financial Services, Insurance; **Function Concentration:** Generalist with a primary focus in Administration, Engineering, Finance/Accounting, General Management, Human Resources, Marketing, Sales, Women/Minorities

Ramsey, John H. — *President*
Mark Stanley/EMA Partners International
2121 Ponce de Leon Boulevard #630
P.O. Box 149071
Coral Gables, FL 33114
Telephone: (305) 444-1612
Recruiter Classification: Retained; **Lowest/Average Salary:** $75,000/$90,000; **Industry Concentration:** Generalist with a primary focus in Financial Services; **Function Concentration:** Generalist with a primary focus in Finance/Accounting, General Management, Human Resources, Sales

Randell, James E. — *Chief Executive Officer*
Randell-Heiken, Inc.
The Lincoln Building
60 East 42nd Street, Suite 2022
New York, NY 10165
Telephone: (212) 490-1313
Recruiter Classification: Retained; **Lowest/Average Salary:** $60,000/$90,000; **Industry Concentration:** Generalist with a primary focus in Financial Services, Insurance; **Function Concentration:** Generalist with a primary focus in General Management, Human Resources, Marketing, Sales, Women/Minorities

Rankin, Jeffrey A. — *Chairman*
The Rankin Group, Ltd
P.O. Box 1120
Lake Geneva, WI 53147
Telephone: (414) 279-5005
Recruiter Classification: Retained; **Lowest/Average Salary:** $90,000/$90,000; **Industry Concentration:** Financial Services

Rankin, M.J. — *President*
The Rankin Group, Ltd
P.O. Box 1120
Lake Geneva, WI 53147
Telephone: (414) 279-5005
Recruiter Classification: Retained; **Lowest/Average Salary:** $90,000/$90,000; **Industry Concentration:** Financial Services

Rasmussen, Timothy — *Associate*
Source Services Corporation
1233 North Mayfair Road, Suite 300
Milwaukee, WI 53226
Telephone: (414) 774-6700
Recruiter Classification: Contingency; **Lowest/Average Salary:** $30,000/$50,000; **Industry Concentration:** Financial Services; **Function Concentration:** Engineering, Finance/Accounting

Ratajczak, Paul — *Managing Director*
Source Services Corporation
15260 Ventura Boulevard, Suite 380
Sherman Oaks, CA 91403
Telephone: (818) 905-1500
Recruiter Classification: Contingency; **Lowest/Average Salary:** $30,000/$50,000; **Industry Concentration:** Financial Services; **Function Concentration:** Engineering, Finance/Accounting

Ravenel, Lavinia — *Executive Recruiter*
MSI International
229 Peachtree Street, NE
Suite 1201
Atlanta, GA 30303
Telephone: (404) 659-5050
Recruiter Classification: Contingency; **Lowest/Average Salary:** $30,000/$75,000; **Industry Concentration:** Generalist with a primary focus in Financial Services; **Function Concentration:** Generalist with a primary focus in Finance/Accounting

Ray, Marianne C. — *Partner*
Callan Associates, Ltd.
2021 Spring Road, Suite 175
Oak Brook, IL 60521
Telephone: (708) 832-7080
Recruiter Classification: Retained; **Lowest/Average Salary:** $90,000/$90,000; **Industry Concentration:** Generalist with a primary focus in Financial Services; **Function Concentration:** Generalist with a primary focus in Administration, Engineering, Finance/Accounting, General Management, Human Resources, Marketing, Research and Development, Sales, Women/Minorities

Raymond, Jean — *Partner*
The Caldwell Partners Amrop International
1840 Sherbrooke Street West
Montreal, Quebec, CANADA H3H 1E4
Telephone: (514) 935-6969
Recruiter Classification: Retained; **Lowest/Average Salary:** $60,000/$90,000; **Industry Concentration:** Generalist with a primary focus in Financial Services; **Function Concentration:** Generalist

Reardon, Joseph — *Associate*
Source Services Corporation
155 Federal Street, Suite 410
Boston, MA 02110
Telephone: (617) 482-8211
Recruiter Classification: Contingency; **Lowest/Average Salary:** $30,000/$50,000; **Industry Concentration:** Financial Services; **Function Concentration:** Engineering, Finance/Accounting

Reddick, David C. — *Managing Director*
Horton International
33 Sloan Street
Roswell, GA 30075
Telephone: (770) 640-1533
Recruiter Classification: Retained; **Lowest/Average Salary:**
$90,000/$90,000; **Industry Concentration:** Generalist with a
primary focus in Financial Services; **Function Concentration:**
Generalist with a primary focus in Engineering,
Finance/Accounting, General Management, Human Resources,
Marketing, Sales, Women/Minorities

Redding, Denise — *Administrative Assistant*
The Douglas Reiter Company, Inc.
1221 S.W. Yamhill, Suite 301A
Portland, OR 97205
Telephone: (503) 228-6916
Recruiter Classification: Executive Temporary; **Lowest/Average
Salary:** $75,000/$90,000; **Industry Concentration:** Generalist
with a primary focus in Financial Services; **Function
Concentration:** Generalist with a primary focus in
Administration, Engineering, Finance/Accounting, General
Management, Human Resources, Marketing

Redler, Rhonda — *Executive Medical Consultant*
National Search, Inc.
2816 University Drive
Coral Springs, FL 33071
Telephone: (800) 935-4355
Recruiter Classification: Contingency; **Lowest/Average Salary:**
$30,000/$50,000; **Industry Concentration:** Insurance;
Function Concentration: Generalist with a primary focus in
Administration, Finance/Accounting, General Management,
Human Resources, Marketing, Research and Development,
Sales, Women/Minorities

Redmond, Andrea — *Managing Director/Area Co-
Manager*
Russell Reynolds Associates, Inc.
200 South Wacker Drive
Suite 3600
Chicago, IL 60606-5823
Telephone: (312) 993-9696
Recruiter Classification: Retained; **Lowest/Average Salary:**
$90,000/$90,000; **Industry Concentration:** Generalist with a
primary focus in Financial Services; **Function Concentration:**
Generalist

Reece, Christopher S. — *Managing Partner*
Reece & Mruk Partners
75 Second Avenue
Needham, MA 02194-2800
Telephone: (617) 449-3603
Recruiter Classification: Retained; **Lowest/Average Salary:**
$75,000/$90,000; **Industry Concentration:** Generalist with a
primary focus in Venture Capital; **Function Concentration:**
Generalist with a primary focus in Engineering,
Finance/Accounting, General Management, Marketing,
Women/Minorities

Reed, Susan — *Associate*
Source Services Corporation
379 Thornall Street
Edison, NJ 08837
Telephone: (908) 494-2800
Recruiter Classification: Contingency; **Lowest/Average Salary:**
$30,000/$50,000; **Industry Concentration:** Financial Services;
Function Concentration: Engineering, Finance/Accounting

Reeves, William B. — *Managing Director*
Spencer Stuart
One Atlantic Center, Suite 3230
1201 West Peachtree Street
Atlanta, GA 30309
Telephone: (404) 892-2800
Recruiter Classification: Retained; **Lowest/Average Salary:**
$90,000/$90,000; **Industry Concentration:** Financial Services,
Insurance; **Function Concentration:** Generalist with a primary
focus in Finance/Accounting, General Management, Human
Resources, Marketing

Regan, Thomas J. — *Vice President and CFO*
Tower Consultants, Ltd.
4195 N.E. Hyline Drive
Jensen Beach, FL 34957
Telephone: (561) 225-5151
Recruiter Classification: Retained; **Lowest/Average Salary:**
$60,000/$90,000; **Industry Concentration:** Generalist with a
primary focus in Financial Services, Insurance; **Function
Concentration:** Administration, Human Resources,
Women/Minorities

Regeuye, Peter J. — *Director*
Accountants Executive Search
535 Fifth Avenue, Suite 1200
New York, NY 10017
Telephone: (212) 682-5900
Recruiter Classification: Executive Temporary; **Lowest/Average
Salary:** $40,000/$60,000; **Industry Concentration:** Generalist
with a primary focus in Financial Services; **Function
Concentration:** Finance/Accounting

Reid, Katherine — *Associate*
Source Services Corporation
150 South Warner Road, Suite 238
King of Prussia, PA 19406
Telephone: (610) 341-1960
Recruiter Classification: Contingency; **Lowest/Average
Salary:** $30,000/$50,000; **Industry Concentration:** Financial
Services; **Function Concentration:** Engineering,
Finance/Accounting

Reid, Scott — *Associate*
Source Services Corporation
Foster Plaza VI
681 Anderson Drive, 2nd Floor
Pittsburgh, PA 15220
Telephone: (412) 928-8300
Recruiter Classification: Contingency; **Lowest/Average
Salary:** $30,000/$50,000; **Industry Concentration:** Financial
Services; **Function Concentration:** Engineering,
Finance/Accounting

Reifel, Laurie — *President*
Reifel & Assocaites
617 Railford Road
Glen Ellyn, IL 60137
Telephone: (630) 469-6651
Recruiter Classification: Retained; **Lowest/Average Salary:**
$75,000/$90,000; **Industry Concentration:** Generalist with a
primary focus in Financial Services; **Function Concentration:**
Generalist with a primary focus in Engineering,
Finance/Accounting, General Management, Marketing,
Women/Minorities

Reifersen, Ruth F. — *Vice President*
The Jonathan Stevens Group, Inc.
116 Village Boulevard
Suite 200
Princeton, NJ 08540-5799
Telephone: (609) 734-7444
Recruiter Classification: Retained; **Lowest/Average Salary:**
$40,000/$75,000; **Industry Concentration:** Generalist
with a primary focus in Financial Services; **Function
Concentration:** Generalist with a primary focus in
Engineering, Finance/Accounting, Human Resources,
Marketing

Reiser, Ellen — *Principal*
Thorndike Deland Associates
275 Madison Avenue, Suite 1300
New York, NY 10016
Telephone: (212) 661-6200
Recruiter Classification: Retained; **Lowest/Average Salary:**
$100,000/$125,000; **Industry Concentration:** Generalist
with a primary focus in Financial Services, Insurance,
Venture Capital; **Function Concentration:** Generalist
with a primary focus in Finance/Accounting, General
Management, Human Resources, Marketing,
Sales

Reisinger, George L. — *President*
Sigma Group International
6551 South Revere Parkway
Suite 125
Englewood, CO 80111-6410
Telephone: (303) 792-9881
Recruiter Classification: Retained; **Lowest/Average Salary:**
$90,000/$90,000; **Industry Concentration:** Generalist with a
primary focus in Financial Services; **Function Concentration:**
Generalist with a primary focus in Administration, Engineering,
Finance/Accounting, General Management, Human Resources,
Marketing

Reiss, Matt — *Insurance Consultant*
National Search, Inc.
2816 University Drive
Coral Springs, FL 33071
Telephone: (800) 935-4355
Recruiter Classification: Contingency; **Lowest/Average Salary:**
$30,000/$50,000; **Industry Concentration:** Insurance;
Function Concentration: Generalist with a primary focus in
Administration, Finance/Accounting, General Management,
Human Resources, Marketing, Research and Development,
Sales, Women/Minorities

Reiter, Douglas — *President*
The Douglas Reiter Company, Inc.
1221 S.W. Yamhill, Suite 301A
Portland, OR 97205
Telephone: (503) 228-6916
Recruiter Classification: Executive Temporary;
Lowest/Average Salary: $75,000/$90,000; **Industry
Concentration:** Generalist with a primary focus in Financial
Services; **Function Concentration:** Generalist with a
primary focus in Administration, Engineering,
Finance/Accounting, General Management, Human
Resources, Marketing

Reiter, Harold D. — *President and COO*
Herbert Mines Associates, Inc.
399 Park Avenue, 27th Floor
New York, NY 10022
Telephone: (212) 355-0909
Recruiter Classification: Retained; **Lowest/Average Salary:**
$90,000/$90,000; **Industry Concentration:** Venture Capital;
Function Concentration: Generalist with a primary focus in
Finance/Accounting, General Management, Human Resources,
Marketing

Remillard, Brad M. — *Vice President*
CJA - The Adler Group
17852 17th Street
Suite 209
Tustin, CA 92780
Telephone: (714) 573-1820
Recruiter Classification: Retained; **Lowest/Average Salary:**
$50,000/$90,000; **Industry Concentration:** Generalist with a
primary focus in Financial Services; **Function Concentration:**
Generalist with a primary focus in Engineering,
Finance/Accounting, General Management, Human Resources,
Marketing, Research and Development, Sales

Renfroe, Ann-Marie — *Associate*
Source Services Corporation
1 Gatehall Drive, Suite 250
Parsippany, NJ 07054
Telephone: (201) 267-3222
Recruiter Classification: Contingency; **Lowest/Average
Salary:** $30,000/$50,000; **Industry Concentration:** Financial
Services; **Function Concentration:** Engineering,
Finance/Accounting

Renick, Cynthia L. — *Manager Insurance/Risk
Management Division*
Morgan Hunter Corp.
6800 College Boulevard, Suite 550
Overland Park, KS 66211
Telephone: (913) 491-3434
Recruiter Classification: Contingency; **Lowest/Average Salary:**
$30,000/$60,000; **Industry Concentration:** Insurance;
Function Concentration: Administration, Engineering, General
Management, Human Resources, Marketing, Sales,
Women/Minorities

Rennell, Thomas — *Associate*
Source Services Corporation
1500 West Park Drive, Suite 390
Westborough, MA 01581
Telephone: (508) 366-2600
Recruiter Classification: Contingency; **Lowest/Average Salary:**
$30,000/$50,000; **Industry Concentration:** Financial Services;
Function Concentration: Engineering, Finance/Accounting

Renner, Sandra L. — *Senior Consultant*
Spectra International Inc.
6991 East Camelback Road, Suite B-305
Scottsdale, AZ 85251
Telephone: (602) 481-0411
Recruiter Classification: Contingency; **Lowest/Average Salary:**
$20,000/$50,000; **Industry Concentration:** Generalist with a
primary focus in Financial Services, Insurance; **Function
Concentration:** Finance/Accounting

Renteria, Elizabeth — *Associate*
Source Services Corporation
15260 Ventura Boulevard, Suite 380
Sherman Oaks, CA 91403
Telephone: (818) 905-1500
Recruiter Classification: Contingency; **Lowest/Average
Salary:** $30,000/$50,000; **Industry Concentration:** Financial
Services; **Function Concentration:** Engineering,
Finance/Accounting

Resnic, Alan — *Associate*
Source Services Corporation
155 Federal Street, Suite 410
Boston, MA 02110
Telephone: (617) 482-8211
Recruiter Classification: Contingency; **Lowest/Average
Salary:** $30,000/$50,000; **Industry Concentration:** Financial
Services; **Function Concentration:** Engineering,
Finance/Accounting

Reticker, Peter — *Unit Manager*
MSI International
229 Peachtree Street, NE
Suite 1201
Atlanta, GA 30303
Telephone: (404) 659-5050
Recruiter Classification: Contingency; **Lowest/Average Salary:**
$30,000/$60,000; **Industry Concentration:** Generalist with a
primary focus in Financial Services; **Function Concentration:**
Administration, Engineering, Finance/Accounting, General
Management, Marketing, Sales

Reuter, Tandom — *Executive Recruiter*
CPS Inc.
One Westbrook Corporate Centre, Suite 600
Westchester, IL 60154
Telephone: (708) 531-8370
Recruiter Classification: Contingency; **Lowest/Average Salary:**
$30,000/$50,000; **Industry Concentration:** Generalist with a
primary focus in Financial Services, Insurance; **Function
Concentration:** Engineering, Research and Development,
Sales, Women/Minorities

Reyman, Susan — *President*
S. Reyman & Associates Ltd.
20 North Michigan Avenue, Suite 520
Chicago, IL 60602
Telephone: (312) 580-0808
Recruiter Classification: Retained; **Lowest/Average Salary:**
$75,000/$90,000; **Industry Concentration:** Generalist with a
primary focus in Financial Services, Insurance; **Function
Concentration:** Generalist with a primary focus in
Administration, Engineering, Finance/Accounting, General
Management, Human Resources, Marketing, Sales

Reynolds, Gregory P. — *Vice President - Account
Executive*
Roberts Ryan and Bentley
7315 Wisconsin Avenue, Suite 333E
Bethesda, MD 20814
Telephone: (301) 469-3150
Recruiter Classification: Retained; **Lowest/Average Salary:**
$90,000/$90,000; **Industry Concentration:** Generalist with a
primary focus in Insurance; **Function Concentration:**
Generalist with a primary focus in Administration,
Engineering, General Management, Marketing,
Women/Minorities

Reynolds, Laura — *Associate*
Source Services Corporation
7730 East Bellview Avenue, Suite 302
Englewood, CO 80111
Telephone: (303) 773-3700
Recruiter Classification: Contingency; **Lowest/Average
Salary:** $30,000/$50,000; **Industry Concentration:** Financial
Services; **Function Concentration:** Engineering,
Finance/Accounting

Rhoades, Michael — *Associate*
Source Services Corporation
One South Main Street, Suite 1440
Dayton, OH 45402
Telephone: (513) 461-4660
Recruiter Classification: Contingency; **Lowest/Average
Salary:** $30,000/$50,000; **Industry Concentration:** Financial
Services; **Function Concentration:** Engineering,
Finance/Accounting

Rice, Marie — *Senior Consultant*
Jay Gaines & Company, Inc.
450 Park Avenue
New York, NY 10022
Telephone: (212) 308-9222
Recruiter Classification: Retained; **Lowest/Average Salary:**
$200,000/$300,000; **Industry Concentration:** Generalist
with a primary focus in Financial Services, Insurance;
Function Concentration: Generalist with a primary focus in
General Management, Human Resources, Marketing,
Sales

Rice, Raymond D. — *President*
Logue & Rice Inc.
8000 Towers Crescent Drive
Suite 650
Vienna, VA 22182-2700
Telephone: (703) 761-4261
Recruiter Classification: Contingency; **Lowest/Average Salary:**
$40,000/$90,000; **Industry Concentration:** Generalist with a
primary focus in Financial Services, Venture Capital; **Function
Concentration:** Generalist with a primary focus in
Administration, Finance/Accounting, General Management,
Human Resources, Women/Minorities

Rich, Kenneth M. — *Geographic Manager/Partner*
Ray & Berndtson
245 Park Avenue, 33rd Floor
New York, NY 10167
Telephone: (212) 370-1316
Recruiter Classification: Retained; **Lowest/Average Salary:**
$90,000/$90,000; **Industry Concentration:** Financial Services;
Function Concentration: Generalist

Rich, Lyttleton — *Principal*
Sockwell & Associates
227 West Trade Street, Suite 1930
Charlotte, NC 28202
Telephone: (704) 372-1865
Recruiter Classification: Retained; **Lowest/Average Salary:**
$90,000/$90,000; **Industry Concentration:** Generalist with a
primary focus in Financial Services; **Function Concentration:**
Generalist with a primary focus in Administration,
Finance/Accounting, General Management, Human Resources,
Marketing, Sales

Richardson, J. Rick — *Senior Director*
Spencer Stuart
Financial Centre
695 East Main Street
Stamford, CT 06901
Telephone: (203) 324-6333
Recruiter Classification: Retained; **Lowest/Average Salary:**
$90,000/$90,000; **Industry Concentration:** Generalist with a
primary focus in Financial Services; **Function Concentration:**
Generalist with a primary focus in General Management,
Marketing

Ridenour, Suzanne S. — *President*
Ridenour & Associates, Ltd.
One East Wacker Drive #3500
Chicago, IL 60601
Telephone: (312) 644-7888
Recruiter Classification: Retained; **Lowest/Average Salary:**
$75,000/$90,000; **Industry Concentration:** Insurance;
Function Concentration: Marketing, Sales

Riederer, Larry — *Executive Recruiter*
CPS Inc.
One Westbrook Corporate Centre, Suite 600
Westchester, IL 60154
Telephone: (708) 531-8370
Recruiter Classification: Contingency; **Lowest/Average Salary:**
$30,000/$50,000; **Industry Concentration:** Generalist with a
primary focus in Financial Services, Insurance; **Function
Concentration:** Engineering, Research and Development,
Sales, Women/Minorities

Rieger, Louis J. — *Managing Director*
Spencer Stuart
1111 Bagby, Suite 1616
Houston, TX 77002-2594
Telephone: (713) 225-1621
Recruiter Classification: Retained; **Lowest/Average Salary:**
$90,000/$90,000; **Industry Concentration:** Generalist with a
primary focus in Financial Services, Venture Capital; **Function
Concentration:** Generalist with a primary focus in
Administration, Finance/Accounting, General Management,
Human Resources, Marketing, Women/Minorities

Rimmel, James E. — *Vice President -
Cleveland/Northeast*
The Hindman Company
123 Lakhani Lane
Canfield, OH 44406
Telephone: (330) 533-5450
Recruiter Classification: Retained; **Lowest/Average Salary:**
$50,000/$90,000; **Industry Concentration:** Generalist with a
primary focus in Financial Services; **Function Concentration:**
Generalist with a primary focus in Administration, Engineering,
Finance/Accounting, General Management, Human Resources,
Marketing, Sales

Rimmele, Michael — *Vice President*
The Bankers Group
10 South Riverside Plaza, Suite 1424
Chicago, IL 60606
Telephone: (312) 930-9456
Recruiter Classification: Contingency; **Lowest/Average Salary:**
$50,000/$75,000; **Industry Concentration:** Generalist with a
primary focus in Financial Services, Insurance, Venture Capital;
Function Concentration: Generalist with a primary focus in
Administration, Finance/Accounting, General Management,
Human Resources, Marketing, Sales, Women/Minorities

Rinker, Jim — *Commercial Finance Specialist*
Southwestern Professional Services
2451 Atrium Way
Nashville, TN 37214
Telephone: (615) 391-2722
Recruiter Classification: Contingency; **Lowest/Average Salary:**
$40,000/$50,000; **Industry Concentration:** Financial Services,
Insurance, Venture Capital; **Function Concentration:**
Administration, Finance/Accounting, General Management,
Marketing, Sales

Rios, Vince — *Managing Director*
Source Services Corporation
1 Corporate Drive, Suite 215
Shelton, CT 06484
Telephone: (203) 944-9001
Recruiter Classification: Contingency; **Lowest/Average Salary:**
$30,000/$50,000; **Industry Concentration:** Financial Services;
Function Concentration: Engineering, Finance/Accounting

Rios, Vincent — *Managing Director*
Source Services Corporation
2 Penn Plaza, Suite 1176
New York, NY 10121
Telephone: (212) 760-2200
Recruiter Classification: Contingency; **Lowest/Average Salary:**
$30,000/$50,000; **Industry Concentration:** Financial Services;
Function Concentration: Engineering, Finance/Accounting

Riotto, Anthony R. — *President*
Riotto-Jones Associates
600 Third Avenue
New York, NY 10016
Telephone: (212) 697-4575
Recruiter Classification: Retained; **Lowest/Average Salary:**
$90,000/$90,000; **Industry Concentration:** Financial Services;
Function Concentration: Administration, Finance/Accounting,
General Management, Marketing, Sales

Rivera, Elba R. — *Principal*
Raymond Karsan Associates
170 So. Warner Road
Wayne, PA 19087
Telephone: (610) 971-9171
Recruiter Classification: Retained; **Lowest/Average Salary:**
$30,000/$90,000; **Industry Concentration:** Generalist with a
primary focus in Insurance; **Function Concentration:**
Generalist

Robb, Tammy — *Associate*
Source Services Corporation
10300 West 103rd Street, Suite 101
Overland Park, KS 66214
Telephone: (913) 888-8885
Recruiter Classification: Contingency; **Lowest/Average Salary:**
$30,000/$50,000; **Industry Concentration:** Financial Services;
Function Concentration: Engineering, Finance/Accounting

Roberts, Carl R. — *Vice President/Director*
Southwestern Professional Services
2451 Atrium Way
Nashville, TN 37214
Telephone: (615) 391-2722
Recruiter Classification: Contingency; **Lowest/Average Salary:**
$20,000/$40,000; **Industry Concentration:** Generalist with a
primary focus in Financial Services, Insurance; **Function
Concentration:** Generalist with a primary focus in
Finance/Accounting, Sales

Roberts, Derek J. — *Partner*
Ward Howell International, Inc.
141 Adelaide Street West
Suite 1800
Toronto, Ontario, CANADA M5H 3L5
Telephone: (416) 862-1273
Recruiter Classification: Retained; **Lowest/Average Salary:**
$75,000/$90,000; **Industry Concentration:** Financial Services,
Insurance; **Function Concentration:** Generalist

Roberts, Kenneth — *Actuarial Specialist*
The Rubicon Group
P.O. Box 2159
Scottsdale, AZ 85252-2159
Telephone: (602) 423-9280
Recruiter Classification: Contingency; **Lowest/Average Salary:**
$40,000/$60,000; **Industry Concentration:** Insurance;
Function Concentration: Generalist with a primary focus in
Administration, Finance/Accounting, Research and
Development

Roberts, Mitch — *Senior Vice President*
A.E. Feldman Associates
445 Northern Boulevard
Great Neck, NY 11021
Telephone: (516) 466-4708
Recruiter Classification: Contingency, Executive Temporary;
Lowest/Average Salary: $60,000/$90,000; **Industry
Concentration:** Generalist with a primary focus in Financial
Services, Venture Capital; **Function Concentration:** Generalist
with a primary focus in Administration, General Management,
Marketing, Sales

Roberts, Nick P. — *President*
Spectrum Search Associates, Inc.
1888 Century Park East, Suite 320
Los Angeles, CA 90067
Telephone: (310) 286-6921
Recruiter Classification: Contingency; **Lowest/Average Salary:**
$40,000/$60,000; **Industry Concentration:** Generalist with a
primary focus in Financial Services, Insurance; **Function
Concentration:** Generalist with a primary focus in
Administration, Finance/Accounting, General Management,
Human Resources

Roberts, Scott — *Vice President*
Jonas, Walters & Assoc., Inc.
1110 North Old World Third St., Suite 510
Milwaukee, WI 53203-1102
Telephone: (414) 291-2828
Recruiter Classification: Retained; **Lowest/Average Salary:**
$60,000/$90,000; **Industry Concentration:** Generalist with a
primary focus in Financial Services; **Function Concentration:**
Generalist with a primary focus in Administration, Engineering,
Finance/Accounting, General Management, Human Resources,
Marketing, Sales

Robertson, Bruce J. — *Partner*
Lamalie Amrop International
200 Park Avenue
New York, NY 10166-0136—
Telephone: (212) 953-7900
Recruiter Classification: Retained; **Lowest/Average Salary:**
$90,000/$90,000; **Industry Concentration:** Generalist with a
primary focus in Financial Services; **Function Concentration:**
Generalist

Robertson, Sherry — *Associate*
Source Services Corporation
5343 North 16th Street, Suite 270
Phoenix, AZ 85016
Telephone: (602) 230-0220
Recruiter Classification: Contingency; **Lowest/Average Salary:**
$30,000/$50,000; **Industry Concentration:** Financial Services;
Function Concentration: Engineering, Finance/Accounting

Robinson, Bruce — *President*
Bruce Robinson Associates
Harmon Cove Towers
Suite 8, A/L Level
Secaucus, NJ 07094
Telephone: (201) 617-9595
Recruiter Classification: Retained; **Lowest/Average Salary:**
$90,000/$90,000; **Industry Concentration:** Generalist with a
primary focus in Financial Services, Insurance; **Function
Concentration:** Generalist with a primary focus in
Administration, Engineering, Finance/Accounting, General
Management, Human Resources, Marketing, Research and
Development, Sales, Women/Minorities

Robinson, Eric B. — *Vice President/Partner*
Bruce Robinson Associates
Harmon Cove Towers
Suite 8, A/L Level
Secaucus, NJ 07094
Telephone: (201) 617-9595
Recruiter Classification: Retained; **Lowest/Average Salary:**
$75,000/$90,000; **Industry Concentration:** Generalist with a
primary focus in Financial Services, Insurance, Venture Capital;
Function Concentration: Generalist with a primary focus in
Women/Minorities

Robinson, Tonya — *Associate*
Source Services Corporation
2850 National City Tower
Louisville, KY 40202
Telephone: (502) 581-9900
Recruiter Classification: Contingency; **Lowest/Average Salary:**
$30,000/$50,000; **Industry Concentration:** Financial Services;
Function Concentration: Engineering, Finance/Accounting

Robles Cuellar, Paulina — *Partner*
Ray & Berndtson
Palo Santo No. 6
Colonia Lomas Altas
Mexico City, D.F., MEXICO 11950
Telephone: (525) 570-7462
Recruiter Classification: Retained; **Lowest/Average Salary:**
$90,000/$90,000; **Industry Concentration:** Generalist with a
primary focus in Financial Services, Insurance; **Function
Concentration:** Generalist with a primary focus in
Administration, Finance/Accounting, General Management,
Human Resources, Marketing, Research and Development,
Sales, Women/Minorities

Rockwell, Bruce — *Managing Director*
Source Services Corporation
One South Main Street, Suite 1440
Dayton, OH 45402
Telephone: (513) 461-4660
Recruiter Classification: Contingency; **Lowest/Average Salary:**
$30,000/$50,000; **Industry Concentration:** Financial Services;
Function Concentration: Engineering, Finance/Accounting

Rodriguez, Manuel — *Associate*
Source Services Corporation
15600 N.W. 67th Avenue, Suite 210
Miami Lakes, FL 33014
Telephone: (305) 556-8000
Recruiter Classification: Contingency; **Lowest/Average Salary:** $30,000/$50,000; **Industry Concentration:** Financial Services; **Function Concentration:** Engineering, Finance/Accounting

Rogan, John P. — *Managing Director*
Russell Reynolds Associates, Inc.
200 Park Avenue
New York, NY 10166-0002
Telephone: (212) 351-2000
Recruiter Classification: Retained; **Lowest/Average Salary:** $90,000/$90,000; **Industry Concentration:** Generalist with a primary focus in Financial Services; **Function Concentration:** Generalist

Rogers, Leah — *Vice President*
Dinte Resources, Inc.
8300 Greensboro Drive
Suite 880
McLean, VA 22102
Telephone: (703) 448-3300
Recruiter Classification: Retained, Executive Temporary; **Lowest/Average Salary:** $75,000/$90,000; **Industry Concentration:** Generalist with a primary focus in Financial Services; **Function Concentration:** Generalist with a primary focus in Finance/Accounting, General Management, Human Resources, Marketing

Rohan, James E. — *Senior Partner*
J.P. Canon Associates
225 Broadway, Ste. 3602, 36th Fl.
New York, NY 10007-3001
Telephone: (212) 233-3131
Recruiter Classification: Contingency; **Lowest/Average Salary:** $40,000/$75,000; **Industry Concentration:** Generalist with a primary focus in Financial Services; **Function Concentration:** Engineering

Rohan, Kevin A. — *Recruiter*
J.P. Canon Associates
225 Broadway, Ste. 3602, 36th Fl.
New York, NY 10007-3001
Telephone: (212) 233-3131
Recruiter Classification: Contingency; **Lowest/Average Salary:** $40,000/$75,000; **Industry Concentration:** Generalist with a primary focus in Financial Services; **Function Concentration:** Engineering

Rojo, Rafael — *Vice President*
A.T. Kearney, Inc.
Ruben Dario 281-Piso 15
Col. Bosques de Chapultepec
Mexico City D.F., MEXICO 11580
Telephone: (525) 282-0050
Recruiter Classification: Retained; **Lowest/Average Salary:** $90,000/$90,000; **Industry Concentration:** Generalist with a primary focus in Financial Services; **Function Concentration:** Generalist with a primary focus in Engineering, Finance/Accounting, General Management

Rollins, Scott — *President*
S.C. International, Ltd.
1430 Branding Lane, Suite 119
Downers Grove, IL 60515
Telephone: (708) 963-3033
Recruiter Classification: Contingency; **Lowest/Average Salary:** $30,000/$50,000; **Industry Concentration:** Insurance; **Function Concentration:** Administration, Human Resources

Rollo, Robert S. — *Partner*
R. Rollo Associates
725 South Figueroa Street, Suite 3230
Los Angeles, CA 90017
Telephone: (213) 688-9444
Recruiter Classification: Retained; **Lowest/Average Salary:** $90,000/$90,000; **Industry Concentration:** Generalist with a primary focus in Financial Services, Insurance, Venture Capital; **Function Concentration:** Generalist with a primary focus in General Management, Human Resources, Marketing, Sales, Women/Minorities

Romanello, Daniel P. — *Senior Director*
Spencer Stuart
Financial Centre
695 East Main Street
Stamford, CT 06901
Telephone: (203) 324-6333
Recruiter Classification: Retained; **Lowest/Average Salary:** $90,000/$90,000; **Industry Concentration:** Venture Capital; **Function Concentration:** Generalist with a primary focus in Engineering, Finance/Accounting, General Management, Human Resources, Marketing, Research and Development, Sales

Romang, Paula — *Account Executive*
Agri-Tech Personnel, Inc.
3113 N.E. 69th Street
Kansas City, MO 64119
Telephone: (816) 453-7200
Recruiter Classification: Contingency; **Lowest/Average Salary:** $20,000/$50,000; **Industry Concentration:** Financial Services; **Function Concentration:** Engineering, Finance/Accounting, General Management, Human Resources, Marketing, Research and Development, Sales

Rorech, Maureen — *Division Vice President*
Romac & Associates
120 Hyde Park Place
Suite 200
Tampa, FL 33606
Telephone: (813) 229-5575
Recruiter Classification: Executive Temporary; **Lowest/Average Salary:** $60,000/$60,000; **Industry Concentration:** Financial Services, Insurance; **Function Concentration:** Finance/Accounting

Rosato, William R. — *President*
W.R. Rosato & Associates, Inc.
61 Broadway, 26th Floor
New York, NY 10006
Telephone: (212) 509-5700
Recruiter Classification: Retained; **Lowest/Average Salary:** $90,000/$90,000; **Industry Concentration:** Financial Services; **Function Concentration:** Administration, Marketing, Research and Development, Sales

Rose, Robert — *Partner*
ESA Professional Consultants
141 Durham Road
Suite 16
Madison, CT 06443
Telephone: (203) 245-1983
Recruiter Classification: Retained; **Lowest/Average Salary:**
$50,000/$75,000; **Industry Concentration:** Venture Capital;
Function Concentration: Engineering, General Management,
Human Resources, Marketing, Research and Development,
Women/Minorities

Rosemarin, Gloria J. — *President*
Barrington Hart, Inc.
20 North Wacker Drive, Suite 2710
Chicago, IL 60606
Telephone: (312) 332-3344
Recruiter Classification: Retained; **Lowest/Average Salary:**
$30,000/$50,000; **Industry Concentration:** Generalist with a
primary focus in Financial Services; **Function Concentration:**
Generalist with a primary focus in Finance/Accounting,
General Management, Marketing, Sales

Rosen, Mitchell — *Associate*
Source Services Corporation
1290 Oakmead Parkway, Suite 318
Sunnyvale, CA 94086
Telephone: (408) 738-8440
Recruiter Classification: Contingency; **Lowest/Average
Salary:** $30,000/$50,000; **Industry Concentration:** Financial
Services; **Function Concentration:** Engineering,
Finance/Accounting

Rosenstein, Michele — *Associate*
Source Services Corporation
120 East Baltimore Street, Suite 1950
Baltimore, MD 21202
Telephone: (410) 727-4050
Recruiter Classification: Contingency; **Lowest/Average
Salary:** $30,000/$50,000; **Industry Concentration:** Financial
Services; **Function Concentration:** Engineering,
Finance/Accounting

Rosenthal, Charles — *Senior Medical Consultant*
National Search, Inc.
2816 University Drive
Coral Springs, FL 33071
Telephone: (800) 935-4355
Recruiter Classification: Contingency; **Lowest/Average Salary:**
$30,000/$50,000; **Industry Concentration:** Insurance;
Function Concentration: Generalist with a primary focus in
Administration, Finance/Accounting, General Management,
Human Resources, Marketing, Research and Development,
Sales, Women/Minorities

Rosin, Jeffrey — *Principal*
Korn/Ferry International
Scotia Plaza
40 King Street West
Toronto, Ontario, CANADA M5H 3Y2
Telephone: (416) 366-1300
Recruiter Classification: Retained; **Lowest/Average Salary:**
$100,000/$150,000; **Industry Concentration:** Generalist with a
primary focus in Financial Services, Insurance; **Function
Concentration:** Generalist

Ross, Curt A. — *Consultant*
Ray & Berndtson
One Allen Center
500 Dallas, Suite 3010
Houston, TX 77002
Telephone: (713) 309-1400
Recruiter Classification: Retained; **Lowest/Average Salary:**
$90,000/$90,000; **Industry Concentration:** Generalist with a
primary focus in Financial Services, Insurance; **Function
Concentration:** Generalist with a primary focus in
Administration, Finance/Accounting, General Management,
Human Resources, Marketing, Research and Development,
Sales, Women/Minorities

Ross, H. Lawrence — *Managing Partner*
Ross & Company
One Gorham Island
Westport, CT 06880
Telephone: (203) 221-8200
Recruiter Classification: Retained; **Lowest/Average Salary:**
$90,000/$90,000; **Industry Concentration:** Venture Capital;
Function Concentration: Generalist with a primary focus in
General Management, Marketing, Sales

Ross, John — *Associate*
Morgan Stampfl, Inc.
6 West 32nd Street
New York, NY 10001
Telephone: (212) 643-7165
Recruiter Classification: Contingency; **Lowest/Average Salary:**
$50,000/$90,000; **Industry Concentration:** Financial Services;
Function Concentration: Finance/Accounting

Ross, Lawrence — *Consultant*
Ray & Berndtson/Lovas Stanley
Royal Bank Plaza, South Tower, Suite 3150
200 Bay Street, P.O. Box 125
Toronto, Ontario, CANADA M5J 2J3
Telephone: (416) 366-1990
Recruiter Classification: Retained; **Lowest/Average Salary:**
$75,000/$90,000; **Industry Concentration:** Generalist with a
primary focus in Financial Services; **Function Concentration:**
Generalist with a primary focus in Finance/Accounting,
General Management, Human Resources, Marketing,
Sales

Ross, Mark — *Consultant*
Ray & Berndtson/Lovas Stanley
Royal Bank Plaza, South Tower, Suite 3150
200 Bay Street, P.O. Box 125
Toronto, Ontario, CANADA M5J 2J3
Telephone: (416) 366-1990
Recruiter Classification: Retained; **Lowest/Average Salary:**
$90,000/$90,000; **Industry Concentration:** Financial Services;
Function Concentration: Generalist with a primary focus in
Finance/Accounting, General Management, Human Resources,
Marketing

Ross, Sheila L. — *Partner*
Ward Howell International, Inc.
141 Adelaide Street West
Suite 1800
Toronto, Ontario, CANADA M5H 3L5
Telephone: (416) 862-1273
Recruiter Classification: Retained; **Lowest/Average Salary:**
$75,000/$90,000; **Industry Concentration:** Financial Services,
Insurance; **Function Concentration:** Generalist

Rotella, Marshall W. — *President*
The Corporate Connection, Ltd.
7202 Glen Forest Drive
Richmond, VA 23226
Telephone: (804) 288-8844
Recruiter Classification: Contingency; **Lowest/Average Salary:** $20,000/$50,000; **Industry Concentration:** Generalist with a primary focus in Financial Services, Insurance; **Function Concentration:** Generalist with a primary focus in Administration, Engineering, Finance/Accounting, General Management, Human Resources, Marketing, Sales, Women/Minorities

Roth, Robert J. — *Partner*
Williams, Roth & Krueger Inc.
20 North Wacker Drive
Chicago, IL 60606
Telephone: (312) 977-0800
Recruiter Classification: Retained; **Lowest/Average Salary:** $90,000/$90,000; **Industry Concentration:** Generalist with a primary focus in Financial Services; **Function Concentration:** Generalist with a primary focus in Engineering, Finance/Accounting, General Management, Human Resources, Marketing, Research and Development, Sales

Roth, William — *Senior Associate*
Harris Heery & Associates
40 Richards Avenue
One Norwalk West
Norwalk, CT 06854
Telephone: (203) 857-0808
Recruiter Classification: Retained; **Lowest/Average Salary:** $75,000/$90,000; **Industry Concentration:** Financial Services, Insurance; **Function Concentration:** General Management, Marketing

Rothenbush, Clayton — *Managing Director*
Source Services Corporation
1105 Schrock Road, Suite 510
Columbus, OH 43229
Telephone: (614) 846-3311
Recruiter Classification: Contingency; **Lowest/Average Salary:** $30,000/$50,000; **Industry Concentration:** Financial Services; **Function Concentration:** Engineering, Finance/Accounting

Rothschild, John S. — *Managing Partner*
Lamalie Amrop International
225 West Wacker Drive
Chicago, IL 60606-1229
Telephone: (312) 782-3113
Recruiter Classification: Retained; **Lowest/Average Salary:** $90,000/$90,000; **Industry Concentration:** Generalist with a primary focus in Financial Services; **Function Concentration:** Generalist

Rowe, Thomas A. — *Principal*
Korn/Ferry International
237 Park Avenue
New York, NY 10017
Telephone: (212) 687-1834
Recruiter Classification: Retained; **Lowest/Average Salary:** $100,000/$150,000; **Industry Concentration:** Generalist with a primary focus in Financial Services; **Function Concentration:** Generalist with a primary focus in Finance/Accounting

Rowe, William D. — *Vice Chairman/Executive Managing Director*
D.E. Foster Partners Inc.
200 Crescent Court, Suite 300
Dallas, TX 75201-1885
Telephone: (214) 754-2241
Recruiter Classification: Retained; **Lowest/Average Salary:** $90,000/$90,000; **Industry Concentration:** Financial Services, Insurance, Venture Capital; **Function Concentration:** Generalist with a primary focus in Finance/Accounting, General Management, Human Resources

Rowland, James — *Associate*
Source Services Corporation
10300 West 103rd Street, Suite 101
Overland Park, KS 66214
Telephone: (913) 888-8885
Recruiter Classification: Contingency; **Lowest/Average Salary:** $30,000/$50,000; **Industry Concentration:** Financial Services; **Function Concentration:** Engineering, Finance/Accounting

Rubenstein, Alan J. — *Legal Search Consultant*
Chicago Legal Search, Ltd.
33 North Dearborn Street, Suite 2302
Chicago, IL 60602-3109
Telephone: (312) 251-2580
Recruiter Classification: Contingency; **Lowest/Average Salary:** $50,000/$90,000; **Industry Concentration:** Venture Capital; **Function Concentration:** Women/Minorities

Rudolph, Kenneth — *Associate*
Kossuth & Associates, Inc.
800 Bellevue Way N.E., Suite 400
Bellevue, WA 98004
Telephone: (206) 450-9050
Recruiter Classification: Retained; **Lowest/Average Salary:** $50,000/$90,000; **Industry Concentration:** Venture Capital; **Function Concentration:** Generalist with a primary focus in Administration, Engineering, Finance/Accounting, General Management, Human Resources, Marketing, Research and Development, Sales, Women/Minorities

Runquist, U.W. — *Managing Director*
Webb, Johnson Associates, Inc.
280 Park Avenue, 43rd Floor
New York, NY 10017
Telephone: (212) 661-3700
Recruiter Classification: Retained; **Lowest/Average Salary:** $90,000/$90,000; **Industry Concentration:** Generalist with a primary focus in Financial Services; **Function Concentration:** Generalist

Rush, Michael E. — *Partner*
D.A.L. Associates, Inc.
2777 Summer Street
Stamford, CT 06905
Telephone: (203) 961-8777
Recruiter Classification: Retained; **Lowest/Average Salary:** $75,000/$90,000; **Industry Concentration:** Generalist with a primary focus in Financial Services; **Function Concentration:** Generalist with a primary focus in Engineering, Finance/Accounting, General Management, Marketing, Sales

Rusher, William H. — *President*
Rusher, Loscavio & LoPresto
180 Montgomery Street, Suite 1616
San Francisco, CA 94104-4239
Telephone: (415) 765-6600
Recruiter Classification: Retained; **Lowest/Average Salary:**
$90,000/$90,000; **Industry Concentration:** Generalist with a
primary focus in Insurance; **Function Concentration:**
Generalist with a primary focus in Administration, Engineering,
Marketing, Sales

Russell, Richard A. — *Vice President*
Executive Search Consultants Corporation
8 South Michigan Avenue, Suite 1205
Chicago, IL 60603
Telephone: (312) 251-8400
Recruiter Classification: Contingency; **Lowest/Average
Salary:** $50,000/$75,000; **Industry Concentration:**
Generalist with a primary focus in Financial Services,
Insurance; **Function Concentration:** Generalist with a
primary focus in Administration, General Management,
Human Resources

Russell, Robin E. — *Vice President*
Kenzer Corp.
6033 West Century Boulevard, Suite 700
Los Angeles, CA 90045
Telephone: (310) 417-8577
Recruiter Classification: Retained; **Lowest/Average Salary:**
$50,000/$90,000; **Industry Concentration:** Financial Services,
Venture Capital; **Function Concentration:** Generalist with a
primary focus in Administration, Finance/Accounting, General
Management, Human Resources, Marketing, Research and
Development, Sales

Russo, Karen — *President*
K. Russo Associates
2 Greenwich Plaza, Suite 100
Greenwich, CT 06830
Telephone: (203) 622-3903
Recruiter Classification: Retained; **Lowest/Average Salary:**
$30,000/$90,000; **Industry Concentration:** Financial
Services, Insurance; **Function Concentration:** Human
Resources

Russo, Karen — *Executive Recruiter*
Maximum Management Corp.
420 Lexington Avenue
Suite 2016
New York, NY 10170
Telephone: (212) 867-4646
Recruiter Classification: Contingency, Executive Temporary;
Lowest/Average Salary: $30,000/$75,000; **Industry
Concentration:** Generalist with a primary focus in Financial
Services, Insurance; **Function Concentration:** Human
Resources

Rustin, Beth — *Senior Vice President*
The Whitney Group
850 Third Avenue, 11th Floor
New York, NY 10022
Telephone: (212) 508-3500
Recruiter Classification: Retained; **Lowest/Average Salary:**
$90,000/$90,000; **Industry Concentration:** Financial Services,
Venture Capital; **Function Concentration:** Generalist with a
primary focus in Finance/Accounting, General Management,
Marketing, Sales

Ryan, David — *Associate*
Source Services Corporation
150 South Wacker Drive, Suite 400
Chicago, IL 60606
Telephone: (312) 346-7000
Recruiter Classification: Contingency; **Lowest/Average
Salary:** $30,000/$50,000; **Industry Concentration:** Financial
Services; **Function Concentration:** Engineering,
Finance/Accounting

Ryan, Kathleen — *Associate*
Source Services Corporation
10300 West 103rd Street, Suite 101
Overland Park, KS 66214
Telephone: (913) 888-8885
Recruiter Classification: Contingency; **Lowest/Average
Salary:** $30,000/$50,000; **Industry Concentration:** Financial
Services; **Function Concentration:** Engineering,
Finance/Accounting

Ryan, Lee — *President*
Ryan, Miller & Associates Inc.
4601 Wilshire Boulevard, Suite 225
Los Angeles, CA 90010
Telephone: (213) 938-4768
Recruiter Classification: Contingency; **Lowest/Average
Salary:** $40,000/$75,000; **Industry Concentration:**
Financial Services; **Function Concentration:**
Administration, Finance/Accounting, Human
Resources

Ryan, Mark — *Associate*
Source Services Corporation
One CityPlace, Suite 170
St. Louis, MO 63141
Telephone: (314) 432-4500
Recruiter Classification: Contingency; **Lowest/Average
Salary:** $30,000/$50,000; **Industry Concentration:** Financial
Services; **Function Concentration:** Engineering,
Finance/Accounting

Sabanosh, Whitney — *Recruiter*
Highland Search Group
565 Fifth Avenue, 22nd Floor
New York, NY 10017
Telephone: (212) 328-1113
Recruiter Classification: Retained; **Lowest/Average Salary:**
$90,000/$90,000; **Industry Concentration:** Financial Services,
Insurance, Venture Capital; **Function Concentration:** Generalist
with a primary focus in Administration, Finance/Accounting,
General Management, Human Resources, Sales,
Women/Minorities

Sabat, Lori S. — *President*
Alta Associates, Inc.
8 Bartles Corner Road, Suite 021
Flemington, NJ 08822
Telephone: (908) 806-8442
Recruiter Classification: Retained; **Lowest/Average Salary:**
$50,000/$90,000; **Industry Concentration:** Generalist
with a primary focus in Financial Services,
Insurance; **Function Concentration:** Finance/
Accounting

Sacerdote, John — *Principal*
Raymond Karsan Associates
18 Commerce Way
Woburn, MA 01801
Telephone: (617) 932-0400
Recruiter Classification: Retained; **Lowest/Average Salary:**
$30,000/$90,000; **Industry Concentration:** Generalist with a
primary focus in Insurance; **Function Concentration:**
Generalist with a primary focus in Administration, Engineering,
Finance/Accounting, General Management, Human Resources,
Marketing, Research and Development, Sales,
Women/Minorities

Sadaj, Michael — *Managing Director*
Source Services Corporation
505 East 200 South, Suite 300
Salt Lake City, UT 84102
Telephone: (801) 328-0011
Recruiter Classification: Contingency; **Lowest/Average
Salary:** $30,000/$50,000; **Industry Concentration:** Financial
Services; **Function Concentration:** Engineering,
Finance/Accounting

Salet, Michael — *Associate*
Source Services Corporation
4170 Ashford Dunwoody Road, Suite 285
Atlanta, GA 30319
Telephone: (404) 255-2045
Recruiter Classification: Contingency; **Lowest/Average
Salary:** $30,000/$50,000; **Industry Concentration:** Financial
Services; **Function Concentration:** Engineering,
Finance/Accounting

Saletra, Andrew — *Executive Recruiter*
CPS Inc.
One Westbrook Corporate Centre, Suite 600
Westchester, IL 60154
Telephone: (708) 531-8370
Recruiter Classification: Contingency; **Lowest/Average Salary:**
$30,000/$50,000; **Industry Concentration:** Generalist with a
primary focus in Financial Services, Insurance; **Function
Concentration:** Engineering, Research and Development,
Sales, Women/Minorities

Sallows, Jill S. — *Manager*
Crowe, Chizek and Company, LLP
330 East Jefferson Boulevard
P.O. Box 7
South Bend, IN 46624
Telephone: (219) 232-3992
Recruiter Classification: Retained; **Lowest/Average Salary:**
$30,000/$50,000; **Industry Concentration:** Financial Services;
Function Concentration: Finance/Accounting, General
Management, Human Resources

Salvagno, Michael J. — *Executive Vice President*
The Cambridge Group Ltd
1175 Post Road East
Westport, CT 06880
Telephone: (203) 226-4243
Recruiter Classification: Contingency; **Lowest/Average Salary:**
$60,000/$75,000; **Industry Concentration:** Generalist with a
primary focus in Financial Services; **Function Concentration:**
Administration, Finance/Accounting, General Management,
Human Resources, Marketing, Research and Development,
Sales, Women/Minorities

Samsel, Randy — *Managing Director*
Source Services Corporation
3 Summit Park Drive, Suite 550
Independence, OH 44131
Telephone: (216) 328-5900
Recruiter Classification: Contingency; **Lowest/Average
Salary:** $30,000/$50,000; **Industry Concentration:** Financial
Services; **Function Concentration:** Engineering,
Finance/Accounting

Samuelson, Robert — *Associate*
Source Services Corporation
520 Post Oak Boulevard, Suite 700
Houston, TX 77027
Telephone: (713) 439-1077
Recruiter Classification: Contingency; **Lowest/Average
Salary:** $30,000/$50,000; **Industry Concentration:** Financial
Services; **Function Concentration:** Engineering,
Finance/Accounting

Sanchez, William — *Associate*
Source Services Corporation
425 California Street, Suite 1200
San Francisco, CA 94104
Telephone: (415) 434-2410
Recruiter Classification: Contingency; **Lowest/Average
Salary:** $30,000/$50,000; **Industry Concentration:** Financial
Services; **Function Concentration:** Engineering,
Finance/Accounting

Sanders, Jason — *Managing Director*
Sanders Management Associates, Inc.
300 Lanidex Plaza
Parsippany, NJ 07054
Telephone: (201) 887-3232
Recruiter Classification: Retained; **Lowest/Average Salary:**
$90,000/$90,000; **Industry Concentration:** Financial
Services

Sanders, Natalie — *Executive Recruiter*
CPS Inc.
One Westbrook Corporate Centre, Suite 600
Westchester, IL 60154
Telephone: (708) 531-8370
Recruiter Classification: Contingency; **Lowest/Average
Salary:** $30,000/$50,000; **Industry Concentration:**
Generalist with a primary focus in Financial Services,
Insurance; **Function Concentration:** Engineering,
Research and Development, Sales, Women/
Minorities

Sanders, Spencer H. — *Senior Vice President*
Battalia Winston International
300 Park Avenue
New York, NY 10022
Telephone: (212) 308-8080
Recruiter Classification: Retained; **Lowest/Average Salary:**
$90,000/$90,000; **Industry Concentration:** Generalist
with a primary focus in Venture Capital; **Function
Concentration:** Generalist with a primary focus in
Engineering, Finance/Accounting, General Management,
Human Resources, Marketing, Research and Development,
Sales

Sandor, Richard J. — *Vice President*
Flynn, Hannock, Incorporated
P.O. Box 8027
Stamford, CT 06905
Telephone: (203) 357-0009
Recruiter Classification: Retained, Executive Temporary;
Lowest/Average Salary: $75,000/$90,000; **Industry Concentration:** Generalist with a primary focus in Financial Services, Insurance; **Function Concentration:** Generalist with a primary focus in Administration, General Management, Marketing, Sales

Saner, Harold — *Branch Manager*
Romac & Associates
1060 North Kings Highway
Suite 653
Cherry Hill, NJ 08034
Telephone: (609) 779-9077
Recruiter Classification: Executive Temporary; **Lowest/Average Salary:** $60,000/$60,000; **Industry Concentration:** Financial Services, Insurance; **Function Concentration:** Finance/Accounting

Sanitago, Anthony — *President*
TaxSearch, Inc.
6102 So. Memorial Drive
Tulsa, OK 74133
Telephone: (918) 252-3100
Recruiter Classification: Retained; **Lowest/Average Salary:** $60,000/$90,000; **Industry Concentration:** Generalist with a primary focus in Financial Services, Insurance, Venture Capital; **Function Concentration:** Generalist with a primary focus in Finance/Accounting

Sanow, Robert — *Search Consultant*
Cochran, Cochran & Yale, Inc.
955 East Henrietta Road
Rochester, NY 14623
Telephone: (716) 424-6060
Recruiter Classification: Retained; **Lowest/Average Salary:** $50,000/$75,000; **Industry Concentration:** Generalist with a primary focus in Financial Services, Venture Capital; **Function Concentration:** Generalist with a primary focus in Engineering, Finance/Accounting, General Management, Human Resources, Marketing, Sales, Women/Minorities

Santiago, Benefrido — *Associate*
Source Services Corporation
879 West 190th Street, Suite 250
Los Angeles, CA 90248
Telephone: (310) 323-6633
Recruiter Classification: Contingency; **Lowest/Average Salary:** $30,000/$50,000; **Industry Concentration:** Financial Services; **Function Concentration:** Engineering, Finance/Accounting

Santimauro, Edward — *Vice President*
Korn/Ferry International
233 South Wacker
Chicago, IL 60606
Telephone: (312) 466-1834
Recruiter Classification: Retained; **Lowest/Average Salary:** $100,000/$150,000; **Industry Concentration:** Generalist with a primary focus in Financial Services, Insurance; **Function Concentration:** Generalist

Sapers, Mark — *Associate*
Source Services Corporation
71 Spit Brook Road, Suite 305
Nashua, NH 03060
Telephone: (603) 888-7650
Recruiter Classification: Contingency; **Lowest/Average Salary:** $30,000/$50,000; **Industry Concentration:** Financial Services; **Function Concentration:** Engineering, Finance/Accounting

Saposhnik, Doron — *Associate*
Source Services Corporation
2029 Century Park East, Suite 1350
Los Angeles, CA 90067
Telephone: (310) 277-8092
Recruiter Classification: Contingency; **Lowest/Average Salary:** $30,000/$50,000; **Industry Concentration:** Financial Services; **Function Concentration:** Engineering, Finance/Accounting

Sardella, Sharon — *Associate*
Source Services Corporation
1500 West Park Drive, Suite 390
Westborough, MA 01581
Telephone: (508) 366-2600
Recruiter Classification: Contingency; **Lowest/Average Salary:** $30,000/$50,000; **Industry Concentration:** Financial Services; **Function Concentration:** Engineering, Finance/Accounting

Sarn, Allan G. — *Managing Director*
Allan Sarn Associates Inc.
230 Park Avenue, Suite 1522
New York, NY 10169
Telephone: (212) 687-0600
Recruiter Classification: Retained; **Lowest/Average Salary:** $75,000/$90,000; **Industry Concentration:** Generalist with a primary focus in Financial Services, Insurance; **Function Concentration:** Human Resources

Sarna, Edmund A. — *Executive Recruiter*
Jonas, Walters & Assoc., Inc.
1110 North Old World Third St., Suite 510
Milwaukee, WI 53203-1102
Telephone: (414) 291-2828
Recruiter Classification: Retained; **Lowest/Average Salary:** $60,000/$60,000; **Industry Concentration:** Financial Services, Insurance; **Function Concentration:** Generalist with a primary focus in Administration, Engineering, Finance/Accounting, General Management, Human Resources, Marketing, Research and Development, Sales

Satenstein, Sloan — *Associate*
Higdon Prince Inc.
230 Park Avenue, Suite 1455
New York, NY 10169
Telephone: (212) 986-4662
Recruiter Classification: Retained; **Lowest/Average Salary:** $150,000/$150,000; **Industry Concentration:** Generalist with a primary focus in Financial Services, Venture Capital; **Function Concentration:** Generalist with a primary focus in Finance/Accounting, General Management, Human Resources, Marketing, Sales, Women/Minorities

Sathe, Mark A. — *President*
Sathe & Associates, Inc.
5821 Cedar Lake Road
Minneapolis, MN 55416
Telephone: (612) 546-2100
Recruiter Classification: Retained; **Lowest/Average Salary:**
$60,000/$75,000; **Industry Concentration:** Financial
Services, Insurance; **Function Concentration:** Generalist
with a primary focus in Administration, Engineering,
Finance/Accounting, General Management, Human
Resources, Marketing, Sales

Sauer, Harry J. — *Managing Partner*
Romac & Associates
1700 Market Street
Suite 2702
Philadelphia, PA 19103
Telephone: (215) 568-6810
Recruiter Classification: Executive Temporary; **Lowest/Average
Salary:** $60,000/$60,000; **Industry Concentration:** Financial
Services, Insurance; **Function Concentration:**
Finance/Accounting

Savage, Edward J. — *Managing Director*
Stanton Chase International
10866 Wilshire Boulevard
Suite 870
Los Angeles, CA 90024
Telephone: (310) 474-1029
Recruiter Classification: Retained; **Lowest/Average Salary:**
$75,000/$90,000; **Industry Concentration:** Generalist with a
primary focus in Insurance, Venture Capital; **Function
Concentration:** Generalist with a primary focus in
Finance/Accounting, General Management, Human
Resources, Marketing, Sales

Savard, Robert F. — *Account Executive*
The Stevenson Group of Delaware Inc.
836 Farmington Avenue, Suite 223
West Hartford, CT 06119-1544
Telephone: (860) 232-3393
Recruiter Classification: Retained; **Lowest/Average Salary:**
$75,000/$90,000; **Industry Concentration:** Financial Services;
Function Concentration: Generalist

Savela, Edward — *Associate*
Source Services Corporation
4170 Ashford Dunwoody Road, Suite 285
Atlanta, GA 30319
Telephone: (404) 255-2045
Recruiter Classification: Contingency; **Lowest/Average
Salary:** $30,000/$50,000; **Industry Concentration:** Financial
Services; **Function Concentration:** Engineering,
Finance/Accounting

Savoy, Michelle — *Director*
Spencer Stuart
One University Avenue
Suite 801
Toronto, Ontario, CANADA M5J 2P1
Telephone: (416) 361-0311
Recruiter Classification: Retained; **Lowest/Average Salary:**
$90,000/$90,000; **Industry Concentration:** Financial Services;
Function Concentration: Finance/Accounting

Sawyer, Deborah — *Principal*
Korn/Ferry International
303 Peachtree Street N.E.
Suite 1600
Atlanta, GA 30308
Telephone: (404) 577-7542
Recruiter Classification: Retained; **Lowest/Average Salary:**
$100,000/$150,000; **Industry Concentration:** Generalist with a
primary focus in Financial Services, Insurance; **Function
Concentration:** Generalist

Sawyer, Patricia L. — *Partner*
Smith & Sawyer Inc.
230 Park Avenue, 33rd Floor
New York, NY 10169
Telephone: (212) 490-4390
Recruiter Classification: Retained; **Lowest/Average Salary:**
$90,000/$90,000; **Industry Concentration:** Generalist with a
primary focus in Financial Services, Venture Capital; **Function
Concentration:** Generalist with a primary focus in General
Management, Marketing, Women/Minorities

Saxon, Alexa — *Associate*
Woodworth International Group
2591 White Owl Drive
Encinitas, CA 92024
Telephone: (760) 634-6893
Recruiter Classification: Retained; **Lowest Salary:** $60,000;
Industry Concentration: Generalist with a primary focus in
Financial Services; **Function Concentration:** Generalist
with a primary focus in Engineering, Finance/Accounting,
General Management, Human Resources, Marketing,
Sales

Scalamera, Tom — *Executive Recruiter*
CPS Inc.
One Westbrook Corporate Centre, Suite 600
Westchester, IL 60154
Telephone: (708) 531-8370
Recruiter Classification: Contingency; **Lowest/Average Salary:**
$30,000/$50,000; **Industry Concentration:** Generalist with a
primary focus in Financial Services, Insurance; **Function
Concentration:** Engineering, Research and Development,
Sales, Women/Minorities

Schaefer, Frederic M. — *Vice President*
A.T. Kearney, Inc.
One Tabor Center, Suite 950
1200 Seventeenth Street
Denver, CO 80202
Telephone: (303) 626-7300
Recruiter Classification: Retained; **Lowest/Average Salary:**
$90,000/$90,000; **Industry Concentration:** Generalist with a
primary focus in Financial Services; **Function Concentration:**
Generalist with a primary focus in General Management,
Marketing, Sales

Schall, William A. — *Vice President and Principal*
The Stevenson Group of New Jersey
560 Sylvan Avenue
Englewood Cliffs, NJ 07632
Telephone: (201) 568-1900
Recruiter Classification: Retained; **Lowest/Average Salary:**
$75,000/$90,000; **Industry Concentration:** Venture Capital;
Function Concentration: Generalist

Schappell, Marc P. — *Consultant*
Egon Zehnder International Inc.
350 Park Avenue
New York, NY 10022
Telephone: (212) 838-9199
Recruiter Classification: Retained; **Lowest/Average Salary:** $90,000/$90,000; **Industry Concentration:** Generalist with a primary focus in Financial Services; **Function Concentration:** Generalist

Schene, Philip — *Technical Recruiter*
A.E. Feldman Associates
445 Northern Boulevard
Great Neck, NY 11021
Telephone: (516) 466-4708
Recruiter Classification: Contingency; **Lowest/Average Salary:** $60,000/$90,000; **Industry Concentration:** Generalist with a primary focus in Financial Services, Venture Capital; **Function Concentration:** Generalist with a primary focus in Administration, General Management, Marketing, Sales

Scherck, Henry J. — *Managing Director*
Ward Howell International, Inc.
99 Park Avenue, Suite 2000
New York, NY 10016-1699
Telephone: (212) 697-3730
Recruiter Classification: Retained; **Lowest/Average Salary:** $75,000/$90,000; **Industry Concentration:** Financial Services; **Function Concentration:** Generalist

Schlesinger, Laurie — *Consultant*
The Whitney Group
850 Third Avenue, 11th Floor
New York, NY 10022
Telephone: (212) 508-3500
Recruiter Classification: Retained; **Lowest/Average Salary:** $90,000/$90,000; **Industry Concentration:** Venture Capital; **Function Concentration:** Generalist with a primary focus in Finance/Accounting, General Management, Marketing, Sales

Schlpma, Christine — *Executive Recruiter*
Advanced Executive Resources
3040 Charlevoix Drive, SE
Grand Rapids, MI 49546
Telephone: (616) 942-4030
Recruiter Classification: Retained; **Lowest/Average Salary:** $30,000/$50,000; **Industry Concentration:** Generalist with a primary focus in Financial Services; **Function Concentration:** Generalist with a primary focus in Engineering, Finance/Accounting, General Management, Human Resources, Marketing, Research and Development, Sales, Women/Minorities

Schmidt, Frank B. — *President*
F.B. Schmidt International
30423 Canwood Place, Suite 239
Agoura Hills, CA 91301
Telephone: (818) 706-0500
Recruiter Classification: Retained; **Lowest/Average Salary:** $60,000/$90,000; **Industry Concentration:** Financial Services; **Function Concentration:** Marketing

Schneider, Thomas P. — *Vice President*
WTW Associates, Inc.
675 Third Avenue, Suite 2808
New York, NY 10017
Telephone: (212) 972-6990
Recruiter Classification: Retained; **Lowest/Average Salary:** $75,000/$90,000; **Industry Concentration:** Generalist with a primary focus in Financial Services; **Function Concentration:** Generalist

Schneiderman, Gerald — *President*
Management Resource Associates, Inc.
P.O. Box 3266
Boca Raton, FL 33427
Telephone: (561) 852-5650
Recruiter Classification: Contingency; **Lowest/Average Salary:** $50,000/$90,000; **Industry Concentration:** Generalist with a primary focus in Financial Services; **Function Concentration:** Generalist with a primary focus in Engineering, Finance/Accounting, General Management, Human Resources, Marketing, Research and Development, Sales

Schroeder, James — *Associate*
Source Services Corporation
One South Main Street, Suite 1440
Dayton, OH 45402
Telephone: (513) 461-4660
Recruiter Classification: Contingency; **Lowest/Average Salary:** $30,000/$50,000; **Industry Concentration:** Financial Services; **Function Concentration:** Engineering, Finance/Accounting

Schroeder, John W. — *Senior Director*
Spencer Stuart
1717 Main Street, Suite 5300
Dallas, TX 75201-4605
Telephone: (214) 658-1777
Recruiter Classification: Retained; **Lowest/Average Salary:** $90,000/$90,000; **Industry Concentration:** Generalist with a primary focus in Financial Services, Insurance, Venture Capital; **Function Concentration:** Generalist with a primary focus in Finance/Accounting, General Management, Human Resources, Marketing, Women/Minorities

Schroeder, Lee — *Partner*
Blau Mancino Schroeder
800 FirsTier Bank Building
Lincoln, NE 68508
Telephone: (402) 434-1494
Recruiter Classification: Retained; **Lowest/Average Salary:** $75,000/$75,000; **Industry Concentration:** Venture Capital; **Function Concentration:** General Management, Marketing, Research and Development

Schroeder, Steven J. — *Vice President Medical Products Group*
Blau Mancino Schroeder
4800 Juan Tabo N.E., Suite D
Albuquerque, NM 87111
Telephone: (505) 271-0702
Recruiter Classification: Retained; **Lowest/Average Salary:** $75,000/$90,000; **Industry Concentration:** Venture Capital; **Function Concentration:** Engineering, General Management, Marketing, Research and Development, Sales

Schueneman, David — *Executive Recruiter*
CPS Inc.
One Westbrook Corporate Centre, Suite 600
Westchester, IL 60154
Telephone: (708) 531-8370
Recruiter Classification: Contingency; **Lowest/Average Salary:**
$30,000/$50,000; **Industry Concentration:** Generalist with a
primary focus in Financial Services, Insurance; **Function
Concentration:** Engineering, Research and Development,
Sales, Women/Minorities

Schuette, Dorothy — *Senior Associate*
Harris Heery & Associates
40 Richards Avenue
One Norwalk West
Norwalk, CT 06854
Telephone: (203) 857-0808
Recruiter Classification: Retained; **Lowest/Average Salary:**
$75,000/$90,000; **Industry Concentration:** Financial Services,
Insurance; **Function Concentration:** General Management,
Marketing

Schultz, Randy — *Associate*
Source Services Corporation
1233 North Mayfair Road, Suite 300
Milwaukee, WI 53226
Telephone: (414) 774-6700
Recruiter Classification: Contingency; **Lowest/Average Salary:**
$30,000/$50,000; **Industry Concentration:** Financial Services;
Function Concentration: Engineering, Finance/Accounting

Schwalbach, Robert — *Associate*
Source Services Corporation
1290 Oakmead Parkway, Suite 318
Sunnyvale, CA 94086
Telephone: (408) 738-8440
Recruiter Classification: Contingency; **Lowest/Average Salary:**
$30,000/$50,000; **Industry Concentration:** Financial Services;
Function Concentration: Engineering, Finance/Accounting

Schwam, Carol — *Vice President*
A.E. Feldman Associates
445 Northern Boulevard
Great Neck, NY 11021
Telephone: (516) 466-4708
Recruiter Classification: Contingency; **Lowest/Average Salary:**
$60,000/$90,000; **Industry Concentration:** Generalist with a
primary focus in Financial Services, Venture Capital; **Function
Concentration:** Generalist with a primary focus in
Administration, General Management, Marketing, Sales

Schwartz, Harry — *Executive Recruiter*
Jacobson Associates
1785 The Exchange, Suite 320
Atlanta, GA 30339
Telephone: (404) 952-3877
Recruiter Classification: Contingency; **Lowest/Average Salary:**
$20,000/$50,000; **Industry Concentration:** Insurance;
Function Concentration: Generalist

Schwartz, Vincent P. — *Vice President*
Slayton International, Inc./I-I-C Partners
181 West Madison Street, Suite 4510
Chicago, IL 60602
Telephone: (312) 456-0080
Recruiter Classification: Retained; **Lowest/Average Salary:**
$90,000/$90,000; **Industry Concentration:** Venture Capital;
Function Concentration: Generalist

Schweichler, Lee J. — *President*
Schweichler Associates, Inc.
200 Tamal Vista, Building 200, Suite 100
Corte Madera, CA 94925
Telephone: (415) 924-7200
Recruiter Classification: Retained; **Lowest/Average Salary:**
$90,000/$90,000; **Industry Concentration:** Venture Capital;
Function Concentration: Engineering, Finance/Accounting,
General Management, Human Resources, Marketing, Research
and Development, Sales

Schwinden, William — *Associate*
Source Services Corporation
500 108th Avenue NE, Suite 1780
Bellevue, WA 98004
Telephone: (206) 454-6400
Recruiter Classification: Contingency; **Lowest/Average Salary:**
$30,000/$50,000; **Industry Concentration:** Financial Services;
Function Concentration: Engineering, Finance/Accounting

Scimone, James — *Managing Director*
Source Services Corporation
15600 N.W. 67th Avenue, Suite 210
Miami Lakes, FL 33014
Telephone: (305) 556-8000
Recruiter Classification: Contingency; **Lowest/Average Salary:**
$30,000/$50,000; **Industry Concentration:** Financial Services;
Function Concentration: Engineering, Finance/Accounting

Scimone, Jim — *Managing Director*
Source Services Corporation
701 West Cypress Creek Road, Suite 202
Ft. Lauderdale, FL 33309
Telephone: (954) 771-0777
Recruiter Classification: Contingency; **Lowest/Average Salary:**
$30,000/$50,000; **Industry Concentration:** Financial Services;
Function Concentration: Engineering, Finance/Accounting

Scodius, Joseph J. — *Manager*
Gregory Michaels and Associates, Inc.
8410 West Bryn Mawr Avenue
Suite 400
Chicago, IL 60631
Telephone: (773) 380-1333
Recruiter Classification: Retained; **Lowest/Average Salary:**
$90,000/$90,000; **Industry Concentration:** Generalist with a
primary focus in Financial Services; **Function Concentration:**
Generalist with a primary focus in Finance/Accounting,
General Management, Human Resources, Marketing, Sales

Scoff, Barry — *Associate*
Source Services Corporation
379 Thornall Street
Edison, NJ 08837
Telephone: (908) 494-2800
Recruiter Classification: Contingency; **Lowest/Average Salary:**
$30,000/$50,000; **Industry Concentration:** Financial Services;
Function Concentration: Engineering, Finance/Accounting

Scothon, Alan — *Managing Partner*
Romac & Associates
6130 Westford Road
Dayton, OH 45426
Telephone: (513) 854-5719
Recruiter Classification: Executive Temporary; **Lowest/Average
Salary:** $60,000/$60,000; **Industry Concentration:** Financial
Services, Insurance; **Function Concentration:**
Finance/Accounting

Scott, Evan — *Executive Vice President/Partner*
Howard Fischer Associates, Inc.
1800 John F. Kennedy Boulevard, 7th Floor
Philadelphia, PA 19103
Telephone: (215) 568-8363
Recruiter Classification: Retained; **Lowest/Average Salary:** $90,000/$90,000; **Industry Concentration:** Generalist with a primary focus in Financial Services, Insurance, Venture Capital; **Function Concentration:** Generalist with a primary focus in Administration, Finance/Accounting, General Management, Human Resources, Marketing, Research and Development, Sales, Women/Minorities

Scott, Gordon S. — *Vice President*
Search Advisors International Corp.
777 South Harbour Island Boulevard
Suite 925
Tampa, FL 33602
Telephone: (813) 221-7555
Recruiter Classification: Retained; **Lowest/Average Salary:** $75,000/$90,000; **Industry Concentration:** Generalist with a primary focus in Financial Services, Insurance; **Function Concentration:** Generalist with a primary focus in Administration, Engineering, Finance/Accounting, General Management, Human Resources, Marketing, Research and Development, Sales, Women/Minorities

Scranton, Lisa — *Professional Recruiter*
A.J. Burton Group, Inc.
120 East Baltimore Street, Suite 2220
Baltimore, MD 21202
Telephone: (410) 752-5244
Recruiter Classification: Contingency; **Lowest/Average Salary:** $40,000/$75,000; **Industry Concentration:** Generalist with a primary focus in Financial Services, Insurance; **Function Concentration:** Generalist with a primary focus in Administration, Finance/Accounting, General Management, Human Resources

Scroggins, Stephen R. — *Managing Director*
Russell Reynolds Associates, Inc.
200 Park Avenue
New York, NY 10166-0002
Telephone: (212) 351-2000
Recruiter Classification: Retained; **Lowest/Average Salary:** $90,000/$90,000; **Industry Concentration:** Generalist with a primary focus in Financial Services; **Function Concentration:** Generalist

Seamon, Kenneth — *Associate*
Source Services Corporation
3 Summit Park Drive, Suite 550
Independence, OH 44131
Telephone: (216) 328-5900
Recruiter Classification: Contingency; **Lowest/Average Salary:** $30,000/$50,000; **Industry Concentration:** Financial Services; **Function Concentration:** Engineering, Finance/Accounting

Seco, William — *Managing Partner*
Seco & Zetto Associates, Inc.
P.O. Box 225
Harrington Park, NJ 07640
Telephone: (201) 784-0674
Recruiter Classification: Contingency; **Lowest/Average Salary:** $60,000/$75,000; **Industry Concentration:** Generalist with a primary focus in Financial Services; **Function Concentration:** Generalist with a primary focus in Marketing, Sales, Women/Minorities

Segal, Eric B. — *President*
Kenzer Corp.
777 Third Avenue, 26th Floor
New York, NY 10017
Telephone: (212) 308-4300
Recruiter Classification: Retained; **Lowest/Average Salary:** $50,000/$90,000; **Industry Concentration:** Financial Services, Venture Capital; **Function Concentration:** Generalist with a primary focus in Administration, Finance/Accounting, General Management, Human Resources, Marketing, Research and Development, Sales

Seiden, Steven A. — *President*
Seiden Krieger Associates, Inc.
375 Park Avenue
New York, NY 10152
Telephone: (212) 688-8383
Recruiter Classification: Retained; **Lowest/Average Salary:** $90,000/$90,000; **Industry Concentration:** Generalist with a primary focus in Financial Services, Venture Capital; **Function Concentration:** Generalist with a primary focus in Finance/Accounting, General Management, Human Resources, Marketing, Sales, Women/Minorities

Selbach, Barbara — *Director*
Spencer Stuart
277 Park Avenue, 29th Floor
New York, NY 10172
Telephone: (212) 336-0200
Recruiter Classification: Retained; **Lowest/Average Salary:** $90,000/$90,000; **Industry Concentration:** Financial Services; **Function Concentration:** Finance/Accounting, Marketing

Selker, Gregory L. — *Vice President*
Christian & Timbers
25825 Science Park Drive, Suite 400
Cleveland, OH 44122
Telephone: (216) 765-5870
Recruiter Classification: Retained; **Lowest/Average Salary:** $90,000/$90,000; **Industry Concentration:** Generalist with a primary focus in Venture Capital; **Function Concentration:** Generalist

Sell, David — *Associate*
Source Services Corporation
7730 East Bellview Avenue, Suite 302
Englewood, CO 80111
Telephone: (303) 773-3700
Recruiter Classification: Contingency; **Lowest/Average Salary:** $30,000/$50,000; **Industry Concentration:** Financial Services; **Function Concentration:** Engineering, Finance/Accounting

Selvaggi, Esther — *Associate*
Source Services Corporation
150 South Warner Road, Suite 238
King of Prussia, PA 19406
Telephone: (610) 341-1960
Recruiter Classification: Contingency; **Lowest/Average Salary:** $30,000/$50,000; **Industry Concentration:** Financial Services; **Function Concentration:** Engineering, Finance/Accounting

Semple, David — *Associate*
Source Services Corporation
4170 Ashford Dunwoody Road, Suite 285
Atlanta, GA 30319
Telephone: (404) 255-2045
Recruiter Classification: Contingency; **Lowest/Average Salary:** $30,000/$50,000; **Industry Concentration:** Financial Services; **Function Concentration:** Engineering, Finance/Accounting

Semyan, John K. — *Partner*
TNS Partners, Inc.
8140 Walnut Hill Lane
Suite 301
Dallas, TX 75231
Telephone: (214) 369-3565
Recruiter Classification: Retained; **Lowest/Average Salary:**
$90,000/$150,000; **Industry Concentration:** Generalist with a
primary focus in Financial Services; **Function Concentration:**
Generalist with a primary focus in Finance/Accounting,
General Management, Marketing, Sales

Sennello, Gendra — *Insurance Consultant*
National Search, Inc.
2816 University Drive
Coral Springs, FL 33071
Telephone: (800) 935-4355
Recruiter Classification: Contingency; **Lowest/Average Salary:**
$30,000/$50,000; **Industry Concentration:** Insurance;
Function Concentration: Generalist with a primary focus in
Administration, Finance/Accounting, General Management,
Human Resources, Marketing, Research and Development,
Sales, Women/Minorities

Serba, Kerri — *Associate*
Source Services Corporation
155 Federal Street, Suite 410
Boston, MA 02110
Telephone: (617) 482-8211
Recruiter Classification: Contingency; **Lowest/Average
Salary:** $30,000/$50,000; **Industry Concentration:** Financial
Services; **Function Concentration:** Engineering,
Finance/Accounting

Sessa, Vincent J. — *Partner*
Integrated Search Solutions Group, LLC
33 Main Street
Port Washington, NY 11050
Telephone: (516) 767-3030
Recruiter Classification: Retained; **Lowest/Average Salary:**
$90,000/$90,000; **Industry Concentration:** Generalist with a
primary focus in Financial Services; **Function Concentration:**
Generalist

Sevilla, Claudio A. — *General Manager*
Crawford & Crofford
15327 NW 60th Avenue, Suite 240
Miami Lakes, FL 33014
Telephone: (305) 820-0855
Recruiter Classification: Contingency; **Lowest/Average Salary:**
$30,000/$50,000; **Industry Concentration:** Generalist with a
primary focus in Financial Services; **Function Concentration:**
Generalist with a primary focus in Administration, Engineering,
Finance/Accounting, General Management, Marketing,
Research and Development, Sales

Shackleford, David — *Associate*
Source Services Corporation
150 South Warner Road, Suite 238
King of Prussia, PA 19406
Telephone: (610) 341-1960
Recruiter Classification: Contingency; **Lowest/Average
Salary:** $30,000/$50,000; **Industry Concentration:** Financial
Services; **Function Concentration:** Engineering,
Finance/Accounting

Shanks, Jennifer — *Associate*
Source Services Corporation
2029 Century Park East, Suite 1350
Los Angeles, CA 90067
Telephone: (310) 277-8092
Recruiter Classification: Contingency; **Lowest/Average Salary:**
$30,000/$50,000; **Industry Concentration:** Financial Services;
Function Concentration: Engineering, Finance/Accounting

Shapanka, Samuel — *Associate*
Source Services Corporation
2 Penn Plaza, Suite 1176
New York, NY 10121
Telephone: (212) 760-2200
Recruiter Classification: Contingency; **Lowest/Average Salary:**
$30,000/$50,000; **Industry Concentration:** Financial Services;
Function Concentration: Engineering, Finance/Accounting

Shapiro, Beth — *Consultant*
Howard Fischer Associates, Inc.
13750 San Pedro Avenue
Suite 810
San Antonio, TX 78232
Telephone: (210) 491-0844
Recruiter Classification: Retained; **Lowest/Average Salary:**
$90,000/$90,000; **Industry Concentration:** Generalist with a
primary focus in Financial Services, Insurance, Venture Capital;
Function Concentration: Generalist

Shapiro, Elaine — *Executive Recruiter*
CPS Inc.
303 Congress Street, 5th Floor
Boston, MA 02210
Telephone: (617) 439-7950
Recruiter Classification: Contingency; **Lowest/Average Salary:**
$30,000/$50,000; **Industry Concentration:** Generalist with a
primary focus in Financial Services, Insurance; **Function
Concentration:** Engineering, Research and Development,
Sales, Women/Minorities

Shawhan, Heather — *Associate*
Source Services Corporation
879 West 190th Street, Suite 250
Los Angeles, CA 90248
Telephone: (310) 323-6633
Recruiter Classification: Contingency; **Lowest/Average Salary:**
$30,000/$50,000; **Industry Concentration:** Financial Services;
Function Concentration: Engineering, Finance/Accounting

Shea, Kathleen M. — *President*
The Penn Partners, Incorporated
117 South 17th Street, Suite 400
Philadelphia, PA 19103
Telephone: (215) 568-9285
Recruiter Classification: Retained; **Lowest/Average Salary:**
$60,000/$90,000; **Industry Concentration:** Generalist with a
primary focus in Financial Services; **Function Concentration:**
Generalist

Shell, John C. — *President*
John Shell Associates, Inc.
115 Atrium Way, Suite 122
Columbia, SC 29223
Telephone: (803) 788-6619
Recruiter Classification: Contingency, Executive Temporary;
Lowest/Average Salary: $20,000/$40,000; **Industry
Concentration:** Generalist with a primary focus in Financial
Services, Insurance; **Function Concentration:**
Finance/Accounting

Shelton, Jonathan — *Associate*
Source Services Corporation
1105 Schrock Road, Suite 510
Columbus, OH 43229
Telephone: (614) 846-3311
Recruiter Classification: Contingency; **Lowest/Average Salary:** $30,000/$50,000; **Industry Concentration:** Financial Services; **Function Concentration:** Engineering, Finance/Accounting

Shelton, Sandra — *Insurance Consultant*
National Search, Inc.
2816 University Drive
Coral Springs, FL 33071
Telephone: (800) 935-4355
Recruiter Classification: Contingency; **Lowest/Average Salary:** $30,000/$50,000; **Industry Concentration:** Insurance; **Function Concentration:** Generalist with a primary focus in Administration, Finance/Accounting, General Management, Human Resources, Marketing, Research and Development, Sales, Women/Minorities

Shemin, Grace — *Executive Recruiter*
Maximum Management Corp.
420 Lexington Avenue
Suite 2016
New York, NY 10170
Telephone: (212) 867-4646
Recruiter Classification: Contingency, Executive Temporary; **Lowest/Average Salary:** $30,000/$75,000; **Industry Concentration:** Generalist with a primary focus in Financial Services, Insurance; **Function Concentration:** Human Resources

Shen, Eugene Y. — *Managing Director*
The Whitney Group
850 Third Avenue, 11th Floor
New York, NY 10022
Telephone: (212) 508-3500
Recruiter Classification: Retained; **Lowest/Average Salary:** $90,000/$90,000; **Industry Concentration:** Financial Services, Venture Capital; **Function Concentration:** Generalist with a primary focus in Finance/Accounting, General Management, Marketing, Sales

Shenfield, Peter — *Vice President*
A.T. Kearney, Inc.
130 Adelaide Street West, Suite 2710
Toronto, Ontario, CANADA M5H 3P5
Telephone: (416) 947-1990
Recruiter Classification: Retained; **Lowest/Average Salary:** $90,000/$90,000; **Industry Concentration:** Generalist with a primary focus in Financial Services; **Function Concentration:** Generalist with a primary focus in Engineering, Finance/Accounting, General Management

Shepard, Michael J. — *Group Vice President*
MSI International
2500 Marquis One Tower
245 Peachtree Center Ave.
Atlanta, GA 30303
Telephone: (404) 659-5236
Recruiter Classification: Contingency; **Lowest/Average Salary:** $30,000/$60,000; **Industry Concentration:** Generalist with a primary focus in Financial Services; **Function Concentration:** Generalist with a primary focus in Administration, Engineering, Finance/Accounting, General Management, Marketing, Sales

Sher, Lawrence — *Managing Director*
M.A. Churchill & Associates, Inc.
Morelyn Plaza #307
1111 Street Road
Southampton, PA 18966
Telephone: (215) 953-0300
Recruiter Classification: Retained; **Lowest/Average Salary:** $50,000/$75,000; **Industry Concentration:** Financial Services, Insurance; **Function Concentration:** Marketing, Research and Development, Sales

Sherman, Robert R. — *President*
Mortgage & Financial Personnel Services
5850 Canoga Avenue, Suite 400
Woodland Hills, CA 91367
Telephone: (818) 710-7133
Recruiter Classification: Contingency, Executive Temporary; **Lowest/Average Salary:** $40,000/$60,000; **Industry Concentration:** Financial Services, Insurance; **Function Concentration:** Finance/Accounting

Shervey, Brent C. — *Consultant*
O'Callaghan Honey/Ray & Berndtson, Inc.
400-400 Fifth Avenue S.W.
Calgary, Alberta, CANADA T2P 0L6
Telephone: (403) 269-3277
Recruiter Classification: Retained; **Lowest/Average Salary:** $75,000/$90,000; **Industry Concentration:** Generalist with a primary focus in Financial Services; **Function Concentration:** Generalist with a primary focus in Administration, Finance/Accounting, General Management, Human Resources, Marketing

Sherwood, Andrew — *Chairman*
Goodrich & Sherwood Associates, Inc.
521 Fifth Avenue
New York, NY 10175
Telephone: (212) 697-4131
Recruiter Classification: Retained; **Lowest/Average Salary:** $60,000/$90,000; **Industry Concentration:** Generalist with a primary focus in Financial Services, Insurance, Venture Capital; **Function Concentration:** Generalist with a primary focus in Administration, Finance/Accounting, General Management, Human Resources, Marketing, Sales

Shield, Nancy — *Vice President*
Maximum Management Corp.
420 Lexington Avenue
Suite 2016
New York, NY 10170
Telephone: (212) 867-4646
Recruiter Classification: Contingency, Executive Temporary; **Lowest/Average Salary:** $30,000/$75,000; **Industry Concentration:** Generalist with a primary focus in Financial Services, Insurance; **Function Concentration:** Human Resources

Shirilla, Robert M. — *Senior Vice President*
F.B. Schmidt International
30423 Canwood Place, Suite 239
Agoura Hills, CA 91301
Telephone: (818) 706-0500
Recruiter Classification: Retained; **Lowest/Average Salary:** $60,000/$90,000; **Industry Concentration:** Financial Services; **Function Concentration:** Marketing

Shore, Earl L. — *President*
E.L. Shore & Associates Ltd.
1201-2 St. Clair Avenue E.
Toronto, Ontario, CANADA M4T 2T5
Telephone: (416) 928-9399
Recruiter Classification: Retained; **Lowest/Average Salary:**
$90,000/$90,000; **Industry Concentration:** Generalist
with a primary focus in Financial Services; **Function
Concentration:** Generalist with a primary focus in
Finance/Accounting, General Management, Human
Resources, Marketing

Shourds, Mary E. — *Executive Vice President*
Houze, Shourds & Montgomery, Inc.
Greater L.A. World Trade Center, Suite 800
Long Beach, CA 90831-0800
Telephone: (562) 495-6495
Recruiter Classification: Retained; **Lowest/Average Salary:**
$90,000/$90,000; **Industry Concentration:** Generalist with a
primary focus in Financial Services; **Function Concentration:**
Generalist

Shufelt, Doug — *Search Consultant*
Sink, Walker, Boltrus International
60 Walnut Street
Wellesley, MA 02181
Telephone: (617) 237-1199
Recruiter Classification: Retained; **Lowest/Average Salary:**
$90,000/$90,000; **Industry Concentration:** Financial Services;
Function Concentration: Engineering, General Management,
Research and Development, Sales

Sibbald, John R. — *President*
John Sibbald Associates, Inc.
7733 Forsyth Boulevard, Suite 2010
St. Louis, MO 63105
Telephone: (314) 727-0227
Recruiter Classification: Retained; **Lowest/Average Salary:**
$90,000/$90,000; **Industry Concentration:** Generalist with a
primary focus in Financial Services; **Function Concentration:**
Generalist with a primary focus in Engineering,
Finance/Accounting, General Management, Human Resources,
Marketing, Research and Development, Sales,
Women/Minorities

Sibul, Shelly Remen — *Legal Search Consultant*
Chicago Legal Search, Ltd.
33 North Dearborn Street, Suite 2302
Chicago, IL 60602-3109
Telephone: (312) 251-2580
Recruiter Classification: Contingency; **Lowest/Average Salary:**
$50,000/$90,000; **Industry Concentration:** Venture Capital;
Function Concentration: Women/Minorities

Siegel, Pamela — *Recruiter*
Executive Options, Ltd.
910 Skokie Boulevard
Suite 210
Northbrook, IL 60068
Telephone: (708) 291-4322
Recruiter Classification: Executive Temporary; **Lowest/Average
Salary:** $30,000/$50,000; **Industry Concentration:** Generalist
with a primary focus in Financial Services; **Function
Concentration:** Generalist with a primary focus in
Finance/Accounting, General Management, Human Resources,
Marketing, Women/Minorities

Siegler, Jody Cukiir — *Vice President*
A.T. Kearney, Inc.
Biltmore Tower
500 South Grand Avenue, Suite 1780
Los Angeles, CA 90071
Telephone: (213) 689-6800
Recruiter Classification: Retained; **Lowest/Average Salary:**
$90,000/$90,000; **Industry Concentration:** Generalist with a
primary focus in Financial Services; **Function Concentration:**
Generalist with a primary focus in Engineering,
Finance/Accounting, General Management

Siegrist, Jeffrey M. — *Managing Director*
D.E. Foster Partners Inc.
2800 Two First Union Center
Charlotte, NC 28282
Telephone: (704) 335-5511
Recruiter Classification: Retained; **Lowest/Average Salary:**
$90,000/$90,000; **Industry Concentration:** Generalist with a
primary focus in Financial Services, Insurance; **Function
Concentration:** Generalist with a primary focus in
Finance/Accounting, General Management, Human Resources,
Marketing, Research and Development

Signer, Julie — *Executive Recruiter*
CPS Inc.
One Westbrook Corporate Centre, Suite 600
Westchester, IL 60154
Telephone: (708) 531-8370
Recruiter Classification: Contingency; **Lowest/Average Salary:**
$30,000/$50,000; **Industry Concentration:** Generalist with a
primary focus in Financial Services, Insurance; **Function
Concentration:** Engineering, Research and Development,
Sales, Women/Minorities

Silcott, Marvin L. — *President*
Marvin L. Silcott & Associates, Inc.
7557 Rambler Road
Suite 1336
Dallas, TX 75231
Telephone: (214) 369-7802
Recruiter Classification: Retained; **Lowest/Average Salary:**
$75,000/$90,000; **Industry Concentration:** Generalist with a
primary focus in Financial Services; **Function Concentration:**
Generalist with a primary focus in Engineering,
Finance/Accounting, General Management, Human Resources,
Research and Development, Women/Minorities

Sill, Igor M. — *Managing Partner*
Geneva Group International
Four Embarcadero Center, Suite 1400
San Francisco, CA 94111
Telephone: (415) 433-4646
Recruiter Classification: Retained; **Lowest/Average Salary:**
$100,000/$100,000; **Industry Concentration:** Venture Capital;
Function Concentration: Engineering, General Management,
Marketing, Research and Development, Sales

Silvas, Stephen D. — *President*
Roberson and Company
10752 North 89th Place, Suite 202
Scottsdale, AZ 85260
Telephone: (602) 391-3200
Recruiter Classification: Contingency; **Lowest/Average Salary:**
$40,000/$60,000; **Industry Concentration:** Generalist with a
primary focus in Financial Services; **Function Concentration:**
Generalist with a primary focus in Engineering,
Finance/Accounting, General Management, Human Resources,
Sales

Silver, Kit — *Associate*
Source Services Corporation
1290 Oakmead Parkway, Suite 318
Sunnyvale, CA 94086
Telephone: (408) 738-8440
Recruiter Classification: Contingency; **Lowest/Average Salary:** $30,000/$50,000; **Industry Concentration:** Financial Services; **Function Concentration:** Engineering, Finance/Accounting

Silver, Lee — *President*
L. A. Silver Associates, Inc.
463 Worcester Road
Farmingham, MA 01701
Telephone: (508) 879-2603
Recruiter Classification: Retained; **Lowest/Average Salary:** $90,000/$90,000; **Industry Concentration:** Generalist with a primary focus in Financial Services, Venture Capital; **Function Concentration:** Generalist with a primary focus in Engineering, Finance/Accounting, General Management, Human Resources, Marketing, Research and Development, Sales

Silverman, Gary W. — *President*
GWS Partners
Two North Riverside Plaza
Chicago, IL 60606
Telephone: (312) 454-5501
Recruiter Classification: Retained; **Lowest/Average Salary:** $90,000/$90,000; **Industry Concentration:** Generalist with a primary focus in Venture Capital; **Function Concentration:** Finance/Accounting, General Management, Human Resources, Marketing, Sales, Women/Minorities

Silverman, Paul M. — *President*
The Marshall Group
1900 East Golf Road, Suite M100
Schaumburg, IL 60173
Telephone: (708) 330-0009
Recruiter Classification: Executive Temporary; **Lowest/Average Salary:** $50,000/$90,000; **Industry Concentration:** Generalist with a primary focus in Financial Services; **Function Concentration:** Generalist

Silverstein, Jackie — *Staffing Consultant*
Don Richard Associates of Charlotte
2650 One First Union Center
301 South College Street
Charlotte, NC 28202-6000
Telephone: (704) 377-6447
Recruiter Classification: Contingency; **Lowest/Average Salary:** $20,000/$30,000; **Industry Concentration:** Generalist with a primary focus in Financial Services; **Function Concentration:** Generalist with a primary focus in Administration, Human Resources, Sales

Simmons, Deborah — *Associate*
Source Services Corporation
10220 SW Greenburg Road, Suite 625
Portland, OR 97223
Telephone: (503) 768-4546
Recruiter Classification: Contingency; **Lowest/Average Salary:** $30,000/$50,000; **Industry Concentration:** Financial Services; **Function Concentration:** Engineering, Finance/Accounting

Simmons, Sandra K. — *Department Manager*
MSI International
229 Peachtree Street, NE
Suite 1201
Atlanta, GA 30303
Telephone: (404) 659-5050
Recruiter Classification: Contingency; **Lowest/Average Salary:** $30,000/$60,000; **Industry Concentration:** Generalist with a primary focus in Financial Services; **Function Concentration:** Administration, Engineering, Finance/Accounting, General Management, Marketing, Sales

Simon, Mary K. — *Senior Consultant*
Gregory Michaels and Associates, Inc.
8410 West Bryn Mawr Avenue
Suite 400
Chicago, IL 60631
Telephone: (773) 380-1333
Recruiter Classification: Retained; **Lowest/Average Salary:** $90,000/$90,000; **Industry Concentration:** Generalist with a primary focus in Financial Services; **Function Concentration:** Generalist with a primary focus in Finance/Accounting, General Management, Human Resources, Marketing, Sales

Simon, Penny B. — *Partner*
Ray & Berndtson
245 Park Avenue, 33rd Floor
New York, NY 10167
Telephone: (212) 370-1316
Recruiter Classification: Retained; **Lowest/Average Salary:** $90,000/$90,000; **Industry Concentration:** Financial Services; **Function Concentration:** Generalist

Simpson, David J. — *Principal*
Simpson Associates, Inc.
1900 Minnesota Court
Suite 118
Mississauga, Ontario Canada, LSN 3C9
Telephone: (905) 821-2722
Recruiter Classification: Retained; **Lowest/Average Salary:** $75,000/$90,000; **Industry Concentration:** Generalist with a primary focus in Financial Services; **Function Concentration:** Generalist with a primary focus in Finance/Accounting, General Management

Simpson, Scott — *Executive Recruiter*
Cendea Connection International
13740 Research Boulevard
Building 0-1
Austin, TX 78750
Telephone: (512) 219-6000
Recruiter Classification: Retained; **Lowest/Average Salary:** $75,000/$90,000; **Industry Concentration:** Generalist with a primary focus in Venture Capital; **Function Concentration:** Generalist with a primary focus in General Management, Marketing, Sales

Sindler, Jay — *Professional Recruiter*
A.J. Burton Group, Inc.
120 East Baltimore Street, Suite 2220
Baltimore, MD 21202
Telephone: (410) 752-5244
Recruiter Classification: Contingency; **Lowest/Average Salary:** $40,000/$75,000; **Industry Concentration:** Generalist with a primary focus in Financial Services, Insurance; **Function Concentration:** Generalist with a primary focus in Administration, Finance/Accounting, General Management, Human Resources

Singleton, Robin — *Senior Vice President*
Tyler & Company
1000 Abernathy Road
Suite 1400
Atlanta, GA 30328-5655
Telephone: (770) 396-3939
Recruiter Classification: Retained; **Lowest/Average Salary:**
$75,000/$90,000; **Industry Concentration:** Insurance;
Function Concentration: Generalist

Sink, Cliff — *Partner*
Sink, Walker, Boltrus International
60 Walnut Street
Wellesley, MA 02181
Telephone: (617) 237-1199
Recruiter Classification: Retained; **Lowest/Average Salary:**
$90,000/$90,000; **Industry Concentration:** Financial Services;
Function Concentration: Engineering, General Management,
Research and Development, Sales

Sirena, Evelyn — *Associate*
Source Services Corporation
925 Westchester Avenue, Suite 309
White Plains, NY 10604
Telephone: (914) 428-9100
Recruiter Classification: Contingency; **Lowest/Average Salary:**
$30,000/$50,000; **Industry Concentration:** Financial Services;
Function Concentration: Engineering, Finance/Accounting

Sitarski, Stan — *Vice President*
Howard Fischer Associates, Inc.
1800 John F. Kennedy Boulevard, 7th Floor
Philadelphia, PA 19103
Telephone: (215) 568-8363
Recruiter Classification: Retained; **Lowest/Average Salary:**
$90,000/$90,000; **Industry Concentration:** Generalist with a
primary focus in Financial Services, Insurance, Venture Capital;
Function Concentration: Generalist with a primary focus in
Administration, Finance/Accounting, General Management,
Human Resources, Marketing, Research and Development,
Sales, Women/Minorities

Skalet, Ira — *Vice President*
A.E. Feldman Associates
445 Northern Boulevard
Great Neck, NY 11021
Telephone: (516) 466-4708
Recruiter Classification: Contingency; **Lowest/Average
Salary:** $60,000/$90,000; **Industry Concentration:**
Generalist with a primary focus in Financial Services,
Venture Capital; **Function Concentration:** Generalist with a
primary focus in Administration, General Management,
Marketing, Sales

Skunda, Donna M. — *Vice President*
Allerton Heneghan & O'Neill
70 West Madison Street, Suite 2015
Chicago, IL 60602
Telephone: (312) 263-1075
Recruiter Classification: Retained; **Lowest/Average Salary:**
$75,000/$90,000; **Industry Concentration:** Generalist
with a primary focus in Financial Services; **Function
Concentration:** Generalist with a primary focus in
Engineering, Finance/Accounting, General Management,
Marketing, Research and Development, Women/
Minorities

Slayton, Richard C. — *President*
Slayton International, Inc./I-I-C Partners
181 West Madison Street, Suite 4510
Chicago, IL 60602
Telephone: (312) 456-0080
Recruiter Classification: Retained; **Lowest/Average Salary:**
$90,000/$90,000; **Industry Concentration:** Venture Capital;
Function Concentration: Engineering, Finance/Accounting,
General Management, Human Resources, Marketing, Research
and Development

Sloan, Scott — *Associate*
Source Services Corporation
150 South Wacker Drive, Suite 400
Chicago, IL 60606
Telephone: (312) 346-7000
Recruiter Classification: Contingency; **Lowest/Average
Salary:** $30,000/$50,000; **Industry Concentration:** Financial
Services; **Function Concentration:** Engineering,
Finance/Accounting

Slocum, Ann Marie — *Vice President*
K.L. Whitney Company
6 Aspen Drive
North Caldwell, NJ 07006
Telephone: (201) 228-7124
Recruiter Classification: Retained; **Lowest/Average Salary:**
$75,000/$90,000; **Industry Concentration:** Financial Services;
Function Concentration: Marketing, Sales

Slosar, John — *Managing Director*
Boyden
375 Park Avenue, Suite 1509
New York, NY 10152
Telephone: (810) 647-4201
Recruiter Classification: Retained; **Lowest/Average Salary:**
$90,000/$90,000; **Industry Concentration:** Generalist with a
primary focus in Financial Services; **Function Concentration:**
Generalist with a primary focus in Engineering,
Finance/Accounting, General Management, Human
Resources, Marketing, Research and Development, Sales,
Women/Minorities

Smead, Michelle M. — *Vice President*
A.T. Kearney, Inc.
222 West Adams Street
Chicago, IL 60606
Telephone: (312) 648-0111
Recruiter Classification: Retained; **Lowest/Average Salary:**
$90,000/$90,000; **Industry Concentration:** Generalist with a
primary focus in Financial Services; **Function Concentration:**
Generalist with a primary focus in Administration,
Finance/Accounting, General Management, Human Resources,
Marketing, Sales

Smirnov, Tatiana — *Vice President*
Allan Sarn Associates Inc.
230 Park Avenue, Suite 1522
New York, NY 10169
Telephone: (212) 687-0600
Recruiter Classification: Retained; **Lowest/Average Salary:**
$75,000/$90,000; **Industry Concentration:** Generalist with a
primary focus in Financial Services, Insurance; **Function
Concentration:** Human Resources

Smith, Ana Luz — *Consultant*
Smith Search, S.C.
Barranca del Muerto No. 472, Col. Alpes
Mexico City, D.F., MEXICO 01010
Telephone: (525) 593-8766
Recruiter Classification: Retained; **Lowest/Average Salary:**
$60,000/$90,000; **Industry Concentration:** Generalist with a
primary focus in Financial Services, Venture Capital; **Function
Concentration:** Generalist with a primary focus in
Administration, Engineering, Finance/Accounting, General
Management, Human Resources, Marketing, Sales

Smith, Brant — *Partner*
Smith Hanley Associates
99 Park Avenue
New York, NY 10016
Telephone: (212) 687-9696
Recruiter Classification: Contingency; **Lowest/Average Salary:**
$75,000/$90,000; **Industry Concentration:** Financial Services;
Function Concentration: Finance/Accounting

Smith, David P. — *President*
HRS, Inc.
P.O. Box 4499
Pittsburgh, PA 15205
Telephone: (412) 331-4700
Recruiter Classification: Retained; **Lowest/Average Salary:**
$90,000/$90,000; **Industry Concentration:** Generalist with a
primary focus in Financial Services, Venture Capital; **Function
Concentration:** Engineering, Finance/Accounting, General
Management, Marketing, Research and Development, Sales,
Women/Minorities

Smith, Ethan L. — *Recruiter*
Highland Search Group
565 Fifth Avenue, 22nd Floor
New York, NY 10017
Telephone: (212) 328-1113
Recruiter Classification: Retained; **Lowest/Average Salary:**
$90,000/$90,000; **Industry Concentration:** Financial Services,
Insurance, Venture Capital; **Function Concentration:** Generalist
with a primary focus in Administration, Finance/Accounting,
General Management, Human Resources, Sales,
Women/Minorities

Smith, Herman M. — *President*
Herman Smith Executive Initiatives Inc.
161 Bay Street, Suite 3600
Box 629
Toronto, Ontario, CANADA M5J 2S1
Telephone: (416) 862-8830
Recruiter Classification: Retained; **Lowest/Average Salary:**
$75,000/$90,000; **Industry Concentration:** Generalist with a
primary focus in Financial Services; **Function Concentration:**
Generalist with a primary focus in Finance/Accounting,
General Management, Marketing, Sales

Smith, John E. — *President*
Smith Search, S.C.
Barranca del Muerto No. 472, Col. Alpes
Mexico City, D.F., MEXICO 01010
Telephone: (525) 593-8766
Recruiter Classification: Retained; **Lowest/Average Salary:**
$75,000/$90,000; **Industry Concentration:** Generalist with a
primary focus in Financial Services; **Function Concentration:**
Generalist with a primary focus in Administration, Engineering,
Finance/Accounting, General Management, Human Resources,
Marketing, Sales

Smith, John F. — *Vice President*
The Penn Partners, Incorporated
117 South 17th Street, Suite 400
Philadelphia, PA 19103
Telephone: (215) 568-9285
Recruiter Classification: Retained; **Lowest/Average Salary:**
$60,000/$90,000; **Industry Concentration:** Generalist with a
primary focus in Financial Services; **Function Concentration:**
Generalist

Smith, Lawrence — *Associate*
Source Services Corporation
One South Main Street, Suite 1440
Dayton, OH 45402
Telephone: (513) 461-4660
Recruiter Classification: Contingency; **Lowest/Average
Salary:** $30,000/$50,000; **Industry Concentration:** Financial
Services; **Function Concentration:** Engineering,
Finance/Accounting

Smith, Lydia — *Sales Recruiter*
The Corporate Connection, Ltd.
7202 Glen Forest Drive
Richmond, VA 23226
Telephone: (804) 288-8844
Recruiter Classification: Contingency; **Lowest/Average Salary:**
$20,000/$30,000; **Industry Concentration:** Generalist with a
primary focus in Financial Services, Insurance; **Function
Concentration:** Generalist with a primary focus in
Administration, Engineering, Finance/Accounting, General
Management, Human Resources, Marketing, Sales,
Women/Minorities

Smith, Matt D. — *Partner*
Ray & Berndtson
Sears Tower, 233 South Wacker Drive, Suite 4020
Chicago, IL 60606-6310
Telephone: (312) 876-0730
Recruiter Classification: Retained; **Lowest/Average Salary:**
$90,000/$90,000; **Industry Concentration:** Generalist with a
primary focus in Financial Services, Insurance; **Function
Concentration:** Generalist with a primary focus in
Administration, Finance/Accounting, General Management,
Human Resources, Marketing, Research and Development,
Sales, Women/Minorities

Smith, Monica L. — *President*
Analysts Resources, Inc.
75 Maiden Lane
New York, NY 10038
Telephone: (212) 755-2777
Recruiter Classification: Contingency; **Lowest/Average
Salary:** $75,000/$90,000; **Industry Concentration:** Financial
Services, Venture Capital; **Function Concentration:**
Generalist with a primary focus in Finance/Accounting,
Marketing, Sales

Smith, R. Michael — *Senior Partner*
Smith James Group, Inc.
11660 Alpharetta Highway, Suite 515
Roswell, GA 30076
Telephone: (770) 667-0212
Recruiter Classification: Retained; **Lowest/Average Salary:**
$40,000/$75,000; **Industry Concentration:** Generalist with a
primary focus in Financial Services; **Function Concentration:**
Generalist

Smith, Richard — *Executive Recruiter*
S.C. International, Ltd.
1430 Branding Lane, Suite 119
Downers Grove, IL 60515
Telephone: (708) 963-3033
Recruiter Classification: Contingency; **Lowest/Average Salary:** $30,000/$50,000; **Industry Concentration:** Insurance; **Function Concentration:** Administration, Human Resources

Smith, Robert L. — *Partner*
Smith & Sawyer Inc.
230 Park Avenue, 33rd Floor
New York, NY 10169
Telephone: (212) 490-4390
Recruiter Classification: Retained; **Lowest/Average Salary:** $90,000/$90,000; **Industry Concentration:** Generalist with a primary focus in Financial Services; **Function Concentration:** Generalist with a primary focus in Finance/Accounting, General Management, Human Resources, Marketing

Smith, Ronald V. — *Executive Search Consultant*
Coe & Company International Inc.
1535 400-3rd Avenue SW
Center Tower
Calgary, Alberta, Canada T20 4H2
Telephone: (403) 232-8833
Recruiter Classification: Retained; **Lowest/Average Salary:** $75,000/$90,000; **Industry Concentration:** Financial Services; **Function Concentration:** Generalist with a primary focus in Administration, Engineering, Finance/Accounting, General Management, Human Resources, Marketing, Research and Development, Sales

Smith, Timothy — *Associate*
Source Services Corporation
155 Federal Street, Suite 410
Boston, MA 02110
Telephone: (617) 482-8211
Recruiter Classification: Contingency; **Lowest/Average Salary:** $30,000/$50,000; **Industry Concentration:** Financial Services; **Function Concentration:** Engineering, Finance/Accounting

Smith, Timothy C. — *Consultant*
Christian & Timbers
25825 Science Park Drive, Suite 400
Cleveland, OH 44122
Telephone: (216) 514-4874
Recruiter Classification: Retained; **Lowest/Average Salary:** $90,000/$90,000; **Industry Concentration:** Generalist with a primary focus in Financial Services, Venture Capital; **Function Concentration:** Generalist with a primary focus in Finance/Accounting, General Management

Smith, W. Guice — *Senior Consultant*
Southwestern Professional Services
2451 Atrium Way
Nashville, TN 37214
Telephone: (615) 391-2722
Recruiter Classification: Contingency; **Lowest/Average Salary:** $40,000/$90,000; **Industry Concentration:** Financial Services; **Function Concentration:** Finance/Accounting

Smock, Cynthia — *Associate*
Source Services Corporation
Foster Plaza VI
681 Anderson Drive, 2nd Floor
Pittsburgh, PA 15220
Telephone: (412) 928-8300
Recruiter Classification: Contingency; **Lowest/Average Salary:** $30,000/$50,000; **Industry Concentration:** Financial Services; **Function Concentration:** Engineering, Finance/Accounting

Smoller, Howard — *Associate*
Source Services Corporation
2 Penn Plaza, Suite 1176
New York, NY 10121
Telephone: (212) 760-2200
Recruiter Classification: Contingency; **Lowest/Average Salary:** $30,000/$50,000; **Industry Concentration:** Financial Services; **Function Concentration:** Engineering, Finance/Accounting

Snelgrove, Geiger — *Manager Operations*
National Search, Inc.
2816 University Drive
Coral Springs, FL 33071
Telephone: (800) 935-4355
Recruiter Classification: Contingency; **Lowest/Average Salary:** $30,000/$50,000; **Industry Concentration:** Insurance; **Function Concentration:** Generalist with a primary focus in Administration, Finance/Accounting, General Management, Human Resources, Marketing, Research and Development, Sales, Women/Minorities

Snowden, Charles — *Associate*
Source Services Corporation
8614 Westwood Center, Suite 750
Vienna, VA 22182
Telephone: (703) 790-5610
Recruiter Classification: Contingency; **Lowest/Average Salary:** $30,000/$50,000; **Industry Concentration:** Financial Services; **Function Concentration:** Engineering, Finance/Accounting

Snowhite, Rebecca — *Associate*
Source Services Corporation
525 Vine Street, Suite 2250
Cincinnati, OH 45202
Telephone: (513) 651-3303
Recruiter Classification: Contingency; **Lowest/Average Salary:** $30,000/$50,000; **Industry Concentration:** Financial Services; **Function Concentration:** Engineering, Finance/Accounting

Snyder, C. Edward — *Managing Director*
Horton International
10 Tower Lane
Avon, CT 06001
Telephone: (860) 674-8701
Recruiter Classification: Retained; **Lowest/Average Salary:** $90,000/$90,000; **Industry Concentration:** Generalist with a primary focus in Insurance, Venture Capital; **Function Concentration:** Generalist with a primary focus in Administration, Engineering, Finance/Accounting, General Management, Human Resources, Marketing, Research and Development, Sales, Women/Minorities

Snyder, James F. — *President*
Snyder & Company
35 Old Avon Village, Suite 185
Avon, CT 06001-3822
Telephone: (860) 521-9760
Recruiter Classification: Retained; **Lowest/Average Salary:** $90,000/$90,000; **Industry Concentration:** Generalist with a primary focus in Financial Services, Insurance; **Function Concentration:** Generalist with a primary focus in Administration, Engineering, Finance/Accounting, General Management, Human Resources, Marketing, Research and Development, Sales

Sochacki, Michael — *Associate*
Source Services Corporation
161 Ottawa NW, Suite 409D
Grand Rapids, MI 49503
Telephone: (616) 451-2400
Recruiter Classification: Contingency; **Lowest/Average Salary:** $30,000/$50,000; **Industry Concentration:** Financial Services; **Function Concentration:** Engineering, Finance/Accounting

Sockwell, J. Edgar — *Owner/Principal*
Sockwell & Associates
227 West Trade Street, Suite 1930
Charlotte, NC 28202
Telephone: (704) 372-1865
Recruiter Classification: Retained; **Lowest/Average Salary:** $90,000/$90,000; **Industry Concentration:** Generalist with a primary focus in Financial Services; **Function Concentration:** Generalist with a primary focus in Administration, Finance/Accounting, General Management, Human Resources, Marketing, Sales

Sondgrass, Stephen — *Managing Principal*
DeFrain, Mayer LLC
6900 College Boulevard
Suite 300
Overland Park, KS 66211
Telephone: (913) 345-0500
Recruiter Classification: Retained; **Lowest/Average Salary:** $40,000/$60,000; **Industry Concentration:** Generalist with a primary focus in Financial Services; **Function Concentration:** Generalist with a primary focus in Finance/Accounting, General Management, Marketing

Song, Louis — *Associate*
Source Services Corporation
4510 Executive Drive, Suite 200
San Diego, CA 92121
Telephone: (619) 552-0300
Recruiter Classification: Contingency; **Lowest/Average Salary:** $30,000/$50,000; **Industry Concentration:** Financial Services; **Function Concentration:** Engineering, Finance/Accounting

Sorgen, Jay — *Associate*
Source Services Corporation
2 Penn Plaza, Suite 1176
New York, NY 10121
Telephone: (212) 760-2200
Recruiter Classification: Contingency; **Lowest/Average Salary:** $30,000/$50,000; **Industry Concentration:** Financial Services; **Function Concentration:** Engineering, Finance/Accounting

Sostilio, Louis — *Associate*
Source Services Corporation
155 Federal Street, Suite 410
Boston, MA 02110
Telephone: (617) 482-8211
Recruiter Classification: Contingency; **Lowest/Average Salary:** $30,000/$50,000; **Industry Concentration:** Financial Services; **Function Concentration:** Engineering, Finance/Accounting

Souder, E.G. — *President*
Souder & Associates
P.O. Box 71
Bridgewater, VA 22812
Telephone: (540) 828-2365
Recruiter Classification: Retained; **Lowest/Average Salary:** $40,000/$75,000; **Industry Concentration:** Generalist with a primary focus in Financial Services; **Function Concentration:** Engineering, General Management, Human Resources, Marketing, Research and Development, Sales

Soutouras, James — *Senior Partner*
Smith James Group, Inc.
11660 Alpharetta Highway, Suite 515
Roswell, GA 30076
Telephone: (770) 667-0212
Recruiter Classification: Retained; **Lowest/Average Salary:** $40,000/$75,000; **Industry Concentration:** Generalist with a primary focus in Financial Services; **Function Concentration:** Generalist

Spadavecchia, Jennifer — *Associate*
Alta Associates, Inc.
8 Bartles Corner Road, Suite 021
Flemington, NJ 08822
Telephone: (908) 806-8442
Recruiter Classification: Retained; **Lowest/Average Salary:** $40,000/$75,000; **Industry Concentration:** Generalist with a primary focus in Insurance; **Function Concentration:** Finance/Accounting

Spann, Richard E. — *Managing Principal*
Goodrich & Sherwood Associates, Inc.
401 Merritt Seven Corporate Park
Norwalk, CT 06851
Telephone: (203) 847-2525
Recruiter Classification: Retained; **Lowest/Average Salary:** $60,000/$90,000; **Industry Concentration:** Generalist with a primary focus in Financial Services, Insurance, Venture Capital; **Function Concentration:** Generalist with a primary focus in Administration, Finance/Accounting, General Management, Human Resources, Marketing, Sales

Spector, Michael — *Associate*
Source Services Corporation
5343 North 16th Street, Suite 270
Phoenix, AZ 85016
Telephone: (602) 230-0220
Recruiter Classification: Contingency; **Lowest/Average Salary:** $30,000/$50,000; **Industry Concentration:** Financial Services; **Function Concentration:** Engineering, Finance/Accounting

Spencer, Bob — *Search Consultant*
Kaye-Bassman International Corp.
18333 Preston Road, Suite 500
Dallas, TX 75252
Telephone: (972) 931-5242
Recruiter Classification: Retained; **Lowest/Average Salary:**
$50,000/$90,000; **Industry Concentration:** Insurance;
Function Concentration: Generalist

Spencer, John — *Managing Director*
Source Services Corporation
879 West 190th Street, Suite 250
Los Angeles, CA 90248
Telephone: (310) 323-6633
Recruiter Classification: Contingency; **Lowest/**
Average Salary: $30,000/$50,000; **Industry**
Concentration: Financial Services; **Function**
Concentration: Engineering, Finance/
Accounting

Spencer, John — *Managing Director*
Source Services Corporation
2029 Century Park East, Suite 1350
Los Angeles, CA 90067
Telephone: (310) 277-8092
Recruiter Classification: Contingency; **Lowest/Average**
Salary: $30,000/$50,000; **Industry Concentration:** Financial
Services; **Function Concentration:** Engineering,
Finance/Accounting

Spera, Stefanie — *Vice President*
A.T. Kearney, Inc.
153 East 53rd Street
New York, NY 10022
Telephone: (212) 751-7040
Recruiter Classification: Retained; **Lowest/Average Salary:**
$90,000/$90,000; **Industry Concentration:** Generalist
with a primary focus in Financial Services; **Function**
Concentration: Generalist with a primary focus in
Engineering, Finance/Accounting, General
Management

Spicehandler, Sheila — *Consultant*
Trebor Weldon Lawrence, Inc.
355 Lexington Avenue
New York, NY 10017
Telephone: (212) 867-0066
Recruiter Classification: Retained; **Lowest/Average Salary:**
$75,000/$90,000; **Industry Concentration:** Financial Services;
Function Concentration: General Management, Marketing,
Sales

Spicher, John — *Division Manager*
M.A. Churchill & Associates, Inc.
Morelyn Plaza #307
1111 Street Road
Southampton, PA 18966
Telephone: (215) 953-0300
Recruiter Classification: Retained; **Lowest/Average**
Salary: $50,000/$75,000; **Industry Concentration:**
Financial Services, Insurance; **Function**
Concentration: Marketing, Research and Development,
Sales

Spiegel, Gayle — *Senior Vice President*
L. A. Silver Associates, Inc.
463 Worcester Road
Farmingham, MA 01701
Telephone: (508) 879-2603
Recruiter Classification: Retained; **Lowest/Average Salary:**
$90,000/$90,000; **Industry Concentration:** Generalist with a
primary focus in Financial Services, Venture Capital; **Function**
Concentration: Generalist with a primary focus in Engineering,
Finance/Accounting, General Management, Human Resources,
Marketing, Research and Development, Sales

Spitz, Grant — *Partner*
The Caldwell Partners Amrop International
999 West Hastings Street
Suite 750
Vancouver, British Columbia, CANADA V6C 2W2
Telephone: (604) 669-3550
Recruiter Classification: Retained; **Lowest/Average Salary:**
$60,000/$90,000; **Industry Concentration:** Generalist with a
primary focus in Financial Services; **Function Concentration:**
Generalist

Sponseller, Vern — *Vice President*
Richard Kader & Associates
7850 Freeway Circle, Suite 201
Cleveland, OH 44130
Telephone: (440) 891-1700
Recruiter Classification: Contingency; **Lowest/Average**
Salary: $40,000/$50,000; **Industry Concentration:** Generalist
with a primary focus in Financial Services; **Function**
Concentration: Generalist with a primary focus in
Finance/Accounting, Sales

Spoutz, Paul — *Associate*
Source Services Corporation
7730 East Bellview Avenue, Suite 302
Englewood, CO 80111
Telephone: (303) 773-3700
Recruiter Classification: Contingency; **Lowest/Average**
Salary: $30,000/$50,000; **Industry Concentration:** Financial
Services; **Function Concentration:** Engineering,
Finance/Accounting

Spriggs, Robert D. — *Partner*
Spriggs & Company, Inc.
1701 East Lake Avenue
Suite 265
Glenview, IL 60025
Telephone: (708) 657-7181
Recruiter Classification: Retained; **Lowest/Average Salary:**
$90,000/$90,000; **Industry Concentration:** Generalist with a
primary focus in Financial Services, Venture Capital; **Function**
Concentration: Generalist with a primary focus in
Administration, Engineering, Finance/Accounting, General
Management, Human Resources, Marketing, Research and
Development, Sales

Springer, Mark H. — *President*
M.H. Springer & Associates Incorporated
5855 Topanga Canyon Boulevard, Suite 230
Woodland Hills, CA 91367
Telephone: (818) 710-8955
Recruiter Classification: Retained; **Lowest/Average Salary:**
$90,000/$90,000; **Industry Concentration:** Financial Services;
Function Concentration: Generalist

Sprowls, Linda — *Assistant Recruiter*
Allard Associates
44 Montgomery Street, Suite 500
San Francisco, CA 94104
Telephone: (800) 291-5279
Recruiter Classification: Retained; **Lowest/Average Salary:**
$40,000/$75,000; **Industry Concentration:** Financial Services;
Function Concentration: Marketing

St. Clair, Alan — *Vice President*
TNS Partners, Inc.
8140 Walnut Hill Lane
Suite 301
Dallas, TX 75231
Telephone: (214) 369-3565
Recruiter Classification: Retained; **Lowest/Average Salary:**
$90,000/$90,000; **Industry Concentration:** Generalist
with a primary focus in Financial Services, Venture Capital;
Function Concentration: Generalist with a primary
focus in Administration, Finance/Accounting, General
Management, Human Resources, Marketing,
Sales

St. Martin, Peter — *Associate*
Source Services Corporation
4170 Ashford Dunwoody Road, Suite 285
Atlanta, GA 30319
Telephone: (404) 255-2045
Recruiter Classification: Contingency; **Lowest/Average
Salary:** $30,000/$50,000; **Industry Concentration:** Financial
Services; **Function Concentration:** Engineering,
Finance/Accounting

Stack, Richard — *Associate*
Source Services Corporation
2 Penn Plaza, Suite 1176
New York, NY 10121
Telephone: (212) 760-2200
Recruiter Classification: Contingency; **Lowest/Average
Salary:** $30,000/$50,000; **Industry Concentration:** Financial
Services; **Function Concentration:** Engineering,
Finance/Accounting

Stahl, Cindy — *Consultant*
Plummer & Associates, Inc.
65 Rowayton Avenue
Rowayton, CT 06853
Telephone: (203) 899-1233
Recruiter Classification: Retained, Executive Temporary;
Lowest/Average Salary: $90,000/$90,000; **Industry
Concentration:** Venture Capital; **Function Concentration:**
Generalist with a primary focus in General
Management

Stampfl, Eric — *Principal*
Morgan Stampfl, Inc.
6 West 32nd Street
New York, NY 10001
Telephone: (212) 643-7165
Recruiter Classification: Contingency; **Lowest/Average
Salary:** $50,000/$90,000; **Industry Concentration:**
Financial Services; **Function Concentration:**
Finance/Accounting

Stanton, John — *Vice President/Managing
Director*
A.T. Kearney, Inc.
3050 Post Oak Boulevard, Suite 570
Houston, TX 77056
Telephone: (713) 621-9967
Recruiter Classification: Retained; **Lowest/Average Salary:**
$90,000/$90,000; **Industry Concentration:** Generalist with a
primary focus in Financial Services; **Function Concentration:**
Generalist with a primary focus in Engineering,
Finance/Accounting, General Management

Stark, Jeff — *Principal*
Thorne, Brieger Associates Inc.
11 East 44th Street
New York, NY 10017
Telephone: (212) 682-5424
Recruiter Classification: Retained; **Lowest/Average Salary:**
$90,000/$90,000; **Industry Concentration:** Generalist with a
primary focus in Financial Services, Insurance; **Function
Concentration:** Generalist with a primary focus in
Administration, Engineering, Finance/Accounting, General
Management, Human Resources, Marketing, Research and
Development, Sales

Steele, Daniel — *Search Consultant*
Cochran, Cochran & Yale, Inc.
1333 W. 120th Avenue, Suite 311
Westminster, CO 80234
Telephone: (303) 252-4600
Recruiter Classification: Retained; **Lowest/Average Salary:**
$50,000/$75,000; **Industry Concentration:** Generalist with a
primary focus in Financial Services, Venture Capital; **Function
Concentration:** Generalist with a primary focus in Engineering,
Finance/Accounting, General Management, Human Resources,
Marketing, Sales, Women/Minorities

Steer, Joe — *Executive Recruiter*
CPS Inc.
One Westbrook Corporate Centre, Suite 600
Westchester, IL 60154
Telephone: (708) 531-8370
Recruiter Classification: Contingency; **Lowest/Average Salary:**
$30,000/$50,000; **Industry Concentration:** Generalist with a
primary focus in Financial Services, Insurance; **Function
Concentration:** Engineering, Research and Development,
Sales, Women/Minorities

Stein, Terry W. — *Partner*
Stewart, Stein and Scott, Ltd.
1000 Shelard Parkway, Suite 606
Minneapolis, MN 55426
Telephone: (612) 595-4456
Recruiter Classification: Retained; **Lowest/Average Salary:**
$75,000/$90,000; **Industry Concentration:** Generalist with a
primary focus in Financial Services, Insurance, Venture Capital;
Function Concentration: Generalist with a primary focus in
Engineering, Finance/Accounting, General Management, Human
Resources, Marketing, Research and Development, Sales

Steinem, Andy — *Principal*
Dahl-Morrow International
12020 Sunrise Valley Drive
Reston, VA 20191
Telephone: (703) 860-6868
Recruiter Classification: Retained; **Lowest/Average Salary:**
$75,000/$90,000; **Industry Concentration:** Venture Capital;
Function Concentration: Generalist with a primary focus in
Engineering, Finance/Accounting, General Management,
Marketing, Sales

Steinem, Andy — *Principal*
Dahl-Morrow International
12110 Sunset Hills Road
Suite 450
Reston, VA 22090
Telephone: (703) 648-1594
Recruiter Classification: Executive Temporary; **Lowest/Average Salary:** $75,000/$90,000; **Industry Concentration:** Generalist with a primary focus in Venture Capital; **Function Concentration:** Generalist

Steinem, Barbara — *President*
Dahl-Morrow International
12110 Sunset Hills Road
Suite 450
Reston, VA 22090
Telephone: (703) 648-1594
Recruiter Classification: Executive Temporary; **Lowest/Average Salary:** $75,000/$90,000; **Industry Concentration:** Generalist with a primary focus in Venture Capital; **Function Concentration:** Generalist

Steinem, Barbra — *Principal*
Dahl-Morrow International
12020 Sunrise Valley Drive
Reston, VA 20191
Telephone: (703) 860-6868
Recruiter Classification: Retained; **Lowest/Average Salary:** $75,000/$90,000; **Industry Concentration:** Venture Capital; **Function Concentration:** Generalist with a primary focus in Engineering, Finance/Accounting, General Management, Marketing, Sales

Steinman, Stephen M. — *President and CEO*
The Stevenson Group of New Jersey
560 Sylvan Avenue
Englewood Cliffs, NJ 07632
Telephone: (201) 568-1900
Recruiter Classification: Retained; **Lowest/Average Salary:** $75,000/$90,000; **Industry Concentration:** Generalist with a primary focus in Financial Services; **Function Concentration:** Generalist with a primary focus in Finance/Accounting, General Management, Human Resources, Marketing, Sales

Stephens, Andrew — *Associate*
Source Services Corporation
8614 Westwood Center, Suite 750
Vienna, VA 22182
Telephone: (703) 790-5610
Recruiter Classification: Contingency; **Lowest/Average Salary:** $30,000/$50,000; **Industry Concentration:** Financial Services; **Function Concentration:** Engineering, Finance/Accounting

Stephens, John — *Associate*
Source Services Corporation
15600 N.W. 67th Avenue, Suite 210
Miami Lakes, FL 33014
Telephone: (305) 556-8000
Recruiter Classification: Contingency; **Lowest/Average Salary:** $30,000/$50,000; **Industry Concentration:** Financial Services; **Function Concentration:** Engineering, Finance/Accounting

Stern, Lester W. — *Managing Director*
Sullivan & Company
20 Exchange Place, 50th Floor
New York, NY 10005
Telephone: (212) 422-3000
Recruiter Classification: Retained; **Lowest/Average Salary:** $90,000/$90,000; **Industry Concentration:** Generalist with a primary focus in Financial Services; **Function Concentration:** Generalist

Stern, Stephen — *Executive Recruiter*
CPS Inc.
One Westbrook Corporate Centre, Suite 600
Westchester, IL 60154
Telephone: (708) 531-8370
Recruiter Classification: Contingency; **Lowest/Average Salary:** $30,000/$50,000; **Industry Concentration:** Generalist with a primary focus in Financial Services, Insurance; **Function Concentration:** Engineering, Research and Development, Sales, Women/Minorities

Sterner, Doug — *Executive Recruiter*
CPS Inc.
One Westbrook Corporate Centre, Suite 600
Westchester, IL 60154
Telephone: (708) 531-8370
Recruiter Classification: Contingency; **Lowest/Average Salary:** $30,000/$50,000; **Industry Concentration:** Generalist with a primary focus in Financial Services, Insurance; **Function Concentration:** Engineering, Research and Development, Sales, Women/Minorities

Stevens, Craig M. — *Partner*
Kirkman & Searing, Inc.
8045 Leesburg Pike
Suite 540
Vienna, VA 22182
Telephone: (703) 761-7020
Recruiter Classification: Retained; **Lowest/Average Salary:** $90,000/$90,000; **Industry Concentration:** Financial Services; **Function Concentration:** Finance/Accounting, General Management, Marketing, Sales

Stevens, Tracey — *Associate*
Don Richard Associates of Washington, D.C., Inc.
1020 19th Street, NW, Suite 650
Washington, DC 20036
Telephone: (202) 463-7210
Recruiter Classification: Contingency; **Lowest/Average Salary:** $20,000/$30,000; **Industry Concentration:** Financial Services; **Function Concentration:** Finance/Accounting

Stevenson, Jane — *Executive Vice President/Partner*
Howard Fischer Associates, Inc.
1800 John F. Kennedy Boulevard, 7th Floor
Philadelphia, PA 19103
Telephone: (215) 568-8363
Recruiter Classification: Retained; **Lowest/Average Salary:** $90,000/$90,000; **Industry Concentration:** Generalist with a primary focus in Financial Services, Insurance, Venture Capital; **Function Concentration:** Generalist with a primary focus in Administration, Finance/Accounting, General Management, Human Resources, Marketing, Research and Development, Sales, Women/Minorities

Stevenson, Jane — *President, Southwest*
Howard Fischer Associates, Inc.
13750 San Pedro Avenue
Suite 810
San Antonio, TX 78232
Telephone: (210) 491-0844
Recruiter Classification: Retained; **Lowest/Average Salary:**
$90,000/$90,000; **Industry Concentration:** Generalist with a
primary focus in Financial Services, Insurance, Venture Capital;
Function Concentration: Generalist

Stewart, Clifford — *Associate*
Morgan Stampfl, Inc.
6 West 32nd Street
New York, NY 10001
Telephone: (212) 643-7165
Recruiter Classification: Contingency; **Lowest/Average Salary:**
$50,000/$90,000; **Industry Concentration:** Financial Services;
Function Concentration: Finance/Accounting

Stewart, Jan J. — *Consultant*
Egon Zehnder International Inc.
1 First Canadian Place
P.O. Box 179
Toronto, Ontario, CANADA M5X 1C7
Telephone: (416) 364-0222
Recruiter Classification: Retained; **Lowest/Average Salary:**
$90,000/$90,000; **Industry Concentration:** Generalist with a
primary focus in Financial Services; **Function Concentration:**
Generalist

Stewart, Jeffrey O. — *Partner*
Stewart, Stein and Scott, Ltd.
1000 Shelard Parkway, Suite 606
Minneapolis, MN 55426
Telephone: (612) 595-4455
Recruiter Classification: Retained; **Lowest/Average Salary:**
$75,000/$90,000; **Industry Concentration:** Generalist with a
primary focus in Financial Services, Insurance, Venture Capital;
Function Concentration: Generalist with a primary focus in
Engineering, Finance/Accounting, General Management,
Human Resources, Marketing, Research and Development,
Sales

Stewart, Ross M. — *Managing Director*
Human Resources Network Partners Inc.
Two Galleria Tower
13455 Noel Road, 10th Floor
Dallas, TX 75240
Telephone: (214) 702-7932
Recruiter Classification: Retained; **Lowest/Average Salary:**
$60,000/$90,000; **Industry Concentration:** Generalist with a
primary focus in Financial Services, Venture Capital; **Function
Concentration:** Generalist with a primary focus in
Administration, Engineering, Finance/Accounting, General
Management, Human Resources, Marketing, Research and
Development, Sales, Women/Minorities

Stivk, Barbara A. — *General Manager*
Thornton Resources
9800 McKnight Road
Pittsburgh, PA 15237
Telephone: (412) 364-2111
Recruiter Classification: Contingency, Executive Temporary;
Lowest/Average Salary: $40,000/$50,000; **Industry
Concentration:** Generalist with a primary focus in Financial
Services; **Function Concentration:** Generalist with a primary
focus in General Management, Human Resources, Marketing

Stone, Robert Ryder — *Partner*
Lamalie Amrop International
Metro Center, One Station Place
Stamford, CT 06902-6800
Telephone: (203) 324-4445
Recruiter Classification: Retained; **Lowest/Average Salary:**
$90,000/$90,000; **Industry Concentration:** Generalist with a
primary focus in Financial Services; **Function Concentration:**
Generalist

Stone, Susan L. — *President*
Stone Enterprises Ltd.
645 North Michigan Avenue, Suite 800
Chicago, IL 60611
Telephone: (312) 404-9300
Recruiter Classification: Contingency; **Lowest/Average Salary:**
$30,000/$90,000; **Industry Concentration:** Generalist with a
primary focus in Financial Services; **Function Concentration:**
Generalist with a primary focus in Engineering,
Finance/Accounting, Marketing, Research and Development,
Sales

Storm, Deborah — *Associate*
Source Services Corporation
150 South Warner Road, Suite 238
King of Prussia, PA 19406
Telephone: (610) 341-1960
Recruiter Classification: Contingency; **Lowest/Average
Salary:** $30,000/$50,000; **Industry Concentration:** Financial
Services; **Function Concentration:** Engineering,
Finance/Accounting

Stoy, Roger W. — *Managing Partner*
Heidrick & Struggles, Inc.
1301 K Street N.W., Suite 500 East
Washington, DC 20005-3317
Telephone: (202) 289-4450
Recruiter Classification: Retained; **Lowest/Average Salary:**
$75,000/$90,000; **Industry Concentration:** Generalist with a
primary focus in Financial Services; **Function Concentration:**
Generalist

Stranberg, James R. — *Associate*
Callan Associates, Ltd.
2021 Spring Road, Suite 175
Oak Brook, IL 60521
Telephone: (708) 832-7080
Recruiter Classification: Retained; **Lowest/Average Salary:**
$90,000/$90,000; **Industry Concentration:** Generalist with a
primary focus in Financial Services; **Function Concentration:**
Generalist with a primary focus in Engineering,
Finance/Accounting, General Management, Human Resources,
Marketing, Research and Development, Sales,
Women/Minorities

Strander, Dervin — *Associate*
Source Services Corporation
5429 LBJ Freeway, Suite 275
Dallas, TX 75240
Telephone: (214) 387-1600
Recruiter Classification: Contingency; **Lowest/Average
Salary:** $30,000/$50,000; **Industry Concentration:** Financial
Services; **Function Concentration:** Engineering,
Finance/Accounting

Strassman, Mark — *Managing Partner*
Don Richard Associates of Washington, D.C., Inc.
1020 19th Street, NW, Suite 650
Washington, DC 20036
Telephone: (202) 463-7210
Recruiter Classification: Contingency, Executive Temporary;
Lowest/Average Salary: $60,000/$75,000; **Industry Concentration:** Financial Services; **Function Concentration:** Finance/Accounting

Stratmeyer, Karin Bergwall — *President*
Princeton Entrepreneurial Resources
600 Alexander Road, P.O. Box 2051
Princeton, NJ 08543
Telephone: (609) 243-0010
Recruiter Classification: Executive Temporary;
Lowest/Average Salary: $75,000/$90,000; **Industry Concentration:** Generalist with a primary focus in Venture Capital; **Function Concentration:** Generalist with a primary focus in Finance/Accounting, General Management, Human Resources, Marketing

Straube, Stanley H. — *President*
Straube Associates
Willows Professional Park
855 Turnpike Street
North Andover, MA 01845-6105
Telephone: (508) 687-1993
Recruiter Classification: Retained; **Lowest/Average Salary:** $60,000/$90,000; **Industry Concentration:** Generalist with a primary focus in Financial Services; **Function Concentration:** Generalist with a primary focus in Engineering, Finance/Accounting, General Management, Human Resources, Marketing, Women/Minorities

Strickland, Katie — *Vice President*
Grantham & Co., Inc.
136 Erwin Road
Chapel Hill, NC 27514
Telephone: (919) 932-5650
Recruiter Classification: Retained; **Lowest/Average Salary:** $85,000/$90,000; **Industry Concentration:** Generalist with a primary focus in Financial Services, Insurance; **Function Concentration:** Generalist with a primary focus in Engineering, Finance/Accounting, General Management, Human Resources, Marketing, Research and Development, Sales

Stringer, Dann P. — *Senior Managing Director*
D.E. Foster Partners Inc.
2001 M Street N.W.
Washington, DC 20036
Telephone: (202) 739-8749
Recruiter Classification: Retained; **Lowest/Average Salary:** $90,000/$90,000; **Industry Concentration:** Generalist with a primary focus in Financial Services; **Function Concentration:** Generalist with a primary focus in Administration, Finance/Accounting, General Management, Marketing, Women/Minorities

Strobridge, Richard P. — *Vice President*
F.L. Taylor & Company, Inc.
300 East 34th Street
New York, NY 10016
Telephone: (212) 679-4674
Recruiter Classification: Retained; **Lowest/Average Salary:** $75,000/$90,000; **Industry Concentration:** Generalist with a primary focus in Financial Services; **Function Concentration:** Generalist with a primary focus in Human Resources, Marketing, Sales

Strom, Mark N. — *President*
Search Advisors International Corp.
777 South Harbour Island Boulevard
Suite 925
Tampa, FL 33602
Telephone: (813) 221-7555
Recruiter Classification: Retained; **Lowest/Average Salary:** $75,000/$90,000; **Industry Concentration:** Generalist with a primary focus in Financial Services, Insurance; **Function Concentration:** Generalist with a primary focus in Administration, Engineering, Finance/Accounting, General Management, Human Resources, Marketing, Research and Development, Sales, Women/Minorities

Struzziero, Ralph E. — *President*
Romac & Associates
183 Middle Street, 3rd Floor
P.O. Box 7040
Portland, ME 04112
Telephone: (207) 773-4749
Recruiter Classification: Executive Temporary; **Lowest/Average Salary:** $60,000/$60,000; **Industry Concentration:** Financial Services, Insurance; **Function Concentration:** Finance/Accounting

Sucato, Carolyn — *Consultant*
Jay Gaines & Company, Inc.
450 Park Avenue
New York, NY 10022
Telephone: (212) 308-9222
Recruiter Classification: Retained; **Lowest/Average Salary:** $200,000/$300,000; **Industry Concentration:** Financial Services, Insurance; **Function Concentration:** Finance/Accounting

Sullivan, Brian M. — *President and CEO*
Sullivan & Company
20 Exchange Place, 50th Floor
New York, NY 10005
Telephone: (212) 422-3000
Recruiter Classification: Retained; **Lowest/Average Salary:** $90,000/$90,000; **Industry Concentration:** Generalist with a primary focus in Financial Services; **Function Concentration:** Generalist

Sullivan, Kay — *Principal*
Rusher, Loscavio & LoPresto
2479 Bayshore Road, Suite 700
Palo Alto, CA 94303
Telephone: (415) 494-0883
Recruiter Classification: Retained; **Lowest/Average Salary:** $75,000/$90,000; **Industry Concentration:** Financial Services; **Function Concentration:** General Management, Human Resources, Marketing, Research and Development, Sales, Women/Minorities

Sumurdy, Melinda — *Vice President*
Kenzer Corp.
Triwest Plaza
3030 LBJ Freeway, Suite 1430
Dallas, TX 75234
Telephone: (972) 620-7776
Recruiter Classification: Retained; **Lowest/Average Salary:** $50,000/$90,000; **Industry Concentration:** Financial Services, Venture Capital; **Function Concentration:** Generalist with a primary focus in Administration, Finance/Accounting, General Management, Human Resources, Marketing, Research and Development, Sales

Susoreny, Samali — *Associate*
Source Services Corporation
5429 LBJ Freeway, Suite 275
Dallas, TX 75240
Telephone: (214) 387-1600
Recruiter Classification: Contingency; **Lowest/Average Salary:** $30,000/$50,000; **Industry Concentration:** Financial Services; **Function Concentration:** Engineering, Finance/Accounting

Sussman, Lynda — *Vice President*
Gilbert Tweed/INESA
415 Madison Avenue
New York, NY 10017
Telephone: (212) 758-3000
Recruiter Classification: Retained; **Lowest/Average Salary:** $90,000/$90,000; **Industry Concentration:** Generalist with a primary focus in Financial Services, Insurance; **Function Concentration:** Generalist with a primary focus in Engineering, Finance/Accounting, General Management, Human Resources, Women/Minorities

Sutter, Howard — *Managing Partner*
Romac & Associates
5900 North Andrews Avenue
Suite 900
Fort Lauderdale, FL 33309
Telephone: (305) 928-0811
Recruiter Classification: Executive Temporary; **Lowest/Average Salary:** $60,000/$60,000; **Industry Concentration:** Financial Services, Insurance; **Function Concentration:** Finance/Accounting

Swanner, William — *Managing Director*
Source Services Corporation
2000 Town Center, Suite 850
Southfield, MI 48075
Telephone: (810) 352-6520
Recruiter Classification: Contingency; **Lowest/Average Salary:** $30,000/$50,000; **Industry Concentration:** Financial Services; **Function Concentration:** Engineering, Finance/Accounting

Swanson, Dick — *Principal*
Raymond Karsan Associates
18 Commerce Way
Woburn, MA 01801
Telephone: (617) 932-0400
Recruiter Classification: Retained; **Lowest/Average Salary:** $30,000/$90,000; **Industry Concentration:** Generalist with a primary focus in Insurance; **Function Concentration:** Generalist with a primary focus in Administration, Engineering, Finance/Accounting, General Management, Human Resources, Marketing, Research and Development, Sales, Women/Minorities

Sweeney, Anne — *Associate*
Source Services Corporation
525 Vine Street, Suite 2250
Cincinnati, OH 45202
Telephone: (513) 651-3303
Recruiter Classification: Contingency; **Lowest/Average Salary:** $30,000/$50,000; **Industry Concentration:** Financial Services; **Function Concentration:** Engineering, Finance/Accounting

Sweeney, Sean K. — *Executive Recruiter*
Bonifield Associates
3003E Lincoln Drive West
Marlton, NJ 08053
Telephone: (609) 596-3300
Recruiter Classification: Contingency; **Lowest/Average Salary:** $40,000/$60,000; **Industry Concentration:** Financial Services, Insurance; **Function Concentration:** Generalist with a primary focus in Administration, Finance/Accounting, General Management, Marketing, Research and Development, Sales

Sweet, Randall — *Associate*
Source Services Corporation
150 South Wacker Drive, Suite 400
Chicago, IL 60606
Telephone: (312) 346-7000
Recruiter Classification: Contingency; **Lowest/Average Salary:** $30,000/$50,000; **Industry Concentration:** Financial Services; **Function Concentration:** Engineering, Finance/Accounting

Swidler, J. Robert — *Managing Partner*
Egon Zehnder International Inc.
1 Place Ville-Marie, Suite 3310
Montreal, Quebec, CANADA H3B 3N2
Telephone: (514) 876-4249
Recruiter Classification: Retained; **Lowest/Average Salary:** $90,000/$90,000; **Industry Concentration:** Generalist with a primary focus in Financial Services; **Function Concentration:** Generalist

Swoboda, Lawrence — *Professional Recruiter*
A.J. Burton Group, Inc.
120 East Baltimore Street, Suite 2220
Baltimore, MD 21202
Telephone: (410) 752-5244
Recruiter Classification: Contingency; **Lowest/Average Salary:** $40,000/$75,000; **Industry Concentration:** Generalist with a primary focus in Financial Services, Insurance; **Function Concentration:** Generalist with a primary focus in Administration, Finance/Accounting, General Management, Human Resources

Taft, David G. — *President*
Techsearch Services, Inc.
6 Hachaliah Brown Drive
Somers, NY 10589
Telephone: (914) 277-2727
Recruiter Classification: Contingency; **Lowest/Average Salary:** $50,000/$75,000; **Industry Concentration:** Financial Services; **Function Concentration:** Finance/Accounting

Tankson, Dawn — *Associate*
Source Services Corporation
1 Gatehall Drive, Suite 250
Parsippany, NJ 07054
Telephone: (201) 267-3222
Recruiter Classification: Contingency; **Lowest/Average Salary:** $30,000/$50,000; **Industry Concentration:** Financial Services; **Function Concentration:** Engineering, Finance/Accounting

Tanner, Frank — *Associate*
Source Services Corporation
520 Post Oak Boulevard, Suite 700
Houston, TX 77027
Telephone: (713) 439-1077
Recruiter Classification: Contingency; **Lowest/Average Salary:** $30,000/$50,000; **Industry Concentration:** Financial Services; **Function Concentration:** Engineering, Finance/Accounting

Tanner, Gary — *Associate*
Source Services Corporation
505 East 200 South, Suite 300
Salt Lake City, UT 84102
Telephone: (801) 328-0011
Recruiter Classification: Contingency; **Lowest/Average Salary:** $30,000/$50,000; **Industry Concentration:** Financial Services; **Function Concentration:** Engineering, Finance/Accounting

Tappan, Michael A. — *Managing Director*
Ward Howell International, Inc.
99 Park Avenue, Suite 2000
New York, NY 10016-1699
Telephone: (212) 697-3730
Recruiter Classification: Retained; **Lowest/Average Salary:** $75,000/$90,000; **Industry Concentration:** Financial Services, Insurance; **Function Concentration:** Generalist

Taylor, Charles E. — *Partner*
Lamalie Amrop International
191 Peachtree Street N.E.
Atlanta, GA 30303-1747
Telephone: (404) 688-0800
Recruiter Classification: Retained; **Lowest/Average Salary:** $90,000/$90,000; **Industry Concentration:** Generalist with a primary focus in Financial Services; **Function Concentration:** Generalist

Taylor, Conrad G. — *Manager*
MSI International
6151 Powers Ferry Road, Suite 540
Atlanta, GA 30339
Telephone: (404) 850-6465
Recruiter Classification: Contingency; **Lowest/Average Salary:** $30,000/$75,000; **Industry Concentration:** Generalist with a primary focus in Financial Services; **Function Concentration:** Generalist with a primary focus in Administration, Engineering, Finance/Accounting, General Management, Marketing, Sales

Taylor, Ernest A. — *Managing Director*
Ward Howell International, Inc.
3350 Peachtree Road N.E.
Suite 1600
Atlanta, GA 30326
Telephone: (404) 261-6532
Recruiter Classification: Retained; **Lowest/Average Salary:** $75,000/$90,000; **Industry Concentration:** Generalist with a primary focus in Financial Services; **Function Concentration:** Generalist with a primary focus in General Management, Marketing, Sales

Taylor, James M. — *Chief Executive Officer*
The HRM Group, Inc.
321 Lorna Square
Birmingham, AL 35216
Telephone: (205) 978-7181
Recruiter Classification: Retained; **Lowest/Average Salary:** $30,000/$50,000; **Industry Concentration:** Generalist with a primary focus in Insurance; **Function Concentration:** Generalist with a primary focus in Finance/Accounting, General Management, Human Resources, Marketing, Sales

Taylor, Kenneth W. — *Consultant*
Egon Zehnder International Inc.
One First National Plaza
21 South Clark Street, Suite 3300
Chicago, IL 60603-2006
Telephone: (312) 782-4500
Recruiter Classification: Retained; **Lowest/Average Salary:** $90,000/$90,000; **Industry Concentration:** Generalist with a primary focus in Financial Services; **Function Concentration:** Generalist

Taylor, R.L. (Larry) — *Partner*
Ray & Berndtson
Sears Tower, 233 South Wacker Drive, Suite 4020
Chicago, IL 60606-6310
Telephone: (312) 876-0730
Recruiter Classification: Retained; **Lowest/Average Salary:** $90,000/$90,000; **Industry Concentration:** Generalist with a primary focus in Financial Services, Insurance; **Function Concentration:** Generalist with a primary focus in Administration, Finance/Accounting, General Management, Human Resources, Marketing, Research and Development, Sales, Women/Minorities

Teger, Stella — *Associate*
Source Services Corporation
2 Penn Plaza, Suite 1176
New York, NY 10121
Telephone: (212) 760-2200
Recruiter Classification: Contingency; **Lowest/Average Salary:** $30,000/$50,000; **Industry Concentration:** Financial Services; **Function Concentration:** Engineering, Finance/Accounting

Telford, John H. — *Managing Principal*
Telford, Adams & Alexander/Telford & Co., Inc.
650 Town Center Drive, Suite 850A
Costa Mesa, CA 92626
Telephone: (714) 850-4354
Recruiter Classification: Retained; **Lowest/Average Salary:** $90,000/$90,000; **Industry Concentration:** Generalist with a primary focus in Financial Services, Insurance; **Function Concentration:** Generalist with a primary focus in Administration, Finance/Accounting, General Management, Human Resources, Marketing, Sales

ten Cate, Herman H. — *President*
Stoneham Associates Corp.
Royal Bank Plaza
200 Bay Street, P.O. Box 105
Toronto, Ontario, CANADA M5J 2J3
Telephone: (416) 362-0852
Recruiter Classification: Retained; **Lowest/Average Salary:** $90,000/$90,000; **Industry Concentration:** Generalist with a primary focus in Financial Services; **Function Concentration:** Generalist with a primary focus in Administration, Engineering, Finance/Accounting, General Management, Marketing

Tenero, Kymberly — *Associate*
Source Services Corporation
111 Founders Plaza, Suite 1501E
Hartford, CT 06108
Telephone: (860) 528-0300
Recruiter Classification: Contingency; **Lowest/Average Salary:** $30,000/$50,000; **Industry Concentration:** Financial Services; **Function Concentration:** Engineering, Finance/Accounting

Terry, Douglas — *Executive Recruiter*
Jacobson Associates
150 North Wacker Drive
Suite 1120
Chicago, IL 60606
Telephone: (312) 726-1578
Recruiter Classification: Contingency; **Lowest/Average Salary:**
$20,000/$50,000; **Industry Concentration:** Insurance;
Function Concentration: Generalist

Teter, Sandra — *Division Manager - Accounting*
The Danbrook Group, Inc.
14180 Dallas Parkway, Suite 400
Dallas, TX 75240
Telephone: (214) 392-0057
Recruiter Classification: Contingency; **Lowest/Average Salary:**
$30,000/$50,000; **Industry Concentration:** Financial Services;
Function Concentration: Generalist with a primary focus in
Administration, Finance/Accounting, General Management,
Sales

Teti, Al — *General Manager*
Chrisman & Company, Incorporated
350 South Figueroa Street, Suite 550
Los Angeles, CA 90071
Telephone: (213) 620-1192
Recruiter Classification: Retained; **Lowest/Average Salary:**
$75,000/$90,000; **Industry Concentration:** Generalist
with a primary focus in Financial Services, Insurance,
Venture Capital; **Function Concentration:** Generalist
with a primary focus in Finance/Accounting, General
Management, Human Resources, Marketing, Sales,
Women/Minorities

Theard, Susan — *Branch Manager*
Romac & Associates
650 Poydras Street, Suite 2523
New Orleans, LA 70130
Telephone: (504) 522-6611
Recruiter Classification: Executive Temporary; **Lowest/Average
Salary:** $60,000/$60,000; **Industry Concentration:** Financial
Services, Insurance; **Function Concentration:**
Finance/Accounting

Theobald, David B. — *President*
Theobald & Associates
1750 Montgomery Street
San Francisco, CA 94111
Telephone: (415) 883-6007
Recruiter Classification: Retained; **Lowest/Average Salary:**
$90,000/$90,000; **Industry Concentration:** Generalist with a
primary focus in Financial Services; **Function Concentration:**
Generalist with a primary focus in Engineering,
Finance/Accounting, General Management, Human Resources,
Marketing, Sales

Thielman, Joseph — *President*
Barrett Partners
100 North LaSalle Street, Suite 1420
Chicago, IL 60602
Telephone: (312) 443-8877
Recruiter Classification: Contingency; **Lowest/Average Salary:**
$30,000/$50,000; **Industry Concentration:** Financial Services,
Insurance; **Function Concentration:** Engineering,
Finance/Accounting

Thomas, Cheryl M. — *Executive Recruiter*
CPS Inc.
One Westbrook Corporate Centre, Suite 600
Westchester, IL 60154
Telephone: (708) 531-8370
Recruiter Classification: Contingency; **Lowest/Average Salary:**
$30,000/$50,000; **Industry Concentration:** Generalist with a
primary focus in Financial Services, Insurance, **Function**
Concentration: Engineering, Research and Development,
Sales, Women/Minorities

Thomas, Jeffrey — *President*
Fairfaxx Corporation
17 High Street
Norwalk, CT 06851
Telephone: (203) 838-8300
Recruiter Classification: Retained; **Lowest/Average Salary:**
$60,000/$90,000; **Industry Concentration:** Venture Capital;
Function Concentration: Generalist with a primary focus in
Engineering, Finance/Accounting, General Management,
Human Resources, Marketing, Sales

Thomas, Kim — *Executive Recruiter*
CPS Inc.
One Westbrook Corporate Centre, Suite 600
Westchester, IL 60154
Telephone: (708) 531-8370
Recruiter Classification: Contingency; **Lowest/Average Salary:**
$30,000/$50,000; **Industry Concentration:** Generalist with a
primary focus in Financial Services, Insurance; **Function**
Concentration: Engineering, Research and Development,
Sales, Women/Minorities

Thomas, Kurt J. — *Vice President*
P.J. Murphy & Associates, Inc.
735 North Water Street
Milwaukee, WI 53202
Telephone: (414) 277-9777
Recruiter Classification: Retained; **Lowest/Average Salary:**
$60,000/$90,000; **Industry Concentration:** Generalist with a
primary focus in Financial Services; **Function Concentration:**
Generalist with a primary focus in Administration,
Finance/Accounting, General Management, Human Resources,
Marketing, Sales

Thomas, Terry — *President*
The Thomas Resource Group
1630 Tiburon Boulevard
Tiburon, CA 94920
Telephone: (415) 435-5123
Recruiter Classification: Retained; **Lowest/Average Salary:**
$90,000/$90,000; **Industry Concentration:** Financial Services,
Venture Capital; **Function Concentration:** Generalist with a
primary focus in Finance/Accounting, General Management,
Marketing

Thompson, Dave — *Director West Coast
Operations*
Battalia Winston International
One Sansome Street, Suite 2100
Citicorp Center
San Francisco, CA 94104
Telephone: (415) 984-3180
Recruiter Classification: Retained; **Lowest/Average Salary:**
$90,000/$90,000; **Industry Concentration:** Financial Services;
Function Concentration: Generalist with a primary focus in
General Management, Human Resources, Marketing, Sales

Thompson, John R. — *Executive Recruiter*
MSI International
229 Peachtree Street, NE
Suite 1201
Atlanta, GA 30303
Telephone: (404) 659-5050
Recruiter Classification: Contingency; **Lowest/Average Salary:**
$30,000/$60,000; **Industry Concentration:** Generalist with a
primary focus in Financial Services; **Function Concentration:**
Administration, Engineering, Finance/Accounting, General
Management, Marketing, Sales

Thompson, Kenneth L. — *Partner*
McCormack & Farrow
695 Town Center Drive
Suite 660
Costa Mesa, CA 92626
Telephone: (714) 549-7222
Recruiter Classification: Retained; **Lowest/Average Salary:**
$75,000/$90,000; **Industry Concentration:** Generalist with a
primary focus in Financial Services; **Function Concentration:**
Generalist with a primary focus in Administration, Engineering,
Finance/Accounting, General Management, Human Resources,
Marketing, Research and Development

Thompson, Leslie — *Associate*
Source Services Corporation
879 West 190th Street, Suite 250
Los Angeles, CA 90248
Telephone: (310) 323-6633
Recruiter Classification: Contingency; **Lowest/Average
Salary:** $30,000/$50,000; **Industry Concentration:** Financial
Services; **Function Concentration:** Engineering,
Finance/Accounting

Thomson, Alexander G. — *Associate*
Russell Reynolds Associates, Inc.
Old City Hall, 45 School Street
Boston, MA 02108-3296
Telephone: (617) 523-1111
Recruiter Classification: Retained; **Lowest/Average Salary:**
$90,000/$90,000; **Industry Concentration:** Generalist with a
primary focus in Financial Services; **Function Concentration:**
Generalist

Thornton, John C. — *President*
Thornton Resources
9800 McKnight Road
Pittsburgh, PA 15237
Telephone: (412) 364-2111
Recruiter Classification: Contingency, Executive Temporary;
Lowest/Average Salary: $40,000/$50,000; **Industry
Concentration:** Generalist with a primary focus in Financial
Services; **Function Concentration:** Generalist with a primary
focus in General Management, Human Resources, Marketing

Thrapp, Mark C. — *Managing Director*
Executive Search Consultants International, Inc.
330 Fifth Avenue
Suite 5501
New York, NY 10118
Telephone: (212) 333-1900
Recruiter Classification: Retained; **Lowest/Average Salary:**
$90,000/$90,000; **Industry Concentration:** Generalist with a
primary focus in Financial Services; **Function Concentration:**
Generalist with a primary focus in Finance/Accounting,
General Management, Human Resources, Marketing

Thrower, Troy — *Associate*
Source Services Corporation
2029 Century Park East, Suite 1350
Los Angeles, CA 90067
Telephone: (310) 277-8092
Recruiter Classification: Contingency; **Lowest/Average
Salary:** $30,000/$50,000; **Industry Concentration:** Financial
Services; **Function Concentration:** Engineering,
Finance/Accounting

Tierney, Eileen — *Managing Director*
The Whitney Group
850 Third Avenue, 11th Floor
New York, NY 10022
Telephone: (212) 508-3500
Recruiter Classification: Retained; **Lowest/Average Salary:**
$90,000/$90,000; **Industry Concentration:** Financial Services,
Venture Capital; **Function Concentration:** Generalist with a
primary focus in Finance/Accounting, General Management,
Marketing, Sales

Tilley, Kyle — *Associate*
Source Services Corporation
10300 West 103rd Street, Suite 101
Overland Park, KS 66214
Telephone: (913) 888-8885
Recruiter Classification: Contingency; **Lowest/Average
Salary:** $30,000/$50,000; **Industry Concentration:** Financial
Services; **Function Concentration:** Engineering,
Finance/Accounting

Tincu, John C. — *Executive Consultant*
Ferneborg & Associates, Inc.
1450 Fashion Island Boulevard, Suite 650
San Mateo, CA 94404
Telephone: (415) 577-0100
Recruiter Classification: Retained; **Lowest/Average Salary:**
$90,000/$90,000; **Industry Concentration:** Generalist
with a primary focus in Financial Services, Insurance;
Function Concentration: Generalist with a primary
focus in Administration, Engineering, Finance/Accounting,
General Management, Human Resources, Marketing,
Sales

Tingle, Trina A. — *Executive Recruiter*
MSI International
1050 Crown Pointe Parkway
Suite 1000
Atlanta, GA 30338
Telephone: (404) 394-2494
Recruiter Classification: Contingency; **Lowest/Average
Salary:** $30,000/$75,000; **Industry Concentration:** Generalist
with a primary focus in Financial Services; **Function
Concentration:** Generalist with a primary focus in
Finance/Accounting

Tipp, George D. — *Vice President*
Intech Summit Group, Inc.
5075 Shoreham Place, Suite 280
San Diego, CA 92116
Telephone: (619) 452-2100
Recruiter Classification: Retained; **Lowest/Average Salary:**
$60,000/$75,000; **Industry Concentration:** Insurance;
Function Concentration: Administration, General
Management, Research and Development, Sales

Tobin, Christopher — *Associate*
Source Services Corporation
One South Main Street, Suite 1440
Dayton, OH 45402
Telephone: (513) 461-4660
Recruiter Classification: Contingency; **Lowest/Average
Salary:** $30,000/$50,000; **Industry Concentration:** Financial
Services; **Function Concentration:** Engineering,
Finance/Accounting

Todres-Bernstein, Margo — *Project Coordinator*
Kaye-Bassman International Corp.
18333 Preston Road, Suite 500
Dallas, TX 75252
Telephone: (972) 931-5242
Recruiter Classification: Retained; **Lowest/Average Salary:**
$40,000/$75,000; **Industry Concentration:** Financial Services,
Insurance; **Function Concentration:** Generalist with a primary
focus in Finance/Accounting, General Management,
Marketing, Research and Development

Tootsey, Mark A. — *Vice President*
A.J. Burton Group, Inc.
4550 Montgomery Avenue, Ste. 325 North
Bethesda, MD 20814
Telephone: (301) 654-0082
Recruiter Classification: Contingency, Executive Temporary;
Lowest/Average Salary: $40,000/$75,000; **Industry
Concentration:** Generalist with a primary focus in Financial
Services, Insurance; **Function Concentration:** Generalist
with a primary focus in Administration, Finance/
Accounting, General Management, Human
Resources

Tornesello, Michael P. — *President*
The Yorkshire Group. Ltd.
182 West Central Street
Natick, MA 01760
Telephone: (508) 853-1222
Recruiter Classification: Retained; **Lowest/Average Salary:**
$60,000/$75,000; **Industry Concentration:** Insurance;
Function Concentration: Generalist

Tovrog, Dan — *Executive Recruiter*
CPS Inc.
One Westbrook Corporate Centre, Suite 600
Westchester, IL 60154
Telephone: (708) 531-8370
Recruiter Classification: Contingency; **Lowest/Average Salary:**
$30,000/$50,000; **Industry Concentration:** Generalist with a
primary focus in Financial Services, Insurance; **Function
Concentration:** Engineering, Research and Development,
Sales, Women/Minorities

Tracey, Jack — *President*
Management Assistance Group, Inc.
10 North Main Street
West Hartford, CT 06107
Telephone: (203) 523-0000
Recruiter Classification: Executive Temporary;
Lowest/Average Salary: $40,000/$60,000; **Industry
Concentration:** Generalist with a primary focus in Financial
Services, Insurance; **Function Concentration:** Generalist
with a primary focus in Administration, Engineering,
Finance/Accounting, General Management, Human
Resources, Marketing, Research and Development,
Sales

Tracy, Ronald O. — *Consultant*
Egon Zehnder International Inc.
One First National Plaza
21 South Clark Street, Suite 3300
Chicago, IL 60603-2006
Telephone: (312) 782-4500
Recruiter Classification: Retained; **Lowest/Average Salary:**
$90,000/$90,000; **Industry Concentration:** Generalist with a
primary focus in Financial Services; **Function Concentration:**
Generalist

Travis, Hallie — *Consultant*
Tyler & Company
1000 Abernathy Road
Suite 1400
Atlanta, GA 30328-5655
Telephone: (770) 396-3939
Recruiter Classification: Retained; **Lowest/Average Salary:**
$75,000/$90,000; **Industry Concentration:** Insurance;
Function Concentration: Generalist

Trefzer, Kristie — *Associate*
Source Services Corporation
150 South Wacker Drive, Suite 400
Chicago, IL 60606
Telephone: (312) 346-7000
Recruiter Classification: Contingency; **Lowest/Average Salary:**
$30,000/$50,000; **Industry Concentration:** Financial Services;
Function Concentration: Engineering, Finance/Accounting

Trewhella, Michael — *Managing Director*
Source Services Corporation
161 Ottawa NW, Suite 409D
Grand Rapids, MI 49503
Telephone: (616) 451-2400
Recruiter Classification: Contingency; **Lowest/Average Salary:**
$30,000/$50,000; **Industry Concentration:** Financial Services;
Function Concentration: Engineering, Finance/Accounting

Trice, Renee — *Associate*
Source Services Corporation
Foster Plaza VI
681 Anderson Drive, 2nd Floor
Pittsburgh, PA 15220
Telephone: (412) 928-8300
Recruiter Classification: Contingency; **Lowest/Average Salary:**
$30,000/$50,000; **Industry Concentration:** Financial Services;
Function Concentration: Engineering, Finance/Accounting

Trieschmann, Daniel — *Associate*
Source Services Corporation
One CityPlace, Suite 170
St. Louis, MO 63141
Telephone: (314) 432-4500
Recruiter Classification: Contingency; **Lowest/Average Salary:**
$30,000/$50,000; **Industry Concentration:** Financial Services;
Function Concentration: Engineering, Finance/Accounting

Trieweiler, Bob — *Consultant*
Executive Placement Consultants, Inc.
2700 River Road, Suite 107
Des Plaines, IL 60018
Telephone: (847) 298-6445
Recruiter Classification: Contingency; **Lowest/Average Salary:**
$40,000/$75,000; **Industry Concentration:** Generalist with a
primary focus in Financial Services; **Function Concentration:**
Generalist with a primary focus in Finance/Accounting, Human
Resources, Marketing

Trimble, Patricia — *Associate*
Source Services Corporation
15260 Ventura Boulevard, Suite 380
Sherman Oaks, CA 91403
Telephone: (818) 905-1500
Recruiter Classification: Contingency; **Lowest/Average Salary:**
$30,000/$50,000; **Industry Concentration:** Financial Services;
Function Concentration: Engineering, Finance/Accounting

Trimble, Rhonda — *Associate*
Source Services Corporation
7730 East Bellview Avenue, Suite 302
Englewood, CO 80111
Telephone: (303) 773-3700
Recruiter Classification: Contingency; **Lowest/Average Salary:**
$30,000/$50,000; **Industry Concentration:** Financial Services;
Function Concentration: Engineering, Finance/Accounting

Trott, Kathryn — *Partner*
Allard Associates
1059 Court Street, Suite 114
Woodland, CA 95695
Telephone: (916) 757-1649
Recruiter Classification: Retained; **Lowest/Average Salary:**
$60,000/$90,000; **Industry Concentration:** Financial Services;
Function Concentration: Generalist with a primary focus in
Administration, General Management, Marketing, Sales,
Women/Minorities

Trott, Kathryn — *Partner*
Allard Associates
44 Montgomery Street, Suite 500
San Francisco, CA 94104
Telephone: (415) 433-0500
Recruiter Classification: Retained; **Lowest/Average Salary:**
$60,000/$90,000; **Industry Concentration:** Financial Services;
Function Concentration: Generalist with a primary focus in
Administration, General Management, Marketing, Research
and Development, Sales, Women/Minorities

Troup, Roger — *Consultant*
The McCormick Group, Inc.
1400 Wilson Boulevard
Arlington, VA 22209
Telephone: (703) 841-1700
Recruiter Classification: Retained; **Lowest/Average Salary:**
$40,000/$75,000; **Industry Concentration:** Insurance;
Function Concentration: Human Resources

Truax, Kevin — *Placement Specialist*
Key Employment Services
1001 Office Park Road, Suite 320
West Des Moines, IA 50265-2567
Telephone: (515) 224-0446
Recruiter Classification: Contingency; **Lowest/Average Salary:**
$30,000/$75,000; **Industry Concentration:** Insurance;
Function Concentration: General Management

Truemper, Dean — *Executive Recruiter*
CPS Inc.
One Westbrook Corporate Centre, Suite 600
Westchester, IL 60154
Telephone: (708) 531-8370
Recruiter Classification: Contingency; **Lowest/Average Salary:**
$30,000/$50,000; **Industry Concentration:** Generalist with a
primary focus in Financial Services, Insurance; **Function
Concentration:** Engineering, Research and Development,
Sales, Women/Minorities

Truex, John F. — *Vice President*
Morton, McCorkle & Associates, Inc.
2190 South Mason Road, Suite 309
St. Louis, MO 63131-1637
Telephone: (314) 984-9494
Recruiter Classification: Retained; **Lowest/Average Salary:**
$30,000/$40,000; **Industry Concentration:** Generalist
with a primary focus in Financial Services; **Function
Concentration:** Generalist with a primary focus in
Administration, Engineering, Finance/Accounting, General
Management, Human Resources, Marketing, Sales,
Women/Minorities

Truitt, Thomas B. — *Senior Manager*
Southwestern Professional Services
2451 Atrium Way
Nashville, TN 37214
Telephone: (615) 391-2722
Recruiter Classification: Contingency; **Lowest/Average Salary:**
$60,000/$90,000; **Industry Concentration:** Financial Services;
Function Concentration: Engineering, Finance/Accounting,
General Management

Tryon, Katey — *Senior Vice President - Managing
Principal*
DeFrain, Mayer LLC
6900 College Boulevard
Suite 300
Overland Park, KS 66211
Telephone: (913) 345-0500
Recruiter Classification: Retained; **Lowest/Average Salary:**
$50,000/$90,000; **Industry Concentration:** Generalist with a
primary focus in Financial Services; **Function Concentration:**
Generalist with a primary focus in Administration, Engineering,
Finance/Accounting, General Management, Human Resources,
Marketing

Tscelli, Maureen — *Associate*
Source Services Corporation
155 Federal Street, Suite 410
Boston, MA 02110
Telephone: (617) 482-8211
Recruiter Classification: Contingency; **Lowest/Average
Salary:** $30,000/$50,000; **Industry Concentration:** Financial
Services; **Function Concentration:** Engineering,
Finance/Accounting

Tschan, Stephen — *Associate*
Source Services Corporation
3 Summit Park Drive, Suite 550
Independence, OH 44131
Telephone: (216) 328-5900
Recruiter Classification: Contingency; **Lowest/Average Salary:**
$30,000/$50,000; **Industry Concentration:** Financial Services;
Function Concentration: Engineering, Finance/Accounting

Tucci, Joseph — *Executive Vice President*
Fairfaxx Corporation
17 High Street
Norwalk, CT 06851
Telephone: (203) 838-8300
Recruiter Classification: Retained; **Lowest/Average Salary:**
$60,000/$90,000; **Industry Concentration:** Generalist with a
primary focus in Venture Capital; **Function Concentration:**
Generalist with a primary focus in Engineering,
Finance/Accounting, General Management, Human Resources,
Marketing, Sales

Tucker, Thomas A. — *Principal*
The Thomas Tucker Company
425 California Street, Suite 2502
San Francisco, CA 94104
Telephone: (415) 693-5900
Recruiter Classification: Retained; **Lowest/Average Salary:**
$90,000/$90,000; **Industry Concentration:** Generalist
with a primary focus in Financial Services, Venture Capital;
Function Concentration: Generalist with a primary focus
in Engineering, Finance/Accounting, General Management,
Human Resources, Marketing, Research and
Development

Tullberg, Tina — *Executive Recruiter*
CPS Inc.
One Westbrook Corporate Centre, Suite 600
Westchester, IL 60154
Telephone: (708) 531-8370
Recruiter Classification: Contingency; **Lowest/Average
Salary:** $30,000/$50,000; **Industry Concentration:**
Generalist with a primary focus in Financial Services,
Insurance; **Function Concentration:** Engineering,
Research and Development, Sales, Women/
Minorities

Tully, Margo L. — *Partner*
Tully/Woodmansee International, Inc.
1088 U.S. 27 North
Lake Placid, FL 33852
Telephone: (941) 465-1024
Recruiter Classification: Retained; **Lowest/Average Salary:**
$60,000/$90,000; **Industry Concentration:** Generalist
with a primary focus in Financial Services, Venture Capital;
Function Concentration: Generalist with a primary
focus in Finance/Accounting, General Management,
Human Resources, Marketing, Sales, Women/
Minorities

Tunney, William — *Vice President*
Grant Cooper and Associates
795 Office Parkway, Suite 117
St. Louis, MO 63141
Telephone: (314) 567-4690
Recruiter Classification: Retained; **Lowest/Average Salary:**
$60,000/$90,000; **Industry Concentration:** Generalist
with a primary focus in Financial Services; **Function
Concentration:** Generalist with a primary focus in
Administration, Engineering, Finance/Accounting,
General Management, Human Resources, Marketing,
Sales

Turner, Edward K. — *President*
Don Richard Associates of Charlotte
2650 One First Union Center
301 South College Street
Charlotte, NC 28202-6000
Telephone: (704) 377-6447
Recruiter Classification: Contingency, Executive Temporary;
Lowest/Average Salary: $40,000/$50,000; **Industry
Concentration:** Generalist with a primary focus in
Financial Services; **Function Concentration:**
Administration, Finance/Accounting, General
Management

Turner, Kimberly — *Senior Consultant*
Barton Associates, Inc.
One Riverway, Suite 2500
Houston, TX 77056
Telephone: (713) 961-9111
Recruiter Classification: Retained; **Lowest/Average Salary:**
$75,000/$90,000; **Industry Concentration:** Generalist with a
primary focus in Financial Services; **Function Concentration:**
Generalist with a primary focus in Administration,
Finance/Accounting, General Management, Human Resources,
Marketing

Turner, Raymond — *Managing Director*
Source Services Corporation
111 Founders Plaza, Suite 1501E
Hartford, CT 06108
Telephone: (860) 528-0300
Recruiter Classification: Contingency; **Lowest/Average
Salary:** $30,000/$50,000; **Industry Concentration:** Financial
Services; **Function Concentration:** Engineering,
Finance/Accounting

Tursi, Deborah J. — *Sales Recruiter*
The Corporate Connection, Ltd.
7202 Glen Forest Drive
Richmond, VA 23226
Telephone: (804) 288-8844
Recruiter Classification: Contingency; **Lowest/Average Salary:**
$20,000/$30,000; **Industry Concentration:** Financial Services,
Insurance; **Function Concentration:** Generalist with a primary
focus in Administration, Engineering, Finance/Accounting,
General Management, Human Resources, Marketing, Sales,
Women/Minorities

Tuttle, Donald E. — *President and CEO*
Tuttle Venture Group, Inc.
5151 Beltline Road, Suite 1018
Dallas, TX 75240
Telephone: (972) 980-1688
Recruiter Classification: Retained; **Lowest/Average Salary:**
$90,000/$90,000; **Industry Concentration:** Venture Capital;
Function Concentration: Generalist

Tutwiler, Stephen — *President*
Don Richard Associates of Tampa, Inc.
100 North Tampa Street, Suite 1925
Tampa, FL 33602
Telephone: (813) 221-7930
Recruiter Classification: Contingency, Executive Temporary;
Lowest/Average Salary: $20,000/$50,000; **Industry
Concentration:** Generalist with a primary focus in Financial
Services, Insurance; **Function Concentration:** Generalist with
a primary focus in Finance/Accounting, General
Management

Tweed, Janet — *Chief Executive Officer*
Gilbert Tweed/INESA
415 Madison Avenue
New York, NY 10017
Telephone: (212) 758-3000
Recruiter Classification: Retained; **Lowest/Average Salary:**
$90,000/$90,000; **Industry Concentration:** Generalist with a
primary focus in Financial Services, Venture Capital; **Function
Concentration:** Generalist with a primary focus in
Engineering, Finance/Accounting, General Management,
Human Resources, Marketing, Research and Development,
Sales

Twiste, Craig — *Senior Consultant*
Raymond Karsan Associates
3725 National Drive, Suite 115
Raleigh, NC 27612
Telephone: (919) 571-1690
Recruiter Classification: Retained; **Lowest/Average Salary:**
$30,000/$90,000; **Industry Concentration:** Generalist with a
primary focus in Insurance; **Function Concentration:**
Generalist

Twomey, James — *Managing Director*
Source Services Corporation
20 Burlington Mall Road, Suite 405
Burlington, MA 01803
Telephone: (617) 272-5000
Recruiter Classification: Contingency; **Lowest/Average
Salary:** $30,000/$50,000; **Industry Concentration:** Financial
Services; **Function Concentration:** Engineering,
Finance/Accounting

Tyler, J. Larry — *President and CEO*
Tyler & Company
1000 Abernathy Road
Suite 1400
Atlanta, GA 30328-5655
Telephone: (770) 396-3939
Recruiter Classification: Retained; **Lowest/Average Salary:**
$75,000/$90,000; **Industry Concentration:** Insurance;
Function Concentration: Generalist

Tyson, Richard L. — *President*
Bonifield Associates
3003E Lincoln Drive West
Marlton, NJ 08053
Telephone: (609) 596-3300
Recruiter Classification: Contingency; **Lowest/Average
Salary:** $40,000/$60,000; **Industry Concentration:** Financial
Services, Insurance; **Function Concentration:** Generalist with
a primary focus in Administration, Finance/Accounting,
General Management, Marketing, Research and
Development, Sales

Ulbert, Nancy — *Director Data Processing/MIS*
Aureus Group
8744 Frederick Street
Omaha, NE 68124-3068
Telephone: (402) 397-2980
Recruiter Classification: Contingency; **Lowest/Average Salary:**
$30,000/$50,000; **Industry Concentration:** Financial Services,
Insurance; **Function Concentration:** Administration,
Engineering, Finance/Accounting, General Management,
Human Resources

Ulrich, Mary Ann — *Partner*
D.S. Allen Associates, Inc.
1119 Raritan Rd., Ste. 2
Clark, NJ 07066
Telephone: (732) 574-1600
Recruiter Classification: Contingency; **Lowest/Average
Salary:** $60,000/$90,000; **Industry Concentration:** Financial
Services; **Function Concentration:** Finance/Accounting,
General Management, Human Resources, Marketing,
Sales

Uzzel, Linda — *Associate*
Source Services Corporation
One South Main Street, Suite 1440
Dayton, OH 45402
Telephone: (513) 461-4660
Recruiter Classification: Contingency; **Lowest/Average
Salary:** $30,000/$50,000; **Industry Concentration:** Financial
Services; **Function Concentration:** Engineering,
Finance/Accounting

Vacca, Domenic — *Managing Partner*
Romac & Associates
1300 North Market Street
Suite 501
Wilmington, DE 19801
Telephone: (302) 658-6181
Recruiter Classification: Executive Temporary; **Lowest/Average
Salary:** $60,000/$60,000; **Industry Concentration:** Financial
Services, Insurance; **Function Concentration:**
Finance/Accounting

Vairo, Leonard A. — *Vice President*
Christian & Timbers
24 New England Executive Park
Burlington, MA 01803
Telephone: (617) 229-9515
Recruiter Classification: Retained; **Lowest/Average Salary:**
$90,000/$90,000; **Industry Concentration:** Generalist with a
primary focus in Venture Capital; **Function Concentration:**
Generalist with a primary focus in Engineering,
Finance/Accounting, General Management, Human Resources,
Marketing, Research and Development, Sales

Valenta, Joseph — *Director*
Princeton Entrepreneurial Resources
600 Alexander Road, P.O. Box 2051
Princeton, NJ 08543
Telephone: (609) 243-0010
Recruiter Classification: Executive Temporary; **Lowest/Average
Salary:** $75,000/$90,000; **Industry Concentration:** Generalist
with a primary focus in Venture Capital; **Function
Concentration:** Generalist with a primary focus in
Finance/Accounting, General Management, Human Resources,
Marketing

Van Alstine, Catherine — *Partner*
Tanton Mitchell/Paul Ray Berndtson
710-1050 West Pender Street
Vancouver, British Columbia, CANADA V6E 3S7
Telephone: (604) 685-0261
Recruiter Classification: Retained; **Lowest/Average Salary:**
$75,000/$90,000; **Industry Concentration:** Generalist with a
primary focus in Financial Services; **Function Concentration:**
Generalist with a primary focus in Finance/Accounting,
Marketing, Sales

Van Biesen, Jacques A.H. — *President*
Search Group Inc.
950 505 Third Street SW
Calgary, Alberta Canada, T2P 3E6
Telephone: (403) 292-0959
Recruiter Classification: Retained; **Lowest/Average Salary:**
$75,000/$90,000; **Industry Concentration:** Generalist with a
primary focus in Financial Services; **Function Concentration:**
Generalist with a primary focus in Engineering,
Finance/Accounting, General Management, Marketing,
Research and Development

Van Campen, Jerry — *Vice President Research and Internal Services*
Gilbert & Van Campen International
Graybar Building, 420 Lexington Avenue
New York, NY 10170
Telephone: (212) 661-2122
Recruiter Classification: Retained; **Lowest/Average Salary:** $90,000/$90,000; **Industry Concentration:** Generalist with a primary focus in Financial Services; **Function Concentration:** Generalist with a primary focus in Finance/Accounting, General Management, Human Resources, Marketing, Sales, Women/Minorities

Van Clieaf, Mark — *Managing Director*
MVC Associates International
36 Toronto Street, Suite 850
Toronto, Ontario, CANADA M5C 2C5
Telephone: (416) 489-1917
Recruiter Classification: Retained; **Lowest/Average Salary:** $50,000/$90,000; **Industry Concentration:** Generalist with a primary focus in Financial Services, Venture Capital; **Function Concentration:** Generalist with a primary focus in General Management, Human Resources, Marketing

Van Norman, Ben — *Associate*
Source Services Corporation
425 California Street, Suite 1200
San Francisco, CA 94104
Telephone: (415) 434-2410
Recruiter Classification: Contingency; **Lowest/Average Salary:** $30,000/$50,000; **Industry Concentration:** Financial Services; **Function Concentration:** Engineering, Finance/Accounting

Van Nostrand, Mara J. — *Senior Consultant*
Barton Associates, Inc.
One Riverway, Suite 2500
Houston, TX 77056
Telephone: (713) 961-9111
Recruiter Classification: Retained; **Lowest/Average Salary:** $75,000/$90,000; **Industry Concentration:** Generalist with a primary focus in Financial Services; **Function Concentration:** Generalist with a primary focus in General Management, Marketing

Van Remmen, Roger — *Partner*
Brown, Bernardy, Van Remmen, Inc.
12100 Wilshire Boulevard, Suite M-40
Los Angeles, CA 90025
Telephone: (310) 826-5777
Recruiter Classification: Contingency; **Lowest/Average Salary:** $30,000/$75,000; **Industry Concentration:** Financial Services; **Function Concentration:** Marketing

Vande-Water, Katie — *Vice President*
J. Robert Scott
27 State Street
Boston, MA 02109
Telephone: (617) 720-2770
Recruiter Classification: Retained; **Lowest/Average Salary:** $75,000/$90,000; **Industry Concentration:** Generalist with a primary focus in Financial Services; **Function Concentration:** Generalist

Vandenbulcke, Cynthia — *Associate*
Source Services Corporation
2029 Century Park East, Suite 1350
Los Angeles, CA 90067
Telephone: (310) 277-8092
Recruiter Classification: Contingency; **Lowest/Average Salary:** $30,000/$50,000; **Industry Concentration:** Financial Services; **Function Concentration:** Engineering, Finance/Accounting

Varney, Monique — *Associate*
Source Services Corporation
500 108th Avenue NE, Suite 1780
Bellevue, WA 98004
Telephone: (206) 454-6400
Recruiter Classification: Contingency; **Lowest/Average Salary:** $30,000/$50,000; **Industry Concentration:** Financial Services; **Function Concentration:** Engineering, Finance/Accounting

Varrichio, Michael — *Managing Director*
Source Services Corporation
5429 LBJ Freeway, Suite 275
Dallas, TX 75240
Telephone: (214) 387-1600
Recruiter Classification: Contingency; **Lowest/Average Salary:** $30,000/$50,000; **Industry Concentration:** Financial Services; **Function Concentration:** Engineering, Finance/Accounting

Velez, Hector — *Associate*
Source Services Corporation
8614 Westwood Center, Suite 750
Vienna, VA 22182
Telephone: (703) 790-5610
Recruiter Classification: Contingency; **Lowest/Average Salary:** $30,000/$50,000; **Industry Concentration:** Financial Services; **Function Concentration:** Engineering, Finance/Accounting

Velten, Mark T. — *Vice President*
Boyden
55 Madison Avenue
Suite 400
Morristown, NJ 07960
Telephone: (201) 267-0980
Recruiter Classification: Retained; **Lowest/Average Salary:** $90,000/$90,000; **Industry Concentration:** Generalist with a primary focus in Financial Services; **Function Concentration:** Generalist with a primary focus in Engineering, Finance/Accounting, General Management, Human Resources, Marketing, Research and Development, Sales, Women/Minorities

Venable, William W. — *Vice President*
Thorndike Deland Associates
275 Madison Avenue, Suite 1300
New York, NY 10016
Telephone: (212) 661-6200
Recruiter Classification: Retained; **Lowest/Average Salary:** $100,000/$125,000; **Industry Concentration:** Generalist with a primary focus in Financial Services, Insurance, Venture Capital; **Function Concentration:** Generalist with a primary focus in Finance/Accounting, General Management, Human Resources, Marketing, Sales

Vergara, Gail H. — *Senior Director*
Spencer Stuart
401 North Michigan Avenue, Suite 3400
Chicago, IL 60611-4244
Telephone: (312) 822-0080
Recruiter Classification: Retained; **Lowest/Average Salary:**
$90,000/$90,000; **Industry Concentration:** Insurance;
Function Concentration: Generalist with a primary
focus in Administration, Finance/Accounting, General
Management, Human Resources, Marketing,
Research and Development, Women/
Minorities

Vergari, Jane — *Senior Vice President*
Herbert Mines Associates, Inc.
399 Park Avenue, 27th Floor
New York, NY 10022
Telephone: (212) 355-0909
Recruiter Classification: Retained; **Lowest/Average Salary:**
$90,000/$90,000; **Industry Concentration:** Venture Capital;
Function Concentration: Generalist with a primary focus in
Marketing

Vernon, Peter C. — *Managing Director*
Horton International
330 Bay Street, Suite 1104
Toronto, Ontario, CANADA M5H 2S8
Telephone: (416) 861-0077
Recruiter Classification: Retained; **Lowest/Average Salary:**
$90,000/$90,000; **Industry Concentration:** Generalist
with a primary focus in Financial Services, Insurance,
Venture Capital; **Function Concentration:** Generalist with a
primary focus in Finance/Accounting, General Management,
Human Resources, Marketing, Research and Development,
Sales

Vilella, Paul — *Managing Director*
Source Services Corporation
1111 19th Street NW, Suite 620
Washington, DC 20036
Telephone: (202) 822-0100
Recruiter Classification: Contingency; **Lowest/Average
Salary:** $30,000/$50,000; **Industry Concentration:** Financial
Services; **Function Concentration:** Engineering,
Finance/Accounting

Villella, Paul — *Managing Director*
Source Services Corporation
8614 Westwood Center, Suite 750
Vienna, VA 22182
Telephone: (703) 790-5610
Recruiter Classification: Contingency; **Lowest/Average
Salary:** $30,000/$50,000; **Industry Concentration:** Financial
Services; **Function Concentration:** Engineering,
Finance/Accounting

Vincelette, Kathy A. — *Senior Consultant*
Raymond Karsan Associates
170 So. Warner Road
Wayne, PA 19087
Telephone: (610) 971-9171
Recruiter Classification: Retained; **Lowest/Average Salary:**
$30,000/$90,000; **Industry Concentration:** Generalist with a
primary focus in Insurance; **Function Concentration:**
Generalist

Vinett-Hessel, Deidre — *Associate*
Source Services Corporation
9020 Capital of Texas Highway
Building I, Suite 337
Austin, TX 78759
Telephone: (512) 345-7473
Recruiter Classification: Contingency; **Lowest/Average Salary:**
$30,000/$50,000; **Industry Concentration:** Financial Services;
Function Concentration: Engineering, Finance/Accounting

Visnich, L. Christine — *Director Executive Search
Consulting*
Bason Associates Inc.
11311 Cornell Park Drive
Cincinnati, OH 45242
Telephone: (513) 469-9881
Recruiter Classification: Retained; **Lowest/Average Salary:**
$60,000/$90,000; **Industry Concentration:** Generalist with a
primary focus in Financial Services, Insurance, Venture Capital;
Function Concentration: Generalist with a primary focus in
Administration, Engineering, Finance/Accounting, General
Management, Human Resources, Marketing, Research and
Development, Sales

Vitale, Amy — *Recruiter*
Highland Search Group
565 Fifth Avenue, 22nd Floor
New York, NY 10017
Telephone: (212) 328-1113
Recruiter Classification: Retained; **Lowest/Average Salary:**
$90,000/$90,000; **Industry Concentration:** Financial Services,
Insurance, Venture Capital; **Function Concentration:** Generalist
with a primary focus in Administration, Finance/Accounting,
General Management, Human Resources, Sales,
Women/Minorities

Viviano, Cathleen — *Associate*
Source Services Corporation
10300 West 103rd Street, Suite 101
Overland Park, KS 66214
Telephone: (913) 888-8885
Recruiter Classification: Contingency; **Lowest/Average Salary:**
$30,000/$50,000; **Industry Concentration:** Financial Services;
Function Concentration: Engineering, Finance/Accounting

Vlcek, Thomas J. — *President*
Vlcek & Company, Inc.
620 Newport Center Drive
Suite 1100
Newport Beach, CA 92660
Telephone: (714) 752-0661
Recruiter Classification: Retained; **Lowest/Average Salary:**
$90,000/$90,000; **Industry Concentration:** Generalist with a
primary focus in Financial Services; **Function Concentration:**
Generalist with a primary focus in Engineering,
Finance/Accounting, General Management, Human Resources,
Marketing, Sales, Women/Minorities

Voigt, John A. — *Managing Partner*
Romac & Associates
4350 North Fairfax Drive
Suite 400
Arlington, VA 22203
Telephone: (703) 351-7600
Recruiter Classification: Executive Temporary; **Lowest/Average
Salary:** $60,000/$60,000; **Industry Concentration:** Financial
Services, Insurance; **Function Concentration:**
Finance/Accounting

Volkman, Arthur — *Search Consultant*
Cochran, Cochran & Yale, Inc.
1333 W. 120th Avenue, Suite 311
Westminster, CO 80234
Telephone: (303) 252-4600
Recruiter Classification: Retained; **Lowest/Average Salary:**
$50,000/$75,000; **Industry Concentration:** Generalist with a
primary focus in Financial Services, Venture Capital; **Function
Concentration:** Generalist with a primary focus in Engineering,
Finance/Accounting, General Management, Human Resources,
Marketing, Sales, Women/Minorities

von Baillou, Astrid — *Principal Managing
Director*
Richard Kinser & Associates
919 Third Avenue, 10th Floor
New York, NY 10022
Telephone: (212) 593-5429
Recruiter Classification: Retained; **Lowest/Average Salary:**
$90,000/$90,000; **Industry Concentration:** Generalist with a
primary focus in Financial Services; **Function Concentration:**
Generalist with a primary focus in General Management,
Marketing, Women/Minorities

Vossler, James — *Professional Recruiter*
A.J. Burton Group, Inc.
4550 Montgomery Avenue, Ste. 325 North
Bethesda, MD 20814
Telephone: (301) 654-0082
Recruiter Classification: Contingency; **Lowest/Average Salary:**
$40,000/$75,000; **Industry Concentration:** Generalist with a
primary focus in Financial Services, Insurance; **Function
Concentration:** Generalist with a primary focus in
Administration, Finance/Accounting, General Management,
Human Resources

Vourakis, Zan — *President*
ZanExec LLC
2063 Madrillon Road
Vienna, VA 22182
Telephone: (703) 734-9440
Recruiter Classification: Retained; **Lowest/Average Salary:**
$90,000/$90,000; **Industry Concentration:** Financial Services,
Venture Capital; **Function Concentration:** Engineering,
Finance/Accounting, General Management, Marketing,
Research and Development, Sales

Waanders, William L. — *President*
ExecuQuest
2050 Breton SE
Suite 103
Grand Rapids, MI 49546-5547
Telephone: (616) 949-1800
Recruiter Classification: Retained; **Lowest/Average Salary:**
$75,000/$90,000; **Industry Concentration:** Financial Services;
Function Concentration: Generalist with a primary focus in
Finance/Accounting, General Management, Human Resources,
Marketing, Sales

Wacholz, Rick — *Vice President*
A.T. Kearney, Inc.
One Memorial Drive, 14th Floor
Cambridge, MA 02142
Telephone: (617) 374-2600
Recruiter Classification: Retained; **Lowest/Average Salary:**
$90,000/$90,000; **Industry Concentration:** Generalist with a
primary focus in Financial Services; **Function Concentration:**
Generalist with a primary focus in Engineering,
Finance/Accounting, General Management

Wade, Christy — *Associate*
Source Services Corporation
520 Post Oak Boulevard, Suite 700
Houston, TX 77027
Telephone: (713) 439-1077
Recruiter Classification: Contingency; **Lowest/Average
Salary:** $30,000/$50,000; **Industry Concentration:** Financial
Services; **Function Concentration:** Engineering,
Finance/Accounting

Waitkus, Karen — *Senior Executive Recruiter*
Richard, Wayne and Roberts
24 Greenway Plaza, Suite 1304
Houston, TX 77046-2493
Telephone: (713) 629-6681
Recruiter Classification: Retained; **Lowest/Average Salary:**
$50,000/$90,000; **Industry Concentration:** Generalist with a
primary focus in Financial Services; **Function Concentration:**
Generalist with a primary focus in Finance/Accounting

Wakefield, Scott — *Insurance Consultant*
National Search, Inc.
2816 University Drive
Coral Springs, FL 33071
Telephone: (800) 935-4355
Recruiter Classification: Contingency; **Lowest/Average Salary:**
$30,000/$50,000; **Industry Concentration:** Insurance;
Function Concentration: Generalist with a primary focus in
Administration, Finance/Accounting, General Management,
Human Resources, Marketing, Research and Development,
Sales, Women/Minorities

Waldman, Noah H. — *Partner*
Lamalie Amrop International
191 Peachtree Street N.E.
Atlanta, GA 30303-1747
Telephone: (404) 688-0800
Recruiter Classification: Retained; **Lowest/Average Salary:**
$90,000/$90,000; **Industry Concentration:** Generalist with a
primary focus in Insurance; **Function Concentration:**
Generalist with a primary focus in Administration,
Finance/Accounting, General Management, Marketing, Sales

Waldoch, D. Mark — *Consultant*
Barnes Development Group, LLC
1017 West Glen Oaks Lane, Suite 108
Mequon, WI 53092
Telephone: (414) 241-8468
Recruiter Classification: Retained; **Lowest/Average Salary:**
$50,000/$75,000; **Industry Concentration:** Insurance;
Function Concentration: Generalist with a primary focus in
Administration, Engineering, Finance/Accounting, General
Management, Human Resources, Marketing, Research and
Development, Sales

Waldrop, Gary R. — *Manager*
MSI International
230 Peachtree Street, N.E.
Suite 1550
Atlanta, GA 30303
Telephone: (404) 653-7360
Recruiter Classification: Contingency; **Lowest/Average Salary:**
$30,000/$60,000; **Industry Concentration:** Generalist with a
primary focus in Financial Services; **Function Concentration:**
Generalist with a primary focus in Administration,
Engineering, Finance/Accounting, General Management,
Marketing, Sales

Walker, Ann — *Associate*
Source Services Corporation
111 Monument Circle, Suite 3930
Indianapolis, IN 46204
Telephone: (317) 631-2900
Recruiter Classification: Contingency; **Lowest/Average Salary:** $30,000/$50,000; **Industry Concentration:** Financial Services; **Function Concentration:** Engineering, Finance/Accounting

Walker, Craig H. — *Professional Recruiter*
A.J. Burton Group, Inc.
120 East Baltimore Street, Suite 2220
Baltimore, MD 21202
Telephone: (410) 752-5244
Recruiter Classification: Contingency; **Lowest/Average Salary:** $40,000/$75,000; **Industry Concentration:** Generalist with a primary focus in Financial Services, Insurance; **Function Concentration:** Generalist with a primary focus in Administration, Finance/Accounting, General Management, Human Resources

Walker, Douglas G. — *Managing Director*
Sink, Walker, Boltrus International
60 Walnut Street
Wellesley, MA 02181
Telephone: (617) 237-1199
Recruiter Classification: Retained; **Lowest/Average Salary:** $90,000/$90,000; **Industry Concentration:** Financial Services, Venture Capital; **Function Concentration:** Engineering, General Management, Research and Development, Sales

Walker, Ewing J. — *Managing Director*
Ward Howell International, Inc.
1000 Louisiana Street
Suite 3150
Houston, TX 77002
Telephone: (713) 655-7155
Recruiter Classification: Retained; **Lowest/Average Salary:** $90,000/$90,000; **Industry Concentration:** Financial Services, Insurance, Venture Capital; **Function Concentration:** Administration, Engineering, Finance/Accounting, General Management, Human Resources, Marketing, Women/Minorities

Walker, Rose — *Associate*
Source Services Corporation
One Park Plaza, Suite 560
Irvine, CA 92714
Telephone: (714) 660-1666
Recruiter Classification: Contingency; **Lowest/Average Salary:** $30,000/$50,000; **Industry Concentration:** Financial Services; **Function Concentration:** Engineering, Finance/Accounting

Wallace, Alec — *Partner*
Tanton Mitchell/Paul Ray Berndtson
710-1050 West Pender Street
Vancouver, British Columbia, CANADA V6E 3S7
Telephone: (604) 685-0261
Recruiter Classification: Retained; **Lowest/Average Salary:** $75,000/$90,000; **Industry Concentration:** Generalist with a primary focus in Financial Services; **Function Concentration:** Generalist with a primary focus in Finance/Accounting, General Management, Human Resources

Wallace, Toby — *Associate*
Source Services Corporation
5429 LBJ Freeway, Suite 275
Dallas, TX 75240
Telephone: (214) 387-1600
Recruiter Classification: Contingency; **Lowest/Average Salary:** $30,000/$50,000; **Industry Concentration:** Financial Services; **Function Concentration:** Engineering, Finance/Accounting

Walsh, Denis — *Senior Staffing Consultant*
Professional Staffing Consultants
1331 Lamar, Suite 1459
Houston, TX 77010
Telephone: (713) 659-8383
Recruiter Classification: Retained; **Lowest/Average Salary:** $50,000/$75,000; **Industry Concentration:** Generalist with a primary focus in Financial Services; **Function Concentration:** Generalist with a primary focus in Engineering, Finance/Accounting, General Management, Human Resources

Walters, William F. — *President*
Jonas, Walters & Assoc., Inc.
1110 North Old World Third St., Suite 510
Milwaukee, WI 53203-1102
Telephone: (414) 291-2828
Recruiter Classification: Retained; **Lowest/Average Salary:** $75,000/$90,000; **Industry Concentration:** Generalist with a primary focus in Financial Services; **Function Concentration:** Generalist with a primary focus in Administration, Engineering, Finance/Accounting, General Management, Human Resources, Marketing, Research and Development, Sales

Ward, Jim — *Executive Recruiter*
F-O-R-T-U-N-E Personnel Consultants of Huntsville, Inc.
3311 Bob Wallace Avenue, Suite 204
Huntsville, AL 35805
Telephone: (205) 534-7282
Recruiter Classification: Contingency; **Lowest/Average Salary:** $30,000/$75,000; **Industry Concentration:** Financial Services

Ward, Les — *President*
Source Services Corporation
5580 LBJ Freeway, Suite 300
Dallas, TX 75240
Telephone: (214) 385-3002
Recruiter Classification: Contingency; **Lowest/Average Salary:** $30,000/$50,000; **Industry Concentration:** Financial Services; **Function Concentration:** Engineering, Finance/Accounting

Ward, Madeleine — *Principal*
LTM Associates
1112 Elizabeth
Naperville, IL 60540
Telephone: (708) 961-3331
Recruiter Classification: Contingency; **Lowest/Average Salary:** $50,000/$90,000; **Industry Concentration:** Financial Services, Venture Capital; **Function Concentration:** Finance/Accounting, General Management, Sales

Ward, Robert — *Associate*
Source Services Corporation
One Park Plaza, Suite 560
Irvine, CA 92714
Telephone: (714) 660-1666
Recruiter Classification: Contingency; **Lowest/Average Salary:** $30,000/$50,000; **Industry Concentration:** Financial Services; **Function Concentration:** Engineering, Finance/Accounting

Ward, Ted — *Vice President*
Korn/Ferry International
237 Park Avenue
New York, NY 10017
Telephone: (212) 687-1834
Recruiter Classification: Retained; **Lowest/Average Salary:**
$100,000/$150,000; **Industry Concentration:** Generalist with a
primary focus in Financial Services; **Function Concentration:**
Generalist

Wardell, Charles W.B. — *Senior Partner*
Nordeman Grimm, Inc.
717 Fifth Avenue, 26th Floor
New York, NY 10022
Telephone: (212) 935-1000
Recruiter Classification: Retained; **Lowest/Average Salary:**
$150,000/$150,000; **Industry Concentration:** Generalist with a
primary focus in Financial Services; **Function Concentration:**
Generalist

Warnock, Phyl — *Associate*
Source Services Corporation
505 East 200 South, Suite 300
Salt Lake City, UT 84102
Telephone: (801) 328-0011
Recruiter Classification: Contingency; **Lowest/Average Salary:**
$30,000/$50,000; **Industry Concentration:** Financial Services;
Function Concentration: Engineering, Finance/Accounting

Warter, Mark — *Senior Recruiter*
Isaacson, Miller
334 Boylston Street, Suite 500
Boston, MA 02111
Telephone: (617) 262-6500
Recruiter Classification: Retained; **Lowest/Average Salary:**
$75,000/$90,000; **Industry Concentration:** Generalist with a
primary focus in Venture Capital; **Function Concentration:**
Administration, Finance/Accounting, General Management,
Human Resources, Women/Minorities

Wasp, Warren T. — *President*
WTW Associates, Inc.
675 Third Avenue, Suite 2808
New York, NY 10017
Telephone: (212) 972-6990
Recruiter Classification: Retained; **Lowest/Average Salary:**
$75,000/$90,000; **Industry Concentration:** Generalist with a
primary focus in Financial Services; **Function Concentration:**
Generalist

Wasson, Thomas W. — *Senior Director*
Spencer Stuart
Financial Centre
695 East Main Street
Stamford, CT 06901
Telephone: (203) 324-6333
Recruiter Classification: Retained; **Lowest/Average Salary:**
$90,000/$90,000; **Industry Concentration:** Financial Services,
Insurance; **Function Concentration:** Generalist

Watkins, Jeffrey P. — *Partner*
Lamalie Amrop International
191 Peachtree Street N.E.
Atlanta, GA 30303-1747
Telephone: (404) 688-0800
Recruiter Classification: Retained; **Lowest/Average Salary:**
$90,000/$90,000; **Industry Concentration:** Generalist with a
primary focus in Financial Services; **Function Concentration:**
Generalist

Watkins, Thomas M. — *Managing Partner*
Lamalie Amrop International
Thanksgiving Tower
1601 Elm Street
Dallas, TX 75201-4768
Telephone: (214) 754-0019
Recruiter Classification: Retained; **Lowest/Average Salary:**
$90,000/$90,000; **Industry Concentration:** Generalist with a
primary focus in Financial Services; **Function Concentration:**
Generalist with a primary focus in Finance/Accounting,
General Management, Human Resources, Marketing

Watkinson, Jim W. — *Vice President*
The Badger Group
4125 Blackhawk Plaza Circle, Suite 270
Danville, CA 94506
Telephone: (510) 736-5553
Recruiter Classification: Retained; **Lowest/Average Salary:**
$90,000/$90,000; **Industry Concentration:** Generalist with a
primary focus in Financial Services; **Function Concentration:**
Generalist with a primary focus in Engineering,
Finance/Accounting, General Management, Human Resources,
Marketing, Research and Development, Sales

Watson, Hanan S. — *President*
Watson International, Inc.
25 West 43rd Street, Suite 914
New York, NY 10036-7406
Telephone: (212) 354-3344
Recruiter Classification: Retained; **Lowest/Average Salary:**
$90,000/$90,000; **Industry Concentration:** Financial Services;
Function Concentration: Generalist with a primary focus in
Administration, Finance/Accounting, General Management,
Human Resources, Marketing, Sales

Watson, James — *Vice President*
MSI International
1050 Crown Pointe Parkway
Suite 1000
Atlanta, GA 30338
Telephone: (404) 394-2494
Recruiter Classification: Contingency; **Lowest/Average Salary:**
$30,000/$60,000; **Industry Concentration:** Generalist with a
primary focus in Financial Services; **Function Concentration:**
Administration, Engineering, Finance/Accounting, General
Management, Marketing, Sales

Waymire, Pamela — *Associate*
Source Services Corporation
One South Main Street, Suite 1440
Dayton, OH 45402
Telephone: (513) 461-4660
Recruiter Classification: Contingency; **Lowest/Average Salary:**
$30,000/$50,000; **Industry Concentration:** Financial Services;
Function Concentration: Engineering, Finance/Accounting

Wayne, Cary S. — *President*
ProSearch Inc.
2550 SOM Center Road
Suite 320
Willoughby Hills, OH 44094
Telephone: (216) 585-9099
Recruiter Classification: Contingency; **Lowest/Average Salary:**
$40,000/$75,000; **Industry Concentration:** Financial Services;
Function Concentration: Administration, Engineering,
Finance/Accounting, General Management, Human Resources,
Marketing, Research and Development, Sales

Webb, George H. — *Managing Director*
Webb, Johnson Associates, Inc.
280 Park Avenue, 43rd Floor
New York, NY 10017
Telephone: (212) 661-3700
Recruiter Classification: Retained; **Lowest/Average Salary:**
$90,000/$90,000; **Industry Concentration:** Generalist with a
primary focus in Financial Services; **Function Concentration:**
Generalist with a primary focus in Administration, Engineering,
Finance/Accounting, General Management, Human Resources,
Marketing, Research and Development, Sales

Webber, Edward — *Associate*
Source Services Corporation
155 Federal Street, Suite 410
Boston, MA 02110
Telephone: (617) 482-8211
Recruiter Classification: Contingency; **Lowest/Average Salary:**
$30,000/$50,000; **Industry Concentration:** Financial Services;
Function Concentration: Engineering, Finance/Accounting

Weber, Ronald R. — *President*
Weber Executive Search
205 East Main Street, Suite 2-3A
Huntington, NY 11743
Telephone: (516) 473-4700
Recruiter Classification: Retained; **Lowest/Average Salary:**
$75,000/$90,000; **Industry Concentration:** Financial Services,
Venture Capital; **Function Concentration:** Generalist

Weeks, Glenn — *Associate*
Source Services Corporation
5343 North 16th Street, Suite 270
Phoenix, AZ 85016
Telephone: (602) 230-0220
Recruiter Classification: Contingency; **Lowest/Average Salary:**
$30,000/$50,000; **Industry Concentration:** Financial Services;
Function Concentration: Engineering, Finance/Accounting

Wein, Michael S. — *President*
Media Management Resources, Inc.
6464 South Quebec Street
Englewood, CO 80111
Telephone: (303) 290-9800
Recruiter Classification: Contingency; **Lowest/Average Salary:**
$50,000/$75,000; **Industry Concentration:** Venture Capital;
Function Concentration: Administration, Engineering, General
Management, Marketing, Research and Development, Sales,
Women/Minorities

Wein, William — *Vice President*
Media Management Resources, Inc.
6464 South Quebec Street
Englewood, CO 80111
Telephone: (303) 290-9800
Recruiter Classification: Contingency; **Lowest/Average Salary:**
$50,000/$75,000; **Industry Concentration:** Venture Capital;
Function Concentration: Administration, Engineering, General
Management, Marketing, Research and Development, Sales,
Women/Minorities

Weinberg, Melvin — *Managing Partner*
Romac & Associates
1001 Craig Road, Suite 260
St. Louis, MO 63146
Telephone: (314) 569-9898
Recruiter Classification: Executive Temporary; **Lowest/Average
Salary:** $60,000/$60,000; **Industry Concentration:** Financial
Services, Insurance; **Function Concentration:**
Finance/Accounting

Weis, Theodore — *Associate*
Source Services Corporation
5343 North 16th Street, Suite 270
Phoenix, AZ 85016
Telephone: (602) 230-0220
Recruiter Classification: Contingency; **Lowest/Average Salary:**
$30,000/$50,000; **Industry Concentration:** Financial Services;
Function Concentration: Engineering, Finance/Accounting

Weisler, Nancy — *Executive Insurance Consultant*
National Search, Inc.
2816 University Drive
Coral Springs, FL 33071
Telephone: (800) 935-4355
Recruiter Classification: Contingency; **Lowest/Average Salary:**
$30,000/$50,000; **Industry Concentration:** Insurance;
Function Concentration: Generalist with a primary focus in
Administration, Finance/Accounting, General Management,
Human Resources, Marketing, Research and Development,
Sales, Women/Minorities

Weiss, Elizabeth — *Associate*
Source Services Corporation
5429 LBJ Freeway, Suite 275
Dallas, TX 75240
Telephone: (214) 387-1600
Recruiter Classification: Contingency; **Lowest/Average Salary:**
$30,000/$50,000; **Industry Concentration:** Financial Services;
Function Concentration: Engineering, Finance/Accounting

Weissman-Rosenthal, Abbe —
President/Consultant
ALW Research International
60 Canterbury Road
Chatham, NJ 07928
Telephone: (201) 701-9700
Recruiter Classification: Retained; **Lowest/Average Salary:**
$60,000/$75,000; **Industry Concentration:** Generalist with a
primary focus in Financial Services; **Function Concentration:**
Generalist with a primary focus in Engineering,
Finance/Accounting, General Management, Human Resources,
Marketing, Research and Development, Sales,
Women/Minorities

Welch, Robert — *Consultant*
Ray & Berndtson
2029 Century Park East, Suite 1000
Los Angeles, CA 90067
Telephone: (310) 557-2828
Recruiter Classification: Retained; **Lowest/Average Salary:**
$90,000/$90,000; **Industry Concentration:** Generalist with a
primary focus in Financial Services, Insurance; **Function
Concentration:** Generalist with a primary focus in
Administration, Finance/Accounting, General Management,
Human Resources, Marketing, Research and Development,
Sales, Women/Minorities

Weller, Paul S. — *Senior Partner*
Mark Stanley/EMA Partners International
1629 K Street N.W.
Suite 1100
Washington, DC 20006-1602
Telephone: (202) 785-6711
Recruiter Classification: Retained; **Lowest/Average Salary:**
$75,000/$90,000; **Industry Concentration:** Generalist with a
primary focus in Financial Services; **Function Concentration:**
Generalist with a primary focus in Finance/Accounting,
General Management, Human Resources, Sales

Wendler, Kambrea R. — *Manager*
Gregory Michaels and Associates, Inc.
8410 West Bryn Mawr Avenue
Suite 400
Chicago, IL 60631
Telephone: (773) 380-1333
Recruiter Classification: Retained; **Lowest/Average Salary:**
$90,000/$90,000; **Industry Concentration:** Generalist
with a primary focus in Financial Services; **Function
Concentration:** Generalist with a primary focus in
Finance/Accounting, General Management, Human
Resources, Marketing, Sales

Wenz, Alexander — *Associate*
Source Services Corporation
4510 Executive Drive, Suite 200
San Diego, CA 92121
Telephone: (619) 552-0300
Recruiter Classification: Contingency; **Lowest/Average
Salary:** $30,000/$50,000; **Industry Concentration:** Financial
Services; **Function Concentration:** Engineering,
Finance/Accounting

Wessling, Jerry — *Associate*
Source Services Corporation
One South Main Street, Suite 1440
Dayton, OH 45402
Telephone: (513) 461-4660
Recruiter Classification: Contingency; **Lowest/Average
Salary:** $30,000/$50,000; **Industry Concentration:** Financial
Services; **Function Concentration:** Engineering,
Finance/Accounting

Westfall, Ed — *Vice President*
Zwell International
300 South Wacker Drive, Suite 650
Chicago, IL 60606
Telephone: (312) 663-3737
Recruiter Classification: Retained; **Lowest/Average Salary:**
$75,000/$90,000; **Industry Concentration:** Generalist
with a primary focus in Financial Services; **Function
Concentration:** Generalist with a primary focus in
Engineering, Finance/Accounting, General
Management, Human Resources, Marketing,
Sales

Weston, Corinne F. — *Director Research*
D.A. Kreuter Associates, Inc.
1100 East Hector Street, Suite 388
Conshohocken, PA 19428
Telephone: (610) 834-1100
Recruiter Classification: Retained; **Lowest/Average Salary:**
$60,000/$90,000; **Industry Concentration:** Financial Services,
Insurance; **Function Concentration:** General Management,
Marketing, Sales

Wheatley, William — *Senior Recruiter*
Drummond Associates, Inc.
50 Broadway, Suite 1201
New York, NY 10004
Telephone: (212) 248-1120
Recruiter Classification: Contingency; **Lowest/Average Salary:**
$40,000/$75,000; **Industry Concentration:** Financial Services;
Function Concentration: Finance/Accounting

Wheeler, Gerard H. — *Executive Vice President*
A.J. Burton Group, Inc.
120 East Baltimore Street, Suite 2220
Baltimore, MD 21202
Telephone: (410) 752-5244
Recruiter Classification: Contingency; **Lowest/Average Salary:**
$40,000/$75,000; **Industry Concentration:** Generalist with a
primary focus in Financial Services, Insurance; **Function
Concentration:** Generalist with a primary focus in
Administration, Finance/Accounting, General Management,
Human Resources

White, Richard B. — *Senior Director*
Spencer Stuart
Financial Centre
695 East Main Street
Stamford, CT 06901
Telephone: (203) 324-6333
Recruiter Classification: Retained; **Lowest/Average Salary:**
$90,000/$90,000; **Industry Concentration:** Generalist with a
primary focus in Financial Services, Venture Capital; **Function
Concentration:** Generalist with a primary focus in General
Management, Marketing, Sales

White, William C. — *President*
Venture Resources Inc.
2659 Townsgate Road, Suite 119
Westlake Village, CA 91361
Telephone: (805) 371-3600
Recruiter Classification: Retained; **Lowest/Average Salary:**
$90,000/$90,000; **Industry Concentration:** Venture Capital;
Function Concentration: Generalist with a primary focus in
Engineering, Finance/Accounting, General Management,
Marketing, Research and Development, Sales

Whitfield, Jack — *Associate*
Source Services Corporation
1233 North Mayfair Road, Suite 300
Milwaukee, WI 53226
Telephone: (414) 774-6700
Recruiter Classification: Contingency; **Lowest/Average
Salary:** $30,000/$50,000; **Industry Concentration:** Financial
Services; **Function Concentration:** Engineering,
Finance/Accounting

Whiting, Anthony — *Partner*
Johnson Smith & Knisely Accord
100 Park Avenue, 15th Floor
New York, NY 10017
Telephone: (212) 885-9100
Recruiter Classification: Retained; **Lowest/Average Salary:**
$90,000/$90,000; **Industry Concentration:** Financial Services,
Insurance, Venture Capital; **Function Concentration:** Generalist
with a primary focus in Administration, Finance/Accounting,
General Management, Human Resources, Marketing, Research
and Development, Sales

Whitley, Sue Ann — *Principal*
Roberts Ryan and Bentley
3206 Sandy Ridge Drive
Clearwater, FL 34621
Telephone: (813) 786-1312
Recruiter Classification: Retained; **Lowest/Average Salary:**
$90,000/$90,000; **Industry Concentration:** Insurance;
Function Concentration: Generalist with a primary
focus in Human Resources, Marketing, Sales,
Women/Minorities

Whitney, David L. — *President*
Whitney & Associates, Inc.
920 Second Avenue South, Suite 625
Minneapolis, MN 55402-4035
Telephone: (612) 338-5600
Recruiter Classification: Contingency, Executive Temporary;
Lowest/Average Salary: $20,000/$50,000; **Industry
Concentration:** Generalist with a primary focus in F
inancial Services, Insurance, Venture Capital;
Function Concentration: Finance/
Accounting

Whitney, Kenneth L. — *Chief Executive Officer*
K.L. Whitney Company
6 Aspen Drive
North Caldwell, NJ 07006
Telephone: (201) 228-7124
Recruiter Classification: Retained; **Lowest/Average Salary:**
$75,000/$90,000; **Industry Concentration:** Financial Services;
Function Concentration: Marketing, Sales

Whitney, William A — *Principal*
Larsen, Whitney, Blecksmith & Zilliacus
888 West 6th Street, Suite 500
Los Angeles, CA 90017
Telephone: (213) 243-0033
Recruiter Classification: Retained; **Lowest/Average Salary:**
$75,000/$90,000; **Industry Concentration:** Generalist
with a primary focus in Financial Services; **Function
Concentration:** Generalist with a primary focus in
Finance/Accounting, General Management, Human
Resources, Marketing, Research and Development, Sales,
Women/Minorities

Whitton, Paula L. — *Associate*
Pearson, Caldwell & Farnsworth, Inc.
250 Park Avenue, 17th Floor
New York, NY 10177
Telephone: (212) 983-5850
Recruiter Classification: Retained; **Lowest/Average Salary:**
$90,000/$90,000; **Industry Concentration:** Financial
Services; **Function Concentration:** Administration,
Finance/Accounting, General Management, Human
Resources, Marketing, Sales

Wier, Daniel — *President*
Daniel Wier & Associates
333 S. Grand Avenue, Suite 1880
Los Angeles, CA 91030
Telephone: (213) 628-2580
Recruiter Classification: Retained; **Lowest/Average Salary:**
$90,000/$90,000; **Industry Concentration:** Generalist with a
primary focus in Financial Services, Venture Capital; **Function
Concentration:** Generalist

Wilbanks, George R. — *Managing Director*
Russell Reynolds Associates, Inc.
200 Park Avenue
New York, NY 10166-0002
Telephone: (212) 351-2000
Recruiter Classification: Retained; **Lowest/Average Salary:**
$90,000/$90,000; **Industry Concentration:** Generalist with a
primary focus in Financial Services; **Function Concentration:**
Generalist

Wilburn, Dan — *Search Consultant*
Kaye-Bassman International Corp.
18333 Preston Road, Suite 500
Dallas, TX 75252
Telephone: (972) 931-5242
Recruiter Classification: Retained; **Lowest/Average Salary:**
$60,000/$60,000; **Industry Concentration:** Financial Services,
Insurance, Venture Capital; **Function Concentration:**
Engineering, Human Resources, Marketing, Research and
Development, Sales

Wilcox, Fred T. — *President*
Wilcox, Bertoux & Miller
100 Howe Avenue, Suite 155N
Sacramento, CA 95825
Telephone: (916) 977-3700
Recruiter Classification: Contingency; **Lowest/Average Salary:**
$50,000/$90,000; **Industry Concentration:** Financial Services;
Function Concentration: Administration, Finance/Accounting,
General Management

Wilder, Richard B. — *Managing Principal*
Columbia Consulting Group
10725 East Cholla Lane
Scottsdale, AZ 85259
Telephone: (602) 451-1180
Recruiter Classification: Retained; **Lowest/Average Salary:**
$75,000/$90,000; **Industry Concentration:** Generalist with a
primary focus in Financial Services, Insurance; **Function
Concentration:** Generalist with a primary focus in
Finance/Accounting, General Management, Human Resources,
Marketing, Sales

Wilkinson, Barbara — *Associate*
Beall & Company, Inc.
535 Colonial Park Drive
Roswell, GA 30075
Telephone: (404) 992-0900
Recruiter Classification: Retained; **Lowest/Average Salary:**
$90,000/$90,000; **Industry Concentration:** Generalist with a
primary focus in Financial Services, Insurance, Venture Capital;
Function Concentration: Generalist with a primary focus in
Administration, Engineering, Finance/Accounting, General
Management, Human Resources, Marketing, Research and
Development, Sales

Wilkinson, Jr. SPHR
The HRM Group, Inc.
321 Lorna Square
Birmingham, AL 35216
Telephone: (205) 978-7181
Recruiter Classification: Retained; **Lowest/Average Salary:**
$30,000/$50,000; **Industry Concentration:** Generalist
with a primary focus in Insurance; **Function Concentration:**
Generalist with a primary focus in Finance/Accounting,
General Management, Human Resources, Marketing,
Sales

Willbrandt, Curt — *Associate*
Source Services Corporation
161 Ottawa NW, Suite 409D
Grand Rapids, MI 49503
Telephone: (616) 451-2400
Recruiter Classification: Contingency; **Lowest/Average
Salary:** $30,000/$50,000; **Industry Concentration:** Financial
Services; **Function Concentration:** Engineering,
Finance/Accounting

Williams, Angie — *Executive Recruiter*
Whitney & Associates, Inc.
920 Second Avenue South, Suite 625
Minneapolis, MN 55402-4035
Telephone: (612) 338-5600
Recruiter Classification: Contingency, Executive Temporary;
Lowest/Average Salary: $20,000/$50,000; **Industry**
Concentration: Generalist with a primary focus in Financial
Services, Insurance, Venture Capital; **Function Concentration:**
Finance/Accounting

Williams, Gary L. — *Consultant*
Barnes Development Group, LLC
1017 West Glen Oaks Lane, Suite 108
Mequon, WI 53092
Telephone: (414) 241-8468
Recruiter Classification: Retained; **Lowest/Average Salary:**
$50,000/$75,000; **Industry Concentration:** Generalist with a
primary focus in Insurance; **Function Concentration:**
Generalist with a primary focus in Administration, Engineering,
Finance/Accounting, General Management, Human Resources,
Marketing, Research and Development, Sales

Williams, Harry D. — *Search Consultant*
Jacobson Associates
Five Neshaminy Interplex
Suite 113
Trevose, PA 19053
Telephone: (215) 639-5860
Recruiter Classification: Contingency; **Lowest/Average Salary:**
$20,000/$40,000; **Industry Concentration:** Financial Services,
Insurance; **Function Concentration:** Generalist with a primary
focus in Administration, Finance/Accounting, General
Management, Marketing, Research and Development, Sales

Williams, Jack — *Vice President*
A.T. Kearney, Inc.
Lincoln Plaza, Suite 4170
500 North Akard Street
Dallas, TX 75201
Telephone: (214) 969-0010
Recruiter Classification: Retained; **Lowest/Average Salary:**
$90,000/$90,000; **Industry Concentration:** Generalist with a
primary focus in Financial Services; **Function Concentration:**
Generalist with a primary focus in Engineering,
Finance/Accounting, General Management

Williams, John — *Associate*
Source Services Corporation
2850 National City Tower
Louisville, KY 40202
Telephone: (502) 581-9900
Recruiter Classification: Contingency; **Lowest/Average Salary:**
$30,000/$50,000; **Industry Concentration:** Financial Services;
Function Concentration: Engineering, Finance/Accounting

Williams, Lis — *Recruiter*
Executive Options, Ltd.
910 Skokie Boulevard
Suite 210
Northbrook, IL 60068
Telephone: (708) 291-4322
Recruiter Classification: Executive Temporary; **Lowest/Average**
Salary: $30,000/$50,000; **Industry Concentration:** Generalist
with a primary focus in Financial Services; **Function**
Concentration: Generalist with a primary focus in
Finance/Accounting, General Management, Human Resources,
Marketing, Women/Minorities

Williams, Roger K. — *Partner*
Williams, Roth & Krueger Inc.
20 North Wacker Drive
Chicago, IL 60606
Telephone: (312) 977-0800
Recruiter Classification: Retained; **Lowest/Average Salary:**
$90,000/$90,000; **Industry Concentration:** Generalist
with a primary focus in Financial Services, Venture Capital;
Function Concentration: Generalist with a primary
focus in Administration, Engineering, Finance/Accounting,
General Management, Human Resources, Marketing,
Sales

Williams, Stephen E. — *Senior Consultant*
Barton Associates, Inc.
One Riverway, Suite 2500
Houston, TX 77056
Telephone: (713) 961-9111
Recruiter Classification: Retained; **Lowest/Average Salary:**
$75,000/$90,000; **Industry Concentration:** Generalist
with a primary focus in Financial Services; **Function**
Concentration: Generalist with a primary focus in
Finance/Accounting, General Management, Human
Resources, Marketing, Sales

Williams, Walter E. — *Partner*
Lamalie Amrop International
10 Post Office Square
Boston, MA 02109-4603
Telephone: (617) 292-6242
Recruiter Classification: Retained; **Lowest/Average Salary:**
$90,000/$90,000; **Industry Concentration:** Generalist with a
primary focus in Financial Services; **Function Concentration:**
Generalist

Willis, William H. — *President/Managing Director*
William Willis Worldwide Inc.
P.O. Box 4444
Greenwich, CT 06831-0408
Telephone: (203) 661-4500
Recruiter Classification: Retained; **Lowest/Average Salary:**
$90,000/$90,000; **Industry Concentration:** Generalist with a
primary focus in Financial Services, Insurance; **Function**
Concentration: Generalist with a primary focus in
Finance/Accounting, General Management, Human Resources,
Marketing, Research and Development

Wilson, Derrick — *Senior Manager Accounts*
Thornton Resources
9800 McKnight Road
Pittsburgh, PA 15237
Telephone: (412) 364-2111
Recruiter Classification: Contingency, Executive Temporary;
Lowest/Average Salary: $40,000/$50,000; **Industry**
Concentration: Generalist with a primary focus in
Financial Services; **Function Concentration:** Generalist with
a primary focus in General Management, Human Resources,
Marketing

Wilson, Harry — *Managing Director*
First Union Executive Search Group
301 S. College Street
Charlotte, NC 28288-0102
Telephone: (704) 383-9969
Recruiter Classification: Retained; **Lowest/Average Salary:**
$75,000/$90,000; **Industry Concentration:** Financial Services;
Function Concentration: Generalist

Wilson, John — *Vice President*
Korn/Ferry International
The Transamerica Pyramid
600 Montgomery Street
San Francisco, CA 94111
Telephone: (415) 956-1834
Recruiter Classification: Retained; **Lowest/Average Salary:**
$100,000/$150,000; **Industry Concentration:** Generalist with a
primary focus in Financial Services, Insurance; **Function
Concentration:** Generalist

Wilson, Joyce — *Associate*
Source Services Corporation
One Park Plaza, Suite 560
Irvine, CA 92714
Telephone: (714) 660-1666
Recruiter Classification: Contingency; **Lowest/Average
Salary:** $30,000/$50,000; **Industry Concentration:** Financial
Services; **Function Concentration:** Engineering,
Finance/Accounting

Wilson, Patricia L. — *Partner*
Leon A. Farley Associates
468 Jackson Street
San Francisco, CA 94111
Telephone: (415) 989-0989
Recruiter Classification: Retained; **Lowest/Average Salary:**
$90,000/$90,000; **Industry Concentration:** Generalist
with a primary focus in Financial Services; **Function
Concentration:** Generalist with a primary focus in
Administration, Finance/Accounting, General
Management, Human Resources, Marketing, Sales,
Women/Minorities

Wilson, T. Gordon — *Partner*
Ray & Berndtson/Lovas Stanley
Royal Bank Plaza, South Tower, Suite 3150
200 Bay Street, P.O. Box 125
Toronto, Ontario, CANADA M5J 2J3
Telephone: (416) 366-1990
Recruiter Classification: Retained; **Lowest/Average Salary:**
$90,000/$90,000; **Industry Concentration:** Financial
Services, Venture Capital; **Function Concentration:**
Finance/Accounting

Wilson, William F. — *Consultant*
Tyler & Company
Chadds Ford Business Campus
Brandywine Two Building, Suite 208
Chadds Ford, PA 19317-9667
Telephone: (610) 558-6100
Recruiter Classification: Retained; **Lowest/Average Salary:**
$75,000/$90,000; **Industry Concentration:** Insurance;
Function Concentration: Generalist

Wingate, Mary — *Associate*
Source Services Corporation
5429 LBJ Freeway, Suite 275
Dallas, TX 75240
Telephone: (214) 387-1600
Recruiter Classification: Contingency; **Lowest/Average
Salary:** $30,000/$50,000; **Industry Concentration:** Financial
Services; **Function Concentration:** Engineering,
Finance/Accounting

Winitz, Joel — *President*
GSW Consulting Group, Inc.
401 B Street
Suite 340
San Diego, CA 92101
Telephone: (619) 696-7900
Recruiter Classification: Retained; **Lowest/Average Salary:**
$60,000/$90,000; **Industry Concentration:** Generalist with a
primary focus in Financial Services; **Function Concentration:**
Generalist with a primary focus in Engineering,
Finance/Accounting, General Management, Marketing,
Research and Development, Sales

Winitz, Marla — *Vice President*
GSW Consulting Group, Inc.
401 B Street
Suite 340
San Diego, CA 92101
Telephone: (619) 696-7900
Recruiter Classification: Retained; **Lowest/Average Salary:**
$60,000/$90,000; **Industry Concentration:** Generalist with a
primary focus in Financial Services; **Function Concentration:**
Generalist with a primary focus in Engineering,
Finance/Accounting, General Management, Marketing,
Research and Development, Sales

Winkowski, Stephen — *Associate*
Source Services Corporation
20 Burlington Mall Road, Suite 405
Burlington, MA 01803
Telephone: (617) 272-5000
Recruiter Classification: Contingency; **Lowest/Average Salary:**
$30,000/$50,000; **Industry Concentration:** Financial Services;
Function Concentration: Engineering, Finance/Accounting

Winnicki, Kimberly — *Associate*
Source Services Corporation
120 East Baltimore Street, Suite 1950
Baltimore, MD 21202
Telephone: (410) 727-4050
Recruiter Classification: Contingency; **Lowest/Average Salary:**
$30,000/$50,000; **Industry Concentration:** Financial Services;
Function Concentration: Engineering, Finance/Accounting

Winograd, Glenn — *Vice President/Division
Manager*
Criterion Executive Search, Inc.
5420 Bay Center Drive, Suite 101
Tampa, FL 33609-3402
Telephone: (813) 286-2000
Recruiter Classification: Contingency; **Lowest/Average Salary:**
$40,000/$90,000; **Industry Concentration:** Generalist with a
primary focus in Financial Services, Insurance; **Function
Concentration:** Generalist with a primary focus in Engineering,
Finance/Accounting, General Management, Research and
Development, Women/Minorities

Winston, Dale — *President*
Battalia Winston International
300 Park Avenue
New York, NY 10022
Telephone: (212) 308-8080
Recruiter Classification: Retained; **Lowest/Average Salary:**
$90,000/$90,000; **Industry Concentration:** Generalist with a
primary focus in Venture Capital; **Function Concentration:**
Generalist with a primary focus in Engineering,
Finance/Accounting, General Management, Human Resources,
Marketing, Research and Development, Sales,
Women/Minorities

Wirtshafter, Linda — *Senior Associate*
Grant Cooper and Associates
795 Office Parkway, Suite 117
St. Louis, MO 63141
Telephone: (314) 567-4690
Recruiter Classification: Retained; **Lowest/Average Salary:**
$60,000/$90,000; **Industry Concentration:** Generalist with a
primary focus in Financial Services; **Function Concentration:**
Generalist

Wisch, Steven C. — *Director*
MB Inc. Interim Executive Division
505 Fifth Avenue
New York, NY 10017
Telephone: (212) 661-4937
Recruiter Classification: Executive Temporary; **Lowest/Average
Salary:** $50,000/$90,000; **Industry Concentration:** Generalist
with a primary focus in Financial Services; **Function
Concentration:** Finance/Accounting, General Management,
Human Resources, Marketing, Sales

Wise, J. Herbert — *Partner*
Sandhurst Associates
4851 LBJ Freeway, Suite 601
Dallas, TX 75244
Telephone: (212) 458-1212
Recruiter Classification: Retained; **Lowest/Average Salary:**
$75,000/$90,000; **Industry Concentration:** Generalist with a
primary focus in Financial Services, Insurance; **Function
Concentration:** Generalist with a primary focus in
Finance/Accounting, Human Resources, Marketing,
Sales

Witzgall, William — *Associate*
Source Services Corporation
525 Vine Street, Suite 2250
Cincinnati, OH 45202
Telephone: (513) 651-3303
Recruiter Classification: Contingency; **Lowest/Average
Salary:** $30,000/$50,000; **Industry Concentration:** Financial
Services; **Function Concentration:** Engineering,
Finance/Accounting

Wold, Ted W. — *Secretary*
Hyde Danforth Wold & Co.
5950 Berkshire Lane, Suite 1600
Dallas, TX 75225
Telephone: (214) 691-5966
Recruiter Classification: Retained; **Lowest/Average Salary:**
$50,000/$75,000; **Industry Concentration:** Generalist
with a primary focus in Financial Services, Venture Capital;
Function Concentration: Generalist with a primary
focus in Administration, Finance/Accounting, Human
Resources, Marketing, Research and
Development

Wolf, Donald — *Associate*
Source Services Corporation
111 Founders Plaza, Suite 1501E
Hartford, CT 06108
Telephone: (860) 528-0300
Recruiter Classification: Contingency; **Lowest/Average
Salary:** $30,000/$50,000; **Industry Concentration:** Financial
Services; **Function Concentration:** Engineering,
Finance/Accounting

Wolf, Stephen M. — *Principal*
Byron Leonard International, Inc.
2659 Townsgate Road, Suite 100
Westlake Village, CA 91361
Telephone: (805) 373-7500
Recruiter Classification: Retained; **Lowest/Average Salary:**
$60,000/$90,000; **Industry Concentration:** Generalist with a
primary focus in Financial Services, Insurance; **Function
Concentration:** Generalist with a primary focus in
Administration, Finance/Accounting, General Management,
Human Resources, Marketing, Research and Development,
Sales

Wolfe, Peter — *Managing Director*
Source Services Corporation
4200 West Cypress Street, Suite 101
Tampa, FL 33607
Telephone: (813) 879-2221
Recruiter Classification: Contingency; **Lowest/Average
Salary:** $30,000/$50,000; **Industry Concentration:** Financial
Services; **Function Concentration:** Engineering,
Finance/Accounting

Womack, Joseph — *Vice President*
The Bankers Group
10 South Riverside Plaza, Suite 1424
Chicago, IL 60606
Telephone: (312) 930-9456
Recruiter Classification: Contingency; **Lowest/Average
Salary:** $50,000/$75,000; **Industry Concentration:** Generalist
with a primary focus in Financial Services, Insurance, Venture
Capital; **Function Concentration:** Generalist with a primary
focus in Administration, Finance/Accounting, General
Management, Human Resources, Marketing, Sales,
Women/Minorities

Wood, Elizabeth — *Recruiter*
Highland Search Group
565 Fifth Avenue, 22nd Floor
New York, NY 10017
Telephone: (212) 328-1113
Recruiter Classification: Retained; **Lowest/Average Salary:**
$90,000/$90,000; **Industry Concentration:** Financial Services,
Insurance, Venture Capital; **Function Concentration:** Generalist
with a primary focus in Administration, Finance/Accounting,
General Management, Human Resources, Sales,
Women/Minorities

Wood, Gary — *Associate*
Source Services Corporation
3 Summit Park Drive, Suite 550
Independence, OH 44131
Telephone: (216) 328-5900
Recruiter Classification: Contingency; **Lowest/Average
Salary:** $30,000/$50,000; **Industry Concentration:** Financial
Services; **Function Concentration:** Engineering,
Finance/Accounting

Wood, John S. — *Consultant*
Egon Zehnder International Inc.
350 Park Avenue
New York, NY 10022
Telephone: (212) 838-9199
Recruiter Classification: Retained; **Lowest/Average Salary:**
$90,000/$90,000; **Industry Concentration:** Generalist with a
primary focus in Financial Services; **Function Concentration:**
Generalist

Wood, Milton M. — *President*
M. Wood Company
10 North Dearborn Street, Suite 700
Chicago, IL 60602
Telephone: (312) 368-0633
Recruiter Classification: Retained; **Lowest/Average Salary:**
$60,000/$90,000; **Industry Concentration:** Generalist with a
primary focus in Financial Services, Insurance; **Function
Concentration:** Generalist with a primary focus in General
Management, Human Resources, Marketing, Sales

Wood, Nicole — *Manager*
Corporate Careers, Inc.
1500 Quail Street, Suite 290
Newport Beach, CA 92660
Telephone: (714) 476-7007
Recruiter Classification: Contingency; **Lowest/Average Salary:**
$30,000/$60,000; **Industry Concentration:** Financial Services;
Function Concentration: General Management, Sales

Woodmansee, Bruce J. — *Partner*
Tully/Woodmansee International, Inc.
7720 Rivers Edge Drive, Suite 101
Columbus, OH 43235
Telephone: (614) 844-5480
Recruiter Classification: Retained; **Lowest/Average Salary:**
$60,000/$90,000; **Industry Concentration:** Generalist with a
primary focus in Financial Services, Insurance; **Function
Concentration:** Generalist with a primary focus in Engineering,
Finance/Accounting, General Management, Human Resources,
Marketing, Sales

Woods, Craig — *Associate*
Source Services Corporation
One Park Plaza, Suite 560
Irvine, CA 92714
Telephone: (714) 660-1666
Recruiter Classification: Contingency; **Lowest/Average Salary:**
$30,000/$50,000; **Industry Concentration:** Financial Services;
Function Concentration: Engineering, Finance/Accounting

Woodworth, Gail — *President*
Woodworth International Group
620 SW 5th Avenue, Suite 1225
Portland, OR 97204
Telephone: (503) 225-5000
Recruiter Classification: Retained; **Lowest/Average Salary:**
$60,000/$90,000; **Industry Concentration:** Generalist with a
primary focus in Financial Services, Insurance, Venture Capital;
Function Concentration: Generalist with a primary focus in
Engineering, Finance/Accounting, General Management,
Human Resources, Marketing, Research and Development,
Sales

Wooldridge, Jeff — *Consultant*
Ray & Berndtson
Texas Commerce Tower
2200 Ross Avenue, Suite 4500W
Dallas, TX 75201
Telephone: (214) 969-7620
Recruiter Classification: Retained; **Lowest/Average Salary:**
$90,000/$90,000; **Industry Concentration:** Generalist with a
primary focus in Financial Services, Insurance; **Function
Concentration:** Generalist with a primary focus in
Administration, Finance/Accounting, General Management,
Human Resources, Marketing, Research and Development,
Sales, Women/Minorities

Wooller, Edmund A.M. — *President*
Windsor International
3350 Cumberland Circle, Suite 1900
Atlanta, GA 30339-3363
Telephone: (770) 438-2300
Recruiter Classification: Retained; **Lowest/Average Salary:**
$50,000/$75,000; **Industry Concentration:** Generalist with a
primary focus in Financial Services, Insurance; **Function
Concentration:** Generalist with a primary focus in
Administration, Engineering, Finance/Accounting, General
Management, Marketing, Sales

Woomer, Jerome — *Associate*
Source Services Corporation
7730 East Bellview Avenue, Suite 302
Englewood, CO 80111
Telephone: (303) 773-3700
Recruiter Classification: Contingency; **Lowest/Average Salary:**
$30,000/$50,000; **Industry Concentration:** Financial Services;
Function Concentration: Engineering, Finance/Accounting

Workman, David — *Associate*
Source Services Corporation
2850 National City Tower
Louisville, KY 40202
Telephone: (502) 581-9900
Recruiter Classification: Contingency; **Lowest/Average
Salary:** $30,000/$50,000; **Industry Concentration:** Financial
Services; **Function Concentration:** Engineering,
Finance/Accounting

Wright, A. Leo — *Vice President - Owensboro*
The Hindman Company
Corporate Center
Fourth and Frederica
Owensboro, KY 42301
Telephone: (502) 688-0010
Recruiter Classification: Retained; **Lowest/Average Salary:**
$50,000/$90,000; **Industry Concentration:** Generalist with a
primary focus in Financial Services; **Function Concentration:**
Generalist with a primary focus in Administration, Engineering,
Finance/Accounting, General Management, Human Resources,
Marketing, Sales

Wright, Carl A.J. — *President*
A.J. Burton Group, Inc.
120 East Baltimore Street, Suite 2220
Baltimore, MD 21202
Telephone: (410) 752-5244
Recruiter Classification: Contingency, Executive Temporary;
Lowest/Average Salary: $40,000/$75,000; **Industry
Concentration:** Generalist with a primary focus in Financial
Services, Insurance; **Function Concentration:** Generalist with a
primary focus in Administration, Finance/Accounting, General
Management, Human Resources

Wright, Charles D. — *Senior Vice President*
Goodrich & Sherwood Associates, Inc.
401 Merritt Seven Corporate Park
Norwalk, CT 06851
Telephone: (203) 847-2525
Recruiter Classification: Retained; **Lowest/Average Salary:**
$60,000/$90,000; **Industry Concentration:** Generalist with a
primary focus in Financial Services, Insurance, Venture Capital;
Function Concentration: Generalist with a primary focus in
Administration, Finance/Accounting, General Management,
Human Resources, Marketing, Sales

Wright, Leslie — *Vice President and Director of Research*
The Stevenson Group of New Jersey
560 Sylvan Avenue
Englewood Cliffs, NJ 07632
Telephone: (201) 568-1900
Recruiter Classification: Retained; **Lowest/Average Salary:** $75,000/$90,000; **Industry Concentration:** Generalist with a primary focus in Financial Services; **Function Concentration:** Generalist with a primary focus in Finance/Accounting, General Management, Human Resources, Marketing, Sales

Wycoff-Viola, Amy — *Associate*
Source Services Corporation
150 South Wacker Drive, Suite 400
Chicago, IL 60606
Telephone: (312) 346-7000
Recruiter Classification: Contingency; **Lowest/Average Salary:** $30,000/$50,000; **Industry Concentration:** Financial Services; **Function Concentration:** Engineering, Finance/Accounting

Wylie, Pamela — *Executive Recruiter*
M.A. Churchill & Associates, Inc.
Morelyn Plaza #307
1111 Street Road
Southampton, PA 18966
Telephone: (215) 953-0300
Recruiter Classification: Retained; **Lowest/Average Salary:** $50,000/$75,000; **Industry Concentration:** Financial Services, Insurance; **Function Concentration:** Marketing, Research and Development, Sales

Wynkoop, Mary — *Vice President*
Tyler & Company
1000 Abernathy Road
Suite 1400
Atlanta, GA 30328-5655
Telephone: (770) 396-3939
Recruiter Classification: Retained; **Lowest/Average Salary:** $75,000/$90,000; **Industry Concentration:** Insurance; **Function Concentration:** Generalist

Yaekle, Gary — *Consultant*
Tully/Woodmansee International, Inc.
7720 Rivers Edge Drive, Suite 101
Columbus, OH 43235
Telephone: (614) 587-7366
Recruiter Classification: Retained; **Lowest/Average Salary:** $60,000/$90,000; **Industry Concentration:** Generalist with a primary focus in Financial Services, Insurance; **Function Concentration:** Generalist with a primary focus in Engineering, Finance/Accounting, General Management, Human Resources, Marketing, Sales

Yeaton, Robert — *Associate*
Source Services Corporation
1500 West Park Drive, Suite 390
Westborough, MA 01581
Telephone: (508) 366-2600
Recruiter Classification: Contingency; **Lowest/Average Salary:** $30,000/$50,000; **Industry Concentration:** Financial Services; **Function Concentration:** Engineering, Finance/Accounting

Yen, Maggie Yeh Ching — *Consultant*
Ray & Berndtson
One Park Plaza, Suite 420
Irvine, CA 92614
Telephone: (714) 476-8844
Recruiter Classification: Retained; **Lowest/Average Salary:** $90,000/$90,000; **Industry Concentration:** Generalist with a primary focus in Financial Services, Insurance; **Function Concentration:** Generalist with a primary focus in Administration, Finance/Accounting, General Management, Human Resources, Marketing, Research and Development, Sales, Women/Minorities

Young, Nick — *Director*
Spencer Stuart
277 Park Avenue, 29th Floor
New York, NY 10172
Telephone: (212) 336-0200
Recruiter Classification: Retained; **Lowest/Average Salary:** $50,000/$75,000; **Industry Concentration:** Financial Services; **Function Concentration:** Finance/Accounting

Youngberg, David — *Managing Director*
Source Services Corporation
1233 North Mayfair Road, Suite 300
Milwaukee, WI 53226
Telephone: (414) 774-6700
Recruiter Classification: Contingency; **Lowest/Average Salary:** $30,000/$50,000; **Industry Concentration:** Financial Services; **Function Concentration:** Engineering, Finance/Accounting

Yungerberg, Steven — *President*
Steven Yungerberg Associates Inc.
P.O. Box 458
Minneapolis, MN 55331-0458
Telephone: (612) 470-2288
Recruiter Classification: Retained; **Lowest/Average Salary:** $75,000/$90,000; **Industry Concentration:** Generalist with a primary focus in Financial Services, Insurance; **Function Concentration:** Generalist with a primary focus in Finance/Accounting, General Management, Human Resources, Marketing, Sales, Women/Minorities

Zadfar, Maryanne — *Vice President*
The Thomas Tucker Company
425 California Street, Suite 2502
San Francisco, CA 94104
Telephone: (415) 693-5900
Recruiter Classification: Retained; **Lowest/Average Salary:** $90,000/$90,000; **Industry Concentration:** Generalist with a primary focus in Venture Capital; **Function Concentration:** Engineering, Human Resources, Research and Development

Zaffrann, Craig S. — *Vice President*
P.J. Murphy & Associates, Inc.
735 North Water Street
Milwaukee, WI 53202
Telephone: (414) 277-9777
Recruiter Classification: Retained; **Lowest/Average Salary:** $60,000/$90,000; **Industry Concentration:** Generalist with a primary focus in Financial Services; **Function Concentration:** Generalist with a primary focus in Administration, Finance/Accounting, General Management, Human Resources, Marketing, Sales

Zahradka, James F. — *Vice President*
P.J. Murphy & Associates, Inc.
735 North Water Street
Milwaukee, WI 53202
Telephone: (414) 277-9777
Recruiter Classification: Retained; **Lowest/Average Salary:**
$60,000/$90,000; **Industry Concentration:** Generalist
with a primary focus in Financial Services; **Function
Concentration:** Generalist with a primary focus in
Administration, Finance/Accounting, General
Management, Human Resources, Marketing,
Sales

Zak, Adam — *President*
Adams & Associates International
463-D W. Russell Street
Barrington, IL 60010
Telephone: (847) 304-5300
Recruiter Classification: Retained; **Lowest/Average Salary:**
$75,000/$75,000; **Industry Concentration:** Generalist with a
primary focus in Venture Capital; **Function Concentration:**
General Management

Zaleta, Andy R. — *Vice President/Managing
Director*
A.T. Kearney, Inc.
One Memorial Drive, 14th Floor
Cambridge, MA 02142
Telephone: (617) 374-2600
Recruiter Classification: Retained; **Lowest/Average Salary:**
$90,000/$90,000; **Industry Concentration:** Generalist
with a primary focus in Financial Services; **Function
Concentration:** Generalist with a primary focus in
Engineering, Finance/Accounting, General
Management

Zamborsky, George — *Managing Partner*
Boyden
12444 Powerscourt Drive
Suite 301
St. Louis, MO 63131
Telephone: (314) 984-2590
Recruiter Classification: Retained; **Lowest/Average Salary:**
$90,000/$90,000; **Industry Concentration:** Generalist
with a primary focus in Financial Services; **Function
Concentration:** Generalist with a primary focus in
Engineering, Finance/Accounting, General
Management, Human Resources, Marketing,
Research and Development, Sales, Women/
Minorities

Zaslav, Debra M. — *Principal*
Telford, Adams & Alexander/Telford & Co., Inc.
650 Town Center Drive, Suite 850A
Costa Mesa, CA 92626
Telephone: (714) 850-4354
Recruiter Classification: Retained; **Lowest/Average Salary:**
$90,000/$90,000; **Industry Concentration:** Generalist
with a primary focus in Financial Services, Insurance;
Function Concentration: Generalist with a primary
focus in Administration, Finance/Accounting, General
Management, Human Resources, Marketing,
Sales

Zavala, Lorenzo — *Executive Director*
Russell Reynolds Associates, Inc.
Arquimedes 130-3
Colonia Polanco
Mexico City, D.F., MEXICO 11560
Telephone: (525) 281-0440
Recruiter Classification: Retained; **Lowest/Average Salary:**
$90,000/$90,000; **Industry Concentration:** Generalist with a
primary focus in Financial Services; **Function Concentration:**
Generalist

Zavat, Marc — *Senior Consultant*
Ryan, Miller & Associates Inc.
790 East Colorado, Suite 506
Pasadena, CA 91101
Telephone: (818) 568-3100
Recruiter Classification: Contingency; **Lowest/Average Salary:**
$40,000/$75,000; **Industry Concentration:** Financial Services;
Function Concentration: Finance/Accounting

Zavrel, Mark — *Associate*
Source Services Corporation
8614 Westwood Center, Suite 750
Vienna, VA 22182
Telephone: (703) 790-5610
Recruiter Classification: Contingency; **Lowest/Average
Salary:** $30,000/$50,000; **Industry Concentration:** Financial
Services; **Function Concentration:** Engineering,
Finance/Accounting

Zay, Thomas C. — *Managing Director*
Boyden/Zay & Company
333 Clay Street
Suite 3810
Houston, TX 77002-4102
Telephone: (713) 655-0123
Recruiter Classification: Retained; **Lowest/Average Salary:**
$90,000/$90,000; **Industry Concentration:** Generalist
with a primary focus in Financial Services, Insurance;
Function Concentration: Generalist with a
primary focus in Finance/Accounting,
General Management, Human Resources,
Marketing

Zay, Thomas C. — *President/Consultant*
Boyden/Zay & Company
Two Midtown Plaza, Suite 1740
1360 Peachtree Street, NE
Atlanta, GA 30309-3214
Telephone: (404) 876-9986
Recruiter Classification: Retained; **Lowest/Average Salary:**
$90,000/$90,000; **Industry Concentration:** Generalist
with a primary focus in Financial Services; **Function
Concentration:** Generalist with a primary focus in
Engineering, General Management, Marketing,
Sales

Zegas, Jeffrey — *Managing Principal*
Zurick, Davis & Co., Inc.
Ten State Street
Woburn, MA 01801
Telephone: (617) 938-1975
Recruiter Classification: Retained; **Lowest/Average Salary:**
$60,000/$90,000; **Industry Concentration:** Venture Capital;
Function Concentration: Generalist

Zegel, Gary — *Associate*
Source Services Corporation
155 Federal Street, Suite 410
Boston, MA 02110
Telephone: (617) 482-8211
Recruiter Classification: Contingency; **Lowest/Average Salary:** $30,000/$50,000; **Industry Concentration:** Financial Services; **Function Concentration:** Engineering, Finance/Accounting

Zetto, Kathryn — *Vice President/Partner*
Seco & Zetto Associates, Inc.
P.O. Box 225
Harrington Park, NJ 07640
Telephone: (201) 784-0674
Recruiter Classification: Contingency; **Lowest/Average Salary:** $60,000/$60,000; **Industry Concentration:** Generalist with a primary focus in Financial Services; **Function Concentration:** Generalist with a primary focus in Marketing, Sales, Women/Minorities

Zila, Laurie M. — *Manager Client Services*
Princeton Entrepreneurial Resources
600 Alexander Road, P.O. Box 2051
Princeton, NJ 08543
Telephone: (609) 243-0010
Recruiter Classification: Executive Temporary; **Lowest/Average Salary:** $75,000/$90,000; **Industry Concentration:** Generalist with a primary focus in Venture Capital; **Function Concentration:** Generalist with a primary focus in Finance/Accounting, General Management, Human Resources, Marketing

Zimbal, Mark — *Associate*
Source Services Corporation
1233 North Mayfair Road, Suite 300
Milwaukee, WI 53226
Telephone: (414) 774-6700
Recruiter Classification: Contingency; **Lowest/Average Salary:** $30,000/$50,000; **Industry Concentration:** Financial Services; **Function Concentration:** Engineering, Finance/Accounting

Zimmerman, Joan C. — *Executive Vice President*
G.Z. Stephens Inc.
One World Trade Center
Suite 1527
New York, NY 10048
Telephone: (212) 321-3040
Recruiter Classification: Retained; **Lowest/Average Salary:** $90,000/$90,000; **Industry Concentration:** Financial Services; **Function Concentration:** Generalist

Zimont, Scott — *Associate*
Source Services Corporation
520 Post Oak Boulevard, Suite 700
Houston, TX 77027
Telephone: (713) 439-1077
Recruiter Classification: Contingency; **Lowest/Average Salary:** $30,000/$50,000; **Industry Concentration:** Financial Services; **Function Concentration:** Engineering, Finance/Accounting

Zivic, Janis M. — *Director*
Spencer Stuart
525 Market Street, Suite 3700
San Francisco, CA 94105
Telephone: (415) 495-4141
Recruiter Classification: Retained; **Lowest/Average Salary:** $90,000/$90,000; **Industry Concentration:** Generalist with a primary focus in Financial Services; **Function Concentration:** Generalist with a primary focus in Administration, Engineering, Finance/Accounting, General Management, Human Resources, Research and Development, Women/Minorities

Zona, Henry F. — *President*
Zona & Associates, Inc.
26 Broadway, Suite 400
New York, NY 10004
Telephone: (212) 837-7878
Recruiter Classification: Contingency; **Lowest/Average Salary:** $50,000/$60,000; **Industry Concentration:** Financial Services, Insurance; **Function Concentration:** Generalist with a primary focus in Administration, Finance/Accounting, General Management, Human Resources, Marketing, Research and Development, Sales

Zonis, Hildy R. — *Manager Placement*
Accountants Executive Search
535 Fifth Avenue, Suite 1200
New York, NY 10017
Telephone: (212) 682-5900
Recruiter Classification: Executive Temporary; **Lowest/Average Salary:** $40,000/$60,000; **Industry Concentration:** Generalist with a primary focus in Financial Services; **Function Concentration:** Finance/Accounting

Zucker, Nancy — *Executive Recruiter*
Maximum Management Corp.
420 Lexington Avenue
Suite 2016
New York, NY 10170
Telephone: (212) 867-4646
Recruiter Classification: Contingency, Executive Temporary; **Lowest/Average Salary:** $30,000/$75,000; **Industry Concentration:** Generalist with a primary focus in Financial Services, Insurance; **Function Concentration:** Human Resources

Zwell, Michael — *President and CEO*
Zwell International
300 South Wacker Drive, Suite 650
Chicago, IL 60606
Telephone: (312) 663-3737
Recruiter Classification: Retained; **Lowest/Average Salary:** $75,000/$90,000; **Industry Concentration:** Generalist with a primary focus in Financial Services, Insurance, Venture Capital; **Function Concentration:** Generalist with a primary focus in Engineering, Finance/Accounting, General Management, Human Resources, Marketing, Sales

Industry Specialization Index by Recruiter

Industry Specialization Index by Recruiter

This index is arranged into 4 business sectors, including the generalist category, and provides a breakdown of the primary and secondary lines of industry specializations of each executive recruiter. Many recruiters have multiple listings in this index depending on the various specializations in which they are engaged. *Recruiters listed in the generalist category serve all industry specializations.*

1. Generalist
2. Financial Services

3. Insurance
4. Venture Capital

1. Generalist

Abbatiello, Christine Murphy — *Winter, Wyman & Company*
Abbott, Peter D. — *The Abbott Group, Inc.*
Abell, Vincent W. — *MSI International*
Abernathy, Donald E. — *Don Richard Associates of Charlotte*
Adams, Amy — *Richard, Wayne and Roberts*
Adams, Jeffrey C. — *Telford, Adams & Alexander/Jeffrey C. Adams & Co., Inc.*
Adler, Louis S. — *CJA - The Adler Group*
Akin, J.R. "Jack" — *J.R. Akin & Company Inc.*
Alexander, John T. — *Telford, Adams & Alexander*
Allen, Jean E. — *Lamalie Amrop International*
Allen, Wade H. — *Cendea Connection International*
Allen, William L. — *The Hindman Company*
Altreuter, Rose — *The ALTCO Group*
Ambler, Peter W. — *Peter W. Ambler Company*
Anderson, Maria H. — *Barton Associates, Inc.*
Anderson, Richard — *Grant Cooper and Associates*
Anderson, Shawn — *Temporary Accounting Personnel, Inc.*
Anderson, Steve — *CPS Inc.*
Anderson, Terry — *Intech Summit Group, Inc.*
Andujo, Michele M. — *Chrisman & Company, Incorporated*
Archer, Sandra F. — *Ryan, Miller & Associates Inc.*
Argentin, Jo — *Executive Placement Consultants, Inc.*
Aronin, Michael — *Fisher-Todd Associates*
Ascher, Susan P. — *The Ascher Group*
Aston, Kathy — *Marra Peters & Partners*
Atkinson, S. Graham — *Raymond Karsan Associates*
Attell, Harold — *A.E. Feldman Associates*
Atwood, Barrie — *The Abbott Group, Inc.*
Aubin, Richard E. — *Aubin International Inc.*
Axelrod, Nancy R. — *A.T. Kearney, Inc.*
Aydelotte, G. Thomas — *Ingram & Aydelotte Inc./I-I-C Partners*
Badger, Fred H. — *The Badger Group*
Baeder, Jeremy — *Executive Manning Corporation*
Bailey, Paul — *Austin-McGregor International*
Baje, Sarah — *Innovative Search Group, LLC*
Baker, Gary M. — *Cochran, Cochran & Yale, Inc.*
Baker, Gary M. — *Temporary Accounting Personnel, Inc.*
Baker, Gerry — *A.T. Kearney, Inc.*
Balbone, Rich — *Executive Manning Corporation*
Balch, Randy — *CPS Inc.*
Baldock, Robert G. — *Ray & Berndtson/Lovas Stanley*
Ballantine, Caroline B. — *Heidrick & Struggles, Inc.*
Baltaglia, Michael — *Cochran, Cochran & Yale, Inc.*
Barbour, Mary Beth — *Tully/Woodmansee International, Inc.*
Barger, H. Carter — *Barger & Sargeant, Inc.*
Barlow, Ken H. — *The Cherbonnier Group, Inc.*
Barnes, Gregory — *Korn/Ferry International*
Barnes, Richard E. — *Barnes Development Group, LLC*
Barnes, Roanne L. — *Barnes Development Group, LLC*

Barnette, Dennis A. — *Heidrick & Struggles, Inc.*
Barnum, Toni M. — *Stone Murphy & Olson*
Barrett, J. David — *Heidrick & Struggles, Inc.*
Barton, Gary R. — *Barton Associates, Inc.*
Bason, Maurice L. — *Bason Associates Inc.*
Bass, M. Lynn — *Ray & Berndtson*
Bassler, John — *Korn/Ferry International*
Battles, Jonathan — *Korn/Ferry International*
Bauman, Martin H. — *Martin H. Bauman Associates, Inc.*
Beall, Charles P. — *Beall & Company, Inc.*
Bearman, Linda — *Grant Cooper and Associates*
Beaudin, Elizabeth C. — *Callan Associates, Ltd.*
Beaver, Bentley H. — *The Onstott Group, Inc.*
Beckvold, John B. — *Atlantic Search Group, Inc.*
Beer, John — *People Management Northeast Incorporated*
Beeson, William B. — *Lawrence-Leiter & Co. Management Conultants*
Belden, Charles P. — *Raymond Karsan Associates*
Belin, Jean — *Boyden*
Bell, Lloyd W. — *O'Brien & Bell*
Bell, Michael — *Spencer Stuart*
Bellano, Robert W. — *Stanton Chase International*
Bender, Alan — *Bender Executive Search*
Bennett, Jo — *Battalia Winston International*
Benson, Kate — *Rene Plessner Associates, Inc.*
Beran, Helena — *Michael J. Cavanagh and Associates*
Berk-Levine, Margo — *MB Inc. Interim Executive Division*
Berman, Mitchell — *Carlyle Group*
Berry, Harold B. — *The Hindman Company*
Bettick, Michael J. — *A.J. Burton Group, Inc.*
Biggins, J. Veronica — *Heidrick & Struggles, Inc.*
Billington, William H. — *Spriggs & Company, Inc.*
Birkhead, Linda — *Zwell International*
Bishop, Barbara — *The Executive Source*
Bladon, Andrew — *Don Richard Associates of Tampa, Inc.*
Bliley, Jerry — *Spencer Stuart*
Bloomer, James E. — *L.W. Foote Company*
Blumenthal, Paula — *J.P. Canon Associates*
Boel, Werner — *The Dalley Hewitt Company*
Bogansky, Amy — *Conex Incorporated*
Bohn, Steve J. — *MSI International*
Bonnell, William R. — *Bonnell Associates Ltd.*
Borland, James — *Goodrich & Sherwood Associates, Inc.*
Bormann, Cindy Ann — *MSI International*
Bourrie, Sharon D. — *Chartwell Partners International, Inc.*
Bovich, Maryann C. — *Higdon Prince Inc.*
Bowden, Otis H. — *BowdenGlobal, Ltd.*
Bowen, Tad — *Executive Search International*
Boyle, Russell E. — *Egon Zehnder International Inc.*
Bradley, Dalena — *Woodworth International Group*
Bradshaw, Monte — *Christian & Timbers*
Brady, Dick — *William Guy & Associates*
Brady, Robert — *CPS Inc.*
Brandeis, Richard — *CPS Inc.*
Brandenburg, David — *Professional Staffing Consultants*
Bratches, Howard — *Thorndike Deland Associates*

Brieger, Steve — *Thorne, Brieger Associates Inc.*

Brindise, Michael J. — *Dynamic Search Systems, Inc.*

Brinson, Robert — *MSI International*

Britt, Stephen — *Keith Bagg & Associates Inc.*

Broadhurst, Austin — *Lamalie Amrop International*

Brocaglia, Joyce — *Alta Associates, Inc.*

Brophy, Melissa — *Maximum Management Corp.*

Brown, Charlene N. — *Accent on Achievement, Inc.*

Brown, Larry C. — *Horton International*

Brown, Lawrence Anthony — *MSI International*

Brown, S. Ross — *Egon Zehnder International Inc.*

Brown, Steffan — *Woodworth International Group*

Brudno, Robert J. — *Savoy Partners, Ltd.*

Bruno, Deborah F. — *The Hindman Company*

Bryant, Richard D. — *Bryant Associates, Inc.*

Bryant, Shari G. — *Bryant Associates, Inc.*

Brzezinski, Ronald T. — *Callan Associates, Ltd.*

Buckles, Donna — *Cochran, Cochran & Yale, Inc.*

Buggy, Linda — *Bonnell Associates Ltd.*

Bump, Gerald J. — *D.E. Foster Partners Inc.*

Burchard, Stephen R. — *Burchard & Associates, Inc.*

Burden, Gene — *The Cherbonnier Group, Inc.*

Burke, John — *The Experts*

Burke, Karen A. — *Mazza & Riley, Inc. (a Korn/Ferry International affiliate)*

Burkhill, John — *The Talley Group*

Burnett-Stohner, Brendan G. — *Sullivan & Company*

Burns, Alan — *The Enns Partners Inc.*

Burns, Terence N. — *D.E. Foster Partners Inc.*

Butterfass, Stanley — *Butterfass, Pepe & MacCallan Inc.*

Byrnes, Thomas A. — *The Search Alliance, Inc.*

Caldwell, C. Douglas — *The Caldwell Partners Amrop International*

Calivas, Kay — *A.J. Burton Group, Inc.*

Call, David — *Cochran, Cochran & Yale, Inc.*

Callan, Robert M. — *Callan Associates, Ltd.*

Cameron, James W. — *Cameron Consulting*

Campbell, Patricia A. — *The Onstott Group, Inc.*

Campbell, Robert Scott — *Wellington Management Group*

Campbell, Robert Scott — *Wellington Management Group*

Campbell, Thomas J. — *Heidrick & Struggles, Inc.*

Campbell, W. Ross — *Egon Zehnder International Inc.*

Cannon, Alexis — *Richard, Wayne and Roberts*

Capizzi, Karen — *Cochran, Cochran & Yale, Inc.*

Carideo, Joseph — *Thorndike Deland Associates*

Carrington, Timothy — *Korn/Ferry International*

Carro, Carl R. — *Executive Search Consultants International, Inc.*

Carrott, Gregory T. — *Egon Zehnder International Inc.*

Carter, Jon F. — *Egon Zehnder International Inc.*

Cary, Con — *Cary & Associates*

Cashen, Anthony B. — *Lamalie Amrop International*

Castillo, Eduardo — *Korn/Ferry International*

Caudill, Nancy — *Webb, Johnson Associates, Inc.*

Cavanagh, Michael J. — *Michael J. Cavanagh and Associates*

Celenza, Catherine — *CPS Inc.*

Chamberlin, Brooks T. — *Korn/Ferry International*

Chamberlin, Joan — *William Guy & Associates*

Chamberlin, Michael A. — *Tower Consultants, Ltd.*

Champion, Geoffrey — *Korn/Ferry International*

Chan, Margaret — *Webb, Johnson Associates, Inc.*

Chappell, Peter — *Robertson & Associates*

Chappell, Peter — *The Bankers Group*

Charles, Ronald D. — *The Caldwell Partners Amrop International*

Chauvin, Ralph A. — *The Caldwell Partners Amrop International*

Cherbonnier, L. Michael — *TCG International, Inc.*

Cherbonnier, L. Michael — *The Cherbonnier Group, Inc.*

Chndler, Brad J. — *Furst Group/MPI*

Cho, Ui — *Richard, Wayne and Roberts*

Chrisman, Timothy R. — *Chrisman & Company, Incorporated*

Christenson, H. Alan — *Christenson & Hutchison*

Christian, Philip — *Ray & Berndtson*

Christiansen, Amy — *CPS Inc.*

Christiansen, Doug — *CPS Inc.*

Citarella, Richard A. — *A.T. Kearney, Inc.*

Citrin, James M. — *Spencer Stuart*

Cizek, John T. — *Cizek Associates, Inc.*

Cizek, Marti J. — *Cizek Associates, Inc.*

Clarey, William A. — *Preng & Associates, Inc.*

Clark, James — *CPS Inc.*

Clark, Julie — *Corporate Recruiters Ltd.*

Clarke Smith, Jamie — *Kaye-Bassman International Corp.*

Clauhsen, Elizabeth A. — *Savoy Partners, Ltd.*

Clayton, Fred J. — *Berkhemer Clayton Incorporated*

Cloutier, Gisela — *Dinte Resources, Inc.*

Cochran, Scott P. — *The Badger Group*

Cohen, Michael R. — *Intech Summit Group, Inc.*

Cohen, Robert C. — *Intech Summit Group, Inc.*

Coleman, J. Gregory — *Korn/Ferry International*

Coleman, J. Kevin — *J. Kevin Coleman & Associates, Inc.*

Coleman, Patricia — *Korn/Ferry International*

Collard, Joseph A. — *Spencer Stuart*

Collis, Martin — *E.L. Shore & Associates Ltd.*

Colman, Michael — *Executive Placement Consultants, Inc.*

Cona, Joseph A. — *Cona Personnel Search*

Conard, Rodney J. — *Conard Associates, Inc.*

Conley, Kevin E. — *Lamalie Amrop International*

Connelly, Kevin M. — *Spencer Stuart*

Conway, Maureen — *Conway & Associates*

Cook, Dennis — *A.T. Kearney, Inc.*

Cooke, Katherine H. — *Horton International*

Cortina Del Valle, Pedro — *Ray & Berndtson*

Coulman, Karen — *CPS Inc.*

Courtney, Brendan — *A.J. Burton Group, Inc.*

Coyle, Hugh F. — *A.J. Burton Group, Inc.*

Cragg, Barbara R. — *Southwestern Professional Services*

Cramer, Paul J. — *C/R Associates*

Crane, Howard C. — *Chartwell Partners International, Inc.*

Crath, Paul F. — *Price Waterhouse*

Ferneborg, John R. — *Ferneborg & Associates, Inc.*
Fields, Fredric — *C.A. Durakis Associates, Inc.*
Fifield, George C. — *Egon Zehnder International Inc.*
Fiorelli, Cheryl — *Tower Consultants, Ltd.*
Fischer, Adam — *Howard Fischer Associates, Inc.*
Fischer, Howard M. — *Howard Fischer Associates, Inc.*
Fischer, John C. — *Horton International*
Fisher, Neal — *Fisher Personnel Management Services*
Fishler, Stu — *A.T. Kearney, Inc.*
Flanagan, Robert M. — *Robert M. Flanagan & Associates, Ltd.*
Fleming, Marco — *MSI International*
Fletcher, David — *A.J. Burton Group, Inc.*
Fogarty, Michael — *CPS Inc.*
Fong, Robert — *Korn/Ferry International*
Foote, Leland W. — *L.W. Foote Company*
Foreman, David C. — *Koontz, Jeffries & Associates, Inc.*
Foreman, Rebecca — *Aubin International Inc.*
Forgosh, Jack H. — *Raymond Karsan Associates*
Foster, Dwight E. — *D.E. Foster Partners Inc.*
Fowler, Edward D.C. — *Higdon Prince Inc.*
Fowler, Susan B. — *Russell Reynolds Associates, Inc.*
Fowler, Thomas A. — *The Hindman Company*
Fox, Amanda C. — *Ray & Berndtson*
Frazier, John — *Cochran, Cochran & Yale, Inc.*
Freedman, Howard — *Korn/Ferry International*
Freier, Bruce — *Executive Referral Services, Inc.*
Frerichs, April — *Ryan, Miller & Associates Inc.*
Fribush, Richard — *A.J. Burton Group, Inc.*
Friedman, Donna L. — *Tower Consultants, Ltd.*
Friedman, Helen E. — *McCormack & Farrow*
Fust, Sheely F. — *Ray & Berndtson*
Gabel, Gregory N. — *Canny, Bowen Inc.*
Gabriel, David L. — *The Arcus Group*
Gaffney, Keith — *Gaffney Management Consultants*
Gaffney, William — *Gaffney Management Consultants*
Gaines, Jay — *Jay Gaines & Company, Inc.*
Galante, Suzanne M. — *Vlcek & Company, Inc.*
Gallagher, Terence M. — *Battalia Winston International*
Gantar, Donna — *Howard Fischer Associates, Inc.*
Gardiner, E. Nicholas P. — *Gardiner International*
Garfinkle, Steven M. — *Battalia Winston International*
Gates, Lucille C. — *Lamalie Amrop International*
Gauthier, Robert C. — *Columbia Consulting Group*
George, Delores F. — *Delores F. George Human Resource Management & Consulting Industry*
Gerber, Mark J. — *Wellington Management Group*
Germain, Valerie — *Jay Gaines & Company, Inc.*
Gestwick, Daniel — *Cochran, Cochran & Yale, Inc.*
Ghurani, Mac — *Gary Kaplan & Associates*
Gibbons, Ronald L. — *Flynn, Hannock, Incorporated*
Gibbs, John S. — *Spencer Stuart*
Gilbert, Jerry — *Gilbert & Van Campen International*

Gilbert, Patricia G. — *Lynch Miller Moore, Inc.*
Gill, Patricia — *Columbia Consulting Group*
Gillespie, Thomas — *Professional Search Consultants*
Gilreath, James M. — *Gilreath Weatherby, Inc.*
Giries, Juliet D. — *Barton Associates, Inc.*
Glass, Lori — *The Executive Source*
Goar, Duane R. — *Sandhurst Associates*
Gobert, Larry — *Professional Search Consultants*
Goedtke, Steven — *Southwestern Professional Services*
Gold, Donald — *Executive Search, Ltd.*
Golde, Lisa — *Tully/Woodmansee International, Inc.*
Goldenberg, Susan — *Grant Cooper and Associates*
Goldsmith, Joseph B. — *Higdon Prince Inc.*
Goldstein, Steven G. — *The Jonathan Stevens Group, Inc.*
Gonye, Peter K. — *Egon Zehnder International Inc.*
Gonzalez, Kristen — *A.J. Burton Group, Inc.*
Gonzalez, Rafael — *Korn/Ferry International*
Goodman, Dawn M. — *Bason Associates Inc.*
Gordon, Gerald L. — *E.G. Jones Associates, Ltd.*
Gotlys, Jordan — *Stone Murphy & Olson*
Gow, Roderick C. — *Lamalie Amrop International*
Graham, Dale — *CPS Inc.*
Grand, Gordon — *Russell Reynolds Associates, Inc.*
Grant, Michael — *Zwell International*
Grantham, John — *Grantham & Co., Inc.*
Grantham, Philip H. — *Columbia Consulting Group*
Grasch, Jerry E. — *The Hindman Company*
Gray, Annie — *Annie Gray Associates, Inc./The Executive Search Firm*
Gray, Betty — *Accent on Achievement, Inc.*
Grayson, E.C. — *Spencer Stuart*
Griffin, Cathy — *A.T. Kearney, Inc.*
Groban, Jack — *A.T. Kearney, Inc.*
Grotenhuis, Dirkten — *Chrisman & Company, Incorporated*
Grotte, Lawrence C. — *Lautz Grotte Engler*
Grzybowski, Jill — *CPS Inc.*
Gulian, Randolph — *Strategic Executives, Inc.*
Gurnani, Angali — *Executive Placement Consultants, Inc.*
Gurtin, Kay L. — *Executive Options, Ltd.*
Guy, C. William — *William Guy & Associates*
Habelmann, Gerald B. — *Habelmann & Associates*
Haberman, Joseph C. — *A.T. Kearney, Inc.*
Hagerty, Kenneth — *Korn/Ferry International*
Hagglund, Karl H. — *Simpson Associates, Inc.*
Hailey, H.M. — *Damon & Associates, Inc.*
Halbrich, Mitch — *A.J. Burton Group, Inc.*
Hall, Peter V. — *Chartwell Partners International, Inc.*
Halladay, Patti — *Intersource, Ltd.*
Hallagan, Robert E. — *Heidrick & Struggles, Inc.*
Hallock, Peter B. — *Goodrich & Sherwood Associates, Inc.*
Hamilton, John R. — *Ray & Berndtson*
Hammond, Karla — *People Management Northeast Incorporated*
Hanes, Leah — *Ray & Berndtson*

Hanley, Alan P. — *Williams, Roth & Krueger Inc.*
Hanley, J. Patrick — *Canny, Bowen Inc.*
Hanley, Maureen E. — *Gilbert Tweed/INESA*
Hannock, Elwin W. — *Flynn, Hannock,*
   Incorporated
Hanson, Grant M. — *Goodrich & Sherwood*
   Associates, Inc.
Hanson, Lee — *Heidrick & Struggles, Inc.*
Harbaugh, Paul J. — *International Management*
   Advisors, Inc.
Harbert, David O. — *Sweeney Harbert &*
   Mummert, Inc.
Hardison, Richard L. — *Hardison & Company*
Hardy, Thomas G. — *Spencer Stuart*
Harfenist, Harry — *Parker Page Group*
Harney, Elyane — *Gary Kaplan & Associates*
Harrell, L. Parker — *Korn/Ferry International*
Harris, Jack — *A.T. Kearney, Inc.*
Harris, Joe W. — *Cendea Connection*
   International
Harris, Seth O. — *Christian & Timbers*
Hart, Robert T. — *D.E. Foster Partners Inc.*
Hartle, Larry — *CPS Inc.*
Harty, Shirley Cox — *Ray & Berndtson*
Harvey, Mike — *Advanced Executive Resources*
Haughton, Michael — *DeFrain, Mayer LLC*
Havener, Donald Clarke — *The Abbott Group,*
   Inc.
Hawksworth, A. Dwight — *A.D. & Associates*
   Executive Search, Inc.
Hay, William E. — *William E. Hay & Co.*
Haystead, Steve — *Advanced Executive Resources*
Hazerjian, Cynthia — *CPS Inc.*
Heafey, Bill — *CPS Inc.*
Heaney, Thomas — *Korn/Ferry International*
Heiken, Barbara E. — *Randell-Heiken, Inc.*
Heinze, David — *Heinze & Associates, Inc.*
Heller, Steven A. — *Martin H. Bauman Associates,*
   Inc.
Hellinger, Audrey W. — *Martin H. Bauman*
   Associates, Inc.
Helminiak, Audrey — *Gaffney Management*
   Consultants
Hendrickson, Jill E. — *Gregory Michaels and*
   Associates, Inc.
Heneghan, Donald A. — *Allerton Heneghan &*
   O'Neill
Henn, George W. — *G.W. Henn & Company*
Hennig, Sandra M. — *MSI International*
Henry, Mary — *Conex Incorporated*
Hensley, Bert — *Morgan Samuels Co., Inc.*
Hensley, Gayla — *Atlantic Search Group, Inc.*
Hergenrather, Richard A. — *Hergenrather &*
   Company
Herman, Pat — *Whitney & Associates, Inc.*
Herman, Shelli — *Gary Kaplan & Associates*
Hewitt, Rives D. — *The Dalley Hewitt Company*
Hewitt, W. Davis — *The Dalley Hewitt Company*
Higbee, Joan — *Thorndike Deland Associates*
Higdon, Henry G. — *Higdon Prince Inc.*
Higgins, Donna — *Howard Fischer Associates,*
   Inc.
Higgins, William — *William Guy & Associates*
Hildebrand, Thomas B. — *Professional Resources*
   Group, Inc.
Hill, Emery — *MSI International*
Hill, Randall W. — *Heidrick & Struggles, Inc.*

Hillen, Skip — *The McCormick Group, Inc.*
Hilliker, Alan D. — *Egon Zehnder International*
   Inc.
Himes, Dirk — *A.T. Kearney, Inc.*
Hindman, Neil C. — *The Hindman Company*
Hockett, William — *Hockett Associates, Inc.*
Hocking, Jeffrey — *Korn/Ferry International*
Hodge, Jeff — *Heidrick & Struggles, Inc.*
Hoevel, Michael J. — *Poirier, Hoevel & Co.*
Hofner, Kevin E. — *Lamalie Amrop International*
Holland, Rose Mary — *Price Waterhouse*
Holmes, Lawrence J. — *Columbia Consulting*
   Group
Holodnak, William A. — *J. Robert Scott*
Honer, Paul E. — *Ingram & Aydelotte Inc./I-I-C*
   Partners
Honey, W. Michael M. — *O'Callaghan*
   Honey/Ray & Berndtson, Inc.
Hoover, Catherine — *J.L. Mark Associates, Inc.*
Hopkins, Chester A. — *Handy HRM Corp.*
Hopp, Lorrie A. — *Gregory Michaels and*
   Associates, Inc.
Hopper, John W. — *William Guy & Associates*
Hoskins, Charles R. — *Heidrick & Struggles, Inc.*
Howard, Lee Ann — *Lamalie Amrop International*
Howard, Leon — *Richard, Wayne and Roberts*
Howard, Susy — *The McCormick Group, Inc.*
Howe, Vance A. — *Ward Howell International,*
   Inc.
Howell, Robert B. — *Atlantic Search Group, Inc.*
Howell, Robert B. — *Atlantic Search Group, Inc.*
Hoyda, Louis A. — *Thorndike Deland Associates*
Hucko, Donald S. — *Jonas, Walters & Assoc., Inc.*
Hudson, Reginald M. — *Search Bureau*
   International
Hughes, Cathy N. — *The Ogdon Partnership*
Hughes, R. Kevin — *Handy HRM Corp.*
Hurd, J. Nicholas — *Russell Reynolds Associates,*
   Inc.
Hussey, Wayne — *Krecklo & Associates Inc.*
Hutchison, William K. — *Christenson &*
   Hutchison
Hutton, Thomas J. — *The Thomas Tucker*
   Company
Hybels, Cynthia — *A.J. Burton Group, Inc.*
Hyman, Linda — *Korn/Ferry International*
Hypes, Richard G. — *Lynch Miller Moore, Inc.*
Imely, Larry S. — *Stratford Group*
Ingram, D. John — *Ingram & Aydelotte Inc./I-I-C*
   Partners
Inguagiato, Gregory — *MSI International*
Irish, Alan — *CPS Inc.*
Issacs, Judith A. — *Grant Cooper and Associates*
Jablo, Steven A. — *Dieckmann & Associates, Ltd.*
Jackowitz, Todd — *J. Robert Scott*
Jackson, Joan — *A.T. Kearney, Inc.*
Jacobs, Martin J. — *The Rubicon Group*
Jacobs, Mike — *Thorne, Brieger Associates Inc.*
Jacobson, Rick — *The Windham Group*
James, Richard — *Criterion Executive Search, Inc.*
Janis, Laurence — *Integrated Search Solutions*
   Group, LLC
Janssen, Don — *Howard Fischer Associates, Inc.*
Januale, Lois — *Cochran, Cochran & Yale, Inc.*
Jazylo, John V. — *Handy HRM Corp.*
Jeffers, Richard B. — *Dieckmann & Associates,*
   Ltd.

Jernigan, Susan N. — *Sockwell & Associates*
Joffe, Barry — *Bason Associates Inc.*
Johnson, Brian — *A.J. Burton Group, Inc.*
Johnson, Harold E. — *Lamalie Amrop International*
Johnson, John W. — *Webb, Johnson Associates, Inc.*
Johnson, Julie M. — *International Staffing Consultants, Inc.*
Johnson, Kathleen A. — *Barton Associates, Inc.*
Johnson, Priscilla — *The Johnson Group, Inc.*
Johnson, Ronald S. — *Ronald S. Johnson Associates, Inc.*
Johnson, S. Hope — *Boyden Washington, D.C.*
Johnson, Stanley C. — *Johnson & Company*
Jones, B.J. — *Intersource, Ltd.*
Jones, Daniel F. — *Atlantic Search Group, Inc.*
Jones, Herschel — *Korn/Ferry International*
Jordan, Jon — *Cochran, Cochran & Yale, Inc.*
Jordan, Stephen T. — *Ray & Berndtson*
Jorgensen, Tom — *The Talley Group*
Joys, David S. — *Heidrick & Struggles, Inc.*
Judge, Alfred L. — *The Cambridge Group Ltd*
Judy, Otto — *CPS Inc.*
Juelis, John J. — *Peeney Associates*
Kacyn, Louis J. — *Egon Zehnder International Inc.*
Kader, Richard — *Richard Kader & Associates*
Kaiser, Donald J. — *Dunhill International Search of New Haven*
Kane, Frank — *A.J. Burton Group, Inc.*
Kane, Karen — *Howard Fischer Associates, Inc.*
Kaplan, Gary — *Gary Kaplan & Associates*
Karalis, William — *CPS Inc.*
Katz, Cyndi — *Search West, Inc.*
Keating, Pierson — *Nordeman Grimm, Inc.*
Kehoe, Mike — *CPS Inc.*
Keitel, Robert S. — *A.T. Kearney, Inc.*
Keller, Barbara E. — *Barton Associates, Inc.*
Kelly, Claudia L. — *Spencer Stuart*
Kelly, Donna J. — *Accountants Executive Search*
Kelly, Elizabeth Ann — *Wellington Management Group*
Kelly, Peter W. — *R. Rollo Associates*
Kelso, Patricia C. — *Barton Associates, Inc.*
Keogh, James — *Sanford Rose Associates*
Kern, Jerry L. — *ADOW's Executeam*
Kern, Kathleen G. — *ADOW's Executeam*
Kershaw, Lisa — *Tanton Mitchell/Paul Ray Berndtson*
Keshishian, Gregory — *Handy HRM Corp.*
Kettwig, David A. — *A.T. Kearney, Inc.*
Keyser, Anne — *A.T. Kearney, Inc.*
Kilcoyne, Pat — *CPS Inc.*
King, Thomas — *Morgan Hunter Corp.*
Kinser, Richard E. — *Richard Kinser & Associates*
Kip, Luanne S. — *Kip Williams, Inc.*
Kishbaugh, Herbert S. — *Kishbaugh Associates International*
Kkorzyniewski, Nicole — *CPS Inc.*
Klages, Constance W. — *International Management Advisors, Inc.*
Klavens, Cecile J. — *The Pickwick Group, Inc.*
Klein, Brandon — *A.J. Burton Group, Inc.*
Klein, Gary — *A.T. Kearney, Inc.*
Klein, Mary Jo — *Cochran, Cochran & Yale, Inc.*
Kleinstein, Jonah A. — *The Kleinstein Group*
Knisely, Gary — *Johnson Smith & Knisely Accord*

Koblentz, Joel M. — *Egon Zehnder International Inc.*
Koehler, Frank R. — *The Koehler Group*
Kohn, Adam P. — *Christian & Timbers*
Kondra, Vernon J. — *The Douglas Reiter Company, Inc.*
Konker, David N. — *Russell Reynolds Associates, Inc.*
Koontz, Donald N. — *Koontz, Jeffries & Associates, Inc.*
Kopsick, Joseph M. — *Spencer Stuart*
Kotick, Maddy — *The Stevenson Group of New Jersey*
Krecklo, Brian Douglas — *Krecklo & Associates Inc.*
Krejci, Stanley L. — *Boyden Washington, D.C.*
Kreutz, Gary L. — *Kreutz Consulting Group, Inc.*
Krieger, Dennis F. — *Seiden Krieger Associates, Inc.*
Krueger, Kurt — *Krueger Associates*
Kucewicz, William — *Search West, Inc.*
Kuhl, Teresa — *Don Richard Associates of Tampa, Inc.*
Kunzer, William J. — *Kunzer Associates, Ltd.*
Kussner, Janice N. — *Herman Smith Executive Initiatives Inc.*
Kvasnicka, Jay Allen — *Morgan Hunter Corp.*
Laba, Marvin — *Marvin Laba & Associates*
Laba, Stuart M. — *Marvin Laba & Associates*
Labrecque, Bernard F. — *Laurendeau Labrecque/Ray & Berndtson, Inc.*
Lachance, Roger — *Laurendeau Labrecque/Ray & Berndtson, Inc.*
Lache, Shawn E. — *The Arcus Group*
Lacoste, Daniel — *The Caldwell Partners Amrop International*
Laird, Cheryl — *CPS Inc.*
Lamb, Angus K. — *Raymond Karsan Associates*
Lang, Sharon A. — *Ray & Berndtson*
Lannamann, Richard S. — *Russell Reynolds Associates, Inc.*
Lapat, Aaron D. — *J. Robert Scott*
Lardner, Lucy D. — *Tully/Woodmansee International, Inc.*
Lasher, Charles M. — *Lasher Associates*
Lauderback, David R. — *A.T. Kearney, Inc.*
Laurendeau, Jean E. — *Laurendeau Labrecque/Ray & Berndtson, Inc.*
Lautz, Lindsay A. — *Lautz Grotte Engler*
Leahy, Jan — *CPS Inc.*
LeComte, Andre — *Egon Zehnder International Inc.*
Ledbetter, Steven G. — *Cendea Connection International*
Lee, Roger — *Montgomery Resources, Inc.*
Leetma, Imbi — *Stanton Chase International*
Leighton, Nina — *The Ogdon Partnership*
Lence, Julie Anne — *MSI International*
Lennox, Charles — *Price Waterhouse*
Leslie, William H. — *Boyden/Zay & Company*
Letcher, Harvey D. — *Sandhurst Associates*
Levine, Alan M. — *MB Inc. Interim Executive Division*
Lewicki, Christopher — *MSI International*
Lewis, Jon A. — *Sandhurst Associates*
Lewis, Marc D. — *Handy HRM Corp.*
Lewis, Sean — *Southwestern Professional Services*

Lezama Cohen, Luis — *Ray & Berndtson*
Lindberg, Eric J. — *MSI International*
Lindholst, Kai — *Egon Zehnder International Inc.*
Lindsay, M. Evan — *Heidrick & Struggles, Inc.*
Linton, Leonard M. — *Byron Leonard International, Inc.*
Little, Suzaane — *Don Richard Associates of Tampa, Inc.*
Livingston, Peter R. — *Livingston, Robert and Company Inc.*
Loeb, Stephen H. — *Grant Cooper and Associates*
Loewenstein, Victor H. — *Egon Zehnder International Inc.*
Lofthouse, Cindy — *CPS Inc.*
Lokken, Karen — *A.E. Feldman Associates*
Lombardi, Nancy W. — *WTW Associates, Inc.*
Long, Helga — *Horton International*
Long, Milt — *William Guy & Associates*
Long, Thomas — *Egon Zehnder International Inc.*
Long, William G. — *McDonald, Long & Associates, Inc.*
Lonneke, John W. — *MSI International*
Looney, Scott — *A.E. Feldman Associates*
Lopis, Roberta — *Richard, Wayne and Roberts*
Loscavio, J. Michael — *Rusher, Loscavio & LoPresto*
Lotufo, Donald A. — *D.A.L. Associates, Inc.*
Lotz, R. James — *International Management Advisors, Inc.*
Loubet, Larry — *Carlyle Group*
Lovas, W. Carl — *Ray & Berndtson/Lovas Stanley*
Lovely, Edward — *The Stevenson Group of New Jersey*
Loving, Vikki — *Intersource, Ltd.*
Lucarelli, Joan — *The Onstott Group, Inc.*
Lucas, Ronnie L. — *MSI International*
Lucht, John — *The John Lucht Consultancy Inc.*
Ludlow, Paula — *Horton International*
Lumsby, George N. — *International Management Advisors, Inc.*
Luntz, Charles E. — *Charles Luntz & Associates. Inc.*
Lupica, Anthony — *Cochran, Cochran & Yale, Inc.*
Lynch, Michael C. — *Lynch Miller Moore, Inc.*
Lynch, Sean E. — *Raymond Karsan Associates*
Lyon, Jenny — *Marra Peters & Partners*
Lyons, Denis B.K. — *Spencer Stuart*
Lyons, J. David — *Aubin International Inc.*
MacCallan, Deirdre — *Butterfass, Pepe & MacCallan Inc.*
Macdonald, G. William — *The Macdonald Group, Inc.*
Mackenna, Kathy — *Plummer & Associates, Inc.*
MacNaughton, Sperry — *McNaughton Associates*
Macomber, Keith S. — *Sullivan & Company*
Magee, Harrison R. — *Bowden & Company, Inc.*
Maglio, Charles J. — *Maglio and Company, Inc.*
Mainwaring, Andrew Brian — *Executive Search Consultants Corporation*
Major, Susan — *A.T. Kearney, Inc.*
Makrianes, James K. — *Webb, Johnson Associates, Inc.*
Malcolm, Rod — *Korn/Ferry International*
Mallin, Ellen — *Howard Fischer Associates, Inc.*
Manassero, Henri J.P. — *International Management Advisors, Inc.*

Mangum, Maria — *Thomas Mangum Company*
Mangum, William T. — *Thomas Mangum Company*
Manns, Alex — *Crawford & Crofford*
Manzo, Renee — *Atlantic Search Group, Inc.*
Maphet, Harriet — *The Stevenson Group of New Jersey*
Marino, Chester — *Cochran, Cochran & Yale, Inc.*
Marino, Jory J. — *Sullivan & Company*
Mark, John L. — *J.L. Mark Associates, Inc.*
Mark, Lynne — *J.L. Mark Associates, Inc.*
Marks, Ira — *Strategic Alternatives*
Marks, Russell E. — *Webb, Johnson Associates, Inc.*
Marra, John — *Marra Peters & Partners*
Marra, John — *Marra Peters & Partners*
Martin, Jon — *Egon Zehnder International Inc.*
Marumoto, William H. — *Boyden Washington, D.C.*
Masserman, Bruce — *Masserman & Associates, Inc.*
Massey, R. Bruce — *Horton International*
Mather, David R. — *Christian & Timbers*
Mathias, Kathy — *Stone Murphy & Olson*
Mattes, Edward C. — *The Ogdon Partnership*
Matthews, Corwin — *Woodworth International Group*
Matthews, Mary — *Korn/Ferry International*
Mayes, Kay H. — *John Shell Associates, Inc.*
Maynard Taylor, Susan — *Chrisman & Company, Incorporated*
Mazor, Elly — *Howard Fischer Associates, Inc.*
Mazza, David B. — *Mazza & Riley, Inc. (a Korn/Ferry International affiliate)*
McAndrews, Kathy — *CPS Inc.*
McAteer, Thomas — *Montgomery Resources, Inc.*
McBride, Jonathan E. — *McBride Associates, Inc.*
McBryde, Marnie — *Spencer Stuart*
McCabe, Christopher — *Raymond Karsan Associates*
McCarty, J. Rucker — *Heidrick & Struggles, Inc.*
McClement, John — *Korn/Ferry International*
McConnell, Greg — *Winter, Wyman & Company*
McCool, Anne G. — *Sullivan & Company*
McCreary, Charles "Chip" — *Austin-McGregor International*
McDermott, Jeffrey T. — *Vlcek & Company, Inc.*
McDonald, Scott A. — *McDonald Associates International*
McDonald, Stanleigh B. — *McDonald Associates International*
McDowell, Robert N. — *Christenson & Hutchison*
McGuire, Pat — *A.J. Burton Group, Inc.*
McKeown, Patricia A. — *DiMarchi Partners, Inc.*
McKnight, Amy E. — *Chartwell Partners International, Inc.*
McLean, B. Keith — *Price Waterhouse*
McLean, E. Peter — *Spencer Stuart*
McManners, Donald E. — *McManners Associates, Inc.*
McManus, Paul — *Aubin International Inc.*
McMillin, Bob — *Price Waterhouse*
McNamara, Catherine — *Ray & Berndtson*
McNamara, Timothy C. — *Columbia Consulting Group*
McNichols, Walter B. — *Gary Kaplan & Associates*

McNulty, Kelly L. — *Gregory Michaels and Associates, Inc.*
McQuoid, David — *A.T. Kearney, Inc.*
McSherry, James F. — *Battalia Winston International*
Mead-Fox, David — *Korn/Ferry International*
Meadows, C. David — *Professional Staffing Consultants*
Meagher, Patricia G. — *Spencer Stuart*
Meany, Brian M. — *Herbert Mines Associates, Inc.*
Medina-Haro, Adolfo — *Heidrick & Struggles, Inc.*
Meier, J. Dale — *Grant Cooper and Associates*
Meiland, A. Daniel — *Egon Zehnder International Inc.*
Meltzer, Andrea Y. — *Executive Options, Ltd.*
Menk, Carl — *Canny, Bowen Inc.*
Mercer, Julie — *Columbia Consulting Group*
Merrigan, Eileen M. — *Lamalie Amrop International*
Mertensotto, Chuck H. — *Whitney & Associates, Inc.*
Messett, William J. — *Messett Associates, Inc.*
Mestepey, John — *A.T. Kearney, Inc.*
Meyer, Stacey — *Gary Kaplan & Associates*
Meyers, Steven — *Montgomery Resources, Inc.*
Meza, Anna — *Richard, Wayne and Roberts*
Michaels, Joseph — *CPS Inc.*
Miller, David — *Cochran, Cochran & Yale, Inc.*
Miller, David — *Temporary Accounting Personnel, Inc.*
Miller, Harold B. — *MSI International*
Miller, Michael R. — *Lynch Miller Moore, Inc.*
Miller, Roy — *The Enns Partners Inc.*
Mingle, Larry D. — *Columbia Consulting Group*
Mirtz, P. John — *Mirtz Morice, Inc.*
Misiurewicz, Marc — *Cochran, Cochran & Yale, Inc.*
Mitchell, Jeff — *A.J. Burton Group, Inc.*
Mitton, Bill — *Executive Resource, Inc.*
Mohr, Brian — *CPS Inc.*
Mondragon, Philip — *A.T. Kearney, Inc.*
Monogenis, Emanuel N. — *Heidrick & Struggles, Inc.*
Montgomery, James M. — *Houze, Shourds & Montgomery, Inc.*
Moodley, Logan — *Austin-McGregor International*
Moore, Janice E. — *MSI International*
Moore, Mark — *Wheeler, Moore & Elam Co.*
Moore, T. Wills — *Ray & Berndtson*
Morgan, Donald T. — *MSI International*
Morice, James L. — *Mirtz Morice, Inc.*
Morris, David A. — *Heidrick & Struggles, Inc.*
Morris, Paul T. — *The Morris Group*
Mortansen, Patricia — *Norman Broadbent International, Inc.*
Morton, Robert C. — *Morton, McCorkle & Associates, Inc.*
Mowatt, Virginia — *Spencer Stuart*
Moyse, Richard G. — *Thorndike Deland Associates*
Mueller-Maerki, Fortunat F. — *Egon Zehnder International Inc.*
Muendel, H. Edward — *Stanton Chase International*
Mulligan, Robert P. — *William Willis Worldwide Inc.*

Murphy, Cornelius J. — *Goodrich & Sherwood Associates, Inc.*
Murphy, Erin — *CPS Inc.*
Murphy, Gary J. — *Stone Murphy & Olson*
Murphy, Patrick J. — *P.J. Murphy & Associates, Inc.*
Murphy, Peter — *Korn/Ferry International*
Murray, Virginia — *A.T. Kearney, Inc.*
Mursuli, Meredith — *Lasher Associates*
Mydlach, Renee — *CPS Inc.*
Myers, Kay — *Signature Staffing*
Nagler, Leon G. — *Nagler, Robins & Poe, Inc.*
Naidicz, Maria — *Ray & Berndtson*
Nair, Leslie — *Zwell International*
Nass, Martin D. — *Lamalie Amrop International*
Nathanson, Barry F. — *Barry Nathanson Associates*
Neelin, Sharon — *The Caldwell Partners Amrop International*
Nees, Eugene C. — *Ray & Berndtson*
Neff, Thomas J. — *Spencer Stuart*
Neher, Robert L. — *Intech Summit Group, Inc.*
Nehring, Keith — *Howard Fischer Associates, Inc.*
Neidhart, Craig C. — *TNS Partners, Inc.*
Nemec, Phillip — *Dunhill International Search of New Haven*
Neuberth, Jeffrey G. — *Canny, Bowen Inc.*
Newman, Lynn — *Kishbaugh Associates International*
Newpoff, Brad L. — *Furst Group/MPI*
Nichols, Gary — *Koontz, Jeffries & Associates, Inc.*
Nielsen, Sue — *Ells Personnel System Inc.*
Noebel, Todd R. — *The Noebel Search Group, Inc.*
Nolte, William D. — *W.D. Nolte & Company*
Norman, Randy — *Austin-McGregor International*
Normann, Amy — *Robert M. Flanagan & Associates, Ltd.*
Norris, Ken — *A.T. Kearney, Inc.*
Norsell, Paul E. — *Paul Norsell & Associates, Inc.*
Norton, James B. — *Lamalie Amrop International*
Nunziata, Peter — *Atlantic Search Group, Inc.*
Nutter, Roger — *Raymond Karsan Associates*
O'Connell, Mary — *CPS Inc.*
O'Halloran, Robert — *MSI International*
O'Hara, Daniel M. — *Lynch Miller Moore, Inc.*
O'Maley, Kimberlee — *Spencer Stuart*
O'Neill, James P. — *Allerton Heneghan & O'Neill*
O'Reilly, John — *Stratford Group*
Ogden, Dayton — *Spencer Stuart*
Ogdon, Thomas H. — *The Ogdon Partnership*
Olin, Robyn — *Richard, Wayne and Roberts*
Olsen, Kristine — *Williams Executive Search, Inc.*
Ongirski, Richard P. — *Raymond Karsan Associates*
Onstott, Joseph E. — *The Onstott Group, Inc.*
Orkin, Ralph — *Sanford Rose Associates*
Orkin, Sheilah — *Sanford Rose Associates*
Oswald, Mark G. — *Canny, Bowen Inc.*
Ott, George W. — *Ott & Hansen, Inc.*
Ottenritter, Chris — *CPS Inc.*
Overlock, Craig — *Ray & Berndtson*
Pace, Susan A. — *Horton International*
Padilla, Jose Sanchez — *Egon Zehnder International Inc.*
Page, G. Schuyler — *A.T. Kearney, Inc.*

Robles Cuellar, Paulina — *Ray & Berndtson*
Rogan, John P. — *Russell Reynolds Associates, Inc.*
Rogers, Leah — *Dinte Resources, Inc.*
Rohan, James E. — *J.P. Canon Associates*
Rohan, Kevin A. — *J.P. Canon Associates*
Rojo, Rafael — *A.T. Kearney, Inc.*
Rollo, Robert S. — *R. Rollo Associates*
Rosemarin, Gloria J. — *Barrington Hart, Inc.*
Rosin, Jeffrey — *Korn/Ferry International*
Ross, Curt A. — *Ray & Berndtson*
Ross, Lawrence — *Ray & Berndtson/Lovas Stanley*
Rotella, Marshall W. — *The Corporate Connection, Ltd.*
Roth, Robert J. — *Williams, Roth & Krueger Inc.*
Rothschild, John S. — *Lamalie Amrop International*
Rowe, Thomas A. — *Korn/Ferry International*
Runquist, U.W. — *Webb, Johnson Associates, Inc.*
Rush, Michael E. — *D.A.L. Associates, Inc.*
Rusher, William H. — *Rusher, Loscavio & LoPresto*
Russell, Richard A. — *Executive Search Consultants Corporation*
Russo, Karen — *Maximum Management Corp.*
Sabat, Lori S. — *Alta Associates, Inc.*
Sacerdote, John — *Raymond Karsan Associates*
Saletra, Andrew — *CPS Inc.*
Salvagno, Michael J. — *The Cambridge Group Ltd*
Sanders, Natalie — *CPS Inc.*
Sanders, Spencer H. — *Battalia Winston International*
Sandor, Richard J. — *Flynn, Hannock, Incorporated*
Sanitago, Anthony — *TaxSearch, Inc.*
Sanow, Robert — *Cochran, Cochran & Yale, Inc.*
Santimauro, Edward — *Korn/Ferry International*
Sarn, Allan G. — *Allan Sarn Associates Inc.*
Satenstein, Sloan — *Higdon Prince Inc.*
Savage, Edward J. — *Stanton Chase International*
Sawyer, Deborah — *Korn/Ferry International*
Sawyer, Patricia L. — *Smith & Sawyer Inc.*
Saxon, Alexa — *Woodworth International Group*
Scalamera, Tom — *CPS Inc.*
Schaefer, Frederic M. — *A.T. Kearney, Inc.*
Schappell, Marc P. — *Egon Zehnder International Inc.*
Schene, Philip — *A.E. Feldman Associates*
Schlpma, Christine — *Advanced Executive Resources*
Schneider, Thomas P. — *WTW Associates, Inc.*
Schneiderman, Gerald — *Management Resource Associates, Inc.*
Schroeder, John W. — *Spencer Stuart*
Schueneman, David — *CPS Inc.*
Schwam, Carol — *A.E. Feldman Associates*
Scodius, Joseph J. — *Gregory Michaels and Associates, Inc.*
Scott, Evan — *Howard Fischer Associates, Inc.*
Scott, Gordon S. — *Search Advisors International Corp.*
Scranton, Lisa — *A.J. Burton Group, Inc.*
Scroggins, Stephen R. — *Russell Reynolds Associates, Inc.*
Seco, William — *Seco & Zetto Associates, Inc.*
Seiden, Steven A. — *Seiden Krieger Associates, Inc.*

Selker, Gregory L. — *Christian & Timbers*
Semyan, John K. — *TNS Partners, Inc.*
Sessa, Vincent J. — *Integrated Search Solutions Group, LLC*
Sevilla, Claudio A. — *Crawford & Crofford*
Shapiro, Beth — *Howard Fischer Associates, Inc.*
Shapiro, Elaine — *CPS Inc.*
Shea, Kathleen M. — *The Penn Partners, Incorporated*
Shell, John C. — *John Shell Associates, Inc.*
Shemin, Grace — *Maximum Management Corp.*
Shenfield, Peter — *A.T. Kearney, Inc.*
Shepard, Michael J. — *MSI International*
Shervey, Brent C. — *O'Callaghan Honey/Ray & Berndtson, Inc.*
Sherwood, Andrew — *Goodrich & Sherwood Associates, Inc.*
Shield, Nancy — *Maximum Management Corp.*
Shore, Earl L. — *E.L. Shore & Associates Ltd.*
Shourds, Mary E. — *Houze, Shourds & Montgomery, Inc.*
Sibbald, John R. — *John Sibbald Associates, Inc.*
Siegel, Pamela — *Executive Options, Ltd.*
Siegler, Jody Cukiir — *A.T. Kearney, Inc.*
Siegrist, Jeffrey M. — *D.E. Foster Partners Inc.*
Signer, Julie — *CPS Inc.*
Silcott, Marvin L. — *Marvin L. Silcott & Associates, Inc.*
Silvas, Stephen D. — *Roberson and Company*
Silver, Lee — *L. A. Silver Associates, Inc.*
Silverman, Gary W. — *GWS Partners*
Silverman, Paul M. — *The Marshall Group*
Silverstein, Jackie — *Don Richard Associates of Charlotte*
Simmons, Sandra K. — *MSI International*
Simon, Mary K. — *Gregory Michaels and Associates, Inc.*
Simpson, David J. — *Simpson Associates, Inc.*
Simpson, Scott — *Cendea Connection International*
Sindler, Jay — *A.J. Burton Group, Inc.*
Sitarski, Stan — *Howard Fischer Associates, Inc.*
Skalet, Ira — *A.E. Feldman Associates*
Skunda, Donna M. — *Allerton Heneghan & O'Neill*
Slosar, John — *Boyden*
Smead, Michelle M. — *A.T. Kearney, Inc.*
Smirnov, Tatiana — *Allan Sarn Associates Inc.*
Smith, Ana Luz — *Smith Search, S.C.*
Smith, David P. — *HRS, Inc.*
Smith, Herman M. — *Herman Smith Executive Initiatives Inc.*
Smith, John E. — *Smith Search, S.C.*
Smith, John F. — *The Penn Partners, Incorporated*
Smith, Lydia — *The Corporate Connection, Ltd.*
Smith, Matt D. — *Ray & Berndtson*
Smith, R. Michael — *Smith James Group, Inc.*
Smith, Robert L. — *Smith & Sawyer Inc.*
Smith, Timothy C. — *Christian & Timbers*
Snyder, C. Edward — *Horton International*
Snyder, James F. — *Snyder & Company*
Sockwell, J. Edgar — *Sockwell & Associates*
Sondgrass, Stephen — *DeFrain, Mayer LLC*
Souder, E.G. — *Souder & Associates*
Soutouras, James — *Smith James Group, Inc.*
Spadavecchia, Jennifer — *Alta Associates, Inc.*

Spann, Richard E. — *Goodrich & Sherwood Associates, Inc.*
Spera, Stefanie — *A.T. Kearney, Inc.*
Spiegel, Gayle — *L. A. Silver Associates, Inc.*
Spitz, Grant — *The Caldwell Partners Amrop International*
Sponseller, Vern — *Richard Kader & Associates*
Spriggs, Robert D. — *Spriggs & Company, Inc.*
St. Clair, Alan — *TNS Partners, Inc.*
Stanton, John — *A.T. Kearney, Inc.*
Stark, Jeff — *Thorne, Brieger Associates Inc.*
Steele, Daniel — *Cochran, Cochran & Yale, Inc.*
Steer, Joe — *CPS Inc.*
Stein, Terry W. — *Stewart, Stein and Scott, Ltd.*
Steinem, Andy — *Dahl-Morrow International*
Steinem, Barbara — *Dahl-Morrow International*
Steinman, Stephen M. — *The Stevenson Group of New Jersey*
Stern, Lester W. — *Sullivan & Company*
Stern, Stephen — *CPS Inc.*
Sterner, Doug — *CPS Inc.*
Stevenson, Jane — *Howard Fischer Associates, Inc.*
Stevenson, Jane — *Howard Fischer Associates, Inc.*
Stewart, Jan J. — *Egon Zehnder International Inc.*
Stewart, Jeffrey O. — *Stewart, Stein and Scott, Ltd.*
Stewart, Ross M. — *Human Resources Network Partners Inc.*
Stivk, Barbara A. — *Thornton Resources*
Stone, Robert Ryder — *Lamalie Amrop International*
Stone, Susan L. — *Stone Enterprises Ltd.*
Stoy, Roger W. — *Heidrick & Struggles, Inc.*
Stranberg, James R. — *Callan Associates, Ltd.*
Stratmeyer, Karin Bergwall — *Princeton Entrepreneurial Resources*
Straube, Stanley H. — *Straube Associates*
Strickland, Katie — *Grantham & Co., Inc.*
Stringer, Dann P. — *D.E. Foster Partners Inc.*
Strobridge, Richard P. — *F.L. Taylor & Company, Inc.*
Strom, Mark N. — *Search Advisors International Corp.*
Sullivan, Brian M. — *Sullivan & Company*
Sussman, Lynda — *Gilbert Tweed/INESA*
Swanson, Dick — *Raymond Karsan Associates*
Swidler, J. Robert — *Egon Zehnder International Inc.*
Swoboda, Lawrence — *A.J. Burton Group, Inc.*
Taylor, Charles E. — *Lamalie Amrop International*
Taylor, Conrad G. — *MSI International*
Taylor, Ernest A. — *Ward Howell International, Inc.*
Taylor, James M. — *The HRM Group, Inc.*
Taylor, Kenneth W. — *Egon Zehnder International Inc.*
Taylor, R.L. (Larry) — *Ray & Berndtson*
Telford, John H. — *Telford, Adams & Alexander/Telford & Co., Inc.*
ten Cate, Herman H. — *Stoneham Associates Corp.*
Teti, Al — *Chrisman & Company, Incorporated*
Theobald, David B. — *Theobald & Associates*
Thomas, Cheryl M. — *CPS Inc.*
Thomas, Kim — *CPS Inc.*
Thomas, Kurt J. — *P.J. Murphy & Associates, Inc.*

Thompson, John R. — *MSI International*
Thompson, Kenneth L. — *McCormack & Farrow*
Thomson, Alexander G. — *Russell Reynolds Associates, Inc.*
Thornton, John C. — *Thornton Resources*
Thrapp, Mark C. — *Executive Search Consultants International, Inc.*
Tincu, John C. — *Ferneborg & Associates, Inc.*
Tingle, Trina A. — *MSI International*
Tootsey, Mark A. — *A.J. Burton Group, Inc.*
Tovrog, Dan — *CPS Inc.*
Tracey, Jack — *Management Assistance Group, Inc.*
Tracy, Ronald O. — *Egon Zehnder International Inc.*
Trieweiler, Bob — *Executive Placement Consultants, Inc.*
Truemper, Dean — *CPS Inc.*
Truex, John F. — *Morton, McCorkle & Associates, Inc.*
Tryon, Katey — *DeFrain, Mayer LLC*
Tucci, Joseph — *Fairfaxx Corporation*
Tucker, Thomas A. — *The Thomas Tucker Company*
Tullberg, Tina — *CPS Inc.*
Tully, Margo L. — *Tully/Woodmansee International, Inc.*
Tunney, William — *Grant Cooper and Associates*
Turner, Edward K. — *Don Richard Associates of Charlotte*
Turner, Kimberly — *Barton Associates, Inc.*
Tutwiler, Stephen — *Don Richard Associates of Tampa, Inc.*
Tweed, Janet — *Gilbert Tweed/INESA*
Twiste, Craig — *Raymond Karsan Associates*
Vairo, Leonard A. — *Christian & Timbers*
Valenta, Joseph — *Princeton Entrepreneurial Resources*
Van Alstine, Catherine — *Tanton Mitchell/Paul Ray Berndtson*
Van Biesen, Jacques A.H. — *Search Group Inc.*
Van Campen, Jerry — *Gilbert & Van Campen International*
Van Clieaf, Mark — *MVC Associates International*
Van Nostrand, Mara J. — *Barton Associates, Inc.*
Vande-Water, Katie — *J. Robert Scott*
Velten, Mark T. — *Boyden*
Venable, William W. — *Thorndike Deland Associates*
Vernon, Peter C. — *Horton International*
Vincelette, Kathy A. — *Raymond Karsan Associates*
Visnich, L. Christine — *Bason Associates Inc.*
Vlcek, Thomas J. — *Vlcek & Company, Inc.*
Volkman, Arthur — *Cochran, Cochran & Yale, Inc.*
von Baillou, Astrid — *Richard Kinser & Associates*
Vossler, James — *A.J. Burton Group, Inc.*
Wacholz, Rick — *A.T. Kearney, Inc.*
Waitkus, Karen — *Richard, Wayne and Roberts*
Waldman, Noah H. — *Lamalie Amrop International*
Waldrop, Gary R. — *MSI International*
Walker, Craig H. — *A.J. Burton Group, Inc.*
Wallace, Alec — *Tanton Mitchell/Paul Ray Berndtson*
Walsh, Denis — *Professional Staffing Consultants*

Walters, William F. — *Jonas, Walters & Assoc., Inc.*
Ward, Ted — *Korn/Ferry International*
Wardell, Charles W.B. — *Nordeman Grimm, Inc.*
Warter, Mark — *Isaacson, Miller*
Wasp, Warren T. — *WTW Associates, Inc.*
Watkins, Jeffrey P. — *Lamalie Amrop International*
Watkins, Thomas M. — *Lamalie Amrop International*
Watkinson, Jim W. — *The Badger Group*
Watson, James — *MSI International*
Webb, George H. — *Webb, Johnson Associates, Inc.*
Weissman-Rosenthal, Abbe — *ALW Research International*
Welch, Robert — *Ray & Berndtson*
Weller, Paul S. — *Mark Stanley/EMA Partners International*
Wendler, Kambrea R. — *Gregory Michaels and Associates, Inc.*
Westfall, Ed — *Zwell International*
Wheeler, Gerard H. — *A.J. Burton Group, Inc.*
White, Richard B. — *Spencer Stuart*
Whitney, David L. — *Whitney & Associates, Inc.*
Whitney, William A — *Larsen, Whitney, Blecksmith & Zilliacus*
Wier, Daniel — *Daniel Wier & Associates*
Wilbanks, George R. — *Russell Reynolds Associates, Inc.*
Wilder, Richard B. — *Columbia Consulting Group*
Wilkinson, Barbara — *Beall & Company, Inc.*
Wilkinson, Jr. SPHR
Wilkinson, Charles E. — *The HRM Group, Inc.*
Williams, Angie — *Whitney & Associates, Inc.*
Williams, Gary L. — *Barnes Development Group, LLC*
Williams, Jack — *A.T. Kearney, Inc.*
Williams, Lis — *Executive Options, Ltd.*
Williams, Roger K. — *Williams, Roth & Krueger Inc.*
Williams, Stephen E. — *Barton Associates, Inc.*
Williams, Walter E. — *Lamalie Amrop International*
Willis, William H. — *William Willis Worldwide Inc.*
Wilson, Derrick — *Thornton Resources*
Wilson, John — *Korn/Ferry International*
Wilson, Patricia L. — *Leon A. Farley Associates*
Winitz, Joel — *GSW Consulting Group, Inc.*
Winitz, Marla — *GSW Consulting Group, Inc.*
Winograd, Glenn — *Criterion Executive Search, Inc.*
Winston, Dale — *Battalia Winston International*
Wirtshafter, Linda — *Grant Cooper and Associates*
Wisch, Steven C. — *MB Inc. Interim Executive Division*
Wise, J. Herbert — *Sandhurst Associates*
Wold, Ted W. — *Hyde Danforth Wold & Co.*
Wolf, Stephen M. — *Byron Leonard International, Inc.*
Womack, Joseph — *The Bankers Group*
Wood, John S. — *Egon Zehnder International Inc.*
Wood, Milton M. — *M. Wood Company*
Woodmansee, Bruce J. — *Tully/Woodmansee International, Inc.*
Woodworth, Gail — *Woodworth International Group*

Wooldridge, Jeff — *Ray & Berndtson*
Wooller, Edmund A.M. — *Windsor International*
Wright, A. Leo — *The Hindman Company*
Wright, Carl A.J. — *A.J. Burton Group, Inc.*
Wright, Charles D. — *Goodrich & Sherwood Associates, Inc.*
Wright, Leslie — *The Stevenson Group of New Jersey*
Yaekle, Gary — *Tully/Woodmansee International, Inc.*
Yen, Maggie Yeh Ching — *Ray & Berndtson*
Yungerberg, Steven — *Steven Yungerberg Associates Inc.*
Zadfar, Maryanne — *The Thomas Tucker Company*
Zaffrann, Craig S. — *P.J. Murphy & Associates, Inc.*
Zahradka, James F. — *P.J. Murphy & Associates, Inc.*
Zak, Adam — *Adams & Associates International*
Zaleta, Andy R. — *A.T. Kearney, Inc.*
Zamborsky, George — *Boyden*
Zaslav, Debra M. — *Telford, Adams & Alexander/Telford & Co., Inc.*
Zavala, Lorenzo — *Russell Reynolds Associates, Inc.*
Zay, Thomas C. — *Boyden/Zay & Company*
Zay, Thomas C. — *Boyden/Zay & Company*
Zetto, Kathryn — *Seco & Zetto Associates, Inc.*
Zila, Laurie M. — *Princeton Entrepreneurial Resources*
Zivic, Janis M. — *Spencer Stuart*
Zonis, Hildy R. — *Accountants Executive Search*
Zucker, Nancy — *Maximum Management Corp.*
Zwell, Michael — *Zwell International*

2. Financial Services

Abbatiello, Christine Murphy — *Winter, Wyman & Company*
Abell, Vincent W. — *MSI International*
Abernathy, Donald E. — *Don Richard Associates of Charlotte*
Abert, Janice — *Ledbetter/Davidson International, Inc.*
Abramson, Roye — *Source Services Corporation*
Ackerman, Larry R. — *Spectrum Search Associates, Inc.*
Adams, Amy — *Richard, Wayne and Roberts*
Adams, Jeffrey C. — *Telford, Adams & Alexander/Jeffrey C. Adams & Co., Inc.*
Adams, Len — *The KPA Group*
Adler, Louis S. — *CJA - The Adler Group*
Agee, Jo Etta — *Chrisman & Company, Incorporated*
Albert, Richard — *Source Services Corporation*
Alexander, John T. — *Telford, Adams & Alexander*
Alford, Holly — *Source Services Corporation*
Allard, Susan — *Allard Associates*
Allen, Jean E. — *Lamalie Amrop International*
Allen, Scott — *Chrisman & Company, Incorporated*
Allen, William L. — *The Hindman Company*
Allgire, Mary L. — *Kenzer Corp.*
Allred, J. Michael — *Spencer Stuart*
Alringer, Marc — *Source Services Corporation*
Altreuter, Rose — *ALTCO Temporary Services*
Altreuter, Rose — *The ALTCO Group*

Ambler, Peter W. — *Peter W. Ambler Company*
Amico, Robert — *Source Services Corporation*
Amilowski, Maria — *Highland Search Group*
Anderson, Maria H. — *Barton Associates, Inc.*
Anderson, Mary — *Source Services Corporation*
Anderson, Matthew — *Source Services Corporation*
Anderson, Richard — *Grant Cooper and Associates*
Anderson, Shawn — *Temporary Accounting Personnel, Inc.*
Anderson, Steve — *CPS Inc.*
Anderson, Terry — *Intech Summit Group, Inc.*
Andre, Jacques P. — *Ray & Berndtson*
Andujo, Michele M. — *Chrisman & Company, Incorporated*
Anwar, Tarin — *Jay Gaines & Company, Inc.*
Archer, Sandra F. — *Ryan, Miller & Associates Inc.*
Argenio, Michelangelo — *Spencer Stuart*
Argentin, Jo — *Executive Placement Consultants, Inc.*
Arms, Douglas — *TOPAZ International, Inc.*
Arms, Douglas — *TOPAZ Legal Solutions*
Aronin, Michael — *Fisher-Todd Associates*
Aronow, Lawrence E. — *Aronow Associates, Inc.*
Ascher, Susan P. — *The Ascher Group*
Aston, Kathy — *Marra Peters & Partners*
Attell, Harold — *A.E. Feldman Associates*
Atwood, Barrie — *The Abbott Group, Inc.*
Austin Lockton, Kathy — *Juntunen-Combs-Poirier*
Axelrod, Nancy R. — *A.T. Kearney, Inc.*
Aydelotte, G. Thomas — *Ingram & Aydelotte Inc./I-I-C Partners*
Bacher, Judith — *Spencer Stuart*
Bader, Sam — *Bader Research Corporation*
Badger, Fred H. — *The Badger Group*
Baeder, Jeremy — *Executive Manning Corporation*
Baer, Kenneth — *Source Services Corporation*
Baglio, Robert — *Source Services Corporation*
Baier, Rebecca — *Source Services Corporation*
Bailey, Paul — *Austin-McGregor International*
Bailey, Vanessa — *Highland Search Group*
Baje, Sarah — *Innovative Search Group, LLC*
Baker, Gary M. — *Cochran, Cochran & Yale, Inc.*
Baker, Gary M. — *Temporary Accounting Personnel, Inc.*
Baker, Gerry — *A.T. Kearney, Inc.*
Bakken, Mark — *Source Services Corporation*
Balbone, Rich — *Executive Manning Corporation*
Balch, Randy — *CPS Inc.*
Balchumas, Charles — *Source Services Corporation*
Baldock, Robert G. — *Ray & Berndtson/Lovas Stanley*
Ballantine, Caroline B. — *Heidrick & Struggles, Inc.*
Baltaglia, Michael — *Cochran, Cochran & Yale, Inc.*
Balter, Sidney — *Source Services Corporation*
Banko, Scott — *Source Services Corporation*
Baranowski, Peter — *Source Services Corporation*
Barbour, Mary Beth — *Tully/Woodmansee International, Inc.*
Barger, H. Carter — *Barger & Sargeant, Inc.*
Barlow, Ken H. — *The Cherbonnier Group, Inc.*
Barnaby, Richard — *Source Services Corporation*
Barnes, Gary — *Brigade Inc.*

Barnes, Gregory — *Korn/Ferry International*
Barnes, Roanne L. — *Barnes Development Group, LLC*
Barnette, Dennis A. — *Heidrick & Struggles, Inc.*
Barnum, Toni M. — *Stone Murphy & Olson*
Barrett, J. David — *Heidrick & Struggles, Inc.*
Bartels, Fredrick — *Source Services Corporation*
Bartfield, Philip — *Source Services Corporation*
Barton, Gary R. — *Barton Associates, Inc.*
Barton, James — *Source Services Corporation*
Bason, Maurice L. — *Bason Associates Inc.*
Bass, M. Lynn — *Ray & Berndtson*
Bass, Nate — *Jacobson Associates*
Bassler, John — *Korn/Ferry International*
Bassman, Robert — *Kaye-Bassman International Corp.*
Bassman, Sandy — *Kaye-Bassman International Corp.*
Bates, Nina — *Allard Associates*
Batte, Carol — *Source Services Corporation*
Battles, Jonathan — *Korn/Ferry International*
Bauman, Martin H. — *Martin H. Bauman Associates, Inc.*
Bearman, Linda — *Grant Cooper and Associates*
Beaudin, Elizabeth C. — *Callan Associates, Ltd.*
Beaulieu, Genie A. — *Romac & Associates*
Beaver, Bentley H. — *The Onstott Group, Inc.*
Beaver, Robert — *Source Services Corporation*
Beckvold, John B. — *Atlantic Search Group, Inc.*
Beer, John — *People Management Northeast Incorporated*
Beeson, William B. — *Lawrence-Leiter & Co. Management Conultants*
Belden, Jeannette — *Source Services Corporation*
Belin, Jean — *Boyden*
Bell, Lloyd W. — *O'Brien & Bell*
Bell, Michael — *Spencer Stuart*
Bender, Alan — *Bender Executive Search*
Benjamin, Maurita — *Source Services Corporation*
Benson, Edward — *Source Services Corporation*
Berger, Jeffrey — *Source Services Corporation*
Berk-Levine, Margo — *MB Inc. Interim Executive Division*
Berman, Mitchell — *Carlyle Group*
Bernard, Bryan — *Source Services Corporation*
Bernas, Sharon — *Source Services Corporation*
Berne, Marlene — *The Whitney Group*
Berry, Harold B. — *The Hindman Company*
Bertoux, Michael P. — *Wilcox, Bertoux & Miller*
Bettick, Michael J. — *A.J. Burton Group, Inc.*
Betts, Suzette — *Source Services Corporation*
Bickett, Nicole — *Source Services Corporation*
Bidelman, Richard — *Source Services Corporation*
Bigelow, Dennis — *Marshall Consultants, Inc.*
Biggins, J. Veronica — *Heidrick & Struggles, Inc.*
Billington, William H. — *Spriggs & Company, Inc.*
Biolsi, Joseph — *Source Services Corporation*
Birkhead, Linda — *Zwell International*
Birns, Douglas — *Source Services Corporation*
Bishop, Barbara — *The Executive Source*
Bladon, Andrew — *Don Richard Associates of Tampa, Inc.*
Blake, Eileen — *Howard Fischer Associates, Inc.*
Bland, Walter — *Source Services Corporation*
Blassaras, Peggy — *Source Services Corporation*

Blecksmith, Edward L. — *Larsen, Whitney, Blecksmith & Zilliacus*
Blickle, Michael — *Source Services Corporation*
Bliley, Jerry — *Spencer Stuart*
Blim, Barbara — *JDG Associates, Ltd.*
Bloch, Suzanne — *Source Services Corporation*
Blocher, John — *Source Services Corporation*
Blumenthal, Paula — *J.P. Canon Associates*
Boel, Werner — *The Dalley Hewitt Company*
Bogansky, Amy — *Conex Incorporated*
Bohn, Steve J. — *MSI International*
Boltrus, Dick — *Sink, Walker, Boltrus International*
Bond, Robert J. — *Romac & Associates*
Bonifield, Len — *Bonifield Associates*
Bonnell, William R. — *Bonnell Associates Ltd.*
Booth, Ronald — *Source Services Corporation*
Borden, Stuart — *M.A. Churchill & Associates, Inc.*
Borkin, Andrew — *Strategic Advancement Inc.*
Borland, James — *Goodrich & Sherwood Associates, Inc.*
Bormann, Cindy Ann — *MSI International*
Bosward, Allan — *Source Services Corporation*
Bourrie, Sharon D. — *Chartwell Partners International, Inc.*
Bovich, Maryann C. — *Higdon Prince Inc.*
Bowen, Tad — *Executive Search International*
Boyle, Russell E. — *Egon Zehnder International Inc.*
Brackenbury, Robert — *Bowman & Marshall, Inc.*
Bradley, Dalena — *Woodworth International Group*
Bradshaw, Monte — *Christian & Timbers*
Brady, Coloin — *Johnson Smith & Knisely Accord*
Brady, Dick — *William Guy & Associates*
Brady, Robert — *CPS Inc.*
Brandeau, John — *Chrisman & Company, Incorporated*
Brandeis, Richard — *CPS Inc.*
Brandenburg, David — *Professional Staffing Consultants*
Brandjes, Michael J. — *Brandjes Associates*
Brandon, Irwin — *Hadley Lockwood, Inc.*
Brassard, Gary — *Source Services Corporation*
Bratches, Howard — *Thorndike Deland Associates*
Bremer, Brian — *Source Services Corporation*
Brennan, Patrick J. — *Handy HRM Corp.*
Brenner, Mary — *Prestige Inc.*
Brewster, Edward — *Source Services Corporation*
Brieger, Steve — *Thorne, Brieger Associates Inc.*
Brindise, Michael J. — *Dynamic Search Systems, Inc.*
Brinson, Robert — *MSI International*
Broadhurst, Austin — *Lamalie Amrop International*
Brocaglia, Joyce — *Alta Associates, Inc.*
Bronger, Patricia — *Source Services Corporation*
Brophy, Melissa — *Maximum Management Corp.*
Brother, Joy — *Charles Luntz & Associates. Inc.*
Brown, Buzz — *Brown, Bernardy, Van Remmen, Inc.*
Brown, Clifford — *Source Services Corporation*
Brown, D. Perry — *Don Richard Associates of Washington, D.C., Inc.*
Brown, Daniel — *Source Services Corporation*

Brown, Franklin Key — *Handy HRM Corp.*
Brown, Gina — *Strategic Alliance Network, Ltd.*
Brown, Lawrence Anthony — *MSI International*
Brown, S. Ross — *Egon Zehnder International Inc.*
Brown, Steffan — *Woodworth International Group*
Brown, Steve — *K. Russo Associates*
Brown, Steven — *Source Services Corporation*
Browne, Michael — *Source Services Corporation*
Bruce, Michael C. — *Spencer Stuart*
Brudno, Robert J. — *Savoy Partners, Ltd.*
Brunner, Terry — *Source Services Corporation*
Bruno, Deborah F. — *The Hindman Company*
Bryant, Richard D. — *Bryant Associates, Inc.*
Bryant, Shari G. — *Bryant Associates, Inc.*
Brzezinski, Ronald T. — *Callan Associates, Ltd.*
Buchalter, Allyson — *The Whitney Group*
Buckles, Donna — *Cochran, Cochran & Yale, Inc.*
Buggy, Linda — *Bonnell Associates Ltd.*
Bump, Gerald J. — *D.E. Foster Partners Inc.*
Burch, Donald — *Source Services Corporation*
Burchard, Stephen R. — *Burchard & Associates, Inc.*
Burden, Gene — *The Cherbonnier Group, Inc.*
Burke, John — *The Experts*
Burkhill, John — *The Talley Group*
Burnett-Stohner, Brendan G. — *Sullivan & Company*
Burns, Alan — *The Enns Partners Inc.*
Burns, Terence N. — *D.E. Foster Partners Inc.*
Bush, R. Stuart — *Russell Reynolds Associates, Inc.*
Busterna, Charles — *The KPA Group*
Butcher, Pascale — *F-O-R-T-U-N-E Personnel Consultants of Manatee County*
Butterfass, Stanley — *Butterfass, Pepe & MacCallan Inc.*
Buttrey, Daniel — *Source Services Corporation*
Buzolits, Patrick — *Source Services Corporation*
Bye, Randy — *Romac & Associates*
Byrnes, Thomas A. — *The Search Alliance, Inc.*
Cafero, Les — *Source Services Corporation*
Caldwell, C. Douglas — *The Caldwell Partners Amrop International*
Caldwell, William R. — *Pearson, Caldwell & Farnsworth, Inc.*
Calivas, Kay — *A.J. Burton Group, Inc.*
Call, David — *Cochran, Cochran & Yale, Inc.*
Callan, Robert M. — *Callan Associates, Ltd.*
Cameron, James W. — *Cameron Consulting*
Campbell, E. — *Source Services Corporation*
Campbell, Gary — *Romac & Associates*
Campbell, Jeff — *Source Services Corporation*
Campbell, Patricia A. — *The Onstott Group, Inc.*
Campbell, Robert Scott — *Wellington Management Group*
Campbell, Robert Scott — *Wellington Management Group*
Campbell, Thomas J. — *Heidrick & Struggles, Inc.*
Campbell, W. Ross — *Egon Zehnder International Inc.*
Cannavino, John J. — *Financial Resource Associates, Inc.*
Cannavino, Matthew J. — *Financial Resource Associates, Inc.*
Cannavo, Louise — *The Whitney Group*
Cannon, Alexis — *Richard, Wayne and Roberts*
Capizzi, Karen — *Cochran, Cochran & Yale, Inc.*

Cappe, Richard R. — *Roberts Ryan and Bentley*
Carideo, Joseph — *Thorndike Deland Associates*
Carlson, Eric — *Source Services Corporation*
Carlson, Judith — *Bowman & Marshall, Inc.*
Carnal, Rick — *Source Services Corporation*
Carrington, Timothy — *Korn/Ferry International*
Carro, Carl R. — *Executive Search Consultants International, Inc.*
Carrott, Gregory T. — *Egon Zehnder International Inc.*
Carter, Jon F. — *Egon Zehnder International Inc.*
Carter, Linda — *Source Services Corporation*
Carvalho-Esteves, Maria — *Source Services Corporation*
Cary, Con — *Cary & Associates*
Casal, Daniel G. — *Bonifield Associates*
Cashen, Anthony B. — *Lamalie Amrop International*
Castillo, Eduardo — *Korn/Ferry International*
Castine, Michael P. — *Highland Search Group*
Castle, Lisa — *Source Services Corporation*
Castriota, Dominic — *Rhodes Associates*
Caudill, Nancy — *Webb, Johnson Associates, Inc.*
Celenza, Catherine — *CPS Inc.*
Cersosimo, Rocco — *Source Services Corporation*
Chamberlin, Brooks T. — *Korn/Ferry International*
Chamberlin, Joan — *William Guy & Associates*
Chamberlin, Michael A. — *Tower Consultants, Ltd.*
Champion, Geoffrey — *Korn/Ferry International*
Chan, Margaret — *Webb, Johnson Associates, Inc.*
Chappell, Peter — *Robertson & Associates*
Chappell, Peter — *The Bankers Group*
Charles, Ronald D. — *The Caldwell Partners Amrop International*
Chase, James — *Source Services Corporation*
Chatterjie, Alok — *MSI International*
Cheah, Victor — *Source Services Corporation*
Cherbonnier, L. Michael — *The Cherbonnier Group, Inc.*
Cho, Ui — *Richard, Wayne and Roberts*
Chrisman, Timothy R. — *Chrisman & Company, Incorporated*
Christenson, H. Alan — *Christenson & Hutchison*
Christian, Philip — *Ray & Berndtson*
Christiansen, Amy — *CPS Inc.*
Christiansen, Doug — *CPS Inc.*
Christman, Joel — *Source Services Corporation*
Chronopoulos, Dennis — *Source Services Corporation*
Citarella, Richard A. — *A.T. Kearney, Inc.*
Citrin, James M. — *Spencer Stuart*
Citrin, Lea — *K.L. Whitney Company*
Cizek, John T. — *Cizek Associates, Inc.*
Cizek, Marti J. — *Cizek Associates, Inc.*
Clark, Donald B. — *Ray & Berndtson*
Clark, Evan — *The Whitney Group*
Clark, James — *CPS Inc.*
Clark, Julie — *Corporate Recruiters Ltd.*
Clark, Steven — *D.A. Kreuter Associates, Inc.*
Clauhsen, Elizabeth A. — *Savoy Partners, Ltd.*
Clawson, Bob — *Source Services Corporation*
Clawson, Robert — *Source Services Corporation*
Clayton, Fred J. — *Berkhemer Clayton Incorporated*
Clemens, Bill — *Spencer Stuart*

Cloutier, Gisella — *Dinte Resources, Inc.*
Cocchiaro, Richard — *Romac & Associates*
Cocconi, Alan — *Source Services Corporation*
Cochran, Scott P. — *The Badger Group*
Cochrun, James — *Source Services Corporation*
Coe, Karen J. — *Coe & Company International Inc.*
Cohen, Michael R. — *Intech Summit Group, Inc.*
Cohen, Pamela — *TOPAZ International, Inc.*
Cohen, Pamela — *TOPAZ Legal Solutions*
Cohen, Robert C. — *Intech Summit Group, Inc.*
Colasanto, Frank M. — *W.R. Rosato & Associates, Inc.*
Cole, Kevin — *Don Richard Associates of Washington, D.C., Inc.*
Cole, Rosalie — *Source Services Corporation*
Coleman, J. Gregory — *Korn/Ferry International*
Coleman, Patricia — *Korn/Ferry International*
Collins, Scott — *Source Services Corporation*
Collins, Stephen — *The Johnson Group, Inc.*
Collis, Martin — *E.L. Shore & Associates Ltd.*
Colman, Michael — *Executive Placement Consultants, Inc.*
Comai, Christine — *Source Services Corporation*
Combs, Stephen L. — *Juntunen-Combs-Poirier*
Combs, Thomas — *Source Services Corporation*
Comstock, Rodger — *Johnson Smith & Knisely Accord*
Cona, Joseph A. — *Cona Personnel Search*
Conard, Rodney J. — *Conard Associates, Inc.*
Coneys, Bridget — *Source Services Corporation*
Conley, Kevin E. — *Lamalie Amrop International*
Connaghan, Linda — *Bowman & Marshall, Inc.*
Connelly, Kevin M. — *Spencer Stuart*
Conway, Maureen — *Conway & Associates*
Cook, Charlene — *Source Services Corporation*
Cook, Dennis — *A.T. Kearney, Inc.*
Cooke, Katherine H. — *Horton International*
Corso, Glen S. — *Chartwell Partners International, Inc.*
Cortina Del Valle, Pedro — *Ray & Berndtson*
Costello, Lynda — *Coe & Company International Inc.*
Cotugno, James — *Source Services Corporation*
Coughlin, Stephen — *Source Services Corporation*
Coulman, Karen — *CPS Inc.*
Courtney, Brendan — *A.J. Burton Group, Inc.*
Coyle, Hugh F. — *A.J. Burton Group, Inc.*
Cramer, Paul J. — *C/R Associates*
Crane, Howard C. — *Chartwell Partners International, Inc.*
Crath, Paul F. — *Price Waterhouse*
Crawford, Cassondra — *Don Richard Associates of Washington, D.C., Inc.*
Crecos, Gregory P. — *Gregory Michaels and Associates, Inc.*
Crist, Peter — *Crist Partners, Ltd.*
Critchley, Walter — *Cochran, Cochran & Yale, Inc.*
Critchley, Walter — *Temporary Accounting Personnel, Inc.*
Cronin, Dolores — *Corporate Careers, Inc.*
Cruz, Catherine — *TOPAZ International, Inc.*
Cruz, Catherine — *TOPAZ Legal Solutions*
Crystal, Jonathan A. — *Spencer Stuart*
Cuddy, Brian C. — *Romac & Associates*

Cuddy, Patricia — *Source Services Corporation*
Cunningham, Lawrence — *Howard Fischer Associates, Inc.*
Cunningham, Robert Y. — *Goodrich & Sherwood Associates, Inc.*
Curren, Camella — *Source Services Corporation*
Curtis, Ellissa — *Cochran, Cochran & Yale, Inc.*
Cushman, Judith — *Judith Cushman & Associates*
Cutka, Matthew — *Source Services Corporation*
Czepiel, Susan — *CPS Inc.*
D'Elia, Arthur P. — *Korn/Ferry International*
Dabich, Thomas M. — *Robert Harkins Associates, Inc.*
Danforth, W. Michael — *Hyde Danforth Wold & Co.*
Daniels, Alfred — *Alfred Daniels & Associates*
Daniels, C. Eugene — *Sigma Group International*
Dankberg, Iris — *Source Services Corporation*
Dannenberg, Richard A. — *Roberts Ryan and Bentley*
Darter, Steven M. — *People Management Northeast Incorporated*
Davis, C. Scott — *Source Services Corporation*
Davis, Elease — *Source Services Corporation*
Davis, Joan — *MSI International*
Davis, Steven M. — *Sullivan & Company*
Dawson, William — *Source Services Corporation*
de Bardin, Francesca — *F.L. Taylor & Company, Inc.*
De Brun, Thomas P. — *Ray & Berndtson*
de Cholnoky, Andrea — *Spencer Stuart*
de Palacios, Jeannette C. — *J. Palacios & Associates, Inc.*
de Tuede, Catherine — *The Search Alliance, Inc.*
De Zara, Max — *Carlyle Group*
Dean, Mary — *Korn/Ferry International*
Deaver, Henry C. — *Ray & Berndtson*
Debus, Wayne — *Source Services Corporation*
Deck, Jack — *Source Services Corporation*
DeCorrevont, James — *DeCorrevont & Associates*
DeCorrevont, James — *DeCorrevont & Associates*
DeHart, Donna — *Tower Consultants, Ltd.*
Del Prete, Karen — *Gilbert Tweed/INESA*
Delaney, Patrick J. — *Sensible Solutions, Inc.*
Delman, Charles — *Korn/Ferry International*
Delmonico, Laura — *A.J. Burton Group, Inc.*
DeMarco, Robert — *Source Services Corporation*
Demchak, James P. — *Sandhurst Associates*
Desai, Sushila — *Sink, Walker, Boltrus International*
Desmond, Dennis — *Beall & Company, Inc.*
Desmond, Mary — *Source Services Corporation*
Dever, Mary — *Source Services Corporation*
Devito, Alice — *Source Services Corporation*
deVry, Kimberly A. — *Tower Consultants, Ltd.*
deWilde, David M. — *Chartwell Partners International, Inc.*
Dewing, Jesse J. — *Don Richard Associates of Charlotte*
Dezember, Steve — *Ray & Berndtson*
Di Filippo, Thomas — *Source Services Corporation*
DiCioccio, Carmen — *Cochran, Cochran & Yale, Inc.*
Dickey, Chester W. — *Bowden & Company, Inc.*
Dickey, Chester W. — *Bowden & Company, Inc.*

Dickson, Duke — *A.D. & Associates Executive Search, Inc.*
Dieckmann, Ralph E. — *Dieckmann & Associates, Ltd.*
Diers, Gary — *Source Services Corporation*
Dietz, David S. — *MSI International*
DiFilippo, James — *Korn/Ferry International*
DiGiovanni, Charles — *Penn Search*
Dingeldey, Peter E. — *Search Advisors International Corp.*
Dingman, Bruce — *Robert W. Dingman Company, Inc.*
Dinte, Paul — *Dinte Resources, Inc.*
DiPiazza, Joseph — *Boyden*
DiSalvo, Fred — *The Cambridge Group Ltd*
Diskin, Rochelle — *Search West, Inc.*
Dittmar, Richard — *Source Services Corporation*
Divine, Robert S. — *O'Shea, Divine & Company, Inc.*
Dixon, Aris — *CPS Inc.*
Do, Sonnie — *Whitney & Associates, Inc.*
Dobrow, Samuel — *Source Services Corporation*
Doele, Donald C. — *Goodrich & Sherwood Associates, Inc.*
Donahue, Debora — *Source Services Corporation*
Dong, Stephen — *Executive Search, Ltd.*
Donnelly, George J. — *Ward Howell International, Inc.*
Donnelly, Patti — *Source Services Corporation*
Dorfner, Martin — *Source Services Corporation*
Dorsey, Jim — *Ryan, Miller & Associates Inc.*
Dotson, M. Ileen — *Dotson & Associates*
Doukas, Jon A. — *Professional Bank Services, Inc. D/B/A Executive Search, Inc.*
Dowdall, Jean — *A.T. Kearney, Inc.*
Dowell, Mary K. — *Professional Search Associates*
Dowlatzadch, Homayoun — *Source Services Corporation*
Downs, James L. — *Sanford Rose Associates*
Downs, William — *Source Services Corporation*
Doyle, James W. — *Executive Search Consultants International, Inc.*
Doyle, John P. — *Ray & Berndtson*
Dreifus, Donald — *Search West, Inc.*
Dressler, Ralph — *Romac & Associates*
Dromeshauser, Peter — *Dromeshauser Associates*
Drummond-Hay, Peter — *Russell Reynolds Associates, Inc.*
Dubbs, William — *Williams Executive Search, Inc.*
Duckworth, Donald R. — *Johnson Smith & Knisely Accord*
Ducruet, Linda K. — *Heidrick & Struggles, Inc.*
Dudley, Craig J. — *Ray & Berndtson*
Duelks, John — *Source Services Corporation*
Dunbar, Marilynne — *Ray & Berndtson/Lovas Stanley*
Duncan, Dana — *Source Services Corporation*
Dunkel, David L. — *Romac & Associates*
Dunlow, Aimee — *Source Services Corporation*
Dunman, Betsy L. — *Crawford & Crofford*
Dunn, Mary Helen — *Ray & Berndtson*
Dupont, Rick — *Source Services Corporation*
Durakis, Charles A. — *C.A. Durakis Associates, Inc.*
Dwyer, Julie — *CPS Inc.*

Fust, Sheely F. — *Ray & Berndtson*
Fyhrie, David — *Source Services Corporation*
Gabler, Howard A. — *G.Z. Stephens Inc.*
Gabriel, David L. — *The Arcus Group*
Gaffney, Megan — *Source Services Corporation*
Gaines, Jay — *Jay Gaines & Company, Inc.*
Gaines, Ronni L. — *TOPAZ International, Inc.*
Gaines, Ronni L. — *TOPAZ Legal Solutions*
Galante, Suzanne M. — *Vlcek & Company, Inc.*
Gallagher, Terence M. — *Battalia Winston International*
Gamble, Ira — *Source Services Corporation*
Gantar, Donna — *Howard Fischer Associates, Inc.*
Gardiner, E. Nicholas P. — *Gardiner International*
Gardner, Michael — *Source Services Corporation*
Garfinkle, Steven M. — *Battalia Winston International*
Garland, Dick — *Dick Garland Consultants*
Garrett, Mark — *Source Services Corporation*
Garzone, Dolores — *M.A. Churchill & Associates, Inc.*
Gates, Lucille C. — *Lamalie Amrop International*
Gauthier, Robert C. — *Columbia Consulting Group*
Geiger, Jan — *Wilcox, Bertoux & Miller*
Gennawey, Robert — *Source Services Corporation*
George, Brenda — *Don Richard Associates of Charlotte*
George, Delores F. — *Delores F. George Human Resource Management & Consulting Industry*
Gerber, Mark J. — *Wellington Management Group*
Germain, Valerie — *Jay Gaines & Company, Inc.*
Gerster, J.P. — *Juntunen-Combs-Poirier*
Gestwick, Daniel — *Cochran, Cochran & Yale, Inc.*
Ghurani, Mac — *Gary Kaplan & Associates*
Giacalone, Louis — *Allard Associates*
Gibbons, Ronald L. — *Flynn, Hannock, Incorporated*
Gibbs, John S. — *Spencer Stuart*
Giesy, John — *Source Services Corporation*
Gilbert, Jerry — *Gilbert & Van Campen International*
Gilbert, Patricia G. — *Lynch Miller Moore, Inc.*
Gilinsky, David — *Source Services Corporation*
Gill, Patricia — *Columbia Consulting Group*
Gill, Susan — *Plummer & Associates, Inc.*
Gillespie, Thomas — *Professional Search Consultants*
Giries, Juliet D. — *Barton Associates, Inc.*
Glass, Lori — *The Executive Source*
Glickman, Leenie — *Source Services Corporation*
Gluzman, Arthur — *Source Services Corporation*
Gnatowski, Bruce — *Source Services Corporation*
Goar, Duane R. — *Sandhurst Associates*
Gobert, Larry — *Professional Search Consultants*
Goedtke, Steven — *Southwestern Professional Services*
Gold, Donald — *Executive Search, Ltd.*
Golde, Lisa — *Tully/Woodmansee International, Inc.*
Goldenberg, Susan — *Grant Cooper and Associates*
Goldsmith, Joseph B. — *Higdon Prince Inc.*
Goldstein, Gary — *The Whitney Group*

Goldstein, Steven G. — *The Jonathan Stevens Group, Inc.*
Gonye, Peter K. — *Egon Zehnder International Inc.*
Gonzalez, Kristen — *A.J. Burton Group, Inc.*
Gonzalez, Rafael — *Korn/Ferry International*
Goodman, Dawn M. — *Bason Associates Inc.*
Goodman, Julie — *Search West, Inc.*
Goodwin, Gary — *Source Services Corporation*
Goodwin, Tim — *William Guy & Associates*
Gordon, Gerald L. — *E.G. Jones Associates, Ltd.*
Gordon, Teri — *Don Richard Associates of Washington, D.C., Inc.*
Gorman, Patrick — *Source Services Corporation*
Gorman, T. Patrick — *Techsearch Services, Inc.*
Gotlys, Jordan — *Stone Murphy & Olson*
Gourley, Timothy — *Source Services Corporation*
Gow, Roderick C. — *Lamalie Amrop International*
Grado, Eduardo — *Source Services Corporation*
Graff, Jack — *Source Services Corporation*
Graham, Craig — *Ward Howell International, Inc.*
Graham, Dale — *CPS Inc.*
Graham, Shannon — *Source Services Corporation*
Grand, Gordon — *Russell Reynolds Associates, Inc.*
Grandinetti, Suzanne — *Source Services Corporation*
Grant, Michael — *Zwell International*
Grantham, John — *Grantham & Co., Inc.*
Grantham, Philip H. — *Columbia Consulting Group*
Grasch, Jerry E. — *The Hindman Company*
Grassl, Peter O. — *Bowman & Marshall, Inc.*
Graves, Rosemarie — *Don Richard Associates of Washington, D.C., Inc.*
Gray, Annie — *Annie Gray Associates, Inc./The Executive Search Firm*
Gray, Betty — *Accent on Achievement, Inc.*
Gray, Heather — *Source Services Corporation*
Gray, Russell — *Source Services Corporation*
Grayson, E.C. — *Spencer Stuart*
Graziano, Lisa — *Source Services Corporation*
Gresia, Paul — *Source Services Corporation*
Griffin, Cathy — *A.T. Kearney, Inc.*
Groban, Jack — *A.T. Kearney, Inc.*
Groner, David — *Source Services Corporation*
Grossman, James — *Source Services Corporation*
Grossman, Martin — *Source Services Corporation*
Grotenhuis, Dirkten — *Chrisman & Company, Incorporated*
Grumulaitis, Leo — *Source Services Corporation*
Grzybowski, Jill — *CPS Inc.*
Guc, Stephen — *Source Services Corporation*
Gudino, Richard — *Keith Bagg & Associates Inc.*
Gulian, Randolph — *Strategic Executives, Inc.*
Gurnani, Angali — *Executive Placement Consultants, Inc.*
Gurtin, Kay L. — *Executive Options, Ltd.*
Guthrie, Stuart — *Source Services Corporation*
Guy, C. William — *William Guy & Associates*
Haas, Margaret P. — *The Haas Associates, Inc.*
Habelmann, Gerald B. — *Habelmann & Associates*
Haberman, Joseph C. — *A.T. Kearney, Inc.*
Hacker-Taylor, Dianna — *Source Services Corporation*

Haddad, Charles — *Romac & Associates*
Hagerty, Kenneth — *Korn/Ferry International*
Hagglund, Karl H. — *Simpson Associates, Inc.*
Haider, Martin — *Source Services Corporation*
Hailey, H.M. — *Damon & Associates, Inc.*
Halbrich, Mitch — *A.J. Burton Group, Inc.*
Hales, Daphne — *Source Services Corporation*
Hall, Peter V. — *Chartwell Partners International, Inc.*
Halladay, Patti — *Intersource, Ltd.*
Hallagan, Robert E. — *Heidrick & Struggles, Inc.*
Haller, Mark — *Source Services Corporation*
Hallock, Peter B. — *Goodrich & Sherwood Associates, Inc.*
Hallstrom, Victoria — *The Whitney Group*
Hamilton, John R. — *Ray & Berndtson*
Hamm, Gary — *Source Services Corporation*
Hamm, Mary Kay — *Romac & Associates*
Hammond, Karla — *People Management Northeast Incorporated*
Hampshire, Kay — *Allard Associates*
Hanes, Leah — *Ray & Berndtson*
Hanley, Alan P. — *Williams, Roth & Krueger Inc.*
Hanley, Maureen E. — *Gilbert Tweed/INESA*
Hanley, Steven — *Source Services Corporation*
Hanna, Remon — *Source Services Corporation*
Hannock, Elwin W. — *Flynn, Hannock, Incorporated*
Hanson, Grant M. — *Goodrich & Sherwood Associates, Inc.*
Hanson, Lee — *Heidrick & Struggles, Inc.*
Harbaugh, Paul J. — *International Management Advisors, Inc.*
Harbert, David O. — *Sweeney Harbert & Mummert, Inc.*
Hardison, Richard L. — *Hardison & Company*
Harfenist, Harry — *Parker Page Group*
Hargis, N. Leann — *Montgomery Resources, Inc.*
Harney, Elyane — *Gary Kaplan & Associates*
Harp, Kimberly — *Source Services Corporation*
Harrell, L. Parker — *Korn/Ferry International*
Harris, Jack — *A.T. Kearney, Inc.*
Harris, Julia — *The Whitney Group*
Harrison, Joel — *D.A. Kreuter Associates, Inc.*
Harrison, Patricia — *Source Services Corporation*
Hart, Andrew D. — *Russell Reynolds Associates, Inc.*
Hart, Crystal — *Source Services Corporation*
Hart, David — *Hadley Lockwood, Inc.*
Hart, James — *Source Services Corporation*
Hart, Robert T. — *D.E. Foster Partners Inc.*
Hartle, Larry — *CPS Inc.*
Harty, Shirley Cox — *Ray & Berndtson*
Harvey, Mike — *Advanced Executive Resources*
Harwood, Brian — *Source Services Corporation*
Haselby, James — *Source Services Corporation*
Hasten, Lawrence — *Source Services Corporation*
Haughton, Michael — *DeFrain, Mayer LLC*
Hawksworth, A. Dwight — *A.D. & Associates Executive Search, Inc.*
Hawley, Robert E. — *Hayden Group, Incorporated*
Hay, William E. — *William E. Hay & Co.*
Hayes, Lee — *Source Services Corporation*
Haystead, Steve — *Advanced Executive Resources*
Hazerjian, Cynthia — *CPS Inc.*
Heafey, Bill — *CPS Inc.*

Healey, Joseph T. — *Highland Search Group*
Heaney, Thomas — *Korn/Ferry International*
Hedlund, David — *Hedlund Corporation*
Heiken, Barbara E. — *Randell-Heiken, Inc.*
Heinrich, Scott — *Source Services Corporation*
Heinze, David — *Heinze & Associates, Inc.*
Hellebusch, Jerry — *Morgan Hunter Corp.*
Heller, Steven A. — *Martin H. Bauman Associates, Inc.*
Hellinger, Audrey W. — *Martin H. Bauman Associates, Inc.*
Hendrickson, Jill E. — *Gregory Michaels and Associates, Inc.*
Heneghan, Donald A. — *Allerton Heneghan & O'Neill*
Henn, George W. — *G.W. Henn & Company*
Henneberry, Ward — *Source Services Corporation*
Hennig, Sandra M. — *MSI International*
Henry, Mary — *Conex Incorporated*
Hensley, Bert — *Morgan Samuels Co., Inc.*
Hensley, Gayla — *Atlantic Search Group, Inc.*
Hergenrather, Richard A. — *Hergenrather & Company*
Herman, Pat — *Whitney & Associates, Inc.*
Herman, Shelli — *Gary Kaplan & Associates*
Hernandez, Ruben — *Source Services Corporation*
Heroux, David — *Source Services Corporation*
Herzog, Sarah — *Source Services Corporation*
Hetherman, Margaret F. — *Highland Search Group*
Hewitt, Rives D. — *The Dalley Hewitt Company*
Hewitt, W. Davis — *The Dalley Hewitt Company*
Higbee, Joan — *Thorndike Deland Associates*
Higdon, Henry G. — *Higdon Prince Inc.*
Higgins, Donna — *Howard Fischer Associates, Inc.*
Higgins, William — *William Guy & Associates*
Hight, Susan — *Source Services Corporation*
Hilbert, Laurence — *Source Services Corporation*
Hildebrand, Thomas B. — *Professional Resources Group, Inc.*
Hilgenberg, Thomas — *Source Services Corporation*
Hill, Emery — *MSI International*
Hill, Randall W. — *Heidrick & Struggles, Inc.*
Hilliker, Alan D. — *Egon Zehnder International Inc.*
Hillyer, Carolyn — *Source Services Corporation*
Himes, Dirk — *A.T. Kearney, Inc.*
Himlin, Amy — *Cochran, Cochran & Yale, Inc.*
Hindman, Neil C. — *The Hindman Company*
Hinojosa, Oscar — *Source Services Corporation*
Hobart, John N. — *Ray & Berndtson*
Hochberg, Brian — *M.A. Churchill & Associates, Inc.*
Hocking, Jeffrey — *Korn/Ferry International*
Hodge, Jeff — *Heidrick & Struggles, Inc.*
Hoevel, Michael J. — *Poirier, Hoevel & Co.*
Hoffman, Stephen — *Source Services Corporation*
Hofner, Andrew — *Source Services Corporation*
Hofner, Kevin E. — *Lamalie Amrop International*
Holland, John A. — *Holland, McFadzean & Associates, Inc.*
Holland, Kathleen — *TOPAZ International, Inc.*

Holland, Kathleen — *TOPAZ Legal Solutions*
Holland, Rose Mary — *Price Waterhouse*
Holmes, Lawrence J. — *Columbia Consulting Group*
Holodnak, William A. — *J. Robert Scott*
Holzberger, Georges L. — *Highland Search Group*
Honer, Paul E. — *Ingram & Aydelotte Inc./I-I-C Partners*
Honey, W. Michael M. — *O'Callaghan Honey/Ray & Berndtson, Inc.*
Hoover, Catherine — *J.L. Mark Associates, Inc.*
Hopkins, Chester A. — *Handy HRM Corp.*
Hopkinson, Dana — *Winter, Wyman & Company*
Hopp, Lorrie A. — *Gregory Michaels and Associates, Inc.*
Hopper, John W. — *William Guy & Associates*
Hoskins, Charles R. — *Heidrick & Struggles, Inc.*
Hostetter, Kristi — *Source Services Corporation*
Houterloot, Tim — *Source Services Corporation*
Howard, Lee Ann — *Lamalie Amrop International*
Howard, Leon — *Richard, Wayne and Roberts*
Howard, Susy — *The McCormick Group, Inc.*
Howe, Theodore — *Romac & Associates*
Howe, Vance A. — *Ward Howell International, Inc.*
Howell, Robert B. — *Atlantic Search Group, Inc.*
Howell, Robert B. — *Atlantic Search Group, Inc.*
Hoyda, Louis A. — *Thorndike Deland Associates*
Hucko, Donald S. — *Jonas, Walters & Assoc., Inc.*
Hudson, Reginald M. — *Search Bureau International*
Hughes, Barbara — *Source Services Corporation*
Hughes, R. Kevin — *Handy HRM Corp.*
Hughes, Randall — *Source Services Corporation*
Hult, Dana — *Source Services Corporation*
Humphrey, Titus — *Source Services Corporation*
Hunter, Steven — *Diamond Tax Recruiting*
Hurd, J. Nicholas — *Russell Reynolds Associates, Inc.*
Hurtado, Jaime — *Source Services Corporation*
Hutchison, William K. — *Christenson & Hutchison*
Hybels, Cynthia — *A.J. Burton Group, Inc.*
Hylas, Lisa — *Source Services Corporation*
Hyman, Linda — *Korn/Ferry International*
Hypes, Richard G. — *Lynch Miller Moore, Inc.*
Illsley, Hugh G. — *Ward Howell International, Inc.*
Imely, Larry S. — *Stratford Group*
Imhof, Kirk — *Source Services Corporation*
Inger, Barry — *Source Services Corporation*
Ingram, D. John — *Ingram & Aydelotte Inc./I-I-C Partners*
Inguagiato, Gregory — *MSI International*
Inskeep, Thomas — *Source Services Corporation*
Intravaia, Salvatore — *Source Services Corporation*
Irish, Alan — *CPS Inc.*
Irwin, Mark — *Source Services Corporation*
Issacs, Judith A. — *Grant Cooper and Associates*
Jablo, Steven A. — *Dieckmann & Associates, Ltd.*
Jackowitz, Todd — *J. Robert Scott*
Jackson, Joan — *A.T. Kearney, Inc.*
Jacobs, Martin J. — *The Rubicon Group*
Jacobs, Mike — *Thorne, Brieger Associates Inc.*
Jacobson, Hayley — *Source Services Corporation*
Jacobson, Rick — *The Windham Group*

Jadulang, Vincent — *Source Services Corporation*
Jaedike, Eldron — *Prestige Inc.*
James, Richard — *Criterion Executive Search, Inc.*
Janis, Laurence — *Integrated Search Solutions Group, LLC*
Jansen, John F. — *Delta Services*
Janssen, Don — *Howard Fischer Associates, Inc.*
Januale, Lois — *Cochran, Cochran & Yale, Inc.*
Januleski, Geoff — *Source Services Corporation*
Jazylo, John V. — *Handy HRM Corp.*
Jazylo, John V. — *Skott/Edwards Consultants, Inc.*
Jeffers, Richard B. — *Dieckmann & Associates, Ltd.*
Jeltema, John — *Source Services Corporation*
Jensen, Robert — *Source Services Corporation*
Jernigan, Susan N. — *Sockwell & Associates*
Joffe, Barry — *Bason Associates Inc.*
Johnson, Brian — *A.J. Burton Group, Inc.*
Johnson, Greg — *Source Services Corporation*
Johnson, Harold E. — *Lamalie Amrop International*
Johnson, John W. — *Webb, Johnson Associates, Inc.*
Johnson, Kathleen A. — *Barton Associates, Inc.*
Johnson, Keith — *Romac & Associates*
Johnson, Priscilla — *The Johnson Group, Inc.*
Johnson, S. Hope — *Boyden Washington, D.C.*
Johnson, Stanley C. — *Johnson & Company*
Johnson, Valerie — *Coe & Company International Inc.*
Johnston, James R. — *The Stevenson Group of Delaware Inc.*
Johnstone, Grant — *Source Services Corporation*
Jones, B.J. — *Intersource, Ltd.*
Jones, Barbara J. — *Kaye-Bassman International Corp.*
Jones, Daniel F. — *Atlantic Search Group, Inc.*
Jones, Herschel — *Korn/Ferry International*
Jones, Jonathan C. — *Canny, Bowen Inc.*
Jones, Rodney — *Source Services Corporation*
Jordan, Jon — *Cochran, Cochran & Yale, Inc.*
Jordan, Stephen T. — *Ray & Berndtson*
Jorgensen, Tom — *The Talley Group*
Joys, David S. — *Heidrick & Struggles, Inc.*
Judge, Alfred L. — *The Cambridge Group Ltd*
Judy, Otto — *CPS Inc.*
Juelis, John J. — *Peeney Associates*
Juratovac, Michael — *Montgomery Resources, Inc.*
Juska, Frank — *Rusher, Loscavio & LoPresto*
Kacyn, Louis J. — *Egon Zehnder International Inc.*
Kader, Richard — *Richard Kader & Associates*
Kaiser, Donald J. — *Dunhill International Search of New Haven*
Kaiser, Elaine M. — *Dunhill International Search of New Haven*
Kalinowski, David — *Jacobson Associates*
Kane, Frank — *A.J. Burton Group, Inc.*
Kane, Karen — *Howard Fischer Associates, Inc.*
Kanovsky, Gerald — *Career Consulting Group, Inc.*
Kanovsky, Marlene — *Career Consulting Group, Inc.*
Kantor, Richard — *Search West, Inc.*
Kaplan, Gary — *Gary Kaplan & Associates*
Kaplan, Traci — *Source Services Corporation*
Karalis, William — *CPS Inc.*

Levenson, Laurel — *Source Services Corporation*
Levine, Alan M. — *MB Inc. Interim Executive Division*
Levine, Irwin — *Source Services Corporation*
Levine, Lawrence — *Trebor Weldon Lawrence, Inc.*
Lewicki, Christopher — *MSI International*
Lewis, Daniel — *Source Services Corporation*
Lewis, Jon A. — *Sandhurst Associates*
Lewis, Marc D. — *Handy HRM Corp.*
Lewis, Sean — *Southwestern Professional Services*
Lezama Cohen, Luis — *Ray & Berndtson*
Liebowitz, Michael E. — *Highland Search Group*
Liebross, Eric — *Source Services Corporation*
Lin, Felix — *Source Services Corporation*
Lindberg, Eric J. — *MSI International*
Lindholst, Kai — *Egon Zehnder International Inc.*
Lindsay, M. Evan — *Heidrick & Struggles, Inc.*
Linton, Leonard M. — *Byron Leonard International, Inc.*
Lipuma, Thomas — *Source Services Corporation*
Litt, Michele — *The Whitney Group*
Little, Elizabeth A. — *Financial Resource Associates, Inc.*
Little, Suzaane — *Don Richard Associates of Tampa, Inc.*
Littman, Stephen — *Rhodes Associates*
Livingston, Peter R. — *Livingston, Robert and Company Inc.*
Loeb, Stephen H. — *Grant Cooper and Associates*
Loewenstein, Victor H. — *Egon Zehnder International Inc.*
Lofthouse, Cindy — *CPS Inc.*
Lokken, Karen — *A.E. Feldman Associates*
Lombardi, Nancy W. — *WTW Associates, Inc.*
Long, Helga — *Horton International*
Long, John — *Source Services Corporation*
Long, Mark — *Source Services Corporation*
Long, Milt — *William Guy & Associates*
Long, Thomas — *Egon Zehnder International Inc.*
Long, William G. — *McDonald, Long & Associates, Inc.*
Lonneke, John W. — *MSI International*
Looney, Scott — *A.E. Feldman Associates*
Loper, Doris — *Mortgage & Financial Personnel Services*
Lopis, Roberta — *Richard, Wayne and Roberts*
Loscavio, J. Michael — *Rusher, Loscavio & LoPresto*
Lotufo, Donald A. — *D.A.L. Associates, Inc.*
Lotz, R. James — *International Management Advisors, Inc.*
Loubet, Larry — *Carlyle Group*
Lovas, W. Carl — *Ray & Berndtson/Lovas Stanley*
Lovely, Edward — *The Stevenson Group of New Jersey*
Loving, Vikki — *Intersource, Ltd.*
Lucarelli, Joan — *The Onstott Group, Inc.*
Lucas, Ronnie L. — *MSI International*
Luce, Daniel — *Source Services Corporation*
Lucht, John — *The John Lucht Consultancy Inc.*
Ludder, Mark — *Source Services Corporation*
Ludlow, Michael — *Source Services Corporation*
Ludlow, Paula — *Horton International*
Lumsby, George N. — *International Management Advisors, Inc.*
Lundy, Martin — *Source Services Corporation*

Luntz, Charles E. — *Charles Luntz & Associates. Inc.*
Lupica, Anthony — *Cochran, Cochran & Yale, Inc.*
Lynam, Joseph V. — *Johnson Smith & Knisely Accord*
Lynch, Michael C. — *Lynch Miller Moore, Inc.*
Lyon, Jenny — *Marra Peters & Partners*
Lyons, Denis B.K. — *Spencer Stuart*
Lyons, Michael — *Source Services Corporation*
MacCallan, Deirdre — *Butterfass, Pepe & MacCallan Inc.*
Macdonald, G. William — *The Macdonald Group, Inc.*
MacDougall, Andrew J. — *Spencer Stuart*
MacIntyre, Lisa W. — *Highland Search Group*
MacMillan, James — *Source Services Corporation*
MacNaughton, Sperry — *McNaughton Associates*
Macomber, Keith S. — *Sullivan & Company*
MacPherson, Holly — *Source Services Corporation*
Macrides, Michael — *Source Services Corporation*
Madaras, Debra — *Financial Resource Associates, Inc.*
Maer, Harry — *Kenzer Corp.*
Magee, Harrison R. — *Bowden & Company, Inc.*
Maggio, Mary — *Source Services Corporation*
Mahmoud, Sophia — *Source Services Corporation*
Mahr, Toni — *K. Russo Associates*
Mairn, Todd — *Source Services Corporation*
Major, Susan — *A.T. Kearney, Inc.*
Makrianes, James K. — *Webb, Johnson Associates, Inc.*
Malcolm, Rod — *Korn/Ferry International*
Mallin, Ellen — *Howard Fischer Associates, Inc.*
Manassero, Henri J.P. — *International Management Advisors, Inc.*
Mangum, Maria — *Thomas Mangum Company*
Mangum, William T. — *Thomas Mangum Company*
Manns, Alex — *Crawford & Crofford*
Mansford, Keith — *Howard Fischer Associates, Inc.*
Manzo, Renee — *Atlantic Search Group, Inc.*
Maphet, Harriet — *The Stevenson Group of New Jersey*
Marino, Chester — *Cochran, Cochran & Yale, Inc.*
Marino, Jory J. — *Sullivan & Company*
Mark, John L. — *J.L. Mark Associates, Inc.*
Mark, Lynne — *J.L. Mark Associates, Inc.*
Marks, Russell E. — *Webb, Johnson Associates, Inc.*
Marks, Sarah J. — *The Executive Source*
Marra, John — *Marra Peters & Partners*
Marra, John — *Marra Peters & Partners*
Marshall, E. Leigh — *Norman Broadbent International, Inc.*
Marsteller, Franklin D. — *Spencer Stuart*
Martin, Jon — *Egon Zehnder International Inc.*
Marumoto, William H. — *Boyden Washington, D.C.*
Marwil, Jennifer — *Source Services Corporation*
Mashakas, Elizabeth — *TOPAZ International, Inc.*
Mashakas, Elizabeth — *TOPAZ Legal Solutions*

Masserman, Bruce — *Masserman & Associates, Inc.*
Massey, R. Bruce — *Horton International*
Mathias, Douglas — *Source Services Corporation*
Mathias, Kathy — *Stone Murphy & Olson*
Mathis, Carrie — *Source Services Corporation*
Mattes, Edward C. — *The Ogdon Partnership*
Matthews, Corwin — *Woodworth International Group*
Matthews, Mary — *Korn/Ferry International*
Mattingly, Kathleen — *Source Services Corporation*
Matueny, Robert — *Ryan, Miller & Associates Inc.*
Mauer, Kristin — *Montgomery Resources, Inc.*
Maxwell, John — *Source Services Corporation*
Mayer, Thomas — *Source Services Corporation*
Mayes, Kay H. — *John Shell Associates, Inc.*
Maynard Taylor, Susan — *Chrisman & Company, Incorporated*
Mazor, Elly — *Howard Fischer Associates, Inc.*
Mazza, David B. — *Mazza & Riley, Inc. (a Korn/Ferry International affiliate)*
McAndrews, Kathy — *CPS Inc.*
McAteer, Thomas — *Montgomery Resources, Inc.*
McBride, Jonathan E. — *McBride Associates, Inc.*
McBryde, Marnie — *Spencer Stuart*
McCallister, Richard A. — *Boyden*
McCann, Cornelia B. — *Spencer Stuart*
McCarthy, Laura — *Source Services Corporation*
McCarty, J. Rucker — *Heidrick & Struggles, Inc.*
McClement, John — *Korn/Ferry International*
McCloskey, Frank D. — *Johnson Smith & Knisely Accord*
McConnell, Greg — *Winter, Wyman & Company*
McCool, Anne G. — *Sullivan & Company*
McCormick, Brian — *The McCormick Group, Inc.*
McCormick, Harry B. — *Hayden Group, Incorporated*
McCormick, Joseph — *Source Services Corporation*
McDermott, Jeffrey T. — *Vlcek & Company, Inc.*
McDonald, Scott A. — *McDonald Associates International*
McDonald, Stanleigh B. — *McDonald Associates International*
McDowell, Robert N. — *Christenson & Hutchison*
McFadden, Ashton S. — *Johnson Smith & Knisely Accord*
McFadzen,, James A. — *Holland, McFadzean & Associates, Inc.*
McGinnis, Rita — *Source Services Corporation*
McGoldrick, Terrence — *Source Services Corporation*
McGuire, Pat — *A.J. Burton Group, Inc.*
McHugh, Keith — *Source Services Corporation*
McIntosh, Arthur — *Source Services Corporation*
McIntosh, Tad — *Source Services Corporation*
McKeown, Patricia A. — *DiMarchi Partners, Inc.*
McKinney, Julia — *Source Services Corporation*
McKnight, Amy E. — *Chartwell Partners International, Inc.*
McLaughlin, John — *Romac & Associates*
McLean, E. Peter — *Spencer Stuart*
McMahan, Stephen — *Source Services Corporation*
McMahan, Stephen — *Source Services Corporation*

McMillin, Bob — *Price Waterhouse*
McNamara, Catherine — *Ray & Berndtson*
McNamara, Timothy C. — *Columbia Consulting Group*
McNamara, Timothy Connor — *Horton International*
McNear, Jeffrey E. — *Barrett Partners*
McNichols, Walter B. — *Gary Kaplan & Associates*
McNulty, Kelly L. — *Gregory Michaels and Associates, Inc.*
McPherson, Stephen M. — *Ward Howell International, Inc.*
McQuoid, David — *A.T. Kearney, Inc.*
Mead-Fox, David — *Korn/Ferry International*
Meadows, C. David — *Professional Staffing Consultants*
Meara, Helen — *Source Services Corporation*
Medina-Haro, Adolfo — *Heidrick & Struggles, Inc.*
Meehan, John — *Source Services Corporation*
Meier, J. Dale — *Grant Cooper and Associates*
Meiland, A. Daniel — *Egon Zehnder International Inc.*
Meltzer, Andrea Y. — *Executive Options, Ltd.*
Mendelson, Jeffrey — *Source Services Corporation*
Mendoza, Guadalupe — *Ward Howell International, Inc.*
Mendoza-Green, Robin — *Source Services Corporation*
Mercer, Julie — *Columbia Consulting Group*
Merrigan, Eileen M. — *Lamalie Amrop International*
Mertensotto, Chuck H. — *Whitney & Associates, Inc.*
Messett, William J. — *Messett Associates, Inc.*
Messina, Marco — *Source Services Corporation*
Mestepey, John — *A.T. Kearney, Inc.*
Meyer, Stacey — *Gary Kaplan & Associates*
Meyers, Steven — *Montgomery Resources, Inc.*
Meza, Anna — *Richard, Wayne and Roberts*
Michaels, Joseph — *CPS Inc.*
Michaels, Stewart — *TOPAZ International, Inc.*
Michaels, Stewart — *TOPAZ Legal Solutions*
Miller, David — *Cochran, Cochran & Yale, Inc.*
Miller, David — *Temporary Accounting Personnel, Inc.*
Miller, Harold B. — *MSI International*
Miller, Larry — *Source Services Corporation*
Miller, Roy — *The Enns Partners Inc.*
Miller, Timothy — *Source Services Corporation*
Milligan, Dale — *Source Services Corporation*
Millonzi, Joel C. — *Johnson Smith & Knisely Accord*
Mills, John — *Source Services Corporation*
Milner, Carol — *Source Services Corporation*
Milstein, Bonnie — *Marvin Laba & Associates*
Mingle, Larry D. — *Columbia Consulting Group*
Miras, Cliff — *Source Services Corporation*
Miras, Cliff — *Source Services Corporation*
Mirtz, P. John — *Mirtz Morice, Inc.*
Misiurewicz, Marc — *Cochran, Cochran & Yale, Inc.*
Mitchell, Jeff — *A.J. Burton Group, Inc.*
Mitchell, John — *Romac & Associates*
Mitton, Bill — *Executive Resource, Inc.*

Mittwol, Myles — *Source Services Corporation*
Mochwart, Donald — *Drummond Associates, Inc.*
Mogul, Gene — *Mogul Consultants, Inc.*
Mohr, Brian — *CPS Inc.*
Molitor, John L. — *Barrett Partners*
Mollichelli, David — *Source Services Corporation*
Molnar, Robert A. — *Johnson Smith & Knisely Accord*
Mondragon, Philip — *A.T. Kearney, Inc.*
Monogenis, Emanuel N. — *Heidrick & Struggles, Inc.*
Moodley, Logan — *Austin-McGregor International*
Moore, Craig — *Source Services Corporation*
Moore, Dianna — *Source Services Corporation*
Moore, Janice E. — *MSI International*
Moore, Suzanne — *Source Services Corporation*
Moore, T. Wills — *Ray & Berndtson*
Moore, Vickie J. — *Kirkman & Searing, Inc.*
Moran, Douglas — *Source Services Corporation*
Morato, Rene — *Source Services Corporation*
Morawetz, Justin A. — *Keith Bagg & Associates Inc.*
Moretti, Denise — *Source Services Corporation*
Morgan, David G. — *Morgan Stampfl, Inc.*
Morgan, Donald T. — *MSI International*
Morgan, Nancy — *K. Russo Associates*
Moriarty, Mike — *Source Services Corporation*
Morice, James L. — *Mirtz Morice, Inc.*
Morris, David A. — *Heidrick & Struggles, Inc.*
Morris, Paul T. — *The Morris Group*
Morris, Scott — *Source Services Corporation*
Morrow, Melanie — *Source Services Corporation*
Morse, Mary — *Travis & Company*
Mortansen, Patricia — *Norman Broadbent International, Inc.*
Moskowitz, Marc — *Kenzer Corp.*
Mott, Greg — *Source Services Corporation*
Mowatt, Virginia — *Spencer Stuart*
Moyse, Richard G. — *Thorndike Deland Associates*
Msidment, Roger — *Source Services Corporation*
Mueller, Colleen — *Source Services Corporation*
Mueller-Maerki, Fortunat F. — *Egon Zehnder International Inc.*
Muendel, H. Edward — *Stanton Chase International*
Muller, Susan — *Corporate Recruiters Ltd.*
Mulligan, Robert P. — *William Willis Worldwide Inc.*
Murphy, Corinne — *Source Services Corporation*
Murphy, Cornelius J. — *Goodrich & Sherwood Associates, Inc.*
Murphy, Erin — *CPS Inc.*
Murphy, Gary J. — *Stone Murphy & Olson*
Murphy, James — *Source Services Corporation*
Murphy, Patrick J. — *P.J. Murphy & Associates, Inc.*
Murphy, Peter — *Korn/Ferry International*
Murray, Virginia — *A.T. Kearney, Inc.*
Murry, John — *Source Services Corporation*
Mursuli, Meredith — *Lasher Associates*
Mydlach, Renee — *CPS Inc.*
Myers, Kay — *Signature Staffing*
Nabers, Karen — *Source Services Corporation*
Nagler, Leon G. — *Nagler, Robins & Poe, Inc.*
Nagy, Les — *Source Services Corporation*

Naidicz, Maria — *Ray & Berndtson*
Nair, Leslie — *Zwell International*
Nass, Martin D. — *Lamalie Amrop International*
Nathanson, Barry F. — *Barry Nathanson Associates*
Necessary, Rick — *Source Services Corporation*
Neckanoff, Sharon — *Search West, Inc.*
Needham, Karen — *Source Services Corporation*
Neelin, Sharon — *The Caldwell Partners Amrop International*
Nees, Eugene C. — *Ray & Berndtson*
Neff, Herbert — *Source Services Corporation*
Neff, Thomas J. — *Spencer Stuart*
Neher, Robert L. — *Intech Summit Group, Inc.*
Nehring, Keith — *Howard Fischer Associates, Inc.*
Nelson, Hitch — *Source Services Corporation*
Nelson, Mary — *Source Services Corporation*
Nelson-Folkersen, Jeffrey — *Source Services Corporation*
Nemec, Phillip — *Dunhill International Search of New Haven*
Nephew, Robert — *Christian & Timbers*
Neuberth, Jeffrey G. — *Canny, Bowen Inc.*
Neuwald, Debrah — *Source Services Corporation*
Newman, Jose L. — *Ward Howell International, Inc.*
Newman, Lynn — *Kishbaugh Associates International*
Nichols, Gary — *Koontz, Jeffries & Associates, Inc.*
Niejet, Michael C. — *O'Brien & Bell*
Noebel, Todd R. — *The Noebel Search Group, Inc.*
Nolan, Robert — *Source Services Corporation*
Nolen, Shannon — *Source Services Corporation*
Nolte, William D. — *W.D. Nolte & Company*
Normann, Amy — *Robert M. Flanagan & Associates, Ltd.*
Norris, Ken — *A.T. Kearney, Inc.*
Norsell, Paul E. — *Paul Norsell & Associates, Inc.*
Norton, James B. — *Lamalie Amrop International*
Nunziata, Peter — *Atlantic Search Group, Inc.*
O'Brien, Susan — *Source Services Corporation*
O'Connell, Mary — *CPS Inc.*
O'Connell, Michael — *Ryan, Miller & Associates Inc.*
O'Halloran, Robert — *MSI International*
O'Hara, Daniel M. — *Lynch Miller Moore, Inc.*
O'Maley, Kimberlee — *Spencer Stuart*
O'Neill, James P. — *Allerton Heneghan & O'Neill*
O'Neill, Stephen A. — *Harris Heery & Associates*
O'Reilly, John — *Stratford Group*
Occhiboi, Emil — *Source Services Corporation*
Ogden, Dayton — *Spencer Stuart*
Ogden, Thomas H. — *The Ogdon Partnership*
Ogilvie, Kit — *Howard Fischer Associates, Inc.*
Ohman, Gregory L. — *Skott/Edwards Consultants, Inc.*
Oldfield, Theresa — *Strategic Alliance Network, Ltd.*
Olin, Robyn — *Richard, Wayne and Roberts*
Olsen, Kristine — *Williams Executive Search, Inc.*
Olsen, Robert — *Source Services Corporation*
Onstott, Joseph — *The Onstott Group, Inc.*
Onstott, Joseph E. — *The Onstott Group, Inc.*
Oppedisano, Edward — *Oppedisano & Company, Inc.*

Price, Carl — *Source Services Corporation*
Price, Kenneth M. — *Messett Associates, Inc.*
Priem, Windle B. — *Korn/Ferry International*
Prince, Marilyn L. — *Higdon Prince Inc.*
Probert, William W. — *Ward Howell International, Inc.*
Proct, Nina — *Martin H. Bauman Associates, Inc.*
Pugrant, Mark A. — *Grant/Morgan Associates, Inc.*
Rabinowitz, Peter A. — *P.A.R. Associates Inc.*
Racht, Janet G. — *Crowe, Chizek and Company, LLP*
Railsback, Richard — *Korn/Ferry International*
Raines, Bruce R. — *Raines International Inc.*
Ramler, Carolyn S. — *The Corporate Connection, Ltd.*
Ramsey, John H. — *Mark Stanley/EMA Partners International*
Randell, James E. — *Randell-Heiken, Inc.*
Rankin, Jeffrey A. — *The Rankin Group, Ltd*
Rankin, M.J. — *The Rankin Group, Ltd*
Rasmussen, Timothy — *Source Services Corporation*
Ratajczak, Paul — *Source Services Corporation*
Ravenel, Lavinia — *MSI International*
Ray, Marianne C. — *Callan Associates, Ltd.*
Raymond, Jean — *The Caldwell Partners Amrop International*
Reardon, Joseph — *Source Services Corporation*
Reddick, David C. — *Horton International*
Redding, Denise — *The Douglas Reiter Company, Inc.*
Redmond, Andrea — *Russell Reynolds Associates, Inc.*
Reed, Susan — *Source Services Corporation*
Reeves, William B. — *Spencer Stuart*
Regan, Thomas J. — *Tower Consultants, Ltd.*
Regeuye, Peter J. — *Accountants Executive Search*
Reid, Katherine — *Source Services Corporation*
Reid, Scott — *Source Services Corporation*
Reifel, Laurie — *Reifel & Assocaites*
Reifersen, Ruth F. — *The Jonathan Stevens Group, Inc.*
Reiser, Ellen — *Thorndike Deland Associates*
Reisinger, George L. — *Sigma Group International*
Reiter, Douglas — *The Douglas Reiter Company, Inc.*
Remillard, Brad M. — *CJA - The Adler Group*
Renfroe, Ann-Marie — *Source Services Corporation*
Rennell, Thomas — *Source Services Corporation*
Renner, Sandra L. — *Spectra International Inc.*
Renteria, Elizabeth — *Source Services Corporation*
Resnic, Alan — *Source Services Corporation*
Reticker, Peter — *MSI International*
Reuter, Tandom — *CPS Inc.*
Reyman, Susan — *S. Reyman & Associates Ltd.*
Reynolds, Laura — *Source Services Corporation*
Rhoades, Michael — *Source Services Corporation*
Rice, Marie — *Jay Gaines & Company, Inc.*
Rice, Raymond D. — *Logue & Rice Inc.*
Rich, Kenneth M. — *Ray & Berndtson*
Rich, Lyttleton — *Sockwell & Associates*
Richardson, J. Rick — *Spencer Stuart*
Riederer, Larry — *CPS Inc.*
Rieger, Louis J. — *Spencer Stuart*
Rimmel, James E. — *The Hindman Company*

Rimmele, Michael — *The Bankers Group*
Rinker, Jim — *Southwestern Professional Services*
Rios, Vince — *Source Services Corporation*
Rios, Vincent — *Source Services Corporation*
Riotto, Anthony R. — *Riotto-Jones Associates*
Robb, Tammy — *Source Services Corporation*
Roberts, Carl R. — *Southwestern Professional Services*
Roberts, Derek J. — *Ward Howell International, Inc.*
Roberts, Mitch — *A.E. Feldman Associates*
Roberts, Nick P. — *Spectrum Search Associates, Inc.*
Roberts, Scott — *Jonas, Walters & Assoc., Inc.*
Robertson, Bruce J. — *Lamalie Amrop International*
Robertson, Sherry — *Source Services Corporation*
Robinson, Bruce — *Bruce Robinson Associates*
Robinson, Eric B. — *Bruce Robinson Associates*
Robinson, Tonya — *Source Services Corporation*
Robles Cuellar, Paulina — *Ray & Berndtson*
Rockwell, Bruce — *Source Services Corporation*
Rodriguez, Manuel — *Source Services Corporation*
Rogan, John P. — *Russell Reynolds Associates, Inc.*
Rogers, Leah — *Dinte Resources, Inc.*
Rohan, James E. — *J.P. Canon Associates*
Rohan, Kevin A. — *J.P. Canon Associates*
Rojo, Rafael — *A.T. Kearney, Inc.*
Rollo, Robert S. — *R. Rollo Associates*
Romang, Paula — *Agri-Tech Personnel, Inc.*
Rorech, Maureen — *Romac & Associates*
Rosato, William R. — *W.R. Rosato & Associates, Inc.*
Rosemarin, Gloria J. — *Barrington Hart, Inc.*
Rosen, Mitchell — *Source Services Corporation*
Rosenstein, Michele — *Source Services Corporation*
Rosin, Jeffrey — *Korn/Ferry International*
Ross, Curt A. — *Ray & Berndtson*
Ross, John — *Morgan Stampfl, Inc.*
Ross, Lawrence — *Ray & Berndtson/Lovas Stanley*
Ross, Mark — *Ray & Berndtson/Lovas Stanley*
Ross, Sheila L. — *Ward Howell International, Inc.*
Rotella, Marshall W. — *The Corporate Connection, Ltd.*
Roth, Robert J. — *Williams, Roth & Krueger Inc.*
Roth, William — *Harris Heery & Associates*
Rothenbush, Clayton — *Source Services Corporation*
Rothschild, John S. — *Lamalie Amrop International*
Rowe, Thomas A. — *Korn/Ferry International*
Rowe, William D. — *D.E. Foster Partners Inc.*
Rowland, James — *Source Services Corporation*
Runquist, U.W. — *Webb, Johnson Associates, Inc.*
Rush, Michael E. — *D.A.L. Associates, Inc.*
Russell, Richard A. — *Executive Search Consultants Corporation*
Russell, Robin E. — *Kenzer Corp.*
Russo, Karen — *K. Russo Associates*
Russo, Karen — *Maximum Management Corp.*
Rustin, Beth — *The Whitney Group*
Ryan, David — *Source Services Corporation*
Ryan, Kathleen — *Source Services Corporation*
Ryan, Lee — *Ryan, Miller & Associates Inc.*

Ryan, Mark — *Source Services Corporation*
Sabanosh, Whitney — *Highland Search Group*
Sabat, Lori S. — *Alta Associates, Inc.*
Sadaj, Michael — *Source Services Corporation*
Salet, Michael — *Source Services Corporation*
Saletra, Andrew — *CPS Inc.*
Sallows, Jill S. — *Crowe, Chizek and Company, LLP*
Salvagno, Michael J. — *The Cambridge Group Ltd*
Samsel, Randy — *Source Services Corporation*
Samuelson, Robert — *Source Services Corporation*
Sanchez, William — *Source Services Corporation*
Sanders, Jason — *Sanders Management Associates, Inc.*
Sanders, Natalie — *CPS Inc.*
Sandor, Richard J. — *Flynn, Hannock, Incorporated*
Saner, Harold — *Romac & Associates*
Sanitago, Anthony — *TaxSearch, Inc.*
Sanow, Robert — *Cochran, Cochran & Yale, Inc.*
Santiago, Benefrido — *Source Services Corporation*
Santimauro, Edward — *Korn/Ferry International*
Sapers, Mark — *Source Services Corporation*
Saposhnik, Doron — *Source Services Corporation*
Sardella, Sharon — *Source Services Corporation*
Sarn, Allan G. — *Allan Sarn Associates Inc.*
Sarna, Edmund A. — *Jonas, Walters & Assoc., Inc.*
Satenstein, Sloan — *Higdon Prince Inc.*
Sathe, Mark A. — *Sathe & Associates, Inc.*
Sauer, Harry J. — *Romac & Associates*
Savard, Robert F. — *The Stevenson Group of Delaware Inc.*
Savela, Edward — *Source Services Corporation*
Savoy, Michelle — *Spencer Stuart*
Sawyer, Deborah — *Korn/Ferry International*
Sawyer, Patricia L. — *Smith & Sawyer Inc.*
Saxon, Alexa — *Woodworth International Group*
Scalamera, Tom — *CPS Inc.*
Schaefer, Frederic M. — *A.T. Kearney, Inc.*
Schappell, Marc P. — *Egon Zehnder International Inc.*
Schene, Philip — *A.E. Feldman Associates*
Scherck, Henry J. — *Ward Howell International, Inc.*
Schlpma, Christine — *Advanced Executive Resources*
Schmidt, Frank B. — *F.B. Schmidt International*
Schneider, Thomas P. — *WTW Associates, Inc.*
Schneiderman, Gerald — *Management Resource Associates, Inc.*
Schroeder, James — *Source Services Corporation*
Schroeder, John W. — *Spencer Stuart*
Schueneman, David — *CPS Inc.*
Schuette, Dorothy — *Harris Heery & Associates*
Schultz, Randy — *Source Services Corporation*
Schwalbach, Robert — *Source Services Corporation*
Schwam, Carol — *A.E. Feldman Associates*
Schwinden, William — *Source Services Corporation*
Scimone, James — *Source Services Corporation*
Scimone, Jim — *Source Services Corporation*
Scodius, Joseph J. — *Gregory Michaels and Associates, Inc.*
Scoff, Barry — *Source Services Corporation*

Scothon, Alan — *Romac & Associates*
Scott, Evan — *Howard Fischer Associates, Inc.*
Scott, Gordon S. — *Search Advisors International Corp.*
Scranton, Lisa — *A.J. Burton Group, Inc.*
Scroggins, Stephen R. — *Russell Reynolds Associates, Inc.*
Seamon, Kenneth — *Source Services Corporation*
Seco, William — *Seco & Zetto Associates, Inc.*
Segal, Eric B. — *Kenzer Corp.*
Seiden, Steven A. — *Seiden Krieger Associates, Inc.*
Selbach, Barbara — *Spencer Stuart*
Sell, David — *Source Services Corporation*
Selvaggi, Esther — *Source Services Corporation*
Semple, David — *Source Services Corporation*
Semyan, John K. — *TNS Partners, Inc.*
Serba, Kerri — *Source Services Corporation*
Sessa, Vincent J. — *Integrated Search Solutions Group, LLC*
Sevilla, Claudio A. — *Crawford & Crofford*
Shackleford, David — *Source Services Corporation*
Shanks, Jennifer — *Source Services Corporation*
Shapanka, Samuel — *Source Services Corporation*
Shapiro, Beth — *Howard Fischer Associates, Inc.*
Shapiro, Elaine — *CPS Inc.*
Shawhan, Heather — *Source Services Corporation*
Shea, Kathleen M. — *The Penn Partners, Incorporated*
Shell, John C. — *John Shell Associates, Inc.*
Shelton, Jonathan — *Source Services Corporation*
Shemin, Grace — *Maximum Management Corp.*
Shen, Eugene Y. — *The Whitney Group*
Shenfield, Peter — *A.T. Kearney, Inc.*
Shepard, Michael J. — *MSI International*
Sher, Lawrence — *M.A. Churchill & Associates, Inc.*
Sherman, Robert R. — *Mortgage & Financial Personnel Services*
Shervey, Brent C. — *O'Callaghan Honey/Ray & Berndtson, Inc.*
Sherwood, Andrew — *Goodrich & Sherwood Associates, Inc.*
Shield, Nancy — *Maximum Management Corp.*
Shirilla, Robert M. — *F.B. Schmidt International*
Shore, Earl L. — *E.L. Shore & Associates Ltd.*
Shourds, Mary E. — *Houze, Shourds & Montgomery, Inc.*
Shufelt, Doug — *Sink, Walker, Boltrus International*
Sibbald, John R. — *John Sibbald Associates, Inc.*
Siegel, Pamela — *Executive Options, Ltd.*
Siegler, Jody Cukiir — *A.T. Kearney, Inc.*
Siegrist, Jeffrey M. — *D.E. Foster Partners Inc.*
Signer, Julie — *CPS Inc.*
Silcott, Marvin L. — *Marvin L. Silcott & Associates, Inc.*
Silvas, Stephen D. — *Roberson and Company*
Silver, Kit — *Source Services Corporation*
Silver, Lee — *L. A. Silver Associates, Inc.*
Silverman, Paul M. — *The Marshall Group*
Silverstein, Jackie — *Don Richard Associates of Charlotte*

Simmons, Deborah — *Source Services Corporation*
Simmons, Sandra K. — *MSI International*
Simon, Mary K. — *Gregory Michaels and Associates, Inc.*
Simon, Penny B. — *Ray & Berndtson*
Simpson, David J. — *Simpson Associates, Inc.*
Sindler, Jay — *A.J. Burton Group, Inc.*
Sink, Cliff — *Sink, Walker, Boltrus International*
Sirena, Evelyn — *Source Services Corporation*
Sitarski, Stan — *Howard Fischer Associates, Inc.*
Skalet, Ira — *A.E. Feldman Associates*
Skunda, Donna M. — *Allerton Heneghan & O'Neill*
Sloan, Scott — *Source Services Corporation*
Slocum, Ann Marie — *K.L. Whitney Company*
Slosar, John — *Boyden*
Smead, Michelle M. — *A.T. Kearney, Inc.*
Smirnov, Tatiana — *Allan Sarn Associates Inc.*
Smith, Ana Luz — *Smith Search, S.C.*
Smith, Brant — *Smith Hanley Associates*
Smith, David P. — *HRS, Inc.*
Smith, Ethan L. — *Highland Search Group*
Smith, Herman M. — *Herman Smith Executive Initiatives Inc.*
Smith, John E. — *Smith Search, S.C.*
Smith, John F. — *The Penn Partners, Incorporated*
Smith, Lawrence — *Source Services Corporation*
Smith, Lydia — *The Corporate Connection, Ltd.*
Smith, Matt D. — *Ray & Berndtson*
Smith, Monica L. — *Analysts Resources, Inc.*
Smith, R. Michael — *Smith James Group, Inc.*
Smith, Robert L. — *Smith & Sawyer Inc.*
Smith, Ronald V. — *Coe & Company International Inc.*
Smith, Timothy — *Source Services Corporation*
Smith, Timothy C. — *Christian & Timbers*
Smith, W. Guice — *Southwestern Professional Services*
Smock, Cynthia — *Source Services Corporation*
Smoller, Howard — *Source Services Corporation*
Snowden, Charles — *Source Services Corporation*
Snowhite, Rebecca — *Source Services Corporation*
Snyder, James F. — *Snyder & Company*
Sochacki, Michael — *Source Services Corporation*
Sockwell, J. Edgar — *Sockwell & Associates*
Sondgrass, Stephen — *DeFrain, Mayer LLC*
Song, Louis — *Source Services Corporation*
Sorgen, Jay — *Source Services Corporation*
Sostilio, Louis — *Source Services Corporation*
Souder, E.G. — *Souder & Associates*
Soutouras, James — *Smith James Group, Inc.*
Spann, Richard E. — *Goodrich & Sherwood Associates, Inc.*
Spector, Michael — *Source Services Corporation*
Spencer, John — *Source Services Corporation*
Spencer, John — *Source Services Corporation*
Spera, Stefanie — *A.T. Kearney, Inc.*
Spicehandler, Sheila — *Trebor Weldon Lawrence, Inc.*
Spicher, John — *M.A. Churchill & Associates, Inc.*
Spiegel, Gayle — *L. A. Silver Associates, Inc.*
Spitz, Grant — *The Caldwell Partners Amrop International*

Sponseller, Vern — *Richard Kader & Associates*
Spoutz, Paul — *Source Services Corporation*
Spriggs, Robert D. — *Spriggs & Company, Inc.*
Springer, Mark H. — *M.H. Springer & Associates Incorporated*
Sprowls, Linda — *Allard Associates*
St. Clair, Alan — *TNS Partners, Inc.*
St. Martin, Peter — *Source Services Corporation*
Stack, Richard — *Source Services Corporation*
Stampfl, Eric — *Morgan Stampfl, Inc.*
Stanton, John — *A.T. Kearney, Inc.*
Stark, Jeff — *Thorne, Brieger Associates Inc.*
Steele, Daniel — *Cochran, Cochran & Yale, Inc.*
Steer, Joe — *CPS Inc.*
Stein, Terry W. — *Stewart, Stein and Scott, Ltd.*
Steinman, Stephen M. — *The Stevenson Group of New Jersey*
Stephens, Andrew — *Source Services Corporation*
Stephens, John — *Source Services Corporation*
Stern, Lester W. — *Sullivan & Company*
Stern, Stephen — *CPS Inc.*
Sterner, Doug — *CPS Inc.*
Stevens, Craig M. — *Kirkman & Searing, Inc.*
Stevens, Tracey — *Don Richard Associates of Washington, D.C., Inc.*
Stevenson, Jane — *Howard Fischer Associates, Inc.*
Stevenson, Jane — *Howard Fischer Associates, Inc.*
Stewart, Clifford — *Morgan Stampfl, Inc.*
Stewart, Jan J. — *Egon Zehnder International Inc.*
Stewart, Jeffrey O. — *Stewart, Stein and Scott, Ltd.*
Stewart, Ross M. — *Human Resources Network Partners Inc.*
Stivk, Barbara A. — *Thornton Resources*
Stone, Robert Ryder — *Lamalie Amrop International*
Stone, Susan L. — *Stone Enterprises Ltd.*
Storm, Deborah — *Source Services Corporation*
Stoy, Roger W. — *Heidrick & Struggles, Inc.*
Stranberg, James R. — *Callan Associates, Ltd.*
Strander, Dervin — *Source Services Corporation*
Strassman, Mark — *Don Richard Associates of Washington, D.C., Inc.*
Straube, Stanley H. — *Straube Associates*
Strickland, Katie — *Grantham & Co., Inc.*
Stringer, Dann P. — *D.E. Foster Partners Inc.*
Strobridge, Richard P. — *F.L. Taylor & Company, Inc.*
Strom, Mark N. — *Search Advisors International Corp.*
Struzziero, Ralph E. — *Romac & Associates*
Sucato, Carolyn — *Jay Gaines & Company, Inc.*
Sullivan, Brian M. — *Sullivan & Company*
Sullivan, Kay — *Rusher, Loscavio & LoPresto*
Sumurdy, Melinda — *Kenzer Corp.*
Susoreny, Samali — *Source Services Corporation*
Sussman, Lynda — *Gilbert Tweed/INESA*
Sutter, Howard — *Romac & Associates*
Swanner, William — *Source Services Corporation*
Sweeney, Anne — *Source Services Corporation*
Sweeney, Sean K. — *Bonifield Associates*
Sweet, Randall — *Source Services Corporation*
Swidler, J. Robert — *Egon Zehnder International Inc.*
Swoboda, Lawrence — *A.J. Burton Group, Inc.*

Taft, David G. — *Techsearch Services, Inc.*
Tankson, Dawn — *Source Services Corporation*
Tanner, Frank — *Source Services Corporation*
Tanner, Gary — *Source Services Corporation*
Tappan, Michael A. — *Ward Howell International, Inc.*
Taylor, Charles E. — *Lamalie Amrop International*
Taylor, Conrad G. — *MSI International*
Taylor, Ernest A. — *Ward Howell International, Inc.*
Taylor, Kenneth W. — *Egon Zehnder International Inc.*
Taylor, R.L. (Larry) — *Ray & Berndtson*
Teger, Stella — *Source Services Corporation*
Telford, John H. — *Telford, Adams & Alexander/Telford & Co., Inc.*
ten Cate, Herman H. — *Stoneham Associates Corp.*
Tenero, Kymberly — *Source Services Corporation*
Teter, Sandra — *The Danbrook Group, Inc.*
Teti, Al — *Chrisman & Company, Incorporated*
Theard, Susan — *Romac & Associates*
Theobald, David B. — *Theobald & Associates*
Thielman, Joseph — *Barrett Partners*
Thomas, Cheryl M. — *CPS Inc.*
Thomas, Kim — *CPS Inc.*
Thomas, Kurt J. — *P.J. Murphy & Associates, Inc.*
Thomas, Terry — *The Thomas Resource Group*
Thompson, Dave — *Battalia Winston International*
Thompson, John R. — *MSI International*
Thompson, Kenneth L. — *McCormack & Farrow*
Thompson, Leslie — *Source Services Corporation*
Thomson, Alexander G. — *Russell Reynolds Associates, Inc.*
Thornton, John C. — *Thornton Resources*
Thrapp, Mark C. — *Executive Search Consultants International, Inc.*
Thrower, Troy — *Source Services Corporation*
Tierney, Eileen — *The Whitney Group*
Tilley, Kyle — *Source Services Corporation*
Tincu, John C. — *Ferneborg & Associates, Inc.*
Tingle, Trina A. — *MSI International*
Tobin, Christopher — *Source Services Corporation*
Todres-Bernstein, Margo — *Kaye-Bassman International Corp.*
Tootsey, Mark A. — *A.J. Burton Group, Inc.*
Tovrog, Dan — *CPS Inc.*
Tracey, Jack — *Management Assistance Group, Inc.*
Tracy, Ronald O. — *Egon Zehnder International Inc.*
Trefzer, Kristie — *Source Services Corporation*
Trewhella, Michael — *Source Services Corporation*
Trice, Renee — *Source Services Corporation*
Trieschmann, Daniel — *Source Services Corporation*
Trieweiler, Bob — *Executive Placement Consultants, Inc.*
Trimble, Patricia — *Source Services Corporation*
Trimble, Rhonda — *Source Services Corporation*
Trott, Kathryn — *Allard Associates*
Trott, Kathryn — *Allard Associates*
Truemper, Dean — *CPS Inc.*
Truex, John F. — *Morton, McCorkle & Associates, Inc.*

Truitt, Thomas B. — *Southwestern Professional Services*
Tryon, Katey — *DeFrain, Mayer LLC*
Tscelli, Maureen — *Source Services Corporation*
Tschan, Stephen — *Source Services Corporation*
Tucker, Thomas A. — *The Thomas Tucker Company*
Tullberg, Tina — *CPS Inc.*
Tully, Margo L. — *Tully/Woodmansee International, Inc.*
Tunney, William — *Grant Cooper and Associates*
Turner, Edward K. — *Don Richard Associates of Charlotte*
Turner, Kimberly — *Barton Associates, Inc.*
Turner, Raymond — *Source Services Corporation*
Tursi, Deborah J. — *The Corporate Connection, Ltd.*
Tutwiler, Stephen — *Don Richard Associates of Tampa, Inc.*
Tweed, Janet — *Gilbert Tweed/INESA*
Twomey, James — *Source Services Corporation*
Tyson, Richard L. — *Bonifield Associates*
Ulbert, Nancy — *Aureus Group*
Ulrich, Mary Ann — *D.S. Allen Associates, Inc.*
Uzzel, Linda — *Source Services Corporation*
Vacca, Domenic — *Romac & Associates*
Van Alstine, Catherine — *Tanton Mitchell/Paul Ray Berndtson*
Van Biesen, Jacques A.H. — *Search Group Inc.*
Van Campen, Jerry — *Gilbert & Van Campen International*
Van Clieaf, Mark — *MVC Associates International*
Van Norman, Ben — *Source Services Corporation*
Van Nostrand, Mara J. — *Barton Associates, Inc.*
Van Remmen, Roger — *Brown, Bernardy, Van Remmen, Inc.*
Vande-Water, Katie — *J. Robert Scott*
Vandenbulcke, Cynthia — *Source Services Corporation*
Varney, Monique — *Source Services Corporation*
Varrichio, Michael — *Source Services Corporation*
Velez, Hector — *Source Services Corporation*
Velten, Mark T. — *Boyden*
Venable, William W. — *Thorndike Deland Associates*
Vernon, Peter C. — *Horton International*
Vilella, Paul — *Source Services Corporation*
Villella, Paul — *Source Services Corporation*
Vinett-Hessel, Deidre — *Source Services Corporation*
Visnich, L. Christine — *Bason Associates Inc.*
Vitale, Amy — *Highland Search Group*
Viviano, Cathleen — *Source Services Corporation*
Vlcek, Thomas J. — *Vlcek & Company, Inc.*
Voigt, John A. — *Romac & Associates*
Volkman, Arthur — *Cochran, Cochran & Yale, Inc.*
von Baillou, Astrid — *Richard Kinser & Associates*
Vossler, James — *A.J. Burton Group, Inc.*
Vourakis, Zan — *ZanExec LLC*
Waanders, William L. — *ExecuQuest*
Wacholz, Rick — *A.T. Kearney, Inc.*
Wade, Christy — *Source Services Corporation*
Waitkus, Karen — *Richard, Wayne and Roberts*
Waldrop, Gary R. — *MSI International*
Walker, Ann — *Source Services Corporation*

Walker, Craig H. — *A.J. Burton Group, Inc.*
Walker, Douglas G. — *Sink, Walker, Boltrus International*
Walker, Ewing J. — *Ward Howell International, Inc.*
Walker, Rose — *Source Services Corporation*
Wallace, Alec — *Tanton Mitchell/Paul Ray Berndtson*
Wallace, Toby — *Source Services Corporation*
Walsh, Denis — *Professional Staffing Consultants*
Walters, William F. — *Jonas, Walters & Assoc., Inc.*
Ward, Jim — *F-O-R-T-U-N-E Personnel Consultants of Huntsville, Inc.*
Ward, Les — *Source Services Corporation*
Ward, Madeleine — *LTM Associates*
Ward, Robert — *Source Services Corporation*
Ward, Ted — *Korn/Ferry International*
Wardell, Charles W.B. — *Nordeman Grimm, Inc.*
Warnock, Phyl — *Source Services Corporation*
Wasp, Warren T. — *WTW Associates, Inc.*
Wasson, Thomas W. — *Spencer Stuart*
Watkins, Jeffrey P. — *Lamalie Amrop International*
Watkins, Thomas M. — *Lamalie Amrop International*
Watkinson, Jim W. — *The Badger Group*
Watson, Hanan S. — *Watson International, Inc.*
Watson, James — *MSI International*
Waymire, Pamela — *Source Services Corporation*
Wayne, Cary S. — *ProSearch Inc.*
Webb, George H. — *Webb, Johnson Associates, Inc.*
Webber, Edward — *Source Services Corporation*
Weber, Ronald R. — *Weber Executive Search*
Weeks, Glenn — *Source Services Corporation*
Weinberg, Melvin — *Romac & Associates*
Weis, Theodore — *Source Services Corporation*
Weiss, Elizabeth — *Source Services Corporation*
Weissman-Rosenthal, Abbe — *ALW Research International*
Welch, Robert — *Ray & Berndtson*
Weller, Paul S. — *Mark Stanley/EMA Partners International*
Wendler, Kambrea R. — *Gregory Michaels and Associates, Inc.*
Wenz, Alexander — *Source Services Corporation*
Wessling, Jerry — *Source Services Corporation*
Westfall, Ed — *Zwell International*
Weston, Corinne F. — *D.A. Kreuter Associates, Inc.*
Wheatley, William — *Drummond Associates, Inc.*
Wheeler, Gerard H. — *A.J. Burton Group, Inc.*
White, Richard B. — *Spencer Stuart*
Whitfield, Jack — *Source Services Corporation*
Whiting, Anthony — *Johnson Smith & Knisely Accord*
Whitney, David L. — *Whitney & Associates, Inc.*
Whitney, Kenneth L. — *K.L. Whitney Company*
Whitney, William A — *Larsen, Whitney, Blecksmith & Zilliacus*
Whitton, Paula L. — *Pearson, Caldwell & Farnsworth, Inc.*
Wier, Daniel — *Daniel Wier & Associates*
Wilbanks, George R. — *Russell Reynolds Associates, Inc.*
Wilburn, Dan — *Kaye-Bassman International Corp.*

Wilcox, Fred T. — *Wilcox, Bertoux & Miller*
Wilder, Richard B. — *Columbia Consulting Group*
Wilkinson, Barbara — *Beall & Company, Inc.*
Willbrandt, Curt — *Source Services Corporation*
Williams, Angie — *Whitney & Associates, Inc.*
Williams, Harry D. — *Jacobson Associates*
Williams, Jack — *A.T. Kearney, Inc.*
Williams, John — *Source Services Corporation*
Williams, Lis — *Executive Options, Ltd.*
Williams, Roger K. — *Williams, Roth & Krueger Inc.*
Williams, Stephen E. — *Barton Associates, Inc.*
Williams, Walter E. — *Lamalie Amrop International*
Willis, William H. — *William Willis Worldwide Inc.*
Wilson, Derrick — *Thornton Resources*
Wilson, Harry — *First Union Executive Search Group*
Wilson, John — *Korn/Ferry International*
Wilson, Joyce — *Source Services Corporation*
Wilson, Patricia L. — *Leon A. Farley Associates*
Wilson, T. Gordon — *Ray & Berndtson/Lovas Stanley*
Wingate, Mary — *Source Services Corporation*
Winitz, Joel — *GSW Consulting Group, Inc.*
Winitz, Marla — *GSW Consulting Group, Inc.*
Winkowski, Stephen — *Source Services Corporation*
Winnicki, Kimberly — *Source Services Corporation*
Winograd, Glenn — *Criterion Executive Search, Inc.*
Wirtshafter, Linda — *Grant Cooper and Associates*
Wisch, Steven C. — *MB Inc. Interim Executive Division*
Wise, J. Herbert — *Sandhurst Associates*
Witzgall, William — *Source Services Corporation*
Wold, Ted W. — *Hyde Danforth Wold & Co.*
Wolf, Donald — *Source Services Corporation*
Wolf, Stephen M. — *Byron Leonard International, Inc.*
Wolfe, Peter — *Source Services Corporation*
Womack, Joseph — *The Bankers Group*
Wood, Elizabeth — *Highland Search Group*
Wood, Gary — *Source Services Corporation*
Wood, John S. — *Egon Zehnder International Inc.*
Wood, Milton M. — *M. Wood Company*
Wood, Nicole — *Corporate Careers, Inc.*
Woodmansee, Bruce J. — *Tully/Woodmansee International, Inc.*
Woods, Craig — *Source Services Corporation*
Woodworth, Gail — *Woodworth International Group*
Wooldridge, Jeff — *Ray & Berndtson*
Wooller, Edmund A.M. — *Windsor International*
Woomer, Jerome — *Source Services Corporation*
Workman, David — *Source Services Corporation*
Wright, A. Leo — *The Hindman Company*
Wright, Carl A.J. — *A.J. Burton Group, Inc.*
Wright, Charles D. — *Goodrich & Sherwood Associates, Inc.*
Wright, Leslie — *The Stevenson Group of New Jersey*
Wycoff-Viola, Amy — *Source Services Corporation*

Wylie, Pamela — *M.A. Churchill & Associates, Inc.*
Yaekle, Gary — *Tully/Woodmansee International, Inc.*
Yeaton, Robert — *Source Services Corporation*
Yen, Maggie Yeh Ching — *Ray & Berndtson*
Young, Nick — *Spencer Stuart*
Youngberg, David — *Source Services Corporation*
Yungerberg, Steven — *Steven Yungerberg Associates Inc.*
Zaffrann, Craig S. — *P.J. Murphy & Associates, Inc.*
Zahradka, James F. — *P.J. Murphy & Associates, Inc.*
Zaleta, Andy R. — *A.T. Kearney, Inc.*
Zamborsky, George — *Boyden*
Zaslav, Debra M. — *Telford, Adams & Alexander/Telford & Co., Inc.*
Zavala, Lorenzo — *Russell Reynolds Associates, Inc.*
Zavat, Marc — *Ryan, Miller & Associates Inc.*
Zavrel, Mark — *Source Services Corporation*
Zay, Thomas C. — *Boyden/Zay & Company*
Zay, Thomas C. — *Boyden/Zay & Company*
Zegel, Gary — *Source Services Corporation*
Zetto, Kathryn — *Seco & Zetto Associates, Inc.*
Zimbal, Mark — *Source Services Corporation*
Zimmerman, Joan C. — *G.Z. Stephens Inc.*
Zimont, Scott — *Source Services Corporation*
Zivic, Janis M. — *Spencer Stuart*
Zona, Henry F. — *Zona & Associates, Inc.*
Zonis, Hildy R. — *Accountants Executive Search*
Zucker, Nancy — *Maximum Management Corp.*
Zwell, Michael — *Zwell International*

3. Insurance

Abbatiello, Christine Murphy — *Winter, Wyman & Company*
Adams, Jeffrey C. — *Telford, Adams & Alexander/Jeffrey C. Adams & Co., Inc.*
Afforde, Sharon Gould — *Jacobson Associates*
Akin, J.R. "Jack" — *J.R. Akin & Company Inc.*
Allen, Scott — *Chrisman & Company, Incorporated*
Altreuter, Rose — *The ALTCO Group*
Amato, Joseph — *Amato & Associates, Inc.*
Amilowski, Maria — *Highland Search Group*
Anderson, Steve — *CPS Inc.*
Andujo, Michele M. — *Chrisman & Company, Incorporated*
Anwar, Tarin — *Jay Gaines & Company, Inc.*
Ascher, Susan P. — *The Ascher Group*
Ashton, Edward J. — *E.J. Ashton & Associates, Ltd.*
Atkinson, S. Graham — *Raymond Karsan Associates*
Attaway, Jana — *Kaye-Bassman International Corp.*
Aydelotte, G. Thomas — *Ingram & Aydelotte Inc./I-I-C Partners*
Baeder, Jeremy — *Executive Manning Corporation*
Bailey, Vanessa — *Highland Search Group*
Baje, Sarah — *Innovative Search Group, LLC*
Baker, Bill — *Kaye-Bassman International Corp.*
Baker, Mark A. — *Kaye-Bassman International Corp.*
Balbone, Rich — *Executive Manning Corporation*
Balch, Randy — *CPS Inc.*

Barch, Sherrie — *Furst Group/MPI*
Barger, H. Carter — *Barger & Sargeant, Inc.*
Barnes, Gregory — *Korn/Ferry International*
Barnes, Richard E. — *Barnes Development Group, LLC*
Barnes, Roanne L. — *Barnes Development Group, LLC*
Barnum, Toni M. — *Stone Murphy & Olson*
Bason, Maurice L. — *Bason Associates Inc.*
Bass, M. Lynn — *Ray & Berndtson*
Bass, Nate — *Jacobson Associates*
Bassler, John — *Korn/Ferry International*
Battles, Jonathan — *Korn/Ferry International*
Beaulieu, Genie A. — *Romac & Associates*
Beer, John — *People Management Northeast Incorporated*
Beeson, William B. — *Lawrence-Leiter & Co. Management Conultants*
Belden, Charles P. — *Raymond Karsan Associates*
Bell, Michael — *Spencer Stuart*
Bellano, Robert W. — *Stanton Chase International*
Bennett, Jo — *Battalia Winston International*
Benson, Kate — *Rene Plessner Associates, Inc.*
Bettick, Michael J. — *A.J. Burton Group, Inc.*
Biddix, Maryanne — *Tyler & Company*
Bigelow, Dennis — *Marshall Consultants, Inc.*
Bishop, Barbara — *The Executive Source*
Blake, Eileen — *Howard Fischer Associates, Inc.*
Boel, Werner — *The Dalley Hewitt Company*
Bond, Robert J. — *Romac & Associates*
Bonifield, Len — *Bonifield Associates*
Bonnell, William R. — *Bonnell Associates Ltd.*
Borden, Stuart — *M.A. Churchill & Associates, Inc.*
Borkin, Andrew — *Strategic Advancement Inc.*
Borland, James — *Goodrich & Sherwood Associates, Inc.*
Bourrie, Sharon D. — *Chartwell Partners International, Inc.*
Bowden, Otis H. — *BowdenGlobal, Ltd.*
Brackenbury, Robert — *Bowman & Marshall, Inc.*
Bradley, Dalena — *Woodworth International Group*
Brady, Dick — *William Guy & Associates*
Brady, Robert — *CPS Inc.*
Brandeis, Richard — *CPS Inc.*
Brannon, Kathy — *Kaye-Bassman International Corp.*
Bratches, Howard — *Thorndike Deland Associates*
Brennan, Patrick J. — *Handy HRM Corp.*
Brenner, Mary — *Prestige Inc.*
Brindise, Michael J. — *Dynamic Search Systems, Inc.*
Britt, Stephen — *Keith Bagg & Associates Inc.*
Brocaglia, Joyce — *Alta Associates, Inc.*
Brophy, Melissa — *Maximum Management Corp.*
Brown, Charlene N. — *Accent on Achievement, Inc.*
Brown, Larry C. — *Horton International*
Brown, Steffan — *Woodworth International Group*
Brown, Steve — *K. Russo Associates*
Bruce, Michael C. — *Spencer Stuart*
Buggy, Linda — *Bonnell Associates Ltd.*
Bump, Gerald J. — *D.E. Foster Partners Inc.*
Burns, Terence N. — *D.E. Foster Partners Inc.*

Butler, Kirby B. — *The Butlers Company Insurance Recruiters*
Butterfass, Stanley — *Butterfass, Pepe & MacCallan Inc.*
Bye, Randy — *Romac & Associates*
Byrnes, Thomas A. — *The Search Alliance, Inc.*
Caldwell, C. Douglas — *The Caldwell Partners Amrop International*
Calivas, Kay — *A.J. Burton Group, Inc.*
Cameron, James W. — *Cameron Consulting*
Campbell, Gary — *Romac & Associates*
Cappe, Richard R. — *Roberts Ryan and Bentley*
Carideo, Joseph — *Thorndike Deland Associates*
Carlson, Judith — *Bowman & Marshall, Inc.*
Carrington, Timothy — *Korn/Ferry International*
Casal, Daniel G. — *Bonifield Associates*
Castillo, Eduardo — *Korn/Ferry International*
Castine, Michael P. — *Highland Search Group*
Castriota, Dominic — *Rhodes Associates*
Celenza, Catherine — *CPS Inc.*
Chamberlin, Brooks T. — *Korn/Ferry International*
Chamberlin, Michael A. — *Tower Consultants, Ltd.*
Champion, Geoffrey — *Korn/Ferry International*
Chappell, Peter — *Robertson & Associates*
Chappell, Peter — *The Bankers Group*
Charles, Ronald D. — *The Caldwell Partners Amrop International*
Chauvin, Ralph A. — *The Caldwell Partners Amrop International*
Chndler, Brad J. — *Furst Group/MPI*
Chrisman, Timothy R. — *Chrisman & Company, Incorporated*
Christenson, H. Alan — *Christenson & Hutchison*
Christian, Philip — *Ray & Berndtson*
Christiansen, Amy — *CPS Inc.*
Christiansen, Doug — *CPS Inc.*
Clake, Bob — *Furst Group/MPI*
Clark, James — *CPS Inc.*
Clark, Julie — *Corporate Recruiters Ltd.*
Clark, Steven — *D.A. Kreuter Associates, Inc.*
Clarke Smith, Jamie — *Kaye-Bassman International Corp.*
Cocchiaro, Richard — *Romac & Associates*
Cohen, Michael R. — *Intech Summit Group, Inc.*
Cohen, Robert C. — *Intech Summit Group, Inc.*
Coleman, Patricia — *Korn/Ferry International*
Collard, Joseph A. — *Spencer Stuart*
Collis, Martin — *E.L. Shore & Associates Ltd.*
Cona, Joseph A. — *Cona Personnel Search*
Connaghan, Linda — *Bowman & Marshall, Inc.*
Cortina Del Valle, Pedro — *Ray & Berndtson*
Coulman, Karen — *CPS Inc.*
Courtney, Brendan — *A.J. Burton Group, Inc.*
Cox, William — *E.J. Ashton & Associates, Ltd.*
Coyle, Hugh F. — *A.J. Burton Group, Inc.*
Cragg, Barbara R. — *Southwestern Professional Services*
Crane, Howard C. — *Chartwell Partners International, Inc.*
Crist, Peter — *Crist Partners, Ltd.*
Crystal, Jonathan A. — *Spencer Stuart*
Cuddy, Brian C. — *Romac & Associates*
Cunningham, Lawrence — *Howard Fischer Associates, Inc.*
Cunningham, Robert Y. — *Goodrich & Sherwood Associates, Inc.*

Czepiel, Susan — *CPS Inc.*
Dannenberg, Richard A. — *Roberts Ryan and Bentley*
Darter, Steven M. — *People Management Northeast Incorporated*
Dawson, Joe — *S.C. International, Ltd.*
De Brun, Thomas P. — *Ray & Berndtson*
de Tuede, Catherine — *The Search Alliance, Inc.*
Dean, Mary — *Korn/Ferry International*
Deaver, Henry C. — *Ray & Berndtson*
DeCorrevont, James — *DeCorrevont & Associates*
DeCorrevont, James — *DeCorrevont & Associates*
DeFuniak, William S. — *DeFuniak & Edwards*
DeHart, Donna — *Tower Consultants, Ltd.*
Del Pino, William — *National Search, Inc.*
Della Monica, Vincent — *Search West, Inc.*
Delmonico, Laura — *A.J. Burton Group, Inc.*
Demchak, James P. — *Sandhurst Associates*
Desgrosellier, Gary P. — *Personnel Unlimited/Executive Search*
Desmond, Dennis — *Beall & Company, Inc.*
deVry, Kimberly A. — *Tower Consultants, Ltd.*
deWilde, David M. — *Chartwell Partners International, Inc.*
Dezember, Steve — *Ray & Berndtson*
Dickerson, Scot — *Key Employment Services*
Dickey, Chester W. — *Bowden & Company, Inc.*
Dickey, Chester W. — *Bowden & Company, Inc.*
Dieckmann, Ralph E. — *Dieckmann & Associates, Ltd.*
DiFilippo, James — *Korn/Ferry International*
DiGiovanni, Charles — *Penn Search*
Dingeldey, Peter E. — *Search Advisors International Corp.*
Dingman, Bruce — *Robert W. Dingman Company, Inc.*
Dixon, Aris — *CPS Inc.*
Do, Sonnie — *Whitney & Associates, Inc.*
Doele, Donald C. — *Goodrich & Sherwood Associates, Inc.*
Doman, Matthew — *S.C. International, Ltd.*
Dong, Stephen — *Executive Search, Ltd.*
Dotson, M. Ileen — *Dotson & Associates*
Dressler, Ralph — *Romac & Associates*
Dunbar, Marilynne — *Ray & Berndtson/Lovas Stanley*
Dunkel, David L. — *Romac & Associates*
Dunman, Betsy L. — *Crawford & Crofford*
Dwyer, Julie — *CPS Inc.*
Eason, Jan C. — *Summit Group International*
Eddy, Terry — *William Guy & Associates*
Edwards, Randolph J. — *DeFuniak & Edwards*
Edwards, Verba L. — *Wing Tips & Pumps, Inc.*
Ehrgott, Elizabeth — *The Ascher Group*
Eldridge, Charles B. — *Ray & Berndtson*
Erlien, Nancy B. — *Jacobson Associates*
Ervin, Darlene — *CPS Inc.*
Esposito, Mark — *Christian & Timbers*
Evan-Cook, James W. — *Jacobson Associates*
Evans, David — *Executive Manning Corporation*
Fancher, Robert L. — *Bason Associates Inc.*
Fennell, Patrick — *Korn/Ferry International*
Ferrari, S. Jay — *Ferrari Search Group*
Fields, Fredric — *C.A. Durakis Associates, Inc.*
Fischer, Adam — *Howard Fischer Associates, Inc.*
Fischer, Howard M. — *Howard Fischer Associates, Inc.*

Hutton, Thomas J. — *The Thomas Tucker Company*
Hybels, Cynthia — *A.J. Burton Group, Inc.*
Hyman, Linda — *Korn/Ferry International*
Ikle, A. Donald — *Ward Howell International, Inc.*
Illsley, Hugh G. — *Ward Howell International, Inc.*
Imely, Larry S. — *Stratford Group*
Ingram, D. John — *Ingram & Aydelotte Inc./I-I-C Partners*
Irish, Alan — *CPS Inc.*
Jablo, Steven A. — *Dieckmann & Associates, Ltd.*
Jacobs, Martin J. — *The Rubicon Group*
Jacobs, Mike — *Thorne, Brieger Associates Inc.*
Jacobson, David — *J. J. & H., Ltd.*
Jacobson, David N. — *Jacobson Associates*
Jacobson, Gregory — *Jacobson Associates*
Jacobson, Jewel — *Jacobson Associates*
Jacobson, Rick — *The Windham Group*
Jaedike, Eldron — *Prestige Inc.*
James, Richard — *Criterion Executive Search, Inc.*
Janssen, Don — *Howard Fischer Associates, Inc.*
Jeffers, Richard B. — *Dieckmann & Associates, Ltd.*
Joffe, Barry — *Bason Associates Inc.*
Johnson, Brian — *A.J. Burton Group, Inc.*
Johnson, Julie M. — *International Staffing Consultants, Inc.*
Johnson, Keith — *Romac & Associates*
Johnson, Priscilla — *The Johnson Group, Inc.*
Johnston, James R. — *The Stevenson Group of Delaware Inc.*
Jones, Mark — *Kaye-Bassman International Corp.*
Judy, Otto — *CPS Inc.*
Juratovac, Michael — *Montgomery Resources, Inc.*
Kalinowski, David — *Jacobson Associates*
Kane, Frank — *A.J. Burton Group, Inc.*
Kane, Karen — *Howard Fischer Associates, Inc.*
Kaplan, Gary — *Gary Kaplan & Associates*
Karalis, William — *CPS Inc.*
Keck, Jason B. — *Kaye-Bassman International Corp.*
Kehoe, Mike — *CPS Inc.*
Keller, Peggy — *The McCormick Group, Inc.*
Kelly, Peter W. — *R. Rollo Associates*
Kennedy, Michael — *The Danbrook Group, Inc.*
Kennedy, Walter — *Romac & Associates*
Kershaw, Lisa — *Tanton Mitchell/Paul Ray Berndtson*
Keshishian, Gregory — *Handy HRM Corp.*
Kilcoyne, Pat — *CPS Inc.*
Kilcullen, Brian A. — *D.A. Kreuter Associates, Inc.*
Kile, Robert W. — *Rusher, Loscavio & LoPresto*
Kiley, Phyllis — *National Search, Inc.*
King, Bill — *The McCormick Group, Inc.*
King, Steven — *Ashway, Ltd.*
Kinser, Richard E. — *Richard Kinser & Associates*
Kirschman, David R. — *Physician Executive Management Center*
Kkorzyniewski, Nicole — *CPS Inc.*
Klein, Brandon — *A.J. Burton Group, Inc.*
Kleinstein, Jonah A. — *The Kleinstein Group*
Koehler, Frank R. — *The Koehler Group*
Kramer, Donald — *Dunhill Professional Search of Tampa*

Kramer, Peter — *Dunhill Professional Search of Tampa*
Kratz, Steve — *Tyler & Company*
Krauser, H. James — *Spencer Stuart*
Krecklo, Brian Douglas — *Krecklo & Associates Inc.*
Kreuter, Daniel A. — *D.A. Kreuter Associates, Inc.*
Krueger, Kurt — *Krueger Associates*
Kucewicz, William — *Search West, Inc.*
Kuo, Linda — *Montgomery Resources, Inc.*
Lache, Shawn E. — *The Arcus Group*
Laderman, David — *Romac & Associates*
Laird, Cheryl — *CPS Inc.*
Lamb, Angus K. — *Raymond Karsan Associates*
Landan, Joy — *Jacobson Associates*
Lang, Sharon A. — *Ray & Berndtson*
LaPierre, Louis — *Romac & Associates*
Larsen, Bruce — *Prestige Inc.*
Larsen, Richard F. — *Larsen, Whitney, Blecksmith & Zilliacus*
Lasher, Charles M. — *Lasher Associates*
Laurendeau, Jean E. — *Laurendeau Labrecque/Ray & Berndtson, Inc.*
LaValle, Michael — *Romac & Associates*
Lawrance, Susanne — *Sharrow & Associates*
Leahy, Jan — *CPS Inc.*
Lee, Roger — *Montgomery Resources, Inc.*
Leetma, Imbi — *Stanton Chase International*
Leighton, Nina — *The Ogdon Partnership*
Leininger, Dennis — *Key Employment Services*
Leonard, Linda — *Harris Heery & Associates*
Leslie, William H. — *Boyden/Zay & Company*
Letcher, Harvey D. — *Sandhurst Associates*
Levine, Lois — *National Search, Inc.*
Levine, Roberta — *Tyler & Company*
Levinson, Lauren — *The Danbrook Group, Inc.*
Lewis, Jon A. — *Sandhurst Associates*
Lezama Cohen, Luis — *Ray & Berndtson*
Line, Joseph T. — *Sharrow & Associates*
Linney, George — *Tyler & Company*
Littman, Stephen — *Rhodes Associates*
Lofthouse, Cindy — *CPS Inc.*
Long, Melanie — *National Search, Inc.*
Long, William G. — *McDonald, Long & Associates, Inc.*
Loper, Doris — *Mortgage & Financial Personnel Services*
Loscavio, J. Michael — *Rusher, Loscavio & LoPresto*
Loving, Vikki — *Intersource, Ltd.*
Lucht, John — *The John Lucht Consultancy Inc.*
Ludlow, Paula — *Horton International*
Luntz, Charles E. — *Charles Luntz & Associates. Inc.*
Lynch, Michael C. — *Lynch Miller Moore, Inc.*
Lynch, Sean E. — *Raymond Karsan Associates*
MacCallan, Deirdre — *Butterfass, Pepe & MacCallan Inc.*
MacDougall, Andrew J. — *Spencer Stuart*
MacIntyre, Lisa W. — *Highland Search Group*
Magee, Harrison R. — *Bowden & Company, Inc.*
Maglio, Charles J. — *Maglio and Company, Inc.*
Mahr, Toni — *K. Russo Associates*
Mainwaring, Andrew Brian — *Executive Search Consultants Corporation*
Malcolm, Rod — *Korn/Ferry International*
Mallin, Ellen — *Howard Fischer Associates, Inc.*

Mansford, Keith — *Howard Fischer Associates, Inc.*
Mark, John L. — *J.L. Mark Associates, Inc.*
Mark, Lynne — *J.L. Mark Associates, Inc.*
Marks, Sarah J. — *The Executive Source*
Marsteller, Franklin D. — *Spencer Stuart*
Masserman, Bruce — *Masserman & Associates, Inc.*
Massey, R. Bruce — *Horton International*
Mathias, Kathy — *Stone Murphy & Olson*
Mattes, Edward C. — *The Ogdon Partnership*
Matthews, Corwin — *Woodworth International Group*
Matthews, Mary — *Korn/Ferry International*
Mauer, Kristin — *Montgomery Resources, Inc.*
Mayes, Kay H. — *John Shell Associates, Inc.*
Maynard Taylor, Susan — *Chrisman & Company, Incorporated*
Mazor, Elly — *Howard Fischer Associates, Inc.*
Mazzuckelli, Katie — *Tyler & Company*
McAndrews, Kathy — *CPS Inc.*
McAteer, Thomas — *Montgomery Resources, Inc.*
McBride, Jonathan E. — *McBride Associates, Inc.*
McCabe, Christopher — *Raymond Karsan Associates*
McClearen, V. Bruce — *Tyler & Company*
McConnell, Greg — *Winter, Wyman & Company*
McCool, Anne G. — *Sullivan & Company*
McCormick, Brian — *The McCormick Group, Inc.*
McDermott, Richard A. — *Ray & Berndtson*
McDonald, Scott A. — *McDonald Associates International*
McDonald, Stanleigh B. — *McDonald Associates International*
McDowell, Robert N. — *Christenson & Hutchison*
McFadden, Ashton S. — *Johnson Smith & Knisely Accord*
McGuire, Pat — *A.J. Burton Group, Inc.*
McKeown, Patricia A. — *DiMarchi Partners, Inc.*
McLaughlin, John — *Romac & Associates*
McLean, B. Keith — *Price Waterhouse*
McManners, Donald E. — *McManners Associates, Inc.*
McMillin, Bob — *Price Waterhouse*
McNamara, Catherine — *Ray & Berndtson*
McNamara, Timothy C. — *Columbia Consulting Group*
McNear, Jeffrey E. — *Barrett Partners*
McNichols, Walter B. — *Gary Kaplan & Associates*
McSherry, James F. — *Battalia Winston International*
Mead-Fox, David — *Korn/Ferry International*
Meagher, Patricia G. — *Spencer Stuart*
Mendoza, Guadalupe — *Ward Howell International, Inc.*
Menk, Carl — *Canny, Bowen Inc.*
Mercer, Julie — *Columbia Consulting Group*
Mertensotto, Chuck H. — *Whitney & Associates, Inc.*
Messett, William J. — *Messett Associates, Inc.*
Meyer, Michael F. — *Witt/Kieffer, Ford, Hadelman & Lloyd*
Meyer, Stacey — *Gary Kaplan & Associates*
Meyers, Steven — *Montgomery Resources, Inc.*
Michaels, Joseph — *CPS Inc.*
Milkint, Margaret Resce — *Jacobson Associates*

Miller, Kenneth A. — *Computer Network Resources, Inc.*
Millonzi, Joel C. — *Johnson Smith & Knisely Accord*
Mingle, Larry D. — *Columbia Consulting Group*
Mirtz, P. John — *Mirtz Morice, Inc.*
Mitchell, Jeff — *A.J. Burton Group, Inc.*
Mitchell, John — *Romac & Associates*
Mogul, Gene — *Mogul Consultants, Inc.*
Mohr, Brian — *CPS Inc.*
Molitor, John L. — *Barrett Partners*
Molnar, Robert A. — *Johnson Smith & Knisely Accord*
Moore, T. Wills — *Ray & Berndtson*
Moore, Vickie J. — *Kirkman & Searing, Inc.*
Morgan, Gary — *National Search, Inc.*
Morgan, Nancy — *K. Russo Associates*
Morice, James L. — *Mirtz Morice, Inc.*
Morris, Paul T. — *The Morris Group*
Morton, Robert C. — *Morton, McCorkle & Associates, Inc.*
Moseley, Micahel A. — *Kaye-Bassman International Corp.*
Moyse, Richard G. — *Thorndike Deland Associates*
Muller, Susan — *Corporate Recruiters Ltd.*
Mulligan, Robert P. — *William Willis Worldwide Inc.*
Murphy, Cornelius J. — *Goodrich & Sherwood Associates, Inc.*
Murphy, Erin — *CPS Inc.*
Murphy, Gary J. — *Stone Murphy & Olson*
Murphy, Peter — *Korn/Ferry International*
Mursuli, Meredith — *Lasher Associates*
Mydlach, Renee — *CPS Inc.*
Myers, Kay — *Signature Staffing*
Nagle, Charles L. — *Tyler & Company*
Naidicz, Maria — *Ray & Berndtson*
Neelin, Sharon — *The Caldwell Partners Amrop International*
Nees, Eugene C. — *Ray & Berndtson*
Neff, Thomas J. — *Spencer Stuart*
Neher, Robert L. — *Intech Summit Group, Inc.*
Nehring, Keith — *Howard Fischer Associates, Inc.*
Nephew, Robert — *Christian & Timbers*
Neri, Gene — *S.C. International, Ltd.*
Newpoff, Brad L. — *Furst Group/MPI*
Nielsen, Sue — *Ells Personnel System Inc.*
Noebel, Todd R. — *The Noebel Search Group, Inc.*
Nolte, William D. — *W.D. Nolte & Company*
Normann, Amy — *Robert M. Flanagan & Associates, Ltd.*
Nutter, Roger — *Raymond Karsan Associates*
O'Connell, Mary — *CPS Inc.*
O'Neill, James P. — *Allerton Heneghan & O'Neill*
O'Neill, Stephen A. — *Harris Heery & Associates*
O'Reilly, John — *Stratford Group*
Ogdon, Thomas H. — *The Ogdon Partnership*
Ogilvie, Kit — *Howard Fischer Associates, Inc.*
Ongirski, Richard P. — *Raymond Karsan Associates*
Ornish, Cindy — *Kaye-Bassman International Corp.*
Oswald, Mark G. — *Canny, Bowen Inc.*
Ottenritter, Chris — *CPS Inc.*
Overlock, Craig — *Ray & Berndtson*

Pace, Susan A. — *Horton International*
Pallman-David, Cynthia — *Bonnell Associates Ltd.*
Palma, Frank R. — *Goodrich & Sherwood Associates, Inc.*
Palmer, Carlton A. — *Beall & Company, Inc.*
Panarese, Pam — *Howard Fischer Associates, Inc.*
Pankratz, Dennis — *Furst Group/MPI*
Papasadero, Kathleen — *Woodworth International Group*
Parker, P. Grant — *Raymond Karsan Associates*
Parkhurst, David R. — *Tyler & Company*
Parry, William H. — *Horton International*
Paynter, Sandra L. — *Ward Howell International, Inc.*
Pedley, Jill — *CPS Inc.*
Pepe, Leonida R. — *Butterfass, Pepe & MacCallan Inc.*
Peretz, Jamie — *Korn/Ferry International*
Pernell, Jeanette — *Norman Broadbent International, Inc.*
Peternell, Melanie — *Signature Staffing*
Peterson, John — *CPS Inc.*
Petty, J. Scott — *The Arcus Group*
Phillips, James L. — *Highland Search Group*
Phipps, Peggy — *Woodworth International Group*
Pickford, Stephen T. — *The Corporate Staff, Inc.*
Pierce, Mark — *Korn/Ferry International*
Pierotazio, John — *CPS Inc.*
Pierson, Edward J. — *Johnson Smith & Knisely Accord*
Pinson, Stephanie L. — *Gilbert Tweed/INESA*
Plazza, Richard C. — *The Executive Source*
Plessner, Rene — *Rene Plessner Associates, Inc.*
Plimpton, Ralph L. — *R L Plimpton Associates*
Poirier, Roland L. — *Poirier, Hoevel & Co.*
Polansky, Mark — *Korn/Ferry International*
Pomerance, Mark — *CPS Inc.*
Poracky, John W. — *M. Wood Company*
Poremski, Paul — *A.J. Burton Group, Inc.*
Potter, Mark W. — *Highland Search Group*
Powers Johnson, Allyson — *Skott/Edwards Consultants, Inc.*
Pratt, Tyler P. — *Furst Group/MPI*
Prencipe, V. Michael — *Raymond Karsan Associates*
Press, Fred — *Adept Tech Recruiting*
Price, Kenneth M. — *Messett Associates, Inc.*
Puckett, Jennifer — *Rene Plessner Associates, Inc.*
Rabinowitz, Peter A. — *P.A.R. Associates Inc.*
Railsback, Richard — *Korn/Ferry International*
Raines, Bruce R. — *Raines International Inc.*
Ramler, Carolyn S. — *The Corporate Connection, Ltd.*
Randell, James E. — *Randell-Heiken, Inc.*
Redler, Rhonda — *National Search, Inc.*
Reeves, William B. — *Spencer Stuart*
Regan, Thomas J. — *Tower Consultants, Ltd.*
Reiser, Ellen — *Thorndike Deland Associates*
Reiss, Matt — *National Search, Inc.*
Renick, Cynthia L. — *Morgan Hunter Corp.*
Renner, Sandra L. — *Spectra International Inc.*
Reuter, Tandom — *CPS Inc.*
Reyman, Susan — *S. Reyman & Associates Ltd.*
Reynolds, Gregory P. — *Roberts Ryan and Bentley*
Rice, Marie — *Jay Gaines & Company, Inc.*

Ridenour, Suzanne S. — *Ridenour & Associates, Ltd.*
Riederer, Larry — *CPS Inc.*
Rimmele, Michael — *The Bankers Group*
Rinker, Jim — *Southwestern Professional Services*
Rivera, Elba R. — *Raymond Karsan Associates*
Roberts, Carl R. — *Southwestern Professional Services*
Roberts, Derek J. — *Ward Howell International, Inc.*
Roberts, Kenneth — *The Rubicon Group*
Roberts, Nick P. — *Spectrum Search Associates, Inc.*
Robinson, Bruce — *Bruce Robinson Associates*
Robinson, Eric B. — *Bruce Robinson Associates*
Robles Cuellar, Paulina — *Ray & Berndtson*
Rollins, Scott — *S.C. International, Ltd.*
Rollo, Robert S. — *R. Rollo Associates*
Rorech, Maureen — *Romac & Associates*
Rosenthal, Charles — *National Search, Inc.*
Rosin, Jeffrey — *Korn/Ferry International*
Ross, Curt A. — *Ray & Berndtson*
Ross, Sheila L. — *Ward Howell International, Inc.*
Rotella, Marshall W. — *The Corporate Connection, Ltd.*
Roth, William — *Harris Heery & Associates*
Rowe, William D. — *D.E. Foster Partners Inc.*
Rusher, William H. — *Rusher, Loscavio & LoPresto*
Russell, Richard A. — *Executive Search Consultants Corporation*
Russo, Karen — *K. Russo Associates*
Russo, Karen — *Maximum Management Corp.*
Sabanosh, Whitney — *Highland Search Group*
Sabat, Lori S. — *Alta Associates, Inc.*
Sacerdote, John — *Raymond Karsan Associates*
Saletra, Andrew — *CPS Inc.*
Sanders, Natalie — *CPS Inc.*
Sandor, Richard J. — *Flynn, Hannock, Incorporated*
Saner, Harold — *Romac & Associates*
Sanitago, Anthony — *TaxSearch, Inc.*
Santimauro, Edward — *Korn/Ferry International*
Sarn, Allan G. — *Allan Sarn Associates Inc.*
Sarna, Edmund A. — *Jonas, Walters & Assoc., Inc.*
Sathe, Mark A. — *Sathe & Associates, Inc.*
Sauer, Harry J. — *Romac & Associates*
Savage, Edward J. — *Stanton Chase International*
Sawyer, Deborah — *Korn/Ferry International*
Scalamera, Tom — *CPS Inc.*
Schroeder, John W. — *Spencer Stuart*
Schueneman, David — *CPS Inc.*
Schuette, Dorothy — *Harris Heery & Associates*
Schwartz, Harry — *Jacobson Associates*
Scothon, Alan — *Romac & Associates*
Scott, Evan — *Howard Fischer Associates, Inc.*
Scott, Gordon S. — *Search Advisors International Corp.*
Scranton, Lisa — *A.J. Burton Group, Inc.*
Sennello, Gendra — *National Search, Inc.*
Shapiro, Beth — *Howard Fischer Associates, Inc.*
Shapiro, Elaine — *CPS Inc.*
Shell, John C. — *John Shell Associates, Inc.*
Shelton, Sandra — *National Search, Inc.*
Shemin, Grace — *Maximum Management Corp.*
Sher, Lawrence — *M.A. Churchill & Associates, Inc.*

Sherman, Robert R. — *Mortgage & Financial Personnel Services*
Sherwood, Andrew — *Goodrich & Sherwood Associates, Inc.*
Shield, Nancy — *Maximum Management Corp.*
Siegrist, Jeffrey M. — *D.E. Foster Partners Inc.*
Signer, Julie — *CPS Inc.*
Sindler, Jay — *A.J. Burton Group, Inc.*
Singleton, Robin — *Tyler & Company*
Sitarski, Stan — *Howard Fischer Associates, Inc.*
Smirnov, Tatiana — *Allan Sarn Associates Inc.*
Smith, Ethan L. — *Highland Search Group*
Smith, Lydia — *The Corporate Connection, Ltd.*
Smith, Matt D. — *Ray & Berndtson*
Smith, Richard — *S.C. International, Ltd.*
Snelgrove, Geiger — *National Search, Inc.*
Snyder, C. Edward — *Horton International*
Snyder, James F. — *Snyder & Company*
Spadavecchia, Jennifer — *Alta Associates, Inc.*
Spann, Richard E. — *Goodrich & Sherwood Associates, Inc.*
Spencer, Bob — *Kaye-Bassman International Corp.*
Spicher, John — *M.A. Churchill & Associates, Inc.*
Stark, Jeff — *Thorne, Brieger Associates Inc.*
Steer, Joe — *CPS Inc.*
Stein, Terry W. — *Stewart, Stein and Scott, Ltd.*
Stern, Stephen — *CPS Inc.*
Sterner, Doug — *CPS Inc.*
Stevenson, Jane — *Howard Fischer Associates, Inc.*
Stevenson, Jane — *Howard Fischer Associates, Inc.*
Stewart, Jeffrey O. — *Stewart, Stein and Scott, Ltd.*
Strickland, Katie — *Grantham & Co., Inc.*
Strom, Mark N. — *Search Advisors International Corp.*
Struzziero, Ralph E. — *Romac & Associates*
Sucato, Carolyn — *Jay Gaines & Company, Inc.*
Sussman, Lynda — *Gilbert Tweed/INESA*
Sutter, Howard — *Romac & Associates*
Swanson, Dick — *Raymond Karsan Associates*
Sweeney, Sean K. — *Bonifield Associates*
Swoboda, Lawrence — *A.J. Burton Group, Inc.*
Tappan, Michael A. — *Ward Howell International, Inc.*
Taylor, James M. — *The HRM Group, Inc.*
Taylor, R.L. (Larry) — *Ray & Berndtson*
Telford, John H. — *Telford, Adams & Alexander/Telford & Co., Inc.*
Terry, Douglas — *Jacobson Associates*
Teti, Al — *Chrisman & Company, Incorporated*
Theard, Susan — *Romac & Associates*
Thielman, Joseph — *Barrett Partners*
Thomas, Cheryl M. — *CPS Inc.*
Thomas, Kim — *CPS Inc.*
Tincu, John C. — *Ferneborg & Associates, Inc.*
Tipp, George D. — *Intech Summit Group, Inc.*
Todres-Bernstein, Margo — *Kaye-Bassman International Corp.*
Tootsey, Mark A. — *A.J. Burton Group, Inc.*
Tornesello, Michael P. — *The Yorkshire Group. Ltd.*
Tovrog, Dan — *CPS Inc.*
Tracey, Jack — *Management Assistance Group, Inc.*
Travis, Hallie — *Tyler & Company*

Troup, Roger — *The McCormick Group, Inc.*
Truax, Kevin — *Key Employment Services*
Truemper, Dean — *CPS Inc.*
Tullberg, Tina — *CPS Inc.*
Tursi, Deborah J. — *The Corporate Connection, Ltd.*
Tutwiler, Stephen — *Don Richard Associates of Tampa, Inc.*
Twiste, Craig — *Raymond Karsan Associates*
Tyler, J. Larry — *Tyler & Company*
Tyson, Richard L. — *Bonifield Associates*
Ulbert, Nancy — *Aureus Group*
Vacca, Domenic — *Romac & Associates*
Venable, William W. — *Thorndike Deland Associates*
Vergara, Gail H. — *Spencer Stuart*
Vernon, Peter C. — *Horton International*
Vincelette, Kathy A. — *Raymond Karsan Associates*
Visnich, L. Christine — *Bason Associates Inc.*
Vitale, Amy — *Highland Search Group*
Voigt, John A. — *Romac & Associates*
Vossler, James — *A.J. Burton Group, Inc.*
Wakefield, Scott — *National Search, Inc.*
Waldman, Noah H. — *Lamalie Amrop International*
Waldoch, D. Mark — *Barnes Development Group, LLC*
Walker, Craig H. — *A.J. Burton Group, Inc.*
Walker, Ewing J. — *Ward Howell International, Inc.*
Wasson, Thomas W. — *Spencer Stuart*
Weinberg, Melvin — *Romac & Associates*
Weisler, Nancy — *National Search, Inc.*
Welch, Robert — *Ray & Berndtson*
Weston, Corinne F. — *D.A. Kreuter Associates, Inc.*
Wheeler, Gerard H. — *A.J. Burton Group, Inc.*
Whiting, Anthony — *Johnson Smith & Knisely Accord*
Whitley, Sue Ann — *Roberts Ryan and Bentley*
Whitney, David L. — *Whitney & Associates, Inc.*
Wilburn, Dan — *Kaye-Bassman International Corp.*
Wilder, Richard B. — *Columbia Consulting Group*
Wilkinson, Barbara — *Beall & Company, Inc.*
Wilkinson, Jr. SPHR
Wilkinson, Charles E. — *The HRM Group, Inc.*
Williams, Angie — *Whitney & Associates, Inc.*
Williams, Gary L. — *Barnes Development Group, LLC*
Williams, Harry D. — *Jacobson Associates*
Willis, William H. — *William Willis Worldwide Inc.*
Wilson, John — *Korn/Ferry International*
Wilson, William F. — *Tyler & Company*
Winograd, Glenn — *Criterion Executive Search, Inc.*
Wise, J. Herbert — *Sandhurst Associates*
Wolf, Stephen M. — *Byron Leonard International, Inc.*
Womack, Joseph — *The Bankers Group*
Wood, Elizabeth — *Highland Search Group*
Wood, Milton M. — *M. Wood Company*
Woodmansee, Bruce J. — *Tully/Woodmansee International, Inc.*

Woodworth, Gail — *Woodworth International Group*
Wooldridge, Jeff — *Ray & Berndtson*
Wooller, Edmund A.M. — *Windsor International*
Wright, Carl A.J. — *A.J. Burton Group, Inc.*
Wright, Charles D. — *Goodrich & Sherwood Associates, Inc.*
Wylie, Pamela — *M.A. Churchill & Associates, Inc.*
Wynkoop, Mary — *Tyler & Company*
Yaekle, Gary — *Tully/Woodmansee International, Inc.*
Yen, Maggie Yeh Ching — *Ray & Berndtson*
Yungerberg, Steven — *Steven Yungerberg Associates Inc.*
Zaslav, Debra M. — *Telford, Adams & Alexander/Telford & Co., Inc.*
Zay, Thomas C. — *Boyden/Zay & Company*
Zona, Henry F. — *Zona & Associates, Inc.*
Zucker, Nancy — *Maximum Management Corp.*
Zwell, Michael — *Zwell International*

4. Venture Capital

Abbott, Peter D. — *The Abbott Group, Inc.*
Allen, Scott — *Chrisman & Company, Incorporated*
Allen, Wade H. — *Cendea Connection International*
Allgire, Mary L. — *Kenzer Corp.*
Allred, J. Michael — *Spencer Stuart*
Amilowski, Maria — *Highland Search Group*
Attell, Harold — *A.E. Feldman Associates*
Aubin, Richard E. — *Aubin International Inc.*
Bailey, Paul — *Austin-McGregor International*
Bailey, Vanessa — *Highland Search Group*
Baker, Gary M. — *Cochran, Cochran & Yale, Inc.*
Baltaglia, Michael — *Cochran, Cochran & Yale, Inc.*
Barlow, Ken H. — *The Cherbonnier Group, Inc.*
Barnes, Gary — *Brigade Inc.*
Barnum, Toni M. — *Stone Murphy & Olson*
Bartholdi, Ted — *Bartholdi & Company, Inc.*
Bartholdi, Theodore G. — *Bartholdi & Company, Inc.*
Bason, Maurice L. — *Bason Associates Inc.*
Bauman, Martin H. — *Martin H. Bauman Associates, Inc.*
Beall, Charles P. — *Beall & Company, Inc.*
Becker, Elizabeth M. — *Caliber Associates*
Bellano, Robert W. — *Stanton Chase International*
Bennett, Jo — *Battalia Winston International*
Beran, Helena — *Michael J. Cavanagh and Associates*
Berne, Marlene — *The Whitney Group*
Bigelow, Dennis — *Marshall Consultants, Inc.*
Bishop, Barbara — *The Executive Source*
Blake, Eileen — *Howard Fischer Associates, Inc.*
Blakslee, Jan H. — *J: Blakslee International, Ltd.*
Bloomer, James E. — *L.W. Foote Company*
Bongiovanni, Vincent — *ESA Professional Consultants*
Borland, James — *Goodrich & Sherwood Associates, Inc.*
Bourrie, Sharon D. — *Chartwell Partners International, Inc.*
Bovich, Maryann C. — *Higdon Prince Inc.*
Brackman, Janet — *Dahl-Morrow International*

Bradley, Dalena — *Woodworth International Group*
Bradshaw, Monte — *Christian & Timbers*
Brady, Dick — *William Guy & Associates*
Bratches, Howard — *Thorndike Deland Associates*
Brennan, Patrick J. — *Handy HRM Corp.*
Brocaglia, Joyce — *Alta Associates, Inc.*
Brown, Charlene N. — *Accent on Achievement, Inc.*
Brown, Franklin Key — *Handy HRM Corp.*
Brown, Larry C. — *Horton International*
Brown, Steffan — *Woodworth International Group*
Brudno, Robert J. — *Savoy Partners, Ltd.*
Buchalter, Allyson — *The Whitney Group*
Buckles, Donna — *Cochran, Cochran & Yale, Inc.*
Burden, Gene — *The Cherbonnier Group, Inc.*
Burfield, Elaine — *Skott/Edwards Consultants, Inc.*
Burke, Karen A. — *Mazza & Riley, Inc. (a Korn/Ferry International affiliate)*
Burkland, Skott B. — *Skott/Edwards Consultants, Inc.*
Burns, Alan — *The Enns Partners Inc.*
Busch, Jack — *Busch International*
Call, David — *Cochran, Cochran & Yale, Inc.*
Campbell, Robert Scott — *Wellington Management Group*
Campbell, Robert Scott — *Wellington Management Group*
Cannavo, Louise — *The Whitney Group*
Capizzi, Karen — *Cochran, Cochran & Yale, Inc.*
Carideo, Joseph — *Thorndike Deland Associates*
Cary, Con — *Cary & Associates*
Castine, Michael P. — *Highland Search Group*
Castriota, Dominic — *Rhodes Associates*
Cavanagh, Michael J. — *Michael J. Cavanagh and Associates*
Chappell, Peter — *Robertson & Associates*
Chappell, Peter — *The Bankers Group*
Cherbonnier, L. Michael — *TCG International, Inc.*
Cherbonnier, L. Michael — *The Cherbonnier Group, Inc.*
Chrisman, Timothy R. — *Chrisman & Company, Incorporated*
Christian, Jeffrey E. — *Christian & Timbers*
Clarey, William A. — *Preng & Associates, Inc.*
Clark, Evan — *The Whitney Group*
Clauhsen, Elizabeth A. — *Savoy Partners, Ltd.*
Coffman, Brian — *Kossuth & Associates, Inc.*
Cohen, Robert C. — *Intech Summit Group, Inc.*
Coleman, J. Kevin — *J. Kevin Coleman & Associates, Inc.*
Combs, Stephen L. — *Juntunen-Combs-Poirier*
Connelly, Kevin M. — *Spencer Stuart*
Crath, Paul F. — *Price Waterhouse*
Crist, Peter — *Crist Partners, Ltd.*
Critchley, Walter — *Cochran, Cochran & Yale, Inc.*
Cruse, O.D. — *Spencer Stuart*
Cuddihy, Paul — *Dahl-Morrow International*
Cunningham, Lawrence — *Howard Fischer Associates, Inc.*
Cunningham, Robert Y. — *Goodrich & Sherwood Associates, Inc.*
Curtis, Ellissa — *Cochran, Cochran & Yale, Inc.*
D'Alessio, Gary A. — *Chicago Legal Search, Ltd.*

Davis, G. Gordon — *Davis & Company*
Del Prete, Karen — *Gilbert Tweed/INESA*
Desmond, Dennis — *Beall & Company, Inc.*
deWilde, David M. — *Chartwell Partners International, Inc.*
DiCioccio, Carmen — *Cochran, Cochran & Yale, Inc.*
Dicker, Barry — *ESA Professional Consultants*
Dickey, Chester W. — *Bowden & Company, Inc.*
Dickey, Chester W. — *Bowden & Company, Inc.*
DiMarchi, Paul — *DiMarchi Partners, Inc.*
DiMarchi, Paul — *DiMarchi Partners, Inc.*
Do, Sonnie — *Whitney & Associates, Inc.*
Doele, Donald C. — *Goodrich & Sherwood Associates, Inc.*
Donath, Linda — *Dahl-Morrow International*
Dowell, Chris — *The Abbott Group, Inc.*
Dromeshauser, Peter — *Dromeshauser Associates*
Drury, James J. — *Spencer Stuart*
Dubbs, William — *Williams Executive Search, Inc.*
Duggan, James P. — *Slayton International, Inc./ I-I-C Partners*
Dunbar, Marilynne — *Ray & Berndtson/Lovas Stanley*
Durakis, Charles A. — *C.A. Durakis Associates, Inc.*
Elder, Tom — *Juntunen-Combs-Poirier*
England, Mark — *Austin-McGregor International*
Enns, George — *The Enns Partners Inc.*
Erder, Debra — *Canny, Bowen Inc.*
Erickson, Elaine — *Kenzer Corp.*
Erikson, Theodore J. — *Erikson Consulting Associates, Inc.*
Esposito, Mark — *Christian & Timbers*
Fancher, Robert L. — *Bason Associates Inc.*
Feldman, Abe — *A.E. Feldman Associates*
Ferneborg, Jay W. — *Ferneborg & Associates, Inc.*
Ferneborg, John R. — *Ferneborg & Associates, Inc.*
Ferrari, S. Jay — *Ferrari Search Group*
Fields, Fredric — *C.A. Durakis Associates, Inc.*
Fischer, Adam — *Howard Fischer Associates, Inc.*
Fischer, Howard M. — *Howard Fischer Associates, Inc.*
Fischer, John C. — *Horton International*
Flood, Michael — *Norman Broadbent International, Inc.*
Foote, Leland W. — *L.W. Foote Company*
Foreman, Rebecca — *Aubin International Inc.*
Fowler, Edward D.C. — *Higdon Prince Inc.*
Frazier, John — *Cochran, Cochran & Yale, Inc.*
Freeman, Mark — *ESA Professional Consultants*
Freier, Bruce — *Executive Referral Services, Inc.*
French, William G. — *Preng & Associates, Inc.*
Fulton, Christine N. — *Highland Search Group*
Furlong, James W. — *Furlong Search, Inc.*
Furlong, James W. — *Furlong Search, Inc.*
Furlong, James W. — *Furlong Search, Inc.*
Gabel, Gregory N. — *Canny, Bowen Inc.*
Gabriel, David L. — *The Arcus Group*
Gaffney, Keith — *Gaffney Management Consultants*
Gaffney, William — *Gaffney Management Consultants*
Gantar, Donna — *Howard Fischer Associates, Inc.*
Garfinkle, Steven M. — *Battalia Winston International*

Gerster, J.P. — *Juntunen-Combs-Poirier*
Gestwick, Daniel — *Cochran, Cochran & Yale, Inc.*
Gibbs, John S. — *Spencer Stuart*
Gilbert, Jerry — *Gilbert & Van Campen International*
Gilbert, Patricia G. — *Lynch Miller Moore, Inc.*
Gill, Patricia — *Columbia Consulting Group*
Gill, Susan — *Plummer & Associates, Inc.*
Gilreath, James M. — *Gilreath Weatherby, Inc.*
Glass, Lori — *The Executive Source*
Gobert, Larry — *Professional Search Consultants*
Goldenberg, Susan — *Grant Cooper and Associates*
Goldsmith, Joseph B. — *Higdon Prince Inc.*
Goldstein, Gary — *The Whitney Group*
Goodman, Dawn M. — *Bason Associates Inc.*
Gorfinkle, Gayle — *Executive Search International*
Gow, Roderick C. — *Lamalie Amrop International*
Grant, Michael — *Zwell International*
Grantham, Philip H. — *Columbia Consulting Group*
Gray, Mark — *Executive Referral Services, Inc.*
Grebenstein, Charles R. — *Skott/Edwards Consultants, Inc.*
Grotte, Lawrence C. — *Lautz Grotte Engler*
Hall, Peter V. — *Chartwell Partners International, Inc.*
Hallock, Peter B. — *Goodrich & Sherwood Associates, Inc.*
Hallstrom, Victoria — *The Whitney Group*
Hanley, J. Patrick — *Canny, Bowen Inc.*
Hanson, Grant M. — *Goodrich & Sherwood Associates, Inc.*
Hardison, Richard L. — *Hardison & Company*
Hardy, Thomas G. — *Spencer Stuart*
Hargis, N. Leann — *Montgomery Resources, Inc.*
Harris, Joe W. — *Cendea Connection International*
Harris, Julia — *The Whitney Group*
Harris, Seth O. — *Christian & Timbers*
Havener, Donald Clarke — *The Abbott Group, Inc.*
Hebel, Robert W. — *R.W. Hebel Associates*
Heinze, David — *Heinze & Associates, Inc.*
Heller, Steven A. — *Martin H. Bauman Associates, Inc.*
Hellinger, Audrey W. — *Martin H. Bauman Associates, Inc.*
Helminiak, Audrey — *Gaffney Management Consultants*
Herman, Pat — *Whitney & Associates, Inc.*
Hetherman, Margaret F. — *Highland Search Group*
Higbee, Joan — *Thorndike Deland Associates*
Higdon, Henry G. — *Higdon Prince Inc.*
Higgins, Donna — *Howard Fischer Associates, Inc.*
Himlin, Amy — *Cochran, Cochran & Yale, Inc.*
Hochberg, Steven P. — *Caliber Associates*
Hockett, William — *Hockett Associates, Inc.*
Holmes, Lawrence J. — *Columbia Consulting Group*
Holt, Carol — *Bartholdi & Company, Inc.*
Holzberger, Georges L. — *Highland Search Group*
Honer, Paul E. — *Ingram & Aydelotte Inc./I-I-C Partners*

Hopkinson, Dana — *Winter, Wyman & Company*
Houchins, William M. — *Christian & Timbers*
Hoyda, Louis A. — *Thorndike Deland Associates*
Hughes, Cathy N. — *The Ogdon Partnership*
Hypes, Richard G. — *Lynch Miller Moore, Inc.*
Imely, Larry S. — *Stratford Group*
Jablo, Steven A. — *Dieckmann & Associates, Ltd.*
Janssen, Don — *Howard Fischer Associates, Inc.*
Januale, Lois — *Cochran, Cochran & Yale, Inc.*
Jazylo, John V. — *Handy HRM Corp.*
Joffe, Barry — *Bason Associates Inc.*
Johnson, Ronald S. — *Ronald S. Johnson Associates, Inc.*
Jones, Edward G. — *E.G. Jones Associates, Ltd.*
Jordan, Jon — *Cochran, Cochran & Yale, Inc.*
Juratovac, Michael — *Montgomery Resources, Inc.*
Juska, Frank — *Rusher, Loscavio & LoPresto*
Kane, Karen — *Howard Fischer Associates, Inc.*
Kassouf, Constance — *The Whitney Group*
Keating, Pierson — *Nordeman Grimm, Inc.*
Kelly, Elizabeth Ann — *Wellington Management Group*
Kelly, Peter W. — *R. Rollo Associates*
Kenzer, Robert D. — *Kenzer Corp.*
Keshishian, Gregory — *Handy HRM Corp.*
King, Margaret — *Christian & Timbers*
Kip, Luanne S. — *Kip Williams, Inc.*
Klein, Mary Jo — *Cochran, Cochran & Yale, Inc.*
Klein, Mel — *Stewart/Laurence Associates*
Knight, Liz — *Plummer & Associates, Inc.*
Knisely, Gary — *Johnson Smith & Knisely Accord*
Kohn, Adam P. — *Christian & Timbers*
Kopsick, Joseph M. — *Spencer Stuart*
Kossuth, David — *Kossuth & Associates, Inc.*
Kossuth, Jane — *Kossuth & Associates, Inc.*
Krauser, H. James — *Spencer Stuart*
Krejci, Stanley L. — *Boyden Washington, D.C.*
Krieger, Dennis F. — *Seiden Krieger Associates, Inc.*
Kuo, Linda — *Montgomery Resources, Inc.*
Kurrigan, Geoffrey — *ESA Professional Consultants*
Labrecque, Bernard F. — *Laurendeau Labrecque/Ray & Berndtson, Inc.*
Lache, Shawn E. — *The Arcus Group*
Lasher, Charles M. — *Lasher Associates*
Lautz, Lindsay A. — *Lautz Grotte Engler*
Lazaro, Alicia C. — *The Whitney Group*
Ledbetter, Steven G. — *Cendea Connection International*
Lee, Roger — *Montgomery Resources, Inc.*
Leetma, Imbi — *Stanton Chase International*
Leighton, Nina — *The Ogdon Partnership*
Leslie, William H. — *Boyden/Zay & Company*
Lewis, Jon A. — *Sandhurst Associates*
Litt, Michele — *The Whitney Group*
Littman, Stephen — *Rhodes Associates*
Lokken, Karen — *A.E. Feldman Associates*
Long, Milt — *William Guy & Associates*
Long, William G. — *McDonald, Long & Associates, Inc.*
Looney, Scott — *A.E. Feldman Associates*
LoPresto, Robert L. — *Rusher, Loscavio & LoPresto*
Lucht, John — *The John Lucht Consultancy Inc.*

Lupica, Anthony — *Cochran, Cochran & Yale, Inc.*
Lynch, Michael C. — *Lynch Miller Moore, Inc.*
Lyons, J. David — *Aubin International Inc.*
Macan, Sandi — *Caliber Associates*
Macdonald, G. William — *The Macdonald Group, Inc.*
MacIntyre, Lisa W. — *Highland Search Group*
Mackenna, Kathy — *Plummer & Associates, Inc.*
Maer, Harry — *Kenzer Corp.*
Magee, Harrison R. — *Bowden & Company, Inc.*
Mallin, Ellen — *Howard Fischer Associates, Inc.*
Mancino, Gene — *Blau Mancino Schroeder*
Mansford, Keith — *Howard Fischer Associates, Inc.*
Marino, Chester — *Cochran, Cochran & Yale, Inc.*
Marks, Ira — *Strategic Alternatives*
Marks, Sarah J. — *The Executive Source*
Marumoto, William H. — *Boyden Washington, D.C.*
Masserman, Bruce — *Masserman & Associates, Inc.*
Massey, R. Bruce — *Horton International*
Mather, David R. — *Christian & Timbers*
Mattes, Edward C. — *The Ogdon Partnership*
Matthews, Corwin — *Woodworth International Group*
Mauer, Kristin — *Montgomery Resources, Inc.*
Maynard Taylor, Susan — *Chrisman & Company, Incorporated*
Mazor, Elly — *Howard Fischer Associates, Inc.*
Mazza, David B. — *Mazza & Riley, Inc. (a Korn/Ferry International affiliate)*
McAteer, Thomas — *Montgomery Resources, Inc.*
McBride, Jonathan E. — *McBride Associates, Inc.*
McCann, Cornelia B. — *Spencer Stuart*
McCreary, Charles "Chip" — *Austin-McGregor International*
McFadden, Ashton S. — *Johnson Smith & Knisely Accord*
McKeown, Patricia A. — *DiMarchi Partners, Inc.*
McManners, Donald E. — *McManners Associates, Inc.*
McManus, Paul — *Aubin International Inc.*
McNamara, Timothy C. — *Columbia Consulting Group*
McSherry, James F. — *Battalia Winston International*
Mead, James D. — *James Mead & Company*
Meany, Brian M. — *Herbert Mines Associates, Inc.*
Mercer, Julie — *Columbia Consulting Group*
Mertensotto, Chuck H. — *Whitney & Associates, Inc.*
Meyers, Steven — *Montgomery Resources, Inc.*
Miller, David — *Cochran, Cochran & Yale, Inc.*
Miller, Michael R. — *Lynch Miller Moore, Inc.*
Miller, Roy — *The Enns Partners Inc.*
Millonzi, Joel C. — *Johnson Smith & Knisely Accord*
Mines, Herbert T. — *Herbert Mines Associates, Inc.*
Mingle, Larry D. — *Columbia Consulting Group*
Misiurewicz, Marc — *Cochran, Cochran & Yale, Inc.*
Molnar, Robert A. — *Johnson Smith & Knisely Accord*

Spann, Richard E. — *Goodrich & Sherwood Associates, Inc.*
Spiegel, Gayle — *L. A. Silver Associates, Inc.*
Spriggs, Robert D. — *Spriggs & Company, Inc.*
St. Clair, Alan — *TNS Partners, Inc.*
Stahl, Cindy — *Plummer & Associates, Inc.*
Steele, Daniel — *Cochran, Cochran & Yale, Inc.*
Stein, Terry W. — *Stewart, Stein and Scott, Ltd.*
Steinem, Andy — *Dahl-Morrow International*
Steinem, Andy — *Dahl-Morrow International*
Steinem, Barbara — *Dahl-Morrow International*
Steinem, Barbra — *Dahl-Morrow International*
Stevenson, Jane — *Howard Fischer Associates, Inc.*
Stevenson, Jane — *Howard Fischer Associates, Inc.*
Stewart, Jeffrey O. — *Stewart, Stein and Scott, Ltd.*
Stewart, Ross M. — *Human Resources Network Partners Inc.*
Stratmeyer, Karin Bergwall — *Princeton Entrepreneurial Resources*
Sumurdy, Melinda — *Kenzer Corp.*
Teti, Al — *Chrisman & Company, Incorporated*
Thomas, Jeffrey — *Fairfaxx Corporation*
Thomas, Terry — *The Thomas Resource Group*
Tierney, Eileen — *The Whitney Group*
Tucci, Joseph — *Fairfaxx Corporation*
Tucker, Thomas A. — *The Thomas Tucker Company*
Tully, Margo L. — *Tully/Woodmansee International, Inc.*
Tuttle, Donald E. — *Tuttle Venture Group, Inc.*
Tweed, Janet — *Gilbert Tweed/INESA*
Vairo, Leonard A. — *Christian & Timbers*
Valenta, Joseph — *Princeton Entrepreneurial Resources*
Van Clieaf, Mark — *MVC Associates International*
Venable, William W. — *Thorndike Deland Associates*
Vergari, Jane — *Herbert Mines Associates, Inc.*
Vernon, Peter C. — *Horton International*
Visnich, L. Christine — *Bason Associates Inc.*
Vitale, Amy — *Highland Search Group*

Volkman, Arthur — *Cochran, Cochran & Yale, Inc.*
Vourakis, Zan — *ZanExec LLC*
Walker, Douglas G. — *Sink, Walker, Boltrus International*
Walker, Ewing J. — *Ward Howell International, Inc.*
Ward, Madeleine — *LTM Associates*
Warter, Mark — *Isaacson, Miller*
Weber, Ronald R. — *Weber Executive Search*
Wein, Michael S. — *Media Management Resources, Inc.*
Wein, William — *Media Management Resources, Inc.*
White, Richard B. — *Spencer Stuart*
White, William C. — *Venture Resources Inc.*
Whiting, Anthony — *Johnson Smith & Knisely Accord*
Whitney, David L. — *Whitney & Associates, Inc.*
Wier, Daniel — *Daniel Wier & Associates*
Wilburn, Dan — *Kaye-Bassman International Corp.*
Wilkinson, Barbara — *Beall & Company, Inc.*
Williams, Angie — *Whitney & Associates, Inc.*
Williams, Roger K. — *Williams, Roth & Krueger Inc.*
Wilson, T. Gordon — *Ray & Berndtson/Lovas Stanley*
Winston, Dale — *Battalia Winston International*
Wold, Ted W. — *Hyde Danforth Wold & Co.*
Womack, Joseph — *The Bankers Group*
Wood, Elizabeth — *Highland Search Group*
Woodworth, Gail — *Woodworth International Group*
Wright, Charles D. — *Goodrich & Sherwood Associates, Inc.*
Zadfar, Maryanne — *The Thomas Tucker Company*
Zak, Adam — *Adams & Associates International*
Zegas, Jeffrey — *Zurick, Davis & Co., Inc.*
Zila, Laurie M. — *Princeton Entrepreneurial Resources*
Zwell, Michael — *Zwell International*

Function Specialization Index
by Recruiter

Function Specialization Index by Recruiter

This index is arranged into 10 selected business functions, including the generalist category, and provides a breakdown of the primary and secondary lines of function specializations of each executive recruiter. Many recruiters have multiple listings in this index depending on the various specializations in which they are engaged. *Recruiters listed in the generalist category serve all function specializations.*

1. Generalist
2. Administration
3. Engineering
4. Finance/Accounting
5. General Management

6. Human Resources
7. Marketing
8. Research/Development
9. Sales
10. Women/Minorities

1. Generalist

Abbatiello, Christine Murphy — *Winter, Wyman & Company*
Abbott, Peter D. — *The Abbott Group, Inc.*
Abell, Vincent W. — *MSI International*
Adams, Amy — *Richard, Wayne and Roberts*
Adams, Jeffrey C. — *Telford, Adams & Alexander/Jeffrey C. Adams & Co., Inc.*
Adler, Louis S. — *CJA - The Adler Group*
Afforde, Sharon Gould — *Jacobson Associates*
Agee, Jo Etta — *Chrisman & Company, Incorporated*
Akin, J.R. "Jack" — *J.R. Akin & Company Inc.*
Alexander, John T. — *Telford, Adams & Alexander*
Allard, Susan — *Allard Associates*
Allen, Jean E. — *Lamalie Amrop International*
Allen, Scott — *Chrisman & Company, Incorporated*
Allen, Wade H. — *Cendea Connection International*
Allen, William L. — *The Hindman Company*
Allgire, Mary L. — *Kenzer Corp.*
Allred, J. Michael — *Spencer Stuart*
Altreuter, Rose — *The ALTCO Group*
Ambler, Peter W. — *Peter W. Ambler Company*
Amilowski, Maria — *Highland Search Group*
Anderson, Maria H. — *Barton Associates, Inc.*
Anderson, Richard — *Grant Cooper and Associates*
Anderson, Terry — *Intech Summit Group, Inc.*
Andre, Jacques P. — *Ray & Berndtson*
Andujo, Michele M. — *Chrisman & Company, Incorporated*
Archer, Sandra F. — *Ryan, Miller & Associates Inc.*
Argenio, Michelangelo — *Spencer Stuart*
Arms, Douglas — *TOPAZ International, Inc.*
Arms, Douglas — *TOPAZ Legal Solutions*
Aronin, Michael — *Fisher-Todd Associates*
Ascher, Susan P. — *The Ascher Group*
Ashton, Edward J. — *E.J. Ashton & Associates, Ltd.*
Aston, Kathy — *Marra Peters & Partners*
Atkinson, S. Graham — *Raymond Karsan Associates*
Attell, Harold — *A.E. Feldman Associates*
Atwood, Barrie — *The Abbott Group, Inc.*
Aubin, Richard E. — *Aubin International Inc.*
Axelrod, Nancy R. — *A.T. Kearney, Inc.*
Aydelotte, G. Thomas — *Ingram & Aydelotte Inc./I-I-C Partners*
Badger, Fred H. — *The Badger Group*
Baeder, Jeremy — *Executive Manning Corporation*
Bailey, Paul — *Austin-McGregor International*
Bailey, Vanessa — *Highland Search Group*
Baje, Sarah — *Innovative Search Group, LLC*
Baker, Gary M. — *Cochran, Cochran & Yale, Inc.*
Baker, Gerry — *A.T. Kearney, Inc.*
Balbone, Rich — *Executive Manning Corporation*
Ballantine, Caroline B. — *Heidrick & Struggles, Inc.*
Baltaglia, Michael — *Cochran, Cochran & Yale, Inc.*
Barbour, Mary Beth — *Tully/Woodmansee International, Inc.*
Barger, H. Carter — *Barger & Sargeant, Inc.*
Barlow, Ken H. — *The Cherbonnier Group, Inc.*
Barnes, Gregory — *Korn/Ferry International*

Barnes, Richard E. — *Barnes Development Group, LLC*
Barnes, Roanne L. — *Barnes Development Group, LLC*
Barnette, Dennis A. — *Heidrick & Struggles, Inc.*
Barnum, Toni M. — *Stone Murphy & Olson*
Barrett, J. David — *Heidrick & Struggles, Inc.*
Bartholdi, Ted — *Bartholdi & Company, Inc.*
Bartholdi, Theodore G. — *Bartholdi & Company, Inc.*
Barton, Gary R. — *Barton Associates, Inc.*
Bason, Maurice L. — *Bason Associates Inc.*
Bass, M. Lynn — *Ray & Berndtson*
Bass, Nate — *Jacobson Associates*
Bassler, John — *Korn/Ferry International*
Bassman, Robert — *Kaye-Bassman International Corp.*
Bassman, Sandy — *Kaye-Bassman International Corp.*
Battles, Jonathan — *Korn/Ferry International*
Bauman, Martin H. — *Martin H. Bauman Associates, Inc.*
Beall, Charles P. — *Beall & Company, Inc.*
Bearman, Linda — *Grant Cooper and Associates*
Beaudin, Elizabeth C. — *Callan Associates, Ltd.*
Beaver, Bentley H. — *The Onstott Group, Inc.*
Beer, John — *People Management Northeast Incorporated*
Beeson, William B. — *Lawrence-Leiter & Co. Management Conultants*
Belden, Charles P. — *Raymond Karsan Associates*
Belin, Jean — *Boyden*
Bell, Lloyd W. — *O'Brien & Bell*
Bell, Michael — *Spencer Stuart*
Bellano, Robert W. — *Stanton Chase International*
Bennett, Jo — *Battalia Winston International*
Benson, Kate — *Rene Plessner Associates, Inc.*
Beran, Helena — *Michael J. Cavanagh and Associates*
Berk-Levine, Margo — *MB Inc. Interim Executive Division*
Berman, Mitchell — *Carlyle Group*
Berne, Marlene — *The Whitney Group*
Berry, Harold B. — *The Hindman Company*
Bettick, Michael J. — *A.J. Burton Group, Inc.*
Biddix, Maryanne — *Tyler & Company*
Biggins, J. Veronica — *Heidrick & Struggles, Inc.*
Billington, William H. — *Spriggs & Company, Inc.*
Birkhead, Linda — *Zwell International*
Bladon, Andrew — *Don Richard Associates of Tampa, Inc.*
Blake, Eileen — *Howard Fischer Associates, Inc.*
Blakslee, Jan H. — *J: Blakslee International, Ltd.*
Blecksmith, Edward L. — *Larsen, Whitney, Blecksmith & Zilliacus*
Bliley, Jerry — *Spencer Stuart*
Bloomer, James E. — *L.W. Foote Company*
Boel, Werner — *The Dalley Hewitt Company*
Bogansky, Amy — *Conex Incorporated*
Bohn, Steve J. — *MSI International*
Bonifield, Len — *Bonifield Associates*
Bonnell, William R. — *Bonnell Associates Ltd.*
Borland, James — *Goodrich & Sherwood Associates, Inc.*
Bormann, Cindy Ann — *MSI International*
Bourrie, Sharon D. — *Chartwell Partners International, Inc.*

Bovich, Maryann C. — *Higdon Prince Inc.*
Bowden, Otis H. — *BowdenGlobal, Ltd.*
Bowen, Tad — *Executive Search International*
Boyle, Russell E. — *Egon Zehnder International Inc.*
Brackman, Janet — *Dahl-Morrow International*
Bradley, Dalena — *Woodworth International Group*
Bradshaw, Monte — *Christian & Timbers*
Brady, Dick — *William Guy & Associates*
Brandenburg, David — *Professional Staffing Consultants*
Brandjes, Michael J. — *Brandjes Associates*
Brandon, Irwin — *Hadley Lockwood, Inc.*
Bratches, Howard — *Thorndike Deland Associates*
Brennan, Patrick J. — *Handy HRM Corp.*
Brenner, Mary — *Prestige Inc.*
Brieger, Steve — *Thorne, Brieger Associates Inc.*
Broadhurst, Austin — *Lamalie Amrop International*
Brother, Joy — *Charles Luntz & Associates. Inc.*
Brown, Franklin Key — *Handy HRM Corp.*
Brown, Larry C. — *Horton International*
Brown, Lawrence Anthony — *MSI International*
Brown, S. Ross — *Egon Zehnder International Inc.*
Brown, Steffan — *Woodworth International Group*
Bruce, Michael C. — *Spencer Stuart*
Brudno, Robert J. — *Savoy Partners, Ltd.*
Bruno, Deborah F. — *The Hindman Company*
Bryant, Richard D. — *Bryant Associates, Inc.*
Bryant, Shari G. — *Bryant Associates, Inc.*
Brzezinski, Ronald T. — *Callan Associates, Ltd.*
Buchalter, Allyson — *The Whitney Group*
Buckles, Donna — *Cochran, Cochran & Yale, Inc.*
Buggy, Linda — *Bonnell Associates Ltd.*
Bump, Gerald J. — *D.E. Foster Partners Inc.*
Burden, Gene — *The Cherbonnier Group, Inc.*
Burke, John — *The Experts*
Burke, Karen A. — *Mazza & Riley, Inc. (a Korn/Ferry International affiliate)*
Burkhill, John — *The Talley Group*
Burnett-Stohner, Brendan G. — *Sullivan & Company*
Burns, Alan — *The Enns Partners Inc.*
Burns, Terence N. — *D.E. Foster Partners Inc.*
Busch, Jack — *Busch International*
Bush, R. Stuart — *Russell Reynolds Associates, Inc.*
Butler, Kirby B. — *The Butlers Company Insurance Recruiters*
Butterfass, Stanley — *Butterfass, Pepe & MacCallan Inc.*
Byrnes, Thomas A. — *The Search Alliance, Inc.*
Caldwell, C. Douglas — *The Caldwell Partners Amrop International*
Calivas, Kay — *A.J. Burton Group, Inc.*
Call, David — *Cochran, Cochran & Yale, Inc.*
Callan, Robert M. — *Callan Associates, Ltd.*
Cameron, James W. — *Cameron Consulting*
Campbell, Patricia A. — *The Onstott Group, Inc.*
Campbell, Robert Scott — *Wellington Management Group*
Campbell, Robert Scott — *Wellington Management Group*
Campbell, Thomas J. — *Heidrick & Struggles, Inc.*

Campbell, W. Ross — *Egon Zehnder International Inc.*
Cannavino, John J. — *Financial Resource Associates, Inc.*
Cannavo, Louise — *The Whitney Group*
Cannon, Alexis — *Richard, Wayne and Roberts*
Capizzi, Karen — *Cochran, Cochran & Yale, Inc.*
Carideo, Joseph — *Thorndike Deland Associates*
Carrington, Timothy — *Korn/Ferry International*
Carro, Carl R. — *Executive Search Consultants International, Inc.*
Carrott, Gregory T. — *Egon Zehnder International Inc.*
Carter, Jon F. — *Egon Zehnder International Inc.*
Cary, Con — *Cary & Associates*
Casal, Daniel G. — *Bonifield Associates*
Cashen, Anthony B. — *Lamalie Amrop International*
Castillo, Eduardo — *Korn/Ferry International*
Castine, Michael P. — *Highland Search Group*
Castriota, Dominic — *Rhodes Associates*
Caudill, Nancy — *Webb, Johnson Associates, Inc.*
Cavanagh, Michael J. — *Michael J. Cavanagh and Associates*
Chamberlin, Brooks T. — *Korn/Ferry International*
Chamberlin, Joan — *William Guy & Associates*
Champion, Geoffrey — *Korn/Ferry International*
Chan, Margaret — *Webb, Johnson Associates, Inc.*
Chappell, Peter — *Robertson & Associates*
Chappell, Peter — *The Bankers Group*
Charles, Ronald D. — *The Caldwell Partners Amrop International*
Chatterjie, Alok — *MSI International*
Chauvin, Ralph A. — *The Caldwell Partners Amrop International*
Cherbonnier, L. Michael — *TCG International, Inc.*
Cherbonnier, L. Michael — *The Cherbonnier Group, Inc.*
Chndler, Brad J. — *Furst Group/MPI*
Cho, Ui — *Richard, Wayne and Roberts*
Chrisman, Timothy R. — *Chrisman & Company, Incorporated*
Christenson, H. Alan — *Christenson & Hutchison*
Christian, Philip — *Ray & Berndtson*
Citarella, Richard A. — *A.T. Kearney, Inc.*
Citrin, James M. — *Spencer Stuart*
Cizek, John T. — *Cizek Associates, Inc.*
Cizek, Marti J. — *Cizek Associates, Inc.*
Clarey, William A. — *Preng & Associates, Inc.*
Clark, Donald B. — *Ray & Berndtson*
Clark, Evan — *The Whitney Group*
Clarke Smith, Jamie — *Kaye-Bassman International Corp.*
Clauhsen, Elizabeth A. — *Savoy Partners, Ltd.*
Clayton, Fred J. — *Berkhemer Clayton Incorporated*
Clemens, Bill — *Spencer Stuart*
Cloutier, Gisella — *Dinte Resources, Inc.*
Cochran, Scott P. — *The Badger Group*
Coe, Karen J. — *Coe & Company International Inc.*
Coffman, Brian — *Kossuth & Associates, Inc.*
Cohen, Michael R. — *Intech Summit Group, Inc.*
Cohen, Pamela — *TOPAZ International, Inc.*
Cohen, Pamela — *TOPAZ Legal Solutions*
Cohen, Robert C. — *Intech Summit Group, Inc.*

Ehrgott, Elizabeth — *The Ascher Group*
Ehrhart, Jennifer — *ADOW's Executeam*
Eldridge, Charles B. — *Ray & Berndtson*
Ellis, Ted K. — *The Hindman Company*
Ellis, William — *Interspace Interactive Inc.*
Emery, Jodie A. — *Lamalie Amrop International*
Engelbert, Kimberly S. — *Watson International, Inc.*
England, Mark — *Austin-McGregor International*
Engler, Peter G — *Lautz Grotte Engler*
Enns, George — *The Enns Partners Inc.*
Epstein, Kathy J. — *Lamalie Amrop International*
Erder, Debra — *Canny, Bowen Inc.*
Erickson, Elaine — *Kenzer Corp.*
Erlien, Nancy B. — *Jacobson Associates*
Esposito, Mark — *Christian & Timbers*
Eustis, Lucy R. — *MSI International*
Evan-Cook, James W. — *Jacobson Associates*
Evans, David — *Executive Manning Corporation*
Fabbro, Vivian — *A.T. Kearney, Inc.*
Fancher, Robert L. — *Bason Associates Inc.*
Farley, Leon A. — *Leon A. Farley Associates*
Fawcett, Anne M. — *The Caldwell Partners Amrop International*
Feder, Gwen — *Egon Zehnder International Inc.*
Fee, J. Curtis — *Spencer Stuart*
Feldman, Abe — *A.E. Feldman Associates*
Fennell, Patrick — *Korn/Ferry International*
Ferneborg, Jay W. — *Ferneborg & Associates, Inc.*
Ferneborg, John R. — *Ferneborg & Associates, Inc.*
Fields, Fredric — *C.A. Durakis Associates, Inc.*
Fifield, George C. — *Egon Zehnder International Inc.*
Fischer, Adam — *Howard Fischer Associates, Inc.*
Fischer, Howard M. — *Howard Fischer Associates, Inc.*
Fischer, Janet L. — *Boyden*
Fischer, John C. — *Horton International*
Fisher, Neal — *Fisher Personnel Management Services*
Fishler, Stu — *A.T. Kearney, Inc.*
Fitzgerald, Diane — *Fitzgerald Associates*
Fitzgerald, Geoffrey — *Fitzgerald Associates*
Flanagan, Robert M. — *Robert M. Flanagan & Associates, Ltd.*
Fleming, Marco — *MSI International*
Fletcher, David — *A.J. Burton Group, Inc.*
Flores, Agustin — *Ward Howell International, Inc.*
Fong, Robert — *Korn/Ferry International*
Foote, Leland W. — *L.W. Foote Company*
Foreman, David C. — *Koontz, Jeffries & Associates, Inc.*
Foreman, Rebecca — *Aubin International Inc.*
Forgosh, Jack H. — *Raymond Karsan Associates*
Fowler, Edward D.C. — *Higdon Prince Inc.*
Fowler, Susan B. — *Russell Reynolds Associates, Inc.*
Fowler, Thomas A. — *The Hindman Company*
Fox, Amanda C. — *Ray & Berndtson*
Frazier, John — *Cochran, Cochran & Yale, Inc.*
Freedman, Howard — *Korn/Ferry International*
French, William G. — *Preng & Associates, Inc.*
Frerichs, April — *Ryan, Miller & Associates Inc.*
Fribush, Richard — *A.J. Burton Group, Inc.*
Friedman, Helen E. — *McCormack & Farrow*
Frock, Suzanne D. — *Brandjes Associates*
Fulton, Christine N. — *Highland Search Group*

Furlong, James W. — *Furlong Search, Inc.*
Furlong, James W. — *Furlong Search, Inc.*
Furlong, James W. — *Furlong Search, Inc.*
Fust, Sheely F. — *Ray & Berndtson*
Gabel, Gregory N. — *Canny, Bowen Inc.*
Gabler, Howard A. — *G.Z. Stephens Inc.*
Gabriel, David L. — *The Arcus Group*
Gaffney, Keith — *Gaffney Management Consultants*
Gaffney, William — *Gaffney Management Consultants*
Gaines, Jay — *Jay Gaines & Company, Inc.*
Gaines, Ronni L. — *TOPAZ International, Inc.*
Gaines, Ronni L. — *TOPAZ Legal Solutions*
Galante, Suzanne M. — *Vlcek & Company, Inc.*
Galinski, Paul — *E.J. Ashton & Associates, Ltd.*
Gallagher, Terence M. — *Battalia Winston International*
Gantar, Donna — *Howard Fischer Associates, Inc.*
Gardiner, E. Nicholas P. — *Gardiner International*
Garfinkle, Steven M. — *Battalia Winston International*
Gates, Lucille C. — *Lamalie Amrop International*
Gauthier, Robert C. — *Columbia Consulting Group*
George, Delores F. — *Delores F. George Human Resource Management & Consulting Industry*
Gerber, Mark J. — *Wellington Management Group*
Germain, Valerie — *Jay Gaines & Company, Inc.*
Gestwick, Daniel — *Cochran, Cochran & Yale, Inc.*
Ghurani, Mac — *Gary Kaplan & Associates*
Gibbons, Ronald L. — *Flynn, Hannock, Incorporated*
Gibbs, John S. — *Spencer Stuart*
Gilbert, Jerry — *Gilbert & Van Campen International*
Gilbert, Patricia G. — *Lynch Miller Moore, Inc.*
Gilchrist, Robert J. — *Horton International*
Gill, Patricia — *Columbia Consulting Group*
Gill, Susan — *Plummer & Associates, Inc.*
Gillespie, Thomas — *Professional Search Consultants*
Gilreath, James M. — *Gilreath Weatherby, Inc.*
Giries, Juliet D. — *Barton Associates, Inc.*
Goar, Duane R. — *Sandhurst Associates*
Gobert, Larry — *Professional Search Consultants*
Golde, Lisa — *Tully/Woodmansee International, Inc.*
Goldenberg, Susan — *Grant Cooper and Associates*
Goldsmith, Joseph B. — *Higdon Prince Inc.*
Goldson, Bob — *The McCormick Group, Inc.*
Goldstein, Gary — *The Whitney Group*
Goldstein, Steven G. — *The Jonathan Stevens Group, Inc.*
Gonye, Peter K. — *Egon Zehnder International Inc.*
Gonzalez, Kristen — *A.J. Burton Group, Inc.*
Gonzalez, Rafael — *Korn/Ferry International*
Goodman, Dawn M. — *Bason Associates Inc.*
Goodwin, Tim — *William Guy & Associates*
Gordon, Gerald L. — *E.G. Jones Associates, Ltd.*
Gorfinkle, Gayle — *Executive Search International*
Gotlys, Jordan — *Stone Murphy & Olson*
Gow, Roderick C. — *Lamalie Amrop International*

Honer, Paul E. — *Ingram & Aydelotte Inc./I-I-C Partners*
Honey, W. Michael M. — *O'Callaghan Honey/Ray & Berndtson, Inc.*
Hoover, Catherine — *J.L. Mark Associates, Inc.*
Hopkins, Chester A. — *Handy HRM Corp.*
Hopp, Lorrie A. — *Gregory Michaels and Associates, Inc.*
Hopper, John W. — *William Guy & Associates*
Hoskins, Charles R. — *Heidrick & Struggles, Inc.*
Houchins, William M. — *Christian & Timbers*
Howard, Lee Ann — *Lamalie Amrop International*
Howard, Leon — *Richard, Wayne and Roberts*
Howard, Susy — *The McCormick Group, Inc.*
Howe, Vance A. — *Ward Howell International, Inc.*
Hoyda, Louis A. — *Thorndike Deland Associates*
Hucko, Donald S. — *Jonas, Walters & Assoc., Inc.*
Hudson, Reginald M. — *Search Bureau International*
Hughes, Cathy N. — *The Ogdon Partnership*
Hughes, Kendall G. — *Hughes & Associates*
Hughes, R. Kevin — *Handy HRM Corp.*
Hurd, J. Nicholas — *Russell Reynolds Associates, Inc.*
Hutchison, William K. — *Christenson & Hutchison*
Hutton, Thomas J. — *The Thomas Tucker Company*
Hybels, Cynthia — *A.J. Burton Group, Inc.*
Hyman, Linda — *Korn/Ferry International*
Hypes, Richard G. — *Lynch Miller Moore, Inc.*
Ikle, A. Donald — *Ward Howell International, Inc.*
Illsley, Hugh G. — *Ward Howell International, Inc.*
Ingram, D. John — *Ingram & Aydelotte Inc./I-I-C Partners*
Inguagiato, Gregory — *MSI International*
Issacs, Judith A. — *Grant Cooper and Associates*
Jablo, Steven A. — *Dieckmann & Associates, Ltd.*
Jackowitz, Todd — *J. Robert Scott*
Jackson, Joan — *A.T. Kearney, Inc.*
Jacobs, Martin J. — *The Rubicon Group*
Jacobs, Mike — *Thorne, Brieger Associates Inc.*
Jacobson, David — *J. J. & H., Ltd.*
Jacobson, David N. — *Jacobson Associates*
Jacobson, Gregory — *Jacobson Associates*
Jacobson, Jewel — *Jacobson Associates*
Jacobson, Rick — *The Windham Group*
Jaedike, Eldron — *Prestige Inc.*
James, Richard — *Criterion Executive Search, Inc.*
Janis, Laurence — *Integrated Search Solutions Group, LLC*
Janssen, Don — *Howard Fischer Associates, Inc.*
Januale, Lois — *Cochran, Cochran & Yale, Inc.*
Jazylo, John V. — *Skott/Edwards Consultants, Inc.*
Jeffers, Richard B. — *Dieckmann & Associates, Ltd.*
Jernigan, Susan N. — *Sockwell & Associates*
Joffe, Barry — *Bason Associates Inc.*
Johnson, Brian — *A.J. Burton Group, Inc.*
Johnson, Harold E. — *Lamalie Amrop International*
Johnson, John W. — *Webb, Johnson Associates, Inc.*

Johnson, Julie M. — *International Staffing Consultants, Inc.*
Johnson, Kathleen A. — *Barton Associates, Inc.*
Johnson, Priscilla — *The Johnson Group, Inc.*
Johnson, Ronald S. — *Ronald S. Johnson Associates, Inc.*
Johnson, S. Hope — *Boyden Washington, D.C.*
Johnson, Stanley C. — *Johnson & Company*
Johnson, Valerie — *Coe & Company International Inc.*
Johnston, James R. — *The Stevenson Group of Delaware Inc.*
Jones, Barbara J. — *Kaye-Bassman International Corp.*
Jones, Edward G. — *E.G. Jones Associates, Ltd.*
Jones, Herschel — *Korn/Ferry International*
Jordan, Jon — *Cochran, Cochran & Yale, Inc.*
Jordan, Stephen T. — *Ray & Berndtson*
Joys, David S. — *Heidrick & Struggles, Inc.*
Juelis, John J. — *Peeney Associates*
Kacyn, Louis J. — *Egon Zehnder International Inc.*
Kader, Richard — *Richard Kader & Associates*
Kaiser, Donald J. — *Dunhill International Search of New Haven*
Kalinowski, David — *Jacobson Associates*
Kane, Frank — *A.J. Burton Group, Inc.*
Kane, Karen — *Howard Fischer Associates, Inc.*
Kaplan, Gary — *Gary Kaplan & Associates*
Kassouf, Constance — *The Whitney Group*
Kaye, Jeffrey — *Kaye-Bassman International Corp.*
Keating, Pierson — *Nordeman Grimm, Inc.*
Keitel, Robert S. — *A.T. Kearney, Inc.*
Keller, Barbara E. — *Barton Associates, Inc.*
Keller, Peggy — *The McCormick Group, Inc.*
Kelly, Claudia L. — *Spencer Stuart*
Kelly, Elizabeth Ann — *Wellington Management Group*
Kelly, Peter W. — *R. Rollo Associates*
Kelso, Patricia C. — *Barton Associates, Inc.*
Kennedy, Michael — *The Danbrook Group, Inc.*
Kenzer, Robert D. — *Kenzer Corp.*
Keogh, James — *Sanford Rose Associates*
Kern, Jerry L. — *ADOW's Executeam*
Kern, Kathleen G. — *ADOW's Executeam*
Kershaw, Lisa — *Tanton Mitchell/Paul Ray Berndtson*
Keshishian, Gregory — *Handy HRM Corp.*
Kettwig, David A. — *A.T. Kearney, Inc.*
Keyser, Anne — *A.T. Kearney, Inc.*
Kiley, Phyllis — *National Search, Inc.*
King, Margaret — *Christian & Timbers*
Kinser, Richard E. — *Richard Kinser & Associates*
Kip, Luanne S. — *Kip Williams, Inc.*
Kishbaugh, Herbert S. — *Kishbaugh Associates International*
Klages, Constance W. — *International Management Advisors, Inc.*
Klavens, Cecile J. — *The Pickwick Group, Inc.*
Klein, Brandon — *A.J. Burton Group, Inc.*
Klein, Gary — *A.T. Kearney, Inc.*
Klein, Mary Jo — *Cochran, Cochran & Yale, Inc.*
Kleinstein, Jonah A. — *The Kleinstein Group*
Knight, Liz — *Plummer & Associates, Inc.*
Knisely, Gary — *Johnson Smith & Knisely Accord*
Koblentz, Joel M. — *Egon Zehnder International Inc.*
Kohn, Adam P. — *Christian & Timbers*

Kondra, Vernon J. — *The Douglas Reiter Company, Inc.*
Konker, David N. — *Russell Reynolds Associates, Inc.*
Koontz, Donald N. — *Koontz, Jeffries & Associates, Inc.*
Kopsick, Joseph M. — *Spencer Stuart*
Kossuth, David — *Kossuth & Associates, Inc.*
Kossuth, Jane — *Kossuth & Associates, Inc.*
Kotick, Maddy — *The Stevenson Group of New Jersey*
Kratz, Steve — *Tyler & Company*
Krauser, H. James — *Spencer Stuart*
Krejci, Stanley L. — *Boyden Washington, D.C.*
Krick, Terry L. — *Financial Resource Associates, Inc.*
Krieger, Dennis F. — *Seiden Krieger Associates, Inc.*
Krueger, Kurt — *Krueger Associates*
Kucewicz, William — *Search West, Inc.*
Kuhl, Teresa — *Don Richard Associates of Tampa, Inc.*
Kunzer, William J. — *Kunzer Associates, Ltd.*
Kussner, Janice N. — *Herman Smith Executive Initiatives Inc.*
Laba, Marvin — *Marvin Laba & Associates*
Laba, Stuart M. — *Marvin Laba & Associates*
Lache, Shawn E. — *The Arcus Group*
Lacoste, Daniel — *The Caldwell Partners Amrop International*
Lamb, Angus K. — *Raymond Karsan Associates*
Lamb, Peter S. — *Executive Resource, Inc.*
Landan, Joy — *Jacobson Associates*
Lang, Sharon A. — *Ray & Berndtson*
Lannamann, Richard S. — *Russell Reynolds Associates, Inc.*
Lapat, Aaron D. — *J. Robert Scott*
Lardner, Lucy D. — *Tully/Woodmansee International, Inc.*
Larsen, Bruce — *Prestige Inc.*
Larsen, Richard F. — *Larsen, Whitney, Blecksmith & Zilliacus*
Lasher, Charles M. — *Lasher Associates*
Lauderback, David R. — *A.T. Kearney, Inc.*
Lautz, Lindsay A. — *Lautz Grotte Engler*
Lazaro, Alicia C. — *The Whitney Group*
LeComte, Andre — *Egon Zehnder International Inc.*
Ledbetter, Steven G. — *Cendea Connection International*
Leetma, Imbi — *Stanton Chase International*
Leighton, Nina — *The Ogdon Partnership*
Lence, Julie Anne — *MSI International*
Lennox, Charles — *Price Waterhouse*
Leslie, William H. — *Boyden/Zay & Company*
Letcher, Harvey D. — *Sandhurst Associates*
Levine, Lois — *National Search, Inc.*
Levine, Roberta — *Tyler & Company*
Levinson, Lauren — *The Danbrook Group, Inc.*
Lewis, Jon A. — *Sandhurst Associates*
Lezama Cohen, Luis — *Ray & Berndtson*
Liebowitz, Michael E. — *Highland Search Group*
Lindberg, Eric J. — *MSI International*
Lindholst, Kai — *Egon Zehnder International Inc.*
Lindsay, M. Evan — *Heidrick & Struggles, Inc.*
Linney, George — *Tyler & Company*

Linton, Leonard M. — *Byron Leonard International, Inc.*
Litt, Michele — *The Whitney Group*
Little, Suzaane — *Don Richard Associates of Tampa, Inc.*
Littman, Stephen — *Rhodes Associates*
Livingston, Peter R. — *Livingston, Robert and Company Inc.*
Loeb, Stephen H. — *Grant Cooper and Associates*
Loewenstein, Victor H. — *Egon Zehnder International Inc.*
Lokken, Karen — *A.E. Feldman Associates*
Lombardi, Nancy W. — *WTW Associates, Inc.*
Long, Helga — *Horton International*
Long, Melanie — *National Search, Inc.*
Long, Milt — *William Guy & Associates*
Long, Thomas — *Egon Zehnder International Inc.*
Long, William G. — *McDonald, Long & Associates, Inc.*
Lonneke, John W. — *MSI International*
Looney, Scott — *A.E. Feldman Associates*
Lopis, Roberta — *Richard, Wayne and Roberts*
Loscavio, J. Michael — *Rusher, Loscavio & LoPresto*
Lotufo, Donald A. — *D.A.L. Associates, Inc.*
Lotz, R. James — *International Management Advisors, Inc.*
Loubet, Larry — *Carlyle Group*
Lovas, W. Carl — *Ray & Berndtson/Lovas Stanley*
Lovely, Edward — *The Stevenson Group of New Jersey*
Lucarelli, Joan — *The Onstott Group, Inc.*
Lucas, Ronnie L. — *MSI International*
Lucht, John — *The John Lucht Consultancy Inc.*
Ludlow, Paula — *Horton International*
Lumsby, George N. — *International Management Advisors, Inc.*
Luntz, Charles E. — *Charles Luntz & Associates. Inc.*
Lupica, Anthony — *Cochran, Cochran & Yale, Inc.*
Lynch, Michael C. — *Lynch Miller Moore, Inc.*
Lynch, Sean E. — *Raymond Karsan Associates*
Lyon, Jenny — *Marra Peters & Partners*
Lyons, Denis B.K. — *Spencer Stuart*
Lyons, J. David — *Aubin International Inc.*
MacCallan, Deirdre — *Butterfass, Pepe & MacCallan Inc.*
Macdonald, G. William — *The Macdonald Group, Inc.*
MacDougall, Andrew J. — *Spencer Stuart*
MacIntyre, Lisa W. — *Highland Search Group*
Mackenna, Kathy — *Plummer & Associates, Inc.*
MacNaughton, Sperry — *McNaughton Associates*
Macomber, Keith S. — *Sullivan & Company*
Maer, Harry — *Kenzer Corp.*
Magee, Harrison R. — *Bowden & Company, Inc.*
Maglio, Charles J. — *Maglio and Company, Inc.*
Mainwaring, Andrew Brian — *Executive Search Consultants Corporation*
Major, Susan — *A.T. Kearney, Inc.*
Makrianes, James K. — *Webb, Johnson Associates, Inc.*
Malcolm, Rod — *Korn/Ferry International*
Mallin, Ellen — *Howard Fischer Associates, Inc.*
Manassero, Henri J.P. — *International Management Advisors, Inc.*

Mangum, Maria — *Thomas Mangum Company*
Mangum, William T. — *Thomas Mangum Company*
Manns, Alex — *Crawford & Crofford*
Mansford, Keith — *Howard Fischer Associates, Inc.*
Maphet, Harriet — *The Stevenson Group of New Jersey*
Marino, Chester — *Cochran, Cochran & Yale, Inc.*
Marino, Jory J. — *Sullivan & Company*
Mark, John L. — *J.L. Mark Associates, Inc.*
Mark, Lynne — *J.L. Mark Associates, Inc.*
Marks, Ira — *Strategic Alternatives*
Marks, Russell E. — *Webb, Johnson Associates, Inc.*
Marra, John — *Marra Peters & Partners*
Marra, John — *Marra Peters & Partners*
Marsteller, Franklin D. — *Spencer Stuart*
Martin, Jon — *Egon Zehnder International Inc.*
Marumoto, William H. — *Boyden Washington, D.C.*
Mashakas, Elizabeth — *TOPAZ International, Inc.*
Mashakas, Elizabeth — *TOPAZ Legal Solutions*
Massey, R. Bruce — *Horton International*
Mather, David R. — *Christian & Timbers*
Mathias, Kathy — *Stone Murphy & Olson*
Mattes, Edward C. — *The Ogdon Partnership*
Matthews, Corwin — *Woodworth International Group*
Matthews, Mary — *Korn/Ferry International*
Maynard Taylor, Susan — *Chrisman & Company, Incorporated*
Mazor, Elly — *Howard Fischer Associates, Inc.*
Mazza, David B. — *Mazza & Riley, Inc. (a Korn/Ferry International affiliate)*
Mazzuckelli, Katie — *Tyler & Company*
McBride, Jonathan E. — *McBride Associates, Inc.*
McBryde, Marnie — *Spencer Stuart*
McCabe, Christopher — *Raymond Karsan Associates*
McCallister, Richard A. — *Boyden*
McCann, Cornelia B. — *Spencer Stuart*
McCarty, J. Rucker — *Heidrick & Struggles, Inc.*
McClearen, V. Bruce — *Tyler & Company*
McClement, John — *Korn/Ferry International*
McConnell, Greg — *Winter, Wyman & Company*
McCool, Anne G. — *Sullivan & Company*
McCreary, Charles "Chip" — *Austin-McGregor International*
McDermott, Jeffrey T. — *Vlcek & Company, Inc.*
McDermott, Richard A. — *Ray & Berndtson*
McDonald, Scott A. — *McDonald Associates International*
McDonald, Stanleigh B. — *McDonald Associates International*
McDowell, Robert N. — *Christenson & Hutchison*
McFadden, Ashton S. — *Johnson Smith & Knisely Accord*
McFadzen,, James A. — *Holland, McFadzean & Associates, Inc.*
McGuire, Pat — *A.J. Burton Group, Inc.*
McKeown, Patricia A. — *DiMarchi Partners, Inc.*
McKnight, Amy E. — *Chartwell Partners International, Inc.*
McLean, B. Keith — *Price Waterhouse*
McLean, E. Peter — *Spencer Stuart*

McManners, Donald E. — *McManners Associates, Inc.*
McManus, Paul — *Aubin International Inc.*
McMillin, Bob — *Price Waterhouse*
McNamara, Catherine — *Ray & Berndtson*
McNamara, Timothy C. — *Columbia Consulting Group*
McNichols, Walter B. — *Gary Kaplan & Associates*
McNulty, Kelly L. — *Gregory Michaels and Associates, Inc.*
McPherson, Stephen M. — *Ward Howell International, Inc.*
McQuoid, David — *A.T. Kearney, Inc.*
McSherry, James F. — *Battalia Winston International*
Mead-Fox, David — *Korn/Ferry International*
Meadows, C. David — *Professional Staffing Consultants*
Meagher, Patricia G. — *Spencer Stuart*
Meany, Brian M. — *Herbert Mines Associates, Inc.*
Medina-Haro, Adolfo — *Heidrick & Struggles, Inc.*
Meier, J. Dale — *Grant Cooper and Associates*
Meiland, A. Daniel — *Egon Zehnder International Inc.*
Meltzer, Andrea Y. — *Executive Options, Ltd.*
Mendoza, Guadalupe — *Ward Howell International, Inc.*
Menk, Carl — *Canny, Bowen Inc.*
Mercer, Julie — *Columbia Consulting Group*
Merrigan, Eileen M. — *Lamalie Amrop International*
Messett, William J. — *Messett Associates, Inc.*
Mestepey, John — *A.T. Kearney, Inc.*
Meyer, Michael F. — *Witt/Kieffer, Ford, Hadelman & Lloyd*
Meyer, Stacey — *Gary Kaplan & Associates*
Meza, Anna — *Richard, Wayne and Roberts*
Michaels, Stewart — *TOPAZ International, Inc.*
Michaels, Stewart — *TOPAZ Legal Solutions*
Milkint, Margaret Resce — *Jacobson Associates*
Miller, David — *Cochran, Cochran & Yale, Inc.*
Miller, Michael R. — *Lynch Miller Moore, Inc.*
Miller, Roy — *The Enns Partners Inc.*
Millonzi, Joel C. — *Johnson Smith & Knisely Accord*
Milstein, Bonnie — *Marvin Laba & Associates*
Mines, Herbert T. — *Herbert Mines Associates, Inc.*
Mingle, Larry D. — *Columbia Consulting Group*
Mirtz, P. John — *Mirtz Morice, Inc.*
Misiurewicz, Marc — *Cochran, Cochran & Yale, Inc.*
Mitchell, Jeff — *A.J. Burton Group, Inc.*
Mogul, Gene — *Mogul Consultants, Inc.*
Molnar, Robert A. — *Johnson Smith & Knisely Accord*
Mondragon, Philip — *A.T. Kearney, Inc.*
Monogenis, Emanuel N. — *Heidrick & Struggles, Inc.*
Montgomery, James M. — *Houze, Shourds & Montgomery, Inc.*
Moodley, Logan — *Austin-McGregor International*
Moore, Janice E. — *MSI International*
Moore, Mark — *Wheeler, Moore & Elam Co.*
Moore, T. Wills — *Ray & Berndtson*

Morgan, Gary — *National Search, Inc.*
Morice, James L. — *Mirtz Morice, Inc.*
Morris, David A. — *Heidrick & Struggles, Inc.*
Morse, Mary — *Travis & Company*
Mortansen, Patricia — *Norman Broadbent International, Inc.*
Morton, Robert C. — *Morton, McCorkle & Associates, Inc.*
Mowatt, Virginia — *Spencer Stuart*
Moyse, Richard G. — *Thorndike Deland Associates*
Mueller-Maerki, Fortunat F. — *Egon Zehnder International Inc.*
Muendel, H. Edward — *Stanton Chase International*
Mulligan, Robert P. — *William Willis Worldwide Inc.*
Murphy, Cornelius J. — *Goodrich & Sherwood Associates, Inc.*
Murphy, Patrick J. — *P.J. Murphy & Associates, Inc.*
Murphy, Peter — *Korn/Ferry International*
Murray, Virginia — *A.T. Kearney, Inc.*
Mursuli, Meredith — *Lasher Associates*
Mustin, Joyce M. — *J: Blakslee International, Ltd.*
Myers, Kay — *Signature Staffing*
Nagle, Charles L. — *Tyler & Company*
Nagler, Leon G. — *Nagler, Robins & Poe, Inc.*
Naidicz, Maria — *Ray & Berndtson*
Nair, Leslie — *Zwell International*
Nass, Martin D. — *Lamalie Amrop International*
Nathanson, Barry F. — *Barry Nathanson Associates*
Neelin, Sharon — *The Caldwell Partners Amrop International*
Nees, Eugene C. — *Ray & Berndtson*
Neff, Thomas J. — *Spencer Stuart*
Neher, Robert L. — *Intech Summit Group, Inc.*
Nehring, Keith — *Howard Fischer Associates, Inc.*
Neidhart, Craig C. — *TNS Partners, Inc.*
Nemec, Phillip — *Dunhill International Search of New Haven*
Nephew, Robert — *Christian & Timbers*
Neuberth, Jeffrey G. — *Canny, Bowen Inc.*
Newman, Jose L. — *Ward Howell International, Inc.*
Newman, Lynn — *Kishbaugh Associates International*
Newpoff, Brad L. — *Furst Group/MPI*
Nichols, Gary — *Koontz, Jeffries & Associates, Inc.*
Niejet, Michael C. — *O'Brien & Bell*
Nielsen, Sue — *Ells Personnel System Inc.*
Nolte, William D. — *W.D. Nolte & Company*
Norman, Randy — *Austin-McGregor International*
Normann, Amy — *Robert M. Flanagan & Associates, Ltd.*
Norris, Ken — *A.T. Kearney, Inc.*
Norsell, Paul E. — *Paul Norsell & Associates, Inc.*
Norton, James B. — *Lamalie Amrop International*
Nutter, Roger — *Raymond Karsan Associates*
O'Halloran, Robert — *MSI International*
O'Hara, Daniel M. — *Lynch Miller Moore, Inc.*
O'Maley, Kimberlee — *Spencer Stuart*
O'Neill, James P. — *Allerton Heneghan & O'Neill*
O'Reilly, John — *Stratford Group*
Ocon, Olga — *Busch International*

Ogden, Dayton — *Spencer Stuart*
Ogdon, Thomas H. — *The Ogdon Partnership*
Ogilvie, Kit — *Howard Fischer Associates, Inc.*
Olin, Robyn — *Richard, Wayne and Roberts*
Olsen, Kristine — *Williams Executive Search, Inc.*
Ongirski, Richard P. — *Raymond Karsan Associates*
Onstott, Joseph — *The Onstott Group, Inc.*
Onstott, Joseph E. — *The Onstott Group, Inc.*
Oppedisano, Edward — *Oppedisano & Company, Inc.*
Orkin, Ralph — *Sanford Rose Associates*
Orkin, Sheilah — *Sanford Rose Associates*
Oswald, Mark G. — *Canny, Bowen Inc.*
Ott, George W. — *Ott & Hansen, Inc.*
Overlock, Craig — *Ray & Berndtson*
Pace, Susan A. — *Horton International*
Padilla, Jose Sanchez — *Egon Zehnder International Inc.*
Page, G. Schuyler — *A.T. Kearney, Inc.*
Palazio, Carla — *A.T. Kearney, Inc.*
Pallman-David, Cynthia — *Bonnell Associates Ltd.*
Palma, Frank R. — *Goodrich & Sherwood Associates, Inc.*
Palmer, Carlton A. — *Beall & Company, Inc.*
Palmer, James H. — *The Hindman Company*
Palmieri, Cathryn C. — *Korn/Ferry International*
Panarese, Pam — *Howard Fischer Associates, Inc.*
Panchella, Joseph J. — *Wellington Management Group*
Pankratz, Dennis — *Furst Group/MPI*
Papasadero, Kathleen — *Woodworth International Group*
Pappas, Christina E. — *Williams Executive Search, Inc.*
Pardo, Maria Elena — *Smith Search, S.C.*
Park, Dabney G. — *Mark Stanley/EMA Partners International*
Parker, P. Grant — *Raymond Karsan Associates*
Parkhurst, David R. — *Tyler & Company*
Parry, William H. — *Horton International*
Parsons, Allison D. — *Barton Associates, Inc.*
Pastrana, Dario — *Egon Zehnder International Inc.*
Paul, Lisa D. — *Merit Resource Group, Inc.*
Payette, Pierre — *Egon Zehnder International Inc.*
Paynter, Sandra L. — *Ward Howell International, Inc.*
Peeney, James D. — *Peeney Associates*
Pelisson, Charles — *Marra Peters & Partners*
Pepe, Leonida R. — *Butterfass, Pepe & MacCallan Inc.*
Peretz, Jamie — *Korn/Ferry International*
Perkey, Richard — *Korn/Ferry International*
Pernell, Jeanette — *Norman Broadbent International, Inc.*
Perry, James — *Strategic Executives, Inc.*
Peternell, Melanie — *Signature Staffing*
Peterson, Eric N. — *Stratford Group*
Pettibone, Linda G. — *Herbert Mines Associates, Inc.*
Petty, J. Scott — *The Arcus Group*
Pfannkuche, Anthony V. — *Spencer Stuart*
Pfau, Madelaine — *Heidrick & Struggles, Inc.*
Pfeiffer, Irene — *Price Waterhouse*

Phillips, Donald L. — *O'Shea, Divine & Company, Inc.*
Phillips, James L. — *Highland Search Group*
Phipps, Peggy — *Woodworth International Group*
Pickering, Dorothy C. — *Livingston, Robert and Company Inc.*
Pickford, Stephen T. — *The Corporate Staff, Inc.*
Pierce, Mark — *Korn/Ferry International*
Pierpont-Engstrom, Elizabeth H. — *Russell Reynolds Associates, Inc.*
Pierson, Edward J. — *Johnson Smith & Knisely Accord*
Pinson, Stephanie L. — *Gilbert Tweed/INESA*
Pittard, Patrick S. — *Heidrick & Struggles, Inc.*
Pitto, Lili — *Ryan, Miller & Associates Inc.*
Platte, John D. — *Russell Reynolds Associates, Inc.*
Plessner, Rene — *Rene Plessner Associates, Inc.*
Pliszka, Donald J. — *Praxis Partners*
Plummer, John — *Plummer & Associates, Inc.*
Poirier, Roland L. — *Poirier, Hoevel & Co.*
Polansky, Mark — *Korn/Ferry International*
Pomeroy, T. Lee — *Egon Zehnder International Inc.*
Poracky, John W. — *M. Wood Company*
Poremski, Paul — *A.J. Burton Group, Inc.*
Porter, Albert — *The Experts*
Poster, Lawrence D. — *Catalyx Group*
Potter, Mark W. — *Highland Search Group*
Potter, Steven B. — *Highland Search Group*
Pratt, Tyler P. — *Furst Group/MPI*
Prencipe, V. Michael — *Raymond Karsan Associates*
Price, Andrew G. — *The Thomas Tucker Company*
Price, Kenneth M. — *Messett Associates, Inc.*
Priem, Windle B. — *Korn/Ferry International*
Prince, Marilyn L. — *Higdon Prince Inc.*
Probert, William W. — *Ward Howell International, Inc.*
Proct, Nina — *Martin H. Bauman Associates, Inc.*
Provus, Barbara L. — *Shepherd Bueschel & Provus, Inc.*
Pryor, Bill — *Cendea Connection International*
Puckett, Jennifer — *Rene Plessner Associates, Inc.*
Rabinowitz, Peter A. — *P.A.R. Associates Inc.*
Railsback, Richard — *Korn/Ferry International*
Raines, Bruce R. — *Raines International Inc.*
Ramler, Carolyn S. — *The Corporate Connection, Ltd.*
Ramsey, John H. — *Mark Stanley/EMA Partners International*
Randell, James E. — *Randell-Heiken, Inc.*
Ravenel, Lavinia — *MSI International*
Ray, Marianne C. — *Callan Associates, Ltd.*
Raymond, Jean — *The Caldwell Partners Amrop International*
Reddick, David C. — *Horton International*
Redding, Denise — *The Douglas Reiter Company, Inc.*
Redler, Rhonda — *National Search, Inc.*
Redmond, Andrea — *Russell Reynolds Associates, Inc.*
Reece, Christopher S. — *Reece & Mruk Partners*
Reeves, William B. — *Spencer Stuart*
Reifel, Laurie — *Reifel & Associates*

Reifersen, Ruth F. — *The Jonathan Stevens Group, Inc.*
Reiser, Ellen — *Thorndike Deland Associates*
Reisinger, George L. — *Sigma Group International*
Reiss, Matt — *National Search, Inc.*
Reiter, Douglas — *The Douglas Reiter Company, Inc.*
Reiter, Harold D. — *Herbert Mines Associates, Inc.*
Remillard, Brad M. — *CJA - The Adler Group*
Reyman, Susan — *S. Reyman & Associates Ltd.*
Reynolds, Gregory P. — *Roberts Ryan and Bentley*
Rice, Marie — *Jay Gaines & Company, Inc.*
Rice, Raymond D. — *Logue & Rice Inc.*
Rich, Kenneth M. — *Ray & Berndtson*
Rich, Lyttleton — *Sockwell & Associates*
Richardson, J. Rick — *Spencer Stuart*
Rieger, Louis J. — *Spencer Stuart*
Rimmel, James E. — *The Hindman Company*
Rimmele, Michael — *The Bankers Group*
Rivera, Elba R. — *Raymond Karsan Associates*
Roberts, Carl R. — *Southwestern Professional Services*
Roberts, Derek J. — *Ward Howell International, Inc.*
Roberts, Kenneth — *The Rubicon Group*
Roberts, Mitch — *A.E. Feldman Associates*
Roberts, Nick P. — *Spectrum Search Associates, Inc.*
Roberts, Scott — *Jonas, Walters & Assoc., Inc.*
Robertson, Bruce J. — *Lamalie Amrop International*
Robinson, Bruce — *Bruce Robinson Associates*
Robinson, Eric B. — *Bruce Robinson Associates*
Robles Cuellar, Paulina — *Ray & Berndtson*
Rogan, John P. — *Russell Reynolds Associates, Inc.*
Rogers, Leah — *Dinte Resources, Inc.*
Rojo, Rafael — *A.T. Kearney, Inc.*
Rollo, Robert S. — *R. Rollo Associates*
Romanello, Daniel P. — *Spencer Stuart*
Rosemarin, Gloria J. — *Barrington Hart, Inc.*
Rosenthal, Charles — *National Search, Inc.*
Rosin, Jeffrey — *Korn/Ferry International*
Ross, Curt A. — *Ray & Berndtson*
Ross, H. Lawrence — *Ross & Company*
Ross, Lawrence — *Ray & Berndtson/Lovas Stanley*
Ross, Mark — *Ray & Berndtson/Lovas Stanley*
Ross, Sheila L. — *Ward Howell International, Inc.*
Rotella, Marshall W. — *The Corporate Connection, Ltd.*
Roth, Robert J. — *Williams, Roth & Krueger Inc.*
Rothschild, John S. — *Lamalie Amrop International*
Rowe, Thomas A. — *Korn/Ferry International*
Rowe, William D. — *D.E. Foster Partners Inc.*
Rudolph, Kenneth — *Kossuth & Associates, Inc.*
Runquist, U.W. — *Webb, Johnson Associates, Inc.*
Rush, Michael E. — *D.A.L. Associates, Inc.*
Rusher, William H. — *Rusher, Loscavio & LoPresto*
Russell, Richard A. — *Executive Search Consultants Corporation*
Russell, Robin E. — *Kenzer Corp.*
Rustin, Beth — *The Whitney Group*
Sabanosh, Whitney — *Highland Search Group*
Sacerdote, John — *Raymond Karsan Associates*

Sanders, Spencer H. — *Battalia Winston International*
Sandor, Richard J. — *Flynn, Hannock, Incorporated*
Sanitago, Anthony — *TaxSearch, Inc.*
Sanow, Robert — *Cochran, Cochran & Yale, Inc.*
Santimauro, Edward — *Korn/Ferry International*
Sarna, Edmund A. — *Jonas, Walters & Assoc., Inc.*
Satenstein, Sloan — *Higdon Prince Inc.*
Sathe, Mark A. — *Sathe & Associates, Inc.*
Savage, Edward J. — *Stanton Chase International*
Savard, Robert F. — *The Stevenson Group of Delaware Inc.*
Sawyer, Deborah — *Korn/Ferry International*
Sawyer, Patricia L. — *Smith & Sawyer Inc.*
Saxon, Alexa — *Woodworth International Group*
Schaefer, Frederic M. — *A.T. Kearney, Inc.*
Schall, William A. — *The Stevenson Group of New Jersey*
Schappell, Marc P. — *Egon Zehnder International Inc.*
Schene, Philip — *A.E. Feldman Associates*
Scherck, Henry J. — *Ward Howell International, Inc.*
Schlesinger, Laurie — *The Whitney Group*
Schlpma, Christine — *Advanced Executive Resources*
Schneider, Thomas P. — *WTW Associates, Inc.*
Schneiderman, Gerald — *Management Resource Associates, Inc.*
Schroeder, John W. — *Spencer Stuart*
Schwam, Carol — *A.E. Feldman Associates*
Schwartz, Harry — *Jacobson Associates*
Schwartz, Vincent P. — *Slayton International, Inc./I-I-C Partners*
Scodius, Joseph J. — *Gregory Michaels and Associates, Inc.*
Scott, Evan — *Howard Fischer Associates, Inc.*
Scott, Gordon S. — *Search Advisors International Corp.*
Scranton, Lisa — *A.J. Burton Group, Inc.*
Scroggins, Stephen R. — *Russell Reynolds Associates, Inc.*
Seco, William — *Seco & Zetto Associates, Inc.*
Segal, Eric B. — *Kenzer Corp.*
Seiden, Steven A. — *Seiden Krieger Associates, Inc.*
Selker, Gregory L. — *Christian & Timbers*
Semyan, John K. — *TNS Partners, Inc.*
Sennello, Gendra — *National Search, Inc.*
Sessa, Vincent J. — *Integrated Search Solutions Group, LLC*
Sevilla, Claudio A. — *Crawford & Crofford*
Shapiro, Beth — *Howard Fischer Associates, Inc.*
Shea, Kathleen M. — *The Penn Partners, Incorporated*
Shelton, Sandra — *National Search, Inc.*
Shen, Eugene Y. — *The Whitney Group*
Shenfield, Peter — *A.T. Kearney, Inc.*
Shepard, Michael J. — *MSI International*
Shervey, Brent C. — *O'Callaghan Honey/Ray & Berndtson, Inc.*
Sherwood, Andrew — *Goodrich & Sherwood Associates, Inc.*
Shore, Earl L. — *E.L. Shore & Associates Ltd.*
Shourds, Mary E. — *Houze, Shourds & Montgomery, Inc.*

Sibbald, John R. — *John Sibbald Associates, Inc.*
Siegel, Pamela — *Executive Options, Ltd.*
Siegler, Jody Cukiir — *A.T. Kearney, Inc.*
Siegrist, Jeffrey M. — *D.E. Foster Partners Inc.*
Silcott, Marvin L. — *Marvin L. Silcott & Associates, Inc.*
Silvas, Stephen D. — *Roberson and Company*
Silver, Lee — *L. A. Silver Associates, Inc.*
Silverman, Paul M. — *The Marshall Group*
Silverstein, Jackie — *Don Richard Associates of Charlotte*
Simon, Mary K. — *Gregory Michaels and Associates, Inc.*
Simon, Penny B. — *Ray & Berndtson*
Simpson, David J. — *Simpson Associates, Inc.*
Simpson, Scott — *Cendea Connection International*
Sindler, Jay — *A.J. Burton Group, Inc.*
Singleton, Robin — *Tyler & Company*
Sitarski, Stan — *Howard Fischer Associates, Inc.*
Skalet, Ira — *A.E. Feldman Associates*
Skunda, Donna M. — *Allerton Heneghan & O'Neill*
Slosar, John — *Boyden*
Smead, Michelle M. — *A.T. Kearney, Inc.*
Smith, Ana Luz — *Smith Search, S.C.*
Smith, Ethan L. — *Highland Search Group*
Smith, Herman M. — *Herman Smith Executive Initiatives Inc.*
Smith, John E. — *Smith Search, S.C.*
Smith, John F. — *The Penn Partners, Incorporated*
Smith, Lydia — *The Corporate Connection, Ltd.*
Smith, Matt D. — *Ray & Berndtson*
Smith, Monica L. — *Analysts Resources, Inc.*
Smith, R. Michael — *Smith James Group, Inc.*
Smith, Robert L. — *Smith & Sawyer Inc.*
Smith, Ronald V. — *Coe & Company International Inc.*
Smith, Timothy C. — *Christian & Timbers*
Snelgrove, Geiger — *National Search, Inc.*
Snyder, C. Edward — *Horton International*
Snyder, James F. — *Snyder & Company*
Sockwell, J. Edgar — *Sockwell & Associates*
Sondgrass, Stephen — *DeFrain, Mayer LLC*
Soutouras, James — *Smith James Group, Inc.*
Spann, Richard E. — *Goodrich & Sherwood Associates, Inc.*
Spencer, Bob — *Kaye-Bassman International Corp.*
Spera, Stefanie — *A.T. Kearney, Inc.*
Spiegel, Gayle — *L. A. Silver Associates, Inc.*
Spitz, Grant — *The Caldwell Partners Amrop International*
Sponseller, Vern — *Richard Kader & Associates*
Spriggs, Robert D. — *Spriggs & Company, Inc.*
Springer, Mark H. — *M.H. Springer & Associates Incorporated*
St. Clair, Alan — *TNS Partners, Inc.*
Stahl, Cindy — *Plummer & Associates, Inc.*
Stanton, John — *A.T. Kearney, Inc.*
Stark, Jeff — *Thorne, Brieger Associates Inc.*
Steele, Daniel — *Cochran, Cochran & Yale, Inc.*
Stein, Terry W. — *Stewart, Stein and Scott, Ltd.*
Steinem, Andy — *Dahl-Morrow International*
Steinem, Andy — *Dahl-Morrow International*
Steinem, Barbara — *Dahl-Morrow International*
Steinem, Barbra — *Dahl-Morrow International*

Steinman, Stephen M. — *The Stevenson Group of New Jersey*

Stern, Lester W. — *Sullivan & Company*

Stevenson, Jane — *Howard Fischer Associates, Inc.*

Stevenson, Jane — *Howard Fischer Associates, Inc.*

Stewart, Jan J. — *Egon Zehnder International Inc.*

Stewart, Jeffrey O. — *Stewart, Stein and Scott, Ltd.*

Stewart, Ross M. — *Human Resources Network Partners Inc.*

Stivk, Barbara A. — *Thornton Resources*

Stone, Robert Ryder — *Lamalie Amrop International*

Stone, Susan L. — *Stone Enterprises Ltd.*

Stoy, Roger W. — *Heidrick & Struggles, Inc.*

Stranberg, James R. — *Callan Associates, Ltd.*

Stratmeyer, Karin Bergwall — *Princeton Entrepreneurial Resources*

Straube, Stanley H. — *Straube Associates*

Strickland, Katie — *Grantham & Co., Inc.*

Stringer, Dann P. — *D.E. Foster Partners Inc.*

Strobridge, Richard P. — *F.L. Taylor & Company, Inc.*

Strom, Mark N. — *Search Advisors International Corp.*

Sullivan, Brian M. — *Sullivan & Company*

Sumurdy, Melinda — *Kenzer Corp.*

Sussman, Lynda — *Gilbert Tweed/INESA*

Swanson, Dick — *Raymond Karsan Associates*

Sweeney, Sean K. — *Bonifield Associates*

Swidler, J. Robert — *Egon Zehnder International Inc.*

Swoboda, Lawrence — *A.J. Burton Group, Inc.*

Tappan, Michael A. — *Ward Howell International, Inc.*

Taylor, Charles E. — *Lamalie Amrop International*

Taylor, Conrad G. — *MSI International*

Taylor, Ernest A. — *Ward Howell International, Inc.*

Taylor, James M. — *The HRM Group, Inc.*

Taylor, Kenneth W. — *Egon Zehnder International Inc.*

Taylor, R.L. (Larry) — *Ray & Berndtson*

Telford, John H. — *Telford, Adams & Alexander/Telford & Co., Inc.*

ten Cate, Herman H. — *Stoneham Associates Corp.*

Terry, Douglas — *Jacobson Associates*

Teter, Sandra — *The Danbrook Group, Inc.*

Teti, Al — *Chrisman & Company, Incorporated*

Theobald, David B. — *Theobald & Associates*

Thomas, Jeffrey — *Fairfaxx Corporation*

Thomas, Kurt J. — *P.J. Murphy & Associates, Inc.*

Thomas, Terry — *The Thomas Resource Group*

Thompson, Dave — *Battalia Winston International*

Thompson, Kenneth L. — *McCormack & Farrow*

Thomson, Alexander G. — *Russell Reynolds Associates, Inc.*

Thornton, John C. — *Thornton Resources*

Thrapp, Mark C. — *Executive Search Consultants International, Inc.*

Tierney, Eileen — *The Whitney Group*

Tincu, John C. — *Ferneborg & Associates, Inc.*

Tingle, Trina A. — *MSI International*

Todres-Bernstein, Margo — *Kaye-Bassman International Corp.*

Tootsey, Mark A. — *A.J. Burton Group, Inc.*

Tornesello, Michael P. — *The Yorkshire Group. Ltd.*

Tracey, Jack — *Management Assistance Group, Inc.*

Tracy, Ronald O. — *Egon Zehnder International Inc.*

Travis, Hallie — *Tyler & Company*

Trieweiler, Bob — *Executive Placement Consultants, Inc.*

Trott, Kathryn — *Allard Associates*

Trott, Kathryn — *Allard Associates*

Truex, John F. — *Morton, McCorkle & Associates, Inc.*

Tryon, Katey — *DeFrain, Mayer LLC*

Tucci, Joseph — *Fairfaxx Corporation*

Tucker, Thomas A. — *The Thomas Tucker Company*

Tully, Margo L. — *Tully/Woodmansee International, Inc.*

Tunney, William — *Grant Cooper and Associates*

Turner, Kimberly — *Barton Associates, Inc.*

Tursi, Deborah J. — *The Corporate Connection, Ltd.*

Tuttle, Donald E. — *Tuttle Venture Group, Inc.*

Tutwiler, Stephen — *Don Richard Associates of Tampa, Inc.*

Tweed, Janet — *Gilbert Tweed/INESA*

Twiste, Craig — *Raymond Karsan Associates*

Tyler, J. Larry — *Tyler & Company*

Tyson, Richard L. — *Bonifield Associates*

Vairo, Leonard A. — *Christian & Timbers*

Valenta, Joseph — *Princeton Entrepreneurial Resources*

Van Alstine, Catherine — *Tanton Mitchell/Paul Ray Berndtson*

Van Biesen, Jacques A.H. — *Search Group Inc.*

Van Campen, Jerry — *Gilbert & Van Campen International*

Van Clieaf, Mark — *MVC Associates International*

Van Nostrand, Mara J. — *Barton Associates, Inc.*

Vande-Water, Katie — *J. Robert Scott*

Velten, Mark T. — *Boyden*

Venable, William W. — *Thorndike Deland Associates*

Vergara, Gail H. — *Spencer Stuart*

Vergari, Jane — *Herbert Mines Associates, Inc.*

Vernon, Peter C. — *Horton International*

Vincelette, Kathy A. — *Raymond Karsan Associates*

Visnich, L. Christine — *Bason Associates Inc.*

Vitale, Amy — *Highland Search Group*

Vlcek, Thomas J. — *Vlcek & Company, Inc.*

Volkman, Arthur — *Cochran, Cochran & Yale, Inc.*

von Baillou, Astrid — *Richard Kinser & Associates*

Vossler, James — *A.J. Burton Group, Inc.*

Waanders, William L. — *ExecuQuest*

Wacholz, Rick — *A.T. Kearney, Inc.*

Waitkus, Karen — *Richard, Wayne and Roberts*

Wakefield, Scott — *National Search, Inc.*

Waldman, Noah H. — *Lamalie Amrop International*

Waldoch, D. Mark — *Barnes Development Group, LLC*

Waldrop, Gary R. — *MSI International*

Walker, Craig H. — *A.J. Burton Group, Inc.*

Wallace, Alec — *Tanton Mitchell/Paul Ray Berndtson*
Walsh, Denis — *Professional Staffing Consultants*
Walters, William F. — *Jonas, Walters & Assoc., Inc.*
Ward, Ted — *Korn/Ferry International*
Wardell, Charles W.B. — *Nordeman Grimm, Inc.*
Wasp, Warren T. — *WTW Associates, Inc.*
Wasson, Thomas W. — *Spencer Stuart*
Watkins, Jeffrey P. — *Lamalie Amrop International*
Watkins, Thomas M. — *Lamalie Amrop International*
Watkinson, Jim W. — *The Badger Group*
Watson, Hanan S. — *Watson International, Inc.*
Webb, George H. — *Webb, Johnson Associates, Inc.*
Weber, Ronald R. — *Weber Executive Search*
Weisler, Nancy — *National Search, Inc.*
Weissman-Rosenthal, Abbe — *ALW Research International*
Welch, Robert — *Ray & Berndtson*
Weller, Paul S. — *Mark Stanley/EMA Partners International*
Wendler, Kambrea R. — *Gregory Michaels and Associates, Inc.*
Westfall, Ed — *Zwell International*
Wheeler, Gerard H. — *A.J. Burton Group, Inc.*
White, Richard B. — *Spencer Stuart*
White, William C. — *Venture Resources Inc.*
Whiting, Anthony — *Johnson Smith & Knisely Accord*
Whitley, Sue Ann — *Roberts Ryan and Bentley*
Whitney, William A — *Larsen, Whitney, Blecksmith & Zilliacus*
Wier, Daniel — *Daniel Wier & Associates*
Wilbanks, George R. — *Russell Reynolds Associates, Inc.*
Wilder, Richard B. — *Columbia Consulting Group*
Wilkinson, Barbara — *Beall & Company, Inc.*
Wilkinson, Jr. SPHR
Wilkinson, Charles E. — *The HRM Group, Inc.*
Williams, Gary L. — *Barnes Development Group, LLC*
Williams, Harry D. — *Jacobson Associates*
Williams, Jack — *A.T. Kearney, Inc.*
Williams, Lis — *Executive Options, Ltd.*
Williams, Roger K. — *Williams, Roth & Krueger Inc.*
Williams, Stephen E. — *Barton Associates, Inc.*
Williams, Walter E. — *Lamalie Amrop International*
Willis, William H. — *William Willis Worldwide Inc.*
Wilson, Derrick — *Thornton Resources*
Wilson, Harry — *First Union Executive Search Group*
Wilson, John — *Korn/Ferry International*
Wilson, Patricia L. — *Leon A. Farley Associates*
Wilson, William F. — *Tyler & Company*
Winitz, Joel — *GSW Consulting Group, Inc.*
Winitz, Marla — *GSW Consulting Group, Inc.*
Winograd, Glenn — *Criterion Executive Search, Inc.*
Winston, Dale — *Battalia Winston International*
Wirtshafter, Linda — *Grant Cooper and Associates*
Wise, J. Herbert — *Sandhurst Associates*
Wold, Ted W. — *Hyde Danforth Wold & Co.*

Wolf, Stephen M. — *Byron Leonard International, Inc.*
Womack, Joseph — *The Bankers Group*
Wood, Elizabeth — *Highland Search Group*
Wood, John S. — *Egon Zehnder International Inc.*
Wood, Milton M. — *M. Wood Company*
Woodmansee, Bruce J. — *Tully/Woodmansee International, Inc.*
Woodworth, Gail — *Woodworth International Group*
Wooldridge, Jeff — *Ray & Berndtson*
Wooller, Edmund A.M. — *Windsor International*
Wright, A. Leo — *The Hindman Company*
Wright, Carl A.J. — *A.J. Burton Group, Inc.*
Wright, Charles D. — *Goodrich & Sherwood Associates, Inc.*
Wright, Leslie — *The Stevenson Group of New Jersey*
Wynkoop, Mary — *Tyler & Company*
Yaekle, Gary — *Tully/Woodmansee International, Inc.*
Yen, Maggie Yeh Ching — *Ray & Berndtson*
Yungerberg, Steven — *Steven Yungerberg Associates Inc.*
Zaffrann, Craig S. — *P.J. Murphy & Associates, Inc.*
Zahradka, James F. — *P.J. Murphy & Associates, Inc.*
Zaleta, Andy R. — *A.T. Kearney, Inc.*
Zamborsky, George — *Boyden*
Zaslav, Debra M. — *Telford, Adams & Alexander/Telford & Co., Inc.*
Zavala, Lorenzo — *Russell Reynolds Associates, Inc.*
Zay, Thomas C. — *Boyden/Zay & Company*
Zay, Thomas C. — *Boyden/Zay & Company*
Zegas, Jeffrey — *Zurick, Davis & Co., Inc.*
Zetto, Kathryn — *Seco & Zetto Associates, Inc.*
Zila, Laurie M. — *Princeton Entrepreneurial Resources*
Zimmerman, Joan C. — *G.Z. Stephens Inc.*
Zivic, Janis M. — *Spencer Stuart*
Zona, Henry F. — *Zona & Associates, Inc.*
Zwell, Michael — *Zwell International*

2. Administration

Abbott, Peter D. — *The Abbott Group, Inc.*
Abell, Vincent W. — *MSI International*
Akin, J.R. "Jack" — *J.R. Akin & Company Inc.*
Alexander, John T. — *Telford, Adams & Alexander*
Allard, Susan — *Allard Associates*
Allgire, Mary L. — *Kenzer Corp.*
Altreuter, Rose — *The ALTCO Group*
Amilowski, Maria — *Highland Search Group*
Anderson, Maria H. — *Barton Associates, Inc.*
Anderson, Richard — *Grant Cooper and Associates*
Aronin, Michael — *Fisher-Todd Associates*
Ascher, Susan P. — *The Ascher Group*
Ashton, Edward J. — *E.J. Ashton & Associates, Ltd.*
Aston, Kathy — *Marra Peters & Partners*
Attell, Harold — *A.E. Feldman Associates*
Atwood, Barrie — *The Abbott Group, Inc.*
Baeder, Jeremy — *Executive Manning Corporation*
Bailey, Vanessa — *Highland Search Group*
Balbone, Rich — *Executive Manning Corporation*
Barlow, Ken H. — *The Cherbonnier Group, Inc.*

Barnes, Richard E. — *Barnes Development Group, LLC*

Barnes, Roanne L. — *Barnes Development Group, LLC*

Barton, Gary R. — *Barton Associates, Inc.*

Bason, Maurice L. — *Bason Associates Inc.*

Bass, M. Lynn — *Ray & Berndtson*

Bass, Nate — *Jacobson Associates*

Bauman, Martin H. — *Martin H. Bauman Associates, Inc.*

Bearman, Linda — *Grant Cooper and Associates*

Beaudin, Elizabeth C. — *Callan Associates, Ltd.*

Benson, Kate — *Rene Plessner Associates, Inc.*

Beran, Helena — *Michael J. Cavanagh and Associates*

Bertoux, Michael P. — *Wilcox, Bertoux & Miller*

Bettick, Michael J. — *A.J. Burton Group, Inc.*

Bladon, Andrew — *Don Richard Associates of Tampa, Inc.*

Bloomer, James E. — *L.W. Foote Company*

Boel, Werner — *The Dalley Hewitt Company*

Bohn, Steve J. — *MSI International*

Bonifield, Len — *Bonifield Associates*

Borkin, Andrew — *Strategic Advancement Inc.*

Borland, James — *Goodrich & Sherwood Associates, Inc.*

Bormann, Cindy Ann — *MSI International*

Brady, Dick — *William Guy & Associates*

Brennan, Patrick J. — *Handy HRM Corp.*

Brieger, Steve — *Thorne, Brieger Associates Inc.*

Brinson, Robert — *MSI International*

Brother, Joy — *Charles Luntz & Associates. Inc.*

Brown, Larry C. — *Horton International*

Brown, Lawrence Anthony — *MSI International*

Brudno, Robert J. — *Savoy Partners, Ltd.*

Burden, Gene — *The Cherbonnier Group, Inc.*

Burke, John — *The Experts*

Burns, Alan — *The Enns Partners Inc.*

Burns, Terence N. — *D.E. Foster Partners Inc.*

Busterna, Charles — *The KPA Group*

Butler, Kirby B. — *The Butlers Company Insurance Recruiters*

Caldwell, William R. — *Pearson, Caldwell & Farnsworth, Inc.*

Calivas, Kay — *A.J. Burton Group, Inc.*

Callan, Robert M. — *Callan Associates, Ltd.*

Cappe, Richard R. — *Roberts Ryan and Bentley*

Cary, Con — *Cary & Associates*

Casal, Daniel G. — *Bonifield Associates*

Castine, Michael P. — *Highland Search Group*

Cavanagh, Michael J. — *Michael J. Cavanagh and Associates*

Chamberlin, Joan — *William Guy & Associates*

Chamberlin, Michael A. — *Tower Consultants, Ltd.*

Chappell, Peter — *The Bankers Group*

Chatterjie, Alok — *MSI International*

Cherbonnier, L. Michael — *The Cherbonnier Group, Inc.*

Christian, Philip — *Ray & Berndtson*

Cizek, John T. — *Cizek Associates, Inc.*

Cizek, Marti J. — *Cizek Associates, Inc.*

Clauhsen, Elizabeth A. — *Savoy Partners, Ltd.*

Clayton, Fred J. — *Berkhemer Clayton Incorporated*

Coffman, Brian — *Kossuth & Associates, Inc.*

Cohen, Robert C. — *Intech Summit Group, Inc.*

Colasanto, Frank M. — *W.R. Rosato & Associates, Inc.*

Cona, Joseph A. — *Cona Personnel Search*

Connelly, Kevin M. — *Spencer Stuart*

Conway, Maureen — *Conway & Associates*

Corso, Glen S. — *Chartwell Partners International, Inc.*

Cortina Del Valle, Pedro — *Ray & Berndtson*

Costello, Lynda — *Coe & Company International Inc.*

Courtney, Brendan — *A.J. Burton Group, Inc.*

Cox, William — *E.J. Ashton & Associates, Ltd.*

Coyle, Hugh F. — *A.J. Burton Group, Inc.*

Cramer, Paul J. — *C/R Associates*

Crath, Paul F. — *Price Waterhouse*

Crystal, Jonathan A. — *Spencer Stuart*

Cunningham, Lawrence — *Howard Fischer Associates, Inc.*

Cunningham, Robert Y. — *Goodrich & Sherwood Associates, Inc.*

Danforth, W. Michael — *Hyde Danforth Wold & Co.*

Daniels, Alfred — *Alfred Daniels & Associates*

Daniels, C. Eugene — *Sigma Group International*

Dannenberg, Richard A. — *Roberts Ryan and Bentley*

Davis, G. Gordon — *Davis & Company*

Dawson, Joe — *S.C. International, Ltd.*

De Brun, Thomas P. — *Ray & Berndtson*

de Cholnoky, Andrea — *Spencer Stuart*

Deaver, Henry C. — *Ray & Berndtson*

DeCorrevont, James — *DeCorrevont & Associates*

DeCorrevont, James — *DeCorrevont & Associates*

DeHart, Donna — *Tower Consultants, Ltd.*

Del Pino, William — *National Search, Inc.*

Delaney, Patrick J. — *Sensible Solutions, Inc.*

Della Monica, Vincent — *Search West, Inc.*

Delmonico, Laura — *A.J. Burton Group, Inc.*

Desmond, Dennis — *Beall & Company, Inc.*

deVry, Kimberly A. — *Tower Consultants, Ltd.*

Dezember, Steve — *Ray & Berndtson*

Dietz, David S. — *MSI International*

Dingeldey, Peter E. — *Search Advisors International Corp.*

Dingman, Bruce — *Robert W. Dingman Company, Inc.*

DiSalvo, Fred — *The Cambridge Group Ltd*

Diskin, Rochelle — *Search West, Inc.*

Doele, Donald C. — *Goodrich & Sherwood Associates, Inc.*

Doman, Matthew — *S.C. International, Ltd.*

Doukas, Jon A. — *Professional Bank Services, Inc. D/B/A Executive Search, Inc.*

Dowell, Chris — *The Abbott Group, Inc.*

Dreifus, Donald — *Search West, Inc.*

Drury, James J. — *Spencer Stuart*

Dunman, Betsy L. — *Crawford & Crofford*

Edwards, Dorothy — *MSI International*

Edwards, Verba L. — *Wing Tips & Pumps, Inc.*

Ehrgott, Elizabeth — *The Ascher Group*

Ehrhart, Jennifer — *ADOW's Executeam*

Eldridge, Charles B. — *Ray & Berndtson*

Engelbert, Kimberly S. — *Watson International, Inc.*

Enns, George — *The Enns Partners Inc.*

Erickson, Elaine — *Kenzer Corp.*

Eustis, Lucy R. — *MSI International*

Evans, David — *Executive Manning Corporation*
Fancher, Robert L. — *Bason Associates Inc.*
Farnsworth, John A. — *Pearson, Caldwell & Farnsworth, Inc.*
Federman, Jack R. — *W.R. Rosato & Associates, Inc.*
Feldman, Abe — *A.E. Feldman Associates*
Ferneborg, Jay W. — *Ferneborg & Associates, Inc.*
Ferneborg, John R. — *Ferneborg & Associates, Inc.*
Fiorelli, Cheryl — *Tower Consultants, Ltd.*
Fischer, Adam — *Howard Fischer Associates, Inc.*
Fischer, Howard M. — *Howard Fischer Associates, Inc.*
Flanagan, Robert M. — *Robert M. Flanagan & Associates, Ltd.*
Fleming, Marco — *MSI International*
Fletcher, David — *A.J. Burton Group, Inc.*
Flora, Dodi — *Crawford & Crofford*
Flynn, Jack — *Executive Search Consultants Corporation*
Foote, Leland W. — *L.W. Foote Company*
Foreman, David C. — *Koontz, Jeffries & Associates, Inc.*
Fribush, Richard — *A.J. Burton Group, Inc.*
Friedman, Donna L. — *Tower Consultants, Ltd.*
Friedman, Helen E. — *McCormack & Farrow*
Fulton, Christine N. — *Highland Search Group*
Fust, Sheely F. — *Ray & Berndtson*
Gabriel, David L. — *The Arcus Group*
Galinski, Paul — *E.J. Ashton & Associates, Ltd.*
Gallagher, Terence M. — *Battalia Winston International*
Gantar, Donna — *Howard Fischer Associates, Inc.*
Geiger, Jan — *Wilcox, Bertoux & Miller*
George, Delores F. — *Delores F. George Human Resource Management & Consulting Industry*
Gerber, Mark J. — *Wellington Management Group*
Germain, Valerie — *Jay Gaines & Company, Inc.*
Gibbons, Ronald L. — *Flynn, Hannock, Incorporated*
Gibbs, John S. — *Spencer Stuart*
Gill, Susan — *Plummer & Associates, Inc.*
Goldenberg, Susan — *Grant Cooper and Associates*
Gonzalez, Kristen — *A.J. Burton Group, Inc.*
Goodman, Dawn M. — *Bason Associates Inc.*
Goodman, Julie — *Search West, Inc.*
Goodridge, Benjamin — *S.C. International, Ltd.*
Goodwin, Tim — *William Guy & Associates*
Gordon, Gerald L. — *E.G. Jones Associates, Ltd.*
Gordon, Teri — *Don Richard Associates of Washington, D.C., Inc.*
Gray, Annie — *Annie Gray Associates, Inc./The Executive Search Firm*
Gray, Mark — *Executive Referral Services, Inc.*
Guy, C. William — *William Guy & Associates*
Haas, Margaret P. — *The Haas Associates, Inc.*
Habelmann, Gerald B. — *Habelmann & Associates*
Halbrich, Mitch — *A.J. Burton Group, Inc.*
Hallock, Peter B. — *Goodrich & Sherwood Associates, Inc.*
Hamilton, John R. — *Ray & Berndtson*
Hanes, Leah — *Ray & Berndtson*
Hanley, J. Patrick — *Canny, Bowen Inc.*

Hannock, Elwin W. — *Flynn, Hannock, Incorporated*
Hanson, Grant M. — *Goodrich & Sherwood Associates, Inc.*
Hart, Robert T. — *D.E. Foster Partners Inc.*
Healey, Joseph T. — *Highland Search Group*
Hellinger, Audrey W. — *Martin H. Bauman Associates, Inc.*
Hennig, Sandra M. — *MSI International*
Hetherman, Margaret F. — *Highland Search Group*
Hewitt, Rives D. — *The Dalley Hewitt Company*
Hewitt, W. Davis — *The Dalley Hewitt Company*
Higdon, Henry G. — *Higdon Prince Inc.*
Higgins, Donna — *Howard Fischer Associates, Inc.*
Hildebrand, Thomas B. — *Professional Resources Group, Inc.*
Hill, Emery — *MSI International*
Hoevel, Michael J. — *Poirier, Hoevel & Co.*
Holland, Rose Mary — *Price Waterhouse*
Holzberger, Georges L. — *Highland Search Group*
Hoover, Catherine — *J.L. Mark Associates, Inc.*
Hopkins, Chester A. — *Handy HRM Corp.*
Hopper, John W. — *William Guy & Associates*
Hucko, Donald S. — *Jonas, Walters & Assoc., Inc.*
Hughes, Cathy N. — *The Ogdon Partnership*
Hughes, R. Kevin — *Handy HRM Corp.*
Hybels, Cynthia — *A.J. Burton Group, Inc.*
Inguagiato, Gregory — *MSI International*
Issacs, Judith A. — *Grant Cooper and Associates*
Jacobs, Martin J. — *The Rubicon Group*
Jacobs, Mike — *Thorne, Brieger Associates Inc.*
James, Richard — *Criterion Executive Search, Inc.*
Janssen, Don — *Howard Fischer Associates, Inc.*
Jazylo, John V. — *Skott/Edwards Consultants, Inc.*
Jernigan, Susan N. — *Sockwell & Associates*
Joffe, Barry — *Bason Associates Inc.*
Johnson, Brian — *A.J. Burton Group, Inc.*
Johnson, John W. — *Webb, Johnson Associates, Inc.*
Johnson, Kathleen A. — *Barton Associates, Inc.*
Johnson, S. Hope — *Boyden Washington, D.C.*
Johnson, Valerie — *Coe & Company International Inc.*
Judge, Alfred L. — *The Cambridge Group Ltd*
Juelis, John J. — *Peeney Associates*
Juska, Frank — *Rusher, Loscavio & LoPresto*
Kader, Richard — *Richard Kader & Associates*
Kaiser, Donald J. — *Dunhill International Search of New Haven*
Kalinowski, David — *Jacobson Associates*
Kane, Frank — *A.J. Burton Group, Inc.*
Kane, Karen — *Howard Fischer Associates, Inc.*
Kantor, Richard — *Search West, Inc.*
Katz, Cyndi — *Search West, Inc.*
Kelly, Peter W. — *R. Rollo Associates*
Kelso, Patricia C. — *Barton Associates, Inc.*
Kennedy, Michael — *The Danbrook Group, Inc.*
Kenzer, Robert D. — *Kenzer Corp.*
Kern, Jerry L. — *ADOW's Executeam*
Kern, Kathleen G. — *ADOW's Executeam*
Kershaw, Lisa — *Tanton Mitchell/Paul Ray Berndtson*
Kile, Robert W. — *Rusher, Loscavio & LoPresto*
Kiley, Phyllis — *National Search, Inc.*

Kishbaugh, Herbert S. — *Kishbaugh Associates International*
Klein, Brandon — *A.J. Burton Group, Inc.*
Klein, Lynn M. — *Riotto-Jones Associates*
Knisely, Gary — *Johnson Smith & Knisely Accord*
Kondra, Vernon J. — *The Douglas Reiter Company, Inc.*
Koontz, Donald N. — *Koontz, Jeffries & Associates, Inc.*
Kreuch, Paul C. — *Skott/Edwards Consultants, Inc.*
Kucewicz, William — *Search West, Inc.*
Kuhl, Teresa — *Don Richard Associates of Tampa, Inc.*
Lachance, Roger — *Laurendeau Labrecque/Ray & Berndtson, Inc.*
Lang, Sharon A. — *Ray & Berndtson*
Laurendeau, Jean E. — *Laurendeau Labrecque/Ray & Berndtson, Inc.*
Lautz, Lindsay A. — *Lautz Grotte Engler*
Lawrance, Susanne — *Sharrow & Associates*
Lence, Julie Anne — *MSI International*
Leslie, William H. — *Boyden/Zay & Company*
Levine, Lois — *National Search, Inc.*
Levinson, Lauren — *The Danbrook Group, Inc.*
Lewicki, Christopher — *MSI International*
Lewis, Jon A. — *Sandhurst Associates*
Lezama Cohen, Luis — *Ray & Berndtson*
Liebowitz, Michael E. — *Highland Search Group*
Lindberg, Eric J. — *MSI International*
Linton, Leonard M. — *Byron Leonard International, Inc.*
Little, Suzaane — *Don Richard Associates of Tampa, Inc.*
Loeb, Stephen H. — *Grant Cooper and Associates*
Lokken, Karen — *A.E. Feldman Associates*
Long, Melanie — *National Search, Inc.*
Long, Milt — *William Guy & Associates*
Long, William G. — *McDonald, Long & Associates, Inc.*
Looney, Scott — *A.E. Feldman Associates*
LoPresto, Robert L. — *Rusher, Loscavio & LoPresto*
Lotufo, Donald A. — *D.A.L. Associates, Inc.*
Lucas, Ronnie L. — *MSI International*
Lucht, John — *The John Lucht Consultancy Inc.*
Luntz, Charles E. — *Charles Luntz & Associates. Inc.*
Lyon, Jenny — *Marra Peters & Partners*
MacIntyre, Lisa W. — *Highland Search Group*
Mackenna, Kathy — *Plummer & Associates, Inc.*
MacNaughton, Sperry — *McNaughton Associates*
Maer, Harry — *Kenzer Corp.*
Mainwaring, Andrew Brian — *Executive Search Consultants Corporation*
Mallin, Ellen — *Howard Fischer Associates, Inc.*
Mangum, Maria — *Thomas Mangum Company*
Mangum, William T. — *Thomas Mangum Company*
Manns, Alex — *Crawford & Crofford*
Mansford, Keith — *Howard Fischer Associates, Inc.*
Mark, John L. — *J.L. Mark Associates, Inc.*
Mark, Lynne — *J.L. Mark Associates, Inc.*
Marks, Russell E. — *Webb, Johnson Associates, Inc.*
Marra, John — *Marra Peters & Partners*
Marra, John — *Marra Peters & Partners*

Mazor, Elly — *Howard Fischer Associates, Inc.*
McBride, Jonathan E. — *McBride Associates, Inc.*
McDonald, Scott A. — *McDonald Associates International*
McDonald, Stanleigh B. — *McDonald Associates International*
McFadden, Ashton S. — *Johnson Smith & Knisely Accord*
McGuire, Pat — *A.J. Burton Group, Inc.*
McManners, Donald E. — *McManners Associates, Inc.*
McMillin, Bob — *Price Waterhouse*
McNamara, Catherine — *Ray & Berndtson*
McNamara, Timothy Connor — *Horton International*
McQuoid, David — *A.T. Kearney, Inc.*
Meagher, Patricia G. — *Spencer Stuart*
Meany, Brian M. — *Herbert Mines Associates, Inc.*
Meier, J. Dale — *Grant Cooper and Associates*
Messett, William J. — *Messett Associates, Inc.*
Mestepey, John — *A.T. Kearney, Inc.*
Miller, Roy — *The Enns Partners Inc.*
Millonzi, Joel C. — *Johnson Smith & Knisely Accord*
Mitchell, Jeff — *A.J. Burton Group, Inc.*
Moore, Mark — *Wheeler, Moore & Elam Co.*
Moore, T. Wills — *Ray & Berndtson*
Morgan, Gary — *National Search, Inc.*
Muendel, H. Edward — *Stanton Chase International*
Murphy, Cornelius J. — *Goodrich & Sherwood Associates, Inc.*
Murphy, Patrick J. — *P.J. Murphy & Associates, Inc.*
Naidicz, Maria — *Ray & Berndtson*
Nathanson, Barry F. — *Barry Nathanson Associates*
Neckanoff, Sharon — *Search West, Inc.*
Nees, Eugene C. — *Ray & Berndtson*
Neher, Robert L. — *Intech Summit Group, Inc.*
Nehring, Keith — *Howard Fischer Associates, Inc.*
Neri, Gene — *S.C. International, Ltd.*
Nichols, Gary — *Koontz, Jeffries & Associates, Inc.*
Nielsen, Sue — *Ells Personnel System Inc.*
Normann, Amy — *Robert M. Flanagan & Associates, Ltd.*
Norsell, Paul E. — *Paul Norsell & Associates, Inc.*
O'Hara, Daniel M. — *Lynch Miller Moore, Inc.*
Ogdon, Thomas H. — *The Ogdon Partnership*
Ogilvie, Kit — *Howard Fischer Associates, Inc.*
Ohman, Gregory L. — *Skott/Edwards Consultants, Inc.*
Onstott, Joseph — *The Onstott Group, Inc.*
Overlock, Craig — *Ray & Berndtson*
Palma, Frank R. — *Goodrich & Sherwood Associates, Inc.*
Palmer, Carlton A. — *Beall & Company, Inc.*
Panarese, Pam — *Howard Fischer Associates, Inc.*
Papciak, Dennis J. — *Accounting Personnel Associates, Inc.*
Papciak, Dennis J. — *Temporary Accounting Personnel*
Pardo, Maria Elena — *Smith Search, S.C.*
Parsons, Allison D. — *Barton Associates, Inc.*
Pearson, John R. — *Pearson, Caldwell & Farnsworth, Inc.*

Peeney, James D. — *Peeney Associates*

Pelisson, Charles — *Marra Peters & Partners*

Pettibone, Linda G. — *Herbert Mines Associates, Inc.*

Pettway, Samuel H. — *Spencer Stuart*

Petty, J. Scott — *The Arcus Group*

Pfeiffer, Irene — *Price Waterhouse*

Phillips, Donald L. — *O'Shea, Divine & Company, Inc.*

Phillips, James L. — *Highland Search Group*

Pickford, Stephen T. — *The Corporate Staff, Inc.*

Pierson, Edward J. — *Johnson Smith & Knisely Accord*

Plessner, Rene — *Rene Plessner Associates, Inc.*

Poirier, Roland L. — *Poirier, Hoevel & Co.*

Poremski, Paul — *A.J. Burton Group, Inc.*

Porter, Albert — *The Experts*

Potter, Mark W. — *Highland Search Group*

Potter, Steven B. — *Highland Search Group*

Powers Johnson, Allyson — *Skott/Edwards Consultants, Inc.*

Press, Fred — *Adept Tech Recruiting*

Price, Kenneth M. — *Messett Associates, Inc.*

Proct, Nina — *Martin H. Bauman Associates, Inc.*

Puckett, Jennifer — *Rene Plessner Associates, Inc.*

Pugrant, Mark A. — *Grant/Morgan Associates, Inc.*

Rabinowitz, Peter A. — *P.A.R. Associates Inc.*

Raines, Bruce R. — *Raines International Inc.*

Ramler, Carolyn S. — *The Corporate Connection, Ltd.*

Ray, Marianne C. — *Callan Associates, Ltd.*

Redding, Denise — *The Douglas Reiter Company, Inc.*

Redler, Rhonda — *National Search, Inc.*

Regan, Thomas J. — *Tower Consultants, Ltd.*

Reisinger, George L. — *Sigma Group International*

Reiss, Matt — *National Search, Inc.*

Reiter, Douglas — *The Douglas Reiter Company, Inc.*

Renick, Cynthia L. — *Morgan Hunter Corp.*

Reticker, Peter — *MSI International*

Reyman, Susan — *S. Reyman & Associates Ltd.*

Reynolds, Gregory P. — *Roberts Ryan and Bentley*

Rice, Raymond D. — *Logue & Rice Inc.*

Rich, Lyttleton — *Sockwell & Associates*

Rieger, Louis J. — *Spencer Stuart*

Rimmel, James E. — *The Hindman Company*

Rimmele, Michael — *The Bankers Group*

Rinker, Jim — *Southwestern Professional Services*

Riotto, Anthony R. — *Riotto-Jones Associates*

Roberts, Kenneth — *The Rubicon Group*

Roberts, Mitch — *A.E. Feldman Associates*

Roberts, Nick P. — *Spectrum Search Associates, Inc.*

Roberts, Scott — *Jonas, Walters & Assoc., Inc.*

Robinson, Bruce — *Bruce Robinson Associates*

Robles Cuellar, Paulina — *Ray & Berndtson*

Rollins, Scott — *S.C. International, Ltd.*

Rosato, William R. — *W.R. Rosato & Associates, Inc.*

Rosenthal, Charles — *National Search, Inc.*

Ross, Curt A. — *Ray & Berndtson*

Rotella, Marshall W. — *The Corporate Connection, Ltd.*

Rudolph, Kenneth — *Kossuth & Associates, Inc.*

Rusher, William H. — *Rusher, Loscavio & LoPresto*

Russell, Richard A. — *Executive Search Consultants Corporation*

Russell, Robin E. — *Kenzer Corp.*

Ryan, Lee — *Ryan, Miller & Associates Inc.*

Sabanosh, Whitney — *Highland Search Group*

Sacerdote, John — *Raymond Karsan Associates*

Salvagno, Michael J. — *The Cambridge Group Ltd*

Sandor, Richard J. — *Flynn, Hannock, Incorporated*

Sarna, Edmund A. — *Jonas, Walters & Assoc., Inc.*

Sathe, Mark A. — *Sathe & Associates, Inc.*

Schene, Philip — *A.E. Feldman Associates*

Schwam, Carol — *A.E. Feldman Associates*

Scott, Evan — *Howard Fischer Associates, Inc.*

Scott, Gordon S. — *Search Advisors International Corp.*

Scranton, Lisa — *A.J. Burton Group, Inc.*

Segal, Eric B. — *Kenzer Corp.*

Sennello, Gendra — *National Search, Inc.*

Sevilla, Claudio A. — *Crawford & Crofford*

Shelton, Sandra — *National Search, Inc.*

Shepard, Michael J. — *MSI International*

Shervey, Brent C. — *O'Callaghan Honey/Ray & Berndtson, Inc.*

Sherwood, Andrew — *Goodrich & Sherwood Associates, Inc.*

Silverstein, Jackie — *Don Richard Associates of Charlotte*

Simmons, Sandra K. — *MSI International*

Sindler, Jay — *A.J. Burton Group, Inc.*

Sitarski, Stan — *Howard Fischer Associates, Inc.*

Skalet, Ira — *A.E. Feldman Associates*

Smead, Michelle M. — *A.T. Kearney, Inc.*

Smith, Ana Luz — *Smith Search, S.C.*

Smith, Ethan L. — *Highland Search Group*

Smith, John E. — *Smith Search, S.C.*

Smith, Lydia — *The Corporate Connection, Ltd.*

Smith, Matt D. — *Ray & Berndtson*

Smith, Richard — *S.C. International, Ltd.*

Smith, Ronald V. — *Coe & Company International Inc.*

Snelgrove, Geiger — *National Search, Inc.*

Snyder, C. Edward — *Horton International*

Snyder, James F. — *Snyder & Company*

Sockwell, J. Edgar — *Sockwell & Associates*

Spann, Richard E. — *Goodrich & Sherwood Associates, Inc.*

Spriggs, Robert D. — *Spriggs & Company, Inc.*

St. Clair, Alan — *TNS Partners, Inc.*

Stark, Jeff — *Thorne, Brieger Associates Inc.*

Stevenson, Jane — *Howard Fischer Associates, Inc.*

Stewart, Ross M. — *Human Resources Network Partners Inc.*

Stringer, Dann P. — *D.E. Foster Partners Inc.*

Strom, Mark N. — *Search Advisors International Corp.*

Sumurdy, Melinda — *Kenzer Corp.*

Swanson, Dick — *Raymond Karsan Associates*

Sweeney, Sean K. — *Bonifield Associates*

Swoboda, Lawrence — *A.J. Burton Group, Inc.*

Taylor, Conrad G. — *MSI International*

Taylor, R.L. (Larry) — *Ray & Berndtson*

Telford, John H. — *Telford, Adams & Alexander/Telford & Co., Inc.*

ten Cate, Herman H. — *Stoneham Associates Corp.*

Teter, Sandra — *The Danbrook Group, Inc.*
Thomas, Kurt J. — *P.J. Murphy & Associates, Inc.*
Thompson, John R. — *MSI International*
Thompson, Kenneth L. — *McCormack & Farrow*
Tincu, John C. — *Ferneborg & Associates, Inc.*
Tipp, George D. — *Intech Summit Group, Inc.*
Tootsey, Mark A. — *A.J. Burton Group, Inc.*
Tracey, Jack — *Management Assistance Group, Inc.*
Trott, Kathryn — *Allard Associates*
Trott, Kathryn — *Allard Associates*
Truex, John F. — *Morton, McCorkle & Associates, Inc.*
Tryon, Katey — *DeFrain, Mayer LLC*
Tunney, William — *Grant Cooper and Associates*
Turner, Edward K. — *Don Richard Associates of Charlotte*
Turner, Kimberly — *Barton Associates, Inc.*
Tursi, Deborah J. — *The Corporate Connection, Ltd.*
Tyson, Richard L. — *Bonifield Associates*
Ulbert, Nancy — *Aureus Group*
Vergara, Gail H. — *Spencer Stuart*
Visnich, L. Christine — *Bason Associates Inc.*
Vitale, Amy — *Highland Search Group*
Vossler, James — *A.J. Burton Group, Inc.*
Wakefield, Scott — *National Search, Inc.*
Waldman, Noah H. — *Lamalie Amrop International*
Waldoch, D. Mark — *Barnes Development Group, LLC*
Waldrop, Gary R. — *MSI International*
Walker, Craig H. — *A.J. Burton Group, Inc.*
Walker, Ewing J. — *Ward Howell International, Inc.*
Walters, William F. — *Jonas, Walters & Assoc., Inc.*
Warter, Mark — *Isaacson, Miller*
Watson, Hanan S. — *Watson International, Inc.*
Watson, James — *MSI International*
Wayne, Cary S. — *ProSearch Inc.*
Webb, George H. — *Webb, Johnson Associates, Inc.*
Wein, Michael S. — *Media Management Resources, Inc.*
Wein, William — *Media Management Resources, Inc.*
Weisler, Nancy — *National Search, Inc.*
Welch, Robert — *Ray & Berndtson*
Wheeler, Gerard H. — *A.J. Burton Group, Inc.*
Whiting, Anthony — *Johnson Smith & Knisely Accord*
Whitton, Paula L. — *Pearson, Caldwell & Farnsworth, Inc.*
Wilcox, Fred T. — *Wilcox, Bertoux & Miller*
Wilkinson, Barbara — *Beall & Company, Inc.*
Williams, Gary L. — *Barnes Development Group, LLC*
Williams, Harry D. — *Jacobson Associates*
Williams, Roger K. — *Williams, Roth & Krueger Inc.*
Wilson, Patricia L. — *Leon A. Farley Associates*
Wold, Ted W. — *Hyde Danforth Wold & Co.*
Wolf, Stephen M. — *Byron Leonard International, Inc.*
Womack, Joseph — *The Bankers Group*
Wood, Elizabeth — *Highland Search Group*

Wooldridge, Jeff — *Ray & Berndtson*
Wooller, Edmund A.M. — *Windsor International*
Wright, A. Leo — *The Hindman Company*
Wright, Carl A.J. — *A.J. Burton Group, Inc.*
Wright, Charles D. — *Goodrich & Sherwood Associates, Inc.*
Yen, Maggie Yeh Ching — *Ray & Berndtson*
Zaffrann, Craig S. — *P.J. Murphy & Associates, Inc.*
Zahradka, James F. — *P.J. Murphy & Associates, Inc.*
Zaslav, Debra M. — *Telford, Adams & Alexander/Telford & Co., Inc.*
Zivic, Janis M. — *Spencer Stuart*
Zona, Henry F. — *Zona & Associates, Inc.*

3. Engineering

Abbott, Peter D. — *The Abbott Group, Inc.*
Abell, Vincent W. — *MSI International*
Abramson, Roye — *Source Services Corporation*
Adler, Louis S. — *CJA - The Adler Group*
Akin, J.R. "Jack" — *J.R. Akin & Company Inc.*
Albert, Richard — *Source Services Corporation*
Alford, Holly — *Source Services Corporation*
Allen, William L. — *The Hindman Company*
Alringer, Marc — *Source Services Corporation*
Altreuter, Rose — *The ALTCO Group*
Ambler, Peter W. — *Peter W. Ambler Company*
Amico, Robert — *Source Services Corporation*
Anderson, Mary — *Source Services Corporation*
Anderson, Matthew — *Source Services Corporation*
Anderson, Richard — *Grant Cooper and Associates*
Anderson, Steve — *CPS Inc.*
Aston, Kathy — *Marra Peters & Partners*
Atwood, Barrie — *The Abbott Group, Inc.*
Axelrod, Nancy R. — *A.T. Kearney, Inc.*
Badger, Fred H. — *The Badger Group*
Baeder, Jeremy — *Executive Manning Corporation*
Baer, Kenneth — *Source Services Corporation*
Baglio, Robert — *Source Services Corporation*
Baier, Rebecca — *Source Services Corporation*
Baje, Sarah — *Innovative Search Group, LLC*
Baker, Gary M. — *Cochran, Cochran & Yale, Inc.*
Baker, Gerry — *A.T. Kearney, Inc.*
Bakken, Mark — *Source Services Corporation*
Balbone, Rich — *Executive Manning Corporation*
Balch, Randy — *CPS Inc.*
Balchumas, Charles — *Source Services Corporation*
Baltaglia, Michael — *Cochran, Cochran & Yale, Inc.*
Balter, Sidney — *Source Services Corporation*
Banko, Scott — *Source Services Corporation*
Baranowski, Peter — *Source Services Corporation*
Barbour, Mary Beth — *Tully/Woodmansee International, Inc.*
Barger, H. Carter — *Barger & Sargeant, Inc.*
Barlow, Ken H. — *The Cherbonnier Group, Inc.*
Barnaby, Richard — *Source Services Corporation*
Barnes, Gary — *Brigade Inc.*
Barnes, Richard E. — *Barnes Development Group, LLC*
Barnes, Roanne L. — *Barnes Development Group, LLC*
Bartels, Fredrick — *Source Services Corporation*

Bartfield, Philip — *Source Services Corporation*
Bartholdi, Ted — *Bartholdi & Company, Inc.*
Bartholdi, Theodore G. — *Bartholdi & Company, Inc.*
Barton, James — *Source Services Corporation*
Bason, Maurice L. — *Bason Associates Inc.*
Batte, Carol — *Source Services Corporation*
Bauman, Martin H. — *Martin H. Bauman Associates, Inc.*
Bearman, Linda — *Grant Cooper and Associates*
Beaudin, Elizabeth C. — *Callan Associates, Ltd.*
Beaver, Bentley H. — *The Onstott Group, Inc.*
Beaver, Robert — *Source Services Corporation*
Belden, Jeannette — *Source Services Corporation*
Belin, Jean — *Boyden*
Bell, Lloyd W. — *O'Brien & Bell*
Benjamin, Maurita — *Source Services Corporation*
Bennett, Jo — *Battalia Winston International*
Benson, Edward — *Source Services Corporation*
Beran, Helena — *Michael J. Cavanagh and Associates*
Berger, Jeffrey — *Source Services Corporation*
Bernard, Bryan — *Source Services Corporation*
Bernas, Sharon — *Source Services Corporation*
Berry, Harold B. — *The Hindman Company*
Betts, Suzette — *Source Services Corporation*
Bickett, Nicole — *Source Services Corporation*
Bidelman, Richard — *Source Services Corporation*
Biolsi, Joseph — *Source Services Corporation*
Birns, Douglas — *Source Services Corporation*
Blakslee, Jan H. — *J: Blakslee International, Ltd.*
Bland, Walter — *Source Services Corporation*
Blassaras, Peggy — *Source Services Corporation*
Blickle, Michael — *Source Services Corporation*
Blim, Barbara — *JDG Associates, Ltd.*
Bloch, Suzanne — *Source Services Corporation*
Blocher, John — *Source Services Corporation*
Bloomer, James E. — *L.W. Foote Company*
Blumenthal, Paula — *J.P. Canon Associates*
Boel, Werner — *The Dalley Hewitt Company*
Bogansky, Amy — *Conex Incorporated*
Bohn, Steve J. — *MSI International*
Boltrus, Dick — *Sink, Walker, Boltrus International*
Bongiovanni, Vincent — *ESA Professional Consultants*
Booth, Ronald — *Source Services Corporation*
Borkin, Andrew — *Strategic Advancement Inc.*
Bormann, Cindy Ann — *MSI International*
Bosward, Allan — *Source Services Corporation*
Bowden, Otis H. — *BowdenGlobal, Ltd.*
Brackman, Janet — *Dahl-Morrow International*
Bradley, Dalena — *Woodworth International Group*
Bradshaw, Monte — *Christian & Timbers*
Brady, Dick — *William Guy & Associates*
Brady, Robert — *CPS Inc.*
Brandeis, Richard — *CPS Inc.*
Brandenburg, David — *Professional Staffing Consultants*
Brassard, Gary — *Source Services Corporation*
Bremer, Brian — *Source Services Corporation*
Brewster, Edward — *Source Services Corporation*
Brieger, Steve — *Thorne, Brieger Associates Inc.*
Brinson, Robert — *MSI International*
Britt, Stephen — *Keith Bagg & Associates Inc.*
Bronger, Patricia — *Source Services Corporation*

Brother, Joy — *Charles Luntz & Associates. Inc.*
Brown, Clifford — *Source Services Corporation*
Brown, Daniel — *Source Services Corporation*
Brown, Lawrence Anthony — *MSI International*
Brown, Steffan — *Woodworth International Group*
Brown, Steven — *Source Services Corporation*
Browne, Michael — *Source Services Corporation*
Brudno, Robert J. — *Savoy Partners, Ltd.*
Brunner, Terry — *Source Services Corporation*
Bruno, Deborah F. — *The Hindman Company*
Bryant, Richard D. — *Bryant Associates, Inc.*
Bryant, Shari G. — *Bryant Associates, Inc.*
Brzezinski, Ronald T. — *Callan Associates, Ltd.*
Buckles, Donna — *Cochran, Cochran & Yale, Inc.*
Burch, Donald — *Source Services Corporation*
Burden, Gene — *The Cherbonnier Group, Inc.*
Burke, John — *The Experts*
Burkhill, John — *The Talley Group*
Busch, Jack — *Busch International*
Buttrey, Daniel — *Source Services Corporation*
Buzolits, Patrick — *Source Services Corporation*
Cafero, Les — *Source Services Corporation*
Call, David — *Cochran, Cochran & Yale, Inc.*
Callan, Robert M. — *Callan Associates, Ltd.*
Cameron, James W. — *Cameron Consulting*
Campbell, E. — *Source Services Corporation*
Campbell, Jeff — *Source Services Corporation*
Capizzi, Karen — *Cochran, Cochran & Yale, Inc.*
Carlson, Eric — *Source Services Corporation*
Carnal, Rick — *Source Services Corporation*
Carter, Linda — *Source Services Corporation*
Carvalho-Esteves, Maria — *Source Services Corporation*
Cary, Con — *Cary & Associates*
Castle, Lisa — *Source Services Corporation*
Cavanagh, Michael J. — *Michael J. Cavanagh and Associates*
Celenza, Catherine — *CPS Inc.*
Cersosimo, Rocco — *Source Services Corporation*
Chase, James — *Source Services Corporation*
Chatterjie, Alok — *MSI International*
Cheah, Victor — *Source Services Corporation*
Cherbonnier, L. Michael — *TCG International, Inc.*
Cherbonnier, L. Michael — *The Cherbonnier Group, Inc.*
Christiansen, Amy — *CPS Inc.*
Christiansen, Doug — *CPS Inc.*
Christman, Joel — *Source Services Corporation*
Chronopoulos, Dennis — *Source Services Corporation*
Cizek, John T. — *Cizek Associates, Inc.*
Cizek, Marti J. — *Cizek Associates, Inc.*
Clark, James — *CPS Inc.*
Clauhsen, Elizabeth A. — *Savoy Partners, Ltd.*
Clawson, Bob — *Source Services Corporation*
Clawson, Robert — *Source Services Corporation*
Cocconi, Alan — *Source Services Corporation*
Cochran, Scott P. — *The Badger Group*
Cochrun, James — *Source Services Corporation*
Coe, Karen J. — *Coe & Company International Inc.*
Coffman, Brian — *Kossuth & Associates, Inc.*
Cohen, Robert C. — *Intech Summit Group, Inc.*
Cole, Rosalie — *Source Services Corporation*
Coleman, J. Kevin — *J. Kevin Coleman & Associates, Inc.*

Collard, Joseph A. — *Spencer Stuart*
Collins, Scott — *Source Services Corporation*
Comai, Christine — *Source Services Corporation*
Combs, Thomas — *Source Services Corporation*
Cona, Joseph A. — *Cona Personnel Search*
Coneys, Bridget — *Source Services Corporation*
Conway, Maureen — *Conway & Associates*
Cook, Charlene — *Source Services Corporation*
Cook, Dennis — *A.T. Kearney, Inc.*
Cooke, Katherine H. — *Horton International*
Costello, Lynda — *Coe & Company International Inc.*
Cotugno, James — *Source Services Corporation*
Coughlin, Stephen — *Source Services Corporation*
Coulman, Karen — *CPS Inc.*
Cragg, Barbara R. — *Southwestern Professional Services*
Crath, Paul F. — *Price Waterhouse*
Critchley, Walter — *Cochran, Cochran & Yale, Inc.*
Cruse, O.D. — *Spencer Stuart*
Cuddihy, Paul — *Dahl-Morrow International*
Cuddy, Patricia — *Source Services Corporation*
Curren, Camella — *Source Services Corporation*
Curtis, Ellissa — *Cochran, Cochran & Yale, Inc.*
Cutka, Matthew — *Source Services Corporation*
Czepiel, Susan — *CPS Inc.*
Daniels, C. Eugene — *Sigma Group International*
Dankberg, Iris — *Source Services Corporation*
Davis, C. Scott — *Source Services Corporation*
Davis, Elease — *Source Services Corporation*
Davis, G. Gordon — *Davis & Company*
Dawson, William — *Source Services Corporation*
de Palacios, Jeannette C. — *J. Palacios & Associates, Inc.*
Debus, Wayne — *Source Services Corporation*
Deck, Jack — *Source Services Corporation*
Delaney, Patrick J. — *Sensible Solutions, Inc.*
DeMarco, Robert — *Source Services Corporation*
Desai, Sushila — *Sink, Walker, Boltrus International*
Desgrosellier, Gary P. — *Personnel Unlimited/Executive Search*
Desmond, Dennis — *Beall & Company, Inc.*
Desmond, Mary — *Source Services Corporation*
Dever, Mary — *Source Services Corporation*
Devito, Alice — *Source Services Corporation*
Di Filippo, Thomas — *Source Services Corporation*
DiCioccio, Carmen — *Cochran, Cochran & Yale, Inc.*
Dicker, Barry — *ESA Professional Consultants*
Dickson, Duke — *A.D. & Associates Executive Search, Inc.*
Diers, Gary — *Source Services Corporation*
Dietz, David S. — *MSI International*
DiMarchi, Paul — *DiMarchi Partners, Inc.*
DiMarchi, Paul — *DiMarchi Partners, Inc.*
Dingeldey, Peter E. — *Search Advisors International Corp.*
Dingman, Bruce — *Robert W. Dingman Company, Inc.*
Dittmar, Richard — *Source Services Corporation*
Divine, Robert S. — *O'Shea, Divine & Company, Inc.*
Dixon, Aris — *CPS Inc.*
Dobrow, Samuel — *Source Services Corporation*

Donahue, Debora — *Source Services Corporation*
Donath, Linda — *Dahl-Morrow International*
Donnelly, Patti — *Source Services Corporation*
Dorfner, Martin — *Source Services Corporation*
Dowdall, Jean — *A.T. Kearney, Inc.*
Dowell, Chris — *The Abbott Group, Inc.*
Dowlatzadch, Homayoun — *Source Services Corporation*
Downs, William — *Source Services Corporation*
Duelks, John — *Source Services Corporation*
Duggan, James P. — *Slayton International, Inc./I-I-C Partners*
Duncan, Dana — *Source Services Corporation*
Dunlow, Aimee — *Source Services Corporation*
Dunman, Betsy L. — *Crawford & Crofford*
Dupont, Rick — *Source Services Corporation*
Dwyer, Julie — *CPS Inc.*
Eason, Jan C. — *Summit Group International*
Eddy, Terry — *William Guy & Associates*
Edwards, Dorothy — *MSI International*
Edwards, Robert — *J.P. Canon Associates*
Edwards, Verba L. — *Wing Tips & Pumps, Inc.*
Eggert, Scott — *Source Services Corporation*
Ehrhart, Jennifer — *ADOW's Executeam*
Eiseman, Joe — *Source Services Corporation*
Eiseman, Joe — *Source Services Corporation*
Eiseman, Joe — *Source Services Corporation*
Elder, Tom — *Juntunen-Combs-Poirier*
Ellis, Patricia — *Source Services Corporation*
Ellis, Ted K. — *The Hindman Company*
Ellis, William — *Interspace Interactive Inc.*
Emerson, Randall — *Source Services Corporation*
England, Mark — *Austin-McGregor International*
Engle, Bryan — *Source Services Corporation*
Ervin, Darlene — *CPS Inc.*
Ervin, Russell — *Source Services Corporation*
Eustis, Lucy R. — *MSI International*
Evans, David — *Executive Manning Corporation*
Evans, Timothy — *Source Services Corporation*
Fagerstrom, Jon — *Source Services Corporation*
Fales, Scott — *Source Services Corporation*
Fancher, Robert L. — *Bason Associates Inc.*
Fanning, Paul — *Source Services Corporation*
Farler, Wiley — *Source Services Corporation*
Farley, Leon A. — *Leon A. Farley Associates*
Fechheimer, Peter — *Source Services Corporation*
Ferguson, Kenneth — *Source Services Corporation*
Field, Andrew — *Source Services Corporation*
Finkel, Leslie — *Source Services Corporation*
Finnerty, James — *Source Services Corporation*
Fischer, Janet L. — *Boyden*
Fisher, Neal — *Fisher Personnel Management Services*
Fishler, Stu — *A.T. Kearney, Inc.*
Fitzgerald, Brian — *Source Services Corporation*
Fleming, Marco — *MSI International*
Flora, Dodi — *Crawford & Crofford*
Florio, Robert — *Source Services Corporation*
Fogarty, Michael — *CPS Inc.*
Foote, Leland W. — *L.W. Foote Company*
Foreman, David C. — *Koontz, Jeffries & Associates, Inc.*
Forestier, Lois — *Source Services Corporation*
Foster, Bradley — *Source Services Corporation*
Foster, John — *Source Services Corporation*
Fotia, Frank — *JDG Associates, Ltd.*
Fowler, Thomas A. — *The Hindman Company*

Francis, Brad — *Source Services Corporation*
Frantino, Michael — *Source Services Corporation*
Frazier, John — *Cochran, Cochran & Yale, Inc.*
Frederick, Dianne — *Source Services Corporation*
Freeh, Thomas — *Source Services Corporation*
Freeman, Mark — *ESA Professional Consultants*
French, William G. — *Preng & Associates, Inc.*
Friedman, Deborah — *Source Services Corporation*
Fuhrman, Dennis — *Source Services Corporation*
Fujino, Rickey — *Source Services Corporation*
Fulger, Herbert — *Source Services Corporation*
Furlong, James W. — *Furlong Search, Inc.*
Furlong, James W. — *Furlong Search, Inc.*
Furlong, James W. — *Furlong Search, Inc.*
Fyhrie, David — *Source Services Corporation*
Gabel, Gregory N. — *Canny, Bowen Inc.*
Gabriel, David L. — *The Arcus Group*
Gaffney, Keith — *Gaffney Management Consultants*
Gaffney, Megan — *Source Services Corporation*
Gaffney, William — *Gaffney Management Consultants*
Galante, Suzanne M. — *Vlcek & Company, Inc.*
Gamble, Ira — *Source Services Corporation*
Gardner, Michael — *Source Services Corporation*
Garfinkle, Steven M. — *Battalia Winston International*
Garrett, Mark — *Source Services Corporation*
Gennawey, Robert — *Source Services Corporation*
Gerster, J.P. — *Juntunen-Combs-Poirier*
Gestwick, Daniel — *Cochran, Cochran & Yale, Inc.*
Ghurani, Mac — *Gary Kaplan & Associates*
Giesy, John — *Source Services Corporation*
Gilchrist, Robert J. — *Horton International*
Gilinsky, David — *Source Services Corporation*
Gillespie, Thomas — *Professional Search Consultants*
Gilreath, James M. — *Gilreath Weatherby, Inc.*
Glickman, Leenie — *Source Services Corporation*
Gluzman, Arthur — *Source Services Corporation*
Gnatowski, Bruce — *Source Services Corporation*
Golde, Lisa — *Tully/Woodmansee International, Inc.*
Goldenberg, Susan — *Grant Cooper and Associates*
Goldstein, Steven G. — *The Jonathan Stevens Group, Inc.*
Goodman, Dawn M. — *Bason Associates Inc.*
Goodwin, Gary — *Source Services Corporation*
Goodwin, Tim — *William Guy & Associates*
Gorman, Patrick — *Source Services Corporation*
Gourley, Timothy — *Source Services Corporation*
Grado, Eduardo — *Source Services Corporation*
Graff, Jack — *Source Services Corporation*
Graham, Dale — *CPS Inc.*
Graham, Shannon — *Source Services Corporation*
Grandinetti, Suzanne — *Source Services Corporation*
Grant, Michael — *Zwell International*
Grantham, John — *Grantham & Co., Inc.*
Grantham, Philip H. — *Columbia Consulting Group*
Grasch, Jerry E. — *The Hindman Company*
Gray, Heather — *Source Services Corporation*
Gray, Russell — *Source Services Corporation*

Graziano, Lisa — *Source Services Corporation*
Grebenstein, Charles R. — *Skott/Edwards Consultants, Inc.*
Gresia, Paul — *Source Services Corporation*
Griffin, Cathy — *A.T. Kearney, Inc.*
Groner, David — *Source Services Corporation*
Grossman, James — *Source Services Corporation*
Grossman, Martin — *Source Services Corporation*
Grotte, Lawrence C. — *Lautz Grotte Engler*
Grumulaitis, Leo — *Source Services Corporation*
Grzybowski, Jill — *CPS Inc.*
Guc, Stephen — *Source Services Corporation*
Guthrie, Stuart — *Source Services Corporation*
Guy, C. William — *William Guy & Associates*
Hacker-Taylor, Dianna — *Source Services Corporation*
Haider, Martin — *Source Services Corporation*
Hales, Daphne — *Source Services Corporation*
Haller, Mark — *Source Services Corporation*
Hamm, Gary — *Source Services Corporation*
Hanley, Alan P. — *Williams, Roth & Krueger Inc.*
Hanley, Steven — *Source Services Corporation*
Hanna, Remon — *Source Services Corporation*
Harbaugh, Paul J. — *International Management Advisors, Inc.*
Harbert, David O. — *Sweeney Harbert & Mummert, Inc.*
Hardison, Richard L. — *Hardison & Company*
Harney, Elyane — *Gary Kaplan & Associates*
Harp, Kimberly — *Source Services Corporation*
Harris, Jack — *A.T. Kearney, Inc.*
Harris, Seth O. — *Christian & Timbers*
Harrison, Patricia — *Source Services Corporation*
Hart, Crystal — *Source Services Corporation*
Hart, James — *Source Services Corporation*
Hartle, Larry — *CPS Inc.*
Harvey, Mike — *Advanced Executive Resources*
Harwood, Brian — *Source Services Corporation*
Haselby, James — *Source Services Corporation*
Hasten, Lawrence — *Source Services Corporation*
Haughton, Michael — *DeFrain, Mayer LLC*
Havener, Donald Clarke — *The Abbott Group, Inc.*
Hawksworth, A. Dwight — *A.D. & Associates Executive Search, Inc.*
Hayes, Lee — *Source Services Corporation*
Haystead, Steve — *Advanced Executive Resources*
Hazerjian, Cynthia — *CPS Inc.*
Heafey, Bill — *CPS Inc.*
Hebel, Robert W. — *R.W. Hebel Associates*
Hedlund, David — *Hedlund Corporation*
Heinrich, Scott — *Source Services Corporation*
Heinze, David — *Heinze & Associates, Inc.*
Hellinger, Audrey W. — *Martin H. Bauman Associates, Inc.*
Helminiak, Audrey — *Gaffney Management Consultants*
Henn, George W. — *G.W. Henn & Company*
Henneberry, Ward — *Source Services Corporation*
Hennig, Sandra M. — *MSI International*
Henry, Mary — *Conex Incorporated*
Hergenrather, Richard A. — *Hergenrather & Company*
Herman, Shelli — *Gary Kaplan & Associates*
Hernandez, Ruben — *Source Services Corporation*
Heroux, David — *Source Services Corporation*

Herzog, Sarah — *Source Services Corporation*
Hewitt, Rives D. — *The Dalley Hewitt Company*
Hewitt, W. Davis — *The Dalley Hewitt Company*
Higgins, William — *William Guy & Associates*
Hight, Susan — *Source Services Corporation*
Hilbert, Laurence — *Source Services Corporation*
Hilgenberg, Thomas — *Source Services Corporation*
Hill, Emery — *MSI International*
Hillen, Skip — *The McCormick Group, Inc.*
Hillyer, Carolyn — *Source Services Corporation*
Himes, Dirk — *A.T. Kearney, Inc.*
Himlin, Amy — *Cochran, Cochran & Yale, Inc.*
Hindman, Neil C. — *The Hindman Company*
Hinojosa, Oscar — *Source Services Corporation*
Hoevel, Michael J. — *Poirier, Hoevel & Co.*
Hoffman, Stephen — *Source Services Corporation*
Hofner, Andrew — *Source Services Corporation*
Holland, John A. — *Holland, McFadzean & Associates, Inc.*
Holland, Rose Mary — *Price Waterhouse*
Holt, Carol — *Bartholdi & Company, Inc.*
Hopper, John W. — *William Guy & Associates*
Hostetter, Kristi — *Source Services Corporation*
Houchins, William M. — *Christian & Timbers*
Houterloot, Tim — *Source Services Corporation*
Hucko, Donald S. — *Jonas, Walters & Assoc., Inc.*
Hudson, Reginald M. — *Search Bureau International*
Hughes, Barbara — *Source Services Corporation*
Hughes, Randall — *Source Services Corporation*
Hult, Dana — *Source Services Corporation*
Humphrey, Titus — *Source Services Corporation*
Hurtado, Jaime — *Source Services Corporation*
Hutton, Thomas J. — *The Thomas Tucker Company*
Hylas, Lisa — *Source Services Corporation*
Imely, Larry S. — *Stratford Group*
Imhof, Kirk — *Source Services Corporation*
Inger, Barry — *Source Services Corporation*
Inguagiato, Gregory — *MSI International*
Inskeep, Thomas — *Source Services Corporation*
Intravaia, Salvatore — *Source Services Corporation*
Irish, Alan — *CPS Inc.*
Irwin, Mark — *Source Services Corporation*
Issacs, Judith A. — *Grant Cooper and Associates*
Jablo, Steven A. — *Dieckmann & Associates, Ltd.*
Jackson, Joan — *A.T. Kearney, Inc.*
Jacobs, Martin J. — *The Rubicon Group*
Jacobs, Mike — *Thorne, Brieger Associates Inc.*
Jacobson, Hayley — *Source Services Corporation*
Jadulang, Vincent — *Source Services Corporation*
James, Richard — *Criterion Executive Search, Inc.*
Jansen, John F. — *Delta Services*
Januale, Lois — *Cochran, Cochran & Yale, Inc.*
Januleski, Geoff — *Source Services Corporation*
Jeltema, John — *Source Services Corporation*
Jensen, Robert — *Source Services Corporation*
Joffe, Barry — *Bason Associates Inc.*
Johnson, Greg — *Source Services Corporation*
Johnson, John W. — *Webb, Johnson Associates, Inc.*
Johnson, Julie M. — *International Staffing Consultants, Inc.*
Johnson, S. Hope — *Boyden Washington, D.C.*
Johnson, Stanley C. — *Johnson & Company*

Johnson, Valerie — *Coe & Company International Inc.*
Johnstone, Grant — *Source Services Corporation*
Jones, Rodney — *Source Services Corporation*
Jordan, Jon — *Cochran, Cochran & Yale, Inc.*
Jorgensen, Tom — *The Talley Group*
Judy, Otto — *CPS Inc.*
Juelis, John J. — *Peeney Associates*
Juska, Frank — *Rusher, Loscavio & LoPresto*
Kader, Richard — *Richard Kader & Associates*
Kaiser, Donald J. — *Dunhill International Search of New Haven*
Kaplan, Gary — *Gary Kaplan & Associates*
Kaplan, Traci — *Source Services Corporation*
Karalis, William — *CPS Inc.*
Kasprzyk, Michael — *Source Services Corporation*
Kehoe, Mike — *CPS Inc.*
Kelly, Robert — *Source Services Corporation*
Kennedy, Craig — *Source Services Corporation*
Kennedy, Paul — *Source Services Corporation*
Kennedy, Walter — *Source Services Corporation*
Kennedy, Walter — *Source Services Corporation*
Kenney, Jeanne — *Source Services Corporation*
Kern, Jerry L. — *ADOW's Executeam*
Kern, Kathleen G. — *ADOW's Executeam*
Keyser, Anne — *A.T. Kearney, Inc.*
Kilcoyne, Pat — *CPS Inc.*
King, Bill — *The McCormick Group, Inc.*
King, Margaret — *Christian & Timbers*
King, Shannon — *Source Services Corporation*
Kinser, Richard E. — *Richard Kinser & Associates*
Kirschner, Alan — *Source Services Corporation*
Kkorzyniewski, Nicole — *CPS Inc.*
Klages, Constance W. — *International Management Advisors, Inc.*
Klein, Gary — *A.T. Kearney, Inc.*
Klein, Mary Jo — *Cochran, Cochran & Yale, Inc.*
Kleinstein, Scott — *Source Services Corporation*
Klusman, Edwin — *Source Services Corporation*
Knoll, Robert — *Source Services Corporation*
Koczak, John — *Source Services Corporation*
Kohn, Adam P. — *Christian & Timbers*
Kondra, Vernon J. — *The Douglas Reiter Company, Inc.*
Koontz, Donald N. — *Koontz, Jeffries & Associates, Inc.*
Kopsick, Joseph M. — *Spencer Stuart*
Kossuth, David — *Kossuth & Associates, Inc.*
Kossuth, Jane — *Kossuth & Associates, Inc.*
Krejci, Stanley L. — *Boyden Washington, D.C.*
Krieger, Dennis F. — *Seiden Krieger Associates, Inc.*
Krueger, Kurt — *Krueger Associates*
Kunzer, William J. — *Kunzer Associates, Ltd.*
Kurrigan, Geoffrey — *ESA Professional Consultants*
Kussner, Janice N. — *Herman Smith Executive Initiatives Inc.*
La Chance, Ronald — *Source Services Corporation*
Lachance, Roger — *Laurendeau Labrecque/Ray & Berndtson, Inc.*
Lache, Shawn E. — *The Arcus Group*
Laird, Cheryl — *CPS Inc.*
Lambert, William — *Source Services Corporation*
Lamia, Michael — *Source Services Corporation*
Lapointe, Fabien — *Source Services Corporation*

Lardner, Lucy D. — *Tully/Woodmansee International, Inc.*
Lasher, Charles M. — *Lasher Associates*
Laskin, Sandy — *Source Services Corporation*
Lautz, Lindsay A. — *Lautz Grotte Engler*
Laverty, William — *Source Services Corporation*
Lazar, Miriam — *Source Services Corporation*
Leahy, Jan — *CPS Inc.*
Leblanc, Danny — *Source Services Corporation*
Lee, Everett — *Source Services Corporation*
Leigh, Rebecca — *Source Services Corporation*
Leighton, Mark — *Source Services Corporation*
Leighton, Nina — *The Ogdon Partnership*
Leininger, Dennis — *Key Employment Services*
Lence, Julie Anne — *MSI International*
Leslie, William H. — *Boyden/Zay & Company*
Levenson, Laurel — *Source Services Corporation*
Levine, Irwin — *Source Services Corporation*
Lewicki, Christopher — *MSI International*
Lewis, Daniel — *Source Services Corporation*
Liebross, Eric — *Source Services Corporation*
Lin, Felix — *Source Services Corporation*
Lindberg, Eric J. — *MSI International*
Linton, Leonard M. — *Byron Leonard International, Inc.*
Lipuma, Thomas — *Source Services Corporation*
Loeb, Stephen H. — *Grant Cooper and Associates*
Lofthouse, Cindy — *CPS Inc.*
Long, John — *Source Services Corporation*
Long, Mark — *Source Services Corporation*
Long, Milt — *William Guy & Associates*
Long, William G. — *McDonald, Long & Associates, Inc.*
LoPresto, Robert L. — *Rusher, Loscavio & LoPresto*
Lotufo, Donald A. — *D.A.L. Associates, Inc.*
Lotz, R. James — *International Management Advisors, Inc.*
Lucarelli, Joan — *The Onstott Group, Inc.*
Lucas, Ronnie L. — *MSI International*
Luce, Daniel — *Source Services Corporation*
Lucht, John — *The John Lucht Consultancy Inc.*
Ludder, Mark — *Source Services Corporation*
Ludlow, Michael — *Source Services Corporation*
Lumsby, George N. — *International Management Advisors, Inc.*
Lundy, Martin — *Source Services Corporation*
Luntz, Charles E. — *Charles Luntz & Associates. Inc.*
Lupica, Anthony — *Cochran, Cochran & Yale, Inc.*
Lyon, Jenny — *Marra Peters & Partners*
Lyons, J. David — *Aubin International Inc.*
Lyons, Michael — *Source Services Corporation*
MacMillan, James — *Source Services Corporation*
MacNaughton, Sperry — *McNaughton Associates*
MacPherson, Holly — *Source Services Corporation*
Macrides, Michael — *Source Services Corporation*
Maggio, Mary — *Source Services Corporation*
Maglio, Charles J. — *Maglio and Company, Inc.*
Mahmoud, Sophia — *Source Services Corporation*
Mairn, Todd — *Source Services Corporation*
Major, Susan — *A.T. Kearney, Inc.*
Manassero, Henri J.P. — *International Management Advisors, Inc.*
Mangum, Maria — *Thomas Mangum Company*

Mangum, William T. — *Thomas Mangum Company*
Manns, Alex — *Crawford & Crofford*
Marino, Chester — *Cochran, Cochran & Yale, Inc.*
Marks, Ira — *Strategic Alternatives*
Marks, Russell E. — *Webb, Johnson Associates, Inc.*
Marra, John — *Marra Peters & Partners*
Marra, John — *Marra Peters & Partners*
Marumoto, William H. — *Boyden Washington, D.C.*
Marwil, Jennifer — *Source Services Corporation*
Mather, David R. — *Christian & Timbers*
Mathias, Douglas — *Source Services Corporation*
Mathias, Kathy — *Stone Murphy & Olson*
Mathis, Carrie — *Source Services Corporation*
Matthews, Corwin — *Woodworth International Group*
Mattingly, Kathleen — *Source Services Corporation*
Maxwell, John — *Source Services Corporation*
Mayer, Thomas — *Source Services Corporation*
McAndrews, Kathy — *CPS Inc.*
McCallister, Richard A. — *Boyden*
McCarthy, Laura — *Source Services Corporation*
McCloskey, Frank D. — *Johnson Smith & Knisely Accord*
McCormick, Brian — *The McCormick Group, Inc.*
McCormick, Joseph — *Source Services Corporation*
McCreary, Charles "Chip" — *Austin-McGregor International*
McDermott, Jeffrey T. — *Vlcek & Company, Inc.*
McDonald, Scott A. — *McDonald Associates International*
McDonald, Stanleigh B. — *McDonald Associates International*
McFadzen,, James A. — *Holland, McFadzean & Associates, Inc.*
McGinnis, Rita — *Source Services Corporation*
McGoldrick, Terrence — *Source Services Corporation*
McHugh, Keith — *Source Services Corporation*
McIntosh, Arthur — *Source Services Corporation*
McIntosh, Tad — *Source Services Corporation*
McKinney, Julia — *Source Services Corporation*
McMahan, Stephen — *Source Services Corporation*
McMahan, Stephen — *Source Services Corporation*
McManners, Donald E. — *McManners Associates, Inc.*
McMillin, Bob — *Price Waterhouse*
McNamara, Timothy C. — *Columbia Consulting Group*
McNamara, Timothy Connor — *Horton International*
McNear, Jeffrey E. — *Barrett Partners*
McNichols, Walter B. — *Gary Kaplan & Associates*
Meadows, C. David — *Professional Staffing Consultants*
Meara, Helen — *Source Services Corporation*
Meehan, John — *Source Services Corporation*
Meier, J. Dale — *Grant Cooper and Associates*
Mendelson, Jeffrey — *Source Services Corporation*

Mendoza-Green, Robin — *Source Services Corporation*
Messett, William J. — *Messett Associates, Inc.*
Messina, Marco — *Source Services Corporation*
Meyer, Stacey — *Gary Kaplan & Associates*
Michaels, Joseph — *CPS Inc.*
Miller, David — *Cochran, Cochran & Yale, Inc.*
Miller, Larry — *Source Services Corporation*
Miller, Timothy — *Source Services Corporation*
Milligan, Dale — *Source Services Corporation*
Mills, John — *Source Services Corporation*
Milner, Carol — *Source Services Corporation*
Miras, Cliff — *Source Services Corporation*
Miras, Cliff — *Source Services Corporation*
Misiurewicz, Marc — *Cochran, Cochran & Yale, Inc.*
Mittwol, Myles — *Source Services Corporation*
Mogul, Gene — *Mogul Consultants, Inc.*
Mohr, Brian — *CPS Inc.*
Molitor, John L. — *Barrett Partners*
Mollichelli, David — *Source Services Corporation*
Mondragon, Philip — *A.T. Kearney, Inc.*
Moore, Craig — *Source Services Corporation*
Moore, Dianna — *Source Services Corporation*
Moore, Mark — *Wheeler, Moore & Elam Co.*
Moore, Suzanne — *Source Services Corporation*
Moran, Douglas — *Source Services Corporation*
Morato, Rene — *Source Services Corporation*
Moretti, Denise — *Source Services Corporation*
Moriarty, Mike — *Source Services Corporation*
Morris, Scott — *Source Services Corporation*
Morrow, Melanie — *Source Services Corporation*
Morton, Robert C. — *Morton, McCorkle & Associates, Inc.*
Mott, Greg — *Source Services Corporation*
Msidment, Roger — *Source Services Corporation*
Mueller, Colleen — *Source Services Corporation*
Muendel, H. Edward — *Stanton Chase International*
Mulligan, Robert P. — *William Willis Worldwide Inc.*
Murphy, Corinne — *Source Services Corporation*
Murphy, Erin — *CPS Inc.*
Murphy, James — *Source Services Corporation*
Murray, Virginia — *A.T. Kearney, Inc.*
Murry, John — *Source Services Corporation*
Mursuli, Meredith — *Lasher Associates*
Mustin, Joyce M. — *J: Blakslee International, Ltd.*
Mydlach, Renee — *CPS Inc.*
Nabers, Karen — *Source Services Corporation*
Nagler, Leon G. — *Nagler, Robins & Poe, Inc.*
Nagy, Les — *Source Services Corporation*
Nair, Leslie — *Zwell International*
Necessary, Rick — *Source Services Corporation*
Needham, Karen — *Source Services Corporation*
Neff, Herbert — *Source Services Corporation*
Neher, Robert L. — *Intech Summit Group, Inc.*
Neidhart, Craig C. — *TNS Partners, Inc.*
Nelson, Hitch — *Source Services Corporation*
Nelson, Mary — *Source Services Corporation*
Nelson-Folkersen, Jeffrey — *Source Services Corporation*
Nemec, Phillip — *Dunhill International Search of New Haven*
Nephew, Robert — *Christian & Timbers*
Neuberth, Jeffrey G. — *Canny, Bowen Inc.*
Neuwald, Debrah — *Source Services Corporation*

Nichols, Gary — *Koontz, Jeffries & Associates, Inc.*
Nolan, Robert — *Source Services Corporation*
Nolen, Shannon — *Source Services Corporation*
Nolte, William D. — *W.D. Nolte & Company*
Norman, Randy — *Austin-McGregor International*
Norris, Ken — *A.T. Kearney, Inc.*
Norsell, Paul E. — *Paul Norsell & Associates, Inc.*
O'Brien, Susan — *Source Services Corporation*
O'Connell, Mary — *CPS Inc.*
Occhiboi, Emil — *Source Services Corporation*
Ocon, Olga — *Busch International*
Olsen, Robert — *Source Services Corporation*
Orr, Stacie — *Source Services Corporation*
Ottenritter, Chris — *CPS Inc.*
Ouellette, Christopher — *Source Services Corporation*
Owen, Christopher — *Source Services Corporation*
Pace, Susan A. — *Horton International*
Pachowitz, John — *Source Services Corporation*
Paliwoda, William — *Source Services Corporation*
Palmer, Carlton A. — *Beall & Company, Inc.*
Palmer, James H. — *The Hindman Company*
Papasadero, Kathleen — *Woodworth International Group*
Paradise, Malcolm — *Source Services Corporation*
Pardo, Maria Elena — *Smith Search, S.C.*
Parente, James — *Source Services Corporation*
Parroco, Jason — *Source Services Corporation*
Patel, Shailesh — *Source Services Corporation*
Paternie, Patrick — *Source Services Corporation*
Paul, Kathleen — *Source Services Corporation*
Peal, Matthew — *Source Services Corporation*
Pedley, Jill — *CPS Inc.*
Peeney, James D. — *Peeney Associates*
Pelisson, Charles — *Marra Peters & Partners*
Perry, Carolyn — *Source Services Corporation*
Peters, Kevin — *Source Services Corporation*
Petersen, Richard — *Source Services Corporation*
Peterson, Eric N. — *Stratford Group*
Peterson, John — *CPS Inc.*
Petty, J. Scott — *The Arcus Group*
Pfeiffer, Irene — *Price Waterhouse*
Phillips, Donald L. — *O'Shea, Divine & Company, Inc.*
Phipps, Peggy — *Woodworth International Group*
Pickering, Dale — *Agri-Tech Personnel, Inc.*
Pickering, Rita — *Agri-Tech Personnel, Inc.*
Pierce, Matthew — *Source Services Corporation*
Pierotazio, John — *CPS Inc.*
Pigott, Daniel — *ESA Professional Consultants*
Pillow, Charles — *Source Services Corporation*
Pineda, Rosanna — *Source Services Corporation*
Pirro, Sheri — *Source Services Corporation*
Plant, Jerry — *Source Services Corporation*
Pliszka, Donald J. — *Praxis Partners*
Poirier, Frank — *Juntunen-Combs-Poirier*
Poirier, Roland L. — *Poirier, Hoevel & Co.*
Pomerance, Mark — *CPS Inc.*
Porter, Albert — *The Experts*
Pototo, Brian — *Source Services Corporation*
Powell, Danny — *Source Services Corporation*
Powell, Gregory — *Source Services Corporation*
Power, Michael — *Source Services Corporation*
Pregeant, David — *Source Services Corporation*
Preusse, Eric — *Source Services Corporation*

Price, Andrew G. — *The Thomas Tucker Company*
Price, Carl — *Source Services Corporation*
Price, Kenneth M. — *Messett Associates, Inc.*
Proct, Nina — *Martin H. Bauman Associates, Inc.*
Ramler, Carolyn S. — *The Corporate Connection, Ltd.*
Rasmussen, Timothy — *Source Services Corporation*
Ratajczak, Paul — *Source Services Corporation*
Ray, Marianne C. — *Callan Associates, Ltd.*
Reardon, Joseph — *Source Services Corporation*
Reddick, David C. — *Horton International*
Redding, Denise — *The Douglas Reiter Company, Inc.*
Reece, Christopher S. — *Reece & Mruk Partners*
Reed, Susan — *Source Services Corporation*
Reid, Katherine — *Source Services Corporation*
Reid, Scott — *Source Services Corporation*
Reifel, Laurie — *Reifel & Assocaites*
Reifersen, Ruth F. — *The Jonathan Stevens Group, Inc.*
Reisinger, George L. — *Sigma Group International*
Reiter, Douglas — *The Douglas Reiter Company, Inc.*
Remillard, Brad M. — *CJA - The Adler Group*
Renfroe, Ann-Marie — *Source Services Corporation*
Renick, Cynthia L. — *Morgan Hunter Corp.*
Rennell, Thomas — *Source Services Corporation*
Renteria, Elizabeth — *Source Services Corporation*
Resnic, Alan — *Source Services Corporation*
Reticker, Peter — *MSI International*
Reuter, Tandom — *CPS Inc.*
Reyman, Susan — *S. Reyman & Associates Ltd.*
Reynolds, Gregory P. — *Roberts Ryan and Bentley*
Reynolds, Laura — *Source Services Corporation*
Rhoades, Michael — *Source Services Corporation*
Riederer, Larry — *CPS Inc.*
Rimmel, James E. — *The Hindman Company*
Rios, Vince — *Source Services Corporation*
Rios, Vincent — *Source Services Corporation*
Robb, Tammy — *Source Services Corporation*
Roberts, Scott — *Jonas, Walters & Assoc., Inc.*
Robertson, Sherry — *Source Services Corporation*
Robinson, Bruce — *Bruce Robinson Associates*
Robinson, Tonya — *Source Services Corporation*
Rockwell, Bruce — *Source Services Corporation*
Rodriguez, Manuel — *Source Services Corporation*
Rohan, James E. — *J.P. Canon Associates*
Rohan, Kevin A. — *J.P. Canon Associates*
Rojo, Rafael — *A.T. Kearney, Inc.*
Romanello, Daniel P. — *Spencer Stuart*
Romang, Paula — *Agri-Tech Personnel, Inc.*
Rose, Robert — *ESA Professional Consultants*
Rosen, Mitchell — *Source Services Corporation*
Rosenstein, Michele — *Source Services Corporation*
Rotella, Marshall W. — *The Corporate Connection, Ltd.*
Roth, Robert J. — *Williams, Roth & Krueger Inc.*
Rothenbush, Clayton — *Source Services Corporation*
Rowland, James — *Source Services Corporation*
Rudolph, Kenneth — *Kossuth & Associates, Inc.*

Rush, Michael E. — *D.A.L. Associates, Inc.*
Rusher, William H. — *Rusher, Loscavio & LoPresto*
Ryan, David — *Source Services Corporation*
Ryan, Kathleen — *Source Services Corporation*
Ryan, Mark — *Source Services Corporation*
Sacerdote, John — *Raymond Karsan Associates*
Sadaj, Michael — *Source Services Corporation*
Salet, Michael — *Source Services Corporation*
Saletra, Andrew — *CPS Inc.*
Samsel, Randy — *Source Services Corporation*
Samuelson, Robert — *Source Services Corporation*
Sanchez, William — *Source Services Corporation*
Sanders, Natalie — *CPS Inc.*
Sanders, Spencer H. — *Battalia Winston International*
Sanow, Robert — *Cochran, Cochran & Yale, Inc.*
Santiago, Benefrido — *Source Services Corporation*
Sapers, Mark — *Source Services Corporation*
Saposhnik, Doron — *Source Services Corporation*
Sardella, Sharon — *Source Services Corporation*
Sarna, Edmund A. — *Jonas, Walters & Assoc., Inc.*
Sathe, Mark A. — *Sathe & Associates, Inc.*
Savela, Edward — *Source Services Corporation*
Saxon, Alexa — *Woodworth International Group*
Scalamera, Tom — *CPS Inc.*
Schlpma, Christine — *Advanced Executive Resources*
Schneiderman, Gerald — *Management Resource Associates, Inc.*
Schroeder, James — *Source Services Corporation*
Schroeder, Steven J. — *Blau Mancino Schroeder*
Schueneman, David — *CPS Inc.*
Schultz, Randy — *Source Services Corporation*
Schwalbach, Robert — *Source Services Corporation*
Schweichler, Lee J. — *Schweichler Associates, Inc.*
Schwinden, William — *Source Services Corporation*
Scimone, James — *Source Services Corporation*
Scimone, Jim — *Source Services Corporation*
Scoff, Barry — *Source Services Corporation*
Scott, Gordon S. — *Search Advisors International Corp.*
Seamon, Kenneth — *Source Services Corporation*
Sell, David — *Source Services Corporation*
Selvaggi, Esther — *Source Services Corporation*
Semple, David — *Source Services Corporation*
Serba, Kerri — *Source Services Corporation*
Sevilla, Claudio A. — *Crawford & Crofford*
Shackleford, David — *Source Services Corporation*
Shanks, Jennifer — *Source Services Corporation*
Shapanka, Samuel — *Source Services Corporation*
Shapiro, Elaine — *CPS Inc.*
Shawhan, Heather — *Source Services Corporation*
Shelton, Jonathan — *Source Services Corporation*
Shenfield, Peter — *A.T. Kearney, Inc.*
Shepard, Michael J. — *MSI International*
Shufelt, Doug — *Sink, Walker, Boltrus International*
Sibbald, John R. — *John Sibbald Associates, Inc.*
Siegler, Jody Cukiir — *A.T. Kearney, Inc.*
Signer, Julie — *CPS Inc.*

Silcott, Marvin L. — *Marvin L. Silcott & Associates, Inc.*
Sill, Igor M. — *Geneva Group International*
Silvas, Stephen D. — *Roberson and Company*
Silver, Kit — *Source Services Corporation*
Silver, Lee — *L. A. Silver Associates, Inc.*
Simmons, Deborah — *Source Services Corporation*
Simmons, Sandra K. — *MSI International*
Sink, Cliff — *Sink, Walker, Boltrus International*
Sirena, Evelyn — *Source Services Corporation*
Skunda, Donna M. — *Allerton Heneghan & O'Neill*
Slayton, Richard C. — *Slayton International, Inc./I-I-C Partners*
Sloan, Scott — *Source Services Corporation*
Slosar, John — *Boyden*
Smith, Ana Luz — *Smith Search, S.C.*
Smith, David P. — *HRS, Inc.*
Smith, John E. — *Smith Search, S.C.*
Smith, Lawrence — *Source Services Corporation*
Smith, Lydia — *The Corporate Connection, Ltd.*
Smith, Ronald V. — *Coe & Company International Inc.*
Smith, Timothy — *Source Services Corporation*
Smock, Cynthia — *Source Services Corporation*
Smoller, Howard — *Source Services Corporation*
Snowden, Charles — *Source Services Corporation*
Snowhite, Rebecca — *Source Services Corporation*
Snyder, C. Edward — *Horton International*
Snyder, James F. — *Snyder & Company*
Sochacki, Michael — *Source Services Corporation*
Song, Louis — *Source Services Corporation*
Sorgen, Jay — *Source Services Corporation*
Sostilio, Louis — *Source Services Corporation*
Souder, E.G. — *Souder & Associates*
Spector, Michael — *Source Services Corporation*
Spencer, John — *Source Services Corporation*
Spencer, John — *Source Services Corporation*
Spera, Stefanie — *A.T. Kearney, Inc.*
Spiegel, Gayle — *L. A. Silver Associates, Inc.*
Spoutz, Paul — *Source Services Corporation*
Spriggs, Robert D. — *Spriggs & Company, Inc.*
St. Martin, Peter — *Source Services Corporation*
Stack, Richard — *Source Services Corporation*
Stanton, John — *A.T. Kearney, Inc.*
Stark, Jeff — *Thorne, Brieger Associates Inc.*
Steele, Daniel — *Cochran, Cochran & Yale, Inc.*
Steer, Joe — *CPS Inc.*
Stein, Terry W. — *Stewart, Stein and Scott, Ltd.*
Steinem, Andy — *Dahl-Morrow International*
Steinem, Barbra — *Dahl-Morrow International*
Stephens, Andrew — *Source Services Corporation*
Stephens, John — *Source Services Corporation*
Stern, Stephen — *CPS Inc.*
Sterner, Doug — *CPS Inc.*
Stewart, Jeffrey O. — *Stewart, Stein and Scott, Ltd.*
Stewart, Ross M. — *Human Resources Network Partners Inc.*
Stone, Susan L. — *Stone Enterprises Ltd.*
Storm, Deborah — *Source Services Corporation*
Stranberg, James R. — *Callan Associates, Ltd.*
Strander, Dervin — *Source Services Corporation*
Straube, Stanley H. — *Straube Associates*
Strickland, Katie — *Grantham & Co., Inc.*

Strom, Mark N. — *Search Advisors International Corp.*
Susoreny, Samali — *Source Services Corporation*
Sussman, Lynda — *Gilbert Tweed/INESA*
Swanner, William — *Source Services Corporation*
Swanson, Dick — *Raymond Karsan Associates*
Sweeney, Anne — *Source Services Corporation*
Sweet, Randall — *Source Services Corporation*
Tankson, Dawn — *Source Services Corporation*
Tanner, Frank — *Source Services Corporation*
Tanner, Gary — *Source Services Corporation*
Taylor, Conrad G. — *MSI International*
Teger, Stella — *Source Services Corporation*
ten Cate, Herman H. — *Stoneham Associates Corp.*
Tenero, Kymberly — *Source Services Corporation*
Theobald, David B. — *Theobald & Associates*
Thielman, Joseph — *Barrett Partners*
Thomas, Cheryl M. — *CPS Inc.*
Thomas, Jeffrey — *Fairfaxx Corporation*
Thomas, Kim — *CPS Inc.*
Thompson, John R. — *MSI International*
Thompson, Kenneth L. — *McCormack & Farrow*
Thompson, Leslie — *Source Services Corporation*
Thrower, Troy — *Source Services Corporation*
Tilley, Kyle — *Source Services Corporation*
Tincu, John C. — *Ferneborg & Associates, Inc.*
Tobin, Christopher — *Source Services Corporation*
Tovrog, Dan — *CPS Inc.*
Tracey, Jack — *Management Assistance Group, Inc.*
Trefzer, Kristie — *Source Services Corporation*
Trewhella, Michael — *Source Services Corporation*
Trice, Renee — *Source Services Corporation*
Trieschmann, Daniel — *Source Services Corporation*
Trimble, Patricia — *Source Services Corporation*
Trimble, Rhonda — *Source Services Corporation*
Truemper, Dean — *CPS Inc.*
Truex, John F. — *Morton, McCorkle & Associates, Inc.*
Truitt, Thomas B. — *Southwestern Professional Services*
Tryon, Katey — *DeFrain, Mayer LLC*
Tscelli, Maureen — *Source Services Corporation*
Tschan, Stephen — *Source Services Corporation*
Tucci, Joseph — *Fairfaxx Corporation*
Tucker, Thomas A. — *The Thomas Tucker Company*
Tullberg, Tina — *CPS Inc.*
Tunney, William — *Grant Cooper and Associates*
Turner, Raymond — *Source Services Corporation*
Tursi, Deborah J. — *The Corporate Connection, Ltd.*
Tweed, Janet — *Gilbert Tweed/INESA*
Twomey, James — *Source Services Corporation*
Ulbert, Nancy — *Aureus Group*
Uzzel, Linda — *Source Services Corporation*
Vairo, Leonard A. — *Christian & Timbers*
Van Biesen, Jacques A.H. — *Search Group Inc.*
Van Norman, Ben — *Source Services Corporation*
Vandenbulcke, Cynthia — *Source Services Corporation*
Varney, Monique — *Source Services Corporation*
Varrichio, Michael — *Source Services Corporation*
Velez, Hector — *Source Services Corporation*

Velten, Mark T. — *Boyden*
Vilella, Paul — *Source Services Corporation*
Villella, Paul — *Source Services Corporation*
Vinett-Hessel, Deidre — *Source Services Corporation*
Visnich, L. Christine — *Bason Associates Inc.*
Viviano, Cathleen — *Source Services Corporation*
Vlcek, Thomas J. — *Vlcek & Company, Inc.*
Volkman, Arthur — *Cochran, Cochran & Yale, Inc.*
Vourakis, Zan — *ZanExec LLC*
Wacholz, Rick — *A.T. Kearney, Inc.*
Wade, Christy — *Source Services Corporation*
Waldoch, D. Mark — *Barnes Development Group, LLC*
Waldrop, Gary R. — *MSI International*
Walker, Ann — *Source Services Corporation*
Walker, Douglas G. — *Sink, Walker, Boltrus International*
Walker, Ewing J. — *Ward Howell International, Inc.*
Walker, Rose — *Source Services Corporation*
Wallace, Toby — *Source Services Corporation*
Walsh, Denis — *Professional Staffing Consultants*
Walters, William F. — *Jonas, Walters & Assoc., Inc.*
Ward, Les — *Source Services Corporation*
Ward, Robert — *Source Services Corporation*
Warnock, Phyl — *Source Services Corporation*
Watkinson, Jim W. — *The Badger Group*
Watson, James — *MSI International*
Waymire, Pamela — *Source Services Corporation*
Wayne, Cary S. — *ProSearch Inc.*
Webb, George H. — *Webb, Johnson Associates, Inc.*
Webber, Edward — *Source Services Corporation*
Weeks, Glenn — *Source Services Corporation*
Wein, Michael S. — *Media Management Resources, Inc.*
Wein, William — *Media Management Resources, Inc.*
Weis, Theodore — *Source Services Corporation*
Weiss, Elizabeth — *Source Services Corporation*
Weissman-Rosenthal, Abbe — *ALW Research International*
Wenz, Alexander — *Source Services Corporation*
Wessling, Jerry — *Source Services Corporation*
Westfall, Ed — *Zwell International*
White, William C. — *Venture Resources Inc.*
Whitfield, Jack — *Source Services Corporation*
Wilburn, Dan — *Kaye-Bassman International Corp.*
Wilkinson, Barbara — *Beall & Company, Inc.*
Willbrandt, Curt — *Source Services Corporation*
Williams, Gary L. — *Barnes Development Group, LLC*
Williams, Jack — *A.T. Kearney, Inc.*
Williams, John — *Source Services Corporation*
Williams, Roger K. — *Williams, Roth & Krueger Inc.*
Wilson, Joyce — *Source Services Corporation*
Wingate, Mary — *Source Services Corporation*
Winitz, Joel — *GSW Consulting Group, Inc.*
Winitz, Marla — *GSW Consulting Group, Inc.*
Winkowski, Stephen — *Source Services Corporation*

Winnicki, Kimberly — *Source Services Corporation*
Winograd, Glenn — *Criterion Executive Search, Inc.*
Winston, Dale — *Battalia Winston International*
Witzgall, William — *Source Services Corporation*
Wolf, Donald — *Source Services Corporation*
Wolfe, Peter — *Source Services Corporation*
Wood, Gary — *Source Services Corporation*
Woodmansee, Bruce J. — *Tully/Woodmansee International, Inc.*
Woods, Craig — *Source Services Corporation*
Woodworth, Gail — *Woodworth International Group*
Wooller, Edmund A.M. — *Windsor International*
Woomer, Jerome — *Source Services Corporation*
Workman, David — *Source Services Corporation*
Wright, A. Leo — *The Hindman Company*
Wycoff-Viola, Amy — *Source Services Corporation*
Yaekle, Gary — *Tully/Woodmansee International, Inc.*
Yeaton, Robert — *Source Services Corporation*
Youngberg, David — *Source Services Corporation*
Zadfar, Maryanne — *The Thomas Tucker Company*
Zaleta, Andy R. — *A.T. Kearney, Inc.*
Zamborsky, George — *Boyden*
Zavrel, Mark — *Source Services Corporation*
Zay, Thomas C. — *Boyden/Zay & Company*
Zegel, Gary — *Source Services Corporation*
Zimbal, Mark — *Source Services Corporation*
Zimont, Scott — *Source Services Corporation*
Zivic, Janis M. — *Spencer Stuart*
Zwell, Michael — *Zwell International*

4. Finance/Accounting

Abbott, Peter D. — *The Abbott Group, Inc.*
Abell, Vincent W. — *MSI International*
Abernathy, Donald E. — *Don Richard Associates of Charlotte*
Abert, Janice — *Ledbetter/Davidson International, Inc.*
Abramson, Roye — *Source Services Corporation*
Ackerman, Larry R. — *Spectrum Search Associates, Inc.*
Adams, Amy — *Richard, Wayne and Roberts*
Adams, Len — *The KPA Group*
Adler, Louis S. — *CJA - The Adler Group*
Agee, Jo Etta — *Chrisman & Company, Incorporated*
Akin, J.R. "Jack" — *J.R. Akin & Company Inc.*
Albert, Richard — *Source Services Corporation*
Alexander, John T. — *Telford, Adams & Alexander*
Alford, Holly — *Source Services Corporation*
Allen, Scott — *Chrisman & Company, Incorporated*
Allen, William L. — *The Hindman Company*
Allgire, Mary L. — *Kenzer Corp.*
Alringer, Marc — *Source Services Corporation*
Altreuter, Rose — *ALTCO Temporary Services*
Altreuter, Rose — *The ALTCO Group*
Ambler, Peter W. — *Peter W. Ambler Company*
Amico, Robert — *Source Services Corporation*
Amilowski, Maria — *Highland Search Group*
Anderson, Maria H. — *Barton Associates, Inc.*
Anderson, Mary — *Source Services Corporation*

Anderson, Matthew — *Source Services Corporation*

Anderson, Richard — *Grant Cooper and Associates*

Anderson, Shawn — *Temporary Accounting Personnel, Inc.*

Anderson, Terry — *Intech Summit Group, Inc.*

Andujo, Michele M. — *Chrisman & Company, Incorporated*

Anwar, Tarin — *Jay Gaines & Company, Inc.*

Archer, Sandra F. — *Ryan, Miller & Associates Inc.*

Argenio, Michelangelo — *Spencer Stuart*

Argentin, Jo — *Executive Placement Consultants, Inc.*

Aronow, Lawrence E. — *Aronow Associates, Inc.*

Ascher, Susan P. — *The Ascher Group*

Ashton, Edward J. — *E.J. Ashton & Associates, Ltd.*

Aston, Kathy — *Marra Peters & Partners*

Austin Lockton, Kathy — *Juntunen-Combs-Poirier*

Axelrod, Nancy R. — *A.T. Kearney, Inc.*

Aydelotte, G. Thomas — *Ingram & Aydelotte Inc./I-I-C Partners*

Bacher, Judith — *Spencer Stuart*

Badger, Fred H. — *The Badger Group*

Baer, Kenneth — *Source Services Corporation*

Baglio, Robert — *Source Services Corporation*

Baier, Rebecca — *Source Services Corporation*

Bailey, Vanessa — *Highland Search Group*

Baje, Sarah — *Innovative Search Group, LLC*

Baker, Gary M. — *Cochran, Cochran & Yale, Inc.*

Baker, Gary M. — *Temporary Accounting Personnel, Inc.*

Baker, Gerry — *A.T. Kearney, Inc.*

Bakken, Mark — *Source Services Corporation*

Balchumas, Charles — *Source Services Corporation*

Baldock, Robert G. — *Ray & Berndtson/Lovas Stanley*

Baltaglia, Michael — *Cochran, Cochran & Yale, Inc.*

Balter, Sidney — *Source Services Corporation*

Banko, Scott — *Source Services Corporation*

Baranowski, Peter — *Source Services Corporation*

Barbour, Mary Beth — *Tully/Woodmansee International, Inc.*

Barch, Sherrie — *Furst Group/MPI*

Barger, H. Carter — *Barger & Sargeant, Inc.*

Barlow, Ken H. — *The Cherbonnier Group, Inc.*

Barnaby, Richard — *Source Services Corporation*

Barnes, Gary — *Brigade Inc.*

Barnes, Richard E. — *Barnes Development Group, LLC*

Barnes, Roanne L. — *Barnes Development Group, LLC*

Barnum, Toni M. — *Stone Murphy & Olson*

Barrett, J. David — *Heidrick & Struggles, Inc.*

Bartels, Fredrick — *Source Services Corporation*

Bartfield, Philip — *Source Services Corporation*

Bartholdi, Ted — *Bartholdi & Company, Inc.*

Bartholdi, Theodore G. — *Bartholdi & Company, Inc.*

Barton, Gary R. — *Barton Associates, Inc.*

Barton, James — *Source Services Corporation*

Bason, Maurice L. — *Bason Associates Inc.*

Bass, M. Lynn — *Ray & Berndtson*

Bass, Nate — *Jacobson Associates*

Batte, Carol — *Source Services Corporation*

Bauman, Martin H. — *Martin H. Bauman Associates, Inc.*

Bearman, Linda — *Grant Cooper and Associates*

Beaudin, Elizabeth C. — *Callan Associates, Ltd.*

Beaulieu, Genie A. — *Romac & Associates*

Beaver, Bentley H. — *The Onstott Group, Inc.*

Beaver, Robert — *Source Services Corporation*

Beckvold, John B. — *Atlantic Search Group, Inc.*

Belden, Jeannette — *Source Services Corporation*

Belin, Jean — *Boyden*

Bell, Lloyd W. — *O'Brien & Bell*

Bellano, Robert W. — *Stanton Chase International*

Benjamin, Maurita — *Source Services Corporation*

Bennett, Jo — *Battalia Winston International*

Benson, Edward — *Source Services Corporation*

Benson, Kate — *Rene Plessner Associates, Inc.*

Beran, Helena — *Michael J. Cavanagh and Associates*

Berger, Jeffrey — *Source Services Corporation*

Bernard, Bryan — *Source Services Corporation*

Bernas, Sharon — *Source Services Corporation*

Berne, Marlene — *The Whitney Group*

Berry, Harold B. — *The Hindman Company*

Bettick, Michael J. — *A.J. Burton Group, Inc.*

Betts, Suzette — *Source Services Corporation*

Bickett, Nicole — *Source Services Corporation*

Bidelman, Richard — *Source Services Corporation*

Biolsi, Joseph — *Source Services Corporation*

Birns, Douglas — *Source Services Corporation*

Bladon, Andrew — *Don Richard Associates of Tampa, Inc.*

Blakslee, Jan H. — *J: Blakslee International, Ltd.*

Bland, Walter — *Source Services Corporation*

Blassaras, Peggy — *Source Services Corporation*

Blickle, Michael — *Source Services Corporation*

Bliley, Jerry — *Spencer Stuart*

Bloch, Suzanne — *Source Services Corporation*

Blocher, John — *Source Services Corporation*

Boel, Werner — *The Dalley Hewitt Company*

Bohn, Steve J. — *MSI International*

Bond, Robert J. — *Romac & Associates*

Bonifield, Len — *Bonifield Associates*

Bonnell, William R. — *Bonnell Associates Ltd.*

Booth, Ronald — *Source Services Corporation*

Borkin, Andrew — *Strategic Advancement Inc.*

Borland, James — *Goodrich & Sherwood Associates, Inc.*

Bormann, Cindy Ann — *MSI International*

Bosward, Allan — *Source Services Corporation*

Bourrie, Sharon D. — *Chartwell Partners International, Inc.*

Bovich, Maryann C. — *Higdon Prince Inc.*

Bowden, Otis H. — *BowdenGlobal, Inc.*

Brackenbury, Robert — *Bowman & Marshall, Inc.*

Brackman, Janet — *Dahl-Morrow International*

Bradley, Dalena — *Woodworth International Group*

Bradshaw, Monte — *Christian & Timbers*

Brady, Dick — *William Guy & Associates*

Brandeau, John — *Chrisman & Company, Incorporated*

Brandenburg, David — *Professional Staffing Consultants*

Brassard, Gary — *Source Services Corporation*

Bratches, Howard — *Thorndike Deland Associates*

Bremer, Brian — *Source Services Corporation*

Brennan, Patrick J. — *Handy HRM Corp.*
Brewster, Edward — *Source Services Corporation*
Brieger, Steve — *Thorne, Brieger Associates Inc.*
Brinson, Robert — *MSI International*
Brocaglia, Joyce — *Alta Associates, Inc.*
Bronger, Patricia — *Source Services Corporation*
Brother, Joy — *Charles Luntz & Associates. Inc.*
Brown, Charlene N. — *Accent on Achievement, Inc.*
Brown, Clifford — *Source Services Corporation*
Brown, D. Perry — *Don Richard Associates of Washington, D.C., Inc.*
Brown, Daniel — *Source Services Corporation*
Brown, Franklin Key — *Handy HRM Corp.*
Brown, Gina — *Strategic Alliance Network, Ltd.*
Brown, Larry C. — *Horton International*
Brown, Lawrence Anthony — *MSI International*
Brown, Steffan — *Woodworth International Group*
Brown, Steven — *Source Services Corporation*
Browne, Michael — *Source Services Corporation*
Brudno, Robert J. — *Savoy Partners, Ltd.*
Brunner, Terry — *Source Services Corporation*
Bruno, Deborah F. — *The Hindman Company*
Bryant, Richard D. — *Bryant Associates, Inc.*
Bryant, Shari G. — *Bryant Associates, Inc.*
Brzezinski, Ronald T. — *Callan Associates, Ltd.*
Buchalter, Allyson — *The Whitney Group*
Buckles, Donna — *Cochran, Cochran & Yale, Inc.*
Buggy, Linda — *Bonnell Associates Ltd.*
Bump, Gerald J. — *D.E. Foster Partners Inc.*
Burch, Donald — *Source Services Corporation*
Burchard, Stephen R. — *Burchard & Associates, Inc.*
Burden, Gene — *The Cherbonnier Group, Inc.*
Burfield, Elaine — *Skott/Edwards Consultants, Inc.*
Burke, John — *The Experts*
Burke, Karen A. — *Mazza & Riley, Inc. (a Korn/Ferry International affiliate)*
Burkhill, John — *The Talley Group*
Burkland, Skott B. — *Skott/Edwards Consultants, Inc.*
Burns, Alan — *The Enns Partners Inc.*
Burns, Terence N. — *D.E. Foster Partners Inc.*
Busch, Jack — *Busch International*
Busterna, Charles — *The KPA Group*
Butcher, Pascale — *F-O-R-T-U-N-E Personnel Consultants of Manatee County*
Butler, Kirby B. — *The Butlers Company Insurance Recruiters*
Butterfass, Stanley — *Butterfass, Pepe & MacCallan Inc.*
Buttrey, Daniel — *Source Services Corporation*
Buzolits, Patrick — *Source Services Corporation*
Bye, Randy — *Romac & Associates*
Byrnes, Thomas A. — *The Search Alliance, Inc.*
Cafero, Les — *Source Services Corporation*
Caldwell, William R. — *Pearson, Caldwell & Farnsworth, Inc.*
Calivas, Kay — *A.J. Burton Group, Inc.*
Call, David — *Cochran, Cochran & Yale, Inc.*
Callan, Robert M. — *Callan Associates, Ltd.*
Cameron, James W. — *Cameron Consulting*
Campbell, E. — *Source Services Corporation*
Campbell, Gary — *Romac & Associates*
Campbell, Jeff — *Source Services Corporation*
Campbell, Robert Scott — *Wellington Management Group*

Campbell, Robert Scott — *Wellington Management Group*
Cannavino, John J. — *Financial Resource Associates, Inc.*
Cannavino, Matthew J. — *Financial Resource Associates, Inc.*
Cannavo, Louise — *The Whitney Group*
Cannon, Alexis — *Richard, Wayne and Roberts*
Capizzi, Karen — *Cochran, Cochran & Yale, Inc.*
Carideo, Joseph — *Thorndike Deland Associates*
Carlson, Eric — *Source Services Corporation*
Carlson, Judith — *Bowman & Marshall, Inc.*
Carnal, Rick — *Source Services Corporation*
Carro, Carl R. — *Executive Search Consultants International, Inc.*
Carter, Linda — *Source Services Corporation*
Carvalho-Esteves, Maria — *Source Services Corporation*
Cary, Con — *Cary & Associates*
Casal, Daniel G. — *Bonifield Associates*
Cashen, Anthony B. — *Lamalie Amrop International*
Castine, Michael P. — *Highland Search Group*
Castle, Lisa — *Source Services Corporation*
Cavanagh, Michael J. — *Michael J. Cavanagh and Associates*
Cersosimo, Rocco — *Source Services Corporation*
Chappell, Peter — *Robertson & Associates*
Chappell, Peter — *The Bankers Group*
Chase, James — *Source Services Corporation*
Chatterjie, Alok — *MSI International*
Cheah, Victor — *Source Services Corporation*
Cherbonnier, L. Michael — *TCG International, Inc.*
Cherbonnier, L. Michael — *The Cherbonnier Group, Inc.*
Chndler, Brad J. — *Furst Group/MPI*
Cho, Ui — *Richard, Wayne and Roberts*
Christenson, H. Alan — *Christenson & Hutchison*
Christian, Philip — *Ray & Berndtson*
Christman, Joel — *Source Services Corporation*
Chronopoulos, Dennis — *Source Services Corporation*
Citarella, Richard A. — *A.T. Kearney, Inc.*
Cizek, John T. — *Cizek Associates, Inc.*
Cizek, Marti J. — *Cizek Associates, Inc.*
Clake, Bob — *Furst Group/MPI*
Clarey, William A. — *Preng & Associates, Inc.*
Clark, Evan — *The Whitney Group*
Clarke Smith, Jamie — *Kaye-Bassman International Corp.*
Clauhsen, Elizabeth A. — *Savoy Partners, Ltd.*
Clawson, Bob — *Source Services Corporation*
Clawson, Robert — *Source Services Corporation*
Clayton, Fred J. — *Berkhemer Clayton Incorporated*
Clemens, Bill — *Spencer Stuart*
Cloutier, Gisella — *Dinte Resources, Inc.*
Cocchiaro, Richard — *Romac & Associates*
Cocconi, Alan — *Source Services Corporation*
Cochran, Scott P. — *The Badger Group*
Cochrun, James — *Source Services Corporation*
Coffman, Brian — *Kossuth & Associates, Inc.*
Cohen, Michael R. — *Intech Summit Group, Inc.*
Cohen, Robert C. — *Intech Summit Group, Inc.*
Cole, Kevin — *Don Richard Associates of Washington, D.C., Inc.*

Cole, Rosalie — *Source Services Corporation*
Coleman, J. Kevin — *J. Kevin Coleman & Associates, Inc.*
Collard, Joseph A. — *Spencer Stuart*
Collins, Scott — *Source Services Corporation*
Collins, Stephen — *The Johnson Group, Inc.*
Colman, Michael — *Executive Placement Consultants, Inc.*
Comai, Christine — *Source Services Corporation*
Combs, Stephen L. — *Juntunen-Combs-Poirier*
Combs, Thomas — *Source Services Corporation*
Cona, Joseph A. — *Cona Personnel Search*
Conard, Rodney J. — *Conard Associates, Inc.*
Coneys, Bridget — *Source Services Corporation*
Connaghan, Linda — *Bowman & Marshall, Inc.*
Connelly, Kevin M. — *Spencer Stuart*
Conway, Maureen — *Conway & Associates*
Cook, Charlene — *Source Services Corporation*
Cook, Dennis — *A.T. Kearney, Inc.*
Cooke, Katherine H. — *Horton International*
Corso, Glen S. — *Chartwell Partners International, Inc.*
Cortina Del Valle, Pedro — *Ray & Berndtson*
Costello, Lynda — *Coe & Company International Inc.*
Cotugno, James — *Source Services Corporation*
Coughlin, Stephen — *Source Services Corporation*
Courtney, Brendan — *A.J. Burton Group, Inc.*
Cox, William — *E.J. Ashton & Associates, Ltd.*
Coyle, Hugh F. — *A.J. Burton Group, Inc.*
Cramer, Paul J. — *C/R Associates*
Crane, Howard C. — *Chartwell Partners International, Inc.*
Crath, Paul F. — *Price Waterhouse*
Crawford, Cassondra — *Don Richard Associates of Washington, D.C., Inc.*
Crecos, Gregory P. — *Gregory Michaels and Associates, Inc.*
Crist, Peter — *Crist Partners, Ltd.*
Critchley, Walter — *Cochran, Cochran & Yale, Inc.*
Critchley, Walter — *Temporary Accounting Personnel, Inc.*
Cruse, O.D. — *Spencer Stuart*
Crystal, Jonathan A. — *Spencer Stuart*
Cuddihy, Paul — *Dahl-Morrow International*
Cuddy, Brian C. — *Romac & Associates*
Cuddy, Patricia — *Source Services Corporation*
Cunningham, Lawrence — *Howard Fischer Associates, Inc.*
Cunningham, Robert Y. — *Goodrich & Sherwood Associates, Inc.*
Curren, Camella — *Source Services Corporation*
Curtis, Ellissa — *Cochran, Cochran & Yale, Inc.*
Cutka, Matthew — *Source Services Corporation*
Dabich, Thomas M. — *Robert Harkins Associates, Inc.*
Daniels, Alfred — *Alfred Daniels & Associates*
Daniels, C. Eugene — *Sigma Group International*
Dankberg, Iris — *Source Services Corporation*
Davis, C. Scott — *Source Services Corporation*
Davis, Elease — *Source Services Corporation*
Davis, G. Gordon — *Davis & Company*
Davis, Joan — *MSI International*
Dawson, William — *Source Services Corporation*
De Brun, Thomas P. — *Ray & Berndtson*
de Cholnoky, Andrea — *Spencer Stuart*

de Palacios, Jeannette C. — *J. Palacios & Associates, Inc.*
Deaver, Henry C. — *Ray & Berndtson*
Debus, Wayne — *Source Services Corporation*
Deck, Jack — *Source Services Corporation*
DeCorrevont, James — *DeCorrevont & Associates*
DeCorrevont, James — *DeCorrevont & Associates*
Del Pino, William — *National Search, Inc.*
Delaney, Patrick J. — *Sensible Solutions, Inc.*
Delmonico, Laura — *A.J. Burton Group, Inc.*
DeMarco, Robert — *Source Services Corporation*
Demchak, James P. — *Sandhurst Associates*
Desgrosellier, Gary P. — *Personnel Unlimited/Executive Search*
Desmond, Dennis — *Beall & Company, Inc.*
Desmond, Mary — *Source Services Corporation*
Dever, Mary — *Source Services Corporation*
Devito, Alice — *Source Services Corporation*
deWilde, David M. — *Chartwell Partners International, Inc.*
Dewing, Jesse J. — *Don Richard Associates of Charlotte*
Dezember, Steve — *Ray & Berndtson*
Di Filippo, Thomas — *Source Services Corporation*
DiCioccio, Carmen — *Cochran, Cochran & Yale, Inc.*
Dickson, Duke — *A.D. & Associates Executive Search, Inc.*
Dieckmann, Ralph E. — *Dieckmann & Associates, Ltd.*
Diers, Gary — *Source Services Corporation*
Dietz, David S. — *MSI International*
DiGiovanni, Charles — *Penn Search*
DiMarchi, Paul — *DiMarchi Partners, Inc.*
DiMarchi, Paul — *DiMarchi Partners, Inc.*
Dingeldey, Peter E. — *Search Advisors International Corp.*
Dingman, Bruce — *Robert W. Dingman Company, Inc.*
Dinte, Paul — *Dinte Resources, Inc.*
DiPiazza, Joseph — *Boyden*
DiSalvo, Fred — *The Cambridge Group Ltd*
Diskin, Rochelle — *Search West, Inc.*
Dittmar, Richard — *Source Services Corporation*
Divine, Robert S. — *O'Shea, Divine & Company, Inc.*
Do, Sonnie — *Whitney & Associates, Inc.*
Dobrow, Samuel — *Source Services Corporation*
Doele, Donald C. — *Goodrich & Sherwood Associates, Inc.*
Donahue, Debora — *Source Services Corporation*
Donath, Linda — *Dahl-Morrow International*
Donnelly, Patti — *Source Services Corporation*
Dorfner, Martin — *Source Services Corporation*
Doukas, Jon A. — *Professional Bank Services, Inc. D/B/A Executive Search, Inc.*
Dowdall, Jean — *A.T. Kearney, Inc.*
Dowell, Chris — *The Abbott Group, Inc.*
Dowell, Mary K. — *Professional Search Associates*
Dowlatzadch, Homayoun — *Source Services Corporation*
Downs, William — *Source Services Corporation*
Doyle, James W. — *Executive Search Consultants International, Inc.*
Dreifus, Donald — *Search West, Inc.*
Dressler, Ralph — *Romac & Associates*

Drury, James J. — *Spencer Stuart*
Dubbs, William — *Williams Executive Search, Inc.*
Ducruet, Linda K. — *Heidrick & Struggles, Inc.*
Duelks, John — *Source Services Corporation*
Dunbar, Marilynne — *Ray & Berndtson/Lovas Stanley*
Duncan, Dana — *Source Services Corporation*
Dunkel, David L. — *Romac & Associates*
Dunlow, Aimee — *Source Services Corporation*
Dunman, Betsy L. — *Crawford & Crofford*
Dupont, Rick — *Source Services Corporation*
Durakis, Charles A. — *C.A. Durakis Associates, Inc.*
Eason, Jan C. — *Summit Group International*
Eddy, Terry — *William Guy & Associates*
Edwards, Dorothy — *MSI International*
Edwards, Ned — *Ingram & Aydelotte Inc./I-I-C Partners*
Edwards, Verba L. — *Wing Tips & Pumps, Inc.*
Eggert, Scott — *Source Services Corporation*
Ehrgott, Elizabeth — *The Ascher Group*
Ehrhart, Jennifer — *ADOW's Executeam*
Eiseman, Joe — *Source Services Corporation*
Eiseman, Joe — *Source Services Corporation*
Eiseman, Joe — *Source Services Corporation*
Elder, Tom — *Juntunen-Combs-Poirier*
Eldridge, Charles B. — *Ray & Berndtson*
Elli-Kirk, Matrice — *Spencer Stuart*
Ellis, David — *Don Richard Associates of Georgia, Inc.*
Ellis, Patricia — *Source Services Corporation*
Ellis, Ted K. — *The Hindman Company*
Ellis, William — *Interspace Interactive Inc.*
Elster, Irv — *Spectrum Search Associates, Inc.*
Emerson, Randall — *Source Services Corporation*
Engelbert, Kimberly S. — *Watson International, Inc.*
England, Mark — *Austin-McGregor International*
Engle, Bryan — *Source Services Corporation*
Enns, George — *The Enns Partners Inc.*
Erder, Debra — *Canny, Bowen Inc.*
Erickson, Elaine — *Kenzer Corp.*
Ervin, Russell — *Source Services Corporation*
Esposito, Mark — *Christian & Timbers*
Eustis, Lucy R. — *MSI International*
Evans, Timothy — *Source Services Corporation*
Fabbro, Vivian — *A.T. Kearney, Inc.*
Fagerstrom, Jon — *Source Services Corporation*
Fales, Scott — *Source Services Corporation*
Fancher, Robert L. — *Bason Associates Inc.*
Fanning, Paul — *Source Services Corporation*
Farler, Wiley — *Source Services Corporation*
Farley, Leon A. — *Leon A. Farley Associates*
Farnsworth, John A. — *Pearson, Caldwell & Farnsworth, Inc.*
Fechheimer, Peter — *Source Services Corporation*
Fee, J. Curtis — *Spencer Stuart*
Feldman, Kimberley — *Atlantic Search Group, Inc.*
Ferguson, Kenneth — *Source Services Corporation*
Ferneborg, Jay W. — *Ferneborg & Associates, Inc.*
Ferneborg, John R. — *Ferneborg & Associates, Inc.*
Ferrari, S. Jay — *Ferrari Search Group*
Field, Andrew — *Source Services Corporation*
Fienberg, Chester — *Drummond Associates, Inc.*
Finkel, Leslie — *Source Services Corporation*

Finnerty, James — *Source Services Corporation*
Fischer, Adam — *Howard Fischer Associates, Inc.*
Fischer, Howard M. — *Howard Fischer Associates, Inc.*
Fischer, Janet L. — *Boyden*
Fischer, John C. — *Horton International*
Fisher, Neal — *Fisher Personnel Management Services*
Fishler, Stu — *A.T. Kearney, Inc.*
Fitzgerald, Brian — *Source Services Corporation*
Fitzgerald, Diane — *Fitzgerald Associates*
Fitzgerald, Geoffrey — *Fitzgerald Associates*
Flanagan, Robert M. — *Robert M. Flanagan & Associates, Ltd.*
Fleming, Marco — *MSI International*
Fletcher, David — *A.J. Burton Group, Inc.*
Flood, Michael — *Norman Broadbent International, Inc.*
Flora, Dodi — *Crawford & Crofford*
Florio, Robert — *Source Services Corporation*
Foote, Leland W. — *L.W. Foote Company*
Ford, Sandra D. — *The Ford Group, Inc.*
Foreman, David C. — *Koontz, Jeffries & Associates, Inc.*
Forestier, Lois — *Source Services Corporation*
Foster, Bradley — *Source Services Corporation*
Foster, Brian Scott — *Don Richard Associates of Charlotte*
Foster, Dwight E. — *D.E. Foster Partners Inc.*
Foster, John — *Source Services Corporation*
Fotia, Frank — *JDG Associates, Ltd.*
Fowler, Edward D.C. — *Higdon Prince Inc.*
Fowler, Thomas A. — *The Hindman Company*
Fox, Amanda C. — *Ray & Berndtson*
Francis, Brad — *Source Services Corporation*
Frantino, Michael — *Source Services Corporation*
Frazier, John — *Cochran, Cochran & Yale, Inc.*
Frederick, Dianne — *Source Services Corporation*
Freeh, Thomas — *Source Services Corporation*
Freier, Bruce — *Executive Referral Services, Inc.*
French, William G. — *Preng & Associates, Inc.*
Frerichs, April — *Ryan, Miller & Associates Inc.*
Fribush, Richard — *A.J. Burton Group, Inc.*
Friedman, Deborah — *Source Services Corporation*
Friedman, Helen E. — *McCormack & Farrow*
Frumess, Gregory — *D.E. Foster Partners Inc.*
Fuhrman, Dennis — *Source Services Corporation*
Fujino, Rickey — *Source Services Corporation*
Fulger, Herbert — *Source Services Corporation*
Fulton, Christine N. — *Highland Search Group*
Furlong, James W. — *Furlong Search, Inc.*
Furlong, James W. — *Furlong Search, Inc.*
Furlong, James W. — *Furlong Search, Inc.*
Fust, Sheely F. — *Ray & Berndtson*
Fyhrie, David — *Source Services Corporation*
Gabel, Gregory N. — *Canny, Bowen Inc.*
Gabriel, David L. — *The Arcus Group*
Gaffney, Megan — *Source Services Corporation*
Gaines, Jay — *Jay Gaines & Company, Inc.*
Galante, Suzanne M. — *Vlcek & Company, Inc.*
Galinski, Paul — *E.J. Ashton & Associates, Ltd.*
Gallagher, Terence M. — *Battalia Winston International*
Gamble, Ira — *Source Services Corporation*
Gantar, Donna — *Howard Fischer Associates, Inc.*
Gardiner, E. Nicholas P. — *Gardiner International*

Gardner, Michael — *Source Services Corporation*
Garfinkle, Steven M. — *Battalia Winston International*
Garland, Dick — *Dick Garland Consultants*
Garrett, Mark — *Source Services Corporation*
Gauthier, Robert C. — *Columbia Consulting Group*
Geiger, Jan — *Wilcox, Bertoux & Miller*
Gennawey, Robert — *Source Services Corporation*
George, Delores F. — *Delores F. George Human Resource Management & Consulting Industry*
Gerber, Mark J. — *Wellington Management Group*
Gerster, J.P. — *Juntunen-Combs-Poirier*
Gestwick, Daniel — *Cochran, Cochran & Yale, Inc.*
Ghurani, Mac — *Gary Kaplan & Associates*
Gibbs, John S. — *Spencer Stuart*
Giesy, John — *Source Services Corporation*
Gilbert, Jerry — *Gilbert & Van Campen International*
Gilbert, Patricia G. — *Lynch Miller Moore, Inc.*
Gilchrist, Robert J. — *Horton International*
Gilinsky, David — *Source Services Corporation*
Gill, Patricia — *Columbia Consulting Group*
Gill, Susan — *Plummer & Associates, Inc.*
Gilreath, James M. — *Gilreath Weatherby, Inc.*
Giries, Juliet D. — *Barton Associates, Inc.*
Glickman, Leenie — *Source Services Corporation*
Gluzman, Arthur — *Source Services Corporation*
Gnatowski, Bruce — *Source Services Corporation*
Goar, Duane R. — *Sandhurst Associates*
Gobert, Larry — *Professional Search Consultants*
Gold, Donald — *Executive Search, Ltd.*
Goldberg, Susan C. — *Susan C. Goldberg Associates*
Golde, Lisa — *Tully/Woodmansee International, Inc.*
Goldenberg, Susan — *Grant Cooper and Associates*
Goldsmith, Joseph B. — *Higdon Prince Inc.*
Goldstein, Gary — *The Whitney Group*
Goldstein, Steven G. — *The Jonathan Stevens Group, Inc.*
Gonzalez, Kristen — *A.J. Burton Group, Inc.*
Goodman, Dawn M. — *Bason Associates Inc.*
Goodman, Julie — *Search West, Inc.*
Goodwin, Gary — *Source Services Corporation*
Goodwin, Tim — *William Guy & Associates*
Gordon, Gerald L. — *E.G. Jones Associates, Ltd.*
Gordon, Teri — *Don Richard Associates of Washington, D.C., Inc.*
Gorman, Patrick — *Source Services Corporation*
Gorman, T. Patrick — *Techsearch Services, Inc.*
Gotlys, Jordan — *Stone Murphy & Olson*
Gourley, Timothy — *Source Services Corporation*
Gow, Roderick C. — *Lamalie Amrop International*
Grado, Eduardo — *Source Services Corporation*
Graff, Jack — *Source Services Corporation*
Graham, Shannon — *Source Services Corporation*
Grandinetti, Suzanne — *Source Services Corporation*
Grant, Michael — *Zwell International*
Grantham, John — *Grantham & Co., Inc.*
Grantham, Philip H. — *Columbia Consulting Group*
Grasch, Jerry E. — *The Hindman Company*

Grassl, Peter O. — *Bowman & Marshall, Inc.*
Graves, Rosemarie — *Don Richard Associates of Washington, D.C., Inc.*
Gray, Betty — *Accent on Achievement, Inc.*
Gray, Heather — *Source Services Corporation*
Gray, Mark — *Executive Referral Services, Inc.*
Gray, Russell — *Source Services Corporation*
Graziano, Lisa — *Source Services Corporation*
Grebenstein, Charles R. — *Skott/Edwards Consultants, Inc.*
Gresia, Paul — *Source Services Corporation*
Griffin, Cathy — *A.T. Kearney, Inc.*
Groban, Jack — *A.T. Kearney, Inc.*
Groner, David — *Source Services Corporation*
Grossman, James — *Source Services Corporation*
Grossman, Martin — *Source Services Corporation*
Grotenhuis, Dirkten — *Chrisman & Company, Incorporated*
Grotte, Lawrence C. — *Lautz Grotte Engler*
Grumulaitis, Leo — *Source Services Corporation*
Guc, Stephen — *Source Services Corporation*
Gudino, Richard — *Keith Bagg & Associates Inc.*
Gurnani, Angali — *Executive Placement Consultants, Inc.*
Gurtin, Kay L. — *Executive Options, Ltd.*
Guthrie, Stuart — *Source Services Corporation*
Guy, C. William — *William Guy & Associates*
Haas, Margaret P. — *The Haas Associates, Inc.*
Habelmann, Gerald B. — *Habelmann & Associates*
Haberman, Joseph C. — *A.T. Kearney, Inc.*
Hacker-Taylor, Dianna — *Source Services Corporation*
Haddad, Charles — *Romac & Associates*
Hagglund, Karl H. — *Simpson Associates, Inc.*
Haider, Martin — *Source Services Corporation*
Halbrich, Mitch — *A.J. Burton Group, Inc.*
Hales, Daphne — *Source Services Corporation*
Hall, Peter V. — *Chartwell Partners International, Inc.*
Halladay, Patti — *Intersource, Ltd.*
Haller, Mark — *Source Services Corporation*
Hallock, Peter B. — *Goodrich & Sherwood Associates, Inc.*
Hallstrom, Victoria — *The Whitney Group*
Hamilton, John R. — *Ray & Berndtson*
Hamm, Gary — *Source Services Corporation*
Hamm, Mary Kay — *Romac & Associates*
Hammond, Karla — *People Management Northeast Incorporated*
Hanes, Leah — *Ray & Berndtson*
Hanley, Alan P. — *Williams, Roth & Krueger Inc.*
Hanley, J. Patrick — *Canny, Bowen Inc.*
Hanley, Maureen E. — *Gilbert Tweed/INESA*
Hanley, Steven — *Source Services Corporation*
Hanna, Remon — *Source Services Corporation*
Hanson, Grant M. — *Goodrich & Sherwood Associates, Inc.*
Hanson, Lee — *Heidrick & Struggles, Inc.*
Harbaugh, Paul J. — *International Management Advisors, Inc.*
Harbert, David O. — *Sweeney Harbert & Mummert, Inc.*
Hardison, Richard L. — *Hardison & Company*
Hargis, N. Leann — *Montgomery Resources, Inc.*
Harney, Elyane — *Gary Kaplan & Associates*
Harp, Kimberly — *Source Services Corporation*

Harris, Jack — *A.T. Kearney, Inc.*
Harris, Julia — *The Whitney Group*
Harris, Seth O. — *Christian & Timbers*
Harrison, Patricia — *Source Services Corporation*
Hart, Crystal — *Source Services Corporation*
Hart, James — *Source Services Corporation*
Hart, Robert T. — *D.E. Foster Partners Inc.*
Harvey, Mike — *Advanced Executive Resources*
Harwood, Brian — *Source Services Corporation*
Haselby, James — *Source Services Corporation*
Hasten, Lawrence — *Source Services Corporation*
Haughton, Michael — *DeFrain, Mayer LLC*
Hauser, Martha — *Spencer Stuart*
Havener, Donald Clarke — *The Abbott Group, Inc.*
Hawksworth, A. Dwight — *A.D. & Associates Executive Search, Inc.*
Hay, William E. — *William E. Hay & Co.*
Hayes, Lee — *Source Services Corporation*
Haystead, Steve — *Advanced Executive Resources*
Healey, Joseph T. — *Highland Search Group*
Hebel, Robert W. — *R.W. Hebel Associates*
Hedlund, David — *Hedlund Corporation*
Heinrich, Scott — *Source Services Corporation*
Heinze, David — *Heinze & Associates, Inc.*
Hellebusch, Jerry — *Morgan Hunter Corp.*
Hellinger, Audrey W. — *Martin H. Bauman Associates, Inc.*
Hendrickson, Jill E. — *Gregory Michaels and Associates, Inc.*
Heneghan, Donald A. — *Allerton Heneghan & O'Neill*
Henn, George W. — *G.W. Henn & Company*
Henneberry, Ward — *Source Services Corporation*
Hennig, Sandra M. — *MSI International*
Hensley, Bert — *Morgan Samuels Co., Inc.*
Hensley, Gayla — *Atlantic Search Group, Inc.*
Hergenrather, Richard A. — *Hergenrather & Company*
Herman, Pat — *Whitney & Associates, Inc.*
Herman, Shelli — *Gary Kaplan & Associates*
Hernandez, Ruben — *Source Services Corporation*
Heroux, David — *Source Services Corporation*
Herzog, Sarah — *Source Services Corporation*
Hetherman, Margaret F. — *Highland Search Group*
Hewitt, Rives D. — *The Dalley Hewitt Company*
Hewitt, W. Davis — *The Dalley Hewitt Company*
Higbee, Joan — *Thorndike Deland Associates*
Higdon, Henry G. — *Higdon Prince Inc.*
Higgins, Donna — *Howard Fischer Associates, Inc.*
Hight, Susan — *Source Services Corporation*
Hilbert, Laurence — *Source Services Corporation*
Hildebrand, Thomas B. — *Professional Resources Group, Inc.*
Hilgenberg, Thomas — *Source Services Corporation*
Hill, Emery — *MSI International*
Hillyer, Carolyn — *Source Services Corporation*
Himes, Dirk — *A.T. Kearney, Inc.*
Himlin, Amy — *Cochran, Cochran & Yale, Inc.*
Hindman, Neil C. — *The Hindman Company*
Hinojosa, Oscar — *Source Services Corporation*
Hockett, William — *Hockett Associates, Inc.*
Hodge, Jeff — *Heidrick & Struggles, Inc.*

Hoevel, Michael J. — *Poirier, Hoevel & Co.*
Hoffman, Stephen — *Source Services Corporation*
Hofner, Andrew — *Source Services Corporation*
Holland, John A. — *Holland, McFadzean & Associates, Inc.*
Holland, Rose Mary — *Price Waterhouse*
Holmes, Lawrence J. — *Columbia Consulting Group*
Holodnak, William A. — *J. Robert Scott*
Holt, Carol — *Bartholdi & Company, Inc.*
Holzberger, Georges L. — *Highland Search Group*
Honer, Paul E. — *Ingram & Aydelotte Inc./I-I-C Partners*
Hoover, Catherine — *J.L. Mark Associates, Inc.*
Hopkins, Chester A. — *Handy HRM Corp.*
Hopkinson, Dana — *Winter, Wyman & Company*
Hopp, Lorrie A. — *Gregory Michaels and Associates, Inc.*
Hostetter, Kristi — *Source Services Corporation*
Houchins, William M. — *Christian & Timbers*
Houterloot, Tim — *Source Services Corporation*
Howard, Leon — *Richard, Wayne and Roberts*
Howe, Theodore — *Romac & Associates*
Howell, Robert B. — *Atlantic Search Group, Inc.*
Howell, Robert B. — *Atlantic Search Group, Inc.*
Hoyda, Louis A. — *Thorndike Deland Associates*
Hucko, Donald S. — *Jonas, Walters & Assoc., Inc.*
Hudson, Reginald M. — *Search Bureau International*
Hughes, Barbara — *Source Services Corporation*
Hughes, Cathy N. — *The Ogdon Partnership*
Hughes, R. Kevin — *Handy HRM Corp.*
Hughes, Randall — *Source Services Corporation*
Hult, Dana — *Source Services Corporation*
Humphrey, Titus — *Source Services Corporation*
Hunter, Steven — *Diamond Tax Recruiting*
Hurtado, Jaime — *Source Services Corporation*
Hutchison, William K. — *Christenson & Hutchison*
Hybels, Cynthia — *A.J. Burton Group, Inc.*
Hylas, Lisa — *Source Services Corporation*
Hypes, Richard G. — *Lynch Miller Moore, Inc.*
Imhof, Kirk — *Source Services Corporation*
Inger, Barry — *Source Services Corporation*
Inguagiato, Gregory — *MSI International*
Inskeep, Thomas — *Source Services Corporation*
Intravaia, Salvatore — *Source Services Corporation*
Irwin, Mark — *Source Services Corporation*
Issacs, Judith A. — *Grant Cooper and Associates*
Jablo, Steven A. — *Dieckmann & Associates, Ltd.*
Jackson, Joan — *A.T. Kearney, Inc.*
Jacobs, Martin J. — *The Rubicon Group*
Jacobs, Mike — *Thorne, Brieger Associates Inc.*
Jacobson, Hayley — *Source Services Corporation*
Jacobson, Rick — *The Windham Group*
Jadulang, Vincent — *Source Services Corporation*
James, Richard — *Criterion Executive Search, Inc.*
Jansen, John F. — *Delta Services*
Janssen, Don — *Howard Fischer Associates, Inc.*
Januale, Lois — *Cochran, Cochran & Yale, Inc.*
Januleski, Geoff — *Source Services Corporation*
Jazylo, John V. — *Handy HRM Corp.*
Jazylo, John V. — *Skott/Edwards Consultants, Inc.*
Jeffers, Richard B. — *Dieckmann & Associates, Ltd.*
Jeltema, John — *Source Services Corporation*

Jensen, Robert — *Source Services Corporation*
Jernigan, Susan N. — *Sockwell & Associates*
Joffe, Barry — *Bason Associates Inc.*
Johnson, Brian — *A.J. Burton Group, Inc.*
Johnson, Greg — *Source Services Corporation*
Johnson, John W. — *Webb, Johnson Associates, Inc.*
Johnson, Kathleen A. — *Barton Associates, Inc.*
Johnson, Keith — *Romac & Associates*
Johnson, Priscilla — *The Johnson Group, Inc.*
Johnson, Stanley C. — *Johnson & Company*
Johnson, Valerie — *Coe & Company International Inc.*
Johnstone, Grant — *Source Services Corporation*
Jones, B.J. — *Intersource, Ltd.*
Jones, Daniel F. — *Atlantic Search Group, Inc.*
Jones, Jonathan C. — *Canny, Bowen Inc.*
Jones, Rodney — *Source Services Corporation*
Jordan, Jon — *Cochran, Cochran & Yale, Inc.*
Jorgensen, Tom — *The Talley Group*
Judge, Alfred L. — *The Cambridge Group Ltd*
Juelis, John J. — *Peeney Associates*
Juratovac, Michael — *Montgomery Resources, Inc.*
Kader, Richard — *Richard Kader & Associates*
Kaiser, Donald J. — *Dunhill International Search of New Haven*
Kaiser, Elaine M. — *Dunhill International Search of New Haven*
Kalinowski, David — *Jacobson Associates*
Kane, Frank — *A.J. Burton Group, Inc.*
Kane, Karen — *Howard Fischer Associates, Inc.*
Kantor, Richard — *Search West, Inc.*
Kaplan, Gary — *Gary Kaplan & Associates*
Kaplan, Traci — *Source Services Corporation*
Kasprzyk, Michael — *Source Services Corporation*
Kassouf, Constance — *The Whitney Group*
Keating, Pierson — *Nordeman Grimm, Inc.*
Keith, Stephanie — *Southwestern Professional Services*
Keller, Barbara E. — *Barton Associates, Inc.*
Kelly, Claudia L. — *Spencer Stuart*
Kelly, Donna J. — *Accountants Executive Search*
Kelly, Peter W. — *R. Rollo Associates*
Kelly, Robert — *Source Services Corporation*
Kennedy, Craig — *Source Services Corporation*
Kennedy, Michael — *The Danbrook Group, Inc.*
Kennedy, Paul — *Source Services Corporation*
Kennedy, Walter — *Romac & Associates*
Kennedy, Walter — *Source Services Corporation*
Kennedy, Walter — *Source Services Corporation*
Kenney, Jeanne — *Source Services Corporation*
Kenzer, Robert D. — *Kenzer Corp.*
Kern, Jerry L. — *ADOW's Executeam*
Kern, Kathleen G. — *ADOW's Executeam*
Kershaw, Lisa — *Tanton Mitchell/Paul Ray Berndtson*
Keshishian, Gregory — *Handy HRM Corp.*
Kettwig, David A. — *A.T. Kearney, Inc.*
Keyser, Anne — *A.T. Kearney, Inc.*
Kien-Jersey, Tammy — *Spencer Stuart*
Kiley, Phyllis — *National Search, Inc.*
King, Bill — *The McCormick Group, Inc.*
King, Margaret — *Christian & Timbers*
King, Shannon — *Source Services Corporation*
King, Thomas — *Morgan Hunter Corp.*
Kinser, Richard E. — *Richard Kinser & Associates*

Kirschner, Alan — *Source Services Corporation*
Kishbaugh, Herbert S. — *Kishbaugh Associates International*
Klages, Constance W. — *International Management Advisors, Inc.*
Klavens, Cecile J. — *The Pickwick Group, Inc.*
Klein, Brandon — *A.J. Burton Group, Inc.*
Klein, Gary — *A.T. Kearney, Inc.*
Klein, Lynn M. — *Riotto-Jones Associates*
Klein, Mary Jo — *Cochran, Cochran & Yale, Inc.*
Kleinstein, Scott — *Source Services Corporation*
Klusman, Edwin — *Source Services Corporation*
Knisely, Gary — *Johnson Smith & Knisely Accord*
Knoll, Robert — *Source Services Corporation*
Koczak, John — *Source Services Corporation*
Kohn, Adam P. — *Christian & Timbers*
Kondra, Vernon J. — *The Douglas Reiter Company, Inc.*
Koontz, Donald N. — *Koontz, Jeffries & Associates, Inc.*
Kopsick, Joseph M. — *Spencer Stuart*
Kossuth, David — *Kossuth & Associates, Inc.*
Kossuth, Jane — *Kossuth & Associates, Inc.*
Kotick, Maddy — *The Stevenson Group of New Jersey*
Kramer, Donald — *Dunhill Professional Search of Tampa*
Kramer, Peter — *Dunhill Professional Search of Tampa*
Krauser, H. James — *Spencer Stuart*
Krejci, Stanley L. — *Boyden Washington, D.C.*
Kreuch, Paul C. — *Skott/Edwards Consultants, Inc.*
Kreutz, Gary L. — *Kreutz Consulting Group, Inc.*
Krick, Terry L. — *Financial Resource Associates, Inc.*
Krieger, Dennis F. — *Seiden Krieger Associates, Inc.*
Krueger, Kurt — *Krueger Associates*
Kuhl, Teresa — *Don Richard Associates of Tampa, Inc.*
Kunzer, William J. — *Kunzer Associates, Ltd.*
Kuo, Linda — *Montgomery Resources, Inc.*
Kussner, Janice N. — *Herman Smith Executive Initiatives Inc.*
Kvasnicka, Jay Allen — *Morgan Hunter Corp.*
La Chance, Ronald — *Source Services Corporation*
Laba, Marvin — *Marvin Laba & Associates*
Laba, Stuart M. — *Marvin Laba & Associates*
Labrecque, Bernard F. — *Laurendeau Labrecque/Ray & Berndtson, Inc.*
Lachance, Roger — *Laurendeau Labrecque/Ray & Berndtson, Inc.*
Lache, Shawn E. — *The Arcus Group*
Laderman, David — *Romac & Associates*
Lamb, Peter S. — *Executive Resource, Inc.*
Lambert, William — *Source Services Corporation*
Lamia, Michael — *Source Services Corporation*
Lang, Sharon A. — *Ray & Berndtson*
LaPierre, Louis — *Romac & Associates*
Lapointe, Fabien — *Source Services Corporation*
Lardner, Lucy D. — *Tully/Woodmansee International, Inc.*
Larsen, Richard F. — *Larsen, Whitney, Blecksmith & Zilliacus*
Lasher, Charles M. — *Lasher Associates*
Laskin, Sandy — *Source Services Corporation*

Lauderback, David R. — *A.T. Kearney, Inc.*
Laurendeau, Jean E. — *Laurendeau Labrecque/Ray & Berndtson, Inc.*
Lautz, Lindsay A. — *Lautz Grotte Engler*
LaValle, Michael — *Romac & Associates*
Laverty, William — *Source Services Corporation*
Lazar, Miriam — *Source Services Corporation*
Lazaro, Alicia C. — *The Whitney Group*
Leblanc, Danny — *Source Services Corporation*
Lee, Everett — *Source Services Corporation*
Lee, Roger — *Montgomery Resources, Inc.*
Leetma, Imbi — *Stanton Chase International*
Leigh, Rebecca — *Source Services Corporation*
Leighton, Mark — *Source Services Corporation*
Leighton, Nina — *The Ogdon Partnership*
Leininger, Dennis — *Key Employment Services*
Lence, Julie Anne — *MSI International*
Leslie, William H. — *Boyden/Zay & Company*
Letcher, Harvey D. — *Sandhurst Associates*
Levenson, Laurel — *Source Services Corporation*
Levine, Alan M. — *MB Inc. Interim Executive Division*
Levine, Irwin — *Source Services Corporation*
Levine, Lois — *National Search, Inc.*
Levinson, Lauren — *The Danbrook Group, Inc.*
Lewicki, Christopher — *MSI International*
Lewis, Daniel — *Source Services Corporation*
Lewis, Jon A. — *Sandhurst Associates*
Lewis, Marc D. — *Handy HRM Corp.*
Lezama Cohen, Luis — *Ray & Berndtson*
Liebowitz, Michael E. — *Highland Search Group*
Liebross, Eric — *Source Services Corporation*
Lin, Felix — *Source Services Corporation*
Lindberg, Eric J. — *MSI International*
Linton, Leonard M. — *Byron Leonard International, Inc.*
Lipuma, Thomas — *Source Services Corporation*
Litt, Michele — *The Whitney Group*
Little, Elizabeth A. — *Financial Resource Associates, Inc.*
Little, Suzaane — *Don Richard Associates of Tampa, Inc.*
Loeb, Stephen H. — *Grant Cooper and Associates*
Long, Helga — *Horton International*
Long, John — *Source Services Corporation*
Long, Mark — *Source Services Corporation*
Long, Melanie — *National Search, Inc.*
Long, William G. — *McDonald, Long & Associates, Inc.*
Lonneke, John W. — *MSI International*
Loper, Doris — *Mortgage & Financial Personnel Services*
Lopis, Roberta — *Richard, Wayne and Roberts*
Lotufo, Donald A. — *D.A.L. Associates, Inc.*
Lotz, R. James — *International Management Advisors, Inc.*
Lovas, W. Carl — *Ray & Berndtson/Lovas Stanley*
Lovely, Edward — *The Stevenson Group of New Jersey*
Loving, Vikki — *Intersource, Ltd.*
Lucarelli, Joan — *The Onstott Group, Inc.*
Lucas, Ronnie L. — *MSI International*
Luce, Daniel — *Source Services Corporation*
Lucht, John — *The John Lucht Consultancy Inc.*
Ludder, Mark — *Source Services Corporation*
Ludlow, Michael — *Source Services Corporation*
Ludlow, Paula — *Horton International*

Lumsby, George N. — *International Management Advisors, Inc.*
Lundy, Martin — *Source Services Corporation*
Luntz, Charles E. — *Charles Luntz & Associates. Inc.*
Lupica, Anthony — *Cochran, Cochran & Yale, Inc.*
Lynam, Joseph V. — *Johnson Smith & Knisely Accord*
Lynch, Michael C. — *Lynch Miller Moore, Inc.*
Lyon, Jenny — *Marra Peters & Partners*
Lyons, Denis B.K. — *Spencer Stuart*
Lyons, J. David — *Aubin International Inc.*
Lyons, Michael — *Source Services Corporation*
MacCallan, Deirdre — *Butterfass, Pepe & MacCallan Inc.*
MacIntyre, Lisa W. — *Highland Search Group*
Mackenna, Kathy — *Plummer & Associates, Inc.*
MacMillan, James — *Source Services Corporation*
MacNaughton, Sperry — *McNaughton Associates*
MacPherson, Holly — *Source Services Corporation*
Macrides, Michael — *Source Services Corporation*
Madaras, Debra — *Financial Resource Associates, Inc.*
Maer, Harry — *Kenzer Corp.*
Maggio, Mary — *Source Services Corporation*
Maglio, Charles J. — *Maglio and Company, Inc.*
Mahmoud, Sophia — *Source Services Corporation*
Mainwaring, Andrew Brian — *Executive Search Consultants Corporation*
Mairn, Todd — *Source Services Corporation*
Major, Susan — *A.T. Kearney, Inc.*
Mallin, Ellen — *Howard Fischer Associates, Inc.*
Manassero, Henri J.P. — *International Management Advisors, Inc.*
Mangum, Maria — *Thomas Mangum Company*
Mangum, William T. — *Thomas Mangum Company*
Manns, Alex — *Crawford & Crofford*
Mansford, Keith — *Howard Fischer Associates, Inc.*
Manzo, Renee — *Atlantic Search Group, Inc.*
Maphet, Harriet — *The Stevenson Group of New Jersey*
Marino, Chester — *Cochran, Cochran & Yale, Inc.*
Mark, John L. — *J.L. Mark Associates, Inc.*
Mark, Lynne — *J.L. Mark Associates, Inc.*
Marks, Russell E. — *Webb, Johnson Associates, Inc.*
Marra, John — *Marra Peters & Partners*
Marra, John — *Marra Peters & Partners*
Marshall, E. Leigh — *Norman Broadbent International, Inc.*
Marumoto, William H. — *Boyden Washington, D.C.*
Marwil, Jennifer — *Source Services Corporation*
Massey, R. Bruce — *Horton International*
Mather, David R. — *Christian & Timbers*
Mathias, Douglas — *Source Services Corporation*
Mathias, Kathy — *Stone Murphy & Olson*
Mathis, Carrie — *Source Services Corporation*
Mattes, Edward C. — *The Ogdon Partnership*
Matthews, Corwin — *Woodworth International Group*
Mattingly, Kathleen — *Source Services Corporation*

Matueny, Robert — *Ryan, Miller & Associates Inc.*
Mauer, Kristin — *Montgomery Resources, Inc.*
Maxwell, John — *Source Services Corporation*
Mayer, Thomas — *Source Services Corporation*
Mayes, Kay H. — *John Shell Associates, Inc.*
Maynard Taylor, Susan — *Chrisman & Company, Incorporated*
Mazor, Elly — *Howard Fischer Associates, Inc.*
Mazza, David B. — *Mazza & Riley, Inc. (a Korn/Ferry International affiliate)*
McAteer, Thomas — *Montgomery Resources, Inc.*
McBride, Jonathan E. — *McBride Associates, Inc.*
McBryde, Marnie — *Spencer Stuart*
McCallister, Richard A. — *Boyden*
McCarthy, Laura — *Source Services Corporation*
McCloskey, Frank D. — *Johnson Smith & Knisely Accord*
McCormick, Brian — *The McCormick Group, Inc.*
McCormick, Joseph — *Source Services Corporation*
McCreary, Charles "Chip" — *Austin-McGregor International*
McDermott, Jeffrey T. — *Vlcek & Company, Inc.*
McDonald, Scott A. — *McDonald Associates International*
McDonald, Stanleigh B. — *McDonald Associates International*
McDowell, Robert N. — *Christenson & Hutchison*
McFadden, Ashton S. — *Johnson Smith & Knisely Accord*
McFadzen,, James A. — *Holland, McFadzean & Associates, Inc.*
McGinnis, Rita — *Source Services Corporation*
McGoldrick, Terrence — *Source Services Corporation*
McGuire, Pat — *A.J. Burton Group, Inc.*
McHugh, Keith — *Source Services Corporation*
McIntosh, Arthur — *Source Services Corporation*
McIntosh, Tad — *Source Services Corporation*
McKeown, Patricia A. — *DiMarchi Partners, Inc.*
McKinney, Julia — *Source Services Corporation*
McKnight, Amy E. — *Chartwell Partners International, Inc.*
McLaughlin, John — *Romac & Associates*
McLean, E. Peter — *Spencer Stuart*
McMahan, Stephen — *Source Services Corporation*
McMahan, Stephen — *Source Services Corporation*
McMillin, Bob — *Price Waterhouse*
McNamara, Catherine — *Ray & Berndtson*
McNamara, Timothy C. — *Columbia Consulting Group*
McNear, Jeffrey E. — *Barrett Partners*
McNichols, Walter B. — *Gary Kaplan & Associates*
McNulty, Kelly L. — *Gregory Michaels and Associates, Inc.*
McQuoid, David — *A.T. Kearney, Inc.*
Meadows, C. David — *Professional Staffing Consultants*
Meagher, Patricia G. — *Spencer Stuart*
Meany, Brian M. — *Herbert Mines Associates, Inc.*
Meara, Helen — *Source Services Corporation*
Meehan, John — *Source Services Corporation*
Meier, J. Dale — *Grant Cooper and Associates*
Meltzer, Andrea Y. — *Executive Options, Ltd.*

Mendelson, Jeffrey — *Source Services Corporation*
Mendoza-Green, Robin — *Source Services Corporation*
Mercer, Julie — *Columbia Consulting Group*
Merrigan, Eileen M. — *Lamalie Amrop International*
Mertensotto, Chuck H. — *Whitney & Associates, Inc.*
Messett, William J. — *Messett Associates, Inc.*
Messina, Marco — *Source Services Corporation*
Mestepey, John — *A.T. Kearney, Inc.*
Meyer, Stacey — *Gary Kaplan & Associates*
Meyers, Steven — *Montgomery Resources, Inc.*
Meza, Anna — *Richard, Wayne and Roberts*
Miller, David — *Cochran, Cochran & Yale, Inc.*
Miller, David — *Temporary Accounting Personnel, Inc.*
Miller, Harold B. — *MSI International*
Miller, Larry — *Source Services Corporation*
Miller, Michael R. — *Lynch Miller Moore, Inc.*
Miller, Roy — *The Enns Partners Inc.*
Miller, Timothy — *Source Services Corporation*
Milligan, Dale — *Source Services Corporation*
Millonzi, Joel C. — *Johnson Smith & Knisely Accord*
Mills, John — *Source Services Corporation*
Milner, Carol — *Source Services Corporation*
Milstein, Bonnie — *Marvin Laba & Associates*
Mines, Herbert T. — *Herbert Mines Associates, Inc.*
Mingle, Larry D. — *Columbia Consulting Group*
Miras, Cliff — *Source Services Corporation*
Miras, Cliff — *Source Services Corporation*
Misiurewicz, Marc — *Cochran, Cochran & Yale, Inc.*
Mitchell, Jeff — *A.J. Burton Group, Inc.*
Mitchell, John — *Romac & Associates*
Mitton, Bill — *Executive Resource, Inc.*
Mittwol, Myles — *Source Services Corporation*
Mochwart, Donald — *Drummond Associates, Inc.*
Molitor, John L. — *Barrett Partners*
Mollichelli, David — *Source Services Corporation*
Mondragon, Philip — *A.T. Kearney, Inc.*
Montgomery, James M. — *Houze, Shourds & Montgomery, Inc.*
Moore, Craig — *Source Services Corporation*
Moore, Dianna — *Source Services Corporation*
Moore, Janice E. — *MSI International*
Moore, Mark — *Wheeler, Moore & Elam Co.*
Moore, Suzanne — *Source Services Corporation*
Moore, T. Wills — *Ray & Berndtson*
Moran, Douglas — *Source Services Corporation*
Morato, Rene — *Source Services Corporation*
Moretti, Denise — *Source Services Corporation*
Morgan, David G. — *Morgan Stampfl, Inc.*
Morgan, Donald T. — *MSI International*
Morgan, Gary — *National Search, Inc.*
Moriarty, Mike — *Source Services Corporation*
Morris, Scott — *Source Services Corporation*
Morrow, Melanie — *Source Services Corporation*
Mortansen, Patricia — *Norman Broadbent International, Inc.*
Morton, Robert C. — *Morton, McCorkle & Associates, Inc.*
Moskowitz, Marc — *Kenzer Corp.*
Mott, Greg — *Source Services Corporation*
Msidment, Roger — *Source Services Corporation*

Mueller, Colleen — *Source Services Corporation*
Muendel, H. Edward — *Stanton Chase International*
Mulligan, Robert P. — *William Willis Worldwide Inc.*
Murphy, Corinne — *Source Services Corporation*
Murphy, Cornelius J. — *Goodrich & Sherwood Associates, Inc.*
Murphy, James — *Source Services Corporation*
Murphy, Patrick J. — *P.J. Murphy & Associates, Inc.*
Murray, Virginia — *A.T. Kearney, Inc.*
Murry, John — *Source Services Corporation*
Mursuli, Meredith — *Lasher Associates*
Mustin, Joyce M. — *J: Blakslee International, Ltd.*
Myers, Kay — *Signature Staffing*
Nabers, Karen — *Source Services Corporation*
Nagler, Leon G. — *Nagler, Robins & Poe, Inc.*
Nagy, Les — *Source Services Corporation*
Naidicz, Maria — *Ray & Berndtson*
Nass, Martin D. — *Lamalie Amrop International*
Nathanson, Barry F. — *Barry Nathanson Associates*
Necessary, Rick — *Source Services Corporation*
Neckanoff, Sharon — *Search West, Inc.*
Needham, Karen — *Source Services Corporation*
Nees, Eugene C. — *Ray & Berndtson*
Neff, Herbert — *Source Services Corporation*
Neher, Robert L. — *Intech Summit Group, Inc.*
Nehring, Keith — *Howard Fischer Associates, Inc.*
Neidhart, Craig C. — *TNS Partners, Inc.*
Nelson, Hitch — *Source Services Corporation*
Nelson, Mary — *Source Services Corporation*
Nelson-Folkersen, Jeffrey — *Source Services Corporation*
Nemec, Phillip — *Dunhill International Search of New Haven*
Nephew, Robert — *Christian & Timbers*
Neuberth, Jeffrey G. — *Canny, Bowen Inc.*
Neuwald, Debrah — *Source Services Corporation*
Newman, Lynn — *Kishbaugh Associates International*
Newpoff, Brad L. — *Furst Group/MPI*
Nichols, Gary — *Koontz, Jeffries & Associates, Inc.*
Nielsen, Sue — *Ells Personnel System Inc.*
Noebel, Todd R. — *The Noebel Search Group, Inc.*
Nolan, Robert — *Source Services Corporation*
Nolen, Shannon — *Source Services Corporation*
Nolte, William D. — *W.D. Nolte & Company*
Norman, Randy — *Austin-McGregor International*
Normann, Amy — *Robert M. Flanagan & Associates, Ltd.*
Norris, Ken — *A.T. Kearney, Inc.*
Norsell, Paul E. — *Paul Norsell & Associates, Inc.*
Nunziata, Peter — *Atlantic Search Group, Inc.*
O'Brien, Susan — *Source Services Corporation*
O'Connell, Michael — *Ryan, Miller & Associates Inc.*
O'Halloran, Robert — *MSI International*
O'Hara, Daniel M. — *Lynch Miller Moore, Inc.*
O'Maley, Kimberlee — *Spencer Stuart*
O'Neill, James P. — *Allerton Heneghan & O'Neill*
O'Neill, Stephen A. — *Harris Heery & Associates*
O'Reilly, John — *Stratford Group*
Occhiboi, Emil — *Source Services Corporation*

Ocon, Olga — *Busch International*
Ogdon, Thomas H. — *The Ogdon Partnership*
Ogilvie, Kit — *Howard Fischer Associates, Inc.*
Ohman, Gregory L. — *Skott/Edwards Consultants, Inc.*
Oldfield, Theresa — *Strategic Alliance Network, Ltd.*
Olin, Robyn — *Richard, Wayne and Roberts*
Olsen, Robert — *Source Services Corporation*
Onstott, Joseph — *The Onstott Group, Inc.*
Onstott, Joseph E. — *The Onstott Group, Inc.*
Oppedisano, Edward — *Oppedisano & Company, Inc.*
Orr, Stacie — *Source Services Corporation*
Ott, George W. — *Ott & Hansen, Inc.*
Ouellette, Christopher — *Source Services Corporation*
Overlock, Craig — *Ray & Berndtson*
Owen, Christopher — *Source Services Corporation*
Pace, Susan A. — *Horton International*
Pachowitz, John — *Source Services Corporation*
Page, G. Schuyler — *A.T. Kearney, Inc.*
Palazio, Carla — *A.T. Kearney, Inc.*
Paliwoda, William — *Source Services Corporation*
Pallman-David, Cynthia — *Bonnell Associates Ltd.*
Palma, Frank R. — *Goodrich & Sherwood Associates, Inc.*
Palmer, Carlton A. — *Beall & Company, Inc.*
Palmer, James H. — *The Hindman Company*
Panarese, Pam — *Howard Fischer Associates, Inc.*
Panchella, Joseph J. — *Wellington Management Group*
Pankratz, Dennis — *Furst Group/MPI*
Papasadero, Kathleen — *Woodworth International Group*
Papciak, Dennis J. — *Accounting Personnel Associates, Inc.*
Papciak, Dennis J. — *Temporary Accounting Personnel*
Pappas, Christina E. — *Williams Executive Search, Inc.*
Paradise, Malcolm — *Source Services Corporation*
Pardo, Maria Elena — *Smith Search, S.C.*
Parente, James — *Source Services Corporation*
Park, Dabney G. — *Mark Stanley/EMA Partners International*
Parroco, Jason — *Source Services Corporation*
Patel, Shailesh — *Source Services Corporation*
Patence, David W. — *Handy HRM Corp.*
Paternie, Patrick — *Source Services Corporation*
Paul, Kathleen — *Source Services Corporation*
Peal, Matthew — *Source Services Corporation*
Pearson, John R. — *Pearson, Caldwell & Farnsworth, Inc.*
Pease, Edward — *Don Richard Associates of Georgia, Inc.*
Peeney, James D. — *Peeney Associates*
Pelisson, Charles — *Marra Peters & Partners*
Pepe, Leonida R. — *Butterfass, Pepe & MacCallan Inc.*
Pernell, Jeanette — *Norman Broadbent International, Inc.*
Perry, Carolyn — *Source Services Corporation*
Peternell, Melanie — *Signature Staffing*
Peters, Kevin — *Source Services Corporation*

Petersen, Richard — *Source Services Corporation*
Peterson, Eric N. — *Stratford Group*
Pettibone, Linda G. — *Herbert Mines Associates, Inc.*
Pettway, Samuel H. — *Spencer Stuart*
Petty, J. Scott — *The Arcus Group*
Pfannkuche, Anthony V. — *Spencer Stuart*
Pfeiffer, Irene — *Price Waterhouse*
Phillips, Donald L. — *O'Shea, Divine & Company, Inc.*
Phillips, James L. — *Highland Search Group*
Phillips, Richard K. — *Handy HRM Corp.*
Phipps, Peggy — *Woodworth International Group*
Pickering, Dale — *Agri-Tech Personnel, Inc.*
Pickering, Rita — *Agri-Tech Personnel, Inc.*
Pickford, Stephen T. — *The Corporate Staff, Inc.*
Pierce, Matthew — *Source Services Corporation*
Pierson, Edward J. — *Johnson Smith & Knisely Accord*
Pillow, Charles — *Source Services Corporation*
Pineda, Rosanna — *Source Services Corporation*
Pirro, Sheri — *Source Services Corporation*
Pitto, Lili — *Ryan, Miller & Associates Inc.*
Plant, Jerry — *Source Services Corporation*
Plessner, Rene — *Rene Plessner Associates, Inc.*
Plimpton, Ralph L. — *R L Plimpton Associates*
Pliszka, Donald J. — *Praxis Partners*
Plummer, John — *Plummer & Associates, Inc.*
Poirier, Frank — *Juntunen-Combs-Poirier*
Poirier, Roland L. — *Poirier, Hoevel & Co.*
Poracky, John W. — *M. Wood Company*
Poremski, Paul — *A.J. Burton Group, Inc.*
Porter, Albert — *The Experts*
Pototo, Brian — *Source Services Corporation*
Potter, Mark W. — *Highland Search Group*
Potter, Steven B. — *Highland Search Group*
Powell, Danny — *Source Services Corporation*
Powell, Gregory — *Source Services Corporation*
Power, Michael — *Source Services Corporation*
Powers Johnson, Allyson — *Skott/Edwards Consultants, Inc.*
Pratt, Tyler P. — *Furst Group/MPI*
Pregeant, David — *Source Services Corporation*
Press, Fred — *Adept Tech Recruiting*
Preusse, Eric — *Source Services Corporation*
Price, Andrew G. — *The Thomas Tucker Company*
Price, Carl — *Source Services Corporation*
Price, Kenneth M. — *Messett Associates, Inc.*
Prince, Marilyn L. — *Higdon Prince Inc.*
Proct, Nina — *Martin H. Bauman Associates, Inc.*
Puckett, Jennifer — *Rene Plessner Associates, Inc.*
Pugrant, Mark A. — *Grant/Morgan Associates, Inc.*
Rabinowitz, Peter A. — *P.A.R. Associates Inc.*
Racht, Janet G. — *Crowe, Chizek and Company, LLP*
Raines, Bruce R. — *Raines International Inc.*
Ramler, Carolyn S. — *The Corporate Connection, Ltd.*
Ramsey, John H. — *Mark Stanley/EMA Partners International*
Rasmussen, Timothy — *Source Services Corporation*
Ratajczak, Paul — *Source Services Corporation*
Ravenel, Lavinia — *MSI International*
Ray, Marianne C. — *Callan Associates, Ltd.*

Reardon, Joseph — *Source Services Corporation*
Reddick, David C. — *Horton International*
Redding, Denise — *The Douglas Reiter Company, Inc.*
Redler, Rhonda — *National Search, Inc.*
Reece, Christopher S. — *Reece & Mruk Partners*
Reed, Susan — *Source Services Corporation*
Reeves, William B. — *Spencer Stuart*
Regeuye, Peter J. — *Accountants Executive Search*
Reid, Katherine — *Source Services Corporation*
Reid, Scott — *Source Services Corporation*
Reifel, Laurie — *Reifel & Assocaites*
Reifersen, Ruth F. — *The Jonathan Stevens Group, Inc.*
Reiser, Ellen — *Thorndike Deland Associates*
Reisinger, George L. — *Sigma Group International*
Reiss, Matt — *National Search, Inc.*
Reiter, Douglas — *The Douglas Reiter Company, Inc.*
Reiter, Harold D. — *Herbert Mines Associates, Inc.*
Remillard, Brad M. — *CJA - The Adler Group*
Renfroe, Ann-Marie — *Source Services Corporation*
Rennell, Thomas — *Source Services Corporation*
Renner, Sandra L. — *Spectra International Inc.*
Renteria, Elizabeth — *Source Services Corporation*
Resnic, Alan — *Source Services Corporation*
Reticker, Peter — *MSI International*
Reyman, Susan — *S. Reyman & Associates Ltd.*
Reynolds, Laura — *Source Services Corporation*
Rhoades, Michael — *Source Services Corporation*
Rice, Raymond D. — *Logue & Rice Inc.*
Rich, Lyttleton — *Sockwell & Associates*
Rieger, Louis J. — *Spencer Stuart*
Rimmel, James E. — *The Hindman Company*
Rimmele, Michael — *The Bankers Group*
Rinker, Jim — *Southwestern Professional Services*
Rios, Vince — *Source Services Corporation*
Rios, Vincent — *Source Services Corporation*
Riotto, Anthony R. — *Riotto-Jones Associates*
Robb, Tammy — *Source Services Corporation*
Roberts, Carl R. — *Southwestern Professional Services*
Roberts, Kenneth — *The Rubicon Group*
Roberts, Nick P. — *Spectrum Search Associates, Inc.*
Roberts, Scott — *Jonas, Walters & Assoc., Inc.*
Robertson, Sherry — *Source Services Corporation*
Robinson, Bruce — *Bruce Robinson Associates*
Robinson, Tonya — *Source Services Corporation*
Robles Cuellar, Paulina — *Ray & Berndtson*
Rockwell, Bruce — *Source Services Corporation*
Rodriguez, Manuel — *Source Services Corporation*
Rogers, Leah — *Dinte Resources, Inc.*
Rojo, Rafael — *A.T. Kearney, Inc.*
Romanello, Daniel P. — *Spencer Stuart*
Romang, Paula — *Agri-Tech Personnel, Inc.*
Rorech, Maureen — *Romac & Associates*
Rosemarin, Gloria J. — *Barrington Hart, Inc.*
Rosen, Mitchell — *Source Services Corporation*
Rosenstein, Michele — *Source Services Corporation*
Rosenthal, Charles — *National Search, Inc.*
Ross, Curt A. — *Ray & Berndtson*

Ross, John — *Morgan Stampfl, Inc.*
Ross, Lawrence — *Ray & Berndtson/Lovas Stanley*
Ross, Mark — *Ray & Berndtson/Lovas Stanley*
Rotella, Marshall W. — *The Corporate Connection, Ltd.*
Roth, Robert J. — *Williams, Roth & Krueger Inc.*
Rothenbush, Clayton — *Source Services Corporation*
Rowe, Thomas A. — *Korn/Ferry International*
Rowe, William D. — *D.E. Foster Partners Inc.*
Rowland, James — *Source Services Corporation*
Rudolph, Kenneth — *Kossuth & Associates, Inc.*
Rush, Michael E. — *D.A.L. Associates, Inc.*
Russell, Robin E. — *Kenzer Corp.*
Rustin, Beth — *The Whitney Group*
Ryan, David — *Source Services Corporation*
Ryan, Kathleen — *Source Services Corporation*
Ryan, Lee — *Ryan, Miller & Associates Inc.*
Ryan, Mark — *Source Services Corporation*
Sabanosh, Whitney — *Highland Search Group*
Sabat, Lori S. — *Alta Associates, Inc.*
Sacerdote, John — *Raymond Karsan Associates*
Sadaj, Michael — *Source Services Corporation*
Salet, Michael — *Source Services Corporation*
Sallows, Jill S. — *Crowe, Chizek and Company, LLP*
Salvagno, Michael J. — *The Cambridge Group Ltd*
Samsel, Randy — *Source Services Corporation*
Samuelson, Robert — *Source Services Corporation*
Sanchez, William — *Source Services Corporation*
Sanders, Spencer H. — *Battalia Winston International*
Saner, Harold — *Romac & Associates*
Sanitago, Anthony — *TaxSearch, Inc.*
Sanow, Robert — *Cochran, Cochran & Yale, Inc.*
Santiago, Benefrido — *Source Services Corporation*
Sapers, Mark — *Source Services Corporation*
Saposhnik, Doron — *Source Services Corporation*
Sardella, Sharon — *Source Services Corporation*
Sarna, Edmund A. — *Jonas, Walters & Assoc., Inc.*
Satenstein, Sloan — *Higdon Prince Inc.*
Sathe, Mark A. — *Sathe & Associates, Inc.*
Sauer, Harry J. — *Romac & Associates*
Savage, Edward J. — *Stanton Chase International*
Savela, Edward — *Source Services Corporation*
Savoy, Michelle — *Spencer Stuart*
Saxon, Alexa — *Woodworth International Group*
Schlesinger, Laurie — *The Whitney Group*
Schlpma, Christine — *Advanced Executive Resources*
Schneiderman, Gerald — *Management Resource Associates, Inc.*
Schroeder, James — *Source Services Corporation*
Schroeder, John W. — *Spencer Stuart*
Schultz, Randy — *Source Services Corporation*
Schwalbach, Robert — *Source Services Corporation*
Schweichler, Lee J. — *Schweichler Associates, Inc.*
Schwinden, William — *Source Services Corporation*
Scimone, James — *Source Services Corporation*
Scimone, Jim — *Source Services Corporation*
Scodius, Joseph J. — *Gregory Michaels and Associates, Inc.*

Scoff, Barry — *Source Services Corporation*
Scothon, Alan — *Romac & Associates*
Scott, Evan — *Howard Fischer Associates, Inc.*
Scott, Gordon S. — *Search Advisors International Corp.*
Scranton, Lisa — *A.J. Burton Group, Inc.*
Seamon, Kenneth — *Source Services Corporation*
Segal, Eric B. — *Kenzer Corp.*
Seiden, Steven A. — *Seiden Krieger Associates, Inc.*
Selbach, Barbara — *Spencer Stuart*
Sell, David — *Source Services Corporation*
Selvaggi, Esther — *Source Services Corporation*
Semple, David — *Source Services Corporation*
Semyan, John K. — *TNS Partners, Inc.*
Sennello, Gendra — *National Search, Inc.*
Serba, Kerri — *Source Services Corporation*
Sevilla, Claudio A. — *Crawford & Crofford*
Shackleford, David — *Source Services Corporation*
Shanks, Jennifer — *Source Services Corporation*
Shapanka, Samuel — *Source Services Corporation*
Shawhan, Heather — *Source Services Corporation*
Shell, John C. — *John Shell Associates, Inc.*
Shelton, Jonathan — *Source Services Corporation*
Shelton, Sandra — *National Search, Inc.*
Shen, Eugene Y. — *The Whitney Group*
Shenfield, Peter — *A.T. Kearney, Inc.*
Shepard, Michael J. — *MSI International*
Sherman, Robert R. — *Mortgage & Financial Personnel Services*
Shervey, Brent C. — *O'Callaghan Honey/Ray & Berndtson, Inc.*
Sherwood, Andrew — *Goodrich & Sherwood Associates, Inc.*
Shore, Earl L. — *E.L. Shore & Associates Ltd.*
Sibbald, John R. — *John Sibbald Associates, Inc.*
Siegel, Pamela — *Executive Options, Ltd.*
Siegler, Jody Cukiir — *A.T. Kearney, Inc.*
Siegrist, Jeffrey M. — *D.E. Foster Partners Inc.*
Silcott, Marvin L. — *Marvin L. Silcott & Associates, Inc.*
Silvas, Stephen D. — *Roberson and Company*
Silver, Kit — *Source Services Corporation*
Silver, Lee — *L. A. Silver Associates, Inc.*
Silverman, Gary W. — *GWS Partners*
Simmons, Deborah — *Source Services Corporation*
Simmons, Sandra K. — *MSI International*
Simon, Mary K. — *Gregory Michaels and Associates, Inc.*
Simpson, David J. — *Simpson Associates, Inc.*
Sindler, Jay — *A.J. Burton Group, Inc.*
Sirena, Evelyn — *Source Services Corporation*
Sitarski, Stan — *Howard Fischer Associates, Inc.*
Skunda, Donna M. — *Allerton Heneghan & O'Neill*
Slayton, Richard C. — *Slayton International, Inc./I-I-C Partners*
Sloan, Scott — *Source Services Corporation*
Slosar, John — *Boyden*
Smead, Michelle M. — *A.T. Kearney, Inc.*
Smith, Ana Luz — *Smith Search, S.C.*
Smith, Brant — *Smith Hanley Associates*
Smith, David P. — *HRS, Inc.*
Smith, Ethan L. — *Highland Search Group*

Smith, Herman M. — *Herman Smith Executive Initiatives Inc.*
Smith, John E. — *Smith Search, S.C.*
Smith, Lawrence — *Source Services Corporation*
Smith, Lydia — *The Corporate Connection, Ltd.*
Smith, Matt D. — *Ray & Berndtson*
Smith, Monica L. — *Analysts Resources, Inc.*
Smith, Robert L. — *Smith & Sawyer Inc.*
Smith, Ronald V. — *Coe & Company International Inc.*
Smith, Timothy — *Source Services Corporation*
Smith, Timothy C. — *Christian & Timbers*
Smith, W. Guice — *Southwestern Professional Services*
Smock, Cynthia — *Source Services Corporation*
Smoller, Howard — *Source Services Corporation*
Snelgrove, Geiger — *National Search, Inc.*
Snowden, Charles — *Source Services Corporation*
Snowhite, Rebecca — *Source Services Corporation*
Snyder, C. Edward — *Horton International*
Snyder, James F. — *Snyder & Company*
Sochacki, Michael — *Source Services Corporation*
Sockwell, J. Edgar — *Sockwell & Associates*
Sondgrass, Stephen — *DeFrain, Mayer LLC*
Song, Louis — *Source Services Corporation*
Sorgen, Jay — *Source Services Corporation*
Sostilio, Louis — *Source Services Corporation*
Spadavecchia, Jennifer — *Alta Associates, Inc.*
Spann, Richard E. — *Goodrich & Sherwood Associates, Inc.*
Spector, Michael — *Source Services Corporation*
Spencer, John — *Source Services Corporation*
Spencer, John — *Source Services Corporation*
Spera, Stefanie — *A.T. Kearney, Inc.*
Spiegel, Gayle — *L. A. Silver Associates, Inc.*
Sponseller, Vern — *Richard Kader & Associates*
Spoutz, Paul — *Source Services Corporation*
Spriggs, Robert D. — *Spriggs & Company, Inc.*
St. Clair, Alan — *TNS Partners, Inc.*
St. Martin, Peter — *Source Services Corporation*
Stack, Richard — *Source Services Corporation*
Stampfl, Eric — *Morgan Stampfl, Inc.*
Stanton, John — *A.T. Kearney, Inc.*
Stark, Jeff — *Thorne, Brieger Associates Inc.*
Steele, Daniel — *Cochran, Cochran & Yale, Inc.*
Stein, Terry W. — *Stewart, Stein and Scott, Ltd.*
Steinem, Andy — *Dahl-Morrow International*
Steinem, Barbra — *Dahl-Morrow International*
Steinman, Stephen M. — *The Stevenson Group of New Jersey*
Stephens, Andrew — *Source Services Corporation*
Stephens, John — *Source Services Corporation*
Stevens, Craig M. — *Kirkman & Searing, Inc.*
Stevens, Tracey — *Don Richard Associates of Washington, D.C., Inc.*
Stevenson, Jane — *Howard Fischer Associates, Inc.*
Stewart, Clifford — *Morgan Stampfl, Inc.*
Stewart, Jeffrey O. — *Stewart, Stein and Scott, Ltd.*
Stewart, Ross M. — *Human Resources Network Partners Inc.*
Stone, Susan L. — *Stone Enterprises Ltd.*
Storm, Deborah — *Source Services Corporation*
Stranberg, James R. — *Callan Associates, Ltd.*
Strander, Dervin — *Source Services Corporation*

Strassman, Mark — *Don Richard Associates of Washington, D.C., Inc.*
Stratmeyer, Karin Bergwall — *Princeton Entrepreneurial Resources*
Straube, Stanley H. — *Straube Associates*
Strickland, Katie — *Grantham & Co., Inc.*
Stringer, Dann P. — *D.E. Foster Partners Inc.*
Strom, Mark N. — *Search Advisors International Corp.*
Struzziero, Ralph E. — *Romac & Associates*
Sucato, Carolyn — *Jay Gaines & Company, Inc.*
Sumurdy, Melinda — *Kenzer Corp.*
Susoreny, Samali — *Source Services Corporation*
Sussman, Lynda — *Gilbert Tweed/INESA*
Sutter, Howard — *Romac & Associates*
Swanner, William — *Source Services Corporation*
Swanson, Dick — *Raymond Karsan Associates*
Sweeney, Anne — *Source Services Corporation*
Sweeney, Sean K. — *Bonifield Associates*
Sweet, Randall — *Source Services Corporation*
Swoboda, Lawrence — *A.J. Burton Group, Inc.*
Taft, David G. — *Techsearch Services, Inc.*
Tankson, Dawn — *Source Services Corporation*
Tanner, Frank — *Source Services Corporation*
Tanner, Gary — *Source Services Corporation*
Taylor, Conrad G. — *MSI International*
Taylor, James M. — *The HRM Group, Inc.*
Taylor, R.L. (Larry) — *Ray & Berndtson*
Teger, Stella — *Source Services Corporation*
Telford, John H. — *Telford, Adams & Alexander/Telford & Co., Inc.*
ten Cate, Herman H. — *Stoneham Associates Corp.*
Tenero, Kymberly — *Source Services Corporation*
Teter, Sandra — *The Danbrook Group, Inc.*
Teti, Al — *Chrisman & Company, Incorporated*
Theard, Susan — *Romac & Associates*
Theobald, David B. — *Theobald & Associates*
Thielman, Joseph — *Barrett Partners*
Thomas, Jeffrey — *Fairfaxx Corporation*
Thomas, Kurt J. — *P.J. Murphy & Associates, Inc.*
Thomas, Terry — *The Thomas Resource Group*
Thompson, John R. — *MSI International*
Thompson, Kenneth L. — *McCormack & Farrow*
Thompson, Leslie — *Source Services Corporation*
Thrapp, Mark C. — *Executive Search Consultants International, Inc.*
Thrower, Troy — *Source Services Corporation*
Tierney, Eileen — *The Whitney Group*
Tilley, Kyle — *Source Services Corporation*
Tincu, John C. — *Ferneborg & Associates, Inc.*
Tingle, Trina A. — *MSI International*
Tobin, Christopher — *Source Services Corporation*
Todres-Bernstein, Margo — *Kaye-Bassman International Corp.*
Tootsey, Mark A. — *A.J. Burton Group, Inc.*
Tracey, Jack — *Management Assistance Group, Inc.*
Trefzer, Kristie — *Source Services Corporation*
Trewhella, Michael — *Source Services Corporation*
Trice, Renee — *Source Services Corporation*
Trieschmann, Daniel — *Source Services Corporation*
Trieweiler, Bob — *Executive Placement Consultants, Inc.*
Trimble, Patricia — *Source Services Corporation*

Trimble, Rhonda — *Source Services Corporation*

Truex, John F. — *Morton, McCorkle & Associates, Inc.*

Truitt, Thomas B. — *Southwestern Professional Services*

Tryon, Katey — *DeFrain, Mayer LLC*

Tscelli, Maureen — *Source Services Corporation*

Tschan, Stephen — *Source Services Corporation*

Tucci, Joseph — *Fairfaxx Corporation*

Tucker, Thomas A. — *The Thomas Tucker Company*

Tully, Margo L. — *Tully/Woodmansee International, Inc.*

Tunney, William — *Grant Cooper and Associates*

Turner, Edward K. — *Don Richard Associates of Charlotte*

Turner, Kimberly — *Barton Associates, Inc.*

Turner, Raymond — *Source Services Corporation*

Tursi, Deborah J. — *The Corporate Connection, Ltd.*

Tutwiler, Stephen — *Don Richard Associates of Tampa, Inc.*

Tweed, Janet — *Gilbert Tweed/INESA*

Twomey, James — *Source Services Corporation*

Tyson, Richard L. — *Bonifield Associates*

Ulbert, Nancy — *Aureus Group*

Ulrich, Mary Ann — *D.S. Allen Associates, Inc.*

Uzzel, Linda — *Source Services Corporation*

Vacca, Domenic — *Romac & Associates*

Vairo, Leonard A. — *Christian & Timbers*

Valenta, Joseph — *Princeton Entrepreneurial Resources*

Van Alstine, Catherine — *Tanton Mitchell/Paul Ray Berndtson*

Van Biesen, Jacques A.H. — *Search Group Inc.*

Van Campen, Jerry — *Gilbert & Van Campen International*

Van Norman, Ben — *Source Services Corporation*

Vandenbulcke, Cynthia — *Source Services Corporation*

Varney, Monique — *Source Services Corporation*

Varrichio, Michael — *Source Services Corporation*

Velez, Hector — *Source Services Corporation*

Velten, Mark T. — *Boyden*

Venable, William W. — *Thorndike Deland Associates*

Vergara, Gail H. — *Spencer Stuart*

Vernon, Peter C. — *Horton International*

Vilella, Paul — *Source Services Corporation*

Villella, Paul — *Source Services Corporation*

Vinett-Hessel, Deidre — *Source Services Corporation*

Visnich, L. Christine — *Bason Associates Inc.*

Vitale, Amy — *Highland Search Group*

Viviano, Cathleen — *Source Services Corporation*

Vlcek, Thomas J. — *Vlcek & Company, Inc.*

Voigt, John A. — *Romac & Associates*

Volkman, Arthur — *Cochran, Cochran & Yale, Inc.*

Vossler, James — *A.J. Burton Group, Inc.*

Vourakis, Zan — *ZanExec LLC*

Waanders, William L. — *ExecuQuest*

Wacholz, Rick — *A.T. Kearney, Inc.*

Wade, Christy — *Source Services Corporation*

Waitkus, Karen — *Richard, Wayne and Roberts*

Wakefield, Scott — *National Search, Inc.*

Waldman, Noah H. — *Lamalie Amrop International*

Waldoch, D. Mark — *Barnes Development Group, LLC*

Waldrop, Gary R. — *MSI International*

Walker, Ann — *Source Services Corporation*

Walker, Craig H. — *A.J. Burton Group, Inc.*

Walker, Ewing J. — *Ward Howell International, Inc.*

Walker, Rose — *Source Services Corporation*

Wallace, Alec — *Tanton Mitchell/Paul Ray Berndtson*

Wallace, Toby — *Source Services Corporation*

Walsh, Denis — *Professional Staffing Consultants*

Walters, William F. — *Jonas, Walters & Assoc., Inc.*

Ward, Les — *Source Services Corporation*

Ward, Madeleine — *LTM Associates*

Ward, Robert — *Source Services Corporation*

Warnock, Phyl — *Source Services Corporation*

Warter, Mark — *Isaacson, Miller*

Watkins, Thomas M. — *Lamalie Amrop International*

Watkinson, Jim W. — *The Badger Group*

Watson, Hanan S. — *Watson International, Inc.*

Watson, James — *MSI International*

Waymire, Pamela — *Source Services Corporation*

Wayne, Cary S. — *ProSearch Inc.*

Webb, George H. — *Webb, Johnson Associates, Inc.*

Webber, Edward — *Source Services Corporation*

Weeks, Glenn — *Source Services Corporation*

Weinberg, Melvin — *Romac & Associates*

Weis, Theodore — *Source Services Corporation*

Weisler, Nancy — *National Search, Inc.*

Weiss, Elizabeth — *Source Services Corporation*

Weissman-Rosenthal, Abbe — *ALW Research International*

Welch, Robert — *Ray & Berndtson*

Weller, Paul S. — *Mark Stanley/EMA Partners International*

Wendler, Kambrea R. — *Gregory Michaels and Associates, Inc.*

Wenz, Alexander — *Source Services Corporation*

Wessling, Jerry — *Source Services Corporation*

Westfall, Ed — *Zwell International*

Wheatley, William — *Drummond Associates, Inc.*

Wheeler, Gerard H. — *A.J. Burton Group, Inc.*

White, William C. — *Venture Resources Inc.*

Whitfield, Jack — *Source Services Corporation*

Whiting, Anthony — *Johnson Smith & Knisely Accord*

Whitney, David L. — *Whitney & Associates, Inc.*

Whitney, William A — *Larsen, Whitney, Blecksmith & Zilliacus*

Whitton, Paula L. — *Pearson, Caldwell & Farnsworth, Inc.*

Wilcox, Fred T. — *Wilcox, Bertoux & Miller*

Wilder, Richard B. — *Columbia Consulting Group*

Wilkinson, Barbara — *Beall & Company, Inc.*

Wilkinson, Jr. SPHR

Wilkinson, Charles E. — *The HRM Group, Inc.*

Willbrandt, Curt — *Source Services Corporation*

Williams, Angie — *Whitney & Associates, Inc.*

Williams, Gary L. — *Barnes Development Group, LLC*

Williams, Harry D. — *Jacobson Associates*

Williams, Jack — *A.T. Kearney, Inc.*
Williams, John — *Source Services Corporation*
Williams, Lis — *Executive Options, Ltd.*
Williams, Roger K. — *Williams, Roth & Krueger Inc.*
Williams, Stephen E. — *Barton Associates, Inc.*
Willis, William H. — *William Willis Worldwide Inc.*
Wilson, Joyce — *Source Services Corporation*
Wilson, Patricia L. — *Leon A. Farley Associates*
Wilson, T. Gordon — *Ray & Berndtson/Lovas Stanley*
Wingate, Mary — *Source Services Corporation*
Winitz, Joel — *GSW Consulting Group, Inc.*
Winitz, Marla — *GSW Consulting Group, Inc.*
Winkowski, Stephen — *Source Services Corporation*
Winnicki, Kimberly — *Source Services Corporation*
Winograd, Glenn — *Criterion Executive Search, Inc.*
Winston, Dale — *Battalia Winston International*
Wisch, Steven C. — *MB Inc. Interim Executive Division*
Wise, J. Herbert — *Sandhurst Associates*
Witzgall, William — *Source Services Corporation*
Wold, Ted W. — *Hyde Danforth Wold & Co.*
Wolf, Donald — *Source Services Corporation*
Wolf, Stephen M. — *Byron Leonard International, Inc.*
Wolfe, Peter — *Source Services Corporation*
Womack, Joseph — *The Bankers Group*
Wood, Elizabeth — *Highland Search Group*
Wood, Gary — *Source Services Corporation*
Woodmansee, Bruce J. — *Tully/Woodmansee International, Inc.*
Woods, Craig — *Source Services Corporation*
Woodworth, Gail — *Woodworth International Group*
Wooldridge, Jeff — *Ray & Berndtson*
Wooller, Edmund A.M. — *Windsor International*
Woomer, Jerome — *Source Services Corporation*
Workman, David — *Source Services Corporation*
Wright, A. Leo — *The Hindman Company*
Wright, Carl A.J. — *A.J. Burton Group, Inc.*
Wright, Charles D. — *Goodrich & Sherwood Associates, Inc.*
Wright, Leslie — *The Stevenson Group of New Jersey*
Wycoff-Viola, Amy — *Source Services Corporation*
Yaekle, Gary — *Tully/Woodmansee International, Inc.*
Yeaton, Robert — *Source Services Corporation*
Yen, Maggie Yeh Ching — *Ray & Berndtson*
Young, Nick — *Spencer Stuart*
Youngberg, David — *Source Services Corporation*
Yungerberg, Steven — *Steven Yungerberg Associates Inc.*
Zaffrann, Craig S. — *P.J. Murphy & Associates, Inc.*
Zahradka, James F. — *P.J. Murphy & Associates, Inc.*
Zaleta, Andy R. — *A.T. Kearney, Inc.*
Zamborsky, George — *Boyden*
Zaslav, Debra M. — *Telford, Adams & Alexander/Telford & Co., Inc.*

Zavat, Marc — *Ryan, Miller & Associates Inc.*
Zavrel, Mark — *Source Services Corporation*
Zay, Thomas C. — *Boyden/Zay & Company*
Zegel, Gary — *Source Services Corporation*
Zila, Laurie M. — *Princeton Entrepreneurial Resources*
Zimbal, Mark — *Source Services Corporation*
Zimont, Scott — *Source Services Corporation*
Zivic, Janis M. — *Spencer Stuart*
Zona, Henry F. — *Zona & Associates, Inc.*
Zonis, Hildy R. — *Accountants Executive Search*
Zwell, Michael — *Zwell International*

5. General Management

Abbott, Peter D. — *The Abbott Group, Inc.*
Abell, Vincent W. — *MSI International*
Abert, Janice — *Ledbetter/Davidson International, Inc.*
Adler, Louis S. — *CJA - The Adler Group*
Agee, Jo Etta — *Chrisman & Company, Incorporated*
Akin, J.R. "Jack" — *J.R. Akin & Company Inc.*
Alexander, John T. — *Telford, Adams & Alexander*
Allard, Susan — *Allard Associates*
Allen, Scott — *Chrisman & Company, Incorporated*
Allen, Wade H. — *Cendea Connection International*
Allen, William L. — *The Hindman Company*
Allgire, Mary L. — *Kenzer Corp.*
Allred, J. Michael — *Spencer Stuart*
Amato, Joseph — *Amato & Associates, Inc.*
Ambler, Peter W. — *Peter W. Ambler Company*
Amilowski, Maria — *Highland Search Group*
Anderson, Maria H. — *Barton Associates, Inc.*
Anderson, Richard — *Grant Cooper and Associates*
Andujo, Michele M. — *Chrisman & Company, Incorporated*
Anwar, Tarin — *Jay Gaines & Company, Inc.*
Argenio, Michelangelo — *Spencer Stuart*
Aronin, Michael — *Fisher-Todd Associates*
Aronow, Lawrence E. — *Aronow Associates, Inc.*
Ascher, Susan P. — *The Ascher Group*
Ashton, Edward J. — *E.J. Ashton & Associates, Ltd.*
Aston, Kathy — *Marra Peters & Partners*
Attell, Harold — *A.E. Feldman Associates*
Austin Lockton, Kathy — *Juntunen-Combs-Poirier*
Axelrod, Nancy R. — *A.T. Kearney, Inc.*
Aydelotte, G. Thomas — *Ingram & Aydelotte Inc./I-I-C Partners*
Badger, Fred H. — *The Badger Group*
Baeder, Jeremy — *Executive Manning Corporation*
Bailey, Vanessa — *Highland Search Group*
Baje, Sarah — *Innovative Search Group, LLC*
Baker, Gary M. — *Cochran, Cochran & Yale, Inc.*
Baker, Gerry — *A.T. Kearney, Inc.*
Balbone, Rich — *Executive Manning Corporation*
Baldock, Robert G. — *Ray & Berndtson/Lovas Stanley*
Baltaglia, Michael — *Cochran, Cochran & Yale, Inc.*
Barbour, Mary Beth — *Tully/Woodmansee International, Inc.*
Barch, Sherrie — *Furst Group/MPI*
Barger, H. Carter — *Barger & Sargeant, Inc.*
Barlow, Ken H. — *The Cherbonnier Group, Inc.*

Barnes, Gary — *Brigade Inc.*
Barnes, Richard E. — *Barnes Development Group, LLC*
Barnes, Roanne L. — *Barnes Development Group, LLC*
Barnum, Toni M. — *Stone Murphy & Olson*
Bartholdi, Ted — *Bartholdi & Company, Inc.*
Bartholdi, Theodore G. — *Bartholdi & Company, Inc.*
Barton, Gary R. — *Barton Associates, Inc.*
Bason, Maurice L. — *Bason Associates Inc.*
Bass, M. Lynn — *Ray & Berndtson*
Bass, Nate — *Jacobson Associates*
Bauman, Martin H. — *Martin H. Bauman Associates, Inc.*
Bearman, Linda — *Grant Cooper and Associates*
Beaudin, Elizabeth C. — *Callan Associates, Ltd.*
Beaver, Bentley H. — *The Onstott Group, Inc.*
Belin, Jean — *Boyden*
Bell, Lloyd W. — *O'Brien & Bell*
Bellano, Robert W. — *Stanton Chase International*
Bender, Alan — *Bender Executive Search*
Bennett, Jo — *Battalia Winston International*
Benson, Kate — *Rene Plessner Associates, Inc.*
Beran, Helena — *Michael J. Cavanagh and Associates*
Berk-Levine, Margo — *MB Inc. Interim Executive Division*
Berne, Marlene — *The Whitney Group*
Berry, Harold B. — *The Hindman Company*
Bertoux, Michael P. — *Wilcox, Bertoux & Miller*
Bettick, Michael J. — *A.J. Burton Group, Inc.*
Billington, William H. — *Spriggs & Company, Inc.*
Birkhead, Linda — *Zwell International*
Blakslee, Jan H. — *J: Blakslee International, Ltd.*
Bliley, Jerry — *Spencer Stuart*
Bloomer, James E. — *L.W. Foote Company*
Boel, Werner — *The Dalley Hewitt Company*
Bogansky, Amy — *Conex Incorporated*
Bohn, Steve J. — *MSI International*
Boltrus, Dick — *Sink, Walker, Boltrus International*
Bongiovanni, Vincent — *ESA Professional Consultants*
Bonifield, Len — *Bonifield Associates*
Bonnell, William R. — *Bonnell Associates Ltd.*
Borkin, Andrew — *Strategic Advancement Inc.*
Borland, James — *Goodrich & Sherwood Associates, Inc.*
Bormann, Cindy Ann — *MSI International*
Bourrie, Sharon D. — *Chartwell Partners International, Inc.*
Bovich, Maryann C. — *Higdon Prince Inc.*
Bowden, Otis H. — *BowdenGlobal, Ltd.*
Bowen, Tad — *Executive Search International*
Brackman, Janet — *Dahl-Morrow International*
Bradley, Dalena — *Woodworth International Group*
Bradshaw, Monte — *Christian & Timbers*
Brady, Dick — *William Guy & Associates*
Brandenburg, David — *Professional Staffing Consultants*
Bratches, Howard — *Thorndike Deland Associates*
Brennan, Patrick J. — *Handy HRM Corp.*
Brieger, Steve — *Thorne, Brieger Associates Inc.*
Brinson, Robert — *MSI International*

Brother, Joy — *Charles Luntz & Associates. Inc.*
Brown, Larry C. — *Horton International*
Brown, Lawrence Anthony — *MSI International*
Brown, Steffan — *Woodworth International Group*
Brudno, Robert J. — *Savoy Partners, Ltd.*
Bruno, Deborah F. — *The Hindman Company*
Bryant, Shari G. — *Bryant Associates, Inc.*
Brzezinski, Ronald T. — *Callan Associates, Ltd.*
Buchalter, Allyson — *The Whitney Group*
Buckles, Donna — *Cochran, Cochran & Yale, Inc.*
Buggy, Linda — *Bonnell Associates Ltd.*
Bump, Gerald J. — *D.E. Foster Partners Inc.*
Burden, Gene — *The Cherbonnier Group, Inc.*
Burfield, Elaine — *Skott/Edwards Consultants, Inc.*
Burke, John — *The Experts*
Burke, Karen A. — *Mazza & Riley, Inc. (a Korn/Ferry International affiliate)*
Burkland, Skott B. — *Skott/Edwards Consultants, Inc.*
Burns, Alan — *The Enns Partners Inc.*
Burns, Terence N. — *D.E. Foster Partners Inc.*
Busch, Jack — *Busch International*
Butler, Kirby B. — *The Butlers Company Insurance Recruiters*
Butterfass, Stanley — *Butterfass, Pepe & MacCallan Inc.*
Byrnes, Thomas A. — *The Search Alliance, Inc.*
Caldwell, William R. — *Pearson, Caldwell & Farnsworth, Inc.*
Calivas, Kay — *A.J. Burton Group, Inc.*
Call, David — *Cochran, Cochran & Yale, Inc.*
Callan, Robert M. — *Callan Associates, Ltd.*
Cameron, James W. — *Cameron Consulting*
Campbell, Patricia A. — *The Onstott Group, Inc.*
Campbell, Robert Scott — *Wellington Management Group*
Campbell, Robert Scott — *Wellington Management Group*
Cannavo, Louise — *The Whitney Group*
Capizzi, Karen — *Cochran, Cochran & Yale, Inc.*
Cappe, Richard R. — *Roberts Ryan and Bentley*
Carideo, Joseph — *Thorndike Deland Associates*
Carro, Carl R. — *Executive Search Consultants International, Inc.*
Casal, Daniel G. — *Bonifield Associates*
Cashen, Anthony B. — *Lamalie Amrop International*
Castine, Michael P. — *Highland Search Group*
Cavanagh, Michael J. — *Michael J. Cavanagh and Associates*
Chappell, Peter — *The Bankers Group*
Chatterjie, Alok — *MSI International*
Cherbonnier, L. Michael — *TCG International, Inc.*
Cherbonnier, L. Michael — *The Cherbonnier Group, Inc.*
Chndler, Brad J. — *Furst Group/MPI*
Christenson, H. Alan — *Christenson & Hutchison*
Christian, Jeffrey E. — *Christian & Timbers*
Christian, Philip — *Ray & Berndtson*
Cizek, John T. — *Cizek Associates, Inc.*
Cizek, Marti J. — *Cizek Associates, Inc.*
Clake, Bob — *Furst Group/MPI*
Clarey, William A. — *Preng & Associates, Inc.*
Clark, Evan — *The Whitney Group*
Clark, Steven — *D.A. Kreuter Associates, Inc.*

Clarke Smith, Jamie — *Kaye-Bassman International Corp.*
Clauhsen, Elizabeth A. — *Savoy Partners, Ltd.*
Clayton, Fred J. — *Berkhemer Clayton Incorporated*
Cloutier, Gisella — *Dinte Resources, Inc.*
Cochran, Scott P. — *The Badger Group*
Coffman, Brian — *Kossuth & Associates, Inc.*
Cohen, Michael R. — *Intech Summit Group, Inc.*
Cohen, Robert C. — *Intech Summit Group, Inc.*
Coleman, J. Kevin — *J. Kevin Coleman & Associates, Inc.*
Collard, Joseph A. — *Spencer Stuart*
Comstock, Rodger — *Johnson Smith & Knisely Accord*
Cona, Joseph A. — *Cona Personnel Search*
Conard, Rodney J. — *Conard Associates, Inc.*
Connelly, Kevin M. — *Spencer Stuart*
Conway, Maureen — *Conway & Associates*
Cook, Dennis — *A.T. Kearney, Inc.*
Cooke, Katherine H. — *Horton International*
Corso, Glen S. — *Chartwell Partners International, Inc.*
Cortina Del Valle, Pedro — *Ray & Berndtson*
Costello, Lynda — *Coe & Company International Inc.*
Courtney, Brendan — *A.J. Burton Group, Inc.*
Cox, William — *E.J. Ashton & Associates, Ltd.*
Coyle, Hugh F. — *A.J. Burton Group, Inc.*
Crane, Howard C. — *Chartwell Partners International, Inc.*
Crath, Paul F. — *Price Waterhouse*
Crecos, Gregory P. — *Gregory Michaels and Associates, Inc.*
Crist, Peter — *Crist Partners, Ltd.*
Critchley, Walter — *Cochran, Cochran & Yale, Inc.*
Cronin, Dolores — *Corporate Careers, Inc.*
Cruse, O.D. — *Spencer Stuart*
Crystal, Jonathan A. — *Spencer Stuart*
Cuddihy, Paul — *Dahl-Morrow International*
Cunningham, Lawrence — *Howard Fischer Associates, Inc.*
Cunningham, Robert Y. — *Goodrich & Sherwood Associates, Inc.*
Curtis, Ellissa — *Cochran, Cochran & Yale, Inc.*
Danforth, W. Michael — *Hyde Danforth Wold & Co.*
Daniels, Alfred — *Alfred Daniels & Associates*
Daniels, C. Eugene — *Sigma Group International*
Davis, G. Gordon — *Davis & Company*
De Brun, Thomas P. — *Ray & Berndtson*
de Cholnoky, Andrea — *Spencer Stuart*
de Palacios, Jeannette C. — *J. Palacios & Associates, Inc.*
de Tuede, Catherine — *The Search Alliance, Inc.*
Deaver, Henry C. — *Ray & Berndtson*
DeFuniak, William S. — *DeFuniak & Edwards*
Del Pino, William — *National Search, Inc.*
Delaney, Patrick J. — *Sensible Solutions, Inc.*
Delmonico, Laura — *A.J. Burton Group, Inc.*
Desai, Sushila — *Sink, Walker, Boltrus International*
Desmond, Dennis — *Beall & Company, Inc.*
deWilde, David M. — *Chartwell Partners International, Inc.*
Dezember, Steve — *Ray & Berndtson*

DiCioccio, Carmen — *Cochran, Cochran & Yale, Inc.*
Dicker, Barry — *ESA Professional Consultants*
Dickerson, Scot — *Key Employment Services*
Dickson, Duke — *A.D. & Associates Executive Search, Inc.*
Dieckmann, Ralph E. — *Dieckmann & Associates, Ltd.*
Dietz, David S. — *MSI International*
DiMarchi, Paul — *DiMarchi Partners, Inc.*
DiMarchi, Paul — *DiMarchi Partners, Inc.*
Dingeldey, Peter E. — *Search Advisors International Corp.*
Dingman, Bruce — *Robert W. Dingman Company, Inc.*
Dinte, Paul — *Dinte Resources, Inc.*
DiSalvo, Fred — *The Cambridge Group Ltd*
Divine, Robert S. — *O'Shea, Divine & Company, Inc.*
Doele, Donald C. — *Goodrich & Sherwood Associates, Inc.*
Donath, Linda — *Dahl-Morrow International*
Donnelly, George J. — *Ward Howell International, Inc.*
Dotson, M. Ileen — *Dotson & Associates*
Doukas, Jon A. — *Professional Bank Services, Inc. D/B/A Executive Search, Inc.*
Dowdall, Jean — *A.T. Kearney, Inc.*
Dowell, Chris — *The Abbott Group, Inc.*
Dowell, Mary K. — *Professional Search Associates*
Doyle, James W. — *Executive Search Consultants International, Inc.*
Dreifus, Donald — *Search West, Inc.*
Dromeshauser, Peter — *Dromeshauser Associates*
Drury, James J. — *Spencer Stuart*
Dubbs, William — *Williams Executive Search, Inc.*
Duckworth, Donald R. — *Johnson Smith & Knisely Accord*
Duggan, James P. — *Slayton International, Inc./ I-I-C Partners*
Dunbar, Marilynne — *Ray & Berndtson/Lovas Stanley*
Dunman, Betsy L. — *Crawford & Crofford*
Durakis, Charles A. — *C.A. Durakis Associates, Inc.*
Eason, Jan C. — *Summit Group International*
Ebeling, John A. — *Gilbert Tweed/INESA*
Eddy, Terry — *William Guy & Associates*
Edwards, Dorothy — *MSI International*
Edwards, Ned — *Ingram & Aydelotte Inc./I-I-C Partners*
Edwards, Randolph J. — *DeFuniak & Edwards*
Edwards, Verba L. — *Wing Tips & Pumps, Inc.*
Ehrgott, Elizabeth — *The Ascher Group*
Ehrhart, Jennifer — *ADOW's Executeam*
Elder, Tom — *Juntunen-Combs-Poirier*
Eldridge, Charles B. — *Ray & Berndtson*
Ellis, Ted K. — *The Hindman Company*
Ellis, William — *Interspace Interactive Inc.*
Engelbert, Kimberly S. — *Watson International, Inc.*
England, Mark — *Austin-McGregor International*
Enns, George — *The Enns Partners Inc.*
Erickson, Elaine — *Kenzer Corp.*
Erikson, Theodore J. — *Erikson Consulting Associates, Inc.*

Eustis, Lucy R. — *MSI International*
Evans, David — *Executive Manning Corporation*
Fancher, Robert L. — *Bason Associates Inc.*
Farley, Leon A. — *Leon A. Farley Associates*
Farnsworth, John A. — *Pearson, Caldwell & Farnsworth, Inc.*
Fee, J. Curtis — *Spencer Stuart*
Feldman, Abe — *A.E. Feldman Associates*
Ferneborg, Jay W. — *Ferneborg & Associates, Inc.*
Ferneborg, John R. — *Ferneborg & Associates, Inc.*
Fischer, Adam — *Howard Fischer Associates, Inc.*
Fischer, Howard M. — *Howard Fischer Associates, Inc.*
Fischer, Janet L. — *Boyden*
Fischer, John C. — *Horton International*
Fisher, Neal — *Fisher Personnel Management Services*
Fishler, Stu — *A.T. Kearney, Inc.*
Fitzgerald, Diane — *Fitzgerald Associates*
Fitzgerald, Geoffrey — *Fitzgerald Associates*
Fleming, Marco — *MSI International*
Fletcher, David — *A.J. Burton Group, Inc.*
Flood, Michael — *Norman Broadbent International, Inc.*
Flora, Dodi — *Crawford & Crofford*
Flynn, Jack — *Executive Search Consultants Corporation*
Foote, Leland W. — *L.W. Foote Company*
Ford, Sandra D. — *The Ford Group, Inc.*
Foreman, David C. — *Koontz, Jeffries & Associates, Inc.*
Foster, Dwight E. — *D.E. Foster Partners Inc.*
Fowler, Edward D.C. — *Higdon Prince Inc.*
Fowler, Thomas A. — *The Hindman Company*
Frazier, John — *Cochran, Cochran & Yale, Inc.*
Freeman, Mark — *ESA Professional Consultants*
Freier, Bruce — *Executive Referral Services, Inc.*
French, William G. — *Preng & Associates, Inc.*
Fribush, Richard — *A.J. Burton Group, Inc.*
Friedman, Helen E. — *McCormack & Farrow*
Fulton, Christine N. — *Highland Search Group*
Furlong, James W. — *Furlong Search, Inc.*
Furlong, James W. — *Furlong Search, Inc.*
Furlong, James W. — *Furlong Search, Inc.*
Fust, Sheely F. — *Ray & Berndtson*
Gabel, Gregory N. — *Canny, Bowen Inc.*
Gabriel, David L. — *The Arcus Group*
Gaffney, Keith — *Gaffney Management Consultants*
Gaffney, William — *Gaffney Management Consultants*
Gaines, Jay — *Jay Gaines & Company, Inc.*
Galante, Suzanne M. — *Vlcek & Company, Inc.*
Galinski, Paul — *E.J. Ashton & Associates, Ltd.*
Gallagher, Terence M. — *Battalia Winston International*
Gantar, Donna — *Howard Fischer Associates, Inc.*
Gardiner, E. Nicholas P. — *Gardiner International*
Garfinkle, Steven M. — *Battalia Winston International*
Garzone, Dolores — *M.A. Churchill & Associates, Inc.*
Gauthier, Robert C. — *Columbia Consulting Group*
Geiger, Jan — *Wilcox, Bertoux & Miller*
George, Delores F. — *Delores F. George Human Resource Management & Consulting Industry*

Gerber, Mark J. — *Wellington Management Group*
Germain, Valerie — *Jay Gaines & Company, Inc.*
Gerster, J.P. — *Juntunen-Combs-Poirier*
Gestwick, Daniel — *Cochran, Cochran & Yale, Inc.*
Ghurani, Mac — *Gary Kaplan & Associates*
Gibbons, Ronald L. — *Flynn, Hannock, Incorporated*
Gibbs, John S. — *Spencer Stuart*
Gilbert, Jerry — *Gilbert & Van Campen International*
Gilbert, Patricia G. — *Lynch Miller Moore, Inc.*
Gilchrist, Robert J. — *Horton International*
Gill, Patricia — *Columbia Consulting Group*
Gill, Susan — *Plummer & Associates, Inc.*
Gilreath, James M. — *Gilreath Weatherby, Inc.*
Gobert, Larry — *Professional Search Consultants*
Golde, Lisa — *Tully/Woodmansee International, Inc.*
Goldenberg, Susan — *Grant Cooper and Associates*
Goldsmith, Joseph B. — *Higdon Prince Inc.*
Goldstein, Gary — *The Whitney Group*
Gonzalez, Kristen — *A.J. Burton Group, Inc.*
Goodman, Dawn M. — *Bason Associates Inc.*
Goodwin, Tim — *William Guy & Associates*
Gordon, Gerald L. — *E.G. Jones Associates, Ltd.*
Gotlys, Jordan — *Stone Murphy & Olson*
Gow, Roderick C. — *Lamalie Amrop International*
Grant, Michael — *Zwell International*
Grantham, John — *Grantham & Co., Inc.*
Grasch, Jerry E. — *The Hindman Company*
Gray, Annie — *Annie Gray Associates, Inc./The Executive Search Firm*
Gray, Mark — *Executive Referral Services, Inc.*
Grebenschikoff, Jennifer R. — *Physician Executive Management Center*
Grebenstein, Charles R. — *Skott/Edwards Consultants, Inc.*
Greco, Patricia — *Howe-Lewis International*
Griffin, Cathy — *A.T. Kearney, Inc.*
Grotenhuis, Dirkten — *Chrisman & Company, Incorporated*
Grotte, Lawrence C. — *Lautz Grotte Engler*
Gulian, Randolph — *Strategic Executives, Inc.*
Gurtin, Kay L. — *Executive Options, Ltd.*
Guy, C. William — *William Guy & Associates*
Haas, Margaret P. — *The Haas Associates, Inc.*
Haberman, Joseph C. — *A.T. Kearney, Inc.*
Hagglund, Karl H. — *Simpson Associates, Inc.*
Hailey, H.M. — *Damon & Associates, Inc.*
Halbrich, Mitch — *A.J. Burton Group, Inc.*
Hall, Peter V. — *Chartwell Partners International, Inc.*
Hallock, Peter B. — *Goodrich & Sherwood Associates, Inc.*
Hallstrom, Victoria — *The Whitney Group*
Hamilton, John R. — *Ray & Berndtson*
Hammond, Karla — *People Management Northeast Incorporated*
Hanes, Leah — *Ray & Berndtson*
Hanley, Alan P. — *Williams, Roth & Krueger Inc.*
Hanley, J. Patrick — *Canny, Bowen Inc.*
Hanley, Maureen E. — *Gilbert Tweed/INESA*
Hannock, Elwin W. — *Flynn, Hannock, Incorporated*

Hanson, Grant M. — *Goodrich & Sherwood Associates, Inc.*
Harbaugh, Paul J. — *International Management Advisors, Inc.*
Harbert, David O. — *Sweeney Harbert & Mummert, Inc.*
Hardison, Richard L. — *Hardison & Company*
Harelick, Arthur S. — *Ashway, Ltd.*
Harney, Elyane — *Gary Kaplan & Associates*
Harris, Jack — *A.T. Kearney, Inc.*
Harris, Joe W. — *Cendea Connection International*
Harris, Julia — *The Whitney Group*
Harris, Seth O. — *Christian & Timbers*
Harrison, Joel — *D.A. Kreuter Associates, Inc.*
Hart, Robert T. — *D.E. Foster Partners Inc.*
Harvey, Mike — *Advanced Executive Resources*
Haughton, Michael — *DeFrain, Mayer LLC*
Hauser, Martha — *Spencer Stuart*
Havener, Donald Clarke — *The Abbott Group, Inc.*
Hawksworth, A. Dwight — *A.D. & Associates Executive Search, Inc.*
Hay, William E. — *William E. Hay & Co.*
Haystead, Steve — *Advanced Executive Resources*
Healey, Joseph T. — *Highland Search Group*
Hebel, Robert W. — *R.W. Hebel Associates*
Heiken, Barbara E. — *Randell-Heiken, Inc.*
Heinze, David — *Heinze & Associates, Inc.*
Hellinger, Audrey W. — *Martin H. Bauman Associates, Inc.*
Helminiak, Audrey — *Gaffney Management Consultants*
Hendrickson, Jill E. — *Gregory Michaels and Associates, Inc.*
Heneghan, Donald A. — *Allerton Heneghan & O'Neill*
Hennig, Sandra M. — *MSI International*
Henry, Mary — *Conex Incorporated*
Hensley, Bert — *Morgan Samuels Co., Inc.*
Hergenrather, Richard A. — *Hergenrather & Company*
Herman, Shelli — *Gary Kaplan & Associates*
Hetherman, Margaret F. — *Highland Search Group*
Hewitt, Rives D. — *The Dalley Hewitt Company*
Hewitt, W. Davis — *The Dalley Hewitt Company*
Higbee, Joan — *Thorndike Deland Associates*
Higdon, Henry G. — *Higdon Prince Inc.*
Higgins, Donna — *Howard Fischer Associates, Inc.*
Hildebrand, Thomas B. — *Professional Resources Group, Inc.*
Hill, Emery — *MSI International*
Hillen, Skip — *The McCormick Group, Inc.*
Himes, Dirk — *A.T. Kearney, Inc.*
Himlin, Amy — *Cochran, Cochran & Yale, Inc.*
Hindman, Neil C. — *The Hindman Company*
Hochberg, Brian — *M.A. Churchill & Associates, Inc.*
Hockett, William — *Hockett Associates, Inc.*
Holland, John A. — *Holland, McFadzean & Associates, Inc.*
Holland, Rose Mary — *Price Waterhouse*
Holmes, Lawrence J. — *Columbia Consulting Group*
Holodnak, William A. — *J. Robert Scott*

Holt, Carol — *Bartholdi & Company, Inc.*
Holzberger, Georges L. — *Highland Search Group*
Honer, Paul E. — *Ingram & Aydelotte Inc./I-I-C Partners*
Hoover, Catherine — *J.L. Mark Associates, Inc.*
Hopkins, Chester A. — *Handy HRM Corp.*
Hopp, Lorrie A. — *Gregory Michaels and Associates, Inc.*
Houchins, William M. — *Christian & Timbers*
Hoyda, Louis A. — *Thorndike Deland Associates*
Hucko, Donald S. — *Jonas, Walters & Assoc., Inc.*
Hudson, Reginald M. — *Search Bureau International*
Hughes, Cathy N. — *The Ogdon Partnership*
Hutchison, William K. — *Christenson & Hutchison*
Hutton, Thomas J. — *The Thomas Tucker Company*
Hybels, Cynthia — *A.J. Burton Group, Inc.*
Hypes, Richard G. — *Lynch Miller Moore, Inc.*
Ikle, A. Donald — *Ward Howell International, Inc.*
Imely, Larry S. — *Stratford Group*
Ingram, D. John — *Ingram & Aydelotte Inc./I-I-C Partners*
Inguagiato, Gregory — *MSI International*
Issacs, Judith A. — *Grant Cooper and Associates*
Jablo, Steven A. — *Dieckmann & Associates, Ltd.*
Jackson, Joan — *A.T. Kearney, Inc.*
Jacobs, Martin J. — *The Rubicon Group*
Jacobs, Mike — *Thorne, Brieger Associates Inc.*
Jacobson, Rick — *The Windham Group*
Janssen, Don — *Howard Fischer Associates, Inc.*
Januale, Lois — *Cochran, Cochran & Yale, Inc.*
Jazylo, John V. — *Handy HRM Corp.*
Jeffers, Richard B. — *Dieckmann & Associates, Ltd.*
Jernigan, Susan N. — *Sockwell & Associates*
Joffe, Barry — *Bason Associates Inc.*
Johnson, Brian — *A.J. Burton Group, Inc.*
Johnson, John W. — *Webb, Johnson Associates, Inc.*
Johnson, Julie M. — *International Staffing Consultants, Inc.*
Johnson, Kathleen A. — *Barton Associates, Inc.*
Johnson, Priscilla — *The Johnson Group, Inc.*
Johnson, S. Hope — *Boyden Washington, D.C.*
Johnson, Stanley C. — *Johnson & Company*
Johnson, Valerie — *Coe & Company International Inc.*
Jordan, Jon — *Cochran, Cochran & Yale, Inc.*
Judge, Alfred L. — *The Cambridge Group Ltd*
Juelis, John J. — *Peeney Associates*
Juska, Frank — *Rusher, Loscavio & LoPresto*
Kaiser, Donald J. — *Dunhill International Search of New Haven*
Kalinowski, David — *Jacobson Associates*
Kane, Frank — *A.J. Burton Group, Inc.*
Kane, Karen — *Howard Fischer Associates, Inc.*
Kaplan, Gary — *Gary Kaplan & Associates*
Kassouf, Constance — *The Whitney Group*
Keating, Pierson — *Nordeman Grimm, Inc.*
Keitel, Robert S. — *A.T. Kearney, Inc.*
Keller, Barbara E. — *Barton Associates, Inc.*
Kelly, Elizabeth Ann — *Wellington Management Group*
Kelly, Peter W. — *R. Rollo Associates*

Kelso, Patricia C. — *Barton Associates, Inc.*
Kennedy, Michael — *The Danbrook Group, Inc.*
Kenzer, Robert D. — *Kenzer Corp.*
Kern, Jerry L. — *ADOW's Executeam*
Kern, Kathleen G. — *ADOW's Executeam*
Kershaw, Lisa — *Tanton Mitchell/Paul Ray Berndtson*
Keshishian, Gregory — *Handy HRM Corp.*
Kettwig, David A. — *A.T. Kearney, Inc.*
Keyser, Anne — *A.T. Kearney, Inc.*
Kilcullen, Brian A. — *D.A. Kreuter Associates, Inc.*
Kile, Robert W. — *Rusher, Loscavio & LoPresto*
Kiley, Phyllis — *National Search, Inc.*
King, Bill — *The McCormick Group, Inc.*
King, Margaret — *Christian & Timbers*
King, Steven — *Ashway, Ltd.*
Kinser, Richard E. — *Richard Kinser & Associates*
Kip, Luanne S. — *Kip Williams, Inc.*
Kirschman, David R. — *Physician Executive Management Center*
Kishbaugh, Herbert S. — *Kishbaugh Associates International*
Klages, Constance W. — *International Management Advisors, Inc.*
Klavens, Cecile J. — *The Pickwick Group, Inc.*
Klein, Brandon — *A.J. Burton Group, Inc.*
Klein, Gary — *A.T. Kearney, Inc.*
Klein, Lynn M. — *Riotto-Jones Associates*
Klein, Mary Jo — *Cochran, Cochran & Yale, Inc.*
Klein, Mel — *Stewart/Laurence Associates*
Knisely, Gary — *Johnson Smith & Knisely Accord*
Kohn, Adam P. — *Christian & Timbers*
Kondra, Vernon J. — *The Douglas Reiter Company, Inc.*
Koontz, Donald N. — *Koontz, Jeffries & Associates, Inc.*
Kopsick, Joseph M. — *Spencer Stuart*
Kossuth, David — *Kossuth & Associates, Inc.*
Kossuth, Jane — *Kossuth & Associates, Inc.*
Kotick, Maddy — *The Stevenson Group of New Jersey*
Krauser, H. James — *Spencer Stuart*
Krejci, Stanley L. — *Boyden Washington, D.C.*
Kreuch, Paul C. — *Skott/Edwards Consultants, Inc.*
Kreuter, Daniel A. — *D.A. Kreuter Associates, Inc.*
Kreutz, Gary L. — *Kreutz Consulting Group, Inc.*
Krieger, Dennis F. — *Seiden Krieger Associates, Inc.*
Krueger, Kurt — *Krueger Associates*
Kunzer, William J. — *Kunzer Associates, Ltd.*
Kurrigan, Geoffrey — *ESA Professional Consultants*
Kussner, Janice N. — *Herman Smith Executive Initiatives Inc.*
Laba, Marvin — *Marvin Laba & Associates*
Laba, Stuart M. — *Marvin Laba & Associates*
Labrecque, Bernard F. — *Laurendeau Labrecque/Ray & Berndtson, Inc.*
Lachance, Roger — *Laurendeau Labrecque/Ray & Berndtson, Inc.*
Lache, Shawn E. — *The Arcus Group*
Lang, Sharon A. — *Ray & Berndtson*
Lardner, Lucy D. — *Tully/Woodmansee International, Inc.*
Larsen, Richard F. — *Larsen, Whitney, Blecksmith & Zilliacus*
Lasher, Charles M. — *Lasher Associates*

Lauderback, David R. — *A.T. Kearney, Inc.*
Laurendeau, Jean E. — *Laurendeau Labrecque/Ray & Berndtson, Inc.*
Lautz, Lindsay A. — *Lautz Grotte Engler*
Lawrance, Susanne — *Sharrow & Associates*
Lazaro, Alicia C. — *The Whitney Group*
Ledbetter, Steven G. — *Cendea Connection International*
Leetma, Imbi — *Stanton Chase International*
Leighton, Nina — *The Ogdon Partnership*
Leininger, Dennis — *Key Employment Services*
Lence, Julie Anne — *MSI International*
Leonard, Linda — *Harris Heery & Associates*
Leslie, William H. — *Boyden/Zay & Company*
Levine, Alan M. — *MB Inc. Interim Executive Division*
Levine, Lawrence — *Trebor Weldon Lawrence, Inc.*
Levine, Lois — *National Search, Inc.*
Levinson, Lauren — *The Danbrook Group, Inc.*
Lewicki, Christopher — *MSI International*
Lewis, Jon A. — *Sandhurst Associates*
Lezama Cohen, Luis — *Ray & Berndtson*
Liebowitz, Michael E. — *Highland Search Group*
Lindberg, Eric J. — *MSI International*
Linton, Leonard M. — *Byron Leonard International, Inc.*
Litt, Michele — *The Whitney Group*
Loeb, Stephen H. — *Grant Cooper and Associates*
Lokken, Karen — *A.E. Feldman Associates*
Long, Helga — *Horton International*
Long, Melanie — *National Search, Inc.*
Long, Milt — *William Guy & Associates*
Long, William G. — *McDonald, Long & Associates, Inc.*
Looney, Scott — *A.E. Feldman Associates*
LoPresto, Robert L. — *Rusher, Loscavio & LoPresto*
Loscavio, J. Michael — *Rusher, Loscavio & LoPresto*
Lotufo, Donald A. — *D.A.L. Associates, Inc.*
Lotz, R. James — *International Management Advisors, Inc.*
Lovas, W. Carl — *Ray & Berndtson/Lovas Stanley*
Lovely, Edward — *The Stevenson Group of New Jersey*
Lucarelli, Joan — *The Onstott Group, Inc.*
Lucas, Ronnie L. — *MSI International*
Lucht, John — *The John Lucht Consultancy Inc.*
Ludlow, Paula — *Horton International*
Lumsby, George N. — *International Management Advisors, Inc.*
Luntz, Charles E. — *Charles Luntz & Associates. Inc.*
Lupica, Anthony — *Cochran, Cochran & Yale, Inc.*
Lynch, Michael C. — *Lynch Miller Moore, Inc.*
Lyon, Jenny — *Marra Peters & Partners*
Lyons, Denis B.K. — *Spencer Stuart*
Lyons, J. David — *Aubin International Inc.*
MacCallan, Deirdre — *Butterfass, Pepe & MacCallan Inc.*
Macdonald, G. William — *The Macdonald Group, Inc.*
MacIntyre, Lisa W. — *Highland Search Group*
Mackenna, Kathy — *Plummer & Associates, Inc.*
Maer, Harry — *Kenzer Corp.*

Maglio, Charles J. — *Maglio and Company, Inc.*
Major, Susan — *A.T. Kearney, Inc.*
Mallin, Ellen — *Howard Fischer Associates, Inc.*
Manassero, Henri J.P. — *International Management Advisors, Inc.*
Mancino, Gene — *Blau Mancino Schroeder*
Mangum, Maria — *Thomas Mangum Company*
Mangum, William T. — *Thomas Mangum Company*
Manns, Alex — *Crawford & Crofford*
Mansford, Keith — *Howard Fischer Associates, Inc.*
Maphet, Harriet — *The Stevenson Group of New Jersey*
Marino, Chester — *Cochran, Cochran & Yale, Inc.*
Mark, John L. — *J.L. Mark Associates, Inc.*
Mark, Lynne — *J.L. Mark Associates, Inc.*
Marks, Ira — *Strategic Alternatives*
Marks, Russell E. — *Webb, Johnson Associates, Inc.*
Marra, John — *Marra Peters & Partners*
Marra, John — *Marra Peters & Partners*
Marumoto, William H. — *Boyden Washington, D.C.*
Massey, R. Bruce — *Horton International*
Mather, David R. — *Christian & Timbers*
Mathias, Kathy — *Stone Murphy & Olson*
Mattes, Edward C. — *The Ogdon Partnership*
Matthews, Corwin — *Woodworth International Group*
Maynard Taylor, Susan — *Chrisman & Company, Incorporated*
Mazor, Elly — *Howard Fischer Associates, Inc.*
Mazza, David B. — *Mazza & Riley, Inc. (a Korn/Ferry International affiliate)*
McBride, Jonathan E. — *McBride Associates, Inc.*
McBryde, Marnie — *Spencer Stuart*
McCallister, Richard A. — *Boyden*
McCloskey, Frank D. — *Johnson Smith & Knisely Accord*
McCormick, Brian — *The McCormick Group, Inc.*
McCreary, Charles "Chip" — *Austin-McGregor International*
McDermott, Jeffrey T. — *Vlcek & Company, Inc.*
McDonald, Scott A. — *McDonald Associates International*
McDonald, Stanleigh B. — *McDonald Associates International*
McDowell, Robert N. — *Christenson & Hutchison*
McFadden, Ashton S. — *Johnson Smith & Knisely Accord*
McFadzen,, James A. — *Holland, McFadzean & Associates, Inc.*
McGuire, Pat — *A.J. Burton Group, Inc.*
McKeown, Patricia A. — *DiMarchi Partners, Inc.*
McLean, E. Peter — *Spencer Stuart*
McManners, Donald E. — *McManners Associates, Inc.*
McMillin, Bob — *Price Waterhouse*
McNamara, Catherine — *Ray & Berndtson*
McNamara, Timothy Connor — *Horton International*
McNichols, Walter B. — *Gary Kaplan & Associates*
McNulty, Kelly L. — *Gregory Michaels and Associates, Inc.*

McSherry, James F. — *Battalia Winston International*
Mead, James D. — *James Mead & Company*
Meadows, C. David — *Professional Staffing Consultants*
Meagher, Patricia G. — *Spencer Stuart*
Meany, Brian M. — *Herbert Mines Associates, Inc.*
Meier, J. Dale — *Grant Cooper and Associates*
Meltzer, Andrea Y. — *Executive Options, Ltd.*
Menk, Carl — *Canny, Bowen Inc.*
Messett, William J. — *Messett Associates, Inc.*
Mestepey, John — *A.T. Kearney, Inc.*
Meyer, Michael F. — *Witt/Kieffer, Ford, Hadelman & Lloyd*
Meyer, Stacey — *Gary Kaplan & Associates*
Miller, David — *Cochran, Cochran & Yale, Inc.*
Miller, Michael R. — *Lynch Miller Moore, Inc.*
Miller, Roy — *The Enns Partners Inc.*
Millonzi, Joel C. — *Johnson Smith & Knisely Accord*
Milstein, Bonnie — *Marvin Laba & Associates*
Mines, Herbert T. — *Herbert Mines Associates, Inc.*
Misiurewicz, Marc — *Cochran, Cochran & Yale, Inc.*
Mitchell, Jeff — *A.J. Burton Group, Inc.*
Mogul, Gene — *Mogul Consultants, Inc.*
Mondragon, Philip — *A.T. Kearney, Inc.*
Montgomery, James M. — *Houze, Shourds & Montgomery, Inc.*
Moore, Mark — *Wheeler, Moore & Elam Co.*
Moore, T. Wills — *Ray & Berndtson*
Moore, Vickie J. — *Kirkman & Searing, Inc.*
Morgan, Gary — *National Search, Inc.*
Mortansen, Patricia — *Norman Broadbent International, Inc.*
Morton, Robert C. — *Morton, McCorkle & Associates, Inc.*
Muendel, H. Edward — *Stanton Chase International*
Mulligan, Robert P. — *William Willis Worldwide Inc.*
Murphy, Cornelius J. — *Goodrich & Sherwood Associates, Inc.*
Murphy, Patrick J. — *P.J. Murphy & Associates, Inc.*
Murray, Virginia — *A.T. Kearney, Inc.*
Mursuli, Meredith — *Lasher Associates*
Mustin, Joyce M. — *J: Blakslee International, Ltd.*
Nagler, Leon G. — *Nagler, Robins & Poe, Inc.*
Naidicz, Maria — *Ray & Berndtson*
Nair, Leslie — *Zwell International*
Nass, Martin D. — *Lamalie Amrop International*
Nathanson, Barry F. — *Barry Nathanson Associates*
Nees, Eugene C. — *Ray & Berndtson*
Neff, Thomas J. — *Spencer Stuart*
Neher, Robert L. — *Intech Summit Group, Inc.*
Nehring, Keith — *Howard Fischer Associates, Inc.*
Neidhart, Craig C. — *TNS Partners, Inc.*
Nemec, Phillip — *Dunhill International Search of New Haven*
Nephew, Robert — *Christian & Timbers*
Neuberth, Jeffrey G. — *Canny, Bowen Inc.*
Newman, Lynn — *Kishbaugh Associates International*

Riotto, Anthony R. — *Riotto-Jones Associates*
Roberts, Mitch — *A.E. Feldman Associates*
Roberts, Nick P. — *Spectrum Search Associates, Inc.*
Roberts, Scott — *Jonas, Walters & Assoc., Inc.*
Robinson, Bruce — *Bruce Robinson Associates*
Robles Cuellar, Paulina — *Ray & Berndtson*
Rogers, Leah — *Dinte Resources, Inc.*
Rojo, Rafael — *A.T. Kearney, Inc.*
Rollo, Robert S. — *R. Rollo Associates*
Romanello, Daniel P. — *Spencer Stuart*
Romang, Paula — *Agri-Tech Personnel, Inc.*
Rose, Robert — *ESA Professional Consultants*
Rosemarin, Gloria J. — *Barrington Hart, Inc.*
Rosenthal, Charles — *National Search, Inc.*
Ross, Curt A. — *Ray & Berndtson*
Ross, H. Lawrence — *Ross & Company*
Ross, Lawrence — *Ray & Berndtson/Lovas Stanley*
Ross, Mark — *Ray & Berndtson/Lovas Stanley*
Rotella, Marshall W. — *The Corporate Connection, Ltd.*
Roth, Robert J. — *Williams, Roth & Krueger Inc.*
Roth, William — *Harris Heery & Associates*
Rowe, William D. — *D.E. Foster Partners Inc.*
Rudolph, Kenneth — *Kossuth & Associates, Inc.*
Rush, Michael E. — *D.A.L. Associates, Inc.*
Russell, Richard A. — *Executive Search Consultants Corporation*
Russell, Robin E. — *Kenzer Corp.*
Rustin, Beth — *The Whitney Group*
Sabanosh, Whitney — *Highland Search Group*
Sacerdote, John — *Raymond Karsan Associates*
Sallows, Jill S. — *Crowe, Chizek and Company, LLP*
Salvagno, Michael J. — *The Cambridge Group Ltd*
Sanders, Spencer H. — *Battalia Winston International*
Sandor, Richard J. — *Flynn, Hannock, Incorporated*
Sanow, Robert — *Cochran, Cochran & Yale, Inc.*
Sarna, Edmund A. — *Jonas, Walters & Assoc., Inc.*
Satenstein, Sloan — *Higdon Prince Inc.*
Sathe, Mark A. — *Sathe & Associates, Inc.*
Savage, Edward J. — *Stanton Chase International*
Sawyer, Patricia L. — *Smith & Sawyer Inc.*
Saxon, Alexa — *Woodworth International Group*
Schaefer, Frederic M. — *A.T. Kearney, Inc.*
Schene, Philip — *A.E. Feldman Associates*
Schlesinger, Laurie — *The Whitney Group*
Schlpma, Christine — *Advanced Executive Resources*
Schneiderman, Gerald — *Management Resource Associates, Inc.*
Schroeder, John W. — *Spencer Stuart*
Schroeder, Lee — *Blau Mancino Schroeder*
Schroeder, Steven J. — *Blau Mancino Schroeder*
Schuette, Dorothy — *Harris Heery & Associates*
Schwam, Carol — *A.E. Feldman Associates*
Schweichler, Lee J. — *Schweichler Associates, Inc.*
Scodius, Joseph J. — *Gregory Michaels and Associates, Inc.*
Scott, Evan — *Howard Fischer Associates, Inc.*
Scott, Gordon S. — *Search Advisors International Corp.*
Scranton, Lisa — *A.J. Burton Group, Inc.*
Segal, Eric B. — *Kenzer Corp.*

Seiden, Steven A. — *Seiden Krieger Associates, Inc.*
Semyan, John K. — *TNS Partners, Inc.*
Sennello, Gendra — *National Search, Inc.*
Sevilla, Claudio A. — *Crawford & Crofford*
Shelton, Sandra — *National Search, Inc.*
Shen, Eugene Y. — *The Whitney Group*
Shenfield, Peter — *A.T. Kearney, Inc.*
Shepard, Michael J. — *MSI International*
Shervey, Brent C. — *O'Callaghan Honey/Ray & Berndtson, Inc.*
Sherwood, Andrew — *Goodrich & Sherwood Associates, Inc.*
Shore, Earl L. — *E.L. Shore & Associates Ltd.*
Shufelt, Doug — *Sink, Walker, Boltrus International*
Sibbald, John R. — *John Sibbald Associates, Inc.*
Siegel, Pamela — *Executive Options, Ltd.*
Siegler, Jody Cukiir — *A.T. Kearney, Inc.*
Siegrist, Jeffrey M. — *D.E. Foster Partners Inc.*
Silcott, Marvin L. — *Marvin L. Silcott & Associates, Inc.*
Sill, Igor M. — *Geneva Group International*
Silvas, Stephen D. — *Roberson and Company*
Silver, Lee — *L. A. Silver Associates, Inc.*
Silverman, Gary W. — *GWS Partners*
Simmons, Sandra K. — *MSI International*
Simon, Mary K. — *Gregory Michaels and Associates, Inc.*
Simpson, David J. — *Simpson Associates, Inc.*
Simpson, Scott — *Cendea Connection International*
Sindler, Jay — *A.J. Burton Group, Inc.*
Sink, Cliff — *Sink, Walker, Boltrus International*
Sitarski, Stan — *Howard Fischer Associates, Inc.*
Skalet, Ira — *A.E. Feldman Associates*
Skunda, Donna M. — *Allerton Heneghan & O'Neill*
Slayton, Richard C. — *Slayton International, Inc./I-I-C Partners*
Slosar, John — *Boyden*
Smead, Michelle M. — *A.T. Kearney, Inc.*
Smith, Ana Luz — *Smith Search, S.C.*
Smith, David P. — *HRS, Inc.*
Smith, Ethan L. — *Highland Search Group*
Smith, Herman M. — *Herman Smith Executive Initiatives Inc.*
Smith, John E. — *Smith Search, S.C.*
Smith, Lydia — *The Corporate Connection, Ltd.*
Smith, Matt D. — *Ray & Berndtson*
Smith, Robert L. — *Smith & Sawyer Inc.*
Smith, Ronald V. — *Coe & Company International Inc.*
Smith, Timothy C. — *Christian & Timbers*
Snelgrove, Geiger — *National Search, Inc.*
Snyder, C. Edward — *Horton International*
Snyder, James F. — *Snyder & Company*
Sockwell, J. Edgar — *Sockwell & Associates*
Sondgrass, Stephen — *DeFrain, Mayer LLC*
Souder, E.G. — *Souder & Associates*
Spann, Richard E. — *Goodrich & Sherwood Associates, Inc.*
Spera, Stefanie — *A.T. Kearney, Inc.*
Spicehandler, Sheila — *Trebor Weldon Lawrence, Inc.*
Spiegel, Gayle — *L. A. Silver Associates, Inc.*
Spriggs, Robert D. — *Spriggs & Company, Inc.*

St. Clair, Alan — *TNS Partners, Inc.*
Stahl, Cindy — *Plummer & Associates, Inc.*
Stanton, John — *A.T. Kearney, Inc.*
Stark, Jeff — *Thorne, Brieger Associates Inc.*
Steele, Daniel — *Cochran, Cochran & Yale, Inc.*
Stein, Terry W. — *Stewart, Stein and Scott, Ltd.*
Steinem, Andy — *Dahl-Morrow International*
Steinem, Barbra — *Dahl-Morrow International*
Steinman, Stephen M. — *The Stevenson Group of New Jersey*
Stevens, Craig M. — *Kirkman & Searing, Inc.*
Stevenson, Jane — *Howard Fischer Associates, Inc.*
Stewart, Jeffrey O. — *Stewart, Stein and Scott, Ltd.*
Stewart, Ross M. — *Human Resources Network Partners Inc.*
Stivk, Barbara A. — *Thornton Resources*
Stranberg, James R. — *Callan Associates, Ltd.*
Stratmeyer, Karin Bergwall — *Princeton Entrepreneurial Resources*
Straube, Stanley H. — *Straube Associates*
Strickland, Katie — *Grantham & Co., Inc.*
Stringer, Dann P. — *D.E. Foster Partners Inc.*
Strom, Mark N. — *Search Advisors International Corp.*
Sullivan, Kay — *Rusher, Loscavio & LoPresto*
Sumurdy, Melinda — *Kenzer Corp.*
Sussman, Lynda — *Gilbert Tweed/INESA*
Swanson, Dick — *Raymond Karsan Associates*
Sweeney, Sean K. — *Bonifield Associates*
Swoboda, Lawrence — *A.J. Burton Group, Inc.*
Taylor, Conrad G. — *MSI International*
Taylor, Ernest A. — *Ward Howell International, Inc.*
Taylor, James M. — *The HRM Group, Inc.*
Taylor, R.L. (Larry) — *Ray & Berndtson*
Telford, John H. — *Telford, Adams & Alexander/Telford & Co., Inc.*
ten Cate, Herman H. — *Stoneham Associates Corp.*
Teter, Sandra — *The Danbrook Group, Inc.*
Teti, Al — *Chrisman & Company, Incorporated*
Theobald, David B. — *Theobald & Associates*
Thomas, Jeffrey — *Fairfaxx Corporation*
Thomas, Kurt J. — *P.J. Murphy & Associates, Inc.*
Thomas, Terry — *The Thomas Resource Group*
Thompson, Dave — *Battalia Winston International*
Thompson, John R. — *MSI International*
Thompson, Kenneth L. — *McCormack & Farrow*
Thornton, John C. — *Thornton Resources*
Thrapp, Mark C. — *Executive Search Consultants International, Inc.*
Tierney, Eileen — *The Whitney Group*
Tincu, John C. — *Ferneborg & Associates, Inc.*
Tipp, George D. — *Intech Summit Group, Inc.*
Todres-Bernstein, Margo — *Kaye-Bassman International Corp.*
Tootsey, Mark A. — *A.J. Burton Group, Inc.*
Tracey, Jack — *Management Assistance Group, Inc.*
Trott, Kathryn — *Allard Associates*
Trott, Kathryn — *Allard Associates*
Truax, Kevin — *Key Employment Services*
Truex, John F. — *Morton, McCorkle & Associates, Inc.*
Truitt, Thomas B. — *Southwestern Professional Services*

Tryon, Katey — *DeFrain, Mayer LLC*
Tucci, Joseph — *Fairfaxx Corporation*
Tucker, Thomas A. — *The Thomas Tucker Company*
Tully, Margo L. — *Tully/Woodmansee International, Inc.*
Tunney, William — *Grant Cooper and Associates*
Turner, Edward K. — *Don Richard Associates of Charlotte*
Turner, Kimberly — *Barton Associates, Inc.*
Tursi, Deborah J. — *The Corporate Connection, Ltd.*
Tutwiler, Stephen — *Don Richard Associates of Tampa, Inc.*
Tweed, Janet — *Gilbert Tweed/INESA*
Tyson, Richard L. — *Bonifield Associates*
Ulbert, Nancy — *Aureus Group*
Ulrich, Mary Ann — *D.S. Allen Associates, Inc.*
Vairo, Leonard A. — *Christian & Timbers*
Valenta, Joseph — *Princeton Entrepreneurial Resources*
Van Biesen, Jacques A.H. — *Search Group Inc.*
Van Campen, Jerry — *Gilbert & Van Campen International*
Van Clieaf, Mark — *MVC Associates International*
Van Nostrand, Mara J. — *Barton Associates, Inc.*
Velten, Mark T. — *Boyden*
Venable, William W. — *Thorndike Deland Associates*
Vergara, Gail H. — *Spencer Stuart*
Vernon, Peter C. — *Horton International*
Visnich, L. Christine — *Bason Associates Inc.*
Vitale, Amy — *Highland Search Group*
Vlcek, Thomas J. — *Vlcek & Company, Inc.*
Volkman, Arthur — *Cochran, Cochran & Yale, Inc.*
von Baillou, Astrid — *Richard Kinser & Associates*
Vossler, James — *A.J. Burton Group, Inc.*
Vourakis, Zan — *ZanExec LLC*
Waanders, William L. — *ExecuQuest*
Wacholz, Rick — *A.T. Kearney, Inc.*
Wakefield, Scott — *National Search, Inc.*
Waldman, Noah H. — *Lamalie Amrop International*
Waldoch, D. Mark — *Barnes Development Group, LLC*
Waldrop, Gary R. — *MSI International*
Walker, Craig H. — *A.J. Burton Group, Inc.*
Walker, Douglas G. — *Sink, Walker, Boltrus International*
Walker, Ewing J. — *Ward Howell International, Inc.*
Wallace, Alec — *Tanton Mitchell/Paul Ray Berndtson*
Walsh, Denis — *Professional Staffing Consultants*
Walters, William F. — *Jonas, Walters & Assoc., Inc.*
Ward, Madeleine — *LTM Associates*
Warter, Mark — *Isaacson, Miller*
Watkins, Thomas M. — *Lamalie Amrop International*
Watkinson, Jim W. — *The Badger Group*
Watson, Hanan S. — *Watson International, Inc.*
Watson, James — *MSI International*
Wayne, Cary S. — *ProSearch Inc.*
Webb, George H. — *Webb, Johnson Associates, Inc.*

Wein, Michael S. — *Media Management Resources, Inc.*
Wein, William — *Media Management Resources, Inc.*
Weisler, Nancy — *National Search, Inc.*
Weissman-Rosenthal, Abbe — *ALW Research International*
Welch, Robert — *Ray & Berndtson*
Weller, Paul S. — *Mark Stanley/EMA Partners International*
Wendler, Kambrea R. — *Gregory Michaels and Associates, Inc.*
Westfall, Ed — *Zwell International*
Weston, Corinne F. — *D.A. Kreuter Associates, Inc.*
Wheeler, Gerard H. — *A.J. Burton Group, Inc.*
White, Richard B. — *Spencer Stuart*
White, William C. — *Venture Resources Inc.*
Whiting, Anthony — *Johnson Smith & Knisely Accord*
Whitney, William A — *Larsen, Whitney, Blecksmith & Zilliacus*
Whitton, Paula L. — *Pearson, Caldwell & Farnsworth, Inc.*
Wilcox, Fred T. — *Wilcox, Bertoux & Miller*
Wilder, Richard B. — *Columbia Consulting Group*
Wilkinson, Barbara — *Beall & Company, Inc.*
Wilkinson, Jr. SPHR
Wilkinson, Charles E. — *The HRM Group, Inc.*
Williams, Gary L. — *Barnes Development Group, LLC*
Williams, Harry D. — *Jacobson Associates*
Williams, Jack — *A.T. Kearney, Inc.*
Williams, Lis — *Executive Options, Ltd.*
Williams, Roger K. — *Williams, Roth & Krueger Inc.*
Williams, Stephen E. — *Barton Associates, Inc.*
Willis, William H. — *William Willis Worldwide Inc.*
Wilson, Derrick — *Thornton Resources*
Wilson, Patricia L. — *Leon A. Farley Associates*
Winitz, Joel — *GSW Consulting Group, Inc.*
Winitz, Marla — *GSW Consulting Group, Inc.*
Winograd, Glenn — *Criterion Executive Search, Inc.*
Winston, Dale — *Battalia Winston International*
Wisch, Steven C. — *MB Inc. Interim Executive Division*
Wolf, Stephen M. — *Byron Leonard International, Inc.*
Womack, Joseph — *The Bankers Group*
Wood, Elizabeth — *Highland Search Group*
Wood, Milton M. — *M. Wood Company*
Wood, Nicole — *Corporate Careers, Inc.*
Woodmansee, Bruce J. — *Tully/Woodmansee International, Inc.*
Woodworth, Gail — *Woodworth International Group*
Wooldridge, Jeff — *Ray & Berndtson*
Wooller, Edmund A.M. — *Windsor International*
Wright, A. Leo — *The Hindman Company*
Wright, Carl A.J. — *A.J. Burton Group, Inc.*
Wright, Charles D. — *Goodrich & Sherwood Associates, Inc.*
Wright, Leslie — *The Stevenson Group of New Jersey*

Yaekle, Gary — *Tully/Woodmansee International, Inc.*
Yen, Maggie Yeh Ching — *Ray & Berndtson*
Yungerberg, Steven — *Steven Yungerberg Associates Inc.*
Zaffrann, Craig S. — *P.J. Murphy & Associates, Inc.*
Zahradka, James F. — *P.J. Murphy & Associates, Inc.*
Zak, Adam — *Adams & Associates International*
Zaleta, Andy R. — *A.T. Kearney, Inc.*
Zamborsky, George — *Boyden*
Zaslav, Debra M. — *Telford, Adams & Alexander/Telford & Co., Inc.*
Zay, Thomas C. — *Boyden/Zay & Company*
Zay, Thomas C. — *Boyden/Zay & Company*
Zila, Laurie M. — *Princeton Entrepreneurial Resources*
Zivic, Janis M. — *Spencer Stuart*
Zona, Henry F. — *Zona & Associates, Inc.*
Zwell, Michael — *Zwell International*

6. Human Resources

Abbott, Peter D. — *The Abbott Group, Inc.*
Abert, Janice — *Ledbetter/Davidson International, Inc.*
Adams, Len — *The KPA Group*
Adler, Louis S. — *CJA - The Adler Group*
Agee, Jo Etta — *Chrisman & Company, Incorporated*
Akin, J.R. "Jack" — *J.R. Akin & Company Inc.*
Alexander, John T. — *Telford, Adams & Alexander*
Allen, William L. — *The Hindman Company*
Allgire, Mary L. — *Kenzer Corp.*
Altreuter, Rose — *ALTCO Temporary Services*
Altreuter, Rose — *The ALTCO Group*
Ambler, Peter W. — *Peter W. Ambler Company*
Amilowski, Maria — *Highland Search Group*
Anderson, Maria H. — *Barton Associates, Inc.*
Anderson, Richard — *Grant Cooper and Associates*
Anderson, Shawn — *Temporary Accounting Personnel, Inc.*
Andujo, Michele M. — *Chrisman & Company, Incorporated*
Argentin, Jo — *Executive Placement Consultants, Inc.*
Ascher, Susan P. — *The Ascher Group*
Aston, Kathy — *Marra Peters & Partners*
Atwood, Barrie — *The Abbott Group, Inc.*
Badger, Fred H. — *The Badger Group*
Baeder, Jeremy — *Executive Manning Corporation*
Bailey, Vanessa — *Highland Search Group*
Baje, Sarah — *Innovative Search Group, LLC*
Baker, Gary M. — *Cochran, Cochran & Yale, Inc.*
Baker, Gary M. — *Temporary Accounting Personnel, Inc.*
Balbone, Rich — *Executive Manning Corporation*
Baltaglia, Michael — *Cochran, Cochran & Yale, Inc.*
Barbour, Mary Beth — *Tully/Woodmansee International, Inc.*
Barch, Sherrie — *Furst Group/MPI*
Barger, H. Carter — *Barger & Sargeant, Inc.*
Barnes, Gary — *Brigade Inc.*
Barnes, Richard E. — *Barnes Development Group, LLC*

Barnes, Roanne L. — *Barnes Development Group, LLC*
Barton, Gary R. — *Barton Associates, Inc.*
Bason, Maurice L. — *Bason Associates Inc.*
Bass, M. Lynn — *Ray & Berndtson*
Bauman, Martin H. — *Martin H. Bauman Associates, Inc.*
Bearman, Linda — *Grant Cooper and Associates*
Beaudin, Elizabeth C. — *Callan Associates, Ltd.*
Beaver, Bentley H. — *The Onstott Group, Inc.*
Belin, Jean — *Boyden*
Bell, Lloyd W. — *O'Brien & Bell*
Bell, Michael — *Spencer Stuart*
Bellano, Robert W. — *Stanton Chase International*
Bennett, Jo — *Battalia Winston International*
Benson, Kate — *Rene Plessner Associates, Inc.*
Beran, Helena — *Michael J. Cavanagh and Associates*
Berk-Levine, Margo — *MB Inc. Interim Executive Division*
Berry, Harold B. — *The Hindman Company*
Bettick, Michael J. — *A.J. Burton Group, Inc.*
Billington, William H. — *Spriggs & Company, Inc.*
Birkhead, Linda — *Zwell International*
Bishop, Barbara — *The Executive Source*
Blakslee, Jan H. — *J: Blakslee International, Ltd.*
Bliley, Jerry — *Spencer Stuart*
Boel, Werner — *The Dalley Hewitt Company*
Bongiovanni, Vincent — *ESA Professional Consultants*
Bonifield, Len — *Bonifield Associates*
Bonnell, William R. — *Bonnell Associates Ltd.*
Borkin, Andrew — *Strategic Advancement Inc.*
Borland, James — *Goodrich & Sherwood Associates, Inc.*
Bourrie, Sharon D. — *Chartwell Partners International, Inc.*
Bovich, Maryann C. — *Higdon Prince Inc.*
Bowden, Otis H. — *BowdenGlobal, Ltd.*
Bradley, Dalena — *Woodworth International Group*
Bradshaw, Monte — *Christian & Timbers*
Brady, Coloin — *Johnson Smith & Knisely Accord*
Brady, Dick — *William Guy & Associates*
Brandenburg, David — *Professional Staffing Consultants*
Bratches, Howard — *Thorndike Deland Associates*
Brennan, Patrick J. — *Handy HRM Corp.*
Brieger, Steve — *Thorne, Brieger Associates Inc.*
Brophy, Melissa — *Maximum Management Corp.*
Brother, Joy — *Charles Luntz & Associates. Inc.*
Brown, Larry C. — *Horton International*
Brown, Steffan — *Woodworth International Group*
Brown, Steve — *K. Russo Associates*
Brudno, Robert J. — *Savoy Partners, Ltd.*
Bruno, Deborah F. — *The Hindman Company*
Bryant, Richard D. — *Bryant Associates, Inc.*
Brzezinski, Ronald T. — *Callan Associates, Ltd.*
Buckles, Donna — *Cochran, Cochran & Yale, Inc.*
Buggy, Linda — *Bonnell Associates Ltd.*
Bump, Gerald J. — *D.E. Foster Partners Inc.*
Burchard, Stephen R. — *Burchard & Associates, Inc.*
Burke, John — *The Experts*
Burkhill, John — *The Talley Group*

Burkland, Skott B. — *Skott/Edwards Consultants, Inc.*
Burns, Alan — *The Enns Partners Inc.*
Burns, Terence N. — *D.E. Foster Partners Inc.*
Busterna, Charles — *The KPA Group*
Butler, Kirby B. — *The Butlers Company Insurance Recruiters*
Butterfass, Stanley — *Butterfass, Pepe & MacCallan Inc.*
Byrnes, Thomas A. — *The Search Alliance, Inc.*
Caldwell, William R. — *Pearson, Caldwell & Farnsworth, Inc.*
Calivas, Kay — *A.J. Burton Group, Inc.*
Call, David — *Cochran, Cochran & Yale, Inc.*
Callan, Robert M. — *Callan Associates, Ltd.*
Cameron, James W. — *Cameron Consulting*
Campbell, Patricia A. — *The Onstott Group, Inc.*
Capizzi, Karen — *Cochran, Cochran & Yale, Inc.*
Carideo, Joseph — *Thorndike Deland Associates*
Carro, Carl R. — *Executive Search Consultants International, Inc.*
Cary, Con — *Cary & Associates*
Castine, Michael P. — *Highland Search Group*
Cavanagh, Michael J. — *Michael J. Cavanagh and Associates*
Chamberlin, Joan — *William Guy & Associates*
Chamberlin, Michael A. — *Tower Consultants, Ltd.*
Chappell, Peter — *Robertson & Associates*
Chappell, Peter — *The Bankers Group*
Cherbonnier, L. Michael — *The Cherbonnier Group, Inc.*
Chndler, Brad J. — *Furst Group/MPI*
Christenson, H. Alan — *Christenson & Hutchison*
Christian, Philip — *Ray & Berndtson*
Cizek, John T. — *Cizek Associates, Inc.*
Cizek, Marti J. — *Cizek Associates, Inc.*
Clake, Bob — *Furst Group/MPI*
Clarey, William A. — *Preng & Associates, Inc.*
Clarke Smith, Jamie — *Kaye-Bassman International Corp.*
Clauhsen, Elizabeth A. — *Savoy Partners, Ltd.*
Clayton, Fred J. — *Berkhemer Clayton Incorporated*
Cloutier, Gisella — *Dinte Resources, Inc.*
Cochran, Scott P. — *The Badger Group*
Coe, Karen J. — *Coe & Company International Inc.*
Coffman, Brian — *Kossuth & Associates, Inc.*
Cohen, Michael R. — *Intech Summit Group, Inc.*
Cohen, Robert C. — *Intech Summit Group, Inc.*
Coleman, J. Kevin — *J. Kevin Coleman & Associates, Inc.*
Collard, Joseph A. — *Spencer Stuart*
Colman, Michael — *Executive Placement Consultants, Inc.*
Comstock, Rodger — *Johnson Smith & Knisely Accord*
Conway, Maureen — *Conway & Associates*
Cooke, Katherine H. — *Horton International*
Cortina Del Valle, Pedro — *Ray & Berndtson*
Costello, Lynda — *Coe & Company International Inc.*
Courtney, Brendan — *A.J. Burton Group, Inc.*
Coyle, Hugh F. — *A.J. Burton Group, Inc.*
Cragg, Barbara R. — *Southwestern Professional Services*

Cramer, Paul J. — *C/R Associates*

Crane, Howard C. — *Chartwell Partners International, Inc.*

Crath, Paul F. — *Price Waterhouse*

Crecos, Gregory P. — *Gregory Michaels and Associates, Inc.*

Critchley, Walter — *Cochran, Cochran & Yale, Inc.*

Critchley, Walter — *Temporary Accounting Personnel, Inc.*

Cunningham, Lawrence — *Howard Fischer Associates, Inc.*

Cunningham, Robert Y. — *Goodrich & Sherwood Associates, Inc.*

Curtis, Ellissa — *Cochran, Cochran & Yale, Inc.*

Danforth, W. Michael — *Hyde Danforth Wold & Co.*

Daniels, C. Eugene — *Sigma Group International*

Davis, G. Gordon — *Davis & Company*

Dawson, Joe — *S.C. International, Ltd.*

de Bardin, Francesca — *F.L. Taylor & Company, Inc.*

De Brun, Thomas P. — *Ray & Berndtson*

de Palacios, Jeannette C. — *J. Palacios & Associates, Inc.*

de Tuede, Catherine — *The Search Alliance, Inc.*

Deaver, Henry C. — *Ray & Berndtson*

DeCorrevont, James — *DeCorrevont & Associates*

DeCorrevont, James — *DeCorrevont & Associates*

DeHart, Donna — *Tower Consultants, Ltd.*

Del Pino, William — *National Search, Inc.*

Delaney, Patrick J. — *Sensible Solutions, Inc.*

Delmonico, Laura — *A.J. Burton Group, Inc.*

Demchak, James P. — *Sandhurst Associates*

Desgrosellier, Gary P. — *Personnel Unlimited/Executive Search*

Desmond, Dennis — *Beall & Company, Inc.*

deVry, Kimberly A. — *Tower Consultants, Ltd.*

deWilde, David M. — *Chartwell Partners International, Inc.*

Dezember, Steve — *Ray & Berndtson*

DiCioccio, Carmen — *Cochran, Cochran & Yale, Inc.*

Dicker, Barry — *ESA Professional Consultants*

Dickson, Duke — *A.D. & Associates Executive Search, Inc.*

Dingeldey, Peter E. — *Search Advisors International Corp.*

Dingman, Bruce — *Robert W. Dingman Company, Inc.*

Dinte, Paul — *Dinte Resources, Inc.*

DiSalvo, Fred — *The Cambridge Group Ltd*

Divine, Robert S. — *O'Shea, Divine & Company, Inc.*

Doele, Donald C. — *Goodrich & Sherwood Associates, Inc.*

Doman, Matthew — *S.C. International, Ltd.*

Doukas, Jon A. — *Professional Bank Services, Inc. D/B/A Executive Search, Inc.*

Dowell, Chris — *The Abbott Group, Inc.*

Dowell, Mary K. — *Professional Search Associates*

Doyle, James W. — *Executive Search Consultants International, Inc.*

Doyle, John P. — *Ray & Berndtson*

Drury, James J. — *Spencer Stuart*

Duckworth, Donald R. — *Johnson Smith & Knisely Accord*

Dunbar, Marilynne — *Ray & Berndtson/Lovas Stanley*

Durakis, Charles A. — *C.A. Durakis Associates, Inc.*

Eason, Jan C. — *Summit Group International*

Ebeling, John A. — *Gilbert Tweed/INESA*

Eddy, Terry — *William Guy & Associates*

Edwards, Verba L. — *Wing Tips & Pumps, Inc.*

Ehrgott, Elizabeth — *The Ascher Group*

Ehrhart, Jennifer — *ADOW's Executeam*

Eldridge, Charles B. — *Ray & Berndtson*

Ellis, David — *Don Richard Associates of Georgia, Inc.*

Ellis, Ted K. — *The Hindman Company*

Ellis, William — *Interspace Interactive Inc.*

Engelbert, Kimberly S. — *Watson International, Inc.*

England, Mark — *Austin-McGregor International*

Enns, George — *The Enns Partners Inc.*

Erder, Debra — *Canny, Bowen Inc.*

Erickson, Elaine — *Kenzer Corp.*

Evans, David — *Executive Manning Corporation*

Fancher, Robert L. — *Bason Associates Inc.*

Farley, Leon A. — *Leon A. Farley Associates*

Farnsworth, John A. — *Pearson, Caldwell & Farnsworth, Inc.*

Ferneborg, Jay W. — *Ferneborg & Associates, Inc.*

Ferneborg, John R. — *Ferneborg & Associates, Inc.*

Fiorelli, Cheryl — *Tower Consultants, Ltd.*

Fischer, Adam — *Howard Fischer Associates, Inc.*

Fischer, Howard M. — *Howard Fischer Associates, Inc.*

Fischer, Janet L. — *Boyden*

Fisher, Neal — *Fisher Personnel Management Services*

Flanagan, Robert M. — *Robert M. Flanagan & Associates, Ltd.*

Fletcher, David — *A.J. Burton Group, Inc.*

Flood, Michael — *Norman Broadbent International, Inc.*

Flora, Dodi — *Crawford & Crofford*

Foote, Leland W. — *L.W. Foote Company*

Ford, Sandra D. — *The Ford Group, Inc.*

Foreman, David C. — *Koontz, Jeffries & Associates, Inc.*

Fowler, Edward D.C. — *Higdon Prince Inc.*

Fowler, Thomas A. — *The Hindman Company*

Fox, Amanda C. — *Ray & Berndtson*

Frazier, John — *Cochran, Cochran & Yale, Inc.*

Freeman, Mark — *ESA Professional Consultants*

French, William G. — *Preng & Associates, Inc.*

Fribush, Richard — *A.J. Burton Group, Inc.*

Friedman, Donna L. — *Tower Consultants, Ltd.*

Friedman, Helen E. — *McCormack & Farrow*

Fulton, Christine N. — *Highland Search Group*

Fust, Sheely F. — *Ray & Berndtson*

Gabel, Gregory N. — *Canny, Bowen Inc.*

Gabriel, David L. — *The Arcus Group*

Galante, Suzanne M. — *Vlcek & Company, Inc.*

Gallagher, Terence M. — *Battalia Winston International*

Gantar, Donna — *Howard Fischer Associates, Inc.*

Garfinkle, Steven M. — *Battalia Winston International*

Gauthier, Robert C. — *Columbia Consulting Group*

George, Delores F. — *Delores F. George Human Resource Management & Consulting Industry*
Gestwick, Daniel — *Cochran, Cochran & Yale, Inc.*
Ghurani, Mac — *Gary Kaplan & Associates*
Gibbs, John S. — *Spencer Stuart*
Gilbert, Jerry — *Gilbert & Van Campen International*
Gilbert, Patricia G. — *Lynch Miller Moore, Inc.*
Gilchrist, Robert J. — *Horton International*
Gill, Patricia — *Columbia Consulting Group*
Gillespie, Thomas — *Professional Search Consultants*
Gilreath, James M. — *Gilreath Weatherby, Inc.*
Giries, Juliet D. — *Barton Associates, Inc.*
Glass, Lori — *The Executive Source*
Goar, Duane R. — *Sandhurst Associates*
Goldenberg, Susan — *Grant Cooper and Associates*
Goldsmith, Joseph B. — *Higdon Prince Inc.*
Goldstein, Steven G. — *The Jonathan Stevens Group, Inc.*
Gonzalez, Kristen — *A.J. Burton Group, Inc.*
Goodman, Dawn M. — *Bason Associates Inc.*
Goodridge, Benjamin — *S.C. International, Ltd.*
Gordon, Teri — *Don Richard Associates of Washington, D.C., Inc.*
Grant, Michael — *Zwell International*
Grantham, John — *Grantham & Co., Inc.*
Grantham, Philip H. — *Columbia Consulting Group*
Grasch, Jerry E. — *The Hindman Company*
Gray, Annie — *Annie Gray Associates, Inc./The Executive Search Firm*
Gray, Mark — *Executive Referral Services, Inc.*
Greco, Patricia — *Howe-Lewis International*
Grotenhuis, Dirkten — *Chrisman & Company, Incorporated*
Grotte, Lawrence C. — *Lautz Grotte Engler*
Gurnani, Angali — *Executive Placement Consultants, Inc.*
Gurtin, Kay L. — *Executive Options, Ltd.*
Guy, C. William — *William Guy & Associates*
Haas, Margaret P. — *The Haas Associates, Inc.*
Haberman, Joseph C. — *A.T. Kearney, Inc.*
Halbrich, Mitch — *A.J. Burton Group, Inc.*
Halladay, Patti — *Intersource, Ltd.*
Hallock, Peter B. — *Goodrich & Sherwood Associates, Inc.*
Hamilton, John R. — *Ray & Berndtson*
Hammond, Karla — *People Management Northeast Incorporated*
Hanes, Leah — *Ray & Berndtson*
Hanley, Alan P. — *Williams, Roth & Krueger Inc.*
Hanley, J. Patrick — *Canny, Bowen Inc.*
Hanley, Maureen E. — *Gilbert Tweed/INESA*
Hanson, Grant M. — *Goodrich & Sherwood Associates, Inc.*
Harbaugh, Paul J. — *International Management Advisors, Inc.*
Harbert, David O. — *Sweeney Harbert & Mummert, Inc.*
Hardison, Richard L. — *Hardison & Company*
Harney, Elyane — *Gary Kaplan & Associates*
Harris, Seth O. — *Christian & Timbers*
Hart, Robert T. — *D.E. Foster Partners Inc.*
Harvey, Mike — *Advanced Executive Resources*

Haughton, Michael — *DeFrain, Mayer LLC*
Hauser, Martha — *Spencer Stuart*
Havener, Donald Clarke — *The Abbott Group, Inc.*
Hawksworth, A. Dwight — *A.D. & Associates Executive Search, Inc.*
Haystead, Steve — *Advanced Executive Resources*
Healey, Joseph T. — *Highland Search Group*
Hebel, Robert W. — *R.W. Hebel Associates*
Heiken, Barbara E. — *Randell-Heiken, Inc.*
Heinze, David — *Heinze & Associates, Inc.*
Hellinger, Audrey W. — *Martin H. Bauman Associates, Inc.*
Helminiak, Audrey — *Gaffney Management Consultants*
Hendrickson, Jill E. — *Gregory Michaels and Associates, Inc.*
Heneghan, Donald A. — *Allerton Heneghan & O'Neill*
Henn, George W. — *G.W. Henn & Company*
Hensley, Bert — *Morgan Samuels Co., Inc.*
Hergenrather, Richard A. — *Hergenrather & Company*
Herman, Shelli — *Gary Kaplan & Associates*
Hetherman, Margaret F. — *Highland Search Group*
Hewitt, Rives D. — *The Dalley Hewitt Company*
Hewitt, W. Davis — *The Dalley Hewitt Company*
Higbee, Joan — *Thorndike Deland Associates*
Higdon, Henry G. — *Higdon Prince Inc.*
Higgins, Donna — *Howard Fischer Associates, Inc.*
Higgins, William — *William Guy & Associates*
Hildebrand, Thomas B. — *Professional Resources Group, Inc.*
Hillen, Skip — *The McCormick Group, Inc.*
Himlin, Amy — *Cochran, Cochran & Yale, Inc.*
Hindman, Neil C. — *The Hindman Company*
Hoevel, Michael J. — *Poirier, Hoevel & Co.*
Holland, John A. — *Holland, McFadzean & Associates, Inc.*
Holland, Rose Mary — *Price Waterhouse*
Holmes, Lawrence J. — *Columbia Consulting Group*
Holodnak, William A. — *J. Robert Scott*
Holzberger, Georges L. — *Highland Search Group*
Hoover, Catherine — *J.L. Mark Associates, Inc.*
Hopkins, Chester A. — *Handy HRM Corp.*
Hopp, Lorrie A. — *Gregory Michaels and Associates, Inc.*
Houchins, William M. — *Christian & Timbers*
Hoyda, Louis A. — *Thorndike Deland Associates*
Hucko, Donald S. — *Jonas, Walters & Assoc., Inc.*
Hudson, Reginald M. — *Search Bureau International*
Hughes, Cathy N. — *The Ogdon Partnership*
Hughes, R. Kevin — *Handy HRM Corp.*
Hutchison, William K. — *Christenson & Hutchison*
Hybels, Cynthia — *A.J. Burton Group, Inc.*
Ingram, D. John — *Ingram & Aydelotte Inc./I-I-C Partners*
Issacs, Judith A. — *Grant Cooper and Associates*
Jacobs, Mike — *Thorne, Brieger Associates Inc.*
Jacobson, Rick — *The Windham Group*
Janis, Laurence — *Integrated Search Solutions Group, LLC*

Jansen, John F. — *Delta Services*
Janssen, Don — *Howard Fischer Associates, Inc.*
Januale, Lois — *Cochran, Cochran & Yale, Inc.*
Jernigan, Susan N. — *Sockwell & Associates*
Joffe, Barry — *Bason Associates Inc.*
Johnson, Brian — *A.J. Burton Group, Inc.*
Johnson, John W. — *Webb, Johnson Associates, Inc.*
Johnson, Kathleen A. — *Barton Associates, Inc.*
Johnson, Priscilla — *The Johnson Group, Inc.*
Johnson, S. Hope — *Boyden Washington, D.C.*
Johnson, Stanley C. — *Johnson & Company*
Johnson, Valerie — *Coe & Company International Inc.*
Jordan, Jon — *Cochran, Cochran & Yale, Inc.*
Judge, Alfred L. — *The Cambridge Group Ltd*
Juelis, John J. — *Peeney Associates*
Kaiser, Donald J. — *Dunhill International Search of New Haven*
Kane, Frank — *A.J. Burton Group, Inc.*
Kane, Karen — *Howard Fischer Associates, Inc.*
Kaplan, Gary — *Gary Kaplan & Associates*
Keating, Pierson — *Nordeman Grimm, Inc.*
Keller, Barbara E. — *Barton Associates, Inc.*
Kelly, Elizabeth Ann — *Wellington Management Group*
Kelly, Peter W. — *R. Rollo Associates*
Kelso, Patricia C. — *Barton Associates, Inc.*
Kenzer, Robert D. — *Kenzer Corp.*
Kern, Jerry L. — *ADOW's Executeam*
Kern, Kathleen G. — *ADOW's Executeam*
Kershaw, Lisa — *Tanton Mitchell/Paul Ray Berndtson*
Keshishian, Gregory — *Handy HRM Corp.*
Kettwig, David A. — *A.T. Kearney, Inc.*
Kiley, Phyllis — *National Search, Inc.*
King, Bill — *The McCormick Group, Inc.*
King, Margaret — *Christian & Timbers*
Kinser, Richard E. — *Richard Kinser & Associates*
Kip, Luanne S. — *Kip Williams, Inc.*
Kishbaugh, Herbert S. — *Kishbaugh Associates International*
Klages, Constance W. — *International Management Advisors, Inc.*
Klavens, Cecile J. — *The Pickwick Group, Inc.*
Klein, Brandon — *A.J. Burton Group, Inc.*
Klein, Mary Jo — *Cochran, Cochran & Yale, Inc.*
Knisely, Gary — *Johnson Smith & Knisely Accord*
Koehler, Frank R. — *The Koehler Group*
Kohn, Adam P. — *Christian & Timbers*
Kondra, Vernon J. — *The Douglas Reiter Company, Inc.*
Koontz, Donald N. — *Koontz, Jeffries & Associates, Inc.*
Kopsick, Joseph M. — *Spencer Stuart*
Kossuth, David — *Kossuth & Associates, Inc.*
Kossuth, Jane — *Kossuth & Associates, Inc.*
Kotick, Maddy — *The Stevenson Group of New Jersey*
Krejci, Stanley L. — *Boyden Washington, D.C.*
Krieger, Dennis F. — *Seiden Krieger Associates, Inc.*
Krueger, Kurt — *Krueger Associates*
Kuhl, Teresa — *Don Richard Associates of Tampa, Inc.*
Kunzer, William J. — *Kunzer Associates, Ltd.*

Kurrigan, Geoffrey — *ESA Professional Consultants*
Kussner, Janice N. — *Herman Smith Executive Initiatives Inc.*
Laba, Marvin — *Marvin Laba & Associates*
Laba, Stuart M. — *Marvin Laba & Associates*
Labrecque, Bernard F. — *Laurendeau Labrecque/Ray & Berndtson, Inc.*
Lachance, Roger — *Laurendeau Labrecque/Ray & Berndtson, Inc.*
Lang, Sharon A. — *Ray & Berndtson*
Lardner, Lucy D. — *Tully/Woodmansee International, Inc.*
Lasher, Charles M. — *Lasher Associates*
Laurendeau, Jean E. — *Laurendeau Labrecque/Ray & Berndtson, Inc.*
Lautz, Lindsay A. — *Lautz Grotte Engler*
Leetma, Imbi — *Stanton Chase International*
Leighton, Nina — *The Ogdon Partnership*
Leininger, Dennis — *Key Employment Services*
Leslie, William H. — *Boyden/Zay & Company*
Letcher, Harvey D. — *Sandhurst Associates*
Levine, Lois — *National Search, Inc.*
Lewis, Jon A. — *Sandhurst Associates*
Lezama Cohen, Luis — *Ray & Berndtson*
Linton, Leonard M. — *Byron Leonard International, Inc.*
Loeb, Stephen H. — *Grant Cooper and Associates*
Long, Helga — *Horton International*
Long, Melanie — *National Search, Inc.*
Long, Milt — *William Guy & Associates*
Long, William G. — *McDonald, Long & Associates, Inc.*
Lotufo, Donald A. — *D.A.L. Associates, Inc.*
Lotz, R. James — *International Management Advisors, Inc.*
Lovely, Edward — *The Stevenson Group of New Jersey*
Loving, Vikki — *Intersource, Ltd.*
Lucarelli, Joan — *The Onstott Group, Inc.*
Lucht, John — *The John Lucht Consultancy Inc.*
Ludlow, Paula — *Horton International*
Lumsby, George N. — *International Management Advisors, Inc.*
Luntz, Charles E. — *Charles Luntz & Associates. Inc.*
Lupica, Anthony — *Cochran, Cochran & Yale, Inc.*
Lyon, Jenny — *Marra Peters & Partners*
Lyons, J. David — *Aubin International Inc.*
MacCallan, Deirdre — *Butterfass, Pepe & MacCallan Inc.*
Macdonald, G. William — *The Macdonald Group, Inc.*
MacIntyre, Lisa W. — *Highland Search Group*
Mackenna, Kathy — *Plummer & Associates, Inc.*
MacNaughton, Sperry — *McNaughton Associates*
Maer, Harry — *Kenzer Corp.*
Maglio, Charles J. — *Maglio and Company, Inc.*
Mahr, Toni — *K. Russo Associates*
Mainwaring, Andrew Brian — *Executive Search Consultants Corporation*
Mallin, Ellen — *Howard Fischer Associates, Inc.*
Manassero, Henri J.P. — *International Management Advisors, Inc.*
Mangum, Maria — *Thomas Mangum Company*

Mangum, William T. — *Thomas Mangum Company*

Manns, Alex — *Crawford & Crofford*

Mansford, Keith — *Howard Fischer Associates, Inc.*

Maphet, Harriet — *The Stevenson Group of New Jersey*

Marino, Chester — *Cochran, Cochran & Yale, Inc.*

Mark, John L. — *J.L. Mark Associates, Inc.*

Mark, Lynne — *J.L. Mark Associates, Inc.*

Marks, Russell E. — *Webb, Johnson Associates, Inc.*

Marks, Sarah J. — *The Executive Source*

Marra, John — *Marra Peters & Partners*

Marra, John — *Marra Peters & Partners*

Marumoto, William H. — *Boyden Washington, D.C.*

Massey, R. Bruce — *Horton International*

Mather, David R. — *Christian & Timbers*

Mathias, Kathy — *Stone Murphy & Olson*

Matthews, Corwin — *Woodworth International Group*

Maynard Taylor, Susan — *Chrisman & Company, Incorporated*

Mazor, Elly — *Howard Fischer Associates, Inc.*

McBride, Jonathan E. — *McBride Associates, Inc.*

McCallister, Richard A. — *Boyden*

McCloskey, Frank D. — *Johnson Smith & Knisely Accord*

McCormick, Brian — *The McCormick Group, Inc.*

McCreary, Charles "Chip" — *Austin-McGregor International*

McDermott, Jeffrey T. — *Vlcek & Company, Inc.*

McDonald, Stanleigh B. — *McDonald Associates International*

McDowell, Robert N. — *Christenson & Hutchison*

McFadden, Ashton S. — *Johnson Smith & Knisely Accord*

McFadzen,, James A. — *Holland, McFadzean & Associates, Inc.*

McGuire, Pat — *A.J. Burton Group, Inc.*

McKeown, Patricia A. — *DiMarchi Partners, Inc.*

McManners, Donald E. — *McManners Associates, Inc.*

McMillin, Bob — *Price Waterhouse*

McNamara, Catherine — *Ray & Berndtson*

McNamara, Timothy C. — *Columbia Consulting Group*

McNamara, Timothy Connor — *Horton International*

McNichols, Walter B. — *Gary Kaplan & Associates*

McNulty, Kelly L. — *Gregory Michaels and Associates, Inc.*

McQuoid, David — *A.T. Kearney, Inc.*

McSherry, James F. — *Battalia Winston International*

Meadows, C. David — *Professional Staffing Consultants*

Meagher, Patricia G. — *Spencer Stuart*

Meany, Brian M. — *Herbert Mines Associates, Inc.*

Meier, J. Dale — *Grant Cooper and Associates*

Meltzer, Andrea Y. — *Executive Options, Ltd.*

Menk, Carl — *Canny, Bowen Inc.*

Mercer, Julie — *Columbia Consulting Group*

Messett, William J. — *Messett Associates, Inc.*

Mestepey, John — *A.T. Kearney, Inc.*

Meyer, Michael F. — *Witt/Kieffer, Ford, Hadelman & Lloyd*

Meyer, Stacey — *Gary Kaplan & Associates*

Miller, David — *Cochran, Cochran & Yale, Inc.*

Miller, David — *Temporary Accounting Personnel, Inc.*

Miller, Roy — *The Enns Partners Inc.*

Millonzi, Joel C. — *Johnson Smith & Knisely Accord*

Milstein, Bonnie — *Marvin Laba & Associates*

Mines, Herbert T. — *Herbert Mines Associates, Inc.*

Mingle, Larry D. — *Columbia Consulting Group*

Misiurewicz, Marc — *Cochran, Cochran & Yale, Inc.*

Mitchell, Jeff — *A.J. Burton Group, Inc.*

Mitton, Bill — *Executive Resource, Inc.*

Montgomery, James M. — *Houze, Shourds & Montgomery, Inc.*

Moore, Mark — *Wheeler, Moore & Elam Co.*

Moore, T. Wills — *Ray & Berndtson*

Morgan, Gary — *National Search, Inc.*

Morgan, Nancy — *K. Russo Associates*

Morris, Paul T. — *The Morris Group*

Mortansen, Patricia — *Norman Broadbent International, Inc.*

Morton, Robert C. — *Morton, McCorkle & Associates, Inc.*

Muendel, H. Edward — *Stanton Chase International*

Mulligan, Robert P. — *William Willis Worldwide Inc.*

Murphy, Cornelius J. — *Goodrich & Sherwood Associates, Inc.*

Murphy, Gary J. — *Stone Murphy & Olson*

Murphy, Patrick J. — *P.J. Murphy & Associates, Inc.*

Mursuli, Meredith — *Lasher Associates*

Mustin, Joyce M. — *J: Blakslee International, Ltd.*

Nagler, Leon G. — *Nagler, Robins & Poe, Inc.*

Naidicz, Maria — *Ray & Berndtson*

Nathanson, Barry F. — *Barry Nathanson Associates*

Nees, Eugene C. — *Ray & Berndtson*

Neher, Robert L. — *Intech Summit Group, Inc.*

Nehring, Keith — *Howard Fischer Associates, Inc.*

Neidhart, Craig C. — *TNS Partners, Inc.*

Nemec, Phillip — *Dunhill International Search of New Haven*

Nephew, Robert — *Christian & Timbers*

Neri, Gene — *S.C. International, Ltd.*

Neuberth, Jeffrey G. — *Canny, Bowen Inc.*

Newpoff, Brad L. — *Furst Group/MPI*

Nichols, Gary — *Koontz, Jeffries & Associates, Inc.*

Nielsen, Sue — *Ells Personnel System Inc.*

Noebel, Todd R. — *The Noebel Search Group, Inc.*

Nolte, William D. — *W.D. Nolte & Company*

Norman, Randy — *Austin-McGregor International*

Normann, Amy — *Robert M. Flanagan & Associates, Ltd.*

Norsell, Paul E. — *Paul Norsell & Associates, Inc.*

O'Hara, Daniel M. — *Lynch Miller Moore, Inc.*

O'Neill, James P. — *Allerton Heneghan & O'Neill*

Ogdon, Thomas H. — *The Ogdon Partnership*

Ogilvie, Kit — *Howard Fischer Associates, Inc.*

Ohman, Gregory L. — *Skott/Edwards Consultants, Inc.*

Onstott, Joseph — *The Onstott Group, Inc.*

Oswald, Mark G. — *Canny, Bowen Inc.*

Ott, George W. — *Ott & Hansen, Inc.*

Overlock, Craig — *Ray & Berndtson*

Pace, Susan A. — *Horton International*

Pallman-David, Cynthia — *Bonnell Associates Ltd.*

Palma, Frank R. — *Goodrich & Sherwood Associates, Inc.*

Palmer, Carlton A. — *Beall & Company, Inc.*

Palmer, James H. — *The Hindman Company*

Panarese, Pam — *Howard Fischer Associates, Inc.*

Papasadero, Kathleen — *Woodworth International Group*

Pardo, Maria Elena — *Smith Search, S.C.*

Park, Dabney G. — *Mark Stanley/EMA Partners International*

Parry, William H. — *Horton International*

Parsons, Allison D. — *Barton Associates, Inc.*

Paul, Lisa D. — *Merit Resource Group, Inc.*

Pearson, John R. — *Pearson, Caldwell & Farnsworth, Inc.*

Pease, Edward — *Don Richard Associates of Georgia, Inc.*

Peeney, James D. — *Peeney Associates*

Pelisson, Charles — *Marra Peters & Partners*

Pepe, Leonida R. — *Butterfass, Pepe & MacCallan Inc.*

Pernell, Jeanette — *Norman Broadbent International, Inc.*

Peterson, Eric N. — *Stratford Group*

Pettibone, Linda G. — *Herbert Mines Associates, Inc.*

Pettway, Samuel H. — *Spencer Stuart*

Petty, J. Scott — *The Arcus Group*

Pfeiffer, Irene — *Price Waterhouse*

Phillips, Donald L. — *O'Shea, Divine & Company, Inc.*

Phillips, James L. — *Highland Search Group*

Phillips, Richard K. — *Handy HRM Corp.*

Phipps, Peggy — *Woodworth International Group*

Pickering, Dale — *Agri-Tech Personnel, Inc.*

Pickering, Rita — *Agri-Tech Personnel, Inc.*

Pickford, Stephen T. — *The Corporate Staff, Inc.*

Pierson, Edward J. — *Johnson Smith & Knisely Accord*

Pigott, Daniel — *ESA Professional Consultants*

Plazza, Richard C. — *The Executive Source*

Plessner, Rene — *Rene Plessner Associates, Inc.*

Plimpton, Ralph L. — *R L Plimpton Associates*

Pliszka, Donald J. — *Praxis Partners*

Plummer, John — *Plummer & Associates, Inc.*

Poirier, Roland L. — *Poirier, Hoevel & Co.*

Poremski, Paul — *A.J. Burton Group, Inc.*

Porter, Albert — *The Experts*

Potter, Mark W. — *Highland Search Group*

Potter, Steven B. — *Highland Search Group*

Pratt, Tyler P. — *Furst Group/MPI*

Price, Andrew G. — *The Thomas Tucker Company*

Price, Kenneth M. — *Messett Associates, Inc.*

Prince, Marilyn L. — *Higdon Prince Inc.*

Proct, Nina — *Martin H. Bauman Associates, Inc.*

Puckett, Jennifer — *Rene Plessner Associates, Inc.*

Racht, Janet G. — *Crowe, Chizek and Company, LLP*

Raines, Bruce R. — *Raines International Inc.*

Ramler, Carolyn S. — *The Corporate Connection, Ltd.*

Ramsey, John H. — *Mark Stanley/EMA Partners International*

Randell, James E. — *Randell-Heiken, Inc.*

Ray, Marianne C. — *Callan Associates, Ltd.*

Reddick, David C. — *Horton International*

Redding, Denise — *The Douglas Reiter Company, Inc.*

Redler, Rhonda — *National Search, Inc.*

Reeves, William B. — *Spencer Stuart*

Regan, Thomas J. — *Tower Consultants, Ltd.*

Reifersen, Ruth F. — *The Jonathan Stevens Group, Inc.*

Reiser, Ellen — *Thorndike Deland Associates*

Reisinger, George L. — *Sigma Group International*

Reiss, Matt — *National Search, Inc.*

Reiter, Douglas — *The Douglas Reiter Company, Inc.*

Reiter, Harold D. — *Herbert Mines Associates, Inc.*

Remillard, Brad M. — *CJA - The Adler Group*

Renick, Cynthia L. — *Morgan Hunter Corp.*

Reyman, Susan — *S. Reyman & Associates Ltd.*

Rice, Marie — *Jay Gaines & Company, Inc.*

Rice, Raymond D. — *Logue & Rice Inc.*

Rich, Lyttleton — *Sockwell & Associates*

Rieger, Louis J. — *Spencer Stuart*

Rimmel, James E. — *The Hindman Company*

Rimmele, Michael — *The Bankers Group*

Roberts, Nick P. — *Spectrum Search Associates, Inc.*

Roberts, Scott — *Jonas, Walters & Assoc., Inc.*

Robinson, Bruce — *Bruce Robinson Associates*

Robles Cuellar, Paulina — *Ray & Berndtson*

Rogers, Leah — *Dinte Resources, Inc.*

Rollins, Scott — *S.C. International, Ltd.*

Rollo, Robert S. — *R. Rollo Associates*

Romanello, Daniel P. — *Spencer Stuart*

Romang, Paula — *Agri-Tech Personnel, Inc.*

Rose, Robert — *ESA Professional Consultants*

Rosenthal, Charles — *National Search, Inc.*

Ross, Curt A. — *Ray & Berndtson*

Ross, Lawrence — *Ray & Berndtson/Lovas Stanley*

Ross, Mark — *Ray & Berndtson/Lovas Stanley*

Rotella, Marshall W. — *The Corporate Connection, Ltd.*

Roth, Robert J. — *Williams, Roth & Krueger Inc.*

Rowe, William D. — *D.E. Foster Partners Inc.*

Rudolph, Kenneth — *Kossuth & Associates, Inc.*

Russell, Richard A. — *Executive Search Consultants Corporation*

Russell, Robin E. — *Kenzer Corp.*

Russo, Karen — *K. Russo Associates*

Russo, Karen — *Maximum Management Corp.*

Ryan, Lee — *Ryan, Miller & Associates Inc.*

Sabanosh, Whitney — *Highland Search Group*

Sacerdote, John — *Raymond Karsan Associates*

Sallows, Jill S. — *Crowe, Chizek and Company, LLP*

Salvagno, Michael J. — *The Cambridge Group Ltd*

Sanders, Spencer H. — *Battalia Winston International*

Sanow, Robert — *Cochran, Cochran & Yale, Inc.*

Sarn, Allan G. — *Allan Sarn Associates Inc.*

Sarna, Edmund A. — *Jonas, Walters & Assoc., Inc.*

Satenstein, Sloan — *Higdon Prince Inc.*

Sathe, Mark A. — *Sathe & Associates, Inc.*
Savage, Edward J. — *Stanton Chase International*
Saxon, Alexa — *Woodworth International Group*
Schlpma, Christine — *Advanced Executive Resources*
Schneiderman, Gerald — *Management Resource Associates, Inc.*
Schroeder, John W. — *Spencer Stuart*
Schweichler, Lee J. — *Schweichler Associates, Inc.*
Scodius, Joseph J. — *Gregory Michaels and Associates, Inc.*
Scott, Evan — *Howard Fischer Associates, Inc.*
Scott, Gordon S. — *Search Advisors International Corp.*
Scranton, Lisa — *A.J. Burton Group, Inc.*
Segal, Eric B. — *Kenzer Corp.*
Seiden, Steven A. — *Seiden Krieger Associates, Inc.*
Sennello, Gendra — *National Search, Inc.*
Shelton, Sandra — *National Search, Inc.*
Shemin, Grace — *Maximum Management Corp.*
Shervey, Brent C. — *O'Callaghan Honey/Ray & Berndtson, Inc.*
Sherwood, Andrew — *Goodrich & Sherwood Associates, Inc.*
Shield, Nancy — *Maximum Management Corp.*
Shore, Earl L. — *E.L. Shore & Associates Ltd.*
Sibbald, John R. — *John Sibbald Associates, Inc.*
Siegel, Pamela — *Executive Options, Ltd.*
Siegrist, Jeffrey M. — *D.E. Foster Partners Inc.*
Silcott, Marvin L. — *Marvin L. Silcott & Associates, Inc.*
Silvas, Stephen D. — *Roberson and Company*
Silver, Lee — *L. A. Silver Associates, Inc.*
Silverman, Gary W. — *GWS Partners*
Silverstein, Jackie — *Don Richard Associates of Charlotte*
Simon, Mary K. — *Gregory Michaels and Associates, Inc.*
Sindler, Jay — *A.J. Burton Group, Inc.*
Sitarski, Stan — *Howard Fischer Associates, Inc.*
Slayton, Richard C. — *Slayton International, Inc./I-I-C Partners*
Slosar, John — *Boyden*
Smead, Michelle M. — *A.T. Kearney, Inc.*
Smirnov, Tatiana — *Allan Sarn Associates Inc.*
Smith, Ana Luz — *Smith Search, S.C.*
Smith, Ethan L. — *Highland Search Group*
Smith, John E. — *Smith Search, S.C.*
Smith, Lydia — *The Corporate Connection, Ltd.*
Smith, Matt D. — *Ray & Berndtson*
Smith, Richard — *S.C. International, Ltd.*
Smith, Robert L. — *Smith & Sawyer Inc.*
Smith, Ronald V. — *Coe & Company International Inc.*
Snelgrove, Geiger — *National Search, Inc.*
Snyder, C. Edward — *Horton International*
Snyder, James F. — *Snyder & Company*
Sockwell, J. Edgar — *Sockwell & Associates*
Souder, E.G. — *Souder & Associates*
Spann, Richard E. — *Goodrich & Sherwood Associates, Inc.*
Spiegel, Gayle — *L. A. Silver Associates, Inc.*
Spriggs, Robert D. — *Spriggs & Company, Inc.*
St. Clair, Alan — *TNS Partners, Inc.*
Stark, Jeff — *Thorne, Brieger Associates Inc.*
Steele, Daniel — *Cochran, Cochran & Yale, Inc.*

Stein, Terry W. — *Stewart, Stein and Scott, Ltd.*
Steinman, Stephen M. — *The Stevenson Group of New Jersey*
Stevenson, Jane — *Howard Fischer Associates, Inc.*
Stewart, Jeffrey O. — *Stewart, Stein and Scott, Ltd.*
Stewart, Ross M. — *Human Resources Network Partners Inc.*
Stivk, Barbara A. — *Thornton Resources*
Stranberg, James R. — *Callan Associates, Ltd.*
Stratmeyer, Karin Bergwall — *Princeton Entrepreneurial Resources*
Straube, Stanley H. — *Straube Associates*
Strickland, Katie — *Grantham & Co., Inc.*
Strobridge, Richard P. — *F.L. Taylor & Company, Inc.*
Strom, Mark N. — *Search Advisors International Corp.*
Sullivan, Kay — *Rusher, Loscavio & LoPresto*
Sumurdy, Melinda — *Kenzer Corp.*
Sussman, Lynda — *Gilbert Tweed/INESA*
Swanson, Dick — *Raymond Karsan Associates*
Swoboda, Lawrence — *A.J. Burton Group, Inc.*
Taylor, James M. — *The HRM Group, Inc.*
Taylor, R.L. (Larry) — *Ray & Berndtson*
Telford, John H. — *Telford, Adams & Alexander/Telford & Co., Inc.*
Teti, Al — *Chrisman & Company, Incorporated*
Theobald, David B. — *Theobald & Associates*
Thomas, Jeffrey — *Fairfaxx Corporation*
Thomas, Kurt J. — *P.J. Murphy & Associates, Inc.*
Thompson, Dave — *Battalia Winston International*
Thompson, Kenneth L. — *McCormack & Farrow*
Thornton, John C. — *Thornton Resources*
Thrapp, Mark C. — *Executive Search Consultants International, Inc.*
Tincu, John C. — *Ferneborg & Associates, Inc.*
Tootsey, Mark A. — *A.J. Burton Group, Inc.*
Tracey, Jack — *Management Assistance Group, Inc.*
Trieweiler, Bob — *Executive Placement Consultants, Inc.*
Troup, Roger — *The McCormick Group, Inc.*
Truex, John F. — *Morton, McCorkle & Associates, Inc.*
Tryon, Katey — *DeFrain, Mayer LLC*
Tucci, Joseph — *Fairfaxx Corporation*
Tucker, Thomas A. — *The Thomas Tucker Company*
Tully, Margo L. — *Tully/Woodmansee International, Inc.*
Tunney, William — *Grant Cooper and Associates*
Turner, Kimberly — *Barton Associates, Inc.*
Tursi, Deborah J. — *The Corporate Connection, Ltd.*
Tweed, Janet — *Gilbert Tweed/INESA*
Ulbert, Nancy — *Aureus Group*
Ulrich, Mary Ann — *D.S. Allen Associates, Inc.*
Vairo, Leonard A. — *Christian & Timbers*
Valenta, Joseph — *Princeton Entrepreneurial Resources*
Van Campen, Jerry — *Gilbert & Van Campen International*
Van Clieaf, Mark — *MVC Associates International*
Velten, Mark T. — *Boyden*
Venable, William W. — *Thorndike Deland Associates*
Vergara, Gail H. — *Spencer Stuart*

Vernon, Peter C. — *Horton International*
Visnich, L. Christine — *Bason Associates Inc.*
Vitale, Amy — *Highland Search Group*
Vlcek, Thomas J. — *Vlcek & Company, Inc.*
Volkman, Arthur — *Cochran, Cochran & Yale, Inc.*
Vossler, James — *A.J. Burton Group, Inc.*
Waanders, William L. — *ExecuQuest*
Wakefield, Scott — *National Search, Inc.*
Waldoch, D. Mark — *Barnes Development Group, LLC*
Walker, Craig H. — *A.J. Burton Group, Inc.*
Walker, Ewing J. — *Ward Howell International, Inc.*
Wallace, Alec — *Tanton Mitchell/Paul Ray Berndtson*
Walsh, Denis — *Professional Staffing Consultants*
Walters, William F. — *Jonas, Walters & Assoc., Inc.*
Warter, Mark — *Isaacson, Miller*
Watkins, Thomas M. — *Lamalie Amrop International*
Watkinson, Jim W. — *The Badger Group*
Watson, Hanan S. — *Watson International, Inc.*
Wayne, Cary S. — *ProSearch Inc.*
Webb, George H. — *Webb, Johnson Associates, Inc.*
Weisler, Nancy — *National Search, Inc.*
Weissman-Rosenthal, Abbe — *ALW Research International*
Welch, Robert — *Ray & Berndtson*
Weller, Paul S. — *Mark Stanley/EMA Partners International*
Wendler, Kambrea R. — *Gregory Michaels and Associates, Inc.*
Westfall, Ed — *Zwell International*
Wheeler, Gerard H. — *A.J. Burton Group, Inc.*
Whiting, Anthony — *Johnson Smith & Knisely Accord*
Whitley, Sue Ann — *Roberts Ryan and Bentley*
Whitney, William A — *Larsen, Whitney, Blecksmith & Zilliacus*
Whitton, Paula L. — *Pearson, Caldwell & Farnsworth, Inc.*
Wilburn, Dan — *Kaye-Bassman International Corp.*
Wilder, Richard B. — *Columbia Consulting Group*
Wilkinson, Barbara — *Beall & Company, Inc.*
Wilkinson, Jr. SPHR
Wilkinson, Charles E. — *The HRM Group, Inc.*
Williams, Gary L. — *Barnes Development Group, LLC*
Williams, Lis — *Executive Options, Ltd.*
Williams, Roger K. — *Williams, Roth & Krueger Inc.*
Williams, Stephen E. — *Barton Associates, Inc.*
Willis, William H. — *William Willis Worldwide Inc.*
Wilson, Derrick — *Thornton Resources*
Wilson, Patricia L. — *Leon A. Farley Associates*
Winston, Dale — *Battalia Winston International*
Wisch, Steven C. — *MB Inc. Interim Executive Division*
Wise, J. Herbert — *Sandhurst Associates*
Wold, Ted W. — *Hyde Danforth Wold & Co.*
Wolf, Stephen M. — *Byron Leonard International, Inc.*
Womack, Joseph — *The Bankers Group*
Wood, Elizabeth — *Highland Search Group*
Wood, Milton M. — *M. Wood Company*

Woodmansee, Bruce J. — *Tully/Woodmansee International, Inc.*
Woodworth, Gail — *Woodworth International Group*
Wooldridge, Jeff — *Ray & Berndtson*
Wright, A. Leo — *The Hindman Company*
Wright, Carl A.J. — *A.J. Burton Group, Inc.*
Wright, Charles D. — *Goodrich & Sherwood Associates, Inc.*
Wright, Leslie — *The Stevenson Group of New Jersey*
Yaekle, Gary — *Tully/Woodmansee International, Inc.*
Yen, Maggie Yeh Ching — *Ray & Berndtson*
Yungerberg, Steven — *Steven Yungerberg Associates Inc.*
Zadfar, Maryanne — *The Thomas Tucker Company*
Zaffrann, Craig S. — *P.J. Murphy & Associates, Inc.*
Zahradka, James F. — *P.J. Murphy & Associates, Inc.*
Zamborsky, George — *Boyden*
Zaslav, Debra M. — *Telford, Adams & Alexander/Telford & Co., Inc.*
Zay, Thomas C. — *Boyden/Zay & Company*
Zila, Laurie M. — *Princeton Entrepreneurial Resources*
Zivic, Janis M. — *Spencer Stuart*
Zona, Henry F. — *Zona & Associates, Inc.*
Zucker, Nancy — *Maximum Management Corp.*
Zwell, Michael — *Zwell International*

7. Marketing

Abbott, Peter D. — *The Abbott Group, Inc.*
Abell, Vincent W. — *MSI International*
Abert, Janice — *Ledbetter/Davidson International, Inc.*
Adler, Louis S. — *CJA - The Adler Group*
Akin, J.R. "Jack" — *J.R. Akin & Company Inc.*
Allard, Susan — *Allard Associates*
Allen, Wade H. — *Cendea Connection International*
Allen, William L. — *The Hindman Company*
Allgire, Mary L. — *Kenzer Corp.*
Allred, J. Michael — *Spencer Stuart*
Altreuter, Rose — *ALTCO Temporary Services*
Altreuter, Rose — *The ALTCO Group*
Amato, Joseph — *Amato & Associates, Inc.*
Ambler, Peter W. — *Peter W. Ambler Company*
Anderson, Maria H. — *Barton Associates, Inc.*
Anderson, Richard — *Grant Cooper and Associates*
Anderson, Terry — *Intech Summit Group, Inc.*
Andujo, Michele M. — *Chrisman & Company, Incorporated*
Anwar, Tarin — *Jay Gaines & Company, Inc.*
Argenio, Michelangelo — *Spencer Stuart*
Argentin, Jo — *Executive Placement Consultants, Inc.*
Aronin, Michael — *Fisher-Todd Associates*
Aronow, Lawrence E. — *Aronow Associates, Inc.*
Ascher, Susan P. — *The Ascher Group*
Ashton, Edward J. — *E.J. Ashton & Associates, Ltd.*
Aston, Kathy — *Marra Peters & Partners*
Attell, Harold — *A.E. Feldman Associates*
Austin Lockton, Kathy — *Juntunen-Combs-Poirier*
Aydelotte, G. Thomas — *Ingram & Aydelotte Inc./I-I-C Partners*

Badger, Fred H. — *The Badger Group*
Baje, Sarah — *Innovative Search Group, LLC*
Baker, Bill — *Kaye-Bassman International Corp.*
Baker, Gary M. — *Cochran, Cochran & Yale, Inc.*
Baltaglia, Michael — *Cochran, Cochran & Yale, Inc.*
Barbour, Mary Beth — *Tully/Woodmansee International, Inc.*
Barch, Sherrie — *Furst Group/MPI*
Barger, H. Carter — *Barger & Sargeant, Inc.*
Barlow, Ken H. — *The Cherbonnier Group, Inc.*
Barnes, Gary — *Brigade Inc.*
Barnes, Richard E. — *Barnes Development Group, LLC*
Barnes, Roanne L. — *Barnes Development Group, LLC*
Barnum, Toni M. — *Stone Murphy & Olson*
Bartholdi, Ted — *Bartholdi & Company, Inc.*
Bartholdi, Theodore G. — *Bartholdi & Company, Inc.*
Barton, Gary R. — *Barton Associates, Inc.*
Bason, Maurice L. — *Bason Associates Inc.*
Bass, M. Lynn — *Ray & Berndtson*
Bass, Nate — *Jacobson Associates*
Bates, Nina — *Allard Associates*
Bauman, Martin H. — *Martin H. Bauman Associates, Inc.*
Bearman, Linda — *Grant Cooper and Associates*
Beaudin, Elizabeth C. — *Callan Associates, Ltd.*
Beaver, Bentley H. — *The Onstott Group, Inc.*
Becker, Elizabeth M. — *Caliber Associates*
Belin, Jean — *Boyden*
Bell, Lloyd W. — *O'Brien & Bell*
Bellano, Robert W. — *Stanton Chase International*
Bender, Alan — *Bender Executive Search*
Bennett, Jo — *Battalia Winston International*
Benson, Kate — *Rene Plessner Associates, Inc.*
Beran, Helena — *Michael J. Cavanagh and Associates*
Berne, Marlene — *The Whitney Group*
Berry, Harold B. — *The Hindman Company*
Bigelow, Dennis — *Marshall Consultants, Inc.*
Billington, William H. — *Spriggs & Company, Inc.*
Blakslee, Jan H. — *J: Blakslee International, Ltd.*
Bliley, Jerry — *Spencer Stuart*
Bloomer, James E. — *L.W. Foote Company*
Boel, Werner — *The Dalley Hewitt Company*
Bogansky, Amy — *Conex Incorporated*
Bohn, Steve J. — *MSI International*
Bongiovanni, Vincent — *ESA Professional Consultants*
Bonifield, Len — *Bonifield Associates*
Bonnell, William R. — *Bonnell Associates Ltd.*
Borden, Stuart — *M.A. Churchill & Associates, Inc.*
Borkin, Andrew — *Strategic Advancement Inc.*
Borland, James — *Goodrich & Sherwood Associates, Inc.*
Bormann, Cindy Ann — *MSI International*
Bourrie, Sharon D. — *Chartwell Partners International, Inc.*
Bovich, Maryann C. — *Higdon Prince Inc.*
Bowden, Otis H. — *BowdenGlobal, Ltd.*
Brackman, Janet — *Dahl-Morrow International*
Bradley, Dalena — *Woodworth International Group*
Bradshaw, Monte — *Christian & Timbers*

Bratches, Howard — *Thorndike Deland Associates*
Brennan, Patrick J. — *Handy HRM Corp.*
Brieger, Steve — *Thorne, Brieger Associates Inc.*
Brinson, Robert — *MSI International*
Brother, Joy — *Charles Luntz & Associates. Inc.*
Brown, Buzz — *Brown, Bernardy, Van Remmen, Inc.*
Brown, Gina — *Strategic Alliance Network, Ltd.*
Brown, Larry C. — *Horton International*
Brown, Lawrence Anthony — *MSI International*
Brown, Steffan — *Woodworth International Group*
Brudno, Robert J. — *Savoy Partners, Ltd.*
Bruno, Deborah F. — *The Hindman Company*
Bryant, Richard D. — *Bryant Associates, Inc.*
Bryant, Shari G. — *Bryant Associates, Inc.*
Brzezinski, Ronald T. — *Callan Associates, Ltd.*
Buchalter, Allyson — *The Whitney Group*
Bump, Gerald J. — *D.E. Foster Partners Inc.*
Burden, Gene — *The Cherbonnier Group, Inc.*
Burfield, Elaine — *Skott/Edwards Consultants, Inc.*
Burke, John — *The Experts*
Burke, Karen A. — *Mazza & Riley, Inc. (a Korn/Ferry International affiliate)*
Burkhill, John — *The Talley Group*
Burkland, Skott B. — *Skott/Edwards Consultants, Inc.*
Burns, Alan — *The Enns Partners Inc.*
Burns, Terence N. — *D.E. Foster Partners Inc.*
Busch, Jack — *Busch International*
Busterna, Charles — *The KPA Group*
Butler, Kirby B. — *The Butlers Company Insurance Recruiters*
Byrnes, Thomas A. — *The Search Alliance, Inc.*
Caldwell, William R. — *Pearson, Caldwell & Farnsworth, Inc.*
Call, David — *Cochran, Cochran & Yale, Inc.*
Callan, Robert M. — *Callan Associates, Ltd.*
Cameron, James W. — *Cameron Consulting*
Campbell, Patricia A. — *The Onstott Group, Inc.*
Campbell, Robert Scott — *Wellington Management Group*
Campbell, Robert Scott — *Wellington Management Group*
Cannavo, Louise — *The Whitney Group*
Capizzi, Karen — *Cochran, Cochran & Yale, Inc.*
Carideo, Joseph — *Thorndike Deland Associates*
Carro, Carl R. — *Executive Search Consultants International, Inc.*
Cary, Con — *Cary & Associates*
Casal, Daniel G. — *Bonifield Associates*
Cashen, Anthony B. — *Lamalie Amrop International*
Cavanagh, Michael J. — *Michael J. Cavanagh and Associates*
Chamberlin, Joan — *William Guy & Associates*
Chappell, Peter — *The Bankers Group*
Chatterjie, Alok — *MSI International*
Cherbonnier, L. Michael — *TCG International, Inc.*
Cherbonnier, L. Michael — *The Cherbonnier Group, Inc.*
Chndler, Brad J. — *Furst Group/MPI*
Chrisman, Timothy R. — *Chrisman & Company, Incorporated*
Christenson, H. Alan — *Christenson & Hutchison*
Christian, Jeffrey E. — *Christian & Timbers*
Christian, Philip — *Ray & Berndtson*

Citarella, Richard A. — *A.T. Kearney, Inc.*
Citrin, Lea — *K.L. Whitney Company*
Cizek, John T. — *Cizek Associates, Inc.*
Cizek, Marti J. — *Cizek Associates, Inc.*
Clake, Bob — *Furst Group/MPI*
Clark, Evan — *The Whitney Group*
Clark, Steven — *D.A. Kreuter Associates, Inc.*
Clarke Smith, Jamie — *Kaye-Bassman International Corp.*
Clauhsen, Elizabeth A. — *Savoy Partners, Ltd.*
Clayton, Fred J. — *Berkhemer Clayton Incorporated*
Cloutier, Gisella — *Dinte Resources, Inc.*
Cochran, Scott P. — *The Badger Group*
Coe, Karen J. — *Coe & Company International Inc.*
Coffman, Brian — *Kossuth & Associates, Inc.*
Cohen, Robert C. — *Intech Summit Group, Inc.*
Colasanto, Frank M. — *W.R. Rosato & Associates, Inc.*
Coleman, J. Kevin — *J. Kevin Coleman & Associates, Inc.*
Collard, Joseph A. — *Spencer Stuart*
Colman, Michael — *Executive Placement Consultants, Inc.*
Combs, Stephen L. — *Juntunen-Combs-Poirier*
Conard, Rodney J. — *Conard Associates, Inc.*
Conway, Maureen — *Conway & Associates*
Cooke, Katherine H. — *Horton International*
Corso, Glen S. — *Chartwell Partners International, Inc.*
Cortina Del Valle, Pedro — *Ray & Berndtson*
Costello, Lynda — *Coe & Company International Inc.*
Cox, William — *E.J. Ashton & Associates, Ltd.*
Crane, Howard C. — *Chartwell Partners International, Inc.*
Crath, Paul F. — *Price Waterhouse*
Crecos, Gregory P. — *Gregory Michaels and Associates, Inc.*
Critchley, Walter — *Cochran, Cochran & Yale, Inc.*
Cruse, O.D. — *Spencer Stuart*
Crystal, Jonathan A. — *Spencer Stuart*
Cuddihy, Paul — *Dahl-Morrow International*
Cunningham, Lawrence — *Howard Fischer Associates, Inc.*
Cunningham, Robert Y. — *Goodrich & Sherwood Associates, Inc.*
Curtis, Ellissa — *Cochran, Cochran & Yale, Inc.*
Daniels, Alfred — *Alfred Daniels & Associates*
Daniels, C. Eugene — *Sigma Group International*
Dannenberg, Richard A. — *Roberts Ryan and Bentley*
Davis, G. Gordon — *Davis & Company*
de Bardin, Francesca — *F.L. Taylor & Company, Inc.*
De Brun, Thomas P. — *Ray & Berndtson*
de Palacios, Jeannette C. — *J. Palacios & Associates, Inc.*
de Tuede, Catherine — *The Search Alliance, Inc.*
Deaver, Henry C. — *Ray & Berndtson*
DeCorrevont, James — *DeCorrevont & Associates*
DeCorrevont, James — *DeCorrevont & Associates*
Del Pino, William — *National Search, Inc.*
Delaney, Patrick J. — *Sensible Solutions, Inc.*
Della Monica, Vincent — *Search West, Inc.*
Demchak, James P. — *Sandhurst Associates*

Desgrosellier, Gary P. — *Personnel Unlimited/Executive Search*
Desmond, Dennis — *Beall & Company, Inc.*
deWilde, David M. — *Chartwell Partners International, Inc.*
Dezember, Steve — *Ray & Berndtson*
DiCioccio, Carmen — *Cochran, Cochran & Yale, Inc.*
Dickson, Duke — *A.D. & Associates Executive Search, Inc.*
Dietz, David S. — *MSI International*
DiMarchi, Paul — *DiMarchi Partners, Inc.*
DiMarchi, Paul — *DiMarchi Partners, Inc.*
Dingeldey, Peter E. — *Search Advisors International Corp.*
Dingman, Bruce — *Robert W. Dingman Company, Inc.*
Dinte, Paul — *Dinte Resources, Inc.*
DiSalvo, Fred — *The Cambridge Group Ltd*
Diskin, Rochelle — *Search West, Inc.*
Divine, Robert S. — *O'Shea, Divine & Company, Inc.*
Doele, Donald C. — *Goodrich & Sherwood Associates, Inc.*
Donath, Linda — *Dahl-Morrow International*
Dotson, M. Ileen — *Dotson & Associates*
Dowell, Chris — *The Abbott Group, Inc.*
Dowell, Mary K. — *Professional Search Associates*
Doyle, James W. — *Executive Search Consultants International, Inc.*
Dreifus, Donald — *Search West, Inc.*
Dromeshauser, Peter — *Dromeshauser Associates*
Drury, James J. — *Spencer Stuart*
Dubbs, William — *Williams Executive Search, Inc.*
Dunbar, Marilynne — *Ray & Berndtson/Lovas Stanley*
Dunman, Betsy L. — *Crawford & Crofford*
Durakis, Charles A. — *C.A. Durakis Associates, Inc.*
Eason, Jan C. — *Summit Group International*
Ebeling, John A. — *Gilbert Tweed/INESA*
Eddy, Terry — *William Guy & Associates*
Edwards, Dorothy — *MSI International*
Edwards, Ned — *Ingram & Aydelotte Inc./I-I-C Partners*
Edwards, Verba L. — *Wing Tips & Pumps, Inc.*
Ehrgott, Elizabeth — *The Ascher Group*
Ehrhart, Jennifer — *ADOW's Executeam*
Eldridge, Charles B. — *Ray & Berndtson*
Ellis, Ted K. — *The Hindman Company*
Ellis, William — *Interspace Interactive Inc.*
Engelbert, Kimberly S. — *Watson International, Inc.*
England, Mark — *Austin-McGregor International*
Engler, Peter G — *Lautz Grotte Engler*
Enns, George — *The Enns Partners Inc.*
Erder, Debra — *Canny, Bowen Inc.*
Erickson, Elaine — *Kenzer Corp.*
Esposito, Mark — *Christian & Timbers*
Eustis, Lucy R. — *MSI International*
Fancher, Robert L. — *Bason Associates Inc.*
Farley, Leon A. — *Leon A. Farley Associates*
Farnsworth, John A. — *Pearson, Caldwell & Farnsworth, Inc.*
Federman, Jack R. — *W.R. Rosato & Associates, Inc.*
Fee, J. Curtis — *Spencer Stuart*
Feldman, Abe — *A.E. Feldman Associates*
Ferneborg, Jay W. — *Ferneborg & Associates, Inc.*
Ferneborg, John R. — *Ferneborg & Associates, Inc.*

Ferrari, S. Jay — *Ferrari Search Group*
Fischer, Adam — *Howard Fischer Associates, Inc.*
Fischer, Howard M. — *Howard Fischer Associates, Inc.*
Fischer, Janet L. — *Boyden*
Fisher, Neal — *Fisher Personnel Management Services*
Fitzgerald, Diane — *Fitzgerald Associates*
Fitzgerald, Geoffrey — *Fitzgerald Associates*
Flanagan, Robert M. — *Robert M. Flanagan & Associates, Ltd.*
Fleming, Marco — *MSI International*
Flood, Michael — *Norman Broadbent International, Inc.*
Foote, Leland W. — *L.W. Foote Company*
Ford, Sandra D. — *The Ford Group, Inc.*
Foreman, David C. — *Koontz, Jeffries & Associates, Inc.*
Fowler, Edward D.C. — *Higdon Prince Inc.*
Fowler, Thomas A. — *The Hindman Company*
Fox, Lucie — *Allard Associates*
Frazier, John — *Cochran, Cochran & Yale, Inc.*
Freeman, Mark — *ESA Professional Consultants*
Freier, Bruce — *Executive Referral Services, Inc.*
French, William G. — *Preng & Associates, Inc.*
Furlong, James W. — *Furlong Search, Inc.*
Furlong, James W. — *Furlong Search, Inc.*
Furlong, James W. — *Furlong Search, Inc.*
Fust, Sheely F. — *Ray & Berndtson*
Gabel, Gregory N. — *Canny, Bowen Inc.*
Gabriel, David L. — *The Arcus Group*
Gaines, Jay — *Jay Gaines & Company, Inc.*
Galante, Suzanne M. — *Vlcek & Company, Inc.*
Galinski, Paul — *E.J. Ashton & Associates, Ltd.*
Gallagher, Terence M. — *Battalia Winston International*
Gantar, Donna — *Howard Fischer Associates, Inc.*
Gardiner, E. Nicholas P. — *Gardiner International*
Garfinkle, Steven M. — *Battalia Winston International*
Garland, Dick — *Dick Garland Consultants*
Garzone, Dolores — *M.A. Churchill & Associates, Inc.*
Gauthier, Robert C. — *Columbia Consulting Group*
George, Delores F. — *Delores F. George Human Resource Management & Consulting Industry*
Germain, Valerie — *Jay Gaines & Company, Inc.*
Gestwick, Daniel — *Cochran, Cochran & Yale, Inc.*
Ghurani, Mac — *Gary Kaplan & Associates*
Giacalone, Louis — *Allard Associates*
Gibbons, Ronald L. — *Flynn, Hannock, Incorporated*
Gibbs, John S. — *Spencer Stuart*
Gilbert, Jerry — *Gilbert & Van Campen International*
Gilchrist, Robert J. — *Horton International*
Gill, Patricia — *Columbia Consulting Group*
Gill, Susan — *Plummer & Associates, Inc.*
Gilreath, James M. — *Gilreath Weatherby, Inc.*
Giries, Juliet D. — *Barton Associates, Inc.*
Goar, Duane R. — *Sandhurst Associates*
Gobert, Larry — *Professional Search Consultants*
Golde, Lisa — *Tully/Woodmansee International, Inc.*
Goldenberg, Susan — *Grant Cooper and Associates*
Goldsmith, Joseph B. — *Higdon Prince Inc.*

Goldstein, Gary — *The Whitney Group*
Goldstein, Steven G. — *The Jonathan Stevens Group, Inc.*
Goodman, Dawn M. — *Bason Associates Inc.*
Gordon, Gerald L. — *E.G. Jones Associates, Ltd.*
Gotlys, Jordan — *Stone Murphy & Olson*
Gow, Roderick C. — *Lamalie Amrop International*
Grant, Michael — *Zwell International*
Grantham, John — *Grantham & Co., Inc.*
Grantham, Philip H. — *Columbia Consulting Group*
Grasch, Jerry E. — *The Hindman Company*
Gray, Mark — *Executive Referral Services, Inc.*
Grebenstein, Charles R. — *Skott/Edwards Consultants, Inc.*
Greco, Patricia — *Howe-Lewis International*
Grotenhuis, Dirkten — *Chrisman & Company, Incorporated*
Grotte, Lawrence C. — *Lautz Grotte Engler*
Gulian, Randolph — *Strategic Executives, Inc.*
Gurnani, Angali — *Executive Placement Consultants, Inc.*
Gurtin, Kay L. — *Executive Options, Ltd.*
Guy, C. William — *William Guy & Associates*
Haas, Margaret P. — *The Haas Associates, Inc.*
Hailey, H.M. — *Damon & Associates, Inc.*
Hall, Peter V. — *Chartwell Partners International, Inc.*
Hallock, Peter B. — *Goodrich & Sherwood Associates, Inc.*
Hallstrom, Victoria — *The Whitney Group*
Hamilton, John R. — *Ray & Berndtson*
Hammond, Karla — *People Management Northeast Incorporated*
Hampshire, Kay — *Allard Associates*
Hanes, Leah — *Ray & Berndtson*
Hanley, Alan P. — *Williams, Roth & Krueger Inc.*
Hanley, Maureen E. — *Gilbert Tweed/INESA*
Hannock, Elwin W. — *Flynn, Hannock, Incorporated*
Hanson, Grant M. — *Goodrich & Sherwood Associates, Inc.*
Harbaugh, Paul J. — *International Management Advisors, Inc.*
Harbert, David O. — *Sweeney Harbert & Mummert, Inc.*
Hardison, Richard L. — *Hardison & Company*
Harney, Elyane — *Gary Kaplan & Associates*
Harris, Joe W. — *Cendea Connection International*
Harris, Julia — *The Whitney Group*
Harris, Seth O. — *Christian & Timbers*
Harrison, Joel — *D.A. Kreuter Associates, Inc.*
Hart, Robert T. — *D.E. Foster Partners Inc.*
Harvey, Mike — *Advanced Executive Resources*
Haughton, Michael — *DeFrain, Mayer LLC*
Havener, Donald Clarke — *The Abbott Group, Inc.*
Hawksworth, A. Dwight — *A.D. & Associates Executive Search, Inc.*
Hay, William E. — *William E. Hay & Co.*
Haystead, Steve — *Advanced Executive Resources*
Hebel, Robert W. — *R.W. Hebel Associates*
Hedlund, David — *Hedlund Corporation*
Heiken, Barbara E. — *Randell-Heiken, Inc.*
Heinze, David — *Heinze & Associates, Inc.*
Hellinger, Audrey W. — *Martin H. Bauman Associates, Inc.*

Helminiak, Audrey — *Gaffney Management Consultants*
Hendrickson, Jill E. — *Gregory Michaels and Associates, Inc.*
Heneghan, Donald A. — *Allerton Heneghan & O'Neill*
Henn, George W. — *G.W. Henn & Company*
Hennig, Sandra M. — *MSI International*
Henry, Mary — *Conex Incorporated*
Hergenrather, Richard A. — *Hergenrather & Company*
Herman, Shelli — *Gary Kaplan & Associates*
Hewitt, Rives D. — *The Dalley Hewitt Company*
Hewitt, W. Davis — *The Dalley Hewitt Company*
Higbee, Joan — *Thorndike Deland Associates*
Higdon, Henry G. — *Higdon Prince Inc.*
Higgins, Donna — *Howard Fischer Associates, Inc.*
Hildebrand, Thomas B. — *Professional Resources Group, Inc.*
Hill, Emery — *MSI International*
Hillen, Skip — *The McCormick Group, Inc.*
Himlin, Amy — *Cochran, Cochran & Yale, Inc.*
Hindman, Neil C. — *The Hindman Company*
Hochberg, Brian — *M.A. Churchill & Associates, Inc.*
Hochberg, Steven P. — *Caliber Associates*
Hockett, William — *Hockett Associates, Inc.*
Hoevel, Michael J. — *Poirier, Hoevel & Co.*
Holland, John A. — *Holland, McFadzean & Associates, Inc.*
Holland, Rose Mary — *Price Waterhouse*
Holmes, Lawrence J. — *Columbia Consulting Group*
Holt, Carol — *Bartholdi & Company, Inc.*
Hoover, Catherine — *J.L. Mark Associates, Inc.*
Hopkins, Chester A. — *Handy HRM Corp.*
Hopp, Lorrie A. — *Gregory Michaels and Associates, Inc.*
Houchins, William M. — *Christian & Timbers*
Hoyda, Louis A. — *Thorndike Deland Associates*
Hucko, Donald S. — *Jonas, Walters & Assoc., Inc.*
Hudson, Reginald M. — *Search Bureau International*
Hughes, Cathy N. — *The Ogdon Partnership*
Hughes, R. Kevin — *Handy HRM Corp.*
Hutchison, William K. — *Christenson & Hutchison*
Hypes, Richard G. — *Lynch Miller Moore, Inc.*
Ingram, D. John — *Ingram & Aydelotte Inc./I-I-C Partners*
Inguagiato, Gregory — *MSI International*
Issacs, Judith A. — *Grant Cooper and Associates*
Jablo, Steven A. — *Dieckmann & Associates, Ltd.*
Jacobs, Martin J. — *The Rubicon Group*
Jacobs, Mike — *Thorne, Brieger Associates Inc.*
Jacobson, Rick — *The Windham Group*
Janis, Laurence — *Integrated Search Solutions Group, LLC*
Jansen, John F. — *Delta Services*
Janssen, Don — *Howard Fischer Associates, Inc.*
Januale, Lois — *Cochran, Cochran & Yale, Inc.*
Jazylo, John V. — *Handy HRM Corp.*
Jeffers, Richard B. — *Dieckmann & Associates, Ltd.*
Jernigan, Susan N. — *Sockwell & Associates*
Joffe, Barry — *Bason Associates Inc.*
Johnson, John W. — *Webb, Johnson Associates, Inc.*
Johnson, Julie M. — *International Staffing Consultants, Inc.*
Johnson, Kathleen A. — *Barton Associates, Inc.*
Johnson, Priscilla — *The Johnson Group, Inc.*
Johnson, Stanley C. — *Johnson & Company*
Johnson, Valerie — *Coe & Company International Inc.*
Jones, Jonathan C. — *Canny, Bowen Inc.*
Jordan, Jon — *Cochran, Cochran & Yale, Inc.*
Judge, Alfred L. — *The Cambridge Group Ltd*
Juelis, John J. — *Peeney Associates*
Kader, Richard — *Richard Kader & Associates*
Kaiser, Donald J. — *Dunhill International Search of New Haven*
Kaiser, Elaine M. — *Dunhill International Search of New Haven*
Kalinowski, David — *Jacobson Associates*
Kane, Karen — *Howard Fischer Associates, Inc.*
Kanovsky, Gerald — *Career Consulting Group, Inc.*
Kanovsky, Marlene — *Career Consulting Group, Inc.*
Kaplan, Gary — *Gary Kaplan & Associates*
Kassouf, Constance — *The Whitney Group*
Keating, Pierson — *Nordeman Grimm, Inc.*
Keck, Jason B. — *Kaye-Bassman International Corp.*
Keller, Barbara E. — *Barton Associates, Inc.*
Kelly, Claudia L. — *Spencer Stuart*
Kelly, Elizabeth Ann — *Wellington Management Group*
Kelly, Peter W. — *R. Rollo Associates*
Kelso, Patricia C. — *Barton Associates, Inc.*
Kennedy, Michael — *The Danbrook Group, Inc.*
Kenzer, Robert D. — *Kenzer Corp.*
Kern, Jerry L. — *ADOW's Executeam*
Kern, Kathleen G. — *ADOW's Executeam*
Kershaw, Lisa — *Tanton Mitchell/Paul Ray Berndtson*
Kettwig, David A. — *A.T. Kearney, Inc.*
Kilcullen, Brian A. — *D.A. Kreuter Associates, Inc.*
Kiley, Phyllis — *National Search, Inc.*
King, Bill — *The McCormick Group, Inc.*
King, Margaret — *Christian & Timbers*
Kinser, Richard E. — *Richard Kinser & Associates*
Kip, Luanne S. — *Kip Williams, Inc.*
Kishbaugh, Herbert S. — *Kishbaugh Associates International*
Klages, Constance W. — *International Management Advisors, Inc.*
Klavens, Cecile J. — *The Pickwick Group, Inc.*
Klein, Lynn M. — *Riotto-Jones Associates*
Klein, Mary Jo — *Cochran, Cochran & Yale, Inc.*
Klein, Mel — *Stewart/Laurence Associates*
Knisely, Gary — *Johnson Smith & Knisely Accord*
Kohn, Adam P. — *Christian & Timbers*
Kondra, Vernon J. — *The Douglas Reiter Company, Inc.*
Koontz, Donald N. — *Koontz, Jeffries & Associates, Inc.*
Kopsick, Joseph M. — *Spencer Stuart*
Kossuth, David — *Kossuth & Associates, Inc.*
Kossuth, Jane — *Kossuth & Associates, Inc.*
Kotick, Maddy — *The Stevenson Group of New Jersey*
Krauser, H. James — *Spencer Stuart*
Krejci, Stanley L. — *Boyden Washington, D.C.*
Kreuch, Paul C. — *Skott/Edwards Consultants, Inc.*

Simpson, Scott — *Cendea Connection International*
Sitarski, Stan — *Howard Fischer Associates, Inc.*
Skalet, Ira — *A.E. Feldman Associates*
Skunda, Donna M. — *Allerton Heneghan & O'Neill*
Slayton, Richard C. — *Slayton International, Inc./I-I-C Partners*
Slocum, Ann Marie — *K.L. Whitney Company*
Slosar, John — *Boyden*
Smead, Michelle M. — *A.T. Kearney, Inc.*
Smith, Ana Luz — *Smith Search, S.C.*
Smith, David P. — *HRS, Inc.*
Smith, Herman M. — *Herman Smith Executive Initiatives Inc.*
Smith, John E. — *Smith Search, S.C.*
Smith, Lydia — *The Corporate Connection, Ltd.*
Smith, Matt D. — *Ray & Berndtson*
Smith, Monica L. — *Analysts Resources, Inc.*
Smith, Robert L. — *Smith & Sawyer Inc.*
Smith, Ronald V. — *Coe & Company International Inc.*
Snelgrove, Geiger — *National Search, Inc.*
Snyder, C. Edward — *Horton International*
Snyder, James F. — *Snyder & Company*
Sockwell, J. Edgar — *Sockwell & Associates*
Sondgrass, Stephen — *DeFrain, Mayer LLC*
Souder, E.G. — *Souder & Associates*
Spann, Richard E. — *Goodrich & Sherwood Associates, Inc.*
Spicehandler, Sheila — *Trebor Weldon Lawrence, Inc.*
Spicher, John — *M.A. Churchill & Associates, Inc.*
Spiegel, Gayle — *L. A. Silver Associates, Inc.*
Spriggs, Robert D. — *Spriggs & Company, Inc.*
Sprowls, Linda — *Allard Associates*
St. Clair, Alan — *TNS Partners, Inc.*
Stark, Jeff — *Thorne, Brieger Associates Inc.*
Steele, Daniel — *Cochran, Cochran & Yale, Inc.*
Stein, Terry W. — *Stewart, Stein and Scott, Ltd.*
Steinem, Andy — *Dahl-Morrow International*
Steinem, Barbra — *Dahl-Morrow International*
Steinman, Stephen M. — *The Stevenson Group of New Jersey*
Stevens, Craig M. — *Kirkman & Searing, Inc.*
Stevenson, Jane — *Howard Fischer Associates, Inc.*
Stewart, Jeffrey O. — *Stewart, Stein and Scott, Ltd.*
Stewart, Ross M. — *Human Resources Network Partners Inc.*
Stivk, Barbara A. — *Thornton Resources*
Stone, Susan L. — *Stone Enterprises Ltd.*
Stranberg, James R. — *Callan Associates, Ltd.*
Stratmeyer, Karin Bergwall — *Princeton Entrepreneurial Resources*
Straube, Stanley H. — *Straube Associates*
Strickland, Katie — *Grantham & Co., Inc.*
Stringer, Dann P. — *D.E. Foster Partners Inc.*
Strobridge, Richard P. — *F.L. Taylor & Company, Inc.*
Strom, Mark N. — *Search Advisors International Corp.*
Sullivan, Kay — *Rusher, Loscavio & LoPresto*
Sumurdy, Melinda — *Kenzer Corp.*
Swanson, Dick — *Raymond Karsan Associates*
Sweeney, Sean K. — *Bonifield Associates*
Taylor, Conrad G. — *MSI International*
Taylor, Ernest A. — *Ward Howell International, Inc.*

Taylor, James M. — *The HRM Group, Inc.*
Taylor, R.L. (Larry) — *Ray & Berndtson*
Telford, John H. — *Telford, Adams & Alexander/Telford & Co., Inc.*
ten Cate, Herman H. — *Stoneham Associates Corp.*
Teti, Al — *Chrisman & Company, Incorporated*
Theobald, David B. — *Theobald & Associates*
Thomas, Jeffrey — *Fairfaxx Corporation*
Thomas, Kurt J. — *P.J. Murphy & Associates, Inc.*
Thomas, Terry — *The Thomas Resource Group*
Thompson, Dave — *Battalia Winston International*
Thompson, John R. — *MSI International*
Thompson, Kenneth L. — *McCormack & Farrow*
Thornton, John C. — *Thornton Resources*
Thrapp, Mark C. — *Executive Search Consultants International, Inc.*
Tierney, Eileen — *The Whitney Group*
Tincu, John C. — *Ferneborg & Associates, Inc.*
Todres-Bernstein, Margo — *Kaye-Bassman International Corp.*
Tracey, Jack — *Management Assistance Group, Inc.*
Trieweiler, Bob — *Executive Placement Consultants, Inc.*
Trott, Kathryn — *Allard Associates*
Trott, Kathryn — *Allard Associates*
Truex, John F. — *Morton, McCorkle & Associates, Inc.*
Tryon, Katey — *DeFrain, Mayer LLC*
Tucci, Joseph — *Fairfaxx Corporation*
Tucker, Thomas A. — *The Thomas Tucker Company*
Tully, Margo L. — *Tully/Woodmansee International, Inc.*
Tunney, William — *Grant Cooper and Associates*
Turner, Kimberly — *Barton Associates, Inc.*
Tursi, Deborah J. — *The Corporate Connection, Ltd.*
Tweed, Janet — *Gilbert Tweed/INESA*
Tyson, Richard L. — *Bonifield Associates*
Ulrich, Mary Ann — *D.S. Allen Associates, Inc.*
Vairo, Leonard A. — *Christian & Timbers*
Valenta, Joseph — *Princeton Entrepreneurial Resources*
Van Alstine, Catherine — *Tanton Mitchell/Paul Ray Berndtson*
Van Biesen, Jacques A.H. — *Search Group Inc.*
Van Campen, Jerry — *Gilbert & Van Campen International*
Van Clieaf, Mark — *MVC Associates International*
Van Nostrand, Mara J. — *Barton Associates, Inc.*
Van Remmen, Roger — *Brown, Bernardy, Van Remmen, Inc.*
Velten, Mark T. — *Boyden*
Venable, William W. — *Thorndike Deland Associates*
Vergara, Gail H. — *Spencer Stuart*
Vergari, Jane — *Herbert Mines Associates, Inc.*
Vernon, Peter C. — *Horton International*
Visnich, L. Christine — *Bason Associates Inc.*
Vlcek, Thomas J. — *Vlcek & Company, Inc.*
Volkman, Arthur — *Cochran, Cochran & Yale, Inc.*
von Baillou, Astrid — *Richard Kinser & Associates*
Vourakis, Zan — *ZanExec LLC*
Waanders, William L. — *ExecuQuest*
Wakefield, Scott — *National Search, Inc.*
Waldman, Noah H. — *Lamalie Amrop International*
Waldoch, D. Mark — *Barnes Development Group, LLC*

Waldrop, Gary R. — *MSI International*
Walker, Ewing J. — *Ward Howell International, Inc.*
Walters, William F. — *Jonas, Walters & Assoc., Inc.*
Watkins, Thomas M. — *Lamalie Amrop International*
Watkinson, Jim W. — *The Badger Group*
Watson, Hanan S. — *Watson International, Inc.*
Watson, James — *MSI International*
Wayne, Cary S. — *ProSearch Inc.*
Webb, George H. — *Webb, Johnson Associates, Inc.*
Wein, Michael S. — *Media Management Resources, Inc.*
Wein, William — *Media Management Resources, Inc.*
Weisler, Nancy — *National Search, Inc.*
Weissman-Rosenthal, Abbe — *ALW Research International*
Welch, Robert — *Ray & Berndtson*
Wendler, Kambrea R. — *Gregory Michaels and Associates, Inc.*
Westfall, Ed — *Zwell International*
Weston, Corinne F. — *D.A. Kreuter Associates, Inc.*
White, Richard B. — *Spencer Stuart*
White, William C. — *Venture Resources Inc.*
Whiting, Anthony — *Johnson Smith & Knisely Accord*
Whitley, Sue Ann — *Roberts Ryan and Bentley*
Whitney, Kenneth L. — *K.L. Whitney Company*
Whitney, William A — *Larsen, Whitney, Blecksmith & Zilliacus*
Whitton, Paula L. — *Pearson, Caldwell & Farnsworth, Inc.*
Wilburn, Dan — *Kaye-Bassman International Corp.*
Wilder, Richard B. — *Columbia Consulting Group*
Wilkinson, Barbara — *Beall & Company, Inc.*
Wilkinson, Jr. SPHR
Wilkinson, Charles E. — *The HRM Group, Inc.*
Williams, Gary L. — *Barnes Development Group, LLC*
Williams, Harry D. — *Jacobson Associates*
Williams, Lis — *Executive Options, Ltd.*
Williams, Roger K. — *Williams, Roth & Krueger Inc.*
Williams, Stephen E. — *Barton Associates, Inc.*
Willis, William H. — *William Willis Worldwide Inc.*
Wilson, Derrick — *Thornton Resources*
Wilson, Patricia L. — *Leon A. Farley Associates*
Winitz, Joel — *GSW Consulting Group, Inc.*
Winitz, Marla — *GSW Consulting Group, Inc.*
Winston, Dale — *Battalia Winston International*
Wisch, Steven C. — *MB Inc. Interim Executive Division*
Wise, J. Herbert — *Sandhurst Associates*
Wold, Ted W. — *Hyde Danforth Wold & Co.*
Wolf, Stephen M. — *Byron Leonard International, Inc.*
Womack, Joseph — *The Bankers Group*
Wood, Milton M. — *M. Wood Company*
Woodmansee, Bruce J. — *Tully/Woodmansee International, Inc.*
Woodworth, Gail — *Woodworth International Group*
Wooldridge, Jeff — *Ray & Berndtson*
Wooller, Edmund A.M. — *Windsor International*
Wright, A. Leo — *The Hindman Company*

Wright, Charles D. — *Goodrich & Sherwood Associates, Inc.*
Wright, Leslie — *The Stevenson Group of New Jersey*
Wylie, Pamela — *M.A. Churchill & Associates, Inc.*
Yaekle, Gary — *Tully/Woodmansee International, Inc.*
Yen, Maggie Yeh Ching — *Ray & Berndtson*
Yungerberg, Steven — *Steven Yungerberg Associates Inc.*
Zaffrann, Craig S. — *P.J. Murphy & Associates, Inc.*
Zahradka, James F. — *P.J. Murphy & Associates, Inc.*
Zamborsky, George — *Boyden*
Zaslav, Debra M. — *Telford, Adams & Alexander/Telford & Co., Inc.*
Zay, Thomas C. — *Boyden/Zay & Company*
Zay, Thomas C. — *Boyden/Zay & Company*
Zetto, Kathryn — *Seco & Zetto Associates, Inc.*
Zila, Laurie M. — *Princeton Entrepreneurial Resources*
Zona, Henry F. — *Zona & Associates, Inc.*
Zwell, Michael — *Zwell International*

8. Research/Development

Abbott, Peter D. — *The Abbott Group, Inc.*
Abert, Janice — *Ledbetter/Davidson International, Inc.*
Adler, Louis S. — *CJA - The Adler Group*
Allgire, Mary L. — *Kenzer Corp.*
Altreuter, Rose — *The ALTCO Group*
Ambler, Peter W. — *Peter W. Ambler Company*
Anderson, Maria H. — *Barton Associates, Inc.*
Anderson, Steve — *CPS Inc.*
Aronin, Michael — *Fisher-Todd Associates*
Aston, Kathy — *Marra Peters & Partners*
Atwood, Barrie — *The Abbott Group, Inc.*
Badger, Fred H. — *The Badger Group*
Baeder, Jeremy — *Executive Manning Corporation*
Baje, Sarah — *Innovative Search Group, LLC*
Balbone, Rich — *Executive Manning Corporation*
Balch, Randy — *CPS Inc.*
Barbour, Mary Beth — *Tully/Woodmansee International, Inc.*
Barch, Sherrie — *Furst Group/MPI*
Barlow, Ken H. — *The Cherbonnier Group, Inc.*
Barnes, Richard E. — *Barnes Development Group, LLC*
Barnes, Roanne L. — *Barnes Development Group, LLC*
Bartholdi, Ted — *Bartholdi & Company, Inc.*
Bartholdi, Theodore G. — *Bartholdi & Company, Inc.*
Bason, Maurice L. — *Bason Associates Inc.*
Bass, M. Lynn — *Ray & Berndtson*
Bass, Nate — *Jacobson Associates*
Bauman, Martin H. — *Martin H. Bauman Associates, Inc.*
Beaudin, Elizabeth C. — *Callan Associates, Ltd.*
Beaver, Bentley H. — *The Onstott Group, Inc.*
Becker, Elizabeth M. — *Caliber Associates*
Benson, Kate — *Rene Plessner Associates, Inc.*
Bladon, Andrew — *Don Richard Associates of Tampa, Inc.*
Blakslee, Jan H. — *J: Blakslee International, Ltd.*
Blim, Barbara — *JDG Associates, Ltd.*
Bloomer, James E. — *L.W. Foote Company*
Boel, Werner — *The Dalley Hewitt Company*

Bogansky, Amy — *Conex Incorporated*
Boltrus, Dick — *Sink, Walker, Boltrus International*
Bongiovanni, Vincent — *ESA Professional Consultants*
Bonifield, Len — *Bonifield Associates*
Borden, Stuart — *M.A. Churchill & Associates, Inc.*
Borkin, Andrew — *Strategic Advancement Inc.*
Bowden, Otis H. — *BowdenGlobal, Ltd.*
Bradley, Dalena — *Woodworth International Group*
Bradshaw, Monte — *Christian & Timbers*
Brady, Dick — *William Guy & Associates*
Brady, Robert — *CPS Inc.*
Brandeis, Richard — *CPS Inc.*
Brieger, Steve — *Thorne, Brieger Associates Inc.*
Britt, Stephen — *Keith Bagg & Associates Inc.*
Brown, Steffan — *Woodworth International Group*
Bryant, Richard D. — *Bryant Associates, Inc.*
Bryant, Shari G. — *Bryant Associates, Inc.*
Brzezinski, Ronald T. — *Callan Associates, Ltd.*
Burden, Gene — *The Cherbonnier Group, Inc.*
Burfield, Elaine — *Skott/Edwards Consultants, Inc.*
Burke, John — *The Experts*
Burkland, Skott B. — *Skott/Edwards Consultants, Inc.*
Busch, Jack — *Busch International*
Butler, Kirby B. — *The Butlers Company Insurance Recruiters*
Byrnes, Thomas A. — *The Search Alliance, Inc.*
Callan, Robert M. — *Callan Associates, Ltd.*
Cameron, James W. — *Cameron Consulting*
Casal, Daniel G. — *Bonifield Associates*
Celenza, Catherine — *CPS Inc.*
Cherbonnier, L. Michael — *TCG International, Inc.*
Cherbonnier, L. Michael — *The Cherbonnier Group, Inc.*
Chndler, Brad J. — *Furst Group/MPI*
Christian, Philip — *Ray & Berndtson*
Christiansen, Amy — *CPS Inc.*
Christiansen, Doug — *CPS Inc.*
Cizek, John T. — *Cizek Associates, Inc.*
Cizek, Marti J. — *Cizek Associates, Inc.*
Clake, Bob — *Furst Group/MPI*
Clark, James — *CPS Inc.*
Cochran, Scott P. — *The Badger Group*
Coffman, Brian — *Kossuth & Associates, Inc.*
Cohen, Robert C. — *Intech Summit Group, Inc.*
Colasanto, Frank M. — *W.R. Rosato & Associates, Inc.*
Conway, Maureen — *Conway & Associates*
Cortina Del Valle, Pedro — *Ray & Berndtson*
Costello, Lynda — *Coe & Company International Inc.*
Coulman, Karen — *CPS Inc.*
Crath, Paul F. — *Price Waterhouse*
Cruse, O.D. — *Spencer Stuart*
Cunningham, Lawrence — *Howard Fischer Associates, Inc.*
Czepiel, Susan — *CPS Inc.*
Daniels, Alfred — *Alfred Daniels & Associates*
Davis, G. Gordon — *Davis & Company*
De Brun, Thomas P. — *Ray & Berndtson*
de Cholnoky, Andrea — *Spencer Stuart*
Deaver, Henry C. — *Ray & Berndtson*
Del Pino, William — *National Search, Inc.*
Desai, Sushila — *Sink, Walker, Boltrus International*

Desmond, Dennis — *Beall & Company, Inc.*
Dezember, Steve — *Ray & Berndtson*
Dickson, Duke — *A.D. & Associates Executive Search, Inc.*
Dingeldey, Peter E. — *Search Advisors International Corp.*
DiSalvo, Fred — *The Cambridge Group Ltd*
Divine, Robert S. — *O'Shea, Divine & Company, Inc.*
Dixon, Aris — *CPS Inc.*
Dowell, Chris — *The Abbott Group, Inc.*
Dunman, Betsy L. — *Crawford & Crofford*
Dwyer, Julie — *CPS Inc.*
Ebeling, John A. — *Gilbert Tweed/INESA*
Edwards, Verba L. — *Wing Tips & Pumps, Inc.*
Elder, Tom — *Juntunen-Combs-Poirier*
Eldridge, Charles B. — *Ray & Berndtson*
England, Mark — *Austin-McGregor International*
Erickson, Elaine — *Kenzer Corp.*
Erikson, Theodore J. — *Erikson Consulting Associates, Inc.*
Ervin, Darlene — *CPS Inc.*
Esposito, Mark — *Christian & Timbers*
Evans, David — *Executive Manning Corporation*
Fancher, Robert L. — *Bason Associates Inc.*
Federman, Jack R. — *W.R. Rosato & Associates, Inc.*
Ferrara, David M. — *Intech Summit Group, Inc.*
Fischer, Adam — *Howard Fischer Associates, Inc.*
Fischer, Howard M. — *Howard Fischer Associates, Inc.*
Fischer, Janet L. — *Boyden*
Fisher, Neal — *Fisher Personnel Management Services*
Fitzgerald, Diane — *Fitzgerald Associates*
Fitzgerald, Geoffrey — *Fitzgerald Associates*
Fogarty, Michael — *CPS Inc.*
Foote, Leland W. — *L.W. Foote Company*
Foreman, David C. — *Koontz, Jeffries & Associates, Inc.*
Fotia, Frank — *JDG Associates, Ltd.*
Freeman, Mark — *ESA Professional Consultants*
French, William G. — *Preng & Associates, Inc.*
Friedman, Helen E. — *McCormack & Farrow*
Fulton, Christine N. — *Highland Search Group*
Furlong, James W. — *Furlong Search, Inc.*
Furlong, James W. — *Furlong Search, Inc.*
Furlong, James W. — *Furlong Search, Inc.*
Fust, Sheely F. — *Ray & Berndtson*
Gabel, Gregory N. — *Canny, Bowen Inc.*
Gabriel, David L. — *The Arcus Group*
Gaffney, Keith — *Gaffney Management Consultants*
Gaffney, William — *Gaffney Management Consultants*
Gantar, Donna — *Howard Fischer Associates, Inc.*
Garfinkle, Steven M. — *Battalia Winston International*
George, Delores F. — *Delores F. George Human Resource Management & Consulting Industry*
Gerster, J.P. — *Juntunen-Combs-Poirier*
Ghurani, Mac — *Gary Kaplan & Associates*
Giries, Juliet D. — *Barton Associates, Inc.*
Goldenberg, Susan — *Grant Cooper and Associates*
Goodman, Dawn M. — *Bason Associates Inc.*
Goodwin, Tim — *William Guy & Associates*
Graham, Dale — *CPS Inc.*

Grant, Michael — *Zwell International*
Grantham, John — *Grantham & Co., Inc.*
Gray, Mark — *Executive Referral Services, Inc.*
Grebenstein, Charles R. — *Skott/Edwards Consultants, Inc.*
Grzybowski, Jill — *CPS Inc.*
Guy, C. William — *William Guy & Associates*
Hamilton, John R. — *Ray & Berndtson*
Hanes, Leah — *Ray & Berndtson*
Hanley, Alan P. — *Williams, Roth & Krueger Inc.*
Harbaugh, Paul J. — *International Management Advisors, Inc.*
Harney, Elyane — *Gary Kaplan & Associates*
Harris, Seth O. — *Christian & Timbers*
Hart, Robert T. — *D.E. Foster Partners Inc.*
Hartle, Larry — *CPS Inc.*
Harvey, Mike — *Advanced Executive Resources*
Havener, Donald Clarke — *The Abbott Group, Inc.*
Hawksworth, A. Dwight — *A.D. & Associates Executive Search, Inc.*
Haystead, Steve — *Advanced Executive Resources*
Hazerjian, Cynthia — *CPS Inc.*
Heafey, Bill — *CPS Inc.*
Hebel, Robert W. — *R.W. Hebel Associates*
Heinze, David — *Heinze & Associates, Inc.*
Hellinger, Audrey W. — *Martin H. Bauman Associates, Inc.*
Helminiak, Audrey — *Gaffney Management Consultants*
Heneghan, Donald A. — *Allerton Heneghan & O'Neill*
Henn, George W. — *G.W. Henn & Company*
Henry, Mary — *Conex Incorporated*
Hergenrather, Richard A. — *Hergenrather & Company*
Herman, Shelli — *Gary Kaplan & Associates*
Hetherman, Margaret F. — *Highland Search Group*
Hewitt, Rives D. — *The Dalley Hewitt Company*
Hewitt, W. Davis — *The Dalley Hewitt Company*
Higgins, Donna — *Howard Fischer Associates, Inc.*
Higgins, William — *William Guy & Associates*
Hochberg, Brian — *M.A. Churchill & Associates, Inc.*
Hochberg, Steven P. — *Caliber Associates*
Hockett, William — *Hockett Associates, Inc.*
Holland, John A. — *Holland, McFadzean & Associates, Inc.*
Holmes, Lawrence J. — *Columbia Consulting Group*
Holt, Carol — *Bartholdi & Company, Inc.*
Hoover, Catherine — *J.L. Mark Associates, Inc.*
Hopkins, Chester A. — *Handy HRM Corp.*
Hopper, John W. — *William Guy & Associates*
Houchins, William M. — *Christian & Timbers*
Hudson, Reginald M. — *Search Bureau International*
Irish, Alan — *CPS Inc.*
Jacobs, Martin J. — *The Rubicon Group*
Jacobs, Mike — *Thorne, Brieger Associates Inc.*
James, Richard — *Criterion Executive Search, Inc.*
Jansen, John F. — *Delta Services*
Janssen, Don — *Howard Fischer Associates, Inc.*
Joffe, Barry — *Bason Associates Inc.*
Johnson, John W. — *Webb, Johnson Associates, Inc.*
Johnson, Julie M. — *International Staffing Consultants, Inc.*

Johnson, Valerie — *Coe & Company International Inc.*
Judge, Alfred L. — *The Cambridge Group Ltd*
Judy, Otto — *CPS Inc.*
Juelis, John J. — *Peeney Associates*
Kalinowski, David — *Jacobson Associates*
Kane, Karen — *Howard Fischer Associates, Inc.*
Kaplan, Gary — *Gary Kaplan & Associates*
Karalis, William — *CPS Inc.*
Keating, Pierson — *Nordeman Grimm, Inc.*
Kehoe, Mike — *CPS Inc.*
Kern, Jerry L. — *ADOW's Executeam*
Kilcoyne, Pat — *CPS Inc.*
Kiley, Phyllis — *National Search, Inc.*
King, Margaret — *Christian & Timbers*
Kinser, Richard E. — *Richard Kinser & Associates*
Kishbaugh, Herbert S. — *Kishbaugh Associates International*
Kkorzyniewski, Nicole — *CPS Inc.*
Klages, Constance W. — *International Management Advisors, Inc.*
Knisely, Gary — *Johnson Smith & Knisely Accord*
Koontz, Donald N. — *Koontz, Jeffries & Associates, Inc.*
Kopsick, Joseph M. — *Spencer Stuart*
Kossuth, David — *Kossuth & Associates, Inc.*
Kossuth, Jane — *Kossuth & Associates, Inc.*
Krejci, Stanley L. — *Boyden Washington, D.C.*
Kreutz, Gary L. — *Kreutz Consulting Group, Inc.*
Krieger, Dennis F. — *Seiden Krieger Associates, Inc.*
Krueger, Kurt — *Krueger Associates*
Kuhl, Teresa — *Don Richard Associates of Tampa, Inc.*
Kunzer, William J. — *Kunzer Associates, Ltd.*
Kurrigan, Geoffrey — *ESA Professional Consultants*
Labrecque, Bernard F. — *Laurendeau Labrecque/Ray & Berndtson, Inc.*
Lache, Shawn E. — *The Arcus Group*
Laird, Cheryl — *CPS Inc.*
Lang, Sharon A. — *Ray & Berndtson*
Lardner, Lucy D. — *Tully/Woodmansee International, Inc.*
Lasher, Charles M. — *Lasher Associates*
Leahy, Jan — *CPS Inc.*
Leininger, Dennis — *Key Employment Services*
Levine, Lois — *National Search, Inc.*
Lezama Cohen, Luis — *Ray & Berndtson*
Linton, Leonard M. — *Byron Leonard International, Inc.*
Lofthouse, Cindy — *CPS Inc.*
Long, Helga — *Horton International*
Long, Melanie — *National Search, Inc.*
LoPresto, Robert L. — *Rusher, Loscavio & LoPresto*
Loscavio, J. Michael — *Rusher, Loscavio & LoPresto*
Lotufo, Donald A. — *D.A.L. Associates, Inc.*
Lotz, R. James — *International Management Advisors, Inc.*
Lucarelli, Joan — *The Onstott Group, Inc.*
Lucht, John — *The John Lucht Consultancy Inc.*
Lumsby, George N. — *International Management Advisors, Inc.*
Luntz, Charles E. — *Charles Luntz & Associates. Inc.*
Lyon, Jenny — *Marra Peters & Partners*
Lyons, J. David — *Aubin International Inc.*
Macan, Sandi — *Caliber Associates*
Macdonald, G. William — *The Macdonald Group, Inc.*

Maer, Harry — *Kenzer Corp.*
Maglio, Charles J. — *Maglio and Company, Inc.*
Mallin, Ellen — *Howard Fischer Associates, Inc.*
Manassero, Henri J.P. — *International Management Advisors, Inc.*
Mancino, Gene — *Blau Mancino Schroeder*
Mangum, Maria — *Thomas Mangum Company*
Mangum, William T. — *Thomas Mangum Company*
Mansford, Keith — *Howard Fischer Associates, Inc.*
Mark, John L. — *J.L. Mark Associates, Inc.*
Mark, Lynne — *J.L. Mark Associates, Inc.*
Marks, Ira — *Strategic Alternatives*
Marks, Russell E. — *Webb, Johnson Associates, Inc.*
Marra, John — *Marra Peters & Partners*
Marra, John — *Marra Peters & Partners*
Marumoto, William H. — *Boyden Washington, D.C.*
Massey, R. Bruce — *Horton International*
Mather, David R. — *Christian & Timbers*
Matthews, Corwin — *Woodworth International Group*
Mazor, Elly — *Howard Fischer Associates, Inc.*
McAndrews, Kathy — *CPS Inc.*
McBride, Jonathan E. — *McBride Associates, Inc.*
McCallister, Richard A. — *Boyden*
McCreary, Charles "Chip" — *Austin-McGregor International*
McFadden, Ashton S. — *Johnson Smith & Knisely Accord*
McFadzen,, James A. — *Holland, McFadzean & Associates, Inc.*
McManners, Donald E. — *McManners Associates, Inc.*
McNamara, Catherine — *Ray & Berndtson*
McNamara, Timothy C. — *Columbia Consulting Group*
McNichols, Walter B. — *Gary Kaplan & Associates*
Meyer, Stacey — *Gary Kaplan & Associates*
Michaels, Joseph — *CPS Inc.*
Millonzi, Joel C. — *Johnson Smith & Knisely Accord*
Mogul, Gene — *Mogul Consultants, Inc.*
Mohr, Brian — *CPS Inc.*
Moore, Mark — *Wheeler, Moore & Elam Co.*
Moore, T. Wills — *Ray & Berndtson*
Morgan, Gary — *National Search, Inc.*
Morris, Paul T. — *The Morris Group*
Morton, Robert C. — *Morton, McCorkle & Associates, Inc.*
Muendel, H. Edward — *Stanton Chase International*
Mulligan, Robert P. — *William Willis Worldwide Inc.*
Murphy, Erin — *CPS Inc.*
Mursuli, Meredith — *Lasher Associates*
Mustin, Joyce M. — *J: Blakslee International, Ltd.*
Mydlach, Renee — *CPS Inc.*
Nagler, Leon G. — *Nagler, Robins & Poe, Inc.*
Naidicz, Maria — *Ray & Berndtson*
Nathanson, Barry F. — *Barry Nathanson Associates*
Nees, Eugene C. — *Ray & Berndtson*
Neher, Robert L. — *Intech Summit Group, Inc.*

Nehring, Keith — *Howard Fischer Associates, Inc.*
Neidhart, Craig C. — *TNS Partners, Inc.*
Nephew, Robert — *Christian & Timbers*
Newman, Lynn — *Kishbaugh Associates International*
Newpoff, Brad L. — *Furst Group/MPI*
Nichols, Gary — *Koontz, Jeffries & Associates, Inc.*
Norman, Randy — *Austin-McGregor International*
Norsell, Paul E. — *Paul Norsell & Associates, Inc.*
O'Connell, Mary — *CPS Inc.*
O'Hara, Daniel M. — *Lynch Miller Moore, Inc.*
Ocon, Olga — *Busch International*
Ogdon, Thomas H. — *The Ogdon Partnership*
Ogilvie, Kit — *Howard Fischer Associates, Inc.*
Ottenritter, Chris — *CPS Inc.*
Overlock, Craig — *Ray & Berndtson*
Palmer, Carlton A. — *Beall & Company, Inc.*
Panarese, Pam — *Howard Fischer Associates, Inc.*
Pankratz, Dennis — *Furst Group/MPI*
Papasadero, Kathleen — *Woodworth International Group*
Parry, William H. — *Horton International*
Pedley, Jill — *CPS Inc.*
Peeney, James D. — *Peeney Associates*
Pelisson, Charles — *Marra Peters & Partners*
Peterson, John — *CPS Inc.*
Phillips, Richard K. — *Handy HRM Corp.*
Phipps, Peggy — *Woodworth International Group*
Pickering, Dale — *Agri-Tech Personnel, Inc.*
Pickering, Rita — *Agri-Tech Personnel, Inc.*
Pierotazio, John — *CPS Inc.*
Pigott, Daniel — *ESA Professional Consultants*
Plessner, Rene — *Rene Plessner Associates, Inc.*
Plimpton, Ralph L. — *R L Plimpton Associates*
Poirier, Frank — *Juntunen-Combs-Poirier*
Pomerance, Mark — *CPS Inc.*
Porter, Albert — *The Experts*
Poster, Lawrence D. — *Catalyx Group*
Pratt, Tyler P. — *Furst Group/MPI*
Price, Andrew G. — *The Thomas Tucker Company*
Proct, Nina — *Martin H. Bauman Associates, Inc.*
Puckett, Jennifer — *Rene Plessner Associates, Inc.*
Raines, Bruce R. — *Raines International Inc.*
Ray, Marianne C. — *Callan Associates, Ltd.*
Redler, Rhonda — *National Search, Inc.*
Reiss, Matt — *National Search, Inc.*
Remillard, Brad M. — *CJA - The Adler Group*
Reuter, Tandom — *CPS Inc.*
Riederer, Larry — *CPS Inc.*
Roberts, Kenneth — *The Rubicon Group*
Robinson, Bruce — *Bruce Robinson Associates*
Robles Cuellar, Paulina — *Ray & Berndtson*
Romanello, Daniel P. — *Spencer Stuart*
Romang, Paula — *Agri-Tech Personnel, Inc.*
Rosato, William R. — *W.R. Rosato & Associates, Inc.*
Rose, Robert — *ESA Professional Consultants*
Rosenthal, Charles — *National Search, Inc.*
Ross, Curt A. — *Ray & Berndtson*
Roth, Robert J. — *Williams, Roth & Krueger Inc.*
Rudolph, Kenneth — *Kossuth & Associates, Inc.*
Russell, Robin E. — *Kenzer Corp.*
Sacerdote, John — *Raymond Karsan Associates*
Saletra, Andrew — *CPS Inc.*
Salvagno, Michael J. — *The Cambridge Group Ltd*

Sanders, Natalie — *CPS Inc.*
Sanders, Spencer H. — *Battalia Winston International*
Sarna, Edmund A. — *Jonas, Walters & Assoc., Inc.*
Scalamera, Tom — *CPS Inc.*
Schlpma, Christine — *Advanced Executive Resources*
Schneiderman, Gerald — *Management Resource Associates, Inc.*
Schroeder, Lee — *Blau Mancino Schroeder*
Schroeder, Steven J. — *Blau Mancino Schroeder*
Schueneman, David — *CPS Inc.*
Schweichler, Lee J. — *Schweichler Associates, Inc.*
Scott, Evan — *Howard Fischer Associates, Inc.*
Scott, Gordon S. — *Search Advisors International Corp.*
Segal, Eric B. — *Kenzer Corp.*
Sennello, Gendra — *National Search, Inc.*
Sevilla, Claudio A. — *Crawford & Crofford*
Shapiro, Elaine — *CPS Inc.*
Shelton, Sandra — *National Search, Inc.*
Sher, Lawrence — *M.A. Churchill & Associates, Inc.*
Shufelt, Doug — *Sink, Walker, Boltrus International*
Sibbald, John R. — *John Sibbald Associates, Inc.*
Siegrist, Jeffrey M. — *D.E. Foster Partners Inc.*
Signer, Julie — *CPS Inc.*
Silcott, Marvin L. — *Marvin L. Silcott & Associates, Inc.*
Sill, Igor M. — *Geneva Group International*
Silver, Lee — *L. A. Silver Associates, Inc.*
Sink, Cliff — *Sink, Walker, Boltrus International*
Sitarski, Stan — *Howard Fischer Associates, Inc.*
Skunda, Donna M. — *Allerton Heneghan & O'Neill*
Slayton, Richard C. — *Slayton International, Inc./I-I-C Partners*
Slosar, John — *Boyden*
Smith, David P. — *HRS, Inc.*
Smith, Matt D. — *Ray & Berndtson*
Smith, Ronald V. — *Coe & Company International Inc.*
Snelgrove, Geiger — *National Search, Inc.*
Snyder, C. Edward — *Horton International*
Snyder, James F. — *Snyder & Company*
Souder, E.G. — *Souder & Associates*
Spicher, John — *M.A. Churchill & Associates, Inc.*
Spiegel, Gayle — *L. A. Silver Associates, Inc.*
Spriggs, Robert D. — *Spriggs & Company, Inc.*
Stark, Jeff — *Thorne, Brieger Associates Inc.*
Steer, Joe — *CPS Inc.*
Stein, Terry W. — *Stewart, Stein and Scott, Ltd.*
Stern, Stephen — *CPS Inc.*
Sterner, Doug — *CPS Inc.*
Stevenson, Jane — *Howard Fischer Associates, Inc.*
Stewart, Jeffrey O. — *Stewart, Stein and Scott, Ltd.*
Stewart, Ross M. — *Human Resources Network Partners Inc.*
Stone, Susan L. — *Stone Enterprises Ltd.*
Stranberg, James R. — *Callan Associates, Ltd.*
Strickland, Katie — *Grantham & Co., Inc.*
Strom, Mark N. — *Search Advisors International Corp.*
Sullivan, Kay — *Rusher, Loscavio & LoPresto*

Sumurdy, Melinda — *Kenzer Corp.*
Swanson, Dick — *Raymond Karsan Associates*
Sweeney, Sean K. — *Bonifield Associates*
Taylor, R.L. (Larry) — *Ray & Berndtson*
Thomas, Cheryl M. — *CPS Inc.*
Thomas, Kim — *CPS Inc.*
Thompson, Kenneth L. — *McCormack & Farrow*
Tipp, George D. — *Intech Summit Group, Inc.*
Todres-Bernstein, Margo — *Kaye-Bassman International Corp.*
Tovrog, Dan — *CPS Inc.*
Tracey, Jack — *Management Assistance Group, Inc.*
Trott, Kathryn — *Allard Associates*
Truemper, Dean — *CPS Inc.*
Tucker, Thomas A. — *The Thomas Tucker Company*
Tullberg, Tina — *CPS Inc.*
Tweed, Janet — *Gilbert Tweed/INESA*
Tyson, Richard L. — *Bonifield Associates*
Vairo, Leonard A. — *Christian & Timbers*
Van Biesen, Jacques A.H. — *Search Group Inc.*
Velten, Mark T. — *Boyden*
Vergara, Gail H. — *Spencer Stuart*
Vernon, Peter C. — *Horton International*
Visnich, L. Christine — *Bason Associates Inc.*
Vourakis, Zan — *ZanExec LLC*
Wakefield, Scott — *National Search, Inc.*
Waldoch, D. Mark — *Barnes Development Group, LLC*
Walker, Douglas G. — *Sink, Walker, Boltrus International*
Walters, William F. — *Jonas, Walters & Assoc., Inc.*
Watkinson, Jim W. — *The Badger Group*
Wayne, Cary S. — *ProSearch Inc.*
Webb, George H. — *Webb, Johnson Associates, Inc.*
Wein, Michael S. — *Media Management Resources, Inc.*
Wein, William — *Media Management Resources, Inc.*
Weisler, Nancy — *National Search, Inc.*
Weissman-Rosenthal, Abbe — *ALW Research International*
Welch, Robert — *Ray & Berndtson*
White, William C. — *Venture Resources Inc.*
Whiting, Anthony — *Johnson Smith & Knisely Accord*
Whitney, William A — *Larsen, Whitney, Blecksmith & Zilliacus*
Wilburn, Dan — *Kaye-Bassman International Corp.*
Wilkinson, Barbara — *Beall & Company, Inc.*
Williams, Gary L. — *Barnes Development Group, LLC*
Williams, Harry D. — *Jacobson Associates*
Willis, William H. — *William Willis Worldwide Inc.*
Winitz, Joel — *GSW Consulting Group, Inc.*
Winitz, Marla — *GSW Consulting Group, Inc.*
Winograd, Glenn — *Criterion Executive Search, Inc.*
Winston, Dale — *Battalia Winston International*
Wold, Ted W. — *Hyde Danforth Wold & Co.*
Wolf, Stephen M. — *Byron Leonard International, Inc.*

Woodworth, Gail — *Woodworth International Group*

Wooldridge, Jeff — *Ray & Berndtson*

Wylie, Pamela — *M.A. Churchill & Associates, Inc.*

Yen, Maggie Yeh Ching — *Ray & Berndtson*

Zadfar, Maryanne — *The Thomas Tucker Company*

Zamborsky, George — *Boyden*

Zivic, Janis M. — *Spencer Stuart*

Zona, Henry F. — *Zona & Associates, Inc.*

9. Sales

Abell, Vincent W. — *MSI International*

Abert, Janice — *Ledbetter/Davidson International, Inc.*

Adler, Louis S. — *CJA - The Adler Group*

Akin, J.R. "Jack" — *J.R. Akin & Company Inc.*

Alexander, John T. — *Telford, Adams & Alexander*

Allard, Susan — *Allard Associates*

Allen, Wade H. — *Cendea Connection International*

Allen, William L. — *The Hindman Company*

Allgire, Mary L. — *Kenzer Corp.*

Allred, J. Michael — *Spencer Stuart*

Amato, Joseph — *Amato & Associates, Inc.*

Ambler, Peter W. — *Peter W. Ambler Company*

Amilowski, Maria — *Highland Search Group*

Anderson, Richard — *Grant Cooper and Associates*

Anderson, Steve — *CPS Inc.*

Anwar, Tarin — *Jay Gaines & Company, Inc.*

Aronin, Michael — *Fisher-Todd Associates*

Aronow, Lawrence E. — *Aronow Associates, Inc.*

Ashton, Edward J. — *E.J. Ashton & Associates, Ltd.*

Aston, Kathy — *Marra Peters & Partners*

Attell, Harold — *A.E. Feldman Associates*

Austin Lockton, Kathy — *Juntunen-Combs-Poirier*

Aydelotte, G. Thomas — *Ingram & Aydelotte Inc./I-I-C Partners*

Badger, Fred H. — *The Badger Group*

Baeder, Jeremy — *Executive Manning Corporation*

Bailey, Vanessa — *Highland Search Group*

Baje, Sarah — *Innovative Search Group, LLC*

Baker, Bill — *Kaye-Bassman International Corp.*

Baker, Gary M. — *Cochran, Cochran & Yale, Inc.*

Baker, Mark A. — *Kaye-Bassman International Corp.*

Balbone, Rich — *Executive Manning Corporation*

Balch, Randy — *CPS Inc.*

Baltaglia, Michael — *Cochran, Cochran & Yale, Inc.*

Barbour, Mary Beth — *Tully/Woodmansee International, Inc.*

Barch, Sherrie — *Furst Group/MPI*

Barlow, Ken H. — *The Cherbonnier Group, Inc.*

Barnes, Richard E. — *Barnes Development Group, LLC*

Barnes, Roanne L. — *Barnes Development Group, LLC*

Bartholdi, Ted — *Bartholdi & Company, Inc.*

Bartholdi, Theodore G. — *Bartholdi & Company, Inc.*

Barton, Gary R. — *Barton Associates, Inc.*

Bason, Maurice L. — *Bason Associates Inc.*

Bass, M. Lynn — *Ray & Berndtson*

Bass, Nate — *Jacobson Associates*

Bauman, Martin H. — *Martin H. Bauman Associates, Inc.*

Bearman, Linda — *Grant Cooper and Associates*

Beaudin, Elizabeth C. — *Callan Associates, Ltd.*

Beaver, Bentley H. — *The Onstott Group, Inc.*

Becker, Elizabeth M. — *Caliber Associates*

Belin, Jean — *Boyden*

Bellano, Robert W. — *Stanton Chase International*

Bender, Alan — *Bender Executive Search*

Bennett, Jo — *Battalia Winston International*

Benson, Kate — *Rene Plessner Associates, Inc.*

Berne, Marlene — *The Whitney Group*

Berry, Harold B. — *The Hindman Company*

Billington, William H. — *Spriggs & Company, Inc.*

Birkhead, Linda — *Zwell International*

Bliley, Jerry — *Spencer Stuart*

Blim, Barbara — *JDG Associates, Ltd.*

Bloomer, James E. — *L.W. Foote Company*

Boel, Werner — *The Dalley Hewitt Company*

Bogansky, Amy — *Conex Incorporated*

Bohn, Steve J. — *MSI International*

Boltrus, Dick — *Sink, Walker, Boltrus International*

Bonifield, Len — *Bonifield Associates*

Bonnell, William R. — *Bonnell Associates Ltd.*

Borden, Stuart — *M.A. Churchill & Associates, Inc.*

Borland, James — *Goodrich & Sherwood Associates, Inc.*

Bormann, Cindy Ann — *MSI International*

Bovich, Maryann C. — *Higdon Prince Inc.*

Brackman, Janet — *Dahl-Morrow International*

Bradley, Dalena — *Woodworth International Group*

Brady, Coloin — *Johnson Smith & Knisely Accord*

Brady, Robert — *CPS Inc.*

Brandeis, Richard — *CPS Inc.*

Bratches, Howard — *Thorndike Deland Associates*

Brieger, Steve — *Thorne, Brieger Associates Inc.*

Brinson, Robert — *MSI International*

Brother, Joy — *Charles Luntz & Associates. Inc.*

Brown, Gina — *Strategic Alliance Network, Ltd.*

Brown, Larry C. — *Horton International*

Brown, Lawrence Anthony — *MSI International*

Brown, Steffan — *Woodworth International Group*

Brudno, Robert J. — *Savoy Partners, Ltd.*

Bruno, Deborah F. — *The Hindman Company*

Bryant, Richard D. — *Bryant Associates, Inc.*

Bryant, Shari G. — *Bryant Associates, Inc.*

Brzezinski, Ronald T. — *Callan Associates, Ltd.*

Buchalter, Allyson — *The Whitney Group*

Buckles, Donna — *Cochran, Cochran & Yale, Inc.*

Buggy, Linda — *Bonnell Associates Ltd.*

Burden, Gene — *The Cherbonnier Group, Inc.*

Burfield, Elaine — *Skott/Edwards Consultants, Inc.*

Burke, John — *The Experts*

Burke, Karen A. — *Mazza & Riley, Inc. (a Korn/Ferry International affiliate)*

Burkhill, John — *The Talley Group*

Burns, Alan — *The Enns Partners Inc.*

Burns, Terence N. — *D.E. Foster Partners Inc.*

Busch, Jack — *Busch International*

Butler, Kirby B. — *The Butlers Company Insurance Recruiters*

Byrnes, Thomas A. — *The Search Alliance, Inc.*

Caldwell, William R. — *Pearson, Caldwell & Farnsworth, Inc.*

Call, David — *Cochran, Cochran & Yale, Inc.*
Callan, Robert M. — *Callan Associates, Ltd.*
Cameron, James W. — *Cameron Consulting*
Campbell, Patricia A. — *The Onstott Group, Inc.*
Campbell, Robert Scott — *Wellington Management Group*
Campbell, Robert Scott — *Wellington Management Group*
Cannavino, Matthew J. — *Financial Resource Associates, Inc.*
Cannavo, Louise — *The Whitney Group*
Capizzi, Karen — *Cochran, Cochran & Yale, Inc.*
Carideo, Joseph — *Thorndike Deland Associates*
Cary, Con — *Cary & Associates*
Casal, Daniel G. — *Bonifield Associates*
Castine, Michael P. — *Highland Search Group*
Celenza, Catherine — *CPS Inc.*
Chamberlin, Joan — *William Guy & Associates*
Chappell, Peter — *The Bankers Group*
Chatterjie, Alok — *MSI International*
Cherbonnier, L. Michael — *TCG International, Inc.*
Cherbonnier, L. Michael — *The Cherbonnier Group, Inc.*
Chndler, Brad J. — *Furst Group/MPI*
Christenson, H. Alan — *Christenson & Hutchison*
Christian, Jeffrey E. — *Christian & Timbers*
Christian, Philip — *Ray & Berndtson*
Christiansen, Amy — *CPS Inc.*
Christiansen, Doug — *CPS Inc.*
Citarella, Richard A. — *A.T. Kearney, Inc.*
Citrin, Lea — *K.L. Whitney Company*
Cizek, John T. — *Cizek Associates, Inc.*
Cizek, Marti J. — *Cizek Associates, Inc.*
Clake, Bob — *Furst Group/MPI*
Clark, Evan — *The Whitney Group*
Clark, James — *CPS Inc.*
Clark, Steven — *D.A. Kreuter Associates, Inc.*
Clarke Smith, Jamie — *Kaye-Bassman International Corp.*
Clauhsen, Elizabeth A. — *Savoy Partners, Ltd.*
Cloutier, Gisella — *Dinte Resources, Inc.*
Cochran, Scott P. — *The Badger Group*
Coe, Karen J. — *Coe & Company International Inc.*
Coffman, Brian — *Kossuth & Associates, Inc.*
Cohen, Robert C. — *Intech Summit Group, Inc.*
Colasanto, Frank M. — *W.R. Rosato & Associates, Inc.*
Collard, Joseph A. — *Spencer Stuart*
Combs, Stephen L. — *Juntunen-Combs-Poirier*
Comstock, Rodger — *Johnson Smith & Knisely Accord*
Conway, Maureen — *Conway & Associates*
Cooke, Katherine H. — *Horton International*
Cortina Del Valle, Pedro — *Ray & Berndtson*
Costello, Lynda — *Coe & Company International Inc.*
Coulman, Karen — *CPS Inc.*
Cox, William — *E.J. Ashton & Associates, Ltd.*
Cragg, Barbara R. — *Southwestern Professional Services*
Crane, Howard C. — *Chartwell Partners International, Inc.*
Crath, Paul F. — *Price Waterhouse*
Crecos, Gregory P. — *Gregory Michaels and Associates, Inc.*

Critchley, Walter — *Cochran, Cochran & Yale, Inc.*
Cronin, Dolores — *Corporate Careers, Inc.*
Cruse, O.D. — *Spencer Stuart*
Crystal, Jonathan A. — *Spencer Stuart*
Cuddihy, Paul — *Dahl-Morrow International*
Cunningham, Lawrence — *Howard Fischer Associates, Inc.*
Cunningham, Robert Y. — *Goodrich & Sherwood Associates, Inc.*
Curtis, Ellissa — *Cochran, Cochran & Yale, Inc.*
Czepiel, Susan — *CPS Inc.*
Danforth, W. Michael — *Hyde Danforth Wold & Co.*
Daniels, Alfred — *Alfred Daniels & Associates*
Davis, G. Gordon — *Davis & Company*
de Bardin, Francesca — *F.L. Taylor & Company, Inc.*
De Brun, Thomas P. — *Ray & Berndtson*
de Cholnoky, Andrea — *Spencer Stuart*
de Palacios, Jeannette C. — *J. Palacios & Associates, Inc.*
de Tuede, Catherine — *The Search Alliance, Inc.*
Deaver, Henry C. — *Ray & Berndtson*
DeCorrevont, James — *DeCorrevont & Associates*
DeCorrevont, James — *DeCorrevont & Associates*
Del Pino, William — *National Search, Inc.*
Delaney, Patrick J. — *Sensible Solutions, Inc.*
Demchak, James P. — *Sandhurst Associates*
Desai, Sushila — *Sink, Walker, Boltrus International*
Desgrosellier, Gary P. — *Personnel Unlimited/Executive Search*
Desmond, Dennis — *Beall & Company, Inc.*
Dezember, Steve — *Ray & Berndtson*
DiCioccio, Carmen — *Cochran, Cochran & Yale, Inc.*
Dickson, Duke — *A.D. & Associates Executive Search, Inc.*
Dietz, David S. — *MSI International*
DiMarchi, Paul — *DiMarchi Partners, Inc.*
DiMarchi, Paul — *DiMarchi Partners, Inc.*
Dingeldey, Peter E. — *Search Advisors International Corp.*
Dingman, Bruce — *Robert W. Dingman Company, Inc.*
DiSalvo, Fred — *The Cambridge Group Ltd*
Divine, Robert S. — *O'Shea, Divine & Company, Inc.*
Dixon, Aris — *CPS Inc.*
Doele, Donald C. — *Goodrich & Sherwood Associates, Inc.*
Donath, Linda — *Dahl-Morrow International*
Dotson, M. Ileen — *Dotson & Associates*
Dowell, Mary K. — *Professional Search Associates*
Dromeshauser, Peter — *Dromeshauser Associates*
Drury, James J. — *Spencer Stuart*
Dubbs, William — *Williams Executive Search, Inc.*
Duckworth, Donald R. — *Johnson Smith & Knisely Accord*
Duggan, James P. — *Slayton International, Inc./ I-I-C Partners*
Dunman, Betsy L. — *Crawford & Crofford*
Dwyer, Julie — *CPS Inc.*
Eason, Jan C. — *Summit Group International*
Ebeling, John A. — *Gilbert Tweed/INESA*

Eddy, Terry — *William Guy & Associates*
Edwards, Dorothy — *MSI International*
Edwards, Verba L. — *Wing Tips & Pumps, Inc.*
Eldridge, Charles B. — *Ray & Berndtson*
Ellis, Ted K. — *The Hindman Company*
Ellis, William — *Interspace Interactive Inc.*
Engelbert, Kimberly S. — *Watson International, Inc.*
England, Mark — *Austin-McGregor International*
Enns, George — *The Enns Partners Inc.*
Erickson, Elaine — *Kenzer Corp.*
Ervin, Darlene — *CPS Inc.*
Esposito, Mark — *Christian & Timbers*
Eustis, Lucy R. — *MSI International*
Evans, David — *Executive Manning Corporation*
Fancher, Robert L. — *Bason Associates Inc.*
Farley, Leon A. — *Leon A. Farley Associates*
Farnsworth, John A. — *Pearson, Caldwell & Farnsworth, Inc.*
Federman, Jack R. — *W.R. Rosato & Associates, Inc.*
Feldman, Abe — *A.E. Feldman Associates*
Ferneborg, Jay W. — *Ferneborg & Associates, Inc.*
Ferneborg, John R. — *Ferneborg & Associates, Inc.*
Ferrari, S. Jay — *Ferrari Search Group*
Fischer, Adam — *Howard Fischer Associates, Inc.*
Fischer, Howard M. — *Howard Fischer Associates, Inc.*
Fischer, Janet L. — *Boyden*
Fischer, John C. — *Horton International*
Fisher, Neal — *Fisher Personnel Management Services*
Fitzgerald, Diane — *Fitzgerald Associates*
Fitzgerald, Geoffrey — *Fitzgerald Associates*
Flanagan, Robert M. — *Robert M. Flanagan & Associates, Ltd.*
Fleming, Marco — *MSI International*
Flood, Michael — *Norman Broadbent International, Inc.*
Flora, Dodi — *Crawford & Crofford*
Fogarty, Michael — *CPS Inc.*
Foote, Leland W. — *L.W. Foote Company*
Foreman, David C. — *Koontz, Jeffries & Associates, Inc.*
Fowler, Edward D.C. — *Higdon Prince Inc.*
Fowler, Thomas A. — *The Hindman Company*
Frazier, John — *Cochran, Cochran & Yale, Inc.*
Fulton, Christine N. — *Highland Search Group*
Furlong, James W. — *Furlong Search, Inc.*
Furlong, James W. — *Furlong Search, Inc.*
Furlong, James W. — *Furlong Search, Inc.*
Fust, Sheely F. — *Ray & Berndtson*
Gabel, Gregory N. — *Canny, Bowen Inc.*
Gaines, Jay — *Jay Gaines & Company, Inc.*
Galante, Suzanne M. — *Vlcek & Company, Inc.*
Galinski, Paul — *E.J. Ashton & Associates, Ltd.*
Gallagher, Terence M. — *Battalia Winston International*
Gantar, Donna — *Howard Fischer Associates, Inc.*
Garfinkle, Steven M. — *Battalia Winston International*
Garland, Dick — *Dick Garland Consultants*
Garzone, Dolores — *M.A. Churchill & Associates, Inc.*
Gauthier, Robert C. — *Columbia Consulting Group*
George, Brenda — *Don Richard Associates of Charlotte*

George, Delores F. — *Delores F. George Human Resource Management & Consulting Industry*
Germain, Valerie — *Jay Gaines & Company, Inc.*
Gestwick, Daniel — *Cochran, Cochran & Yale, Inc.*
Gibbons, Ronald L. — *Flynn, Hannock, Incorporated*
Gibbs, John S. — *Spencer Stuart*
Gilbert, Jerry — *Gilbert & Van Campen International*
Gill, Patricia — *Columbia Consulting Group*
Gillespie, Thomas — *Professional Search Consultants*
Giries, Juliet D. — *Barton Associates, Inc.*
Goar, Duane R. — *Sandhurst Associates*
Goedtke, Steven — *Southwestern Professional Services*
Golde, Lisa — *Tully/Woodmansee International, Inc.*
Goldenberg, Susan — *Grant Cooper and Associates*
Goldsmith, Joseph B. — *Higdon Prince Inc.*
Goldstein, Gary — *The Whitney Group*
Goodman, Dawn M. — *Bason Associates Inc.*
Gordon, Gerald L. — *E.G. Jones Associates, Ltd.*
Gotlys, Jordan — *Stone Murphy & Olson*
Gow, Roderick C. — *Lamalie Amrop International*
Graham, Dale — *CPS Inc.*
Grant, Michael — *Zwell International*
Grantham, John — *Grantham & Co., Inc.*
Grantham, Philip H. — *Columbia Consulting Group*
Grasch, Jerry E. — *The Hindman Company*
Gray, Mark — *Executive Referral Services, Inc.*
Grebenstein, Charles R. — *Skott/Edwards Consultants, Inc.*
Grotenhuis, Dirkten — *Chrisman & Company, Incorporated*
Grotte, Lawrence C. — *Lautz Grotte Engler*
Grzybowski, Jill — *CPS Inc.*
Gulian, Randolph — *Strategic Executives, Inc.*
Haas, Margaret P. — *The Haas Associates, Inc.*
Hailey, H.M. — *Damon & Associates, Inc.*
Hall, Peter V. — *Chartwell Partners International, Inc.*
Hallock, Peter B. — *Goodrich & Sherwood Associates, Inc.*
Hallstrom, Victoria — *The Whitney Group*
Hamilton, John R. — *Ray & Berndtson*
Hammond, Karla — *People Management Northeast Incorporated*
Hanes, Leah — *Ray & Berndtson*
Hanley, Alan P. — *Williams, Roth & Krueger Inc.*
Hanley, Maureen E. — *Gilbert Tweed/INESA*
Hannock, Elwin W. — *Flynn, Hannock, Incorporated*
Hanson, Grant M. — *Goodrich & Sherwood Associates, Inc.*
Harris, Joe W. — *Cendea Connection International*
Harris, Julia — *The Whitney Group*
Harris, Seth O. — *Christian & Timbers*
Harrison, Joel — *D.A. Kreuter Associates, Inc.*
Hart, Robert T. — *D.E. Foster Partners Inc.*
Hartle, Larry — *CPS Inc.*
Harvey, Mike — *Advanced Executive Resources*
Haughton, Michael — *DeFrain, Mayer LLC*

Hauser, Martha — *Spencer Stuart*
Hawksworth, A. Dwight — *A.D. & Associates Executive Search, Inc.*
Haystead, Steve — *Advanced Executive Resources*
Hazerjian, Cynthia — *CPS Inc.*
Heafey, Bill — *CPS Inc.*
Healey, Joseph T. — *Highland Search Group*
Hebel, Robert W. — *R.W. Hebel Associates*
Heiken, Barbara E. — *Randell-Heiken, Inc.*
Heinze, David — *Heinze & Associates, Inc.*
Hellinger, Audrey W. — *Martin H. Bauman Associates, Inc.*
Helminiak, Audrey — *Gaffney Management Consultants*
Hendrickson, Jill E. — *Gregory Michaels and Associates, Inc.*
Hennig, Sandra M. — *MSI International*
Henry, Mary — *Conex Incorporated*
Hergenrather, Richard A. — *Hergenrather & Company*
Hetherman, Margaret F. — *Highland Search Group*
Hewitt, Rives D. — *The Dalley Hewitt Company*
Hewitt, W. Davis — *The Dalley Hewitt Company*
Higbee, Joan — *Thorndike Deland Associates*
Higdon, Henry G. — *Higdon Prince Inc.*
Higgins, Donna — *Howard Fischer Associates, Inc.*
Higgins, William — *William Guy & Associates*
Hill, Emery — *MSI International*
Hillen, Skip — *The McCormick Group, Inc.*
Himlin, Amy — *Cochran, Cochran & Yale, Inc.*
Hindman, Neil C. — *The Hindman Company*
Hochberg, Brian — *M.A. Churchill & Associates, Inc.*
Hochberg, Steven P. — *Caliber Associates*
Hockett, William — *Hockett Associates, Inc.*
Hoevel, Michael J. — *Poirier, Hoevel & Co.*
Holland, John A. — *Holland, McFadzean & Associates, Inc.*
Holland, Rose Mary — *Price Waterhouse*
Holmes, Lawrence J. — *Columbia Consulting Group*
Holt, Carol — *Bartholdi & Company, Inc.*
Holzberger, Georges L. — *Highland Search Group*
Hoover, Catherine — *J.L. Mark Associates, Inc.*
Hopkins, Chester A. — *Handy HRM Corp.*
Hopp, Lorrie A. — *Gregory Michaels and Associates, Inc.*
Hopper, John W. — *William Guy & Associates*
Houchins, William M. — *Christian & Timbers*
Hoyda, Louis A. — *Thorndike Deland Associates*
Hucko, Donald S. — *Jonas, Walters & Assoc., Inc.*
Hudson, Reginald M. — *Search Bureau International*
Hughes, Cathy N. — *The Ogdon Partnership*
Hughes, David — *Southwestern Professional Services*
Hughes, R. Kevin — *Handy HRM Corp.*
Hutchison, William K. — *Christenson & Hutchison*
Imely, Larry S. — *Stratford Group*
Ingram, D. John — *Ingram & Aydelotte Inc./I-I-C Partners*
Inguagiato, Gregory — *MSI International*
Irish, Alan — *CPS Inc.*
Issacs, Judith A. — *Grant Cooper and Associates*

Jablo, Steven A. — *Dieckmann & Associates, Ltd.*
Jacobs, Mike — *Thorne, Brieger Associates Inc.*
Jacobson, Rick — *The Windham Group*
Janis, Laurence — *Integrated Search Solutions Group, LLC*
Jansen, John F. — *Delta Services*
Janssen, Don — *Howard Fischer Associates, Inc.*
Januale, Lois — *Cochran, Cochran & Yale, Inc.*
Jazylo, John V. — *Handy HRM Corp.*
Jeffers, Richard B. — *Dieckmann & Associates, Ltd.*
Jernigan, Susan N. — *Sockwell & Associates*
Joffe, Barry — *Bason Associates Inc.*
Johnson, John W. — *Webb, Johnson Associates, Inc.*
Johnson, Julie M. — *International Staffing Consultants, Inc.*
Johnson, Kathleen A. — *Barton Associates, Inc.*
Johnson, Priscilla — *The Johnson Group, Inc.*
Johnson, Stanley C. — *Johnson & Company*
Johnson, Valerie — *Coe & Company International Inc.*
Jones, Jonathan C. — *Canny, Bowen Inc.*
Jordan, Jon — *Cochran, Cochran & Yale, Inc.*
Judge, Alfred L. — *The Cambridge Group Ltd*
Judy, Otto — *CPS Inc.*
Juelis, John J. — *Peeney Associates*
Kader, Richard — *Richard Kader & Associates*
Kaiser, Donald J. — *Dunhill International Search of New Haven*
Kaiser, Elaine M. — *Dunhill International Search of New Haven*
Kalinowski, David — *Jacobson Associates*
Kane, Karen — *Howard Fischer Associates, Inc.*
Kanovsky, Gerald — *Career Consulting Group, Inc.*
Kanovsky, Marlene — *Career Consulting Group, Inc.*
Kaplan, Gary — *Gary Kaplan & Associates*
Karalis, William — *CPS Inc.*
Kassouf, Constance — *The Whitney Group*
Keating, Pierson — *Nordeman Grimm, Inc.*
Keck, Jason B. — *Kaye-Bassman International Corp.*
Kehoe, Mike — *CPS Inc.*
Keller, Barbara E. — *Barton Associates, Inc.*
Kelly, Elizabeth Ann — *Wellington Management Group*
Kelso, Patricia C. — *Barton Associates, Inc.*
Kennedy, Michael — *The Danbrook Group, Inc.*
Kershaw, Lisa — *Tanton Mitchell/Paul Ray Berndtson*
Kettwig, David A. — *A.T. Kearney, Inc.*
Kilcoyne, Pat — *CPS Inc.*
Kilcullen, Brian A. — *D.A. Kreuter Associates, Inc.*
Kiley, Phyllis — *National Search, Inc.*
King, Bill — *The McCormick Group, Inc.*
King, Margaret — *Christian & Timbers*
Kip, Luanne S. — *Kip Williams, Inc.*
Kishbaugh, Herbert S. — *Kishbaugh Associates International*
Kkorzyniewski, Nicole — *CPS Inc.*
Klein, Lynn M. — *Riotto-Jones Associates*
Klein, Mary Jo — *Cochran, Cochran & Yale, Inc.*
Klein, Mel — *Stewart/Laurence Associates*
Knisely, Gary — *Johnson Smith & Knisely Accord*
Kohn, Adam P. — *Christian & Timbers*

Koontz, Donald N. — *Koontz, Jeffries & Associates, Inc.*
Kopsick, Joseph M. — *Spencer Stuart*
Kossuth, David — *Kossuth & Associates, Inc.*
Kossuth, Jane — *Kossuth & Associates, Inc.*
Kotick, Maddy — *The Stevenson Group of New Jersey*
Krejci, Stanley L. — *Boyden Washington, D.C.*
Kreuch, Paul C. — *Skott/Edwards Consultants, Inc.*
Kreuter, Daniel A. — *D.A. Kreuter Associates, Inc.*
Krieger, Dennis F. — *Seiden Krieger Associates, Inc.*
Kunzer, William J. — *Kunzer Associates, Ltd.*
Kussner, Janice N. — *Herman Smith Executive Initiatives Inc.*
Laba, Marvin — *Marvin Laba & Associates*
Laba, Stuart M. — *Marvin Laba & Associates*
Labrecque, Bernard F. — *Laurendeau Labrecque/Ray & Berndtson, Inc.*
Lache, Shawn E. — *The Arcus Group*
Laird, Cheryl — *CPS Inc.*
Lang, Sharon A. — *Ray & Berndtson*
Lardner, Lucy D. — *Tully/Woodmansee International, Inc.*
Lasher, Charles M. — *Lasher Associates*
Lauderback, David R. — *A.T. Kearney, Inc.*
Lautz, Lindsay A. — *Lautz Grotte Engler*
Lawrance, Susanne — *Sharrow & Associates*
Lazaro, Alicia C. — *The Whitney Group*
Leahy, Jan — *CPS Inc.*
Ledbetter, Steven G. — *Cendea Connection International*
Leetma, Imbi — *Stanton Chase International*
Leighton, Nina — *The Ogdon Partnership*
Leininger, Dennis — *Key Employment Services*
Lence, Julie Anne — *MSI International*
Letcher, Harvey D. — *Sandhurst Associates*
Levine, Alan M. — *MB Inc. Interim Executive Division*
Levine, Lawrence — *Trebor Weldon Lawrence, Inc.*
Levine, Lois — *National Search, Inc.*
Levinson, Lauren — *The Danbrook Group, Inc.*
Lewicki, Christopher — *MSI International*
Lewis, Jon A. — *Sandhurst Associates*
Lewis, Sean — *Southwestern Professional Services*
Lezama Cohen, Luis — *Ray & Berndtson*
Liebowitz, Michael E. — *Highland Search Group*
Lindberg, Eric J. — *MSI International*
Linton, Leonard M. — *Byron Leonard International, Inc.*
Litt, Michele — *The Whitney Group*
Little, Elizabeth A. — *Financial Resource Associates, Inc.*
Loeb, Stephen H. — *Grant Cooper and Associates*
Lofthouse, Cindy — *CPS Inc.*
Lokken, Karen — *A.E. Feldman Associates*
Long, Helga — *Horton International*
Long, Melanie — *National Search, Inc.*
Long, William G. — *McDonald, Long & Associates, Inc.*
Looney, Scott — *A.E. Feldman Associates*
LoPresto, Robert L. — *Rusher, Loscavio & LoPresto*
Lotufo, Donald A. — *D.A.L. Associates, Inc.*
Lovely, Edward — *The Stevenson Group of New Jersey*

Lucarelli, Joan — *The Onstott Group, Inc.*
Lucas, Ronnie L. — *MSI International*
Lucht, John — *The John Lucht Consultancy Inc.*
Ludlow, Paula — *Horton International*
Luntz, Charles E. — *Charles Luntz & Associates. Inc.*
Lupica, Anthony — *Cochran, Cochran & Yale, Inc.*
Lyon, Jenny — *Marra Peters & Partners*
Lyons, J. David — *Aubin International Inc.*
Macan, Sandi — *Caliber Associates*
MacIntyre, Lisa W. — *Highland Search Group*
MacNaughton, Sperry — *McNaughton Associates*
Maer, Harry — *Kenzer Corp.*
Maglio, Charles J. — *Maglio and Company, Inc.*
Mallin, Ellen — *Howard Fischer Associates, Inc.*
Manns, Alex — *Crawford & Crofford*
Mansford, Keith — *Howard Fischer Associates, Inc.*
Maphet, Harriet — *The Stevenson Group of New Jersey*
Marino, Chester — *Cochran, Cochran & Yale, Inc.*
Mark, John L. — *J.L. Mark Associates, Inc.*
Mark, Lynne — *J.L. Mark Associates, Inc.*
Marks, Ira — *Strategic Alternatives*
Marks, Russell E. — *Webb, Johnson Associates, Inc.*
Marra, John — *Marra Peters & Partners*
Marra, John — *Marra Peters & Partners*
Marumoto, William H. — *Boyden Washington, D.C.*
Massey, R. Bruce — *Horton International*
Mather, David R. — *Christian & Timbers*
Mathias, Kathy — *Stone Murphy & Olson*
Mattes, Edward C. — *The Ogdon Partnership*
Matthews, Corwin — *Woodworth International Group*
Mazor, Elly — *Howard Fischer Associates, Inc.*
Mazza, David B. — *Mazza & Riley, Inc. (a Korn/Ferry International affiliate)*
McAndrews, Kathy — *CPS Inc.*
McBride, Jonathan E. — *McBride Associates, Inc.*
McBryde, Marnie — *Spencer Stuart*
McCallister, Richard A. — *Boyden*
McCloskey, Frank D. — *Johnson Smith & Knisely Accord*
McCormick, Brian — *The McCormick Group, Inc.*
McCreary, Charles "Chip" — *Austin-McGregor International*
McDermott, Jeffrey T. — *Vlcek & Company, Inc.*
McDonald, Scott A. — *McDonald Associates International*
McDonald, Stanleigh B. — *McDonald Associates International*
McDowell, Robert N. — *Christenson & Hutchison*
McFadden, Ashton S. — *Johnson Smith & Knisely Accord*
McFadzen,, James A. — *Holland, McFadzean & Associates, Inc.*
McKeown, Patricia A. — *DiMarchi Partners, Inc.*
McKnight, Amy E. — *Chartwell Partners International, Inc.*
McMillin, Bob — *Price Waterhouse*
McNamara, Catherine — *Ray & Berndtson*
McNulty, Kelly L. — *Gregory Michaels and Associates, Inc.*
McSherry, James F. — *Battalia Winston International*

Mead, James D. — *James Mead & Company*
Meagher, Patricia G. — *Spencer Stuart*
Meany, Brian M. — *Herbert Mines Associates, Inc.*
Meier, J. Dale — *Grant Cooper and Associates*
Mercer, Julie — *Columbia Consulting Group*
Merrigan, Eileen M. — *Lamalie Amrop International*
Messett, William J. — *Messett Associates, Inc.*
Mestepey, John — *A.T. Kearney, Inc.*
Michaels, Joseph — *CPS Inc.*
Miller, David — *Cochran, Cochran & Yale, Inc.*
Miller, Kenneth A. — *Computer Network Resources, Inc.*
Miller, Roy — *The Enns Partners Inc.*
Millonzi, Joel C. — *Johnson Smith & Knisely Accord*
Milstein, Bonnie — *Marvin Laba & Associates*
Mingle, Larry D. — *Columbia Consulting Group*
Misiurewicz, Marc — *Cochran, Cochran & Yale, Inc.*
Mogul, Gene — *Mogul Consultants, Inc.*
Mohr, Brian — *CPS Inc.*
Moore, Mark — *Wheeler, Moore & Elam Co.*
Moore, T. Wills — *Ray & Berndtson*
Moore, Vickie J. — *Kirkman & Searing, Inc.*
Morawetz, Justin A. — *Keith Bagg & Associates Inc.*
Morgan, Gary — *National Search, Inc.*
Morris, Paul T. — *The Morris Group*
Mortansen, Patricia — *Norman Broadbent International, Inc.*
Morton, Robert C. — *Morton, McCorkle & Associates, Inc.*
Moseley, Micahel A. — *Kaye-Bassman International Corp.*
Moyse, Richard G. — *Thorndike Deland Associates*
Muendel, H. Edward — *Stanton Chase International*
Murphy, Cornelius J. — *Goodrich & Sherwood Associates, Inc.*
Murphy, Erin — *CPS Inc.*
Murphy, Patrick J. — *P.J. Murphy & Associates, Inc.*
Mursuli, Meredith — *Lasher Associates*
Mydlach, Renee — *CPS Inc.*
Nagler, Leon G. — *Nagler, Robins & Poe, Inc.*
Naidicz, Maria — *Ray & Berndtson*
Nair, Leslie — *Zwell International*
Nathanson, Barry F. — *Barry Nathanson Associates*
Nees, Eugene C. — *Ray & Berndtson*
Neher, Robert L. — *Intech Summit Group, Inc.*
Nehring, Keith — *Howard Fischer Associates, Inc.*
Neidhart, Craig C. — *TNS Partners, Inc.*
Nemec, Phillip — *Dunhill International Search of New Haven*
Nephew, Robert — *Christian & Timbers*
Newman, Lynn — *Kishbaugh Associates International*
Newpoff, Brad L. — *Furst Group/MPI*
Nichols, Gary — *Koontz, Jeffries & Associates, Inc.*
Niejet, Michael C. — *O'Brien & Bell*
Nolte, William D. — *W.D. Nolte & Company*
Norman, Randy — *Austin-McGregor International*
Normann, Amy — *Robert M. Flanagan & Associates, Ltd.*

Norsell, Paul E. — *Paul Norsell & Associates, Inc.*
O'Connell, Mary — *CPS Inc.*
O'Hara, Daniel M. — *Lynch Miller Moore, Inc.*
O'Maley, Kimberlee — *Spencer Stuart*
Ocon, Olga — *Busch International*
Ogdon, Thomas H. — *The Ogdon Partnership*
Ogilvie, Kit — *Howard Fischer Associates, Inc.*
Oldfield, Theresa — *Strategic Alliance Network, Ltd.*
Onstott, Joseph — *The Onstott Group, Inc.*
Onstott, Joseph E. — *The Onstott Group, Inc.*
Ornish, Cindy — *Kaye-Bassman International Corp.*
Ornstein, Robert — *Trebor Weldon Lawrence, Inc.*
Ott, George W. — *Ott & Hansen, Inc.*
Ottenritter, Chris — *CPS Inc.*
Overlock, Craig — *Ray & Berndtson*
Pace, Susan A. — *Horton International*
Pallman-David, Cynthia — *Bonnell Associates Ltd.*
Palma, Frank R. — *Goodrich & Sherwood Associates, Inc.*
Palmer, Carlton A. — *Beall & Company, Inc.*
Palmer, James H. — *The Hindman Company*
Panarese, Pam — *Howard Fischer Associates, Inc.*
Pankratz, Dennis — *Furst Group/MPI*
Papasadero, Kathleen — *Woodworth International Group*
Papoulias, Cathy — *Pendleton James and Associates, Inc.*
Pardo, Maria Elena — *Smith Search, S.C.*
Park, Dabney G. — *Mark Stanley/EMA Partners International*
Parker, Gayle — *Trebor Weldon Lawrence, Inc.*
Parry, William H. — *Horton International*
Patence, David W. — *Handy HRM Corp.*
Pearson, John R. — *Pearson, Caldwell & Farnsworth, Inc.*
Pedley, Jill — *CPS Inc.*
Peeney, James D. — *Peeney Associates*
Pelisson, Charles — *Marra Peters & Partners*
Pernell, Jeanette — *Norman Broadbent International, Inc.*
Peroff, Michael — *Trebor Weldon Lawrence, Inc.*
Perry, James — *Strategic Executives, Inc.*
Peterson, Eric N. — *Stratford Group*
Peterson, John — *CPS Inc.*
Pettibone, Linda G. — *Herbert Mines Associates, Inc.*
Pettway, Samuel H. — *Spencer Stuart*
Petty, J. Scott — *The Arcus Group*
Pfeiffer, Irene — *Price Waterhouse*
Phillips, Donald L. — *O'Shea, Divine & Company, Inc.*
Phillips, James L. — *Highland Search Group*
Phipps, Peggy — *Woodworth International Group*
Pickering, Dale — *Agri-Tech Personnel, Inc.*
Pickering, Rita — *Agri-Tech Personnel, Inc.*
Pickford, Stephen T. — *The Corporate Staff, Inc.*
Pierotazio, John — *CPS Inc.*
Pierson, Edward J. — *Johnson Smith & Knisely Accord*
Plessner, Rene — *Rene Plessner Associates, Inc.*
Poirier, Roland L. — *Poirier, Hoevel & Co.*
Pomerance, Mark — *CPS Inc.*
Poracky, John W. — *M. Wood Company*
Porter, Albert — *The Experts*

Potter, Mark W. — *Highland Search Group*
Potter, Steven B. — *Highland Search Group*
Powers Johnson, Allyson — *Skott/Edwards Consultants, Inc.*
Price, Kenneth M. — *Messett Associates, Inc.*
Prince, Marilyn L. — *Higdon Prince Inc.*
Proct, Nina — *Martin H. Bauman Associates, Inc.*
Provus, Barbara L. — *Shepherd Bueschel & Provus, Inc.*
Pryor, Bill — *Cendea Connection International*
Puckett, Jennifer — *Rene Plessner Associates, Inc.*
Raines, Bruce R. — *Raines International Inc.*
Ramler, Carolyn S. — *The Corporate Connection, Ltd.*
Ramsey, John H. — *Mark Stanley/EMA Partners International*
Randell, James E. — *Randell-Heiken, Inc.*
Ray, Marianne C. — *Callan Associates, Ltd.*
Reddick, David C. — *Horton International*
Redler, Rhonda — *National Search, Inc.*
Reiser, Ellen — *Thorndike Deland Associates*
Reiss, Matt — *National Search, Inc.*
Remillard, Brad M. — *CJA - The Adler Group*
Renick, Cynthia L. — *Morgan Hunter Corp.*
Reticker, Peter — *MSI International*
Reuter, Tandom — *CPS Inc.*
Reyman, Susan — *S. Reyman & Associates Ltd.*
Rice, Marie — *Jay Gaines & Company, Inc.*
Rich, Lyttleton — *Sockwell & Associates*
Ridenour, Suzanne S. — *Ridenour & Associates, Ltd.*
Riederer, Larry — *CPS Inc.*
Rimmel, James E. — *The Hindman Company*
Rimmele, Michael — *The Bankers Group*
Rinker, Jim — *Southwestern Professional Services*
Riotto, Anthony R. — *Riotto-Jones Associates*
Roberts, Carl R. — *Southwestern Professional Services*
Roberts, Mitch — *A.E. Feldman Associates*
Roberts, Scott — *Jonas, Walters & Assoc., Inc.*
Robinson, Bruce — *Bruce Robinson Associates*
Robles Cuellar, Paulina — *Ray & Berndtson*
Rollo, Robert S. — *R. Rollo Associates*
Romanello, Daniel P. — *Spencer Stuart*
Romang, Paula — *Agri-Tech Personnel, Inc.*
Rosato, William R. — *W.R. Rosato & Associates, Inc.*
Rosemarin, Gloria J. — *Barrington Hart, Inc.*
Rosenthal, Charles — *National Search, Inc.*
Ross, Curt A. — *Ray & Berndtson*
Ross, H. Lawrence — *Ross & Company*
Ross, Lawrence — *Ray & Berndtson/Lovas Stanley*
Rotella, Marshall W. — *The Corporate Connection, Ltd.*
Roth, Robert J. — *Williams, Roth & Krueger Inc.*
Rudolph, Kenneth — *Kossuth & Associates, Inc.*
Rush, Michael E. — *D.A.L. Associates, Inc.*
Rusher, William H. — *Rusher, Loscavio & LoPresto*
Russell, Robin E. — *Kenzer Corp.*
Rustin, Beth — *The Whitney Group*
Sabanosh, Whitney — *Highland Search Group*
Sacerdote, John — *Raymond Karsan Associates*
Saletra, Andrew — *CPS Inc.*
Salvagno, Michael J. — *The Cambridge Group Ltd*
Sanders, Natalie — *CPS Inc.*
Sanders, Spencer H. — *Battalia Winston International*

Sandor, Richard J. — *Flynn, Hannock, Incorporated*
Sanow, Robert — *Cochran, Cochran & Yale, Inc.*
Sarna, Edmund A. — *Jonas, Walters & Assoc., Inc.*
Satenstein, Sloan — *Higdon Prince Inc.*
Sathe, Mark A. — *Sathe & Associates, Inc.*
Savage, Edward J. — *Stanton Chase International*
Saxon, Alexa — *Woodworth International Group*
Scalamera, Tom — *CPS Inc.*
Schaefer, Frederic M. — *A.T. Kearney, Inc.*
Schene, Philip — *A.E. Feldman Associates*
Schlesinger, Laurie — *The Whitney Group*
Schlpma, Christine — *Advanced Executive Resources*
Schneiderman, Gerald — *Management Resource Associates, Inc.*
Schroeder, Steven J. — *Blau Mancino Schroeder*
Schueneman, David — *CPS Inc.*
Schwam, Carol — *A.E. Feldman Associates*
Schweichler, Lee J. — *Schweichler Associates, Inc.*
Scodius, Joseph J. — *Gregory Michaels and Associates, Inc.*
Scott, Evan — *Howard Fischer Associates, Inc.*
Scott, Gordon S. — *Search Advisors International Corp.*
Seco, William — *Seco & Zetto Associates, Inc.*
Segal, Eric B. — *Kenzer Corp.*
Seiden, Steven A. — *Seiden Krieger Associates, Inc.*
Semyan, John K. — *TNS Partners, Inc.*
Sennello, Gendra — *National Search, Inc.*
Sevilla, Claudio A. — *Crawford & Crofford*
Shapiro, Elaine — *CPS Inc.*
Shelton, Sandra — *National Search, Inc.*
Shen, Eugene Y. — *The Whitney Group*
Shepard, Michael J. — *MSI International*
Sher, Lawrence — *M.A. Churchill & Associates, Inc.*
Sherwood, Andrew — *Goodrich & Sherwood Associates, Inc.*
Shufelt, Doug — *Sink, Walker, Boltrus International*
Sibbald, John R. — *John Sibbald Associates, Inc.*
Signer, Julie — *CPS Inc.*
Sill, Igor M. — *Geneva Group International*
Silvas, Stephen D. — *Roberson and Company*
Silver, Lee — *L. A. Silver Associates, Inc.*
Silverman, Gary W. — *GWS Partners*
Silverstein, Jackie — *Don Richard Associates of Charlotte*
Simmons, Sandra K. — *MSI International*
Simon, Mary K. — *Gregory Michaels and Associates, Inc.*
Simpson, Scott — *Cendea Connection International*
Sink, Cliff — *Sink, Walker, Boltrus International*
Sitarski, Stan — *Howard Fischer Associates, Inc.*
Skalet, Ira — *A.E. Feldman Associates*
Slocum, Ann Marie — *K.L. Whitney Company*
Slosar, John — *Boyden*
Smead, Michelle M. — *A.T. Kearney, Inc.*
Smith, Ana Luz — *Smith Search, S.C.*
Smith, David P. — *HRS, Inc.*
Smith, Ethan L. — *Highland Search Group*
Smith, Herman M. — *Herman Smith Executive Initiatives Inc.*

Smith, John E. — *Smith Search, S.C.*
Smith, Lydia — *The Corporate Connection, Ltd.*
Smith, Matt D. — *Ray & Berndtson*
Smith, Monica L. — *Analysts Resources, Inc.*
Smith, Ronald V. — *Coe & Company International Inc.*
Snelgrove, Geiger — *National Search, Inc.*
Snyder, C. Edward — *Horton International*
Snyder, James F. — *Snyder & Company*
Sockwell, J. Edgar — *Sockwell & Associates*
Souder, E.G. — *Souder & Associates*
Spann, Richard E. — *Goodrich & Sherwood Associates, Inc.*
Spicehandler, Sheila — *Trebor Weldon Lawrence, Inc.*
Spicher, John — *M.A. Churchill & Associates, Inc.*
Spiegel, Gayle — *L. A. Silver Associates, Inc.*
Sponseller, Vern — *Richard Kader & Associates*
Spriggs, Robert D. — *Spriggs & Company, Inc.*
St. Clair, Alan — *TNS Partners, Inc.*
Stark, Jeff — *Thorne, Brieger Associates Inc.*
Steele, Daniel — *Cochran, Cochran & Yale, Inc.*
Steer, Joe — *CPS Inc.*
Stein, Terry W. — *Stewart, Stein and Scott, Ltd.*
Steinem, Andy — *Dahl-Morrow International*
Steinem, Barbra — *Dahl-Morrow International*
Steinman, Stephen M. — *The Stevenson Group of New Jersey*
Stern, Stephen — *CPS Inc.*
Sterner, Doug — *CPS Inc.*
Stevens, Craig M. — *Kirkman & Searing, Inc.*
Stevenson, Jane — *Howard Fischer Associates, Inc.*
Stewart, Jeffrey O. — *Stewart, Stein and Scott, Ltd.*
Stewart, Ross M. — *Human Resources Network Partners Inc.*
Stone, Susan L. — *Stone Enterprises Ltd.*
Stranberg, James R. — *Callan Associates, Ltd.*
Strickland, Katie — *Grantham & Co., Inc.*
Strobridge, Richard P. — *F.L. Taylor & Company, Inc.*
Strom, Mark N. — *Search Advisors International Corp.*
Sullivan, Kay — *Rusher, Loscavio & LoPresto*
Sumurdy, Melinda — *Kenzer Corp.*
Swanson, Dick — *Raymond Karsan Associates*
Sweeney, Sean K. — *Bonifield Associates*
Taylor, Conrad G. — *MSI International*
Taylor, Ernest A. — *Ward Howell International, Inc.*
Taylor, James M. — *The HRM Group, Inc.*
Taylor, R.L. (Larry) — *Ray & Berndtson*
Telford, John H. — *Telford, Adams & Alexander/Telford & Co., Inc.*
Teter, Sandra — *The Danbrook Group, Inc.*
Teti, Al — *Chrisman & Company, Incorporated*
Theobald, David B. — *Theobald & Associates*
Thomas, Cheryl M. — *CPS Inc.*
Thomas, Jeffrey — *Fairfaxx Corporation*
Thomas, Kim — *CPS Inc.*
Thomas, Kurt J. — *P.J. Murphy & Associates, Inc.*
Thompson, Dave — *Battalia Winston International*
Thompson, John R. — *MSI International*
Tierney, Eileen — *The Whitney Group*
Tincu, John C. — *Ferneborg & Associates, Inc.*
Tipp, George D. — *Intech Summit Group, Inc.*
Tovrog, Dan — *CPS Inc.*

Tracey, Jack — *Management Assistance Group, Inc.*
Trott, Kathryn — *Allard Associates*
Trott, Kathryn — *Allard Associates*
Truemper, Dean — *CPS Inc.*
Truex, John F. — *Morton, McCorkle & Associates, Inc.*
Tucci, Joseph — *Fairfaxx Corporation*
Tullberg, Tina — *CPS Inc.*
Tully, Margo L. — *Tully/Woodmansee International, Inc.*
Tunney, William — *Grant Cooper and Associates*
Tursi, Deborah J. — *The Corporate Connection, Ltd.*
Tweed, Janet — *Gilbert Tweed/INESA*
Tyson, Richard L. — *Bonifield Associates*
Ulrich, Mary Ann — *D.S. Allen Associates, Inc.*
Vairo, Leonard A. — *Christian & Timbers*
Van Alstine, Catherine — *Tanton Mitchell/Paul Ray Berndtson*
Van Campen, Jerry — *Gilbert & Van Campen International*
Velten, Mark T. — *Boyden*
Venable, William W. — *Thorndike Deland Associates*
Vernon, Peter C. — *Horton International*
Visnich, L. Christine — *Bason Associates Inc.*
Vitale, Amy — *Highland Search Group*
Vlcek, Thomas J. — *Vlcek & Company, Inc.*
Volkman, Arthur — *Cochran, Cochran & Yale, Inc.*
Vourakis, Zan — *ZanExec LLC*
Waanders, William L. — *ExecuQuest*
Wakefield, Scott — *National Search, Inc.*
Waldman, Noah H. — *Lamalie Amrop International*
Waldoch, D. Mark — *Barnes Development Group, LLC*
Waldrop, Gary R. — *MSI International*
Walker, Douglas G. — *Sink, Walker, Boltrus International*
Walters, William F. — *Jonas, Walters & Assoc., Inc.*
Ward, Madeleine — *LTM Associates*
Watkinson, Jim W. — *The Badger Group*
Watson, Hanan S. — *Watson International, Inc.*
Watson, James — *MSI International*
Wayne, Cary S. — *ProSearch Inc.*
Webb, George H. — *Webb, Johnson Associates, Inc.*
Wein, Michael S. — *Media Management Resources, Inc.*
Wein, William — *Media Management Resources, Inc.*
Weisler, Nancy — *National Search, Inc.*
Weissman-Rosenthal, Abbe — *ALW Research International*
Welch, Robert — *Ray & Berndtson*
Weller, Paul S. — *Mark Stanley/EMA Partners International*
Wendler, Kambrea R. — *Gregory Michaels and Associates, Inc.*
Westfall, Ed — *Zwell International*
Weston, Corinne F. — *D.A. Kreuter Associates, Inc.*
White, Richard B. — *Spencer Stuart*
White, William C. — *Venture Resources Inc.*

Whiting, Anthony — *Johnson Smith & Knisely Accord*
Whitley, Sue Ann — *Roberts Ryan and Bentley*
Whitney, Kenneth L. — *K.L. Whitney Company*
Whitney, William A — *Larsen, Whitney, Blecksmith & Zilliacus*
Whitton, Paula L. — *Pearson, Caldwell & Farnsworth, Inc.*
Wilburn, Dan — *Kaye-Bassman International Corp.*
Wilder, Richard B. — *Columbia Consulting Group*
Wilkinson, Barbara — *Beall & Company, Inc.*
Wilkinson, Jr. SPHR
Wilkinson, Charles E. — *The HRM Group, Inc.*
Williams, Gary L. — *Barnes Development Group, LLC*
Williams, Harry D. — *Jacobson Associates*
Williams, Roger K. — *Williams, Roth & Krueger Inc.*
Williams, Stephen E. — *Barton Associates, Inc.*
Wilson, Patricia L. — *Leon A. Farley Associates*
Winitz, Joel — *GSW Consulting Group, Inc.*
Winitz, Marla — *GSW Consulting Group, Inc.*
Winston, Dale — *Battalia Winston International*
Wisch, Steven C. — *MB Inc. Interim Executive Division*
Wise, J. Herbert — *Sandhurst Associates*
Wolf, Stephen M. — *Byron Leonard International, Inc.*
Womack, Joseph — *The Bankers Group*
Wood, Elizabeth — *Highland Search Group*
Wood, Milton M. — *M. Wood Company*
Wood, Nicole — *Corporate Careers, Inc.*
Woodmansee, Bruce J. — *Tully/Woodmansee International, Inc.*
Woodworth, Gail — *Woodworth International Group*
Wooldridge, Jeff — *Ray & Berndtson*
Wooller, Edmund A.M. — *Windsor International*
Wright, A. Leo — *The Hindman Company*
Wright, Charles D. — *Goodrich & Sherwood Associates, Inc.*
Wright, Leslie — *The Stevenson Group of New Jersey*
Wylie, Pamela — *M.A. Churchill & Associates, Inc.*
Yaekle, Gary — *Tully/Woodmansee International, Inc.*
Yen, Maggie Yeh Ching — *Ray & Berndtson*
Yungerberg, Steven — *Steven Yungerberg Associates Inc.*
Zaffrann, Craig S. — *P.J. Murphy & Associates, Inc.*
Zahradka, James F. — *P.J. Murphy & Associates, Inc.*
Zamborsky, George — *Boyden*
Zaslav, Debra M. — *Telford, Adams & Alexander/Telford & Co., Inc.*
Zay, Thomas C. — *Boyden/Zay & Company*
Zetto, Kathryn — *Seco & Zetto Associates, Inc.*
Zona, Henry F. — *Zona & Associates, Inc.*
Zwell, Michael — *Zwell International*

10. Women/Minorities

Agee, Jo Etta — *Chrisman & Company, Incorporated*
Akin, J.R. "Jack" — *J.R. Akin & Company Inc.*

Allard, Susan — *Allard Associates*
Allen, Scott — *Chrisman & Company, Incorporated*
Altreuter, Rose — *ALTCO Temporary Services*
Amilowski, Maria — *Highland Search Group*
Anderson, Maria H. — *Barton Associates, Inc.*
Anderson, Steve — *CPS Inc.*
Andujo, Michele M. — *Chrisman & Company, Incorporated*
Arms, Douglas — *TOPAZ International, Inc.*
Arms, Douglas — *TOPAZ Legal Solutions*
Aronin, Michael — *Fisher-Todd Associates*
Ascher, Susan P. — *The Ascher Group*
Atwood, Barrie — *The Abbott Group, Inc.*
Baeder, Jeremy — *Executive Manning Corporation*
Bailey, Vanessa — *Highland Search Group*
Baje, Sarah — *Innovative Search Group, LLC*
Baker, Gary M. — *Cochran, Cochran & Yale, Inc.*
Balbone, Rich — *Executive Manning Corporation*
Balch, Randy — *CPS Inc.*
Baltaglia, Michael — *Cochran, Cochran & Yale, Inc.*
Barbour, Mary Beth — *Tully/Woodmansee International, Inc.*
Barnes, Gary — *Brigade Inc.*
Bass, M. Lynn — *Ray & Berndtson*
Bauman, Martin H. — *Martin H. Bauman Associates, Inc.*
Beaudin, Elizabeth C. — *Callan Associates, Ltd.*
Belin, Jean — *Boyden*
Bender, Alan — *Bender Executive Search*
Bennett, Jo — *Battalia Winston International*
Blakslee, Jan H. — *J: Blakslee International, Ltd.*
Bongiovanni, Vincent — *ESA Professional Consultants*
Bourrie, Sharon D. — *Chartwell Partners International, Inc.*
Bovich, Maryann C. — *Higdon Prince Inc.*
Bowden, Otis H. — *BowdenGlobal, Ltd.*
Brady, Dick — *William Guy & Associates*
Brady, Robert — *CPS Inc.*
Brandeau, John — *Chrisman & Company, Incorporated*
Brandeis, Richard — *CPS Inc.*
Brown, Larry C. — *Horton International*
Brudno, Robert J. — *Savoy Partners, Ltd.*
Bruno, Deborah F. — *The Hindman Company*
Brzezinski, Ronald T. — *Callan Associates, Ltd.*
Buckles, Donna — *Cochran, Cochran & Yale, Inc.*
Buggy, Linda — *Bonnell Associates Ltd.*
Burns, Terence N. — *D.E. Foster Partners Inc.*
Butterfass, Stanley — *Butterfass, Pepe & MacCallan Inc.*
Byrnes, Thomas A. — *The Search Alliance, Inc.*
Call, David — *Cochran, Cochran & Yale, Inc.*
Callan, Robert M. — *Callan Associates, Ltd.*
Campbell, Patricia A. — *The Onstott Group, Inc.*
Capizzi, Karen — *Cochran, Cochran & Yale, Inc.*
Castine, Michael P. — *Highland Search Group*
Celenza, Catherine — *CPS Inc.*
Chamberlin, Joan — *William Guy & Associates*
Chamberlin, Michael A. — *Tower Consultants, Ltd.*
Chappell, Peter — *Robertson & Associates*
Chappell, Peter — *The Bankers Group*
Chrisman, Timothy R. — *Chrisman & Company, Incorporated*

Hawksworth, A. Dwight — *A.D. & Associates Executive Search, Inc.*
Hay, William E. — *William E. Hay & Co.*
Haystead, Steve — *Advanced Executive Resources*
Hazerjian, Cynthia — *CPS Inc.*
Heafey, Bill — *CPS Inc.*
Healey, Joseph T. — *Highland Search Group*
Heiken, Barbara E. — *Randell-Heiken, Inc.*
Hellinger, Audrey W. — *Martin H. Bauman Associates, Inc.*
Helminiak, Audrey — *Gaffney Management Consultants*
Heneghan, Donald A. — *Allerton Heneghan & O'Neill*
Hetherman, Margaret F. — *Highland Search Group*
Higdon, Henry G. — *Higdon Prince Inc.*
Higgins, Donna — *Howard Fischer Associates, Inc.*
Higgins, William — *William Guy & Associates*
Himlin, Amy — *Cochran, Cochran & Yale, Inc.*
Hoevel, Michael J. — *Poirier, Hoevel & Co.*
Holland, Kathleen — *TOPAZ International, Inc.*
Holland, Kathleen — *TOPAZ Legal Solutions*
Holzberger, Georges L. — *Highland Search Group*
Houchins, William M. — *Christian & Timbers*
Hudson, Reginald M. — *Search Bureau International*
Hughes, Cathy N. — *The Ogdon Partnership*
Imely, Larry S. — *Stratford Group*
Irish, Alan — *CPS Inc.*
James, Richard — *Criterion Executive Search, Inc.*
Janssen, Don — *Howard Fischer Associates, Inc.*
Januale, Lois — *Cochran, Cochran & Yale, Inc.*
Jazylo, John V. — *Handy HRM Corp.*
Jeffers, Richard B. — *Dieckmann & Associates, Ltd.*
Johnson, Priscilla — *The Johnson Group, Inc.*
Johnson, S. Hope — *Boyden Washington, D.C.*
Jordan, Jon — *Cochran, Cochran & Yale, Inc.*
Judge, Alfred L. — *The Cambridge Group Ltd*
Judy, Otto — *CPS Inc.*
Juelis, John J. — *Peeney Associates*
Kader, Richard — *Richard Kader & Associates*
Kane, Karen — *Howard Fischer Associates, Inc.*
Karalis, William — *CPS Inc.*
Kehoe, Mike — *CPS Inc.*
Kelly, Claudia L. — *Spencer Stuart*
Kelly, Elizabeth Ann — *Wellington Management Group*
Kern, Jerry L. — *ADOW's Executeam*
Kern, Kathleen G. — *ADOW's Executeam*
Kilcoyne, Pat — *CPS Inc.*
Kiley, Phyllis — *National Search, Inc.*
Kip, Luanne S. — *Kip Williams, Inc.*
Kkorzyniewski, Nicole — *CPS Inc.*
Klages, Constance W. — *International Management Advisors, Inc.*
Klavens, Cecile J. — *The Pickwick Group, Inc.*
Klein, Mary Jo — *Cochran, Cochran & Yale, Inc.*
Knisely, Gary — *Johnson Smith & Knisely Accord*
Kohn, Adam P. — *Christian & Timbers*
Koontz, Donald N. — *Koontz, Jeffries & Associates, Inc.*
Kossuth, Jane — *Kossuth & Associates, Inc.*
Krejci, Stanley L. — *Boyden Washington, D.C.*
Kreutz, Gary L. — *Kreutz Consulting Group, Inc.*

Krieger, Dennis F. — *Seiden Krieger Associates, Inc.*
Kurrigan, Geoffrey — *ESA Professional Consultants*
Laird, Cheryl — *CPS Inc.*
Lang, Sharon A. — *Ray & Berndtson*
Lautz, Lindsay A. — *Lautz Grotte Engler*
Leahy, Jan — *CPS Inc.*
Leininger, Dennis — *Key Employment Services*
Levine, Lois — *National Search, Inc.*
Lewis, Marc D. — *Handy HRM Corp.*
Lezama Cohen, Luis — *Ray & Berndtson*
Liebowitz, Michael E. — *Highland Search Group*
Lofthouse, Cindy — *CPS Inc.*
Long, Helga — *Horton International*
Long, Melanie — *National Search, Inc.*
Long, Milt — *William Guy & Associates*
Long, William G. — *McDonald, Long & Associates, Inc.*
Lotz, R. James — *International Management Advisors, Inc.*
Loving, Vikki — *Intersource, Ltd.*
Lucarelli, Joan — *The Onstott Group, Inc.*
Lucht, John — *The John Lucht Consultancy Inc.*
Lumsby, George N. — *International Management Advisors, Inc.*
Luntz, Charles E. — *Charles Luntz & Associates. Inc.*
Lupica, Anthony — *Cochran, Cochran & Yale, Inc.*
MacCallan, Deirdre — *Butterfass, Pepe & MacCallan Inc.*
MacIntyre, Lisa W. — *Highland Search Group*
MacNaughton, Sperry — *McNaughton Associates*
Mainwaring, Andrew Brian — *Executive Search Consultants Corporation*
Mallin, Ellen — *Howard Fischer Associates, Inc.*
Manassero, Henri J.P. — *International Management Advisors, Inc.*
Mansford, Keith — *Howard Fischer Associates, Inc.*
Marino, Chester — *Cochran, Cochran & Yale, Inc.*
Mark, John L. — *J.L. Mark Associates, Inc.*
Mark, Lynne — *J.L. Mark Associates, Inc.*
Marks, Ira — *Strategic Alternatives*
Marumoto, William H. — *Boyden Washington, D.C.*
Mashakas, Elizabeth — *TOPAZ International, Inc.*
Mashakas, Elizabeth — *TOPAZ Legal Solutions*
Mathias, Kathy — *Stone Murphy & Olson*
Maynard Taylor, Susan — *Chrisman & Company, Incorporated*
Mazor, Elly — *Howard Fischer Associates, Inc.*
McAndrews, Kathy — *CPS Inc.*
McBride, Jonathan E. — *McBride Associates, Inc.*
McCallister, Richard A. — *Boyden*
McCreary, Charles "Chip" — *Austin-McGregor International*
McDermott, Jeffrey T. — *Vlcek & Company, Inc.*
McDonald, Scott A. — *McDonald Associates International*
McDonald, Stanleigh B. — *McDonald Associates International*
McKeown, Patricia A. — *DiMarchi Partners, Inc.*
McKnight, Amy E. — *Chartwell Partners International, Inc.*
McManners, Donald E. — *McManners Associates, Inc.*

Slosar, John — *Boyden*
Smith, David P. — *HRS, Inc.*
Smith, Ethan L. — *Highland Search Group*
Smith, Lydia — *The Corporate Connection, Ltd.*
Smith, Matt D. — *Ray & Berndtson*
Snelgrove, Geiger — *National Search, Inc.*
Snyder, C. Edward — *Horton International*
Steele, Daniel — *Cochran, Cochran & Yale, Inc.*
Steer, Joe — *CPS Inc.*
Stern, Stephen — *CPS Inc.*
Sterner, Doug — *CPS Inc.*
Stevenson, Jane — *Howard Fischer Associates, Inc.*
Stewart, Ross M. — *Human Resources Network Partners Inc.*
Stranberg, James R. — *Callan Associates, Ltd.*
Straube, Stanley H. — *Straube Associates*
Stringer, Dann P. — *D.E. Foster Partners Inc.*
Strom, Mark N. — *Search Advisors International Corp.*
Sullivan, Kay — *Rusher, Loscavio & LoPresto*
Sussman, Lynda — *Gilbert Tweed/INESA*
Swanson, Dick — *Raymond Karsan Associates*
Taylor, R.L. (Larry) — *Ray & Berndtson*
Teti, Al — *Chrisman & Company, Incorporated*
Thomas, Cheryl M. — *CPS Inc.*
Thomas, Kim — *CPS Inc.*
Tovrog, Dan — *CPS Inc.*
Trott, Kathryn — *Allard Associates*
Trott, Kathryn — *Allard Associates*
Truemper, Dean — *CPS Inc.*
Truex, John F. — *Morton, McCorkle & Associates, Inc.*
Tullberg, Tina — *CPS Inc.*
Tully, Margo L. — *Tully/Woodmansee International, Inc.*
Tursi, Deborah J. — *The Corporate Connection, Ltd.*

Van Campen, Jerry — *Gilbert & Van Campen International*
Velten, Mark T. — *Boyden*
Vergara, Gail H. — *Spencer Stuart*
Vitale, Amy — *Highland Search Group*
Vlcek, Thomas J. — *Vlcek & Company, Inc.*
Volkman, Arthur — *Cochran, Cochran & Yale, Inc.*
von Baillou, Astrid — *Richard Kinser & Associates*
Wakefield, Scott — *National Search, Inc.*
Walker, Ewing J. — *Ward Howell International, Inc.*
Warter, Mark — *Isaacson, Miller*
Wein, Michael S. — *Media Management Resources, Inc.*
Wein, William — *Media Management Resources, Inc.*
Weisler, Nancy — *National Search, Inc.*
Weissman-Rosenthal, Abbe — *ALW Research International*
Welch, Robert — *Ray & Berndtson*
Whitley, Sue Ann — *Roberts Ryan and Bentley*
Whitney, William A — *Larsen, Whitney, Blecksmith & Zilliacus*
Williams, Lis — *Executive Options, Ltd.*
Wilson, Patricia L. — *Leon A. Farley Associates*
Winograd, Glenn — *Criterion Executive Search, Inc.*
Winston, Dale — *Battalia Winston International*
Womack, Joseph — *The Bankers Group*
Wood, Elizabeth — *Highland Search Group*
Wooldridge, Jeff — *Ray & Berndtson*
Yen, Maggie Yeh Ching — *Ray & Berndtson*
Yungerberg, Steven — *Steven Yungerberg Associates Inc.*
Zamborsky, George — *Boyden*
Zetto, Kathryn — *Seco & Zetto Associates, Inc.*
Zivic, Janis M. — *Spencer Stuart*

Geographic Index

Alabama
Birmingham
Taylor, James M. — *The HRM Group, Inc.*
Wilkinson, Jr. SPHR — *The HRM Group, Inc.*
Huntsville
Ward, Jim — *F-O-R-T-U-N-E Personnel Consultants of Huntsville, Inc.*

Arizona
Phoenix
Balchumas, Charles — *Source Services Corporation*
Booth, Ronald — *Source Services Corporation*
Cizek, Marti J. — *Cizek Associates, Inc.*
Collins, Scott — *Source Services Corporation*
Debus, Wayne — *Source Services Corporation*
Graff, Jack — *Source Services Corporation*
Howe, Vance A. — *Ward Howell International, Inc.*
Jones, B.J. — *Intersource, Ltd.*
Meyer, Michael F. — *Witt/Kieffer, Ford, Hadelman & Lloyd*
Petersen, Richard — *Source Services Corporation*
Robertson, Sherry — *Source Services Corporation*
Spector, Michael — *Source Services Corporation*
Weeks, Glenn — *Source Services Corporation*
Weis, Theodore — *Source Services Corporation*
Scottsdale
Bartholdi, Theodore G. — *Bartholdi & Company, Inc.*
Jacobs, Martin J. — *The Rubicon Group*
Renner, Sandra L. — *Spectra International Inc.*
Roberts, Kenneth — *The Rubicon Group*
Silvas, Stephen D. — *Roberson and Company*
Wilder, Richard B. — *Columbia Consulting Group*

California
Agoura Hills
Schmidt, Frank B. — *F.B. Schmidt International*
Shirilla, Robert M. — *F.B. Schmidt International*
Auburn
Norsell, Paul E. — *Paul Norsell & Associates, Inc.*
Beverly Hills
Hensley, Bert — *Morgan Samuels Co., Inc.*
Corte Madera
Schweichler, Lee J. — *Schweichler Associates, Inc.*
Costa Mesa
Friedman, Helen E. — *McCormack & Farrow*
Telford, John H. — *Telford, Adams & Alexander/Telford & Co., Inc.*
Thompson, Kenneth L. — *McCormack & Farrow*
Zaslav, Debra M. — *Telford, Adams & Alexander/Telford & Co., Inc.*
Cupertino
Barnes, Gary — *Brigade Inc.*
King, Margaret — *Christian & Timbers*
Mather, David R. — *Christian & Timbers*
Danville
Badger, Fred H. — *The Badger Group*
Cochran, Scott P. — *The Badger Group*
Watkinson, Jim W. — *The Badger Group*
Dublin
Paul, Lisa D. — *Merit Resource Group, Inc.*
Encinitas
Saxon, Alexa — *Woodworth International Group*

Encino
Inguagiato, Gregory — *MSI International*
Garden Grove
Dowell, Mary K. — *Professional Search Associates*
Irvine
DeBrun, Thomas P. — *Ray & Berndtson*
Gennawey, Robert — *Source Services Corporation*
Guthrie, Stuart — *Source Services Corporation*
Hart, Crystal — *Source Services Corporation*
Herzog, Sarah — *Source Services Corporation*
Jadulang, Vincent — *Source Services Corporation*
Jeltema, John — *Source Services Corporation*
Kennedy, Paul — *Source Services Corporation*
Ludlow, Michael — *Source Services Corporation*
Mollichelli, David — *Source Services Corporation*
Paternie, Patrick — *Source Services Corporation*
Pierce, Matthew — *Source Services Corporation*
Walker, Rose — *Source Services Corporation*
Ward, Robert — *Source Services Corporation*
Wilson, Joyce — *Source Services Corporation*
Woods, Craig — *Source Services Corporation*
Yen, Maggie Yeh Ching — *Ray & Berndtson*
La Jolla
Daniels, Alfred — *Alfred Daniels & Associates*
Long Beach
Montgomery, James M. — *Houze, Shourds & Montgomery, Inc.*
Shourds, Mary E. — *Houze, Shourds & Montgomery, Inc.*
Los Altos
Busch, Jack — *Busch International*
Furlong, James W. — *Furlong Search, Inc.*
Hockett, William — *Hockett Associates, Inc.*
Ocon, Olga — *Busch International*
Los Angeles
Ackerman, Larry R. — *Spectrum Search Associates, Inc.*
Allen, Scott — *Chrisman & Company, Incorporated*
Andujo, Michele M. — *Chrisman & Company, Incorporated*
Archer, Sandra F. — *Ryan, Miller & Associates Inc.*
Bellano, Robert W. — *Stanton Chase International*
Blecksmith, Edward L. — *Larsen, Whitney, Blecksmith & Zilliacus*
Brown, Buzz — *Brown, Bernardy, Van Remmen, Inc.*
Bruce, Michael C. — *Spencer Stuart*
Chrisman, Timothy R. — *Chrisman & Company, Incorporated*
Clayton, Fred J. — *Berkhemer Clayton Incorporated*
Cutka, Matthew — *Source Services Corporation*
Dorsey, Jim — *Ryan, Miller & Associates Inc.*
Dreifus, Donald — *Search West, Inc.*
Elster, Irv — *Spectrum Search Associates, Inc.*
Fifield, George C. — *Egon Zehnder International Inc.*
Fishler, Stu — *A.T. Kearney, Inc.*
Frerichs, April — *Ryan, Miller & Associates Inc.*
Fust, Sheely F. — *Ray & Berndtson*
Groban, Jack — *A.T. Kearney, Inc.*
Grotenhuis, Dirkten — *Chrisman & Company, Incorporated*
Hanes, Leah — *Ray & Berndtson*
Hanna, Remon — *Source Services Corporation*

Neher, Robert L. — *Intech Summit Group, Inc.*
Song, Louis — *Source Services Corporation*
Tipp, George D. — *Intech Summit Group, Inc.*
Wenz, Alexander — *Source Services Corporation*
Winitz, Joel — *GSW Consulting Group, Inc.*
Winitz, Marla — *GSW Consulting Group, Inc.*

San Francisco
Adams, Jeffrey C. — *Telford, Adams & Alexander/Jeffrey C. Adams & Co., Inc.*
Agee, Jo Etta — *Chrisman & Company, Incorporated*
Amato, Joseph — *Amato & Associates, Inc.*
Anderson, Mary — *Source Services Corporation*
Austin Lockton, Kathy — *Juntunen-Combs-Poirier*
Bates, Nina — *Allard Associates*
Bourrie, Sharon D. — *Chartwell Partners International, Inc.*
Brandeau, John — *Chrisman & Company, Incorporated*
Brown, S. Ross — *Egon Zehnder International Inc.*
Cafero, Les — *Source Services Corporation*
Caldwell, William R. — *Pearson, Caldwell & Farnsworth, Inc.*
Campbell, Jeff — *Source Services Corporation*
Carter, Jon F. — *Egon Zehnder International Inc.*
Combs, Stephen L. — *Juntunen-Combs-Poirier*
Corso, Glen S. — *Chartwell Partners International, Inc.*
Crane, Howard C. — *Chartwell Partners International, Inc.*
deWilde, David M. — *Chartwell Partners International, Inc.*
Engler, Peter G — *Lautz Grotte Engler*
Farley, Leon A. — *Leon A. Farley Associates*
Farnsworth, John A. — *Pearson, Caldwell & Farnsworth, Inc.*
Fox, Lucie — *Allard Associates*
Friedman, Deborah — *Source Services Corporation*
Gorman, Patrick — *Source Services Corporation*
Grayson, E.C. — *Spencer Stuart*
Grotte, Lawrence C. — *Lautz Grotte Engler*
Hall, Peter V. — *Chartwell Partners International, Inc.*
Hampshire, Kay — *Allard Associates*
Hanson, Lee — *Heidrick & Struggles, Inc.*
Hargis, N. Leann — *Montgomery Resources, Inc.*
Hocking, Jeffrey — *Korn/Ferry International*
Hodge, Jeff — *Heidrick & Struggles, Inc.*
Hutton, Thomas J. — *The Thomas Tucker Company*
Juratovac, Michael — *Montgomery Resources, Inc.*
Juska, Frank — *Rusher, Loscavio & LoPresto*
Kenney, Jeanne — *Source Services Corporation*
Kile, Robert W. — *Rusher, Loscavio & LoPresto*
Kuo, Linda — *Montgomery Resources, Inc.*
Lautz, Lindsay A. — *Lautz Grotte Engler*
Lee, Roger — *Montgomery Resources, Inc.*
Loscavio, J. Michael — *Rusher, Loscavio & LoPresto*
MacPherson, Holly — *Source Services Corporation*
Mahmoud, Sophia — *Source Services Corporation*
Mauer, Kristin — *Montgomery Resources, Inc.*
McAteer, Thomas — *Montgomery Resources, Inc.*
McKnight, Amy E. — *Chartwell Partners International, Inc.*

McLaughlin, John — *Romac & Associates*
Meyers, Steven — *Montgomery Resources, Inc.*
O'Maley, Kimberlee — *Spencer Stuart*
Pearson, John R. — *Pearson, Caldwell & Farnsworth, Inc.*
Price, Andrew G. — *The Thomas Tucker Company*
Rusher, William H. — *Rusher, Loscavio & LoPresto*
Sanchez, William — *Source Services Corporation*
Sill, Igor M. — *Geneva Group International*
Sprowls, Linda — *Allard Associates*
Theobald, David B. — *Theobald & Associates*
Thompson, Dave — *Battalia Winston International*
Trott, Kathryn — *Allard Associates*
Tucker, Thomas A. — *The Thomas Tucker Company*
Van Norman, Ben — *Source Services Corporation*
Wilson, John — *Korn/Ferry International*
Wilson, Patricia L. — *Leon A. Farley Associates*
Zadfar, Maryanne — *The Thomas Tucker Company*
Zivic, Janis M. — *Spencer Stuart*

San Jose
McManners, Donald E. — *McManners Associates, Inc.*

San Mateo
Ferneborg, Jay W. — *Ferneborg & Associates, Inc.*
Ferneborg, John R. — *Ferneborg & Associates, Inc.*
Pickford, Stephen T. — *The Corporate Staff, Inc.*
Tincu, John C. — *Ferneborg & Associates, Inc.*

Santa Clara
Campbell, Robert Scott — *Wellington Management Group*
Holland, John A. — *Holland, McFadzean & Associates, Inc.*
McFadzen, James A. — *Holland, McFadzean & Associates, Inc.*

Santa Clarita
Parry, William H. — *Horton International*

Sherman Oaks
Biolsi, Joseph — *Source Services Corporation*
Chamberlin, Joan — *William Guy & Associates*
Cook, Charlene — *Source Services Corporation*
Eddy, Terry — *William Guy & Associates*
Fanning, Paul — *Source Services Corporation*
Goodwin, Tim — *William Guy & Associates*
Guy, C. William — *William Guy & Associates*
Hasten, Lawrence — *Source Services Corporation*
Heroux, David — *Source Services Corporation*
Higgins, William — *William Guy & Associates*
Hopper, John W. — *William Guy & Associates*
Long, Milt — *William Guy & Associates*
Ratajczak, Paul — *Source Services Corporation*
Renteria, Elizabeth — *Source Services Corporation*
Trimble, Patricia — *Source Services Corporation*

So. Pasadena
Coleman, J. Kevin — *J. Kevin Coleman & Associates, Inc.*

Sunnyvale
Beaver, Robert — *Source Services Corporation*
Bosward, Allan — *Source Services Corporation*
Fechheimer, Peter — *Source Services Corporation*

Fujino, Rickey — *Source Services Corporation*
Gamble, Ira — *Source Services Corporation*
Gray, Russell — *Source Services Corporation*
Hoffman, Stephen — *Source Services Corporation*
Hughes, Barbara — *Source Services Corporation*
Humphrey, Titus — *Source Services Corporation*
Nelson, Hitch — *Source Services Corporation*
Pregeant, David — *Source Services Corporation*
Rosen, Mitchell — *Source Services Corporation*
Schwalbach, Robert — *Source Services Corporation*
Silver, Kit — *Source Services Corporation*

Tiburon
Thomas, Terry — *The Thomas Resource Group*

Tustin
Adler, Louis S. — *CJA - The Adler Group*
Remillard, Brad M. — *CJA - The Adler Group*

Westlake Village
Della Monica, Vincent — *Search West, Inc.*
Dingman, Bruce — *Robert W. Dingman Company, Inc.*
Diskin, Rochelle — *Search West, Inc.*
Kantor, Richard — *Search West, Inc.*
Linton, Leonard M. — *Byron Leonard International, Inc.*
Neckanoff, Sharon — *Search West, Inc.*
White, William C. — *Venture Resources Inc.*
Wolf, Stephen M. — *Byron Leonard International, Inc.*

Woodland
Allard, Susan — *Allard Associates*
Trott, Kathryn — *Allard Associates*

Woodland Hills
Loper, Doris — *Mortgage & Financial Personnel Services*
Sherman, Robert R. — *Mortgage & Financial Personnel Services*
Springer, Mark H. — *M.H. Springer & Associates Incorporated*

Colorado
Boulder
DiMarchi, Paul — *DiMarchi Partners, Inc.*

Denver
DiMarchi, Paul — *DiMarchi Partners, Inc.*
Hoover, Catherine — *J.L. Mark Associates, Inc.*
Mark, John L. — *J.L. Mark Associates, Inc.*
Mark, Lynne — *J.L. Mark Associates, Inc.*
McKeown, Patricia A. — *DiMarchi Partners, Inc.*
Schaefer, Frederic M. — *A.T. Kearney, Inc.*

Englewood
Daniels, C. Eugene — *Sigma Group International*
Davis, C. Scott — *Source Services Corporation*
Ellis, Patricia — *Source Services Corporation*
Field, Andrew — *Source Services Corporation*
Francis, Brad — *Source Services Corporation*
Graham, Shannon — *Source Services Corporation*
Haider, Martin — *Source Services Corporation*
Harp, Kimberly — *Source Services Corporation*
Reisinger, George L. — *Sigma Group International*
Reynolds, Laura — *Source Services Corporation*
Sell, David — *Source Services Corporation*
Spoutz, Paul — *Source Services Corporation*
Trimble, Rhonda — *Source Services Corporation*
Wein, Michael S. — *Media Management Resources, Inc.*

Wein, William — *Media Management Resources, Inc.*
Woomer, Jerome — *Source Services Corporation*

Greenwood Village
Plimpton, Ralph L. — *R L Plimpton Associates*

Westminster
Lupica, Anthony — *Cochran, Cochran & Yale, Inc.*
Marino, Chester — *Cochran, Cochran & Yale, Inc.*
Steele, Daniel — *Cochran, Cochran & Yale, Inc.*
Volkman, Arthur — *Cochran, Cochran & Yale, Inc.*

Connecticut
Avon
Beer, John — *People Management Northeast Incorporated*
Brown, Larry C. — *Horton International*
Cooke, Katherine H. — *Horton International*
Darter, Steven M. — *People Management Northeast Incorporated*
Fischer, John C. — *Horton International*
Gilchrist, Robert J. — *Horton International*
Hammond, Karla — *People Management Northeast Incorporated*
Pace, Susan A. — *Horton International*
Snyder, C. Edward — *Horton International*
Snyder, James F. — *Snyder & Company*

Darien
Nolte, William S. — *W.D. Nolte & Company*

Greenwich
Brown, Steve — *K. Russo Associates*
Ducruet, Linda K. — *Heidrick & Struggles, Inc.*
Livingston, Peter R. — *Livingston, Robert and Company Inc.*
Mahr, Toni — *K. Russo Associates*
Morgan, Nancy — *K. Russo Associates*
Mulligan, Robert P. — *William Willis Worldwide Inc.*
Pickering, Dorothy C. — *Livingston, Robert and Company Inc.*
Russo, Karen — *K. Russo Associates*
Willis, William H. — *William Willis Worldwide Inc.*

Hartford
Brown, Clifford — *Source Services Corporation*
Harwood, Brian — *Source Services Corporation*
McCormick, Joseph — *Source Services Corporation*
Needham, Karen — *Source Services Corporation*
Tenero, Kymberly — *Source Services Corporation*
Turner, Raymond — *Source Services Corporation*
Wolf, Donald — *Source Services Corporation*

Madison
Bongiovanni, Vincent — *ESA Professional Consultants*
Dicker, Barry — *ESA Professional Consultants*
Freeman, Mark — *ESA Professional Consultants*
Kurrigan, Geoffrey — *ESA Professional Consultants*
Pigott, Daniel — *ESA Professional Consultants*
Rose, Robert — *ESA Professional Consultants*

New Haven
Kaiser, Donald J. — *Dunhill Search International*
Kaiser, Elaine M. — *Dunhill Search International*

Nemec, Phillip — *Dunhill International Search of New Haven*

Norwalk

Byrnes, Thomas A. — *The Search Alliance, Inc.*
de Tuede, Catherine — *The Search Alliance, Inc.*
Hallock, Peter B. — *Goodrich & Sherwood Associates, Inc.*
Leonard, Linda — *Harris Heery & Associates*
O'Neill, Stephen A. — *Harris Heery & Associates*
Roth, William — *Harris Heery & Associates*
Schuette, Dorothy — *Harris Heery & Associates*
Spann, Richard E. — *Goodrich & Sherwood Associates, Inc.*
Thomas, Jeffrey — *Fairfaxx Corporation*
Tucci, Joseph — *Fairfaxx Corporation*
Wright, Charles D. — *Goodrich & Sherwood Associates, Inc.*

Rowayton

Knight, Liz — *Plummer & Associates, Inc.*
MacKenna, Kathy — *Plummer & Associates, Inc.*
Plummer, John — *Plummer & Associates, Inc.*
Stahl, Cindy — *Plummer & Associates, Inc.*

Shelton

Rios, Vince — *Source Services Corporation*

Southport

Bonnell, William R. — *Bonnell Associates Ltd.*
Buggy, Linda — *Bonnell Associates Ltd.*
Pallman-David, Cynthia — *Bonnell Associates Ltd.*

Stamford

Broadhurst, Austin — *Lamalie Amrop International*
Citrin, James M. — *Spencer Stuart*
Clemens, Bill — *Spencer Stuart*
Emery, Jodie A. — *Lamalie Amrop International*
Gulian, Randolph — *Strategic Executives, Inc.*
Hart, Robert T. — *D.E. Foster Partners Inc.*
Howard, Lee Ann — *Lamalie Amrop International*
Kanovsky, Gerald — *Career Consulting Group, Inc.*
Kanovsky, Marlene — *Career Consulting Group, Inc.*
Kelly, Claudia L. — *Spencer Stuart*
Kien-Jersey, Tammy — *Spencer Stuart*
Krauser, H. James — *Spencer Stuart*
Lotufo, Donald A. — *D.A.L. Associates, Inc.*
Mirtz, P. John — *Mirtz Morice, Inc.*
Morice, James L. — *Mirtz Morice, Inc.*
Murphy, Peter — *Korn/Ferry International*
Ogden, Dayton — *Spencer Stuart*
Perry, James — *Strategic Executives, Inc.*
Richardson, J. Rick — *Spencer Stuart*
Romanello, Daniel P. — *Spencer Stuart*
Rush, Michael E. — *D.A.L. Associates, Inc.*
Sandor, Richard J. — *Flynn, Hannock, Incorporated*
Stone, Robert Ryder — *Lamalie Amrop International*
Wasson, Thomas W. — *Spencer Stuart*
White, Richard B. — *Spencer Stuart*

West Hartford

Gibbons, Ronald L. — *Flynn, Hannock, Incorporated*
Goldberg, Susan C. — *Susan C. Goldberg Associates*

Hannock, Elwin W. — *Flynn, Hannock, Incorporated*
Johnston, James R. — *The Stevenson Group of Delaware Inc.*
Savard, Robert F. — *The Stevenson Group of Delaware Inc.*
Tracey, Jack — *Management Assistance Group, Inc.*

Westport

Judge, Alfred L. — *The Cambridge Group Ltd.*
Masserman, Bruce — *Masserman & Associates, Inc.*
Mead, James D. — *James Mead & Company*
Ross, H. Lawrence — *Ross & Company*
Salvagno, Michael J. — *The Cambridge Group Ltd.*

Wilton

Johnson, Stanley C. — *Johnson & Company*

Delaware

Wilmington

Vacca, Domenic — *Romac & Associates*

District of Columbia

Washington

Brudno, Robert J. — *Savoy Partners, Ltd.*
Clauhsen, Elizabeth A. — *Savoy Partners, Ltd.*
Crawford, Cassondra — *Don Richard Associates of Washington, D.C., Inc.*
Hagerty, Kenneth — *Korn/Ferry International*
Harrell, L. Parker — *Korn/Ferry International*
Johnson, S. Hope — *Boyden Washington, D.C.*
Krejci, Stanley L. — *Boyden Washington, D.C. Ltd./Boyden*
Marumoto, William H. — *Boyden Washington, D.C.*
McBride, Jonathan E. — *McBride Associates, Inc.*
Stevens, Tracey — *Don Richard Associates of Washington, D.C., Inc.*
Stoy, Roger W. — *Heidrick & Struggles, Inc.*
Strassman, Mark — *Don Richard Associates of Washington, D.C., Inc.*
Stringer, Dann P. — *D.E. Foster Partners Inc.*
Vilella, Paul — *Source Services Corporation*
Weller, Paul S. — *Mark Stanley/EMA Partners International*

Florida

Altamonte Springs

Cannavino, John J. — *Financial Resource Associates, Inc.*
Cannavino, Matthew J. — *Financial Resource Associates, Inc.*
Krick, Terry L. — *Financial Resource Associates, Inc.*
Little, Elizabeth A. — *Financial Resource Associates, Inc.*
Madaras, Debra — *Financial Resource Associates, Inc.*

Boca Raton

Marra, John — *Marra Peters & Partners*
Schneiderman, Gerald — *Management Resource Associates, Inc.*

Clearwater

Butler, Kirby B. — *The Butlers Company Insurance Recruiters*
Whitley, Sue Ann — *Roberts Ryan and Bentley*

Coral Gables
Park, Dabney G. — *Mark Stanley/EMA Partners International*
Ramsey, John H. — *Mark Stanley/EMA Partners International*

Coral Springs
Del Pino, William — *National Search, Inc.*
Kiley, Phyllis — *National Search, Inc.*
Levine, Lois —, *National Search, Inc.*
Long, Melanie — *National Search, Inc.*
Morgan, Gary — *National Search, Inc.*
Redler, Rhonda — *National Search, Inc.*
Reiss, Matt — *National Search, Inc.*
Rosenthal, Charles — *National Search, Inc.*
Sennello, Gendra — *National Search, Inc.*
Shelton, Sandra — *National Search, Inc.*
Snelgrove, Geiger — *National Search, Inc.*
Wakefield, Scott — *National Search, Inc.*
Weisler, Nancy — *National Search, Inc.*

Fort Lauderdale
Baeder, Jeremy — *Executive Manning Corporation*
Baer, Kenneth — *Source Services Corporation*
Balbone, Rich — *Executive Manning Corporation*
Belin, Jean — *Boyden*
Bloch, Suzanne — *Source Services Corporation*
Evans, David — *Executive Manning Corporation*
Lasher, Charles M. — *Lasher Associates*
Mursuli, Meredith — *Lasher Associates*
Scimone, Jim — *Source Services Corporation*
Sutter, Howard — *Romac & Associates*

Fort Myers
Akin, J.R. "Jack" — *J.R. Akin & Company Inc.*

Jacksonville
Hoskins, Charles R. — *Heidrick & Struggles, Inc.*
Keith, Stephanie — *Southwestern Professional Services*

Jensen Beach
Chamberlin, Michael A. — *Tower Consultants, Ltd.*
Friedman, Donna L. — *Tower Consultants, Ltd.*
Regan, Thomas J. — *Tower Consultants, Ltd.*

Jupiter
Mingle, Larry D. — *Columbia Consulting Group*

Lake Placid
Golde, Lisa — *Tully/Woodmansee International, Inc.*
Tully, Margo L. — *Tully/Woodmansee International, Inc.*

Largo
DeCorrevont, James — *DeCorrevont & Associates*

Longwood
Bohn, Steve J. — *MSI International*
Fleming, Marco — *MSI International*

Miami
Harfenist, Harry — *Parker Page Group*
Messett, William J. — *Messett Associates, Inc.*
Mestepey, John — *A.T. Kearney, Inc.*
Palazio, Carla — *A.T. Kearney, Inc.*
Price, Kenneth M. — *Messett Associates, Inc.*

Miami Lakes
Dunman, Betsy L. — *Crawford & Crofford*
Flora, Dodi — *Crawford & Crofford*
Grossman, Martin — *Source Services Corporation*

Hernandez, Ruben — *Source Services Corporation*
Hylas, Lisa — *Source Services Corporation*
La Chance, Ronald — *Source Services Corporation*
Lamia, Michael — *Source Services Corporation*
Manns, Alex — *Crawford & Crofford*
Morato, Rene — *Source Services Corporation*
Neff, Herbert — *Source Services Corporation*
Rodriguez, Manuel — *Source Services Corporation*
Scimone, James — *Source Services Corporation*
Sevilla, Claudio A. — *Crawford & Crofford*
Stephens, John — *Source Services Corporation*

Orlando
Kennedy, Walter — *Romac & Associates*

Palmetto
Butcher, Pascale — *F-O-R-T-U-N-E Personnel Consultants of Manatee County*

Tampa
Bladon, Andrew — *Don Richard Associates of Tampa, Inc.*
Dickey, Chester W. — *Bowden & Company, Inc.*
Dingeldey, Peter E. — *Search Advisors International Corp.*
Dittmar, Richard — *Source Services Corporation*
Dunkel, David L. — *Romac & Associates*
Grebenschikoff, Jennifer R. — *Physician Executive Management Center*
Harbert, David O. — *Sweeney Harbert & Mummert, Inc.*
Hughes, Randall — *Source Services Corporation*
James, Richard — *Criterion Executive Search, Inc.*
Kirschman, David R. — *Physician Executive Management Center*
Kramer, Donald — *Dunhill Personnel of Tampa, Inc.*
Kramer, Peter — *Dunhill Personnel of Tampa, Inc.*
Kuhl, Teresa — *Don Richard Associates of Tampa, Inc.*
Little, Suzaane — *Don Richard Associates of Tampa, Inc.*
Long, John — *Source Services Corporation*
Miller, Larry — *Source Services Corporation*
Nelson-Folkersen, Jeffrey — *Source Services Corporation*
Rorech, Maureen — *Romac & Associates*
Scott, Gordon S. — *Search Advisors International Corp.*
Strom, Mark N. — *Search Advisors International Corp.*
Tutwiler, Stephen — *Don Richard Associates of Tampa, Inc.*
Winograd, Glenn — *Criterion Executive Search, Inc.*
Wolfe, Peter — *Source Services Corporation*

Winter Park
Cary, Con — *Cary & Associates*

Georgia
Alpharetta
McCabe, Christopher — *Raymond Karsan Associates*

Atlanta
Abbatiello, Christine Murphy — *Winter, Wyman & Company*
Allred, J. Michael — *Spencer Stuart*

Baje, Sarah — *Innovative Search Group, LLC*
Biddix, Maryanne — *Tyler & Company*
Biggins, J. Veronica — *Heidrick & Struggles, Inc.*
Boel, Werner — *The Dalley Hewitt Company*
Brinson, Robert — *MSI International*
Brown, Lawrence Anthony — *MSI International*
Bump, Gerald J. — *D.E. Foster Partners Inc.*
Campbell, Gary — *Romac & Associates*
Carrington, Timothy — *Korn/Ferry International*
Citarella, Richard A. — *A.T. Kearney, Inc.*
Curren, Camella — *Source Services Corporation*
Dankberg, Iris — *Source Services Corporation*
Dezember, Steve — *Ray & Berndtson*
Dickson, Duke — *A.D. & Associates Executive Search, Inc.*
Dobrow, Samuel — *Source Services Corporation*
Downs, William — *Source Services Corporation*
Duckworth, Donald R. — *Johnson Smith & Knisely Accord*
Duelks, John — *Source Services Corporation*
Edwards, Douglas W. — *Egon Zehnder International Inc.*
Eldridge, Charles B. — *Ray & Berndtson*
Ellis, David — *Don Richard Associates of Georgia, Inc.*
Ferguson, Kenneth — *Source Services Corporation*
Freeh, Thomas — *Source Services Corporation*
Hales, Daphne — *Source Services Corporation*
Harty, Shirley Cox — *Ray & Berndtson*
Hauser, Martha — *Spencer Stuart*
Hawksworth, A. Dwight — *A.D. & Associates Executive Search, Inc.*
Hennig, Sandra M. — *MSI International*
Hewitt, Rives D. — *The Dalley Hewitt Company*
Hewitt, W. Davis — *The Dalley Hewitt Company*
Jacobson, Gregory — *Jacobson Associates*
Koblentz, Joel M. — *Egon Zehnder International Inc.*
Kratz, Steve — *Tyler & Company*
Leslie, William H. — *Boyden/Zay & Company*
Lindberg, Eric J. — *MSI International*
Lindsay, M. Evan — *Heidrick & Struggles, Inc.*
Mazzuckelli, Katie — *Tyler & Company*
McCarty, J. Rucker — *Heidrick & Struggles, Inc.*
McClearen, V. Bruce — *Tyler & Company*
McConnell, Greg — *Winter, Wyman & Company*
Miller, Harold B. — *MSI International*
Milligan, Dale — *Source Services Corporation*
Moore, Janice E. — *MSI International*
Moore, T. Willis — *Ray & Berndtson*
Morgan, Donald T. — *MSI International*
Murphy, James — *Source Services Corporation*
Nagle, Charles L. — *Tyler & Company*
Norton, James B. — *Lamalie Amrop International*
O'Halloran, Robert — *MSI International*
Parkhurst, David R. — *Tyler & Company*
Pease, Edward — *Don Richard Associates of Georgia, Inc.*
Perkey, Richard — *Korn/Ferry International*
Pettway, Samuel H. — *Spencer Stuart*
Pittard, Patrick S. — *Heidrick & Struggles, Inc.*
Ravenel, Lavinia — *MSI International*
Reeves, William B. — *Spencer Stuart*
Reticker, Peter — *MSI International*
Salet, Michael — *Source Services Corporation*
Savela, Edward — *Source Services Corporation*
Sawyer, Deborah — *Korn/Ferry International*

Schwartz, Harry — *Jacobson Associates*
Semple, David — *Source Services Corporation*
Shepard, Michael J. — *MSI International*
Simmons, Sandra K. — *MSI International*
Singleton, Robin — *Tyler & Company*
St. Martin, Peter — *Source Services Corporation*
Taylor, Charles E. — *Lamalie Amrop International*
Taylor, Conrad G. — *MSI International*
Taylor, Ernest A. — *Ward Howell International, Inc.*
Thompson, John R. — *MSI International*
Tingle, Trina A. — *MSI International*
Travis, Hallie — *Tyler & Company*
Tyler, J. Larry — *Tyler & Company*
Waldman, Noah H. — *Lamalie Amrop International*
Waldrop, Gary R. — *MSI International*
Watkins, Jeffrey P. — *Lamalie Amrop International*
Watson, James — *MSI International*
Wooller, Edmund A.M. — *Windsor International*
Wynkoop, Mary — *Tyler & Company*
Zay, Thomas C. — *Boyden/Zay & Company*

Marietta
Gill, Susan — *Plummer & Associates, Inc.*

Roswell
Beall, Charles P. — *Beall & Company, Inc.*
Desmond, Dennis — *Beall & Company, Inc.*
Loving, Vikki — *Intersource, Ltd.*
Palmer, Carlton A. — *Beall & Company, Inc.*
Reddick, David C. — *Horton International*
Smith, R. Michael — *Smith James Group, Inc.*
Soutouras, James — *Smith James Group, Inc.*
Wilkinson, Barbara — *Beall & Company, Inc.*

Stone Mountain
Eason, Jan C. — *Summit Group International*

Illinois
Arlington Heights
Brindise, Michael J. — *Dynamic Search Systems, Inc.*

Barrington
Bryant, Richard D. — *Bryant Associates, Inc.*
Bryant, Shari G. — *Bryant Associates, Inc.*
Delaney, Patrick J. — *Sensible Solutions, Inc.*
Zak, Adam — *Adams & Associates International*

Chicago
Afforde, Sharon Gould — *Jacobson Associates*
Allgire, Mary L. — *Kenzer Corp.*
Ballantine, Caroline B. — *Heidrick & Struggles, Inc.*
Barnette, Dennis A. — *Heidrick & Struggles, Inc.*
Berman, Mitchell — *Carlyle Group*
Birkhead, Linda — *Zwell International*
Burns, Terence N. — *D.E. Foster Partners Inc.*
Chappell, Peter — *Robertson & Associates*
Chappell, Peter — *The Bankers Group*
Clark, Donald B. — *Ray & Berndtson*
Clawson, Robert — *Source Services Corporation*
Cocchiaro, Richard — *Romac & Associates*
Cocconi, Alan — *Source Services Corporation*
Cole, Rosalie — *Source Services Corporation*
Coleman, Patricia — *Korn/Ferry International*
Connelly, Kevin M. — *Spencer Stuart*
Crecos, Gregory P. — *Gregory Michaels and Associates*
Crist, Peter — *Crist Partners, Ltd.*

Wendler, Kambrea R. — *Gregory Michaels and Associates*
Westfall, Ed — *Zwell International*
Williams, Roger K. — *Williams, Roth & Krueger Inc.*
Womack, Joseph — *The Bankers Group*
Wood, Milton M. — *M. Wood Company*
Wycoff-Viola, Amy — *Source Services Corporation*
Zwell, Michael — *Zwell International*

DeKalb
Clark, James — *CPS Inc.*

Des Plaines
Argentin, Jo — *Executive Placement Consultants, Inc.*
Colman, Michael — *Executive Placement Consultants, Inc.*
Gurnani, Angali — *Executive Placement Consultants, Inc.*
Trieweiler, Bob — *Executive Placement Consultants, Inc.*

Downers Grove
Dawson, Joe — *S.C. International, Ltd.*
Doman, Matthew — *S.C. International, Ltd.*
Goodridge, Benjamin — *S.C. International, Ltd.*
Neri, Gene — *S.C. International, Ltd.*
Rollins, Scott — *S.C. International, Ltd.*
Smith, Richard — *S.C. International, Ltd.*

Evanston
Conway, Maureen — *Conway & Associates*

Glen Ellyn
Reifel, Laurie — *Reifel & Associates*

Glendale Heights
Gaffney, Keith — *Gaffney Management Consultants*
Gaffney, William — *Gaffney Management Consultants*
Helminiak, Audrey — *Gaffney Management Consultants*

Glenview
Billington, William H. — *Spriggs & Company, Inc.*
Spriggs, Robert D. — *Spriggs & Company, Inc.*

Lake Forest
Kreutz, Gary L. — *Kreutz Consulting Group, Inc.*
McDonald, Stanleigh B. — *McDonald Associates International*

Lake Zurich
Ashton, Edward J. — *E.J. Ashton & Associates, Ltd.*
Cox, William — *E.J. Ashton & Associates, Ltd.*
Galinski, Paul — *E.J. Ashton & Associates, Ltd.*

Naperville
Ward, Madeleine — *LTM Associates*

Northbrook
Gurtin, Kay L. — *Executive Options, Ltd.*
Meltzer, Andrea Y. — *Executive Options, Ltd.*
Siegel, Pamela — *Executive Options, Ltd.*
Williams, Lis — *Executive Options, Ltd.*

Oak Brook
Beaudin, Elizabeth C. — *Callan Associates, Ltd.*
Brzezinski, Ronald T. — *Callan Associates, Ltd.*
Callan, Robert M. — *Callan Associates, Ltd.*
Cizek, John T. — *Cizek Associates, Inc.*
Keogh, James — *Sanford Rose Associates*

Kunzer, William J. — *Kunzer Associates, Ltd.*
Ray, Marianne C. — *Callan Associates, Ltd.*
Stranberg, James R. — *Callan Associates, Ltd.*

Rockford
Barch, Sherrie — *Furst Group/MPI*
Clake, Bob — *Furst Group/MPI*
Newpoff, Brad L. — *Furst Group/MPI*
Pankratz, Dennis — *Furst Group/MPI*
Pratt, Tyler — *Furst Group/MPI*

Rolling Meadows
Clawson, Bob — *Source Services Corporation*
Fyhrie, David — *Source Services Corporation*
Hayes, Lee — *Source Services Corporation*
Jensen, Robert — *Source Services Corporation*
Power, Michael — *Source Services Corporation*
Price, Carl — *Source Services Corporation*

Schaumburg
Silverman, Paul M. — *The Marshall Group*

Springfield
Cona, Joseph A. — *Cona Personnel Search*

Westchester
Anderson, Steve — *CPS Inc.*
Balch, Randy — *CPS Inc.*
Brady, Robert — *CPS Inc.*
Brandeis, Richard — *CPS Inc.*
Christiansen, Amy — *CPS Inc.*
Christiansen, Doug — *CPS Inc.*
Coulman, Karen — *CPS Inc.*
Dixon, Aris — *CPS Inc.*
Dwyer, Julie — *CPS Inc.*
Ervin, Darlene — *CPS Inc.*
Fogarty, Michael — *CPS Inc.*
Graham, Dale — *CPS Inc.*
Grzybowski, Jill — *CPS Inc.*
Hartle, Larry — *CPS Inc.*
Heafey, Bill — *CPS Inc.*
Irish, Alan — *CPS Inc.*
Judy, Otto — *CPS Inc.*
Karalis, William — *CPS Inc.*
Kehoe, Mike — *CPS Inc.*
Kilcoyne, Pat — *CPS Inc.*
Kkorzyniewski, Nicole — *CPS Inc.*
Laird, Cheryl — *CPS Inc.*
Leahy, Jan — *CPS Inc.*
Lofthouse, Cindy — *CPS Inc.*
McAndrews, Kathy — *CPS Inc.*
Michaels, Joseph — *CPS Inc.*
Mohr, Brian — *CPS Inc.*
Murphy, Erin — *CPS Inc.*
Mydlach, Renee — *CPS Inc.*
Ottenritter, Chris — *CPS Inc.*
Pedley, Jill — *CPS Inc.*
Peterson, John — *CPS Inc.*
Pierotazio, John — *CPS Inc.*
Pomerance, Mark — *CPS Inc.*
Reuter, Tandom — *CPS Inc.*
Riederer, Larry — *CPS Inc.*
Saletra, Andrew — *CPS Inc.*
Sanders, Natalie — *CPS Inc.*
Scalamera, Tom — *CPS Inc.*
Schueneman, David — *CPS Inc.*
Signer, Julie — *CPS Inc.*
Steer, Joe — *CPS Inc.*
Stern, Stephen — *CPS Inc.*
Sterner, Doug — *CPS Inc.*
Thomas, Cheryl M. — *CPS Inc.*

Thomas, Kim — *CPS Inc.*
Tovrog, Dan — *CPS Inc.*
Truemper, Dean — *CPS Inc.*
Tullberg, Tina — *CPS Inc.*

Wilmette
Krueger, Kurt — *Krueger Associates*

Indiana
Indianapolis
Bickett, Nicole — *Source Services Corporation*
Blassaras, Peggy — *Source Services Corporation*
Brassard, Gary — *Source Services Corporation*
Emerson, Randall — *Source Services Corporation*
Houterloot, Tim — *Source Services Corporation*
Long, Mark — *Source Services Corporation*
Necessary, Rick — *Source Services Corporation*
Walker, Ann — *Source Services Corporation*

Long Beach
DeFuniak, William S. — *DeFuniak & Edwards*

South Bend
Racht, Janet G. — *Crowe, Chizek and Company, LLP*
Sallows, Jill S. — *Crowe, Chizek and Company, LLP*

Iowa
West Des Moines
Dickerson, Scot — *Key Employment Services*
Hildebrand, Thomas B. — *Professional Resources Group, Inc.*
Leininger, Dennis — *Key Employment Services*
Truax, Kevin — *Key Employment Services*

Kansas
Overland Park
Berger, Jeffrey — *Source Services Corporation*
Blocher, John — *Source Services Corporation*
Brackenbury, Robert — *Bowman & Marshall, Inc.*
Carlson, Judith — *Bowman & Marshall, Inc.*
Connaghan, Linda — *Bowman & Marshall, Inc.*
Grassl, Peter O. — *Bowman & Marshall, Inc.*
Grossman, James — *Source Services Corporation*
Haselby, James — *Source Services Corporation*
Haughton, Michael — *DeFrain, Mayer, Lee & Burgess LLC*
Hellebusch, Jerry — *Morgan Hunter Corp.*
Hillyer, Carolyn — *Source Services Corporation*
King, Thomas — *Morgan Hunter Corp.*
Kvasnicka, Jay Allen — *Morgan Hunter Corp.*
Msidment, Roger — *Source Services Corporation*
Myers, Kay — *Signature Staffing*
Peternell, Melanie — *Signature Staffing*
Renick, Cynthia L. — *Morgan Hunter Corp.*
Robb, Tammy — *Source Services Corporation*
Rowland, James — *Source Services Corporation*
Ryan, Kathleen — *Source Services Corporation*
Sondgrass, Stephen — *DeFrain, Mayer, Lee & Burgess LLC*
Tilley, Kyle — *Source Services Corporation*
Tryon, Katey — *DeFrain, Mayer, Lee & Burgess LLC*
Viviano, Cathleen — *Source Services Corporation*

Shawnee-Mission
Beeson, William B. — *Lawrence-Leiter and Company*

Kentucky
Crestview Hills
Kern, Jerry L. — *ADOW's Executeam*

Louisville
Allen, William L. — *The Hindman Company*
Berry, Harold B. — *The Hindman Company*
Bruno, Deborah F. — *The Hindman Company*
Doukas, Jon A. — *Professional Bank Services, Inc. D/B/A Executive Search, Inc.*
Grasch, Jerry E. — *The Hindman Company*
Hindman, Neil C. — *The Hindman Company*
Mattingly, Kathleen — *Source Services Corporation*
Moore, Dianna — *Source Services Corporation*
Moriarty, Mike — *Source Services Corporation*
Palmer, James H. — *The Hindman Company*
Parroco, Jason — *Source Services Corporation*
Robinson, Tonya — *Source Services Corporation*
Williams, John — *Source Services Corporation*
Workman, David — *Source Services Corporation*

Owensboro
Wright, A. Leo — *The Hindman Company*

Lousiana
New Orleans
Dietz, David S. — *MSI International*
Eustis, Lucy R. — *MSI International*
Lence, Julie Anne — *MSI International*
Theard, Susan — *Romac & Associates*

Maine
Portland
Beaulieu, Genie A. — *Romac & Associates*
LaPierre, Louis — *Romac & Associates*
Struzziero, Ralph E. — *Romac & Associates*

Maryland
Annapolis
Abbott, Peter D. — *The Abbott Group, Inc.*
Atwood, Barrie — *The Abbott Group, Inc.*
Havener, Donald Clarke — *The Abbott Group, Inc.*

Baltimore
Balter, Sidney — *Source Services Corporation*
Bettick, Michael J. — *A.J. Burton Group, Inc.*
Brandjes, Michael J. — *Brandjes Associates*
Calivas, Kay — *A.J. Burton Group, Inc.*
Campbell, E. — *Source Services Corporation*
Courtney, Brendan — *A.J. Burton Group, Inc.*
Coyle, Hugh F. — *A.J. Burton Group, Inc.*
Delmonico, Laura — *A.J. Burton Group, Inc.*
Edwards, Randolph J. — *DeFuniak & Edwards*
Engle, Bryan — *Source Services Corporation*
Fletcher, David — *A.J. Burton Group, Inc.*
Fribush, Richard — *A.J. Burton Group, Inc.*
Frock, Suzanne D. — *Brandjes Associates*
Gauthier, Robert C. — *Columbia Consulting Group*
Gonzalez, Kristen — *A.J. Burton Group, Inc.*
Grantham, Philip H. — *Columbia Consulting Group*
Halbrich, Mitch — *A.J. Burton Group, Inc.*
Holmes, Lawrence J. — *Columbia Consulting Group*
Hybels, Cynthia — *A.J. Burton Group, Inc.*
Johnson, Brian — *A.J. Burton Group, Inc.*
Klein, Brandon — *A.J. Burton Group, Inc.*

Lazar, Miriam — *Source Services Corporation*
McNamara, Timothy C. — *Columbia Consulting Group*
McNamara, Timothy Connor — *Horton International*
Mercer, Julie — *Columbia Consulting Group*
Muendel, H. Edward — *Stanton Chase International*
Poremski, Paul — *A.J. Burton Group, Inc.*
Rosenstein, Michele — *Source Services Corporation*
Scranton, Lisa — *A.J. Burton Group, Inc.*
Sindler, Jay — *A.J. Burton Group, Inc.*
Swoboda, Lawrence — *A.J. Burton Group, Inc.*
Walker, Craig H. — *A.J. Burton Group, Inc.*
Wheeler, Gerard H. — *A.J. Burton Group, Inc.*
Winnicki, Kimberly — *Source Services Corporation*
Wright, Carl A.J. — *A.J. Burton Group, Inc.*

Bethesda
Kane, Frank — *A.J. Burton Group, Inc.*
McGuire, Pat — *A.J. Burton Group, Inc.*
Mitchell, Jeff — *A.J. Burton Group, Inc.*
Pugrant, Mark A. — *Grant/Morgan Associates, Inc.*
Reynolds, Gregory P. — *Roberts Ryan and Bentley*
Tootsey, Mark A. — *A.J. Burton Group, Inc.*
Vossler, James — *A.J. Burton Group, Inc.*

Columbia
Durakis, Charles A. — *C.A. Durakis, Inc.*
Fields, Fredric — *C.A. Durakis, Inc.*
Houchins, William M. — *Christian & Timbers*

Landover
Graves, Rosemarie — *Don Richard Associates of Washington, D.C., Inc.*

Lutherville
Gordon, Gerald L. — *E.G. Jones Associates, Ltd.*
Jones, Edward G. — *E.G. Jones Associates, Ltd.*

Rockville
Blim, Barbara — *JDG Associates, Ltd.*
Brown, D. Perry — *Don Richard Associates of Washington, D.C., Inc.*
Fotia, Frank — *JDG Associates, Ltd.*

Towson
Cappe, Richard R. — *Roberts Ryan and Bentley*
Dannenberg, Richard A. — *Roberts Ryan and Bentley*

Massachusetts
Andover
Kishbaugh, Herbert S. — *Kishbaugh Associates International*
Newman, Lynn — *Kishbaugh Associates International*

Boston
Beckvold, John B. — *Atlantic Search Group, Inc.*
Birns, Douglas — *Source Services Corporation*
Bond, Robert J. — *Romac & Associates*
Celenza, Catherine — *CPS Inc.*
Conley, Kevin E. — *Lamalie Amrop International*
Cuddy, Brian C. — *Romac & Associates*
Czepiel, Susan — *CPS Inc.*
Epstein, Kathy J. — *Lamalie Amrop International*
Feldman, Kimberley — *Atlantic Search Group, Inc.*
Gourley, Timothy — *Source Services Corporation*
Hallagan, Robert E. — *Heidrick & Struggles, Inc.*

Hawley, Robert E. — *Hayden Group, Incorporated*
Hazerjian, Cynthia — *CPS Inc.*
Hensley, Gayla — *Atlantic Search Group, Inc.*
Holodnak, William A. — *J. Robert Scott*
Hopkinson, Dana — *Winter, Wyman & Company*
Howell, Robert B. — *Atlantic Search Group, Inc.*
Howell, Robert B. — *Atlantic Search Group, Inc.*
Hurd, J. Nicholas — *Russell Reynolds Associates, Inc.*
Jackowitz, Todd — *J. Robert Scott*
Jones, Daniel F. — *Atlantic Search Group, Inc.*
Lapat, Aaron D. — *J. Robert Scott*
Manzo, Renee — *Atlantic Search Group, Inc.*
McCormick, Harry B. — *Hayden Group, Incorporated*
McMahan, Stephen — *Source Services Corporation*
Mead-Fox, David — *Korn/Ferry International*
Nunziata, Peter — *Atlantic Search Group, Inc.*
O'Connell, Mary — *CPS Inc.*
Orr, Stacie — *Source Services Corporation*
Oswald, Mark G. — *Canny, Bowen Inc.*
Ouellette, Christopher — *Source Services Corporation*
Papoulias, Cathy — *Pendleton James and Associates, Inc.*
Rabinowitz, Peter A. — *P.A.R. Associates Inc.*
Reardon, Joseph — *Source Services Corporation*
Resnic, Alan — *Source Services Corporation*
Serba, Kerri — *Source Services Corporation*
Shapiro, Elaine — *CPS Inc.*
Smith, Timothy — *Source Services Corporation*
Sostilio, Louis — *Source Services Corporation*
Thomson, Alexander G. — *Russell Reynolds Associates, Inc.*
Tscelli, Maureen — *Source Services Corporation*
Vande-Water, Katie — *J. Robert Scott*
Warter, Mark — *Isaacson, Miller*
Webber, Edward — *Source Services Corporation*
Williams, Walter E. — *Lamalie Amrop International*
Zegel, Gary — *Source Services Corporation*

Burlington
Browne, Michael — *Source Services Corporation*
Cheah, Victor — *Source Services Corporation*
Chronopoulos, Dennis — *Source Services Corporation*
Di Filippo, Thomas — *Source Services Corporation*
Finnerty, James — *Source Services Corporation*
Glickman, Leenie — *Source Services Corporation*
Harris, Seth O. — *Christian & Timbers*
Inger, Barry — *Source Services Corporation*
Lundy, Martin — *Source Services Corporation*
Macrides, Michael — *Source Services Corporation*
Moore, Craig — *Source Services Corporation*
Murry, John — *Source Services Corporation*
Nephew, Robert — *Christian & Timbers*
Twomey, James — *Source Services Corporation*
Vairo, Leonard A. — *Christian & Timbers*
Winkowski, Stephen — *Source Services Corporation*

Cambridge
Keyser, Anne — *A.T. Kearney, Inc.*
Wacholz, Rick — *A.T. Kearney, Inc.*
Zaleta, Andy R. — *A.T. Kearney, Inc.*

McQuoid, David — *A.T. Kearney, Inc.*
Mertensotto, Chuck H. — *Whitney & Associates, Inc.*
Murphy, Gary J. — *Stone Murphy & Olson*
Olsen, Kristine — *Williams Executive Search, Inc.*
Pappas, Christina E. — *Williams Executive Search, Inc.*
Sathe, Mark A. — *Sathe & Associates, Inc.*
Stein, Terry W. — *Stewart, Stein and Scott, Ltd.*
Stewart, Jeffrey O. — *Stewart, Stein and Scott, Ltd.*
Whitney, David L. — *Whitney & Associates, Inc.*
Williams, Angie — *Whitney & Associates, Inc.*
Yungerberg, Steven — *Steven Yungerberg Associates, Inc.*

Minnetonka
Nielsen, Sue — *Ells Personnel System Inc.*

Mississippi
Ridgeland
Barlow, Ken H. — *The Cherbonnier Group, Inc.*

Missouri
Chesterfield
Brother, Joy — *Charles Luntz & Associates, Inc.*
Luntz, Charles E. — *Charles Luntz & Associates, Inc.*

Kansas City
Howe, Theodore — *Romac & Associates*
Pickering, Dale — *Agri-Tech Personnel, Inc.*
Pickering, Rita — *Agri-Tech Personnel, Inc.*
Romang, Paula — *Agri-Tech Personnel, Inc.*

St. Louis
Albert, Richard — *Source Services Corporation*
Anderson, Richard — *Grant Cooper and Associates*
Bearman, Linda — *Grant Cooper and Associates*
Burchard, Stephen R. — *Burchard & Associates, Inc.*
Deck, Jack — *Source Services Corporation*
Garrett, Mark — *Source Services Corporation*
Goldenberg, Susan — *Grant Cooper and Associates*
Gray, Annie — *Annie Gray Associates, Inc./The Executive Search Firm*
Hart, James — *Source Services Corporation*
Issacs, Judith A. — *Grant Cooper and Associates*
Knoll, Robert — *Source Services Corporation*
Loeb, Stephen H. — *Grant Cooper and Associates*
Meier, J. Dale — *Grant Cooper and Associates*
Milner, Carol — *Source Services Corporation*
Morton, Robert C. — *Morton, McCorkle & Associates, Inc.*
Paul, Kathleen — *Source Services Corporation*
Ryan, Mark — *Source Services Corporation*
Sibbald, John R. — *John Sibbald Associates, Inc.*
Trieschmann, Daniel — *Source Services Corporation*
Truex, John F. — *Morton, McCorkle & Associates, Inc.*
Tunney, William — *Grant Cooper and Associates*
Weinberg, Melvin — *Romac & Associates*
Wirtshafter, Linda — *Grant Cooper and Associates*
Zamborsky, George — *Boyden*

Nebraska
Lincoln
Schroeder, Lee — *Blau Kaptain Schroeder*

Omaha
Ulbert, Nancy — *Aureus Group*

Nevada
Las Vegas
Benson, Edward — *Source Services Corporation*
Bidelman, Richard — *Source Services Corporation*

New Hampshire
Center Harbor
Barger, H. Carter — *Barger & Sargeant, Inc.*
Exeter
Bartholdi, Ted — *Bartholdi & Company, Inc.*
Nashua
Amico, Robert — *Source Services Corporation*
Baranowski, Peter — *Source Services Corporation*
Conard, Rodney J. — *Conard Associates, Inc.*
Hult, Dana — *Source Services Corporation*
McMahan, Stephen — *Source Services Corporation*
Paradise, Malcolm — *Source Services Corporation*
Sapers, Mark — *Source Services Corporation*
Rye
McDonald, Scott A. — *McDonald Associates International*

New Jersey
Chatham
Christenson, H. Alan — *Christenson & Hutchison*
Hutchison, William K. — *Christenson & Hutchison*
McDowell, Robert N. — *Christenson & Hutchison*
Weissman-Rosenthal, Abbe — *ALW Research International*
Cherry Hill
Dressler, Ralph — *Romac & Associates*
Saner, Harold — *Romac & Associates*
Clark
Ulrich, Mary Ann — *D.S. Allen Associates, Inc.*
Edison
Abramson, Roye — *Source Services Corporation*
Altreuter, Rose — *ALTCO Temporary Services*
Altreuter, Rose — *The ALTCO Group*
Carvalho-Esteves, Maria — *Source Services Corporation*
Castle, Lisa — *Source Services Corporation*
Cuddy, Patricia — *Source Services Corporation*
Frantino, Michael — *Source Services Corporation*
Jones, Rodney — *Source Services Corporation*
Miras, Cliff — *Source Services Corporation*
Reed, Susan — *Source Services Corporation*
Scoff, Barry — *Source Services Corporation*
Englewood Cliffs
Kotick, Maddy — *The Stevenson Group of New Jersey*
Lovely, Edward — *The Stevenson Group of New Jersey*
Maphet, Harriet — *The Stevenson Group of New Jersey*
Schall, William A. — *The Stevenson Group of New Jersey*
Steinman, Stephen M. — *The Stevenson Group of New Jersey*

New Mexico
Albuquerque
Schroeder, Steven J. — *Blau Kaptain Schroeder*

New York
Buffalo
Cramer, Paul J. — *C/R Associates*
Fayetteville
Atkinson, S. Graham — *Raymond Karsan Associates*
Great Neck
Attell, Harold — *A.E. Feldman Associates*
Bender, Alan — *Bender Executive Search*
Feldman, Abe — *A.E. Feldman Associates*
Lokken, Karen — *A.E. Feldman Associates*
Looney, Scott — *A.E. Feldman Associates*
Nathanson, Barry F. — *Barry Nathanson Associates*
Roberts, Mitch — *A.E. Feldman Associates*
Schene, Philip — *A.E. Feldman Associates*
Schwam, Carol — *A.E. Feldman Associates*
Skalet, Ira — *A.E. Feldman Associates*
Huntington
Weber, Ronald R. — *Weber Executive Search*
Jericho
Mogul, Gene — *Mogul Consultants, Inc.*
New York
Abert, Janice — *Ledbetter/Davidson International, Inc.*
Adams, Len — *The KPA Group*
Allen, Jean E. — *Lamalie Amrop International*
Amilowski, Maria — *Highland Search Group*
Andre, Jacques P. — *Paul Ray Berndtson*
Anwar, Tarin — *Jay Gaines & Company, Inc.*
Argenio, Michelangelo — *Spencer Stuart*
Aronin, Michael — *Fisher-Todd Associates*
Aronow, Lawrence E. — *Aronow Associates, Inc.*
Aydelotte, G. Thomas — *Ingram & Aydelotte Inc.*
Bacher, Judith — *Spencer Stuart*
Bader, Sam — *Bader Research Corporation*
Bailey, Vanessa — *Highland Search Group*
Barrett, J. David — *Heidrick & Struggles, Inc.*
Bassler, John — *Korn/Ferry International*
Bauman, Martin H. — *Martin H. Bauman Associates, Inc.*
Bennett, Jo — *Battalia Winston International*
Benson, Kate — *Rene Plessner Associates, Inc.*
Berk-Levine, Margo — *MB Inc. Interim Executive Division*
Berne, Marlene — *The Whitney Group*
Bigelow, Dennis — *Marshall Consultants, Inc.*
Bishop, Barbara — *The Executive Source*
Blumenthal, Paula — *J.P. Canon Associates*
Bogansky, Amy — *Conex Incorporated*
Borland, James — *Goodrich & Sherwood Associates, Inc.*
Bovich, Maryann C. — *Higdon Prince Inc.*
Boyle, Russell E. — *Egon Zehnder International Inc.*
Brady, Coloin — *Johnson Smith & Knisely Accord*
Brandon, Irwin — *Hadley Lockwood, Inc.*
Bratches, Howard — *Thorndike Deland Associates*
Brennan, Patrick J. — *Handy HRM Corp.*
Brieger, Steve — *Thorne, Brieger Associates Inc.*
Brophy, Melissa — *Maximum Management Corp.*

Brown, Franklin Key — *Handy HRM Corp.*
Buchalter, Allyson — *The Whitney Group*
Burnett-Stohner, Brendan G. — *Sullivan & Company*
Busterna, Charles — *The KPA Group*
Cannavo, Louise — *The Whitney Group*
Carideo, Joseph — *Thorndike Deland Associates*
Carro, Carl R. — *Executive Search Consultants International*
Cashen, Anthony B. — *Lamalie Amrop International*
Castine, Michael P. — *Highland Search Group*
Castriota, Dominic — *Rhodes Associates*
Caudill, Nancy — *Webb, Johnson Associates, Inc.*
Chamberlin, Brooks T. — *Korn/Ferry International*
Chan, Margaret — *Webb, Johnson Associates, Inc.*
Clark, Evan — *The Whitney Group*
Colasanto, Frank M. — *W.R. Rosato & Associates, Inc.*
Coleman, J. Gregory — *Korn/Ferry International*
Collins, Stephen — *The Johnson Group, Inc.*
Comstock, Rodger — *Johnson Smith & Knisely Accord*
Cunningham, Robert Y. — *Goodrich & Sherwood Associates, Inc.*
D'Elia, Arthur P. — *Korn/Ferry International*
Davis, Steven M. — *Sullivan & Company*
de Bardin, Francesca — *F.L. Taylor & Company, Inc.*
de Cholnoky, Andrea — *Spencer Stuart*
Del Prete, Karen — *Gilbert Tweed/INESA*
Delman, Charles — *Korn/Ferry International*
DiFilippo, James — *Korn/Ferry International*
DiPiazza, Joseph — *Boyden*
Dotson, M. Ileen — *Dotson & Associates*
Doyle, James W. — *Executive Search Consultants International*
Drummond-Hay, Peter — *Russell Reynolds Associates, Inc.*
Dunn, Mary Helen — *Ray & Berndtson*
Early, Alice C. — *Russell Reynolds Associates, Inc.*
Edwards, Ned — *Ingram & Aydelotte Inc./I-I-C Partners*
Edwards, Robert — *J.P. Canon Associates*
Ellis, William — *Interspace Interactive Inc.*
Engelbert, Kimberly S. — *Watson International, Inc.*
Erder, Debra — *Canny, Bowen Inc.*
Erickson, Elaine — *Kenzer Corp.*
Erikson, Theodore J. — *Erikson Consulting Associates, Inc.*
Esposito, Mark — *Christian & Timbers*
Feder, Gwen — *Egon Zehnder International Inc.*
Federman, Jack R. — *W.R. Rosato & Associates, Inc.*
Fienberg, Chester — *Drummond Associates, Inc.*
Flood, Michael — *Norman Broadbent International*
Forestier, Lois — *Source Services Corporation*
Foster, Dwight E. — *D.E. Foster Partners Inc.*
Fowler, Edward D.C. — *Higdon Prince Inc.*
Fowler, Susan B. — *Russell Reynolds Associates, Inc.*
Freedman, Howard — *Korn/Ferry International*
Frumess, Gregory — *D.E. Foster Partners Inc.*
Fulton, Christine N. — *Highland Search Group, L.L.C.*

McPherson, Stephen M. — *Ward Howell International, Inc.*
Meany, Brian M. — *Herbert Mines Associates, Inc.*
Meiland, A. Daniel — *Egon Zehnder International Inc.*
Mendelson, Jeffrey — *Source Services Corporation*
Menk, Carl — *Canny, Bowen Inc.*
Merrigan, Eileen M. — *Lamalie Amrop International*
Millonzi, Joel C. — *Johnson Smith & Knisely Accord*
Mines, Herbert T. — *Herbert Mines Associates, Inc.*
Mochwart, Donald — *Drummond Associates, Inc.*
Molnar, Robert A. — *Johnson Smith & Knisely Accord*
Monogenis, Emanuel N. — *Heidrick & Struggles, Inc.*
Morgan, David G. — *Morgan Stampfl, Inc.*
Moskowitz, Marc — *Kenzer Corp.*
Moyse, Richard G. — *Thorndike Deland Associates*
Mueller-Maerki, Fortunat F. — *Egon Zehnder International Inc.*
Nass, Martin D. — *Lamalie Amrop International*
Ness, Eugene C. — *Ray & Berndtson*
Neff, Thomas J. — *Spencer Stuart*
Neuberth, Jeffrey G. — *Canny, Bowen Inc.*
Ogdon, Thomas H. — *The Ogdon Partnership*
Ohman, Gregory L. — *Skott/Edwards Consultants, Inc.*
Oppedisano, Edward — *Oppedisano & Company, Inc.*
Ornstein, Robert — *Trebor Weldon Lawrence, Inc.*
Palmieri, Cathryn C. — *Korn/Ferry International*
Parker, Gayle — *Trebor Weldon Lawrence, Inc.*
Patence, David W. — *Handy HRM Corp.*
Peretz, Jamie — *Korn/Ferry International*
Peroff, Michael — *Trebor Weldon Lawrence, Inc.*
Pettibone, Linda G. — *Herbert Mines Associates, Inc.*
Phillips, James L. — *Highland Search Group, L.L.C.*
Phillips, Richard K. — *Handy HRM Corp.*
Pierpont-Engstrom, Elizabeth H. — *Russell Reynolds Associates, Inc.*
Pierson, Edward J. — *Johnson Smith & Knisely Accord*
Pineda, Rosanna — *Source Services Corporation*
Platte, John D. — *Russell Reynolds Associates, Inc.*
Plazza, Richard C. — *The Executive Source*
Plessner, Rene — *Rene Plessner Associates, Inc.*
Polansky, Mark — *Korn/Ferry International*
Pomeroy, T. Lee — *Egon Zehnder International Inc.*
Poster, Lawrence D. — *Catalyx Group*
Potter, Mark W. — *Highland Search Group*
Potter, Steven B. — *Highland Search Group, L.L.C.*
Powers Johnson, Allyson — *Skott/Edwards Consultants*
Priem, Windle B. — *Korn/Ferry International*
Prince, Marilyn L. — *Higdon Prince Inc.*
Proct, Nina — *Martin H. Bauman Associates, Inc.*
Puckett, Jennifer — *Rene Plessner Associates, Inc.*

Railsback, Richard — *Korn/Ferry International*
Raines, Bruce R. — *Raines International Inc.*
Randell, James E. — *Randell-Heiken, Inc.*
Regeuye, Peter J. — *Accountants Executive Search*
Reiser, Ellen — *Thorndike Deland Associates*
Reiter, Harold D. — *Herbert Mines Associates, Inc.*
Rice, Marie — *Jay Gaines & Company, Inc.*
Rich, Kenneth M. — *Paul Ray Berndtson*
Rios, Vincent — *Source Services Corporation*
Riotto, Anthony R. — *Riotto-Jones Associates*
Robertson, Bruce J. — *Lamalie Amrop International*
Rogan, John P. — *Russell Reynolds Associates, Inc.*
Rohan, James E. — *J.P. Canon Associates*
Rohan, Kevin A. — *J.P. Canon Associates*
Rosato, William R. — *W.R. Rosato & Associates, Inc.*
Ross, John — *Morgan Stampfl, Inc.*
Rowe, Thomas A. — *Korn/Ferry International*
Runquist, U.W. — *Webb, Johnson Associates, Inc.*
Rustin, Beth — *The Whitney Group*
Sabanosh, Whitney — *Highland Search Group*
Sanders, Spencer H. — *Battalia Winston International*
Sarn, Allan G. — *Allan Sarn Associates Inc.*
Satenstein, Sloan — *Higdon Prince Inc.*
Sawyer, Patricia L. — *Smith & Sawyer Inc.*
Schappell, Marc P. — *Egon Zehnder International Inc.*
Scherck, Henry J. — *Ward Howell International, Inc.*
Schlesinger, Laurie — *The Whitney Group*
Schneider, Thomas P. — *WTW Associates*
Scroggins, Stephen R. — *Russell Reynolds Associates, Inc.*
Segal, Eric B. — *Kenzer Corp.*
Seiden, Steven A. — *Seiden Krieger Associates, Inc.*
Selbach, Barbara — *Spencer Stuart*
Shapanka, Samuel — *Source Services Corporation*
Shemin, Grace — *Maximum Management Corp.*
Shen, Eugene Y. — *The Whitney Group*
Sherwood, Andrew — *Goodrich & Sherwood Associates, Inc.*
Shield, Nancy — *Maximum Management Corp.*
Simon, Penny B. — *Paul Ray Berndtson*
Slosar, John — *Boyden*
Smirnov, Tatiana — *Allan Sarn Associates Inc.*
Smith, Brant — *Smith Hanley Associates*
Smith, Ethan L. — *Highland Search Group, L.L.C.*
Smith, Monica L. — *Analysts Resources, Inc.*
Smith, Robert L. — *Smith & Sawyer Inc.*
Smoller, Howard — *Source Services Corporation*
Sorgen, Jay — *Source Services Corporation*
Spera, Stefaine — *A.T. Kearney, Inc.*
Spicehandler, Sheila — *Trebor Weldon Lawrence, Inc.*
Stack, Richard — *Source Services Corporation*
Stampfl, Eric — *Morgan Stampfl, Inc.*
Stark, Jeff — *Thorne, Brieger Associates Inc.*
Stern, Lester W. — *Sullivan & Company*
Stewart, Clifford — *Morgan Stampfl, Inc.*
Strobridge, Richard P. — *F.L. Taylor & Company, Inc.*
Sucato, Carolyn — *Jay Gaines & Company, Inc.*

Sullivan, Brian M. — *Sullivan & Company*
Sussman, Lynda — *Gilbert Tweed/INESA*
Tappan, Michael A. — *Ward Howell International, Inc.*
Teger, Stella — *Source Services Corporation*
Thrapp, Mark C. — *Executive Search Consultants International*
Tierney, Eileen — *The Whitney Group*
Tweed, Janet — *Gilbert Tweed/INESA*
Van Campen, Jerry — *Gilbert & Van Campen International*
Venable, William W. — *Thorndike Deland Associates*
Vergari, Jane — *Herbert Mines Associates, Inc.*
Ward, Ted — *Korn/Ferry International*
Wardell, Charles W.B. — *Nordeman Grimm, Inc.*
Wasp, Warren T. — *WTW Associates*
Webb, George H. — *Webb, Johnson Associates, Inc.*
Wheatley, William — *Drummond Associates, Inc.*
Whiting, Anthony — *Johnson Smith & Knisely Accord*
Whitton, Paula L. — *Pearson, Caldwell & Farnsworth, Inc.*
Wilbanks, George R. — *Russell Reynolds Associates, Inc.*
Winston, Dale — *Battalia Winston International*
Wisch, Steven C. — *MB Inc. Interim Executive Division*
Wood, Elizabeth — *Highland Search Group*
Wood, John S. — *Egon Zehnder International Inc.*
Young, Nick — *Spencer Stuart*
Zimmerman, Joan C. — *G.Z. Stephens Inc.*
Zona, Henry F. — *Zona & Associates, Inc.*
Zonis, Hildy R. — *Accountants Executive Search*
Zucker, Nancy — *Maximum Management Corp.*

North Salem
Flanagan, Robert M. — *Robert M. Flanagan & Associates, Ltd.*
Normann, Amy — *Robert M. Flanagan & Associates, Ltd.*

Port Washington
Janis, Laurence — *Integrated Search Solutions Group LLC*
Sessa, Vincent J. — *Integrated Search Solutions Group LLC*

Rochester
Anderson, Shawn — *Temporary Accounting Personnel, Inc.*
Baker, Gary M. — *Cochran, Cochran & Yale, Inc.*
Baker, Gary M. — *Temporary Accounting Personnel, Inc.*
Baltaglia, Michael — *Cochran, Cochran & Yale, Inc.*
Buckles, Donna — *Cochran, Cochran & Yale, Inc.*
Call, David — *Cochran, Cochran & Yale, Inc.*
Capizzi, Karen — *Cochran, Cochran & Yale, Inc.*
Critchley, Walter — *Temporary Accounting Personnel, Inc.*
Curtis, Ellissa — *Cochran, Cochran & Yale, Inc.*
Frazier, John — *Cochran, Cochran & Yale, Inc.*
Himlin, Amy — *Cochran, Cochran & Yale, Inc.*
Jordan, Jon — *Cochran, Cochran & Yale, Inc.*
Klein, Mary Jo — *Cochran, Cochran & Yale, Inc.*
Miller, David — *Cochran, Cochran & Yale, Inc.*
Miller, David — *Temporary Accounting Personnel, Inc.*

Misiurewicz, Marc — *Cochran, Cochran & Yale, Inc.*
Murphy, Cornelius J. — *Goodrich & Sherwood Associates, Inc.*
Sanow, Robert — *Cochran, Cochran & Yale, Inc.*

Scarsdale
Long, William G. — *McDonald, Long & Associates, Inc.*
Press, Fred — *Adept Tech Recruiting*

Somers
Gorman, T. Patrick — *Techsearch Services, Inc.*
Taft, David G. — *Techsearch Services, Inc.*

White Plains
Bland, Walter — *Source Services Corporation*
Burch, Donald — *Source Services Corporation*
Devito, Alice — *Source Services Corporation*
Eiseman, Joe — *Source Services Corporation*
Laskin, Sandy — *Source Services Corporation*
Maggio, Mary — *Source Services Corporation*
Occhiboi, Emil — *Source Services Corporation*
Paliwoda, William — *Source Services Corporation*
Parente, James — *Source Services Corporation*
Patel, Shailesh — *Source Services Corporation*
Sirena, Evelyn — *Source Services Corporation*

Williamsville
Critchley, Walter — *Cochran, Cochran & Yale, Inc.*
DiCioccio, Carmen — *Cochran, Cochran & Yale, Inc.*
Gestwick, Daniel — *Cochran, Cochran & Yale, Inc.*
Januale, Lois — *Cochran, Cochran & Yale, Inc.*

North Carolina
Chapel Hill
Grantham, John — *Grantham & Co., Inc.*
Strickland, Katie — *Grantham & Co., Inc.*

Charlotte
Abernathy, Donald E. — *Don Richard Associates of Charlotte*
Buttrey, Daniel — *Source Services Corporation*
Coughlin, Stephen — *Source Services Corporation*
Dewing, Jesse J. — *Don Richard Associates of Charlotte*
Downs, James L. — *Sanford Rose Associates*
Foster, Brian Scott — *Don Richard Associates of Charlotte*
George, Brenda — *Don Richard Associates of Charlotte*
Hill, Emery — *MSI International*
Jernigan, Susan N. — *Sockwell & Associates*
Kelly, Robert — *Source Services Corporation*
Linney, George — *Tyler & Company*
Lyon, Jenny — *Marra Peters & Partners*
MacMillan, James — *Source Services Corporation*
McKinney, Julia — *Source Services Corporation*
Murphy, Corinne — *Source Services Corporation*
Rich, Lyttleton — *Sockwell & Associates*
Siegrist, Jeffrey M. — *D.E. Foster Partners, Inc.*
Silverstein, Jackie — *Don Richard Associates of Charlotte*
Sockwell, J. Edgar — *Sockwell & Associates*
Turner, Edward K. — *Don Richard Associates of Charlotte*
Wilson, Harry — *First Union Executive Search Group*

Raleigh
Bye, Randy — *Romac & Associates*
Twiste, Craig — *Raymond Karsan Associates*

Winston-Salem
LaValle, Michael — *Romac & Associates*

Ohio

Blue Ash
Ehrhart, Jennifer — *ADOW's Executeam*

Canfield
Rimmel, James E. — *The Hindman Company*

Cincinnati
Bason, Maurice L. — *Bason Associates Inc.*
Brown, Gina — *Strategic Alliance Network, Ltd.*
Christman, Joel — *Source Services Corporation*
Davis, Elease — *Source Services Corporation*
Dong, Stephen — *Executive Search, Ltd.*
Fancher, Robert L. — *Bason Associates Inc.*
Florio, Robert — *Source Services Corporation*
Frederick, Dianne — *Source Services Corporation*
Gold, Donald — *Executive Search, Ltd.*
Goodman, Dawn M. — *Bason Associates Inc.*
Hacker-Taylor, Dianna — *Source Services Corporation*
Haller, Mark — *Source Services Corporation*
Joffe, Barry — *Bason Associates Inc.*
Johnson, Greg — *Source Services Corporation*
Kern, Kathleen G. — *ADOW's Executeam*
Koczak, John — *Source Services Corporation*
Lambert, William — *Source Services Corporation*
Laverty, William — *Source Services Corporation*
Nutter, Roger — *Raymond Karsan Associates*
Oldfield, Theresa — *Strategic Alliance Network, Ltd.*
Snowhite, Rebecca — *Source Services Corporation*
Sweeney, Anne — *Source Services Corporation*
Visnich, L. Christine — *Bason Associates Inc.*
Witzgall, William — *Source Services Corporation*

Cleveland
Bell, Lloyd W. — *O'Brien & Bell*
Bowden, Otis H. — *BowdenGlobal, Ltd.*
Bradshaw, Monte — *Christian & Timbers*
Christian, Jeffrey E. — *Christian & Timbers*
Dickey, Chester W. — *Bowden & Company, Inc.*
Ferrari, S. Jay — *Ferrari Search Group*
Imely, Larry S. — *Stratford Group*
Kader, Richard — *Richard Kader & Associates*
Kohn, Adam P. — *Christian & Timbers*
Lauderback, David R. — *A.T. Kearney, Inc.*
Magee, Harrison R. — *Bowden & Company, Inc.*
Niejet, Michael C. — *O'Brien & Bell*
Peterson, Eric N. — *Stratford Group*
Selker, Gregory L. — *Christian & Timbers*
Smith, Timothy C. — *Christian & Timbers*
Sponseller, Vern — *Richard Kader & Associates*

Columbus
Eggert, Scott — *Source Services Corporation*
Giesy, John — *Source Services Corporation*
Henn, George W. — *G.W. Henn & Company*
Hostetter, Kristi — *Source Services Corporation*
Mills, John — *Source Services Corporation*
Morris, Scott — *Source Services Corporation*
O'Brien, Susan — *Source Services Corporation*
Pirro, Sheri — *Source Services Corporation*
Rothenbush, Clayton — *Source Services Corporation*

Shelton, Jonathan — *Source Services Corporation*
Yaekle, Gary — *Tully/Woodmansee International, Inc.*

Dayton
Blickle, Michael — *Source Services Corporation*
Marwil, Jennifer — *Source Services Corporation*
McGoldrick, Terrence — *Source Services Corporation*
Rhoades, Michael — *Source Services Corporation*
Rockwell, Bruce — *Source Services Corporation*
Schroeder, James — *Source Services Corporation*
Scothon, Alan — *Romac & Associates*
Smith, Lawrence — *Source Services Corporation*
Tobin, Christopher — *Source Services Corporation*
Uzzel, Linda — *Source Services Corporation*
Waymire, Pamela — *Source Services Corporation*
Wessling, Jerry — *Source Services Corporation*

Euclid
Orkin, Ralph — *Sanford Rose Associates*
Orkin, Sheilah — *Sanford Rose Associates*

Fairlawn
Jacobson, Rick — *The Windham Group*

Independence
Banko, Scott — *Source Services Corporation*
Barnaby, Richard — *Source Services Corporation*
Bernas, Sharon — *Source Services Corporation*
Carnal, Rick — *Source Services Corporation*
Fulger, Herbert — *Source Services Corporation*
Gilinsky, David — *Source Services Corporation*
Mayer, Thomas — *Source Services Corporation*
Miller, Timothy — *Source Services Corporation*
Morrow, Melanie — *Source Services Corporation*
Samsel, Randy — *Source Services Corporation*
Seamon, Kenneth — *Source Services Corporation*
Tschan, Stephen — *Source Services Corporation*
Wood, Gary — *Source Services Corporation*

Miamisburg
O'Reily, John — *Stratford Group*

Willoughby Hills
Wayne, Cary S. — *ProSearch Inc.*

Oklahoma

Tulsa
Santiago, Anthony — *TaxSearch, Inc.*

Oregon

Hillsboro
Furlong, James W. — *Furlong Search, Inc.*

Portland
Belden, Jeannette — *Source Services Corporation*
Bradley, Dalena — *Woodworth International Group*
Brown, Steffan — *Woodworth International Group*
Diers, Gary — *Source Services Corporation*
Ervin, Russell — *Source Services Corporation*
Irwin, Mark — *Source Services Corporation*
Kennedy, Craig — *Source Services Corporation*
Kondra, Vernon J. — *The Douglas Reiter Company, Inc.*
Mathias, Douglas — *Source Services Corporation*
Matthews, Corwin — *Woodworth International Group*
Moran, Douglas — *Source Services Corporation*
Papasadero, Kathleen — *Woodworth International Group*

Phipps, Peggy — *Woodworth International Group*
Redding, Denise — *The Douglas Reiter Company, Inc.*
Reiter, Douglas — *The Douglas Reiter Company, Inc.*
Simmons, Deborah — *Source Services Corporation*
Woodworth, Gail — *Woodworth International Group*

Pennsylvania
Bryn Mawr
Morris, Paul T. — *The Morris Group*
Chadds Ford
Hoffmeir, Patti — *Tyler & Company*
Levine, Roberta — *Tyler & Company*
Wilson, William F. — *Tyler & Company*
Conshohocken
Clark, Steven — *D.A. Kreuter Associates, Inc.*
Harrison, Joel — *D.A. Kreuter Associates, Inc.*
Kilcullen, Brian A. — *D.A. Kreuter Associates, Inc.*
Kreuter, Daniel A. — *D.A. Kreuter Associates, Inc.*
Weston, Corinne F. — *D.A. Kreuter Associates, Inc.*
Ephrata
Dabich, Thomas M. — *Robert Harkins Associates, Inc.*
King of Prussia
Donnelly, Patti — *Source Services Corporation*
Finkel, Leslie — *Source Services Corporation*
Hight, Susan — *Source Services Corporation*
Inskeep, Thomas — *Source Services Corporation*
Januleski, Geoff — *Source Services Corporation*
Moretti, Denise — *Source Services Corporation*
Nolan, Robert — *Source Services Corporation*
Reid, Katherine — *Source Services Corporation*
Selvaggi, Esther — *Source Services Corporation*
Shackleford, David — *Source Services Corporation*
Storm, Deborah — *Source Services Corporation*
Monroeville
Belden, Charles P. — *Raymond Karsan Associates*
Philadelphia
Battles, Jonathan — *Korn/Ferry International*
Blake, Eileen — *Howard Fischer Associates, Inc.*
Campbell, Robert Scott — *Wellington Management Group*
Cunningham, Lawrence — *Howard Fischer Associates, Inc.*
Fischer, Adam — *Howard Fischer Associates, Inc.*
Fischer, Howard M. — *Howard Fischer Associates, Inc.*
Gantar, Donna — *Howard Fischer Associates, Inc.*
Gerber, Mark J. — *Wellington Management Group*
Higgins, Donna — *Howard Fischer Associates, Inc.*
Janssen, Don — *Howard Fischer Associates, Inc.*
Kane, Karen — *Howard Fischer Associates, Inc.*
Kelly, Elizabeth Ann — *Wellington Management Group*
Koehler, Frank R. — *The Koehler Group*
Mallin, Ellen — *Howard Fischer Associates, Inc.*
Mansford, Keith — *Howard Fischer Associates, Inc.*
Marsteller, Franklin D. — *Spencer Stuart*
Mazor, Elly — *Howard Fischer Associates, Inc.*

McCann, Cornelia B. — *Spencer Stuart*
Nehring, Keith — *Howard Fischer Associates, Inc.*
Ogilvie, Kit — *Howard Fischer Associates, Inc.*
Panarese, Pam — *Howard Fischer Associates, Inc.*
Panchella, Joseph J. — *Wellington Management Group*
Sauer, Harry J. — *Romac & Associates*
Scott, Evan — *Howard Fischer Associates, Inc.*
Shea, Kathleen M. — *The Penn Partners, Incorporated*
Sitarski, Stan — *Howard Fischer Associates, Inc.*
Smith, John F. — *The Penn Partners, Incorporated*
Stevenson, Jane — *Howard Fischer Associates, Inc.*

Pittsburgh
Cersosimo, Rocco — *Source Services Corporation*
Dorfner, Martin — *Source Services Corporation*
Farler, Wiley — *Source Services Corporation*
Papciak, Dennis J. — *Accounting Personnel Associates, Inc.*
Papciak, Dennis J. — *Temporary Accounting Personnel*
Reid, Scott — *Source Services Corporation*
Smith, David P. — *Smith & Latterell (HRS, Inc.)*
Smock, Cynthia — *Source Services Corporation*
Stivk, Barbara A. — *Thornton Resources*
Thornton, John C. — *Thornton Resources*
Trice, Renee — *Source Services Corporation*
Wilson, Derrick — *Thornton Resources*
Southampton
Borden, Stuart — *M.A. Churchill & Associates, Inc.*
Garzone, Dolores — *M.A. Churchill & Associates, Inc.*
Hochberg, Brian — *M.A. Churchill & Associates, Inc.*
Sher, Lawrence — *M.A. Churchill & Associates, Inc.*
Spicher, John — *M.A. Churchill & Associates, Inc.*
Wylie, Pamela — *M.A. Churchill & Associates, Inc.*
Strafford
DiGiovanni, Charles — *Penn Search*
Trevose
Bass, Nate — *Jacobson Associates*
Kalinowski, David — *Jacobson Associates*
Williams, Harry D. — *Jacobson Associates*
Valley Forge
Hamm, Mary Kay — *Romac & Associates*
Villanova
DeHart, Donna — *Tower Consultants, Ltd.*
deVry, Kimberly A. — *Tower Consultants, Ltd.*
Fiorelli, Cheryl — *Tower Consultants, Ltd.*
Wayne
Becker, Elizabeth M. — *Caliber Associates*
Ford, Sandra D. — *Phillips & Ford, Inc.*
Forgosh, Jack H. — *Raymond Karsan Associates*
Hochberg, Steven P. — *Caliber Associates*
Laderman, David — *Romac & Associates*
Lynch, Sean E. — *Raymond Karsan Associates*
Macan, Sandi — *Caliber Associates*
Ongirski, Richard P. — *Raymond Karsan Associates*
Parker, P. Grant — *Raymond Karsan Associates*

Rivera, Elba R. — *Raymond Karsan Associates*
Vincelette, Kathy A. — *Raymond Karsan Associates*

Puerto Rico
San Juan
de Palacios, Jeannette C. — *J. Palacios & Associates, Inc.*

South Carolina
Columbia
Mayes, Kay H. — *John Shell Associates, Inc.*
Shell, John C. — *John Shell Associates, Inc.*

Tennessee
Memphis
Haddad, Charles — *Romac & Associates*

Nashville
Cragg, Barbara R. — *Southwestern Professional Services*
Goedtke, Steven — *Southwestern Professional Services*
Hughes, David — *Southwestern Professional Services*
Lewis, Sean — *Southwestern Professional Services*
Rinker, Jim — *Southwestern Professional Services*
Roberts, Carl R. — *Southwestern Professional Services*
Smith, W. Guice — *Southwestern Professional Services*
Truitt, Thomas B. — *Southwestern Professional Services*

Texas
Austin
Allen, Wade H. — *Cendea Connection International*
Brewster, Edward — *Source Services Corporation*
Cochrun, James — *Source Services Corporation*
Halladay, Patti — *Intersource, Ltd.*
Harris, Joe W. — *Cendea Connection International*
Hebel, Robert W. — *R.W. Hebel Associates*
Hilbert, Laurence — *Source Services Corporation*
Ledbetter, Steven G. — *Cendea Connection International*
Leigh, Rebecca — *Source Services Corporation*
Nabers, Karen — *Source Services Corporation*
Pryor, Bill — *Cendea Connection International*
Simpson, Scott — *Cendea Connection International*
Vinett-Hessel, Deidre — *Source Services Corporation*

Dallas
Alford, Holly — *Source Services Corporation*
Ambler, Peter W. — *Peter W. Ambler Company*
Attaway, Jana — *Kaye-Bassman International Corp.*
Baier, Rebecca — *Source Services Corporation*
Bailey, Paul — *Austin-McGregor International*
Baker, Bill — *Kaye-Bassman International Corp.*
Baker, Mark A. — *Kaye-Bassman International Corp.*
Bakken, Mark — *Source Services Corporation*
Bassman, Robert — *Kaye-Bassman International Corp.*
Bassman, Sandy — *Kaye-Bassman International Corp.*

Brannon, Kathy — *Kaye-Bassman International Corp.*
Brown, Steven — *Source Services Corporation*
Bush, R. Stuart — *Russell Reynolds Associates, Inc.*
Carter, Linda — *Source Services Corporation*
Clarke Smith, Jamie — *Kaye-Bassman International Corp.*
Cruse, O.D. — *Spencer Stuart*
Danforth, W. Michael — *Hyde Danforth Wold & Co.*
Demchak, James P. — *Sandhurst Associates*
Duncan, Dana — *Source Services Corporation*
Dunlow, Aimee — *Source Services Corporation*
Dupont, Rick — *Source Services Corporation*
Elli-Kirk, Matrice — *Spencer Stuart*
England, Mark — *Austin-McGregor International*
Fitzgerald, Brian — *Source Services Corporation*
Gabriel, David L. — *The Arcus Group*
Goar, Duane R. — *Sandhurst Associates*
Grado, Eduardo — *Source Services Corporation*
Grumulaitis, Leo — *Source Services Corporation*
Hailey, H.M. — *Damon & Associates, Inc.*
Hamm, Gary — *Source Services Corporation*
Harrison, Patricia — *Source Services Corporation*
Hill, Michael S. — *Tyler & Company*
Hinojosa, Oscar — *Source Services Corporation*
Jones, Barbara J. — *Kaye-Bassman International Corp.*
Jones, Mark — *Kaye-Bassman International Corp.*
Jordan, Stephen T. — *Paul Ray Berndtson*
Kaye, Jeffrey — *Kaye-Bassman International Corp.*
Keck, Jason B. — *Kaye-Bassman International Corp.*
Kennedy, Michael — *The Danbrook Group, Inc.*
Konker, David N. — *Russell Reynolds Associates, Inc.*
Lache, Shawn E. — *The Arcus Group*
Leblanc, Danny — *Source Services Corporation*
Lee, Everett — *Source Services Corporation*
Letcher, Harvey D. — *Sandhurst Associates*
Levinson, Lauren — *The Danbrook Group, Inc.*
Lewis, Jon A. — *Sandhurst Associates*
Mathis, Carrie — *Source Services Corporation*
McCreary, Charles "Chip" — *Austin-McGregor International*
McGinnis, Rita — *Source Services Corporation*
McIntosh, Arthur — *Source Services Corporation*
McIntosh, Tad — *Source Services Corporation*
McNamara, Catherine — *Ray & Berndtson*
Mitchell, John — *Romac & Associates*
Moodley, Logan — *Austin-McGregor International*
Moore, Mark — *Wheeler, Moore & Elam Co.*
Moseley, Micael A. — *Kaye-Bassman International*
Mott, Greg — *Source Services Corporation*
Mueller, Colleen — *Source Services Corporation*
Neidhart, Craig C. — *TNS Partners, Inc.*
Noebel, Todd L. — *The Noebel Search Group, Inc.*
Norman, Randy — *Austin-McGregor International*
Ornish, Cindy — *Kaye-Bassman International*
Page, G. Schuyler — *A.T. Kearney, Inc.*
Pfau, Madelaine — *Heidrick & Struggles, Inc.*
Pillow, Charles — *Source Services Corporation*
Rowe, William D. — *D.E. Foster Partners Inc.*
Schroeder, John W. — *Spencer Stuart*
Semyan, John K. — *TNS Partners, Inc.*

McLean

Cloutier, G. — *Dinte Resources, Inc.*
Cole, Kevin — *Don Richard Associates of Washington, D.C., Inc.*
Dinte, Paul — *Dinte Resources, Incorporated*
Gordon, Teri — *Don Richard Associates of Washington, D.C., Inc.*
Rogers, Leah — *Dinte Resources, Incorporated*

Reston

Brackman, Janet — *Dahl-Morrow International*
Cuddihy, Paul — *Dahl-Morrow International*
Donath, Linda — *Dahl-Morrow International*
Holt, Carol — *Bartholdi & Company, Inc.*
Steinem, Andy — *Dahl-Morrow International*
Steinem, Barbara — *Dahl-Morrow International*

Richmond

Pliszka, Donald J. — *Praxis Partners*
Ramler, Carolyn S. — *The Corporate Connection, Ltd.*
Rotella, Marshall W. — *The Corporate Connection, Ltd.*
Smith, Lydia — *The Corporate Connection, Ltd.*
Tursi, Deborah J. — *The Corporate Connection, Ltd.*

Stanton

Burkhill, John — *The Talley Group*
Estes, Susan — *The Talley Group*
Jorgensen, Tom — *The Talley Group*

Vienna

Abell, Vincent W. — *MSI International*
Baglio, Robert — *Source Services Corporation*
Benjamin, Maurita — *Source Services Corporation*
Chatterjie, Alok — *MSI International*
Coneys, Bridget — *Source Services Corporation*
Dawson, William — *Source Services Corporation*
Dowell, Chris — *The Abbott Group, Inc.*
Foster, John — *Source Services Corporation*
Gaffney, Megan — *Source Services Corporation*
Gnatowski, Bruce — *Source Services Corporation*
Gresia, Paul — *Source Services Corporation*
Hanley, Steven — *Source Services Corporation*
Kaplan, Traci — *Source Services Corporation*
Kasprzyk, Michael — *Source Services Corporation*
Lewicki, Christopher — *MSI International*
Ludder, Mark — *Source Services Corporation*
McCarthy, Laura — *Source Services Corporation*
Meehan, John — *Source Services Corporation*
Moore, Suzanne — *Source Services Corporation*
Moore, Vickie J. — *Kirkman & Searing, Inc.*
Nelson, Mary — *Source Services Corporation*
Owen, Christopher — *Source Services Corporation*
Powell, Gregory — *Source Services Corporation*
Rice, Raymond D. — *Logue & Rice Inc.*
Snowden, Charles — *Source Services Corporation*
Stephens, Andrew — *Source Services Corporation*
Stevens, Craig M. — *Kirkman & Searing, Inc.*
Velez, Hector — *Source Services Corporation*
Villella, Paul — *Source Services Corporation*
Vourakis, Zan — *Zan Exec LLC*
Zavrel, Mark — *Source Services Corporation*

Williamsburg

DiSalvo, Fred — *The Cambridge Group Ltd*

Washington

Bellevue

Bloomer, James E. — *L.W. Foote Company*
Bronger, Patricia — *Source Services Corporation*
Brown, Daniel — *Source Services Corporation*
Burden, Gene — *The Cherbonnier Group, Inc.*
Carlson, Eric — *Source Services Corporation*
Coffman, Brian — *Kossuth & Associates, Inc.*
Foote, Leland W. — *L.W. Foote Company*
Fuhrman, Dennis — *Source Services Corporation*
Heinrich, Scott — *Source Services Corporation*
Henneberry, Ward — *Source Services Corporation*
Kossuth, David — *Kossuth & Associates, Inc.*
Kossuth, Jane — *Kossuth & Associates, Inc.*
Messina, Marco — *Source Services Corporation*
Rudolph, Kenneth — *Kossuth & Associates, Inc.*
Schwinden, William — *Source Services Corporation*
Varney, Monique — *Source Services Corporation*

Isaquah

Cushman, Judith — *Judith Cushman & Associates*

Seattle

Barbour, Mary Beth — *Tulley/Woodmansee International*
Fong, Robert — *Korn/Ferry International, Inc.*
Jones, Herschel — *Korn/Ferry International*

Spokane

Desgrosellier, Gary P. — *Personnel Unlimited/Executive Search*
Hergenrather, Richard A. — *Hergenrather & Company*

Wisconsin

Brookfield

Maglio, Charles J. — *Maglio and Company, Inc.*

Hartland

Lamb, Peter S. — *Executive Resource, Inc.*
Mitton, Bill — *Executive Resource, Inc.*

Lake Geneva

Rankin, Jeffrey A. — *The Rankin Group, Ltd.*
Rankin, M.J. — *The Rankin Group, Ltd.*

Mequon

Barnes, Richard E. — *Barnes Development Group, LLC*
Barnes, Roanne L. — *Barnes Development Group, LLC*
Waldoch, D. Mark — *Barnes Development Group, LLC*
Williams, Gary L. — *Barnes Development Group, LLC*

Milwaukee

Hilgenberg, Thomas — *Source Services Corporation*
Hucko, Donald S. — *Jonas, Walters & Assoc., Inc.*
Murphy, Patrick J. — *P.J. Murphy & Associates, Inc.*
Neuwald, Debrah — *Source Services Corporation*
Pachowitz, John — *Source Services Corporation*
Rasmussen, Timothy — *Source Services Corporation*
Roberts, Scott — *Jonas, Walters & Assoc., Inc.*
Sarna, Edmund A. — *Jonas, Walters & Assoc., Inc.*
Schultz, Randy — *Source Services Corporation*
Thomas, Kurt J. — *P.J. Murphy & Associates, Inc.*
Walters, William F. — *Jonas, Walters & Assoc., Inc.*

Whitfield, Jack — *Source Services Corporation*
Youngberg, David — *Source Services Corporation*
Zaffrann, Craig S. — *P.J. Murphy & Associates, Inc.*
Zahradka, James F. — *P.J. Murphy & Associates, Inc.*
Zimbal, Mark — *Source Services Corporation*

Reedsburg
Brenner, Mary — *Prestige Inc.*
Jaedike, Eldron — *Prestige Inc.*
Larsen, Bruce — *Prestige Inc.*

Canada
Calgary, Alberta
Coe, Karen J. — *Coe & Company International, Inc.*
Costello, Lynda — *Coe & Company International, Inc.*
Honey, W. Michael M. — *O'Callaghan Honey/Paul Ray Berndtson, Inc.*
Johnson, Valerie — *Coe & Company International, Inc.*
Pfeiffer, Irene — *Price Waterhouse*
Shervey, Brent C. — *O'Callaghan Honey/Ray Berndtson, Inc.*
Smith, Ronald V. — *Coe & Company International, Inc.*

Edmonton, Alberta
Holland, Rose Mary — *Price Waterhouse*

Mississauga, Ontario Canada
Hagglund, Karl H. — *Simpson Associates, Inc.*
Simpson, David J. — *Simpson Associates, Inc.*

Montreal, Quebec
Krecklo, Brian Douglas — *Krecklo & Associates, Inc.*
Labrecque, Bernard F. — *Laurendeau, Labrecque/Ray Berndtson, Inc.*
Lachance, Roger — *Laurendeau, Labrecque/Ray Berndtson, Inc.*
Lacoste, Daniel — *The Caldwell Partners Amrop International*
Laurendeau, Jean E. — *Laurendeau, Labrecque/Ray Berndtson, Inc.*
LeComte, Andre — *Egon Zehnder International Inc.*
Payette, Pierre — *Egon Zehnder International Inc.*
Raymond, Jean — *The Caldwell Partners Amrop International*
Swidler, J. Robert — *Egon Zehnder International Inc.*

North York, Ontario
Nagy, Les — *Source Services Corporation*

Toronto, Ontario
Baker, Gerry — *A.T. Kearney, Inc.*
Baldock, Robert G. — *Ray & Berndtson/Lovas Stanley*
Bell, Michael — *Spencer Stuart*
Beran, Helena — *Michael J. Cavanagh and Associates*
Bliley, Jerry — *Spencer Stuart*
Britt, Stephen — *Keith Bagg & Associates, Inc.*
Burns, Alan — *The Enns Partners Inc.*
Caldwell, C. Douglas — *The Caldwell Partners Amrop International*
Campbell, W. Ross — *Egon Zehnder International Inc.*

Carrott, Gregory T. — *Egon Zehnder International, Inc.*
Cavanagh, Michael J. — *Michael J. Cavanagh and Associates*
Charles, Ronald D. — *The Caldwell Partners Amrop International*
Chauvin, Ralph A. — *The Caldwell Partners Amrop International*
Collis, Martin — *E.L. Shore & Associates Ltd.*
Cook, Dennis — *A.T. Kearney, Inc.*
Crath, Paul F. — *Price Waterhouse*
Dunbar, Marilynne — *Ray & Berndtson/Lovas Stanley*
Enns, George — *The Enns Partners Inc.*
Fawcett, Anne M. — *The Caldwell Partners Amrop International*
Fennell, Patrick — *Korn/Ferry International*
Graham, Craig — *Ward Howell International, Inc.*
Gudino, Richard — *Keith Bagg & Associates, Inc.*
Harris, Jack — *A.T. Kearney, Inc.*
Hussey, Wayne — *Krecklo & Associates, Inc.*
Illsley, Hugh G. — *Ward Howell International, Inc.*
Kussner, Janice N. — *Herman Smith Executive Initiatives Inc.*
Lennox, Charles — *Price Waterhouse*
Long, Thomas — *Egon Zehnder International Inc.*
Lovas, W. Carl — *Ray & Berndtson/Lovas Stanley*
MacDougall, Andrew J. — *Spencer Stuart*
Malcolm, Rod — *Korn/Ferry International*
Martin, Jon — *Egon Zehnder International Inc.*
Massey, R. Bruce — *Horton International*
McLean, B. Keith — *Price Waterhouse*
Miller, Roy — *The Enns Partners Inc.*
Morawetz, Justin A. — *Keith Bagg & Associates, Inc.*
Murray, Virginia — *A.T. Kearney, Inc.*
Neelin, Sharon — *The Caldwell Partners Amrop International*
Paynter, Sandra L. — *Ward Howell International, Inc.*
Probert, William W. — *Ward Howell International, Inc.*
Roberts, Derek J. — *Ward Howell International, Inc.*
Rosin, Jeffrey — *Korn/Ferry International*
Ross, Lawrence — *Ray & Berndtson/Lovas Stanley*
Ross, Mark — *Ray & Berndtson/Lovas Stanley*
Ross, Sheila L. — *Ward Howell International, Inc.*
Savoy, Michelle — *Spencer Stuart*
Shenfield, Peter — *A.T. Kearney, Inc.*
Shore, Earl L. — *E.L. Shore & Associates Ltd.*
Smith, Herman M. — *Herman Smith Executive Initiatives Inc.*
Stewart, Jan J. — *Egon Zehnder International Inc.*
ten Cate, Herman H. — *Stoneham Associates Corp.*
Van Clieaf, Mark — *MVC Associates International*
Vernon, Peter C. — *Horton International*
Wilson, T. Gordon — *Ray & Berndtson/Lovas Stanley*

Vancouver, British Columbia
Clark, Julie — *Corporate Recruiters Ltd.*
Kershaw, Lisa — *Tanton Mitchell/Paul Ray Berndtson*
McMillin, Bob — *Price Waterhouse*

Muller, Susan — *Corporate Recruiters Ltd.*
Spitz, Grant — *The Caldwell Partners Amrop International*
Van Alstine, Catherine — *Tanton Mitchell/Paul Ray Berndtson*
Wallace, Alec — *Tanton Mitchell/Paul Ray Berndtson*

Mexico
Mexico City, D.F.
Cortina Del Valle, Pedro — *Ray & Berndtson*
Dudley, Craig J. — *Paul Ray Berndtson*
Flores, Agustin — *Ward Howell International, Inc.*
Gonzalez, Rafael — *Korn/Ferry International*
Lezama Cohen, Luis — *Ray & Berndtson*
Medina-Haro, Adolfo — *Heidrick & Struggles, Inc.*
Mendoza, Guadalupe — *Ward Howell International, Inc.*
Newman, Jose L. — *Ward Howell International, Inc.*
Padilla, Jose Sanchez — *Egon Zehnder International Inc.*
Pardo, Maria Elena — *Smith Search, S.C.*
Pastrana, Dario — *Egon Zehnder International Inc.*
Robles Cuellar, Paulina — *Ray & Berndtson*
Smith, Ana Luz — *Smith Search, S.C.*
Smith, John E. — *Smith Search, S.C.*
Zavala, Lorenzo — *Russell Reynolds Associates, Inc.*

Monterrey, N.L.
Castillo, Eduardo — *Korn/Ferry International*

Appendix: Job-Search Resources

If you would like more information about executive recruiters, or if you would like to order other career strategy guides and subscribe to our online *Job-Seekers Network*, please refer to the following Hunt-Scanlon publications. To learn more about these products and ordering information, please call (800) 477-1199 toll free today!

- Executive Recruiters of North America
- Executive Search Review
- Headhunter News (at www.job-seekers.com)
- The Job-Seekers Network (at www.job-seekers.com)
- The Kingmaker
- The Select Guide to Human Resource Executives
- Silicon Valley Recruiters
- Wall $treet Recruiters
- Workplace America (at www.job-seekers.com)